Mary Bo Bannister
Mary Bo.
You are an academic inspiration
and you will always be
a member of the "cast" at
Bazareth College.

fondly, the Naz
family

THE
SHOWS
OF
LONDON

THE
SHOWS
❧ OF ❧
LONDON

RICHARD D. ALTICK

THE BELKNAP PRESS OF
HARVARD UNIVERSITY PRESS
CAMBRIDGE, MASSACHUSETTS
AND LONDON, ENGLAND · 1978

Library of Congress Cataloging in Publication Data

Altick, Richard Daniel, 1915-
    The shows of London.

    Includes bibliographical references and index.
      1. London—Exhibitions—History. I. Title.
T395.5.G7A45   942.1   77-2755
ISBN 0-674-80731-6

The Public Exhibitions of a Nation, principally form and establish that *peculiar character,* which the rest of Mankind agree in annexing to their general ideas concerning them. —Look around you, in this extraordinary Country, and contemplate the various Shows and Diversions of the People, and then say, whether their temper or mind at various periods of our History, may not be collected from them?

> —Prefatory page, signed "G.S., Peckham, 1840," in British Library scrapbook, *Exhibitions of Mechanical and Other Works of Ingenuity*

Contents

Acknowledgments

The debts incurred in writing this book reach all the way back to the antiquarians and hobbyists—a few, like Daniel Lysons, known by name, the identities of the rest long since lost—who, from the end of the eighteenth century onward, gathered into ponderous scrapbooks and filing boxes the countless newspaper clippings, handbills, programs, sixpenny souvenir guides, and prints that have served as the indispensable raw material of my research. Few of their contemporaries can have sympathized with their eccentric zeal to preserve the records of a neglected part of the London entertainment scene, but it is to be hoped that their foresight and industry find their belated justification in these pages.

The list of more recent benefactors begins with the staffs of the libraries where I worked: the London Library; the British Library and its cotenant in Bloomsbury, the British Museum; the Guildhall Library, where Ralph Hyde, the keeper of prints and maps, gave me valuable guidance over an extended period of time; the Westminster City Libraries' local archives in Buckingham Palace Road; the Marylebone Public Library; the Enthoven Theatre Collection at the Victoria and Albert Museum (eventually to become a part of the projected British Theatre Museum) and its director, George Nash; the library of the Victoria and Albert Museum; the library of the Museum of London; the John Johnson Collection of Printed Ephemera at the Bodleian Library, Oxford, where the curator, Dr. Michael Turner, was of much help; and the Harvard Theatre Collection. I have taken constant advantage of the wide resources of my headquarters library at the Ohio State University, where I am especially grateful to Clara Goldslager for her perseverance in obtaining books on interlibrary loan and to Jacqueline Sisson for the hospitality of the Fine Arts Library of which she has charge.

Two successive chairmen of the Department of English at the university, John B. Gabel and Julian Markels, helped me in a number of ways. Through their good offices I was able to enjoy the services of several research assistants, most notably Karen Neslund Atwood, whose tireless searching of bibliographies and the indexes of periodicals turned up many obscure but valuable pieces of information, and Larry Long, who checked most of the facts, quotations, and references. Two of my colleagues, James R. Kincaid and Christian K. Zacher, subjected the penultimate draft of my manuscript to the most stringent criticism it has ever been my humbling privilege to receive, and my dedicated and expert editor, Nancy Clemente, did her tactful best to improve the final version. But of course, like Claudius's, all remaining imperfections are on my head.

Every reader, I am sure, will share my admiration for the work of the book's designer, Marianne Perlak. Others who have aided in one way or another include James J. Barnes, Jerome H. Buckley, John Clubbe, George H. Ford, Francis R. Hart, Park Honan, Peter Jackson, E. D. H. Johnson, U. C. Knoepflmacher, Carl Woodring, and Andrew Wright. Several other courtesies are acknowledged in the notes at the back of the book. Once more, June Johnson's typing was literally flawless. Travel expenses were defrayed in part by generous grants from the American Council of Learned Societies and the American Philosophical Society (Penrose Fund). The Graduate School and the College of Humanities at the Ohio State University picked up the bills for the photography. But among institutions my greatest immediate debt is to the John Simon Guggenheim Memorial Foundation for a fellowship that enabled me to finish the book sooner and in more comfortable circumstances than would otherwise have been possible.

Whether accompanying me on tours of innumerable English and continental museums (an amateur interest in museology provides a most agreeable pretext for travel) or helping with the proofs, my wife tolerated with unfailing cheer what proved to be a six-year preoccupation with the shows of London. My final thanks, necessarily and most deservedly, go to her.

Grateful acknowledgment is made to the following institutions and individuals for permission to reproduce pictures in their possession:

The British Library Board: 15, 91, 112, 113, 114.
The Trustees of the British Museum: Department of Prints and Drawings: 1, 3, 6, 8, 12, 16, 19, 20, 21, 22, 23, 24, 25, 26, 27, 30, 31, 55, 66, 70, 71, 78, 79, 80, 82, 84, 85, 86, 87, 100, 101, 109, 122, 133, 135, 136, 144, 145, 147, 152, 153, 155, 156, 173; Natural History Museum: 67.
Guildhall Library, City of London: 2, 4, 9, 13, 14, 17, 29, 32, 33, 34, 35, 36, 37, 38, 39, 40, 41, 42, 43, 44, 48, 49, 50, 52, 53, 56, 57, 58, 62, 63, 68, 69, 72, 73, 74, 75, 77, 88, 89, 90, 92, 93, 94, 95, 96, 97, 99, 102, 103, 105, 106, 107, 110, 111, 116, 117, 118, 119, 123, 124, 128, 129, 130, 131, 132 (left), 138, 139, 140, 141, 143, 146, 150, 151, 154, 157, 158, 159, 160, 161, 164, 165, 166, 167, 168, 169, 170, 171, 172, 174, 175, 178, 179, 180, 181.
Harvard Theatre Collection: 61.
Illustrated London News: 18.
John Johnson Collection, Bodleian Library: 5, 45, 46, 47, 51, 64, 76, 120, 121, 137.
Dr. David Mayer: 59.
Musée d'Art et d'Histoire, Neuchâtel, Switzerland: 10.
Professor Harry Stone: 115.
University of London Library: 60.
Victoria and Albert Museum (Crown Copyright): 65, 98, 163.
Westminster City Libraries (Archives Department): 7, 11, 28, 54, 81, 83, 104, 108, 125, 126, 127, 132 (right), 134, 142, 148, 149, 176, 177.

R. D. A.

THE
SHOWS
OF
LONDON

Introduction

Well might the great Napoleon say, we trafficked in every thing; but he was little aware that to "a nation of shopkeepers," he might have added, of show-keepers.
　　　　　—Letter to the *Examiner,* 7 March 1824

. . . that love for shows,
Which stamps us as the "Staring Nation."
　　　　　—Bulwer, *The Siamese Twins,* 1831

In effect, though certainly not by intention, this book complements my *The English Common Reader: A Social History of the Mass Reading Public, 1800–1900* (Chicago, 1957). There, I dealt with what the English people paid to read; here, I am concerned with what Londoners paid to gaze at. Both volumes, therefore, are studies in the history of English popular culture. The present one, however, has (except for being confined to London) a considerably wider scope. It is concerned with the habits and experience not only of that portion of the population who had access to the printed word and took advantage of it, but also of that much larger number of people who either could not read or simply were disinclined to do so.

My subject this time is the broad stream of urban culture which ran parallel to and sometimes mingled with that of the printed word: a great variety of public nontheatrical entertainments, here called exhibitions, that ministered to the same widespread impulses and interests to which print also catered—the desire to be amused or instructed, the indulgence of curiosity and the sheer sense of wonder, sometimes a rudimentary aesthetic sensibility. While books and magazines proliferated, becoming an ever more familiar part of everyday life and resulting eventually in the Victorians' adoption of Caxton as a culture hero, exhibitions were simultaneously giving practical realization to Bacon's advocacy of things over words as instruments of knowledge. They were, in fact, an alternative medium to print, reifying the word; through them, the vicarious became the immediate, the theoretical and general became the concrete and specific. They were the occasion for a communal exercise, not restricted to the literate, that was to the life of London society at large what the private practice of purposeful or casual reading was to some members of it. To those who could and did read, exhibitions served as a supplement to books, particularly to illustrate in tangible form some of the most popular kinds of informational literature in various periods: narratives of exploration and travel (later including ethnography), treatises on pseudo-science and science (especially natural history), histories (including the stories of momentous recent events), works describing successive centers of archaeological discovery. To the uneducated, exhibitions served as surrogates for such books, telling them as much about those subjects of civilized human interest as they were likely ever to know. To both the literate and the illiterate, they were a prime means by which the mind and the imagination could be exercised and daily routine experience given occasional welcome patches of variety and color. They were an indispensable way of momentary escape from the dullness, the mental vacuity, the constriction of horizons, the suppression of the imagination which were too often the price of life in the enveloping city.

In *Notes and Queries* (1899) a correspondent remarked that "the subject of exhibitions in London is of great interest, and so far as I know, is one of the few subjects of which no reasonably comprehensive history has been published."[1] He evidently made no effort to remedy the lack, nor did anyone else. This wide expanse of English social history therefore has remained unsurveyed until now, a circumstance that has had, from my point of view, advantages and disadvantages. Among the latter is the fact that I have had to define the boundaries of the subject more or less empirically and not always with strict attention to logic or consistency. The term "exhibition" as used in these pages (along with "show," here employed as a synonym, devoid of its colloquial connotation of "theatrical performance") has the same broad application it had when Regency and early Victorian newspaper editors used it to head columns devoted to public entertainments that were neither dramatic nor musical. For convenience, though with no historical warrant ("exhibition" for some time referred only to annual shows of art, beginning with that of the Society of Artists in 1760), the word has been applied retrospectively in the same way.

In general, exhibitions are defined as displays of pictures, objects, or living creatures, including human beings, that people as a rule paid to see. In the last-named category of sights, the concentration is on what the animals or humans were—their remarkable physical peculiarities—rather than what they did. Shows having performance of some kind—conjuring, tumbling, fire-eating, mind-reading—as their principal raison d'être are generally excluded, but this omission applies more strictly to human beings in action than to talented animals. Thus Shakespeare's calculating and climbing horse and Dr. Johnson's learned pig are awarded a paragraph or two, whereas the Victorian "Wizard of the North," a magician named John Henry Anderson, appears only as the proprietor of a controversial exhibition of Aztec Lilliputians. But neither a desire for consistency nor scholarly austerity could be stretched so far as to leave out such memorable human performers as the fireproof Ivan Ivanitz Chabert, Richardson's Original Rock Band, and the gifted Michael Boai, who played operatic overtures on his chin.

Although the history of London shows has not previously been told, it adjoins four areas about which a good deal has been written and whose borders it often overlaps: the history of fairs, freaks, and itinerant showmen; the history of the theatre, especially the pantomime, the spectacle, and the music hall; the history of art, particularly of art exhibitions and galleries; and the history of scientific collecting, both private and institutional. Some borderline regions, such as the histories of puppet and Punch and Judy shows, the circus, hippodrama, pantomime, balloon ascensions, and fireworks displays, have already been described by others, in most instances adequately. They are therefore omitted here except for a few glancing references. Such London sights as the Royal Exchange and Guildhall are not dealt with, but the Tower, Westminster Abbey, and St. Paul's Cathedral are, for the sufficient reason that they were operated like catchpenny commercial exhibitions and were often likened—not with approval—to Bartholomew Fair and Madame Tussaud's. Spectacular official ceremonies such as the Lord Mayor's Show, royal marriages, state funerals, and celebrations of military victories have been entirely excluded.

Limiting this study to London rather than extending it to the whole of Britain can be justified on grounds other than the obvious one, that it makes a huge subject a little less unmanageable. In the seventeenth and eighteenth centuries, exhibitions were mainly confined to London, although, of course, wandering showmen did take their peepshows, curiosities, freaks, and performers into the country in season. But it is not unfair to say that Londoners' tastes in such matters as exhibitions accurately reflected the tastes of most provincial people as well, excluding only those who were entirely and inextricably attached to the purely rural tradition. To a degree unmatched in larger countries, the capital was in essential respects a microcosm of the whole nation's culture. It has recently been observed that in the middle of the eighteenth century "about one in six of all English men and women were either living in London [which held ten percent of the total population of England and Wales] or had once lived there and had thus been directly exposed to the social, political, and cultural influence of the capital."[2] In 1801, the year of the first official census, the population of Greater London (1,117,000) was approximately 13 percent of that of England and Wales; by 1861, it was some 16 percent (3,227,000). As transport improved, notably with the completion of railways from every direction, a steadily larger proportion of the people living outside London were able to participate directly in its social and cultural life. Thus, even though the booming provincial cities in time became miniature Londons, with their own museums and a constant traffic of various kinds of exhibitions brought down from London, it was in the metropolis itself that the nation's popular cultural interest remained focused.

The time span covered in this volume is somewhat different from that of *The English Common Reader,* which dealt only in quick summary with the development of the mass reading public before 1800 and devoted the rest of its space to the nineteenth century, resolutely concluding at the edge of the twentieth. Here, the story begins in the afterglow of the Middle Ages, with "scientific" and "historical" rarities replacing, as objects of curiosity, the religious relics which lent credibility to Scripture and hagiography. It ends, for a number of reasons which will become clear in the final chapters, with the decade following that exhilarating apotheosis of the London exhibition, the Crystal Palace of 1851. Symbolically as well as chronologically, the narrative landscape reaches from the Tudor and Stuart mountebank booths at Bartholomew Fair to the museum complex in South Kensington, whose first building rose in the mid-1850s.

The history of London exhibitions demonstrates, as Neil Harris has observed specifically of P. T. Barnum's career, "the involvement of the politics of entertainment with the politics of life."[3] In the extremely diversified body of historical information gathered here, three main themes can be recognized. One, needless to say, is the unfolding story of popular taste itself—of Londoners' preferences when they had an idle hour, a few pennies or a shilling in pocket, and a choice of interesting objects to inspect. As will become evident, those preferences were an ever unstable mixture, in which an insatiable appetite for novelty contended with a perennial loyalty to staple attractions such as waxworks and freaks. Earlier, the old and the new were just about equally sought after, but under the altered conditions of life in nineteenth-century London, stimulated in part by the first stirrings of the mass communication industry, there was an increasingly restless demand for innovation, and, except among the most easily satisfied part of the audience, a concomitant decline from favor of the old standbys. In every era the showmen staked their livelihood on a shrewd perception, if not anticipation, of what the public wanted at a given moment.

A second phenomenon that can be traced through the history of the London shows is the cultural interplay between the several classes that was a prelude to the slowly evolving social democracy of the Victorian period. At all times, curiosity was a great leveler. Exhibitions that engaged the attention of the "lower ranks" also attracted the cultivated and, perhaps to a lesser extent, vice versa. The spectrum of available shows was not divided into one category that was exclusively for the poor and unschooled and another, entirely separate, for the well-to-do and educated. Pepys, Evelyn, and the other founding luminaries of the Royal Society in one generation, and the Duke of Wellington and England's most distinguished lord of maritime law in another, mixed unaffectedly, though perhaps not always comfortably, with the common people wherever rarities and spectacles were to be seen. And numerous exhibitions intended for an elite audience, such as Philippe Jacques de Loutherbourg's miniature moving light-and-sound show called the Eidophusikon, soon were made accessible, sometimes in modified form, to a wider public at a reduced rate. As more than a few foreign visitors noted, no English trait was more widespread throughout the entire social structure than the relish for exhibitions, and, one might add, none was more effective in lowering, however briefly, the conventional barriers that kept class and class at a distance.

But this well-nigh universal participation in the ·shows of London, embracing as it did both the cultured and the illiterate, implied a variety of motives. If shows brought the classes together, they were also the scene of the perennial conflict between the claims of amusement and those of earnest instruction. Aware as the showmen were of the value the English temper placed upon knowledge, if only by way of lip service, at no time did their publicity wholly lack some promise of instruction; "scientific" interest was attributed even to exhibitions of palpably contrived mermaids. But with the Enlightenment, the desirability of "rational amusement"—education sugarcoated with entertainment—became an article of social faith, and with the arrival of the early Victorian commitment to the instruction of the population at large, it became of paramount importance. The ineradicable presence of the Old Adam in the masses of people—their stubborn insistence on being amused, whether or not they also learned something—taxed all the ingenuity that public men infected with the reforming spirit of the times could muster as they sought to harness shows to the cause of social improvement, and the search for the elusive acceptable balance between instruction and diversion became the recurrent motif (a melancholy one, it might be added) in the history of London exhibitions during the first half of the nineteenth century. As every reader will reflect upon finishing this book, the magic formula is still to seek, over a hundred years later.

A more or less direct outgrowth of the confrontation between amusement and instruction was government's eventual arrival on the London show scene. Hitherto, exhibitions were a virtual monopoly of the London entertainment industry, put on as frank money-making enterprises with no thought of the public weal. When it became apparent in the early Victorian era that commercial or proprietary sponsorship could not, or would not, supply uplift, the state, goaded by liberal reformers, assumed responsibility for the instructional side of the exhibition business as part of its larger, reluctant acceptance of responsibility for providing schools and teachers for the masses. The age of exhibitions, conducted for profit, gave way to the modern age of museums, established and maintained by public funds for the benefit of all.

Perhaps the widest value a study of this kind, and of these dimensions, has is the light it sheds on the limitations, contours, and texture of the popular mind in a given place and time. As the epigraph to this volume, quoted from some nameless but thoughtful resident of Peckham in 1840, suggests, and as present-day social philosophers like Eric Hoffer affirm, it is possible to infer pretty much about the nature of a society from the ways in which it chooses to spend its leisure and whatever money it has for self-indulgent purposes. Like the history of the theatre and of the reading public, the history of exhibitions is a valuable indicator of what went on inside ordinary Londoners' minds— the atmosphere of their imagination—in any period between the late sixteenth century and the mid-Victorian era. It is, indeed, a more comprehensive key to the popular consciousness than those other, more familiar histories, because the people who attended exhibitions of all kinds clearly outnumbered those who went to the theatre, and they included hundreds of thousands of nonreaders whose mental bent was never reflected in best-seller or magazine circulation statistics.

Although the main outlines of the story told in these pages can be relied on, no blanket guarantee can be made of the multitudinous particulars. Many of the claims cited without comment—the attendance at various shows, the rarity, dimensions, provenance, or other extraordinary attributes of the persons or things displayed—are derived from advertisements or what are in all likelihood showmen's puffs posing as reviews or news stories; and of all the classes of documents that historians may be called on to deal with, few are more engagingly disingenuous or downright mendacious than show-business publicity, where honesty possesses neither virtue nor advantage. In addition, the annals of the London entertainment business as a whole are a notorious breeding ground of error and legend. Although the modern historian is oppressively aware of the weight of accumulated misinformation, sanctified by time and repetition, with which he must cope, there is little he can do about it beyond maintaining his own skepticism and encouraging that of his readers, because in most cases there is no way of confronting a suspected falsehood with a demonstrable fact. Despite its ambition to be a reliable history, therefore, this book doubtless contains more than a few statements that would have been reconsidered or expunged had the countervailing truth been available. Under these shadowed circumstances, the best I can hope is that I have not swelled the irreducible number of inherited but undetected errors with many of my own inadvertent devising.

From Cabinets to Museums, I: 1600-1750

1

Two oddly assorted figures, separated by three centuries, stand at the gateway of our view: an engaging clerical rogue out of Chaucer and a very real seventeenth-century gentleman. Their differences are more conspicuous than their resemblances. One, a mendicant friar with the mercenary instincts of a true showman, appealed to the superstitious credulity of the common "lewed" man of the late Middle Ages; the other, a founder of the Royal Society, was concerned to spread the new learning among his own superior class in seventeenth-century England. But both, for our purposes, are symbolic and prophetic. Chaucer's Pardoner, his glass case filled with dubious relics of cloth and bones, including a miraculous "sholder-boon . . . of an hooly Jewes sheep," exploited a vein of gullibility among the masses which would prove so durable as to afford a living to numberless London showmen in the centuries to come. John Evelyn, a man of insatiable curiosity and a devotee of Bacon, exemplified the quickening eagerness for knowledge that would lead to the Enlightenment and eventually to museums and other exhibitions catering to all classes of society. From our perspective late in the twentieth century, the Pardoner looks backward, into an age of uncritical wonder; Evelyn forward, into an age of scientific explanation. And it is the tension between these two climates of mind that forms much of the early background to the history of London exhibitions.

The medieval church was the common man's first museum. Its stock of holy relics, of which the Pardoner's repertory was in a sense a portable exten-

sion, testified to the strength, persistence, and profitability of the people's appetite for tangible objects to be gazed upon in awe. Especially at those churches belonging to the various orders of friars, the devout came to receive the spiritual benefits of religious treasures, and by custom, enforced by vigorous pleading such as the Pardoner was a master of, they left a bit of money as an offering. It was certain monks who first came to the advantageous realization that people would gladly pay to have their sense of wonder indulged in the presence of things with legendary associations, whether the legend lay in Scripture, the annals of the saints, the lore of the classics or the folk, or sober history. In the Middle Ages, of course, the first categories predominated. Special sermons, under auspices considerably more dignified than the Pardoner's, were devised to stress the extraordinary benefits to be derived from contemplation of holy objects:

Syrres, than on relike Sonday next commyng we shall reverens, honour, and worship the precius sacrament of the awter, verey Goddis body, . . . and in generall all the reverent relikes of patriackes, prophetes, apostelles, martirs, confessours, and virtuous virgins, and other holy and devoute men and women, whoos blessid bodyes, holy bones, and other relikes th[t] be left in erth to cristen mannes socour, comfort, and recreacion, and their names be regestrede in the boke of life.[1]

The more infrequently some relics were shown, the greater, presumably, their drawing power at the Offertory. About 1314 the authorities of St. Paul's

Cathedral had the good fortune to discover a cache of holy objects in the old cross on the steeple, placed there, it was thought, to serve as the ghostly equivalent of a lightning rod. These were typical of many such collections, though others had a less lofty abode: "A piece of the true Cross, a stone of the Holy Sepulchre, other stones from the place of Ascension and the Mount of Calvary, bones of martyred Virgins . . . 'These relics Master Robert de Clothale (Chancellor of the Cathedral) showed to the people during his preaching on the Sunday, before the Feast of St. Botolph, and after the same the relics were replaced in the cross' "—to be rediscovered, one may be confident, on another occasion.[2]

Evidently, England never possessed a collection of richly enshrined relics as great as the celebrated ones at the Royal Abbey of St. Denis in France, of which a catalogue drawn up by Abbot Suger in the twelfth century survives, or at St. Omer, whose inventory as of 1346 also exists. There, as elsewhere, relics with specifically religious significance were shown side by side with natural curiosities: a drop of the Virgin's milk, a pot that figured in the miracle at Cana, a scrap of a martyr's shroud, nails or a fragment of wood from the true cross, a cameo with a portrait of the Queen of Sheba, a crystal goblet from King Solomon's temple, souvenirs brought back from distant lands by pilgrims and crusaders, "thunderstones," griffins' eggs, tortoise shells, unicorns' horns, antediluvian giants' bones and teeth.[3] But the "visitations" of English religious houses that Thomas Cromwell supervised in 1535–1540 at the behest of Henry VIII revealed that hardly a house was without its prized relics, most of them enclosed in reliquaries of precious metals and stones. Although part of the duty laid on Cromwell's agents was to eradicate all traces of "the abomination of idolatry," it was these settings, rather than the relics themselves, which led to their being sent up to the Tower of London, the national collection point. From Bath Abbey, for example, came the girdle of St. Peter and the combs of Mary Magdalene, St. Dorothy, and St. Margaret; from Bristol, God's coat, Our Lady's smock, "part of God's supper on the Lord's table, part of the stone [of the manger] in which was born Jesus in Bethlehem"; from Bury St. Edmunds, "the coals that Saint Lawrence was toasted withal, the parings of S. Edmund's nails, S. Thomas of Canterbury's pen knife and his boots"; from Dover, "Malchus' ear that Peter struck off as it is written"; from Reading, "the holy dagger that killed king Henry [VI], and the holy knife that killed saint Edward [the Martyr]."[4]

One piece of booty seized during this crusade against the monasteries has particular relevance to a much later phase of London show business. Early in 1538 one of Cromwell's agents reported that in the course of dismantling and defacing the Cistercian abbey at Boxley, Kent,

I found in the image of the Rood called the Rood of Grace, the which heretofore hath been held in great veneration of people, certain engines and old wire, with old rotten sticks in the back of the same, that did cause the eyes of the same to move and stare in the head thereof like unto a living thing; and also the nether lip in likewise to move as though it should speak; which, so famed was not a little strange to me and others that was present at the plucking down of same. . . . [I] did convey the said image unto Maidstone this present Thursday, then being the market day, and in the chief of the market time, did show it openly unto all the people there being present, to see the false, crafty, and subtle handling thereof, to the dishonour of God, and illusion of the said people.[5]

Later this magical cross was brought to London, where "it was made to perform again outside St. Paul's, while Bishop Hilsey of Rochester preached to the people and exposed the abuse; after which he broke up the mechanism and flung the image among the people, who further broke it to pieces."[6] Centuries later, the descendants of these same Londoners would willingly pay sixpence or more to see improved models of this primitive automaton in action.

During the long winnowing process at the Tower, the miscellaneous venerable relics, including an incalculable number of rotting saints' and martyrs' bones, were wrenched from their reliquaries and thrown away. But it is not improbable that a certain number of relics—one or more of Our Lady's and Mary Magdalene's girdles, Malchus's ear, or reasonable facsimiles thereof—were preserved, to find their way eventually into collectors' cabinets.

In spite of the general depredation, some London churches, including parish churches as well as Cromwell's primary targets, the monasteries and collegiate churches, managed to retain their treasures until the iconoclastic campaign resumed following the brief Romish interval under Mary Tudor. The richest collection was that of St. Stephen Walbrook, "kept," we are told, "in a little 'fosser' or chest covered with black and blue satin and containing twenty-two 'relics of God' and of his saints. Among them was a relic of the place where God appeared to St. Mary Magdalene, relics of St. Stephen, of the rock where the Lord spoke to Moses, of Mt. Calvary, a piece of the stone whereon

Christ's body was washed when taken from the Cross, a finger of one of the Holy Innocents, a piece of bone of one of the 11,000 virgins, and a piece of stone from the spot where Christ ascended to heaven."[7]

But soon after Elizabeth I's reign began, the last objects of veneration that had been used for "increase of lucre" had been disposed of, and along with them had gone not only the superb reliquaries which were themselves works of art but also most of the wall paintings, tapestries, statuary, and liturgical accessories that had made the pre-Reformation church a gallery of art as well as a museum. Such art as escaped mutilation or outright destruction then was merely reprieved, to become the victim of Puritans' hammers, whitewash brushes, and torches in a later epoch. What also remained for a while were the natural curiosities that the churches also exhibited, without direct reference to any biblical or later religious event but simply as evidence of the marvelousness of God's creation. At the very end of the sixteenth century, that indispensable chronicler of old London, John Stow, wrote:

I my selfe more then 70. yeares since haue seene in this church [St. Lawrence Jewry] the shanke bone of a man (as it is taken) and also a tooth of a very greate bignes hanged vp for shew in chaines of iron, vppon a pillar of stone, the tooth (being aboute the bignes of a mans fist) is long since conveyed from thence: the thigh or shanke bone of 25. inches in length by the rule, remayneth yet fastened to a post of timber, and is not so much to be noted for the length, as for the thicknes, hardnes and strength thereof, for when it was hanged on the stone pillar, it fretted with mouing the said pillar, and was not itself fretted, nor as seemeth, is not yet lightned by remayning drie: but where or when this bone was first found or discovered I haue not heard.[8]

Under the new dispensation, London churches evidently retained the spirit of rivalry that had pitted one order of friars against another, now taking the form of zeal to display the biggest and most astonishing natural curiosities, with special attention to the reputed Age of Giants. Of St. Mary Aldermanbury, Stow observed:

in the . . . cloyster is hanged and fastned a shanke bone of a man (as is said) very great and larger by three inches and a halfe then that which hangeth in S.Lawrence church in the Iury, for it is in length 28 inches and a halfe of assise, but not so hard and steely, like as the other, for the same is light and somewhat Porie and spongie. This bone is said to bee found amongst the bones of men remoued from the charnel house of Powles, or rather from the cloyster of Powls church, of both which reportes I doubt, for that the late Reyne Wolfe Stationer (who paid for the carriage of those bones from the charnell to the Morefieldes) tolde mee of some thousandes of

Carrie loades and more to be conueighed, whereof hee wondred, but neuer told of any such bone in eyther place to bee found, *neyther would the same haue beene easily gotten from him, if hee had heard thereof, except he had reserued the like for himselfe, being the greatest preseruer of antiquities in those partes for his time.*[9]

Already London was supplied with a few men who enthusiastically swept together the stuff of which museums are made.

But museums themselves still were far in the future, and in the meantime rarity-showing was thrown open to candidly commercial enterprise. The official Protestant desanctifying of relics, although ending the practice of veneration, had in no way diminished the people's innate hunger for marvels; it had only completed its secularization. This hunger in fact increased as, after the middle of the sixteenth century, English ships began to explore remote regions of the world and bring back tales and objects testifying to the existence of places and races formerly undreamed of, or at best merely the subject of unverified rumor. Now that edification was no longer involved, showmen were free to exploit the popular sense of wonder in its pure state, so to speak. In taking up where the monks had left off, they gradually broadened the scope of their shows to include anything marvelous without reference to its possible didactic value. One of the earliest records of a London exhibition dates from 1578, when a smith named Mark Scaliot showed, as proof of his skill, "a Lock, of iron, steel, and brass, of eleven several pieces, and a pipe key, all which weighed but one grain of gold. He also made a chain of gold, of forty-three links, which chain being fastned* to the lock and key, and put about a Flea's neck, the Flea drew them with ease. Chain, key, lock, and flea, weighed but one grain and a half."[10] All this proved was that a certain man was capable of a certain kind of scarcely credible mechanical achievement; but, in the developing atmosphere of confidence in human capability, that was enough to guarantee the gifted artisan a hearing or, more precisely, a showing.

By 1611 Londoners had at their disposal an impressive range of sights, as Henry Peacham testily remarked:

Why doe the rude vulgar so hastily post in a madnesse
To gaze at trifles, and toyes not worthy the viewing?
And thinke them happy, when may be shew'd for a penny
The Fleet-streete Mandrakes, that heauenly Motion of
 Eltham,
Westminster monuments, and Guildhall huge Corinaeus,
That horne of Windsor (of a Unicorne very likely,)

* The intrusive and often pedantic "[*sic*]" will be used sparingly in these pages. Generally speaking, irregularities of spelling and grammar in quoted matter may be assumed to occur in the original documents.

The caue of Merlin, the skirts of old Tom a Lincolne,
King Johns sword at Linne, with the cup the Fraternity
   drinke in,
The Tombe of Beauchampe, and sword of Sir Guy a War-
   wicke:
The great long Dutchman, and roaring Marget a Barwicke,
The Mummied Princes, and Caesars wine yet; 'Douer,
Saint James his Ginney Hens, the Cassawarway moreouer,
The Beauer i' the Parke (strange beast as ere any man saw)
Downe-shearing willowes with teeth as sharpe as a hand-
   saw.
The Lance of John a Gaunt, and Brandons still i' the Tower;
The fall of Niniue, with Norwich built in an hower.
King Henries slip-shoes, the sword of valiant Edward.
The Couentry Boares-shield, and fire-workes seen but to
   bedward.[11]

It would be a wearisome task to try to identify all these sights, and indeed a few probably could not now be identified at all; but this early Amusement Guide to London makes plain enough that the show-going subjects of James I had an adequate variety of objects of historical, legendary, scientific, and mechanical interest to occupy their attention and empty their purses. In the same year that Peacham wrote, Shakespeare had a play performed before the king at Whitehall in the course of which a jester named Trinculo stumbled upon a grotesque half-man half-beast on the island of Bermuda: "A strange fish!" he exclaimed. "Were I in England now, as once I was, and had but this fish painted, not a holiday fool there but would give a piece of silver; there would this monster make a man; any strange beast there makes a man; when they will not give a doit to relieve a tame beggar, they will lay out ten to see a dead Indian." Ten years later, and in the same vein, Henry Farley, in a "poetic effusion" urging repairs to old St. Paul's, contrasted the public's parsimony in good causes with what it spent for amusements:

> To see a strange out-landish Fowle,
> A quaint Baboon, an Ape, an Owle,
> A dancing Beare, a Gyants bone,
> A foolish Ingin move alone,
> A Morris-dance, a Puppit play,
> Mad Tom to sing a Roundelay,
> A woman dancing on a Rope,
> Bull-baiting also at the Hope;
> A Rimers Jests, a Juglers cheats,
> A Tumbler shewing cunning feats,
> Or Players acting on the Stage,
> There goes the bounty of our Age;
>   But unto any pious motion,*
>   There's little coine, and lesse devotion.[12]

Throughout the seventeenth century, gentlemen joined with artisans, tradesmen, apprentices, laborers, and their families in frequenting the taverns and fairs where such entertainments could be seen. But in the century's earlier decades there was little sign of an equivalent cluster of exhibitions appealing to the nominally more sophisticated interests of the handful of scientific and artistic amateurs who were appearing among the aristocracy and higher gentry. In this respect, as in others, the Renaissance came late to England.[13] There had been no counterpart of the fifteenth-century Jean de France, Duc de Berry, who had collected artistic rarities and books on a magnificent scale. In the sixteenth and early seventeenth centuries there still were no English equivalents of the French and Italian cardinals and dukes and the German princelings whose booty from conquests and the gifts of ambassadors and visiting sovereigns filled to overflowing the rooms set apart for them—*cabinets des curieux* in France, *Wunderkammern* or *Kunstkammern* in Germany.

Such private museums were status symbols above all. Hence their emphasis was on rare coins and medals, elaborately decorated objets d'art, armor, works of gold, silver, and glass—things that were obviously very costly. But this "magpiety," to borrow the art historian Francis Henry Taylor's word, often extended to materials more closely related to the developing scientific concerns of the age. Indeed, the multiplying of encyclopedic collections, not limited to objects of art, is a fairly accurate index of the spread of modern culture during the Renaissance. A typical cabinet or *Wunderkammer* comprised all manner of rarities that happened to be sent or attracted in its direction. Seldom was there any specialization. The abnormal, the strange, the rare, the exotic, the tour de force—all appealed to the indiscriminate sense of wonder, and therefore could be mixed together in a mad potpourri without reference to kind. Classification, if attempted at all, went only so far as to group separately "natural curiosities" (including "animal" ones, which in turn embraced ethnographical materials), antiquities, coins, pictures, works of art in other media, and "artificial" rarities—"artificial" here being used in a sense now obsolete, to designate manmade objects that were the products of great skill or ingenuity.

Nor were most collectors disposed to ask many searching questions, such as those bearing on authenticity, probability, or provenance. A given curio was what tradition or the inventive imagination said it was. But even while credulity continued to reign, the

* Evidently a pun. "Motion," as will be seen in Chapter 4, meant "puppet show" or "automaton" (the latter is possibly what the "foolish Ingin" of the fourth line alludes to). So the emphasis should rest on "pious."

ambiguous Faustian spirit which brooded over the Northern Renaissance was affecting some collectors with a zeal for fresh observation and analysis, for logical hypothesizing, liberated from what was considered to be the dogmatism, superstition, and abject veneration of ancient authority that survived from the Middle Ages.

Such was the mixed atmosphere in which the idea of the modern museum germinated in western Europe before the English began to collect on their own. By the last years of Elizabeth's reign there were at least enough collectors at work in England to earn the robust disrespect of Thomas Nashe, in his *Pierce Penilesse his Svpplication to the Divell* (1592):

I know many wise Gentlemen of this mustie vocation, who, out of loue with the times wherein they liue . . . will blow their nose in a boxe, & say it is the spettle that Diogenes spet in ones face . . . Let their Mistresse (or some other woman) giue them a feather of her fanne for her fauour, and if one aske them what it is, they make an answer, a plume of the Phenix, whereof there is but one in all the whole world. A thousand guegawes and toyes haue they in their chambers, which they heape vp together, with infinite expence, and are made beleeue of them that sell them, that they are rare and pretious thinges, when they haue gathered them vpon some dunghill, or rakte them out of the kennell by chance. I know one sold an old rope with foure knots on it for foure pound, in that he gaue it out, it was the length and breadth of Christs Tombe. Let a Tinker take a peece of brasse worth a halfe penie, and set strange stamps on it, and I warrant he may make it more worth to him of some fantasticall foole, than all the kettels that euer he mended in his life. This is the disease of our newfangled humorists, that know not what to doe with their welth. It argueth a very rusty witte, so to doate on worme-eated Elde.[14]

We cannot tell whether Nashe had any particular "newfangled humorist" in mind, but we know one or two by name in more serious contexts. The journal of the Duke of Stettin, who visited London in 1602, describes his visit to the cabinet of a wealthy man of affairs, Sir Walter Cope:*

Some crowns worn by the Queen in America, a number of shields and swords. A dagger entirely made of steel had a scabbard made wholly of black lac or Spanish wax. Further, two teeth of the sea-horse, the horn of a rhinoceros, was not long but bent upwards, also the tail with very coarse hair. Many strange worms, birds, and fishes, a salamander scolopendra, a little Indian bird phosphorescent by night; the celebrated little fish, Remoram, had scales almost square like a stone perch, a head like an eel-pout; also a cauda Delphini, and a mummy. We further saw many Indian manuscripts and books, a passport given by the King of Peru to the English, neatly written on wood, various strange cucumber plants. The musical instrument celebrated in ancient times, and called cymbalum, was round like a globe of brass or steel; when touched it gave forth a sound like a triangle, but it is not known how it was used in early times.[15]

If this, one of the earliest English cabinets, was smaller than those on the continent, it yielded little to them in miscellaneity. The characteristic emphasis of English collectors at this time, however, as Nashe suggested, was antiquarian rather than scientific. It is true that Cope's contemporary, Sir Robert Bruce Cotton, went in for natural curiosities to some extent; he possessed, for example, a "fossilized skeleton of a colossal sea-fish." But, for reasons not dissimiliar to those of Italian antiquaries with their passion for the memorabilia of ancient Rome, as well as the special Protestant need to find a substitute for the now discredited worship of a past dominated by saints, Cotton concentrated on the relics of ancient pre-Christian Britain—coins, medals, inscribed stones, and, above all, manuscripts.

Alongside the antiquarian existed another product of the time, the virtuoso: an anglicized and expanded version of the Italian courtier, a gentleman-scholar dedicated to the pursuit of learning for its own sake as an ornament of the "courtly" character.[16] Deep though their interest was in the intellectual affairs suitable to the English-blooded Renaissance man, virtuosi were not themselves collectors at first, although the name came to be applied to collectors by the end of the seventeenth century. They were devoted to polite learning as found in books, not to the external world of nature and society as represented by things. But it was their intellectual curiosity as much as that of the antiquarians and, more recently, the "natural philosophers" which fed the English appetite for collecting that became acute by the time of the Restoration.

John Evelyn belonged, like a number of his contemporaries, to all three communities of scientists, antiquarians, and virtuosi. Not himself a collector of first consequence except for the specimens he cultivated in his extensive garden and arboretum, he reveals in his diary how strong an impetus the presence of so many opulent treasure-houses on the continent lent to the new English inclination. It is significant that in the course of all he says about the collections he inspected during his extended continental tour in the 1640s, Evelyn makes no comparison with any back home. Although he must at this time have known of Cope's and Cotton's, and perhaps also of the beginnings of the museum-making urge at the universities, his diary im-

* Called "Kopf" in the original, this man was formerly identified—by G. B. Harrison—as Sir Robert Cotton. But Cotton's biographer, Hope Mirrlees, makes a persuasive case for Cope. (*A Fly in Amber: Being an Extravagant Biography of the Romantic Antiquary Sir Robert Bruce Cotton*, London, 1962, pp. 73–74.)

plies that he was on a journey of continual discovery. In Italy and elsewhere—in the Low Countries and France, but above all at Venice, Florence, and Rome—Evelyn visited scores of places where accumulated curiosities of various kinds were to be seen. There were, of course, the churches, which maintained here, as they no longer did in England, their immemorial character of museums, enriched by the precious treasures, the jewels and gold and silver objects that had accrued to the church over the centuries as a tribute to her supremacy over the affairs of men. These were for the most part locked away in strong rooms, but the merely extraordinary exhibits—holy relics and natural rarities—were open to public gaze.

In addition to the churches, there were the collections of cardinals, aristocrats, wealthy merchants, and savants. Although the common people were excluded, these were normally accessible to the growing number of travelers who belonged to the international freemasonry of the curious-minded. Typified by Evelyn himself, these men went from city to city on a regular round of collections, carrying printed itineraries and guidebooks which were compiled for them and whose very existence testifies to the prevalence of the custom. Indeed, Evelyn derived many of his descriptions from such books. By this time, specialization was well under way. In addition to the collections without fixed limitations, which remained in the majority, there were many devoted to antiquities and works of art, and others (some 250 had been counted in Italy alone in the preceding century) which concentrated on natural history. Some collections observed regular hours of opening; some charged a small admission fee; some displayed sets of rules and regulations governing the behavior of visitors. In short, Evelyn, like other English travelers on the continent, discovered the vital role that cabinets could play in a nation's cultural life, serving as informal centers where like-minded men of inquiring bent could meet, compare notes, exchange specimens, and, in effect, pursue their education. Such visitors from an island country that in recent times had had relatively little cultural intercourse with the nations of the continent must have envied the cosmopolitanism of this great chain of well-filled cabinets, where humanistic and scientific learning knew no national boundaries.

In England there were a number of reasons, apart from the desire to participate more fully in European intellectual life, why conditions now were favorable for the planting of the museum idea. The increase of wealth and leisure among the educated encouraged them to take up collecting as a worthy avocation. As on the continent, a livelier sense of the past gave new impetus to the antiquarianism that had sprung up in the Elizabethan age. The broader the historical perspective, the broader the range of artifacts to be studied. At the same time, the zeal to collect specimens and rarities of nature was fed by the response to Baconian empiricism, which belatedly came into its own by mid-century. As naturalists in their search for scientific truth ceased to defer to the superstitious authority of fable and legend and the bookish authority of the ancients in matters relating to the physical world, they increasingly turned to observation and experiment. The first requisite for the systematic study of nature was availability of materials to be studied, and for this the cabinets and museums of continental collectors served as models for English endeavor.

In Evelyn's time, Oxford had more collectors than did London. His diary for 1654 describes the curiosities kept at the various colleges, notably at Wadham, where the "universaly Curious" Dr. John Wilkins kept adding to a collection that included a transparent aviary, automatons, a speaking figure, thermometers, magnets, optical devices, and, says Evelyn, "many other artificial, mathematical [i.e., mechanical], and Magical curiosities."[17]

Although London had fewer individual collectors than any comparable European capital or seat of learning, by the middle of the century it possessed what was widely regarded as the finest and largest natural history museum anywhere.[18] This was the famed "Tradescant's Ark," whose founder, John Tradescant, was a professional gardener successively in the employment of Lord Salisbury, Lord Wotton, and the Duke of Buckingham. In 1618 he had voyaged to Archangel with Sir Dudley Digges and brought back the first specimens of Russian flora known in England; two years later, he brought from Algiers, among other spoils, the first apricot trees to be planted in England. When, after Buckingham's assassination in 1628, Tradescant entered the service of James I, he settled at Turret House, South Lambeth, at the present site of Walberswick Street and Tradescant Road. Here he established a garden and museum, with the avowed intention of assembling and displaying every rarity "he can hear of in any place in Christendom, Turkey, yea, or the whole world." He kept up a voluminous correspondence with fellow gardeners "in forrin partes" who sent him specimens, and these donations were augmented, as the years passed, by plants and fruits brought to Lambeth by captains, ordinary sailors, and

1. Tradescant's house, Lambeth (engraving by J. T. Smith, 1773).

merchants newly returned from one of the Americas, the East Indies, or Cathay. The house and garden became one of the obligatory sights of London. Not only the king and queen came bearing gifts, but other noble benefactors as well, naturalists like John Ray and, of course, the ubiquitous Evelyn.

Izaak Walton's allusion to the museum in *The Compleat Angler* illustrates the fascination it had for natural history enthusiasts. Writing of the marvels attributed to various sea monsters, Walton—by trade a London ironmonger—remarks how Tradescant's rarities sometimes appeared to substantiate the hitherto unverified assertions of travelers:

I know, we Islanders are averse to the belief of these wonders: but there be so many strange Creatures to be now seen (many collected by John Tradescant . . .) as may get some belief of some of the other wonders I mentioned. I will tell you some of the wonders that you may now see, and not till then believe, unless you think fit.

You may there see the Hog-fish, the Dog-fish, the Dolphin, the Cony-fish, the Parrot-fish, the Shark, the Poyson-fish, sword-fish, and not only other incredible fish! but you may there see the Salamander, several sorts of Barnacles, of Solan Geese, the bird of Paradise, such sorts of Snakes, and such birds-nests, and of so various forms, and so

wonderfully made, as may beget wonder and amusement in any beholder: and so many hundred of other rarities in that collection, as will make the other wonders I spake of, the less incredible; for, you may note, that the waters are natures store-house, in which she locks up her wonders.[19]

Tradescant's son, also named John, contributed to the collection bearskin garments, wampum girdles, tobacco pipes, "a Bracelet made of thighes of Indian flyes," and Powhatan's "habit all embroidered with shells," which he acquired on an expedition to Virginia in 1637. The next year he succeeded to the ownership of the Ark on the death of his father. The *Musaeum Tradescantium* that he published in 1656 was the first printed catalogue of a British collection. Omitting the hundreds of "whole birds," "four-footed beasts," fishes, shells, reptiles, fossils, stones, fruits, and roots with which the pages abound, these were some of the Tradescant treasures, a fair representation of what was deemed collectible and worthy of preservation in the mid-seventeenth century:

"Mechanick artificiall Works in Carvings, Turnings, Sowings, and Paintings": carvings in coral, amber, agate; miniatures (such as a cherrystone holding ten dozen tortoise shell combs); "flea chains of silver and gold with 300 links a piece and yet but an inch long"; a "nest of 52 wooden-cups turned within each other as thin as paper"; a set of chessmen in a peppercorn turned in ivory.

"Variety of Rarities": a circumcision knife of stone; "Blood that rained in the Isle of Wight"; a piece of stone from the Oracle of Apollo; "a Brazen-ball to warme the Nunnes hands"; "a Trunion of Capt: Drake's Ship"; "an Orange gathered from a Tree that grew over Zebulon's Tombe"; "a choice piece of perspective in a black Ivory case."

"Warlike instruments": China armor, "Tamahack, 6 sorts"; German poleaxes; "Ginny [Guinea] Drum made of one piece"; poisoned daggers and arrows; "a Damascus knife perfum'd in the casting."

"Utensils": "Gurgolets to poure water into their [whose?] mouthes without touching it"; "an Umbrella"; "a copper Letter-case an inch long, taken in the Isle of Ree with a Letter in it, which was swallowed by a Woman, and found."

. . . All these, and "a natural Dragon, above two inches long," "two feathers of the Phoenix tayle," a white blackbird, and a "dodar, from the Island Mauritius; it is not able to flie being so big."[20]

At his death in 1662, the younger Tradescant left the "closet of Rarities" to his wife and, upon her death, to either of the universities. Mrs. Tradescant immediately was sued by the antiquarian-astrologer-solicitor Elias Ashmole, a graduate of Oxford, who maintained that her husband had bequeathed the rarities to him. The Court of Chancery decided in his favor, although allowing her to retain the museum during her lifetime. A sordid struggle ensued, in the course of which Ashmole alleged, apparently with some justification, that Mrs. Tradescant was selling valuable specimens to collectors. He built a house next to the Ark and met her public defamations with a campaign of harassment, with the result that in 1674 he was able to move all the collection, except for the pictures, to his own house. Four years later the distracted widow drowned herself in her pond, and Ashmole acquired the pictures as well. Pursuant to a pledge he had made to the University of Oxford, in 1677 he delivered the whole collection to that institution, which housed it in a building expressly designed for it. Most of its contents were dispersed among various other Oxford collections during the nineteenth century, but a select few continue to be shown in the "Tradescant lobby" of the museum which bears Ashmole's name. The inscription on the family tomb (next to the grave of Captain Bligh) in the churchyard of St. Mary Lambeth summa-

rizes with a touch of period wit the Tradescants' claim to lasting remembrance as their contemporaries saw it:

Know stranger ere thou pass beneath this stone
Lye John Tradescant grandsire father son:
The last dy'd in his spring, the other two
Liv'd till they travell'd Art and Nature through;
As by their choice Collections may appear,
Of what is rare in land in sea in air;
Whilst they (as Homer's Iliad in a nut)
A world of wonders in one closet shut
These famous antiquarians that had been
Both Gardiners to the Rose and Lily Queen,
Transplanted now themselves sleep here, and when
Angels shall with their trumpets waken men,
And fire shall purge the world, these hence shall rise,
And change this Garden for Paradise.

D3-✳-Ɛꓷ

By the closing years of the seventeenth century, the activities of the Royal Society, chartered in 1662, had spread interest in science beyond the elite circle of the virtuosi. The society's membership and the mixed character of its widely distributed correspondents had proved that no heavy erudition was necessary to share in the pleasures of scientific demonstration and speculation—that it was an intellectual game any amateur of some education, wealth, and leisure could play. Making cabinets of rarities and performing experiments with newly devised apparatus became as much the sign of a cultivated Londoner as attending the playhouse or gathering with wits at one of the modish coffeehouses. Periodicals like John Dunton's *Athenian Gazette,* a question-and-answer paper on scientific as well as superstitious topics, and hundreds of popularized books catered to this audience that sought to mingle amusement with instruction.

Situated as it was at a crossroads of the sea traffic between western Europe and the exotic lands of the southern and western hemispheres, the port of London was an unsurpassed place to inspect and obtain the materials with which cabinets were filled. In 1664 Evelyn saw a collection of rarities sent in East Indiamen by Jesuits in Japan and China and now being transshipped on its way to their order in Paris. It was, he declared, "such a Collection . . . as in my life I had not seene." Among the items were rhinoceros' horns, gorgeous costumes, fans, drugs, and pictures, including some "rarely painted on a sort of gumm'd Calico transparant as glasse."[21] Londoners were advantageously located, also, to importune outward-bound travelers to remember the collector at home. The spirit of every man of science intent on forming a collection was expressed by the words of the herbalist James Petiver, whom we shall meet in a moment: "I humbly entreat that all practitioners in Physick, Sea-Surgeons or other curious persons, who travel into foreign countries, will be pleased to make collections for me of whatever plants, shells, insects &c they shall meet with, preserving them according to directions that I have made so easie as the meanest capacity is able to perform, the which I am ready to give to such as shall desire them."[22]

Several sources attest how numerous private museums had become by Queen Anne's time. The Leeds antiquarian and collector Ralph Thoresby periodically traveled to London, partly on business but mainly in pursuit of his absorbing hobby. In the 1670s his diary seldom mentions such cabinets, but about the turn of the century references to them become commonplace. Another sure evidence of the popularity of curio collecting was the appearance of its materials in the ordinary channels of commerce. In the middle of the century, Evelyn had noted the existence, at Amsterdam, Paris, and elsewhere, of shops supplying collectors with coins, medals, and other antiquities and the treasure trove brought back by explorers and merchants. One such shop, in Paris, was called "Noahs-Arke, where are to be had for mony all the Curiosities naturall or artificial imaginable, Indian or Europan, for luxury or Use, as Cabinets, Shells, Ivorys, Purselan [porcelain], Dried fishes, rare Insects, Birds, Pictures, & a thousand exotic extravagances."[23] Although there seemingly was as yet no shop like this in London, as early as 1664 a ready-made collection was offered for sale, composed, as the title of the catalogue put it, of "many Natural Rarities, with great Industry, Cost, and Thirty Years' Travel in Foraign Countries, Collected by Robert Hubert alias Forges, Gent. and Sworn Servant to His Majesty." Hubert alias Forges, unknown by either name to the *Dictionary of National Biography,* displayed his collection daily at "the place called the Musick-House, at the Miter, near the West End of St. Paul's Church." Among its contents were

a mummy; a giant's thigh-bone, more than four feet in length, found in Syria: a haget, that sleeps for six months; it is a creature of the island Mayonto in the lake Yondarro: the hornes of a dog of a land near China: the ribb of a Triton or Mereman, taken by Captain Finney on the shoutts [rapids?] of Brazil, 500 leagues from the Maine: the vein of the tongue of that whale, that was taken up at Greenwich a little before Cromwel's death: a manucodiata or bird of Paradise with

feet, for it hath great feet, to shew that it perches on trees in a land as yet unknown, for they are never seen alive, but are always found dead in the Malaccos Islands, by reason of a continual wind that bloweth six months one way and six months the other way, and because of their sharp head, little body, and a great feathered tayle, they are blown up so high that they fall dead in another climate or country: a pelican's head, bill, and bag, to prove that it is a water-fowle; he does not make himself to bleed a purpose for his young ones, but by accident, by carrying of shell-fishes in his thin bag makes it to bleed: a great crocodile, given by noble Squire Courtene, a lover of vertue and ingenuity.

Hubert, already in full command of the colorful language that would enliven London show business for the next two centuries, forbore specifying many additional rarities in his collection, but promised that if he did "sell them to any noble-minded party, he then, God willing, will write at large a more ample declaration, to the expression of each thing in particular, to honour that vertuous person that shall buy them!"[24]

The history of the trade in curios can never be adequately narrated, because apart from occasional auction catalogues the dealers left few records. But it is certain, at least, that parallel with the commerce in exotic animals and birds which served the scattering of noblemen and wealthy gentlemen who kept small menageries and aviaries on their estates, there sprang up, toward the end of the seventeenth century, a similar trade in inanimate objects suitable for cabinets. An advertisement published in 1700 reveals that one early device for selling rarities to collectors—a nice indication both of the social standing of the clientele at this time and of the tact necessary when they were invited to a commercial transaction—was a combination raffle and sale disguised as a social occasion. At the White Head inn facing the Haymarket was "a collection of several curiosities to be sold and raffled for . . . every Monday and Friday . . . those days being appointed the public raffling-days, besides a great variety of rarities: and to entertain the nobility and gentry (who, the undertakers hope, will countenance them with the honour of their company) there shall be on Wednesday the 14th instant (Jan.) a concert of musick by the best performers; and if all these diversions please such for whom they are intended, there shall be from time to time great additions made."[25]

Among the first London dealers in rarities was a Charing Cross cutler named Campe, who filled two rooms with antiquities and what the German bibliophile Zacharias von Uffenbach, visiting London in 1710, described as "an extremely elegant cabinet of coins" and "a superabundance of statues . . . on var-nished wooden pedestals. . . . I believe," he said, "that there were as many as 200 to 250 of all kinds of statuettes, idols, 'utensilibus' and other such things, all of which we looked at with much pleasure." Campe's prices, however, were "monstrous," and the visitor doubted whether all the objects were genuine.[26]

Hubert himself did not have to wait long for a buyer. The year after he advertised (1665), his collection was bought to form the basis of the "repository" the Royal Society established at Gresham House. To it was added a large assortment of contributions by various individual members. The inventory of the collection as described in Nehemiah Grew's printed catalogue (1681) makes clear that this first, and for a long time only, institutional collection in London was no more rigorous in its principles of selection and exclusion than any private one. It abounded in specimens that were, to put it mildly, absurdly identified, or, if correctly named, of no conceivable scientific or antiquarian significance. Ned Ward, writing as "the London Spy" at the turn of the century, described a tour of the repository, which he called a "Ware-House of Aegyptian Mummies, Old Musty Skeletons, and other Antiquated Trumpery": magnets, "a parcel of Shell-Flies almost as big as Lobsters, Arm'd with Beaks as big as those of Jack-Daws," "an Aviary of Dead Birds, Collected from the Extream parts of Europe, Asia, Africa, and America, amongst which was an East-Indian Owl, a West-India Bat, and a Bird of Paradise"; "sundry sort of Serpents" including rattlesnakes, crocodiles, and alligators; "Skeleton[s] of Men, Women, and Monkeys, Birds, Beasts, and Fishes; Abortives put up in Pickle, and abundance of other Memorandums of Mortality." These "Rusty Reliques and Philosophical Toys" were explained by the "Elaboratory-keeper," a "Raree-Show Interpreter . . . who, like the crooked Orator to the Abby-Tombs, made a Notable Harangue upon every Bauble in this Store-House."[27]

Von Uffenbach was no more favorably impressed by the museum's contents, its condition, or its curator. Like many foreigners, he had been led to entertain an "exalted idea" of the collection by reading Grew's catalogue and the *Philosophical Transactions*. But he was amazed to discover "how wretchedly all is now ordered. . . . It consists of what appear to be two long narrow chambers, where lie the finest instruments and other arts (which Grew describes), not only in no sort of order or tidiness but covered with dust, filth, and coal-smoke, and many of them broken and utterly

ruined. If one inquires for anything, the operator who shows strangers round . . . will usually say: 'A rogue had it stolen away,' or he will show you pieces of it, saying: 'It is corrupted or broken'; and such is the care they take of things! Hardly a thing is to be recognized, so wretched do they all look."[28] On the whole, it is doubtful if the nation gained much when the decrepit collection was presented to the British Museum in 1779.

ᴆᴣ✳ᴈᴅ

Native visitors were more enthusiastic about some of the principal private collections in London. Once Evelyn had acquired the taste on the continent, his admiration of varied and rich cabinets never cooled, and he continued to inspect them to the end of his life. In 1690, when he was seventy years old, he wrote of one London cabinet that it was "doubtlesse one of the most perfect assemblys of rarities that can be any where seene."[29] This was the accumulation made over the considerable part of a lifetime by William Courten (1642–1702), who had inherited the collections of his father (the "noble Squire Courtene" who gave Hubert his crocodile) and his grandfather, members of a family of rich traders and colonizers in the West Indies. Unfortunately, along with their rarities the younger Courten inherited his father's and grandfather's tangled finances, with the result that to satisfy their creditors, he renounced his claims on their estate and left the country. For the next twenty-five years he traveled extensively throughout Europe on what was, in effect, one long collecting expedition. About 1684 he returned to England under the assumed name of William Charleton and settled himself and his curiosities in ten rooms in the Temple. The naturalist John Ray, who spent a week in 1687 inspecting the foreign seeds and nuts, called the museum "a repository of rare and select objects of natural history and art so curiously and elegantly arranged and preserved that you could hardly find the like in all Europe."[30] Thoresby, visiting the Temple eight years later, agreed. Charleton, he recorded, "very courteously showed me his museum, which is perhaps the most noble collection of natural and artificial curiosities, of ancient and modern coins and medals, that any private person in the world enjoys; it is said to have cost him 7,000*l.* or 8,000*l.* sterling; there is, I think, the greatest variety of insects and animals, corals, shells, petrifactions, &c. that ever I beheld. . . . But," he concluded, "before I was half satisfied an unfortunate visit from the Countess of Pembroke, and other ladies from court, prevented further queries, &c."[31]—sufficient evidence of the social cachet which the vogue of visiting cabinets enjoyed, following the example of royalty at Tradescant's.

Another prominent London collector of the time was James Petiver, who began as an apothecary's apprentice at St. Bartholomew's Hospital, later setting up in the same occupation in Aldersgate Street and acting as apothecary to the Charterhouse.[32] Sir Hans Sloane, though conceding that "he had taken great pains to gather together the productions of nature in England, and by his correspondents and acquaintance all over the world procured, I believe, a greater quantity than any man before him," added that "he did not take equal care to keep them, but put them into heaps, with sometimes small labels of paper, where they were many of them injured by dust, insects, rain &c."[33] Petiver disappointed Von Uffenbach as keenly as did the Royal Society's repository. This man, whose collection was known throughout the world of learning, turned out to be "wretched both in looks and actions and he had no parts, speaking very poor and deficient Latin and scarce able to string a few words together. . . . Everything is kept in true English fashion in prodigious confusion in one wretched cabinet and in boxes. . . . He offers all foreigners who come to him a sample of his collection; but he takes care to ask a vast sum for it, so I declined with thanks."[34]

The difference in character between Charleton and Petiver is exemplified by the way they disposed of their respective collections. Charleton, dying in 1702, bequeathed his to Sloane, whom he had first met in Montpellier many years before and with whom he had kept up a busy correspondence during his years of exile. Petiver, dying in 1718, was not so generous. Sloane, who knew the worth of his collection no matter how disorderly it was, had to pay £4,000 for it.[35]

With the Charleton and Petiver collections, among others, added to his own immense one, which he had begun during the year and a half he spent in his late twenties in Jamaica as the governor general's physician, Sir Hans Sloane (as he became in 1716) emerged as the first collector in London.[36] He divided his long life between the practice of medicine and the enlargement and care of his museum, which was housed first at his home in Great Russell Street and, after 1742, in the large Manor House in Cheyne Walk. There, in nine spacious rooms, one of them 110 feet long, were assembled 79,575 objects, including some 32,000 medals and coins and 12,506 "vegetables, as seed, gums,

woods, roots, &c," in addition to the contents of an enormous herbarium. According to Sir Gavin de Beer, Sloane's biographer, "Taken as a whole, with all the subjects which they covered, Sloane's collections were more extensive than any others of the time, although some may and did excel his in particular fields. In natural history, Sloane's collection was probably unique."[37]

The diary entry of a visitor, Sir Erasmus Philipps, gives a fair idea of the scope of the collection while it was still in Bloomsbury (1730):

vast No. of Curiosities in the Animal, Vegetable, and Mineral way; a Swedish owl, 2 Crain Birds, a dog; vast No. of Agats, an Owel in one, exact, orange; Tobacco in others, Lusus Naturae; an opal here; Catalogue of Books, ab^t 40 volumes; 250 large Folios, Horti Sicci; Butterflies in Nos.; 23,000 Medals; Inscriptions, one exceeding fair from Caerleon; A foetus cut out of a Woman's belly, thought she had the dropsy; lived afterwards, and had several Children; Fine Injections of the Brain by Rhuish of Amsterdam.[38]

Von Uffenbach's depreciation of the English museum-keeping habit ("prodigious confusion") was not applicable to Sloane, who took pains to classify, arrange, and protect his specimens as systematically as a collector blessed with scientific intelligence and adequate money could. When Pehr Kalm, Linnaeus' pupil, visited Chelsea he was impressed by the advanced methods of preservation, mounting, and display. The insects were preserved in boxes, with wooden sides and glass top and bottom; the stuffed birds "often stood fast on small bits of board as naturally as if they still lived"; the West Indian hummingbirds were "set in their nests under glass as though they had been living."[39]

Like modern scientific museums, Sloane's was for use as well as mere display; it was a working institution, to which other scientists as well as interested amateurs were freely admitted. "Very friendly," noted Sir Erasmus Philipps, "and seemed to take delight in shewing his things." The Gentleman's Magazine for July 1748 preserves an account of a visit the Prince and Princess of Wales made to the collection in that year, four years before Sloane, "antient and infirm," died at the age of ninety-three. Nor did Sloane ever regard the collection as finished; he was constantly acquiring new specimens. Among his incidental sources was the young journeyman printer Benjamin Franklin, who wrote to him in 1725: "Sir, Having lately been in the Northern Parts of America, I have brought from hence a Purse made of the Stone Asbestus, a Piece of the same Nature, and a Piece of Wood, the Pithy Part of which is of the same Nature, and call'd by the Inhabitants, Salamander Cotton. As you are noted to be a Lover of Curiosities, I have inform'd you of these; and if you have any Inclination to purchase them, or see 'em, let me know your Pleasure by a Line directed for me at the Golden Fan in Little Britain, and I will wait upon you with them."[40] In the original manuscript of his memoirs, however, Franklin, perhaps forgetting that he had written the letter or merely neglecting to reveal who had taken the initiative, said that "Sir Hans Sloane heard of it [the asbestos purse], came to see me, and invited me to his House in Bloomsbury Square; where he show'd me all his Curiosities, and persuaded me to let him add that to the Number, for which he paid me handsomely."[41] The purse is now to be seen in the Natural History Museum, South Kensington.

But not even the great Sir Hans Sloane was exempt from the ridicule to which virtuosi and collectors had been subjected from their first appearance in Nashe's day. The poet Edward Young viewed Sloane's professional enthusiasm from the distant, distorting perspective of Augustan decorum:

> But what in oddness can be more sublime
> Than Sloane, the foremost toyman of his time?
> His nice ambition lies in curious fancies:
> His daughter's portion a rich shell enhances;
> And Ashmole's baby-house is, in his view,
> Britannia's golden mine, a rich Peru!
> How his eyes languish! how his thoughts adore
> That painted coat which Joseph *never* wore!
> He shows, on holidays, a sacred pin,
> That touch'd the ruff that touch'd Queen Bess's chin.
> "Since that great dearth our chronicles deplore,
> Since that great plague that swept as many more,
> Was ever year unbless'd as this?" he'll cry;
> "It has not brought us one new butterfly!"[42]

This is not very good poetry. But it is typical of the less than reverential attitude which unscientific men of the Restoration and the early eighteenth century entertained toward collectors in general, failing to make the crucial distinction between true scholars of Sloane's breed and dilettantes who collected curiosities and played at being scientists because it was the fashionable thing to do. The latter stereotype had been molded as early as 1676, when Thomas Shadwell, in his play *The Virtuoso,* introduced the character of Sir Nicholas Gimcrack. Sir Nicholas reappears in one of Steele's *Tatler* papers (no. 216) as the virtuoso who bequeaths to various relatives, with appropriate explanations,

such items as (to his wife) "One box of butterflies, One drawer of shells, A female skeleton, A dried cockatrice"; and to others, crocodile's eggs, a hummingbird's nest, and "English weeds pasted on royal paper, With my large folio of Indian cabbage."[43]

Ned Ward pursued the theme in his *London Spy* when he wrote of a certain fictitious virtuoso:

He's a wonderful Antiquary, and has a Closet of Curiosities out-does Gresham-Colledge [i.e., the Royal Society]: He tells ye, that he has a Tooth-Pick of Epicurus, which he always us'd after Eating; it is made of the Claws of an American Humming-Bird; and is to be us'd like a Rake, and will pick four Teeth at once. He has Diogenes's Lanthorn which he carry'd about Athens at Noon-Day to seek for an Honest Man. He says he has some of Heraclitus's Tears, which drop'd from him in a hard Winter, and are Frozen into Christial; they are set in a Locket, and every time any Body looks upon it, they cannot forbear Weeping. Also a Ten-penny Nail drawn out of the Ark; and tho' it's Iron, toss it into a Tub of Water, and 'twill swim like a Feather; he pretends to have one of Judas's Thirty Pence; and every time he looks upon't, he is ready to Hang himself. A mighty Collection of these sort of Trinkets, he tells the World he's Master of, and some give Credit to his Ridiculous Romances.[44]

Such satire of witless collectors threads through the literature of the time. In *Gulliver's Travels* Swift has Gulliver, who has himself lately been a curiosity in Brobdingnag, leave that country with a collection of what, in the outside world with its different scale of magnitude, are unquestionable rarities—combs made from the stubble of the king's beard and a paring of the queen's thumbnail, a corn, large as a Kentish apple, cut from a maid of honor's toe, a servant's foot-long tooth.[45] One may well believe that Gulliver found a ready market for his collection when he returned to England on 3 June 1706.

As is true of most satire, however, there was a solid kernel of truth beneath the hyperbole. Von Uffenbach described the mishmash accumulated by Claudius du Puy, a French-Swiss calico-printer and "an extremely strange creature." Surely no set of rooms in London was crammed with a more miscellaneous assortment of curios. One selects almost at random from Von Uffenbach's lengthy inventory: "five very elegantly carved mother-of-pearl shells in black frames, on which the story of Lot in the case, etc. was excessively well depicted"; various idols, among them "a large wooden one with an ass's head, the body as hollow as a baker's oven"; "an elegant ship of Chariophyllis put together, about an ell long"; various urns; magnets; a snake skin sixteen feet long; the head of Oliver Cromwell (M. Du Puy was confident he could get sixty guineas for it);* ancient musical instruments; a goblet "on which were engraved in relief, with the most uncommon elegance, various Bible stories, such as those of Esther, Susanna, etc." Alongside this last, in Von Uffenbach's inventory at any rate, was "a marble Priapium an ell high." Still more medals, dirty and in no order whatsoever; twenty wax dolls, in nun's habits, made by the sisters of Brabant; a hollow walking stick containing not only a sword but a gun; "all kinds of snakes and beasts in spirit." Upstairs were a dozen waxwork figures, to which we will return in another connection. In still another room were "all kinds of plaster casts," two mummies, a portrait of Christ made of feathers (another product of the Brabant nunnery), a model of Christ's tomb, "also," concluded Von Uffenbach, "a prodigious quantity of all kinds of trifles and common articles, and, as I said before, all strewn about in great disorder."[46]

ᗡᕒ✳ᕒᗡ

Du Puy may have been among the first of the English breed of eccentric pack rats, but he was assuredly not the last. Collecting curious odds and ends just because they were "curious," without reference to any intellectual principle or purpose, became an ingrained habit on which no amount of satire could have its vaunted corrective effect. Cabinets—museums in embryo—were there to stay, and they multiplied throughout the eighteenth century. But ordinary citizens, those with no particular cultural or social credentials, seldom had an opportunity to visit the collections that were among the sights to which foreign visitors, among others, routinely repaired. Londoners' experience of curiosities was confined in general to those they could see at fairs and throughout the rest of the year at taverns, which, as the centers of middle-class social life and conversation, were the logical places where rarities could be displayed. Like the old friars, innkeepers competed with one another to obtain curious objects that would draw custom to their establishments. In the 1670s, we are told by a historian of London life writing more than a century later,

an elm plank was exhibited to the King and the credulous of London, which, being touched with a hot iron, invariably produced a sound resembling deep groans.† This sensible, and very irritable board, received numbers of noble visitors; and other boards, sympathising with their afflicted brother, demonstrated how much affected they might be by similar means. The publicans in different parts of the city immedi-

ately applied ignited metal to all the wood work of their houses, in hopes of finding sensitive timber; but I do not perceive any were so successful as the landlord of the Bowman tavern in Drury Lane, who had a mantle tree so extremely prompt and loud in its responses, that the sagacious observers were nearly unanimous in pronouncing it part of the same trunk which had afforded the original plank.[47]

When, during the Restoration, coffeehouses provided comfortable and sedate alternatives to taverns, they too became the sites of individual displays. It was only natural, therefore, that when large private collections of rarities become familiar places of London resort for the privileged, it was at a coffeehouse that the disadvantaged were provided with a cabinet of their own, which they could inspect whenever, and at whatever length, they desired, and for the mere price of a cup of coffee.

Don Saltero's coffeehouse was London's first public museum.[48] (By its use in this connection the very word "museum," hitherto restricted to a collection by and for the literati, was launched on a long career of vulgarization which ended only when it became a glib showman's term for any collection of two or more objects.) The cheeky Don, who was so dubbed by Admiral Sir John Munden, had begun life as plain James Salter. He had been bred to the conjoint trades of "scraper" (barber) and tooth-puller, both of which services were available gratis to his customers. Reputedly, he had been a servant of Sir Hans Sloane, and when he set up his coffeehouse business near Chelsea Church in 1695, Sloane gave him duplicates from his collection to embellish the room and draw customers. From 1708 to 1717 the coffeehouse was in Danvers Street, from which it then was transferred to a new building at 18 Cheyne Walk, where the present terrace house still bears the legend "Don Saltero's." Saltero's association with Sloane was now closer than ever, because the new premises adjoined the Manor House, which Sloane bought in 1712 and to which he was to move his own huge collection in 1742. Thus London's first popular museum and its greatest scientific collection were, for a number of years, next-door neighbors.

Few eighteenth-century London places of resort are better documented than Don Saltero's: naturally enough, because he was a master of publicity. In 1723, for example, he ran the following advertisement in *Mist's Weekly Journal:*

> Monsters of all sorts here are seen,
>   Strange things in nature as they grew so;
> Some relics of the Sheba Queen,
>   And fragments of the famed Bob Crusoe.

* This grisly relic was destined to reappear time and again down through the years; it might be called, except for the obvious unsuitability, the King Charles's head of the London show business. For twenty-five years after the Lord Protector's execution in 1658, his head was impaled atop Westminster Hall, until it was blown down in a storm and picked up by a sentry who secreted it, revealing its hiding place only on his deathbed. His family sold it to another, and somehow it arrived in Du Puy's possession. Later it was acquired by a "needy and careless man" named Samuel Russell, who exhibited it near Clare Market. From him it is said to have been bought by James Cox, proprietor of a famous museum to be visited in Chapter 5. (Cox's part in the story is suspect, because no contemporary record seems to involve him with Cromwell's head, and it is not the sort of exhibit he specialized in.) The head next went, for £230, to three brothers, one of whom was John Cranch, a self-taught painter from Devonshire. "His whole time and thoughts," wrote John Constable to a friend in 1799, "are occupied in exhibiting an old, rusty, fusty head, with a spike in it, which he declares to be the real embalmed head of Oliver Cromwell! Where he got it I know not; 'tis to be seen in Bond Street, at half a crown admittance." Each of the three brothers is reported to have met sudden death. The head then fell into other hands and finally was bequeathed to Cromwell's college, Sidney Sussex, Cambridge, near whose chapel it is now buried. The weight of modern scientific evidence is that this is indeed Cromwell's skull. Of course, there is a possibility that more than one head figured in the line of descent described. For the story in general, see the *Times,* 31 December 1874, and Antonia Fraser, *Cromwell: Our Chief of Men* (London, 1973), pp. 697–98. On the Cranches, see *John Constable's Correspondence,* ed. R. B. Beckett, II (Suffolk Records Society, IV, 1964), 23.

† "Groaning board" was among the first of the numerous contributions the London show trade made

2. Don Saltero's coffeehouse, Cheyne Walk, Chelsea (anonymous watercolor, ca. 1800).

Knick-knacks, too, range round the wall,
  Some in glass-cases, some on shelf;
But, what's the rarest sight of all,
  Your humble servant shows himself.[49]

Just as the Tradescant and Royal Society collections were dignified by printed catalogues, so, on a more popular level, was Don Saltero's. His sold for a modest threepence. Among the 293 rarities listed in the 1732 edition were a nun's penitential whip, four evangelists' heads carved on a cherry stone, "the Pope's infallible candle" (whatever that may have been), a starved cat found many years earlier between the walls of Westminster Abbey, William the Conqueror's flaming sword, Queen Elizabeth's strawberry dish, a cockatrice, petrified rain, barnacles, a rose from Jericho, a piece of "Asbestus" stone, a giant's tooth, belts of wampum, Muscovy gloves, a necklace made of Job's tears, "a whale's pizzle," "a wooden clock, with a man a mowing the grass from the top," manna from Canaan, a petrified oyster, a pair of garter snakes from South Carolina, an Indian ladies' back scratcher, a

fifteen-inch-long frog, and the horns of a "shamway" (chamois).[50]

Sir Richard Steele devoted the *Tatler* of 28 June 1709 (no. 34) to a visit to Don Saltero's:

When I came into the coffee-house, I had not time to salute the company, before my eye was diverted by ten thousand gimcracks round the room and on the ceiling. When my first astonishment was over, comes to me a sage of a thin and meagre countenance; which aspect made me doubt, whether reading or fretting had made it so philosophic: but I very soon perceived him to be of that sect which the ancients call Gingivistae, in our language, tooth-drawers. I immediately had a respect for the man; for these practical philosophers go upon a very rational hypothesis, not to cure, but to take away the part affected. My love of mankind made me very benevolent to Mr. Salter, for such is the name of this eminent barber and antiquary. Men are usually, but unjustly, distinguished rather by their fortunes, than their talents, otherwise this personage would make a great figure in that class of men which I distinguish under the title of Odd Fellows. But it is the misfortune of persons of great genius, to have their faculties dissipated by attention to too many things at once. Mr.

to the English vocabulary. The *Oxford English Dictionary* explains the term by quoting from Grew's *Anatomy of Plants* (1673/74): "The Planks commonly called Groaning-Boards, lately exposed, as a kind of Prodigy . . . were of Elm. The Aer-Vessels of this Wood, being . . . more ample, than in any other Timber . . . upon the application of the Red-hot-Iron . . . every vessel became, as it were a little Wind-Pipe . . . a great many of these pipes playing together, might make a kind of big or groaning noyse."

Salter is an instance of this: if he would wholly give himself up to the string, instead of playing twenty beginnings to tunes, he might before he dies play "Roger de Caubly" quite out. I heard him go through his whole round, and indeed I think he does play the "Merry Christ-Church Bells" pretty justly; but he confessed to me, he did that rather to show he was orthodox, than that he valued himself upon the music itself. . . . You see the barber in "Don Quixote," is one of the principal characters in the history, which gave me satisfaction in the doubt, why Don Saltero writ his name with a Spanish termination; for he is descended in a right line, not from John Tradescant, as he himself asserts, but from that memorable companion of the Knight of Mancha. . . . Though I go thus far in favour of Don Saltero's great merit, I cannot allow a liberty he takes of imposing several names (without my license) on the collections he has made, to the abuse of the good people of England; one of which is particularly calculated to deceive religious persons, to the great scandal of the well disposed, and may introduce heterodox opinions. He shows you a straw hat, which I know to be made by Madge Peskad, within three miles of Bedford; and tells you, it is Pontius Pilate's wife's chambermaid's sister's hat. To my knowledge of this very hat, it may be added, that the covering of straw was never used among the Jews, since it was demanded of them to make bricks without it. Therefore this is really nothing, but under the specious pretence of learning and antiquity, to impose upon the world.[51]

Among other visitors was Benjamin Franklin, who recorded in his memoirs that he went by water to Chelsea with "some Gentlemen from the Country" to see the "College" (Chelsea Hospital) and "Don Saltero's Curiosities."[52] Just before this (1723), the elderly Thoresby had made a visit of inspection which resulted in the condescending comment—a professional judging an upstart—that the collection was "really very surprising considering his circumstances as a coffee-man; but several persons of distinction have been benefactors."[53]

This, however, was only one man's opinion, and a biased one at that. In *Peregrine Pickle* (1751) Smollett—or his eponymous hero, at any rate—found Don Saltero's a cause of honest patriotic pride. Peregrine's friends visited a Dutch virtuoso whose pitiable cabinet was "decorated with a few paltry figures in plaister of Paris, two or three miserable landscapes, the skins of an otter, seal, and some fishes stuffed; and in one corner stood a glass-case, furnished with newts, frogs, lizzards, and serpants, preserved in spirits; a human foetus, a calf with two heads, and about two dozen of butterflies pinned upon paper." They had to listen to his "tedious commentary" for two hours, after which he "desired that the English gentlemen would frankly and candidly declare whether his cabinet, or that of mynheer Sloane, at London, was the most valuable. When this request was signified in English to the company, the painter instantly exclaimed, 'By the Lard! they are not to be named of a day. And as for that matter, I would not give one corner of Saltero's coffee-house, at Chelsea, for all the trash he hath shewn!'"[54]

The Don, unfortunately, did not live to appreciate this fresh burst of publicity from a writer who, in the early 1760s, lived around the corner, dined and drank punch at the house, and contributed curiosities to the museum.[55] Salter died in 1728. But his son-in-law continued to operate the coffeehouse for the next thirty years, after which it fell into other hands. It was finally closed in January 1799, and the sadly deteriorated collection was sold at auction for a paltry £50, a figure which contrasts most unfavorably with the £80,000 at which Saltero's benefactor valued his own.

Not far from Don Saltero's, in Jew's Row, stood the almost equally celebrated Chelsea Bun House.[56] On one Good Friday in the eighteenth century it was reputed to have attracted a riotous crowd of fifty thousand bun-hungry customers. Swift was there in 1711, expecting to enjoy one of those "Rrrrrrrrrare Chelsea buns" but, as he reported to Stella, getting only a stale one for his penny.[57] This was no ordinary bakery. Its interior was fitted up in a grotesque style, with a number of foreign clocks, and shelves and cases housing a mélange of natural and artificial rarities. Among these were a cardboard model of St. Mary Redcliffe Church in Bristol, celebrated for its association with the teen-aged literary forger Thomas Chatterton, but not very faithfully reproduced ("the upper towers, pinnacles &c resemble more an eastern mosque than a Christian church"); a model of the house itself, "with painted masquerade figures on two circles, turned round by a bird whilst on its perch in a cage at the back of the model"; a colored lead statue, eighteen inches high, of the Duke of Cumberland, taken after the Battle of Culloden; "a model of a British soldier, in the stiff costume of the same age, and some grotto-works"; a pair of lead grenadier guards, four feet high and weighing 200 pounds each; and a full-length portrait, by an unknown Italian artist, of Aurengzebe. Although many of the curios had disappeared long before, the Bun House survived until 1839.

On the other side of town, the Royal Swan tavern in Kingsland Road housed Adams's Museum. The proprietor was as devout a believer in advertising as Don

3. The Chelsea Bun House: exterior and interior (woodcuts, *Mirror of Literature,* 33, 1839, 209).

* Especially those near the wharves, where they would acquire conversation pieces from arriving seamen. Some of them must have built up considerable collections in this way. No record seems to exist of museum pubs in the eighteenth century, but we know of a number in the nineteenth, among them the Edinburgh Castle, Regent's Park; the Vale of Health, Hampstead Heath; the Bell and Mackerel, Mile End Road, which acquired the entire collection of a local naturalists' society; and the Hole in the Wall, Borough High Street. As late as the 1920s Charley Brown's Railway Tavern in Limehouse had a notable collection, and the Whitbread "theme" pubs of the present day continue the tradition in a fashion, although their exhibitions are ready-made, not built by accretion. See Charles E. Lawrence, "Public-House Museums," *The Ludgate* (1895?); copy at GL. (Short forms of citation used in these notes are explained on p. 512.)

Saltero had been, and his style was even more sprightly, if less informative. For half a dozen years about the middle of the century he ran advertisements in the London newspapers, of which this is a fair sample:

To be seen Gratis;
at Adams's, the Royal Swan, just in the middle of Kingsland Road, leading from Shoreditch-church, the greatest Collection of your oh Laws and Lackedazees! Oh Dears! Goodlacks! Bless mees! Oh la! Dear mees! Heyday! Believe me! Dear la! Ods me! Hah! Odso! Looke-there! Aye Eh! Hi! Oh! Umph! Well I vow! See there now! Well-a-day! So they say! Well to be sure! Nay-but-there! Dear Heart! For my Part! Pon-my-Honour! I protest! Pon-my-Word! I'm amaz'd! Pon-my-life! I'm surprised! Who would think it? I'm astonish'd! Who cou'd a thought it? Take my word for 't! I-never-see-the-like! Didn't I tell yo so? 'Tis-very-fine! That-ever-any-Body-saw! Rais'd chiefly by Presents, more than Purchase, being the generous Gifts of worthy Benefactors; Daily Increasing, Hourly a Pleasing, Accounts on Sight told, and Catalogues sold.

Note, a large quantity of oh Jemminies! Are lately arrived.[58]

We learn from the third edition of Adams's catalogue what this expletive-evoking collection consisted of in 1756. Among the 567 items were "Charles of Swedeland's boots; Harry the 8th's spurs; a tobacco stopper made from the royal oak King Charles was hid in at Boscobello Grove in Staffordshire; Vicar of Bray's clogs; caps, gloves, and shoes from Hudson's Bay; Mandarin's hubble-bubble from Gambroon in Persia; Chinese chop-sticks; Star and Garter made of Indian arrows, with a George in the middle; a corn-mill in a

bottle, that goes without wind, water, or clock work; thunderbolt stones, and many relics of the risings of 1715 and 1745."[59]

As at some other museums, there was a constant inflow of objects of timely interest. On 30 March 1752, only five days after the captain of a West Indiaman had been hanged at Execution Dock for murdering one of his crew, Adams announced the exhibition of "all the whole identic, authentick, original and real Rope that hang'd Capt. Lowry . . . together with one-third of the Cord that pinion'd his hands." This fresh relic evidently was on loan from its fortunate owner, who had been offered a guinea an inch for the rope, which "actually and effectually cured the Captain of the Head-Ach, Tooth-Ach, Ear-Ach, and Belly-Ach." But he was "happily endowed with such strict honour, honesty, and integrity, that he was not to be bribed by Lucre, Interest, nor Gain." How much, if anything, Adams charged for a view of the celebrated rope does not appear.[60]

There must have been a number of informal museums like these in the eighteenth century, adjuncts to coffeehouses or taverns* or, in some cases, separate entities. An instance of the latter is probably represented by a pamphlet tentatively dated 1766 and entitled *A Catalogue of a Great Variety of Natural and Artificial Curiosities, Now Exhibiting at the Large House, the Corner of Queen's Row, facing the Road, at Pimlico.* No proprietor's name is given. This was a typical miscellaneous show, composed mostly of birds, but containing also a few snakes, shrimps, monkeys, butterflies, insects, the model of a horse, two fragments of a painting from Herculaneum, a picture of the Nativity claimed to be by Dürer, a model of an Indian canoe, and—coming events cast their shadows before!—a 20,000-piece model of a "Chrystal Palace" "began for the late Emperor of Germany."[61]

Of these exhibitions of miscellaneous curiosities, the most inconsequential and charming, to judge from what small record it left, was a peripatetic one, "The Iron House" that was trundled from place to place in the greater London area in 1750–1755. This was a caravan whose roof, ends, and sides were covered with plate iron. On the roof was a pigeon house, and elsewhere on the outside of the premises, a cage containing an owl, a hawk, and a pigeon living in perfect amity, additional cages of singing birds, and a "Turkey gun" and several other kinds of firearms. The room inside was equipped with sash windows, a clock, a cooking jack, and a fireplace, and on its walls were engravings of Versailles, Blenheim, Venice, and the Battle of Culloden. The proprietor and occupant was one "Batchelor Dick," who also had mastered the art of chatty advertising; he kept interest in his mobile exhibition alive by such remarks as "God knows where it goes next, for the Batchelor can't tell."[62]

By the middle of the century, therefore, the cabinets of the virtuosi had been, if not exactly duplicated, then at least roughly imitated for the delectation of a larger

4. The Iron House (woodcut, *Mirror of Literature,* 32, 1838, 441).

public. For every nobleman and savant who was given a tour of Sloane's celebrated collection there were thousands of middle-class citizens, including gentlemen of the rank of Steele and professional men like Smollett, who examined the curios over a cup of coffee and a pipe at Don Saltero's. No doubt there were many from the trading and artisan class as well. The filter-down process which was to characterize so many aspects of the London museum and exhibition trade in the next century was well under way.

From Cabinets to Museums, II: 1750–1800

2

Precisely at the midpoint of the century, on 29 December 1750 and 1 January 1751, Samuel Johnson devoted two numbers of *The Rambler* to the virtuoso.[1] Three quarters of a century had elapsed since Shadwell had written his play about Sir Nicholas Gimcrack, and in the interval scores of satirists and moralists had had their repetitious say about the type which the character represented; yet the subject remained timely—evidence enough of how persistent was the enthusiasm for collecting in this age of enlightenment.

In the first of the *Rambler* papers, no. 82, Johnson, writing in the person of "Quisquilius," the self-described "most laborious and zealous virtuoso that the present age has had the honour of producing," recalls that he was a collector from earliest childhood. When he came into his inheritance as a landowner he collected his rent from farmers in the form of butterflies ("till I had exhausted the papilionaceous tribe"), earthworms ("I have three species . . . not known to the naturalists") and "four wasps that were taken torpid in their winter quarters." As an antiquarian, "I have ransacked the old and the new world, and been equally attentive to past ages and the present . . . . The Persian monarchs are said to have boasted the greatness of their empire, by being served at their tables with drink from the Ganges and the Danube: I can shew one vial, of which the water was formerly an icicle on the crags of Caucasus, and another that contains what once was snow on top of the Atlas; in a third is dew brushed from a banana in the gardens of Ispahan; and, in another, brine that has rolled in the Pacific Ocean." The complacent inventory continues: "a snail that has crawled upon the wall of China; a humming bird which an American princess wore in her ear; the tooth of an elephant who carried the queen of Siam; the skin of an ape that was kept in the palace of the great mogul; a ribbon that adorned one of the maids of a Turkish sultana; and a symeter once wielded by a soldier of Abas the great."

In the next paper Johnson, writing *in propria persona,* offers moral reflections on the text "All useless science is an empty boast."

There are, indeed, many subjects of study which seem but remotely allied to useful knowledge, and of little importance to happiness or virtue. . . . Yet it is dangerous to discourage well-intended labours, or innocent curiosity. . . . It is impossible to determine the limits of enquiry, or to foresee what consequences a new discovery may produce. . . . The virtuoso therefore cannot be said to be wholly useless; but perhaps he may be sometimes culpable for confining himself to business below his genius, and losing in petty speculations, those hours by which if he had spent them in nobler studies, he might have given new light to the intellectual world. . . . Collections of this kind are of use to the learned, as heaps of stones and piles of timber are necessary to the architect. But to dig the quarry or to search the field, requires not much of any quality, beyond stubborn perseverance; and though genius must often lye inactive without this humble assistance, yet this can claim little praise because every man can afford it. To mean understandings, it is sufficient honour to be numbered amongst the lowest labourers of learning; but different abilities must find different tasks. To hew stone, would have been unworthy of Palladio; and to have rambled in search of shells and flowers, had but ill-suited with the capacity of Newton.

This may or may not have been what Johnson's contemporaries, if they sought any rationalization for their inoffensive hobby, wanted to hear; it depended on the size of their individual ambitions. More and more men with some degree of learning were assembling cabinets. The virtuoso impulse, confined at the beginning of the century to a few gentlemen, now had acquired, in many cases, a more distinctly scientific flavor and had spread to a wider social circle. The zest for inquiry and the faith in empirical knowledge that had led to the founding of the Royal Society, the exciting possibilities of a slowly developing technology, the intensified interest in remote regions and peoples that resulted from the nation's economic expansionism, the popularity of the Grand Tour as a routine event in the education of aristocratic and upper-middle-class Englishmen—all stimulated the pursuit of knowledge, of which keeping a cabinet was one significant symptom. The private museum was as faithful a manifestation of the spirit of the age as were the public scientific lectures that had begun to be offered early in the century.

The eighteenth century was the great age of the encyclopedia, and as it progressed it witnessed as well the publication of thousands of books, written for every level of understanding and priced for every purse, on the various branches of science, on antiquities, history, exploration, ethnography. Magazines specially intended to convey information in popular form multiplied. Circulating libraries and book clubs made it possible for single copies of books to serve a score of readers. It was not only the printed word they relied upon for their information, but the printed image as well. Engravings copied from paintings and drawings added visual force to written accounts of new areas of human interest and experience; graphic art, indeed, was becoming almost as influential a disseminator of information as was language. For the descriptions and images to which the eighteenth-century public resorted for its instruction, the materials of cabinets supplied tangible documentation. No matter how vivid a printed account may have been, or how detailed a picture, the *realia* of a subject—stuffed animals and birds, fossils, small artifacts, articles of costume and weaponry, religious accessories, mechanical devices, even wax models—were unsurpassed for immediacy and, allowing for an irreducible element of deception, authenticity.

Knowledge, however conveyed, had become a prof-

itable commodity. Just as authors, printers, booksellers, artists, and engravers benefited from the popular desire for wider intellectual horizons, so, from the same source, came added support for the trade in curios and natural history specimens. Disposing of private (noncommercial) collections became a thriving business in the course of the century. Virtuosi died, or tired of their toys, or suddenly needed ready cash, or went to the country or abroad, to the profit of both brokers and auctioneers. The clockmaker and inventor Christopher Pinchbeck, whom we shall meet more formally later on, not only showed and sold his own inventions but dealt in the general materials of museums and exhibitions as a broker and commission merchant. In 1744 he began to devote two large rooms over his shop to "a Repository for the Reception of such Things as are worthy the Inspection of the Virtuosi, without any Expence to the Proprietors till sold," when he would charge a 5 percent commission. In 1750 his inventory included "several good Pictures, a great choice of fine old China . . . some old coins, medals; a fine parcel of clay models."[2] When his unsold stock was auctioned at Christie's in 1784, it contained, among other categories of art objects, 916 "bijoux curieux," 94 pictures, 41 porcelains, and 24 prints.[3]

The great bulk of the collections figuring in the scores of sales that were held in London each year comprised the usual kinds of art objects favored by contemporary taste—paintings, statuary, coins, medals, miniatures, prints, drawings, pieces of furniture, porcelain, bric-a-brac. From time to time, however, natural curiosities were included. A few years before her death, the insatiable Dowager Duchess of Portland, one of the greatest collectors of her time, abandoned her previous concentration on art objects in favor of natural specimens. "Her collection in that walk," wrote Horace Walpole, "was supposed to have cost her fifteen thousand pounds." Ninety percent of the collection, auctioned in 1786 for almost £11,000 (of which £300 was Walpole's), consisted of "Shells, Corals, Petrifactions," "Spars, Ores, and Chrystals," "Fishes and Parts of Ditto," and similar items.[4]

Often the surviving records do not tell us whether a given collection, offered at auction, was that of a bona fide collector or of a speculative trader. We do not know, for instance, whether Sidney Kennon, a midwife, was a genuine virtuoso or a shrewd businesswoman—she may of course have been both—but we do know the sort of things her collection, sold in 1755, contained, because Horace Walpole was among the bidders. "You would laugh," he wrote a correspondent, "if you saw in the midst of what trumpery I am writing. Two porters have just brought home my purchases from Mrs. Kennon the midwife's sale. Brobdingnag combs, old broken pots, pans, and pipkins, a lanthorn of scraped oyster-shells, scimitars, Turkish pipes, Chinese baskets, etc. etc." Walpole's bill adds more specifics: "two large clumbs [clam shells] with mahogany stands," "an India bow, eight arrows, a dagger, etc.," "a Chinese lanthorn and an India basket," "a basso relievo in ivory and a large comb," and "a large and curious crucifix."[5] Walpole's booty, for which he paid £15 19s., was nothing if not eclectic. Nor, one suspects, was Mrs. Kennon's stock untypical of the auction sales which facilitated the migration of curiosities from one collection to another.

The "cause of a very curious nature" tried before the Middlesex sheriff's court half a century later (1802) sheds additional light on the flourishing commerce in curios. From one viewpoint, *Hurst* v. *Halford* provides a belated real-life satire on addle-pated virtuosi; from another, although it does not involve a public exhibition, it supplies a rare glimpse of the sometimes picturesque transactions by which showmen as well as private collectors obtained their curios.

The plaintiff in this cause [reported the *Annual Register*] was of a profession technically called a Nicknackitorian, that is, a dealer in all manner of curiosities, such as Egyptian mummies, Indian implements of war, arrows dipped in the poison of the upas tree, bows, antique shields, helmets, &c. and was described as possessing the skin of the cameleopard exhibited in the Roman amphitheatre, the head of the spear used by king Arthur, and the breech of the first cannon used at the siege of Constantinople, and, in short, almost every rarity that the most ardent virtuoso would wish to possess.

The defendant was the executor of a widow lady of the name of Morgan, who, in the enjoyment of a considerable fortune, indulged her fancy and amused herself in collecting objects of natural and artificial curiosity. She had been in the habit of purchasing a variety of rare articles of the plaintiff. She had bought of him models of the temple of Jerusalem and the Alexandrian library, a specimen of the type invented by Memnon* the Egyptian, and a genuine manuscript of the first play acted by Thespis and his company in a waggon. For all these she had in her life-time paid most liberally. It appeared also she had erected a mausoleum, in which her deceased husband was laid, and that she projected the depositing her own remains, when death should overtake her, by the side of him. The plaintiff was employed in fitting it up, and ornamenting it with a tesselated pavement. This was also paid for, and constituted no part of the present demand. This action was brought against the defendant, her executor, to

recover the sum of 40l. for stuffing and embalming a bird of paradise, a fly bird, an ourang-outang, an inchneumon, and a cassowary. The defendant did not deny that the plaintiff had a claim on the estate of the deceased, but he had let judgment go by default, and attempted merely to cut down the amount of the demand. The plaintiff's foreman or assistant proved that the work had been done by the direction of Mrs. Morgan, and that the charge was extremely reasonable. On the contrary, the defendant's solicitor contended that the charge was most extravagant. He stated, that the museum of the deceased virtuoso had been sold by public auction, and, including the models of the temple of Jerusalem and the Alexandrian library, the antique type, Thespian manuscript, spear-head, and everything else she had been all her life collecting, it had not netted more than 110l. As to the stuffed monkeys and birds, which constituted the foundation of the plaintiff's claim, they scarcely defrayed the expense of carrying them away—they were absolute rubbish. The plaintiff's attorney replied, that his client's labour was not to be appreciated by what the objects of it produced at a common sale, attended perhaps by brokers, who were as ignorant as the stuffed animals they were purchasing.

The under sheriff observed, that in matters of taste the intrinsic value of an article was not the proper medium of ascertaining the compensation due to the labour which produced it. A virtuoso frequently expended a large sum of money for what another man would kick out of his house as lumber. If Mrs. Morgan, who it was proved was a lady of fortune, wished to amuse the gloomy hours of her widowhood by stuffing apes and birds, her executor was at least bound to pay the expense she had incurred in indulging her whimsical fancy. He saw no reason why a single shilling of the plaintiff's demand should be subtracted.

The jury accordingly soon after gave a verdict for the plaintiff—damages 40l.[6]

In 1770 Walpole, writing to Sir Horace Mann of a London novelty, three competing art exhibitions (the Royal Academy, the Royal Incorporated Society of Artists, and the Society of Artists Associated for the Relief of Their Distressed Brethren), observed, "The rage to see these exhibitions is so great, that sometimes one cannot pass through the streets where they are. But it is incredible what sums are raised by mere exhibitions of anything; a new fashion, and to enter at which you pay a shilling or half a crown."[7] Although there may not really have been so marked an increase in the number of London exhibitions of all sorts at that moment, Walpole certainly thought so, and his testimony is not to be ignored, because he had a special instinct and penchant for shows. The leading virtuoso-antiquarian of his time, he was as representative of its particular tastes as Sloane had been of those of the preceding generation. He began collecting in 1741, at the sale of the great library of the first and second Earls of Oxford, Robert and Edward Harley, and six years later he bought the lease of Strawberry Hill from the proprietress of a toy and trifle shop in Pall Mall: "a little play-thing house that I got out of Mrs. Chenevix's shop," he told his cousin Henry Conway, "and is the prettiest bauble you ever saw."[8] Once he was firmly in possession, he transformed the plaything house into a "compact little Gothic villa" and then, by successive additions over the next twenty years, more than doubled its size with an Armory, Chapel, Cloister, Gallery, Great Parlour, Holbein Chamber, Library, and Round Tower. Strawberry Hill was a showplace in two distinct senses: by virtue of its architecture and decoration—an eighteenth-century Gothick mansion in a confusion of styles—and by virtue of its contents, which made it a combination art gallery and museum. Indeed, as Walpole expanded it, it became the first purpose-built exhibition structure in the London area.

Walpole, child of his age that he was, was a compulsive collector.[9] Despite his repeated protestations that he lacked both of the collector's requisites, money and space, he kept on buying to the end of his life—antiquarian relics, paintings, sculpture, armor, down to the ordinary truck of curio shops such as he brought home from Mrs. Kennon's sale—oddments that would not have been out of place at Don Saltero's a mile or two down the Thames. Inescapably, as the national custom of visiting stately homes began to take root, this ever-growing and much spoken of museum-mansion also attracted sightseers, and Walpole, the first of many similarly situated house-owners to do so, printed a full catalogue, from which he extracted a shortened version for the use of servants who acted as guides. As Strawberry Hill's fame spread, Walpole's initial pleasure turned to something like panic; parties of sightseers began to overrun the place. He therefore was forced to draw up a set of rules to govern his tourist attraction: tickets to be applied for a day or two in advance, only one party per day and each to be limited to four persons (no children), limited hours of opening. Sometimes, when he felt like it, he took visitors through the house himself. His experience was that of every such proprietor; in general, things worked smoothly, but sometimes there was trouble, as with a Mr. Perkins who was "very rude, abused James, gave Margaret nothing, because his servant had been made to wait while I was at dinner."

Walpole's museological experience came too late for him to have been of any practical assistance to the first administrators of the British Museum.[10] Still, his fleeting connection with that institution at the moment of its birth qualifies him as the firmest symbolic link between the well-established world of the eighteenth-century collector and the nascent one of the public museum. He wrote to Mann on 14 February 1753:

You will scarce guess how I employ my time; chiefly at present in the guardianship of embryos and cockleshells. Sir Hans Sloane is dead, and has made me one of the trustees to his museum, which is to be offered for twenty thousand pounds to the King, the Parliament, the royal academies of Petersburg, Berlin, Paris and Madrid. He valued it at fourscore thousand, and so would anybody who loves hippopotamuses, sharks with one ear, and spiders as big as geese! It is a rent charge to keep the foetuses in spirits! You may believe that those, who think money the most valuable of all curiosities, will not be purchasers. The King has excused himself, saying he did not believe that there are twenty thousand pounds in the treasury. We are a charming wise set, all philosophers, botanists, antiquarians and mathematicians; and adjourned our first meeting, because Lord Macclesfield, our chairman, was engaged to a party for finding out the longitude.[11]

Although the royal treasury was bare, Parliament was persuaded to allow a lottery to finance the purchase of the Sloane Collection. Of the £300,000 to be raised, £200,000 was reserved for prizes. The rest was to buy not only the Sloane collection but the Harleian collection of books and manuscripts and a building to house these, as well as the antiquarian collection of Sir Robert Cotton, which his grandson had bequeathed to the nation in 1700. Despite a fair amount of chicanery—a swindler named Peter Leheup sold black market tickets with great advantage to himself—the scheme succeeded. Once the money was in hand, it was decided to purchase Montagu House in Bloomsbury, the property of the Earl of Halifax. This elegant mansion, built late in the seventeenth century in imitation of a Parisian *hôtel,* was itself a showplace, but its unsuitability for exhibition purposes illustrated the fateful contemporary fallacy—one that would shadow the history of museums and libraries well into the twentieth century—that in respect to architecture, arrangement, and décor such public institutions could not do better than to be replicas of palaces and private mansions.

Opened in January 1759, the refurbished Montagu House retained its palatial air, with a forecourt, a garden behind, and a quadrangular court with a colonnade of Ionic columns. It had parquetry floors, and its ceilings bore allegorical paintings executed by Huguenot artists. One entered by way of a cupola-topped hall, which in the ensuing decades would become congested with "oriental idols, marble busts, elephants and sponges; polar bears, portraits, fossils, and meteorites . . . and several stuffed giraffes."[12] The upstairs saloon was "furnished with a curious selection of miscellaneous objects . . . including the first of the Museum's famous collection of mummies, various specimens of coral, a vulture's head in spirits, and the stuffed flamingo." In the remaining rooms there was more semblance of system, although the display space immediately became overcrowded. In six rooms on the east side of the main floor were the manuscripts, medals, and coins; in the corresponding apartments on the west side were the "natural and artificial productions" comprising the Sloane collection; and on the ground floor, the Sloane books and the bulk of the King's Library, given by George II in 1757.[13]

This was the first museum in Europe to be explicitly open to the people. According to the act of incorporation, it was intended "not only for the inspection and entertainment of the learned and the curious, but for the general use and benefit of the public." Nowhere on the continent was any such provision made, although the great collections in Paris, Milan, Madrid, and elsewhere were sometimes accessible under certain conditions. In France one of the goals of the Enlightenment was to give all people continuous access to the royal collections, but this was to be achieved only when the revolutionary government threw open the Louvre.

The principle of the national museum therefore was, somewhat surprisingly, established in England fully forty years before it was in France. But the reality was another matter. From the beginning, the British Museum trustees, a deeply conservative body drawn from the ranks of ecclesiastics and "persons of rank and fortune," maintained that the museum's overriding obligation was to promote "Science and the Arts," not to cater to "the curiosity of . . . multitudes . . . in quest of amusement."[14] Even before the museum opened, one of the trustees, Dr. John Ward, antiquarian and professor of rhetoric at Gresham College, declared that

a general liberty to ordinary people of all ranks and denominations, is not to be [i.e., cannot be] kept within bounds. Many irregularities will be committed that cannot be prevented by a few librarians who will soon be insulted by such people, if they offer to control or contradict them. . . . If any such people are in liquor and misbehave, they are rarely without their accomplices . . . who out of an Idle vanity in exerting what they will call their liberty will side with

them and promote mischiefs that are to be more easily suppressed than . . . prevented. . . . No persons of superior degree will care to come on such days . . . a great concourse of ordinary people will never be kept in order. . . . If public days should be allowed, then it will be necessary for the Trustees to have the presence of a Committee of themselves attending, with at least two Justices of the Peace and the constables of the division of Bloomsbury . . . supported by a guard such a one as usually attends at the Play-House, and even after all this, Accidents must and will happen.[15]

In response to such fears as these, the world's first "public" museum instituted rules that effectively frustrated its stated purpose. Tickets of admission were required. One had to appear at the door in person and request the porter to write one's name, social rank, and address in his book. The application then went through channels at a leisurely rate, and some days, weeks, or months later one could call back and get the ticket. In 1776 persons who applied for tickets in April were still waiting for them in August. As a consequence, scalpers appeared who sold the tickets they had had the patience to obtain to visitors who could not wait. The list of closed days was formidable: Saturdays and Sundays; the weeks following Christmas, Easter, and Whitsunday (the very times when ordinary people were most likely to have leisure); Good Friday and all other feast and fast days appointed by public authority. On such days as remained, the building was open between 9 A.M. and 3 P.M., except that on Mondays and Fridays between May and August it was open only from 4 to 8 P.M.

Not surprisingly, therefore, in its first years no more than sixty visitors a day visited the British Museum. But even so, the officials complained that guiding tours took up most of their time. The fatigue of four hours' attendance on visitors, they claimed, prevented their using to advantage the two hours left for their other duties. But they could not avoid giving tours, because tours were the only means of seeing the museum; free browsing among the exhibits was forbidden.

There was considerable question whether, under such conditions, looking in at the British Museum was worth the bother. The officials seem to have made reasonably clear to visitors that they were unwelcome intruders. The visitors, for their part, disliked the guides as—in the words of a German clergyman—"venal praters who ten times a day repeat the same dull lesson they have got by heart."[16] Other guides seem not to have talked at all. In 1784 a substantial citizen from Birmingham, William Hutton, fulfilled a long-standing dream of seeing the museum and its treasures. On a brief visit to London he was lucky enough to be offered a black market ticket. He gladly paid for it, and presented himself at Montagu House with glorious expectations. The party of ten (five more than the regulations allowed) to which he belonged

began to move pretty fast, when I asked with some surprize, whether there were none to inform us what the curiosities were as we went on? A tall genteel young man *in person,* who seemed to be our conductor, replied with some warmth, "What! would you have me tell you every thing in the Museum? How is it possible? Besides, are not the names written upon many of them?" I was too much humbled by this reply to utter another word. The company seemed influenced; they made haste, and were silent. No voice was heard but in whispers.

If a man pass two minutes in a room, in which are a thousand things to demand his attention, he cannot find time to bestow on them a glance each.

When our leader opens the door of another apartment, the silent language of that action is, *come along.* . . .

It grieved me to think how much I lost for want of information. In about thirty minutes we finished our silent journey through this princely mansion, which would well have taken thirty days. I went out much about as wise as I went in. . . . I had . . . paid two shillings for a ticket, been hackneyed through the rooms with violence, had lost the little share of good humour I brought in, and came away completely disappointed.

Hope is the most active of all the human passions. It is the most delusive. I had laid more stress on the British Museum, than on any thing I should see in London. It was the only sight that disgusted me. . . .

In my visit to Don Saltero's curiosities, at Chelsea, they furnished me with a book, explaining every article in the collection. Here I could take my own time, and entertain myself.[17]

The unfavorable comparison of the British Museum with Don Saltero's was the cruelest cut of all.

Whatever hope there may have been for an improvement in conditions had already, by 1784, been damped by outside events, which convinced the authorities that admitting the public indiscriminately posed a much graver threat than mere insults to the staff. Dr. Ward's fear of the mob, far from being a mere eccentricity, was shared by many trustees, and it was melodramatically justified in the summer of 1780, when the Gordon rioters swept through Bloomsbury and burned Lord Mansfield's house with his irreplaceable manuscripts and library. Although no attempt was made to harm the museum, the York Regiment

belatedly summoned to quell the riots was bivouacked in the garden, and parts of the basement were turned over to the officers on duty. When the troops withdrew a month later, they left behind a sergeant's guard at the gates—a military presence that would remain until 1863, as a constant symbolic reminder that the museum was vulnerable to the destructive caprice of the London populace, as well as an implicit rebuke to the liberal public men of a later generation who advocated free access to such national institutions.

Furthermore, the temper of the country toward the end of the museum's first half-century did not favor the idea of public educational institutions. A writer in the *Quarterly Review* in 1850 recalled the effect of the Napoleonic Wars, when the survival of the nation took priority over any effort to instruct the public. "Nor did the nation at large take a tithe of the present interest in purely intellectual subjects. Few comparatively thirsted after knowledge or hungered after education—the modern panacea. The childlike uninstructed curiosity of the many was well pleased with the sort of exhibitions provided for them by our fathers; and the government, compelled to be prodigal in warlike expenditure, grudged grants to an institution whose ends and objects flourish best in peace."[18] For well over fifty years, the government's funding of the British Museum was minimal; it spent about £2,500 a year on officials' salaries and, at best, a few hundred pounds on purchases. One of the few exceptions to this parsimony was the granting of £8,400 to buy part of Sir William Hamilton's collection of Greek and Roman antiquities in 1772.

Thus such ordinary Londoners as had some desire for additional knowledge were hardly better off after the British Museum opened than they had been before. Although private collections had multiplied in the wake of Tradescant's Ark, none of them was readily accessible. Entrée could be had only with credentials of some sort, such as a letter of introduction to the owner. In the case of three famous collections in the second half of the century, only qualified medical men and scientists, and sometimes laymen of superior social standing, were admitted. In ascending order of size and celebrity, these were the anatomical museums of three eminent surgeons, Joshua Brookes, William Hunter, and John Hunter. Brookes, a pupil of William Hunter, in the course of a long career taught more than 5,000 students. At his demonstration rooms in Great Marlborough Street he maintained a steadily growing collection and experimented so successfully with means of preserving color and staying decomposition in his specimens as to win a fellowship in the Royal Society on that ground. His 6,000 items were said to have cost him, first and last, some £30,000.[19]

William Hunter's museum, containing large assortments of minerals, fossils, and shells in addition to the specimens most closely connected with his medical work, was housed in what a contemporary admired as a "magnificent room, fitted up with great elegance and propriety" at Hunter's anatomical theatre at 16 Great Windmill Street. His hope was to obtain a government appropriation to build a separate museum and medical school, in return for which he would bequeath his collection to the nation. The government failed to respond, with the result that Hunter, reputedly at the suggestion of Dr. Johnson, left it (1783) to the University of Glasgow.[20]

Hunter's younger brother, John, a surgeon and medical researcher with many interests, began his museum of comparative anatomy in the 1770s at his house in Jermyn Street.[21] The collection soon outgrew the accommodations, and in 1783 Hunter, who like his brother had achieved wealth as well as renown in their profession, took the lease of 28 Leicester Square, where, in the garden between two existing large houses, he built a third. In this he arranged a great variety of animal and vegetable preparations in scientific order, not according to species but by function—motor apparatus, digestive and sensory organs, reproductive parts, and so on—"each series ranging the evolutionary scale from the simplest mechanisms to the most complex," a thematic emphasis which anticipated a basic principle of modern educational museology. In addition to this encyclopedic display of comparative anatomy, the museum contained thousands of pathological specimens and congenital monstrosities and, under a glass canopy outside the building, the skeleton of a forty-foot bottlenose whale.

The Hunterian Museum, which by the time of its owner's death contained 13,682 specimens, was famed not only in Britain but throughout Europe. For scope of contents and rationality of display it had no equal anywhere. Intended primarily for teaching purposes, it was open to outsiders only in two months of the year—to "noblemen and gentlemen" in May, to scientists in October. The enthusiasm with which John Hunter collected (typified by his excited request one day that a bookseller-patient join him in buying a dying tiger from a menagerie) ran him deeply into debt. After he died in 1793, three sales of other parts of his estate were insufficient to pay his creditors, and his executors sold the museum to the government for £15,000, about a fifth of its estimated cost. The collection was then transferred to the Royal College of Surgeons, which provided it with a permanent home in Lincoln's Inn Fields.

It was typical of the time that both Hunter brothers, far from limiting their collecting to their professional interests, built up "gentlemen's collections" as well. Each had his own preferences. William's ran to pictures—he eventually possessed forty-three Old Masters as well as three Chardins—and to books (12,000), ancient manuscripts (600), and old coins (30,000). John, by contrast, was a magpie who indiscriminately swept together "waxworks, portraits of freaks, Oriental scrimshaw, exotic weapons, scraps of tapestry, electromechanical novelties." Before he branched out from anatomical collecting on his own account, he scouted for pictures and bric-a-brac on behalf of his former pupil and friend, Edward Jenner, then a country doctor in Gloucestershire. In a number of letters to Jenner, Hunter mentions his luck in picking up what he called "Don Salteros" for his correspondent, among them a picture by George Stubbs which he acquired for a thrifty five guineas.

D⅗✳⅗꘎

When the Hunterian Museum was finished and occupied in 1785, it faced, diagonally across Leicester Square, an already well established museum of another kind, one which had been founded in the spirit of Sir Hans Sloane and was at that moment beginning to be affected by the spirit of Don Saltero. This was the Holophusikon, as it had been dignified upon its transfer to London, though it continued to be more commonly referred to as Sir Ashton Lever's Museum.[22] An enthusiastic naturalist and curio collector, Lever had conceived, in his own words, an ambition "to pursue Natural History and carry the exhibition of it to such an height as no one can imagine; and to make it the most wonderful sight in the world." At Alkrington Hall, his seat near Manchester, he had begun collecting on a grand scale. By late 1772 his aviary-cum-museum comprised 60 species of quadrupeds, 160 of English birds, 100 of foreign birds, similar numbers of English and foreign quadrupeds, and 1,100 fossils. Among the "imperfect conceptions, or what are improperly called Lusus Naturae," according to a correspondent in the *Gentleman's Magazine,* were a pig with eight legs, two tails, but only a single backbone and one head; a leveret (no relation) with seven legs and eight feet; and "a Pupp with two mouths and one head." The inevitable "artificial curiosities" included "a few pictures of birds in straw, very natural," a basket of flowers cut in paper, and the head of George III cut in cannel coal.[23]

The presence of the latter oddities did not obscure the scientific value that the rest of the specimens possessed. Gilbert White of Selborne, who knew Lever through his brother, the Rev. John White, vicar of a parish near Alkrington, considered Lever "a very adroit *natural* Naturalist," although he added that "it is . . . pity he does not . . . call in the assistance of system." In several letters exchanged by the brothers there is warm mention of the help Lever lent the clergyman in his scientific studies, in gratitude for which Gilbert gave Lever free use of his papers: "he is a man of honor and will not suffer them to be transcribed."[24]

Lever's generosity was not translated into all-embracing hospitality, however. On 13 September 1773 he advertised:

This is to inform the Publick that being tired out with the insolence of the common People, who I have hitherto indulged with a sight of my museum at Alkrington, I am now come to the resolution of refusing admittance to the lower class except they come provided with a ticket from some Gentleman or Lady of my acquaintance. And I hereby authorize every friend of mine to give a ticket to any orderly Man to bring in eleven Persons, besides himself whose behaviour he must be answerable for, according to the directions he will receive before they are admitted. They will not be admitted during the time of Gentlemen and Ladies being in the Museum. If it happens to be inconvenient when they bring their ticket, they must submit to go back and come some other day, admittance in the morning *only* from eight o'clock to twelve.[25]

Another rule excluded all would-be visitors who came on foot, but this was circumvented on one occasion by a gentleman who, being denied entrance, went down a country lane and returned aboard a cow.

Within the next year, finding that his expenditures were outrunning his income and intent on steadily enlarging his collection, Lever moved it to London, where he spread it through sixteen rooms and numerous corridors of Leicester House. Dominating the north side of Leicester Square, this mansion, built in the 1630s, was owned by the Sidney family (the Earls of Leicester) and had long been a royal residence, occupied by a succession of princes and dukes. It now was turned into a pay-as-you-enter museum, the admission charge ranging from 2s. 6d. upward to 5s. 3d.—a scale sufficiently high to exclude the "common People" who had outworn their welcome at Alkrington and were *personae non gratae* at the British Museum.

The Holophusikon at once was the talk of the town. Apart from Sloane's collection, which had been open only to selected visitors during its owner's lifetime and now was beyond the reach of most of the public in Bloomsbury, London had never known so extensive a museum of natural history, ethnography, and miscellany.

The well-to-do crowd came in abundance. Its enthusiasm for this novel show may possibly be gauged from a set of "Verses addressed to Sir Ashton Lever by a little Boy of ten Years old, on being favoured with a Sight of his Museum, November 6, 1778," which was printed in the *Gentleman's Magazine* the following spring. Writing from Kennington, the infant poetaster began,

> If I had Virgil's judgment, Homer's fire,
> And could with equal rapture strike the lyre,
> Could drink as largely of the Muse's spring,
> Then would I of Sir Ashton's merits sing.
> Look here, look there, above, beneath, around
> Sure great Apollo consecrates the ground.
> Here stands a tiger—[26]

The rest can easily be imagined. For more spontaneous inventories of the collection we may comfortably turn to two wide-eyed ladies.[27] In a letter to her sister Fanny, Susan Burney described what she saw on a visit some months before the precocious rhymer from Kennington:

The birds of paradise, and the humming birds, were I think among the most beautiful—There are several pelicans—flamingoes—peacocks (one quite white)—a penguin. Among the beasts a hippopotamus (sea-horse) of an immense size, an elephant, a tyger from the Tower—a Greenland bear and its cub—a wolf—two or three leopards—an Otaheite dog, a very coarse ugly looking creature—a camelion—a young crocodile—a room full of monkeys—one of which presents the company with an Italian Song—another is reading a book—another, the most horrid of all, is put in the attitude of *Venus de Medicis,* and is scarce fit to be look'd at. Lizards, bats, toads, frogs, scorpions and other filthy creatures in abundance. There were a great many things from Otaheite—the compleat dress of a Chinese Mandarine, made of blue and brown sattin—of an African Prince—A suit of armour that they say belonged to Oliver Cromwel—the Dress worn in Charles 1st's time—etc—etc.[28]

The "room full of monkeys" was what chiefly caught the eye of the young American scientist Benjamin Silliman when he visited the museum, then removed to Lambeth, some years later. It would seem that, despite his concluding comment, the display provoked more laughter than thought:

Not satisfied with what the Creator has done, in making these animals so very ludicrous in their appearance and manners; so much like men that we must acknowledge the resemblance; so much like a brute's that we cannot but be disgusted at it; the artist has employed them as busied about various human employments.
  The taylor monkey sits, cross legged, threading his needle, with his work in his lap, and his goose, scissors, and bodkin by his side.
  The watchman stands at a corner, with his cane and lanthorn in his hands.
  The house carpenter monkey is driving tne plane over the bench.
  The ballad singer, with his ballad in his hand, is very gravely composing his muscles to sing.
  The clerk of the monkey room sits writing at a desk.
  The shaver has one of his own species seated in a chair;—his beard lathered, and the razor just beginning to slide over his face.
  The dentist holds the patient by the chops, while he strains the turnkey, and produces all the grimace and contortion of features, which tooth-drawing can extort.
  Crispin is pushing the awl and pointing the bristle to the shoe, and thus we have our rivals in form actually placed erect, and emulating human employments. Nothing is wanting but Lord Monboddoe's aid to free them from an appendage which this philosopher says our species have been so fortunate as to drop, and they might perhaps aspire even to the wool sack.[29]

From this, it would be only a step to the Museum of Humorous Taxidermy in Brighton, two centuries later.
  Eight years after Susan Burney's visit (September 1786), a German lady, Sophie von la Roche, wrote her own impressions of the Leverian Museum. She remembered most vividly the "heap of old armour and guns from every age and corner of the globe" at the foot of the staircase; the "dried sea-monsters of every description" that festooned the surrounding walls; the "excellently stuffed young elephant" that welcomed her to the first room; and the collection of "musical instruments of all nations, ancient and modern, and . . . different types of music since the discovery of notes." She also "enjoyed seeing dresses belonging to kings and queens, lords and ladies three hundred years ago or more, offering a splendid selection of models for masked fancy dress; some of their weird trimmings are just as preposterous as those of the Chinese, Turks, or Tahiti in the adjoining room."[30]
  Sophie liked "good Sir Ashton," who took her

about in person: "a good friendly man of some fifty years or so" (actually he was fifty-seven). But Sophie was prepared to like most people; whereas Fanny Burney, when she inspected the museum with her father several years earlier, on the last day of 1782, had brought with her the cool and critical eye for human foibles that won her celebrity as a novelist of manners.

Sir Ashton came and talked to us a good while. He may be an admirable natural*ist,* but I think if in other matters you leave the *ist* out, you will not much wrong him. He looks full sixty years old [it is perhaps typical that Fanny exaggerated Lever's age, while Sophie underestimated it], yet he had dressed not only two young men, but himself, in a green jacket, a round hat, with green feathers, a bundle of arrows under one arm, and a bow in the other, and thus, accoutred as a forester, he pranced about; while the younger fools, who were in the same garb, kept running to and fro in the garden, carefully contriving to shoot at some mark, just as any of the company appeared at any of the windows.* After such a specimen of his actions, you will excuse me if I give you none of his conversation.[31]

  Even though it was often remarked that the Leverian Museum was superior in accessibility and arrangement to the British Museum, Sir Ashton's hope that it would pull him out of debt and finance new purchases was not realized. The novelty wore off, and the supply of fashionable visitors just as inevitably diminished. Although between February 1775 and February 1784 Lever took in some £13,000 at the door, most of this was earned in the earlier years. In 1781 he twice tried to sell the collection, which he was not reluctant to advertise as "the First Museum in the Universe," but there were no takers. Two years later he offered it to the trustees of the British Museum at a price far below the £50,000 at which it had been valued, but again he was unsuccessful. He now had recourse to the device by which the British Museum had been brought into being, a lottery. An act of Parliament in 1784 permitted him to offer to the public 36,000 tickets at a guinea apiece, the winner to take all. But only 7,000 or 8,000 were sold.[32] When, five weeks after the drawing, no one claimed the prize, Lever and his friends, as he told Sophie von la Roche, "thought some magnanimous soul had won it and had decided not to put in an appearance, either to enable the owner to retain it or let him make some profitable deal." But this hope was disappointed when a law stationer and estate agent to noblemen named James Parkinson (evidently not a barrister, as he was said to be) appeared with the winning ticket, which his late wife had

* This performance was not put on merely for the diversion of the paying customers; Lever was a dedicated toxophilite. The American John Adams, visiting the museum in 1783 while in London on a diplomatic mission, "saw Sir Ashton and some other knights, his friends, practising the ancient but as I thought long forgotten art of archery. In his garden, with their bows and arrows they hit as small a mark and at as great a distance as any of our sharpshooters could have done with their rifles." (*Diary and Autobiography of John Adams,* ed. L. H. Butterfield, Cambridge, Mass., 1961, III, 151.)

5. Rotunda of the Leverian Museum, Blackfriars Road (engraving by Miss Stone and C. Ryley, undated).

bought and which he had come upon when going through her effects. "Popular sympathy," wrote Sophie, "was so hot on Sir Ashton's side that some went to see the collection ten to twenty times to contribute an equal number of shillings towards his losses [evidently the former price scale no longer held]; and nearly all showed a certain aversion to the barrister who had destroyed the fine ideal of generosity entertained for so many weeks, during which time all had rejoiced at Sir Ashton's returning good fortune."

The rest of the story is a sad anticlimax. While Parkinson attempted, unsuccessfully, to sell the museum en bloc to two interested buyers, the Queen of Portugal and the Empress of Russia,[33] he allowed Lever to remain in possession for a while; as we have just seen, he was there in 1786, when Sophie made her visit. But at length Lever departed, to die in January 1788 at the Bull's Head inn, Manchester. A month earlier, having decided that the rent paid for Leicester House was prohibitive, Parkinson, or a company of speculators he had formed, moved the collection to a new location across the river, a specially designed building at the corner of Blackfriars Road and Albion Street. Here, in a dozen rooms in addition to the rotunda that gave the structure its name, the "Museum Leveriarum" survived, in increasing neglect, for some twenty years.[34] The early Victorian journalist William Jerdan remembered it as "a most heterogeneous medley of stuffed animals, without order or classification, and savage costumes, weapons, and products," a visit to which could possibly provide one with "a few desultory facts . . . but as a means for solid or lasting instruction, its miscellaneous and aimless character rendered it useless."[35]

The collection was, however, sufficiently valuable to induce a German prince to offer Parkinson £12,000 for it, with the title of Baron for his son thrown in. Thomas Holcroft, the dramatist, heard at this time (1798) that Parkinson refused the offer because he planned to move the museum to Bond Street, "make scientific arrangements, &c., and exhibit it at half-a-crown, or by annual tickets"—in other words, to restore it to the *status quo ante*.[36] But this did not work out, and the institution continued to lose money. In 1804 or 1805 Parkinson offered the collection to the British Museum, but to no avail. A renewed offer, in 1806, was informally accepted on condition that the maximum price be £20,000. But now Pitt's cabinet balked and sought the advice of Sir Joseph Banks, president of the Royal Society and an influential trustee of the British Museum, who recommended against the

purchase. Parkinson was said to believe that Banks "hated" Lever and so hated his collection (though Banks had nothing against Parkinson, and indeed gave him specimens).[37] If so, the animosity may have been traceable to the two naturalists' rivalry over the artifacts and natural curiosities brought back from Captain Cook's voyages. Banks, who had sailed on the first voyage as official naturalist, may have resented Lever's possessing so many objects from Cook's expeditions that a separate room at Leicester House was set apart for them.

The British Museum being deprived of the collection, Parkinson proceeded to disperse it at a sixty-day auction.[38] He probably got the ten or twelve thousand pounds he counted on. Although the war prevented agents for continental museums from attending, British collectors were present in force. Many of the lots they bought eventually found their way to public museums; some other lots went in another direction. As late as 1829 a portion of the Leverian collection was exhibited at Camberwell Fair by an agent for "a Society of Gentlemen," which probably means a cut-price syndicate of speculators. "Several commodious caravans" were advertised as holding 1,600 cases of stuffed birds alone, as well as twenty-five serpents, an eleven-foot swordfish, the usual assortment of fossils and shells, and the heads of two chieftain warriors from the South Pacific.[39] Thus the tag ends of a once-distinguished museum wound up as a cheapjack attraction at a suburban fair; it was a pattern often to be repeated in one variation or another.*

It was on this not particularly auspicious note that London museums entered the nineteenth century. The virtuoso's cabinet, in a way, had "gone public." Collections of natural history and manmade curiosities had entered the world of show business. The growing popular interest in the stuff of which museums are composed had made evident the commercial value of such collections. That museums should become a concern of the government, in behalf of the people at large, was a notion entertained, if at all, only by those few observers who took literally the lofty sentiments expressed in the founding instrument of the British Museum.

In any event, the museum as a cultural idea and institution had become so well embedded in educated men's consciousness as to serve as a convenient and graphic metaphor for the variety of the world in which men lived. Suffering from a hangover on the first of April, 1775, James Boswell went, he recorded, "to Old Slaughter's Coffee-house, and drank some brandy and

* So too was the subsequent career of the Rotunda, which probably went through a wider gamut of metamorphoses than any other single London exhibition place. After the Leverian collection left, it was first occupied by the lecture rooms, library, and laboratory of the Surrey Institution, the South Bank counterpart of the Royal Institution. When this hopeful venture collapsed in 1820, the building became a wine cellar and concert hall. During the Reform Bill crisis in the early thirties, as the headquarters of the National Union of the Working Classes, it was a hotbed of radicalism. Thereafter, until 1858, it was a place of miscellaneous and not infrequently disreputable entertainment, housing waxworks, wild beast shows, and penny gaffs, the lowest form of the early Victorian theatre.

water; was a sad being for while, but recovered pretty well by walking in the streets of London, which is really to me a high entertainment of itself. I see a vast museum of all objects, and I think with a kind of wonder that I see it for nothing."[40] Attendance at showplaces, too, was beginning to produce a new kind of human experience, museum fatigue. When she was at Sir Ashton Lever's, Sophie von la Roche complained, "All the wonders of nature, and all the incredible artistic conceptions of form and colour, pleasant and unpleasant, are so tightly packed, that the mind and eye are quite dazzled by them, and in the end both are overwhelmed and retain nothing at all."[41] When he came to write *The Prelude,* William Wordsworth was to seize on this novel affliction of urban life to image his unsystematic intellectual progress during his "residence at Cambridge" in those same years toward the end of the century:

Carelessly
I gazed, roving as through a cabinet
Or wide museum (thronged with fishes, gems,
Birds, crocodiles, shells) where little can be seen
Well understood, or naturally endeared,
Yet still does every step bring something forth
That quickens, pleases, stings; and here and there
A casual rarity is singled out,
And has its brief perusal, then gives way
To others, all supplanted in their turn.
Meanwhile, amid this gaudy congress, framed
Of things by nature most unneighbourly,
The head turns round and cannot right itself;
And though an aching and a barren sense
Of gay confusion still be uppermost,
With few wise longings and but little love,
Yet something to the memory sticks at last,
Whence profit may be drawn in times to come.[42]

Monster-Mongers and Other Retailers of Strange Sights

3

For I have always lookt upon it as a high Point of Indiscretion in Monster-mongers and other Retailers of strange Sights; to hang out a fair large Picture over the Door, drawn after the Life, with a most eloquent Description underneath: This hath saved me many a Threepence, for my Curiosity was fully satisfied, and I never offered to go in, tho' often invited by the urging and attending Orator, with his last moving and standing Piece of Rhetorick; *Sir, Upon my Word, we are just going to begin.*
—Swift, *A Tale of a Tub,* 1704

While museumlike exhibitions of curious natural and "artificial" objects brought something of the Enlightenment spirit to the relatively uneducated members of the middle class, on a lower social level displays of living beings (and of beings which had once been alive) were catering to what today would be called the mass audience. At the end of the sixteenth century the population of London and Westminster had been about 125,000; at the end of the seventeenth, despite the ravages of the plague in 1665, the whole metropolitan area held some 750,000 people; and in the course of the eighteenth century this figure would approach a million. Although the new affluence which marked the century benefited almost exclusively the already wealthy and a fortunate minority of nouveaux riches, it trickled down to the extent that most working people had an occasional copper or two, sometimes a shilling, to spend on amusement. And amusement they sought, as a means of escape from their overcrowded dwellings and the general penury and emptiness of their everyday existence. Since few could read, books were of no use to them, and so they sought their diversion in the streets, at taverns, pleasure gardens, fairs—at all of which, exhibitions of one kind or another were a prominent feature. In the aggregate this widening mass audience was large enough and possessed sufficient purchasing power to encourage showmen to supply it with what it quite plainly wanted, which was amusement with blunt, immediate impact uncomplicated by thought or the tenderer feelings.

Although Londoners constituted most of the audience for the shows, the number of provincial visitors must not be underestimated. The midlands and north being as yet sparsely settled, the English population was concentrated in the southern counties, so that most English families lived relatively close to London. It was to London that they traveled if they needed, for any reason, to be in a city, because London was the single metropolis in the kingdom, four times larger than Bristol, its closest rival. The great difficulty, of course, was transport. As Macaulay showed in a famous passage in his *History of England,* the conditions of travel in late seventeenth-century England were deplorable, and they seem, unbelievably, to have got even worse until improvements in highway engineering began to have some effect after the 1750s. Nevertheless, there was considerable traffic in and out of town. County families arrived for the season in their springless coaches, and rustics with mud-caked boots carted produce or drove cattle into the capital's markets. Ned Ward wrote of the "Reports of . . . Inticing Rarities, to be visited at a small Expence," which were taken back to the country by "Boobily Bumpkins, who had stolen so much time from their Waggons and Hay-Carts, as to be spectators of these surprizing Curiosities."[1]

These could be found in many places. The humblest and cheapest shows, and the least recorded because they never attained the minimum dignity of handbills, let alone newspaper advertisements, were those in the streets—human freaks, tame bears which often danced, monkeys, even tigers and other wild animals. An edict in 1697 had forbidden the display of "lions, lionesses, leopards, or any other beasts which are ferae natura" on the ground that this was a monopoly reserved for the keeper of His Majesty's lions at the Tower of London, but the prohibition was largely ineffective.[2] Three years later Ned Ward observed that tigers were "grown now so common they are scarce worth mentioning,"[3] and in 1773 a catalogue of London sights asserted, no doubt with some exaggeration, that there were "Lions, Tygers, Elephants, &c. in every Street in Town."[4]

Itinerant showmen wandered through the thoroughfares, setting up their pitches wherever pedestrian traffic was heaviest. One favorite stopping place was the vicinity of inns, where they competed head-on with their brethren inside. In the absence of structures specially built for the purpose, taverns were ideally suited to be exhibition places, as Chaucer's Pardoner had discovered centuries earlier. They were, by definition, places of entertainment, with a constant turnover of patrons; they had large rooms, and their yards and stables could accommodate remarkable animals. Throughout the seventeenth and eighteenth centuries, therefore, inns at Charing Cross, in the Strand and Fleet Street, and at various other locations in the City and Westminster rented to exhibitors both space and, in effect, an established clientele as the nucleus of a larger custom drawn from passersby.

Paradoxically, the most authentic particulars we have of show-business practices at the beginning of the eighteenth century are found, not in any historical source, but in *Gulliver's Travels*. Seeking to endow his flights of fantastic invention with verisimilitude and his narrator with credibility, Swift was at pains to provide a base of realistic detail to which every reader in touch with London life at the moment could give his instant assent. In the middle of the second chapter of the voyage to Brobdingnag, Gulliver is a living curiosity described by his showman-master as "a strange creature . . . not so big as a *splacknuck* (an animal in that country very finely shaped, about six foot long) and in every part of the body resembling a human creature, could speak several words, and perform an hundred diverting tricks"—the familiar idiom of showmen's publicity. A crier is hired to advertise the living rarity's presence at the Sign of the Green Eagle, where he is exhibited in the largest room, twenty-five feet square.* Only about thirty persons are admitted at one time to witness Gulliver's performances, of which there are ten or a dozen a day, and which consist of tricks actually done by lower primates on show in London. He stands on a table five feet in diameter, and for his protection benches are placed round it to keep him out of the spectators' reach. Like many actual exhibits in Swift's England, the tiny Gulliver is taken on tour, being exhibited for ten weeks "in eighteen large towns, besides many villages and private families." In Gulliver's case, the London (Lorbrulgrud) run is the climax of the country tour. Often, however, shows went on the road only after they had exhausted, at least temporarily, the London market.

Had he been brought to the capital at the end of August instead of October, Gulliver in all probability would have been exhibited at the Lorbrulgrudian equivalent of Bartholomew Fair, which was held annually for two weeks beginning on 24 August—the biggest and longest-lived of the London fairs, which also included "May fair" (in the district that now bears its name) and those at Southwark, Stepney, Greenwich, Tottenham, and elsewhere. It was a raucous, free-spending fortnight, during which Londoners flocked to Smithfield by the tens of thousands, to eat, drink, gamble, brawl—and, above all, to gawk. To these littered precincts gravitated exhibitors from all over the country as well as those who at other times operated in taverns and other hired rooms in London itself. There the booths of living rarities had their place among all the other performers and fair-haunters: conjurors, acrobats, rope dancers, religious fanatics, quacks, whores, ballad singers, beer sellers, cutpurses, sharpers, and gamesters. Wordsworth's panoramic description of Bartholomew Fair as it was in 1802, when Charles Lamb took him to see it, might, granting the difference in literary style and the presence of a few novelties, have been written by Ben Jonson. Like Hogarth's painting of Southwark Fair, it is accurate as well as graphic social history:

* "Three hundred feet square," says Gulliver. To convert Brobdingnagian dimensions to London scale they must be divided by twelve.

. . . the open space, through every nook
Of the wide area, twinkles, is alive
With heads; the midway region, and above,
Is thronged with staring pictures and huge scrolls,
Dumb proclamations of the Prodigies;
And chattering monkeys dangling from their poles,
And children whirling in their roundabouts;
With those that stretch the neck and strain the eyes,
And crack the voice in rivalship, the crowd
Inviting; with buffoons against buffoons
Grimacing, writhing, screaming,—him who grinds
The hurdy-gurdy, at the fiddle weaves,
Rattles the salt-box, thumps the kettle-drum,
And him who at the trumpet puffs his cheeks,
The silver-collared Negro with his timbrel,
Equestrians, tumblers, women, girls, and boys,
Blue-breeched, pink-vested, and with towering plumes.—
All moveables of wonder, from all parts,
Are here—Albinos, painted Indians, Dwarfs,
The Horse of knowledge, and the learned Pig,
The Stone-eater, the man that swallows fire,
Giants, Ventriloquists, the Invisible Girl,
The Bust that speaks and moves its goggling eyes,
The Wax-work, Clock-work, all the marvellous craft
Of modern Merlins, Wild Beasts, Puppet-shows,
All out-o'-the-way, far-fetched, perverted things,
All freaks of nature, all Promethean thoughts
Of man; his dulness, madness, and their feats
All jumbled up together to make up
This Parliament of Monsters. Tents and Booths
Meanwhile, as if the whole were one vast mill,
Are vomiting, receiving, on all sides,
Men, Women, three-years' Children, Babes in arms.[5]

Although the fairs and at least some of the taverns
where freaks were shown were primarily patronized
by the working class, they also attracted aristocratic
amateurs and learned men. Virtuosi's cabinets and the
booths at the fair were on the same route in the educated man's quest of oddities. A common curiosity
erased social distinctions: the quality and the rabble,
the cultivated and the ignorant mingled to see the latest
marvel. Although most came because their innate relish for the sensational, the mysterious, and the grotesque was titillated by stridently announced new importations, some—the educated minority—came out
of genuinely scientific motives, to amplify and verify
the descriptions they had read in learned treatises.*
Evelyn offers a striking example of this catholicity of
interest. On 17 September 1657 we find him visiting
Tradescant's Ark. Two days earlier he had been
inspecting, with equal if not greater attention, a perennial attraction among the London freak shows:

the hairy Maid, or Woman whom twenty years before I had
also seene when a child: her very Eyebrowes were combed
upward, & all her forehead as thick & even as growes on any
womans head, neatly dress'd: There come also two locks
very long out of Each Eare: she had also a most prolix beard,
& *mustachios,* with long locks of haire growing on the very
middle of her nose, exactly like an Island [Iceland] Dog; the
rest of her body not so hairy, yet exceeding long in comparison, armes, neck, breast & back; the Colour of a bright
browne, & fine as well dressed flax: She was now married, &
told me had one Child, that was not hairy, as nor were any of
her parents or relations: she was borne at Ausburg in Ger-
manie, & for the rest very well shaped, plaied well on the
Harpsichord &c.[6]

Pepys, too, made the rounds, even more compul-
sively than his friend Evelyn. Thus we have him
inspecting the bearded lady eleven years after the elder
man had looked his fill; and going also

to Charing-cross, there to see the great Boy and Girle that
are lately come out of Ireland; the latter, eight, the former
but four years old, of most prodigious bigness for their age. I
tried to weigh them in my arms, and find them twice as
heavy as people almost twice their age; and yet I am apt to
believe they are very young—their father a little sorry
fellow, and their mother an old Irish woman. They have had
four children of this bigness and four of ordinary growth,
whereof two of each are dead. If (as my Lord Ormond cer-
tifies) it be true that they are no older, it is very monstrous.[7]

Four months later Pepys was back at the show, where
the giants had been joined by their normal-sized
siblings: "but Lord, how strange it is to observe the
difference between the same children, come out of the
same little woman's belly."[8]

On these excursions Evelyn and Pepys would often
have met fellow members of the Royal Society, such as
Robert Hooke, whose diary jottings referring to his
attendance at shows, while more terse, further illustrate the variety of exhibitions to which men of science
repaired: "saw India catt, Japan Peacock, Porcupine,
Upupa, Vultur, Great Owl, 3 Cassawaris" (1672);
"Saw Elephant 3sh" (1675); "saw tigre in Bartholomew Fair 2d" (1677);† "Saw Elephant wave colours,
shoot a gun, bend and kneel, carry a castle and a man,
etc." (1679); "To fire[e]ater in Gracechurch Street"
(1675/76); "saw the Dutch woeman in Bartholmew
fair, very strange" (1677: she was a giantess); "saw
bonelesse child" (1677).[9] This last was "a girl, above
Sixteen Years of Age, born in Cheshire, and not above
Eighteen inches long, having shed the Teeth seven several Times, and not a perfect Bone in any part of her,

only the Head[!]; yet she hath all her senses to Admiration, and Discourses, Reads very well, Sings, Whistles, and all very pleasant to hear."[10]

Thus, too, Sir Hans Sloane studied the animals at Bartholomew Fair and sent a draftsman to record their physical characteristics. But the most extensive illustration of the overlapping of the world of the Royal Society and that of Bartholomew Fair, and of the fact that all things then were grist for scientific pondering, is found in the many volumes of the society's *Philosophical Transactions*. Few of the freaks, human and subhuman, exhibited in London between 1665 and 1800 go unmentioned in those grave and lively pages.* Sometimes it was there, or at the society's meetings, that a new marvel was first heralded, before it went on show. Shortly after a letter describing them was read before the Royal Society (12 May 1708), Helena and Judith, the phenomenal seven-year-old Hungarian sisters, went on display at the Angel, Cornhill. These were Siamese twins, although the term would not be invented until another such pair, actually coming from Siam, were the sensation of London in 1829. "One of the greatest Wonders in Nature that ever was seen," ran the publicity, "being Born with their Backs fastn'd to each other, and the Passages of their Bodies are both one way. These children are very Handsome and Lusty, and Talk three different Languages. . . . Those who see them, may very well say, they have seen a Miracle, which may pass for the 8th Wonder of the World."[11] The sight, as Swift remarked a month after the twins went on display, "causes a great many speculations; and raises abundance of questions in divinity, law, and physic."[12] Few of those questions occurred to the ordinary sensation seekers who crowded into the Angel, but the philosophical and scientific implications of many such exhibitions were reason enough why savants joined servants in visiting the shows and, no doubt, gazed slack-jawed with the best of them.

D₃✦ʃɑ

The demand for human and animal freaks kept well abreast of the increasing supply.† The ships that brought botanical specimens to Petiver and Sloane also had as cargo a colorful variety of birds, animals, reptiles, and sea creatures—some ferocious, some mighty in size, some distinguished by singular physical attributes or habits, but all possessed of the glamor of distance, tangible living evidence of the still largely mysterious regions to which English explorers and traders now were penetrating. One of the huge volumes of handbills, prints, and newspaper clippings relating to London exhibitions that were assembled by the antiquarian Daniel Lysons is encyclopedic on the subject of living creatures alone: elephants, tigers, lions, rhinoceroses, orangutans, dromedaries, American elk, buffalo, beavers, bears, hippopotamuses, zebras, chimpanzees, cassowaries, ostriches, pelicans, black swans, vultures, electric eels, grampuses, dogfish, crocodiles, porpoises, sea hogs, whales—the list is almost as long as the whole roster of the then known animal kingdom.

Of all these importations, the one that most excited Restoration London was "the strange Beast called the Rynnoceros." Evelyn, like most of the learned, identified the breed with the fabled unicorn, although the reality somewhat belied the myth, for "it more ressembled a huge enormous Swine, than any other Beast amongst us."[13] Arriving aboard an East Indiaman in August 1684, the "Rhinincerous" (the spelling presented insuperable difficulties to contemporary pens) was valued at £2,000—an impressive indication of its worth as a commercial showpiece. The Rhinenceras was immediately put up for sale and was "bought for £2320 by Mr. Langley one of those that bought Mr. Sadlers well at Islington & in a day or two will be seen in Bartholomew faire." But Mr. Langley was unable to raise the money and lost his £500 deposit; whereupon the owners took back their Rhinonceros and put it up for resale, "but noe person bid a farthing soe lyes upon their hands." By the end of September the Rhynonceros was at the Belle Sauvage inn at the foot of Ludgate Hill, where the proprietor was said to take in £15 a day at a price of 12d. for a look and 2s. for a ride. The Rhynoceros continued to attract crowds until its premature death two years later (September 1686); "the severall proprietors haveing Ensured £1200 on her life the Ensurers are catched for much money."[14]

Apart from its putative identification with a legendary animal, the rhino's value derived from its sheer size, ugliness, and, of course, rarity. In the days before scientific nomenclature and taxonomy were established or had descended to the common understanding, much of the charm of these show beasts resided in the aura of mystery or romance in which the showmen diligently wrapped them. Whatever scientific rigor the advertisements lacked was often atoned for by a pleasing touch of poetry. In the records are found such creatures as "a Murino dear, one of the seven sleepers," "the Noble Histix from the West Indies," and "the little Whifler, admired for his

* Thus providing the showmen with valuable publicity in the form of borrowed scientific prestige. Another handbill in the BL collection cited previously (551.d.18) announced "a fresh, lively Country Lad, just come from Suffolk, who is cover'd all over his Body with Bristles like a Hedge Hog, as hard as Horn, which shoot off Yearly." It went on to refer to "the PHILOSOPHICAL TRANSACTIONS, (Numb. 424, Pag. 299), publish'd by the ROYAL SOCIETY, under the Direction of Sir HANS SLOANE, and other eminent Men of all Nations, where they will find a full and particular Account of this surprising Lad, from the Time of his Birth. But though most People are acquainted with the Credit of the PHILOSOPHICAL TRANSACTIONS, yet, as many are not furnish'd with them, we think it proper to transcribe the following Lines for their Satisfaction; by which it will appear to every one, that the various Things expos'd for many Years past (under the title of Curiosities) have all been far inferior to the Lad we are speaking of." Actually, the short excerpt given does not make any explicit comparisons; it merely remarks that "it is not easy to think of any Sort of Skin or natural Integument that exactly resembled it."

† Indeed, on at least one occasion there was a serious oversupply. Sir Edmund Verney, a Royalist soldier and M.P., wrote to his son in 1636: "A merchant of lundon wrote to a factor of his beyound sea, desired him by the next shipp to send him 2 or 3 Apes; he forgot the r, and then it was 203 Apes. His factor has sent him fower scoare, and sayes hee shall have the rest by the next shipp, conceiving the merchant had sent for two hundred and three apes; if yoʳself or frends will buy any to breede on, you could never have had such a chance as now." (*Memoirs of the Verney Family during the Seventeenth Century,* ed. Frances P. Verney and Margaret M. Verney, 2nd ed., London, 1907, I, 82.)

extraordinary Scent."[15] In 1703, the Coach and Horses tavern, Charing Cross, displayed

Two Kaamas's, Male and Female, lately arrived from the Bear-Bishes; being the strangest Creatures that ever was seen alive in Europe; being as tame as a Lamb, having a Trunk like an Elephant, Teeth like a Christian, and Eyes like a Rhinoceros; Ears with a white Furr round them like Sable, Neck and Main like a Horse, and Skin as thick as a Bouffler [buffalo?], a Voice like a Bird, stranger Feet than any Creature that ever has been seen; live as well in Water as on Land.[16]

A decade later, at the Duke of Marlborough's Head, Fleet Street, an especially busy showplace, one could view a "noble and majestick Lion" from Barbary and a younger specimen from Algiers, "so wonderful tame that any Person may handle him as well as his Keeper"; a "noble Panther, lately brought from Egypt, one of the beautifullest Creatures in the World for variety of Spots of divers Colours," and a "noble Pelican or Vulture, lately arriv'd from America . . . the Head like a Griffin, Neck like a Swan."[17]

The familiar hypothesis of the "missing link"—the as yet unidentified occupant of the twilight zone between human beings and the rest of the animal world—was recurrently invoked when creatures suitable for the role turned up. There was, for example, the "Man Teger, lately brought from the East Indies, a most strange and wonderful Creature, the like never seen before in England, it being of Seven several Colours, from the Head downwards resembling a Man, its fore parts clear, and his hinder parts all Hairy; having a long Head of Hair, and Teeth two or three Inches long; taking a Glass of Ale in his hand like a Christian, Drinks it, also plays at Quarter Staff."[18] This probably was a West African baboon. Another candidate for the role of neither-man-nor-beast was the "little Black Hairy Pigmey, bred in the Desarts of Arabia," who was shown at the White Horse inn, Fleet Street, early in the century. Two feet high, with "a Natural Ruff of Hair about his Face," he was said to walk upright, drink a glass of ale or wine, and do "several other things to admiration."[19] The "pigmey" was also, in all likelihood, a member of the monkey family. Toward the end of the century was displayed still another "monster"—this one from "Mount Tibet"—which was said to "approach the Human Species nearer than any hitherto exhibited, and is supposed to be the long lost link between the Human and Brute Creation." A quadruped five feet high, it was unknown to Buffon, but its great beauty and sagacity, "affability, friendship, and good-nature" had led the natives to call it "The Child of the Sky" or "Wonder of the East."[20] Perhaps it was the Abominable Snowman?

Once in a while a specimen of a creature much valued for its exhibition potential came up the river under its own power. In 1702 the skeleton of a whale caught in the Thames was exhibited in a field near King Street, Bloomsbury; the head alone was alleged to weigh forty hundredweight.[21] A decade later one could visit, on a barge near Blackfriars, a "Royal Parmacitty Whale taken in the Thames . . . the noblest Fish ever seen in England." When it got inconveniently ripe, it was auctioned off and demolished, and Thoresby, visiting its skeleton on the Isle of Dogs, measured it at forty-eight yards long and thirty-five round.[22] Still another specimen, displayed sometime in the 1730s, was billed as "the largest Thames-Monster, or miraculous man-eater, that was ever in the World."[23]

Except for the Tower of London, there was no fixed site for the public display of whole menageries until the 1770s, when Exeter Change began to be associated in Londoners' minds with the idea of wild animals on show.* The building has been erected in the last quarter of the seventeenth century with materials salvaged from old Exeter House, which had stood on the same site in the Strand.[24] (The area is now covered by Burleigh Street and the Strand Palace Hotel.) On the ground floor, flanking an arcade which incorporated the Strand footway, was a double line of forty-eight stalls occupied at first by hosiers, milliners, seamsters, and the like. Slowly the nature of the goods and services offered changed. So-called toy shops eventually predominated—mini-boutiques for the sale of fans, china, lacquer ware, tea, silks, brocades, watches, snuff boxes, cutlery, purses, heads of canes, trinkets and baubles of a thousand kinds. These shops, by the nature of their trade, became informal meeting places for the fashionable and idle of both sexes; it was there, for example, that members of Miss Arabella Fermor's set, in Pope's *The Rape of the Lock,* doubtless went for their hair-styling equipment. While the extravagantly coiffeured habitués of Exeter Change gossiped, flirted, and haggled over the costly trifles on display, the large well-lighted room above housed a long succession of exhibitions,† among them Mrs. Mills's waxwork show, a sixteen-foot-high bed adorned with "the most beautiful feathers of divers Colours woven into a Stuff," architectural models, and exhibitions of art and miscellaneous objects prior to sale by auction. One such exhibition included an electrifying machine, a

* Joshua Brookes had a "vivarium" with a menagerie adjacent to his anatomical museum near Oxford Street, but this of course was not public except insofar as passersby could peer through the iron gate at the animals chained to pieces of Gibraltar rock. The night the nearby Pantheon burned down (16 January 1792), "the heat was so violent . . . that his doors and sash-frames were blistered, and the eagle, hawks, raccoons, foxes, and other animals, terrified by the scene and incommoded by the heat, were panting and endeavouring to break their chains. The mob assembled, and fancying that the poor animals were roasting alive, kept up an alarming yell, and threatened to pull the house about his ears." (*Reminiscences of Henry Angelo,* London, 1904, I, 72–73.) Brookes's brother at one time kept a menagerie at 242 Piccadilly, and it was from him that the anatomist got some of his specimens.

† Thus inaugurating an association between exhibitions and "bazaars" which would persist into the mid-Victorian period. More will be said about this later (Chapter 30).

Cremona violin, "a fine groupe of heads drawn with a red-hot poker," and Indian bows and arrows—a sufficient microcosm of eighteenth-century taste.

Some time in the 1770s Exeter Change was taken over by a longtime tenant, a businessman named Thomas Clark who had expanded his stick shop to include cutlery and other hardware and a complete line of equipment for military and naval officers en route to their foreign stations. Eventually he accumulated a fortune of £300,000 and paid the then enormous sum of £7,000 a year in income tax; but never was he known to spend more than a shilling for dinner.[25] Clark put the multipurpose hall to a new use, as a theatre for the popular one-man "entertainments" (songs and recitations) of the elder Charles Dibdin, the composer and dramatist. Subsequently, under Dibdin's management (1776–1781), the hall was occupied by a puppet acting company, the Patagonian Theatre, which had originated in Dublin and during its long London run performed some forty plays, half of which, chiefly ballad operas, were adapted by Dibdin from the human theatre.

From time to time in these years, probably between Dibdin's and the Patagonian puppets' seasonal engagements, the large room at Exeter Change was the London headquarters of the small traveling menagerie belonging to Gilbert Pidcock, who took it to the London fairs and into the provinces during the summer. It was during one of the earliest years of this arrangement that George Stubbs painted a picture, made from sketches at Pidcock's, of an Indian rhinoceros and another of a baboon and an albino macaque monkey, both for John Hunter, who obtained pictures of animals of which he was unable to acquire actual specimens.[26] On another occasion, according to a contemporary anecdote, Stubbs got word at 10 P.M. that there was a dead tiger at Pidcock's which he could buy for a song. "His coat was hurried on, and he flew towards the well-known place and presently entered the den where the dead animal lay extended; this was a precious moment; three guineas were given the attendant, and the body was instantly conveyed to the painter's habitation, where in the place set apart for his muscular pursuits, Mr. S[tubbs] spent the rest of the night carbonading the once tremendous tyrant of the jungle."[27]

At some point, Clark had himself become a dealer in wild animals and birds. In 1793 Pidcock bought Clark's stock to add to his own. The exhibits at this moment, housed in rooms whose walls were painted with appropriate scenery, included a "unicorn" (rhinoceros), a zebra, a kangaroo from Botany Bay, an African ram, a "Sagittaire [secretary] bird that kills the snakes," a "Fiery Lynx," and a "ravenous wolf from Algiers," along with such timely but unrelated items as a "French Beheading Machine." Four years later they were joined by elephants and tigers.[28]

The Exeter Change menagerie never had any overtones of the sideshow or the circus: the wild animals were there simply for their own sake, as examples of what might be seen in the jungle and on the veldt. But although exoticism was never to be underrated as a drawing card, showmen found domestic animals to be quite satisfactory exhibition material so long as they were either monstrous or talented. Presumably because pork, roasted on the spot, was the traditional *plat de la fête* at Bartholomew Fair, a gigantic hog was a standard attraction there, indeed the show's virtual emblem—"the Genius of Smithfield," as Henry Morley, the historian of the fair, called it.[29] Each successive specimen had more grandiose dimensions claimed for it. Early in the century a Buckinghamshire hog on show was ten feet long, thirteen hands (four feet four inches) high, and seven and a half feet in girth; in 1748 the current monarch was twelve feet long and weighed 120 stone; by 1779 either the progress of husbandry or an elastic measuring tape had elongated the newest specimen to fourteen feet. "When he rises from the ground for the spectators to see him, he roars in such a manner that his voice seems to mix, as it were, with the earth."[30] Nor were hogs the only gigantic farm animals to be shown. At the White Horse inn, late the "place where the great Elephant was seen," could be viewed a Lincolnshire ox nineteen hands (six feet four inches) high and four yards long; it had previously been shown at Cambridge University "with great Satisfaction to all that saw him." Later the same hostelry featured a Worcestershire mare that stood as tall as the ox.[31]

The anomalous, deformed, or superabundantly equipped animal was as commonplace in the London shows as it has been until recently at country fairs. Nature's mistakes and aberrations had a morbid attraction for a popular mind that was steeped in superstition and avid for crude shocks, even outright revulsion. Not that the educated mind was any less fascinated. In 1654 Evelyn recorded seeing a six-legged sheep, which "made use of five of them to walke," and, at the same show, a generously endowed goose "that had four legs, two Cropps, & as many Vents."[32] Early in the next century an advertisement called attention to a similarly equipped "strange Cock from Hamborough, having Three proper Legs, Two Fundaments, and makes use of them both at one time. Vivat Reginae."[33] Vivat indeed. Even more complexly constructed was a lamb, shown in 1753, which "has no Vent under his tail, but dungs through each Buttock, and waters through two Pizzels at once."[34] In addition to which, there were one-eyed pigs, four-horned sheep, two-headed heifers, white crows, and seemingly every other anomaly that either Nature or a resourceful showman could contrive.

Performing animals and birds, especially dancing bears, had been staples of London entertainment as early as Tudor times. The showman Banks's trained horse Morocco (Marocco), exhibited for a number of years toward the end of the sixteenth century, was so celebrated that he was mentioned in numerous contemporary plays and books, including *Love's Labour's Lost, Every Man out of His Humor,* and Dekker's *The Wonderful Yeare.* "If Banks had lived in older times," wrote Sir Walter Ralegh, "he would have shamed all the enchanters of the world, for whosoever was most famous of them could never master or instruct any beast as he did."[35] According to Sir Kenelm Digby, Morocco would restore a glove to its owner "after his master had whispered the man's name in his ear; would tell the just number of pence in any silver coin, newly shewn him by his master; and even obey presently his command, in discharging himself of his excrements, whensoever he had bade him."[36] (Alongside this, Morocco's further reputed feat of climbing the steeple of St. Paul's is almost anticlimatic. But it is also apocryphal, because in the new Protestant dispensation the holy relics stowed in the cross had proved an ineffective safeguard against acts of God; the steeple was struck by lightning and burned in 1561 and was never rebuilt.) It was perhaps from this gifted creature, in any event, that the "learned horse" (or horses: there may have been more than one) which was put through its intellectual paces at Exeter Change in 1760 and 1772 descended; among the several human faculties, according to its owner, it "only want[ed] speech."[37]

The variety of creatures proving amenable to instruction increased with the years. A "little Marmazet from Bengal . . . dance[d] the Cheshire Rounds, and Exercise[d] at the Word of Command";[38] hares played the tabor;[39] Chinese birds played cards and told the time by clock or watch.[40] Between 1766 and 1773 Daniel Wildman's troupe of trained bees performed at several London rooms and tea gardens. Wildman was an equestrian as well as an apiarist. In one act, he rode about a ring with one foot on the saddle and the other on the horse's neck, "with a curious mask of bees on his head and face." So adorned, he would drink a glass of wine, and when he fired a pistol, the bees would break ranks, half of them marching over a table and the others returning to the hive.[41] Equally celebrated, somewhat later, were Breslaw's birds, of whose performance Joseph Strutt, the early historian of English sports and pastimes, left an eyewitness account:

A number of little birds, to the amount, I believe, of twelve or fourteen, being taken from different cages, were placed upon a table in the presence of the spectators; and there they formed themselves into ranks like a company of soldiers: small cones of paper bearing some resemblance to grenadiers' caps were put upon their heads, and diminutive imitations of muskets made with wood, secured under their left wings. Thus equipped, they marched to and fro several times; when a single bird was brought forward, supposed to be a deserter, and set between six of the musketeers, three in a row, who conducted him from the top to the bottom of the table, on the middle of which a small brass cannon charged with a little gunpowder had been previously placed, and the deserter was situated in the front part of the cannon; his guards then divided, three retiring on one side, and three on the other, and he was left standing by himself. Another bird was immediately produced; and, a lighted match being put into one of his claws, he hopped boldly on the other to the tail of the cannon, and, applying the match to the priming, discharged the piece without the least appearance of fear or agitation. The moment the explosion took place, the deserter fell down, and lay, apparently motionless, like a dead bird; but, at the command of his tutor he rose again; and the cages being brought, the feathered soldiers were stripped of their ornaments, and returned into them in perfect order.[42]

Of the Learned Pig, "well versed in all Languages, perfect Arethmatician & Composer of Musick," Robert Southey wrote that he was "in his day a far greater object of admiration to the English nation than ever was Sir Isaac Newton."[43] This prodigy of erudition made his London debut at 55 Charing Cross early in 1785, after triumphs at York, Scarborough, and elsewhere the preceding summer. According to his publicity, "he reads, writes, and casts accounts by means of typographical cards, in the same manner that a printer composes and by the same method . . . sets down any capital or surname; solves questions in the four rules of Arithmetic," tells time, and so on, *ad baccalaureatum.*[44] He figures in contemporary prints, including Rowlandson's *The Wonderful Pig* of April 1785, and in Dr. Johnson's conversation. Boswell records that on one of her last visits to Johnson in the preceding year, Anna Seward told him

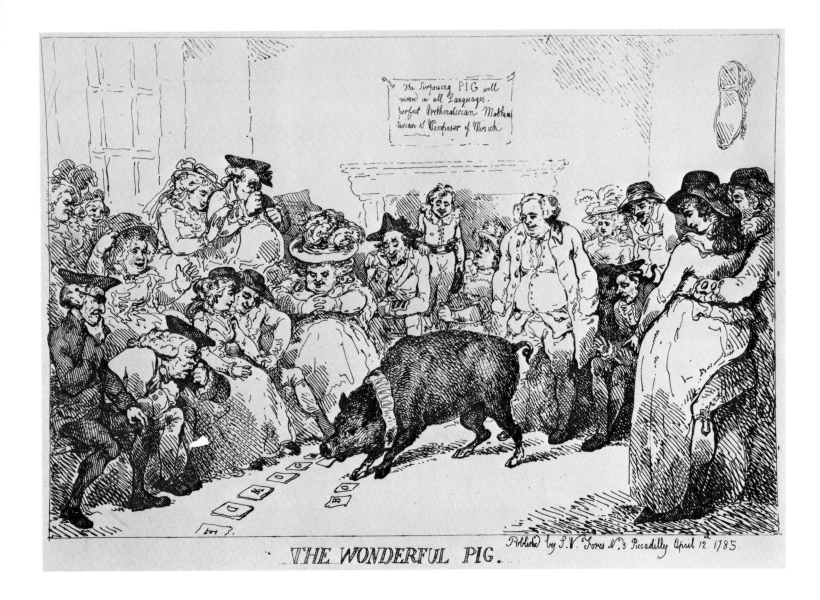

The Surprising PIG well versed in all Languages, perfect Arethmatician Mothematician & Composer of Musick

THE WONDERFUL PIG.

Published by S.V. Fores N.3 Piccadilly April 12 1785.

of a wonderful learned pig, which I [Miss Seward] had seen at Nottingham; and which did all that we have observed exhibited by dogs and horses. The subject amused him. "Then, (said he,) the pigs are a race unjustly calumniated. *Pig* has, it seems, not been wanting to *man*, but *man* to *pig*. We do not allow *time* for his education, we kill him at a year old." Mr. Henry White, who was present, observed that if this instance had happened in or before Pope's time, he would not have been justified in instancing the swine as the lowest degree of groveling instinct. Dr. Johnson seemed pleased with the observation, while the person who made it proceeded to remark, that great torture must have been employed, ere the indocility of the animal could have been subdued.—"Certainly, (said the Doctor;) but, (turning to me,) how old is your pig?" I told him, three years old. "Then, (said he,) the

pig has no cause to complain; he would have been killed the first year if he had not been *educated,* and protracted existence is a good recompence for very considerable degrees of torture."[45]

Johnson died on 13 December, just before the pig began his London engagement. On 6 April of the following year, these verses, not in the best taste, were printed in the *Public Advertiser:*

On the Learned Pig

Though Johnson, learned Bear, is gone,
    Let us no longer mourn our loss,
For lo, a learned Hog is come,
    And wisdom grunts at Charing Cross.

6. *The Wonderful Pig* (engraving by Thomas Rowlandson, 1785).

> Happy for Johnson—that he died
>   Before this wonder came to town,
> Else had it blasted all his pride
>   *Another* brute should gain renown.

◁◦❋◦▷

In one of his scrapbooks Daniel Lysons collected hand-bills and clippings referring to another copious source of London amusement, human freaks; specifically, to quote his manuscript index, "exhibitions of giants, gigantic children, large men, dwarfs, giants and dwarfs exhibited together, masculine women, persons without arms and legs, monstrous births, strange formations and diseases"—as well as persons with bizarre accomplishments, who do not often figure in these pages: "grimacers, strong persons, fire eaters &c., eaters of raw flesh—cats, &c., stone eaters, calculating boys . . ."

There were giants galore, attributed to a dozen nations, including Ireland, France, Holland, Germany, Sweden, and China. Hooke saw a "tall Dutchwoman" at the fair in 1677,[46] and there was an Italian giantess, over seven feet tall and weighing more than 475 pounds, in the Fleet Street taverns.[47] Toward the end of the eighteenth century two Irish giants dominated the scene, one enjoying a long run, the other a lamentably brief one. The latter was Charles Byrne, eight feet four inches tall, wearing shoes fifteen inches long, an ill-favored, flabby-fleshed, stooped wreck of a man before he arrived in London at the age of twenty-one. Evidently, he had taken to poteen the moment he was parted from his mother's breast. Immediately conceiving designs upon his skeleton, and shrewdly estimating that not much of his life expectancy remained, John Hunter is said to have had him kept under surveillance at each successive exhibition place in order to acquire his bones the moment alcohol completed its task. That moment came at the end of May 1783, when Byrne, additionally distressed by the loss of his total savings by mischance or robbery (while in a drunken stupor), was clearly *in extremis* at 23 Cockspur Street. Hunter conducted intensive negotiations with the attending "corpse watcher," who kept raising the asking price for his patient's prospective remains. The upshot was that Hunter had to pay £500 cash—a sum he borrowed from Pidcock at Exeter Change. Hunter transported the dead giant in triumph to his laboratory at Earl's Court and emerged with a skeleton as fine as any anatomist could desire. It became one of the showpieces at his Leicester Square museum and subse-

quently at the Royal College of Surgeons, where it can still be viewed (see Chapter 19).[48]

The more durable and altogether more fortunate member of the pair was Patrick Cotter, born in 1760 in the County Cork, who abandoned the bricklaying trade at the age of eighteen and, adding the name of the legendary Irish giant, O'Brien, to his own, entered the English show business. He was visible in London and the provinces for some twenty-six years, retiring on his savings in 1804. Rowlandson memorialized this good-looking, well-proportioned man in the same year that he portrayed the Learned Pig. No absolutely attested record of his height is preserved, the estimates ranging from eight feet seven and one-half inches to a comparatively diminutive seven feet ten. Contemplating his rival's posthumous destiny and the assiduity with which "resurrection men"—ghouls who supplied anatomists with cadavers—plied their trade, O'Brien had an understandable horror of ending up in the Hunterian Museum. To foil the resurrectionists, therefore, he saw to it that when he died he was to be buried twelve feet down, in a grave carved out of solid rock, guarded by iron bars and arched over with brickwork.[49]

At the other end of the scale were midgets and dwarfs. (The distinction between the two—midgets retaining normal physical proportions despite their miniature size, while dwarfs are characterized by abnormalities of various kinds—was seldom recognized in the show business.) The "Little Family" described in the *Spectator* for 10 January 1711/12 was put together for exhibition purposes from an Italian "Fairy Queen" not three feet high, a West Indian Negro of similar stature, and a "little Turkey Horse 2 Foot odd Inches high . . . that shews several diverting and surprising Actions, at the Word of Command."[50] The extra attractiveness of this show stemmed from the fact that the woman was pregnant, "being the least Woman that ever was with Child in Europe." She was eventually delivered by Queen Caroline's personal physician.[51]

The gallery of malformed human beings who were shown for money might have been painted by Hieronymus Bosch inspired by photographs of the Thalidomide babies born in the 1960s. As early as 1588 a pamphlet described a sixty-year-old Welshwoman "in the middest of whose forehead by the wonderfull woorke of GOD, there groweth out a Croked horne of 4 ynches longe." She was sent up to London to be inspected by the Privy Council and supposedly was also "nowe to be seene" at some public exhibition.[52] A century later a "mail child" was distinguished by an excrescence of another sort, "a Bear growing on his back alive."[53]

Most such human show creatures, like their barnyard counterparts, were marked by either superfluity or deprivation. On the one hand, one could see "the Admirable Work of Nature, a Woman having three Breasts," along with her daughter, similarly endowed;[54] a thirty-week-old suckling from Guernsey with a head a yard in circumference;[55] two-headed men,[56] hermaphrodites,[57] and both children and adults with either one head and two bodies (heteradelphi) or two heads and one body.[58] On the other hand, there were the hideously crippled, who somehow managed to perform a few human acts: a "High German woman without hands or feet, who could sew, thread needles, spin fine thread, and fire pistols" and an armless man who combed his hair and shaved with his feet and saluted visitors by removing his hat with his toes.[59] The most accomplished of these was Mathew Buchinger, a twenty-nine-inch dwarf who had been born without hands, legs, or even thighs; it was said that he could play an oboe, write and draw with a pen, play cards, and dance a hornpipe in highland dress.[60]

Such were some of the attractions visited by Londoners sharing the insatiable curiosity of men like Pepys, who once wrote of himself that he was "with child to see any strange thing."[61] In the generation following Pepys's, a London visitor sometimes to be observed at the freak shows, despite his ironic assertion that his curiosity could be satisfied at no expense without going inside, was Jonathan Swift. The impact of London's dwarfs and giants on the imagination that created the Lilliputians and Brobdingnagians need hardly be remarked. It has been demonstrated that Swift uses the shows of contemporary London constantly and variously in the episodes, motifs, and structure of Gulliver's Travels.[62] During his stay in Lilliput, Gulliver is, in effect, the showman before whom a community of midgets go through their laughable tricks; but in Brobdingnag, as we have seen, the erstwhile showman becomes the show. The most impressive borrowing Swift made from the show trade was the box in which Gulliver, a curious exhibit, is carried about Brobdingnag: a physical object, drawn from everyday London observation, transformed into a complex literary device. Dwarfs were taken about London in just such boxes. One famous passenger was a thirty-one-inch Swiss dwarf named Hans Worrenbergh or John Womberg, "the little mannikin that was lately carried about in a box," as Evelyn called him, who could be seen at various taverns in 1688–89.[63] The Little Family too was transported on the showman's back, in the manner of a peepshow. To contemporary readers the implication of the human being Gulliver's being transported in a box while in Brobdingnag was darkened by the fact that the contents of London showmen's boxes often were not pleasant to look upon. A "Little Farey Woman, lately come from Italy, being but Two Foot Two Inches high," was recommended to the attention of the public not only because she was thirteen inches shorter than the competition but on the additional ground that she was "in no ways Deform'd, as the other two Women are, that are carried about the Streets in Boxes from House to House, for some years past."[64]

Gulliver's sufferings as he is conveyed from place to place in Brobdingnag, before the queen buys him for a pet, echo the plight of those whose inherent misery was compounded by the indignities visited upon them by their exhibitors and, scarcely less, by the normal men and women who paid to see and handle them. Some preferred to do so in private. The proprietors of the "Farey Woman," who was more presentable than her box-borne sisters in this deplorable trade, advertised that "if any Person has a desire to see her at their own Houses, we are ready to wait upon them at any Hour of the Day."[65] Or, by a compromise arrangement, a private showing could be held at the regular places of business. Helena and Judith, the incorporate Hungarian twins mentioned earlier, were available in this fashion, at double the charge for the public generally.[66] Gulliver's exhibitor showed him at his own lodgings, charging a private party, regardless of number, as much as he would make from a full room at an inn.

The compassion for human indignity and outright suffering that is implicit in Gulliver's reflections of the trade in freaks was a harbinger of the fashion of sensibility—extreme, self-indulgent feelings of sympathy and pity—that began to make itself felt in the middle third of the eighteenth century. This reaction from the tyranny of Reason had at least something to do with the declining attendance of the "superior ranks" at the popular shows as the century wore on. Another compelling influence, certainly, was social: the dictates of decorum became more binding, and as the risk of unpleasant confrontations with the unruly and disrespectful mob increased, the nobility and gentry were more cautious in their patronage. Exhibitors seeking to attract them provided discreet ways to approach and leave their booths at fairs and promised suitable care for their comfort while they were there. In 1728, for example, the operators of a theatrical booth at Southwark Fair, one of whom was Henry Fielding, advertised that "there is a commodious Passage for the Quality, and Coaches through the Half-Moon Inn, and care will be taken that there shall be Lights, and People to conduct them to their Places."[67]

This desire on the part of the crowd-shunning but insatiably curious to eat their cake and have it too resulted, in one instance after the middle of the eighteenth century, in carrying the private-show policy to its logical extreme, the general avoidance of public exhibition. The object of interest was the midget "Count" Boruwlaski, actually an untitled member of the minor Polish aristocracy who was the protégé of a succession of countesses until he struck out on his own, at the age of forty, in 1780.[68] An account given to the Académie des Sciences when he was twenty put his height at twenty-eight inches; since then, he had grown only eleven more. Already a favorite at various European courts, including Vienna and Versailles, the tiny count arrived in London in June 1782 under the protection of the Duke and Duchess of Devonshire and the Duke of Gloucester, through whom he met, and was petted by, royalty and most of the nobility. Thenceforward, until he retired, he divided his time between England and the continent.

Boruwlaski was set apart from his fellow freaks both physically and intellectually. The only abnormality of his frame and features was their miniature size; he was well proportioned, had a bright and expressive countenance, and enjoyed perfect health. He was a witty conversationalist, full of high spirits, the life of any small fashionable gathering. Forced by circumstances to exhibit himself for money, Boruwlaski successfully avoided the stigma of Charing Cross and Bartholomew Fair, at first giving private "concerts" on his guitar. Later even this pretense of paid entertainment was abandoned. During appointed hours he kept to his house, with a butler to open the door to his "friends" who left a tip—originally half a guinea but later reduced as low as a shilling when the pool of instant friends shrank. Or alternately, as John Gibson Lockhart recalled, he would go from house to house in a sedan chair, "with a servant in livery following him who took the fee—M. le Comte himself (dressed in a scarlet coat and bag wig) being ushered into the room like any ordinary visitor."[69] George IV and Lockhart's father-in-law, Sir Walter Scott, were among his loyal acquaintances, as were Mr. and Mrs. Charles Mathews of the theatre. When he visited the latter, as he did

whenever he came to London in his later years, Mrs. Mathews would seat him beside her at dinner and, it is recorded, "sometimes in doing so put a playful kiss upon his delicate little cheek, round the rosy softness of which a profusion of snow-white hair curled and waved like that of a fair child."[70] He was then in his eighties.*

D3✳Ɛꓷ

The most populous and diverting of all London's freak shows (as it was widely regarded) could not, however, be moved to people's houses for private showing; nor was it approved of by many who had no compunction about inviting the bearers of stunted and deformed human beings to bring their boxes into the drawing room. The public opposition to Bethlehem (or, as it came to be spelled, Bethlem) Hospital's open-door policy, however inconsistent with the toleration of commercial freak exhibits, was among the earliest manifestations of English humanitarianism, although many years would pass before it had any effect.[71]

Bedlam, as this asylum for the insane at Bishopsgate was universally called, was an entertainment center as early in 1609, when it figured in Ben Jonson's *Epicoene, or The Silent Woman*. In that same year a typical upper-crust family party, that of Lord Percy, paid ten shillings to watch inmates of Bedlam's twenty-one rooms perform their unrehearsed antics.[72] Closed for a period during the Commonwealth, Bedlam was reopened after the Restoration and in 1676 moved to its new building in Moorfields, a structure so imposing as to be likened to the Louvre and as unsuited to its purpose as Montagu House was later to prove when it became the home of the British Museum. Here the "poor, distracted" lunatics were on show, resulting, as the governors repeatedly pointed out when the practice was criticized, in gate receipts of £400 a year as well as publicity which, they maintained, attracted gifts and bequests.

There are numerous contemporary descriptions of Bedlam and its inmates, by Ned Ward, Tom Brown, Sir Richard Steele, and Henry Mackenzie (*The Man of Feeling*) among others. Unfortunately for the historian, madmen and their odd conduct were all too convenient a vehicle for the kind of satire in which writers of the period delighted, so that descriptions of Bedlam are characterized by imaginative and pointed wit, rather than by sober factual detail. What begins as "a visit to Bedlam" quickly loses its descriptive value as it

* Boruwlaski lived the last decades of his life at Durham, where a wealthy tradesman had made what he deemed a shrewd investment by selling the already elderly midget a life annuity in expectation of his imminent decease. Instead, while the speculator grew older and older, the count retained the bloom and buoyancy of youth. The latter won the longevity race by a number of years, surviving until the age of ninety-nine. When he died in 1837, *Bentley's Miscellany* (2, 484) contrived a sprightly epitaph:

A spirit brave, yet gentle, has dwelt,
    as it appears,
Within three feet of flesh for near
    one hundred years;
Which causes wonder, like his consti-
    tution, strong,
That one *so short alive* should be *alive
    so long!*

becomes a free exercise in caricature. Still, the tumultuous atmosphere seems captured faithfully enough in the beginning of Ned Ward's narrative: "We were admitted in thro' an Iron-Gate, within which sat a Brawny Cerberus, of an Indico-Colour, leaning upon a Money-box; we turned in thro' another Iron-Barricade, where we heard such a rattling of Chains, drumming of Doors, Ranting, Hollowing, Singing, and Ratling, that I could think of nothing but Don Quevedo's Vision, where the Damn'd broke loose, and put Hell in an Up-roar."[73] The cells were arranged in galleries, in the manner of cages in a menagerie or booths at a fair, and in each one was a chained lunatic, whose behavior, if it were not sufficiently entertaining to begin with, was made so by the spectators' prodding him or her with their sticks or encouraging further wildness by ridicule, gestures, and imitations.

The milder patients, however—those whom Von Uffenbach, another visitor, described as "not mad but only deprived of their wits or simple"—were allowed to mingle with one another, though separated by sex, in an open space, where they provided a show less violent than those of their caged fellows. Von Uffenbach remembered especially a man who crowed all day like a cock, and another who "imagined that he was a Captain and wore a wooden sword at his side and had several cock's feathers stuck into his hat. He wanted to command the others and did all sorts of tomfoolery; we threw a shilling or two down to him, with which he appeared highly delighted."[74] This comparatively inoffensive transaction, however, was the exception rather then the rule, and other accounts suggest that the atmosphere inside Bedlam during visiting hours resembled that of Bartholomew Fair, with nuts, fruit, and cheesecakes being hawked, beer brought in from nearby taverns, and pickpockets hard at work. "Mistresses, we found," wrote Ned Ward, "were to be had of all Ranks, Qualities, Colours, Prices, and Sizes, from the Velvet Scarf to the Scotch-Plad Petticoat; Commodities of all sorts went off, for there wanted not a Suitable Jack to every Jill. Every fresh comer was soon engaged in an Amour; tho' they came in Single they went out by Pairs. . . . all that I can say of it, is this, 'Tis an Alms-house for Madmen, a Showing Room for Whores, a sure Market for Lechers, a dry Walk for Loiterers."[75]

The full horror of Bedlam was depicted by Hogarth in the eighth plate of *A Rake's Progress.* By then the humanitarian spirit was making itself felt more positively. The young lady who was the putative writer of the model letters Samuel Richardson published as *Letters Written to and for Particular Friends* (1741) expressed a revulsion that was becoming more general:

Instead of the concern I think unavoidable at such a sight, a sort of mirth appeared on their [the visitors'] countenances; and the distemper'd fancies of the miserable patients most unaccountably provoked mirth, and loud laughter, in the unthinking auditors; and the many hideous roarings, and wild motions of others, seemed equally entertaining to them. Nay, so shamefully inhuman were some, among whom (I am sorry to say it!) were several of my own sex, as to endeavour to provoke the patients into rage to make them sport. I have been told, this dreadful place is often used for the resort of lewd persons to meet and make assignments: But that I cannot credit.[76]

It was symptomatic of the new feeling that when another asylum, St. Luke's Hospital, was established in 1751, its articles of foundation specified that "the patients shall not be exposed to public view." Finally (1770), the governors of Bedlam required that admission be by ticket only, and one venerable source of merriment was deleted from London's list.

D₃✳₤◖

The same ships that brought exotic plants to Tradescant and rhinoceroses to the showmen also occasionally delivered specimens of strange human beings from distant shores—not freaks (though they were necessarily regarded as such, being so rare) but typical members of other races. Three Eskimos seem to have been brought to Bristol as early as 1501, and a Brazilian chieftain appeared in Henry VIII's Whitehall some three decades later, but it was not until after the middle of the sixteenth century, when the English age of exploration really got under way, that American and African savages were added to the list of London exhibitions. Frobisher brought one American Indian back from his first expedition and two from his second, and the dead body of one, if we may believe Trinculo in *The Tempest,* was shown in London. From 1584 onward, Indians were imported, partly for the exhibition trade, from Virginia and New England.[77]

These persons, physically so different from Anglo-Saxons, speaking an unintelligible tongue, bearing with them evidence of strange customs and superstitions, did more than merely cater to the curiosity of the London populace; in time they fed the rising philosophical interest in the origin, nature, and significance of distant races. The ordinary Londoner staring at a dark-skinned tribesman in a Charing Cross tavern had no notion that he was participating in what modern historians of ideas were to call the study of primitivism, nor would he have cared. The cultivated Londoner had a somewhat clearer idea: the exhibit was a Noble Savage, an exotic type of hero, the concept of whom had been imported from France after the Restoration and who now was appearing, as an Aztec or a Peruvian, in the plays of Davenant, Howard, and Dryden and the romances of Aphra Behn. More than half a century later, under the influence of Rousseau, the Noble Savage was romanticized as a living exemplar of the personal innocence and innate resistance to the corruption of civilization's institutions and customs which flourished in a state of nature, a living reproach to what were taken to be the affectations and arid systematizing of the Age of Reason. And so, though the grounds of their interest could scarcely have been farther apart, both the illiterate and the sophisticated flocked to see the newest arrival from halfway round the world.

The nobility that was attributed to the savage of eighteenth-century philosophical theory was as much social—a matter of rank—as moral. Common jungle specimens of exotic manhood were less interesting or significant than the negroid or Polynesian equivalent of dukes and marquesses. Hence, "noblemen" were particularly prized, whether or not it was possible to document their exalted station in their homeland. One such was brought to London by the navigator William Dampier, who described him in *A New Voyage round the World* (1697). The claim was that this "nobleman" had been shipwrecked off his native land of Mindanao and, with his mother, sold and sent to Europe. The quality could inspect him privately, by appointment, at their houses; ordinary people could find him at the Blue Boar's Head, Fleet Street. If we are to believe a handbill describing this "Painted Prince," as he came to be called, he was a walking exemplification of "the whole Mystery of Painting or Staining upon Human Bodies. . . . The more admirable Back-parts afford us a lively Representation of one quarter part of the World, upon and betwixt his Shoulders, where the Arctic and Tropic Circles centre in the North Pole on his Neck."[78] He seems, in fact, to have been an ambulant map, though how such up-to-date knowledge of geography as included the Arctic and Tropic circles—even if the latter was grossly misplaced—had penetrated to the Philippines is not for us to inquire. Prince Giolo, to give him the more formal name he acquired, died of smallpox after a few years, and his place in the ethnological limelight was taken by another sav-

age of high degree. This was "the Indian King, who was betrayed on Board of an English Interloper, and barbarously abused on Board of that Ship, by one Waters and his Men, and put in Irons; from thence carried to Jamaica, and sold there for a slave, and now Redeem'd by a Merchant in London." He could be seen for twopence at the Golden Lion, Smithfield.[79]

In 1710 arrived four Iroquois sachems on what was, by design and in effect, a state visit in behalf of both diplomacy and public relations.[80] The trip was part of a strategy devised by the governors of the northern colonies to recruit home support for a renewed expedition against the French in Canada—a previous one had ended disastrously—and to impress these influential savages from the Mohawk Valley, on whose future good offices much depended, with the strength and majesty of the nation to which they owed fealty. Although public display for gain was obviously not to be thought of in this case, otherwise London gave the chiefs the full treatment. "They appeared," writes Richmond P. Bond, the historian of the episode, "in newspaper accounts and periodical comments, diplomatic dispatches, official notations, letters and diaries; and they found their way into such varied publications as epilogue, ballad, occasional poem, prose tract, annal, and essay, composed on demand of purse or self by Anonymous of Grub and Mr Hack of Fleet Street as well as by Steele and Addison"—the former in the *Tatler,* the latter in the *Spectator*. One evidence of their fame was a production which the leading puppet impresario, Martin Powell, staged for the occasion: "A New Opera, Performed by a Company of Artificial Actors . . . an incomparable Entertainment call'd The Last Year's Campaigne" (the Duke of Marlborough's engagement with the French near Blaguiers). When they turned up at another playhouse, the mob would not let the performance begin until the Iroquois were seated on the stage: "since we have paid our money, the Kings we will have." Momentarily, therefore, the Iroquois monarchs figured in London entertainment; they had a similar glancing contact with the coeval world of London collecting, in that they brought for Sir Hans Sloane's museum, in Bond's words, "a thin, sword-like purification stick for inciting the eruption of foodstuffs, and tump-lines, with headband plain and headband decorated by dyed porcupine quill work, thought by their hosts to be cords for tying prisoners."

The Iroquois were followed to London over fifty years later (1762) by three Cherokee chiefs from the Carolina-Tennessee mountains, accompanied by two young veterans of George Washington's campaign in the American interior—Henry Timberlake and Sergeant Thomas Sumter, who was destined to be the last surviving general officer of the Revolution.[81] According to Timberlake, the journey was undertaken at the behest of one of the chiefs, a friend of the Jefferson family, who, being shown a picture of George III while at Williamsburg, expressed a wish to see "the king my father" in person. During their London stay, from mid-June to mid-August, one of them was painted by Reynolds, Oliver Goldsmith waited three hours for the privilege of an interview with them, magazines published their copperplate portraits, a ribald song "on the Cherokee Chiefs, Inscribed to the Ladies of Great Britain" went on sale at sixpence, and, it was rumored, puppet showmen transformed Punch into the likeness of a Cherokee.

There were accusations, which Timberlake heatedly denied, that he admitted sightseers to the Indians' Suffolk Street lodgings only upon payment of a fee. (Actually, it was the lodginghouse keeper who profited in this respect from their presence.) They attracted crowds wherever they went—at the Tower, St. Paul's, the Houses of Parliament, Woolwich arsenal, and the other standard sights—and they were much in evidence at various taverns and pleasure gardens, whose proprietors, when they had advance notice of the Cherokees' coming, ran newspaper advertisements announcing that fact and raised their prices. On their second visit to Vauxhall Gardens, 10,000 persons flocked to watch the copper-skinned visitors, adorned with shells, feathers, and earrings, get riotously drunk. "Swallowing by wholesale Bumpers of Frontiniac," said one newspaper, "they entertained themselves and the gaping multitude by sounding the keys of the Organ, scraping upon the Strings of a Violin, clapping their Hands in Return for the Claps of Applause bestowed upon them." They committed several graver "irregularities" which Timberlake, in his narrative of the visit, forbore to specify, but which, he said, "ought rather to be attributed to those that enticed them, than to the simple Indians, who drank only to please them." The party, in any case, broke up between two and three o'clock in the morning.

The wanton exploitation of the Americans evoked severe criticism in the press. A letter purporting to come from an envious tavern owner described his wife's insistence that he emulate another innkeeper who posted signs at his door, "July 25. This day the King of the Cherokees and his two Chiefs drink Tea here," and proposed to ensconce the king in the inn's "club-chair" (the sort of throne Dr. Johnson would have occupied). The writer went to the rival tavern to see how the celebrities' appearance was managed, but, he said, "I was too much shocked to stay long . . . reflecting upon a very just, though shocking remark, made by a vulgar fellow, in the room whilst I was present; 'They are brought here,' says he, 'to be shewn like wild beasts.'" The letter went on to describe the arrangements proposed for the Indians' visit to the writer's own establishment. The beer on that occasion would be more expensive and of poorer quality than usual, "as people will be too much taken up with the Cherokees to mind their liquor. We are . . . to have a man stand at the door with a Constable's staff, who is to cry, *'Walk in, Gentlemen, see 'em alive!'*"

Further protest, couched in nonsatirical terms, appeared in the *London Chronicle:*

What . . . can apologize for people running in such shoals to all public places, at the hazard of health, life, or disappointment, to see the savage chiefs that are come among us? . . . These poor creatures make no more than theatrical figures, and can be seen with no satisfaction from the pressure of a throng: why then are people mad in their avidity to behold them? . . . to read in the papers, how these poor wild hunters were surrounded by as wild gazers on them at Vauxhall, and that three hundred eager crouders were made happy by shaking hands with them . . . I should like to read a letter (if they could write one) on that subject, to their friends at home, in order to learn what they think of the mad savages of Great Britain.

As a consequence of the commotion at Vauxhall, if not of the criticism in the press, the authorities forbade the Indians to be taken to any more places of entertainment.

The government intervened on another ground three years later (1765), when two Mohawks went on exhibition for a shilling at the Sun tavern, Strand. The day after the first advertisement appeared, the innkeeper and the impresario were hauled before the House of Lords. Evidently, there was no law on the books to cover their offense, so the Lords promptly passed one, not to ban such exhibitions, but "to prevent any free Indian, under his Majesty's Protection, from being carried by Sea from any of his Majesty's Colonies in America, without a proper License for that Purpose."[82]

After the Cherokees, the next sensation of the sort was the arrival in December 1772 of Captain George Cartwright with a company of Eskimos.[83] Cartwright, the scion of an old Nottinghamshire family, was an army officer, retired on half pay, who had gone to Labrador two years earlier as partner in a London trading firm. Now, on his first visit home, he brought an Eskimo and one of his several wives, her daughter, his youngest brother, and the brother's wife. At Westminster Bridge, according to Cartwright's journal, they were "immediately surrounded by a great concourse of people; attracted not only by the uncommon appearance of the Indians who were in their sealskin dresses, but also by a beautiful eagle, and an Esquimau dog; which had much the resemblance of a wolf, and a remarkable wildness of look." Cartwright and his troupe took lodgings in Leicester Street, but so many visitors clamored to see the Eskimos that he rented a house in Little Castle Street, Oxford Market, where they could be inspected on Tuesdays and Fridays. "On these days," Cartwright wrote, "not only my house was filled, even to an inconvenience, but the street was so much crowded with carriages and people, that my residence was a great nuisance to the neighborhood." Among the sightseers was the indefatigable Boswell, who reported to Dr. Johnson that he "had carried on a short conversation by signs . . . particularly with one of them who was a priest." Dr. Johnson refused to believe they understood him.[84]

The inconvenience Cartwright noted was intensified by the foul odor of the Eskimos' skin dresses (as well, one might hazard, as their persons). Cartwright therefore had the women make new costumes out of broadcloth. Thus fashionably appareled, they went to a performance of *Cymbeline* at Covent Garden, where, like the Iroquois chiefs many years earlier, they were greeted with "thundering applause." But they were little impressed by the standard sights of London except the view from the dome of St. Paul's. At John Hunter's anatomical museum, the head of the group was disturbed by the bones. "Are these the bones of Esquimaux whom Mr. Hunter has killed and eaten?" he inquired. "Are we to be killed? Will he eat us, and put our bones there?" But their spirits revived when Cartwright took them to his family's estate near Newark.

After a refreshing interval in the country, where they enjoyed a fox hunt, Cartwright brought his Eskimos back to London. They were summoned before royalty and taken also to the houses of "several of the nobility and people of fashion." They embarked for Labrador in May 1773, but not all reached home: both men died of smallpox at the very outset of the voyage.

The noblest savage of them all, however, taking the term in its fullest Rousseauistic connotation, was

Omai, the Tahitian youth whom Captain Furneaux, Cook's second in command during his second voyage, brought back in the *Adventurer* in July 1775, two years after the Eskimos departed.[85] Announced in the press first as a "wild Indian, that was taken on an island in the South Seas" but soon promoted to the rank of "a private Gentleman of a small fortune," Omai was an instant hit with the nobility and the literati, to all of whom he appeared to exemplify everything that was right in unspoiled society: full of agreeable sensibility, equipped with unexceptionable social manners and tact, unaffectedly dignified, considerate, cheerful, sympathetic, he was, in short, a true "nature's gentleman." He was entertained by Lord Sandwich, Sir Joseph Banks, the Burneys (Fanny left a famous description of him), George Colman the playwright, and Mrs. Thrale. Dr. Johnson approved of "the elegance of his behavior." Crowds followed Omai in the streets, as they had the Eskimos. But eventually his novelty wore off, and after two years of lionizing, which stopped short only of formal exhibition, he was returned to the South Seas on Cook's next voyage.

ᗞᎫ☀Ꭼᗞ

The authenticity of the Iroquois and Cherokee sachems, Cartwright's Eskimos, and Omai was beyond question, but they were not, after all, the subjects of commercial exhibitions. No exhibit, live or inanimate, that was shown for profit was wholly free of suspicion, and with good reason: deception was rife in the London exhibition trade. Although the possibility, indeed in many cases the probability, of chicanery had long been taken for granted by more sophisticated observers—witness Trinculo's doubts about the painted fish, Sir Richard Steele on Don Saltero, and every satirical description ever written of a virtuoso's cabinet—the presence of some skeptics among the showgoers did little to reduce the chances of deceit. The learned, we know, often were taken in as completely as the credulous masses or, to put the best face on it, were sometimes divided in their opinions. In March 1701 Evelyn saw on view near Somerset House

a little Dutch Boy, of about eight or nine years old, who was by his parents carried about to shew, that had about the Circle or Iris of his Eyes, in one of them these letters *Deus meus,* & in that of his left Iris *Elohim* in the Hebrew Character: how this was impress'd, or don by artifice none could imagine, his parents affirming him to be so born, nor did it at all prejudice his sight, for flinging a small pin on the floore, he immediatly took it up, & seemed to be a lively playing boy: Everybody went to see this unusual phenomena: Physitians & philosophers with greate accuracy examining it, some affirmed it artificial, others tooke it for something almost supernaturall.[86]

Seldom do we find reports of particular deceptions being exposed—of showmen treated as, for example, Swift dealt with the astrologer John Partridge. Nonsense was more acceptable in the exhibition field than elsewhere, or at least less fuss was made about it. In view of what were unquestionably more flagrant deceptions, it seems a little hard that through the agency of a physician-antiquary named James Parsons a showman was "turned out of town" for exhibiting in a glass case what he claimed was a mermaid taken on the coast of Acapulco, but what was in fact a human fetal monstrosity.[87]

In the total absence of any code of ethics and in the presence of an urban population ignorant of the very meaning of *caveat emptor* and furthermore with an almost stubborn desire to be deceived, exhibitors had a clear field, of which they took the utmost advantage. They had no obligation to tell the truth in their advertising, with the result that we, who depend largely on such evidence, are as ill informed as their customers. Apart from those objects and creatures that could not possibly have been what they purported to be, how many were genuine and how many fabricated or misrepresented? It is impossible to tell. But if there is any disposition to overestimate the effect that the gradual dissemination of scientific ways of thinking had at this time upon the show business and its clientele, it can easily be corrected by reference to Goldsmith's *The Citizen of the World* (1762), in which the fictive author, a Chinese philosopher resident in London, dilates upon popular curiosity and popular credulity and the hazards and rewards involved in serving them.

"From the highest to the lowest," he says, "this [English] people seem fond of sights and monsters. I am told of a person here who gets a very comfortable livelihood by making wonders, and then selling or shewing them to the people for money, no matter how insignificant they were in the beginning; by locking them up close, and shewing for money, they soon become prodigies!" First this resourceful showman exhibited himself as a waxwork automaton, a venture prematurely concluded by an untimely sneeze. Then he painted himself as an Indian warrior, frightening ladies and children with his war whoop until he was arrested for a debt contracted while he was a waxwork.

After some time, being freed from gaol, he was now grown wiser, and instead of making himself a wonder, was resolved only to make wonders. He learned the art of pasting up mummies: was never at a loss for an artificial *lusus naturae;* nay, it has been reported that he has sold seven petrified lobsters of his own manufacture to a noted collector of rarities; but this the learned Cracovius Putridus has undertaken to refute in a very elaborate dissertation. . . .

By their fondness of sights, one would be apt to imagine, that instead of desiring to see things as they should be, they are rather solicitous of seeing them as they ought not to be. A cat with four legs is disregarded, though never so useful; but if it has but two, and is consequently incapable of catching mice, it is reckoned inestimable, and every man of taste is ready to raise the auction. A man, though in his person faultless as an aerial genius, might starve; but if stuck over with hideous warts like a porcupine, his fortune is made for ever, and he may propagate the breed with impunity and applause.

Goldsmith cites an ordinary mantua-maker who could not get work until by an accident her arms were cut off above the elbow. "She now was thought more fit for her trade than before: business flowed in a-pace, and all people paid for seeing the mantua-maker who wrought without hands." So too with a gentleman showing his collection of pictures and stopping before one which his auditors regarded as "the most paltry piece of the whole collection." No such thing: "The painter drew the whole with his foot, and held the pencil between his toes: I bought it at a very great price; for peculiar merit should ever be rewarded."

But these people are not more fond of wonders than liberal in rewarding those who shew them. From the wonderful dog of knowledge under the patronage of the nobility, down to the man with the box, who professes to shew *the most imitation of Nature that was ever seen:* they all live in luxury. A singing woman shall collect subscriptions in her own coach and six; a fellow shall make a fortune by tossing a straw from his toe to his nose; one in particular has found that eating fire was the most ready way to live; and another who jingles several bells fixed to his cap, is the only man I know of who has received emolument from the labours of his head.[88]

Waxwork and Clockwork

4

While some exhibitions were bringing to seventeenth- and eighteenth-century London tangible evidence of Nature's variety and man's ingenuity, others depicted an illusory reality. Hovering sometimes on the distant periphery of the theatre, with antecedents rooted in earlier centuries, these exhibitions fascinated visitors by their mimetic effects and often, as well, by the mechanical means by which those effects were produced.

Of these, wax figures of human beings had the most enduring popularity, as the prosperity of elaborate waxwork museums in today's world bears witness. In Protestant England waxworks were vestiges of a form of religious art which had flourished in pre-Reformation times and which continued to do so in the Roman Catholic nations on the continent. Small wax figures then had been a kind of votive offering, and much of the early statuary of saints had been in wax. As we shall see in Chapter 7, effigies of English monarchs, made of wax as well as of wood, had been carried at their funerals, and since this custom did not smack of Romish idolatry, it survived into the Restoration. Waxworks with more emphatic religious associations, however, caused scandal when they were brought into the country by diplomatic missions under the tolerance of Charles II. In 1672 Evelyn "went to see the fopperies of the Papists at Somerset house & York house, where now the French Ambassador had caused to be represented our Blessed Saviour, at the Pascal Supper, with his Disciples, in figures & puppets made as big as the life, of wax work, curiously clad, & sitting round a large table, the roome nobly hung, & shining with innumerable Lamps & Candles, this exposed, to the whole world, all the City came to see; such liberty had the Roman Catholics at this time obtained."[1]

There were secular waxworks in England as early as the middle of the seventeenth century; the Tradescant catalogue lists, in its typically unelaborated way, "Several sorts of impost [embossed, hence high or low relief?] wax-works curious" and "Phaëton with his Chariot and Horses, excellent waxworks." The presence of waxworks at Bartholomew Fair is first recorded in 1647.[2] Half a century later, Ned Ward visited a waxwork booth there. Billed as "the Temple of Diana," it drew trade with a barker in the form of "a Comical Figure Gaping and Drumming," which may indicate a primitive clockwork mechanism. He and the two wax babies flanking him, said Ward,

appear'd very Natural, insomuch that it induced us to Walk in and take a sight of their whole Works; being much astonish'd upon our first entrance of the Room, at the Liveliness of the Figures, who sat in such easie Postures, and their hands dispos'd with such a becoming freedom, that Life, it self could not have appear'd less stiff, or the whole Frame more regular; the Eyes being fix'd with that Tenderness, which I apprehend as a great difficulty; so that the most experienc'd of our Charming Ladies could not, after an Hours practice in her Glass, have look'd more Soft and Languishing.[3]

The first artist-showman in wax to appear by name in the English records seems to have been Johann

Heinrich Schalch (1623–ca. 1704), a native of Schaffhausen, who obtained from the Lord Mayor of London in 1685 "a Permitt to make Shew within this City and liberties of divers peeces of wax worke representing severall Monarchs and potentates of Europe he doeing nothing prejudituall to his Majesties peace."[4] Schalch worked for the royal family and made a death mask of Queen Mary in 1694. Evidently he modeled, in addition, a tableau of the queen on her deathbed, "surrounded by many persons, some of them important personages at the Court of Denmark," which he toured extensively.[5] Not surprisingly, in view both of the early association of wax modeling with funeral effigies and the fact that wax more closely approximated the color of corpses than of living human flesh, representations of recently deceased royalty and other famous persons lying on their biers would be a staple of waxwork shows well into the Victorian era.

Another artist in wax to portray royalty and members of the nobility was a Mrs. Goldsmith, whose best-known work was the funeral effigy she executed of the Duchess of Richmond, a famous beauty. She also made effigies of William III and Queen Mary, the former, according to a letter to a newspaper in 1702, "dressed in coronation robe, with so majestic a mien that nothing seems wanting but life and motion." (The last seven words soon hardened into a formula which was to occur in waxwork advertising for the next two centuries.) These were displayed, along with figures of several other persons of quality, such as the Duke of Gloucester in garter robes, at Mrs. Goldsmith's premises in Green Court, Old Jewry.[6] In those same early years of the eighteenth century, another lady, Mrs. Mills, had a similar show of the reigning English court and other notable characters. Most of what we know about it is contained in the striking handbill reproduced here.

An early waxwork collection, its origin unknown, was absorbed into the unspeakable clutter of Du Puy's house, where Von Uffenbach saw it in 1710. There were "more than a dozen life-size wax figures, all made excellently and most natural," including

Cleopatra lying on a couch, clasping the asp to her bosom. Opposite was a quite incomparable representation of her maid weeping. Her eyes were all swollen, as if she had been crying them out, and tears were coursing down her cheeks, while she wrung her hands most piteously. Nearby was Mark Antony stabbing himself. There was also the whole of the well-known story of the madness of Rosamond, the mistress of one of the English kings. She was represented kneeling before Queen Elionor (Eleonora), who was offering

To be seen in Exeter Change in the Strand, as well in Christmas and other Holidays, and at all other Times, tho' the Change be shut, only then you must go in at that end towards Charing Cross.

Just finish'd, and to be seen. The present COURT of ENGLAND, in Wax, after (and as big as) the Life, in the Inner-Walk of Exeter Change in the Strand, much exceeding, tho' both made by the most deservedly famous Mrs. MILLS, whom in that Art all ingenious Persons own had never yet an equal. The Names of the Chief Persons, are the Queen, his Royal Highness Prince George, the Princess Sophia, his Grace the Duke of Marlborough, the Countess of Manchester, the Countess of Kingston, the Countess of Musgrave, &c. As likewise the Effigies of Mark Anthony, naturally acting that which rendered him remarkable to the World: Cleopatra, his Queen; one of her Egyptian Ladies. Oliver Cromwell in Armour: the Count Tollemach: with many others too tedious here to mention. To be seen from 9 in the Morn, till 9 at Night. You may go in at any of the Doors in the Change, and pass thro' the Hatter's Shop in the Outward Walks.

Note.—The Prices are Six Pence—Four Pence, and Two Pence a-Piece.

There is the Effigies of a Comedian, walking behind the Queen.

☞ Persons may have their Effigies made of their deceas'd Friends, on moderate Terms.

7. Handbill (undated) advertising Mrs. Mills's Waxwork.

her rival either the dagger or the poisoned cup. The wounded King was near her, lying on the ground with a gash on his forehead. There was also Princess Sophia of Hanover, the Heiress of England, when still young, sleeping by a table. On the side was Queen Anne, well made but flattered.[7]

This mixed cast of characters was to be typical of all waxwork shows to come, culminating in the splendid and ever changing variety of Madame Tussaud. Royalty and statesmen, both domestic and foreign, would never cease to be prominently featured, both because of their topicality—these full-length representations were the equivalent, with color and a third dimension added, of the engraved portraits most people could not afford to buy—and because of the opportunity they offered for rich costuming. But soon the waxworks' subjects came to include every kind of person that engaged the popular imagination: familiar biblical and literary characters, heroes and villains of history, characters from folklore and legend, even, by a kind of intramural rivalry, famous freaks such as one could see in the flesh in nearby rooms or fair booths. And increasingly, the individual figures were displayed in episodic groups: formal studio poses, so to speak, were well enough in the case of royalty, but the dramatic instincts of the people were most engaged by what were, in effect, frozen theatrical scenes.

If one can infer the astuteness of the proprietor from the protracted life of the establishment, the shrewdest judge of popular taste among the eighteenth-century waxwork impresarios was Mrs. Salmon. We do not have her first name, but we know she was the widow of a Mr. Salmon, "the famous waxwork man," who was in business before 1693 and died in mid-December 1718.[8] Until 1710 their exhibition was housed at the Golden Ball, St. Martin's-le-Grand, where Von Uffenbach saw it—"six rooms full of all kinds of wax figures, mostly life-size and representing ancient tales, specially English ones. . . . We could see that her work is very accurate from her figure of the Queen as well as one of herself. She has represented herself holding a child on her lap."[9]

In 1711 the Salmons' change of address to the north side of Fleet Street, near Chancery Lane, received free publicity from the great Addison in the *Spectator* (no. 28). Commenting on the standard practice of advertising one's business on a board over the door, he remarked: "When the Name gives an Occasion for an ingenious Sign-post, I would likewise advise the Owner to take that Opportunity of letting the World know who he is. It would have been ridiculous for the ingenious Mrs. *Salmon* to have lived at the Sign of the

Trout; for which Reason she has erected before her House, the Figure of the Fish that is her Name-Sake."[10] When she remarried and became Mrs. Steers, she might well have put up a new pictorial sign, but, no doubt wisely, for business purposes she kept to the end of her life the style of "Mrs. Salmon," to which the London public had become accustomed.

In the early years, at least, she also exhibited her waxworks at Southwark Fair and at the Golden Lion, Smithfield, during Bartholomew Fair. A sideline was the sale of molds and glass eyes. Schalch, too, we are told, was a glass-eye maker,[11] but in his case these objects were intended for the medical profession, whereas Mrs. Salmon sold them to the students who learned "the full art" of wax portraiture from her.

Soon after its arrival in Fleet Street, the show was described in a handbill:

The Royal Off Spring: Or, the Maid's Tragedy Represented in Wax Work, with many Moving Figures and these Histories Following. King Charles the First upon the Fatal Scaffold, attended by Dr. Juxon the Bishop of London, and the Lieutenant of the Tower, with the Executioner and Guards waiting upon our Royal Martyr. The Royal Seraglio, or the Life and Death of Mahomet the Third, with the Death of Ireniae Princess of Persia, and the fair Sultaness Urania. The Overthrow of Queen Voaditia [Boadicea], and the Tragical Death of her two Princely Daughters. The Palace of Flora or the Roman superstition. The Rites of Moloch, or the Unhumane Cruelty, with the manner of the Canaanitish Ladies, Offering up their First-born Infants, in Sacrifice to that ugly Idol, in whose Belly was a burning Furnace, to destroy those Unhappy Children. Margaret Countess of Heningbergh, Lying on a Bed of State, with her Three hundred and Sixty-Five Children, all born at one Birth, and baptized by the Names of Johns and Elizabeths, occasioned by the rash Wish of a poor beggar Woman. Hermonia a Roman Lady, whose Father offended the Emperor, was sentenced to be starved to Death, but was preserved by Sucking his Daughter's Breast. Old Mother Shipton the Famous English Prophetess, which fortold the Death of the White King; All richly dress'd and composed with so much variety of Invention, that it is wonderfully Diverting to all Lovers of Art and Ingenuity.[12]

Of all these wonders, a particularly memorable one was the mechanized figure of Mother Shipton, who administered a farewell kick to Mrs. Salmon's patrons as they left. The floor of the exhibition was booby-trapped with hidden treadles, which, when stepped on, not only set Mother Shipton kicking but threw another figure into a threatening attitude with an uplifted broom.[13]

Mrs. Salmon seems, indeed, to have possessed what

Henry Angelo, a memoirist of a later epoch, called a "singular humour." Some of her waxen groups, he said, "were exceedingly humorous, particularly two subjects, one entitled the *Old Bachelor's Conversazione,* and the other, the *Old Maid's Coterie.* . . . Hogarth bore testimony to their merit, by saying, that when he was an apprentice, 'he frequently loitered at old Mother Salmon's, when he was sent of an errand into the city, to take a peep at these humorous pieces.'"[14] There appears to be no independent substantiation for the Hogarth story, but it is credible enough.

Mrs. Salmon—or Mrs. Steers—died in 1760 at the great age of ninety. A Chancery Lane surgeon named Clarke then took over the exhibition, which was continued after his death by his widow. On 4 July 1763 Boswell spent a pleasant quarter hour there.[15] Happily, we have a record, in a handbill of that very moment, of the recently introduced figures he saw:

A fine new Press, the Representation of the Christening of his Royal Highness George Prince of Wales, with her Royal Highness the Princess Dowager of Wales, his Royal Highness the Duke of Cumberland, and his Highness the Prince of Mecklenburgh, Sponsor; with a new Press of the Cherokee King, with his two chiefs, in their Country Dress, and Habilments; and also a fine new Press of Mark Antony and Cleopatra with their two Children, and the large Rock, finely ornamented and embellished; all the other Presses richly dressed and beautified; with many new Figures of various Sorts. There are four Rooms. Price One Shilling each Person.[16]

In later years, if the recollection of a man who visited the show in 1793 can be trusted, the proprietor went in heavily for the sort of display that would later make Madame Tussaud's fortune:

I remember in the collection was a representation (and a horrible one it was!) of Ankerstrom stabbing the king of Sweden; also, the Cherokee Chiefs [holdovers from Boswell's time]; Renwick Williams, called the Monster, cutting the Miss Porters, &c. &c.* I was then quite a youth, and the hideous copper countenance of the chiefs, together with the bloody appearances of the Swedish king, and the Miss Porters, contrasting so frightfully with the sweaty death-like faces of the principal figures, rivetted the scene so firmly on my memory, that I have it now as fresh in my mind's eye as when I first beheld it, forty-four years since.[17]

In 1795, when the house it had occupied for so long was about to be pulled down, the exhibition moved across Fleet Street to the corner of Inner Temple Lane—the still extant half-timbered structure with an overhanging upper story that was reputed to have

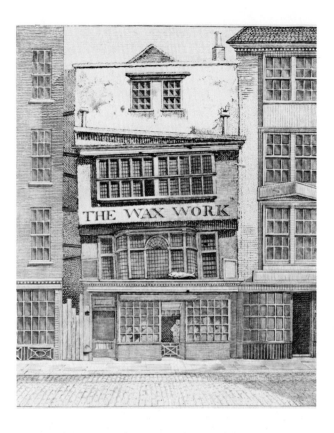

8. Mrs. Salmon's Waxwork, Fleet Street (engraving by John Thomas Smith, 1793).

been the palace of Henry VIII and Cardinal Wolsey, but was more likely the council chamber of the Duchy of Cornwall under James I's eldest son, Prince Henry. There Mrs. Salmon's, as it continued to be called, remained a landmark until Dickens's time.

Throughout the eighteenth century small waxwork shows came and went: here today (in a rented room or in a booth at the fair), gone tomorrow to another location, and quite possibly, another proprietor. These exhibitions were so obscure and rootless as to have left little record.[18] One was at the Roebuck inn, Cheapside, in 1718, another in Berwick Street, Soho, in 1731. In 1758 the big waxwork show of the year, at the corner of Pall Mall and the Haymarket, was the Prussian court. Twenty years later, someone showed three figures of a single personage, the late King of Prussia, in Cockspur Street. It is regrettable that we lack particulars of a show at the corner of Shoe Lane and Fleet Street in 1745. In April, three months before Joseph Highmore's well-known set of twelve engraved illustrations was issued, the waxwork proprietor advertised a series of tableaux depicting, with one hundred "figures in miniature," Pamela; or Virtue Rewarded, here renamed "the low life of Pamela," and in De-

* Renwick Williams was convicted in December 1790 of "maliciously tearing, cutting, spoiling, and defacing the garments" of a young lady he met in St. James's Street. This conviction was set aside on a technicality, and he was then tried and convicted on the charge of assaulting with the intent to kill, even though Miss Porter evidently suffered little physical injury. The case caused a sensation, not least because there was widespread suspicion that she identified the wrong man.

cember it added a sequel, Pamela in High Life. This is as impressive evidence as could be wished of the phenomenal popularity of Richardson's novel, adding credence to such familiar stories as that of the village which rang the church bell when the latest volume arrived with news of Pamela's marriage.

Toward the end of the century, the best-known name among the commercial waxwork artists was that of Mr. and Mrs. Sylvester, whose "Cabinet of Royal Figures, most curiously moulded in wax, as large as Nature," was shown at the Lyceum* between 1786 and 1789 and later on tour.[19] In addition to the complete British and French royal families, the show included a sleeping full-length Venus, Warren Hastings, Franklin, Voltaire, and the Countess de la Motte (of Diamond Necklace fame). During a brief stand at Mr. Ansell's Large Room,† Spring Gardens, in 1788, "an Exact Representation of a Seraglio" was an added attraction. The Sylvesters, like Mrs. Mills and Mrs. Goldsmith at the beginning of the century, accepted private commissions for wax likenesses; full-length effigies being no longer in demand, they specialized in portraits, probably of the medallion sort. Each product was accompanied by a money-back guarantee: "Should the Portraits not be thought the most striking, and correct Likenesses, he will not expect any thing for his Trouble."[20]

Portrait modeling in wax was no mere commercial craft in the latter part of the century. Examples of the art were often included in the annual exhibitions of the Royal Academy and the Society of Artists. Among the artists represented were such aristocratic ladies as Horace Walpole's lifelong friend Anne Damer, daughter of Field Marshal Henry Conway, and Lady Diana Beauclerk, daughter of the third Duke of Marlborough and friend of Dr. Johnson.[21] From Philadelphia came, in 1772, Patience Wright, a tall, sallow, masculine-featured widow with three children who had toured the colonies with a show of waxworks of her own making until it burned in New York.[22] Introduced to London society by Benjamin Franklin, she soon attracted the attention of the Walpole circle; the talent of this "artistress," as Walpole called her, was such that Lady Aylesbury "literally spoke to a waxen figure of a housemaid" planted in a drawing room.[23] Mrs. Wright was also a friend of Benjamin West, who often painted her daughter Phoebe, a famous beauty who later married John Hoppner. For a time, until she became too outspoken on the subject of the American war, Mrs. Wright was on familiar terms with the king and queen, whom she addressed, American-egalitarian fashion, as

"George and Charlotte." Thanks to these manifold social contacts, she built up a thriving business in the modeling of wax portraits, busts, and life-size figures. Some of these, along with historical groups, she exhibited at her residence in Cockspur Street. An often-repeated story has it that she passed on to Franklin military information she picked up from her fashionable and presumably well-informed acquaintances. This cannot be substantiated, but a recent writer credits another story, that she smuggled secret intelligence into Philadelphia inside wax figures shipped to her sister, who was running a wax museum there.

Whatever her accomplishments as a spy, Mrs. Wright was not universally admired as a person; the forthright Abigail Adams called her "the queen of sluts."[24] She was not lacking, certainly, in aggressiveness. In 1779 she proposed to Franklin, then at Passy, that he help her set up business in Paris, but that gentleman discouraged her, saying that the city already had two or three professors of the art (Madame Tussaud's uncle, Dr. Christopher Curtius, was already conducting a popular museum in the Boulevard du Temple). Six years later she wrote to Thomas Jefferson, in Paris with the American delegation appointed to sign the peace treaty, suggesting that she come over to model the delegation for display in some public building in the United States. Jefferson apparently did not reply. Mrs. Wright died in London in 1786; her only surviving work, as we shall have occasion to note in Chapter 7, is the effigy of the elder Pitt in Westminster Abbey.

Waxworks occurred in still another region of London life far removed from the fair booths, Mrs. Salmon's Fleet Street establishment, the art exhibitions, and the drawing rooms. By the end of the seventeenth century it had been proved that expertly prepared and durable anatomical pieces molded in wax were superior for medical teaching purposes to the customary debris from the dissecting room. Cadavers, in addition, were in chronic short supply (hence the prosperity of the illicit and much denounced resurrectionist trade). Among the leading makers of pathological-anatomical models in Paris was a surgeon, Guillaume Desnoués.[25] In 1727 and again in 1730 Desnoués brought numerous examples of his art to London for exhibition and sale; in the latter year they were shown, at the stiff admission price of five shillings, at a chemist's at the corner of Pall Mall and the Haymarket.[26] Desnoués seems to have done a good trade in these waxen representations of the human frame in health, disease, and dissolution, but eventu-

* The Lyceum, in the Strand a few yards east of Exeter Change, was built in 1772 by the Society of Artists for art exhibitions, but it served only briefly in that capacity. In the 1780s and 1790s, it housed a large variety of exhibitions—astronomical demonstrations, air balloons, waxworks, "philosophical fireworks," boxing matches, circuses, programs of humorous recitations, and concerts.

† The term "large [or great] room," so often found in the records of London exhibitions in the eighteenth and early nineteenth centuries, was applied to any rentable room large enough to accommodate concerts or exhibitions.

ally the collection became something of a white elephant. In 1739 "the present proprietor," whoever he may have been, sent it to Dublin "for the instruction of the curious," and a friend of his wrote to Swift begging him to encourage "such of your acquaintance as are curious to see these figures" so that they would "excite the curiosity of the others."[27] Seven years later the collection was back in London, displayed at the reduced rate of a shilling. In 1753 Viscount Fitzmaurice bought it for the University of Dublin. Before being removed to Ireland, it was shown at "Mr. Rackstrow's, Statuary, facing Sergeant's Inn, Fleet Street." After a prolonged teaser campaign in the newspapers, designed to squeeze every profitable penny from the exhibition before it entered academic life, Desnoués's models were duly sent back to Ireland and thus swim out of our ken.[28]

We are left behind at Rackstrow's "Museum of Anatomy and Curiosities," as it came to be called, a combination of Don Saltero's knicknackatory and the reproductive-organ department of Dr. John Hunter's museum. Benjamin Rackstrow was a well-known modeler and a substantial citizen. In the latter capacity he held the rank of colonel in the Trained Bands (militia) of the City of London and narrowly escaped having under his command Samuel Johnson, who was once drawn for duty and, though he did not serve, kept in his closet the musket, sword, and belt he bought for the occasion.[29] Rackstrow's figures evidently set the standard by which others were judged. In 1763 Walpole, writing of Anne Conway's "progress in waxen statuary," predicted, perhaps not without humor, that "by next winter she may rival Rackstrow's old man"—an allusion to a particularly realistic colored plaster figure of a seated elderly man which Rackstrow showed in that year at the exhibition of the Free Society of Artists.[30]

The museum occupied a pair of Tudor houses at the sign of Sir Isaac Newton, in Fleet Street between Temple Bar and Chancery Lane. It was thus a near neighbor of Mrs. Salmon's, with whose show Rackstrow (or his successor) was at some pains that his own not be confused. "This Museum," a newspaper advertisement emphasized, "is not called the Waxwork"[31]—the implication being that "Wax-work" was synonymous with "Mrs. Salmon's," as in fact it largely was in eighteenth-century London. But Rackstrow's was a waxwork nonetheless, and some of his figures were in direct rivalry with Mrs. Salmon —Mother Shipton telling the fortunes of a young lady and child, a Chinese mandarin, Coan the Norfolk

dwarf, and Bamford, the seven foot–four inch Staffordshire giant who was buried at nearby St. Dunstan's. In time, the wax figures came to be surrounded with all kinds of oddments, from a whale skeleton to a perpetual motion machine. There was the usual miscellany of fish, birds, shells, skulls, skeletons, fossils, and so forth, as well as a mummy (said to be of Pharaoh's daughter), two stuffed crocodiles, a rhinoceros hide, a pair of snow shoes, and Cromwell's and Newton's death masks.[32]

Rackstrow himself died in 1772, but the museum, or what purported to be his (there is some mention of the dispersal of the original collection in 1779), continued in business for a number of years. Irrespective of the unrelated objects it absorbed, from beginning to end Rackstrow's collection specialized in three-dimensional anatomical illustration, waxen and real. The void left by the departure of Desnoués's collection was quickly filled. One of the chief attractions in the early years was a wax model of a woman eight months pregnant. This was a dramatic piece indeed, because, according to a handbill, "the Circulation of the Blood is imitated (by Liquors resembling the Arterial and Veinous Blood, flowing through Glass Vessels whose Figure and Situation exactly correspond with the natural Blood Vessels) also the action of the Heart and Motion of the Lungs in Breathing. The whole making a most wonderful and beautiful Appearance."[33]

Later there were two full-sized anatomical wax figures, one of a man and the other of a woman; the latter, showing all the musculature, was modeled during the dissection of a woman who had been hanged. In one room were concentrated, preserved in spirits, a variety of fetuses, human and animal abortions, and placentas; figures "coloured to nature, and moulded from women who have died undelivered (occasioned by extraordinary and preternatural causes) shewing various positions of the child in the womb, at nine months, and other periods of pregnancy, &c."; "an anatomical representation (in wax) of the urinary bladder, and penis of a man," and a similar representation of "the urinary parts, and parts of generation of a woman"; and—not representations, but the actuality—"the real parts of generation of a woman about thirty years old" and of a seventeen-year-old virgin, as well as of a penis "injected to the state of erection."

Whatever unwholesome instincts Rackstrow's may have obliged are not recognized in the establishment's guidebook, which discusses all the examples of obstetrical pathology and sexual anatomy in the most brisk scientific language available at the time. Nowhere does one find any explanation, pious or otherwise, of the rationale behind the display except the obvious one of its educational value. Nothing is even implied about the audience to which it was meant to appeal. The obvious *argumentum ab silentio* is that ladies and gentlemen alike were expected to find it instructive, and neither embarrassing nor revolting. Only at the very end of the museum's career, perhaps reflecting the slow but inexorable rise of pre-Victorian prudery, do we find Rackstrow's advertising that "a Gentlewoman attends the Ladies separately."[34]

⊅⊰✳⊱⊄

No less familar to eighteenth-century Londoners than waxworks were peepshows, a representational entertainment of a different sort which had at least as long a history, though it can be only vaguely and fitfully discerned in the scattered records. It is at least certain that, just as waxworks served both art and Mammon, peepshows at one stage existed on two distinct levels. At the end of the sixteenth century an Augsburg clockmaker named Marggraf made a number of combination clocks and peepshows, three examples of which are preserved in the Kunsthistorisches Museum, Vienna. The peepshow, framed and artificially lighted, consisted of modeled groups of figures placed against a painted background; they were seen not directly, but as reflected in a slanted mirror on the principle of the camera obscura.[35] Such perspective boxes were a striking novelty at a time when discoveries in optics were inviting adventurous artists to experiment with fresh devices and effects. In 1656 Evelyn, in London, was shown "a pretty Perspective & well represented in a triangular Box, the greate Church at Harlem in Holland, to be seene thro a small hole at one of the Corners, & contrived into an handsome Cabinet: It was so rarely don, that all the Artists & Painters in Towne, came flocking to see & admire it."[36] A similar *trompe l'oeil* box by Samuel van Hoogstraten (1627–1678), portraying the interior of a Dutch house by paintings on the sides and bottom, is in the National Gallery.*

Simple versions and variations of these show boxes were made both for home use as toys and for catchpenny shows.[37] Wandering showmen carried them on their backs or in donkey carts to the remotest districts of western Europe and the British Isles, and like all other portable entertainments, they found their way to the streets and fairs of London. They were, in fact, one of the archetypal forms of post-sixteenth-century pop-

ular amusement, and as such the popular name applied to them acquired, in educated usage, an indelible suggestion of derision. To call any new form of visual entertainment or instruction a "raree show" was to dismiss any expectation that it be taken seriously.† The device and the name were sufficiently current by 1681 for the term to serve as the title of a pamphlet which portrayed Charles II as "a raree-show man with his pack on his back, a peep-show containing the Parliament which he is carrying off to Oxford."[38]

The earliest portable peepshows seem to have been cut-out cardboard Nativity scenes, set in front of colored isinglass lighted from behind by a candle; later an oil lamp might be used. Unlike the Marggraf and Van Hoogstraten boxes, these peepshows usually provided for the spectator's looking at the scene directly, not as reflected in mirrors. Mirrors were used, but only to enhance the perspective. The scenes were made of various materials—painted wood or board, engravings mounted on board, or (possibly) cloth transparencies. As the box evolved, various designs and devices were employed to achieve the combined illusion of perspective and life size. Some elaborate models had scenes painted in translucent colors on glass panels and mounted in a series to provide the illusion of depth; others, representing, for example, the long vista of a formal palace garden with baroque fountains and statuary, were made of opaque and translucent papers, elaborately cut and folded, sometimes concertina-fashion. It was frequently astonishing how many spectacular or delicate effects could be attained in the narrow confines of a box. The illusion of life size, achieved primarily by excluding the external surroundings and thus enabling the scene to have a scale of its own, independent of the outside world, was assisted by magnifying glasses set in the apertures. With larger models, several people could look in at the same time. Hogarth's picture of Southwark Fair, for example, depicts a two-hole peepshow ready for customers, and later on there were four-aperture boxes. Often a penny bought a performance consisting of a series of scenes that the showman successively lowered into view as the spectator kept his eyes glued to the hole.

Sometimes the box contained not a stationary scene but one with moving figures. Here the peepshow adopted another kind of visual entertainment that had developed independently, the clockwork figure. Although these mechanical figures and scenes also were exhibited separately, it is not unlikely that they were enclosed in peepshows oftener than the advertisements, our chief source of information, reveal. No ad-

* The seventeenth-century *trompe l'oeil* vogue had another bearing on the history of exhibitions. Illusionistic paintings depicting cupboards crowded with typical rarities were sometimes hung on the walls of virtuosi's cabinets, where they were prized for two reasons: they were themselves "artificial curiosities" and they appeared to enlarge the collection's scope, including as they did representations of rarities which the collection did not in fact possess. Sometimes, however, the pictures portrayed actual components of a collection which were kept in a vault because of their great monetary value. See Martin Battersby, *Trompe l'Oeil: The Eye Deceived* (New York, 1974), pp. 12–13, 91–95.

† "Raree show" entered the language toward the end of the seventeenth century; the first occurrence cited by the *Oxford English Dictionary* is in the title of the pamphlet mentioned in the text. Dr. Johnson, aware that many peepshow proprietors were Savoyards, explained that "this word is formed in imitation of the foreign way of pronouncing *rare* show."

vantage was to be had in admitting that one was operating a mere raree show when the carefully evasive wording of the advertisement allowed the public to expect something grander.

The first English clockwork figures, those whose motive power was supplied by actual clocks, were called "jacks" in English (from the French *jaquemarts*) and had an ancestry reaching back to the mid-fourteenth century in Milan, Padua, and Orvieto. They performed their characteristic drills when clocks struck in cathedrals or churches at Wells (the best-known and most elaborate English example still working), York, Oxford, Exeter, Evesham, Rye, Bristol, Norwich, Leicester, and elsewhere. As early as 1478, according to Stow, there was a clock mechanism in Fleet Street near Shoe Lane, the figures being angels with hammers striking hymn tunes. From 1671 onward, Londoners knew well and affectionately the jacks at St. Dunstan's in the West, Fleet Street—two wooden life-size figures of savages, each with a club in his right hand which struck the quarters on two suspended bells as he moved his head.[39] After a hiatus of a century (1830–1935), they are back at work at the old location.

By Elizabethan times derivatives of the clock jack, whether powered by water or a wind-up mechanism, had been adapted to secular entertainment, elaborated into scenes, and given a troublesome name, "motion."[40] To the permanent confusion of the record, "motion," along with related words such as "movement" and "mechanical," was applied indiscriminately to exhibitions of clockwork figures and to puppet plays. The explicit distinction made in a document of the Master of the Revels dated 1663, which refers to "clock-work motions, ordinary motions [puppets], and extra motions," whatever they may have been, was seldom observed in practice, so that often it is impossible to tell which is meant. A few references, however, are reasonably unambiguous. In 1573 the Privy Council asked the Lord Mayor to allow "certain Italian players to make show of an instrument of strange motions," and between 1619 and 1640 there are repeated allusions to "Italian motions" touring the countryside. These shows have been interpreted as being boxes divided into compartments, in each of which small figures were moved by clockwork on the turning of a handle, the scenes depicting incidents from the Gospels or the lives of saints. In June 1661 Pepys wrote of eating and drinking at the Globe tavern, Greenwich, where he "saw the simple motion that is there, of a woman with a rod in her hand, keeping

time to the music while it plays—which is simple methinks."[41] As Pepys's editors and others have pointed out, Donne alludes to moving figures attached to an organ in his *Satyre II:* "As in some Organ, Puppets dance above / And bellows pant below, which them do move." (In this instance, clockwork was aided, or replaced, by air power.) In August 1663 Pepys attended "a puppet-play in Lincolnes Inn fields; where there was the story of Holofernes and other clockwork, well done."[42] The next month, at Bartholomew Fair, after inspecting "munkys dancing on the ropes" ("such dirty sport that I was not pleased with it") and a four-footed goose, Pepys went "to another place and saw some German clocke-works, the Salutacion of the Virgin Mary and several Scripture stories; but above all, there was at last represented the Sea, with Neptune, Venus, mermaids, and Cupid [actually Arion] on a Dolphin, the sea rolling; so well done, that had it been in a gaudy* manner and place and at a good distance, it had been admirable."[43] At the same fair four years later, he saw a native product of the same kind: "a piece of Clocke-work made by an Englishman, indeed, very good, wherein all the several states of man's age, to 100 year old, is shown very pretty and solemne, and several other things more cheerful."[44] These clockwork performances seem to have been early examples of the mechanical theatre, to which we will turn in a moment.

Almost from the beginning, Mrs. Salmon had wax figures moved by wound-up clockwork in addition to the spring-actuated Mother Shipton. An early handbill refers to her "Temple of Ephesus, of Apollo, the Vision of Augustus and the Six Sybyls, moving figures. Also an old woman flying from time who shakes his head and hour-glass with sorrow at seeing age so unwilling to die."[45] The concurrent vogue in the new century's first decades for comedies and operas performed by marionettes (puppets on strings or wires), which Addison made much of, naturally encouraged men of the theatre to work out fresh novelties. From their normal miniature size the figures were enlarged to almost true human height and clockwork was substituted for wires. These apparently self-acting figures impressed a visiting Frenchman in 1734 with the realism with which they performed "entire tragedies . . . with dress, gestures, walk, and living lips and eyes, in every way resembling human beings."[46] In the same year, at Southwark Fair, the long-established firm of Pinchbeck and Fawkes exhibited such a cast performing "the comical tragedy of *Tom Thumb*. With several scenes out of *The Tragedy of*

* Presumably, Pepys meant "had it been presented in a more brilliant or colorful manner." The word "gaudy" did not then possess its modern disparaging connotation.

Tragedies."[47] As George Speaight, the modern historian of puppet shows, observes, figures as tall as those advertised—five feet—must almost of necessity have been made of wax rather than the conventional wood, since wooden figures would have been too heavy to manipulate either by strings or by concealed clockwork. The actions in any case must have been very rudimentary. As Speaight says, "The secret of these almost life-sized puppets—veritable *Übermarionetten*—has now been lost, and perhaps they died, like the dinosaur, from lack of movement."[48]

But if there were practical limitations to the further development of these play-acting "automatons"—a term, originally designating clockwork figures, which was immediately compromised by puppet masters' adopting it to add timeliness, mystery, and meretricious novelty to their traditional art of hand-manipulation—the showmen were not reluctant to make do with what they had. One form of waxwork exhibition at the fairs represented a royal procession, with life-size figures, richly dressed in robes bedight with tinsel finery and paste jewels, moving slowly across the stage—in effect, the funeral effigies of Mrs. Goldsmith and Mrs. Mills not only stood upright but given motion. This court scene remained a favorite of fairgoers for many years; between 1779 and 1794, for instance, the showman Jobson attended Bartholomew Fair with "a display of moving waxwork figures five feet high representing a foreign Court."[49]

The alternative direction taken by makers of clockwork figures had wider practical possibilities, because it did not present the dead end of unmanageable size and weight. This was the mechanical theatre. It, too, owed its origin partly to the puppet shows, because in its earliest form it was simply a mechanized version of a standard part of the puppet-show repertory. From the 1620s onward, puppets had often performed what amounted to fragments of the medieval mystery cycles: a series of episodes from Scripture beginning with the creation of Adam and Eve, running through the stories of Cain and Abel, Abraham and Isaac, and Joseph and Mary and the Christ Child, and ending, in one version performed at Bartholomew Fair in 1701, with "Rich Dives in Hell, and Lazarus in Abraham's Bosom, seen in a most glorious Object, all in machines, descending in a Throne, Guarded with multitudes of Angels, with the Breaking of the Clouds, discovering the Palace of the Sun, in double and treble Prospects, to the Admiration of all Spectators."[50]

A clockwork adaptation of the Creation scene was performed in 1661, at the Two Wreathed Posts tavern in Shoe Lane, by one Christopher Whitehead. The title of this show, according to a pamphlet written in that year by "I.H., gent," was *Paradise Transplanted and Restored, in a Most Artfull and Lively Representation of the Severall Creatures, Plants, Flowers, and Other Vegetables, in Their Full Growth, Shape, and Colour,*—a "Representation," the text said, "of that Beautiful Prospect Adam had in Paradice." "Adam appeared naming the animals, which ranged from the elephant to the mouse and from the crocodile to the glowworm, and Eve appeared, taking the apple from the serpent."[51] Evelyn saw the same show, or an imitation, on 23 September 1673: "we went to see Paradise, a room in Hatton Garden furnished with the representations of all sorts of animals, handsomely painted on boards or cloth, & so cut out & made to stand & move, fly, crawll, roare & make their severall cries, as was not unpretty: though in it selfe a meere bauble, whilst the man who shew'd, made us Laugh heartily at his formal poetrie."[52] (Might the poetry have been excerpts from *Paradise Lost* or *Paradise Regained*, published respectively six and two years earlier?) In 1680 a revival of the entertainment entitled *Creatio Mundi; or, The World Made in Six Days,* was performed twice daily, again in Hatton Garden. Thoresby saw it then ("multitudes of beasts and birds are lively represented both in shapes and notes")* and again in 1683 "(an ingenious and innocent show"). His religious scruples led him to prefer it to the playhouse, a bias which must have been shared by many.[53]

What was billed as a "new" form of mechanical entertainment, the invention of a German artist named Jacobus Morian, was introduced to London early in 1709 at the Duke of Marlborough's Head, Fleet Street, by William Pinkethman (Penkethman), a popular low comedian who was also a fair-booth impresario in season. The "moving [or mechanical] picture," as it was regularly called from the start, probably was not as complete a novelty as it was claimed to be. It certainly had affinities with the Creation entertainments as well as with the clockwork shows Pepys saw in the same period, and if we had more information on these, the family resemblance between them and Morian's device would no doubt be clear. From such evidence as we have, including several considerably later examples in modern museums,† it appears that in the moving picture, if not in its immediate antecedents, a frame enclosed a painted background against which a variety of cut-out figures, activated by hidden clockwork, performed characteristic repetitive motions, either fixed in one place or traveling across the scene.

* That is, both in physical form and with imitated sound (at least of bird song)?

† Three *tableaux animés* dating from the mid- or late eighteenth century are in the Conservatoire National des Arts et Métiers, Paris. The picture space enclosed by each elaborate gilt frame ranges from about 24 × 18 inches to 30 × 24. The mechanized figures and objects, arranged on two or three separate vertical planes, are between three and six inches tall.

On the continent, such a mechanical picture was called a Theatrum Mundi. The closest modern analogies no doubt would be the moving figures that act as targets or incidental decorations in shooting galleries at fairs and amusement parks or, more elaborately, the animated displays assembled in department store show windows at Christmas. One of Pinkethman's pictures was said to consist of "above 100" figures, which "move their Heads, Legs, Arms and Fingers . . . like living creatures," as well as "Ships, Beasts, Fish, Fowl and other Embellishments, some near a Foot in height."[54] This gives us some indication of scale.

Pinkethman's first moving picture was described in the greatest detail in a handbill:

Part of this fine Picture represents a Landskip, and the other part the Water or Sea: In the Landskip you see a Town, out of the Gates of which, cometh a Coach riding over a Bridge through the country, behind, before and between the Trees till out of sight; coming on the Bridge, a Gentleman sitting on the Coach, civilly salutes the Spectating Company, the turning of the Wheels and Motions of the Horses are plainly seen as if natural and Alive. There cometh also from the Town Gate a Hunter on Horseback, with his Doggs behind him, and his Horn at his side, coming to the Bridge he taketh up his Horn and Blows it that it is distinctly heard by all the spectators. Another Hunter painted as if sleeping, and by the said blowing of the Horn awaking, riseth up his Head, looks about, and then lays down his Head again to sleep, to the great Amazement and Diversion of the Company. There are also represented and Painted, Country men and Women, Travellers, Cows and Pack horses going along the Road till out of sight. And at a seeming distance on the Hills are several Windmills continually Turning and Working. From a River or Sea port, you see several sorts of Ships and Vessels putting to Sea, which ships by degrees lessen, to the sight as they seem to sail further off. Many more Varieties too long to be inserted here, are Painted and Represented in this Picture to the greatest Admiration, Diversion and Satisfaction of all Ingenious Spectators. The Artist Master of this Piece hath employed above five years in contriving, making and perfecting it. It was designed for a present to a great Prince in Germany [the Elector of Bavaria], to be put into his chiefest Cabinet of Greatest Rarities, but that Prince Dying, the maker kept it to himself, and now presents it to the View and Diversion of all ingenious Persons.[55]

Among the first to see the show was Thoresby, who wrote in his diary on 11 February 1708/9, "The landscape looks as an ordinary picture till the clock-work behind the curtain be set at work, and then the ships move and sail distinctly upon the sea till out of sight; a coach comes out of the town, the motion of the horses and wheels are very distinct, and a gentleman in the coach that salutes the company; a hunter also and his dogs, &c. keep their course till out of sight."[56] In other words, Pinkethman's animated painting did what the advertisements claimed.*

Pinkethman's first show was an immediate success. In May 1709 he moved it to the Hospital Tavern, Greenwich, next to his summer theatre,[57] but he returned with it to the Duke of Marlborough's Head for the winter season. By that time several rivals, or "impostures" as he called them in his advertisements, had appeared. One, exhibited at the Great House, Strand, near Hungerford Market, was the work of "a famous engineer from the camp." Nominally it depicted the siege of Lille in 1708,† but in some particulars it bore a striking resemblance to its unlocalized prototype:

First, it doth represent the confederate camp, and the army lying intrenched before the town; secondly, the convoys and the mules with prince Eugene's baggage; thirdly, the English forces commanded by the duke of Marlborough; likewise, several vessels, laden with provisions for the army, which are so artificially done as to seem to drive the water before them. The city and the citadel are very fine, with all its outworks, ravelins, hornworks, counter-scarps, half-moons, and palisados; the French horse marching out at one gate, and the confederate army marching in at the other; the prince's travelling coach with two generals in it, one saluting the company as it passes by; then a trumpeter sounds a call as he rides, at the noise whereof a sleeping centinel starts, and lifts up his head, but, not being espied, lies down to sleep again.[58]

Other rival shows in the 1709–10 season included one "next Door to the Grecian's Head Coffee-House, over against Cecil-street in the Strand": "a PICTURE finely drawn, by an extraordinary Master, which has many curious and wonderfully pleasing and surprising Motions in it, all natural."[59] Still other moving pictures, subjects unrecorded, could be seen at the Green Man tavern, King Street, Bloomsbury Square, and at David Randall's—earlier, if not still, a dealer in wild animals—in Channel Row, Westminster.[60]

Pinkethman soon confronted the competition with a new picture of his own, which was advertised in the *Postman* for 1–3 March 1709/10 in such general terms ("drawn by the best hand . . . has the general approbation of all who see it, and far exceeds the original formerly shown at the same place")[61] as to leave us in ignorance of its subject. This show may or may not have been the one advertised in the spring of 1711 as "Mr. Penkethman's Wonderful Invention, call'd the Pantheon: Or, the Temple of the Heathen-gods . . . being a most surprizing and Magnificent

* Equally uninformative so far as the operative details are concerned is Swift's brief report to Stella on this or a very similar exhibition in 1713: "I went . . . to see a famous moving Picture, & I never saw anything so pretty. You see a Sea ten miles wide, a Town on tothr end, & Ships sailing in the Sea, & discharging their Canon. You see a great Sky with Moon & Stars &c." (*Journal to Stella,* ed. Harold Williams, Oxford, 1948, II, 647.)

† This subject reflected the growing tendency of popular London shows to have topical content or at least frequent topical allusions. In 1692 Evelyn recorded that "this [earthquake] of Jamaica, being prophanely & Ludicrously represented in a puppet play, or some such lewd pass-time in the Faire of Southwarke, caused the Queene to put-downe & abolish that idle & vicious mock-shew." (*Diary,* V, 115–16.) In 1704 the puppet "opera" added to its biblical scenes an afterpiece, "the Glorious Battle obtained over the French and Spaniards, by his Grace the Duke of Marlborough" (Blenheim), and the next year a droll at Bartholomew Fair capitalized on the Earl of Peterborough's victory the previous October with *The Siege of Barcelona, or The Soldier's Fortune: with the Taking of Fort Mont-Jouy.* (John Ashton, *Social Life in the Reign of Queen Anne,* London, 1883, pp. 193–94; Sybil Rosenfeld, *The Theatre of the London Fairs in the Eighteenth Century,* Cambridge, 1960, p. 144.)

Machine, consisting of five several curious Pictures."[62] It was this which claimed over a hundred figures, some almost a foot high. In later years (1717–1724) Pinkethman exhibited an elaborated derivative of the mechanical picture at his summer stands. Called a "musical Picture . . . the like of which has never been seen in England," it was described as "a machine in a cabinet" with the Muses shown hovering about the royal family, portrayed here in paintings by Pieter Tillemans of Antwerp, scene designer for the King's Opera.[63]

At this time, Pinkethman acquired a formidable rival in the person of Christopher Pinchbeck, who, with his sons Edward and Christopher junior, belonged equally to show business and the clockmaking trade. As a clockmaker he participated in that remarkable surge of creativeness, initiated by Thomas Tompion, which resulted in English astronomical clocks, chronometers, and other marine instruments being recognized as the best in the world and gave English seamen the accurate navigational tools they needed. Pinchbeck himself, however, was less interested in making such instruments than in producing barrel organs for country churches and musical automatons such as singing birds. The inclination that led him to specialize in clockwork machinery for public consumption also led him directly toward show business; and alone or in partnership with a veteran of the entertainment trade, one Fawkes, he was a well-known figure at the fairs. While Pinkethman displayed his moving musical picture of the royal family, Pinchbeck showed "that most Delightful and Surprizing Piece of ART, the GRAND THEATRE of the MUSES."[64] Valued for publicity purposes at 700 guineas, this masterpiece of the creative clockmaker's art was to be seen for a number of years at various locales—Bartholomew Fair in summer, at other times at the Great Room in Panton Street and the old Tennis Court Theatre, James Street. It was most fully described in an advertisement of 1729, inviting visitors to the former South Sea coffeehouse, Bishopsgate Street:

This Wonderful and Magnificent MACHINE has in the Front Two most beautiful moving Pictures. The One is ORPHEUS in a Forest, playing on his Lyre, and beating exact Time with his Head and Foot to every Tune, among a great number of wild Beasts, who, by their various Motions, seem to be animated and charm'd by his Harmony.

At the same Time it performs on several Instruments, great Variety of fine Pieces of MUSICK, composed by Mr. HANDEL[,] CORELLI, and other celebrated Masters, in so excellent a Manner, that scarce any Hand can equal. Likewise

* Like some other words coined in the London exhibition trade, "panopticon" is incompletely traced in the Oxford English Dictionary. The Pinchbeckian occurrence is not noted, the earliest citation referring to an optical instrument mentioned by Benjamin Franklin in 1768. Jeremy Bentham used the word considerably later for his model prison.

the sweet Harmony of an Aviary of Birds, which is imitated to so great Perfection, as not to be distinguished from Nature itself.

The other Picture is a Landscape, with a View of the Sea, terminating insensibly at a very great Distance; with Ships sailing, plying to Windward, and diminishing by Degrees, as they seem to go further from the Eye, till at length they disappear, with Fish playing or tumbling in the Sea at the same Time.

On the Land are Horse-men, Carts, Chaises, &c., passing along, the Wheels turning round as tho' on the Road, the Men and Horses altering their Position, to keep themselves upright, as they come down a steep Hill, and pass through a Valley.

Then, in a fresh Water River are seen Swans swimming, fishing and feathering themselves, their Motions as natural as tho' really alive. Likewise the sporting of the Dog and Duck is highly diverting.[65]

Pinchbeck died in 1732 and his business passed to his sons, who inherited both their father's mechanical ingenuity and his showmanship. About 1742 they produced a new version of the musical clock, the Panopticon:* a "Triangular Musical Machine with six moving Pictures, which is universally allowed, from its beautiful Structure, the vast Variety of its Motions, and the Harmony of its Music, to be the first Piece of Mechanism of its Magnitude in Europe."[66] In addition to a representation of a concert at a country fair, there were scenes of a shipbuilding yard, a founder's shop, a smithy, a stonemason's yard, all in action, and a landscape with mills working, carriages passing, and a dog and duck hunting.[67]

The Pinchbecks had started a fashion which merged the utilitarian (sophisticated clockwork mechanisms, easily adapted to practical uses) with the artistic (baroque elaboration, with particular use of classical themes). While a "Grand Theatre of Arts, or Musical Machine Clock . . . which for its surprising Movements, and beautiful Musick on the Organ surpasses all that was ever made of the kind" was on display at Mile End Fair in 1738,[68] other craftsmen were constructing exhibition pieces in which the mechanical aspect was subordinated to the artistic. The clock and the musical and figure-activating mechanisms having been developed as far as present resources allowed, attention now shifted to the cabinet. At the Mitre, Charing Cross, was shown in 1741 "The Microcosm, or The World in Miniature, Built in the Form of a Roman Temple" by Henry Bridges, who is variously described as the architect or the carpenter of Waltham Abbey. This was a complicated astronomical showpiece, the "outward structure" being "a most beautiful

9. Henry Bridges's Microcosm (engraving, 1744). The medallions at the top somewhat cheekily associate the inventor with Sir Isaac Newton.

composition of Architecture, Sculpture, and Painting."[69] Some twelve hundred wheels and pinions combined to keep things moving. To a musical accompaniment, the stars and planets went through their respective evolutions, including a solar eclipse; the nine muses played on musical instruments; Orpheus was seen in a forest, playing his lyre, as in Pinchbeck's earlier machine; in a carpenter's yard, a number of workmen addressed themselves to their various tasks; birds flew, perched, twittered, and warbled in a "delightful grove"; and across a capacious landscape moved the by now standard array of ships under sail, coaches and carts with their wheels revolving, swans swimming and feathering themselves, dogs and ducks sporting.[70] The makers' inventiveness seems not to have extended very far in the direction of new subjects. "That noble pile," as a later advertisement called it, was displayed periodically in London, as well as throughout England, Europe, and "the English America" for the next forty years. The music that Handel was said to have written for it actually was composed for an organ of the Earl of Bute, to which cylinders had been added in the Microcosm manner.[71]

Another such edifice, unveiled the same year (1741) as the Microcosm, was the "Temple of Arts and Sciences" built by Nathaniel Edmunds of St. Saviour's Dock Head, Southwark: a mahogany Roman temple representing, on its four sides, the Palace of Harmony (geography and astronomy), Night (music), Phoebus Going through the Twelve Signs (mathematics), and the School of Athens (painting).[72] How much action occurred is not clear, but the Handelian musical accompaniment, at least, was driven by clockwork. Contemporary newspaper clippings reflect a massive lack of public encouragement. No doubt there was a limit to the number of Temples of Arts people would pay to see and hear. Even so, these imposing machines continued to be exhibited at the fairs. As late as 1789 a mixed bill at Bartholomew Fair that included conjuring tricks, fantoccini (marionettes), and a miniature "opera" ended with the showman Flockton's display of his "grand and inimitable MUSICAL CLOCK, at first view, a curious organ, exhibited three times before their Majesties." Nine hundred figures, it was said, could be seen working at their various trades.[73]

But it was the older mechanical theatres and moving pictures, usually devoid of musical accompaniment, which had the most durable appeal to fairgoers. In 1719 a Mr. De Lepine exhibited a clockwork theatre which performed a pantomimic opera.[74] At both Bartholomew and Tottenham fairs in 1731 the veteran showman Yeates (Yates) had "a curious piece of Italian machinery, nine feet high and eight feet wide" with either two or three hundred figures—the sources differ—moved by clockwork. Ten years later Fawkes and a Pinchbeck son had "a machine showing the Siege of Carthagena" at Southwark Fair, and at Bartholomew Fair in 1747 there were mechanical representations of the siege of Bergen op Zoom and of unbesieged Venice. At the same fair in 1758 the capture of Louisburg and Cape Breton was depicted.[75]

Although after the early decades of the century mechanical pictures were seen mainly at the fairs, they occasionally reappeared indoors. At Exeter Change in 1769, for instance, there was a "Grand Illuminated Exhibition in the Italian Taste" portraying the death of Sisera. The "figures in relief as large as the life" moved against a background of "mechanical perspective" including "ruins, water-falls, woods, hills, lawns. . . . The whole illuminated with an innumerable quantity of lamps on a new construction."[76] A later show at Exeter Change (1772) belonged to the same genre. The scene was a gentleman's estate, with buildings, grottoes, temples, alcoves, cascades, ponds, and so on, and the two-inch-high figures were of ladies walking in the gardens, artisans plying their trades, deer running in the park, and a six-horse chariot going at full speed.[77]

There was a distinct revival of interest in moving pictures in the 1770s. In 1776 a member of a famous family of Swiss clockwork specialists, Henri-Louis Jaquet-Droz, opened his Spectacle Mécanique, or Mechanical Exhibition, at the Great Room, 6 King Street, Covent Garden. The more traditional attraction was what must have been one of the most elaborate mechanical pictures ever devised, though it had an area of no more than four and a half feet square. Spread across the lower part, or foreground, were a palace and formal garden, with fountains playing and a clock striking the hours. But most of the action occurred in what was called a "grotto," behind and above the palace. Here scores of miniature figures went through an intricate program against the pasteboard-and-clay background of a Swiss landscape. The sun rose and proceeded across the sky in accordance with the seasons of the year; a shepherd and shepherdess played tunes on a flute and guitar; a dog barked and frisked, sheep grazed and bleated, a cow fed her calf, a loaded donkey plodded along a path, singing birds flew through a wood, fruit trees blossomed and bore fruit. Flanking all these activities were a chalet and a mill with a running stream.[78]

In addition to this busy scene, Jaquet-Droz exhibited three separate, almost life-size automaton figures; according to a newspaper advertisement, "one figure writes whatever is dictated to it, another draws and finishes in a masterly manner several curious designs; another plays divers Airs on the Harpsichorde."[79] "The *tout ensemble*," wrote Henry Angelo, the fencing master whose *Reminiscences* are a useful but sometimes unreliable source of information on some of the shows of the period, "was an object of curiosity to all the amateurs of mechanical inventions, and must have been very lucrative to the ingenious artist, who could not have been more than twenty-five."[80] (He was actually twenty-four.) Whether the exhibition drew as many patrons as it deserved, we have no way of knowing. But Jaquet-Droz's show proved to have been the prelude to a new chapter in the history of London's automaton exhibitions.

Exhibitions of Mechanical Ingenuity

5

Jaquet-Droz's Spectacle Mécanique exhibited together what previously had been two rather distinct species in the broad genus of automatons.[1] The moving-picture, musical-clock tradition represented by his Swiss landscape involved a number of miniature figures, representing both living beings and inanimate objects, which were part of a composition and were activated by a central power source, usually a clockwork. Although the program might be fairly elaborate, on the whole the action of the figures was so repetitious as to forestall any illusion that they were actually alive. There was little attempt at verisimilitude. By contrast, the automaton writer, draftsman, and musician were independent figures, each with its own mechanism and belonging to no composition; they approached life size; their actions were less repetitive, more "realistic"; and they were explicitly intended to give the illusion of life. The fundamental difference between the two categories, therefore, was the relative emphasis placed on mimesis and mechanism. Which was the spectator to admire more, the illusive representation of life or the sheer gadgetry involved in producing that illusion?

The choice was typical of the age. The ill-educated who gaped at automatons at the eighteenth-century London fairs still retained vestiges of the superstitious awe with which their forefathers had looked on the Boxley cross with its crude motions. The sophisticated, on the other hand, regarded the automatons and other machines to be described in this chapter as dramatic evidence of their age's unprecedented technical ingenuity. "To collect the productions of art [i.e., invention], and examples of mechanical science or manual ability," wrote Dr. Johnson in the *Rambler* (no. 83), "is unquestionably useful, even when the things themselves are of small importance, because it is always advantageous to know how far the human powers have proceeded, and how much experience has found to be within the reach of diligence. . . . It may sometimes happen that the greatest efforts of ingenuity have been exerted in trifles, yet the same principles and expedients may be applied to more valuable purposes, and the movements which put into action machines of no use but to raise the wonder of ignorance, may be employed to drain fens, or manufacture metals, to assist the architect, or preserve the sailor."[2]

Despite England's eminence in clockwork manufacture, the first notable self-acting figure, like Pinkethman's first moving picture, came from abroad. Its inventor was Jacques de Vaucanson, of whom Voltaire wrote,

> Le hardi Vaucanson, rival de Prométhée,
> Semblait, de la nature imitant les ressorts,
> Prendre le feu des cieux pour animer les corps.[3]

No mere charlatan, Vaucanson was a serious scientist and inventor who deserved the high regard in which contemporary savants held him. He belongs to the history of French science and technology rather than of English showmanship, where his fame rests solely on the figures he displayed in action four times daily in the Long Room of the Opera House, Haymarket, in

1742: a flute player, a performer on the tabor (drum) and pipe, and a duck.

The flute player had evoked much skepticism when it was shown in Paris six years earlier, because people still remembered an "automaton" harpsichord player which had taken in the learned men and the court until Louis XV, insisting on examining the hidden works, discovered a five-year-old girl inside. Vaucanson disarmed his potential critics by allowing a committee of the Académie des Sciences to inspect the flute player's machinery for themselves. Having done so, they promptly concluded in astonishment that no trickery was involved. The inventor went on to create a more complicated figure, of which we have a fuller account, because Vaucanson's own description of it was copied in Diderot's and d'Alembert's *Encyclopédie* and published in an English translation by the Prince of Wales's chaplain.[4] This figure, dressed like a dancing shepherd, held a pipe in one hand and a stick in the other, "with which he strikes on the Tabor single and double strokes, Rollings varied for all the Tunes, and keeping Time with what is play'd with the Pipe in the other Hand. . . . The Mechanism for this consists in an infinite Combination of Levers, and different Springs, all moved with Exactness to keep true to the Tune." The flageolet, though it had only three holes, was capable of twenty tunes, which were made possible by variations of the force of the wind, produced by a miniature bellows, and the different degrees with which the holes were covered. The effect, it was said, was superior to that of human performers, whose tongue could not articulate the notes with the speed of the machine.[5]

Vaucanson's gilded-copper duck was even more marvelous. "It executed accurately all [a natural bird's] movements and gestures, it ate and drank with avidity, performed all the quick motions of the head and throat which are peculiar to the living animal, and like it, it muddled the water which it drank with its bill."[6] It also quacked. But its most spectacular accomplishment was digestion.

I represent [Vaucanson wrote] the Mechanism of the Intestines which are employed in the operations of Eating, Drinking, and Digestion: Wherein the Working of all the Parts necessary for those Actions is exactly imitated. The Duck stretches out its Neck to take Corn out of your Hand; it swallows it, digests it, and discharges it digested by the usual Passage. You see all the Actions of a Duck that swallows greedily, and doubles the Swiftness in the Motion of its Neck and Throat or Gullet to drive the Food into its Stomach, copied from Nature: The Food is digested as in real

Animals, by Dissolution, not Trituration, as some natural Philosophers will have it. . . . I only pretend to imitate the Mechanism of that Action in three Things, Viz. First, to swallow the Corn; secondly, to macerate or dissolve it; thirdly, to make it come out sensibly changed from what it was.

Nevertheless, it was no easy Matter to find Means for those three Actions, and those Means may perhaps deserve some Attention from those that may expect more. They will see what Contrivances have been made use of to make this artificial Duck take up the Corn, and suck it up quite to its Stomach; and there in a little Space to make a Chymical Elaboratory to decompound or separate the Integrant Parts of the Food, and then drive it away at Pleasure thro' Circumvolutions of Pipes, which discharge it at the other End of the Body of the Duck.[7]

For an explanation of how it was actually done, however, we must turn to the great nineteenth-century French conjuror Robert-Houdin, who makes it sound embarrassingly simple:

A vase, containing seed steeped in water, was placed before the bird. The motion of the bill in dabbling crushed the food, and facilitated its introduction into a pipe placed beneath the lower bill. The water and seed thus swallowed fell into a box placed under the bird's stomach, which was emptied every three or four days. The other part of the operation was thus effected: Bread-crumb, colored green, was expelled by a forcing pump, and carefully caught on a silver salver as the result of artificial digestion. This was handed round to be admired, while the ingenious trickster laughed in his sleeve at the credulity of the public.[8]

Robert-Houdin may not have shown sufficient respect for his illustrious predecessor, but there is pleasure in the notion of a group of French or English scientists gravely examining the end product of an artificial duck; it is too bad that by 1742 Swift's mind had deteriorated so far that he was incapable of appreciating the scene. We do, however, possess the reaction of Hogarth, who was unable to perceive even praiseworthy realism, let alone a scientific marvel, in Vaucanson's invention:

There was brought from France some years ago, a little clock-work machine, with a duck's head and legs fixed to it, which was so contrived as to have some resemblance to that fowl standing upon one foot, and stretching back its leg, turning its head, opening and shutting its bill, moving its wings, and shaking its tail; all of them the plainest and easiest directions in living movements, yet for the poorly performing of these few motions, this silly, but much extolled machine, being uncovered, appeared a most complicated, confused, and disagreeable object: nor would its being covered with a skin closely adhering to its parts, as that of a real duck does, have much mended its figure; at best, a bag of hob-nails, broken hinges, and patten-rings, would have looked as well, unless by other means it had been stuffed out to bring it into form.[9]

The accomplished and indefatigable duck was toured for the rest of the century. Goethe saw it at Helmstadt in 1805, by which time it could eat its oats but not digest them. Its condition worsened until it was rescued by the owners of a traveling museum of automatons in Prague (1839) and rehabilitated by a specialist in clockwork who required three and a half years for the job. Thereafter it resumed its travels, which ended obscurely at Dresden early in the twentieth century.[10]

The second European mechanician to excite London with his automatons, thirty-four years later, was Henri-Louis Jaquet-Droz. His three figures—the writer, draftsman, and harpsichord player—represented the highest state of complexity and sophistication the art of automaton making had yet attained. When they were exhibited in Paris before being brought to London in 1776, Vaucanson, it was said, would have exclaimed, "Jeune homme, vous commencez par où j'aurais voulu finir!"[11] After their London run, these first-generation Jaquet-Droz figures, along with the mechanical picture of the Swiss landscape, went on tour on the continent, spent the years of the Napoleonic Wars in Spain, then resumed their wanderings through western Europe; they evidently never returned to England.* But replicas, built by the firm of Jaquet-Droz and Leschot in Geneva (makers also of elaborate clocks and watches, mechanical singing birds, and other novelties lavishly fashioned from clockwork, gems, and precious metals), were shown in London well into the nineteenth century. Their proprietor in earlier years was Henri Maillardet, another Swiss clock- and automaton-artificer who managed the London branch of the Geneva firm from 1783 to about 1790, when it was forced into liquidation.

The harpsichord-playing automaton Maillardet exhibited was familiarly known as "The Musical Lady" in allusion to a popular farce derived from George Colman's *The Jealous Wife* (1761). Valued at £420, she was described in the accounts of Jaquet-Droz and Leschot as "an organ mechanism with two registers and bellows; the figure of a girl automaton playing a harpsichord under instruction with wheel train, hand movements, etc."[12] The advertising and the testimony of eyewitnesses flesh out this prosaic description. Seated at the keyboard, she began by bowing to her auditors. "She is apparently agitated with an anxiety and diffidence not always felt in real life," wrote one spectator; "her eyes then seem intent on the notes, her bosom heaves."[13] Apart from the "anxiety and diffidence," this was no mere fancy; the figure's eyes did move, her bosom did heave, her fingers did alight on the appropriate keys, her feet did beat time. She had a repertory of sixteen or eighteen tunes, the natural notes of which she produced at the keyboard and the sharps and flats by pressing the pedal. At the end of a selection she rose and bowed again.

The automaton writer was a figure of a boy about eight years old, seated at a desk. With a card or sheet of paper before him, he dipped a pen into an inkstand, shook off the excess ink, and proceeded to copy a sentence from a specimen of handwriting on the desk, leaving the proper spaces between words and lines, differentiating between capitals and small letters, and meticulously going back to dot the *i*'s and cross the *t*'s. The draftsman was capable of filling six successive cards of "Dutch vellum" with different pictures, beginning with portraits of the king and queen facing each other. Maillardet subsequently exhibited a combination writer-draftsman of his own creation, which was capable, in the course of an hour, of inscribing three landscapes and four pieces of writing in English and French.

To the three classic Jaquet-Droz figures Maillardet added a fourth, a magician, which sat holding a wand in one hand and a book of necromancy in the other. A spectator chose one of a score of oval medallions, each of which had a different question inscribed on it (for example, "What is the most universal passion?"), and inserted it into a slot. The magician then rose, bowed, waved his wand, and consulted the book. Raising the wand again, he struck it against the wall behind him and a pair of doors flew open, displaying the answer ("Love"). When the doors closed, the medallion was returned to stock. One winding of the machinery was good for an hour. The secret was a simple one: "The medallions had holes, which did not precisely correspond, and these were brought into contact with needles, so as to produce a different result with each medallion."[14]

Maillardet's rival in the mid-1790s was a man named Haddock, who had a show at 38 Norfolk Street, Strand, under the interchangeable names of the Mechanic Theatre and the Androides. Several of the automaton figures here had a lineage reaching all the way back to a show by one Balducci which was at the Red Lion inn, Pall Mall, in 1738 and subsequently toured

* After extensive tours during the rest of the nineteenth century, the three automatons settled permanently in 1909 at the Musée d'Art et d'Histoire, Neuchâtel, not far from their birthplace at La Chaux-de-Fonds. In perfect repair, they give public performances on the first Sunday of every month. The mechanical landscape seems to have disappeared during the troupe's stay in Spain.

up and down the country for the next thirty years;[15] others seem to have been inspired by Jaquet-Droz or, in one case, by current events. This last was the figure of a volunteer soldier which appeared at the gate of an old building labeled the Temple of Mars, went through the manual of arms accompanied by a drum beaten by another automaton, and concluded by firing his musket. Haddock's writing and drawing automaton drew clear outlines of a bear, lion, elephant, tiger, horse, camel, or stag, whichever was requested. A highland oracle gave a "rational Answer (by Motion) to any Question proposed, calculate[d] Sums in Arithmetic, etc., etc."[16] But the most elaborate performance was that of the fruitery. Outside a rural mansion stood a porter who, upon being addressed, rang a bell; the door opened and a fruitress emerged, to receive orders from the onlookers for any of a dozen different kinds of fruit, which she then fetched. As the fruits were given away, a watch dog sitting in front of the house began to bark, and could not be quieted until they were returned. A chimney sweep, coming from behind the house, entered the door, reappeared at the top of the chimney, cried "Sweep!" several times, went back down the chimney, and came out with a bag full of soot.[17]

There may well have been some doubt whether all these activities were accomplished without discreet human intervention. Londoners' skepticism had been sharpened a decade earlier (1784) when a pamphlet, *The Speaking Figure and the Automaton Chess-Player Exposed and Detected,* rebuked a gullible public which allowed a foreigner to "call a Toy-Shop Doll a *Speaking Figure,* and demand HALF-A-CROWN apiece admittance to hear it, and find within a hundred yards another Foreigner who imposes double that sum to see what he calls an AUTOMATON *Chess-Player.*"[18] The "speaking figure," exhibited by a Frenchman, was a twenty-two-inch effigy of a child, suspended from a ribbon or held in the hand, which answered questions in French, English, or Dutch.[19] Dr. Johnson, in his best avuncular-didactic manner, explained to little Hester Maria ("Queeney") Thrale:

11. Kempelen's automaton chess player (*Illustrated London News*, 20 December 1845).

*Johnson may have been referring either to the original figure or to an imitation made in London by Thomas Denton, formerly a tinman in Yorkshire and a bookseller in York, who after touring it to various parts of the country sold it to a printer in the City. A man of diverse skills, Denton also built a writing figure, plated coach harnesses, and minted counterfeit coins which, it was said at the time, "deceived the best judges." As a consequence of this last occupation he was hanged before Newgate in 1789. (*Gentleman's Magazine*, 59, 1789, 757–58.)

The Speaking Image, about which you enquire, is a very subtle and wonderful deception. The answer to the question is doubtless made by ventriloquy, or the art of directing the voice in what [way] the speaker wills, but [how] the question is conveyed to the Speaker, wherever he is, has not yet been discovered. The statue is of wax, and incapable of any mechanical operation. Besides that, no mechanism can provide answers to arbitrary questions. No chimes can be set to play any tune that may be called. The artifice is according to all accounts astonishing, yet it will some time [be] resolved into some petty trick.[20]

It was—by the author of the pamphlet, who showed that the trick was done by a series of speaking tubes.*

The more celebrated of these two artificial persons, however, was the automaton chess player exhibited in 1783–84 at 8 Savile Row, Burlington Gardens.[21] Invented by Wolfgang von Kempelen, a native of Presburg, to gratify a whim of Empress Maria Theresa, like Jaquet-Droz's trio it had been exhibited at courts and in public places across western Europe. Behind a chest, four feet wide, two deep, and three high, sat a half-size figure of a man, turbaned and clad in the Turkish cos-

tume, suggestive of an Oriental sorcerer, that was the conventional garb of automaton magicians. In his right hand was a long Turkish pipe. Before he began a game with a human challenger, his exhibitor made an elaborate ritual of opening the doors of the three compartments into which the chest was divided and holding a candle at the back, to show that nothing was inside but a mass of clockwork machinery. The showman then wound up the machinery, which could be heard in operation as play progressed. During a game, the adversary was seated at a chessboard a little distance away; each move he made was duplicated by the exhibitor on the Turk's board laid atop the chest. The Turk responded by raising his left hand, turning his head and eyes from left to right, and then moving his own piece. The showman would make the same move in his behalf on the human player's board. And so the game went on, the Turk shaking his head and impatiently rapping his fingers on the board when his opponent made a false move, nodding his head three times when he checkmated the king. With periodic rewinding of the mechanism, a game might last as long as an hour. The automaton usually won, although once in a while an exceptionally good player would beat him.

The author of the denunciatory pamphlet, a former military man and controversialist named Philip Thicknesse, argued that the alleged automaton figure was merely window dressing, as was the complicated but functionless mechanism inside the chest, and that the true chess player was a child concealed in the cabinet, who could see every move his opponent made. But in view of the owner's understandable refusal to let anyone inspect the box, this "explanation" had to remain a hypothesis. It was to be revived in London some forty years later, as we shall see.

⊃Ʒ·❋·Ʒ⊂

None of these automatons, or what purported to be such, had any pretense to beauty; they were, at base, mere mechanisms, to be admired for what they did rather than how they looked. Automatons that were also splendid works of art—self-acting "bijoux," though the size of some belied the name, for they included gigantic examples as much as sixteen feet in height—were the special province of Cox's Museum, the most elegant of eighteenth-century London exhibitions in respect to both contents and clientele.[22] James Cox, the proprietor, had been in business as early as 1751 as a jeweler and maker of baubles for the rich. His novelties were designed by such artists as Joseph Nollekens and Johann Zoffany and manufactured by Cox's own artificers as well as those of Jaquet-Droz and Leschot in Geneva. The principal market for these luxurious curios, with their encrustations of gold and silver, inlays of gems, and intricate systems of springs, wheels, and escapements, was—or until recently had been—the Orient. By selling the mandarins these expensive "sing-songs," as they were called, either for themselves or as gifts to higher officials and the court at Peking, Britain sought to redress the balance of payments between the two countries, which was decidedly in China's favor. Britain bought from the Chinese great quantities of tea, most of which she had to pay for in precious bullion rather than goods, because her Oriental creditors were proudly self-sufficient.

For a while, apparently, the sing-songs did help reduce Britain's trade deficit. But Cox and others sent them out in such numbers that the market became glutted and the price the mandarins were willing to pay fell sharply. In 1771 the Hong merchants, the middlemen between the British traders and the mandarins, protested to the East India Company's council that they were caught in a profit squeeze.[23] And so the sing-song trade fell off, and Cox found himself burdened with a heavy capital investment and short of cash. He was forced to liquidate some of his stock through two sales at Christie's in July and December 1772.[24]

At the beginning of the same year Cox also set up a display of twenty-three of his most imposing pieces in the Great Room, Spring Gardens, which for the ensuing half-century was to be one of London's busiest exhibition halls. Cox's occupancy was so memorable that for many years the building was customarily identified as "the Great Room, Spring Gardens, formerly Cox's Museum." Located on a site adjacent to today's Admiralty Arch (a short byway in the vicinity preserves the name of Spring Gardens), this former Huguenot chapel, measuring fifty-eight by forty-four feet, had also served as a concert hall. In 1764, for instance, Johann Christian Bach had directed concerts there, and in the same year it had been the scene of young Mozart's London debut.

The décor of the Great Room for Cox's tenancy was worthy of its contents. The ceiling of the dome had chiaroscuro paintings representing the Liberal Arts; five crystal lusters provided the lighting; crimson curtains set off the jeweled objects enshrined behind railings. Cox charged admission at the unprecedented and subsequently unmatched rate of 10s. 6d. There was some grumbling about this even among the patrons who could best afford it, but in the interests of security Cox was required to limit the number of people in the room at any one time. The announced value of the precious metals and jewels in these cunning *objets de luxe* was enormous, £197,000.

The museum was the talk of London for three full years. Boswell visited it on 6 April 1772, soon after it opened, on the recommendation of Dr. Johnson, who evidently had already been there. "For power of mechanism and splendour of show," Johnson told him, "[it] was a very fine exhibition." Boswell agreed: "The mechanism and rich appearance of the jewels were both very wonderful and very pleasing."[25] A peacock (now in the Hermitage, Leningrad) screeched and spread its tail when the hour struck, while a cock crowed and a cage with an owl inside revolved and twelve bells rang.[26] A silver swan with an articulated neck glided across a surface of "artificial water." A gilt throne thirty-two feet in circumference was equipped

12. The Great Room, Spring Gardens, often called "Late Cox's Museum" (drawing by C. Bigot, 1820). The building, soon to be demolished, was then rented for exhibition and entertainment purposes by Charles Wigley, a jeweler.

with a "band of mechanical music" which performed "God Save the King" on kettle drums and trumpets. Sixteen elephants supported a pair of seven-foot-high temples adorned with 1,700 pieces of jewelry; rhinoceroses, standing on rocks of gold stone, similarly upheld cabinets of onyx and gold; and silver turtles bore gilded and jeweled vases on their backs. Gorgeously caparisoned bulls and goats with pearl housings upheld nothing. A chronoscope inlaid with 100,000 precious stones evidently needed no animal guise.

Not all of this riot of brilliance, movement, and sound was to everyone's taste, but a visit to Cox's Museum, the air filled with the warble of mechanical birds and the many-voiced tinkle and clangor of splendidly elaborated clocks, was an experience not to be missed. In *Evelina* (1778) Fanny Burney, who seems to have looked on most exhibitions with a cool eye, used it to stage a confrontation between advocates of utility and of art. "This Museum," wrote the heroine, "is very astonishing, and very superb; yet, it afforded me but little pleasure, for it is a mere show, though a wonderful one."

Sir Clement Willoughby, in our walk round the room, asked me what my opinion was of this brilliant *spectacle!*

"It is very fine, and very ingenious," answered I, "and yet—I don't know how it is—but I seem to miss something."

"Excellently answered!" cried he, "you have exactly defined my own feelings, tho' in a manner I should never have arrived at. But I was certain your taste was too well formed, to be pleased at the expence of your understanding."

"Pardie," cried Madame Duval, "I hope you two is difficult enough! I'm sure if you don't like this, you like nothing;

for it's the grandest, prettiest, finest sight that ever I see, in England."

"What," (cried the Captain, with a sneer), "I suppose this may be in your French taste? it's like enough, for it's all *kickshaw* work. But, pr'ythee, friend," (turning to the person who explained the devices), "will you tell me the *use* of all this? for I'm not enough of a conjurer to find it out."

"Use, indeed!" (repeated Madame Duval disdainfully) "Lord, if every thing's to be useful!"

"Why, Sir, as to that, Sir," said our conductor, "the ingenuity of the mechanism,—the beauty of the workmanship,—the—undoubtedly, Sir, any person of taste may easily discern the utility of such extraordinary performances."

"Why then, Sir," answered the Captain, "your person of taste must be either a coxcomb, or a Frenchman; though for the matter of that, 'tis the same thing."

Just then, our attention was attracted by a pine-apple, which, suddenly opening, discovered a nest of birds, who immediately began to sing. "Well," cried Madame Duval, "this is prettier than all the rest! I declare, in all my travels, I never see nothing eleganter."

"Hark ye, friend," said the Captain, "hast never another pine-apple?"

"Sir?—"

"Because, if thou hast, pr'ythee give it us without the birds; for d'ye see, I'm no Frenchman, and should relish something more substantial."

The entertainment concluded with a concert of mechanical music: I cannot explain how it was produced, but the effect was pleasing.[27]

Cox's Museum served satirists in more than one way. In an attack on governmental corruption, the "Epistle to Dr. Shebbeare," William Mason used it for a simile which Horace Walpole excessively praised as "a far more brilliant piece of poetic Machinery than what it describes . . . a Chef d'oeuvre of Poetry . . . as difficult to match . . . as it was to compose":

> Tax then, ye greedy ministers, your fill:
> No matter, if with ignorance or skill.
>
> . . . .
> Ye know, whate'er is from the public prest,
> Will sevenfold sink into your private chest.
> For he, the nursing father, that receives,
> Full freely tho' he takes, as freely gives.
> So when great Cox, at his mechanic call,
> Bids orient pearls from golden dragons fall,
> Each little dragonet, with brazen grin,
> Gapes for the precious prize, and gulps it in.
> Yet when we peep behind the magic scene,
> One master-wheel directs the whole machine:
> The self-same pearls, in nice gradation, all

> Around one common centre, rise and fall:
> Thus may our state-museum long surprise. . .[28]

Although an artificer-merchant by trade, Cox was as adept an advertiser as any professional showman. He issued a ninety-two-page pamphlet entitled *A Collection of Various Extracts, in Prose and in Verse, from the London Publications, Relative to the Museum, in Spring-Gardens; Containing Many Favourable Testimonies and Judicious Observations, on That Superb and Singular Display of Art.*[29] Its contents, mostly letters to the editor and verse effusions, were drawn from London newspapers published between January and September 1772. It is not impossible that Cox planted at least some of them. Presumably genuine, however, was a friendly testimonial from Christopher Pinchbeck, who vowed in future to call his own show (Chapter 6) "the *Minor* Mechanical Exhibition." As well he might have, because in sheer effulgence Cox's Museum wholly outdid his own, just as true gold outshone the alloy that bore his name.

Another, unsolicited tribute to the museum occurred in the second act of Sheridan's *The Rivals,* when Sir Anthony Absolute thundered to his son, who professed reluctance to marry Lydia Languish: "Zounds! sirrah! the lady shall be as ugly as I choose: she shall have a hump on each shoulder; she shall be as crooked as the crescent; her one eye shall roll like the bull's in Cox's Museum; she shall have a skin like a mummy, and the beard of a Jew—she shall be all this, sirrah!" These lines were first uttered on the Covent Garden stage on 17 January 1775. On the following 7 April the collection was removed from Spring Gardens to grace a "grand rout" given by the Lord Mayor at the Mansion House, preliminary to the collection's being disposed of by lottery.[30]

Still asserting that "the present distress and scarcity of money in the East Indies" required his stock to be liquidated, Cox advertised the event by composing a song to the tune of "Roast Beef of Old England":

> Whoe'er in this season of public distress,
> Would court Lady Fortune with certain success,
> To her shrine let him now with alacrity press,
> For tickets in Cox's new lottery,
> Let him haste, and buy tickets of Cox.
>
> The sly slippery Goddess here plays you no tricks,
> Nor smiles in your face, while your pocket she picks;
> A method is found out her wheel how to fix,
> If we buy into Cox's new lottery,
> Then let us buy tickets from Cox.

And so on for seven more stanzas, the initial appeal to the prospective ticket buyer's cupidity giving way in the conclusion to nobler sentiments:

If genius or splendor with pleasure you view,
See here more than Athens or Rome ever knew,
And feel for those Arts, which pour honour on you;
   O haste then, and buy in the Lott'ry,
   O haste, and buy tickets from Cox.

Thus Britain's white sails shall be kept unfurl'd,
And our commerce extend, as our thunders are hurl'd,
Till the Empress of Science is Queen of the World,
   If we haste to buy into the Lott'ry
   If we haste to buy tickets from Cox.[31]

Not only the star pieces at the museum but all the items Cox owned were evidently to be raffled off. Of the 120,404 tickets printed, each of the top two winners was worth £5,000 in merchandise, and the next two £3,000 each, and so on down to number 212, whose holder was entitled to £150 worth.[32] How many were sold and who, if anyone, got the prizes is not known. Cox survived this attempted liquidation and remained in business, but only as a retailer, not a manufacturer. He died late in 1791 or early in 1792, and what was left of his stock—fifty-five "bijoux curieux et horloges"—was sold at Christie's for 12,000 guineas.[33]

Some years after the lottery, Cox's Museum was succeeded in the same Spring Gardens building by "Davies's Grand Museum."* This evidently was the undertaking of one of Cox's assistants who had helped fashion the original pieces and who now (according to a newspaper item on 13 May 1782) "executed, to a small scale, a truly curious representation of many of the most capital pieces in that astonishing Collection, in the same elegance of design and richness of composition as the originals." Among the exhibits were a golden throne, a silver-plumaged swan, "a Gardener's Boy, with a Pine-Apple on his Head, which opens and discovers a Nest of Birds" (a miniature replica of the one Fanny Burney mentions), a palm tree "representing a serpent creeping round one way, and an eagle moving the other," and a mechanical star with 3,000 precious stones "in spiral and circular motion."[34]

The presence of these small-scale reproductions of Cox's original pieces confuses the record henceforth: it may be that some of the items attributed to Cox's Museum in later years were Davies's instead. The enduring celebrity of Cox's collection would have been sufficient reason for his name, rather than Davies's, to appear in the advertising. However, there

is no reason to doubt that many of the "Cox" pieces were actually Cox's. Maillardet had several in his automaton exhibition, and one group remained intact for many years at Weeks's Museum, which we will visit later.

◻⅜✳⅜◻

Some time in the 1760s Cox acquired, as an assistant and eventually his "chief mechanic," a Belgian named John Joseph Merlin, who had come to London in (according to one writer) the suite of the Spanish Ambassador Extraordinary, the Count de Fuentes.[35] Merlin made some clockwork novelties in the familiar mode, among them fifteen-inch-high figures of women that performed "almost every motion and inclination of the human body; viz. of the head, the breasts, the neck, the arms, the fingers, the legs, &c. even to the motion of the eye-lids, and the lifting up of the hands and fingers to the face"; a mechanical garden with figures of ladies and gentlemen on horseback and fountains playing; and a Circus of Cupid, showing fishermen in a boat, Fortune on a wheel, flying doves drawing Venus in a shell, and the Goddess of Love coyly shooting arrows at the lady onlookers. But these were the least novel and the least characteristic of his many productions. Merlin was a gadgeteer par excellence, and with him we leave the world of self-acting jeweled playthings made for monarchs and return to the more recognizably English world of imaginative practicality. Most of Merlin's creations would have won the ungrudging approval of Fanny Burney's Captain Mirvan.

It is through Fanny's eyes that we see Merlin most vividly. On the whole, he pleased her—certainly he amused her—more than did Sir Ashton Lever. "He is a great favourite in our house," she wrote in her diary in May 1775. "He is very diverting also in conversation. There is a singular simplicity in his manners. . . . He speaks his opinion upon all subjects and about all persons with the most undisguised freedom. He does not, though a foreigner, want *words;* but he *arranges* and *pronounces* them very comically. [He had an unerring habit of stressing the wrong syllable.] He is humbly grateful for all civilities that are shown him; but is warmly and honestly resentful for the least slight."[36] On another occasion, however, Fanny spoke of him, more sharply, as "that ridiculous Merlin . . . with his inconceivable absurdities."[37]

Leaving Cox's employ in 1772 or 1773, Merlin set up shop on his own at 11 Princes Street, Hanover

* The building was rented by a succession of entrepreneurs after Cox relinquished it. One such occupant was Davies; another was a jeweler, Charles Wigley, during whose tenancy it was called "Wigley's Auction Rooms" and "Wigley's Great Promenade Room." Between 1809 and 1820 it was used for three months of the year by the Society of Artists in Water-Colours, who, says the society's historian, "had to take their turn there with the proprietors of a variety of entertainments of all kinds, often affording more popular, though much less intellectual attractions, than those which they themselves were able to offer." (John Lewis Roget, *A History of the "Old Water-Colour" Society,* London, 1891, I, 401–402.) Among the more popular ones were Maillardet's automatons, waxworks, and panoramas of Boulogne and Waterloo. The building was pulled down in the mid-1820s. See *Survey of London,* XX (1940), 67–68, for a concise history.

Square. By 1783, if not earlier, the establishment was styled "Merlin's Mechanical Museum," where, according to the charming little catalogue, "Ladies and Gentlemen, who honour Mr. Merlin with their Company, may be accommodated with TEA and COFFEE, AT ONE SHILLING EACH."[38] Morning admission (11 A.M. to 3 P.M.) was 2s. 6d.; evening (7–9 P.M.), 3s. At first the evening session was limited to private parties, but later the public was admitted to these soirées.

Merlin's stock in trade was what Horace Walpole called "scientific toys,"[39] each of the words to be taken in its broad eighteenth-century meaning, ranging as the objects did from musical instruments and clockwork novelties to labor-saving household devices and sickroom equipment. Fanny's father, Dr. Charles Burney, the organist, composer, and historian of music, acquired a Merlin-made harpsichord about 1774 or 1775, at the same time that Merlin patented a combined harpsichord-pianoforte. Soon after this, Burney commissioned from him, for use in "duets à Quatre Mains," a pianoforte with a compass of six octaves, an extension of the keyboard that was encouraged by the necessity of accommodating two hoopskirts before one instrument. Here Merlin was in the vanguard of innovation, because Broadwood's first piano with a five-and-a-half-octave span was not made until 1790. He participated with much enthusiasm in the developing vogue of mechanical instruments, putting together a barrel organ–harpsichord capable of playing nineteen tunes and a one-man orchestra best described by lines in a long versified inventory of Merlin's creations, the rest of which the reader will be spared:

> Five instruments always in tune,
> It's a sight you can't always survey;
> Composed in one instrument's une,
> All of which one Musician can play.[40]

There was also a Welsh harp played with keys; according to the museum's catalogue, it "displays a celestial body of sound, resembles the human voice, gives the effect of Fiddles and Bases, and is most admirably calculated for the Expressivo." Among Merlin's other contributions to musical technology were "a machine for notating music, which he sent to Prince Galitzin, in St. Petersburg" (unsuccessful, because the signs were too hard to translate), and, in the words of Burney's will, "a Table, which may be formed into desks for 8 performers, with brass furniture for Candle light: by a winch it can be elevated to

any height, for writing or playing standing, with drawers and various contrivances for secret deposits."[41] This evidently was one of the numerous devices which catered to the era's delight in multiple-use contrivances, including furniture. Merlin also invented a novel tea table. Sitting behind it, the hostess could rotate the round surface by a pedal, bringing before her in sequence each cup to be filled; by touching another pedal, she could open and close the cock of the urn.[42]

The genial inventor was as anxious to reduce the labor of servants as he was that of their mistress. In his house he had installed, according to Sophie von la Roche,

an arrangement whereby the servants should know immediately the bell rang in their master's room what was required, by a means of a list fastened to the latter's bell similar to a barometer, registering the orders which so constantly recur—water, broth, coffee, chocolate and the like. Now since whoever pulls the bell simultaneously moves the pencil connected with the list and fastened in the servants' room, so this, the sound of the small bell, announces the employer's requests to the servants—all of which is a great saving for the staff and results in rapid service, as English kitchens are in the basement with the servants' quarters.[43]

Merlin was equally dedicated to the advancement of locomotion. On Sundays in Hyde Park he attracted much attention as he drove a "mechanical chariot" loaded with optional equipment, including a mechanical whip operated by a cord and spring and a "way wise," the ancestor of the modern odometer. (The way wise, however, was not his own invention. Evelyn saw one at Dr. Wilkins's as early as 1654.) Another of his inventions was a kind of roller skate. An often-repeated anecdote reports that he once appeared aboard a pair, with a violin tucked under his arm, at a masquerade in Soho Square. He glided over the polished floor and, having neglected to equip the skates with brakes, smashed into a valuable mirror, which, like the violin, was demolished. Merlin himself suffered some injury.

Inventors who held formal exhibitions in late eighteenth-century London seemingly had a special concern to alleviate the handicaps of deformity or illness. Just as Jaquet-Droz momentarily deserted his own specialty to make a prosthetic device—"Hands for a Person born with Stumps only" which enabled him to use a knife and fork, manage the reins in riding or driving, "and even write with great Freedom"[44]—so Merlin manufactured a whole line of such apparatus. The most famous were the Morpheus

13. John Joseph Merlin and his mechanical chariot (engravings in *Kirby's Wonderful and Scientific Museum*, 1803).

14. Merlin's mechanical chair (engraving in *Ackermann's Repository of Arts*, 1811).

(or rather, to use his own pronunciation, "Morfus") chair, the Merlin or "gouty" chair, and the Valetudinarian Bedstead. It is not certain how many distinct pieces of equipment these represented, because the terms were used loosely; but one was a wheelchair with an adjustable cradle for the patient's legs, a reclining back, and a small table, and another was an invalid's chair convertible into a bed. Other Merlinian inventions in this line were a "Hygeian Air-Pump" to "draw foul air out of Ships, Hospitals, Bedclothes, etc." and a "Balance Sanctorius" which measured weight and height.

Still other exhibits in Princes Street were a gambling machine, on which a game of odd or even could be played for four hours at one winding up; a set of whist cards for the blind, which may well have been an anticipation of the Braille system; the bust of a Turk which chewed and swallowed an artificial stone (the automaton chess player crossed with Vaucanson's duck?); and an "Aerial Cavalcade," four wooden horses on a structure supported by six pillars, "on which the Ladies and Gentlemen may ride, perfectly safe, over the heads of the rest of the company." This last was unquestionably an early carousel, complete with brass rings ("Whoever takes most rings off fair, / With the title of Hero'll be graced").

As the roller-skating incident suggests, Merlin did not shrink from advertising his wares even on social occasions. It was proper enough, no doubt, for him to demonstrate at the museum itself an indoor Fortune's Chariot that enabled him to scoot hither and thither in the room, but that did not necessarily give him license to turn up inside Fortune's Wheel at the Prince of Wales's masquerade or, at a party at the Burneys', in his Morpheus chair. Indeed, there was something tiresome about these antics. As Fanny's sister Charlotte wrote her in April 1780, when Merlin appeared as a sick man at a Pantheon masquerade, "He was a very good mask . . . but the newsmongers are not so good natured to him, for *they* say that there was a sick man in his Chair who made everybody sick of him!"[45] To vary the routine, Merlin also arrived at masquerades in the combined character of Cupid and Vulcan, "forging his own darts, for which he had a fire and a forge, and these he likewise very successfully aimed against the fair sex."

By a pleasant gesture of his favorite goddess, part of Merlin's fortune was his name.* He spent eighty guineas having his mechanized carriage painted with "various emblematical figures" of his legendary namesake. Although he seems never to have applied the name to his existing museum, he did, at one time, propose to raise a subscription of £5,040, at twelve guineas a share, to install a totally new "Merlin's Necromancic Cave" on the premises.

On Entrance [said the prospectus], the Company will be accommodated in a CIRCULAR SALOON, most judiciously adapted to its Uses, and ornamented with uncommon Taste. In the Centre of the SALOON will be the NECROMANCIC CAVE, on which the Automaton Figure of AMBROSIUS MERLIN will be seated; holding in his Right-hand a Leaden Sceptre, or conjuring Rod, a Symbol of his absolute Power, by which he will apparently animate all inanimated Things, such as Chairs, Paintings, and Magical Looking-Glasses; all which will obey his Commands; he will likewise tell the Fortunes of the Ladies. Two AUTOMATON FIGURES will then walk in a Gallery to the Saloon, and play on ancient Instruments of Music, by Means of a wonderful Exertion of Mechanism, presenting Refreshments to the Ladies only.

Under the Entrance to the Cave will be a dark subterraneous Cavern ten Feet deep, wherein the Author will make Use of his supposed Necromancic Power, in imitation of the celebrated AMBROSIUS MERLIN, called the NECROMANCER. A Variety of Phantoms, red and white Dragons, Rattle-snakes, all Sorts of Reptiles, creeping Animals and nocturnal Birds, will be seen and heard making the most horrid mournful Shrieks and Noise, so as to strike the Beholders with the utmost Astonishment; the Goddess of Darkness will also appear in a sable Habit, wearing Bat's Wings. By an extraordinary Display of Mechanical Ingenuity, the Prince of Darkness and Chief of the Devils, will be discovered in a deep, extensive and tremendous Cavern, which will also contain all the Furies and infernal Harpies.

After having explored this dark Recess, the Company will be desired to walk into a Circus, richly adorned and ornamented with the Temple of Apollo, where a Concert will be performed, entirely the Effect of an amazing Effort of Mechanical Invention, and so well directed as nearly to equal, both in Vocal and Instrumental Music, FIVE or SIX HUNDRED PERFORMERS, in a Selection of the most approved Works of the most celebrated Masters that have appeared throughout Europe.[46]

This imaginative contribution to London entertainment never got beyond the planning stage, nor did another Merlinian project, bearing the same name, which involved a structure to be built at Paddington. In addition to housing the inventor's mechanical collection, it would have three circular ballrooms, "a grand Orchestra to imitate the Band at the Abbey; and two alcoves for the reception of a pair of Automaton figures as large as life." But Merlin's notions plainly were greater than his resources. He died in 1803, leaving orders in his will that his thirty-year-old horse be shot.

* "Merlin's Cave," with its ancient associations of native British magic, was well established in the nomenclature of the eighteenth-century London entertainment business. In 1735 Queen Caroline commissioned William Kent to build a showplace of her own at Richmond: Merlin's Cave, a strange thatched mixture of Gothic and Palladian architecture and décor which housed wax figures representing Merlin and his "secretary," Queen Elizabeth and her nurse, Henry VII's queen, and Minerva. The resident guide was the Wiltshire thresher-poet Stephen Duck. This royal folly was much talked of, and several taverns capitalized on its fame by adopting the name Merlin's Cave. At the Crown coffeehouse in King Street was to be seen "Merlin in Miniature; or, a Lively Representation of Merlin in his Cave, as in the Royal Gardens at Richmond, Being, a New and Entertaining Piece of Moving Machinery, such as never before appeared in Publick". The theme of Merlin's Cave was used by the living theatre also, in both the drolls at the fairs and the operas on the regular stage. (B. Sprague Allen, *Tides in English Taste (1619–1800)*, Cambridge, Mass., 1937, II, 135–38.)

* To others, though, the magic remained, only the source being changed. Citing an enormous German predecessor of Brewster's little volume, Johann Christian Wiegleb's *Unterricht in der natürlichen Magie oder zu allerhand belustigenden und nützlichen Kunststücken* (20 vols., 1779–1805), Grete de Francesco has argued that despite all the efforts of such expositors, the crowds still wanted mystery, not elucidation. "The men of the Enlightenment strove to explain tricks in order to dissipate the power and spoil the business of the quacks who peddled scientific marvels," but "the mythology they drove out and expelled was not gone from the world; it hid itself and became entrenched where the Enlightened least expected it and where it therefore remained most invisibly concealed: behind modern science itself, behind technology. Science and technology became magical." "A disappointed society," she concludes, "sought to recapture in technology the supernatural world it had lost." (*The Power of the Charlatan,* trans. Miriam Beard, New Haven, 1939, pp. 233–35, 241.)

† Brewster is referring to the gimbals, a device for mounting a navigational instrument so that it retains its equilibrium despite the angle the ship assumes. But his statement is inaccurate. The gimbals were not originally a showman's mechanism, but were first used about 1530 for ships' lamps and compasses; thus the showman evidently got them from the sailor. Moreover, the first successful chronometer, made by John Harrison, did not use gimbals, although he had incorporated them in three preceding models. (Rupert T. Gould, *The Marine Chronometer: Its History and Development,* 1923, reprinted London, 1960, pp. 28, 50.)

It was. The museum lasted another five years, closing in the summer of 1808.[47]

◙⫶✳⫶◙

Thus, in the course of the century, the London exhibitions faithfully reflected the transition from "natural philosophy," with its lingering rack of mystery, to the Industrial Revolution, in which all things seemed possible to the practical inventive mind. What happened was tersely summarized by the phrase *Natural Magic,* which occurs in the title of a book the Scottish scientist Sir David Brewster addressed to Sir Walter Scott in 1832, explaining how a number of the automatons described in this and later chapters worked. To some, perhaps most, of the people to whom the creations of Vaucanson, Jaquet-Droz, Maillardet, and Cox appealed, "magic" was stripped of the occult and became a simple matter of mechanics, accessible to anyone with sufficient brain and manual skill to make such miraculous machines.*

Of the machines displayed in these exhibitions, only Merlin's—and, obviously, not all of these—had discernible utilitarian value; the rest, notwithstanding the museum guide's spirited defense of Cox's productions in the scene in *Evelina,* were intended solely to amuse. Yet, as Dr. Johnson intimated, the principles they embodied, and the craftsmanship required to build them, could readily be adapted to useful purposes. Even where technology could not be directly transferred, the mere example of clever mechanic-showmen, or men who purported to be such, might serve to inspire practical inventors. On holiday at Matlock in the summer of 1784, the Reverend Edmund Cartwright, brother of the man who brought the Eskimos to London, fell into conversation with some gentlemen from Manchester on the subject of

Arkwright's spinning machinery and the necessity of inventing a "weaving mill" to make cloth out of the thread it produced. They maintained it could not be done. But Cartwright had just seen the automaton chess player in London, and he replied, "Now, you will not assert, gentlemen, that it is more difficult to construct a machine that shall weave than one which shall make all the variety of moves which are required in that complicated game." In this case, credulity served where scepticism would have been fruitless. A true believer in the chess player's automatism, Cartwright went home to Kent, got to work, and three years later received a patent for his completed power loom.[48]

The full contribution the automatons made to the progress of English invention would reward study. Brewster was not disposed to underestimate it:

The passion for automatic exhibitions which characterized the 18th century, gave rise to the most ingenious mechanical devices, and introduced among the higher order of artists [i.e., artisans] habits of nice and neat execution in the formation of the most delicate pieces of machinery. The same combination of the mechanical powers which made the spider crawl, or which waved the tiny rod of the magician, contributed in future years to purposes of higher import. Those wheels and pinions, which almost eluded our senses by their minuteness, reappeared in the stupendous mechanism of our spinning-machines, and our steam-engines. The elements of the tumbling puppet were revived in the chronometer, which now conducts our navy through the ocean;† and the shapeless wheel which directed the hand of the drawing automaton has served in the present age to guide the movements of the tambouring engine. Those mechanical wonders which in one century enriched only the conjuror who used them, contributed in another to augment the wealth of the nation; and those automatic toys which once amused the vulgar, are now employed in extending the power and promoting the civilization of our species.[49]

Water, Fire, Air, and a Celestial Bed

6

The serious world of learning and the lighter world of entertainment shared the latest fruits of man's progress in studying and beginning to master his environment. While the clockwork pictures and automatons adapted for the purposes of amusement some of the mechanical principles that were ushering in the age of industrialism, London shows mirrored some of the advances being made in such diverse fields as astronomy, chemistry, microscopy, aeronautics, and engineering. Here, as in the popular versions of virtuosi's cabinets, the distinction between sheer entertainment and the satisfaction of intellectual curiosity often was blurred. Sometimes, one imagines, the diversion-seeking showgoers picked up a scrap or two of knowledge in spite of themselves and the learned, some amusement.

The seventeenth century's ambivalent interest in hydraulics well typified the indistinctness of that borderline. Although in the long run the primary treatises on the subject, the records of experiment and invention, were most important for their eventual contribution to the Industrial Revolution, in their own time a few also served in effect as handbooks of magical illusion—how-to-do-it repositories of tricks involving, among other things, the use of water to produce startling and mysterious effects. This newly acquired scientific knowledge of the properties of water had reverberations, as well, in the life of the court and aristocracy in both France and England. Playing with water was a delightful occupation for the leisured class, harnessing as it did the principles of science and engineering for the sake of beauty. In their formal gardens, water, channeled into canals and basins and expelled from fountains, was as vital to the total aesthetic effect as the work of the gardener and the topiarist; later, when taste turned away from the classical style, the same water was diverted into cleverly constructed "natural" cascades. Evelyn's diary often reflects the rage for this typically Renaissance merging of science and spectacle. At Amsterdam in 1641 he visited a rich Anabaptist who had

divers pretty Water workes . . . here were many quaint devices, fountaines, artificiall musique, noyses of beasts & chirping of birds etc.; but what I most admir'd then, was a lamp of brasse, projecting eight sockketts from the middle stemm, like to those we use in Churches, which having counterfeit lights or Tapers in them, had streames of Water issuing, as out of their Wieekes or Snuffs: the whole branch hanging all this while loose upon a [s]talk in the middst of a beame, and without any other perceptible commerce with any pipe; so that unlesse it were by compression of the ayre with a syringe, I could not comprehend how it should be done.[1]

In view of the widespread enthusiasm for scientific and technological novelties, especially if they were accompanied by a piquant air of mystification, it would have been odd if no attempt had been made to produce effects such as Evelyn described for a paying public. One such venture was actually undertaken some years before the first clockwork moving picture was introduced in London. Although it seems to have been fairly successful, it left little record, and we have less practical knowledge of how it worked than we would wish. The inventor, a retired mercer named William Winstanley, was an amateur mechanist. At his estate at Littlebury, Essex, he passed his time inventing various parlor tricks—a method of raising a ghost from the floor, an armchair that imprisoned anyone who sat in it—as well as designing a fantastic pagoda-shaped lighthouse, which was erected at the Eddystone rocks off the Cornish coast in 1696.[2] This "Merlin of his day," as he once was called, also experimented with hydraulics. In the same year the lighthouse was built, Evelyn recorded that he visited Lord Cheyne at Chelsea, where he "saw those ingenious Water works invented by Mr. Vinstanley wherein were some things very surprising & extraordinary."[3]

What these were can only be inferred from such evidence as we have of "Winstanley's Water Theatre," which was open in London at least as early as May 1703, six months before the inventor was swept away in a storm that destroyed his lighthouse. Thenceforward, the theatre, with a windmill atop it to operate the pumps, was managed by Winstanley's widow and his former employees. Von Uffenbach visited it in June 1710:

It is immediately behind St. James Park and is an Ordinary theater, in which all kinds of water effects are represented. They all depend on the vat that stands in the middle, but the inner mechanism could not be seen. All kinds of tubes may be set on the vat, just as one pleases, and pulled towards the end of the theatre, while some fellow blows into them from above. In the vat they have put a tea- and coffee-pot, from the top of which water is tapped, as though it were springing up out of it. Above on the ceiling there were pulleys, to which a coffee-tray was fastened with ropes, so that it could be drawn hither and thither in the theatre and offered to the people of highest rank. Finally all the jets played on the stage, and that, with the glass candle-sticks in which candles were burning, looked very well. The theatre is elegant, although it is only made of painted wood.[4]

The "magic barrel" trick, which is none too satisfactorily described by Von Uffenbach, was always the main attraction. Usually a variety of beverages was dispensed from it—"seven sorts of Liquors both hot and cold," promised one advertisement—but sometimes "the Curious Barril" was enlarged into a "Spring Garden, entertaining the Boxes and Pit with Cool Tankards, Spaw Waters, Bisquits, Milk, Ale, Beer, Sullibubs, Cake, and Cheese Cakes," and when it was made into a dairy, "several sorts of Creams,

Milk, Whey . . . New Butter, [and] Butter Milk" were added to the menu.[5]

The water theatre's program included a number of other hydraulic and pyrotechnic performances, some of which required, if the advertisements are to be trusted, as much as 800 tuns (200,000 gallons) of water. There were "two flying Boys with a flaming Torch, playing of Water out of the Burning Flame"; "a flying fiery Dragon, out of whose Mouth comes great Fire Balls, flames of Fire," and perfumes; a "Garland of Wheat playing of Water in a curious manner"; and "Bacchus squeezing the purple Juice out of the Grapes." The bill was heavily mythological in theme: there were sea gods and goddesses, nymphs, mermaids, and satyrs galore, a flying Zepherus, a Flora who presented the spectators with a basket of fruit, and "Galuthetis's [Galatea's] Flight from Polypheme . . . carried in state by Neptune attended by many Figures playing of Water, and some with Fire mingling with it." The last program offered at the water theatre before its lease expired and it was forced to close (August 1720) seems to have been the most elaborate of all:

. . . a Harvest Field, with Corn and Reapers, Fruit and sweet Flowers, playing Water, which a flying Cupid presents to the Spectators, with good Brandy, cool Tankards, Biskets, Beer, Ale, Milk, Syllabubs, Coffee and Tea. The curious Barrel plays its Part, then is broke in Pieces, leaving a Flame of Fire that burns in the Water. Venus is with her flaming Heart that burns in the Water, after that she appears with the Golden Ball in the triumphant Chariot, the Graces attending her with Garlands; Apollo is bathing; they are attended by Cupids, Doves and Swans; Daphny is turnd to a Tree, and Narcissus to Flowers; with many more Metamorphoses; Jupiter is there with his Thunder and Lightning; god Rivers and his Daughters; Gods, and Goddesses, Nymphs, Mermaids, and Satyrs, from Hills, Groves, and Fountains, meet in Triumph, all playing Water mingled with Fire, which falls into delightful Cascades, to the Expence of 100 Tons of Water extraordinary.[6]

The "curious barrel," so prolific, so inexhaustible, so versatile, seems to have been a sophisticated model of a device apparently first described in English in a classic work on conjuring, *Mathematicall Recreations* (1633). The text ("Problem LXIII: Of a vessell which containes three severall kinds of liquor, all put in at one bung-hole, and drawne out at one tappe severally without mixture") and the accompanying illustration reveal that the vessel was divided into partitions and that the separation of the several liquors was maintained by a system of stopcocks. Only three liquors could be accommodated in the vessel shown, but the principle could easily be applied to as many as promised in the Winstanley publicity.

As for the busy mythological characters and their feats with water and flame, sometimes accompanied by sound effects, a work published the very next year after *Mathematicall Recreations,* John Bate's *The Mysteryes of Nature and Art,* provides clues enough, although Winstanley obviously elaborated upon the rudimentary devices described there. Bate gives instructions for creating numerous effects by using systems of pipes, glass or brass vessels, pumps, cisterns, floats, and fire to produce water under pressure or in the form of steam. The animals and mythological figures were, in every case, introduced merely to lend dramatic color to a series of conjuring tricks based on hydraulic principles; in form and function they were not far removed from clock jacks. Thus, appropriate combinations of apparatus could make Hercules draw a bow at a hissing dragon, birds chirp, trumpets sound, and wheels turn. Weather glasses and water clocks, too, could be adapted to theatrical use; for example, a figure of Time or Death (a skeleton with an hour glass) pointed with his dart to a pillar on which the hours were inscribed, and "the dropping of the water out of the cock thorow the hole of the board wheron the image standeth, causeth the same to ascend little by little."

The most elaborate trick Bate describes, the one which brings us closest to what happened in Winstanley's Water Theatre, was produced by a complicated device involving a "leaden moat," several cisterns, a three-level frame, pumps, jacks, weights, springs, and piping. When the machine was working, the water could be seen "breaking out into the fashions and formes of Dragons, Swans, Whales, Flowers, and such like pretty conceits"; other streams turned wheels, and at the top of the structure could be seen "Neptune riding on a Whale, out of whose nostrils, as also out of Neptune's Trident, the water may be made to spin through small pin-holes."

The second part of Bate's treatise deals with fireworks, with special attention to devices which went off in or atop water, "Rockets, Dolphins, Ships, Tumbling Balls." Particularly appropriate for displays involving mythological figures would have been "flying dragons" such as were actually seen at Winstanley's. They were made with a painted framework of light wood or thin whalebones and energized by rockets whose flames emerged from both the mouth and the tail. Bate concludes with directions for constructing a dolphin: Make a pasteboard body, fill it with rockets, smear it all over with "pap" made of gunpowder, sulphur, and so on; then "binde unto it a large Rocket for the water, which Rocket must be armed . . . that the water may not hurt it, then ballast it with a wyre, hauing at each end a piece of lead of weight sufficient, and it is done."

From such suggestions, found in these and possibly later books, Winstanley evidently developed water-and-fire tricks on a scale large enough to be seen by all who paid 2s. 6d. to sit in a box, 2s. for a place in the pit, and 1s. 6d. for one in the first gallery. Since a draft of the beverage of one's choice from the bottomless barrel was included in the price, this would seem to have been fair enough.

Winstanley had no monopoly on his devices. In 1710, a variation of the curious barrel, called the "new Mathematical Fountain," was exhibited at the Black Horse tavern, Hosier Lane, West Smithfield. A handbill described it as "a large piece of Water Work, twelve foot long and nine foot high . . . made in white flint glass, in which is a Tavern, a Coffee house and a Brandy shop, which at your command runs at one Cock hot and Cold liquor, as Sack, White wine, Claret, Coffee, Tea, Content, plain, cherry and Rasberry Brandy, Geneva, Usquebaugh [distilled spirits], and Punch. All these liquors of themselves rising much higher than their level, and each liquor drawn singly at one Cock." The proprietor, Charles Butcher, concluded, in the poetic vein of Don Saltero on the other side of town:

> For satisfaction your own eyes believe,
> Art cannot blind you, nor your taste deceive;
> Com, and welcom my friends, and tast e're you pass,
> It's but 6d. to see 't and 2d. each glass.[7]

In one version or another, this automated cocktail lounge lasted down to the end of the century and beyond. In 1796–97 one of the automatons at Haddock's Androides exhibition was a liquor merchant standing at a cask from which it drew, "at the choice of the Company, any of the following Liquors, Rum, Brandy, Gin, Whisky, Port, Mountain Shrub, Raisin Wine, Peppermint, Aniseed, Caraway, and Usquebah."[8] Two decades later (1816–1818) a distiller who drew eight different kinds of liquor from a single barrel was among the automatons displayed by Jack Bologna, member of a well-known family of acrobats

15. *Hydraulick Water Works (as Exhibited at Exeter-Change in the Strand) by Mr. Jas. Bourier, Mechanist to the King of Poland* (unsigned, undated chalk sketch).

and clowns who occasionally exploited his fame as a star in pantomime by putting on miscellaneous exhibitions in the off season.[9]

Other hydraulic tricks turned up here and there. Early in the century, for example, a revival of the *Creation of the World* show at Bartholomew Fair added an episode dealing with Noah's flood, during which "several fountains play[ed] water."[10] But on the whole there is less evidence of water effects than of pyrotechnics, which were widely used in spectacular entertainments and in conjunction with water, as we shall see, in the mimic representations of sea engagements which became popular toward the end of the eighteenth century. Seemingly the only full-dress water show recorded in London after Winstanley's, however, was at Exeter Change in 1771. Instead of combining the antithetical elements of fire and water, the engineer, James Bourier, "Mechanist to the King of Poland," imitated pyrotechnic effects in water: "the art of imitating by water what the greatest Fire-workers have been able to perform as yet by Powder . . . representing Piramids, Turning Columns, Turning Rocks, Turning Suns, the Game of the Ring, Cascades, Blazing Stars, and many other Pieces too tedious to insert; the whole being composed of about 500 different Pieces, entirely thru' the Effects of Water."[11] A later advertisement mentions other images supposedly pro-

duced hydraulically: "in a very large bason, a vast number of ducks, of a natural size, spouting the water, as well as a dog who pursues and dives after them." The whole show was "illuminated by a great quantity of reverberatories [reflector lamps] which the Sieur Bourier has imported from Paris." The engineer added that he was available for consultation with noblemen who contemplated installing hydraulic displays at their country houses.[12]

⊅⦂⁕⦂⊄

While one branch of the exhibition business was intermittently exploiting the spectacular possibilities of water and fire, another, much more didactically inclined, was exploring infinite space in a little room. Its popular appeal, too, depended upon recently developed technology. The orrery, a machine for exhibiting the relative positions and motions of the planets with respect to the sun and to one another by means of globes appropriately distributed on slender rotatory rods, had been invented by a Dutch mechanist, Christiaan Huygens, in 1682, but the most famous was built by John Rowley for the fourth Earl of Orrery, whence the name. The device immediately delighted cultivated men and women, to whom, as Sir Richard Steele wrote in 1713, "it is like the receiving a new

Sense. . . . It administers the Pleasure of Science to any one. . . . All Persons, never so remotely employed from a learned Way, might come into the Interests of Knowledge, and taste the Pleasure of it by this Intelligible Method." Every family, he concluded, should have one.[13] Few families, of course, did; but the orrery made it possible for natural philosophers to give demonstration-lectures to small groups of leisure-class men, women, and children.* The well-known painting by Joseph Wright of Derby, *A Philosopher Giving That Lecture on the Orrery, in Which a Lamp Is Put in the Place of the Sun* (1766), affords an excellent idea of what those demonstrations were like—of the darkness in which the orrery operated, so as to give maximum effect to the place of the sun in the system, and of the fascination with which children watched the demonstration.

The best known of these popularizers was Adam Walker (1731?–1821), a self-taught inventor who, after making false starts in several occupations, became a peripatetic lecturer on astronomy.[14] He came to the attention of Joseph Priestley, who arranged for him to deliver a course of lectures at the Haymarket Theatre in 1778. These were successful enough to encourage him to take a house in George Street, Hanover Square, where he conducted a lecture series each winter. Through them, he came to the notice of London's intelligentsia; he dined with Fanny Burney and her father, Sir Joshua Reynolds, and the literary brothers Joseph and Thomas Warton in 1783 (Fanny found him, "though modest in science . . . vulgar in conversation").[15] Walker also became a visiting lecturer at Westminster, Winchester, and other schools where science was not yet (nor would it be for many years) part of the formal curriculum. At Syon House Academy and again at Eton, one of his rapt auditors was Percy Bysshe Shelley, who, as a recent biographer of the poet says, was "completely captivated" by Walker's discourses, as entertaining as they were speculative, not only on astronomy but on electricity, chemistry, magnetism, and hydrostatics. Some of his leading notions reappeared in Shelley's poetry.[16]

By the time Walker was striking sparks in Shelley's mind, his inventive talent, which also was responsible for his development of a number of machines for agricultural use, had enabled him to overcome the orrery's deficiency as a teaching device. Instruments such as Wright of Derby portrayed could be used, of course, only in small gatherings. But about 1781 Walker succeeded in building an orrery he named the Eidouranion, a twenty-foot-high model with transpar-

ent, luminous (candle-lighted?) globes of various sizes to represent the planets. The workings of the solar system could thus be seen by everyone in a darkened auditorium the size of the Lyceum, for example. A newspaper noted that the machine "exhibits the diurnal and annual motions of every planet, and satellite in the solar system, without any apparent cause or support. Day, night, twilight, winter, summer, long and short days; the waxing and waning of the moon; solar and lunar eclipses; the causes of tides; the transit of Venus and Mercury; and the descent of a comet, are so like nature, that a bare inspection of the machine gives the clearest idea of these phenomena."[17] The Eidouranion and similar instruments were featured in astronomical lectures at London theatres and in provincial towns for many years. To judge from the syllabi, the discourses themselves must have been pretty heavy going for the average audience, but additional illustrative devices to be introduced shortly after the turn of the century would sustain their popularity with that portion of the show-going public which consciously required to be instructed.

Those who needed only a thin veil of Enlightenment terminology to legitimate their attendance at exhibitions that were scarcely more than a series of conjurors' acts were well taken care of. Shows billed as "philosophical recreations" consisting (as the publicity for such an exhibition in the mid–1780s had it) of "all the most favourite, surprising, and pleasing Philosophical, Physical, and Mechanical Pieces,"[18] merely shifted the nominal emphasis from old-fashioned magic to new-fashioned science. "Philosophical" meant "scientific"; conjurors' tricks were dignified as "experiments" or "demonstrations," as if rational explanations accompanied them—which they normally did not. The programs consisted mostly of familiar optical illusions, mind reading, prestidigitation, and mechanical effects, but recent advances in the production of inflammable gas and electricity were responsible for some novelties under the heading of "philosophical fireworks." In 1788 the Lyceum, then the particular home of shows with scientific pretensions, housed Diller's Philosophical Fireworks, an apparatus innocent of "smoke, smell, or detonation" that produced, among other effects, "a fixed flower—a sun turning round, varying in figure, a star varying, a triangle, a dragon pursuing a serpent—a star of knighthood." "A central piece is exhibited on the grand apparatus, that undergoes 120 changes of figure, which it performs by a multitude of intersecting circles, each having a rotatory motion on its own axis. To this

* Orreries were sometimes built into the baroque display pieces —clocks cum organs cum a number of other things—which were mentioned in Chapter 4. In 1738, for example, one could see at the Great Room, Panton Street, "an organ combined with a harpsichord played by clock-work, which exhibited the movements of an orrery and air-pump, besides solving astronomical and geographical problems on two globes, and shewing the moon's age with the Copernican system in motion; in the canopy, Apollo, and the Muses, &c., &c." (J. P. Malcolm, *Anecdotes of the Manners and Customs of London during the Eighteenth Century*, London, 1808, p. 360).

are added eight Cadrilles, consisting of eighty different flames each, rose-colored and green. The last display of this piece produces several thousand flames, representing all colours imaginable, and in the most strict symmetry."[19]

The familiar quackish custom of invoking science, both to take advantage of its growing prestige and to add sometimes factitious novelty to whatever was exhibited, was carried to memorable lengths by two self-styled "doctors" who were the talk of London between 1780 and 1783. Their respective exhibitions and lectures were in a class by themselves.

James Graham was a Scotsman who, having spent some years in America administering milk baths, massages, and electrical treatments to the ailing colonists, arrived in London in 1780 and opened, in a handsome house in Adelphi Terrace, the Templum Æsculapio Sacrum, which, being translated for the commonalty, meant "Temple of Health."[20] The portals were guarded by tall attendants decked out in splendid livery, as befitted an establishment that charged two guineas for admission. Inside, one found a suite of apartments whose lavish furnishings and décor made Cox's Museum seem a slum by comparison. Here, Dr. Graham delivered lectures on "health," including what would today be known as sexology. Assisting him, as blooming exemplars of perfect physical fitness, was a series of Goddesses of Youth and Health, hired by way of newspaper advertisements, who posed in white silk robes and perhaps, on occasion, in less than that. One such "Hebe Vestina" was a sixteen-year-old domestic servant named Amy (Emma) Lyons, who was destined to rise in the world as Lady Hamilton.

But the lectures and illustrative poses were mere appendages to the Temple of Health's main attraction, the celebrated Celestial Bed, which was enshrined in a room of its own, with a private entrance from the street. Here, at a fee of £50 for a night's occupancy, sterility was purportedly cured in sybaritic luxury. Reputed to have cost £10,000 to build and equip, the bed was twelve feet long and nine wide, its domed canopy "supported by forty pillars of brilliant glass of the most exquisite workmanship, in richly variegated colours." Only Graham's own prose is adequate to describe it in all its imposing glory:

The super-celestial dome of the bed, which contains the odoriferous, balmy and ethereal spices, odours and essences, which is the grand reservoir of those reviving invigorating influences which are exhaled by the breath of the music and by the exhilarating force of electrical fire, is covered on the other side with brilliant panes of looking-glass.

On the utmost summit of the dome are placed two exquisite figures of Cupid and Psyche, with a figure of Hymen behind, with his torch flaming with electrical fire in one hand and with the other, supporting a celestial crown, sparkling over a pair of living turtle doves, on a little bed of roses.

The other elegant group of figures which sport on the top of the dome, having each of them musical instruments in their hands, which by the most expensive mechanism, breathe forth sound corresponding to their instruments, flutes, guitars, violins, clarinets, trumpets, horns, oboes, kettle drums, etc.

The post or pillars too, which support the grand dome are groups of musical instruments, golden pipes, etc., which in sweet concert breathe forth celestial sounds, lulling the visions of Elysian Joys.

At the head of the bed appears sparkling with electrical fire a great first commandment: "BE FRUITFUL, MULTIPLY AND REPLENISH THE EARTH." Under that is an elegant sweet-toned organ in front of which is a fine landscape of moving figures, priest and bride's procession entering the Temple of Hymen.

In the Celestial Bed no feather bed is employed but sometimes mattresses filled with sweet new wheat or oat straw mingled with balm, rose leaves, lavender flowers and oriental spices. The sheets are of the richest and softest silk, stained of various colours suited to the complexion. Pale green, rose colour, sky blue, white and purple, and are sweetly perfumed in oriental manner with the tudor rose, or with rich gums or balsams.

The chief principle of my Celestial Bed is produced by artificial lodestones. About 15 cwt. of compound magnets are continually pouring forth in an ever flowing circle.

The bed is constructed with a double frame, which moves on an axis or pivot and can be converted into an inclined plane.

Sometimes the mattresses are filled with the strongest, most springy hair, produced at vast expense from the tails of English stallions which are elastic to the highest degree.

In short, a most bountifully enriched Microcosm or Temple of the Arts, dedicated to procreation. One might wonder how, enwrapped as they were by the manifold pleasures comprehended within the bed's magnetic field, the fifty-pound-a-night couple managed to fight distraction with determination. But they were assured that the various sensuous luxuries were all a well-calculated scientific means to the desired end: "the barren must certainly become fruitful when they are powerfully agitated in the delights of love." After coition had been accomplished, and the band played on, the bed tilted in order to assist conception.

There is no record of how effective the Celestial Bed was, either in its original location or at the one to which the Temple of Health moved the following

16. Caricature of Dr. Graham and Dr. Katterfelto (anonymous engraving, 1783).

year—Schomberg House, Pall Mall, a mansion divided into artists' homes and studios. Now the advertising stressed the eugenic idea to which the bed was dedicated, nothing less than "the propagating of beings rational, and far stronger and more beautiful in mental as well as bodily endowment, than the present puny, feeble and nonsensical race of probationary mortals, which crawl, fret and politely play at cutting one another's throats for nothing at all, on most parts of this terraqueous globe." Glum reflections on the fallen state of man were, however, dissipated by the magnificence of the apartments, to which admission was now 2s. 6d. during the day and 5s. in the evening. In this "grand Elysian promenade" one might savor all the delights save the ultimate one, which was reserved for the bed. Aromatic wax candles loaded the air with perfume, the "harmonious strains of wind instruments" were wafted from hidden openings in the staircase, and the "electrical apparatus which is infinitely larger and more magnificent than any other that ever was erected in the world" gave off arcs and sparks that were reflected in the mirrors and the crystals of the chandeliers. Here, too, Dr. Graham delivered his hygienic lectures, with musical preludes and postludes offered by the reigning Hebe.

Despite the Temple's fame and the crowds it attracted, it was not a financial success, and in 1783 it was sold up. Graham then prepared a new exhibition in Panton Street, where the Celestial Bed was replaced by a pile of wet earth. His new specialty was mud baths, the virtues of which he extolled to his audience as, *tout nu,* he sat encased in one. But after the bed, anything else was bound to be an anticlimax, as was, surely, Graham's next step—his belatedly attending

17. Lunardi's balloon exhibited at the Pantheon, 1784 (engraving by Francis Jukes and Valentine Green, from a painting by F. G. Byron).

medical lectures at Edinburgh University. He toured the country thereafter, lapsed into religious mania, and died in 1794.

While Graham held forth at Schomberg House and then in Panton Street, he had to endure the competition of a quite different kind of charlatan, Dr. Katterfelto.[21] Katterfelto's origins are obscure, but he was working the Gloucester region by 1777, and in December 1780 he began lecturing at Cox's late museum in Spring Gardens. According to his flamboyant publicity, his "lectures" and "experiments"—a different program each evening of the week—drew on "mathematics, optics, magnetism, electricity, chemistry, pneumatics, hydraulics, hydrostatics," and such obscure realms of knowledge as "proetics," "stynacraphy," and "caprimancy." The latter actually existed

only in the time-honored jargon of the quack; unlike some other coinages that were about to be introduced in the London exhibition business, these hifalutin names never took hold, even momentarily, in the English vocabulary.

Identifying himself as "the greatest philosopher in this kingdom since Sir Isaac Newton" and heading his newspaper advertisements "WONDERS! WONDERS! WONDERS!" Katterfelto claimed to have improved, if not invented, the solar microscope, an instrument inspired by the camera obscura, whereby the field of a microscope was projected on a white surface to be viewed by a number of people simultaneously. (The fact was that the device was invented by a Dr. Lieberkuhn, who exhibited it to members of the Royal Society in 1739.) Needing more sunlight for its employment than the Spring Gardens room afforded, in the summer of 1782 Katterfelto moved it, along with the rest of his show, to 22 Piccadilly, where he used the microscope to reveal to an astonished audience the "insects" which had caused a recent epidemic of influenza in the metropolis. They were "as large as a bird, and in a drop of water the size of a pin's head, there will be seen above 50,000 insects."[22] To immunize his high-society auditors against a visitation of the insects, Katterfelto hawked the remedy which had lately cured him, Dr. Bato's medicine, at five shillings a bottle. Indeed, his services after the formal lecture-demonstration ended were as valuable and various as any information the lectures may have contained; for in addition he sold phosphorus matches, another invention to which he laid claim, and gave advice on how to win at dice, cards, billiards, and O.E. (roulette).

Except for Graham, whose star had in any case begun to set, there was no more famous person in London in 1782–83 than Dr. Katterfelto, what with his saturation advertising, his use of necromantic black cats for electrical tricks in the course of which they gave off sparks, the rumor that he had ordered a £25,000 carriage from a Long Acre coachmaker, and his appearance in at least eight different satirical prints.[23] But his prosperity, like Graham's, was as brief as it was feverish. By the end of 1783 he was offering the whole of his "philosophical and mathematical apparatus" for sale at £2,500. There were no takers, and so, to revive business, Katterfelto announced that he had discovered the secret of perpetual motion. There were few believers, and in the end Katterfelto was reduced to a mere mountebank, traveling from town to town with his cats, what remained of his apparatus, and a small miscellaneous museum of natural and artificial curiosities. He died in 1799.

No sooner had Katterfelto left London than the public had a new sensation to discuss and watch: man-carrying balloons. Like the automatons which had materialized the ancient legends of mechanical men and beasts, balloons, by making it possible for human beings to soar like birds, realized a millennium-old dream. In this excitement of 1784–85 the indoor exhibitors played only a minor role. The main action was at the open spaces where the balloons were launched and wherever else a good view could be had of their miraculous progress across the English sky. Still, the showmen did all they could to profit from the rage.[24]

In 1784 a minor functionary at the London embassy of the Kingdom of Naples named Vincenzo Lunardi, ambitious to match the first successful flight of the Montgolfier brothers' balloon over Paris the preceding year, built a hydrogen balloon paid for by subscription. Every subscriber was entitled to see it being built and then exhibited suspended from the Lyceum dome: a red- and white-striped bag made from 520 yards of oiled silk, thirty-three feet across, and with a gondola eleven feet long and four feet wide. After more than 20,000 people, most of whom had paid a straight admission fee rather than taking out a subscription, had stared their fill, a contretemps occurred: the Lyceum's manager locked up the balloon until Lunardi paid him a royalty on the subscriptions received. It took the police to rescue the balloon, after which the first London ascent was finally made before a crowd of 150,000 at Moorfields (15 September). The pioneer aeronaut and the cat accompanying him landed at Ware, Hertfordshire, and the historic balloon, obviously unwelcome at the Lyceum, then went on display at the Pantheon.* There, too, Lunardi had bad luck, when part of the dome's skylight broke and punctured the envelope.[25]

Fantastic new "aerostatic machines" at once competed with Lunardi's at other London showplaces. At the Great Room in the King's Arms tavern, Cornhill, in July 1785, was displayed a "flying fish"—a fifty-foot structure designed, said the inventor, "to imitate, as near as can be, in the Air the Motion of that Animal in the Water. It is covered with Persian Silk, coloured after Nature."[26] The motive power was to be provided by working the fins like oars. But it is unlikely that making this fish out of water behave like a fowl was ever attempted—and still less likely that it would have worked. The next year another hopeful aeronaut, a Mr. Uncles, exhibited an even more arresting prototype at the Pantheon. This machine too was shaped like a fish, with a gondola suspended from it "triumphal in form and magnificent beyond description in appearance," but its forward motion was to be supplied by four eagles which "Mr. Uncles has so trained, as in their flight for the purpose of guiding the machine, or return to the car, to be perfectly subservient to his pleasure." Unlike the man-powered flying fish, this remarkable vehicle was given a chance to prove itself. Before a crowd of ten thousand gathered at Ranelagh on 18 July, Mr. Uncles "mounted his seat with eagles harnessed, and made an effort to ascend." He went up about eight feet, dropped to the ground, and that was that.[27]

How seriously did people take these weird contrivances? Probably no more so than they did some of

* Built in the same year as the Lyceum (1772), the elegantly decorated Pantheon, in Oxford Street at the corner of Poland Street, is often said to have been one of the principal London exhibition rooms. It was famous enough in its time, but mainly as the scene of masquerades, concerts, operas, and fashionable assemblies. Apart from housing flying apparatus and occasional displays of such wares as stained glass and lightning conductors, neither it nor the building which replaced it after it was destroyed in a spectacular fire in January 1792 was notable for its exhibitions.

Water, Fire, Air, and a Celestial Bed 85

John Joseph Merlin's fanciful devices. But the eighteenth-century enthusiasm for inventions of genuine practical utility was sometimes manifested in exhibitions, especially from the fifties onward. The Society of Arts, to be discussed in Chapter 8, exhibited new inventions in its rooms. The younger Christopher Pinchbeck was prolific in them, among his productions being a candlestick that kept the candle always in an upright position, a device for writing memoranda in the dark, and a pneumatic safety brake for shipyard cranes. In the late sixties he put on what was advertised as "UTILE & DULCE, or the Much Improved Mechanical Exhibition; Universally esteemed to be the most entertaining, cheap, and instructive Amusement offered to the Public." Alongside the Panopticon, which served as centerpiece, were shown other Pinchbeckian creations—a "pyromatical Thermometer," a patent fire escape, safety devices for mines, and "an actual book-case, or real circulating-library, for making a small Closet hold as many books as a Large Room."[28] The whole collection was for sale, piecemeal or en bloc.

Occasionally we read of displays presumably arranged to attract venture capital for some sort of engineering enterprise. A Dutch windmill, alleged to have the power of six "common" ones, was at the Black Bear inn, Piccadilly, in 1750,[29] and a model of the pile driver used to build Westminster and Blackfriars bridges, having served its original advertising purpose, was included in Pinchbeck's "Utile et Dulce" package. At the Horn tavern, Palace Yard, in 1791 there was a model to illustrate a scheme for raising the flagship *Royal George,* which had sunk in Portsmouth Harbor nine years earlier.[30]

But it was solely for public information, not in the prospect of selling shares in a new commercial scheme, that two devices much in the news in the century's last decade were exhibited in London. Both, as it happened, were French inventions. One was the "Telegraph upon Mechanical Principles," a semaphore system devised by Claude Chappe in 1792. Philip Astley, the proprietor of the famous equestrian amphitheatre, who, as the *Times* said, was "always employed in the production of something new," first exhibited it at the Lyceum two years later.[31] Toward the end of 1797, after it had served England well by speeding to London the message that the Dutch fleet was out and thus enabling Admiral Duncan to receive the orders that led to his victory off Camperdown, a replica of the device, "with the Cabin underneath, where the Officer sits to work it," was a timely addition to Haddock's Androides show.[32]

Equally timely and considerably more fearsome was another instrument illustrated in two London locales early in 1793. An added attraction at the printseller Fores's shop, where hundreds of satirical prints, both French and English, on the bloody events across the Channel were on display, was "a correct Model of the Guillotine 6 feet high."[33] This seems, however, not to have been a working model, a deficiency rectified a few steps away in the Haymarket.

The unhappy fate of the Sovereign of a neighbouring Kingdom having excited universal compassion in this country [ran an advertisement], it is presumed that the curiosity of the public will be gratified by the view and effect of an instrument like that by which he suffered. Accordingly, a guillotine has been constructed under the immediate direction of a gentleman who very minutely examined the original, which is exactly similar in every respect. And in order that the effect of the machine may be the better conveyed to the spectator the execution is performed on a figure as large as life. The head is severed from the body by the tremendous fall of the axe, and the illusion is complete.[34]

There were no demonstrations on Sundays.

The Sights and Resorts
of Eighteenth-Century London

7

In 1709 "Isaac Bickerstaff" (Sir Richard Steele) wrote in the *Tatler* (no. 30) of taking "three lads who are under my guardianship a rambling in an hackney-coach, to show them the town, as the lions, the tombs, Bedlam, and the other places which are entertainments to raw minds."[1] The lions and the tombs are next on our itinerary. Then, since we have already looked in at Bedlam, we shall let the momentum of eighteenth-century sightseeing carry us instead across the river to Vauxhall Gardens, which, though scarcely to be deprecated by Steele's phrase, were as obligatory a London sight as the Tower and the Abbey.

The Tower of London was the city's supreme historical monument. A great deal of dramatic English history was preserved within those grim walls, the stories of conspiracy, betrayal, fall from favor, and execution known to every child. The historical associations of the place would alone have been enough to make it a goal of every sight-seeker, but it had several specific attractions which made it an exhibition place as well. The oldest of these dated from 1235, when, in Stow's words,

Fredericke the Emperour sent to Henrie the third three Leopards, in token of his regal shield of armes, wherein three Leopards were pictured, since the which time, those Lions and others haue been kept in a part of this bulwarke, now called the Lion tower, and their keepers there lodged. King Edward the second in the twelft of his raigne, commaunded the shiriffes of London to pay to the keepers of the kings Leopard in the tower of London vi. d. the day, for the suste-nance of the Leopard, and three halfe pence a day for diet of the said keeper, out of the fee farme of the sayd Citie.

More, the 16. of Edward the third [1342–43], one Lion, one Lionesse, one Leopard, and two Cattes Lions, in the said tower, were committed to the custodie of Robert, the sonne of Iohn Bowre.[2]

Besides housing the royal menagerie, the Tower came to be the stronghold of the crown jewels, first exhibited after the Restoration, and of a formidable store of arms and armor, ancient and modern.

Among the first to record what the Tower held for the sightseer was the Duke of Würtemberg in 1592. His journal, kept for him by a secretary, remarked that the armory "is not indeed to be compared with the German armouries, for, although there are many fine cannon in it, yet they are full of dust, and stand about in the greatest disorder. At the top of the armoury there is an unspeakable number of arrows, which is a sufficient proof that the English used such things in battle in former times." The duke also saw, "in separate small houses made of wood," "six lions and lionesses, two of them upwards of a hundred years old," as well as a "lean, ugly wolf."[3]

A century later, the tireless Ned Ward wrote a typically vivacious account of the Tower sights. At the entrance he found "a parcel of Bulky Warders, in old Fashion'd Lac'd Jackets, and in Velvet Flat-Caps, hung round with divers colour'd Ribbons, like a Fools Hat upon a Holiday." (Their uniform was identical with their present dress, except that under their caps they wore periwigs.) Under the guidance of one of them, Ward was shown the usual points of historical interest—the Traitor's Gate, the White Tower, and St. Peter's Church. Then, as if he were amidst the banners and signboards of Bartholomew Fair, he came upon a picture of a lion's head, advertising "the Royal Palace, where the King of Beasts keeps his court." This shed, he discovered, "smelt as Frowzily as a Dove-House, or a Dog-Kennel." Among the inhabitants were a tiger, a "Cat-a-Mountain," a hyena, owls, and a two-legged dog. A special attraction, costing an extra penny to view, was a leopard, whose offensive behavior throws an interesting sidelight on the hazards of visiting Bedlam as well: "as a Madman will be apt to Salute you with a Bowl of Chamber-Lie, so will the Leopard, if you come near him, stare in your Face, and Piss upon you, his Urine being as Hot as Aqua Fortis, and stinks worse than a Pole-Cats." At the armory, "now placed under a New and Modish Name the Arsenal," Ward was particularly delighted to see that "at the Corner of every Lobby, and turning of the Stairs, stood a Wooden Granadier as Sentinel, Painted in his proper Colours, cut out with as much Exactness upon Board. . . . The first Figure at our coming in, that most affected the Eye, by reason of its Bigness, was a long Range of Muskets and Carbines, that run the length of the Armory, which was distinguished by a Wilderness of Arms, whose Locks and Barrels were kept in that Admirable Order, that they shone as Bright as a Good Housewifes Spits and Pewter in the Christmas-Holidays: On each side of these were Pistols, Baggonets, Scimiters, Hangers, [etc., etc.,] and in the middle of all, Pillars of Pikes, and turn'd Pillars of Pistols; and at the end of the Wilderness, Fire-Arms plac'd in the Order of a great Organ."[4]

Ward had no taste for statistics, but from other sources we learn that the "volunteer armoury" and the "sea armoury" contained between them muskets for 80,000 soldiers and marines, which were arranged so that any one piece could be removed without disturbing the rest. The "small armoury" had arms for an additional 150,000 men. Von Uffenbach, following Ward at a distance of a decade, also marveled at the cleanliness of the weapons—obviously someone had been at work since the Duke of Würtemberg complained about the dust—and went on, like Ward, to describe the decorative arrangement, which was a singular reflection of eighteenth-century taste: "they have played about with the pistols, bayonets, and swords, which are all unsheathed, arranging them so as to form all kinds of stars, the sun and other objects, and even the

insignia of the order of the garter, which is certainly elegant but looks rather fantastic in an armoury."[5]

Some effort was made to show the armor on cardboard cut-outs or wooden dummies. "The most notable" of the figures thus accoutered, said Von Uffenbach, was King Henry VIII, "whose armour is of a prodigious size. The headpiece, like the stomach-piece and breeches, is lined with red velvet. For a jest countless pins have been stuck into this velvet, and any young persons, especially females, who come here, are presented with one, because they are supposed to be a charm against impotency and barrenness."[6]

Whether through a defect of observation or translation, or through prudery, Von Uffenbach misrepresents this most famous of all exhibits in the Tower of the time.* "Headpiece" indeed! Ned Ward sets us straight:

King Henry the Eighths Codpiece, which was Lin'd with Red, hung gaping like a Maiden-Head at full Stretch, just Consenting to be Ravish'd: This, says [the guide], "is the Codpiece of that Great Prince, who never spar'd Woman in his Lust, nor Man in his Anger; and in it, to this Day, remains this Vertue, That if any Married Woman, tho' she has for many Years been Barren, if she but sticks a Pin in this Member-Case, the next time she uses proper means, let her but think of her Tower Pin-Cushion, and she need not fear Conception."[7]

All this was explained, says Ward, by the "Principal Orator" of the group of armorers' substitutes who awaited visitors. He "advanc'd before us, Cap in Hand, with as much Ceremony as a Dancing-Master Ushers the Parents of his Pupils into the School upon a Ball-Day; beginning to tell us, at our Entrance, with an Audible Voice, the Signification of those Figures which first presented to our View; having every thing as ready at his Fingers-ends, as the Fellow that shows the Tombs at Westminster, or as a Savoy Vagabond has the Explanation of his Raree-Show." "Our little Holder-forth having done his Blundering Lecture upon the King-killing Blunderbuss," Ned and his companions made for the exit, where stood "a Bulky Frizzle-Pate (who we might guess by his Fatness, could Write himself no less than Servant to Her Majesty) in a readiness to receive the Accustomary Purchase Money for that Sight which had given our Eyes such an extraordinary Satisfaction."

Then to the Horse Armory, presided over by "two or three Smugfaced Vulcans" with powder-blackened visages—"Smutty Interpreter[s] of this Raree-Show." One of them "told us to whom each Suit of Armour

* A Swiss visitor in 1725 recorded that this prime curiosity was mechanized. "If you press a spot on the floor with your feet," he wrote, "you will see something surprising with regard to this figure; but I will not say more, and leave you to guess what it is." (César de Saussure, *A Foreign View of England in the Reigns of George I and George II*, ed. Madame Van Muyden, London, 1902, p. 88.)

did belong Originally, adding some short Memorandums out of History, to every empty Iron-side; some True, some False, supplying that with Invention which he wanted in Memory. He now and then endeavoured to break a Jest to divert his Customers, but did it so like an Irishman, that I had much ado to forbear telling the Fellow what a Fool he was in endeavouring to be Witty." After this "War-like Opera, we Paid our Money, and made our Exit; our Stuttering Perambulator turning his Head over his Shoulder, like a Fox that had Stole a Goose, ask'd us Whether we would see the Crowns, or no?" No fools, Ward and his friends cozened the tout into describing the regalia and crown jewels, and then, reckoning they had as good as seen them, like Swift on other occasions they declined to enter and thus saved eighteen pence apiece.[8]

Von Uffenbach, however, not being one to miss anything, paid his money and went in. When his description is compared with those of several later visitors, it appears that nothing much changed in the course of the century except that the lighting, which to Von Uffenbach made the jewels "sparkle charmingly," was reduced to "two wretched candles." The twelve-foot-square room, "a dismal hole resembling the cell of the condemned," according to one account, was divided down the middle by an iron palisade reaching from floor to ceiling. While a sentry guarded the door, the visitors were seated on benches, and on the other side of the bars the woman attendant drew forth the jewels from what Sophie von la Roche called "an old smoky cupboard"[9] and—this from another visitor about the same time, William Hutton of Birmingham—"in that tone of voice universally adopted by raree showmen, observed, 'This is the imperial crown of England, with which all the kings have been crowned, from Edward the Confessor, in 1042.'"[10] Another German visitor, several decades earlier, complained that the attendant then on duty "recites her lesson faster than a nun repeats her psalms."[11] Whereas Von Uffenbach had merely considered the possibility of getting one's hands through the grate and picking up the jewels, Hutton actually did so; he was even invited to try on the spurs and bracelets used during the coronation ceremony.

But the menagerie remained the center of attraction. During the reign of James I lions and tigers were baited with dogs in a semicircular enclosure, but this sport of kings was not open to commoners. In 1644 Evelyn used the menagerie as a standard by which to judge the exhibition of wild animals he saw at Florence,[12] and in May 1662 Pepys took the children of Sir Thomas Crewes and of Lord and Lady Sandwich "to the Tower and showed them the lions and all that was to be shown."[13] Though often a dispirited lot, so tame that they could be handled with impunity, the lions had by this time become so familiar a London sight as to inspire a word, a hoax, and a superstition. The use of "lion" in the sense of a celebrity, a walking showpiece, derives, of course, from the fact that the Tower lions were a sight not to be missed; as early as 1590 (Greene's *Never Too Late*) and 1600 (Jonson's *Cynthia's Revels*) the word was so used. Being sent to see the lions washed at the Tower was a popular April Fool hoax, the point no doubt being that, as numerous reports of their odor attest, the lions did not in fact get washed. And the death of a Tower lion was interpreted as a portent of some calamity, just as the continuing presence of the ravens today is said to be a guarantee against such an event.

The unsanitary cages and dens held a constantly changing variety of other animals, depending on what the London captains and merchants brought back and in particular on what foreign envoys presented to the king. Horace Walpole referred in 1760 to "the Shahgoest, the strange Indian beast,"[14] a kind of lynx which the Nabob of Bengal had presented to General Clive, who had sent it to Pitt, who had passed it on to the king, who, after making suitable acknowledgment, gave it according to custom to the Tower menagerie. Toward the end of the eighteenth century the population dwindled, until at one time it consisted of but a single elephant, a grizzly bear, and a lonely bird or two.[15]

ロ₹❋₹ロ

If the Tower was redolent of dark passages in English history and an abiding symbol of the nation's armed strength, Westminster Abbey was the great monument of monarchy and the national spirit, the coronation and burial place of its kings and queens, a pantheon of heroes and poets. Visiting it and showing foreigners its tombs, chapels, and windows was the obligation of every patriotic Englishman. The spirit of simple reverence noted by a French visitor in 1765 probably was never wholly absent. "The abbey," he wrote, ". . . is incessantly filled with crowds, who contemplate [the monuments]; I have seen herb-women holding a little book, which gives an account of them; I have seen milk-women getting them explained, and testifying, not a stupid admiration, but a lively and most significant surprize. I have seen the vulgar weep at the sight of Shakespeare's beautiful and expressive statue."[16] Even Ned Ward, who had little emotional energy to spare for piety and even less fitting language with which to express it, wrote of his visit in a general elevation of soul, though he was forced to add that he disliked allowing the parish poor of St. Margaret's to beg in the aisles, even at prayer time, and was disturbed "that the Monuments should be defac'd, some with their Hands off, and some with their Feet off, lying by them without Reparation."[17] And, as we have already seen, he could not forget "the crooked Orator to the Abby-Tombs," of whom the guide at the Tower and the "Raree-Show Interpreter" at the Royal Society's repository both reminded him.

The management of the Abbey as a showplace, especially the attendants' avarice and the ignorance and unintelligibility of their rote speeches, was already the subject of scandal in Elizabethan times. In his *Epigram 30* (1597) Sir John Davies, satirizing a fellow poet who may have been Drayton, wrote that

> could he neuer make an English rime,
> But some prose speeches I haue heard of his,
> Which haue been spoken many an hundreth time;
> The man that keeps the Elephant hath one,
> Wherein he tells the wonders of the beast;
> Another Bankes pronounced long agon,
> When he his curtailes qualities exprest:*
> He first taught him that keepes the monuments
> At Westminster, his formall tale to say,
> And also him which Puppets represents,
> And also him which with the Ape doth play . . .[18]

So early, then, were the vergers at the Abbey classed with common showmen. They belonged to London lore even more firmly than the gabbling woman who presided over the crown jewels at the Tower. Their importunate greed was legendary. In 1617 a foreigner, peering with great interest at the inscriptions on the monuments, was approached by a verger who offered him a printed collection of epitaphs, for which, "after the manner of his nation, eaten up with avarice, he demanded a great price."[19] Henry Peacham observed, less reproachfully but not without irony, that in London at that time a penny could buy, among other things, a sight of "any Monster, Jacknapes; or those roaring boys, the Lions"—or an earful of "a most eloquent oration upon our English Kings and Queens, if, keeping your hands off, you will seriously listen to DAVID OWEN, who keeps the Monuments at Westminster."[20]

These "guides," "conductors," or "interpreters," as they were called, were the beneficiaries of a minor species of ecclesiastical graft. A series of acts, beginning in Elizabeth I's reign and concluding in 1662, had established the principle that every member of the Abbey should share in the revenues of land and other property the church owned. The dean and chapter, however, had not abided by this understanding, with the result that the functionaries, thus deprived of income, were forced to "descend to the disgraceful practice of showing the church, and of collecting wax-work, models, etc. to induce the public to come and pay." The authorities willingly legitimated this activity by giving the minor canons and "gentlemen of the choir" a monopoly on it, with the proviso that in return they should keep the monuments clean. Thereupon the canons and choir men hired "ignorant persons" who did the actual showing of the Abbey and split their take with them.[21] The tombs, as every witness attests, were kept neither clean nor in repair. The best contemporary description of what resulted from this practice of leasing and subleasing the Abbey's box-office revenue is Goldsmith's, in *The Citizen of the World* (1762). As soon as he entered the building, the Chinese philosopher who was the putative author of these letters met "a gentleman, dressed in black, [who], perceiving me to be a stranger came up, entered into conversation, and politely offered to be my instructor and guide through the temple." Lien Chi Altangi accepted the courteous offer, and the tour began. All went well until after the Poets' Corner had been viewed. Then:

we made up to an iron gate, through which my companion told me we were to pass in order to see the monuments of the kings. Accordingly I marched up without further ceremony, and was going to enter, when a person who held the gate in his hand, told me I must pay first. I was surprised at such a demand; and asked the man whether the people of England kept a *show*? Whether the paltry sum he demanded was not a national reproach? Whether it was not more to the honour of the country to let their magnificence or their antiquities be openly seen, than thus meanly to tax a curiosity which tended to their own honour? As for your questions, replied the gate-keeper, to be sure they may be very right, because I don't understand them, but as for that there three-pence, I farm it from one, who rents it from another, who hires it from a third, who leases it from the guardians of the temple, and we all must live. I expected upon paying here to see something extraordinary, since what I had seen for nothing filled me with so much surprise; but in this I was disappointed; there was little more within than black coffins, rusty armour, tattered standards, and some few slovenly figures in wax. I was sorry I had paid, but I comforted myself

* Davies refers here to the proprietor of the educated horse ("curtail": one with a docked tail) mentioned in Chapter 3.

by considering it would be my last payment. A person attended us, who, without once blushing, told a hundred lies; he talked of a lady who died by pricking her finger, of a king with a golden head, and twenty such pieces of absurdity; Look ye there, gentlemen, says he, pointing to an old oak chair, there's a curiosity for ye; in that chair the kings of England were crowned; you see also a stone underneath, and that stone is Jacob's pillow. I could see no curiosity either in the oak chair or the stone; could I, indeed, behold one of the old kings of England seated in this, or Jacob's head laid upon the other, there might be something curious in the sight; but in the present case, there was no more reason for my surprise than if I should pick a stone from the streets, and call it a curiosity, merely because one of the kings happened to tread upon it as he passed in a procession.[22]

In his book *Nollekens and His Times* (1828) the sculptor Joseph Nollekens's one-time pupil John Thomas Smith narrated a (no doubt imaginary) scene in the Abbey about 1786.[23] In the course of his conversation with a verger and the resident mason, the peppery Nollekens enumerated the various reasons for the derision the Abbey evoked as an ill-maintained, ill-managed tourist trap. One was the woeful condition of the monumental effigies, many of which lacked hands and feet, fingers and noses—damage attributed, rightly or wrongly, to the Westminster School boys, who ran rampant in the church and the cloisters and often needed odd fragments of stone to play games with. They also were blamed for chalking all over the monuments; Nollekens asserted that the graffiti could not be removed by "pudding, grease, lard, butter, kitchen-stuff, and I don't know what all."

"And then," he said to the verger, "for you to take money for this foolish thing, and that foolish thing, so that nobody can come in to see the fine works of art, without being bothered with Queen Catherine's bones,* the Spanish Ambassador's coffin, the Lady who died by pricking her finger. . . ." Mrs. Nollekens, he continued, "wants to know what you've done with the wooden figures, with wax masks, all in silk tatters, that the Westminster boys called the 'Ragged Regiment': she says they was always carried before the corpse formerly."

Mrs. Nollekens was correct. From the fourteenth century onward, in emulation of a Roman custom, the English carried in the funeral processions of royalty a black-hung platform ("herse") bearing an effigy of the deceased, the hands and head being shaped from wax or wood and the body simulated by some sort of framework, covered with royal raiment.[24] After the funeral, the effigy was kept at the tomb until extreme

dilapidation had set in. The ragged regiment, as it came down to modern times, consisted of Edward III and Queen Philippa (actually, it is now thought, Mary Tudor), Queen Katherine, Queen Anne of Bohemia, Henry VII and Queen Elizabeth of York, Henry Frederick, Prince of Wales, Elizabeth I, and James I and his queen, Anne of Denmark. These ancient things of wax and patches, already in a sad state of disrepair, were part of the routine tour of the Abbey from the early seventeenth century onward. About 1643 they were gathered in a closet on the upper level of Bishop Islip's chapel. A pair of quatrains from *The Mysteries of Love and Eloquence* (1658) suggests the headlong dismissiveness with which they were shown at the time:

> Henry the Seventh and his fair Queen,
>   Edward the First [*sic*] and his Queen;
> Henry the Fifth here stands upright.
>   And his fair Queen was this Queen.
>
> The noble prince, Prince Henry,
>   King James's eldest son;
> King James, Queen Anne, Queen Elizabeth,
>   And so this Chapel's done.[25]

At the turn of the century Tom Brown, Ned Ward's fellow London perambulator, was conducted to the Islip chapel.

As soon as we ascended half a score stone steps in a dirty cobweb hole, and in old worm-eaten presses, whose doors flew open on our approach, here stood Edward III, as they told us, which was a broken piece of wax-work, a battered head, and a straw-stuffed body, not one quarter covered with rags. His beautiful queen stood by, not better in repair: and so to the number of half a score kings and queens, not near so good figures as the king of the beggars makes, and the begging crew would be ashamed of their company. Their rear was brought up with good Queen Bess, with the remnants of an old dirty ruff, and nothing to cover her majesty's nakedness.[26]

Often identified as part of the ragged regiment but actually distinct from it were what were often referred to as the Abbey waxworks. These consisted partly of later funeral effigies (Charles II, the Duke and Duchess of Richmond, and the Duchess of Buckingham and her sons, the Marquess of Normanby and the last Duke of Buckingham) and partly of ordinary wax figures. The most notable of the former group was that of the Duchess of Richmond, who was determined that her celebrated beauty should last beyond the grave. In her will she had commanded that her "Effigie [be] . . . well done in Wax . . . and set up . . . in a presse by itselfe . . . with cleare crowne glasse before

* The "bones" were the skeleton and dessicated body of Henry V's queen, Katherine of Valois, which were kept in a chest near her husband's tomb and which, "by perticular favour," Pepys was allowed to touch when he took his country cousins to the Abbey on 23 February 1668/69. "I had her upper part of her body in my hands. And I did kiss her mouth, reflecting upon it that I did kiss a Queen, and that this was my birthday, 36 year old, that I did first kiss a Queen." (*Diary,* IX, 457.)

18. The royal effigies in the Henry V Chantry, Westminster Abbey (drawing by John Carter, 1786).

it and dressed in my Coronation Robes and Coronett." Mrs. Goldsmith was paid the great sum of £260 to execute the figure, which was installed in Henry VII's Chapel in August 1703.[27] Eighty years later Sophie von la Roche had only praise for it, despite what must have been its seediness by that time: "A beautiful Duchess of Richmond," she wrote, "seems to come towards one, when the doors of her cupboard have been opened, fan in hand, in her court-dress of green velvet embroidered in gold, as seen a hundred years ago; her stuffed dog and parrot are by her side."[28]

In their decrepitude,* the old effigies were no credit to London showmanship. The more recent figures, devoid of ceremonial significance and commissioned by the vergers, as Horace Walpole put it in 1761, "to draw visits and money from the mob,"[29] were more presentable; and it was these that placed the Abbey most decidedly in the category of catchpenny shows. As Nollekens exclaimed to the verger he was conversing with, "I wonder you keep such stuff: why, at Antwerp, where my father was born, they put such things in silks outside in the streets. I don't mind going to Mrs. Salmon's Wax-work, in Fleet Street, where Mother Shipton gives you a kick as you are going out. Oh, dear! you should not have such rubbish in the Abbey."[30] Still, there they were: Queen Anne, installed in 1714–15; William and Mary (1725, probably by Mrs. Goldsmith); Elizabeth I (1760, perhaps using part of the original effigy); and the elder Pitt (finished in 1775, set up in 1779: the work of Patience Wright, to whom Pitt sat for the purpose).

Presiding over the Westminster show was a suit of armor with, incongruously, a ducal robe thrown over it. This was the funeral armor (now in the Abbey museum) of General Monck, the Cromwellian officer otherwise known to history as the first Duke of Albemarle, which the vergers used as their final collection point. From the armed fist hung what Nollekens feelingly referred to as "that nasty cap of General Monk's you beg of people to put money into." All accounts agree that it was a filthy object. Dirt apart, it was a perennial cause of offense, serving as it did as the climax of the Abbey tour. Goldsmith's Chinese philosopher described his experience, which was that of countless others:

[The guide] desired me to consider attentively a certain suit of armour, which seemed to shew nothing remarkable. This armour, said he, belonged to general Monk. *Very surprising, that a general should wear armour.* And pray, added he, observe this cap, this is general Monk's cap. *Very strange indeed,*

very strange, that a general should have a cap also! Pray friend, what might this cap have cost originally? That, Sir, says he, I don't know, but this cap is all the wages I have for my trouble. *A very small recompence, truly,* said I. Not too small, replied he, for every gentleman puts some money into it, and I spend the money. *What, more money! still more money!* Every gentleman gives something, Sir. I'll give thee nothing, returned I; the guardians of the temple should pay you your wages, friend, and not permit you to squeeze thus from every spectator. When we pay our money at the door to see a show, we never give more as we are going out. Sure the guardians of the temple can never think they get enough. Shew me the gate; if I stay longer I may probably meet with more of those ecclesiastical beggars.[31]

But the ecclesiastical beggars, enduring this recurrent criticism with steadfast spirit, continued for many more years to practice their specialty among the seven deadly sins.

London's other great church, St. Paul's Cathedral, was not yet as much of an attraction as the Abbey. It was, after all, a comparatively recent building, and its historical associations were still few. Nevertheless, it already possessed a tradition, inherited from the old structure, which united its vergers with the Abbey's in sympathetic communion. As early as 1606 a foreign visitor, speaking of the King of Denmark's ascent to the base of the former steeple of old St. Paul's in the company of James I, remarked, "No German is admitted to it, unless he pays his money beforehand, so intense is the avarice of the English, and I don't know whether the reason be not the simplicity of the Germans!"[32] While Wren's building was still under construction—it had been opened for service in 1697, but would not be completed until 1710—the great dome, commanding as it did a superlative view of the ever growing metropolis, was already a sightseeing attraction. Access to it could be had only by paying a fee ("stairs-foot money") imposed by the contracting carpenters, who earmarked the proceeds for a fund to aid workmen injured during the last phases of construction and their families. In time, in emulation of the Abbey, the initial single fee to visit the dome proliferated into a number, each governing a different part of the building, and the revenue, no longer required for a workmen's compensation fund, was diverted to the pockets of the vergers.[33]

⋈⊹⋈

One famous eighteenth-century London showplace, however, incurred no reproach on the score of inap-

19. *Frontispiece to the Wax Work and Monumental Records in Westminster Abbey* (engraving by Richard Newton, 1792). In effect, a double satire, associating the notorious miserliness of George III and Queen Charlotte with the avarice of the Abbey guides.

propriate commercialism. Vauxhall Gardens were neither eleemosynary-custodial (Bedlam), historic (the Tower), nor ecclesiastical; they were a pleasure resort pure and simple, and as such the management was entitled to charge whatever the traffic would bear. Actually, the entrance fee of one shilling was remarkably modest in view of the value received. The result was that the gardens throughout most of the century attracted a clientele notable, indeed virtually unique in its time, for its democratic spread: nobility, sometimes even royalty, mingled in perfect amity with commoners, eventually including those as low in the social scale as servants and ordinary soldiers.

Vauxhall Gardens ("New Spring Gardens" as they were first called, to distinguish them from the older Spring Gardens near Whitehall) were opened about 1660 on a twelve-acre plot on the Surrey side of the Thames, upstream from Lambeth.[34] Originally they were simply a well-landscaped promenade ground, with walks, arbors, hedges, and an orchard—an English adaptation of the kind of public garden already familiar in France. At first there was no charge for admission, the proprietor depending for his profit on the sale of refreshments at his house. During the last dec-

ades of the seventeenth century Vauxhall, with its convenient winding paths and secluded groves, was a favorite site for the gallantry and sexual intrigue that enlivened Restoration London society, and as the moral atmosphere of society changed in Queen Anne's day it acquired an unpleasant notoriety.

From this it was redeemed by Jonathan Tyers, an entrepreneur of entertainment who proved to have almost as great and wholesome an influence on eighteenth-century manners as did the better-remembered Beau Nash at Bath. Having rented the grounds in 1728—he later bought them outright—Tyers thoroughly rehabilitated them, transforming them into an elegantly designed and equipped resort which he opened in 1732 with a grand "Ridotto al fresco" to which four hundred leaders of society, headed by the Prince of Wales, were invited. His formula was a simple one, and it was perfectly adapted to the age. He provided in one spacious locale, for the enjoyment of all who could pay, the amenities of the private gardens that were so essential an accompaniment to fashionable eighteenth-century life and so characteristic a manifestation of contemporary taste. In the latter role Vauxhall reflected the eclecticism of the time. Its architecture was a medley of styles, Gothick, classic, and Chinese; its fountains and cascades—the "fairy cataracts" Wordsworth praised in *The Prelude*—exemplified, as did Winstanley's Water Theatre, the contemporary application of hydraulic principles to artistic spectacle; but its layout, conservative in light of the current fashion for "natural" landscaping, retained, in general, the formalism of the seventeenth-century French garden, though it was not without its groves and serpentine paths.

Open from 5 P.M. onward during the summer months, Vauxhall offered a diversity of delights: straight unbroken lines of trees and gravel paths to invite the stroller, triumphal arches, semicircular colonnades and domed pavilions, artificial ruins, statuary, open-air tea shops and restaurants, platforms for *concerts d'été,* and thousands of lamps and lanterns, which after nightfall transformed the grounds into a park quite like the Tivoli Gardens in modern Copenhagen. No other London showplace accommodated as many activities—promenading, flirting, dining, drinking, listening to music, admiring vistas, pictures, and statuary—and no other one figures as often in the literary record, from Smollett, Goldsmith, and Fanny Burney all the way to Thackeray.

One Vauxhall attraction mentioned by almost all contemporary writers was a "whimsical mechanism" that evidently was an offshoot of the moving picture: the much ridiculed "tin cascade," as it was called by Smollett in *Humphry Clinker* and by several mid-century essayists.* At nine o'clock each evening, the pleasure-seekers were summoned by a bell accompanied by perhaps not wholly facetious cries of "Take care of your pockets!" At the end of an avenue at the north side of the gardens a curtain rose to reveal a lighted landscape scene. In the foreground were a miller's house and a waterfall down which what appeared to be water flowed to turn the wheel of the mill. The illusion of falling water evidently was produced by strips of tin shimmering in the light of concealed lamps. The other moving parts were faithful adaptations of components of the old clockwork theatre, and these, along with the painted background, underwent numerous metamorphoses as the years passed. Among the familiar accessories was a bridge, which, when Benjamin Silliman saw it in 1805, was thinly disguised as London Bridge, with the ever adaptable cascade and mill wheel serving as the waterworks beneath that familiar old structure. "An old woman," he wrote, "was sitting and spinning at the foot of the bridge; the mail and heavy coach passed over into town, and a fierce bull followed driving before him an ass. The thing was very well done, and it was at once so odd, unexpected and puerile, that it afforded us more diversion than a fine strain of wit could have done." Shortly afterward, revisiting the gardens when they were illuminated for the Prince of Wales's birthday, Silliman found that the current threat of French invasion had resulted in some topical modification: now "a distant view of the enemy's camp was given, and detachments of English volunteers were represented as marching over London bridge to the attack."[35] Six years later, shortly before the apparatus was dismantled, another American, the painter Samuel F. B. Morse, wrote that in its final version the performance lasted a full fifteen minutes.[36]

Framed by trees, the vista down the paths, one of them 900 feet long, provided a fine opportunity for perspective effects, sometimes assisted by *trompe l'oeil* paintings. At the terminus of the south walk, for example, were three arches through which could be seen a painted Temple of Neptune, with the god surrounded by tritons. Sometimes the subjects were topical: in 1745 strollers along the walk were persuaded that in the distance they could see the ruins of Palmyra, a locality much talked about after the appearance the preceding year of Robert Wood's book describing it.[37]

At night, promenaders could also pause to admire the transparent pictures installed, often with an eye to surprise, throughout the grounds. Transparencies—pictures made with translucent paints on materials like calico, linen, or oiled paper and lighted from behind in the manner of stained glass—were a favorite form of eighteenth-century public art, much seen on occasions of national rejoicing, such as military victories and royal weddings and births, when they were placed in the parks and in the windows of shops and dwellings as part of general "illuminations." At Vauxhall they were either representational or allegorical in intent, mainly the latter. A typical example was the elaborate picture (1791) of the Prince of Wales, a frequent visitor, leaning against his horse held by Britannia, while "Minerva bore his helmet; Providence fixed his spurs, and Fame blew a trumpet and crowned him with laurel."[38]

Vauxhall was also a picture gallery on a grand scale. Each of the fifty supper boxes surrounding the central quadrangle contained a painting, usually eight feet in width, and larger canvases were spotted elsewhere. In the Prince's Pavilion were four paintings by Francis Hayman illustrating scenes from *King Lear, Hamlet, Henry V,* and *The Tempest.* Four other large pictures

* It also appears in *The Citizen of the World* (letter 62) and in Fanny Burney's *Evelina* (ch. 46).

by Hayman, on themes of contemporary history, decorated the music room that was built adjoining the rotunda. Hogarth was represented by his picture of *Henry VIII and Anne Boleyn* and possibly—the attribution is much debated—by *Fairies Dancing on the Green by Moonlight*. He was additionally known to the garden's patrons by Hayman's copies of his *Four Times of Day*.[39]

◁⊰✻⊱▷

Eager as they were to keep abreast of popular taste, it is odd that Jonathan Tyers and his descendants, who retained ownership of Vauxhall Gardens after his death in 1767, were so tardy in putting on fireworks displays. Only at the very end of the century (1798) did pyrotechnics appear there, and they became a regular feature only in 1813. Meanwhile they were a chief means by which several other pleasure gardens, lacking Vauxhall's abundant permanent resources of landscaping, buildings, and art, drew crowds.[40] Fireworks were shown at Marylebone Gardens as early as 1718 and cascades and showers of fire and "air-balloons" became standard fare there by midcentury, sometimes in conjunction with transparencies. In 1772 Marylebone had a spectacular show devised by Morel Torré, former pyrotechnician at Versailles—a half theatrical, half scenic display called "The Forge of Vulcan," produced to honor the king's birthday. After the fireworks proper, "a curtain which covered the base of the mountain rose, and discovered Vulcan leading the Cyclops to work at their forge; the fire blazed, and Venus entered with Cupid at her side, who begged them to make for her son those arrows which are said to be the causes of love in the human breast: they assented, and the mountain immediately appeared in eruption with lava rushing down the precipices."[41]

It appears that this show was regularly produced at Marylebone for some years thereafter. A similar exhibition was produced at Ranelagh Gardens in Chelsea, in a building expressly designed for the purpose.* The scene, painted by G. Marinari, painter to the Opera, showed Etna and the Cavern of Vulcan. Accompanied by the music of Gluck, Haydn, Giardini, and Handel, the Cyclops went to work forging Mars's armor. "The smoke," according to one breathless advertisement, "thickens, the crater on the top of Etna vomits forth flames, and the lava rolls dreadful along the side of the mountain. This continues with increasing violence till

there is a prodigious eruption, which finishes with a tremendous explosion."[42]

These eruptions and explosions were destined to reverberate throughout the London show scene, indoor as well as outdoor, for the next half-century and beyond. Of the various manifestations of nature's sublime violence which showmen, sharing the taste of romantic artists, sought to portray, volcanic action was second only to sea storms in popularity. In Great Hart Street, Covent Garden, in 1780 the landscape artist Hugh Dean(e) exhibited, as a means of attracting possible buyers for his black chalk drawings, a quarter-hour performance of Mount Vesuvius, with transparencies, "machinery," and the sound of rumbling underground convulsions and peals of thunder.[43] This show, however, was not a success, probably because within a few months of its opening Loutherbourg's far more elaborate and sophisticated miniature spectacle, the Eidophusikon (Chapter 9), was unveiled in Lisle Street.

Two decades later, Silliman saw a representation of Vesuvius's 1771 eruption at Dubourg's display of cork models of Roman buildings and ruins (Chapter 8):

We were conducted behind a curtain where all was dark, and through a door or window, opened for the purpose, we perceived Mount Vesuvius throwing out fire, red hot stones, smoke and flame, attended with a roaring noise like thunder; the crater glowed with heat, and, near it, the lava had burst through the side of the mountain, and poured down a torrent of liquid fire, which was tending toward the town of Portici, at the foot of the mountain, and toward the sea, on the margin of which this town stands. The waves of the sea are in motion—the lava is a real flood of glowing and burning matter, which this ingenious artist contrives to manage in such a manner as not to set fire to his cork mountain. The flames, cinders, fiery stones, &c. are all real . . .

In the eruption of 1771, the lava ran down a precipice of 70 or 80 feet, and presented the awful view of a cataract of fire. This, also, by shifting his machinery, Du Bourg has contrived to exhibit in a very striking manner. He has not forgotten to appeal to the sense of smell as well as to those of sight and hearing, for, the spectator is assailed by the odour of burning sulphur, and such other effluvia as volcanoes usually emit: I suppose they are set on fire by some one behind the scene, for the double purpose of producing the smell and the fiery eruptions.[44]

Indoor resorts frequently tried to create the characteristic Vauxhall spirit of relaxed festivity by installing novel decorations and attractions. In 1742 a Chelsea establishment called Perrott's Luminous Amphitheatre offered for sixpence an opportunity to enjoy a room filled with a hundred fountains playing simulta-

* Although it was Vauxhall's chief rival, Ranelagh (1741–1803) was not as distinguished for scenic effects. Throughout its history its main feature was the enormous rotunda, comparable in size to the present-day British Library reading room: "an immense amphitheatre," Walpole said, "with balconies full of little alehouses [i.e., fifty-two boxes, each with a "droll painting," accommodating seven or eight people] . . . finely gilt, painted and illuminated; into which everybody that loves eating, drinking, staring, or crowding, is admitted for twelvepence." Dr. Johnson, who went there often, declared that the rotunda's *coupe d'oeil* was "the finest thing he had ever seen." Outside, there was a formal garden, and at the end of the main walk, a circular Temple of Pan and a canal with "a Temple indifferently described as the Chinese House and the Venetian Temple." (Warwick Wroth, *London Pleasure Gardens*, London, 1896, pp. 199–218).

neously, their reflections caught in eighteen pier glasses "beautifully illuminated with shell-work and festoons." The entrance fee also entitled one to "as good Liquor as can be procur'd."[45] Forty years later the centrally heated building that had formerly housed Cox's Museum was transformed for a brief time into an indoor flower garden, a "Paradise in miniature" as the advertisements declared. Four thousand plants, flowers, shrubs, and trees were said to be "in bud and blossom at one instant"; there were herbaceous borders and a hothouse, as well as a specimen of the American aloe, a plant of perennial interest to Englishmen.[46] (Aloes were exhibited in London from the 1740s onward, and when two specimens bloomed at Bagnigge Wells spa in 1785, half a crown was charged to see them.) In 1786, three years after the Spring Gardens show, its proprietor, one Harvey, erected a building in St. George's Fields, on the Surrey side of Westminster Bridge, to house a replica of an elaborate display he had created for a recent "Grand Gala" at Ranelagh. Called "the British Elysium" or "the Temple of Flora," this resort boasted a summer garden, a winter garden, an orange grove, a hothouse with a statue of Pomona, a Chinese pagoda, goldfish ponds, and a grotto complete with the indispensable hermit. An automaton gardener was on hand to answer questions in what was advertised as "an astonishing manner."[47]

Across Oakley Street from the Temple of Flora was another new resort, the Apollo Gardens, operated by the former lessee of the Pantheon. Here, in addition to various horticultural displays, could be seen both paintings and transparencies of the royal family, "descriptive of the greatest national, and most signal blessing ever experienced, viz. the first interview between our beloved Monarch, his amiable Royal Consort, and the six Princesses, immediately after his recovery" from an attack of madness.[48]

There were no fireworks at either of these gardens, only the music of bands, the singing of birds in aviaries, and the plash of fountains and "natural" cascades; but despite the decorous setting and, in the case of the latter at least, the blend of patriotism and domestic sentiment represented in the transparencies, both the Temple of Flora and the Apollo Gardens soon failed. An originally respectable, if not fashionable, clientele gave way to low-life characters whose riotous behavior got the managements in trouble with the neighbors and the magistrates. The proprietor of the Temple of Flora was sentenced to six months' imprisonment for keeping a disorderly house, and within a few years both places were closed.[49]

Of the numerous eighteenth-century satellites of Vauxhall, the tea garden and spa at Bermondsey offered the most varied attractions.[50] Formerly the Waterman's Arms tavern, the premises were taken over in 1765 by a self-taught artist named Thomas Keyes (Keyse), who is reputed to have been "a cheery, ingenious landlord, remarkable among other things for his preparation of cherry-brandy." When a chalybeate spring was discovered in 1770, the tavern became also a spa; when a music license was obtained fourteen years later, it expanded still further and became a concert room.

Among the "improvements" on which Keyes spent £4,000 at this time was an outdoor spectacle portraying the Battle of Gibraltar (1782), when the British fleet under Lord Howe lifted the three-year-long siege of the garrison by the French and Spanish. It was an event whose inspiriting effect upon the national morale, depressed by the loss of the American war, was to persist down at least to the greater victories of the Nile and Trafalgar. A number of paintings, by Wright of Derby and Copley among others, commemorated the battle. In 1786 Keyes built, in a field separated by a ha-ha from a three-acre lawn which served as a spectators' gallery, a huge model of the rock of Gilbraltar, 200 feet long and 50 feet high. Here, during a performance, lights showed in the town, vehicles moved, and the "fictitious water" of the bay was filled with an assortment of miniature naval vessels assaulting the fortifications. We may assume that the fireworks representing the gunfire were brilliant and loud.

This was one of the first appearances in the London entertainment business of what, in the patriotic fervor aroused by the heroic encounters between the French and British fleets during the Napoleonic Wars, was to become a dependably popular spectacle: the naumachia. A mimic battle, in real water, between fleets of model ships, the naumachia was often staged in ancient Rome, where the Colosseum was flooded for the purpose, and in the Renaissance it had a part in the courtly "magnificences." Beginning with Nelson's exploits in 1794, it appeared in various forms in the London theatres.*

Adjacent to the original tavern Keyes built a picture gallery, admission sixpence, in which he showed, not Hogarths or Haymans, but the products of his own brush. The *pièces de résistance* in this one-man show were several enormous paintings representing a fishmonger's, a poulterer's, a greengrocer's, and a butcher's shop. Only the last-named survived to be shown at a gallery in Leicester Square in 1818, eighteen years

* Among these, in addition to (or possibly identical with) "Mr. Turner's" exhibition in Silver Street (see below, Chapter 9), was a "Grand Nautical Moving Spectacle of the Naumachia": "Splendid Victories achieved by Lord Nelson, with the Elements and Ships in Motion; L'Artemise, L'Orient, and L'Achille on fire; the masts falling by the board; the three Lines of English and French exchanging Broadsides; the Explosion of the L'Orient, and the Boats out saving the People: Depicting the Havock and Destruction which took place, with all the majestic Horrors which characterised those great Events." (Undated handbill, WCL, F137/Princes St.) In 1804 Sadler's Wells reached back to the siege of Gibraltar to inaugurate its sensational novelty, a stage area consisting of a tank holding 8,000 cubic feet of water. Here playgoers watched the combined forces of France and Spain, represented by 117 miniature men-of-war and floating batteries built and rigged by artisans from His Majesty's dockyards, besieging and then being vanquished by the British garrison. This was the first of a long series of mimic naval encounters performed at Sadler's Wells. Outside the world of commercial entertainment, the most memorable naumachia took place in Hyde Park in the summer of 1814, to celebrate Napoleon's defeat and his flight to Elba. On the anniversary of the Battle of the Nile (1 August) model men-of-war clashed in desperate combat in the Serpentine and the whole thunderous engagement ended in a fireworks display which Lamb described to Wordsworth in a letter written two weeks later. (*Letters of Charles Lamb . . . ,* ed. E. V. Lucas, New Haven, 1935, II, 128.)

after the artist-publican's death and fourteen after the gardens closed. At that time it was described by a writer in a weekly paper. The picture was, he wrote,

about eight feet in height, and twelve or fourteen feet in length, and exhibits the whole range of a butcher's shop, hung with joints of beef, mutton, veal, and lamb. These are so perfectly executed, that not only at a few yards distance is the spectator inclined to believe them real, but even when he approaches near enough to touch them, to swear, as Lord Peter did about the brown loaf, "by ———— it is substantial mutton as ever was sold in Leadenhall Market." Nothing that ever was painted surpasses this extraordinary performance in regard to the exact representation of *still life,* as we trust *dead meat* may very properly be called. There is also another merit belonging to this picture; the pigment employed in producing the appearance of cawls, white fat, &c. is wonderfully pure and natural. The softness, which does not impair its brilliancy as a colour, though it subdues it to a tone of perfect truth in its local application, is of a description which we rather think it would puzzle the greatest painters of the day to parallel.[51]

The last two sentences pinpoint Keyes's single claim to celebrity as a painter. He was fond of saying that Sir Joshua Reynolds, who paid two visits to the Bermondsey gallery, could not understand why, since he and Keyes used the same pigment, his whites faded and Keyes's—chiefly used, it seems, to portray animal fat—remained bright. The difference, Keyes patiently explained to Reynolds, lay in the fact that his own canvases enjoyed constant exposure to fresh air. However that may be, Keyes's forte seems to have resided in the difficult art of portraying butcher's meat; and he and his clientele may have been pleased to contemplate how far superior his pictorial meat was to the pitiful slices of ham, themselves so thin as to be almost illusory, in the sandwiches that were notorious for a century as the house specialty at Vauxhall Gardens upstream.

Art on Display

8

In 1788 a newspaper advertisement announced: "There is now added to the elegant exhibition adjoining Somerset House, in the Strand (consisting of Automaton Figures which move in a great variety of descriptions, by clockwork, with the Diamond Beetle, scarce and valuable paintings, Needlework, Shells, Flies, Water Fall, etc., etc., so universally admired) some of the most beautiful and striking Pencil and Chalk Drawings in the Kingdom, by Mr. Lawrence, late of Bath, now at 41 Jermyn Street."[1]

One could not wish for more satisfactory symbolism. Here in the Strand were juxtaposed two popular kinds of late eighteenth-century shows, the link between them being supplied by the nineteen-year-old Thomas Lawrence. Moving his family from Bath, where his son had already earned a reputation as an artist, the elder Lawrence had used a £200 legacy of his daughter's to buy a small museum next to Somerset House, headquarters of the Royal Academy and site of its annual exhibition. Two new worlds of London shows thus impinged: the world of the small catch-penny museum of automatons, natural history specimens, and miscellaneous curiosities, and the more exclusive, not to say more exalted, one of the art exhibition. Not only did they abut: to the distress of some conservative inhabitants of the latter world, the two were already tending to overlap. A public which patronized exhibitions of "natural and artificial rarities" and examples of "mechanical ingenuity" now also had the means of indulging its recently acquired taste for pictorial beauty—in the case of Lawrence's museum,

under the same roof. In the year before the Lawrence advertisement, a newspaper proudly observed that there were "no less than six places . . . open for the exhibition of ancient and modern paintings."[2] This was a great step forward, and it had been achieved only in the past thirty years.

In the early golden age of the virtuoso, ordinary Londoners had had little access to art; indeed, London, in contrast with cities on the continent, had little "public" art of any sort apart from the pictorial signs of shops and taverns. Most of the stained glass, wall paintings, tapestries, and sculpture that had enriched churches at the beginning of the Tudor period had perished with the Reformation, and much of what survived—those elements of ecclesiastical art not so closely identified with "superstitious idolatry"—had been destroyed by the widened Puritan assault on every form of religious imagery that the church fabric contained. In London, the Great Fire of 1666 completed the devastation. These losses were not made good when Wren built his City churches, because in the aftermath of Puritan iconoclasm an influential portion of the clergy continued to oppose pictorial art as an adjunct to devotion. Churches might be elegant and chastely splendid, as Wren's were, but in general paintings and, even more, statuary were disapproved. It is true that Sir James Thornhill's painted cupola crowned St. Paul's, but it was too high to be seen well, and below it the bareness of the cathedral contrasted unfavorably with the rich exterior.

In vain did English artists, as their sense of community and power grew, protest this scanting of art by ecclesiastical policy. When a proposal was made in the early 1760s to erect a monument in St. Paul's to a former Lord Mayor, the Bishop of London, Richard Osbaldeston, was obdurate: "there had been no monuments in all the time before he was bishop, and in his time there should be none."[3] Some years later several members of the Royal Academy, led by Benjamin West, offered to paint a series of historical pictures, fifteen to twenty feet high, to fill the wall spaces Wren had provided for the purpose. The dean and chapter welcomed the proposal, the dean, Dr. Thomas Newton, maintaining that "whatever might have been the case in the days of our first reformers, there was surely no danger now of pictures seducing our people into popery and idolatry; they would only make Scripture history better known and remembered." But the new bishop, Dr. Terrick, took the same view as had his predecessor: the artists' project "would occasion a great noise and clamour against it, as an artful intrusion of popery."[4] And so it too was dropped.

Small reparation had been supplied for the losses the Londoner's eye for pictorial beauty had suffered across more than two full centuries. Such wall painting as was done in the late seventeenth and early eighteenth centuries—and there was, to be sure, a goodly amount of it—was confined to the royal palaces and the mansions of the nobility, where only the privileged could walk. It was a noteworthy, but isolated, breakthrough when Hogarth painted the murals of the pool of Bethesda and the Good Samaritan in the great staircase of St. Bartholomew's Hospital, to which the public had free access.

There were no public art collections. The same forces which had made the nation so long unreceptive to the Renaissance itself had delayed the advent of art collecting. Only with Charles I did the nation have a monarch who possessed and exercised a taste already identified with many rulers on the continent. But he at least made up for lost time. In 1625 Rubens called the Prince of Wales, as he then was, "the most enthusiastic amateur of painting in the world," and Charles was, in fact, a true connoisseur of the arts and a collector of the first rank. When political events put a stop to his collecting, he owned 1,387 pictures and 399 sculptures, including the rich hereditary collections of the Duke of Mantua and the Raphael cartoons. But in a series of sales ordered by Cromwell's Parliament between 1649 and 1653, this first and perhaps greatest of all English private collections was dispersed, most of it going back to the continent.

Two English noblemen also had built up extensive collections. At York House the Duke of Buckingham, John Tradescant's employer, possessed nineteen Titians, seventeen Tintorettos, fifteen Veroneses, six Holbeins, and numerous other pictures of similar quality; but he was assassinated in 1628, and his collection, like the king's, was confiscated and sold. The third of the great seventeenth-century art collectors, the Earl of Arundel, had brought back from his many trips to Italy six hundred pictures and two hundred objets d'art as well as a valuable array of Grecian antiquities. But when he went into exile in 1642 he took most of the former with him, and the antiquities he left behind at Arundel House were severely damaged by neglect and what Evelyn called "the corrosive aire of London."[5]

The tide was reversed to some extent when Charles II came to the throne in 1660. Using as a nucleus the small group of his father's works of art which Cromwell had reserved for Hampton Court Palace, he built the royal collection to about one hundred pictures and one hundred sculptures, distributed among the palaces of St. James, Whitehall, Hampton Court, and Windsor. But the temper of the time was not markedly aesthetic, and the virtuosi, those exemplars of Restoration and early eighteenth-century culture, were little concerned with beauty. For the most part they regarded paintings and drawings as they did coins, inscriptions, and other antiquities: as documentary representations or historical *realia,* not aesthetic objects. It is significant that when Evelyn returned from his extended European tour in 1647 he found a cultured society that was beginning to amass cabinets; when Horace Walpole returned from the same tour almost exactly a century later, he found a society which now boasted an abundance of such collections, Sir Hans Sloane's indeed being unmatched in all Europe, but except among a few men of taste there was no comparable passion to accumulate works of art. The Royal Society was flourishing, and its influence was pervasive, but there was no Royal Academy of Arts.

Those few men of taste, however, included Walpole's father, Sir Robert, who spent huge sums furnishing his Norfolk mansion, Houghton, with treasures of art, and the Duke of Marlborough, who similarly filled the cavernous rooms at Blenheim. Once such influential men turned to connoisseurship and collecting, many followed, encouraged by the spread of "taste" as a fashionable attribute and by the wealth that their fortunate participation in the nation's expanded trade brought them, to spend, if they wished, on luxuries such as art. Throughout England the stately homes began to include picture galleries; by 1776 the Duke of Devonshire had four, including one at Devonshire House, London.

In addition to the gentlemen who did their own collecting as they toured Europe and the agents who collected for others, speculators bought up stock in the continental art centers and consigned it to the London auction houses, which, from the late seventeenth century onward, served as the main channel through which works of art destined for English ownership flowed. Thus ordinary Londoners, if they lacked a permanent gallery, still could momentarily see pictures, sculpture, and other objets d'art before they disappeared into the great private collections. The auction galleries were open two or three days before each sale, and at these times they became a kind of London equivalent of the Paris Salon, where persons of fashion gathered as much for conversation as to see the pictures. There was no admission charge, but a police officer was stationed at the door to exclude the mob—a portentous figure, because the apprehensions of disorder which caused his presence were destined to color thinking about the public's right of access to art for more than a century.

Among those who qualified for admission, these brief shows unquestionably sharpened interest in art as well as the appetite for possessing it.[6] How lively that interest had become by the 1740s was revealed by the fortuitous success of Captain Coram's new Foundling Hospital as an art gallery. William Hogarth, still at the beginning of his career, was one of the foundation's original governors, and when, in 1740, he presented to the hospital his portrait of the benevolent captain, he set in motion a chain of events which resulted, within a generation, in London's witnessing a veritable "picture mania," as it was later to be called. Hogarth prevailed upon fifteen of his fellow artists to contribute works of their own to the hospital, and in 1746 no fewer than twenty artists were formally appointed governors. Once every year they dined at the institution, as a body which today would probably call itself "the Friends of the Foundling," and by the end of the seventies a notable collection of donated art had accumulated there: paintings by Hogarth, Gainsborough, Allan Ramsay, Benjamin West, and Richard Wilson, and sculpture by Rysbrack and Roubiliac. The Foundling's gallery and court room became a rendezvous for all ranks except the working class, and, although no charge was made for admission, most people left a contribution in appreciation of the privilege.

The artists' willingness to donate pictures to the Foundling sprang, of course, from healthy self-interest: it was an admirable way to bring their talents to the attention of prospective patrons. Hitherto, they had done so only by displaying their new pictures privately, in their own home-studios. Hogarth showed *A Harlot's Progress* at his house in the Great Piazza, Covent Garden, in 1730–1732, and after his removal to the Golden Head, Leicester Square, he exhibited his successive pictures there. In 1749 and 1751 Canaletto had taken newspaper advertisements inviting the nobility and gentry to see his latest canvases of London at his lodgings in Silver Street, Golden Square. Observing the success of the Foundling Hospital as a public showcase for their work, the artists who gathered for the 1759 dinner of the governors took the next logical step. They undertook to hold a free exhibition of their newest canvases from 21 April to 8 May 1760 at a room in the Strand occupied by the newly formed Society for the Encouragement of Arts, Manufactures, and Commerce in Great Britain, a title immediately abbreviated in ordinary usage to the Society of Arts. One hundred and thirty pictures were hung, and a sixpenny catalogue was available—good value for the money, because its frontispiece and tailpiece were by Hogarth. According to modern estimates, based on the sale of 6,582 catalogues, some 20,000 persons attended the show, but this figure does not include the undeterminable number who entered without buying a catalogue and did not belong to a group who shared one.[7]

Sharing the nervousness the proprietors of the auction galleries had felt over the indiscriminate admission of the public, the officials of the Society of Arts, the host organization, laid down strict rules. The attendants hired by the exhibiting artists were empowered "to exclude all persons whom they shall think improper to be admitted, such as livery servants, foot soldiers, porters, women with children, etc., and to prevent all disorders in the Room, such as smoking, drinking, etc., by turning the disorderly persons out."[8] Despite these rules, window glass to the value of 13s. 6d. was broken, and the artists complained of "the intrusion of great numbers whose stations and education made them no proper judges of statuary or painting and who were made idle and tumultuous by the opportunity of a show."[9] Modern historians of the Society of Arts suggest that some visitors misbehaved out of "sheer excitement at discovering the works of Reynolds, Richard Wilson, Cosway, Morland, Roubiliac, Paul Sandby, and sixty-three others,"[10] but such ecstasy in the presence of art does not seem very true to the eighteenth-century character, and the probable explanation is just what it was said to be: "the opportunity of a show" attracted, among others, persons who had no idea of decorum, let alone of art, but shared the universal enthusiasm for seeing something for nothing.

In order to ensure propriety at the next year's exhibition the artists insisted that an admission fee be charged, but the Society of Arts demurred and most of the group, now formally organized as the Society of Artists of Great Britain, rented instead the Great Room, Spring Gardens, which a decade later would house Cox's Museum. In the catalogue that was given with every shilling admission the artists, noting that "an exhibition of the works of art [was] a spectacle new in this kingdom," explained why an entrance fee had to be charged:

Though we are far from wishing to diminish the pleasures, or depreciate the sentiments of any class of the community, we know, however, what everyone knows, that all cannot be judges or purchasers of works of art. Yet we have already found by experience, that all are desirous to see an exhibition. When the terms of admission were low, our room was throng'd with such multitudes, as made access dangerous, and frightened away those, whose approbation was most desired.[11]

Under this arrangement, the attendance was kept under control; whereas the first show drew well over 20,000 persons, this one attracted a more manageable 13,000. The Society also made more money, £650 from entrance fees, as contrasted with the £164 received from the sale of catalogues the year before. Meanwhile, the artists who did not secede to Spring Gardens, mediocrities except for Nollekens and Cosway, banded together as the Free Society of Artists and exhibited at the Society of Arts for four more years, then in a succession of rooms elsewhere until the organization was dissolved in 1783. From 1772 onward they too charged admission.*

The next in this series of organizations and projects proved to be the most momentous of all. In 1768 some influential members of the Incorporated Society of Artists, as the original group was now called to distinguish it from the Free Society, formed a new organization for both the exhibition of the work of British artists at large and the training of promising young ones. The king granted it an "instrument of foundation" on 10 December and the Royal Academy came into being.

The Academy's first show, held in 1769 in a building in Pall Mall which had formerly been an auction room and printseller's shop, drew 18,000 persons at a shilling each. Here, too, the catalogue explained why an admission fee had to be charged; the question was the more pertinent because the Academy was "supported by royal munificence." The Academicians' answer was that "they have not been able to suggest any other Means than that of receiving Money for Admittance to prevent the Room from being fill'd by improper Persons, to the entire exclusion of those for whom the Exhibition is apparently intended."[12] Henceforth the annual Academy exhibition, held at Somerset House beginning in 1781, was the great event of the art year, as it also became one of the obligatory social events of the London season. Since the history of the Royal Academy, in large part the story of British art itself from 1769 onward, is a familiar one, it needs no re-telling here. The occurrence of the summer exhibition (to many persons down through the years, the very word "exhibition" referred to this show and no other) must be assumed to be a punctual and ritual accompaniment to all the other kinds of shows chronicled in these chapters.

As the Royal Academy set the style and the circle of collectors continued to grow, the art market expanded and the number of London shows increased. In addition to the seasonal exhibitions of the several artists' societies, there were more auctions. The two venerable auction houses which have survived into our own time had been established even before the Academy was founded—Sotheby's about 1744 (though initially its main trade was in "literary properties") and Christie's in 1762. Sometimes dealers, emulating the artists' groups, charged admission to their preauction shows. In 1787, for instance, an American-born auctioneer, Thomas Greenwood, charged a shilling to see *The Adoration of the Magi,* then attributed to Dürer but later identified as the work of Jean Mabuse.[13] Two years later another displaced American, a self-styled "Loyalist from Charleston, South Carolina" named John Wilson, founded in King Street, St. James's Square, the European Museum "for the Promotion of the Fine Arts, and the Encouragement of British Artists." These lofty aims, which seemed to place the establishment on an equal footing with the Royal Academy, were actually window dressing for a merchandising venture. For a commission of 5 percent of the selling price, an artist or other owner could exhibit a picture there for as long as a year. The public was admitted for an annual subscription of a guinea.[14]

As a commercial enterprise the European Museum

* In 1762 the rivalry of the exhibitions in the Strand and Spring Gardens inspired the wit Bonnell Thornton to hold a parody show at his home in Bow Street. A preliminary teaser in the *St. James's Chronicle* announced: "The Society of Sign-Painters are . . . preparing a most magnificent collection of portraits, landscapes, fancy-pieces, flower-pieces, history-pieces, night-pieces, Scripture-pieces, &c. &c. designed by the ablest masters, and executed by the best hands in these kingdoms. The virtuosi will have a new opportunity to display their taste on this occasion, by discovering the different styles of the several masters employed, and pointing out by what hand each piece is drawn." The room, according to another paper, was "hung round with green baize, on which [a] curious collection of wooden originals is fixed flat, and from whence hang keys, bells, swords, poles, sugar-loaves, tobacco-rolls, candles, and other ornamental figures, carved in wood, which commonly dangled from the pent-houses of the different shops in our streets." Among the subjects were the Vicar of Bray, the Irish Arms (Patrick O'Blarney *pinxit*), the Scotch Fiddle (M'Pherson *pinxit*), A Man (showing nine tailors at work), and A Man Loaded with Mischief (a woman, a magpie, and a monkey on his back). Numbers 49 and 50 were concealed by blue curtains, in the manner of "indecent pictures in some collections." When one of the curtains was lifted, the curious connoisseur beheld a board reading "Ha! ha! ha!" or "he! he! he!" (John Pye, *Patronage of British Art: An Historical Sketch . . . ,* London, 1845, pp. 109–14n.) A decade later, advertisements appeared for a similar show, which burlesqued not only the art exhibitions but the name of Sir Ashton Lever's museum: "The Drol-o-phusikon, a whimsical and original exhibition of sign-painting." (Tom Taylor, *Leicester Square: Its Associations and Its Worthies,* London, 1874, p. 451n.)

20. The Royal Academy exhibition in Pall Mall, 1771 (mezzotint by Charles Brandoin).

seems to have been fairly successful; it lasted until 1823, when its building was taken over and remodeled by James Christie, who moved his auction business there from Pall Mall. But most of the pictures that passed through it during those thirty-four years were of modern origin, and meanwhile London had continued to be largely deprived of the sight of Old Masters,* examples of which might only be seen in the auction rooms or as they were inadequately reproduced in engravings.

London awakened to what it had been missing when, in the spring of 1793, part of the Duc d'Orléans's great collection went on display.[15] Having correctly read the handwriting on the revolutionary wall, "Philippe Égalité," the "sans-culotte Duke," had sold his treasure the previous year to two speculators, one Belgian and the other English. The latter's share,

composed of Flemish, Dutch, and German paintings, was exhibited for sale at the Royal Academy's former room in Pall Mall under the direction of John Wilson of the European Museum. This was the first exhibition of Old Masters ever held in England, and it was a great success; during the last week alone, more than £100 a day was taken in, at a shilling a person. The remainder of the collection, consisting of French and Italian masterpieces, was sold privately to three collectors, the Duke of Bridgewater, the Earl of Carlisle, and the Earl of Gower. They selected what they wanted, and at the end of December 1798 they opened a six-month exhibition of these pictures, as well as the residue which they wished to sell, at two locations, the room in Pall Mall and the Lyceum.

The two Orleans exhibitions—the accent mark did not survive the channel crossing—were a major mile-

* Or what passed for Old Masters. The *London Magazine* in 1737 vilified the "picture-jobbers from abroad" whose trade was "importing, by ship-loads, Dead Christs, Holy Families, Madonnas, and other dismal, dark subjects, on which they scrawl the names of Italian masters, and fix on us poor Englishmen the character of universal dupes." This flourishing business, which worked hand in glove with resident manufacturers and "restorers" of putative Masters, was satirized by Samuel Foote in a play called *Taste* (1752). (Pye, *Patronage of British Art,* pp. 27–28n., 68–73.) Hogarth's *Time Smoking a Picture* is on the same theme. On the whole, spurious Raphaels, Correggios, and Andrea del Sartos seem to have been at least as numerous in English private galleries as alleged shipments from Captain Cook were to be in museums toward the end of the century.

21. The Royal Academy exhibition at Somerset House, 1787 (engraving by J. H. Ramberg). The Prince of Wales (later George IV) is in the center, holding hat, cane, and catalogue. The figure with the ear trumpet is Sir Joshua Reynolds.

stone in the art education of the upper- and middle-class public, who now could steep themselves as had never before been possible in the idiom of schools other than the native one. Their impact is best described by William Hazlitt, who visited the 1799 show at the age of twenty:

My first initiation in the mysteries of the art was at the Orleans Gallery: it was there I formed my taste, such as it is. . . . I was staggered when I saw the works there collected, and looked at them with wondering and with longing eyes. A mist passed away from my sight; the scales fell off. A new sense came upon me, a new heaven and a new earth stood before me. I saw the soul speaking in the face. . . . We had all heard the names of Titian, Raphael, Guido, Domenichino, the Caracci—but to see them face to face, to be in the same room with their deathless productions, was like

breaking some mighty spell—was almost an effect of necromancy! From that time I lived in a world of pictures.[16]

Faced with this sharpening competition from their celebrated continental predecessors, British artists sought and found additional ways to promote their own work. Already they had put on one-man shows. In 1775 the minor painter Nathaniel Hone had exhibited one hundred of his pictures and designs in St. Martin's Lane. An early manifestation of anti-Academicism—Hone's picture of *The Conjuror,* which was reputed to contain a satire on Sir Joshua Reynolds, the Academy's president, had been rejected for the annual exhibition—this show was a *succès de scandale* if nothing else.[17] Personal pique, this time arising from the Academy's unsatisfactory hanging of his portrait of the three royal princesses, also prompted Gainsborough's decision to exhibit twenty-five of his paintings in his Pall Mall house in 1784. This exhibition remained open, with additions and rearrangements, until his death four years later. Barry and West had similar exhibitions during the same period, and in May 1793 the debt-ridden George Morland showed sixty of his pot-boilers in King Street, Covent Garden.

One-man shows were soon joined by one-picture exhibitions. The latter were an invention of John Singleton Copley, an American with a fully developed exploitative sense who, several years after arriving in London, undertook to paint the dramatic scene that had occurred in the House of Lords in 1778 when the elder Pitt suffered a stroke while speaking.[18] The picture was awaited with great interest because of its subject, and Copley did not underestimate its commercial possibilities. Most of the fifty-five noblemen included in the scene sat to him; they and their families and friends could be expected not only to come to see the finished picture but to constitute a large market for the engraving that would be made of it. Furthermore, the presence in the picture of so many notable public men of the day, painted from life, would lend it extraordinary interest apart from the episode itself. Therefore, instead of sending the canvas to the Royal Academy when it was finished in the spring of 1781, Copley decided to exhibit it on his own. The Academy having just vacated its Pall Mall room and moved to Somerset House, Copley arranged to sublet the room from the lessee, the auctioneer James Christie.

Outraged by Copley's cool appropriation for commercial purposes of the house so firmly associated with the Academy in the public mind, its treasurer, Sir William Chambers, acidulously wrote him: "No one wishes Mr. Copley greater success, or is more sensible of his merit, than his humble servant, who, if he may be allowed to give his opinion, thinks no place so proper as the Royal Exhibition to promote either the sale of prints or the raffle for the picture, which he understands are Mr. Copley's motives. Or, if that be objected to, he thinks no place so proper as Mr. Copley's own house, where the idea of a raree-show will not be quite so striking as in any other place, and where his own presence will not fail to be of service to his views."[19] At the same time, Chambers successfully pressured Christie to revoke his agreement with Copley. Copley then hired the Great Room, Spring Gardens, and in six weeks *The Death of the Earl of Chatham* attracted more than 20,000 persons at a shilling each. He was said to have made £5,000 from

the exhibition, as well as 5,000 enemies, because his competition reduced attendance at the Academy's show by a third and the gate receipts by £1,000, despite the presence that year of seven Gainsboroughs and fifteen Reynoldses. In addition to his financial coup, Copley enjoyed invaluable publicity for future use, especially in the form of long press notices copied from the explanatory brochure handed out at the door. Three years later the *Chatham* was shown again, along with the more recent *Death of Peirson,* and again the public responded in a most profitable manner.

In 1791 Copley had fresh trouble finding a suitable gallery, this time not because of Academic outrage at his presumption but because of the new painting's size: *The Floating Batteries at Gibraltar* measured 25 by 18 feet, larger than any available room could accommodate. With the permission of the Crown, Copley erected an eighty-foot-long tent in the Green Park, only to meet opposition from the aristocratic neighbors in Arlington Street, who were reminded all too vividly of Bartholomew Fair and its mountebank booths. The painter moved his tent to another site in the park but again ran into objections. Finally he found refuge near Buckingham House, where, it is said, the king urged him, "Push it up nearer to my wife's house—she won't complain." Indeed, the royal family gladly came to see the picture, along with other sightseers to the number of 60,000. Their attendance was worth £3,000 to Copley. Eight years later, denied permission to use the park, he pitched his tent in the garden of Lord Sheffield's house in Albemarle Street and showed a triple bill consisting of *The Death of Chatham, Charles I Demanding the Five Impeached Members,* and *Admiral Duncan's Victory at Camperdown.*

DƷ✴Ʒꟼ

The new economics of art as it had developed by the end of the century is tersely summarized by the formal agreement by which the Corporation of London commissioned Copley to paint *The Floating Batteries.* It acknowledged that the price of £1,000 was low for so ambitious a canvas, but it expressed the hope that "the advantages of an Exhibition of the Picture and the publication of a Print from it will compensate him for the time and study requisite for completing so large a work."[20] Copley was the first artist to appreciate the value of both engravings *and* exhibitions as a direct source of income, supplementing whatever a picture itself might bring, and as a medium of publicity. He may have made more from what today would be called the subsidiary rights to a picture than from the sale of the actual canvas. In this he went beyond Hogarth, who, shrewd entrepreneur though he was, had realized only the potential profitability of engravings and overlooked that of an admission-charging exhibition. When Hogarth showed *A Rake's Progress* and *Marriage à la Mode,* for instance, at his Leicester Square studio, he charged no admission and was interested only in attracting subscriptions for the prospective engravings. In the case of such later pictures as *Industry and Idleness* and *Beer Street and Gin Lane,* the engravings of which were not sold by subscription but (more democratically) over the counter, the exhibition was still only an advertising device. And so for a long time, down to Copley's day in fact, the display of a painting that was to be engraved continued to be only a means to an end rather than a profitable end in itself.

The engravings to which exhibitions drew attention were an increasingly important source of artists' income. Earlier, publishers had commissioned paintings from which engravings could be made to embellish expensive books. Now the popularity of Hogarth's pictures and, in a quite different direction, the widened public interest in art generated by the annual shows enlarged the market for separate prints, to be bought as one bought a copy of a book or pamphlet. Popular artists like Reynolds, Gainsborough, and Stothard could make several hundred pounds per picture from engraving rights, even though such rights were not as valuable as they were later to become, when the market had expanded still further and it was mechanically possible to produce editions larger than the thousand copies to which eighteenth-century prints were limited.[21] As popular demand caused more and more new pictures to be engraved, the site for exhibiting the original picture was moved from the artist's studio to the prospective publisher's shop if there was space, or else to a hired room. Among the earliest commissioned paintings to be exhibited to advertise the engraving was Stothard's *Death of Lord John Manners,* shown by Thomas Macklin in a room in Cockspur Street in 1783; "the Proprietor," a newspaper said, "is to pay the greatest price for the engraving ever given in this country"—£700.[22]

As yet, a publisher's right to show the picture was implicit in the engraving fee; exhibition rights would become a separate consideration in the transaction between the publisher and the artist only in the early nineteenth century. This was due in part to a development in the decade 1790–1800, when the popularity of engravings made from paintings as well as the growing demand for illustrated books resulted in a new genre in publishing, books composed of a large series of specially commissioned pictures and advertised by a long-term exhibition of those paintings. It was then that the potentialities of the exhibition as the chief way of promoting the sale of engravings were first realized by the projectors of various "galleries" —the word here meaning both exhibition places and, by extension, folio volumes serving the same purpose in the home (André Malraux's "museums without walls").

Of these galleries in the double sense, the most ambitious, as it was the most celebrated, was Boydell's Shakespeare Gallery.[23] John Boydell ("Alderman" as he was often called: he acquired that title in 1782, and would become Lord Mayor in 1790) was the doyen of England's print publishers. During his career he had managed completely to reverse the flow of the international trade in prints. Whereas in the middle of the century, when he began business, England had imported most of her prints from France, by 1786 she was supplying the whole continent at a rate of £200,000 worth a year, and most of these prints were from Boydell's own shop. Toward the end, he had 4,432 copperplates in his catalogue. Though holding only a third share in the engraving rights to the picture, in fifteen years he had made £15,000 from prints of West's *Death of General Wolfe.* All told, his attentive catering to the rising public enthusiasm for art at home and abroad had earned him a fortune of £350,000.

Dining with West, Romney, and others late in 1786, Boydell, then sixty-seven years old, expressed his intention to help Britain acquire what she notoriously lacked, a school of history painting. And, as he subsequently declared, "no subject seem[ed] so proper to form an English School of Historical Paintings, as the scenes of the immortal Shakespeare." This was the germ of the Shakespeare Gallery, which as the plan developed was to be composed of a long series of oil paintings, some small and some large, of Shakespearean scenes and characters. These would be exhibited in a permanent gallery designed for the purpose, and from them Boydell would make engravings, the large ones to be gathered in an imperial folio edition with no text and the small ones in a typographically magnificent edition of Shakespeare's works. In a gesture combining commercial interest and altruism that was not to be matched in English publishing until George Smith, of the firm of Smith, Elder, underwrote the *Dictionary of National Biography* a century later, Boydell proposed to leave to the nation both the paintings and the gallery that housed them.

Thirty-five artists received commissions. Headed by Reynolds, Romney, West, Fuseli, Opie, and Northcote, the list reached as far toward forgettable mediocrity as William Hamilton, Smirke, Westall, and Wheatley, who among them were to produce half of the total of 170 illustrations. By June 1789 the first batch of thirty-four paintings was ready, and the Shakespeare Gallery opened at 52 Pall Mall, in a building formerly occupied by Dodsley's famous bookshop. Rebuilt under the supervision of George Dance the younger and entirely sheathed in copper, it had on its façade a relief of Shakespeare reclining against a rock, flanked by the Dramatic Muse and the Genius of Painting and bearing the bardolatrous inscription: "He was a Man, take him for all in all, I shall not look upon his like again." On the ground floor was a suite 130 feet long, with an iron-plated ceiling for fireproofing; above it were three rooms with a wall area of over 4,000 square feet.

The gallery immediately became a headquarters of London literary and artistic life. Thirty-three paintings were added in 1790, and at the beginning of the next year appeared the first parts of the edition of Shakespeare, with engravings from the small-sized pictures. But ambition as grandiose as Boydell's always entails risk, and his gallery's fair prospects, which were substantially dependent on the continued prosperity of the firm, soon were blighted by circumstances beyond his control. When the war with France broke out in 1793, his lucrative European market for prints was cut off. The dislocations of the war also were hard on his subscribers, many of whom were unable to make good on their commitments to buy one or the other of the expensive editions. His return from the sale of the books was slow and far below expectations. To make things worse, imitators quickly invaded the market, and a public appetite which in 1790 may have been as keen as Boydell thought was sated by 1800.

Boydell's outlay for the paintings, the engravings, and the Pall Mall building exceeded £100,000. The Shakespeare edition would not be completed until 1805, and the folio containing the large-size pictures would not be published at all until that year. Faced with bankruptcy, in 1804 Boydell obtained an act of Parliament enabling him, like James Cox and Sir Ashton Lever before him, to try to recoup his losses by a lottery.[24] Twenty-two thousand tickets were sold at three guineas each. Each one entitled the purchaser to a print from Boydell's large stock; there were several grades of prizes, topped by the entire collection of commissioned pictures and the *alto relievo* on the gal-

22. Boydell's Shakespeare Gallery, Pall Mall (engraving by S. Rawle; frontispiece to *European Magazine,* 1804).

lery's façade. The winner of this supreme prize, valued at £30,000, was a Mr. Tassie, nephew of a well-known cameo maker. He sold the paintings for the small sum of £6,182 (the ninety by Smirke, Westall, Hamilton and Wheatley, which went for an average of £20, doubtless had a depressant effect). The lease of the building was sold to a new artists' group, the British Institution, which occupied it until it was pulled down in 1868–69.

Boydell's magnanimous and, as it proved, ruinous effort to establish a British school of history painting and, equally, to honor British poetic genius received sufficient praise; at a Royal Academy dinner the year the gallery opened, the Prince of Wales, prompted by Reynolds and Burke, toasted the alderman as "an English tradesman who patronizes art better than the

Grand Monarque, . . . the Commercial Maecenas." But gratitude lines no coffers, and in any case the undertaking was not without its critics. James Gillray lampooned Boydell and his works in a famous print, *Shakespeare Sacrificed; or The Offering to Avarice,* and the reaction among literary men was generally cool. Horace Walpole wrote to Lord Hailes a year after the exhibition opened, "The Shakespeare Gallery is truly most inadequate to its prototypes; but how should it be worthy of them? If we could recall the brightest luminaries of painting, could they do justice to Shakespeare? Was Raphael himself as great a genius in his art as the author of *Macbeth?* and who could draw Falstaff, but the writer of Falstaff?"[25] Charles Lamb was no Walpole, but his reaction was similar. "What injury (short of the theatres) did not Boydell's 'Shakespeare Gallery' do me with Shakespeare!" Lamb later wrote. "To have Opie's Shakespeare, Northcote's Shakespeare, light-headed Fuseli's Shakespeare, heavy-headed Romney's Shakespeare, wooden-headed West's Shakespeare (though he did the best in 'Lear'), deaf-headed Reynolds' Shakespeare, instead of my, and everybody's Shakespeare. To be tied down to an authentic face of Juliet! To have Imogen's portrait! To confine the illimitable!"[26] For better or worse, however, the Shakespeare Gallery influenced the taste of a steadily widening reading public for many years. It determined their visual conception of Shakespeare's characters and scenes as fatefully as Bowdler's edition, published in 1818, formed their notion of what he wrote.

Boydell's first rival in commissioning and then exhibiting pictures intended to illustrate books with literary content was Thomas Macklin, printer and publisher at 192 Fleet Street, who issued the *Poets' Gallery* (1788–1799) and the *Illustrated Bible* (1791–1800).[27] The English poets whose works were illustrated were Shakespeare, Collins, Gray, Pope, Shenstone, Thomson, Somerville, Spenser, Chaucer, Mrs. Barbauld, Gay, Jerningham, Mallet, Prior, and Goldsmith —a selection thoroughly consonant with the taste of the times, as a comparison of Dr. Johnson's own gallery in his *Lives of the Poets* shows. (Milton, Prior, Young, Dryden, Jago, and Parnell were represented in the text, but not engraved.) The list of artists, fifteen in all, was headed by Reynolds, Gainsborough, Fuseli, Opie, Stothard, and Loutherbourg, who also did twenty-two of the seventy-one pictures required for the *Illustrated Bible.* In December 1794 the students of the Royal Academy chipped in a shilling apiece to take a newspaper advertisement thanking both Macklin and Boy-

dell "for the privilege granted them to go into the picture Galleries without expence."[28]

When the Swiss-born artist Henry Fuseli was about to finish his commission for Boydell, the publisher John Johnson engaged him to paint thirty pictures to be engraved for a projected de luxe edition of Milton, with annotations by William Cowper.[29] But when Cowper suffered one of his periods of insanity and Boydell protested that he was planning his own edition of Milton, Johnson dropped the scheme. Fuseli, however, continued to cherish the idea of the paintings if not of the book. For the latter there was no urgent need, because twenty-one editions of Milton were published between 1788 and 1801 alone; but pictures illustrating Milton were not similarly overabundant. During the 1790s, therefore, supported by annual subsidies of £50 from each of six friends who expected either to receive one of the pictures or to share in the profits from the gallery, Fuseli worked steadily on, eventually completing forty paintings. The resulting Gallery of the Miltonic Sublime opened on 20 May 1799, in the Royal Academy's former room in Pall Mall. The admission fee was the customary shilling, and the sixpenny catalogue included the relevant passages from Milton's poems. Evidently, some people did not buy it. "On one occasion," says Fuseli's early biographer, "a coarse-looking man left his party, and coming up to him, said, 'Pray, Sir, what is that picture?' Fuseli answered, 'It is the bridging of Chaos: the subject from Milton.'—'No wonder,' said he, 'I did not know it, for I never read Milton, but I will.'—'I advise you not,' said Fuseli, 'for you will find it a d——d tough job.'"[30]

Fuseli's receipts the first month were only £117, and they declined thereafter. When the show closed at the end of July, he had sustained a net loss. But he reopened the next season (21 March 1800) with seven additional pictures. Even holding a dinner of the Academy on the gallery premises two months later failed to stimulate interest, and the show closed for good on 18 July, unable to compete, as Fuseli wrote, with the topical panorama of Seringapatam (Chapter 10) and "the posies of Portraits & knicknacks of Somerset-house."[31]

Also in the "gallery" competition during the 1790s was the fashionable miniature painter Robert Bowyer, who enlisted the usual roster of artists, including West, Loutherbourg, and Smirke, for a sumptuously illustrated edition of Hume's *History of England.*[32] In 1792 he opened a gallery on the top floor of his house in Pall Mall. The edition got only as far as the year 1688. Its nine heavy folio volumes are said to have cost Bowyer

£30,000, and in 1805 he followed Boydell down the lottery path, with what success is not known.[33]

The last in this melancholy procession of expensive and doomed attempts to enlist showmanship in the service of art was Robert John Thornton's Temple of Flora.[34] Thornton, the son of the well-known wit and man-about-the-theatre Bonnell Thornton, who had conceived the idea of the Society of Sign-Painters exhibition, was a botanist and physician who commissioned paintings from Opie, Raeburn, and others to illustrate his *New Illustration of the Sexual System of Linnaeus,* a ponderous folio issued in parts between 1799 and 1807. To stimulate subscriptions to the third and last portion, entitled *The Temple of Flora, or Garden of Nature, Being Picturesque Plates of the Choicest Flowers of Europe, Asia, Africa, and America,* Thornton opened in 1804, at 49 New Bond Street, an exhibition called successively the Botanical Exhibition and the Temple of Flora (not to be confused with the late amusement place in the Westminster Bridge Road). Here, in an indoor bower composed of "backgrounds expressive of the country of each flower" and "agreeably decorated with birds, in the attitudes of life, butterflies, transparencies, etc.," he displayed thirty-one paintings from which engravings had been or were to be made. Most were studies of flowers, but there also were allegorical subjects (*Flora Dispensing Her Favours on the Earth, Cupid Inspiring Plants with Love*) and portraits of eminent botanists, including Erasmus Darwin, Linnaeus, and Thornton himself.

In 1805 the exhibition, now called the Linnaean Gallery, was moved to Thornton's house in Manchester Square. Neither the pictures, which represented an early burst of lush romanticism, nor the carefully contrived setting sufficed to rescue Thornton, who had invested the whole of his patrimony in the *New Illustrations* with what Geoffrey Grigson describes as its "splendid plates, splendid calligraphic title pages, splendid typography, splendid expanses of Whatman's wove [paper]." In 1811 Thornton too received permission to hold a lottery, this one called the Royal Botanical Lottery. ("BRITONS!" cried the advertisement, "join Hand and Heart in promoting the ARTS and SCIENCES of your COUNTRY, by the IMMEDIATE PURCHASE OF A TICKET".) To promote the sale of the two-guinea tickets the pictures were again displayed, this time at the European Museum. When the public still proved reluctant to buy, further inducements were added, such as prints of the Emperor of Russia, the hero of the moment following Napoleon's retreat from Moscow. But all was to no avail. The drawing was held finally in May 1813, but the lottery was a fiasco, and Thornton spent the rest of his life in poverty.[35]

Although most of the men and women who paid their shillings to see the pictures in these several galleries were in no position to buy the expensive books for which they were commissioned—each part of *The Temple of Flora,* for example, cost twenty-five shillings and the whole, some fifty guineas—their visits would certainly have enlarged their experience of art. In addition, the exhibitions, which unlike the Royal Academy shows had no fixed term but continued as long as the public patronized them, were an important half-way station on the road to permanent, year-round art exhibitions, a goal to be first realized in the National Gallery.

D3✳E3

Eventually disastrous though they were, the gallery ventures of Boydell, Fuseli, Bowyer, Macklin, and Thornton were a prominent aspect of an expanding and prosperous London trade, that of printselling, whose shop windows were often called "the poor man's picture gallery." Print shops were no novelty on the London scene. Ned Ward saw them at the beginning of the eighteenth century in his "Loitering Perambulation round the outside of St. Pauls," where he "came to a Picture-sellers Shop, where as many Smutty Prints were staring the Church in the Face, as a Learned Debauchee ever found in Aretine's Postures. I observ'd there were more People gazing at these loose Fancies of some Leacherous Graver, than I could see reading of Sermons at the Stalls of all the Neighbouring Booksellers."[36] It need not be supposed that all the window displays were of the same character; here, as usual, Ward saw only what his compulsive rake's eye prompted him to see. In general, the stock of early eighteenth-century print shops consisted chiefly of engraved copies of old and modern masters, topographical scenes, portraits, and other subjects appealing to cultivated taste. As painters, especially portraitists like Kneller, came to realize how useful engravings could be in attracting new commissions, they saw to it that mezzotints of recently completed works were displayed in the shop windows. The increased timeliness of these free sidewalk shows naturally enhanced their attractiveness to the public. In addition, the passage in 1735 of an act to protect copyright in pictures, which put the print publishing business on a more solid footing, encouraged more people to enter it, and so the number of shops grew.

One popular specialized branch of the trade was that of satirical prints. By Hogarth's time, toward the middle of the eighteenth century, caricatures were already well on the way to replacing ballads as a common weapon of political controversy. It was Hogarth's peculiar genius, of course, which created a mass market for satirical and moralistic prints in general. His own, priced as low as sixpence and illustrating contemporary London life with unmatched realistic detail, appealed to an audience much larger than had been affected by art of any kind since the churches lost their picture-stories. With him, as Sir John Rothenstein has said, "art became not a plutocratic luxury but spontaneous expression. And it is not too much to say that he created, and for the first time since the Reformation, a subject-matter understood both by artist and layman, a circumstance which powerfully favours a flourishing condition of the arts."[37] No one needed a classical education to understand the moral and satirical themes of eighteenth-century prints in the Hogarthian vein. But pictorial satire on political and social themes appealed to the sophisticated as well as the man on the street. It was the most democratic form of art in eighteenth-century Britain. And the fortunate coincidence of inventive geniuses like Gillray and Rowlandson with events worthy of their mordant attention resulted in an unprecedented torrent of prints by the time of the French Revolution and the Napoleonic Wars.

Thus, to all the other places of public entertainment in London were added numerous printsellers' windows, which constantly drew appreciative audiences of men laughing their fill at the latest impudent pictorial lampoon and explaining its finer points to their more lumpish companions. The caricaturists themselves drew spirited drawings of these sidewalk assemblies. Of such house advertisements, the best known is Gillray's *Very Slippy-Weather* (1808), showing the St. James's Street shop of Mrs. Hannah Humphrey, who had a fortunate monopoly on the artist's services.

Caricature shops were part of the daily round of the man of fashion, a place to meet friends and exchange gossip as well as to inspect the newest prints. It was natural, therefore, that the proprietors should look upon their salesrooms proper as a kind of exhibition for which the many-paned window served as an advertisement. As early as 1773, Matt Darly of the Macaroni Print Shop, 39 Strand, anticipated the Boy-

dells and Macklins of a later day by holding a show of the original drawings for 233 of the prints he sold.[38] For a decade beginning in the mid-eighties two of the largest shops, seeking to reap some profit from the crowds enjoying the free show outside, enticed them with comprehensive exhibitions of their stock, and sometimes of original drawings, to which they charged a shilling admission. (One must allow, however, for the possibility that they were not so much interested in actual cash profit as in keeping out the free lookers. The admission charged may have been imposed in self-defense, as it had been at the regular art exhibitions.) For a number of years the radical William Holland, first in Drury Lane and then at 50 Oxford Street, advertised that "Holland's Caricature Rooms are now open, presenting a general Exhibition of all the distinguished Caricatures that have been published the last Ten Years, with many original Paintings and Drawings of high celebrity."[39] In 1790 a change in the wording at the bottom of Holland's prints reflected the impact of events on the trade: "In Holland's Caricature Exhibition Rooms may be seen the largest Collection in Europe of Political and other Humorous Prints with those Published in Paris on the French Revolution."[40]

While some shops charged admission to their exhibitions, others, such as Aitken's Exhibition Room in Castle Street, Leicester Square, advertised that admittance was gratis.[41] Not for nothing did the printsellers conduct their business in the midst of a city thickly dotted with catchpenny shows. At one juncture W. Humphrey, at his shop at 227 Strand, used as bait a "Museum of Natural and Artificial Curiosities" to which every purchaser of a shilling print was admitted free.[42] In Piccadilly, S. W. Fores added spice to his caricature gallery ("the Compleatest Collection in the Kingdom") by exhibiting both a six-foot model of the guillotine and the head and hand of Count Struenzee,* a Danish statesman who had been executed for treason in 1772.[43]

⁂

While attendance swelled at the exhibitions of paintings, workers and dealers in the subsidiary arts also found a profitable sideline in showing their wares for an admission fee. Among these were the stained glass artists, whose several displays enjoyed a vogue that entitled them for a while to be mentioned in the same breath with more famous or customary London sights. (Samuel Foote's play *The Cozeners*, 1774: "I promised precisely at twelve to call on Lady Frolic, to take a turn

* Presumably these were of wax. At least, waxen replicas of the same kind were exhibited in London in 1778 and 1782 as a bonus to purchasers of controversial books by Philip Thicknesse, the writer who had "exposed" the automaton chess player. (George, VI, 641).

in Kensington Gardens, to see both the [art] exhibitions, the stain'd glass, dwarf, giant, and Cox's museum.") In the last quarter of the century three craftsmen dominated this field, Thomas Jervais and Mr. and Mrs. James Pearson.[44]

Jervais held several exhibitions. In one of the earliest, at Exeter Change in 1772, he displayed fifteen works, including portraits of contemporary figures and two compositions after Teniers, *Smokers* and *Boys Blowing Up a Bladder*. Seven years later crowds came to see his windows for New College chapel, Oxford, after designs by Reynolds. Walpole admired the Nativity scene that Jervais had adapted from Correggio by way of Reynolds: "The room being darkened," he wrote, "and the sun shining through the transparencies, realizes the illumination that is supposed to be diffused from the glory, and has a magic effect."[45] Unfortunately, when they were installed at Oxford, none of the windows proved as dramatically effective as they had been in Pall Mall.

Although the New College windows and the large window of the Resurrection he made after a design by Benjamin West for St. George's Chapel, Windsor, were Jervais's most celebrated productions, at his shows he also offered for sale a variety of other subjects. One display had something for almost every taste: the Madonna, Hebe, nymphs bathing, a fortune teller, several pictures of cattle, an assortment of frost scenes "with and without snow," a sea storm, a ship on fire, an episode in *Gil Blas,* an angel delivering St. Peter from prison.[46]

Jervais's chief competitors, James Pearson and his wife, Eglington Margaret, exhibited their work at a succession of locations: the Pantheon in 1779, the Society of Arts' former rooms in the Strand in 1780, and the Pearsons' house in Great Newport Street, Long Acre, in 1790. One of their best-known windows, subsequently installed in Salisbury Cathedral, portrayed the raising of the brazen serpent in the wilderness. In the 1790 show appeared life-size portraits of the Prince of Wales, after Barry, and of Charles James Fox, after Reynolds. But the Pearsons' particular forte was making glass copies of Old Masters—Carlo Marotti's *Salutation of the Virgin,* Teniers's *Temptation of St. Anthony,* and Raphael's *Transfiguration* and *Descent from the Cross.*

Others besides workers in stained glass benefited from the burgeoning public enthusiasm for the fine arts. Exhibitions of celebrated paintings copied in needlework likewise sought to cater to this taste. Needlework had inherited some of the dignity attached to its ancestor-art of tapestry making, and like wax modeling it was a form of creative activity that enjoyed considerable popularity among eighteenth-century ladies, some forty of whom exhibited needlework pictures at both the Incorporated and the Free Societies of Artists between 1761 and 1791.[47] Among these artists was Lady Aylesbury, the wife of Henry Conway, whose pictures in worsted Walpole praised in his *Anecdotes of Painting.* But although persons of Lady Aylesbury's social rank would not have been involved in commercial shows, less blue-blooded artists of the needle were. One was a Miss Atkinson, whose work could be viewed, about 1787, at successive addresses in Golden Square, Bloomsbury, and Holborn; another was a Miss Thomson, who in 1802 exhibited copies in wool of pictures by Carracci, Titian, Van Dyck, Reynolds, Gainsborough, Opie, and others at 17 Old Bond Street.[48] The needlewoman who soon dominated the field, however, was Mary Linwood. Although she first exhibited in London in 1776, the gallery which made her name a household word was not established in Leicester Square until 1806. Accordingly, we shall delay our visit until a later chapter.

At least one practitioner of xylopyrography, as it would be called in the next century, exhibited at this time: a lady in reduced circumstances named Mrs. Nelson, who in 1788 took a room next to the Lyceum to display an assortment of drawings made by a hot poker on wood. These included copies of paintings by Guido, Carracci, Teniers, Murillo, Claude, and Reynolds. "They appear," said an advertisement hopefully, "like Original Sketches of those Great Masters."[49]

Associated in another way with the progress of taste in the eighteenth century were the constructions made of shells, a reflection of the Augustan fad for grottoes that was definitively typified by Pope's subterranean showplace at Twickenham. Between 1745 and 1747 the Golden Head coffeehouse, near Buckingham House, boasted (in its garden?) a piece of artificial rock-and-shellwork twenty-six feet round and six feet high, topped by a temple from which various avenues led away, with fountains playing and beds of coral growing. At a joiner's shop next to the Serjeants' Inn coffeehouse in 1752, one could see shells and other petrifactions assembled into a cavern, palaces, castles, gardens, walks, statues, cascades, and even a representation of the sea.[50]

The longest running of all such fossil-and-shell exhibitions was a side attraction at the Tower of London for which the yeomen of the guard acted as touts. Going down a path from the Tower proper in 1786,

23. Darly's Macaroni Print Shop
(engraving by E. Topham, 1772).

24. Humphrey's Print Shop:
T. Lane's *Honi Soit Qui Mal Y
Pense,* 1821. The crowd is looking at some of the many satirical
prints evoked by the scandal-
filled trial of Queen Caroline and
her frustrated attempt to join her
husband, George IV, at his coronation.

25. Humphrey's Print Shop: James Gillray's *Very Slippy-Weather,* 1808. All the prints displayed in the window are Gillray's.

Sophie von la Roche paid her sixpence and was admitted to "the shellwork of some honest lass, who by this means helps to feed her poor mother's many children. This thought in itself would have lent beauty to the work, had it not been so pretty and varied in any case. It is hard to know which to admire more—the charm of thousands of shells or the industry with which the good creature composes lovely buildings, half-relief pictures, birds and flowers. . . . Miss Phillips is very modest and simple with all this. The inscription on the wall, where she applied a ground of black shells on which she announced in white ones that there was something to see, we thought a clever invention."[51] The impressionable and sentimental Sophie was obviously easy to please. Still, an attraction that lasted forty years in one location must have existed on something more substantial than sightseers' charitable impulses.

It was, as Sophie said, a question of which to admire more, the intrinsic "charm" of a show or the sheer patient labor that had been devoted to the exhibits. Certainly this was true also of the assemblages of miniature objects that were shown from time to time. Whether they were done well was less to the point than that they were done at all. So it must have been in 1745 at a watchmaker's shop near the New Exchange, where one could inspect through a magnifying glass a complete set of dining room furniture from chairs and table to two dozen dishes, twenty dozen plates, thirty dozen spoons, all contained in a single cherry stone; a landau, including four passengers, a coachman, two footmen, and a postilion, the entire equipage capable of being drawn by a flea; a flea attached to a chain made of two hundred links; a camel that confounded Prophecy by passing through the head of a medium-sized needle; and scissors so tiny that six of the kind could be wrapped up in a fly's wing.[52]

These feats of miniaturization were among the standard curios which found their way into virtuosi's cabinets and, as here, into public exhibitions. In another category of reductive art, with a different class of subjects and made to a different scale, were architectural models. Tradescant possessed a number of such objects, including models of the Tower of Strasbourg and the Holy Sepulcher; a model of the latter was also among Du Puy's collection of oddments. Such models of buildings and cities constituted the most numerous class of reduced-scale objects shown in London exhibitions, and their popularity never waned. At their best, their foundations rested in two worlds—the world of utility and that of art. At their most typical, they were both a curio pure and simple—a demonstration of an artisan's deftness, like a frigate assembled in a bottle, but hardly more—and an important aid to the art of architecture and the science of engineering. There were two main reasons for their perennial attraction, apart from sheer admiration of the artificer's patient skill: they were three-dimensional, and thus superior, for representational purposes, to flat pictures; and, while incorporating great detail, they compressed much into a small space, permitting one to envision large buildings or whole topographical areas more comprehensively than did pictures.

Architectural models, either of buildings already in existence or of projected ones, were late in coming to England. An extant papier-mâché model of the church of St. Maclou, Rouen, dates from about 1432, and Vasari and other chroniclers give considerable evidence of models' being made in Italy from the fourteenth century onward. It may have been through the recommendation (1624) of Sir Henry Wotton, stationed in Venice as a diplomat, that English architects adopted the model as a means of envisioning what a finished building would look like and of foreseeing—and solving—difficulties in its construction. Wren made a model of Pembroke College chapel, Cambridge, in 1663, and in the same year exhibited one of the Sheldonian Theatre, Oxford, before the Royal Society. Later he made models of Emmanuel and Trinity Colleges, Cambridge, of Greenwich Hospital, and a whole series of the new St. Paul's.[53]

At this same time, architectural and topographical models were becoming popular exhibition pieces, wholly apart from their professional uses. A government notice in 1682 included displayers of "models," not further described, among the "Mountebanks, Ballad Singers, Newshawkers, Scotch Pedlers" and other showmen who had to be licensed to ply their trade.[54] Five years later could be seen, at the newly built Exeter Change, an imported model of Versailles palace, twenty-four by eighteen feet, made of copper "gilt over with silver and gold."[55] The gardens and fountains that surrounded the palace must have been of compelling interest to everyone who was aware of Le Nôtre's recent work for the French king. Equally timely would have been the models of the Dutch palaces of Britain's king-by-adoption, William III. In 1701, at the White Hart inn facing the Haymarket, certain "outlandish men" (foreigners) exhibited models of Loo, Keswick, and Hunslaerdike.[56]

Henceforth, models thread their way through the history of London exhibitions in two streams, one composed of faithful miniature reproductions, the other of mere curiosities, devoid of authenticity or power to instruct. Specimens of the latter were found at the Chelsea Bun House, which, as we have seen, had a cut-paper model of St. Mary Redcliffe, Bristol, as well as one of itself.[57] In 1741, at a butcher's shop near Hyde Park Corner, patrons gazed upon a five-foot-high Tower of Babylon, made entirely of cards, "neither sew'd, stitch'd, nor pasted."[58] At mid-century Adams's Museum in the Kingsland Road displayed a model of Lord Burlington's seat at Chiswick made of "Baccopipe Clay."[59] A "Tower of Mark Antony built by Herod the Great," five feet high and equipped with 2,500 figures made of enameled china, was at the Golden Head, Haymarket, in 1756.[60]

In lack of particulars, it is often hard to differentiate between such oddities and models in conventional materials that were meant to be faithful representations in miniature, although one probably may rely on the advertisers' calling attention to any peculiarities of material or construction if they were present. Among the displays not distinguished in this manner was the elaborate model of Amsterdam, between twenty and thrity feet long and twenty feet wide, that was shown at the Bell Yard, Fleet Street, in 1710, "with all the Churches, Chappels, Stadt house, Hospitals, noble Buildings, Streets, Trees, Walks, Avenues, with the Sea, Shipping, Sluices, Rivers, Canals, &c., most exactly built to admiration."[61]

The subjects of these eighteenth-century exhibition models add a trifle to our awareness of contemporary popular interests. Scriptural sites were frequently represented in the first half of the century; there were models of the Temple of Solomon, thirteen feet high and eighty in circumference, with 2,000 windows and 7,000 pillars (1729),[62] the Tabernacle of Moses (1747), and the Holy Sepulcher (1752).[63] From the 1740s onward, models of English buildings and cities were in particular evidence: the Mansion House while it was being constructed (1741–1742), the Radcliffe Camera, Oxford, and the Queen's Pavilion in Richmond Gardens (both 1753).[64] One Signor Grimani, "Professor of Mathematicks," exhibited a model of London and Westminster at the Fantoccini Room, Panton Street, Haymarket, in 1774.[65] As Bath basked in its reputation as the most fashionable watering place in the kingdom, it too was depicted to stay-at-home Londoners. The Circus there was shown at Spring Gardens in 1782,[66] and in 1790 there were two competing models of the town as a whole, one at the Pantheon, the other at Spring Gardens. The latter had

the ample dimensions of twenty-five by fifteen feet, but visitors still were urged to bring opera glasses so that they could appreciate the detail.[67]

After mid-century, the fashion in models also turned toward the continent. A wood-and-pasteboard representation of Paris, eighteen feet square, with 50,000 houses as well as 20,000 trees fashioned from green silk—surely an impressive sight if it lived up to its billing—was in James Street, Haymarket, in 1764.[68] Another Paris model, of wood only and on a scale of 62 feet to the inch, could be seen at Exeter Change in 1769.[69] When the French royal family were imprisoned at the Tour du Temple in 1793, a model of that building was immediately placed on show at 1 Rupert Street.[70]

Although the Alps would not figure prominently in English imaginations for several more decades, a model of the region, twenty feet long, six wide, and eight high, was on display at a cabinetmaker's in Piccadilly about 1770.[71] More attuned to the cultural interests of the moment were the several models of Italian cities and buildings, among them Signor Grimani's Rome and Venice (Pantheon, 1788)[72] and a model of Rome that was cofeatured with the circus at Bath in 1782.[73]

Like most objects that figured in eighteenth-century commercial exhibitions, these models were not attached to any permanent show. They appeared in some suitable rented room, were advertised, attracted as much custom as they could, and then vanished from view. Only one established London exhibition was devoted principally to models. This was the Classical Exhibition, which first appears in the records in 1778 at 24 St. Albans Street, Pall Mall: a collection of cork models of sites associated with classical literature, the twenty-year labor of a native of St. Pancras parish, Richard Dubourg. In April 1785 a miscalculated experiment with a Vesuvius effect started a fire which destroyed the whole show. A public subscription was taken for the unfortunate proprietor, who became a pensioner of the Royal Academy.[74]

In 1798 a new collection of cork models was at 17 Duke Street, Manchester Square. By what seems to be no more than a coincidence, the proprietor again was named Dubourg; he was said to be a Frenchman who had lived in Italy for nine years. Benjamin Silliman was enthralled by his "perfect copies of some of the most admired ruins of antiquity." To the models themselves, made from cork with a little help from cement and paint, Dubourg added theatrical effects in the best manner of London shows as they were developing

* It is surprising that one other kind of model seldom figures in eighteenth-century exhibition records. Although warfare was sufficiently present in Englishmen's minds throughout the period—this was, after all, the time when Corporal Trim built miniature earthworks on the bowling green of Tristram Shandy's Uncle Toby—they were not provided with models of fortifications or battlefields. One of the few references to such objects is in Von Uffenbach's journal and it is disparaging at that: "We drove to a bookseller's in Common [Covent] Garden, who had made great boast in the news-sheets of a model of a fortification, which was to be shown for half a crown. But when we came in, we perceived that it was not worth sixpence, for it was a model of a most ordinary kind, made of wood and lacking proportion and accuracy." (*London in 1710 . . .*, London, 1934, pp. 78–79.)

at the turn of the century. The cascade of Tivoli was represented pouring down the precipice, "with copious foam and spray," by mechanical means which doubtless owed something to Vauxhall Gardens.[75] Undeterred by his predecessor's misfortune, the second Dubourg, as we saw in the last chapter, also put on a sensational volcanic eruption. This exhibition continued for a number of years at various locations, and the name Dubourg itself would be retained by another kind of show well into the Victorian era.*

Though architectural and topographical models do not appear in histories of eighteenth-century culture, their influence on the English imagination was by no means negligible. As would be true also of the panoramas that were yet to come, inspecting the models of Paris and the Alps, of Roman ruins and the buildings mentioned in Scripture was a substitute for the wide-ranging travel that was denied to most. In addi-

tion models provided a useful visual supplement to books. It was with good reason that Wordsworth praised the mind-expanding service of the model maker, a "mechanic artist" who represented

By scale exact, in model, wood or clay
From shading colours also borrowing help,
Some miniature of famous spots and things,—
Domestic or the boast of foreign realms;
The Firth of Forth, and Edinburgh throned
On crags, fit empress of that mountain land;
St. Peter's Church; or, more aspiring aim,
In microscopic vision, Rome itself;
Or else, perhaps, some rural haunt,—the Falls
Of Tivoli; and, high upon that steep,
The Temple of the Sibyl! every tree
Through all the landscape, tuft, stone, scratch minute,
And every cottage, lurking in the rocks—
All that the traveller sees when he is there.[76]

The Eidophusikon

9

Exhibitors of moving pictures must often have regretted that no technical advance had as yet made it possible to bathe their scenes in appropriate lighting. The illusion created by peepshows had long been enhanced by concealed candles or oil lamps which lighted the miniature paintings or colored engravings from the front or the transparencies from behind. Why could not the principle of the lighted peepshow be adapted for displays on at least as large a scale as that of the mechanical theatres, with an audience of scores, perhaps even hundreds, rather than the mere handful (at most) of spectators possible for the peepshow?

The magic lantern with its scenes painted on glass "sliders," which suggested in part the direction such a development might take, was already in existence.[1] Pepys recorded seeing one in 1666, and among the many souvenirs the Six Nations sachems took back with them from their London visit in 1710 was a "Magick Lanthorn with Pictures."[2] Although there is some evidence that wandering showmen carried small magic lanterns with them as an alternative to the more familiar peepshow, the lack of a sufficiently powerful light source prevented the device from becoming a general public entertainment. Instead, it remained for many years nothing more than a domestic toy specializing in horrific effects. Edward Phillips's *The New World of English Words* (1696) defined the "magic lanthorn" as "a certain small Optical Macheen, that shews by a gloomy Light upon a white Wall, Spectres and Monsters so hideous that he who knows not the Secret, believes it to be perform'd by Magic Art."

From the mid-1770s, for some reason, interest in the lantern became more lively. Though records of performances before audiences outside the home are lacking, the existence of some sort of vogue is indicated by the facts that in 1775 an exhibition of caricatures at the Great Room, Panton Street, was called the Magick Lantern,[3] and that satirical printmakers, always alert for timely topics, were repeatedly using the magic lantern as a central accessory.* Between 1774 and 1809 at least half a dozen caricatures appeared which prominently featured it.[4] It is tempting to think that this increased interest had some connection with the invention in 1782 of the Argand lamp, which, by replacing the customary oil-lamp wick with a hollow incandescent cylinder, provided a source of concentrated light such as was required to project images on a wall or screen from a moderate distance.

A second type of optical entertainment which depended on lighting was the shadow show, otherwise known as the Schattenspiel, Italian shadows, or Ombres Chinoises.[5] The principle behind it was illustrated at the end of Ben Jonson's play *A Tale of a Tub* (1633), when, at a private merrymaking, a cooper projected shadows from an empty barrel across the top of which was stretched oiled paper with cut-out silhouettes pasted on it. Behind the paper was a light whose heat caused it to revolve, and as it did so, the cooper "interpreted" each of the five tableaux the silhouettes represented. A similar kind of show was occasionally brought to England by the Savoyards. At Bartholomew Fair in 1737, for example, could be seen

* One of these caricatures (on the trial of Warren Hastings, 1788) was titled *Galante Show:* a term which now was joining "raree show" as a common token of disparagement. The 1788 use antedates by thirty-three years the first cited in the *Oxford English Dictionary,* and the term probably is much older. It seemingly was derived from the old French *galer,* "to make a show."

26. *The Magic Lantern* (engraving by C. Williams, 1822). Another political satire: the mandarin is George IV, flanked by several political figures of the day. The man with the sword is the Duke of Wellington.

a shadow play "by the best Masters from Italy . . . which have not been seen here these Twenty years."[6] But these were isolated instances, and the shadow show was introduced (or reintroduced, if we count Jonson's play) into London indoor entertainment by different routes. About the middle of the century, the celebrated fencing master Domenico Angelo, father of the Henry Angelo who has already been quoted in these pages, saw a little pictorial drama, entitled *Le tableau mouvant,* at a carnival in Venice. "He was so delighted with its effect," says the son, "the scenes being painted as transparencies, and the figures being all black profiles, that he constructed a stage on the same plan, and it was greatly admired by Gainsborough, Wilson, and other English landscape painters."[7] At the request of the Princess Dowager, he and Giovanni Girolami Servandoni, the master illusionist of the French stage, who was in London to produce the fireworks celebrating the treaty of Aix-la-Chapelle and to design scenery for Covent Garden, produced such a show for the young princes and their guests. Inspired by this novelty, David Garrick introduced moving shadows at the end of his new and, as it proved, popular pantomime *Harlequin's Invasion* (1759). According to the original script, a concluding

transparency represented "the Powers of Pantomime going to Attack Mount Parnassus. A Storm comes on [and] destroys the Fleet."[8] It was evidently then that, in the younger Angelo's words, "visionary figures were seen flitting across, upon the plan of the *Tableau Mouvant.*" The "visionary figures" were jointed cut-outs worked with strings or sticks by manipulators. As the little genre developed, the unseen showmen came to speak lines for the figures and even burst into song. Thus the shadow play was a hybrid entertainment deriving from both the puppet show and the magic-lantern principle, with (in the latter case) the relation between the audience, the light source, and the translucent curtain or reflective wall or sheet reversed.

As a separate entertainment, the Chinese shadows, as they were usually called at this time, were introduced to London in 1775, after successful engagements in France. An Italian showman, originally named Ambrogio but rechristened Ambroise for French and English audiences, joined with the English impresarios Brunn and Breslaw to present at the Great Room, Panton Street, what "a contemporary paragraphist" described as "absolutely the greatest Amusements that ever were exhibited in the Metropolis."[9] For the unusually high admission price of five shillings the audience saw seventeen scenes, the most memorable of which was a representation of a shipwreck accompanied by effects of thunder and lightning. They evidently got their money's worth, because during the show's second season in Panton Street (1776–77) a rival company operated at the Great Room, St. Albans Street.[10]

Then Philip Astley, the future impresario of the hippodrama, added shadow shows to his popular variety entertainment, first at Ambroise's location after the original company ended its season, then at 22 Piccadilly, and finally, from March 1779, at his permanent headquarters, the Amphitheatre Riding House at the foot of Westminster Bridge.[11] Here the Chinese shadows remained a standard feature of the bill for a decade. An early Astley's program is probably typical of them all, a series of brief comic scenes played out in silhouette: Diversions of a Certain Public Garden (in Paris); The Beggar and His Wife; The Humourous Courtship, or The Travelling Knifegrinder; The Sportsman, or The Duck-Hunting; The Weaver, or Militia Man, a Comic Opera; The Rope Dancer; The Cat, or The Downfall of the Porridge Pot; The Lion Catchers; The Traveller Benighted; The Broken Bridge, or The Insolent Carpenter Rewarded; The Shipwreck; The Metamorphoses of a Magician; and a Hornpipe "in a Surprising Manner." Also on the bill were a conjuring horse, a human conjuror, and a Signor Rossignol (a *nom de théâtre,* obviously) who played a concert on a stringless violin and imitated bird songs.[12]

In retrospect it is clear that during the 1770s a number of separate little genres were existing side by side in the London show business, only awaiting someone who would put them together. There were, first of all, the magic lantern and the Chinese shadows, both depending for their effect upon strong light—in the one case to illuminate and enlarge scenes painted on glass slides, in the other to illuminate transparencies which served as the illusory background for sketches performed by shadow figures. Then there was the increasingly elaborate use of transparencies not only during public celebrations and at the pleasure gardens, but—most important for present purposes—in the theatre, especially the pantomime.* In these same years, the several exhibitions of Jervais's and the Pearsons' stained glass also dramatized the spectacular possibilities of light flowing through a painted, translucent medium. Finally, there were the clockwork mechanical theatres. Some of them, descendants of the original moving pictures of Addison's time, were still being shown at fairs and once in a while in London

rooms. Now a new wave of interest in mechanical figures and scenes was stimulated to some extent by the fame of Cox's Museum of jeweled automatons and, more directly, by the Spectacle Mécanique through which Jaquet-Droz publicized the clockwork marvels his family manufactured in Switzerland.

From 1770 onward, at an inn at Versailles and then in the palace itself, another maker of automatons, François Dominique Séraphin, displayed a shadow show in which the silhouetted figures were activated by clockwork rather than by concealed human agents. Included in its repertory were such scenes as "Le Chasse aux canards," "Le Magicien Rothomago," "Le Pont cassé," "L'Embarras du ménage," and "Arlequin corsair."[13] The program, in fact, bore a striking resemblance to those of the unmechanized Ombres Chinoises. Although Séraphin's show seems never to have come to England, it may well have been seen at Versailles by Philippe Jacques de Loutherbourg, the distinguished artist who was to synthesize the clockwork picture, the transparency, and one of the principles of the magic lantern and the Chinese shadows—the concentration of lighting in a confined space—into a new and memorable kind of show. Loutherbourg, in any case, had been acquainted with Servandoni (who died in 1766) and would have seen many of the sixty spectacular productions he mounted at the Paris Opéra, replete with clever mechanical contrivances, fountains, and movable colored sources of light. There is every reason, therefore, to believe Loutherbourg's statement, in 1781, that the Eidophusikon he introduced to London in that year realized a dream of twenty years' standing.[14] But it might not have come to fruition except for two fortunate circumstances: his acquaintance with John Joseph Merlin and Henri-Louis Jaquet-Droz, master mechanicians, about which we know nothing beyond the bare report that it occurred, and his long experience as London's premier scene designer.

Loutherbourg came to London late in 1771 as a man of thirty-one.[15] Born in Strasbourg, he had already acquired considerable reputation as an artist in France, where he first exhibited at the Salon in 1763 and, though several years under age for the honor, was elected in 1767 to the Académie Royale. As a painter of landscapes, battles, and sea scenes he won numerous commissions and the public praise of Diderot. Despite this early and continuing success, however, he left his large family behind in Paris and, armed with a letter to Garrick at Drury Lane from Jean Monnet, manager of the Opéra Comique, sought a new career in the English theatre. He arrived at a lucky moment. During

* Transparencies had been employed in the theatre as early as Inigo Jones's masques in the first half of the seventeenth century. The most spectacular of all Restoration plays, Purcell's *The Fairy Queen* (1692), an operatic version of *A Midsummer Night's Dream* adapted by Elkanah Settle, had a memorable transparent scene of a Chinese garden. Transparent scenes were introduced to the mass audience at Bartholomew Fair in another of Settle's productions, *The Siege of Troy,* which portrayed the burning of the city. After falling into disuse except on rare occasions, transparencies had become quite common by the 1770s.

his sojourn in Paris several years earlier Garrick had been deeply impressed by Servandoni's theatrical magic and wished to emulate it on his own stage. Nor had he forgotten how much the success of *Harlequin's Invasion* owed to the spectacular effects suggested by the elder Angelo—the Chinese shadows, realized by his principal designer, John French, and the positioning of scarlet, crimson, and bright blue screens, lighted from behind, in such a way as to bathe the sets in a succession of rich colors.[16] Garrick was prepared to pay well for a talent that promised to accomplish great things in the scenic department, even though he prevailed upon Loutherbourg to accept a salary £100 lower than the £600 Servandoni had received at the opera and Loutherbourg at first demanded.

To his new life at Drury Lane—or, rather, this additional one, since he continued his prolific career as a gallery painter, exhibiting at the Royal Academy from 1772 and becoming an Academician in 1781, the year he left Drury Lane—Loutherbourg brought what the changing theatrical taste at the moment most required, a strong bent for pictorial naturalism. The public was now coming to some plays as much for the scenery as for the actors, and in reviews the press devoted more and more space to the spectacle—settings whose fidelity to nature was heightened by imitations of changing light. In the thirty-odd pantomimes and serious dramas Loutherbourg designed, he initiated a revolution whose full effects were to be felt only by the middle of the next century.

From the clockwork moving pictures, he borrowed the idea of adding moving objects—not necessarily flat pasteboard cut-outs but three-dimensional models—to the sets. Thus for the 1773 revival of Thomson's and Mallet's *The Masque of Alfred* he introduced a timely allusion to the naval display attending the king's visit to Spithead a few months earlier, in the form of fully rigged models of ships passing across the rear of the stage. For the final tableau of Henry Woodward's *Queen Mab* (1775) he staged an elaborate miniature regatta with moving barges and rowers keeping time to the music. In Sheridan's "musical entertainment" *The Camp* (1778), capitalizing upon the fad of military dress and drill briefly stirred by the American war, Loutherbourg mounted a climactic scene of army maneuvers employing mechanical figures.

More fundamental, however, were Loutherbourg's innovations in scenery and lighting. For the act drop of a pantomime, *The Wonders of Derbyshire* (1779), he painted a "terrific" landscape of mountains and waterfalls in that most proto-romantic of English counties.

It was so well received that it remained standard equipment at Drury Lane until the house was pulled down in 1791. The scenic innovations revealed when the curtain rose on this and other productions were exciting. Turning decisively away from the artificial perspectives and formal outdoor settings of the baroque tradition, Loutherbourg broke up the back flat and wings into free-standing raking pieces which could be set at various angles, instead of being confined to the rigid parallelism of fixed grooves. The result was a more natural perspective and an illusion of depth such as the London stage had never before seen.

Loutherbourg constantly experimented with the distribution and control of light, liberating this element of production from long uninspired convention and using it to produce effects of chiaroscuro—substituting carefully plotted shadow-and-light patterns for the usual uniform lighting—and to heighten the physical atmosphere of a scene. He made free and imaginative use of transparencies, employed in conjunction with the flexible lighting—screens, reflectors, colored slides—that always fascinated him. In the second of his productions for Garrick, *A Christmas Tale* (1773), he transformed a forest scene from the green of spring to the russet of autumn by pivoting silk screens of different colors before concentrated lights stationed in the wings, and created a fog scene by placing dim lights behind a scrim. In another pantomime, anticipating by many years the "double effect" of Daguerre's Diorama (Chapter 12), he produced the obligatory transformation scene by a wholly novel technique: the "Cavern of Despair" visible when the light fell on the front of the transparency became the Temple of Virtue when the light came from behind and revealed the picture painted on the back of the same transparency. In *The Wonders of Derbyshire,* not content with designing eleven scenes showing particular localities, he varied these by lighting them according to different times of the day.[17]

Loutherbourg's most extravagant spectacle was his last, and the only one he designed for Covent Garden (1785): O'Keeffe's *Omai, or A Trip Round the World,* recalling at a remove of ten years the fame of Captain Cook's well-bred savage and deriving timeliness from the current popularity of published narratives of Cook's voyages.[18] The *Daily Universal Register,* soon to become the *Times,* went all out in its tribute:

The scenery is infinitely beyond any designs or paintings the stage has ever displayed. To the rational mind what can be more entertaining than to contemplate prospects of countries in their natural colourings and tints.—To bring into living action, the customs and manners of distant nations! To see exact representations of their buildings, marine vessels, arms, manufactures, sacrifices, and dresses? These are the materials which form the grand spectacle before us—a spectacle the most magnificent that modern times has produced, and which must fully satisfy not only the mind of the philosopher, but the curiosity of every spectator.

This wrap-up of the world was also a grand recapitulation of all that Loutherbourg had contributed to the theatre. It consisted of no fewer than nineteen scenes, one of which, that of a frozen ocean, was composed of forty-two different pieces. Among the devices and effects were a moon which was reddened by pivoting screens, moving ships, a violent storm, a fire, a flying machine in the form of a fantastic balloon, a verdant spring scene, and a crimson-hued "burning cave of the devil spirit." The topographical locales ranged from London (one scene representing the house where the Learned Pig was showing) to Kamtschatka, the Sandwich Islands, and Otaheite.

But the truly remarkable distillation of Loutherbourg's innovative theatrical career had been placed before the public some years before. During his ten years at Drury Lane he had discovered that he could produce, as theatrical spectacle, effects that as yet no painter had attempted within the confines of a framed picture. As a writer put it in the *European Magazine* in 1782, probably on Loutherbourg's own authority:

He resolved to add motion to resemblance. He knew that the most exquisite painting represented only one moment of time of action, and though we might justly admire the representation of the foaming surge, the rolling ship, the gliding water, or the running steed; yet however well the action was depicted, the heightened look soon perceived the object to be at rest, and the deception lasted no longer than the first glance. He therefore planned a series of moving pictures, which should unite the painter and the mechanic; by giving natural motion to accurate resemblance.[19]

The result of this effort to add the dimension of time (as well as a more convincing illusion of depth) to painting was the "Eidophusikon, or Representation of Nature," alternatively called "Various Imitations of Natural Phenomena, represented by Moving Pictures," which was presented to its first audience on 26 February 1781 at Loutherbourg's house in Lisle Street, Leicester Square.[20] The company was select (130 persons at five shillings each), the setting luxurious.* After gathering in a foyer hung with a number of Loutherbourg's oils, the audience ascended a staircase to a splendid little theatre. "This room," wrote a witness, "is the most beautiful that can be conceived; the panels painted in the richest style with festoons of flowers, musical instruments, etc. heightened in gold; where taste seems to have banished tawdriness and elegance takes complete possession. The seats for the spectators are crimson stuff, and at the upper end is a seat of state between two pillars of the Ionic order, fit for a princely visitor."[21]

What the visitor beheld was a stage—or box—ten feet wide, six high, and eight deep. Here, when the salon was darkened, was performed a series of scenes:

1. Aurora; or, the Effects of the Dawn, with a View of London from Greenwich Park.
2. Noon; the Port of Tangier in Africa, with the distant View of the Rock of Gibraltar and Europa Point.
3. Sunset, a View near Naples.
4. Moonlight, a View in the Mediterranean, the Rising of the Moon contrasted with the Effect of Fire.
5. The Conclusive Scene, a Storm at Sea, and Shipwreck.

This last scene marked one of the first appearances in London shows of a theme that was to become a veritable obsession with English romantic painters and, transposed downward, one of the staple subjects of pictorial entertainments. As we will see, tempests and shipwrecks became as common in the commercial shows as they were on the walls of the Academy exhibitions.

At some point during the run, the Tangier-Gibraltar scene was replaced by a more timely subject, an episode in the recently declared war against the Dutch: "The Bringing of French and Dutch Prizes into the Port of Plymouth." In the intervals necessary for changing scenes, transparencies were displayed: An Incantation, A Sea Port ("conversation of Sailors of different Nations"), A View in the Alps (woodcutter attacked by wolves), and Summer Evening, with Cattle and Figures. Between the second and third scenes Michael Arne, son of the composer, and his wife presented musical selections.

The Eidophusikon's first season, with three performances a week, ended in May. The second season began on the tenth of December (1781) with the same program, but a new one was substituted for it on 31 January:†

1. The Sun rising in the Fog, an Italian Seaport.
2. The Cataract of Niagara, in North America.

* The report of the opening night in the *Morning Herald* (1 March) gives interesting particulars. The room was crowded and the ladies complained of the heat, "but by a contrivance of machinery, the ventelators instantly removed the inconvenience. It is a pity," continued the writer, "that at a spectacle so well contrived to gratify the sight, the audience will not keep their seats; the eagerness of curiosity is so great, that as the scenes follow each other in a quick succession, the spectators too frequently rise from their seats so suddenly, as to destroy the perspective effects of the pictures."

† It is conceivable that the delay in introducing the new bill had something to do with a mysterious episode in Loutherbourg's life that Christmas season. William Beckford, son of a former Lord Mayor of London and master of Fonthill Abbey, having celebrated his coming of age the preceding summer with a tremendous three-day fête at Fonthill, had determined to outdo himself with a Christmas revel. To a friend he wrote that "every preparation is going forwards that our much admired and admiring Loutherbourg . . . in all the wildness of his fervid imagination can suggest or contrive—to give our favourite apartments the strangeness and novelty of a fairy world. This very morning he sets forth with his attendant genii, and swears by one of his principal Imps . . . that in less than three weeks from time present a mysterious something—a something that eye has not yet seen or heart of man conceived, shall be created (his own unhallowed words) purposely for our especial delight and recreation." (Guy Chapman, *Beckford*, London, 1952, p. 99.) There seems to be no contemporary description of what went on at Fonthill then, but a note Beckford wrote many years later (1838) suggests that Loutherbourg surpassed himself in scenic and lighting effects, to which were added exotic perfumes and foods, and atmospheric music provided by three famous singers. "It was," wrote Beckford, "the realization of romance in all its fervours, in all its

27. The Eidophusikon, presenting the scene in Pandemonium (watercolor by Edward Francis Burney).

extravagance. . . . I wrote *V[athek]* [his famous Oriental romance] immediately upon my return to London at the close of this romantic villegiatura." (Chapman, pp. 105–106, 102.) Some of Beckford's biographers, prepared to assume the worst, have believed that the "voluptuous festival," as one of them has Beckford calling it, consisted of proceedings which, if not unspeakably orgiastic, were, at the very least, occult and necromantic. (John W. Oliver, *The Life of William Beckford,* London, 1932, p. 92; André Parreaux, *William Beckford,* Paris, 1960, p. 204.) More reasonably, Boyd Alexander (*England's Wealthiest Son,* London, 1962, pp. 83–84) believes that Loutherbourg's chief contribution to the extravaganza was a preview of the Pandemonium scene which was added to the Eidophusikon program a few weeks later. How it led to the composition of *Vathek* is not clear, although, as Alexander says, Beckford had a taste for Milton as, indeed, he had for visions of hell.

3. The Setting of the Sun, after a Rainy Day, with a View of the Castle, Town and Cliffs of Dover.
4. The Rising of the Moon, with a Water Spout, exhibiting the Effect of three different Lights, with a View of a Rocky Shore on the Coast of Japan.
5. Satan arraying his Troops on the Banks of the Fiery Lake, with the Raising of Pandemonium, from Milton.

After 7 March the storm at sea was restored to the bill, presumably by popular demand. During this season, which ended on 31 May, Dr. Burney accompanied the scenes at the harpsichord with music of his own composing, and Mrs. Sophia Baddeley, who sang at Vauxhall and Ranelagh during the summer, added a "vocal Part."

Of the five scenes which constituted the first bill, the Greenwich is the most fully described in contemporary sources.[22] The view, from One-Tree Hill, was a perspective which had in the foreground Flamsteed House and Greenwich Hospital and then, increasingly distant, the towns of Deptford and Greenwich, the Thames with its busy shipping, London from Poplar to Chelsea, and, farthest away, Hampstead, Highgate, and Harrow hills. First a faint glow appeared on the horizon, to be succeeded by a vaporish gray and then by a saffron color that tinged the light clouds; then the sun rose, its rays touching the tops of the trees and glancing off the vanes of the buildings' cupolas. Cattle and horsemen moved across the fields and roads and ships sailed up and down the river. The illumination was brightest at noon, and the effects were probably less dynamic at that time. With the fading of light at sunset, the landscape, buildings, and ships reflected a series of modulated tints. As darkness fell and the moon rose, "peasants" (gypsies?) were seen sitting about a fire. In the final phase of the scene, a storm rose and the picture was racked with wind and rain and fitfully illuminated by forked lightning.

The other scenes in the first program are described

less fully; but for the second bill we have a complete account. The Italian sunrise scene followed, in general, the scenario of the Greenwich one, with the addition of a thick Mediterranean fog. In the Niagara scene, the admired effects were the tumbling of a cataract over several obstacles, the torrent that roared in from the bottom right, and the "spungy foam" where the two streams joined. The picture of Dover Castle at sunset was lighted successively in red, purple, and blue tones reflected from the clouds and castle walls. In the fourth scene, set on the coast of Japan, a lighthouse beam played on the waves and moonlight silvered the clouds, followed by a blue waterspout and a climactic tempest.

The final portion of the second bill, the scene in Pandemonium, was the most spectacular of all. Contemporary witnesses ransacked their vocabulary of the sublime in vain, they said, to convey the awful effect. "Here, in the fore-ground of a vista, stretching an immeasurable length between mountains, ignited from their bases to their lofty summits, with many-coloured flame, a chaotic mass rose in dark majesty, which gradually assumed form until it stood, the interior of a vast temple of gorgeous architecture, bright as molten brass, seemingly composed of unconsuming and unquenchable fire."[23] Beelzebub and Moloch, advancing from the burning lake with their thousands of demons, occupied Pandemonium as the lightning flashed and the thunder rolled. In this palace of the devils, serpents were entwined around the Doric pillars, and as the fires rose the intense red gave way to a transparent white, "expressing thereby the effect of fire upon metal"—a significant gesture toward eighteenth-century scientific literalism. It was a scene, all in all, which everyone agreed added a new dimension of terror to the Miltonic narrative.*

All this, it must be remembered, was accomplished in a box with a vertical picture area of sixty square feet at most, and a depth of no more than eight feet. How were these effects managed? First, there must have been a back flat to portray the most remote part of the vista, and in many scenes there were cut-out wings and raked rows, graduated in size according to distance: pasteboard miniatures of the pieces Loutherbourg had designed in such abundance at Drury Lane. It was these which provided the several distinct stages of perspective in the Greenwich scene. The clouds were painted in semitransparent colors on long strips of linen, stretched on frames and operated by a windlass. Each cloth contained a series of different cloud effects. As it rose diagonally, the clouds appeared from below

the horizon, rose to the meridian, "and floated fast or slow, according to their supposed density, or the power of the wind."

Although some of the large objects represented in motion were cut from pasteboard, others were actual three-dimensional models. The ships were correctly rigged and carried only as much sail as real ones would have done in the circumstances portrayed. Their speed was regulated according to their size and their distance from the point of viewing, so that small vessels, for instance, would pass more quickly across the foreground than would larger ones in a fleet near the horizon. The coloring of distant ones was modified to take into account the effect of the atmosphere. The waves were first modeled in clay, then carved in soft wood and colored and varnished, so as to reflect the light of the sun or moon. Each row turned on its own axis to produce the illusion of alternate crests of foam, and the size of the rows diminished, with appropriate modification of color, as they receded in the distance. The whole ensemble was worked by one machine, the motion being regulated according to the effect intended, a calm moonlit sea or a rising storm. To enhance the illusion, in some land scenes, as in modern museum "dioramas," suitable materials, shaped, colored, and arranged, represented natural characteristics in the foreground. Thus, once again in the Greenwich scene, the heath was represented by "cork, broken into the rugged and picturesque forms of a sand-pit, covered with minute mosses and lichens."

But these were minor touches compared with Loutherbourg's resourceful handling of light and sound. The lighting of his miniature stage owed much to his Drury Lane experiments. William Henry Pyne, author of the fullest contemporary description of the Eidophusikon, alleges that he used the Argand lamp, but if he did, it was only in a later season, because the lamp had not yet been invented when the Eidophusikon was first demonstrated. It is certain, however, that Loutherbourg did wonders with such sources of light as he possessed; and he had the advantage of being able to concentrate the light in a small area rather than having to diffuse it over a whole large theatrical stage. As at Drury Lane, he mounted a batten of lamps above the proscenium, concealed from the audience and throwing all their light on the scene. Before these he placed stained glass slips of yellow, red, green, purple, and blue, which were changed and mixed as the passage of time and the representation of altering atmospheric conditions required. For a moonlight scene a lamp, mounted in a tin box with an inch-wide

* It was the one inevitably chosen for reenactment when a half-size working model of the Eidophusikon was displayed at Kenwood House, London, in the summer of 1973 as part of a Loutherbourg exhibition. Through the aperture was seen, first, the "asphaltick lake" with a mountain glowing ruddily in the background; the scrim at the very rear varied in tint and patterns of color as the lights played upon it. The second set—a model of the Palace of Pandemonium dominated by Satan—rose in front of the former one (which could still be seen through the columns of the palace) and deployed in it were some fifty or sixty small figures representing the satanic army. These were mounted on a kind of grilled platform, and gave the appearance of movement because of their intentionally loose mounting. During the four-minute presentation, powered by a phase motor, a recorded voice read the relevant passage from *Paradise Lost* to the accompaniment of tempestuous sound. At the end, the model of the palace sank from view, along with its devils, and the sounds of the Cimmerian wind were replaced by the tape of a harpsichord playing interval music.

Exhibition Rooms, over Exeter'Change, Strand.

(Sunday excepted) every Day will be prefented at the above Rooms,

A Miſcellaneous Exhibition,

Compriſing a Series of Beautiful Pictures in Stained Glaſs, repreſenting the moſt ſtriking Effects of Nature; the Works of that admired Artiſt Mr. JERVAIS, and purchaſed from him at a very great Expence.

A Collection of Mr. DEAN's Tranſparent Paintings of Mount Veſuvius, and the Conflagrations in London during the Riots.

And a Variety of novel and pleaſing Optical Effects in STORER's Delineators and other Inſtruments.

To be opened for public Inſpection from ELEVEN till SIX.

*** Admiſſion One Shilling.

And in the EVENING will be prefented,
That elegant and highly favored SPECTACLE,

The EIDOPHUSIKON,

Invented and Painted by Mr. DE LOUTHERBOURG.

In the courſe of which will be introduced the celebrated Scene of

The STORM & SHIPWRECK.

The other SCENES as uſual.

TO CONCLUDE WITH THE

Grand Scene from Milton.

With the uſual Accompaniments.

Firſt Seats, 3s.   Second Seats, 2s.

The Doors to be opened at Seven, and the Performance to begin at Half paſt Seven.

*** The Proprietors have paid the utmoſt Attention to the elegant Accommodations of the Company.

Printed by H. REYNELL, (No. 21,) Piccadilly, near the Hay-Market.

28. Handbill advertising the Eidophusikon and added attractions, 1786.

circular aperture, played on the moving cloud-cloth from behind, as the proscenium lights with bluish-green slips played on it from above and before; when the coloring of the clouds was semitransparent, the moon could be seen through it, and when the coloring was opaque, the moon lighted only the clouds' edges.

In the Pandemonium as well as the sea-storm pictures, the spectacular lighting was accompanied by auditory effects which Pyne called "the picturesque of sound." In contrast to the perfunctory off-stage noises common to the regular theatre, the sound effects in the Eidophusikon not only were more realistic than any hitherto produced: they were carefully orchestrated with the visual action, being modulated and continued as long as the action demanded. Like the lightning, the thunder was produced in a number of forms to suit the occasion. This was the function of a thin sheet of copper suspended by a chain and expertly shaken by one of the lower corners, in conjunction with a machine that "hurled balls and stones with indescribable rumbling and noise." So realistic were the thunder and lightning combined that, according to one anecdote among the several told of the Eidophusikon, when a genuine thunderstorm passed over the theatre during a performance some edgy members of the audience, more impressed by the celestial display than by Loutherbourg's, denounced his exhibition as "presumptuous," while the more empirically inclined went out on a balcony, compared the two storms, and concluded that Loutherbourg's thunder was best.

The rush of waves and the sound of rain and hail were produced by revolving or agitating cylinders loaded with small shells, peas, beads, or seeds, depending on the effect desired. The whistling of the wind came from pressing together, in a swift motion, two circular frames covered with tightly strained silk; and to enhance the "awful din" large silken balls were rubbed over a drumhead. This "vast tambourine," when struck with a sponge at the end of a whalebone spring, imitated, with suitable variations of loudness, the sound of distress signals from a foundering ship, the answering shore gun, and the echoes they produced. The same versatile drumhead, when an assistant ran his thumb over it, emitted what purported to be the groans of the infernal spirits on the burning lake in the Pandemonium scene.

It is hard to tell how seriously Loutherbourg took all this, although a later passage in his extra-artistic career, when he acquired considerable notoriety as a self-proclaimed faith healer, suggests that there was a definite streak of showmanship in his character. In the Eidophusikon, of course, no charlatanry was involved; the machine did, and evidently did well, what it was advertised to do. But when the *European Magazine* proclaimed it to be a "new species of painting . . . one of the most remarkable inventions in the art, and one of the most valuable, that ever was made," we may perhaps detect a Loutherbourgian puff.[24] Even if ridiculously oversold, however, as constituting a revolution in art, the Eidophusikon did captivate many of the cognoscenti of the day, including more than one celebrated artist. Sir Joshua Reynolds, Pyne tells us, was often in the audience, and recommended that young ladies be encouraged to attend in order to cultivate their talent for drawing from nature. Pyne also declares that Gainsborough, an old friend of Loutherbourg—they painted portraits of each other—was so entranced "that for a time he thought of nothing else—he talked of nothing else—and passed his evenings at that exhibition in long succession. Gainsborough, himself a great experimentalist, could not fail to admire scenes wrought to such perfection by the aid of so many collateral inventions."*

Except for one or two hints that it was on tour, nothing more is heard of the Eidophusikon from its closing in Lisle Street in May 1782 to its opening at Exeter Change on 30 January 1786.[25] It now was owned by Loutherbourg's former assistant, a man named Chapman, whose wife was a minor actress at Covent Garden. The auditorium at Exeter Change was just right for this show. Its capacity was two hundred—larger than the Lisle Street salon and probably accommodating as many people as could conveniently witness a performance on so small a scale.

Here the Pandemonium scene again was the finale, but the sea storm it had temporarily replaced was retained. Introduced only three weeks after the East Indiaman *Halsewell* had been wrecked off Dorsetshire with heavy loss of life, and modified to suit this news sensation, it was billed as providing an "exact, awful, and tremendous Representation of that lamentable Event," a printed narrative of which might be bought from a bookseller downstairs.[26] To publicize the nightly performance, during the daylight hours the auditorium was used as an exhibition room for Jervais's stained glass, "representing the most striking Effects of Nature," and for the late Hugh Dean's transparent paintings of Vesuvius and of the Gordon riots six years earlier.[27] As we have seen, the Vesuvius pictures had been shown with sound effects in 1780; now, however, they were motionless and silent, the greater wonders of the Eidophusikon having eclipsed their

modest pretensions. In the performances themselves, the introduction of a topical note with the *Halsewell* wreck was only one of a number of devices intended to increase patronage. The program was changed from time to time, and for the former musical interludes of Arne and Burney were substituted readings and recitations. It was appropriate, in a way, that on the night the show closed, 12 May 1786, the Pandemonium scene was preceded by the diminutive Count Boruwlaski playing the guitar.

The Eidophusikon turned up again at the Great Room, Spring Gardens, in February 1793. Evidently Loutherbourg's scenes alone were insufficient to attract audiences, because the show's advertising was devoted chiefly to the live entertainment that took over in the intervals. A "Master Hummell," singing to his own pianoforte accompaniment, had a brief engagement,† followed by George Saville Cary's "Comic Songs, Readings, and Imitations," the latter being of "many characters of the past and present age" including contemporary actors and actresses. In May the Eidophusikon featured, for one week only, "the Sieur Comus, who will display his astonishing performance on Cards, Caskets, Rings, Watches, Medals, Sympathetick Clocks, and many Magical Deceptions." The next month the whole show was moved to the King's Arms Hall, Cornhill, for a limited engagement, after which it vanished from the advertising columns. No doubt the Eidophusikon itself, if not Sieur Comus, went on tour.[28]

Six years later, in 1799, Chapman exhibited a "New" Eidophusikon in a room in Panton Street, Haymarket. He made clear in his advertising that this was not Loutherbourg's show. Without saying what had happened to it, he declared that he had "been enabled to trace out its beauty, on a scale infinitely superior in size, and, by the aid of accumulated light, and power of mechanism, to exhibit the most interesting operations of nature."[29] The program, suggesting that Chapman had no intention of deviating from Loutherbourg's formula, included a view of the setting sun from Dublin Bay, "Moonlight Contrasted with Fire from a Light House," the town and harbor of Liverpool with "gradual effect of dawning day," and the requisite storm at sea and shipwreck.[30] A planted news item in April averred that there were "no less than seventy-four movements of action and reaction in the moving canvas of the Eidophusikon; and so voluminous are the component parts, as to take the Machinists nine weeks in putting it together fit for public inspection." On the same bill were a Mr. Wilkinson,

* It is often said that the Eidophusikon was the inspiration for Gainsborough's famous show box, now in the Victoria and Albert Museum: an oak box equipped with candle holders and a silk screen for back lighting, in which could be inserted painted glass slides to be viewed through a movable magnifying lens. This supposition, however, seems to have originated with Gainsborough's early biographer, George Fulcher (1856); Pyne does not mention the box. Another, more plausible origin of the show box was also suggested by Fulcher and, much earlier, by Edward Edwards (1808): Jervais's exhibitions of stained glass in the 1770s and 1780s, in which some small works illustrating the effects of candlelight and moonlight were included. Gainsborough's peepshow was no mere toy; preoccupied as he was in his later years with problems of lighting, he intended the box and the slides he painted for it, ten of which are displayed at the Victoria and Albert, to help him design his paintings. The most authoritative treatment of the show box is Jonathan Mayne, "Thomas Gainsborough's Exhibition Box," *Victoria and Albert Museum Bulletin,* 1, no. 3 (July 1965), 16–24.

† Barring a coincidence of name, this was Johann Nepomuk Hummel (1778–1837), a child prodigy and pupil of Mozart, who had been in London concertizing and studying with Clementi. He would later achieve considerable celebrity as a composer and teacher.

* No account of the Eidophusikon mentions the fact that its fame soon crossed the Atlantic. The Philadelphia artist Charles Willson Peale, already an expert painter of transparencies as well as something of a showman—a role he would fully realize later on—somehow learned of Loutherbourg's exhibition in the summer of 1784. Evidently his informant had actually seen how the Eidophusikon worked, because no printed description went into the backstage mechanics of the show. In the following autumn Peale added to his existing gallery of portraits of contemporary military heroes a room to house the equipment, the gallery itself serving as auditorium, and in May 1785 he opened his "Perspective Views with Changeable Effects; or, Nature Delineated, and in Motion" (simplified a year later to "Moving Pictures"). This New World Eidophusikon, like the original, presented five scenes, complete with movement and sound effects, in a performance lasting two hours. The climactic scene was, not surprisingly, Pandemonium, with Milton's text printed in the program and additional verse by Peale that was recited as the picture evolved. As at Exeter Change and in Panton Street, the intervals were occupied by variety entertainment, notably readings from classic English authors relieved by humorous pieces. Encouraged by popular success, Peale went on to air-condition his showplace by hanging twelve large fans from the ceiling and swinging them by machinery, and added a barrel organ armed with thirty tunes. In February 1786, he created a maritime scene, this one on the patriotic theme of the battle between the *Bonhomme Richard* and the *Seraphis*. After a spectacular, noisy encounter the American ship, of course, triumphed. Eventually, mechanical difficulties occurred too often for the comfort of the audience, and after presenting occasional shows during the Constitutional Convention of 1787, Peale sold the whole outfit to a peripatetic showman and returned to his great project of assembling a national museum of natural history. (Charles Coleman Sellers, *Charles Willson Peale,* New York, 1969, pp. 188–211.) Some additional details,

performer on harmonic glasses; a young lady making her debut in several songs; a twenty-eight-year-old solicitor's clerk named John Britton, who was later to become well known as an antiquary and topographical artist, performing songs and recitations; and "Le Chien Savant, or, the Learned Dog."[31]

This second-generation Eidophusikon came to a sudden end on the night of 21 March 1800, when Chapman was burned out. There may be more than coincidence in the fact that he had just installed a Mount Etna scene; might not the eruption have got out of hand, just as Dubourg's Vesuvius had done fifteen years earlier? One newspaper, it is true, reported that the fire started in a nearby brothel and not in the Eidophusikon room. But start it did, in any case, and by the time it was quenched it had destroyed these buildings as well as the Hole in the Wall public house, several dwellings, and the house of a tallow chandler. Chapman's loss, uninsured, was said to have been £600.[32]

During the same season of 1799–1800 at least one other Eidophusikon-type exhibition was current, in Silver Street, Fleet Street: a miniature naumachia in the general tradition of the Bermondsey Spa's outdoor Siege of Gibraltar but framed (twenty-nine feet wide and twelve high) and evidently with added motion and noise:

BLOWING UP OF L'ORIENT, with the Representation of the whole of the BATTLE OF THE NILE, aided by the united Powers of Mechanics, Painting, and Optics, from its commencement on the Evening of Attack, until its glorious termination on the ensuing morning. The whole in motion, the respective vessels taking their stations in the order in which the combat began, with the State of the Fleets on the ensuing Morning; part of the French Fleet effecting their Escape; the zealous Capt. Hood bearing down on them, and firing and receiving their Broadsides as she passes; the English boats rowing in different directions, taking possession of the vanquished ships, and saving the Frenchmen from the wrecks.[33]

This advertisement appeared on 13 June 1799. Later in the year the bill included "BUONAPARTE'S LAST AND MOST DESPERATE ASSAULT UPON ACRE" and a Loutherbourgian tempest, and in the following February, inspiring the rivalry which led Chapman to produce his ill-fated Etna eruption, another fearsome "ERUPTION OF MOUNT VESUVIUS VOMITING forth Torrents of Fire." "The whole," it was said, was "designed and executed by, and under the direction of Mr. Turner." Two modern

authorities on J. M. W. Turner[34] have argued from a variety of circumstantial details that the Fleet Street show was a hitherto unrecognized and admittedly untypical episode in the painter's career, but the evidence against this hypothesis is fairly strong. In the Academy show of 1800 another Turner—George—exhibited a painting of the same subject, the destruction of *L'Orient;*[35] a third Turner was associated with Loutherbourg in the mounting of *Omai* (1785);[36] and, perhaps most conclusive, a certain "M. Turner, Jun." is mentioned by Charles Dibdin the younger as "a Gentleman who had invented an extraordinary naumachial exhibition, illustrative of the Battle of the Nile . . . which had attracted all the curiosity hunters in London."[37] Although Loutherbourg's influence on *the* Turner, especially in the dynamic handling of light and the dramatic treatment of storms at sea, may well have been profound, it was exerted by way of his gallery paintings, not the Eidophusikon.

The fate of the original Eidophusikon is unknown.* More certain is the persistence with which Loutherbourg's complicated toy was remembered and referred to in the next several decades. The Eidophusikon so deeply impressed itself on London memory that it became a veritable legend; its fame was disproportionate to the number of persons who could actually have seen it. As will be noted in a later chapter, exhibitions purporting to use its unique combination of mechanical action and lighting and sound effects would reappear from time to time down into the early Victorian era.

As far as the theatre itself was concerned, the Eidophusikon would prove to have been a model for the future. Loutherbourg drew upon his fruitful experience at Drury Lane, but went far beyond it, to construct a fully operative mechanical maquette representing what might be further accomplished as theatrical craftsmanship progressed beyond the point to which he had brought it. He achieved on a miniature scale a series of spectacles uniting form, perspective, color, movement, and sound such as was yet impossible in the theatre, despite the advances represented by *The Wonders of Derbyshire* and *Omai*. In effect, the little Eidophusikon was the way-station between the theatre of Garrick and that of Phelps and the younger Kean, producers of the most elaborate spectacles the nineteenth-century London stage was to witness. It raised the sights of stage designers, giving them a new magnitude and audacity of effect to aspire to when the means became available in the form of more powerful and controllable lighting and of more efficient machinery. To a large extent, the history of English theatrical staging during the next half-century would represent the realization of the Loutherbourgian ambitions.

Outside the theatre, apart from the minor result of giving the old clockwork theatre a tenuous extension of life, the general result of the Eidophusikon was to intensify interest in other forms of pictorial entertainment which created, above all, the illusion of reality. With one exception (the Cosmorama) the miniature scale of the Eidophusikon was abandoned and magnitude became a desideratum: the bigger the picture, the better. The illusion of perspective was sought, not by ranging successive ranks of objects and side scenes to give the effect of distance, but by experimentation with *trompe l'oeil* techniques on a flat surface. When Chapman's New Eidophusikon was burned in 1800, the age of the panorama had already arrived.

drawn from Peale's unpublished letters, diaries, and autobiography, have recently appeared in Kenneth Silverman, *A Cultural History of the American Revolution* (New York, 1976), pp. 452–54, 571–72.

The Panorama in Leicester Square

10

Shortly after Louterbourg first exhibited his miniature solutions to certain problems of theatrical perspective and lighting, an Edinburgh portrait painter was developing, on a grand scale, another novel means of producing the illusion of reality. Drawing upon two older artistic techniques—the portrayal of landscapes on interior walls and of wide outdoor scenes in engraved "prospects"—he added his own discovery, the trick of painting a broad scene on a cylindrical canvas, and the result was the panorama.[1] Insofar as the new method was immediately put to commercial use, the episode belongs to the history of entertainment rather than of art.

The idea of decorating interior walls to give the impression of outdoor space had attracted artists as early as the fourteenth century B.C. and again in Roman times.[2] In Renaissance Italy, particularly as the new art of scene design influenced domestic decoration, a room with walls painted to represent a continuous landscape or a series of vistas—thus denying that it was a confined space—was frequently found in villas. The earliest surviving English example, at Eastbury, Barking, Essex, dates from the first half of the seventeenth century. A room so treated at a Fleet Street tavern is briefly described in the title of a poem by Henry Vaughan (1646): "A Rhapsodie. Occasionally written upon a meeting with some of his friends at the Globe Taverne, in a Chamber painted over head with a Cloudy Skie, and some few dispersed Starres, and on the sides with Land-scapes, Hills, Shepheards, and Sheep." Such landscapes were a part of the general vogue of illusionistic painting in the middle of the seventeenth century. In 1663–64 both Pepys and Evelyn recorded their admiration of the "perspectives" a Mr. Povey had had painted at his house in Lincoln's Inn Fields—one a deceptive vista of porphyry vases and fountains on the garden wall, the other, hung on the wall of a small room, an interior view down a long corridor. The latter, still extant at Dyrham Park, Gloucestershire, is thought to have been the work of Samuel van Hoogstraten. One can savor the moment when the proud Mr. Povey dramatically opened the door for Pepys, "and there I saw that there is nothing but only a plain picture hung upon the wall."[3]

Elaborate landscapes were included in the décor at Montagu House (later the British Museum) and in Sir James Thornhill's *trompe l'oeil* work in the saloon at Roehampton House, Surrey. At Standlych (now Trafalgar) House near Salisbury, about 1766, the neoclassical painter Cipriani omitted the usual architectural framing and painted a continuous landscape around the four walls. Another Cipriani room, this one at Norbury Park, near Dorking, was described by William Gilpin, the peripatetic connoisseur of the picturesque, as representing "a bower or arbour, admitting a *fictitious* sky through a large oval at the top, and covered at the angles with trellis-work."

Sir George Beaumont, the art patron and friend of poets, was so much impressed by the room at Norbury that in the 1770s he commissioned the artist Thomas Hearne to paint a similar one for the banqueting room at his seat near Keswick, with the significant difference that the room, instead of having the rectangular shape which prevented the accomplishment of total illusion when surrounded by a painted landscape, was circular. Robert Southey, who saw Hearne's twenty-foot-long sketch, regretted that the painting was never made. "If the execution had not always been procrastinated," he wrote many years later, "here would have been the first panorama."[4]

Meanwhile, the same technique of representing wide vistas in perspective had been adopted elsewhere, by gardeners and artist-engravers. At the end of long walks, seventeenth-century French landscape designers had placed painted canvases extending the view still farther. These false perspectives became a valued feature of formal gardens, and at Vauxhall, as we have seen, there were a number of such outdoor deceptions. These were necessarily limited in the breadth of the scene portrayed. But during those same years, topographical representations of much greater compass were being produced in the form of elongated drawings and engravings. As early as 1543–1550, Anthony van den Wyngaerde had produced a "prospect" of London, Westminster, and Southwark ten feet long and seventeen inches high. This was followed in the next century by more famous bird's-eye views of London and its vicinity—J. C. Visscher's in 1616 and Wenceslaus Hollar's numerous renditions in the middle decades of the century, among them prospects of the city both before and after the Great Fire.

As heavy folios of local historical and topographical works proliferated in the eighteenth century, among their distinctive features was one or more fold-out engravings illustrating broad expanses of country or town. These engravings had an obvious affinity with Canaletto's paintings of London and the Thames, of which the two classic examples, the view of Westminster from Somerset House and that of the Thames from Somerset House toward the City, were engraved in 1750–51. None of these, however, attempted to portray the entire circle of the horizon from an elevated vantage point. They were limited by the conventional "rule of forty-five [or at most, sixty] degrees," which allowed a view to embrace only as much as the painter could see without moving his head. But their role as precursor of the panorama was recognized as soon as the panorama itself was invented. Immediately, and retrospectively, the word "panorama" was applied by extension and, one might say, by diminution, to these painted and engraved representations of a wide topographical sweep, in time replacing the word "prospect," by which they had formerly been designated. As early as 1804 an advertisement in the *Times* listed among pictures for sale "Cannalletti's Panorama of Venice."[5]

The first artist who discovered how to paint a realistic landscape on a cylindrical surface was Robert Barker, born at Kells in 1739, who had become a successful portraitist at Edinburgh.[6] There are at least three versions of how the discovery was made in the mid-1780s, but the essential point is that Barker, walking atop Calton Hill (or sitting under an umbrella, according to one account), conceived the idea of fixing a square frame on the spot and then rotating it, so that he could sketch segments of the entire 360° view in an unbroken sequence. He put his twelve-year-old son, Henry Aston Barker, to work on the project and in due time possessed a view of Edinburgh and its environs from the observatory on Calton Hill. But when these flat drawings were hung in a circle, the horizontal lines appeared curved except at exact eye level. This was the crucial problem presented by circularity; and Barker solved it by inventing a system of curved lines which would neutralize the distortion created by a concave surface.*

Having proved that it was possible to paint a circular picture without sacrificing realism, Barker began to consider the commercial possibilities of his discovery. On 19 June 1787 he received a patent for "an entire new Contrivance or Apparatus, called by him *La Nature à Coup d'Oeil,* for the Purpose of displaying Views of Nature at large, by Oil-Painting, Fresco, Watercolours, Crayons, or any other Mode of painting or drawing." The specifications included a circular building; lighting admitted exclusively from the top; an enclosure to prevent the observer from going too near the painting; over the enclosure, a shade or roof "to prevent an observer seeing above the drawing or painting when looking up"—so as to conceal the direct-light source—and a similar obstruction, such as a wall or paling, at the bottom; an entrance to the enclosure from below, so that no door would interrupt the continuity of the scene; and adequate ventilation without the use of windows.[7] Obviously, Barker had thought it out completely. But between the conception and the execution intervened the problem of capital.

It appears that at this point, or possibly before he took out his patent, he went to London and laid his plans before Sir Joshua Reynolds, whose approval would go a long way toward getting Barker the sponsors he needed. Reynolds listened politely but doubted that the scheme was practical. Barker, undeterred, returned to Edinburgh and, using the guard

* Two other contemporary artists, one American and one German, conceived the idea of panorama painting independently of Barker. In New York City in the winter of 1784–85 the painter William Dunlap was conversing with "an English gentleman," most unfortunately not identified, who "asked me," Dunlap later wrote, "if I had any idea of a picture which should represent all surrounding objects as they appear in nature when we turn and look from a central spot? I answered, 'Yes. It has been familiar with me from childhood, though I do not think I have ever before spoken of it. Often when standing on an eminence, and looking around me on the bright and glorious objects, here a landscape, there a bay and shipping—a city glittering in light—all the tints of a sky from the setting sun to the sober colors of the opposite horizon—I have imagined myself surrounded by an upright circular canvas, and depicting the scene just as nature displayed it, and I have regretted that I could not make the experiment.' '*That's it!*' was his unintelligible exclamation. He then told me, as a thing unknown, that an artist in Edinburgh had conceived the plan, made the drawings, and was executing such a picture; that he had helped him with funds, and by that means became acquainted with the fact. This was the first time I ever heard of a panorama, a species of pictures then unknown to the world." (Dunlap, *A History of the Rise and Progress of the Arts of Design in the United States,* ed. Frank W. Bayley and Charles E. Goodspeed, Boston, 1918, I, 315–16.) Dunlap, however, did not attempt to solve the technical problems involved, as did the German artist Johann Adam Breysig (1766–1831) at the very end of the century; see S. Hausmann, "Der Erfindung der Panoramen," *Kunst für Alle,* 4 (1889), 198–202. There is no question that Barker painted the first panorama and designed the first structure to house such pictures.

29. Panorama of London from the Albion Mills, Southwark (six aquatint engravings by Robert Barker, from original sketches by Henry Aston Barker, 1791). Notice that the left margin of the first segment coincides with the right margin of the last segment. The six parts constitute a 360° view.

room at Holyrood Palace as a studio, painted on the paper-covered surface of a circular canvas, twenty-five feet in diameter, a watercolor view of Edinburgh and vicinity. This he exhibited first at two locations in Edinburgh and then at Glasgow. In November 1788 he took the picture to London and in the following spring exhibited it, still without any of the housing refinements the patent described, at 28 Haymarket. By now he had attracted the requisite financial backing, from a joint stock company organized by Lord Elcho, son of the Earl of Wemyss; and, just as important, Reynolds, the lawgiver of British art, was won over. Earlier, he had assured Barker that "he would cheerfully leave his bed at any time in the night to inspect such a work of art" as Barker proposed; now, according to a story which one is at liberty to doubt, he left his breakfast table, walked to the Haymarket in his dressing gown and slippers, and having inspected the picture, congratulated its creator. "I find I was in error in supposing your invention could never succeed," he is quoted as saying, "for the present exhibition proves it is capable of producing effects and representing nature in a manner far superior to the limited scale of pictures in general." Reynolds in fact became, in the painter Northcote's words, a "prodigious admirer" of Barker's invention, and returned time after time to see it, often with friends.* He took Lord Lansdowne and his young son on one occasion,[8] and urged Northcote to go, "saying it would surprise me more than anything of the kind I had ever seen in my life, and I found it to be as he had said."[9] Benjamin West, too, as Barker was proud to advertise, gave him permission "freely to make use of his name, in asserting Mr. Barker's idea and mode of description to be the greatest improvement to the art of painting that has ever yet been discovered"[10]—hyperbole that would seem to place Barker somewhat ahead of Loutherbourg.†

With such distinguished sponsors, Barker was well launched on the way to success as a London showman. He had, however, to convince the public that his was not merely one more tired variation on the visual entertainments with which they were familiar. Although he advertised his picture as an "exhibition," he stressed that it was not a model and that glasses were not needed to examine it—a good indication of what the London showgoer was accustomed to at this time.[11] A distinctive name was required; and one of Barker's "classical friends" supplied him with one, which came into use in 1791. The speed with which the word "panorama" (Greek: all-embracing view) entered the

common vocabulary and acquired applications far removed from Barker's circular picture testifies not only to the initial popularity of his show but to the fact that the word filled a need that was not met by such older words as "prospect."

In the winter of 1790–91 Barker sent his son, then sixteen, to the roof of the highest landmark between St. Paul's and Westminster Abbey, the Albion sugar mills at the Southwark end of Blackfriars Bridge, to sketch as much as he could see from that vantage point. The choice of subject was as astute as the choice of moment was fortunate. Londoners' taste for detailed pictorial representations of their metropolis had been sharpened by the many paintings Samuel Scott had made of the Thames from Greenwich to Twickenham, as well as by Canaletto's much-admired portrayals.[12] The site was utilized just in time, for the Albion mills burned to the ground on 3 March, just after the young man completed his sketches. From these his father painted a canvas of 1,479 square feet, showing not only all architectural and topographical features but such homely touches as workmen repairing the road at the approach to the bridge, a man carrying a sack on his back, and a woman looking down from the window of a house in nearby Albion Place at someone on the doorstep. Originally the painting was only somewhat "more than half a circle," but later it was made into a complete one. This was shown in the spring of 1792 at a new location, a rough building behind 28 Castle Street, Leicester Square, opposite Hunter's anatomical museum.

Soon, however, Barker was able to abandon the makeshift quarters where he had been exhibiting thus far and to build the structure called for in his patent. He acquired a site on the east side of Leicester Place, between Cranbourne Street and Lisle Street, within a few steps of the former Leverian Museum and the first Eidophusikon salon, and there erected what would become for over sixty years one of the several buildings that made Leicester Square the center of London's popular entertainment industry.[13]

Opened in 1794, the circular building, eventually to be surrounded by other structures, was entered from Cranbourne Street through a narrow passage that led to the lower level, ninety feet in diameter. A short flight of steps delivered spectators to a raised and balustraded circular platform thirty feet wide. From here they could view the principal canvas, hung on the circumference of the building's wall at a uniform distance of thirty feet from the edge of the platform and reaching several feet below it. Atop this platform, sup-

* Although two independent sources testify to Reynolds's enthusiasm, it must be weighed against the fact that by 1789, when he first saw Barker's canvas, his sight was partially gone. Since he died in February 1792, he never saw the panorama in its fully developed form, in Barker's new Leicester Square building.

† The relationship between West and Barker went beyond the mere proffer of a testimonial; they seem to have been well acquainted. In 1808 Colonel John Trumbull, the American artist, to whom West had been, as he said, "for thirty years . . . more than a father," brought back from America some sketches of Niagara Falls which he hoped Barker would convert into a panorama. When Barker rejected them, Trumbull, on the basis of a report he got of an overheard conversation between West and Barker at a theatre, bitterly blamed his compatriot for influencing Barker's decision. (Dunlap, History of the Arts of Design, II, 51–52.)

ported by the column which rose from the center of the ground floor, was a smaller platform, reached from that level by three flights of stairs placed at one side of the building. (These staircases were reputed to be among the hardest climbs in a city which also contained the Monument and the dome of St. Paul's. At a desperate point in his love affair with Fanny Bolton, Thackeray's Pendennis climbs them, arriving, panting, at the top only to discover that "care had come up with him, and was bearing him company.") A second picture was hung around this smaller circumference. In the center of the roof was a skylight, which was the only source of illumination for either picture. A black canopy concealed it from the spectators on the upper platform, so that the picture was lighted by an unseen sun. The floor of the upper platform served a similar purpose for the area below. The building was so designed that two of the forces which militate against perfect illusion in a gallery painting—the limiting

frame and standards of size and distance external to the picture itself—were eliminated in the panorama, as they were, perhaps more crudely and at the opposite end of the scale of magnitude, in well-made peepshows. The intrusive elements of the spectators' surroundings being blacked out, the world in which they were enwrapped consisted exclusively of the landscape or cityscape depicted on the canvas suspended thirty feet away, in the case of the large circle.*

While the building was still under construction, Barker and his son had painted in a temporary wooden shed in the center of the rotunda a panorama, based on sketches made at the scene, of the grand fleet lying at Spithead, with a capsizing boat in the foreground and Portsmouth and the Isle of Wight in the distance. This, hung in the lower circle, and the London picture in the upper circle constituted the new house's first bill. The royal family came for a preview. "The king," Henry Barker recalled many years later, "asked many

30. Burford's Panorama, Leicester Square: cross section (aquatint from Robert Mitchell's *Plans and Views in Perspective of Buildings Erected in England and Scotland,* 1801). Mitchell was the panorama's architect.

* In 1841 a third circle, smaller than the others, was added, but it was not a success. The reduced wall space prevented the full panoramic effect, and the spectators were brought too close to the painting. The circle was retained, however, until the building closed.

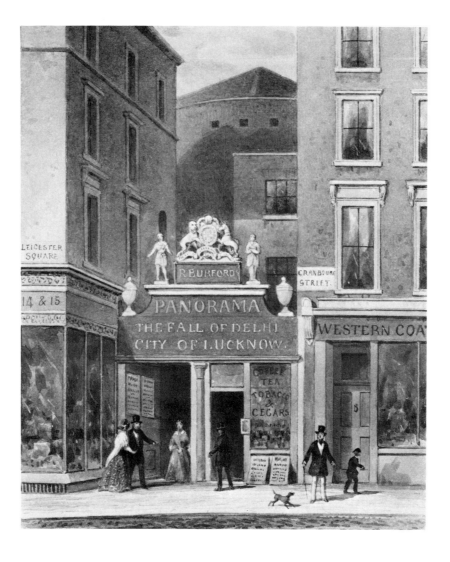

31. Burford's Panorama, Leicester Square: The entrance from Cranbourne Street, 1858 (unsigned pencil sketch). The surrounding buildings were erected some time after the rotunda was completed in 1794.

* In 1823 the *European Magazine* (83, 447n.) said that "the first Panorama ever seen [in Paris] was one of London, painted by Mr. Barker, and sold to a person who took it over to France on speculation." Nothing more is known of this transaction, if it actually took place; but it is certain that a "person" took the panorama *idea* to France in 1797. This was none other than the American painter-inventor Robert Fulton, who went from London to Paris in that year, primarily in an effort to interest the Directoire in his scheme for submarine navigation. In April 1799 he and his close friend Joel Barlow, the

questions; and when answered, turned round to Lord Harcourt, to whom he gave the answer verbatim, always beginning with 'He says' so-and-so. His majesty had a large gold-headed cane, which he pointed with, and sometimes put into my hand, making me stoop down in a line with it, to be informed of an object so small that I could not otherwise understand him." Queen Charlotte said she felt seasick.

From London the panorama vogue spread across the continent, to Paris, Berlin, and as far away as St. Petersburg—an episode in the history of European urban culture in the nineteenth century which has yet to be described authoritatively and in detail.* In London, the original panorama soon had competition from quickly painted imitations. In 1796, for example, at the Great Room, Spring Gardens, under the title "Campus Nautica" a 100-foot canvas depicted the fleet at Spithead on

1 May 1795, as it got under sail to escape the vicinity of the warship *Boyne,* which had caught fire. The proprietor claimed that the artist, a marine painter named Robert Dodd, had out-Barkered Barker. He gave no reason for this assertion, but perhaps the sort of people who accepted his classic etymology did not expect reasons. "The peculiar manner in which [the painting] is exhibited, as well as the richness of the subject, is superior to whatever has hitherto been shewn under the title of PANORAMA (or great sight) as spectators may suppose themselves looking through a window at real objects."[14] It is possible that this may have been a kind of uneasy blend of panorama and large-scale peepshow.

Among the young artists who turned their skill to panorama painting at the turn of the century were two friends of Henry Aston Barker who were, like him, enrolled in the school of the Royal Academy: Robert Ker Porter and Thomas Girtin. Porter's contribution to the panorama vogue in 1800 is best recounted in the enthusiastic words of his sister Jane, soon to become a best-selling novelist (*Thaddeus of Warsaw, The Scottish Chiefs*):

The historical picture of the *Taking of Seringapatam* [in the fourth Mysore War, 1799] was painted by my dear brother Robert, at the age of nineteen. It was two hundred and odd feet long; the proportioned height I have now forgotten. But I remember, when I first saw the vast expanse of vacant canvas stretched along, or rather in a semicircle, against the wall of the great room in the Lyceum, where he painted it, I was terrified at the daring of his undertaking. I could not conceive that he could cover that immense space with the subject he intended, under a year's time at least, but—and it is indeed marvellous!—he did it in SIX WEEKS! But he worked on it every day (except Sundays) during those weeks, from sunrise until dark. It was finished during the time the committees of the Royal Academy were sitting at Somerset-house, respecting the hanging of the pictures there for that year's exhibition; therefore, it must have been towards the latter end of April. No artist had seen the painting of Seringapatam during its progress; but when it was completed, my brother invited his revered old friend Mr. West (the then President of the Royal Academy) to come and look at the picture, and give him his opinion of it, ere it should be opened to the public view. . . . He went over from the Lyceum, on the morning on which he had called to see my brother and his finished painting, to Somerset-house, where the Committee had been awaiting his presence above an hour. "What has detained our President so long?" enquired Sir Thomas Lawrence of him, on his entrance. "A WONDER!" returned he, "a WONDER OF THE WORLD!—I never saw anything like it!—a picture of two hundred foot dimensions, painted by that boy KER PORTER, in six weeks! and as admirably done as it could have been by the best historical painter amongst us in as many months!"[15]

The bibliophile Thomas Frognall Dibdin, the writer for whom, many years later, Jane Porter set down her memories of that heady season, described the huge picture which caused all the excitement:

The learned were amazed, and the unlearned were enraptured. I can never forget its first impression upon my own mind. It was as a thing dropped down from the clouds—all fire, energy, intelligence, and animation. You looked a second time, the figures moved, and were commingled in hot and bloody fight. You saw the flash of the cannon, the glitter of the bayonet, the gleam of the falchion. You longed to be leaping from crag to crag with Sir David Baird, who is hallooing his men on to victory! Then, again, you seemed to be listening to the groans of the wounded and the dying—and

more than one female was carried out swooning. The oriental dress, the jewelled turban, the curved and ponderous scymitar—these were among the prime objects with Sir Robert's pencil: and he touched and treated them to the very spirit and letter of the truth. The colouring, too, was good and sound throughout. The accessories were strikingly characteristic—rock, earth, and water, had its peculiar and happy touch; and the accompaniments about the sally-port, half choked up with the bodies of the dead, made you look on with a shuddering awe, and retreat as you shuddered. The public poured in by hundreds and thousands for even a transient gaze—for such a sight was altogether as marvellous as it was novel. You carried it home, and did nothing but think of it, talk of it, and dream of it. And all this by a young man of NINETEEN![16]

Little wonder that the young man immediately went on to paint, on a similar scale, the siege of Acre (1800), the battles of Agincourt and Alexandria (both shown in 1801), the battle of Lodi (1803), and General Suvorov's defeat of the French at Novi and crossing the Alps by way of Mount St. Gothard (1804). None of these, however, was as popular as the first, and Porter soon cut back his production to easel paintings and became a professional traveler, serving fourteen years as British consul in Venezuela and wandering through Persia, Armenia, and Russia, where he died in 1842.

In Porter's room, which had been Reynolds's studio, gathered a sketching club to which belonged the prolific and extremely talented watercolorist Thomas Girtin. Turner's remark, "If Girtin had lived I should have starved," is probably apocryphal, but his estimate of his friend's genius is sustained by modern opinion. Given the delicacy of both his physical constitution and his watercolor art, there is some irony in the fact that at the very end of his life—he died of consumption in November 1802, at the age of twenty-seven—the particular work of his which was before the London public was a huge oil painting, measuring 108 feet by 18: the Eidometropolis or Panorama of London from the terrace adjoining the British Plate Glass Manufactory, shown from 2 August at the Lyceum.[17] Displayed in the Lyceum's foyer as an advertisement of the next attraction, which was never to materialize, were the sketches he had made in Paris for a panorama intended to compete with a view of the city which had been showing at the Haymarket Theatre since May.[18] This was the work of James DeMaria, formerly a scene painter at the Birmingham Theatre, who was also a student at the Royal Academy and a friend of Turner. Among other so-called panoramas on display in these years was one of Edin-

American poet, diplomat, and businessman then residing in Paris, received a French patent of ten years' duration to exploit Barker's invention. In the following December, Fulton assigned his rights to another American businessman, James Thayer, who was adding to his already considerable fortune by developing land in central Paris. Among the commercial buildings Thayer erected on the Boulevard Montmartre, lending their name to the still existing Passage and Rue des Panoramas, were twin "cupoles" in which were shown, in 1800, two panoramas painted by Jean Mouchet, Denis Fontaine, Pierre Prévost, and Constant Bourgeois. One depicted Paris seen from the central dome of the Tuileries, the other the British fleet evacuating Toulon in 1793. Thayer and his wife managed the two houses, sending a portion of the receipts to Fulton, who used them to resume his marine engineering experiments at Le Havre. (H. W. Dickinson, *Robert Fulton: Engineer and Artist: His Life and Works,* London, 1913, pp. 95–97, 103; Germain Bapst, *Essai sur l'histoire des panoramas et des dioramas,* Paris, 1891, pp. 14–15; Heinz Buddemeier, *Panorama/Diorama/Photographie,* Munich, 1970, pp. 167–70; Yvon Bizardel, *American Painters in Paris,* trans. Richard Howard, New York, 1960, pp. 65–67.)

burgh, the work of a young artist named Saunders, which was shown at the Great Room, Spring Gardens, in 1803.[19] Two years later, at the same place, the attraction was John Thomas Serres's 150-foot canvas of Boulogne, showing the staging facilities for Napoleon's projected invasion of England and the flotilla he had assembled for that frustrated venture.[20]

None of Barker's rivals, it must be noted, exhibited pictures that could be called panoramas in the strict original sense of the word, that is, paintings hung around the entire circumference of a wall. Ker Porter's *Seringapatam* was a semicircle or, according to one writer, three quarters of a circle. The others probably were either mildly concave or else unambiguously flat. But at least they could claim the other attribute of panoramas: they did use up a large expanse of cloth.

That complete circularity soon ceased to be part of the popular definition of the new word was due to the panorama's affinity with another current fashion, that of large historical paintings. In practice, the distinction between the two often was blurred. Panoramas represented logical extensions—or magnifications—of the recently developed school of English historical art in two respects. There was, for one thing, the matter of size: epic subjects, it was agreed, demanded epic scale, and no scale could conveniently be larger than the one Barker and his rivals adopted. Moreover, a new subgenre of history-painting had emerged, a kind of pictorial journalism that portrayed contemporary events, often subjects so current they were still in the newspapers. This combination of physical magnitude and topicality had been responsible for the popularity of West's *Death of General Wolfe* in 1771 and of Copley's *Death of Chatham* a decade later. The violent turn of events in the mid-nineties added pertinence to this thriving branch of British art. Every year brought new battles whose critical importance to the nation's survival made them prime material for artistic exploitation. In 1794–95 crowds paid a shilling a head to enter the Historic Gallery, where the newest of Loutherbourg's canvases were hung: *The Battle of Valenciennes*, to paint which he had followed the allied armies in the company of James Gillray, and *Lord Howe's Victory, or, The Battle of the Glorious First of June 1794*.

What the first panoramists did, in effect, was to bring this kind of instant-history painting to a somewhat broader public—to translate the drama of the great struggle into huge pictures which, whatever their artistic merits might be, had the forthright appeal of topicality realistically and dramatically presented. Benjamin Silliman no doubt expressed the preference of many when he wrote in 1805, "I am fond of panoramas, especially of battles. Their magnitude, the consequent distinctness of the objects, and the circular position of the canvass, corresponding with the real horizon, all tend to give one the strongest impression of the reality of the scene."[21] Panoramas became the newsreels of the Napoleonic era. When Robert Barker met Nelson at Palermo in 1799, the admiral told him that he was indebted to him "for keeping up the fame of his victory in the battle of the Nile for a year longer than it would have lasted in the public estimation."[22] Nelson was too modest, but he did understand the panorama's value as a means of sustaining and gratifying the London public's absorption in the events of the war. The roll of panoramic subjects in those years echoes, but goes far beyond, the roster that would be inscribed half a century later on Wellington's funeral car: the Glorious First of June . . . the Battle of the Nile . . . the Siege of St. Jean d'Acre . . . Alexandria . . . Malta . . . the Straits of Messina . . . Copenhagen . . . Lodi . . . St. Gothard . . . Boulogne . . . Trafalgar . . . Flushing . . . Corunna . . . Badajoz . . . Lisbon . . . Salamanca . . . Vittoria . . . Paris . . . Waterloo.

Not all the subjects were depicted in the Leicester Square panorama; a few were shown elsewhere. Nor were all the early panoramas devoted to military topics. Some, such as those of Windsor, Weymouth, Brighton, Dublin, Rome, Berlin, Naples, and Florence, were purely topographical in interest. But it was upon its portrayal of the events and places of the Napoleonic Wars that the initial prosperity of Barker's panorama rested, and a solid foundation it proved to be. In time Barker was able to buy out his backers, and to Londoners in the next several decades his was "*the* panorama," just as the Royal Academy's annual show was "*the* exhibition." There were several reasons why it continued to flourish when so many imitators and appropriators of the name came and went. Being first in the field was not necessarily one of them; in show business as in other fields of endeavor the mortality rate among the pioneers is as high as among the followers. To be sure, once established, the Barker panorama had the advantage of being a familiar institution, such as Madame Tussaud's would later become. But even so, it would not have been proof against the notorious fickleness of entertainment fashion had not the managers had a constantly reliable sense of the subjects their clientele were interested in at the moment. They could scarcely have gone wrong by presenting pictures of wartime subjects, but in 1815 they faced a problem: what would most profitably attract a peace-time public? Their guesses over the years, as we shall see in Chapter 13, proved accurate enough. Barker and his successors kept a steady finger on the public pulse.

But above all it was their ability to provide a superior illusion that guaranteed a steady box office. How thoroughly the artist-proprietors were able to monopolize the secret of Barker's distortion-correcting technique is hard to tell; probably most of it could have been mastered fairly quickly by experienced scene painters. But even if the method could easily be copied, it would have been useless without the kind of building specified in Barker's patent, which expired in 1801. With no more than one or two exceptions, notably the Colosseum in Regent's Park (Chapter 11) and perhaps the secessionary establishment in the Strand, to be mentioned in a moment, the rotunda in Leicester Square was the only structure having complete facilities for showing a picture that portrayed, without any extraneous elements to dispel the illusion, what an observer might see in all directions as he stood on an elevation. Other exhibition halls, such as the Lyceum and the Great Room, Spring Gardens, may have provided a rudimentary and makeshift imitation of the arrangements at Barker's, but structurally they could not be adapted to provide the panorama's full effect.*

In 1801 or 1802 Barker's elder son, Thomas Edward, who was associated with him in the business although not himself an artist, left Leicester Square and set up a rival panorama in the Strand, near Surrey Street, in partnership with Ramsay Richard Reinagle, artist son of an artist father, Philip Reinagle. Both Reinagles seem to have done some painting at the original panorama; the son did most of it for the Strand house. By an accident of circumstance, the younger Reinagle had lately (1799–1800) been the intimate friend of John Constable, freshly arrived from Suffolk, with whom he shared rooms off Portland Place. Constable the idealist quickly took the moral measure of Reinagle, an unprincipled and cunning operator. (Not only was Reinagle involved, like his father, in questionable transactions by way of buying, restoring, and selling paintings; in 1848 he sent to the Academy, under his own name, a picture he bought at a broker's, and was forced to resign his membership.) Although the two soon drifted apart, Constable was invited to a preview of Reinagle's panorama of Rome, to which his reaction was lukewarm—as regarded both the panorama as a form of art and Reinagle's personal talent: "I should think he has taken his view favourably, and it is executed with the greatest care and fidelity. This style of

painting suits his ideas of the art itself, and his defects are not so apparent in it—that is, great principles are neither expected nor looked for in this mode of describing nature. He views Nature minutely and *cunningly*, but with no greatness or breadth. The defects of the picture at present are a profusion of high lights, and too great a number of abrupt patches of shadow. But it is not to be considered as a whole."[23]

Robert Barker died in 1806, and his painter son, Henry Aston, took over the business, assisted by John Burford, who had been his father's pupil and, in addition to helping paint panoramas in the following years, was an occasional exhibitor at the Academy shows (1812–1829). Meanwhile, the rival operation in the Strand got into difficulties. On 1 January 1807, T. E. Barker dissolved his partnership with Reinagle. The latter told Constable, who told Farington, that he "lost a great deal of money" in the venture.[24] A decade later, in 1817, Henry Aston Barker and John Burford bought the Strand house and continued to operate it, exchanging pictures back and forth between the two houses. Barker (who, incidentally, was married to the daughter of Captain Bligh of the *Bounty*) retired early on a competence (1822), though he would live on until 1856, leaving both businesses in the hands of Burford and his son, Robert, who also exhibited at the Royal Academy.† Upon his father's retirement in 1826, Robert Burford became sole proprietor of the Leicester Square panorama. The Strand panorama closed in 1831, and the building soon thereafter was occupied by the much longer-lived Strand Theatre; the Aldwych Underground station is on the site today.

During their various terms as proprietors and artistic directors of the panorama, Henry Barker and both Burfords were constantly in the field making drawings for their next big picture. In the earlier years especially, Barker's travels brought him into contact with some of the most famous people of the age. On the way to Turkey to make drawings for the panorama of Constantinople (1799) he called upon Sir William Hamilton, the ambassador at the Court of Naples. Sir William was not at home, but Barker dined that evening with Lady Hamilton and Lord Nelson. He met Napoleon in Paris in May 1802, and again on Elba.

Each of these panoramists had his share of adventures. Robert Burford could tell of being locked in the spire of the Karlskirche, Vienna, from which he had been making sketches of the surrounding territory, and finally being rescued when passersby saw his frantically waved handkerchief; of being snowed in for forty-eight hours in a chalet in the Bernese Alps; and

* In 1830 a panorama of Madras painted by William Daniell, R. A., a prolific topographical artist, and E. T. Parris, painter of the London panorama at the Colosseum, was shown at a specially constructed building designed by Parris in Coromandel Place, New Road. It was said to be of "most ingenious construction, and, by raising the base of the platform a few feet, the staircase is so contrived as to admit the visitor directly into the centre of the platform." (*Athenaeum*, 30 October 1830, p. 684; see also *Literary Gazette*, 2 and 30 October 1830, pp. 642–43, 707, and *Times*, 30 October 1830.) Another unusual feature of this wooden structure was that it could be taken apart and reassembled within a few hours. Although the panorama was well received in the press, surprisingly little more is reported of it or of the building. The show closed in February 1832, some sixteen months after it opened. (*Literary Gazette*, 4 February 1832, p. 78.)

† Some accounts say Robert was John's younger brother, but the date of his birth (1791 or 1792) seems to substantiate the assertion of others that he was John's son. There is an appreciation of their easel landscapes in M. H. Grant, *A Chronological History of the Old English Landscape Painters* (London, 1926–1943), II, 317–18.

32. Burford's Panorama: Naples by moonlight (painted by Robert Burford and H. C. Selous; engraving in *Illustrated London News,* 11 January 1845).

of being arrested as a trespasser when he was drawing Salzburg and its vicinity from the heights of the castle. In all, over thirty of the Leicester Square panoramas were painted from drawings made by one or another of the proprietors: Messina, Flushing, Lisbon, Badajoz, Vittoria, Elba, Waterloo, Dover, Paris, Venice, Naples, Lausanne, the Bernese Alps, Pompeii, Malta, Edinburgh, Constantinople, Amsterdam, Geneva, Florence, Milan, Antwerp, Stirling, New York City, Niagara Falls, Lago Maggiore, Mont Blanc, Rome, the Roman Colosseum, Coblenz, Vienna, Switzerland from the Rigi, Killarney, and Salzburg. The remainder were painted from sketches brought back by travelers. Some of these contributors to the edification of stay-at-home Londoners belonged to the numerous early nineteenth-century breed of artist-travelers who, moved by the romantic passion for the remote, the sublime, the picturesque, and the antique, wandered across the continents in search of subjects.[25] Probably the only one whose name is recognized today was Frederick Catherwood, the antiquary-architect who spent a number of years sketching Egyptian sites and contributed the drawings for Burford's panoramas of Jerusalem, Thebes, Karnak, and Baalbec.[26] Other sketches were provided by men who were abroad for

other reasons and had art as an avocation: soldiers, naval officers, government officials on foreign station.

The proprietors painted most of the panoramas themselves, with the assistance of subordinates such as Ramsay Reinagle before he seceded. From 1844 onward almost every canvas at Leicester Square was the work, at least in part, of Henry Courtney Selous, a well-known painter and illustrator who during his long career showed some sixty pictures at the annual exhibitions in addition to painting thirty panoramas. Except for the two earliest panoramas, which were painted in distemper and thus gave rise to the complaint that panoramas were nothing more than enlarged examples of theatrical scenery, all the Barker-Burford-Selous productions were done in oil and varnished like gallery pictures. Painting them, of course, required special equipment of the kind Copley had used when painting his mammoth *Defeat of the Floating Batteries at Gibraltar*—a platform and a roller by which the canvas could be raised or lowered as required. The Leicester Square panoramas were painted in large structures expressly built or adapted for such work: first a wooden rotunda near Barker's home at 14 West Square, St. George's Fields, and later a tall building that was long a landmark in Kentish Town. In such cav-

33. Burford's Panorama: Cairo (painted by Robert Burford and H. C. Selous from drawings made especially for them by David Roberts; engraving in *Illustrated London News*, 20 March 1847).

ernous rooms, working from sketches which divided the circle of the horizon into eight sections, the master panoramists and their assistants painted with a care that the detractors of their novel art refused to acknowledge.

The canvas used for the purpose [said a writer in *Chambers's Journal* in 1860] is of the very finest description that is manufactured. The broad brushes with which the sky is painted are of the finest French hair; and even with these delicate implements, the direction, horizontal or perpendicular, in which the brush might be used would be distinctly visible, owing to the fineness of the canvas and the strength of the light, were it not softened down with the utmost elaboration. Indeed, the escape of a single hair from the brush, if it were suffered to remain on the surface, would be a distinctly perceptible blemish. The more important parts of the panorama are painted with pencils of the finest sable, so delicate as to make lines as fine as a hair, each of which, however, is perceptible by the eye of the spectator. Zinc-white is used instead of lead, and the oils employed are of the purest quality that can be manufactured.[27]

One wonders how the finished painting was transported to Leicester Square; supposedly it was carted there in several bulky rolled-up segments. Once it arrived, a painting could go through the process of being

set up in one circle while the other remained open to the public. Hung from a hoop about 283 feet in circumference, in the case of the lower, larger circle, the canvas was attached to a similar hoop at the bottom and tightly stretched.

Since all the illumination came through the skylight, the panorama was open only in the daytime, and even then its effectiveness depended on the season and the weather. (Robert Burford once toyed with the idea of illuminating the canvas with gas, from below. But there were practical obstacles as well as the obvious danger from fire, and so the scheme was never put to the test.) The spring and autumn were deemed the best times to see a panorama; during the winter the daylight was insufficient to do justice to the painting, and in summer it was too intense, bringing out blemishes that were otherwise unnoticed. A dull London day was no time to go to Leicester Square, and a foggy one was the worst of all. In 1832 the *Athenaeum* apologized for not reviewing Burford's new painting of Stirling in the appropriate issue because "on the day appointed for the private view we had one of those fleecy-hosiery atmospheres, which make it impossible to see anything."[28] The time of day, too, affected the impression the picture made. Reviewing the Damascus scene in

34. The building at 14 West Square, St. George's Fields, where Barker's and Burford's early panoramas were painted (unsigned wash drawing, 1827).

1841, the same journal commented that "our favourable judgment [may be] ascribed to having visited it in the afternoon, when the waning sunshine and lessening light gave the scene a crowning charm of reality."[29] Despite the limited hours of daylight in the winter, the Leicester Square panorama remained open, its advertisements assuring the public that there was heat "in the circles"—a phrase which seems not to have had any Dantean suggestion in that context.

The length of the runs of individual panoramas varied greatly, but as the contemporary penciled annotations in a file of the printed guides in the library of the Museum of London show, the average for the Burford productions in the late forties and fifties was about twelve months. The picture of Athens seems to have been retained for a full three years (1845–1848), the Lucerne two years (1850–1852), and the Nimrud that followed it, eighteen months. On the other hand, revivals, either an old painting reshown, or an old subject repainted, seem to have had limited appeal. The

1846 Constantinople lasted only two months, and the Waterloo, requisitely reshown at the time of Wellington's death, was on display merely from 17 November 1852 to 12 March 1853. After Burford died in 1861, his successors, evidently unable or unwilling to obtain fresh canvases, sought to squeeze still more drops of revenue from the old ones. Following a series of triple bills, the Leicester Square panorama closed forever on 12 December 1863.

Such was the history and nature of a London exhibition which added a familiar word to the language, a landmark to Leicester Square, and an influential concept to the entertainment world. Much more remains to be said about it, but in the wider context of the other pictorial entertainments that competed with it. "The" panorama, though first in the field, was but one among many that bore that capaciously categorical name. And of these, one in particular, created in the late 1820s at the southeastern corner of Regent's Park, spectacularly outdid Barker and Burford. We must now turn to it.

A Panorama in a Pleasure Dome

11

This City now doth, like a garment, wear
The beauty of the morning; silent, bare,
Ships, towers, domes, theatres, and temples lie
Open unto the fields, and to the sky;
All bright and glittering in the smokeless air.
—Wordsworth, "Composed Upon Westminster
Bridge, September 3, 1802"

While business at Burford's rotunda proceeded in its quiet, uneventful course, a pleasure palace in a new section of London to the northwest, Regent's Park, housed a panorama that allegedly was forty times the size of the one in the smaller circle at Leicester Square.[1] As the Colosseum lurched toward what would seem to have been its foreordained fate and its successive managers led lives of quiet desperation, its supreme attraction, the vast panorama of London, remained intact, an ironic symbol of permanence in the ever fluctuating ambience of this intended monument of—or to—the Age of Elegance.

The panorama and the pleasure palace were conceived separately. In 1821 the dean and chapter of St. Paul's Cathedral undertook a thorough repair and restoration of the building's great dome and its surmounting ball and cross—the highest point in London, from which, for many years, sightseers had looked out on a view that embraced a horizon of some 120 miles when the weather was perfect. For this purpose a scaffolding was put up around the topmost part of the building. Seeing it, a land surveyor named Thomas Hornor recognized a once-in-a-lifetime

opportunity to make a complete graphic record of all that could be discerned from this vantage point. His reward would be the proceeds of a set of four panoramic engravings to be made from his sketches.

Not much is known of Hornor. A Yorkshireman, he specialized in depicting country estates by a combination of maps and watercolor sketches: "pictorial surveying" was the phrase he used in an advertisement in 1814 recommending his services to the landed gentry. A protracted stay in Wales resulted in some 300 or 400 watercolors of estates in that region.[2] One of Hornor's clients was a wealthy banker and member of Parliament named Rowland Stephenson, who engaged him to make camera lucida sketches of his acres at Marshalls, near Romford, Essex. Many years after Hornor disappeared from public view a magazine averred that "a Quaker professedly, he was in reality a compound of Barnum and [Beau] Nash,—as great a dandy as the one and as great a humbug as the other."[3]

It is at least plain that Hornor had no fear of heights. Having received the necessary permission, he made the top of St. Paul's his second home, day after day climbing the stairway through the shell of the cupola, then a series of exterior ladders past the additional scaffolding fanned out as a safety net, and finally, more and more perilously, creeping past the ball and cross to the "Observatory"—a tiny shack, rigged over the cross on fragile poles, where he worked. Assisted by powerful telescopes and some sort of apparatus he had invented "by which the most distant and intricate scenery may be delineated with mathematical accuracy,"

Hornor slowly sketched his way around the complete circle.[4] He had to be at work at sunrise, to get as much done as he could before London's countless chimneys began to cast a sooty cloud between him and his subject. He tried to work in all weathers and all seasons, so long as visibility permitted; sometimes the wind was so high that he had to cling to the scaffolding, like a mariner at the mast-head. He spent one whole night in his precarious shanty, but one night only, for the cold was unbearable. Even under the best conditions, moreover, he had to contend with the London outdoor artist's constant bane, the varying intensity and shifting direction of light. So great was his passion for accuracy that after he had sketched a certain tiny segment of the view from aloft, he went by foot to every street, every building, every open space to verify and amplify his drawings.*

In 1823 Hornor issued an elaborate prospectus of his engraving project, complete with a cross section of the dome showing the route he had taken every day to the summit.[5] Never unappreciative of the value of publicity, he planted lengthy descriptions of his exploit in at least two magazines, the newly founded *Mirror of Literature* and the venerable *European Magazine*. Despite the fanfare, however, the engravings were never made. Instead, the 2,000 sketches Hornor brought down from the golden cross were diverted to serve as raw material for what he conceived to be the climax, the culmination, the *ne plus ultra* of the panoramic art: a permanent installation, the biggest in the world, designed to provide London showgoers with a facsimile of the view from St. Paul's without their having to make the long, arduous climb only, as too often happened, to find the city below hidden in smoke and fog when they got there.

The building to house the panorama was already being projected. We cannot be sure how Hornor's panorama plans became attached to someone else's palace plans, but there is every likelihood that the man who brought them together was his former employer, the banker Rowland Stephenson. One of the most desirable sites in London at the moment was the southeastern corner of the newly developed Regent's Park, adjacent to the terraces then rising as a climax to the sequence of wide dignified streets—Regent Street, the Quadrant, Langham Place, and Portland Place—by which the architect John Nash proposed to link Pall Mall with the park. Here a group of speculators planned to build a magnificent palace-for-profit, dedicated to the more seemly pleasures of Regency society.

There doubtless was also in the minds of Stephenson and his associates the idea that the Colosseum would be a kind of public counterpart of Carlton House, the sumptuous mansion in Pall Mall on which the Prince Regent, now George IV, had squandered a fortune. As *à la mode* as Carlton House in decoration and appointments, the Colosseum would afford subscribing members and their families "the advantages of a club-house in town with the attractions of a rural villa."[6]

Construction began in the summer of 1824 on a site between Albany Street and Cambridge Terrace, now occupied by the Royal College of Physicians; the name of the adjacent Colosseum Terrace memorializes the earlier building. The brilliant twenty-three-year-old architect Decimus Burton designed the building around the proposed panorama. It was a polygon of brick overlaid with stucco, each of its sixteen sides being twenty-five feet long and sixty-four high, with a six-columned Doric portico facing westward across the southern edge of the park. The center of the structure was a rotunda, topped by a dome thirty feet wider than that of St. Paul's and rising 112 feet above the ground.[7]

The rotunda was finished first. The dome's 15,000 square feet were painted to represent the sky, and at a distance of three feet from the wall at its base was hung a circle of canvas 134 feet in diameter (as against the ninety feet of Burford's large circle) and measuring, from dome to floor, sixty-four feet; at the bottom of this expanse, the canvas was curved inward, accounting for 4,000 more square feet. The total surface of canvas to be painted, therefore, was about 46,000 square feet. Hornor quickly discovered that it was one thing to draw two thousand sketches at the top of St. Paul's and quite another to translate them into a continuous painting of such enormous dimensions, involving hitherto unfaced problems of linear and aerial perspective in addition to those that Barker had confronted—the distortion of horizontal lines when painted on a curved canvas; the unrealistic nearness of the horizon at eye level and the concomitant diminution of foreground. This last difficulty was more acute in Hornor's case because of his subject and the point from which it was depicted. At eye level from the top of St. Paul's, the viewer saw only the distant horizon; the foreground—the area of the city nearest the cathedral—was much lower and, in reality, less distinct than suited the purpose of the panoramist, bent on reproducing every detail of architecture.

* Writing in *Sketches by Boz* ("Greenwich Fair") of the pensioners who set up telescopes on the hospital grounds at fair time, Dickens said they were "requested to find out particular houses in particular streets, which it would have been a task of some difficulty for Mr. Horner (not the young gentleman who ate mince-pies with his thumb, but the man of Colosseum notoriety) to discover." In view of what happened to Hornor—as we will shortly see—Dickens's first readers would have found more than meets the casual eye in his use of the word "notoriety."

Hornor solved this problem by deliberately exaggerating the foreground, bringing it, in effect, closer to the spectator than the original actually was.

Apart from these problems of craft, there was the sheer practical difficulty of working on a canvas which was always in motion from the movement of air or some other cause, such as someone's leaning on it, and the awkwardness, not to say danger, of painting from a platform fifty or sixty feet above ground. To the rescue, as he was not reluctant to put it in subsequent accounts, came Edmund Thomas Parris.[8] A thirty-one-year-old painter who had just made his first appearance at the Academy exhibition (1824), he was known to Hornor through having invented an apparatus to enable artists to rise into the dome of St. Paul's to restore Thornhill's paintings. The cathedral authorities had run out of money and so his offer was not accepted, but Hornor's impasse inside the dome of the Colosseum provided a fresh challenge to Parris's ingenuity and an alternate use for his equipment. He now provided access to the hanging canvas by a variety of scaffoldings, rigging, bridges, and platforms. Sometimes the painter was hung from the roof in a basket or a kind of bosun's chair; at other times, he stood on a perilously swaying little stage "supported from the floor by two or three long and slender spars, which vibrated with every motion of his arm." Parris fell only twice, and escaped serious injury both times.

Now that the canvas had been made completely accessible, all that remained was to find a way to transfer Hornor's 2,000 raw sketches to it. On 12 December 1825 Parris began what proved to be the five months' task of chalking the outlines, enlarged sixteen times, onto the cloth. Conceding that even he could not singlehandedly chalk and then paint the entire panorama, he accepted Hornor's offer of several easel-trained assistants, but soon found that they were almost more bother than they were worth. When they were set to work on their allotted rectangles, the result was what Parris later called "a kind of Dutch concert," in which each performer played a distinct and separate tune. Each also was anxious that his allotment, whatever it might be, should be conspicuous; "like some Rosencrantz or Guildenstern, seeking to render his character as prominent and effective as that of Hamlet." One individualist made his smoke blow in a direction opposite to that shown in an adjoining panel; another lighted his buildings with sunshine from the north. An additional perplexity, unrelated to the system of parceling out work, was the change various colors under-

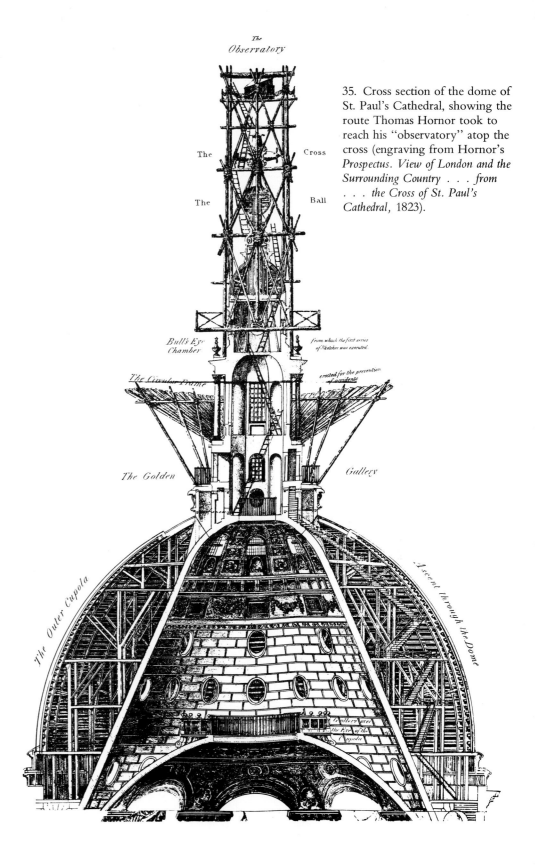

35. Cross section of the dome of St. Paul's Cathedral, showing the route Thomas Hornor took to reach his "observatory" atop the cross (engraving from Hornor's Prospectus. *View of London and the Surrounding Country . . . from . . . the Cross of St. Paul's Cathedral*, 1823).

36. The Colosseum: painting the panorama of London (lithograph by Ackermann, 1829). The "geometrical ascent" (stairway enclosing elevator) is in the foreground; Parris's crew of painters are seen at work on platforms, boatswain's chairs, and other equipment. The covered area at the bottom was to become the "salon for the exhibition of works of art."

37. The Colosseum: the panorama of London seen from a painter's platform (lithograph by Ackermann, 1829). The column containing the staircase and "ascending platform" (elevator), surmounted by the viewing galleries, is on the left. The view past the (painted) twin towers of the cathedral, in the right foreground, is to the west, down Fleet Street and the Strand. The scaffolding in the left foreground was permanent, being a replica of that erected around the top of the real building at the time Hornor made his sketches.

* In his report on his personal achievement, Parris overlooked one who did. This was George Chambers (1803–1840), a native of Whitby who had left school at the age of eight to become, successively, a coal heaver, a seaman, and a ship and house painter. In 1823 his landlord, proprietor of a Wapping pub, took him to see Hornor. On the strength of the easel paintings he was producing in his spare time and, equally important, the head for heights he had acquired as a sailor, Chambers was hired and put to work under Parris. His admittedly partisan early biographer, describing Parris's "conceit" and "jealousy" when confronted with the work of a superior artist, offers us a revealing insight into the personal politics that soured the Colosseum project: "Parris being the head man, reserved all the best things,—such as the churches and public buildings—to himself, and grieved the gentle spirit of Chambers by painting after him, and putting the finishing touches to his work. Parris had a politic design in this—it gave him a colour to declare that Chambers was merely engaged to do the subordinate or mechanical portions of the work, and that the credit of this magnificent view belonged chiefly, if not wholly, to himself. Nay, so far did Parris envy the touches of others in this great public work, that he hid what they had done by painting smoke over it, although by so doing he spoiled the picture. But he could not disfigure or obscure the River Thames, which was Chambers's work, although his name is not personally associated with the praises bestowed upon it." After the job, for which Chambers was never paid in full, was finished, he worked as a scene painter at the Pavilion Theatre and gained a modest reputation as a marine artist. (John Watkins, *Life and Career of George Chambers*, London, 1841, esp. pp. 26–32; David Cordingly, *Marine Painting in England, 1700–1800*, London, 1974, pp. 162–64.)

went, according to their distance from the spectator and the angle at which they were seen. Red bricks turned blue and blue slates turned red, the result being a vast patchwork of unharmonized hues. In the end, Parris again took over the job himself, leaving only "the more laborious parts of the task" to a platoon of specially trained house painters who presumably had no untoward artistic aspirations.*

While all this was going on under the dome, London's curiosity mounted. A barrage of articles in newspapers and magazines, designed to reinforce the publicity Hornor's feat atop St. Paul's had already received, described the marvels that the new building and its gardens would contain. At the same time, the inexplicably slow progress in construction—a mystery the more tantalizing and conspicuous because of the Colosseum's exposed site in an especially newsworthy region of London—raised questions; and the questions generated confident rumors. To judge from Hornor's attempts to squelch them, they had to do with the general impression that the speculators (of questionable repute?) who were behind this grandiose project were getting cold feet. How much truth there was in this rumor it is impossible to say, but Hornor flatly denied it. A full column in the *Times* for 2 August 1827, almost surely inspired by him, sought to contradict a report that "the money was furnished by capitalists, who had felt some doubt about advancing the requisite funds as it proceeded." No, the writer maintained: the long delay in completion was solely due to Hornor's insistence that the panorama be painted with minute accuracy. The Colosseum as a whole was his own venture. A year later, however, this time in a signed letter, Hornor found it necessary to counter fresh gossip arising from the fact that visitors were not allowed to inspect the premises. Their exclusion, he wrote the *Times* (23 September 1828), had led to "rumors of obstacles that never occurred, and to ideas that never existed." No stock company was involved in the Colosseum; he and "a few private friends" were the sole proprietors. The principal difficulty had been to find artists capable of working on so novel a project as the giant panorama, and then to train them. But now, thanks to Parris's "artistical ability and mechanical ingenuity," the end was in sight, and a prospectus inviting subscriptions would soon be ready for circulation.

On 13 December 1828 the *Times* ran an article predicting that the Colosseum would be finished by February. Sixteen days later, in its Police News columns, it announced that a warrant had been issued for the ar-

rest of Rowland Stephenson, partner in the Lombard Street firm of Remington, Stephenson, and Company and treasurer of St. Bartholomew's Hospital, who had disappeared with £40,000 in government securities deposited with his firm by various clients and double that amount in cash. (Later the amount of the defalcation was several times revised upward.) Thenceforward, the Stephenson story vied for newspaper space with the concurrent sensation of Burke and Hare, the Edinburgh body snatchers. Stephenson was reported seen here, there, and everywhere, especially in the west of England. As the days passed, the consensus grew that he had fled to America by way of Bristol. Hornor had suffered the abrupt loss of his financial backer. Evidently, Hornor had relied upon Stephenson's backing to pay the heavy expenses of completing the Colosseum and its panorama, and when Stephenson decamped, Hornor was left with large bills and no credit.

Hornor's manifold connections with the London press were never more useful than now. In immediate response to the crisis, the *Literary Gazette* came out with a two-part article (17, 31 January) on the Colosseum; the February issue of the *London Magazine* carried a descriptive essay on the coming wonders, somewhat in the discursive manner of Leigh Hunt; the *Mirror of Literature* also had an article in its issue for 14 February. The *Athenaeum* for 21 January limited its coverage of the private view to two paragraphs, but wished Hornor success, hoping that "when through perils as numerous as those in the Apostolic list, and after having been in jeopardy of every kind every hour, he has put the last touch to his astounding work, he may have nothing to do but rest from his labours." But Hornor had already put his last touch to the "astounding work." In the second week of February, he too was on his way to the United States.

Stephenson, it turned out, had in fact preceded him there. Soon after his arrival at Savannah, the absconding financier was kidnapped by local "ruffians" who had read of the rewards for his capture posted in New York. They delivered him to the New York authorities as planned, but in the absence of an extradition treaty between Britain and the United States he could not be surrendered to the British authorities. As an international incident brewed, Stephenson was released on a writ of habeas corpus. A year later he was said to be living in hunt-country luxury at Bristol, Virginia, and still later (December 1833) he was reported to be in prison for a debt of $80,000 owed to a former sheriff of London who was in the same jail.[9]

Meanwhile, Hornor had arrived in New York, where he set up as a free-lance artist.[10] Apart from later rumors that he had died insane and "by the roadside," nothing more is heard of him, except for the recently discovered fact that he died in New York on 14 March 1844 and was buried in the Friends' Burial Ground there.[11]

Back at the Colosseum, Hornor's creditors had moved in, retaining Parris to finish work on the panorama. In the spring and summer of 1829, while workmen busied themselves staining the stucco to give it "the massive and weather-exposed effect of hard material and antiquity," the Colosseum, still far from finished, was opened to patrons at five shillings a head. These had, among other attractions, the privilege of watching Parris and his crew still dangling from the dome on suspended scaffolds and balancing themselves on catwalks. Soon four hundred persons a day were being admitted, including the Duchess of Clarence in repeated visits, the Duke of Wellington with his constant companion Lady Conyngham, and Prince Lieven, the Russian ambassador, and his wife. In June the printseller Ackermann, at whose shops, along with other agencies, the admission tickets could be purchased, issued a set of five handsome lithographs, *Graphic Illustrations of the Colosseum, Regent's Park,* which had a large sale and remain today a vivid record both of the building itself as it was—or was purported to be—on the eve of its opening and of the engineering work that went into the panorama.

Over three years more would be needed to bring the Colosseum to a state of official completion, "not indeed upon the scale of magnitude contemplated originally," said the *Times* on 25 October 1832, "but still upon a scale which far exceeds anything of the kind which has hitherto been attempted." It was imposing enough to call forth praise from the aged poet Samuel Rogers, whose sympathies still were rooted in classical antiquity. The Colosseum, he said, "is a noble building,—finer than any thing among the remains of ancient architectural art in Italy. It is ridiculous to hear Englishmen who have been at Rome talking with such rapture of the ancient buildings they have seen there: in fact, the old Romans were but indifferent architects."[12] One hopes this opinion reached Decimus Burton.

In the center of the building, approached from the Doric portico through a vestibule, was a spacious rotunda called "the Saloon of Arts" or "the Hall of Sculpture." Here, by invitation of the "committee of management" (Hornor's creditors), "professors of the ingenious and fine arts" exhibited their works. Alongside recent productions there stood casts of Phidias's *Diana,* the *Venus de Medici,* the *Apollo Belvedere,* Canova's *Three Graces,* and replicas of Michaelangelo's *Moses* and *Lorenzo of the Medicis.* Adjoining this room on the south was a glass-enclosed conservatory.[13]

Outside, mainly on the south toward the New Road, Hornor had (according to the first guidebook to the Colosseum) exercised his landscaper's art, which "had the necromantic, or talismanic power of creating mountains, dells, cascades, and the most delicious scenes of Paradise, from and within a small and limited piece of flat ground."[14] Assisted by mirrors and other illusionistic devices, he had transformed the four acres of Marylebone soil into what appeared to be a garden several times as large. By excavating ravines and forming high sloping banks with the spoil, he had contrived a series of terraces planted with exotic plants and flowers and with twenty-foot trees which effectively enclosed the garden from outside view. A winding "valley" led to the conservatory entrance; a subterranean passage in the form of a series of grottoes—the last component to be finished (October 1832)—delivered one to a Swiss cottage erected on the north side of the building. From the cottage's windows could be seen a rushing cataract, which an optical illusion made to seem much higher than the fifty feet it was said actually to measure, and a "lake" of real water. Chained on the property rocks brooded a despondent eagle, which was reported to have been acquired from the Exeter Change menagerie when it closed and which became a longtime fixture of the Colosseum. The four rooms of the cottage were completely furnished for the use of a typical Swiss family, but it seems to have been occupied by an employee with a strong Cockney—others said Irish—accent who kept the refreshment concession there by day and watched by night.

Not all of Hornor's envisioned attractions, mentioned in preliminary press descriptions, were realized in the finished Colosseum. The original plan contemplated an additional garden of fourteen acres in front of the building, connected with the other by a tunnel. Here were to be more shrubbery and trees, with fountains and temples in the manner of an elaborate pleasure garden. On some evenings the gardens were to be lighted by lamps concealed in the flower beds. There was also to be an artificial moon atop the building. This last innovation came into being, but for one night only, when on 4 August 1835 one Alexander Gordon mounted a limelight on the roof. It could be seen from

38. The Colosseum: the west front, facing Regent's Park (engraving from *A Picturesque Guide to the Regent's Park,* 1829).

39. The Colosseum: south side of the grounds, seen from the conservatory (lithograph by Ackermann, 1829). This view is an imaginative rendering, presumably made from architect's sketches. Since it was made and offered for sale before the building was finished, it does not represent the Colosseum as it actually was after Hornor's sudden departure required a curtailment of the original lavish plans.

many points in the park and as far away as Baker Street.[15]

❧❋❧

But the supreme experience at the Colosseum was to see the imitation London from the top of the imitation St. Paul's. From the floor of the rotunda rose a circular structure of timber which supported the viewing galleries, the first of which was higher than the four-story terraces in nearby Portland Place. If they wished, visitors could make the ascent by conventional means, one of the two spiral staircases enclosed within the shaft, each of which led to a separate gallery. The climb possibly was not as constricted as the familiar one in the Monument or as steep as the one in Leicester Square, and it was certainly less taxing than the sequence of tight staircases and rude ladders that Hornor had negotiated so many times in the real St. Paul's. But it did not have to be attempted at all, because inside the core of the staircase was a miraculous "ascending room," the very first passenger elevator in London. Holding ten or twelve persons, it was worked by hydraulic power.*

The ascent by foot had a considerable advantage in verisimilitude, because on the way up one could look out at the lower part of the panorama through an imitation of the scaffolding that had enclosed St. Paul's when Hornor was working. Whether arriving by stairway or by lift, spectators stepped out on the lower of the two circular balustraded galleries from which they could inspect the panorama at their leisure. These galleries corresponded with those at the cathedral itself. Extending umbrellalike from underneath the lower one was a replica of a portion of the outer dome of St. Paul's, so that, bending over the railing, a spectator would see it closest at hand and then, beyond it in the immediate foreground—the three-dimensional mockup blending into the painting—those portions of the cathedral's roof and towers which would be seen from the corresponding place on the real gallery.

The second gallery was thirty feet above the other, with a corresponding alteration in perspective. The city below and the horizon were farther away, though the detail of the portrayal was no less sharp; and above, to extend the illusion, was the original ball which had been replaced during the repair work in 1821–22, surmounted by a facsimile of the cross. The final touch of verisimilitude was provided by Hornor's frail hut, which was rigged atop the cross. In the earliest designs

and prospectuses, provision was made for still another viewing gallery, as well as for two levels of entertainment rooms adjacent to the ball and cross, one for a "refectory" serving ices and other refreshments lifted from the cool cellar, the other for music or balls, though the space would have been, to say the least, rather restricted. These top-of-the-dome extras seem never to have been installed.

All the lighting came from a seventy-five-foot skylight at the top of the dome, which was concealed from the spectators. The picture, of course, was brightest at the top, the light diminishing toward the bottom. The gradation of lighting enhanced the illusion, but nothing could be done, by way of movable shadows, to imitate the changing direction of the sunlight according to the time of day or the season of the year. In this vision of London, as in the land of Tennyson's lotos-eaters, it always seemed afternoon.

The painted canvas represented London and its environs as they could be seen for twenty miles in all directions, under absolutely ideal conditions, cloudless, smokeless, and fogless (though Hornor introduced a suggestion of mist in the far distance). Benches were provided on each of the galleries, as well as spyglasses by which one could discover distant details that would have been invisible to the naked eye either *in situ* or from this substitute vantage point. From the City to Windsor Castle, Epping Forest, and Greenwich, everything was depicted with microscopic particularity. An American naval officer summarized as well as anyone, in those early years, the hypnotic effect of the whole arrangement:

You insensibly draw back from the balustrade, separating the spectators from [the picture], as from the fearful parapet, from which, on the cathedral itself, you cast a glance into the terrific depth around. And are obliged almost to reason with yourself, to be persuaded that it is not nature, instead of a work of art, upon which you are bestowing your admiration.

The winding river, with its craft and numerous bridges; the undulating sea of brick and mortar, sweeping widely on every hand; the long vistas here and there, marking the grand avenues—by Fleet street and the Strand, Oxford street, and the new road—through the city; the unnumbered public edifices; the parks, the palaces, the gardens, and the distant, but lovely regions encircling the whole, for twenty miles in every direction, are all presented to the view, as distinctly and minutely, as faithfully to themselves and to their colouring in the finest shades of the purest atmosphere, as if seen under the best possible advantages, from the giddy height itself.[16]

* This was Hornor's own invention, announced as early as 1826, in the August issue of the *Gentleman's Magazine* (96, part 2, pp. 160–61). "It will be furnished with various objects sufficiently amusing to excite the curiosity of the company for a few moments. In the mean time, by a strong mechanical power, and by a movement wholly imperceptible, the spectator will be raised to a proper elevation for viewing the painting. The novelty and surprise which this must produce in the minds of persons who a few moments before were setting in a carriage, or sauntering in the park, can hardly be imagined, and cannot fail to add to the attraction and interest which the panorama is, of itself, well calculated to excite."

So compelling was the illusion that more than a few spectators insisted that the people depicted in the streets and the parks actually moved. A visiting Persian (whose account of the sights of London in 1836, to be sure, is the most fanciful one can conceive), claimed in addition to have heard "a great noise . . . of carriages, coaches and horses."[17] For this latter fancy there is some independent evidence, because a writer in the *People's Journal* in the mid-forties said, "there is a low murmuring, as of a busy countless multitude, in eager motion far down beneath you," as well as "sound of numerous clocks striking the hour simultaneously, or in quick succession, and occasionally you hear a merry peal of bells from a church steeple near or distant."[18]

When Hornor made his sketches, the site of the future Post Office in St. Martin's-le-Grand was empty, and he so represented it. By the time the panorama was painted, however, the Post Office had been built, and he and Parris decided that it would be "more interesting" to compromise and show it still scaffolded. Parris therefore went up to the Golden Gallery at St. Paul's, made sketches, and in seventeen days painted in the unfinished edifice, minutely portraying every plinth and frieze.[19] Apart from this addition, the finished panorama showed London as it was in 1821–22. This meant that the Colosseum itself was missing—an omission of no little importance, because this massive building, with its "heavy, huge, and dome-crowned walls," was now conspicuous in the middle distance as one looked west-northwest from atop the real St. Paul's.

But if, *at* the Colosseum, the Colosseum could not be seen from St. Paul's, *from* the Colosseum one could see St. Paul's. From the very top of the rotunda, even above the ball and cross, a final short stairway led to an open-air gallery that ran along the circumference of the dome. From this breezy vantage point could be inspected the newest "improvements" in fashionable Regent's Park; in the opposite direction, Hyde Park and Westminster Abbey; and, not least, the real St. Paul's, its dome and cross shining atop Ludgate Hill.

This, then, was the Colosseum in its first years: a London sensation, the most celebrated entertainment spot of the moment. How far it pervaded the public consciousness is illustrated by the quite different uses that were made of its topicality. As early as 1827, a scene in the Covent Garden pantomime, *Harlequin and Number Nip,* had a quartet of beggar boys singing a "sad complaint" against a backcloth depicting the Colosseum.[20] No such dimly implied social criticism was present in another use made of the building some-

what later: the completed structure, as shown in architectural drawings, was the *mise en scène* for a group of engravings illustrating the season's fashions.[21] An equally bright side of the Colosseum's presence was stressed to a different audience in 1833, when the *Penny Magazine,* a new weekly dedicated to enlisting the minds and wills of the working class in the cause and conviction of British Progress, interpreted the Colosseum as symbolizing "the best possessions of civilization" and the accumulated advantages of the British people.[22] It was, in short, a sermon in stucco.

But it did not pay. If, as was said at the time, Hornor left £60,000 in debts behind him, it would have taken an extraordinary flood of five-shilling patrons, coming day after day and year after year, to put the Colosseum in the black. After the first flurry of excitement, the novelty wore off, a development that must have been hastened by the nervous public climate of the moment. The agitation for electoral reform had thrown England into a fever of political anxiety. The nation had not recovered from the financial crisis of 1825–26, and the amusement industry was in a particularly depressed condition, as the general lowering of prices at the theatres demonstrated. The reduction of the Colosseum's admission fee in 1832 to two shillings (one for the panorama, the other for the rest of the building and grounds), though required by the special circumstances in which the establishment found itself, was part of a widespread trend.* In addition, the Colosseum's well-publicized association with the peculating Stephenson did not noticeably contribute to its prestige; it is possible that among the potential subscribers who did not sign up were members of the nobility and gentry who had had money with Remington, Stephenson, and Company.

After only two years, therefore, the managing committee was glad to unload the Colosseum on the famous tenor John Braham, who paid £40,000 for it out of the considerable fortune he had amassed from his singing career and from the first English production of *Der Freischütz* and other popular operas. When Braham and his partner, the actor-manager Frederick Henry Yates, took over, the Colosseum's future was predicated on its ability to compete with other popular entertainments on their own terms. Thus they added, for example, a "Panoramic Painting" of the South African Kaffir country, showing, among other subjects, the massacre in 1829 of a party led by the aptly named Lieutenant Farewell. Entrance to this exhibition was through an African glen, a reconstruction of wild and rocky scenery populated by stuffed young animals

* Late in 1829, notwithstanding the lesson one would think Hornor's catastrophe had taught prospective speculators, plans were announced to build an equally ambitious hall with special emphasis on the drama. A singing master at 11 Liverpool Street with the charming name of Gesualdo Lanza circulated a prospectus for a "Panarmonion," which would include a "grand panorama" not further described, a subscription theatre, an "academic" theatre for aspiring actors, an assembly and concert room, and an exhibition room for works of art. (JJ Coll., London Play Places box 7.) Nothing more is heard of the Panarmonion or of Signor Lanza.

40. The Colosseum: the Hall of Mirrors (drawing by C. Marshall).

and ingeniously lighted to represent the successive effects of dawn, noon, and evening.[23] The marine grotto leading from the garden to the Swiss chalet likewise was equipped with mechanical pictures and sound effects, one such display portraying a bark heading for shore to the accompaniment of rolling waves and the pounding of breakers.[24]

Hornor's pipedream of the building as a resort of the rich and fashionable was not quite abandoned, however. In 1835 Braham added to the building, on the Albany Street side, a "Grand Reception or Banqueting Room of Mirrors, supported by Crystal Columns, and Lined with Looking Glass." It was opened in July with a charity fete in aid of three London hospitals, patronized by the king and queen and other members of the royal family, including Princess Victoria. Two thousand persons were there, resplendent in military, naval, diplomatic, and court garb. Presumably the price of tickets, twenty-five shillings, discouraged the attendance of what the *Times* called "persons who had no pretensions to respectability." Some said the event

compared favorably with the famous fancy-dress balls at Almack's, the elegant "assembly room" in King Street, St. James's, which since 1765 had been the scene of innumerable fashionable occasions. According to the newspapers, the Hall of Mirrors was supplemented by "the Splendid Salon de Danse, Egyptian Tent, and Illuminated Terraces," as well as an Indian Supper Room "overhanging the waterfalls"; but these probably were areas of the original building renamed for the occasion, as the Saloon of Arts was temporarily converted into the "Salon de Nations."[25]

Another attempt to sustain—or revive—the Colosseum's ultra-respectability was made in January 1838, when it was the site of the first noteworthy series of English prom concerts—an importation from France, where the institution was known as the *concerts à la Musard,* after the composer and conductor who had introduced the idea five years earlier.* A sixty-piece orchestra played a program of overtures, quadrilles, and waltzes as the attending music lovers strolled and had light refreshments, in the manner of old Ranelagh and

* The Colosseum, however, did not *introduce* the prom concert to England, as is sometimes said. That distinction seemingly belonged to Madame Tussaud in her temporary quarters in the Gray's Inn Road, 1833—the same year the concerts began in Paris. A placard reproduced in J. T. Tussaud's *The Romance of Madame Tussauds* (London, 1920), p. 72, announces "a Musical Promenade every Evening from Half-past Seven till Ten, when a selection of Music will be performed by the Messrs. Tussaud and Fishers; the Promenade will be lighted with a profusion of lamps, producing, with the variety of rich costumes, special decorations, etc., an unequalled coup d'oeil." There is no question that the Colosseum had a bigger orchestra.

Vauxhall. The experiment was successful enough to warrant a daily performance for several weeks, after which the concerts were moved to a succession of other locales.[26]

These repeated gestures toward restoring the tone that had been built into the Colosseum's prospectus but seldom had been realized in practice did nothing to arrest its decline. By this time it was plainly the victim of oversanguine enterpreneurial hopes, the show-going public's fickleness, and slack management. From 1835 onward Braham was deeply involved in another expensive enterprise, the St. James's Theatre, which he built and managed to the accompaniment of frequent lawsuits. At one point he had to tour America for two years to recoup his losses, and his wife was constantly interfering with Yates's management at Regent's Park, to the latter's great annoyance.[27]

In the summer of 1838 Yates and Braham turned the Albany Street hall for the nonce into the Royal Colosseum Saloon under the aegis of the low comedian Charles Sloman, who had entered show business over thirty years earlier as "Master Solomon, the Comic Roscius." Sloman was then pioneering, in singing or concert saloons, the new kind of variety entertainment which would later be institutionalized as the music hall. When it is noted that during this same season he was "chairman" (compère) at the Duke's Head tavern in Whitechapel, little further evidence is needed of the depth to which the former pretensions of the Colosseum had by this time sunk. One paper, selecting another example for comparison, commented that "this splendid and aristocratic establishment has in its entertainments come down to the level of the Eagle in the City-Road. . . . At either place the public are admitted on payment of a shilling, having sixpenn'orth of grog out of the same. The following has been composed by Mr. Braham:

Now pay your bob, and take your grog, in my vast Colos-
    seum—
I've sung all songs in Opera, and chaunted in Te Deum,
But times are changed, and we must stoop, although we are
    unwilling,
Down from the grand half-guinea to the very humble
    shilling."[28]

The variety turns offered as the waiters circulated among the customers, bawling "Give your orders, gents," included (not necessarily all on the same bill) a burletta entitled *The Little Tiger*, starring a "Lilliputian Roscius," Master Hutchings, aged four; a vaudeville of *The Weathercock;* a concert by "The Minstrel Family"

with such songs as "The Hunter of the Tyrol," "Widow Mahony," "Old Robin Gray," and "Vive le Roi"; the "laughable Ballet" of *The Dancing Scotchman or Jockey and Jannie;* a ventriloquist, Mr. Alexandre, doing seven roles in his own piece, *Le coche d'Auxerre;* fireless fireworks ("a sort of combination of optics and mechanics"); waltzing; and so on.

Sloman lasted only one season at the Colosseum Saloon. Perhaps his following felt uncomfortable in what had started out as so emphatically posh an establishment, however faded its glories had by now become.* Braham and Yates therefore decided to seek the Colosseum's salvation elsewhere—in the current rage for popularized science and technology—by converting the protean premises into a Marylebone version of the newly opened Polytechnic Institution not far away in Regent Street (Chapter 27). The Colosseum earned good marks from the press for the contribution its "Gallery of Natural Magic" made to the culture of the masses. There was a fair amount to see and marvel over, in addition to optical illusions and scary ventures into "the World of Spirits," the former marine cavern, where a performance entitled "Phantoms of a Witches' Sabbath" was put on for children. Especially admirable were the achromatic solar microscope, magnifying (it was said) up to 4,665,600 times; a Gregorian reflecting telescope; and a "plate machine" with "electric surface of upwards of 80 square feet . . . so constructed as to give a striking distance or length of spark, hitherto unattainable."[29] But if the metropolis could support one hall of astounding magnifications and immense spark gaps, it could not, or would not, support two; and the Colosseum's show, unlike that at the Polytechnic, was a hastily conceived and slapdash enterprise.

And so, in 1840, the summer variety bill was restored in what now was called the Royal Colosseum Theatre and Saloon of Mirrors. The opening night was a disaster. The room was not one-fifth filled, and those who incautiously did attend had to suffer through an execrable program headed, or burdened, by one Mr. Carroll, of whom it was said that "if this aspirant to metropolitan fame rest his pretensions upon his capabilities to play and sing buffo parts, the sooner he retires the better." He sang a duet—entering three bars prematurely—with another debutante, a Miss Hamilton, whose talent, such as it was, "was wholly marred and annihilated by the worse than buffoonery of her coadjutor."[30] Still worse: Braham, like Loutherbourg when he added musical interludes to his Eidophusikon program, ran into trouble with the magis-

* If it was Greek Revival magnificence they were looking for, they could have found it in its pristine state and at no expense at all at Euston station, which opened in 1837. Its Doric arch alone cost £35,000, and its sixty-foot high "Regal Hall" (main waiting room) was adorned with statuary and other Colosseumlike amenities. About the same time, the patent theatres, which would lose their monopoly on legitimate drama in 1843, were seeking to bolster their fortunes by converting themselves into concert promenades during the summer season, the auditoriums being decorated with masses of hot-house plants, fountains playing real water, and statuary. So the Colosseum had strong competition from more than one direction.

41. The "Colossal Electrical Apparatus" at the Colosseum's Gallery of Natural Magic (*Mirror of Literature*, 34, 1839, 18).

trates on the ground that he lacked a music license.[31] But whereas the magistrates had benignly allowed Loutherbourg to proceed, they "suppressed," in the words of a letter to the *Times*, "the sink of vice the Colosseum had become."[32] The much-tried Braham belatedly learned that he had influential neighbors to contend with; one ran a concert saloon on the edge of Regent's Park at one's own risk.

But there was evidently no objection to a skating rink. The next season (1841), Braham opened the Glacarium, a rink of artificial ice produced by a chemical mixture consisting chiefly of soda and supposed to last two years with only routine maintenance. It was reported that the Skating Club gave the new rink its approval when the surface held at an indoor temperature of eighty-five degrees—a statement which, as regards London either indoors or outdoors, strains credulity, or would have before the summer of 1976.[33] The artificial ice may have held firm, but the next year the figurative ice gave way under Braham and Yates, and the Colosseum was put up for sale. In a fit of mel-

ancholy Byronesque verse entitled "Childe Snobson's Pilgrimage" the fledgling *Punch* celebrated "the chain'd eagle, with a broken wing, / The type of liberty for ever lost," "the land of artificial ice," and the chalet where "the pseudo Swiss doth . . . dwell." It concluded:

> While stands the Colosseum London stands;
> When falls the Colosseum London falls
> (They mean the picture done by many hands,
> Which decorates the Colosseum's walls:)
> Alas! this prophecy the sense appals,
> For Robins—auctioneer of vast renown—
> Has issued a prospectus where he calls
> The whole attention of the astonished town,
> To his intent to knock the Colosseum down.[34]

The prospectus issued by Robins, the famous auctioneer, was indeed worthy of mention—and of its subject. The flawed magniloquence began by alluding to the Colosseum as "the Most Classical Building throughout Europe . . . This Mighty Labour, The

42. The Colosseum, 1845: the Glyptotheka, or Museum of Sculpture (*Illustrated London News,* 26 April 1845).

Modern Wonder of Architecture . . . this Great Leviathan." After which, Robins's prose burst forth in drenching spate, with occasional intervals of verse:

The Colosseum, A Building which stands proudly preeminent amid all and everything that has been erected throughout Europe. Its renown obviates the necessity of a lengthened announcement, and the individual to whom the conduct of the Sale is committed is fully aware that it is on Classic Ground He is about to enter, and, therefore, he may well fear that by his imperfect attempt to strengthen and define its worth, he may but weaken the sensation that has so long existed. The Colosseum, in the Regent's Park, Is so designed from Its Colossel Dimensions, Which equal, if not exceed, in "Gigantic Elegance" The most celebrated Construction of Antiquity. It will be difficult to condense, in the usual space of a Particular of Sale, even the most prominent features connected with this Cyclopaean Structure, where Description Fails to Portray "Its eloquent proportions, / Its mighty gradations," which, even when seen, "Thou seest not all, but piecemeal thou must break, / To separate contemplation, the great whole." The Exquisite Proportions of the

Classic Portico, One of the finest specimens of the Greek Doric, together with "The Dome, the vast and wondrous Dome," which Proudly "——Vies / In air with earth's chief structures," Win our admiration, while there is nothing of ancient or modern days that can compete with it either in Classic Elegance, Grandeur of Effect, or Beauty of Proportion; And it must remain to future ages a monument of the genius of the architect, as an "Outshining and o'erwhelming edifice." The Dome, it is believed, is of larger dimensions than that of any other of a similar nature, and it is as admirable for the scientific principles of its internal construction as for the grandeur of its external effect; being "To art a model, / Simple, erect, severe, austere, sublime, / It looks tranquility."[35]

When the sale took place in May 1843, all the auctioneer's rhetoric could bring was 23,000 guineas, not much more than half of Braham's original investment. The purchaser was David Montague, a member of a firm of cement merchants, who closed down the whole dilapidated establishment and commissioned William Bradwell, a mainstay of the Covent Garden scenery department, to give it a thorough face-lifting.[36]

When the Colosseum reopened in 1845, it was evident that Bradwell had worked hard and to good effect.[37] Upon entering, the patron was first impressed by the fresh luxury of the rotunda, now renamed the Glyptotheka. Hung with silk instead of the former calico, it was encircled with a 300-foot frieze of the Panathenaic procession in the Elgin marbles, below which were "nine large Looking Glasses in handsome Gilt Frames, seats covered with Utrecht velvet, and twelve three-light gas branches supported by Groups of Cupid and Psyche." Placed about the room were statues and busts of Canute, Bacon, Chaucer, Caractacus, Richard the Lion-Hearted, Nelson, and other personages ancient and modern; all of the works of art displayed, amounting to some two hundred items, were for sale. The ascending room had been converted to steam power (supplied by a sixteen-horsepower engine housed in a shed in the north garden) and redecorated in Tudor style, with stained glass panels in its ceiling and its walls covered with crimson draperies. It provided, wrote one visitor, "the notion of being inclosed in a large and very gorgeous Chinese lantern." The former conservatory had become an aviary, half-Gothic, half-Moorish in tendency.

In the grounds, which had become a "weedy desolation," Bradwell retained Hornor's devices that made the four acres seem many more, but with new centers of attention: a scattering of property antique ruins—the Arch of Titus, the Temples of Theseus and Vesta. The former marine grotto now was a replica of the caves at Adelsberg, filled with fantastically shaped stalactites and stalagmites. The Swiss cottage remained, but from one of its windows could now be seen a magnified working model of a silver mine.

The panorama of London had been especially in need of attention. Once the top drawing card of the Colosseum, it had latterly proved something of a liability. Whereas Burford could, and did, change the subject of his picture at least once a year, Parris's panorama still depicted a rapidly changing London as it had been in 1822. It therefore attracted little of the repeat business which kept the Leicester Square operation prosperous. Except for those small portions accessible to broom or cloth, the canvas had been untouched since it was finished in 1829, and the sky was so badly cracked that a whole new plastering and repainting job was required. Parris was therefore called back to the scene of his early labors. Assisted by his son, he spent a year repainting the extreme and middle distance of the panorama, the parts which had been worst obscured by smoke and dirt. No attempt was made to bring the scene up to date.[38] The new management, however, hedged its bets—and sought to get more use out of the attraction, which hitherto had been open only during the daylight hours—by commissioning from the theatrical scene painter George Danson a new panorama, *London by Night*. This was made by tracing the whole of Parris's picture on linen, with apertures cut at numerous places where windows and street lamps were represented, and then transferring the new picture, section by section, to twenty-eight frames that folded out of sight below the day picture. At the end of the afternoon these frames were drawn up to the horizon, across the original picture, with space left behind to illuminate the cut-out windows and lamps. On the sky (the dome) a magic lantern projected clouds which passed over a lighted canvas moon. The *Examiner* was delighted by the show:

We see the lighted streets and shops; the people clustering and crowding in the roads and footways; the warm firesides of private dwellings shining forth a jovial red upon the outer night; skylights of factories and warehouses bright with the busy life within; church towers and steeples rising up like ghosts among the short-lived creatures fluttering about them; and, over all, a bright moon sailing proudly through the sky, and winking stars attending it. There are clouds, too; not obdurate masses of wood and canvas [as in the theatre], but mere shadowy vapour, flying fast before the moon, and for the moment quenching the lustre of its reflection in the moving water, and in the stagnant mud where the tide is out.[39]

"How sweet the moonlight sleeps upon the Bank," as a character in one of Planché's extravaganzas murmured.[40]

London by Night seems to have drawn fairly well at a half-crown admission. (During the day the building and grounds, including the original London panorama, could be seen for two shillings, with the stalactite cavern one shilling extra.) But a timely new canvas was already in preparation. In February 1848 Louis Philippe had been dethroned, and Paris was plunged into revolution. The English watched the bloody course of events with horrified fascination; they were the more at liberty to do so after they survived the threat of a Chartist takeover of London in April and felt their own institutions to be secure. Both the Colosseum management and that in Leicester Square immediately put their painters to work. At virtually the same moment in May that Burford opened a panorama of *Paris*

43. The Colosseum, 1845: the conservatory (*Illustrated London News*, 3 May 1845).

44. The Colosseum, 1845: "Ruins of the Temple of Vesta" (*Illustrated London News,* 3 May 1845).

by Daylight, the Colosseum replaced the *London by Night* show with one of *Paris by Night.*

As the revolution continued into the summer, spectators could locate the action on the canvas. Even those with no interest in current events were delighted by the painting, which assumed that they were hovering over the Tuileries in a balloon; so assiduous was the attention to detail that the cords hanging from the balloon's netting intervened between them and the view below.[41] An American black man named William Wells Brown, in England to promote the abolitionist cause, wrote:

There, all brilliant with gas-lights, and favored by the shining moon, Paris lay spread far out beneath us, though the canvas on which the scene was painted was but half a dozen feet from where we gazed in wonder. [This probably is an error.] The moon herself seemed actually in the heavens. Nay, bets were laid that she had risen since we entered. Nothing can

surpass the uniformity of appearance which every spire, and house, and wood, and river—yea, which every shop-window, ornamented, presented. All seemed natural, from the twinkling of the stars above us, to the monkey of the organ-man in the market-place below.[42]

In this busy year, however, there was a still more sensational novelty at the Colosseum. On the Albany Street side the Royal Colosseum Saloon and Hall of Mirrors, of tarnished memory, gave way to a new building called the Cyclorama.[43] Entered through a corridor lighted by twenty-six bronzed tripods, and a "rustic armory" foyer in which refreshments were sold, this was a luxurious little auditorium laden with the embellishments proper to early Victorian taste. The eighteen benches and tier of boxes were arranged to suggest "the vestibule of a regal mansion, fitted up for the performance of a masque, or play." The stage area, separated from the seating by an entablature ex-

45. The Colosseum, 1845: entrance to the Stalactite Cavern (watercolor). The artist wrote: "It was seen only by candle light. The glistening of the spar, added to the sound of the water dripping from the roof into the deep pools surrounding you, seen by an artistically arranged light, was most striking."

tending the entire width of the auditorium, was flanked on each side by six Roman-Ionic columns of Siena scagliola, interspersed with gas lusters. On a level with the floor of the stage were four lions couchant, looking as if they were watching the proceedings along with the audience. The walls and ceiling bore copies of classic pictures—Raphael's *School of Athens* and *Constantine Delivering Up His Authority to the Pope; Minerva with Prudence Directing the Arts; The Triumph of Alexander;* and *Jupiter Demanding a Solemn Council of the Gods.*

The show for which this building was erected was a re-creation of the Lisbon earthquake of 1755—in essence, an enlarged Eidophusikon, with horrific effects which Loutherbourg would have heartily envied. The four daily performances abounded with violent action, spectacular lighting, and almost deafening noise. As the show began, the audience found itself seemingly aboard a vessel floating down the Tagus and eventually reaching the Grand Square of Lisbon. Then things began to happen, as Thackeray recounted in *Punch:* "Ships were tossed and dashed about the river before us in a frightful manner. Convents and castles toppled down before our eyes and burst into flames. We heard the shrieks of the mariners in the storm, the groans of the miserable people being swallowed up or smashed in the rocking, reeling ruins—tremendous darkness, lurid lightning flashes, and the awful booming of thunderbolts roared in our ears, dazzled our eyes, and frightened our senses so, that I protest I was more dead than alive when I quitted the premises, and don't know how I found myself in my carriage."[44]

Edmund Yates, son of Braham's partner, remembered that "the manner in which the earth heaved and was rent, the buildings toppled over, and the sea rose, was most cleverly contrived, and had a most terrifying effect upon the spectators; frightful rumblings, proceeding apparently from under your feet, increased the horror, which was anything but diminished by accompanying musical performances on that awful instrument, the apollonicon. Never was better value in fright given for the money."[45]

One of the most monstrous products of the nineteenth-century penchant for replacing men, in this case musicians, with machinery, was the Apollonicon, constructed by Messrs. Bevington and Sons, Greek Street. It had sixteen pedals and 2,407 pipes which actuated and gave vent to the sounds of contrabasses,

46. The Colosseum, 1845: entrance to the Swiss cottage (unsigned watercolor).

47. The Colosseum, 1845: view from the balcony of the Swiss cottage (unsigned watercolor).

48. The Cyclorama at the Colosseum: Swiss Armory refreshment room (*Illustrated London News*, 30 December 1848).

* The Lisbon show was the stuff of which legend was made. In 1905, Bradwell's nephew, who had assisted his uncle in renovating the Colosseum, reminisced that at the press preview, "the earthquake was proceeding with every sort of contrivance for thunder and lightning, and in the midst of the din, there came suddenly a tremendous crash, which shook the visitors in their seats. They thought that was the finest effect of all. My uncle, who was sitting with them, jumped up and went round to the back. When he returned he said he was sorry they would not be able to repeat *that* effect again. He explained that a gas explosion had just taken place in a shop in Albany Street, and blown out nearly the whole front of a house opposite the exhibition." (*N & Q*, 10th ser. 3, 1905, 189–90.) This was one of Victorian London's major disasters, the explosion of illuminating gas in a Berlin wool merchant's house, which devastated a portion of Albany Street, but left the Colosseum unscathed. The story is a good one, and it is too bad that it is not true. The fact is that the explosion, which, miraculously, caused only one fatality, occurred on the evening of 7 August 1848, and the preview was held five months later, on 23 December.

cellos, violins, fagotts, oboes, clarinets, flutes, piccolos, flageolets, and other instruments. The tranquil opening of the earthquake show was accompanied by the first movement of Beethoven's Pastoral Symphony. Then as the cataclysm got under way—while the earth rumbled, buildings tottered and collapsed, trapped victims shrieked, and the turbulent sea roared—the Apollonicon poured forth selections from *Don Giovanni, Masaniello,* and *Moses in Egypt.*[46]

Despite the name "Cyclorama," coined about a decade earlier to designate a wrap-around canvas like Parris's London, the scenery was divided into flat segments. In view of the sensational popularity at the moment of Banvard's immense "rolling" panorama of the Mississippi River (Chapter 15), the *Times* made a point of the difference. "The machinery," it said, "is so contrived that no portion of the picture is rolled upon drums or cylinders, but is moved on and off the stage by means of apparatus by which it is kept continually extended, so that no bending or collapsing takes place on the canvass, and nothing, as heretofore at exhibi-

tions of this class, occurs to destroy the pictorial illusion and discover the artificial effects."[47] Against this frequently changing background was enacted a series of episodes involving not mere cardboard cut-outs but real objects, moved by machinery. The inventory of the equipment used suggests how elaborate and massive the effects were:

One back frame, 160 ft by 43—Three Telescope Frames, 190 ft. varying in height from 20 to 40 feet—One frame, 70 ft by 43—Truck with sea, 80 ft long and 4 ft wide, running on twelve 22-inch wheels, containing working machinery for ships and waves. —One large Felucca. —One Life Boat—One double-purchase Crab with long shaft and 4 barrels—Levers to throw in and out of gear—Two single-purchase Crabs—Two Wood Barrels—and 1520 feet of iron rails and sleepers for working same.[48]

The results doubtless were worth all the ingenuity and labor that went into their creation.*

The Cyclorama's immediate success brought the Colosseum a new but brief lease on life. At Christmas

49. The Cyclorama at the Colosseum: the theatre where the Lisbon Earthquake show was presented (*Illustrated London News,* 30 December 1848).

1850 the Paris panorama gave way to one of the Lake of Thun, but the London show was restored for the Crystal Palace crowds the following summer. In the Cyclorama itself, the Lisbon production was after a long run replaced successively by a series of huge paintings of the Crystal Palace and the dependable old subject of Vesuvius in eruption. In the latter show, an attempt was made to recapture the excitement of the Lisbon earthquake, with offstage voices and machines imitating the thunder of the explosion and the cries of the victims, but the *Times,* at least, found the sound effects "in bad taste, and in no way aid[ing] the efforts of the painter."[49]

Again the Colosseum found itself in straits. In 1855, after being closed for some months, it was put up for sale again, this time in connection with a suit in Chancery, Phillipson and another versus Joseph Turner, evidently David Montague's partner, and twenty-five others. The auctioneer declared that "150,000 persons have paid for admission in One Year and as much as £20,000 been received during the same period,"

conveniently neglecting to state that the period in question probably was more than twenty years earlier and omitting to specify how much of that sum was earmarked to pay off the creditors. In the event, the property failed to make the reserve price of £20,000 and was withdrawn.[50] Once more a salvage operation was mounted, this time under the auspices of a paper group calling itself the Colosseum of Science and Art Company, Ltd., and consisting chiefly of the prospective managing director, George Bachhoffner, Ph.Dr., F.C.S., etc., former professor of natural philosophy at the negligible institution of Queen's College, Guernsey, and for many years a well-known figure in the educational entertainment field. The company was to be capitalized at £10,000, with shares, entitling the owner to free admission, offered at £10. Despite the failure of the "Gallery of Natural Magic" in 1839 Bachhoffner evidently wanted to make another stab at imitating the Polytechnic Institution and for that purpose proposed to spend £2,000 on scientific equipment.[51]

But if the equipment was actually bought and used, it made no difference. By the Christmas season of 1859 the Colosseum was once more a variety house with a bill including dissolving views of China, a magician, and a clairvoyant.[52] Though otherwise undistinguished, the program was memorable for one item, a pair of playlets entitled *Distant Relations* and *Home for the Holidays* and starring two daughters of the Terry family, late of the Princess's Theatre. One girl, Nelly (later Ellen), was cast as a "fly-by-night, cigar-smoking schoolboy," and when not on stage she could be found studying the part of Juliet in the old stalactite cavern. "To me," she wrote in her autobiography, "the gloomy horror of the place was a perfect god-send! Here I could cultivate a creepy, eerie sensation, and get into a fitting frame of mind for the potion scene. Down in this least imposing of subterranean abodes I used to tremble and thrill with passion and terror. Ah, if only in after years, when I played Juliet at the Lyceum, I could have thrilled an audience to the same extent!"[53]

In thirty nights the Terry family played to 30,000 persons, but this success was too late to save the Colosseum. Even the arrival of the Underground Railway, with a nearby station at Portland Road, could not do so. If the crowds wanted music hall programs, such as the Colosseum presented during its last season (1863: Burford's panorama closed almost simultaneously)—"Neapolitan Minstrels," dissolving views, conjurors, comic monologists, juvenile flutists, "chansonettes" by a "Swiss comique," and so on—they had a larger choice at the more conveniently located houses in Leicester Square and the Strand. And so the building stood sadly moldering, its stucco crumbling to expose the rough bricks underneath, until it was again put up for sale, along with all its contents, in August 1868. *Punch* solemnized the occasion—this time inspired not by Byron but by Thomas Hood:

> I remember, I remember,
>   When I was a little boy,
> How I came home in December
>   My fond parents to annoy.
> But my pretty maiden Aunty
>   Was kind and gave to me
> A sort of show galanty,
>   A funny thing to see.
>
> I remember I was taken
>   By my aunt's peculiar cabby,

> For to hear the rafters shaken
>   By the Choir in the Abbey.
> Nor the service, nor Te Deum,
>   Nor the sights of Christmas time,
> Could approach the Colosseum,
>   Save, perhaps, the Pantomime.
>
> I remember, I remember,
>   All those Ruins in the grounds,
> And the classic broken pillars
>   (Sold for something like three pounds.)
> And the statues! One of Jason
>   Was a noble work of art;
> They were knocked down to a mason,
>   Who removed them in his cart.
>
> At the Panorama great I'm
>   Looking back with sad delight,
> It was London Seen by Day-Time,
>   It was London Seen by Night.
> But it suited no one's coffers
>   On the selling afternoon,
> And I heard of no great offers,
>   For old MISTER BRADWELL'S "Moon."
>
> A statue of KING WIL-LI-AM
>   THE FOURTH was then knocked down,
> I weep—perhaps I silly am—
>   The bid was a half-a-crown.
> The auctioneer declined to let
>   It go for next to nix,
> But took the highest he could get—
>   It fetched just one-pound-six.
>
> SIR ROBERT PEEL, ten feet in height,
>   From pedestal to nob,
> 'Twas stone or marble, purely white,
>   It fetched—ah, me!—ten bob.
> The end—five pounds or under
>   Bought a lot which all ears dinned,
> "Three Rain Barrels and One Thunder,"
>   "Then Two Crashes and One Wind."
>
> Fit ending, awful, fright'ning!
>   For the place now gone to smash,
> Stricken down by resin-lightning,
>   And the iron thunder-crash.
> But sunk in thunder crashes
>   It lies on Regent's plain;
> Like a Phoenix from its ashes,
>   Shall it ever rise again?[54]

Although the demolition may have begun in 1868, it was not completed, and the site cleared, until 1875.[55] Whenever the great dome was brought down, the panorama of London vanished with the rest of the debris.

The Diorama

12

On 10 February 1824 John Arrowsmith, of Air Street, Piccadilly, was granted a patent for "an improved Mode of publicly exhibiting Pictures or Painted Scenery of every Description, and of distributing or directing the Day-light upon or through them, so as to produce many beautiful Effects of Light and Shade, which he denominates Diorama. Partly communicated to him by certain Foreigners residing Abroad."[1] The Diorama, arriving in England thirty-seven years after Barker had taken out a patent for his panorama, took pictorial entertainment in a different direction. Like the panorama, it required a specially designed building for a fully realized performance; but it went beyond the panorama in its capacity for dynamic effects. The Diorama was, in essence, a flat picture with an illusion of depth and, most important, capable of changes in lighting so dramatic as to alter its whole aspect.

It originated in the vogue for panoramas that swept Paris following Robert Fulton's introduction of Barker's invention there. One of the leading French panorama painters was Pierre Prévost, whose huge canvases of European cities and Napoleonic events (the camp at Boulogne, the conference at Tilsit, the Battle of Wagram) were shown in Thayer's twin rotundas and later (from 1807?) in Prévost's own building in the Boulevard des Capucines. Among Prévost's assistants was a theatrical scene designer named Louis Jacques Mandé Daguerre, who was achieving considerable reputation as a worthy successor—at long remove—of the great Servandoni and would, in his later years, become one of the fathers of photography.[2] His scenery

and effects for thirteen melodramas at the Théâtre Ambigu-Comique were masterpieces of *trompe l'oeil* realism, and his sunbathed sets for Nicolò's *Aladin ou la lampe merveilleuse,* produced at the Opéra in February 1822, were destined to be remembered for decades. When Daguerre conceived the idea of his Diorama, therefore, he brought to the project the same impressive experience that Loutherbourg had amassed in the London theatre before he embarked on his Eidophusikon. And like Loutherbourg, he was fascinated by the dramatic potentialities of light.*

On 11 July 1822, Daguerre's Diorama opened in an expressly constructed building at 4 Rue Sanson, now the Rue de la Douane, just off the Place de la République. It was an immediate sensation, and Daguerre and his partner, Charles-Marie Bouton, a pupil of David who had also been one of Prévost's assistants, proceeded at once to establish a similar exhibition in London. Daguerre had English connections by marriage. His wife, Louise Georgina, belonged to an English family settled in Paris; its true name, Arrowsmith, was sometimes shortened in French to "Smith."† Early in 1823 one of Madame Daguerre's brothers, Charles Arrowsmith, an artist, was sent to London to find an architect and a location for the branch Diorama. The architect chosen was the émigré Augustus Charles Pugin, father of a more celebrated son. Pugin was then working for John Nash, who was building terraces of mansions in Park Square and Park Crescent, respectively north and south of the New Road at the southeast corner of Regent's Park. Since

* His inspiration may have been due at least partially to a Swiss pictorial entertainment, the Diaphanorama, which was exhibited in Paris in 1821. The invention of a Swiss landscape painter and scene designer named Franz Niklaus König, it involved transparencies painted with watercolor on sheets of paper and shown in a darkened room. The novelty seems to have been that König "achieved various degrees of transparency . . . by oiling and partly scraping away the back of the paper." (Helmut and Alison Gernsheim, *L. J. M. Daguerre,* New York, 1968, p. 14.)

† The connection, if any, between the English patentee, John Arrowsmith, and the French family is uncertain. A John Arrowsmith (1790–1873) was a prominent London mapmaker. Another of the name, one of Mme Daguerre's brothers, was a Parisian art dealer. He often visited London in these years, but since he presumably was a French citizen he would not have been eligible to receive a patent. As a British subject, the London John Arrowsmith could have taken one out in behalf of "certain Foreigners residing abroad."

50. The Diorama and Colosseum buildings, viewed from the southwest (the Marylebone Road) (aquatint, ca. 1830). The entrance to the Diorama (extreme right) was in the middle of the long residential terrace.

this was the most fashionable neighborhood on the outskirts of London at the moment—a consideration which, at the same time, was also determining Hornor's choice of site for the Colosseum—it was almost inevitable that Pugin, Arrowsmith, and Daguerre should have decided to locate the Diorama there, with the entrance hall occupying the center of the west-facing terrace in Park Square East and the show building proper in the space behind, toward Albany Street. Assisted by a civil engineer named James Morgan, Pugin built the new Diorama at a cost of £10,000, reportedly in the short span of four months.

The show opened on 29 September 1823, and thus was the first in the field of the two famous Regent's Park pictorial exhibitions; ground was broken for the Colosseum, a few hundred feet to the north, only the next summer, and during the next five years (1824–1829), while the imposing Greek revival building was going up and Parris and his house painters were doggedly working away at the London panorama, the Diorama was open and flourishing. It is

likely that its swift erection and conspicuous prosperity contributed to the rumor-breeding impatience with which the London public watched the Colosseum's slow progress.

Although some refinements may have been introduced in the design of the new building and the technique of the exhibition, in all important respects except capacity the Regent's Park Diorama was a duplicate of the original.[3] In the circular viewing area 200 persons could be accommodated—a significant reduction from the Paris building's capacity of 350, probably because experience had proved that the picture was too small to be satisfactorily viewed at the required distance by so large an audience. (It will be recalled that the Exeter Change room where the Eidophusikon was displayed also seated 200.)

The ceiling was of transparent fabric painted in colors, with portraits of Reynolds, West, Poussin, Ruisdael, Rembrandt, Vernet, Claude Lorrain, Berghem, Leonardo, Teniers, Rubens, Raphael, and Gainsborough: a combined pantheon of Old Masters and modern British ones was invoked to consecrate this latest attempt to expand the boundaries of fine art. Although there was a skylight above them, these portraits were only dimly visible, because the show's success depended heavily on darkness in the viewing area. Just as the patrons of the Leicester Square panorama were required to climb dark stairways before they emerged on the viewing platform, so the people who came to see the Diorama were conducted to their seats through a corridor lighted by a single lamp. Almost every eyewitness account mentions the odd, sometimes disquieting experience of either groping or being led by an attendant to a place inside the darkened amphitheatre. There were two reasons for this exclusion of light apart from that which emanated from or was reflected by the picture itself. One was that by contrast it permitted maximum use of the available natural lighting: illumination concentrated on a single area is brighter, and also capable of greater variations in intensity, than light that has competition from elsewhere. The other, more important, reason was that, as in the panorama, it eliminated from the spectator's consciousness all the extraneous objects by which size and distance could be measured and the illusion thereby destroyed. In Barker's and Parris's panoramas, the painted scene enveloped the spectator, and with the source of light in the top of the cupola concealed from him by an umbrella structure, he was cut off from the "reality" in which he had existed before entering the place. In the Diorama, the same end was attained in part by another means. The effect on the showgoers of the time was all the more dramatic because they were not accustomed to it. In the regular theatre the auditorium lights were not extinguished during a performance; not until late in the century did it become standard practice to darken the hall so that the audience's attention would be fixed upon the brightly lighted picture area, as it was in the Diorama.

The amphitheatre was the inner one of two concentric rotundas. Mounted on a ten-foot-square platform built on eighteen-foot piles, and so delicately balanced that, even when loaded with a capacity audience, it could be moved by a boy and a ram engine, it could pivot on a 73° arc. In the portion of the wall the audience faced was an aperture resembling the picture frame opening then being adopted on the London stage. During a performance, this aperture was successively aligned with two similar apertures in the wall of the enclosing shell. Each of these two rectangular windows, which were adjacent to each other, served as a frame for a tunnel, thirty or forty feet long, ex-tending at a slight angle toward Albany Street. These corridors were so contrived as to obliterate themselves from the spectators' consciousness. Perhaps their walls were painted black. Their ceilings, invisible to the viewer, were ground-glass skylights which threw all illumination on the flat picture mounted at the far end.

Each picture, measuring (according to which source one consults) 72 by 42 feet, 70 by 50 feet, or 69 by 45 feet, was made of calico or lawn, painted partly in translucent, partly in opaque colors. The opaque portions were lighted by frontal reflection from the skylights over the corridors. In the wall of the building wing behind each picture—that is, at the end of the corridors—were tall ground-glass windows, the light from which shone through the translucent portions of the picture. Thus the Diorama artist had at his command a greater intensity and flexibility of lighting than was available to painters of gallery pictures or to the makers of panoramas, who worked only with opaque surfaces. The combination of reflected and mediated illumination resulted in the impression that the brilliance was inherent in the picture itself.

The Diorama's dynamic effects were produced by working, according to a predetermined program, a combination of lines and cords, pulleys and counterweights, that activated an elaborate system of screens, shutters, and curtains positioned at both sources of light—the skylights in front of the picture and the windows behind it. Some of these interceptors were opaque, to shut off light completely from certain portions of the picture; others, made of colored fabrics, served to modify the color and intensity of the light. The various shutters and shades could be made to pass by and overlay one another, thus producing an unlimited number of momentary colors. The same mechanisms also made possible variations in the distribution of color, light, and shade on the wide picture, depending on the manipulation of the contrasts between the opaque and translucent details. There was no artificial lighting. Mere daylight was all that was needed; the colored screens and curtains seem to have provided the effect of sunlight even on a cloudy day—an advantage over the panoramas that the Diorama's proprietors were not loath to stress. London fog, however, was as much a bane to the Diorama as to the panorama, and when it hung heavy over Regent's Park on the day a new picture, *Ruins in a Fog,* was being previewed inside the building, one can understand the remark of a *Times* critic that conditions prevented an accurate evaluation of the artist's effect.[4]

When the show was under way, the single aperture

51. The Diorama: floor plan (from Pugin and Britton's *Illustrations of the Public Buildings of London*, 1838). The circular salon in the center, enclosed in a shell, is seen positioned so that the spectators on the three rows of benches and in the boxes at the rear of the room could view, through an aperture in the wall, the painting stretched across the far end of the "tunnel." When the second scene was to be viewed, the salon pivoted clockwise until the aperture faced the right-hand tunnel, the one on the left now being concealed by the salon's wall. The rotating salon could be entered when one of its doors coincided with one in the enclosing shell.

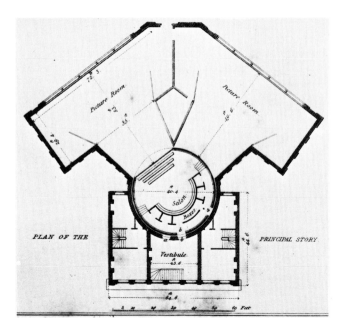

PLAN OF THE ⋯ PRINCIPAL STORY

of the inner room was aligned with one of the two openings in the wall of the enclosing shell. The audience thus would see the picture at the far end of the "invisible" tunnel. After the fifteen-minute performance featuring that picture was completed, the viewing room rotated, swinging its single aperture away from the first of the twin frames, which then disappeared, and toward the second; when the two coincided, the second picture was wholly in view and its display commenced.

These, then, were the novelties which brought crowds to the Diorama in its first years in London —the location of the picture, the only visible area in a world of darkness, isolated from all means by which "real" size and distance could be estimated and the illusion thus dispelled; and the imitation of numerous natural and artificial lighting effects. On its first Easter Monday (1824) it took in £200, and later it was reported to gross £3,000 to £4,000 a year.[5] The press greeted it as warmly as it had the Eidophusikon. But praise from leading artists was not forthcoming. Whereas Loutherbourg's show had been admired by his fellow Academicians West, Reynolds, and Gainsborough, among the painters of this new epoch only John Constable seems ever to have expressed an opinion. Constable was invited to the preview of the Diorama because John Arrowsmith, the Parisian art dealer who was about to introduce the English landscapist to the French public by exhibiting three of his paintings at the 1824 Salon, was Daguerre's brother-

in-law. Like his judgment of Reinagle's panorama of Rome, Constable's opinion of the Diorama was ambiguous. To his friend Archdeacon Fisher he wrote: "I was on Saturday at the private view of the 'Diorama'—it is a transparency, the spectator in a dark chamber—it is very pleasing & has great illusion—it is without the pale of Art because its object is deception—Claude's never was—or any other great landscape painter's. The style of the pictures is French, which is decide[d]ly against them. Some real stones, as bits of brown paper & a bit of silver lace turned on a wheel glides through the stone—to help. The place," Constable, the bluff countryman from Suffolk, was obliged to add, "was filled with foreigners—& I seemed to be in a cage of magpies."[6]

Every year from 1823 to 1830, except for 1825 when part of the previous year's bill was retained, the Diorama brought over a pair of pictures from the Paris house, one by Daguerre and the other by Bouton. Most of the subjects were landscapes, with particular emphasis on architectural interiors and Swiss scenes: the Valley of Sarnen and Canterbury Cathedral (1823); Brest and Chartres Cathedral (1824); Holyrood Castle (1825); Roslyn Abbey and Rouen Cathedral (1826); Ruins in a Fog and St. Cloud, Paris (1827); the Valley of Unterseen and the Cloisters of St. Wandrille (1828); the village of Thiers and the Basilica of St. Peter's, Rome (1829); Mt. St. Gothard and Rheims Cathedral (1830, continued in 1831–32, probably because the July Revolution of 1830 prevented the completion of the scheduled pictures); and Paris from Montmartre and the Campo Santo, Pisa (1832). In contrast to the subjects of the panoramas shown in London during the Napoleonic Wars, the Diorama's were seldom topical. They catered instead, as the panoramas also now were doing, though somewhat less consistently, to the public taste for romantic topography, the stuff of picturesque art and of sentimental antiquarianism. The shows at Park Square East were the colorful spectacular counterpart of the albums of engraved scenes that were so popular as the Regency faded into the Victorian era.

The opening bill was typical of those to come.[7] First, the interior of Canterbury Cathedral was seen undergoing repair, with two or three workmen resting and planks of wood strewn on the floor. The building was alternately bathed in sunlight and cast into shadow as clouds were understood to be passing; when the sun shone through the windows, it threw colored shadows on the floor, and remote objects, otherwise hidden, were momentarily illuminated. After the audience had taken in all the details, even to the damp-stains on the pillars and arches, there were sounds underneath the round little theatre (less alarming, to be sure, than those of a Lisbon earthquake), and the cathedral seemed to be moving out of the field of vision. Actually, it was the theatre that was in motion, as it turned from the opening of one tunnel to the other. Slowly a new picture came into view, the Valley of Sarnen in Switzerland, with a lake in the foreground and snow-capped mountains beyond. Initially, it was seen in the serenity of a summer afternoon, but gradually the sky became overcast as a storm approached. On the surface of the lake the reflection of the sunshine gave way to a dark shadow; the rivulets that flowed into the lake developed a glassy black tinge; and the snow on the mountains stood out more distinctly in contrast with the gloom. The performance ended as the storm was about to break.

This was the sort of annual double bill that would occupy the Diorama for the next decade. Each picture offered variations on a single basic scenario, the fleeting changes caused by the alternation of sunlight, moonlight, and shadow on diverse surfaces. In the Roslyn Chapel scene, for example, as a German visitor, Prince Pückler-Muskau, described it, one saw

the interior of a large abbey-church, appearing perfectly in its real dimensions. A side door is open, ivy climbs through the windows, and the sun occasionally shines through the door, and lightens with a cheering beam the remains of coloured windows, glittering through the cobwebs. Through the opposite window at the end you see the neglected garden of the monastery, and above it, single clouds in the sky, which, flitting stormily across, occasionally obscure the sunlight, and throw deep shadows over the church—tranquil as death; where the crumbled but magnificent remains of an ancient knight repose in gloomy majesty.[8]

Similarly, in Daguerre's *Interior of the Cloisters of St. Wandrill,* a portion of the desolate ruin was seen as lighted by the midday sun, while the rest was thrust into darkness. Outside, as fleecy clouds passed across the sun, the leaves of the shrubs that half-covered the decaying mullions rustled in the wind and their shadows were reflected on the adjoining columns.[9] In the Rouen scene, following an early morning storm, a rainbow appeared and the roofs of the buildings shone as if recently wetted by the rain.[10] The next season's picture of a ruined chapel began with a thick February fog enveloping everything beyond the wall; then gradually, as if dispersed by the wind, the fog lifted, the tops of the trees and the snow on the distant mountains be-

came visible, and at the end the whole valley, with its variety of tints and shades, was revealed.[11]

ロ3✳Σロ

Like the panorama, the Diorama soon had its imitators. Since the tunnel wings and the lighting equipment were protected for some years by Arrowsmith's patent, these could not be adopted elsewhere, even if an entrepreneur wished to make so substantial a capital investment; but there were no property rights in the word "diorama" nor in the general idea it connoted—pictures shown under variable lighting.*Accordingly, a "diorama" was set up late in 1827 or early in 1828 at the Bazaar in Baker Street, Portman Square. It showed two pictures, one of the recent Battle of Navarino, the other of the interior of St. Peter's. The latter, according to one critic, was in some ways superior to Daguerre's.[12]

This exhibition, however, was immediately outshone by the British Diorama at the Royal Bazaar, Oxford Street. The bazaar, which opened in the spring of 1828, was the undertaking of Thomas Hamlet, a silversmith with a high-society clientele who intended it to be the premier "fashionable lounge" in the metropolis. The British Diorama consisted of four pictures by the well-known theatrical scenery painters Clarkson Stanfield and David Roberts: *St. George's Chapel at Windsor, The Ruins of Tintern Abbey, The Kent East Indiaman Afire,* and *Lago Maggiore.* Each scene was twenty-seven feet high and thirty-eight feet in width.[13] A year later the same team painted four new scenes for the bazaar—*The Temple of Apollonopolis* and *The Interior of St. Sauveur, Caen,* both by Roberts, and *The Entrance to the Italian Village of Virex* and *The Burning of York Minster*—a recent news event—by Stanfield.[14]

This last subject was admirably suited for the kind of spectacular treatment the diorama provided. "A faint reddish light," wrote a witness, "betrays itself through some of the windows of the minster; by degrees it increases in vividness; until at length the flame from which it proceeds bursts fiercely forth, illuminating the adjacent towers, and mingled volumes of smoke, and masses of brilliant sparks, now rapidly ascend to the skies; a great portion of the roof of the building falls in; and the dreadful conflagration is at its height when the scene closes."[15] Most of these effects could not have been produced by the Daguerre machinery, even if it had been available for use at the Royal Bazaar; but the Oxford Street showmen, more resourceful than prudent, knew other ways of repre-

* To minimize confusion, "diorama" as a generic term will not be capitalized, "Diorama" being reserved for the original exhibition at Regent's Park.

52. The Diorama: the Roslyn Chapel scene (engraving in the *Mirror of Literature*, 7, 1826, 129, after the picture painted by Daguerre).

senting a fierce conflagration, and one of these proved fatal to the show. During a performance on 27 May, less than a month after the York Minster scene was first presented, some blazing turpentine ignited the "transparency," and within hours the elegant new bazaar was in ruins.[16]

Hazardous though the dioramic depiction of great fires was, the subject was too well adapted to the medium and too popular to be abandoned. Five years later (1834) another conflagration of the era was the subject of a dioramic exhibition, as it was also of a famous picture from Turner's luminous palette. At the Cosmorama Rooms, Regent Street, could be seen Kenny Meadows's "Grand Tableaux, of the Interiors of the Houses of Lords & Commons, As They Appeared Previous to Their Destruction by Fire, with a Correct Moonlight View, of the Exteriors of the Late Houses, from the River Thames, And a Splendid Representation of the Conflagration with Dioramic & Mechanical Effect. Also a View of the Ruins, as Visited by their Majesties."[17]

Presumably all the dioramic presentations except the original one used gas rather than daylight for illumina-

tion. This was commercially, if not artistically, a decided advantage, for it enabled the show to be presented at night as well as during the day, and without regard to weather. An initial shortcoming, which probably was remedied as gas technology improved, was the flickering of the jets. And, of course, there was the ever present danger of fire. In July 1841 Charles Marshall's "Kineorama" at 121 Pall Mall, a combination panorama and diorama showing views of Turkey, Syria, and Egypt, caught fire during a matinee. The audience, composed mostly of ladies, including the Countess of Blessington, escaped in good order, and workmen managed to put out the blaze before the fire brigades arrived, so that the Kineorama was spared the fate of the second edition of the British Diorama. From the press reports of the incident we learn something of the dioramic technique employed by the rivals of the Regent's Park operation. The picture was lighted from above by a batten of 150 gas jets, below which was "a piece of machinery called a medium . . . comprised of several large frames of coloured oiled silk," which was operated by pulleys.[18] This sounds like a simplified adaptation of Daguerre's mechanism; it is unlikely

53. The Diorama: "Ruins in a Fog" (engraving in the *Mirror of Literature,* 8, 1827, 425, after the picture painted by Daguerre). The representations of the workmen's tools and pieces of masonry in the foreground were meant to achieve the realistic effect produced by the same details in the earlier picture of Canterbury Cathedral.

to have been as flexible as the original or as capable of detailed and dynamic effects. Apart from exceptional cases like the York Minster turpentine, we do not hear much of backlighting being supplied in the other dioramas.

Although John Arrowsmith's patent specifically excluded the revolving amphitheatre, no diorama imitated the original in this respect. Even if other showmen had deemed it economically feasible to build such a structure, they evidently had reason to believe the public did not particularly care for it. A handbill advertising the British Diorama, after observing that "Fine Weather or Sun Shine is not at all necessary" for the presentation of the four pictures, stressed the "ingenious mechanism" which enabled the audience to enjoy them "without the disagreeable sensation of a turning saloon." This device was nothing more or less than a rudimentary camera shutter; each change of picture within the frame was accomplished by "four boards closing up from each side, and then receding from a point of light to the full space of the scene."[19] More commonly used, no doubt, was a simple drop curtain, such as the Regent's Park house itself eventu-

ally installed across each aperture to make more decisive the transition from one picture to the other.

These were the ways in which the rival dioramas sought to improve on the original. It took less than a decade for the Regent's Park show to lose its appeal. There were, after all, limits to the variations that could be played on the two standard Diorama subjects—Swiss landscapes, and cathedrals and abbeys whether intact or in ruins—and York Minster and Westminster fires were more exciting than either. As the show's novelty faded and innovative competition appeared, repeat business fell off. Daguerre therefore cast about for some genuine novelty, and he found it in the "double-effect" technique he conceived with his new collaborator Hippolyte Sébron, who in 1830 replaced Bouton, now the manager of the London house.[20] The idea of painting the picture on both sides was not strictly theirs, since Loutherbourg had long ago employed it in some of the transformation scenes he designed for the Drury Lane pantomime; but the Diorama facilities permitted more elaborate spectacles than had been possible for either Loutherbourg or his successors in the theatre. The artist first painted the front, in a combination of opaque and transparent effects; then, working on the back, he devoted himself to the transparent spaces, either preserving them as they were or painting them in translucent colors. The result was that, in a sense, two pictures of the same scene were superimposed. The managed lighting acted successively on the opaque and translucent portions of the cloth. When only the front scene was to be displayed, the backlighting was cut off, so that the illumination came exclusively from the skylight in front of the picture and made only the opaquely painted sections visible, as if the subject were seen by external, or reflected, light. Conversely, illumination from behind, through the translucent portions, suggested internal lighting only. Essentially, the difference between the original Diorama performance and the double-effect one was that in the former, the scene was merely modified, while in the latter, it was transformed.

The first pictures embodying the new technique, shown in Paris in 1834, were *The Central Basin of Commerce at Ghent* and the *Midnight Mass at St. Étienne du Mont*. In the St. Étienne scene, the church, lighted from the front, was seen by day, devoid of worshipers. Then the gradual reduction of reflected light and the simultaneous substitution of light from behind, effected by the closing of the front skylights and the opening of the rear light sources, represented the coming of night. When the front lights were completely extinguished, the backlighting, shining through the painted cloth, revealed the sanctuary filled with people and illuminated by candles and hanging lamps.[21]

Neither the Ghent nor the St. Étienne picture, however, was ever brought to London, where Bouton's pictures were displayed exclusively during the middle and late thirties.* But Bouton adopted Daguerre's technique, and so Londoners were not deprived of the transformation scenes then being enjoyed in Paris. Typical of Bouton's productions was the double bill described with great particularity—far too much to quote—by the novelist Lady Morgan, who saw it in 1836.[22] She brought an especially educated eye to the first scene, a representation of the avalanche that buried the Swiss village of Alagna in 1820, because she had herself been at the site of the disaster the day after it happened. First, she said, the Alpine village and the mountains beyond were seen lying tranquil in the moonlight, with a little lake in the foreground, reflecting the glow of a hearth inside a cottage. As the moonlight diminished, the pinpoints of light elsewhere in the village became more visible. Then, as the villagers retired, the lights were extinguished, one by

one. Backstage sounds of thunder and wind warned of the impending catastrophe, followed by the clangor of the church bell as someone in the village awoke (as represented by the reappearance of a single tiny light) and gave the alarm. The avalanche descended with a roar; the bell in the spire suddenly ceased ringing; and suddenly the whole picture was blacked out. When it reappeared, the sunrise first clothed the distant mountains, then, advancing into the valley, revealed that the village was now totally buried, the cottage in the foreground visible only in outline and the church spire alone protruding from the sea of snow.

The other half of the bill Lady Morgan described portrayed the Florentine church of Santa Croce in long interior perspective. First it was seen in the brightness of noon, the windows resplendent with "a thousand coloured hues," and Michaelangelo's sarcophagus, the Galileo monument, and the tombs of Alfieri and Machiavelli standing out in sharp relief. As the sun set, these conspicuous details gradually faded, until the church grew completely dark. Then suddenly it reappeared, but now it seemed to be illuminated from within, by the chandeliers suspended from the roof and columns and the candelabras deployed on the altar. What had been empty chairs in the daylight scene now were occupied by the congregation; the organ pealed, and the bell tinkled for the elevation of the Host. In the last phases of the performance, the artificial lights were extinguished and the church was lighted only by the cold gray dawn. But then the sun rose, and the spectators again saw the church as it had first appeared.†

Among the other dramatic transformations the London Diorama depicted (1837, with reruns in 1838 and 1843) was the scene of the Roman basilica of St. Paul, which had burned in 1823. First the church was portrayed intact, one wall covered with paintings bathed in the moonlight streaming in through the windows on the opposite side. "But as we gaze," wrote a witness, "the dark cedar roof disappears, and we see nothing but the pure blue Italian sky, whilst below, some of the pillars have fallen—the floor is covered with wrecks; the whole, in short, has almost instantaneously changed to a perfect and mournful picture of the church after the desolation wrought by the fire."[23]

In 1839 the original Paris Diorama itself burned, and Bouton was summoned back to supervise the construction of a new building on the Boulevard Bonne-Nouvelle (which was also to burn, nine years later). During the next several years the London house showed pictures, most of them double-effect, by

* Meanwhile, New York had the advantage of seeing some pictures from the Paris house that were not taken to London. Daguerre's and Sébron's diorama of "Jerusalem, the Crucifixion, Calvary, etc." was shown there in 1839–40, and in the next season Daguerre's *Venice* and *St. Étienne*. At the end of the decade (1848–49) two old pictures that had been seen in London in the Diorama's first years (1824–25) arrived in New York. (Odell, IV, 420, 514; V, 500.)

† A copy (at EC) of the leaflet describing the Alagna–Santa Croce show preserves the notes of a spectator: "The *groping* of *groups* on entering the dark room and seating themselves back to the picture." "I see one pillar—I now see *2* etc as scene changed." "A chalet and some smoke from its chimney." "The whole room turns round with its inmates—reminds one of all his *sea* voyages." "*The incense.*" This last was no figment of an oversuggestible imagination. Incense was actually burned as the picture went through its transformation, a touch which, combined with the musical accompaniment that will be mentioned later (Chapter 14), made this a genuine multimedia show.

Charles Caïus Renoux. The first, opening in September 1840, was a then-and-now portrayal of the Shrine of the Nativity. Other Renoux subjects were the cathedral of Auch (1841), Notre Dame (1843), Rouen (1844), and Heidelberg (1845). Renoux died in 1846, and the fresh pictures in the next two years (St. Mark's and the Valley of Rosenlaui) were painted by one of Daguerre's pupils, a man named Diosse. In 1848 the Diorama finally got around to portraying that old faithful subject of London pictorial exhibitions, the eruption of a volcano, in this case Mount Etna. This was a triple-effect show. The mountain, said the *Athenaeum*, was

first beheld at evening, under the effect of serene moonlight. Day breaks, and the morning sun reveals the features of the landscape,—till at noon it is seen under the full blaze of meridian light. Day declines—and the shades of night descend; when fitful bursts of light issuing from the mountain bespeak the coming eruption. The obscuring masses which the clouds roll rapidly over it have their forms impinged by the burning colours that the lava, as it is thrown up, reflects on them;—while streams of liquid fire rush down the sides of the mountain, and reveal by their own light the work of desolation which they do.[24]

But the Diorama's Etna had the misfortune to have its thunder stolen, not merely in a figurative sense, by the new Cyclorama attached to the Colosseum, where the Lisbon earthquake began to rumble at the end of 1848. By now, the two showplaces had been rivals for almost twenty years. In respect to the pictorial exhibition that was the Colosseum's chief attraction and the Diorama's sole one, the competition had been even: the Colosseum's panorama of London had the advantage of size, but the Diorama had the lighting and dynamic quality that its huge rival lacked, apart from the recent introduction of the London and Paris by night shows. The Diorama, however, was strictly limited in the variety of entertainment it could provide on its premises. Unlike the Colosseum, with its refurbished main building and grounds, it was committed, by virtue of its peculiar configuration and equipment, to a single type of show, which in turn was adaptable to only a restricted range of subjects.

Although Thackeray's dyspeptic view of the Diorama as it was in 1850 may have been due chiefly to his abiding solicitude for children's sensibilities, it is not unlikely that he also reflected a now jaded public taste. His account in *Punch* of a visit to the "Tenebrorama," as he called it, written in the persona of an elderly country gentleman giving his five grand-

children a treat, is a salutary corrective to the uncritical descriptions which abound in the newspapers and magazines of the time. The current bill was composed of the Shrine of the Nativity, then in its fourth run, and the Castle of Stolzenfels, painted by the German artist Simon Meister:

I paid my money at the entrance of the building, and entered with my unsuspicious little charges into the interior of the building. Sir, it is like the entrance to the Eleusinian mysteries, or what I have been given to understand is the initiation into Freemasonry. We plunged out of the light into such a profound darkness, that my darling Anna Maria instantly began to cry. We felt we were in a chamber, Sir, dimly creaking and moving underneath us—a horrid sensation of sea-sickness and terror overcame us, and I was almost as frightened as my poor innocent Anna Maria.

The first thing we saw was a ghastly view of a church—the Cathedral of Saint Sepulchre's, at Jericho, I believe it was called—a dreary pile, with not a soul in it, not so much as a pew-opener or verger to whom one could look for refuge from the solitude of the dismal . . . death's heads, and I own that I thought a walk in the Park would have been more cheerful than this.

As we looked at the picture, the dreary church became more dreary; the shadows of night (by means of curtains and contrivances, which I heard in the back part of the mystery making an awful flapping and pulling) fell deeply and more terribly on the scene. It grew pitch dark; my poor little ones clung convulsively to my knees; an organ commenced playing a dead march—it was midnight—tapers presently began to flicker in the darkness—the organ to moan more dismally—and suddenly, by a hideous optical delusion, the church was made to appear as if full of people, the altar was lighted up with a mortuary illumination, and the dreadful monks were in their stalls.

I have been in churches. I have thought the sermon long. I never thought the real service so long as that painted one which I witnessed at the Tenebrorama. My dear children whispered, "Take us out of this place, Grandpapa." I would have done so. I started to get up—(the place being now dimly visible to our eyes, accustomed to the darkness, and disclosing two other wretches looking on in the twilight besides ourselves)—I started, I say, to get up, when the chamber began to move again, and I sank back on my seat, not daring to stir.

The next view was the Summit of Mount Ararat, I believe, or else of a mountain in Switzerland just before dawn. I can't bear looking down from mountains or heights; when taken to St. Paul's by my dear mother, as a child, I had well-nigh fainted when brought out into the outer gallery; and this view of Mount Ararat is so dreadful, so lonely, so like nature, that it was all I could do to prevent myself from dashing down the peak and plunging into the valley below. A storm, the thunderous rumble of which made me run cold, the fall of an avalanche destroying a village, some lightning, and an eclipse I believe of the sun, were introduced as ornaments to this picture, which I would as lief see again as undergo a nightmare.[25]

In his description of the second scene, Thackeray uses artistic license, substituting for the actual subject at that time, the castle on the Rhine, the famous Alagna avalanche, last seen at the Diorama in 1842. But no matter: Thackeray makes his point. The Diorama was no longer the magical place it once had been—or as it had never been, perhaps, to illusion-resistant eyes like Thackeray's. And if there really were only two other "wretches" in the house for that performance, the Diorama had fallen upon evil days indeed.

In truth, it had. By the time of Thackeray's visit it had already changed owners twice in two years. In September 1848 the building, machinery, and fifteen rolled-up pictures had brought £6,750 at auction. The next year, the same package brought only £4,800. Shortly after Thackeray's visit it was up for auction a third time, on which occasion the going price declined to a derisory £3,000. Meanwhile the show went on; the pictures of St. Mark's, Santa Croce, and the Shrine of the Nativity were restored to the bill until the summer of 1851, when the Mount Etna and Stolzenfels shows replaced them. At the end of that season, the Diorama closed forever. At a fourth sale, in 1853, it was bought by Sir Samuel Peto, the construction magnate, who as a very young man had built the Colosseum to Decimus Burton's designs.[26] Peto converted the premises into a Baptist chapel, adding ecclesiastical buttresses to the walls whose tall windows had admitted light to the back of the pictures. The Diorama building remained a chapel until 1921, subsequently becoming an annex to a division of the University of London. It survives today, in the center of the original terrace in Park Square East, as the only building associated with the shows of London that remains, at least as far as the façade is concerned, in a condition recognizable to the early Victorian pleasure seeker. But as this book was passing through the press, governmental permission was sought for Pugin's show place to be converted again—this time into a mosque for the Aga Khan.

Panoramas: Topics of the Times

13

The shows introduced by Barker, Hornor, and Daguerre had numerous progeny. As a distinct though variegated kind of mass entertainment, these pictorial exhibitions were a highly characteristic product of their time. Much if not most of their popularity derived from their topicality—their involvement with the preoccupations and tastes of the day. They were also topical in another way, for they were themselves a recurrent fad for more than half a century. Or, more accurately, their entrepreneurs sought to give them constantly fresh, though largely factitious, novelty through elastic applications of the time-tested names "panorama" and "diorama" or the invention of new ones.

Within a few years after their respective appearances, "panorama" (originally designating Barker's and Hornor's circular paintings) and "diorama" (originally designating the illuminated show presented in a specially designed building by Daguerre and Bouton), along with the adjectives derived from them, had acquired a wide range of additional applications; so many, in fact, that in everyday practice they came to mean whatever exhibitors wanted them to mean, irrespective of the actual nature of the entertainment in question. Never was there a more bountiful example of easygoing semantics. Not only were the terms applied to shows whose sole resemblance to the prototypes was that they inferentially, though by no means always in fact, involved large pictures, or even a series of ordinary-sized ones, that had some sort of mechanical or optical peculiarity; in addition, they set the style

for innumerable coinages ending in the magic Greek root "-orama" (sight). In sheer numbers, if not ingenuity, the rank growth of "-oramas" eclipsed the pseudo-scientific coinages typified by Katterfelto's jargon, and in general they lasted no longer. In 1830 it was observed, apropos of a show called the Octorama, "The family of Ramas is already large, but it will soon increase to an extent which no verbal Malthus will be able either to limit or to predict, if its members are to be distinguished, like the streets of Washington, by numerical prefixes."[1] Although, apart from Octorama, numerical prefixes did not have to be resorted to, the Greek and Latin lexicons being adequate to the demand for new if not necessarily accurate words to yoke with "-orama," the Malthusian reference, as we will have ample occasion to see, was accurate enough.* From the pictorial exhibitions the craze spread to other parts of the entertainment business—the comedian Charles Mathews's popular one-man "At Home" shows were called "Mathew-oramas"—and beyond: in 1806 a monthly magazine called the *Literary Panorama* began publication.

The implication of magnitude was especially useful when showmen advertised what were, in actuality, pictures no bigger than could be accommodated in a caravan or booth at the fair or in a tavern room. Thus, between 1807 and 1823, Richardson, the veteran theatrical impresario of Bartholomew Fair, announced as an after-piece to his bill of variety acts and severely abridged melodramas a set of "grand panorama views" of such subjects—there was a new group every

* Nor was the fad confined to England. In Paris in 1829 Pückler-Muskau found (pp. 498–99), in addition to the Panorama and the Diorama, the Georama, the Neorama, the Uranorama, and the Cosmorama. Five years later, in Balzac's *Père Goriot,* a young painter infected his fellow-boarders *chez Vauquer* with "la plaisanterie de parler en *rama*" that was raging in artistic circles. The ensuing combat of demi-wit around the dinner table resulted in "santérama" (how are you?), "froitorama" (cold feet), "soupeaurama," "Goriorama," and "cornorama." The United States was not immune, either. When he returned after many years in Paris and London, Joel Barlow, Fulton's erstwhile partner in the Paris panorama, named his home on the outskirts of Washington "Kalorama." The ever adaptable suffix has been revived and put to many uses in the present-day promotional vocabulary, few of them—"Cinerama" is a familiar exception—having to do with visual entertainment. In modern Paris, sightseeing excursions are billed as the Parisorama, the Cityrama, the Chateaurama, and the Seinorama.

year or so—as Montevideo, Amsterdam, Gibraltar, Niagara, Glamorganshire, St. Helena, Paris, and Lake Como.[2] These may have been ordinary opaque paintings or they may have been transparencies. By the sixties a so-called panorama, such as Hamilton's Tour of Europe, might consist of fifty successive scenes, larger than the usual run of gallery pictures, perhaps, but not otherwise related to Barker's invention. In addition, "panorama" might designate a mechanical-picture type of show which was hardly more elaborate than the moving picture of a century earlier. The word was so widely applied, in fact, that it sometimes served as a generic name for all pictorial shows, including dioramas—thus giving us historical warrant for the convenience of so using it in the title of this chapter and at certain points in the following pages.

The initially very specific meaning of "diorama" disintegrated even more quickly than did that of "panorama." Only six years after the word was introduced to London in 1823, a brochure entitled *A Picturesque Guide to the Regent's Park* acknowledged a *fait accompli:* "The term *Diorama* has . . . been strangely corrupted since its successful adoption in the Regent's Park—it being now almost indefinitely applied to any number or description of paintings." The speed with which the theatre picked it up and gave it new application will be described in Chapter 15. In the exhibition business, just as "panorama" was meant to connote magnitude, so "diorama" implied lighting tricks, transparency in particular, with the addition, following theatrical usage, of movement; but often the words were used almost interchangeably, and in many cases, so far as we can tell, no peculiarity was present to justify use of either term. Thus a handbill of about 1836 advertised a Bartholomew Fair "Exhibition of Beautiful Paintings, Forming a Splendid Diorama," its subjects being the recent "Attempt to Destroy the King of the French," including the execution of the assassins; a battle between the troops of the Queen of Spain and of Don Carlos; and the tantalizingly undescribed "Adventures of the Female Sailor."[3] It is possible that some of these Bartholomew Fair "dioramas" were nothing more than peepshows. The word was certainly used in such a connection by 1843, when Albert Smith, the future star of a famous pictorial entertainment, *The Ascent of Mont Blanc,* recalled his childhood at Chertsey: "Even the humble peep-shows were not without enjoying a share of our patronage; and we listened with the most juvenile credulity to the exhibitor's descriptions, as we stood behind the green-baize curtain, on the little low form that raised our eyes to a level with the wondrous

lenses. At the time we write of, Mr. Weare's murder furnished abundant material for these migrating dioramas; and we perfectly recollect the series of peep-show views that the event gave birth to."[4] By the early fifties, "diorama" was applied to programs of dissolving (magic-lantern) views, as in the "Arctic Diorama" shown in Leicester Square in 1851[5] and the "Magnificent Dissolving Dioramas Illuminated by the Newly Invented Electric Light" that were displayed at the former Linwood Gallery in the same neighborhood.[6] In view of this lexical anarchy, where showmen simply attached to their exhibitions whatever labels they deemed most likely to draw customers, we can seldom be sure what a given show was really like when we have only its advertised title.*

⧫

The panorama's claim to dignity as a quasi-cultural institution and to patronage as a respectable alternative to the theatre lay in its vaunted educational value. It was one of the several nineteenth-century commercial enterprises that were dedicated, on paper at least, to the dissemination of useful knowledge: "a pictorial chart, describing facts, and illustrating the writings of historians and travelers," as a writer succinctly but not very enthusiastically characterized it in 1847.[7] Less Gradgrindian in spirit was Ruskin's assertion twenty years later, when the popularity of panoramas had faded, that at their best they had displayed "an attention to truth and a splendour and care in the execution" which made them "very truly a school both in physical geography and in art."[8] Whatever their aesthetic merit, panoramas instructed adults and children alike in a manner that was indisputably agreeable if not necessarily beneficial. The educational effect of the pictures was reinforced by sixpenny booklets, such as could be bought at every Barker-Burford show, to serve first as a guide to the picture while one viewed it—there was no lecturer—and then as a permanent souvenir, to be added to one's collection of informative reading matter. In addition to an outline sketch of the picture, these pamphlets contained a dozen or so pages of text, summarizing the history, geography, and current interest of the scene depicted.

Almost from the beginning, the panorama was meant to illustrate history as it was being made. No sooner was Barker's invention well established in its permanent home than the war with France broke out, and excitement over military affairs and the precarious destiny not only of Britain but of all Europe came to

* Literary usages of the word throw additional light on the versatile role it had in the Victorian vocabulary, as well as on the contribution the diorama made to the imagistic resources of contemporary writers. George Eliot's "The memory has as many moods as the temper, and shifts its scenery like a diorama" (*Middlemarch,* Ch. 79) more or less retains the original connotation. Hardy's use, in the gambling scene with Diggory Venn and Wildeve in *The Return of the Native* (Book 3, Ch. 8), is more subtle: "The aspect of the two opponents was now singular. Apart from motions, a complete diorama of the fluctuations of the game went on in their eyes. A diminutive candle-flame was mirrored in each pupil, and it would have been possible to distinguish therein between the moods of hope and the moods of abandonment, even as regards the reddleman, though his facial muscles betrayed nothing at all." The fluctuating play of light suggests the Regent's Park Diorama, but the diminution of the whole scene, with the mention of the single candle flame, introduces a hint of the peepshow. Thackeray, by contrast, takes "diorama" to mean what "panorama" in loose usage also meant—a series of more or less connected paintings, in the manner of George Cruikshank's *The Bottle.* In *Pendennis* (Ch. 51) he wrote that "the rents in the Temple will begin to fall from the day of the publication of the dismal diorama." Thackeray's choice of "diorama" here was clearly suggested by a sentence earlier in the same paragraph: "A committee of marriageable ladies, or of any Christian persons interested in the propagation of the domestic virtues, should employ a Cruikshank or a Leech, or some other kindly expositor of the follies of the day, to make a series of Designs representing the horrors of a bachelor's life in chambers, and leading the beholder to think of better things, and a more wholesome condition."

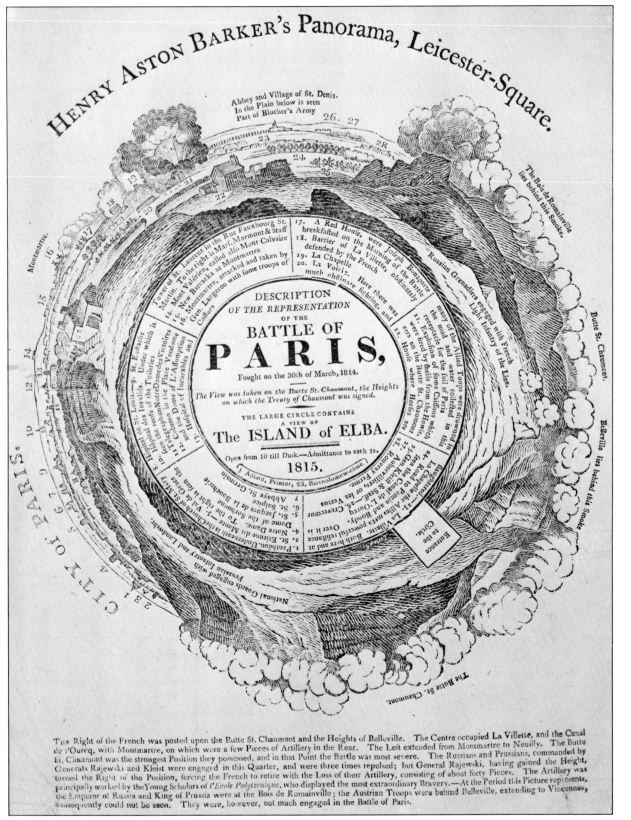

The drawing within the panorama contains the following text:

HENRY ASTON BARKER's Panorama, Leicester-Square.

Abbey and Village of St. Denis.
In the Plain below is seen
Part of Blucher's Army

DESCRIPTION
OF THE REPRESENTATION
OF THE
BATTLE OF
PARIS,
Fought on the 30th of March, 1814.

*The View was taken on the Butte St. Chaumont, the Heights
on which the Treaty of Chaumont was signed.*

THE LARGE CIRCLE CONTAINS
A VIEW OF
The ISLAND of ELBA.

Open from 10 till Dusk.—Admittance to each 1s.

1815.

J. Adlard, Printer, 23, Bartholomew-close.

The Right of the French was posted upon the Butte St. Chaumont and the Heights of Belleville. The Centre occupied La Villette, and the Canal de l'Ourcq, with Montmartre, on which were a few Pieces of Artillery in the Rear. The Left extended from Montmartre to Neuilly. The Butte St. Chaumont was the strongest Position they possessed, and in that Point the Battle was most severe. The Russians and Prussians, commanded by Generals Rajewski and Kleist were engaged in this Quarter, and were three times repulsed; but General Rajewski, having gained the Height, turned the Right of the Position, forcing the French to retire with the Loss of their Artillery, consisting of about forty Pieces. The Artillery was principally worked by the Young Scholars of l'Ecole Polytecnique, who displayed the most extraordinary Bravery.—At the Period this Picture represents, the Emperor of Russia and King of Prussia were at the Bois de Romainville; the Austrian Troops were behind Belleville, extending to Vincennes, consequently could not be seen. They were, however, not much engaged in the Battle of Paris.

54. Barker's Panorama: descriptive drawing in the souvenir guide to the panorama of the Battle of Paris, 1815.

dominate the public mind for twenty years. This concern with current events was fed, in the first instance, by newspapers, but these were not illustrated, nor would they be for several more decades. Thus it fell to two forms of entertainment, the theatre and the new panorama, to give pictorial realization to events. At Sadler's Wells and Astley's Amphitheatre, military triumphs supplied admirable opportunities to exploit the respective specialties of the two houses, a tank of water at Sadler's Wells, which therefore put on a string of naumachias, and trained horses at Astley's, which produced a series of land engagements featuring the cavalry.[9] Between Astley's production in mid-1801 of *The British Glory in Egypt,* showing the defeat of the French by the Highlanders, with "REAL CAVALRY and INFANTRY," and Sadler's Wells's *The Battle of the Nile* in 1815, a score or more of such war-inspired spectacles were performed for London audiences.

Even when they ceased to be timely they continued to be performed. One practical reason was that they kept those theatres, with their peculiar, and in other respects limited, facilities, in business (although they sometimes could be seen elsewhere, at Covent Garden, the Haymarket, and the Coburg, for instance). But the predominant reason was that in peace, as in war, London audiences had an insatiable appetite for patriotic spectacles. In the very season, nine years after the event, that a paper remarked, "London is sick to death of Waterloo,"[10] Astley's *The Battle of Waterloo,* replete with cavalry advances, bugle calls, and cannon fire, ran for 144 consecutive performances and then went into the repertory to become the second most frequently performed show in the house's history, excelled only by *Mazeppa.* The same situation prevailed in the panorama business. No more than two days before this production opened on 19 April 1824, another paper, reporting on the opening of a Waterloo panorama in Spring Gardens, had commented that "there have been so many daubs of this national 'set-to,' that people . . . would now almost as soon wish to be in such a battle itself, as to visit representations of it."[11] Nevertheless, the panorama prospered along with the live competition at Astley's, and representations of Waterloo would continue to draw crowds both to the theatres and to the panoramas for many more years.

In the theatre, the resemblance between the staged versions and the battles they were billed as representing was minimal; in the panorama, by contrast, fidelity to fact was a prime consideration. Here the literate public repaired to visualize what it read about in the newspapers, with the same expectations with which, in the twentieth century, it would watch first newsreels and then newsreels' successors, television news programs.

Unlike the heroic-scale gallery paintings that were produced on the same themes by leading artists, the panoramas had no expectation of permanence. As with other forms of journalism, their singular merit lay not in the durability of their documentation but in the speed with which they laid it before the public. The fortune went to the fleetest, and the panoramists sometimes vied with the theatrical scene painters to be first in London to portray some recent sensational event. When the Houses of Parliament burned on the night of 16 October 1834, the scenery man at the Victoria Theatre, Charles Marshall, proved to have the fastest brush—his "panoramic view" was on display at the theatre within a week; but it was not long afterward, in early December, that E. Lambert's "dioramic" version, with the flames reflected on the water and "brilliantly though fitfully illuminating the rich Gothic tracery of the magnificent and venerable Abbey," could be seen at the former Royal Bazaar in Oxford Street, now rebuilt after its destruction by fire in 1829 and renamed the Queen's Bazaar.[12]

So also with battles. Climactic episodes in post-Napoleonic conflicts continued to stir both theatrical people and panoramists into action. When London learned late in November 1827 of Admiral Codrington's destruction of the Turkish and Egyptian fleets at Navarino, the scene designers at both Drury Lane and Covent Garden quickly created appropriate pictures to insert into their Christmas pantomimes, and by January there were two competing panoramas: Burford's, painted, it was justly said, "with extraordinary rapidity" from drawings made at the scene and plans lent by the Admiralty; and the diorama in the Bazaar, King Street, Portman Square.[13] Six years later, Burford again won critical applause for "chronicling the times on canvas,"[14] on this occasion his portrayal, only a few weeks after the event, of the capitulation of Antwerp to the French after a month's siege. He was equally prompt, given the distances involved, with his picture of the bombardment and capture of Acre (3 November 1840); "little more than three months have elapsed since the brilliant deed," remarked the *Mirror of Literature,* "and scarcely have Parliament voted thanks to the conquerors, when here we have a perfect pictorial representation of the terrific scene."[15] (It was a little too terrific for some tastes. Two Bombay naval architects, who lived in London for over two years and recorded their impressions of a number of shows they saw, wrote in their journal: "we observed some of the Egyptian troops lying here and there killed, and wounded, while others were busy in firing at the ships. The blowing up of the powder magazine, which was supposed to have taken place by one of the shells from the steamers finding its way into it, and which killed nearly three thousand Egyptians, it was a terrible sight as we saw hands, legs, &c., of these unfortunate beings flung into the air. The town of Acre also presented a galling and heart-rending spectacle, it was a mass of ruin and every house was shattered to pieces."[16])

The Leicester Square portrayal of the Battle of Sobraon in the Punjab War (1846) was yet another example of Burford's alert and energetic showmanship; its details were determined by the dispatches received as it was being painted. The Sobraon picture was one of a number of panoramas, military or topographical, which took up the imperial theme in those confident early Victorian years. Burford portrayed the Battle of Kabul in the Afghan War—one of the few British defeats to be commemorated in a panorama—in 1842. India figured in half a dozen other Leicester Square shows: Calcutta (1830), Bombay (1831), Benares (1840), the Himalayas (1847), and two focal points of the Sepoy Mutiny, Delhi and Lucknow (1857–58). Indian places and events were also prominent among the subjects of the moving panoramas that achieved popularity at mid-century. Another topic that repeatedly found its way onto Burford's canvases was the British campaign to open China to western trade. Canton, the only Chinese port open to such trade until after the Opium War, was portrayed in 1838; Macao, the Portuguese dependency to which the Canton merchants repaired during the summer season, was shown on the eve of the war, in 1840; and Hong Kong and Nanking in 1844–45, after the war had been brought to a satisfactory conclusion. Canton was shown again at Burford's in 1859–60, when the city was the center of the military actions that led to the sack of the Summer Palace in 1860.

A group of popular panorama topics which had no overt military or imperialistic significance were inspired by the several Arctic expeditions that engaged the peacetime British navy.[17] Early in 1834 the return of Sir John Ross and his men after three years' captivity in the ice at the magnetic North Pole called forth one of Burford's superior efforts ("Boothia"). The Times, in an unusually long appreciation, singled out for special praise the representation of the aurora borealis and stars of "refulgent brightness."[18] In the three years beginning late in 1849, the already pro-

tracted search for Sir John Franklin—it would go on for another twenty years—was the subject of several panoramas. The quest was one in which the nation had a deep emotional involvement: not only was British prestige at stake, but the shock of Franklin's total disappearance, after the confidence that had surrounded the departure of his elaborately equipped expedition, was an upsetting national experience. At Leicester Square, Burford provided a pictorial supplement to the growing literature on Arctic exploration which the Franklin drama had evoked by producing a show composed of two "hemiramas," as the diarist Crabb Robinson called them, one portraying Ross, a would-be rescuer, on the coast of Greenland in July, the other showing his ships, the Enterprise and the Investigator, iced in during the winter at Port Leopold.[19] The existence of rival panoramas led Lieutenant Brown, an officer of the Enterprise, to notify the press (doubtless prompted by Burford) that he alone had made any sketches during the late expedition, and that it was these sketches the Admiralty had given Burford exclusive permission to use.[20] Later (1852) Vauxhall Gardens erected an enormous outdoor "diorama" of Arctic scenery.

Popular though martial and naval subjects were, the panoramists wisely put some of their eggs in other baskets. Henry Aston Barker's biggest success, which grossed £10,000 and doubtless helped him retire at the early age of forty-eight, was his panorama of the coronation of George IV in July 1821. The splendid event attracted extraordinary interest, not only because it was the first ceremony of its kind in sixty years but because of the new king's unkingly character and the scandal which reached its climax in Queen Caroline's frustrated attempt to join him inside the Abbey on the great day. Confident that the public's interest would last, Barker took his time preparing his canvas. A handwritten note at the back of the Museum of London's copy of the souvenir booklet preserves some anonymous showgoer's awe at the announced statistics: "There are 30,000 figures introduced in this Panorama, 14,000 of whom are in costume for the occasion, including the Military. It took 12 Months in painting." While the picture was in preparation, the topic was kept before the public by the highly successful Drury Lane reenactment of the coronation, upon which the lessee-manager of the house, Robert William Elliston, who played the king, spent £5,000— a great sum for a single theatrical spectacle at the time, though George IV had laid out £250,000 on the original. Barker's immediate rival seems also to have done well.

The Moving Panorama — or Spring Garden Rout.

55. Crowd outside Marshall's panorama of the coronation of George IV (engraving by C. Williams, *The Moving Panorama—or Spring Garden Rout,* 1823).

At the Great Room, Spring Gardens, Marshall's 10,000-square-foot version was announced as containing not a mere 30,000 figures but a cool 100,000, of which 500 were life size.[21]

Despite their early emphasis on recent events and their frequent return to such subjects later on, from the outset panoramas were, almost by definition, portrayals of scenes rather than of actions; in the long run, they were more topographical than topical. Ideally, of course, the two interests were combined in a single picture. At Leicester Square, as elsewhere, there was a

strong representation of what modern journalistic jargon would call "places in the news"—scenes that were of intrinsic interest by virtue of their exoticism or well-publicized picturesqueness or historical associations, but that acquired added interest from the current headlines. In addition to following the headlines as expeditiously as possible, Burford had a happy knack of anticipating them. Repeatedly, his choice of topographical subjects was praised for its almost uncanny timeliness. In 1840 the *Athenaeum* spoke of his current show, the picture of Macao, as "singularly well-timed." "Who is there," it demanded, "taking the most indolent interest in the storm now brewing in 'the world's Teapot,' that will not be eager to take a look at Macao?"[22] Later in the same year, the *Mirror of Literature* found the new panorama, Damascus, "another convincing proof of Mr. Burford's judicious selection; for, it is impossible he could have chosen one in all respects so vitally interesting, particularly at the present moment, when the East is pregnant with such startling events."[23] (The Quadruple Alliance of Russia, Britain, Prussia, and Austria was helping Turkey confront Mehemet Ali in the ever restless Middle East.)

More frequent, however, were topographical subjects whose time had already arrived or whose interest was perennial. Such a one was Constantinople, which entered the panoramic repertory in 1801, Barker having made drawings for it on the scene two years earlier. The subject recurred no fewer than three times at Leicester Square (1804, 1846, and 1853–54), as well as once at the Strand house after Barker and Burford took over. At the time of the Strand run (1829) it drew crowds because, as one reviewer wrote, of "the present critical situation of the Turkish Empire, when no one can tell how soon this magnificent city, with its splendid palaces, superb kiosks, swelling domes, extensive terraces, lofty mosques, pointed minarets, glittering crescents, and populous seraglios, may be exposed to the ravages of an almost barbarous army."[24]

Paris was another city of constant interest, appealing as it did to a complexity of emotions ranging from fear and distrust (on political grounds) to envy (for its architecture and, among less parochial Londoners, its "civilization"). In the midst of the Napoleonic Wars, in 1802, two panoramas of the city were displayed in London—DeMaria's and Barker's—and a third, Girtin's, was promised, though it never materialized. The Battle of Paris in 1814 was duly illustrated at Leicester Square. In 1828 the Strand panorama had a Paris painting on its bill, possibly one or the other of Barker's old canvases. In 1832 the Queen's Bazaar displayed "eight grand diorama views, painted on many thousand feet of canvas," of events during the three-day revolt in July 1830, among them the battle at the Porte St. Denis, the attack on the Hôtel de Ville, the taking of the Louvre and the Tuileries, and the French troops' embarcation at Toulon.[25] In July 1832 the Diorama presented a view of Paris from Montmartre. And in 1848, as has been noted, the Colosseum had one of its few bits of good fortune when it opened a view of Paris by night during the season when that city was convulsed by revolution. As the *Illustrated London*

News commented in August, "All the points where barricades were erected in the June insurrection, and where the carnage was hottest, are clearly indicated, thus giving a greater degree of historical interest to this great picture."[26]

In the absence of a detailed record of Burford's activities in the early months of 1848, it is hard to tell whether his twin successes that year were the result of luck or of his demonstrable instinct for impending events. When his own Paris panorama was put on view late in May, it displayed, according to the *Times,* the city as it was on "the fourth instant," when the Republic was proclaimed from the steps of the Assembly. "The view on every side is animated by groups characteristic of the present state of France. The Pont de la Révolution and the front of the Chamber are thronged by a multitude hastening to hear the determination of the Assembly. In another part a group is parading a tree of liberty, which is about to be erected."[27] Perhaps Burford had begun to paint the canvas soon after the revolt broke out in late February and added fresh timely touches as he worked on. The result, in any case, was a twin bill of surpassing timeliness, for in the second Leicester Square circle Burford had already installed a panorama of Vienna—at the end of March, when the newspapers were full of the "revolutionary proceedings" in the Habsburg capital.

Recurrently, the state visits of royalty provided occasions for topical panoramas. Burford's *Valetta* (1839) acquired most of its interest from the recent visit there of the Queen Dowager. His Christmas show in 1843 was "Tréport, the Surrounding Country, and the Château d'Eu; with the Arrival of Her Majesty Queen Victoria on Her Visit to His Majesty Louis Philippe, on Saturday, September 2, 1843." The queen's visit to Ireland in 1849 was portrayed the next year at the Chinese Gallery. Sometimes advertisements reached inordinately far to locate a topical tie-in; the Diorama's picture of the Rhine from the Castle of Stolzenfels (1850), for example, was recommended because the queen and Prince Albert happened to have toured the vicinity several years earlier.[28]

◖◈◗

That the panoramas flourished as long as they did, in spite of the emerging competition in the 1840s of illustrated print-journalism that could produce engraved representations of current events far faster than the speediest painter, was due to an abiding interest in foreign lands for reasons other than their prominence

56. Robert Burford's panorama
of Vienna, 1848 (*Illustrated
London News,* 5 March 1848).

in the headlines. Throughout the period reaching from James Cook's voyages in the 1770s to Thomas Cook's pioneer conducted tours of the continent in the mid-1850s, the English mind had a particular interest in geography, manifested, among other ways, by the enthusiasm for travel which eventually was democratized into "tourism." In part, this was due to a recognition that the sources of the nation's present and prospective supremacy, economic as well as geopolitical, lay overseas. She was, above all, the workshop of the world, the imperial trader, the guardian of the sea lanes: this was her manifest destiny. The popularity of shows like Burford's, therefore, reflected a marked strain of curiosity about all the realms lying beyond the tight little island in which her power was felt and upon which her prosperity largely depended.

Equally important, the topographical panoramas as a group were a bourgeois public's substitute for the Grand Tour, that seventeenth- and eighteenth-century cultural *rite de passage* of upper-class society. Although it gained a new fashionable motivation and a changed perspective with the spread of enthusiasm for the picturesque and sublime, the Grand Tour for the most part could not be undertaken in the war conditions of 1793–1815, and persons in quest of natural beauty and antiquarian ruins had to limit their wanderings to their

homeland. Many, however, could only afford to visit the panoramas, which fed upon this frustrated yearning for romantic experience among those who were, to borrow Keats's phrase, in city pent.

The yearning spread as the middle class grew more prosperous and more receptive to the appeal of foreign places. To a few, the end of the war and the consequent freedom to travel in Europe meant that their ambition could be realized; to many who were less well off, the same aspiration could be satisfied only vicariously, as before. One obvious means was through print. Every year saw more engravings of foreign scenes—landscape vistas, picturesque or stately cities, architectural monuments—on sale in the print shops. Hundreds of volumes appeared that were devoted solely to topographical or architectural illustration or else were the travel narratives of antiquarians, artists, soldiers, diplomats, copiously interlarded with plates. Pictures of scenes designed to stir the romantic sensibility were a main attraction of the silk-bound "keepsakes" that adorned the drawing room tables of the relatively well-to-do during the Regency and the early Victorian years. The convergence of these two streams of cultivated public interest—the subjects of romantic topographical and landscape art, and travel to the scenes themselves—was exemplified by the appearance of series of gift books specifically devoted to landscape and travel: the *Landscape Annual,* the *Picturesque Annual, Turner's Annual Tour, Campbell's Scenic Annual,* the *Annual of British Landscape Scenery.*

The panorama was the show-business equivalent of this literature and art of travel. Its painters depicted, on the scale of stage scenery, the same subjects that families dreamed over in their illustrated books: Lago Maggiore, the Rhine, the Alhambra, Milan, Lucerne, St. Petersburg, Mount Rigi, Venice, Cairo, Athens, Lausanne, Niagara. It is significant that none of the panoramas showing locales like Ramsgate, Brighton, Bath, St. Michael's Mount, Killarney, and Stirling made much impression. Such places were accessible with relative ease, the more so as railways reached them, and the true province of the panoramist was the remote scene which relatively few favored travelers, such as families of unlimited means and leisure, itinerant artists, soldiers and seamen, and foreign merchants, could hope to visit.*

But travel, however delightful in the contemplation, had definite drawbacks in practice, and it was often remarked of panoramas that they offered the pleasures of tourism without its cost or hardships; it permitted xenophobes to enjoy its adventures comfortably and safely at home.

Panoramas [wrote an unidentified contributor to *Blackwood's Magazine* in 1824] are among the happiest contrivances for saving time and expense in this age of contrivances. What cost a couple of hundred pounds and half a year half a century ago, now costs a shilling and a quarter of an hour. Throwing out of the old account the innumerable miseries of travel, the insolence of public functionaries, the roguery of innkeepers, the visitations of banditti, charged to the muzzle with sabre, pistol, and scapulary, and the rascality of the custom-house officers, who plunder, passport in hand, the indescribable *désagrémens* of Italian cookery, and the insufferable annoyances of that epitome of abomination, an Italian bed.

Now the affair is settled in a summary manner. The mountain or the sea, the classic vale or the ancient city, is transported to us on the wings of the wind. And their location here is curious. We have seen Vesuvius in full roar and torrent, within a hundred yards of a hackney-coach stand, with all its cattle, human and bestial, unmoved by the phenomenon. Constantinople, with its bearded and turbaned multitudes, quietly pitched beside a Christian thoroughfare, and offering neither persecution nor proselytism. Switzerland, with its lakes covered with sunset, and mountains capped and robed in storms; the adored of sentimentalists, and the refuge of miry metaphysics; the *Demisolde* of all nations, and German geology—stuck in a corner of a corner in London, and forgotten in the tempting vicinage of a cook-

shop;—and now Pompeii, reposing in its slumber of two thousand years, in the very buzz of the Strand. There is no exaggeration in talking of those things as really existing. Berkeley was a metaphysician; and therefore his word goes for nothing but waste of brains, time, and printing-ink; but if we have not the waters of the Lake of Geneva, and the bricks and mortar of the little Greek town, tangible by our hands, we have them tangible by the eye—the fullest impression that can be purchased, by our being parched, passported, pummelled, plundered, starved, and stenched, for twelve hundred miles east and by south, could not be fuller than the work of Messrs Barker's and Burford's brushes. The scene is absolutely alive, vivid, and true; we feel all but the breeze, and hear all but the dashing of the wave. Travellers recognize the spot where they plucked grapes, and fell sick of the *miasmata;* the draughtsman would swear to the very stone on which he stretched himself into an ague; the man of half-pay, the identical *casa* in which he was fleeced into a perfect knowledge that roguery was as expensive as taxation at home.[29]

To put it in less philistine terms, the panoramas were an expression in popular art of the spirit which permeated much of literate English life in those decades. In painting and poetry, romantic artists sought to fix for their audiences, to make permanent for constant refreshment, the emotions both tranquil and turbulent which contemplation of nature—and of old buildings—inspired in the heightened sensibility of the era. In their necessarily cruder form, panoramas of romantic locales—an Alpine pass, Roman ruins, a Niagara cataract, an Irish lake, a medieval French town, a Levantine city—appealed to the same tastes that were drawn to the poetry of Wordsworth, Scott, Byron, and Moore. But except insofar as such scenes evoked recollections of favorite authors, the romanticism of the Leicester Square panorama and the Diorama was almost exclusively pictorial. (It is curious that no scene in the Lake District, famous as its poets had made it, seems ever to have been transferred to a panorama. Perhaps, like the native locales that were actually depicted in the earlier years, the lakes lacked the necessary glamor of distance.) While English painting in the first Victorian decades was tending heavily to literary subjects—scenes from Shakespeare, Goldsmith, Fielding, Scott, Tennyson, Molière, Cervantes—the panoramas generally avoided specific literary reference.

Milton, to be sure, was a possibility, and the scene in Pandemonium had been one of Loutherbourg's most admired creations.† Burford took courage in 1829 and produced his own version for Leicester Square.

* At a certain expense of cab fare, in addition to separate admission fees, it was possible to "visit" half a dozen such places in the course of a day. A chatty verse-letter "From a Young Lady in Town to Her Friend in the Country," printed in the *Comic Almanack* for 1842, tells how it was done:

. . . You cannot conceive, if 'tis not pointed out,
How quickly in London you travel about;
So I'll tell you, all fabulous narratives scorning,
The various places we saw *in one morning!*
Our lodgings we left about half after nine,
And, taking a coach, we drove off to the Shrine
Of the Chapel at Bethlehem, whence we could glance
At the fine church of Auch, which you know is in France.
Next, into the famed Polytechnic we dropp'd,
And there, a few minutes, at Canton we stopp'd;
Then quitting this spot, with despatch just the same,
By the route of Pall Mall, into Syria we came
At the Kineorama—a tour rather fleet,
Since to Egypt you pass, without quitting your seat,
From whose ancient relics, time-worn and corroded,
We reach'd St. Jean d'Acre just as it exploded.
(To make my accounts with localities tally,
The fortress *I* mean overlooks Cranbourne-alley.)
And after we'd travell'd these scenes to explore,
We got home to dine, at our lodgings, by four.

† Perhaps Byron had something of the sort vaguely in mind when, writing of *Don Juan* as a proposed "epic poem," he promised among the other episodes "a panoramic view of hell's in training." (*Don Juan,* I, cc.)

During the forty years that this species of painting has been so liberally patronized [he explained, not without pomposity, in the souvenir guide], the Views have consisted of cities, remarkable for the magnificence of their public buildings, the beauty of their situation, or circumstances connected with their history, which rendered them objects of general attention, varied occasionally by the most striking and interesting events of the day; such as battles, naval engagements &c in which his countrymen have gloriously supported the fame of British valour, and immortalised their names by the most splendid and honourable achievements. It having been long and generally admitted that no style of painting could portray these subjects with so much interest and appearance of reality, it occurred to him that it might be adapted to the higher branches of the art with increased effect, and embody, with unrivalled boldness and grandeur, the most sublime and stupendous imagery. With this view he was induced to seek in works of imagination for a subject like the present, for which the Panorama is peculiarly adapted, offering a field of sufficient magnitude to do ample justice to the most vivid and splendid conceptions. With this impression solely, the present attempt (in the execution of which he has received the most valuable assistance from the abilities of Mr. SLOUS) has been made, the success of which he leaves to the impartial judgment of his best friends, a liberal and enlightened public.

The liberal and enlightened public's impartial judgment was discouraging. Reviewers suspected, with reason, that Burford and Mr. Slous—whose name was soon afterward euphonized into "Selous"—had sought to take advantage of the current popularity of John Martin's huge, calamitous canvases. As the *Athenaeum* wrote,

Milton's painting is historical, the panorama is landscape; in the former, the animate objects are principal; the scenery and architecture are accessory; in the latter, the view of the infernal abyss forms the picture, its inmates act a subordinate part. The panorama, in fact, as those more penetrating divined it would be, is a picture of the capital of Satan, somewhat in the style of Martin.* It abounds in massive architecture and lofty and rugged mountains, floods and rocks of every hue, and of every temperature, from the fiery Phlegethon to the cold and oblivious Lethe.[30]

The *Times* dismissed the show in a paragraph. Burford, who had learned the hard way what Fuseli discovered twenty-nine years earlier, that the public would not patronize a Pandemonium when there was a Seringapatam—or, in the present case, Martin's new *Fall of Nineveh*—to see, never attempted another excursion into literature.

Sites associated with antiquity were a bit more common. Reinagle showed his picture of Rome at the Strand house in 1804, and Burford had panoramas of Pompeii (1824), Karnak and Thebes (1835), the interior of the Roman Colosseum (1839), and Baalbek (1844).† The strongest impact the progress of archaeological discovery made upon the entertainment world, however, was in 1851–1853, as a result of the publication of Sir Austen Henry Layard's works *Nineveh and Its Remains* and *Nineveh and Babylon*. The immediate celebrity of these books and the arrival of the famed winged bulls of Nineveh at the British Museum touched off a brief but intense vogue of Assyriana. While Kean's production of Byron's *Sardanapalus* drew crowds who, like Crabb Robinson, wanted to view the lavish scenery,[31] Burford displayed a panorama of Nimrud which had an unusually long run, and at the Gothic Hall, Lower Grosvenor Street, a diorama of Nineveh was presented, with an accompanying lecture by F. C. Cooper, "the Artist sent out by the Trustees of the British Museum to assist Dr. Layard."[32]

In the British population during these years there were hundreds of thousands of Evangelical and Dissenting families whose scruples forbade their entering a playhouse, but whose Scripture-centered religion made them a natural clientele for panoramas illustrating the Holy Land. In the forties, the Middle East was replacing Rome and Pompeii as the favorite locale of artists specializing in historical topography. Burford's picture of Damascus thus had a double attractiveness, as a topographical show and as an illustration of the Bible. "The sacred interest of the subject," it was reported some time later, "attracted thousands of visitors who were not profane enough to enjoy ordinary sights."[33] Renoux's double-effect picture of the Shrine of the Nativity at the Diorama had a similar appeal. But the peak of business in Holy Land panoramas occurred in the Crystal Palace year, when three such exhibitions were available to the heavily Nonconformist throngs from the provinces. One was Burford's, probably the old one (1835) reshown. Another, the work of the resident scenic artist at the Lyceum and the Princess's Theatre, William Roxby Beverley, was at the St. George's Gallery, Hyde Park Corner. The third, first seen at the Society of Painters in Water-Colours gallery in Pall Mall and then moved to the Egyptian Hall, was painted from original sketches by three artists—Henry Warren, Joseph Fahey, and Joseph Bonomi, "the distinguished traveller in the East." It

* Martin's mezzotint of Pandemonium had been among the engravings of *Paradise Lost* he published in 1825.

† Panoramas had the additional, if incidental, advantage of serving as a handy means by which a traveler or topographer could further expatiate upon his subject to a group of acquaintances. At Thomas Moore's behest, John Gardner Wilkinson, whose book *The Topography of Thebes, and General View of Egypt* had just been published, took him and several other friends to the Thebes panorama for a fuller explanation. "Nothing," wrote Moore, "could be more intelligent, satisfactory, and at the same time unaffected, than his manner of explaining to us all the localities, antiquities, &c., of the place, which he has every reason to be familiar with, having remained no less than twelve years in Egypt." In the same diary Moore also noted a similar, though rather more personal, use Mary Shelley made of a panorama. After visiting the Academy exhibition in June 1827 he and she went to Burford's Geneva show, where she "pointed out to me the place where Lord B[yron] lived." (*Memoirs, Journal, and Correspondence of Thomas Moore,* ed. Lord John Russell, London, 1856, VII, 150; V, 178.)

was this last show, bitterly competing with the one at Hyde Park Corner, which evoked from the *Times* the comment that "some of the scenes exhibited (for instance, that of Mount Sinai) trench so closely on the descriptions of Sacred Writ as to be decidedly improper."[34] It is not easy to imagine what impropriety could have been introduced into a picture of Sinai, but the criticism illustrates the truth that the lot of a Victorian panoramist was never a predictable one. Among all the geographical subjects he could select from, the Holy Land would seem to have had the most nearly universal appeal. If it was not invulnerable to criticism, what, then, was left?

The Theatrical Art of the Panorama

14

Writing *The Prelude* in 1804, William Wordsworth, recalling his first residence in London thirteen years before,* briefly mentioned what can only have been the Exeter Change menagerie and then went on to describe the panorama:

> At leisure let us view, from day to day,
> As they present themselves, the spectacles
> Within doors, troops of wild beasts, birds and beasts
> Of every nature, from all climes convened;
> And, next to these, those mimic sights that ape
> The absolute presence of reality,
> Expressing, as in mirror, sea and land,
> And what earth is, and what she has to show;
> I do not here allude to subtlest craft,
> By means refined attaining purest ends,
> But imitations, fondly made in plain
> Confession of man's weakness and his loves.
> . . . the Painter, fashioning a work
> To Nature's circumambient scenery,
> And with his greedy pencil taking in
> A whole horizon on all sides, with power,
> Like that of angels or commissioned spirits,
> Plant[s] us upon some lofty pinnacle,
> Or in a ship on waters, with a world
> Of life, and life-like mockery, to east,
> To west, beneath, behind us, and before . . .[1]

A lofty concept indeed, this linking of the panoramic art with the "subtlest craft" of the imaginative easel painter. If "imitations" were not themselves fine art, Wordsworth attributes to them a dignity of their own, inferior no doubt, but scarcely to be dismissed as ig-

noble fakery. This of a branch of picture making which detractors in those same years, and later, dismissed as glorified theatrical scene painting!

The truth was that panoramas did derive from, or reflect, two worlds. They were a commercial entertainment which appealed to both the playgoer and the art fancier, a unique blend of the spectacular and romantic impulses that characterized English theatrical and pictorial art during the first half of the nineteenth century. The panorama's affinity with the stage was plain enough. The topical and topographical bent that it shared with the pantomime in particular was actually the least important link between the two kinds of entertainment. Not only did they have a large audience in common; the panorama also served as a much-needed alternative to the theatre in a period when playgoing was unthinkable to the "serious" families of London. The Evangelical fervor which reached its peak in those decades had revived the old Puritan hostility toward the stage. Even those middle-class families who had no such scruples still had their comfort and their respectability to consider, and both were imperiled when many theatrical audiences largely consisted, as they then did, of rowdy and sometimes actually riotous working-class men and women, whose proximity was offensive to ear, eye, and nose, and when, in addition, prostitutes haunted the premises. At the panorama, by contrast, morality and respectability were not in question; any head of a family could treat his wife and children to a visit, secure in the knowledge that they would be edified, never corrupted, by the sight and the

* The date need not be taken too literally. In general, Book VII of *The Prelude,* where this passage occurs, describes Wordsworth's experiences and observations during his first extended stay in London in 1791. By the time of writing, however, these had probably coalesced in memory with some later ones. The only panorama in London in 1791 was Barker's picture of Edinburgh, but this was soon replaced by the London picture and by the scene of the fleet at Spithead. By 1804, of course, there were a number of so-called panoramas on display.

surroundings. Thus panoramas enabled the public to enjoy at least one of the charms of the contemporary theatre without any of the risks that going there entailed.

That charm was the spectacular scenery. One of the inexorable facts of their profession with which managers had somehow to cope was the cavernous size of the two patent theatres. Drury Lane, rebuilt after it burned in February 1809, seated 3,200, and Elliston raised the capacity to 3,590 in 1821. Covent Garden, rebuilt at the same time, held well over 3,000. Both had huge stages: Drury Lane's was ninety feet deep. These imposing theatrical barns were too big for the comparatively subtle effects of traditional acting. As the address delivered at the opening of the much smaller New English Opera House on the site of the Lyceum in 1816 put it, this was a house, unlike the Big Two,

> Where you can see the *Stage* and *hear* the *Play*.
> Where you with ease can mark our real faces.
> Without the aid of glasses or grimaces!
> And each inflection of the voice is heard,
> Your ears preserved, and our poor lungs are spared![2]

In these circumstances the managers of Drury Lane and Covent Garden had little choice but to supplement the broad acting now required with spectacular scenery; nothing less would succeed in such theatres. Thus Loutherbourg's pioneering between 1771 and 1785 had the unforeseen result of providing the stage with an attraction which threatened to overshadow the acting. In pantomimes and extravaganzas especially, much of the appeal henceforth would reside in the elaborate settings, which could be appreciated from the farthest seats, where the actors could be seen and heard only with difficulty. Unconverted playgoers who regretted the consequent downgrading of acting and of the divertissements and mechanical novelties that were a staple of pantomime would have subscribed to the obviously exaggerated statement in the twenties, "Pantomimes are now virtually extinct; Stanfield and Roberts have made picture galleries of them."[3]

To many, at all events, the proper place for lavish scenic effects was not the theatre but the panorama. In 1830 the *Examiner* commented, "beautiful as these [theatrical] paintings are . . . we feel that they interfere with the business in hand; we can see as splendid works in the Strand and Leicester Square for one shilling; more beautiful at the Diorama; and most beautiful at the Colosseum, which last place, with its fairy-like enchantments, leaves all the pantomime scenic illusions we ever beheld in the distance."[4] There

was, furthermore, this important difference: stage scenery, theoretically at least, was subordinate to the action; it was not meant to be closely inspected but was intended simply to provide a general effect of locality and atmosphere, and anyway it was too far from most of the seats to be subjected to close examination except by spyglasses. Panoramas, on the other hand, were expressly meant to be studied close-up. None of the places where panoramas were shown approached the dimensions or the capacity of the patent theatres. At Leicester Square and the Colosseum, the spectators' area was only a few feet from the canvas, as was true also of the "great rooms" where panoramas and dioramas were shown. As the center of attention rather than the background, they had to be painted with greater care than stage scenery; coarse effects acceptable at Drury Lane would be intolerable at Leicester Square, where a single painting was intended to be examined for as long as one wished.

It is true that the theatrical scenery men had at their disposal technical resources which enabled them to mount three-dimensional spectacles that were beyond the capability of the panoramists. To the painted scenery, consisting not merely of backcloths but of wings, raking pieces, ground rows, and other devices for creating perspective, were added various kinds of Loutherbourgian lighting tricks. The introduction of gas about 1817 made it possible to light the stage more brilliantly, more flexibly, and (in time) more steadily than ever before, and the later addition of limelight enhanced these advantages. Portions of the stage could be highlighted while others were cast into shadow; the brightness of sunshine could be contrasted with the subdued illumination of interiors; changing times of day could be indicated. Outside the theatre, only the best of the dioramas, perhaps only the original one, were able to use manipulated lighting with anything like the same effectiveness. The theatres, however, largely wasted this superiority by keeping the auditorium fully illuminated throughout a performance.*

The panorama's greatest influence on the stage was its encouragement of the realistic tendency already set in motion by Loutherbourg. The panoramists' original insistence on topographical accuracy, typified first by Barker's work and then, unsurpassably, by Hornor and Parris, had much to do with the developing zeal for antiquarian authenticity in staging. Although no other panorama attempted the sharpness and wealth of detail that made the Colosseum's picture of London such a marvel, every panoramist knew that the public expected to be shown places and events as they actu-

* The comparative economics of the situation is worth a note. From the viewpoint of management, the panoramists had the better of their rivals; their capital investment was confined to the picture, and their running expenses included no more than the rental and maintenance of the exhibition room, whereas the theatrical men had not only to maintain large theatres but to lay out substantial sums for every new spectacle and to pay the large companies and expensive stars that were required by the triple bills then customary. For the amusement seeker, a shilling bought admission to a single panorama, which might be good for perhaps a half-hour's amusement, whereas a theatrical evening lasting from seven o'clock to well past midnight would cost one or two shillings in the galleries at Drury Lane and Covent Garden, much more (up to 7s. 6d.) in the better seats. Prices were lower in the minor theatres; by mid-century a leading East End theatre, the Britannia, had a scale from 1s. 6d. down to 4d. and 3d. for the galleries, and the Victoria, 1s. to 3d. (Michael R. Booth et al., *The Revels History of Drama in English*, VI, London, 1975, pp. 9–10.)

ally were. Hence Barker's and Burford's constant stress, in their advertising, on the fact that their pictures were based on drawings made on the spot and, in the case of some battles, from official maps and dispatches. In the theatre, this graphic source material had its first counterparts in the sketches that Loutherbourg made in the field for *The Wonders of Derbyshire* and William Capon made of the Tower and Westminster for the series of plays on medieval themes he mounted for Kemble at Drury Lane early in the century.

The zenith of drama-as-panorama was reached in the 1850s, when the settings in Charles Kean's and Samuel Phelps's Shakespearean productions, whose antiquarian details were correct down to the finest point of shape and color, led to the remark that the plays consisted of a succession of magnificent pictures periodically interrupted by recitations from Shakespeare. Their cumulative effects clearly outdid anything a panorama was capable of achieving. But by that very fact the theatrical producers overreached themselves. Of Kean's production of Byron's *Sardanapalus* (1853), George Henry Lewes wrote:

among those who think scenery and costume the "be-all and the end-all" of the drama . . . I will suppose the spectacle to be as effective as to us it was wearisome; I will suppose the winged bulls (in flats) to have had a truly massive grandiose effect; I will suppose the conflagration at the end to be something more than a rival of the eruptions of Etna and Vesuvius at the Surrey Zoo Gardens [see below, Chapter 23]—something more than red fire and collapsing "flies"—and still say *cui bono?* Is the Drama nothing more than a Magic Lantern on a large scale? Was Byron only a pretext for a panorama? It is a strange state of Art when the mere *accessories* become the aim and purpose of representation—when truth of archaeology supplants truth of human passion—when "winged bulls" dwarf heroic natures![5]

And so, in the opinion of many amateurs of the theatre, the ultimate effect of the panorama on the London stage was to degrade it. Acceding to the taste of audiences brought up on the panorama (and now returning to the theatre itself as conditions improved), Kean and Phelps pushed the spectacular element of drama beyond endurance.* After the fifth-act "grand panoramic procession" in Kean's *Henry VIII* (1855), representing a sweep of the Thames from the City to Greenwich that seemingly covered as much territory as the eastern view from the Colosseum St. Paul's, the stage had little left to do by way of scenic coverage, and most managers quickly returned to what was generally regarded as their proper line of work. It may not have been accidental that at this same time the pan-

orama itself was declining. The public had finally become sated with large theatrical pictures wherever found.

ᗡ꒳꙰ꗥ꒒ᗡ

The panorama's other affinity, with the fine art of painting, was also, in part, a matter of size. The "cult of immensity," as the art historian T. S. R. Boase called it,[6] dated from the time of Copley's *Defeat of the Floating Batteries* (1786–1791: 25 by 18 feet); Fuseli's series of Milton paintings (1793–1800), which ranged in size from 10 by 7 to 13 by 12 feet; and Benjamin West's *Christ Rejected by Caiaphas* (1814: 34 by 16 feet), which led to the remark, attributed to Hazlitt, that West was "only good by the acre." In 1815 the British Institution offered a prize of £1,000 for a canvas, 16 by 21 feet, "expressing in an allegorical spirit the triumph of Wellington." James Ward, thinking to give the donors good value for their money, produced a picture whose final measurements were 35 by 22 feet. The prize was his, and the canvas therefore was the British Institution's; but this body, unable to accommodate it, gave it to the Chelsea Hospital, where the antiquarian and topographer John Thomas Smith saw it, "not only suspended without a frame, (just as a showman in a fair would put out his large canvass to display 'the true and lively portraiture' of a giant, the Pig-faced Lady, or the Fire-eater,) but with its lower part projecting over a gallery, just like the lid of a kitchen salt-box."[7]

Before it went to Chelsea, however, Ward's formidable picture was exhibited at the Egyptian Hall in Piccadilly, which in those years housed a succession of immense canvases: Le Thière's *Judgment of Brutus* (1816: 26 by 10 feet), Chevalier Wicar's *Son of the Widow of Naim* (1817: 30 by 21), and David's *Coronation of Napoleon* (1822: 33 by 21), which was claimed to be "the largest picture ever painted,"[8] but which, in fact, was seventy-seven square feet smaller than Ward's canvas. Although no contemporary British painter of any eminence attempted canvases on quite the same extravagant scale, several had excellent credentials as members of the cult of immensity: Haydon (*The Judgment of Solomon*, 12 feet 10 inches by 10 feet 10 inches; *The Raising of Lazarus*, 15 by 10 feet); John Martin (*The Fall of Nineveh*, 11 feet 2 inches by 7 feet; *The Last Judgment*, 10 feet 8 inches by 6 feet 6 inches); Francis Danby (*The Deluge*, 15 by 9 feet); and William Etty (*The Combat*, 13 feet 3 inches by 10 feet 4 inches; *Beniah*, 13 by 10 feet; *Ulysses and the Sirens*, 14 feet 6 inches by 9 feet 9 inches). Many of these pictures

* The most lavish use of panoramic techniques, however, occurred not on the restricted contemporary stage but later, in the illimitable visual imagination of Thomas Hardy as he composed his epic drama, *The Dynasts* (published 1904–1908). *The Dynasts* owed much of its spectacular, fluid staging (never realized, of course, in practice) to the various nineteenth-century pictorial entertainments, which had made a profound impression on Hardy. He described the work as "a panoramic show" and "the diorama of a dream," and this conception is borne out in his directions for the settings of many of the 130 scenes, which were to encompass not only battlefields but enormous geographical tracts—"panoramic" or "bird's-eye views" as he called them—and in his indications of dioramic effects such as changes of lighting, the use of transparencies, and transformations of scene. Equally conspicuous in *The Dynasts* is the phantasmagoria or magic-lantern show (see below, Chapter 16), represented not only by the chorus-characters or "spirits" as they constantly materialize and fade away but in metaphorical references to the device (Part I, Act IV, Scene 5). Older forms of pictorial entertainment also figure in *The Dynasts*. In addition to a number of allusions to puppet shows, Hardy refers at least twice to mechanical pictures (Part II, Act IV, Scene 5, and Part III, "After Scene"). In the latter passage, constituting the last lines of the vast drama, the Spirit Ironic climactically refers to the Immanent Will as "the dreaming, dark, dumb Thing / That turns the handle of this idle Show!"

were shown individually, at a shilling admission, in the manner of panoramas. An even bigger canvas by a minor artist, Pieneman's *Battle of Waterloo* (27 by 18 feet), was exhibited in 1825 in an ugly shed in Hyde Park. In such circumstances it was inescapable that the contemporary mind would belittle the commercial exploitation of big paintings as a branch of show business. The *Literary Gazette* dourly predicted that Pieneman, if not restrained, would set a precedent which would result in "booths spread from the Ride [Rotten Row] to the Serpentine, to receive and exhibit pictures of a similar kind."[9]

The demarcation between such exhibitions and those of panoramas was hardly perceptible. Was a painting occupying, say, three or four hundred square feet of canvas an object of fine art or a small-scale panorama? The charge made to see it was the same, at least. The relationship between the panorama and products of the cult of immensity deserves to be looked into. Gerald Reitlinger, the historian of the economics of taste, correctly remarks that "the logical progeny" of enormous exhibition pieces such as West's *Christ Rejected by Caiaphas* and *Death on the Pale Horse* "was not a picture at all but a panorama," and he may also be right in believing that once the initial estimation in some quarters of panoramas as a legitimate form of fine art had subsided, "it became unwise to drag historical painting down to the same level in competing exhibitions."[10] Unwise or not, there was money in such exhibitions, as we shall see in a later chapter, and large pictures continued to be shown as commercial speculations well past the middle of the century.

As Boase observes, immensity was an important attribute of romantic art. Sheer magnitude, combined with the powerful feeling inherent in the subject and amplified by the artist, was intended to overwhelm the spectator. Size was the chief characteristic which tended to draw the panorama toward the stream of contemporary romantic art, but it was not the only one. Another was its frequent subject: not primarily great battles or public events, for these were as much the topic of classical (more currently, historical) art as of romantic, but picturesque or sublime topography. Panoramas were, in effect, the magnified continuators, in popular art, of the tradition stemming from Paul Sandby, Richard Wilson, Joseph Wright, Loutherbourg, and Gainsborough; in their most prosperous early years they were contemporary with Turner and Constable. It was hardly accidental that some of the favorite subjects at the Diorama—Alpine scenes, ava-

lanches, tempests—were also portrayed time and again by Turner. No one, of course, ever claimed that even the most impressive panorama had the poetic quality of a landscape by either master; by Ruskin's useful definition, panoramas were examples of "simple" or "historical" topographical painting—that is, they merely recorded, as contrasted with the "Turnerian" or "poetical" mode, which interpreted the scene through the painter's sensibility. But it must not be forgotten that many panoramas originated in sketches made by artists whose intentions reached beyond simple documentation, members of the numerous breed of pilgrim-painters—Roberts, Bonington, Prout, Holland, Lewis, and the rest—who roamed through Europe and Asia in the first half of the century. It was such artists who provided the Barkers and Burfords with drawings of locales which the panoramists did not visit personally.

But were they really art, these mass entertainment equivalents of the topographical engravings that were lingered over in London drawing rooms? Those who dismissed them as mere scenic backcloths looking for a theatre or as monstrous gallery paintings fit only to be exhibited in a Hyde Park shed obviously did not think so. In 1830 the *Times* asserted that "the persons employed upon them have, for the most part, had no reputation to sustain as artists, and their chief object seems to have been to emulate, by very gaudy and exaggerated colouring, those paintings which are introduced into the Christmas pantomimes, where red and yellow blaze in the lamplight, and, at the distance from which they are seen, produce an effect which is more pleasing to the eye than satisfactory to persons of taste."[11]

On the other hand, Wordsworth was far from disparaging them, and Ruskin conceded their legitimacy. Both the quantity and the tone of press comment, especially in the first decades of the century, suggest that panoramas usually were granted the possibility of aesthetic appeal. When the Diorama opened in London, it was regarded in some quarters as a highly promising new form of art, as is evidenced by the comparisons a writer in the *European Magazine* chose when he looked forward to its further refinement: "In unskilful hands it would degenerate into a mere child's galantee-show, from which de Loutherbourg's Eidophusikon was as remote as the acting of Garrick [was] from that of the wretchedest mummer at Bartholomew-fair, or as 'The Last Supper' of Raphael Morghen, from the coarsest wood-cut ever prefixed to a St. Giles's ballad."[12] If the show in its present form was not itself great art, it clearly contained the seeds of greatness.

In those years, critics in the daily and weekly papers reported on and judged the newest panoramas with the same earnestness and, in general, the same criteria that they brought to their reviews of the annual shows of the Royal Academy, the British Institution, and the Water-Colour Society. Their notices of panoramas are in no way inferior to their criticism of gallery art. This, in the context of contemporary art journalism, may appear to be faint praise, and it is. But the point is that panoramas as an artistic genre were taken seriously, even if, sometimes, the ultimate decision was against them. Most reviews, naturally, were routine and perfunctory, but they were seldom frivolous. On a few occasions, moreover, the anonymous critics showed genuine perspicacity, the panorama under discussion suggesting important questions of aesthetic intention and effect. The *Times*'s full-column review (5 April 1828) of the new Diorama show of the Cloisters of St. Wandrill and the Village of Unterseen, for instance, was as careful and judicious as an article by Hazlitt; the writer, whoever he was, approached the pictures as new examples of a form of representational art which merited and demanded his full attention and his best analytical powers.

At a conservative estimate, 90 percent of the criticism of panoramas throughout their history was concerned with their success or failure as realistic representation. Of the literally hundreds of assertions, across the years, that the artistic purpose of panoramas was to convey the illusion of reality, this one, occurring in a rapturous *Times* review of Burford's Geneva picture in 1827, was typical: "The efforts of art were never, perhaps, directed to a more enchanting result than in the painting of panoramas, presenting, as they do, so perfect and illusive a representation of nature. . . [T]he pictorial beauties of the present view could not well be exceeded by those of the original. . . . The beholder is involuntarily transported to the identical scene of his admiration—he believes himself contemplating not a draught, but in reality the overpowering majesty of Mont Blanc and the luxuriance of the vallies and hills which are strewed at its feet."[13]

The insistence on verisimilitude which was a cardinal tenet of nineteenth-century English aesthetic doctrine was intensified by the special conditions under which panoramas and dioramas were shown. By its very nature, the circular panorama enjoyed in this respect a great advantage over conventional art as well as theatrical scene painting: it had no frame. Instead, the heart of Barker's novelty was the special precautions taken to obliterate all physical circumstances that would detract from the panorama's illusion. So long as a picture has discernible edges, no matter how overwhelming its size, it remains a palpable counterfeit; no one mistakes it for a manifestation of the real world. It has, instead, its own integral reality, a circumscribed world existing only within the boundaries of the canvas. But a circular panorama, far from being an artist's flat, rectangular insert in the limitless surface of the spectator's world, purported to be that reality itself, enwrapping the spectator on all sides. The fact that the "reality" existed only on painted canvas was obscured by the absence of anything *besides* the canvas. Barker's illusion consisted of substituting for the *real* reality an artificial, but, so long as no outside elements intruded, a complete one. At the Colosseum, the illusion was strengthened by the elaborate structure which imitated the top of St. Paul's. Spectators were persuaded that they were, in fact, atop the real dome and not inside a totally different building two or three miles away, looking, not into space, but at a circular canvas wall. At the Diorama the illusion of reality was sought by the blacked-out tunnel which erased the surroundings of the picture and enforced single-minded concentration upon the scene itself.

The result was what Constable called, in effect, the art of deception. True art, he said in denying the Diorama's claim to such dignity, "pleases by *reminding, not by deceiving*."[14] Had he written about the special effect of the panorama, Constable perhaps would have expatiated in the vein of Sir Ernst Gombrich's discussion of the "ambiguities of the third dimension" when he speaks of

. . . the power of a curved surface to create that illusion of reality we experience in the circular panorama painting beloved of the nineteenth century, or under the vaulted dome of the Zeiss Planetarium, beloved of the twentieth. Here there are two illusions interacting which must be carefully separated. The first is the illusion that the real sky is vaulted or even (though less obviously so) that a real panorama from a mountain top is circular. What is real in such life situations is our freedom to turn round and to assign imaginary equal distances to all remote objects in our field of vision. Enjoying the same freedom of movement in the panorama or planetarium, we experience the second illusion that even to the arrested gaze the curved picture will be more truthful than the flat one. This is not so.[15]

The raison d'être of the panorama, however, was precisely this: that, no matter at what expense in illusion (the falsifying of experience), the artist should depict a scene faithful in every detail to what one would behold if he were actually there. The more minute and accurate its detail and the more credible its perspective, the better the picture was. Intrinsic beauty—the true aesthetic consideration—was almost entirely neglected in criticism of panoramas. Here, in fact, Truth *was* Beauty; the aesthetic satisfaction received from viewing a panorama resided in the conviction that the picture was utterly faithful to external reality. The panorama in fact was the largest conceivable expression of the *trompe l'oeil* principle. If it looked like a picture, it was a failure. One criticism of the Diorama's Chartres scene was that its distances were "too unreal and pictorial to confirm the prepossession with which the foreground fills the spectator's mind, that it is actually a building you see, and not a painted superficies without depths or other perspective than the skill of the artist has given it."[16] Even when a so-called panorama was nothing more than a great flat canvas, shown under conditions in which the ideal suppression of any conflicting "reality" was neither sought nor achieved, verisimilitude was insisted on, to the near-neglect of all other qualities.

The anecdotes told of the panorama's effect on spectators belong to the vein of *trompe l'oeil* stories stemming from that of Zeuxis, the artist whose painted cherries and grapes were so "real" that birds came to peck at them. Indeed, the anecdote of an imperious lady at Burford's panorama who demanded that her escort pluck some of the painted flowers and fruits for her was obviously inspired by that ancient fable. At the same Spithead show of Barker's at which Queen Charlotte felt queasy when she beheld a capsized boat with sailors struggling in the waves, a gentleman's Newfoundland dog was said to have sprung over the rail of the platform, bent on rescuing the drowning men. Many visitors to the Diorama's first bill could not believe that the workmen's tools, planks, and mounds of mortar in the foreground of the Canterbury Cathedral picture were merely painted. To be sure, when the picture was first shown in Paris, some of these *were* real, for, as a writer in *Blackwood's Magazine* reported, the building was still unfinished, "full of masons and bricklayers, and their *matériel de guerre.*"[17] It was hard to distinguish the real workmen and their debris from those in the picture. ("Maman," piped a little girl, "pourquoi met-on toute cette cochonnerie-là devant le tableau?") But the illusion needed no extraneous aid. The *Blackwood's* writer affirmed that the Paris newspaper reports of the surpassingly realistic appearance of "the scaffolding on the Chapel view,—and the workmen at which the French General threw stones,—and the pots, and the tools, and the broken marble" were "true enough. The workmen," he continued, "certainly did not deceive me; but I confess that I took the planks and trowels, (they are at a distance, understand, from the figures of the men,) to be part of the preparations used in putting up the picture." The illusion was just as persuasive when the picture was presented in London. Like the French general, a London spectator was reported to have been "so convinced that the two workmen were actually flesh and blood, that he threw some halfpence at the lazy fellows to rouse them."[18]

Anything that endangered the illusion was of course to be deplored. The only recorded criticism made of the Eidophusikon (in the *Morning Herald* and the *Whitehall Evening Post,* 1 March 1781) bore on this point. The waves in the tempest scene, represented by wooden cut-outs turned on opposing axes by a windlass, were "too abruptly angular"; the ruddy reflection on the buildings in the Greenwich scene persisted too long after the sun had set; and the shipping "frequently sailed . . . in the wind's eye when all their sails were filled a-back!" This set the tone for virtually all of the adverse criticism the panoramas later evoked. Eyes far less captious than those which today spot small anachronisms in films on historical themes noticed inconsistencies. A reviewer of the second half of the Diorama's opening bill, the Valley of Sarnen, pointed out that only the stream appeared to move. "But the question immediately and naturally arises,—why is this the only moving thing? Especially as the storm comes on, why do not the trees wave? Why is not the lake agitated? Why are not the clouds hurried forward in dense and voluminous grandeur? Either the current of the brook should be arrested, or, which would be infinitely better, motion should be imparted to every object in the scene that is susceptible of it."[19] In one picture on the following bill, Daguerre's *City and Harbor of Brest,* the play of light made the water seem to move and one or two chimneys to smoke. "Now this," said another critic, "is a mixture of principles in extremely bad taste. The diorama ought to stand upon its own ground of affording a more irresistible deception to the eye, and through the eye to the understanding, than any other disposition of painting; but it should not attempt to go beyond this. For example in this picture, when the waves rise and fall, why are the vessels stationary? When one chimney smokes, why are the other ten thousand houses of Brest condemned to show no sign of firing within? The artists must either do more, or be content with doing less, and that less quite enough to satisfy the public."[20]

The trouble was that the artists' attempts to do more were sometimes misguided. Not content to let the lighting apparatus do the work, Bouton used a mechanical device to create the effect of a gentle breeze on the trees in the St. Wandrill picture. This struck some, though possibly not the man who regretted the motionlessness of the trees in the Sarnen scene, as a gratuitous and unconvincing detail. In the course of the performance of the same picture, a door suddenly opened and a "beautiful perspective" was revealed. This was clearly too much. The reviewer in the *Literary Gazette,* finding the event "destitute of meaning or consequence," bluntly recommended that the door be nailed up.[21] It was generally thought that such touches detracted from the overall effect.

The leaves [wrote someone in the *Mechanics' Magazine*] are *not* agitated, though they may seem to be so—it is an optical deception accomplished by very simple and obvious means, and though a door does open and close in view of the spectator, it reveals nothing to his sight.* The less the proprietors of the Diorama say about such mechanical devices as the shaking leaves and opening door, the better. Either the brush and canvas should have been left to produce their own impression (with the help always of the coloured screens, which are very allowable auxiliaries), or mechanical motion, if called in at all, should have been employed to far more purpose than it has ever yet been at these exhibitions.[22]

Although modern museum "dioramas," particularly natural habitat scenes with their meticulous simulation of the physical environment, make extensive use of real objects in the foreground, the original Diorama had none. The repairmen's litter in the Canterbury picture was almost certainly painted in; Constable's mention of "some real stones" may imply that he was deceived, just as the little Parisienne was. Within a few years, however, Daguerre felt that the addition of three-dimensional objects would enhance the Diorama's realism. In 1828, for his *View of Mont Blanc Taken from the Valley of Chamonix,* he brought to Paris a complete chalet and outbuildings and erected them at the end of the tunnel as a framing foreground to the picture. A live goat eating hay in the shed provided the final touch. Wits remarked that "only the front half of the goat was real and . . . the rest formed part of the back-cloth."† But the Mont Blanc show was not sent to London, and Daguerre sought novelty in a new and, as it turned out, more profitable direction, toward the double-effect technique.

Constable also mentioned Daguerre's use of "a bit of silver lace turned on a wheel" to represent flowing water in the Sarnen scene. This represented Daguerre's effort to cope with the most intractable problem every panoramist had to face: the representation of light on water. This difficulty was most acute when some attempt also was made to suggest water in motion. Vauxhall's tin cascade had been much oftener ridiculed than admired. Loutherbourg's varnished wooden waves in the sea scenes were not among the effects singled out for praise, and for all we know, the Niagara cataract in his second program may have been no more sophisticated technically than the one at Vauxhall. Reflecting the romantic infatuation with bodies of water, a remarkable number of painted panoramas, which had no moving parts or manipulated lighting, portrayed a sea, lake, bay, river, or waterfall. To critics, the standard touchstone of an artist's success was the realism of his representation of water, with its motion, its limpidity and liquidity, and its constantly shifting reflection of light. Although no panorama painter sought to imitate Turner, if the panoramist mastered water effects as well as any scenery painter or gallery artist could do in the pre-Turnerian mode, he usually was home clear.

Measured in square feet, one of the more daring efforts to come to grips with this recurrent problem was the pair of pictures of Niagara, each thirty-two by forty feet, which an artist named Sintzenick painted for display in 1832 at the Pantechnicon, the newly built "lounge" and salesroom in Belgravia. It was a true diorama of sorts, its effects being produced by playing various hues of light on the scenes.[23]

We confess [said the *Athenaeum*] that we were startled on hearing of the attempt—we could not conceive how a few feet of motionless canvas could, by the hand of art, be made to represent, or even to convey an idea of a scene which is sublime from the very life and energy of nature, and strikes with awe and astonishment beyond all others, from the tremendous power which is made visibly and audibly present by the rush, and whirl, and thunder of a mighty torrent of uncontrollable waters. We regret to add, that the justice of our opinion has been proved.[24]

Burford's portrayal of the same subject, displayed a few months later, was more kindly received. These Niagara shows were part of a short-lived vogue for cascade scenes initiated in 1829 at Covent Garden, where the leading marine artist of the period, Clarkson Stanfield, painted a scene of the Falls of Virginia Water for the pantomime *Jack in the Box; or, Harlequin and the Princess of the Hidden Island.* Its sensational novelty lay in the fact that it featured real water, thirty-nine tuns of

---

* Apparently, he missed the "beautiful perspective" that the critics noted.

† This bold but unsuccessful use of real objects was trumped in 1830 by Daguerre's near neighbor in the Rue des Marais, Colonel Jean-Charles Langlois, who physically involved the spectators in his panorama of the Battle of Navarino by fitting up the approach to the viewing area to represent the interior of a ship and disguising the platform itself as the poop (a real one, extracted from an old man-of-war). In the foreground, before the painted picture, were a rigging made of real cords which faded into the "fictif" rigging, deck swabs that were half real and half image, and other such palpable accessories. (Helmut and Alison Gernsheim, *L. J. M. Daguerre,* London, 1956, p. 32n; Heinz Buddemeier, *Panorama/Diorama/Photographie,* Munich, 1970, p. 187.) But Langlois was not running a changing-light diorama, and there were practical as well as aesthetic objections to emulating him at Daguerre's establishment. Possibly Langlois had been inspired by the similar imitation of actual surroundings at the Colosseum, where the panorama of London with its mock-up of the topmost elements of St. Paul's had opened the preceding year.

which (almost ten thousand gallons) gushed forth at each performance. Rival houses immediately retaliated with representations of Niagara, followed shortly by the panoramas. In April 1830 the new Diorama bill included Daguerre's *Mount Saint Gothard,* with a mighty cataract depicted by what the *Times* described as "the trickling of a small fountain."[25] Such effects, it said, were better left to the imagination. But the Diorama continued to experiment with real water. As late as 1838, Bouton's Tivoli show included a wet simulacrum of that famous garden's cascades. It, too, failed to impress anyone with its realism.

But motionless ships at sea, smokeless chimneys on land, leaves that were unconvincingly fluttered by machine, doors that opened without the intervention of a hand, and cataracts insufficiently supplied with water (if, indeed, they were not merely composed of wrinkled silver paper or tin) were comparatively small details that militated against the panorama's artful effort to deceive. More important were the two linked considerations mentioned by the painter Charles Robert Leslie in a lecture at the Royal Academy in 1849:

I would ask whether others have not felt what has always occurred to me in looking at a Panorama,—that exactly in the degree in which the eye is deceived the stillness of the figures and the silence of the place produces a strange and somewhat unpleasant effect, and the more so if the subject places us in a city. We then want the hum of population, and the din of carriages, and the few voices heard in the room have an unnatural sound as not harmonizing with the scene. Even in the Diorama, where the light and shade is varied by movement and the water is made to ripple, there are still many wants to be supplied, and these are indeed suggested the more in proportion to the attainment of deception. I have no wish to disparage the ingenuity of these contrivances; the Panorama is an admirable mode of conveying much information which by no other means can so well be given.* My object is merely to ascertain how it is that there is always something unsatisfactory—to speak from my own feelings I should say *unpleasant*—in all Art of every kind of which deception is an object.[26]

Leslie here restated, specifically in respect to human figures, a criticism already noted in connection with the Diorama's Sarnen picture. No one objected to the presence of unmoving people in any other kind of pictorial art except that ultimate form of realism, *trompe l'oeil,* where it was agreed that they endangered if they did not actually destroy the illusion. But it was different with panoramas, which did, after all, aspire to the *trompe l'oeil* effect. With the comparatively few ex-

ceptions of pure landscapes, panoramas had subjects that necessarily implied the presence of human beings, worshiping in a cathedral, walking the streets of an Italian town, fighting a battle. Sometimes the people rather than the topography were the center of interest. Of Burford's picture of Paris in 1828 the *Examiner* said, "You not only see Paris before you, but a good specimen of its lively, helter-skelter, joyous, gallant, good-natured, intelligent, out-of-door living but not over-cleanly population. The Artist has presented to the eye a variety of groups, which are exceedingly picturesque and characteristic, and which, even more than the style of architecture, give you the idea of standing in the midst of a foreign people."[27] In a concurrent panorama of Sydney, New South Wales, were seen not only "many European figures [and] several groups of Natives, employed in their exercises and sports," but "that useful animal the kangaroo . . . playfully sporting on the turf."[28] Under the special assumptions of the panorama, the convention which permitted frozen action in an ordinary picture offered some difficulty. To accept a kangaroo arrested in mid-bounce as part of a living scene or to assume that one was watching an actual battle when neither man nor horse moved and the smoke issuing from the silent cannons never blew away, required a considerable suspension of disbelief. Fortunately, all but the most literal-minded spectators were capable of this assent to deception; otherwise the panorama would not have lasted as long as it did.

To judge from the number of times it was mentioned in reviews, the problem of the presence or absence of life was most vexatious at the Diorama. The one element in the Village of Unterseen picture that destroyed an otherwise perfect illusion, according to one critic, was the unlikelihood that "on so beautiful a day, and in so lovely a neighborhood, no human being was moving about in any direction."[29] But there could be trouble if human beings were introduced. In the midst of the ruins of Holyrood Chapel, for example, Daguerre represented "a female, dressed in a white robe, with a black girdle, praying near a tomb on which she has placed her lamp." The *Times* reviewer observed that it was improbable that a woman, however deeply bereaved, would remain "standing perfectly motionless, and *not* in an attitude of repose,— without moving a muscle, for half an hour together."[30] The Diorama sought to enhance the effect of the praying figure by having a flute played softly behind the scene, "breath[ing] forth an old Scotch air."[31] This doubtless was an admissible touch, but it did not really

* Leslie had expressed a less reserved opinion much earlier (1812) after seeing three panoramas, including Barker's *Lisbon.* "They are certainly perfect in their way," he wrote to his sister. "The objects appear so real, that it is impossible to imagine at what distance the canvas is from the eye." (*Autobiographical Recollections,* ed. Tom Taylor, Boston, 1860, p. 174.)

57. The Diorama: ruins of Holy-rood Chapel (engraving in the *Mirror of Literature,* 5, 1825, 193, after the painting by Daguerre). On the right is the figure of the praying woman which caused some controversy.

58. The Diorama: view of the village of Unterseen (engraving in the *Mirror of Literature,* 11, 1828, 193, after the painting by Daguerre).

meet Leslie's other objection, that the silence enveloping what was supposed to be a place in the real world, with the sounds natural to it, was as destructive of the illusion as the motionlessness of the human figures. The Diorama occasionally adopted elements of Loutherbourg's "picturesque of sound." In the scene of the avalanche at Alagna one heard the raging of the wind and the thunder accompanying the torrent of snow as it overwhelmed the sleeping village,[32] and in the Tivoli scene, since the feeble fountains of tap water did not make a plausible noise, the realism was supplied by backstage effects.[33]

Daguerre introduced Swiss songs and the deep note of the Alpenhorn in his Mont Blanc show at the Paris house, but this was not taken to London.[34] Like other cathedral scenes, the St. Peter's Basilica picture at the Regent's Park Diorama in 1828–29 obviously called for music, and one visitor, a young Newcastle mining engineer named Thomas Sopwith, regretted its absence. "An organ playing some of the beautiful symphonies of the Italian service," he wrote in his diary, "would have added much to the interest of the scene, and by partly attracting the imagination would in some measure heighten the pictorial illusion by diverting the eye from the sole employment of scrutinizing it."[35] This deficiency was at length made good with Bouton's first double-effect picture, the interior of Santa Croce (1835), when, in addition to the tinkling of the acolyte's bell at the elevation of the Host, the audience heard the Kyrie from Haydn's Mass Number One played on an organ provided by Messrs. Robson of St. Martin's Lane.[36] A later Diorama production, St. Mark's Cathedral (1847), had an extensive accompaniment played on a "Grand Machine-Organ"—a portion of Clari's "Laetatus Sum" from the Fitzwilliam Music, the Gloria from Beethoven's Mass in C, and the Kyrie from Mozart's Twelfth Mass.[37]

Meanwhile, other forms of pictorial entertainment had added music to the performance. Marshall's panorama of the coronation in 1821 was accompanied by a full military band assisted by "finger organ, trumpets, etc.,"[38] and three years later his twelve-scene narrative of Napoleon's career included "a symphony supplied by a band of music up stairs, which plays a dead march, or battle air, just as circumstances call for the visitor's sympathy."[39] At such shows the accompaniment was inserted not only at the places where verisimilitude recommended it—scenes where a band would have been playing in real life—but at others where mood music was desirable.* Thus, even though

it was unlikely that bands would actually have struck up in the heat of battle at Navarino and Seringapatam, Marshall cued them in during his panoramic portrayals of those events. The representation of Napoleon's reinterment at Les Invalides, shown at the Bazaar, St. James's Street, in 1841, was considerably more faithful to historic fact: in addition to the Mozart Requiem, it was accompanied by funeral marches composed for the late occasion by Auber, Adam, and Halévy.[40]

At regular panoramas of the Barker kind, however, almost no sound effects were attempted. At the Colosseum, London's clocks were heard striking the hour, but evidence is scant that similar incidental sounds were provided at Leicester Square. There, as at other big-picture shows, people simply stood and looked. Apart from the sound of their own voices, they heard nothing. The scene that surrounded them was as devoid of animation as Coleridge's painted ship upon a painted ocean.

One infrequent accident, wholly out of the management's control, which compromised the illusion was the introduction of an extraneous element into the picture. After visiting Burford's Athens panorama in 1845, a journalist reported that "the alighting of a large fly on one of the blue mountains of the horizon startled us back from the Piraeus, and the Acropolis, and the Temple of Theseus, and the Monument of Philopappus, to reality and Leicester Square!"[41] In a front corner of the Diorama's representation of Chartres Cathedral there was a famous cobweb, but it was not as out of harmony with the setting as the fly on the Greek mountain distinctly was, and a good deal of debate occurred over whether it had been spun by a Regent's Park spider or painted there by Bouton.[42]

Notwithstanding these deficiencies and occasional incongruities, to most spectators panoramas at their best, especially when seen under controlled conditions, did provide the illusion for which they were designed. The complaints in the press from time to time that a given picture (seldom one at Leicester Square) fooled nobody, that it was too obviously a contrivance of canvas and paint rather than an alternate reality, may well be interpreted as the exceptions that proved the rule. These failed but more succeeded. After all, the public's eagerness to be deceived met the panoramist at least halfway. Sometimes the image became the measure by which reality was judged. In an advertisement of a panorama of Constantinople and the Crimean War in 1854, the eastern correspondent of the Daily News was quoted as writing from the war scene, "Had it not been for the cold, I could have believed that I saw the

* The references in the advertisements and elsewhere to "bands" must, of course, be read in the most minimal sense: a combination of instruments no larger than that of an itinerant sidewalk band, or even a mechanical one. Similarly, except for the mighty Apollonicon at the Cyclorama, the organs were of a modest machine variety, as befitted show premises that bore no resemblance to the Abbey and St. Paul's, where nobler instruments were employed.

Diorama at the Egyptian Hall, with the restless tide of London street life surging around me."[43] In effect, the picture became the substitute actuality, and the true actuality was merely a reminiscent reflection of the picture.*

But by this time the panoramic image was being measured, to its cost, by another image. With the arrival of photography in the early forties, the panorama, the graphic medium which had up to that moment been most esteemed for its fidelity to fact, was now judged by a new one which surpassed it. In a brief notice of Burford's panorama of the queen's arrival at Edinburgh on a state visit (1843) the *Athenaeum* observed, "The view has almost the literal and lineal truth of a Daguerréotype, not merely as regards the aspect of the city . . . but as giving the rainy, variable atmosphere of the North."[44] In this instance, the panorama survived the comparison; but the shape of things to come was plain in a notice, two years later in the same journal, of the Diorama's representation of the Castle of Heidelberg: "Even the Daguerreotype pictures—Nature's own transcript of herself—leave us something to desire;—how much then must the most cunning of mortals fall short when dealing with the evanescent changes of light and shadow!"[45] A photograph might not be a perfect reproduction of physical actuality, but it was nevertheless more faithful than the panorama.

D3❋ƐD

It is clear from the past several pages that we possess considerable evidence of how the panoramists' creations struck their contemporaries. If the result were worth the trouble, one might compile a substantial anthology of panorama criticism from the press. But this is to see art only through others' eyes rather than through one's own. There is only one obstacle to arriving at an independent estimate of the panorama as a form of art, but it is an insuperable one: no examples remain. No English ones, that is, from the period when they flourished as a major form of mass entertainment, down to the early 1860s.† All of the circular panoramas, or cycloramas, which can be seen today in North America (Gettysburg, Atlanta, Ste. Anne de Beaupré), the Netherlands (The Hague), Austria (Innsbruck), Switzerland (Lucerne), and the Soviet Union (Moscow), were painted late in the nineteenth century or in the present one, and from them we can infer only in general terms what the older ones were like. Nor does any existing London building repro-

duce the steep staircases and the umbrella-canopied platform at Burford's, or the Colosseum's indoor imitation of St. Paul's scaffolded dome, or the rotatory amphitheatre and the complicated apparatus of lines, pulleys, shutters, and colored translucent screens which produced the unique effects of the Diorama.

Although photography was available in the last two decades in which the panorama flourished, the rudimentary cameras, not to say such factors as lighting, did not permit pictures to be taken of such huge indoor objects. The only remaining graphic evidence of the pictures consists of reproductions of sketches, which fall into several categories. There are, first, engravings made from the preliminary drawings for two of the early panoramas of London: Robert Barker's aquatints in six sheets, and twenty etchings made from Girtin's watercolors. Several later sets of drawings made by Barker, including four sketches for the Constantinople panorama and six for the Waterloo, were engraved. A number of the drawings, made abroad by free-lance artists, which formed the basis of other Leicester Square panoramas were subsequently engraved to make up albums or to illustrate books on their respective subjects. Each of the souvenir pamphlets sold at Leicester Square and the Strand contained a rough outline drawing, circular in the early years, of the painting to which it served as a key (as shown in Fig. 54, p. 175). Illustrated papers such as the *Mirror of Literature* and the *Illustrated London News* often ran woodcuts or engravings of current pictures at Burford's and the Diorama. Finally, one easel picture painted from a Diorama scene survives: Daguerre's *Holyrood Chapel,* in the Walker Art Gallery, Liverpool. But none of these brings us within visible distance of the panoramas themselves. None, naturally, contains any clue to the special tricks of perspective, of curvilinear treatment, or of light manipulation and distribution which produced so persuasive an illusion when the great picture was shown in its proper setting, nor can we learn from them what special techniques, say, of brushwork or coloring, the panoramist employed.

What happened to all the panoramas? Some, perhaps most, suffered the fates common to theatrical scenery: they were cut up for other purposes when their value as show material was exhausted, or they were thriftily repainted, sometimes more than once. An American who saw Barker's *Malta* in 1811 wrote, "We learned, with much regret, that the panorama of Dover, which we admired so much last year, was painted on this identical cloth. Malta is laid over Dover, and Dover covers half-a-dozen more *chefs d'oeuvre!* I should be

* There is other testimony to the manner in which a panoramic scene fixed the expectations of travelers, so that when they beheld the original they instinctively compared it with the copy. Mrs. Charles Mathews, the actor's wife, wrote their son from New York City in 1834, "I have not yet been out, but . . . the street is as gay as represented in Mr. Burford's Panorama," which she must have seen just before leaving London. (*Memoirs of Charles Mathews, Comedian,* London, 1838–1839, IV, 293.) Similarly, Thackeray described Constantinople by reference to a theatrical panorama. "Stanfield's panorama," he wrote in *Notes of a Journey from Cornhill to Grand Cairo* (1846), "used to be the realization of the most intense youthful fancy. I puzzle my brains and find no better likeness for the place. The view of Constantinople resembles the *ne plus ultra* of a Stanfield diorama, with a glorious accompaniment of music, spangled houris, warriors, and winding processions, feasting the eyes and the soul with light, splendour, and harmony."

† At least three panoramas of American origin survive in the United States: the Dickeson-Egan panorama of the Mississippi at the City Art Museum, St. Louis; the Russell-Purrington *Whaling Voyage round the World* at the Whaling Museum, New Bedford, Massachusetts; and Vanderlyn's panorama of the palace and gardens of Versailles, in storage at the Metropolitan Museum of Art, New York. The first two, however, are of the rolling type to be discussed in the next chapter, and throw no light on the peculiarities of the Barker-Parris wrap-around canvas. Vanderlyn's obviously comes closest to the original mode.

much tempted to rescue a few of them if I could, and carry off some of Mr. Parker's [sic] canvas as Lord Elgin has done Phidias's marbles."[46] Disappearance under a fresh coat of paint was one of three different fates ascribed to Barker's first picture of Waterloo. According to one account, communicated to *Notes and Queries* twice in twenty years, the writer when a boy had actually seen Barker "painting 'Spitzbergen' over the 'Battle of Waterloo.' He was then, with his long brush, obliterating a charge of cuirassiers with icebergs and white bears that quite chilled you to look at."[47] But an obituary of Barker in 1856, testifying to the popularity of the Waterloo scene, declared, "It had been painted on an older picture, but was not painted out, being laid by and re-exhibited some years later, and was even then so attractive, that it hung on the walls until, from decay, it fell from its fastenings and was removed piecemeal."[48] A third source asserts that the picture was taken to India.[49] In 1851 it was said that Barker's London panorama had been found "not many years back . . . rolled up in a loft over a carpenter's shop," but this conflicts with another report that it was taken to France.[50] When the Diorama was sold at auction, the inventory included fifteen pictures. What happened to these is unknown. Porter's *Agincourt* ended up in the cellar at Guildhall. His *Alexandria* and *Lodi* went to America; they were shown in New York in 1804.[51] About a dozen of the Barker-Burford panoramas also went to the United States, where they toured the larger cities and eventually must have disintegrated or been destroyed. Those of Jerusalem and Thebes perished when Frederick Catherwood's rotunda in New York burned down in July 1842.[52]

Since there are no data for the comparative eye, the tantalizing question of the influence panorama painting may have had on British gallery art in the first half of the nineteenth century can only be approached by the speculative mind.* Some artists of the period unquestionably visited panoramas. In the earlier years, the seriousness with which Reynolds, West, and Gainsborough regarded this new form of art would have communicated itself to the next generation. How far, if at all, was Turner's revolutionary management of light affected by dioramas? What significance can be found in the fact that numerous panorama painters (Henry Aston Barker, both Burfords, Reinagle, Chambers) and creators of dioramas for the theatre (Stanfield, Roberts, Beverley) also exhibited at the Royal Academy and elsewhere: in what ways was their practice as easel painters affected by their work on huge canvases? May not the superabundance of detail

in the panoramas have contributed to the growing literalism of landscape painting and of Pre-Raphaelite art? Except for such meager information as may be gathered from memoirs and other biographical material deriving from showgoers, the answers to such questions constitute, and in all likelihood must remain, a lost chapter in the history of Victorian art.

We can be slightly more positive in the case of the once popular Francis Danby. Recent scholarship has revealed that he had a close if fleeting connection with the panorama trade in the middle and late twenties when, having lately arrived in London from Bristol, he proposed to paint and house a panorama of a mountainous landscape, of which he went so far as to make a model. He was deterred from proceeding by the cost of the large quantity of muslin required and by the lukewarm response of his patron at Bristol, who commented that the projected panorama was "only an exhibition of transparent pictures, things long known, and ill-executed, so will never do. We have had too many such exhibitions. The Great Pantheon [the Colosseum] will fail, I am well informed." Danby's biographer argues plausibly, though somewhat overenthusiastically, that the artist's peculiar tricks of lighting and illusionism were derived from the panorama and the Diorama, in particular the latter's pictures of Canterbury Cathedral, the Valley of Sarnen, and Holyrood Chapel. "It is easy," he writes of Danby's vast landscape in *The Delivery of Israel,* "to imagine that it reflected some of the evocative magic, as distinct from the mere conjuring, of the diorama. . . . Danby early discovered the power of light to lift material objects onto an imaginative plane, and he never outgrew or discarded this discovery"—an aesthetic principle the demonstration of which may well have been the Diorama's main contribution to English art.[53]

If the attempt to define the effect of panoramic painting upon regular art is bound to be highly speculative, any similar effort to determine how it influenced the English way of looking at paintings is hardly less so. According to Leslie, Sir George Beaumont was of the opinion that "the effect of panorama painting has been injurious to the taste, both of the artists and the public, in landscape," but since he seems not to have elaborated, this does not take us very far.[54] To what extent, for instance, did the Diorama sensitize the gallery-goer to dramatic contrasts and changes of lighting, and thus help govern his responses at the annual exhibitions and elsewhere, especially when Turner's latest audacious works were on display? To what extent, again, did the practice cultivated at the

* It would scarcely be possible to write an equivalent, for British art, of the suggestive chapter on "The Panoramic Style" in Wolfgang Born's *American Landscape Painting: An Interpretation* (New Haven, 1948). The originator of the style, Thomas Cole, saw Burford's *Pandemonium* when he was in London in 1829 and used it as a pattern for one of the pictures in his monumental series, *The Course of Empire.* In 1836 he painted his first panoramic landscape, *Oxbow* (a scene on the Connecticut River). From Cole the style spread to Durand, Doughty, Bierstadt, Moran, and Church. No such development could be traced in the history of British landscape art during the same period; for various reasons, the panoramic style of gallery painting was, as Born says, "a uniquely American phenomenon."

panoramas, of "reading" every square foot of the canvas in order to get one's shilling's worth of details, affect the habit of visitors to shows of gallery paintings: did not they tend to scrutinize those works more intently? Certainly they were encouraged to do so; artists like Haydon and Martin provided printed "keys" to their crowded pictures when they exhibited them separately, just as similar guides were available at the panoramas.

What contribution, to take a famous case in point, did repeated attendance at Burford's panorama make to the development of Ruskin's aesthetic faculty? We know that Ruskin was among those whose mental images of various locales were formed at the panorama (as well as by paintings and engravings) before the scenes were themselves visited. Late in life he recalled the impact his first view of Milan had on him as a boy of fourteen:

I had been partly prepared for this view by the admirable presentment of it in London, a year or two before, in an exhibition, of which the vanishing has been in later life a greatly felt loss to me,—Burford's panorama in Leicester Square, which was an educational institution of the highest and purest value, and ought to have been supported by the Government as one of the most beneficial school instruments in London. There I had seen, exquisitely painted, the view from the roof of Milan Cathedral, when I had no hope of ever seeing the reality, but with a joy and wonder of the deepest;—and now to be there indeed, made deep wonder become fathomless.[55]

Tantalizingly, he says no more; our estimate of the panoramas' artistic quality would be much more confident if he had elaborated upon the phrase "exquisitely painted." But there is reason to assume that many impressionable visitors to the panorama came away, as Ruskin seems to have done, with a heightened appreciation of the real scenery that was so appealingly imaged on those great canvases, as well as of landscape art itself.

Marcel Brion, touching on the panorama in his book on romantic art, distinguishes—following Ruskin—between the "landscape of feeling" and the "landscape of instruction."[56] It was the latter which was the panoramists' forte, and though it was a lower form of art, it was more comprehensible and acceptable to a large portion of the public than were the subjective interpretations of a Constable or a Turner. As the anonymous author of a guide to London put it in 1851, in the course of an extended discussion of the several panoramas then being exhibited, "The same feeling that makes [the Englishman] prefer Shakspere to every

other poet, leads him to portraiture and landscape, in which he recognises old acquaintances or sympathies; from the same cause, panoramas, that combine information and the recognised beauties of nature, have become the favourite exhibitions of the present time."[57]

By then, it had become generally agreed that as both Leslie (quoted above) and Ruskin said, panoramas were welcome contributors to "the great object of communicating useful knowledge in a delightful manner."[58] There was no more agreeable way of learning geography and history.* But the panoramas' educative value might reach beyond this, since "useful knowledge," liberally defined, had room for a cautious, nonaddictive smattering of aesthetic experience. In an era when more and more people were being added to the potential audience for exhibitions of all kinds, the panorama was the form of pictorial art that was most accessible, in two senses of the word. During the earlier years of the nineteenth century, in the absence of permanent art galleries and other institutions where paintings could be viewed by the London public at large, regularly and at no expense, panoramas were the only means by which it could indulge whatever interest it had in art. To most ordinary Londoners, not accustomed to attending the annual exhibitions, paintings of any size were a novelty. At the same time—and much was made of this point—the panorama was a form of art that was readily intelligible to the untutored mind and the unrefined sensibility. James Baillie Fraser, the man who escorted the exiled Persian princes from show to show in 1835 and 1836, expected that because they were so delighted by the Diorama and the London panorama at the Colosseum they would derive equal pleasure from the summer show at the Royal Academy. By no means:

Had I reflected on the important difference which must subsist to an unpractised eye, between an immense collection of works of art, to appreciate which requires a species of positive education,—and a single chef d'oeuvre, the great merit of which depends less on strict adherence to rules of art, than on presenting to the senses, by a very wonderful optical illusion, a fac-simile of reality, and is therefore palpable to all, I should have probably calculated upon the disappointment which I experienced in seeing the feeble impression which this magnificent exhibition produced. . . . They were bewildered rather than delighted.[59]

Angled somewhat differently, this was also the opinion an unnamed "memoirist" attributed to the American artist John Vanderlyn, who painted a well-received panorama of Versailles. Vanderlyn, he said, concluded from observing the popularity of pan-

* "The wars of Marlborough," remarked a journalist at mid-century, when a diorama of Napoleon's career was on exhibition in Regent Street, "were perpetuated in Art by the skill of workers in tapestry and Arras,—and the wars of Wellington and Napoleon are now commemorated and in part made intelligible to the public by the dexterous brush of the theatrical scene-painter." (Athenaeum, 26 February 1853, p. 264.)

oramas in London and Paris in the first years of the century that "panoramic exhibitions possess so much of the magic deceptions of the art, as irresistibly to captivate all classes of spectators, which gives them a decided advantage over every other description of pictures; for no study or cultivated taste is required fully to appreciate the merits of such representations."[60]

In the progressive climate of the day, however, this was not enough. Some of those who had no illusions that panoramas were a new form of fine art still clung to the hope that on their modest level they would encourage a taste for something better. Their acceptance by a large public which had no prior experience of art and no means of judging it was a healthy sign that people could be pleased by *some* kind of art, inferior though it might be. Beginning with the same premise as the preceding writers, a review of the new bill at the Diorama in the *Examiner* (30 September 1832) went on to express the cautious hope that the Diorama would lead to the improvement of popular taste in art, if, indeed, it had not already done so:

In proportion, as works of art are capable of arousing the sympathy of the uncultivated, so do they require artistical powers of an inferior grade, to those which higher branches of art demand . . . The introduction of Dioramic paintings we do not regard as evidence of any advance in art, but they may be considered as a useful and general vehicle of pleasure, particularly to large classes whose education may not have induced in them much taste for works of a superior kind, and it is not unlikely that many would be tempted to notice the imitation, who would have passed the original without observation, and may thus receive a gratification by a secondary process, which they would not have received from the primary object projecting even always before them. The Diorama seems to be a division of art, expressly invented for the gratification of the many—the general dissemination of taste, and *a means of stimulating the appetite, for the enjoyment of the higher branches of art;* their popularity is an evidence of the improvement and extension of a taste, and that too, amongst many, who, a few years ago, were wholly indifferent to such subjects [italics supplied].

Or, as the same paper had put it more tersely a few months earlier, "It is no small step towards the improvement of taste for the Fine Arts, to know of a beginning which may lead to the enjoyment of the luxury physical and mental, which the higher branches

of art offer, but which is not appreciated by the untutored eye."[61]

Such was the feeling at a moment when faith in the redemptive powers of education for the adult masses was nearing its peak. But irrespective of their nominal commitment to the linked causes of *utile* and *dulce,* for practical purposes the panoramists regarded themselves not as educators but as members of the highly competitive London amusement trade. If they were to make money on their speculation they had to keep up with the competition, whatever form it took, and surpass it whenever possible. Burford alone seems to have been exempt from this pressure; even Daguerre responded to it by devising the double effect, and failure to introduce any novelty into the London panorama at the Colosseum—even to dust it off—was responsible in part for that establishment's decline. Apart from the unsuccessful addition of the third circle in 1841, the Leicester Square house remained in 1860 what it had been in 1795, a place for the exhibition of large circular paintings, with no gimmicks or frills such as motion or sound. That this operation prospered as long as it did is proof of the existence of a dependable, self-renewing clientele which preferred the panorama in its pure state—a public intent on deriving from it the socially and culturally approved benefits it was widely pronounced to offer, and needing only a periodic change of bill for it to be brought back year after year. As the proprietor of an old-established London institution, Burford could afford not to keep up with the times except in choice of subjects. But London evidently had room for only one such show, and Burford's fellow entrepreneurs soon learned that unadulterated, sedate instruction was not good box office. The truth that Albert Smith discovered when his *Ascent of Mont Blanc* became an instant hit in 1852 had been apparent to veteran pictorial showmen for many years: "the diffusion of knowledge, instead of entertainment, was getting rather tiresome; in fact, there was great danger of instruction becoming a bogie to frighten people away rather than attract them."[62] During all the years that the Leicester Square panorama went its routine way, therefore, a ceaseless search was on for novelties that would keep pictorial shows competitive with the liveliest forms of entertainment London could offer.

Panoramas in Motion

15

In their early decades, panoramas were repeatedly if somewhat unfairly compared with the Eidophusikon, and they came off second best in two respects. One was their lack of motion. This point was made about 1815 in the advertising of a mechanical picture: "Painting is one of the attractive arts cultivated by the ingenuity of man; but in order to complete the pleasure to be derived from it, it's necessary that motion should be imparted to the Sublime Scenery it copies." Wherefore, "every object with which [the landscapes in the show] are embellished appears animated. The Man, the Horse, the Carriage, and the Vessel, are emphatically impressed with movements peculiarly [sic] to each, so as to imitate precisely the operations of Nature."[1] The panorama's second shortcoming was somewhat related to the absence of motion: it offered little variety. One scene, or at the most two, was all that a single admission bought. Various as the contents of one large canvas might have been, they all belonged to a single locale. At the pantomime, meanwhile, one could see a rapid succession of pictures, thanks in part to Loutherbourg's inventiveness.

As a result, "moving panoramas" soon were announced. What these were, it is sometimes hazardous to speculate, because the nature of the new devices, if they were in fact new, is hidden in the cloudy terminology of which complaint has already been made. Both parts of the term were used elastically. "Moving" was stretched so far as to mean "in quick succession" as well as "in actual motion," and "panorama" could refer to virtually any kind of picture, with no necessary suggestion of circularity or even of unusual size. Most often, in earlier years at least, "moving panorama" seems to have referred to nothing more than an old-fashioned moving picture, perhaps with Eidophusikon accessories. This was certainly true of a show thus advertised in 1808 in New York City, which lagged behind English usage only by the time it took a ship to sail there from Liverpool;[2] and it was true also of the "animated Panorama" shown in the Strand in 1814: "the Town and Fort of St. Sebastian at the period of the Bombardment, with the Troops and Vessels in Motion, performing the whole of the Maneuvers of that Celebrated Siege."[3]

Exhibitions competing with the painted panorama made a special point of advertising the element of motion as early as 1799. A planted news item on 25 April reported, without elaboration or explanation, that there were "no less than 74 movements of action and reaction in the moving canvas" of Chapman's New Eidophusikon.[4] In 1800, "moving panorama" was used to describe the series of topographical scenes in the Christmas pantomime at Drury Lane, *Harlequin Amulet:* "a moving Panorama of the most magnificent buildings in London," said the *European Magazine.*[5] The rival pantomime that season at Covent Garden, Thomas Dibdin's *Harlequin's Tour; or, The Dominion of Fancy,* had scenes of "Margate Pier, Dandelion, Road from Margate to Tunbridge, Tunbridge Wells, Charing Cross, Scarborough, Ullswater Lake, Bath, Weymouth, Forest Landscape and Fancy's Pavilion."[6] Both productions, then, featured a succession of topographical and architectural scenes. The "moving pan-orama" could have consisted of a series of flats, opaque or transparent, for which the constructing and changing technique had been available at least since Loutherbourg's *Wonders of Derbyshire* and *Omai,* if not before. (The scenes were changed behind a drop curtain.) Or it could have been a continuous strip of canvas which was rolled horizontally across the stage from one large spool to another, an enlargement, in effect, of the Eidophusikon's clouds-over-Greenwich device. Either type of "moving panorama" would have been suitable for the series of discrete scenes in both pantomimes, the continuous strip being required only if the scenery portrayed was consecutive, as in the representation of a journey.

One or the other of these two devices was used in 1802 in a self-described "new species of entertainment" performed in the Lyceum's upper room, renamed for the occasion the Scenic Theatre.[7] *Ægyptiana* was produced by Mark Lonsdale, a well-known figure in the London theatre who had been employed for a number of years as resident director and producer at Sadler's Wells and more recently in a similar capacity at Covent Garden. The name was derived from the first portion of the program, a three-part spectacle consisting of "eighteen scenic pictures, upon a large scale, with explanatory readings." The pictures, commissioned from several leading scene painters, were based on prints contained in a recently published book, Dominique Vivant Denon's *Travels in Upper and Lower Egypt in Company with Several Divisions of the French Army,* which was among the first products of the large complement of scientists and archaeologists who had accompanied Napoleon in 1798. One handbill continued: "This Part of the Evening's Entertainment, intended to give an amusing Turn to Information, and to exhibit Fact in its most picturesque Form, will be relieved by a few Productions of Fancy, uniting the more sportive Efforts of Poetry, Painting and Spectacle." These included an "intermezzo" of readings from Gothic romances "Illustrated by Machinery and Painting, in Six Picturesque Changes" and, as the climax of the bill, "an Embellished Recitation of Milton's L'Allegro, Including a Scenic View of the Imagery of the Poet. In Ten Successive Pictures, produced by a System of Machinery upon a plan entirely new." The Milton pictures were composed of "the Poet's Study; A Rural Scene, at Daybreak; Sun-rise—An Open Landscape; A Rustic Noontide Repast; The Upland Hamlet and Holiday Sports; Evening—The Cottage Fireside; A Splendid Tournament; An Ancient Hall,

with a Banquet; a Theatre—Scenes from Johnson [*sic;* Ben Jonson was meant] and Shakespeare; A Music Saloon—Opening to a View of the Elysian Fields."

All this constituted what John Britton, who had provided the songs and recitations at Chapman's ill-fated Eidophusikon and soon afterward wrote and delivered the script for *Ægyptiana,* was to call in his autobiography a "moving panorama."[8] Unfortunately, he does not specify what the "System of Machinery upon a plan entirely new" consisted of. By the time he wrote in 1850, "moving panorama" had come to mean primarily a lengthy series of related scenes painted on a single cloth. But there is no way to tell whether Lonsdale's pictures were of this kind, or whether, on the contrary, they were individually mounted. Given the date, the latter is more likely. In any case, *Ægyptiana* was a resounding commercial failure; it made, as Britton said, "a pleasing and rational exhibition, but was not sufficiently attractive to draw remunerating houses; indeed the unfortunate adventurer was unable to pay his creditors."

And so it was at the pantomime, rather than at exhibitions, that the so-called moving panorama developed in the next two decades.[9] By 1820 there is no question that a rolling cloth was used. In Covent Garden's *Harlequin and Friar Bacon; or, The Brazen Head* a cut-out vessel was drawn across the stage while, behind it, a painted scene rolled in the opposite direction to represent the crossing from Holyhead Bay to Dublin. "Twilight darkens," wrote a magazine critic, "and still the packet sweeps along, and still remote vessels pass her; the steam-boat is seen smoking on its way; the moon rises, throws its rays upon the water, and with it midnight is gone; the sky brightens, and morning shews the mountains round the bay of Dublin. . . . this whole scene received great applause."[10]

Henceforth the theatres vied with one another in mounting such panoramas and inventing variations. Drury Lane's "extravaganza opera" *Giovanni in Ireland* at Christmas 1821 had a "moving Panoramic view of the coast to Milford Haven."[11] The 1822 Covent Garden pantomime, *Harlequin and the Ogress,* had two moving panoramas of the king's recent trip from London to Edinburgh, and its successor the next year, *Harlequin and Poor Robin,* came up with a vertical cloth "representing bird's eye views of London and Paris supposed to be seen from a balloon." The balloon ascended from Vauxhall Gardens, the chief launching pad for this popular kind of spectator sport. After it passed over the main sites between London and the channel, the stage was blacked out to represent the

GRAND MOVING PANORAMA.
Painted by the MESSᴿˢ GRIEVE, in the Pantomime of
PUSS IN BOOTS.

CALAIS.   FLEET UNDER WEIGH   THE DOWNS

17, Cathedral	15 Collonnade of Lovis XVIII.	13 Hotel de Ville.	11 Calais Cliffs	9 Donegal	7 Fleet at Anchor.	5 Shakespeare Cliff.	3 Castle	1 Deal
18 Talbot	16 Pier	14 Light House	12 Fort Rouge	10 Napoleons Column.	8 Suffren.	6 Folkestone	4 Dover.	2 South Foreland

OSTEND   SQUADRON IN FULL SAIL.   DUNKIRK.   GRAVELINES

39 Vessels making for the Hd. 36 Town House.	33 Talavera	Spartiate	Meedée	Vernon.	26 Pier	24 Pilot Tower.	22 Cathedral	20 L'Ariane	19 Gravelines.
38 Pier	37 St Martins.	35 De Groote kirck	Revenge	Melpomene	Calypso	&c &c &c. 25 Dutch Vessels.	23 Harbour.	21 Castor.	

FLUSHING.   ANTWERP.   CITADEL   GALE.

17 Cathedral	62 Steam Ship Zeeuw.	60 Gun Boats	58 St. Pauls	50 Hotel de Ville.	45 French Ship	43 Verom	41 Talavera
46 Dutch Ships	61 Tête de Flandres	59 Fort du Nord.	57 La Boucherie	55 St James.	44 Revolving Light	42 Snake	40 Calypso
	54 Cathedral de Notre Dame.	53 Porte de l'Escaut	52 St Michaels.	51 Arsenal	50 Dock Yard.	49 Citadel	48 Scheldt	39 Dutch Vessel making for the Harbour.

Printed at Nᵒ 1 Gt Castle St

59. Diorama of a trip from Dover to Antwerp, in the Covent Garden pantomime *Puss in Boots,* 1832 (engraved, from a painting by the Grieve family, in the show's "Book of Songs and Choruses").

coming of night; when light was restored, the balloon was over Paris and descended into the Tuileries Gardens.[12] The Drury Lane competition that season, *Harlequin and the Flying Chest,* had a 272-foot-long painting, by Clarkson Stanfield, of the Plymouth Breakwater, a massive engineering project that had been much in the news.

It was in connection with this Drury Lane production (1823) that the moving panorama acquired the new name by which it would henceforth be most often known in stage parlance, although the older term re-

mained in alternate use. The word "diorama" had been introduced to London through press coverage of Daguerre and Bouton's Paris show, which opened 11 July 1822, and it had become naturalized, so to speak, with the opening of their Regent's Park house in September 1823. With extraordinary swiftness—a matter of no more than four months—the Drury Lane management seized upon it to apply to the new pantomime: the term "Moving Diorama" appeared in the printed book of songs. "Diorama" was a pleasantly modish term, now that "moving panorama" had lost its pristine novelty and become more or less commonplace (and abused). It had the advantage of reinforcing the connotation of "moving," since although the scene in the Diorama did not itself move, the changes of light produced the illusion of time passing. The *Times,* however, was reluctant to go along, alluding rather sniffily in its issue for 27 December to "last night's 'diorama' as they were pleased to call it." Actually, there seems to have been nothing in the performance to justify the adoption of the new term with its specific connotation of dynamic lighting effects.

Although during those years the theatrical diorama was found chiefly in pantomime, its popularity was increased by the sensational use made of it in the revival of *Mazeppa* at Astley's Amphitheatre in April 1831. At the beginning of the second act, Cassimir, bound to a horse, hurtled along on a treadmill between a ground row representing the banks of the Dnieper and a moving cloth of the stormy countryside, the whole effect being enhanced by copious thunder and lightning. Thanks to this wild ride with moving pictorial accompaniment, *Mazeppa* remained in the repertory of the English and American stage for the next half century.[13] The diorama reached the highest level of the drama eight years later, when Macready's production of *Henry V* included three much-praised pictures by Stanfield—the English fleet's voyage from Southampton to the siege of Harfleur, the French and English camps on the eve of Agincourt, and the king's triumphal return to London.

In the exhibition world, meanwhile, the moving panorama was appearing under the newly invented term "peristrephic" ("turning round, revolving, rotatory"—*Oxford English Dictionary*). The show bearing that name, belonging to one Marshall,* was appearing in provincial towns as early as 1819.[14] In 1823 it was Marshall who exhibited in London the "Original Grand New Peristrephic or Moving Panorama" of George IV's coronation with its alleged 100,000 figures. The show evidently consisted of three separate pictures, one of the interior of the Abbey at the moment of the crowning, another of the grand procession from the Abbey, and a third of the banquet in Westminster Hall "at the interesting moment His Majesty's Champion is giving the Challenge"—an ancient ritual then performed for the last time.[15] The coronation show was succeeded in the spring of 1824 by a twelve-view survey of the battles of Ligny, Les Quatres Bras, and Waterloo,[16] and this gave way, in December of the same year, to another Napoleonic exhibition, beginning with four scenes of the Battle of

60. Vertical diorama of an aerial journey, in the Drury Lane pantomime *Harlequin and Old Gammer Gurton,* 1836 (design by J. H. Grieve).

* This Marshall has not been identified. Charles Marshall, who had a long career as principal scene painter in the London theatres, was born only in 1806. He was also identified with the panorama trade, however, as the painter of several such canvases in the fifties. The fact that the Kineorama exhibited by a Charles Marshall in Pall Mall in 1841 was described as being a show in which "the picture passes before the spectators, in the manner of the scenic displays in our pantomimes of late years" (*Mirror of Literature,* 7, 1841, 253) suggests not only that the former peristrephic panorama had been rechristened but that the peristrephic and kineoramic Marshalls were related, perhaps as father and son.

61. Clarkson Stanfield's diorama of Venice, in the Drury Lane pantomime *Harlequin and Little Thumb,* 1831 (engraving in the show's "Book of Songs and Choruses").

Trafalgar and proceeding through salient episodes of the emperor's subsequent career to his surrender, his exile on St. Helena, and his funeral.[17] A conflation of the two shows seems later to have gone on the road.[18]

Prince Pückler-Muskau saw Marshall's version of the Battle of Navarino in Dublin in August 1828, and it is from his account that we discover what a "peristrephic panorama" was like:

You enter a small theatre,—the curtain draws up, and behind it is discovered the pictures which represent, in a grand whole, the series of the several incidents of the fight. The canvas does not hang straight down, but is stretched in a convex semicircle, and moved off slowly upon rollers, so that the pictures are changed almost imperceptibly, and without any break between scene and scene. A man describes aloud the objects represented; and the distant thunder of cannon, military music, and the noise of the battle, increase the illusion. By means of panoramic painting, and a slight undulation of that part which represents the waves and the ships, the imitation almost reaches reality. . . [The first scene is described in some detail. Then:] In the distance, just at the extremity of the horizon, the allied fleets are faintly

descried. This picture slowly disappears, and is succeeded by the open sea,—the entrance to the bay of Navarino then gradually succeeds. You distinguish the armed men on the rocks, and at length see the allied fleet forcing the passage. By some optical deception everything appears of its natural size; and the spectator seems to be placed in the Turkish position in the bay, and to see the admiral's ship, the Asia, bearing down upon him with all sails set.[19]

By an immutable law of London showmanship, these "moving" and "dioramic" novelties (the names at least, if seldom the genuine articles) soon turned up at the fairs. In 1831 a "Grand Original Peristrephic; or Moving Panorama" showing a voyage from Brighton through the Mediterranean and ending with, once more, the Battle of Navarino was the finale to a pictorial bill at Bartholomew Fair which also included a view of London through the arch of Waterloo Bridge and eight oil paintings "Descriptive of the Manners and Customs of the Russians." The Navarino portion, at least, had, according to the handbill, been viewed by ten thousand persons at Portsmouth, including the port admiral and five or six hundred officers and men, who "testified their unqualified Satisfaction and Delight" and "pronounced it to be as complete and correct a delineation of that Glorious Adventure as was possible to be."[20] The next year, under the banner of "M. de Berar's OPTIKALI ILLUSIO!" an indifferently spelled handbill invited fairgoers to "The Grand Moving Dioramic Collosseum Introducing a variety of British Views of Clifton Rocks &c. TOMB OF DEATH with a variety of subjects too numerous to mention." On the same program was "an entire, new and elegant medium, 6 feet by 6," showing "a variety of subjects consisting of Fun, Wit, Wim, Humour, and Laughter," to wit, Joey Grimaldi, "the Phenomenen of Pantomime," Death on the Pale Horse (from West's painting), Earl Grey ("the Staunch and Patrotic friend of the People of England in the Cause of Reform"), the Bleeding Nun of Lindenburgh, Lord Brougham, and the Enchanted Skeleton, with appropriate music and fireworks afterward.[21]

D3❈Ɛꓷ

In the pantomimes, the miniature tours by rolling diorama were no more than divertissements, fanciful pictorial cameos attached to a larger entertainment, just as a quick tour of the Clyde was appended as an afterpiece to Marshall's coronation show. The idea of a journey as the sole subject of a panoramic exhibition seems to have occurred first to the German theatrical artist Carl Wilhelm Gropius, who had opened a Berlin version of the Diorama in 1827. Five years later, Gropius installed in his small auditorium, renamed the Pleorama, a replica of an excursion boat, and in it presented an hour-long pictorial voyage around the Bay of Naples or down the Rhine. Perhaps because the show failed to pay—the ship's capacity was limited to a mere thirty persons—Gropius soon restored the diorama.[22]

But the Pleorama may have inspired a show at the Baker Street Bazaar in 1834. The Padorama, as it was called, was a combination mechanical-pictorial exhibition. The background consisted of a 10,000-square-foot dioramic strip wound on drums, showing "the most interesting parts of the country traversed by the Liverpool and Manchester Railway," the first passenger line, which had been opened four years earlier. In front of this moving scenery were miniature mockups, also in motion, of various kinds of rolling stock—locomotive engines and wagons filled with goods, cattle, and passengers.[23] "The mechanism of

Barthlomew Fair 1831

Unequalled Exhibition. During the Fair!

A COLLECTION of most superb PAINTINGS in OIL, By an Artist attached to the Royal Academy of St. Petersburgh.

Descriptive of the Manners and Customs of the Russians, and illustrative of their Physiognomical Character, Stature, Religious Rites, and Ceremonies, Amusements, Punishments, and the mode of Travelling in those inclement Regions.

View 1.—The Frozen Market of Podneski
View 2.—Portraits of Two Russian Ladies of Rank and an Infant Noble.
View 3.—The Church and Burial Ground of Smolenski.
View 4.—The City of St. Petersburgh. With a most beautiful Portrait from Life of his late Imperial Highness, Alexander,

Late EMPEROR of all the RUSSIANS. And others of his Suite.
View 5.—A View in the City of Simberski
View 6.—A Tartar Camp in Siberia.
View 7.—Interior of a Lapland Wizard's Hut. Who is telling a Lady's Fortune.
View 8.—Samoyedes Armed for the Chase.

A View of London THROUGH AN ARCH OF **WATERLOO BRIDGE.**

After which, a Grand Original Peristrephic; or Moving **DIORAMA,** EMBRACING A VIEW OF The CHAIN PIER at BRIGHTON, Together with the PALACE.--The STEYNE and **TOWN OF BRIGHTON.**

THE CONTINUATION OF WHICH REPRESENTS A **VOYAGE UP THE MEDITERANEAN,** Passing BEACHY HEAD,—SHIPS SAILING UP AND DOWN CHANNEL, (SUNSET.) DISTANT VIEW OF THE **ROCK OF GIBRALTER,** (MOONLIGHT.) EXTENSIVE EXPANSE OF OCEAN AND VARIETY OF SHIPPING, Until the Arrival at the Grand Point of Destination.

The TOWN, HARBOUR and FLEET at NAVARINO. Vessels Sailing about, taking their Station previous to the Action,—together with a Magnificent Representation of the

BATTLE OF NAVARINO

In which amongst other interesting objects, is displayed, the dangerous situation of the **Asia, commanded by Admiral Sir Edward Codrington,** Anchored between the Ships commanded by the **TURKISH AND EGYPTIAN ADMIRALS,** And Engaged in the full Vigour of Action with Both, And includes Portraits of the **GENOA, the DARTMOUTH, the GLASGOW, the ALBION,** And other Vessels engaged in that Memorable Contest, together with Ships of War, Gallies, Galliots, Explosion of Fire Ships, Turkish, Egyptian, English, French, & Russian Men of War, **FLOATING WRECKS, &c.** The above was Exhibited at Portsmouth in the course of a Fortnight to upwards of **TEN THOUSAND PERSONS,** INCLUDING The Right Honorable the Port Admiral, And between Five and Six Hundred of the Officers, Marines & Seamen, Who were on Board the respective Ships, and bore a most conspicuous part in the Action at Navarino, all of whom testified their unqualified Satisfaction and Delight, and pronounced it to be as complete and correct a delineation of that Glorious Achievement as was possible to be.

62. Handbill advertising dioramas at Bartholomew Fair, 1831.

the steam-engines," said the *Times*, "is accurately represented, and the pigmy passengers by whom the carriages are crowded might easily . . . be mistaken for living people of the full size of life."[24] An advertisement added its praise: "The Locomotive Engines . . . give a more correct idea of the mode of transit on this great work of art and science than can be conveyed by any description, however elaborate. Every one of our juvenile friends ought in particular to see it, as it is very instructive for youth."[25] Ingenious and instructive though it was, however, the Padorama set no fashion.*

This is rather odd, not only because the railway, a revolutionary kind of transport, was a lively topic of the moment, but because it was the railway which, by democratizing travel, lent additional relevance to certain kinds of exhibitions. As extended travel, initially within Britain and then abroad, came within the reach of more and more people, popular interest in the scenes depicted in panoramas increased. There is little sign, however, that the London entertainment industry realized what attractive possibilities lay in dramatizing in pictorial form the idea of an extended journey—that is, of stretching into a full-length program what had hitherto been an incidental feature of the pantomime. The showmen awoke only when an American entrepreneur brought across the Atlantic a moving panorama of a trip down the Mississippi—a canvas so big and so stridently advertised that Londoners, forgetting that the mechanical principle was the same as that of the by now familiar theatrical diorama, were persuaded to believe the rolling panorama was an American invention.

Panoramas of the original one-piece, static variety had arrived in the United States not much more than a year after Robert Barker opened for business in Leicester Square.[26] A set of the aquatints made from the drawings for the panorama of London was brought to New York City by a man named Laing, who lent them to William Winstanley, an Englishman of "good family [and] gentlemanly education" who "was understood to have come to New York on some business connected with the Episcopal Church." Winstanley immediately copied the pictures on canvas, which he exhibited in Greenwich Street in 1795.[27] A number of other panoramas, including two of Ker Porter's, were shown in New York in the following twenty years, and in 1818 a special rotunda was built to house Vanderlyn's panorama of Versailles. This was the first of a number of such structures to rise in American cities during the first half of the century.

The first moving panorama to be seen in America (May 1828) was the "Moving Panoramic View from Calais to Dover, by various Painted Flats to the Scene" featured in Planché's and Moncrieff's *Paris and London; or, A Trip to Both Cities,* which had been performed several months earlier at the Adelphi in London.[28] In November of the same year William Dunlap's *A Trip to Niagara*—written, as he said, simply to provide a vehicle for "dioramic scenery"—portrayed a steamboat journey up the Hudson (with storm and fog effects), through the moonlit Catskills, and then by way of the Erie Canal to Niagara.[29]

This show's success led to the painting of similar rolling canvases to be displayed separately. The doyen of the trade was John Banvard, a self-styled "poor, untaught" New York–born painter whose panorama of the Mississippi set the London entertainment world of 1848–1850 in a turmoil.[30] The picture, Banvard claimed, was the largest ever painted: a full three miles long. Evidently no disinterested party was ever allowed to measure it, but simple arithmetic suggests that if a strip of that length were unrolled during a two-hour performance, without any intermission, it would have had to pass before the audience at the rate of 132 feet a minute. Furthermore, so big a roll of canvas would have been extremely hard to transport and mount in any existing hall, even if cut into sections. The leading authority on the Mississippi panoramas has said, without giving a source for his information, that the pictorial cloth "sometimes attained a length of more than 1,200 yards (actual, not claimed length) by four yards in height."[31]

It was indisputable, at least, that the canvas depicted no fewer than thirty-six scenes of the Mississippi from the mouth of the Missouri River to New Orleans. Banvard had painted it at Louisville, Kentucky, where he made expenses by doing decorating jobs for the local Odd Fellows Lodge. On the opening night, he recounted, not a single person turned up to see it. But by distributing free passes among river boatmen he managed to attract audiences, and the word-of-mouth publicity thus generated turned the tide.

The subsequent American tour was a triumph. At Boston, to which special trains brought customers from all over New England, Banvard cleared $50,000 in six months. In New York the picture—one must make constant allowance for the fact that these claims were made in a day when Barnum had no monopoly on exaggeration—attracted 400,000 customers in nine months, enriching Banvard by $200,000. State legislatures and the United States Congress passed res-

* The show relocated in the summer of 1835 in a purpose-built structure at the foot of Pierpont Street, Brooklyn, New York. From the publicity at that time we gain extra details: the field of view was between forty and fifty feet long and twenty-four high, and the miniature rolling stock was propelled by a steam engine. The expanse of canvas now was said to be 15,000 square feet instead of the former 10,000. (Odell, IV, 48–49.)

olutions applauding this stupendous enterprise, as patriotic as it was artistic.[32]

In the autumn of 1848, Banvard brought his mammoth canvas to London, where it opened at the Egyptian Hall shortly before Christmas. It was an immediate sensation. The London audience was treated to a comprehensive view of a portion of western America in all its incredible variety. There were scenes of bluffs with lonely cabins perched on their edges, and prairies with bison grazing in the thick grass; rice swamps, corn fields, levees, cotton fields, sugar plantations with their slave quarters and imposing mansions; there were rough waterside hamlets thrown together, it seemed, overnight, and thriving little cities with steeples and domes, theatres and warehouses; there were Indian encampments with their wigwams and campfires. Many "episodal groups" showed Indians, emigrants, and settlers in their characteristic activities, and, to add the indispensable spice of excitement, there were steamboat races and wrecks. For still further variety, the painter portrayed the various locales under different aspects of light—dawn, full daylight, moonlight, an approaching storm.

As the canvas passed across the stage (instead of rewinding it after every performance, Banvard simply reversed the direction of the trip for the next show), the artist, perched on a little platform at the side, explained the points of interest and, as one reviewer put it, interspersed his narrative "with Jonathanisms and jokes, poetry and patter, which delight his audience mightily." The performance, the writer concluded, not without condescension, was "well worth the patronage of all who delight in doing justice to self-taught genius."[33] The attendance at the two shows daily left no doubt that there were many such generous spirits in the London public.

Apart from the novelty of so gigantic a panorama, Banvard's success owed something to the fact that American subjects were more or less unhackneyed as far as panoramas were concerned. Down to this time, besides a few pictures of New York and Niagara, there had only been such ephemeral attractions as the "American Exhibition" in 1843 at 218 High Holborn. This "grand Moving Panorama," "the MICROCOSM of the Shores beyond the Atlantic," consisted of eleven scenes, eight of New York City and its environs and the rest portraying such decidedly fringe subjects as the Bay of Gibraltar and the York Minster fire.[34]

But it soon became evident that Banvard was running scared. He had had news of a rival on his way across the Atlantic, John Rowson Smith, son and great-grandson of English painters, who had been a scene painter successively at New Orleans, St. Louis, and New York.[35] In the summer of 1848 Smith had introduced his own Mississippi panorama at Saratoga, New York, and that autumn had gone into partnership with a Professor Risley, a New Jersey-born, internationally famous acrobat, for the purpose of challenging John Banvard.[36]

Banvard alerted London by an advertisement headed "CAUTION TO THE PUBLIC," which quoted "several late American papers" as warning England to be on guard against "a spurious copy of Banvard's great painting . . . which has been got up by a party of speculators, who had already sailed for Europe with the intention of palming it off on the British public as the original."[37] Smith and Risley opened on schedule (26 March 1849) at "the Grand American Hall" in Savile House, their "ORIGINAL GIGANTIC AMERICAN PANORAMA" being advertised as "extending over four miles of canvas, and depicting nearly four thousand miles of American scenery, being one-third larger than any other moving panorama in the world."[38]

This intra-American rivalry engaged the attention of all London. Banvard won at least a temporary advantage over his competitors by ostentatiously closing his room at the Egyptian Hall for several days so that the canvas could be taken to Windsor for a command showing. Smith and Risley, for their part, met Banvard's accusations of plagiarism by flourishing letters from Baron von Humboldt and the Indian painter George Catlin, himself a seasoned veteran of the London exhibition business, attesting to the originality and authenticity of *their* canvas and denouncing Banvard's as "an utter imagination" filled with "glaring omissions and incongruities."[39] Later on in this acrimonious exchange in the *Times*'s advertisement columns, Banvard quoted an item from a Boston paper reporting a meeting in that city of a "fashionable assemblage of ladies and gentlemen," who evidently had convened for the sole purpose of attesting their admiration of his painting.[40] To this unanimous expression of confidence, according to Banvard's souvenir booklet, was added the authority of Charles Dickens, who had once inspected a stretch of the upper Mississippi from Cairo, Illinois, to St. Louis. Dickens's testimonial, which reads as if someone wrote it for him, ran, "I . . . cannot refrain from saying that I was in the highest degree interested and pleased by your picture, by its truthfulness, by your account of it,

63. How to paint a monster panorama. These drawings, from *Punch*, 14 July 1849, illustrated a brief sketch, "The Monster Panorama Manias," inspired by the preliminary publicity for the Warren-Fahey-Bonomi panorama of the Nile. "We can imagine the exertions made by the artists in their process of taking their sketches from the spot, and we can fancy one of them mounted on a camel, the camel's hair being from time to time cut to replenish the brushes, while the hump of the brute might be converted into a sort of easel very easily. Whatever may be the intrinsic merits of the forthcoming picture . . . we ought to take into consideration the courage of the artists in exploring such a river as the Nile, and looking all its perilous fea-tures in the face, particularly when some of those features include the mouth and teeth of that dental phenomenon —whom we should not like accidentally to encounter—the Crocodile. . . . We cannot, of course, look for any high degree of finish in these paintings, whose merit is measured by their mileage rather than by the talent the artists have displayed, for we presume that the colours can be laid on with nothing more delicate than a mop in the production of these works, which literally illustrate the maxim as to Art being long and Life being short, for he must have a long life indeed who hopes to see the end of the lengths which our modern artists are going to."

by its remarkable characteristics, by the striking and original manner in which the scenes it represents are plainly presented to the spectator."[41]

While the feuding Americans lobbed defamatory shells at each other between Piccadilly and Leicester Square, the London panorama industry, which for years had been languishing for want of novelties, quickly came to life.[42] All this publicity over lengthy moving panoramas was too valuable to waste. The first feature-length British-made panoramic river trip, the work of the Warren-Fahey-Bonomi team, who were shortly to paint the Holy Land panorama mentioned in Chapter 13, opened in another room of the Egyptian Hall on 16 July 1849. This, appropriately enough, was a panorama of the Nile. Unlike Banvard's opaque cloth, it was a transparency. During the first half of the show, going upstream, the audience saw the west bank of the Nile. When the head of navigation at the second cataract was reached, there was an intermission, after which the return journey passed places of interest on the east bank. Two of the most admired scenes were a tableau of the interior of the Abu Simbel temple, seen by torchlight, and a representation of a sandstorm overtaking a caravan in the Libyan desert.[43]

The *Athenaeum* devoted a warm and unusually long review to the show, commenting that "in all the qualities of Art the English work far surpasses its transatlantic compeers."[44] (Dickens, writing in the *Examiner*, had earlier taken this same patriotic line in respect to Banvard. The American's splashy art, he said, had no resemblance to "those delicate and beautiful pictures by Mr. Stanfield which used, once upon a time, to pass before our eyes in like manner."[45] It may be noted that his testimonial had said nothing about the specifically artistic qualities of the panorama.) Despite the picture's critical and popular success, the proprietors found it advantageous to sell it to George Gliddon, a noted Egyptologist, to show during his forthcoming American lecture tour. But they immediately painted a duplicate, and the Nile trip resumed.

Moving panoramas multiplied in the 1849–50 season. The brazen rivalry and puffery of the Mississippi shows, said the *Illustrated London News*,

has excited what would appear to be insatiate taste for that class of artistic productions in our own metropolis. Strange it is that we should have received such a hint from a nation by no means distinguished for its school of painting; and we suspect the explanation will be traceable to certain broad effects which alike characterize Transatlantic scenery and manners. How far this species of attraction will be realized in the success of the English Moving Panoramas and Dioramas which have just burst upon the town for its holiday novelties, we will not venture to predict. As regards composition, drawing, colour, and other means of art, our own pictures are, unquestionably, of the highest class; whilst they are as remarkable for their freedom from exaggeration, and adherence to nature, as their American prototypes were characterized by these equivocal recommendations.[46]

So much for Messrs. Banvard, Smith, and Risley, and the nation whose art they represented for better or worse. By this time, Banvard was seeking to duplicate the success of the Mississippi panorama with one of the Ohio River. Its accuracy also was challenged, but, as one paper said, "in the absence of any authentic evidence of imposition, the public flocked in crowds" to see it.[47] Another American importation fared less well: a four-part journey from Washington, D.C., to Oregon, the "Overland Route" of Colonel Fremont, indifferently painted by three American artists named Kyle, Dallas, and Lee. One chilly notice complained that it was merely "a clever map or survey of a tract of land richly diversified with wood, water, and noble and fantastic shaped mountains."[48] The topical interest of this show was heightened when news arrived of the gold strike in California, and the route was altered accordingly.

Although the Fremont show presumably had been in preparation earlier, its name, "the Overland Route," was chosen in an obvious attempt to participate in the fame of another panorama which had opened just a month earlier, Easter 1850: the *Overland Route to India,* at the new Gallery of Illustration, 14 Regent Street.* The *Illustrated London News* found this production "superior to any work of its class hitherto produced in this country," and Edmund Yates, a professional man-about-town closely associated with the entertainment world, later declared in his autobiography that the *Overland Route to India* was "by far the best of all these panoramic shows."[49] By the first anniversary of its opening, it had been shown 900 times and there had been over 200,000 admissions.[50] Before it finally closed, the number of performances had exceeded 1,600 and the attendance, a quarter of a million.[51]

The man whose achievement this show commemorated—an achievement which also was partly responsible for the fresh interest in Egypt, so profitably catered to by the Nile panorama—had died in

mid-January. He was Thomas Waghorn, an officer in the Bengal naval service and later in the Royal Navy, who had made the direct route between Britain and India, via the Mediterranean, Alexandria, and Suez, more practicable by setting up a chain of resting places and hotels at strategic locations along the rigorous desert portion of the route. He had thus cut the time of the journey from the three to four months required on the longer but less uncomfortable voyage by way of the Cape of Good Hope to less than a month. Waghorn therefore, like the engineers Brunel and Stephenson, was a culture hero of the day. Thackeray fancifully reported glimpsing him at Cairo: "The bells are ringing prodigiously; and Lieutenant Waghorn is bouncing in and out of the courtyard full of business. He only left Bombay yesterday morning, was seen in the Red Sea on Tuesday, is engaged to dinner this afternoon in the Regent's Park, and (as it is about two minutes since I saw him in the courtyard) I make no doubt he is by this time at Alexandria, or at Malta, say, perhaps, at both. *Il en est capable.* If any man can be at two places at once (which I don't believe or deny) Waghorn is he."[52]

It was Waghorn's route that the panorama at the Gallery of Illustration illustrated in paintings made by a consortium of artists, the theatrical scenery specialists Thomas Grieve and William Telbin, the Academician (and collaborator in the British Diorama) David Roberts, and assistants who painted the human figures and the animals. The program began with stationary views of the earlier stages of the journey, at Gibraltar and Malta; then a moving panorama took over for the segment (the overland route proper) between Cairo and Suez, and the final stages, Ceylon and Calcutta, were represented by further flats. "The great feature of this work," declared the *Times*, ". . . is the combination of the vastness of the American dioramas with the artistic perfection belonging to the best English productions."[53] Another paper praised the "sublime and picturesque scenery, beautiful aërial effects, characteristic grouping, variety of incident, richness of color, and tone or atmosphere skilfully varied with the several countries."[54]

That would seem to cover it. But there was more. Down to this point in the history of panoramas, we hear little of lecturers. Although Pückler-Muskau mentions one at the peristrephic Battle of Navarino when it was showing in Dublin, there is no evidence of their presence at Burford's—the sixpenny booklets were meant to serve their purpose—nor were there any at the Diorama. The first expositor to be singled

* The show was called, almost as often, the *Overland Mail to India.* "Route" will be used here to avoid confusion with Albert Smith's entertainment the *Overland Mail to India,* which opened two months later (28 May) and will be discussed in Chapter 23. Part of the Overland Route's success was due to the elegance of the setting. The Gallery of Illustration was the house which John Nash had built as his home, and the exhibition room had been furnished and decorated by him in the style of one of the Vatican galleries. Under its conveniently evasive title, it became a little playhouse where middle-class families could enjoy the more innocent pleasures of the contemporary stage, such as one-man entertainments and *readings* from the drama, secure in the knowledge that they were not inside a real theatre listening to performers who were identified as actors and actresses. See Jane W. Stedman, *Gilbert before Sullivan* (Chicago, 1967), Introduction, especially pp. 5–6.

out in the press for his contribution to the proceedings was Banvard, with his "Jonathanisms and jokes, poetry and patter," and he would shortly prove to have set an important precedent. But his novel role was obscured by the larger novelty of the canvas's monstrous length, and it was at the Overland Route show that the lecturer's presence first was as noteworthy as the panorama itself. The affable guide there was Joachim Heyward Stocqueler (pen name: J. H. Siddons), whom a recent writer credits with being "the Baedeker of early Victorian India."[55] Having gone out to India in 1819, at the age of nineteen, Stocqueler spent twenty-four years there as a journalist and author of books, including a guide to the overland route. On his return to London in 1843 he set up an "East India Institute" and general information office. He was therefore well qualified to be the tour guide at the Gallery of Illustration. Yates wrote that the "clear, concise, and most pleasantly delivered descriptive comment on the passing scene by Mr. Stocqueler . . . enhanced the success, which was tremendous."[56] After the long run of the Overland Route show, he appeared as narrator in a short-lived sequel, the Oriental Diorama (not a travel show, but a pictorial representation of the social life of the English in India). Subsequently, after a brief bout of bankruptcy in 1851, he lectured at panoramas of Wellington's campaigns (1852), the Ocean Mail to India (1853), and the Danube and the Black Sea (1854).

Although Stocqueler's lecturing style seems to have been devoid of any suggestion of mere "entertainment," his prominence at the Overland Route panorama, coinciding as it did with other developments, signaled that the panorama business had come to a fork in the road. Panoramas had always hesitated between the claims of education and amusement, reconciling them as best they could. The spirit of popular education which had lent the panorama a utilitarian rationale a generation earlier was still alive, and to some confirmed believers the panorama, now turned into a pictorial tour, continued to represent a welcome contribution to the edification of the masses. Reviewing the season ending in August 1850, the *Illustrated London News* declared that "the extraordinary increase in the number and variety of pictorial exhibitions illustrative of scenery in various parts of the world" was a wholesome sign of "the anxiety for information when conveyed through this most effectual and impressive medium."[57] That the didactic value of the panorama remained strong after the passage of fifty years was also the opinion of the elderly "Mr. Booley," a world-

wide traveler who never left London's amusement district, and whom, a few months earlier, Dickens had represented as saying, in a sketch in *Household Words:* *

When I was a boy . . . the gigantic-moving-panorama or diorama mode of conveyance, which I have principally adopted (all my means of conveyance have been pictorial), had then not been attempted. It is a delightful characteristic of these times, that new and cheap means are continually being devised, for conveying the results of actual experience, to those who are unable to obtain such experiences for themselves; and to bring them within the reach of the people—emphatically of the people; for it is they at large who are addressed in these endeavours, and not exclusive audiences. Hence . . . even if I see a run on an idea, like the panorama one, it awakens no ill-humor within me, but gives me pleasant thoughts. Some of the best results of actual travel are suggested by such means to those whose lot it is to stay at home. New worlds open out to them, beyond their little worlds, and widen their range of reflection, information, sympathy, and interest. The more man knows of man, the better for the common brotherhood among us all.[58]

A program composed exclusively of travel pictures, however, involved more unrelieved instruction and more concentration on the purely visual than most audiences were capable of at a single sitting. To lighten and diversify the show, as at the Eidophusikon half a century earlier, live entertainment had to be introduced in the form of recitations and music, even if their tone and content were not always in keeping with the relatively sedate nature of the pictorial production. Theoretically, this did not necessarily mean the new panoramic show had to be vulgarized. Shortly before Stocqueler began escorting his audiences to Calcutta, some distance up Regent Street another journey was undertaken in what was described as "an elegant little theatre, capable of holding some 250 persons." This was the Picturesque Exhibition, a scenic trip from Primrose Hill to Holyhead by way of the London & North Western and Chester & Holyhead railways, with stops at, among other places, Wolverhampton, Coventry, Chester (by moonlight), and two new bridges.[59] The scenery was well spoken of, but the accompanying "*viva voce* precis" was regretted, not because it was facetious in the Banvard manner but because, on the contrary, it was couched in fine language. "We could spare the story of Godiva and the rapture about Shakespeare," said the *Athenaeum,* recommending that the blanks be filled with "some figures and facts less transcendental."[60]

The paper was only half right. The taste of the day among showgoers bent on amusement decidedly did not run to Elegant Extracts; on the other hand, there is no reason to think it ran to figures and facts, either, even if the show was, as is not impossible, a covert promotion for a pair of railways. The picture-and-beautiful-prose formula had not worked for poor Lonsdale at the Lyceum, and it did not work for the proprietors of the Picturesque Tour, the very title of which was outdated. The show soon closed, and the Overland Route began to draw crowds down the street.

The truth was that, faced with ever livelier competition from the theatre, where spectacular effects were outdoing anything the panoramas could manage, and from the saloon theatres that were about to evolve into music halls, pictorial showmen had to bait their bills with anything that would attract and keep their clientele. Music, for example: The elaborate musical script for the Lisbon earthquake show at the Cyclorama typified the increasingly important role which background or descriptive music now was acquiring in the panoramas. Banvard's trip down the Mississippi was accompanied on the pianoforte and "seraphine" (harmonium), and, like some modern motion pictures, it had its own songs, sheet music for which was on sale. There were the *Mississippi Waltzes, Played during the Moving of Banvard's Three Mile Picture of the Mississippi River,* composed by Thomas Bricher and originally published by Oliver Ditson of Boston, and *The White Fawn of the Mississippi River,* words by John Banvard, Esq., music by Madame Schwieso, price 2s. 6d.[61] Not to be outdone, the Nile panorama featured "characteristic musical illustrations" including "the famous boat-song, 'Hèy, hèy, hò heelèysa,' a barcarolle with which the boatmen of the Nile cheer their voyage."[62] A main element in the competition between the Holy Land tours in 1851–52 was the music supplied by voices singing hymns behind the scenes with organ accompaniment. The St. George's Gallery panorama provided "Grand Sacred Vocal Music by the Great Masters," while its Egyptian Hall rival had one Herr Krausz de Feher, who was alleged to be able to sing in thirty-six languages, devoting himself and a "full choir" to Hebrew melodies during the show. Afterward, this talented gentleman presented "his unique entertainment, 'A Musical Journey Round the World,' being the Music and Melodies of every land in every language."[63] The camel of variety entertainment had thrust its nose underneath the panoramic tent.*

There was also a renewed quest for gadgetry of the sort that produced unmotivated opening of doors and unconvincing trembling of leaves in the Diorama's St. Wandrill scene. Commenting in 1851 on a sequel to the Overland Route panorama, a guidebook author voiced the conservative opinion that a panoramist should stick to his last: "whilst we praise the amount of skill and talent, we object strongly to the abuse of both; shifting scenes and dioramic effects, instead of modestly assisting nature and art, are here made, in many instances, to out-step them, and destroy all faith and illusion." In the exhibition reviewed, an ill-considered lighting effect represented a river "as running at the rate of three or four hundred miles per hour. . . . We are severe on these inconsistencies and claptraps," the critic continued, "because they tend to corrupt public taste, and to bring into contempt and disrepute an otherwise valuable and commendable mode of imparting knowledge. This Panorama is indeed an example of what can be done, and what ought to be left alone; with an abundance of ability and contrivance in every department, art is recklessly made to supersede nature, and mechanical tricks to supersede art, in the most indiscreet manner."[64] The "besetting sin of obtrusive skill," as this anonymous author phrased it—an excellent capsule aesthetic—was perhaps inescapable in a situation in which showmen eager for momentary sensations, like declamatory actors bent on making "points," allowed cheap effects to obscure whatever more solid merits their exhibitions contained.

In view of the panoramic tours' increasing tendency to borrow their tone from the light-hearted entertainments that surrounded—and drew patrons away from—Burford's sedate rotunda in Leicester Square, it was fitting that in one of the concert saloons of the moment "The Age of Panoramas" was the topic of a comic song with a Jim Crow refrain:

> The world indeed is on the move,
>   You must with me engage,
> This truly is a Dio—— and
>   A Panoramic age.
> Trav'lings now so moderate,
>   To the world's end you can go,
> As cheap as cabby takes you
> From the Op'ra to Soho.
>   So wheel about and turn about,
>   Join the motley throng,
>   And see the panoramas,
>   Eight or ten miles long!
>
> The route to India Overland,
>   Thro' Waterloo Place lies,
> But I think if males go overland,
>   *Fe*-males should likewise.

* As far as music was concerned, this may have been a two-way development. Was there not a more than coincidental relationship between the succession of scenes that constituted the Victorian moving panorama and the popularity of "pictorial" music in the concert hall? Fantasias from well-known operas were intended to evoke various scenes and actions in the memories of operagoers. The elder Johann Strauss's "Potpourri Le Bouquet des Dames," played at a *concert d'été* at Drury Lane in 1841, included "such effects as Chinese Chimes, sledge party, post horn, cracking of whips, description of an earthquake, coronation procession, God save the Queen, firing of cannon, flourishing of trumpets, ringing of bells, and shouts of thousands of spectators"—the auditory equivalent of a multiscened panorama. The great specialist in this line of art, who conducted the Drury Lane performance, was the French musician Jullien. (His given names were too numerous to cite, because he reputedly was named for all the members of the Philharmonic Society in the Basses Alpes village where he was born.) Presented in 1844 under still another name—his nom de plume of "Ruch-Albert"—Jullien's own "descriptive fantasia," "The Destruction of Pompeii," was as rousing as any pictorial representation of a volcanic eruption, ending with "the explosion of the crater, falling temples, and total destruction of the city." Given such material, as well as the enormous size of Jullien's human and instrumental forces (see below, Chapter 23), it is clear that the term "program music" does not do justice to these productions; "panoramic" would better suit their scale and their material. As *Punch* observed more than once, Jullien's ensembles were the equivalent in sound of the three-mile panorama. In his portly person the "cult of immensity," having earlier linked the art-gallery and panorama worlds, now embraced music as well. See Adam Carse, *The Life of Jullien* (Cambridge, 1951), especially pp. 43, 48–49.

Prince Albert dropp'd in t'other day,
    And paid a handsome fare, O,
Altho' his stay, he said, was short,
    To *See long* (Ceylon) he should *care, O* (Cairo).
      So wheel about [etc.]

At the Egyptian Hall, you'll California
    Find—my jolly sorts,
The lecturer will *pint* out where
    You'll find the gold in *quartz*.
The stuff is mighty plentiful,
    The wittles tarnal mean,
And the ladies are excruciating
    Few and far between.
      So wheel about [etc.][65]

Now that they were in motion and offering vicarious tours laced with variety entertainment, panoramas flourished as never before. But their prosperity rested on the uncertain foundation of novelty; adjustments and innovations had constantly to be made to sustain public interest in the heatedly competitive world of London entertainment. We now for a time leave the panorama, hesitating between further success and swift decline, and examine what had meanwhile been happening elsewhere in the industry. Londoners had been looking at a good many other sights during the five busy decades since the century began.

Scenes Optical, Mechanical, and Spectral

16

Far from rendering the older forms of pictorial entertainment obsolete, the panorama gave them a new lease on life, if only by reinvigorating popular interest in all kinds of pictures-for-show. Some of the peepshows and mechanical pictures exhibited during the first part of the nineteenth century technically were no more advanced than their predecessors many decades earlier, even though they now often possessed a name ending in "-orama." But with others, the novelty went beyond mere nomenclature.

Among these retailored old favorites of the London exhibition business, one of the most prominent was the Cosmorama, a high-toned indoor version of the old peepshow. The first London exhibition with this title* opened in 1820 in St. James's Street, but the premises proving unsuitable, it moved in May 1823 to 209 Regent Street, where adequate natural lighting was available.[1] Here the "Cosmorama Rooms," like the future Royal Bazaar in Oxford Street and similar exhibition halls elsewhere, served as a fashionable meeting place where, in addition to the advertised shows, paintings and other objects of art were offered for sale and light refreshments were available for those who chose to drop in and idle away an hour or so in casually inspecting whatever was on display and gossiping with acquaintances.

Let into each of two facing walls in the salon was a row of seven glasses, which were in fact large convex lenses.[2] Behind each lens was a small picture whose size and distance from the viewer the lens magnified. The pictures were generally superior to the coarse col-

ored prints and the daubs, bought for a few shillings from decrepit tenement artists, which were to be seen in the itinerant peepshows.† The Cosmorama, instead, commissioned respectable little oil paintings—panoramas writ small. To produce the illusion of a separate reality, a black frame, the equivalent of the Diorama's dark tunnel, was interposed between the lens and the picture. Various perspective effects were created through mirrors, which were doubtless put to more sophisticated uses than they had been, and continued to be, in the old-fashioned portable boxes. As soon as the Diorama began to captivate London, the Cosmorama adopted dynamic lighting effects as well.

Initially it had a mixed press. To some papers it seemed the height of pretentiousness, this array of fourteen peepshows set up in a room whose appointments were designed to attract the patronage of what the advertisements addressed as "Cosmopolite Society." In a spasm of facetiousness the *Literary Gazette* declared that after its move to Regent Street the Cosmorama was

a more agreeable lounge than ever for the various ranks which may be comprised under the titles of Idlers, Lovers, Young Folks, Amusement-seekers, Ice-eaters, &c. &c. &c. Here, by looking through a glass, you can see Mont-blanc as true as reality; and then, by just turning round, you may indulge in that cooling element which constitutes its eternal cap, commingled with the sweets of the luscious strawberry or the torrid pine[apple]. From a view of the great Square at Cairo, the transition is momentary to a nice little square cake; and from contemplating the ruins of Palmyra in the

* The first Cosmorama was opened in Paris in 1808, and a "superb Optical Cosmorama, or Promenade round the world, just arrived from Paris" was shown in New York in 1815. (Odell, II, 445.) Earlier (1807) the word had been used to designate an astronomical exhibition at the Pantheon. After its adoption as a synonym for a superior grade of peepshow, it was quickly absorbed into the entertainment business lexicon, theatres occasionally using it to refer to what was oftener called a diorama. In 1840–41 it was among the words considered for the title of a new comic weekly which ultimately appeared as *Punch*. (R. G. G. Price, *A History of "Punch"*, London, 1957, p. 353.)

† The quality of these is well suggested by Nathaniel Hawthorne in his description ("Ethan Brand," 1850) of the "diorama" the German Jew showman brought on his back to the village at the foot of Mount Graylock. One infers from the subjects of the various scenes that this was a second-hand property acquired in England, perhaps from a street showman such as Henry Mayhew would be interviewing a few years later: "a series of the most outrageous scratchings and daubings, as specimens of the fine arts," wrote Hawthorne, "that ever an itinerant

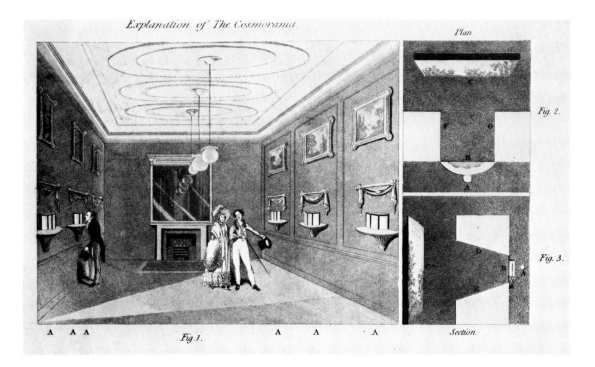

Explanation of The Cosmorama.

Plan

Fig. 2.

Fig. 3.

Fig. 1.

Section

64. The Cosmorama: interior and plan (from *La belle assemblée,* 1 December 1821). *A* in Fig. 1 represents six of the fourteen viewing apertures. Fig. 2 shows one of the optical arrangements from above: the lens is at the bottom of the diagram, and the flanking rectangles are the "bounding screens" which created the tunnel effect. The picture is at the top. Fig. 3 is a horizontal view of the same arrangement, with the lens at the right and the picture at the left.

showman had the face to impose upon his circle of spectators. The pictures were worn out, moreover, tattered, full of cracks and wrinkles, dingy with tobacco-smoke, and otherwise in a most pitiable condition. Some purported to be cities, public edifices, and ruined castles, in Europe; others represented Napoleon's battles, and Nelson's sea-fights; and in the midst of these would be seen a gigantic, brown, hairy hand—which might have been mistaken for the Hand of Destiny, though, in truth, it was only the showman's—pointing its forefinger to various scenes of the conflict, while its owner gave historical illustrations."

Desert, the twinkling of an eye transports you to the demolition of jellies in this place of abundance.[3]

Some observers were offended by the price of admission, which initially was a shilling for each of the two sides. Although a shilling was a standard price at the panoramas, the going rate for the street peepshow had always been a penny or less. But the elegance of the premises counted for something, and here, in contrast to the maximum of two scenes available at Leicester Square or the Diorama, there was ample variety. "The sensation," one paper remarked, "is curious, when, by walking two or three steps, we pass from a stormy ocean, on which we seemed just about to embark, to the dimly-lighted nave of a noble church, thence again to a Swiss valley surrounded by Alps, whose summits seek the skies, and so on through all the varieties here presented to the eye."[4]

One considerable advantage the Lilliputian Cosmorama had over its Brobdingnagian rivals was the flexibility of its programing. Whereas the shows at Leicester Square and Regent's Park could be changed only once or at most twice a year, the fourteen scenes at the Cosmorama had to be kept only as long as the attendance warranted; pictures of the required size could always be obtained on short notice to freshen the bill or provide a completely new one. In the earliest years, at least, there was a partial turnover of scenes on the first Monday of every month. The subjects were, in general, of the same architectural and topographical kinds favored in the panoramas. An 1825 catalogue listed seven views in the "Gallery of Europe": the Place Royale at Brussels, a general view of Rome, the interiors of St. Peter's and Milan cathedrals, the cities of Geneva and Seville, and the marketplace at Valencia. Across the room, in the "Gallery of Asia and Africa," one could see Grand Cairo, the Pyramids and the Sphinx, the Great Temple of Edfou, monuments on the island of Phyloe, and two views of Kailaca, at Elora, Hindostan.[5]

In subsequent years the Cosmorama, sometimes also called the Dioramic and Panoramic Exhibition, displayed on the European side such scenes as the Trinity Chapel at Canterbury (a miniature version of the early Diorama picture), Lucerne, Baden, Berne, the interior of the Pantheon in Paris, the Grande Chartreuse, the lake of Thun, the palace and gardens of Versailles, the ruins of Paestum, Mont Blanc, Mount St. Bernard, the interior of St. Gudule's Cathedral in Brussels, and the new Devil's Bridge on the St. Gothard Pass. On the Asian-African side, meanwhile, were portrayals of the Palace of the Sultana Hadige, Constantinople (general view, the Hippodrome, and the court of the Seraglio), Antioch (the city, ramparts, and Iron Gate), the statue of Memnon, the Palace of Zenobia at Palmyra, and the Syrian village of Bedan.[6]

As might have been expected, this miniature diorama, like its full-size counterparts, was strong on fires. At different times it depicted the burning of a theatre at Le Havre, of the Houses of Parliament, and of a considerable part of Constantinople. The most praised of this series, however, was the first, a dramatic representation of a large fire at Edinburgh in November 1824. Dr. Neil Arnott, a physician and scientist who later described the Cosmorama in the *Penny Magazine,* was among its admirers.

First [he wrote] that fine city was seen sleeping in darkness while the fire began, then the conflagration grew and lighted up the sky, and soon at short intervals, as the wind increased, or as roofs fell in, there were bursts of flame towering to heaven, and vividly reflected from every wall or spire which caught the direct light—then the clouds of smoke were seen rising in rapid succession and sailing northward upon the wind, until they disappeared in the womb of distant darkness. No one can have viewed that appalling scene with indifference, and the impression left by the representation, on those who knew the city, can scarcely have been weaker than that left on those who saw the reality.[7]

Pückler-Muskau agreed: "You saw the flames stream upwards; then clouds of black smoke ascend; while the view of the whole landscape incessantly changed with the changes of this fearful light, just as in a real fire. Probably," he added on a less appreciative note, "the proprietor's kitchen was behind the picture, and the fire which heated the fancy of credulous spectators like myself, roasted the leg of mutton which our shillings paid for."[8]

Like the panorama, the Cosmorama was judged primarily by the success of its illusion. The usual feeble anecdotes were told of accidental harmless deception. Dr. Arnott wrote that "one day . . . a schoolboy visitor exclaimed, with fearful delight, that he saw a monstrous tiger coming from its den among the rocks; it was a kitten belonging to the attendant, which, by accident, had strayed among the paintings. And another young spectator was heard calling out that he saw a horse galloping up the mountain side;—it was a minute fly crawling slowly up the canvas."[9] Adults like Pückler-Muskau tended to be more critical, sometimes on other grounds. The prince objected to the scene of Charles X's coronation in Rheims Cathedral: "what tasteless costume, from the King to the lowest courtier! New and old mixed in the most ludicrous and offensive manner! If people will perform such farces, the least they can do is to make them as pretty as those at Franconi's"—the celebrated Paris amphitheatre specializing in circuses and spectacles.[10] As at the

Diorama, providing an illusion of movement was risky business, for the presence of motion in one part of the painting called attention to its unrealistic absence elsewhere. In 1838, for instance, the *Athenaeum* remarked, "if the machinist could only contrive to render his masses of salt water as moveable as his cascades and cabin-smoke, the deception would be perfect: but at present the bays of Algiers and Havre look like creeks of the Frozen Ocean."[11]

Still, such quibbles occurred only to the most captious, and peepshows, whether called cosmoramas or by some other quirkily pedantic name, continued to be a popular Regency and early Victorian entertainment. At the Egyptian Hall in 1826 was the Poecilorama ("Why so called, we leave the learned to determine," said a paper), a group of cosmoramic paintings by Clarkson Stanfield which included scenes of Turin, the Castle of Chillon, London in 1590, Rouen (with a dioramic effect of a rainbow) and Netley Abbey (with moonrise).[12] To tie in with the Burmese State Carriage, which was displayed there at the same time (Chapter 18), there were also views of Burma and India, "over which," as Pückler-Muskau noted, "the light is ingeniously thrown so as to produce very lively and varied effects."[13] When the Royal Bazaar was reopened after its fire, it offered, in addition to the new four-scene diorama, a Physiorama, which was nothing more than an array of cosmoramic views of such subjects as the Grand Canal at Venice, the opening that year of Rennie's new London Bridge, the interior of Fingal's Cave, Joshua Commanding the Sun to Stand Still upon Gibeon (a drastic reduction of John Martin's recent huge painting of the same subject), places along the Rhône and the Rhine, and the classic Regent's Park Diorama subject of the Village of Unterseen.[14]

The new dignity the peepshow enjoyed as a result of its appearance in fashionable haunts and the classical-sounding names applied to it was not, however, always deserved. A raree show moved indoors and priced at sixpence or a shilling might still be only a raree show worth a penny at most. A "Naturorama" shown in 1824 in a room in Bond Street was typical of the way the Cosmorama's respectability immediately drew flies to the feast. Of it, the *Literary Gazette* commented in fairly high dudgeon: "The halfpenny shows in the streets are creditable performances of the fine arts in comparison with this trashy exhibition, which resembles them in character. You are allowed to look through glasses at miserable *models* of places, persons, and landscapes; while two or three nasty people sit eating onions and oranges [cf. the Cosmorama's "sweets of the luscious strawberry or the torrid pine"!] in a corner of the room. In the Sights, the trees are less like nature than the worst artificial flowers ever worn by a May-day sweeper; the figures are contemptible, and the whole affair is wretched."[15]

⋈

Another old standby of London showcraft was the mechanical picture, which, except insofar as it borrowed ideas from the Eidophusikon, seems not to have undergone the improvement that distinguished the Cosmorama from the pavement peepshow.* In the first post-Waterloo years there was an Eidophusikon-type show which went from location to location in London under successive names: Le Fort's Mechanical and Picturesque Cabinet when it was at 35 Piccadilly; Miller's Mechanical and Beautiful Picturesque Representations when at Savile House, Leicester Square; and Thiodon's (or Theodon's) Grand Original Mechanical and Picturesque Theatre of Arts when at Wigley's Great Room, Spring Gardens. Edmund Kean saw it in 1819 when he was preparing to act Lear at Drury Lane, and was so much impressed by the neo-Loutherbourgian storm scene that he determined to include a comparable tempest "After the Manner of Loutherbourg's Eidophusikon" in the production.[16] The comedian Joe Cowell, who was present on the first night (24 April 1820), remembered the uproar with considerable relish:

the sea was introduced in the back-ground, the billows, painted after nature, "curling their monstrous heads and hanging them with deafening clamours"—trees were made to see-saw back and forth, accompanied with the natural creak! creak! attending the operation; Winston [the assistant manager] had hunted up, *without any expense to the management,* every infernal machine that was ever able to spit fire, spout rain, or make thunder, and together were brought into full play behind the entrances. Over head were revolving prismatic coloured transparencies, to emit a continual-changing supernatural tint, and add to the unearthly character of the scene. King Lear would one instant appear a beautiful pea-green, and the next sky-blue, and, in the event of a momentary cessation of the rotary motion of the magic lantern, his head would be purple and his legs Dutch-pink. . . . [E]very carpenter who was intrusted to shake a sheet of thunder, or turn a rain-box, was determined that his element should be the most conspicuous of the party, and, together, they raised a hurly-burly sufficient to "strike flat the thick rotundity o' the world."[17]

What with lights that never were on sea or land, and a deafening "picturesque of sound," it was a production

the ghost of Loutherbourg would have reveled in. But Kean and Eidophusikon did not mix, and the production was withdrawn after a few nights.

This fresh spurt of publicity strengthened the Eidophusikon legend. In 1824, at the same theatre where Kean's storm had raged, the Eidophusikon was remembered again, and by name. In Act 1, Scene 6, of W. T. Moncrieff's extravaganza *Zoroaster; or, The Spirit of the Star,* the back part of the scene disappeared and revealed

THE
ΕΙΔΟΦΥΣΙΚΟΝ
or
Καλοσκηνητεκνηφυσικινεων

"commencing," said the stage directions, "with the Great Desert by Twilight, and Arab Encampment: . . . A caravan of Merchants who sing, depart, followed by The Pyramids and the head of the Sphinx, which give place to The Great Temple of Apollinopolis Magna, Colossus of Rhodes, with all its animated Scenery, which leads to a View of the beautiful Bay of Naples, then Mount Vesuvius, by Moonlight—a terrific eruption—burning lava descends, an obscure sky disperses and discovers an allegorical vista, a momentary glimpse of 'Home, Sweet Home,' the Grand Falls of Tivoli, The City of Babylon, the Destruction of Babylon, which closes the Eidophusikon, and ends Act the First."[18] How much this spectacle owed to genuinely Loutherbourgian devices does not appear.

Notwithstanding the Le Fort–Miller–Thiodon show's claim that it was based on "an improved principle of de Loutherbourg's Eidophusikon," it seems not to have advanced beyond its prototype in any significant respect. Such small novelty as it possessed resided in the fact that some of the scenes got a new habitation every time the exhibition got a new name. What had been the sunrise over Coblenz under one proprietor became the sunrise over the ruins of Troy under another, and the sunrise over Marseilles under a third. When Miller was in charge, the bill consisted of: (1) the rising sun near Coblenz; (2) "Rome, with the Castle and Bridge of St. Angelo, where are seen a great variety of Carriages, &c. passing and repassing each in its regular motion, sometime making a noise and appearance truly surprising"; (3) the forest of Fontainebleau: "several Sportsmen pursuing and killing of game, with Dogs fetching it to their Masters"; (4) St. Helena, with Napoleon landing, "also Ships of War saluting the Forts as they pass, and the Forts returning the Salutes"; (5) Geneva, "ornamented with several Episodic

* Since "mechanical" retained its earlier ambiguity, some so-called mechanical theatres or exhibitions were actually puppet shows. This was the case, for instance, with the "Mechanical and Optical Theatre" in Catherine Street, Strand, which Crabb Robinson attended in 1812, dryly commenting that "the expression given to some of the waxen figures confirmed Schlegel's suggestion in favour of the use of masks by the Ancients in the Drama." (*The London Theatre, 1811–1866,* p. 47.) Similarly, "Middleton's Mechanical and Automaton Theatre" at Bartholomew Fair in 1831, a show that claimed to be a century old, was composed of marionettes four feet high in an "opera" called *The Election; or, The Choice of a Husband.* (Handbill, GL, Fairs box.)

scenes . . . several Swans diving, fishing, fluttering their Wings, &c., a Sportsman in a Boat will fire at a Water Fowl, and his Dog will jump into the Water, swim after the Bird and bring it to his Master"; (6) Wellington reviewing troops in the Grand Square of the Tuileries; (7) "Representation of a Sea-Storm, Accompanied with all its awful effects, which Captain Cook, encountered on a Voyage round the World. At the rising of the Curtain the sound of distant Thunder is heard, the Skies darken with heavy Clouds and Rain, the Thunder progressively increasing, until the Elements open with a Thunder Bolt darting through a SHIP, which instantly blows up, when the Seamen are perceived Swimming to the surrounding Rocks, which a few get upon, waiting the Return of fine Weather, when Boats are seen going and returning, with the sufferers safe to Shore."[19] It is obvious that some of those scenes could be traced all the way back to Pinkethman's moving picture at the Duke of Marlborough's Head, more than a hundred years earlier. The storm at sea, of course, was Loutherbourg's, as it was also the popular theatre's, for tempests and shipwrecks were staples of the era's melodrama. Whatever superficial changes were made elsewhere in the program, a storm was the indispensable finale in this or any other mechanical exhibition.

Heavily reliant as we are upon the exhibitions' own publicity, we must constantly guard against accepting them at their proprietors' valuation. In a few instances, such as the present one, the testimony of eyewitnesses enables us to cut them down to their actual, very modest, aesthetic size. Although, as usual, the publicity made no mention of the physical dimensions of the pictures, we learn from the press that the viewing area was no larger than that of a good-sized window. With ponderous irony one writer conceded that the figures did move, as advertised; they "represent nature in the most astonishing manner! For example, individuals, squadrons, and coaches, *sail* over a bridge; boats and barges *jirk* through the yielding medium of the stream below; while on the foreground a beggar absolutely uncovers his head, horses legs twirl like spindles, and the wheels of carriages bona fide go round! These phenomena were witnessed with great applause."

To Dresden [he continued], succeeded the passage of Great St. Bernard, which consisted of a multitude of puppets swimming round and round some fantastic looking snow balls. These are justly described as "Mountains which seem inaccessible, and what is more frightful is, (quoth Mr. Thiodon) that they are perpetually covered with snow and surrounded by dreadful precipices." Nevertheless we ob-

served with infinite delight that no accident befel the Lilliputian paper heroes, who wound their toilsome way over these cold and comfortless hillocks. To crown the scene, Bounaparte with two Aides-de-Camp trotted along the foreground. This we take it is a sly cut at the Ex-Emperor, who always left his men to their own difficulties, and took the safest route for himself—a practice which Mr. Thiodon declares to be, at least in his way of representing it, "surprising beyond description." The fourth piece would by most children, young or old, be reckoned pretty: it consists of several temples, &c. in Chinese artificial fire-works. The last is entitled "Homage to England," during the exhibition of which the orchestra, videlicet, a cracked pianoforte and a sound hurdy-gurdy performed *Moll Brook* to admiration.

As for the climactic storm at sea:

We were glad to see a storm almost as terrible as the imagination creates from Lord Thurlow's famous expression of "a storm in a—wash-hand bason!" The agitated sea is as large as half a blanket, and is memorable for preserving a fine uniformity of wave even in its wildest agitation—(thus it is that the highest Art improves upon nature)—six lamps afford a noble change of sky from the gloom of Tartarus to the shining light of Heaven—the ships leap awfully from place to place, sometimes on their prows, at others on their sterns—a cracker plays the part of Thunderbolt, and a squib explodes one poor ship's magazine—the astonishing efforts she makes to keep on the surface of the water, after experiencing these calamities, is miraculous.—At last she goes down, and a parcel of pasteboard seamen on a pasteboard sea perform a burlesque on Akenside's sublime description of a shipwreck.[20]

After a period when it may have been on tour, this much (and no doubt justly) maligned exhibition turned up (1833) at the Cosmorama Rooms. In the interval, London's lingering taste for mechanical theatres had been served by several other shows of the same kind. In 1826, also at the Cosmorama Rooms, one C. Bullock showed his Panstereomachia, a "picto-mechanical representation," as the *Times* called it, availing itself of "the same liberty in coining a compound as Mr. Bullock." The subject was the Battle of Poitiers, depicted by 1,500 figures "beautifully modelled in plastic marble," whatever that may have been. Although the accuracy of the weapons and costumes, it was said, left little to be desired, the illusion was destroyed by the spectators' proximity to the foreground figures.[21] In 1830–31, at the Gothic Rooms, opposite the new St. Marylebone Church, the "Grand Mechanical Exhibition of Arts" advertised itself as "not a Transparency or a Flat Picture, but a real Imitation of Nature! Each piece is animated by a variety of

Figures, Carriages, Horses, and other Animals, &c." The scenes were of "His late majesty landing in Scotland," the village of Tivoli, Alexandria and the Turkish Fleet, Osaka with a "beautiful Elephant," and the inevitable tempestuous finale.[22] During the same season, Dalberg's Udorama at the Savile House Bazaar, Leicester Square, presented "a model from nature" of the Valley of Grindelwald. A reviewer, this time in the *Athenaeum,* described the dismal reality of a show which evidently tried to imitate the lighting and miniature modeling techniques of the Eidophusikon but had little, if any, mechanical action:

The snow-capped mountains looked to us very like furniture stowed away, and covered with table-cloths to keep off the dust—the glaciers like dirty dough in a baker's trough—the lake we did not see at all until it was pointed out to us—the waterfall is something less (we speak literally) than the rushing stream of an average tea-pot—the whole very like a giant ornament for a twelfth-cake [i.e., a one-twelfth slice of a cake prepared for Twelfth Night]. As to morning, noon, evening, and night, and the various atmospheric changes, there are certainly tricks played with the windows, and bodies are interposed to cast shadows; but the most powerful shadow was of the performer himself, which covered the whole mountain, and ridiculously enough betrayed all his actions.[23]

By now, more than half a century had passed since the term "Eidophusikon" was first used, but the very name retained its box-office power; or so, at least, thought the proprietor of a mechanical theatre in 1837, who exhibited the Eidephusikon (as he consistently spelled it), first at the Gallery of British Artists in Suffolk Street and later at Savile House. This was evidently the only mechanical show to perform a literary story. The subject was Queen Mary's escape from Lochleven Castle in Scott's *The Abbot,* and a synopsis of the action in a handbill suggests that the novelist had provided the exhibitor with a story that happily enabled him to utilize the by now ageless components of his mechanical theatre:

The scene opens in a Summer's afternoon, and is animated with Fishing and Sailing Boats plying on the Lake, the constant passing of Peasants to and from the Town of Kinross, the Abbot disguised as a Soldier making signal with Horn and Flag for a Boat, which takes him to the Castle. The Travelling Tinker Blowing his Fire and mending a Can brought to him by an Old Woman affords much Amusement. A Beautiful Swan gracefully swimming on the Lake, and The Sportsman Firing his Gun! Excite much admiration for the correctness of their action and ingenuity of the mechanism.

Evening & Night arrive, exhibiting All the Gradations of Light, and its Varied Effects, Moon Rise succeeds, and the soft grey light which is thrown over the whole scene, gives it the most natural appearance, and leads the imagination to identify it with reality. Signal Lights at the Castle answered from the Cottage. Firing from the Alarmed Garrison now indicates the Escape, and the Boat is seen conveying the Party to the Gardener's Cottage. The Queen surrounded by her adherents on Horseback finally departs from the scene of her confinement.[24]

Another narrative presentation, this time (1839) from recent headlines rather than from a widely read novel, was the "Pictorial and Mechanical Exhibition . . . on the plan of De Loutherbourg's Eidophusikon" at the Egyptian Hall, showing the deed of Grace Darling, a Northumbrian lighthouse keeper's daughter who, early in the morning of 7 September 1838, helped her father rescue the survivors of a wrecked steamship. Grace was one of the very first instant celebrities created by the machinery of modern publicity.[25] Although her feat was not as heroic as the press claimed, she was immediately idolized in a surge of mass hysteria. She was the subject of knicknacks, broadsheets, and a dozen or more popular engravings, the target of autograph hounds and summer trippers, and the recipient of innumerable gifts—money, Bibles, tracts, clothing, and even an offer, which she did not accept, to appear for a quarter of an hour at each performance of a drama which the Adelphi Theatre's resident playwright had hastily cobbled to portray the story. The mechanical show at the Egyptian Hall was merely one small manifestation of the Grace Darling craze, but it was foreordained; what showman could neglect the opportunity to offer the public still another version of Loutherbourg's famous scene? And so, the show featured what a handbill described as a "terrific STORM AT SEA!"[26] The curtain rose on a rugged coast, where various ships were fighting a storm, and one of them, after firing distress signals, promptly sank. Another, the *Forfarshire,* then was shown hitting a rock and going to pieces. "It would be impossible," wrote one critic, "to speak too highly of the representation of the sea, for the undulating and troubled motion of the waves are given with a fidelity never yet excelled in a mechanical exhibition: the thunder and lightning are also well managed; and the howling of the wind was astonishingly true to nature. The puppets also worked well, and performed their parts with great accuracy. Indeed the *tout ensemble* presented as faithful a picture of a storm at sea, as it is possible to be represented by pictorial mechanism."[27]

At the same location the following year there was an animated picture of a Swiss village with sailboats plying on the lake and peasants passing on the way to Lugano. Into this setting, rather surprisingly, wandered the queen in her Windsor uniform, Prince Albert, Wellington, and the one-legged veteran of Waterloo, the Marquis of Anglesey, on holiday no doubt. After they passed from view, a "beautiful stag" went across the scene, followed by a sportsman with his dog pursuing and killing a hare, a swan swimming, a lady with her parasol opening and closing, and "harvest home with the antics of an unruly donkey."[28] Another production of the sort in the same year, "The City of Shau-Chew-Fu in China," surpassed it in timeliness if nothing else.[29]

Jawbreaking names continued to be adopted to divert attention from the staleness of the show. The Akolouthorama (1844, at 213 Piccadilly) presented a "Novel Mechanical and Pictorial Exhibition" entitled "The Shipwreck, Depicting the various Perils in the Adventurous Life of a Sailor."[30] The following year, the Alethorama, at the Princess's Concert Room, Castle Street, advertised "ANIMATED ILLUSIONS" in five scenes: the Palace of Santa Felice, the Maas at Rotterdam, St. Martin's Dyke in Iceland, the Castle of Doornwerd, and the S----at S--. There were 2,000 figures "employed in their several pursuits of pleasure or business" as well as ships, carriages, and horses.[31] But "the eye," reported the *Times,* "was continually annoyed by seeing the machinery which worked it," and in any case the admission charged—four shillings for front seats, two for the rest—was far too steep for the scarcely novel entertainment it bought.[32]

As always, the obsolescence of a show-type made least difference at the fairs. At Bartholomew Fair in 1836, for example, there was a booth called Brown's Theatre of Arts, "consisting of Battles, &c. both by Sea and Land, together with several beautiful Foreign Views, enlivened with upwards of 40,000 Beautiful and Chaste Figures, and Upwards of Seventy Sail of the Line." The scenes portrayed Napoleon crossing the Alps, the Marble Palace of St. Petersburg with people, carriages, and a funeral procession "passing and repassing," and "three beautiful swans swimming upon the river," the ascent of a balloon, and the Battle of Trafalgar, when "each ship will move and fire distinctly from itself."[33] Two years later, at the Hyde Park coronation fair, the variety program of Tanner's Mechanical Victoria Pantheon had at least a few animated pictures, notably a new version of storm and

shipwreck: the foundering near Boulogne of the *Amphitrite,* laden with female convicts.[34]

D3❋E3

About 1796 Jack Bologna, the young theatrical man of many trades, put on a show at the Lyceum called the Phantoscopia. Nothing more seems to be known about it, but the name suggests that it resembled the Phantasmagoria, a scare show then on view in Paris, which was freshly exploiting the specialty for which the magic lantern had always been valued, the production of supernatural effects.[35] This improved version of the magic lantern, the invention of a Belgian professor of physics named Étienne Gaspard Robert (later Briticized to Robertson), gave audiences delicious chills by calling up, in eerie clouds of smoke, the ghosts of such heroes and celebrities of revolutionary France as Voltaire, Rousseau, Marat, and Lavoisier. The Phantasmagoria, under that name, was first exhibited in London in late 1801 or early 1802 by a French showman named Paul de Philipstal. Shown in the downstairs room at the Lyceum, it was an immediate hit, profiting from the same popular relish for managed spectral visitations that was to have been catered to by one of the rooms in Merlin's Necromancic Cave, and that was, in fact, the reason why Gothic novels, crammed with ghosts and events against nature, had been bestsellers in the past few years.

The Phantasmagoria's operation was simple enough. The source of light was a magic lantern placed at a distance behind a semitransparent screen, which was more dependable and controllable than the smoke used in Paris. A movable carriage and adjustable lenses enabled the images to be increased or decreased as the effect (the illusion of ominously advancing or retreating figures) required. The ghostly figures were painted on glass "sliders," the extraneous portions of which were blacked out so as to concentrate the light, and the audience's fearful attention, on the luminous images. Sir David Brewster described the performance thus:

The small theatre of exhibition was lighted only by one hanging lamp, the flame of which was drawn up into an opaque chimney or shade when the performance began. In this "darkness visible" the curtain rose and displayed a cave with skeletons and other terrific figures in relief upon its walls. The flickering light was then drawn up beneath its shroud, and the spectators in total darkness found themselves in the middle of thunder and lightning. A thin transparent screen had, unknown to the spectators, been let down after the disappearance of the light, and upon it the flashes of lightning and all the subsequent appearances were represented. This screen being half-way between the spectators and the cave which was first shown, and being itself invisible, prevented the observers from having any idea of the real distance of the figures, and gave them the entire character of aërial pictures. The thunder and lightning were followed by the figures of ghosts, skeletons, and known individuals, whose eyes and mouth were made to move by the shifting of combined sliders. After the first figure had been exhibited for a short time, it began to grow less and less, as if removed to a great distance, and at last vanished in a small cloud of light. Out of this same cloud the germ of another figure began to appear, and gradually grew larger and larger, and approached the spectators till it attained its perfect developement. In this manner, the head of Dr. Franklin was transformed into a skull; figures which retired with the freshness of life came back in the form of skeletons, and the retiring skeletons returned in the drapery of flesh and blood.

The exhibition of these transmutations was followed by spectres, skeletons, and terrific figures, which, instead of receding and vanishing as before, suddenly advanced upon the spectators, becoming larger as they approached them, and finally vanished by appearing to sink into the ground. The effect of this part of the exhibition was naturally the most impressive. The spectators were not only surprised but agitated, and many of them were of opinion that they could have touched the figures.[36]

While this *frisson*-filled communion with visible spirits drew audiences to Philipstal's room night after night, upstairs Mark Lonsdale's *Ægyptiana,* with its "moving panorama" and recitations from the poets, played to meager houses. Lonsdale thus was impelled to fight ghosts with ghosts in the form of a "Spectrographia," described in a handbill as "the effect of Supernatural Appearances as described in popular Stories, and credited by Weak Minds, . . . produced to the eye of the Spectator by a system of Machinery connected with a series of Experiments . . . forming a varied and amusing picture of TRADITIONARY GHOST WORK!"[37] The bill consisted of a series of specter raisings, accompanied by suitable readings and recitations of poetry: Julius Caesar appearing to Brutus; the murdered princes appearing to Richard III; the apparition of the murdered Sir George Villiers, first Duke of Buckingham; Margaret's ghost, and the ghost of the young woman at sea, both from popular ballads; an encounter with a churchyard ghost; and the procession of spirits called before Macbeth by the witches. Bidding for the custom of the timorous, Lonsdale added: "The Public are respectfully informed that as the above specimen of Phantomimic Appear-

ances is materially connected with Scenery and General Effect, the Total Extinction of Light in the Theatre is unnecessary." But here he certainly miscalculated. The very attractiveness of Philipstal's show downstairs resided in the fact that the room was thrust into total darkness for the sake of the maximum thrill; nobody looking for a genuinely spine-tingling experience would settle for an innocuous substitute such as Lonsdale proposed. Despite the attempted salvage operation, the *Ægyptiana* show soon sank, the Spectrographia along with it, while the Phantasmagoria ran until April 1803.

Not much more than a year after the original Phantasmagoria opened in London, a writer in the *European Magazine* offered a sample of the spiel which, one hopes, was more typical of the subsequent cut-rate operations than of the one at the Lyceum. Coming before the curtain, the showman announced: "Ladies and gentlemen, Hin the hurly hages of hignorance, there wasn't no such thing as a Phantastigrorium; it is a quite spick span new invention, never invented before. Here you will see, Ladies and Gentlemen, your friends and relations, dead and alive, present or absent, above or below. You'll excuse my descending into particulars. Never mind; we'll put ye in spirits, I warrant ye, and keep ye in them too; proof spirits for the Ladies, and choice spirits for the Gentlemen. I should have no objection to a drop of brandy myself . . ."[38]

Londoners with appetites that the staid panoramas could never satisfy supported a number of phantasmagoria shows in the next two decades.* Philipstal's show was succeeded at the Lyceum, now informally renamed the "Phantoscopic Theatre," by an exhibition boasting "a great variety of Optical Eidothaumata" along with "some surprising Capnophoric Phantoms."[39] In 1805, while the room formerly occupied by *Ægyptiana* housed an "Ergascopia—an exhibition of 'Musical, Mechanical, Aerostatic, Acoustic, and Optical Novelties'" put on by two German "Professors of Physic" (probably a conjuring show), downstairs Jack Bologna was managing an exhibition which was forthrightly advertised as being "upon the same elegant plan of Mr. de Philipstal."[40] Soon phantasmagorias became parts of variety bills. At the Catherine Street Theatre in 1812 Crabb Robinson saw a specter show along with the performance of waxen puppets mentioned above. "In an age in which the process was familiar but not known to the people," he wrote, alluding to the tradition that the Jesuit scientist-inventor Athanasius Kircher had devised a magic lantern in the seventeenth century, "it must have

* Like the magic lantern in the preceding decades, the phantasmagoria served the caricaturists well, supplying an up-to-the-minute metaphor to use in their political satire. The persistence of imitations and variations of the show, as well as the memories people had of their experience in the darkened room, kept the phantasmagoria topical down to the time of Waterloo at least. Between 1803, when Gillray satirized the Peace of Amiens in *A Phantasmagoria;—Scene—Conjuring-Up an Armed-Skeleton,* and 1816, when *Phantasmagoria. A View in Elephanta* was one of the plates in Rowlandson's *The Grand Master or Adventures of Qui Hi in Hindostan,* the phantasmagoria was the metaphorical vehicle in at least half a dozen prints. (George, VIII, 129, 133, 175, 323, 832; IX, 648.)

been very easy to raise spirits from the dead apparently by means of good likenesses, for the eyes &c. may be easily made to move—the artificial luminous and coloured wheels coats of arms &c. very splendid."[41]

Some years later, on a bill that also included "Lilliput Island; or Ombres Chinoises," the familiar magic barrel and "mechanical fruiterer and confectioner's shop," and "artificial or mechanical fireworks," Bologna offered "a new and pleasing Experiment in Optics, after the manner of the Phantasmagoria," which had, in addition to routine phantoms, portraits of Kean as Bajazet in *Tamburlaine,* the late Princess Amelia, and General Blücher.[42] The specific association of the phantasmagoria with ghosts apparently lasted longest at the fairs. In 1833 De Berar's "Optikali Illusio" at Bartholomew Fair included a series of phantasmagoric pictures that included Death on the Pale Horse and other favorite subjects evoking horror and fear.[43] But some time before this, the term, with its vogue value, had begun to be applied also to ordinary magic-lantern exhibitions, without any necessary implication of ghost work.

Like that other, closely contemporary neologism, "panorama," the word "phantasmagoria" quickly was absorbed into the common vocabulary; it, too, filled a need which was much wider than that of simply labeling a new kind of entertainment. Byron used it in *The Vision of Judgment* (1822)—"The man was a phantasmagoria in / Himself—he was so volatile and thin"—and Carlyle, to whom the Gothic and now-you-see-it-now-you-don't resonances of the word were especially attractive, employed it time after time, as in *The French Revolution:* "Phantasmagories, and loud-gibbering Spectral Realities" and (the idea without the precise word) "new quick-changing Phantasms, which shift like magic-lantern figures more spectral than ever!"

The phantasmagoria also made it possible to put into words perceptions and effects new in human experience. The available fund of comparisons was inadequate to describe the unprecedented sensations incident to traveling on the railway or watching a train go by. And so a spectator at the opening of the Liverpool and Manchester railway in 1830 resourcefully drew upon the phantasmagoria to describe a peculiar optical effect:

The long continuous lines of spectators . . . seemed to glide away, like painted figures swiftly drawn through the tubes of a magic lantern. . . . In the rapid movement of these engines, there is an optical deception worth noticing. A spectator observing their approach, when at extreme speed, can scarcely divest himself of the idea, that they are not enlarging and increasing in size rather than moving. I know not how to explain my meaning better, than by referring to the enlargement of objects in a phantasmagoria. At first the image is barely discernible, but as it advances from the focal point, it seems to increase beyond all limit. Thus an engine, as it draws near, appears to become rapidly magnified, and as if it would fill up the entire space between the banks, and absorb everything within its vortex.[44]

Most important, the phantasmagoria moved entertainment a step closer to the cinema. Like the Eidophusikon, it added to optical illusion the revolutionary element of movement. Perhaps Daguerre was inspired to some extent by whatever shows of the kind he had seen in Paris at the turn of the century; in any case, in the Diorama he emulated the dynamics of a phantasmagoric show, though its spectral subject matter was replaced by the more earthly, instructive, "rational," and aesthetically pleasing subjects of architecture and topography.

It was under the loosely applied name of "phantasmagoria" that the oil-lighted magic lantern was introduced into the regular theatre, where it was occasionally used for special effects. In Fitzball's *The Flying Dutchman* (Adelphi, 1826), for example, it provided the phantom ship which appeared in a peal of thunder on a totally darkened stage—a foretaste of the lavish use of projections in some modern Wagnerian productions.[45] By this time, the magic lantern's effectiveness and flexibility as a form of entertainment had been notably increased by the invention and perfection (1807–1818) of the "dissolving views." The new device, later to be adopted for the same purpose by some dioramas, was a metallic shutter which, by closing upon one projected image and opening on another, made it unnecessary for the audience to see one scene being pushed from the screen by the next, though a brief interval of darkness still occurred between the two. It was invented by Henry Langdon Childe (1781–1874), a former slide painter for Philipstal who devoted his entire life to improving and presenting magic-lantern shows.[46]

A second technical improvement, this one originating outside the exhibition field, advanced the art of the magic lantern still further: Sir Goldsworthy Gurney's invention of the limelight (more often referred to at the time as the oxyhydrogen, or hydro-oxygen, light). Gas made by applying a mixture of oxygen and hydrogen to a small ball of lime produced an intense, steady light equivalent to that of a dozen

Argand lamps. After this new source of illumination was first used in lighthouses in 1826 by Lieutenant Thomas Drummond of the Royal Engineers (by whose name it also came to be known), it was quickly adopted by the show trade. As will be seen later on, it supplied light to the projecting microscopes that revealed the wonders of the subvisible world to London audiences. In ordinary slide shows, it not only made possible the projection of brighter images across larger spaces; it enabled the views to "dissolve" more smoothly, in the manner of the modern motion picture technique known by that word. In the Biscenascope, invented by Edward Marmaduke Clarke, an optician in the Strand, a single lantern incorporated two separate optical units, each with its own lens and oxyhydrogen lamp.* When the picture projected from one lens was to be faded into another, a stopcock simultaneously reduced the light from the first source and increased that from the source supplying the other lens. Thus one image faded from view as another was first superimposed on it and then replaced it. The resemblance to the operation of the Diorama is obvious. Two difficulties, however, remained: the gas had to be manufactured on the spot, requiring big rubber bags for storage and cumbersome apparatus for maintaining pressure; and the hand-painted slides, which were sometimes as much as eight inches wide and required proportionately large lenses, cost up to twenty pounds apiece.

Childe's slides were used in astronomical lectures as early as 1830, and about the same time and in a lighter vein they were cofeatured with automatons, a demonstration of laughing gas, and a "Physioramic Pyrotechnicon" (undescribed) in a bill at the Royal Bazaar, Leicester Square.[47] In 1837 the New Strand Theatre's program concluded with "a grand display of a beautiful series of new Phantom Views, imperceptibly melting into each other in a most pleasing and surprising manner, before the eyes of the spectator."[48] At one point the device acquired the name of "Eidoprotean," but this was one of the numerous show-business coinages that failed to catch on.[49]

As perfected, the dissolving views made possible the creation of a much wider range of effects than could be achieved in the Diorama, to whose decline Childe's and Clarke's inventions undoubtedly contributed. The replacement of the Argand (oil) lamp by the more brilliant limelight meant that slides which hitherto were painted in bold lines and colors now could be drawn more finely and tinted more delicately. Toward the middle of the century the chromatrope was introduced: a pair of circular slides, one of which rotated in front of the other to produce brilliant color effects of such phenomena as Chinese fireworks and volcanic eruptions.

The limelight-assisted dissolving views appeared just in time to be of great usefulness in the two new establishments dedicated to popularizing scientific and technical knowledge, the Adelaide Gallery and the Polytechnic Institution. As we shall see in Chapter 27, dissolving-view lectures on all manner of subjects, from the dead serious to the sentimental and facetious, were a regular feature at both places for many years. From about 1850 onward, in addition, they provided a cheap, convenient, portable, and flexible alternative to the moving panorama. The framed area across which the cloth passed could now be filled instead with a white screen on which an unlimited number of scenes could be projected from glass slides. This meant that any room large enough to hold the anticipated audience, anywhere in London or the country—not necessarily a regular entertainment building—could be used for pictorial tours.

Thus dissolving views became a familiar "engine of public instruction" in Victorian years, adding welcome glamor to dull subjects. But they were employed for other purposes as well. Evangelists and temperance lecturers used picture-talks to impart their respective messages in schoolrooms and chapels; teetotal societies, the Salvation Army, and proselytizing religious groups opened their own circulating libraries of slide shows, complete with prepared lectures, devoted to their particular cause. But most popular of all were the magic-lantern shows devoted to sheer amusement, usually in conjunction with comic lectures. By the 1860s they were well on the way to becoming one of the most widely attended of all forms of Victorian entertainment. They were most popular, no doubt, in rural communities where there were few other means of indoor recreation, but their impact on commercial London entertainment must have been substantial. A large portion of the mass audience would have gone to neighborhood dissolving-view shows more frequently than to most other kinds of exhibitions.

* Clarke said he got the idea from his father, a Dublin optician. According to information he gave the *Mirror of Literature* (n. s. 1, 1842, 97–100), after a successful showing of the Phantasmagoria in London, Philipstal embarked for Ireland. But during the stormy passage he lost nearly all of his equipment overboard, including his "magic lanthorn." (Hence, said the waggish author of the article, the term "dissolving views.") His slides, however, were saved, and when he arrived at Dublin he commissioned the elder Clarke to make a new lantern. While it was being made, Philipstal conceived the notion of producing the standard illusion of the Witch of Endor raising the ghost of Samuel by using two lanterns, lowering the wick of one while raising that of the other, thus superseding the old effect of the phantom's rising from the ground by making it appear out of the mist instead.

Entr'acte: Exhibitions and London Life

17

Alongside the London pictorial entertainments in the first half of the nineteenth century existed many other kinds of shows. Before turning to them, however, we must survey the place they and other kinds of exhibitions occupied in everyday London life during the decades when their popularity reached its peak. Exhibitions then were as much of an institution as the theatre, and some were as widely publicized and as much talked about as any popular play or actor. The press regularly reported on them as a distinct genre of London sights. In theatrical pantomimes and extravaganzas, specific current shows often were more or less wittily alluded to, as subjects of timely interest. Caricaturists used a dozen or more of them as familiar and vibrantly topical metaphors. Similarly with popular poets: Thomas Hood referred to the exhibitions of the moment time after time in his humorous verse-journalism, and Thomas Moore once couched some political sentiments in the form of a barker's routine entitled "New Grand Exhibition of Models of the Two Houses of Parliament."* Like other timely subjects, shows inspired E. Moses and Sons, drapers and outfitters, whose rhymed ads lightened the pages of London papers for many years:

CHRISTMAS EXIBITIONS

Once more the glad season of Christmas is here,
And folks from the country in London appear,
Some have come to a relative, some to a friend—
To pass a few days ere the season shall end,
And visit the fam'd "exibitions" of Town,
Which have ever enjoy'd such a matchless renown.

Some view the Museum—and others, St. Paul's—
But there's ONE "Exibition" where ev'ry one calls
'Tis a place to which thousands with eagerness run—
And that is the warehouse of MOSES and SON. . . .[1]

There are ten more lines, but enough is enough.

Seeing the London sights continued to be the ritual it had been since Elizabethan times, and now there were both more sights to see and more people to see them. In 1801, the year of the first official census, the population of metropolitan London—that is, the built-in market for exhibitions—was not much short of a million (958,863). By 1861 it exceeded three million. To this great potential audience was added the indeterminable number of visitors from abroad who made the round of the sights,[2] as well as the equally uncertain, but unquestionably large, number of people who came up from the country on business or for pleasure. The latter category sharply increased as railways were completed into London from every direction; between 1836 and 1848 no fewer than eight terminals were opened. As a consequence, the proportion of non-Londoners at any exhibition grew year by year.

What the routine of London sightseeing consisted of about 1820 is clear from Thackeray's description, written many years later, of a child's circuit of the leading attractions, beginning with Miss Linwood's gallery of needlework pictures in Leicester Square.

Another exhibition used to be West's Gallery, where the pleasing figures of Lazarus in his grave-clothes, and Death on

* The form of Moore's poem was perhaps inspired by William Hone's invective-laden pamphlet *The Political Showman—at Home! Exhibiting his Cabinet of Curiosities and Creatures—All Alive!* published in 1821 with twenty-four caricatures by George Cruikshank. This radical bestiary began with a pitch by the showman, which doubtless conveys the authentic manner and accents of barkers standing before actual London exhibitions: "Walk *up!* walk *up!* and see the CURIOSITIES and CREATURES—all alive! alive O! Walk *up!*—now's your time!—*only a* shilling. Please to walk up! Here is the strangest and most wonderful *artificial* CABINET in Europe!—made of NOTHING—but *lacker'd brass, turnery,* and *papier mâché*—all FRET *work* and *varnish,* held together by *steel points!*—very CRAZY, but very CURIOUS! . . . Ladies and Gentlemen,—these animals have been exhibited *at Court,* before the KING, and all the Royal Family! Indeed His Majesty is so *fond* of 'em that he often sees 'em *in private,* and *feeds* 'em; and he is so *diverted* by 'em that he has been pleased to express his gracious approbation of all their *motions.* But they're as cunning as the *old one* himself! Bless you, *he* does not know a thousandth part of their *tricks!* " The text proper of the pamphlet imitated the souvenir guides sold at such shows, with a picture and scientific description (duly credited to the authorities) of each creature on display.

the pale horse, used to impress us children. The tombs of Westminster Abbey, the vaults at St. Paul's, the men in armour at the Tower, frowning ferociously out of their helmets, and wielding their dreadful swords; that superhuman Queen Elizabeth at the end of the room, a livid sovereign with glass eyes, a ruff, and a dirty satin petticoat, riding a horse covered with steel; who does not remember these sights in London in the consulship of Plancus? and the waxwork in Fleet Street, not like that of Madame Tussaud's, whose chamber of death is gay and brilliant, but a nice old gloomy waxwork, full of murderers; and as a chief attraction, the dead baby and the Princess Charlotte lying in state.[3]

This juvenile party might well have wound up at the theatre where Charles Mathews was performing the third of his long series of one-man "At Home" entertainments, *Country Cousins and the Sights of London* (1820). In the course of his program of songs and recitations Mathews celebrated the view from St. Paul's, the museum of the Royal College of Surgeons (John Hunter's), the art exhibition at Somerset House, Westminster Abbey, and the panorama of the North Pole. Possibly the most quotable passage in the text is this unaffected tribute to London:

> Oh! what a town!
> What a wonderful metropolis!
> Such a town as this was never seen;
> Folks are so gay,
> And the crowds so obstrepolis.[4]

The itinerary of Thomas Sopwith, the mining engineer and railway surveyor from Newcastle, is typical of scores at the time (1830). Dutifulness shines from every sentence:

. . . went through the museum of the Zoological Gardens in Bruton Street, and a very admirable museum it is. I next spent an hour at the Western Bazaar, and saw Haydon's pictures of Eucles and Punch, with which I was much pleased, and also with the sculptured figures of Tam o' Shanter and Souter Johnnie [see below, Chapter 29]. . . . I then visited the beautiful and extensive exhibition of paintings, models, and sculpture at the galleries of the Society of British Artists; and after much too hasty an inspection of these, which well deserve a whole day's examination, I went to the Royal Menagerie at Charing Cross (removed from Exeter Change),—I saw the lions and other principal animals fed. The collection is very interesting, and the ravenous disposition excited by hunger, in most of the animals, is truly terrible.

On another day,

I visited the Excise Office in Broad Street, and spent some time at the East India House, the museum of which was cer-

tainly among the most curious and interesting sights I saw in London. The Eastern manuscripts in particular are highly deserving the attention of the stranger.

I went to see the animals in the Tower, and as a menagerie the thing was much more confined and insignificant than I expected. I deferred seeing the armouries and jewels to another visit.[5]

In that age of freely indulged enthusiasms, there were several well-known public figures who made a special hobby of going the rounds of the exhibitions. Their hon. patroness was young Queen Victoria herself, a devotee of the theatre who also liked to keep au courant with other kinds of shows. In 1838–39 she made three visits to Van Amburgh's lions at Drury Lane, and after marriage and the conventions that hedge a queen limited her public appearances at places of entertainment, she and Prince Albert often had popular London exhibitions brought to one or another of the royal residences. Occasionally, however, when the sheer size of the display, such as the Chinese Exhibition of 1841, made this impracticable, the couple came to a private view on the premises.

Next in rank below the queen in the order of exhibition-goers was the Duke of Wellington. A living legend among Londoners for upward of thirty years, a familiar figure on horseback in the main thoroughfares, he was nowhere oftener seen than at exhibitions. His presence at show after show is so amply documented in contemporary news reports, letters, and diaries that one is surprised to find his biographers making little if any mention of this penchant. From the Royal Academy summer exhibitions to displays of new inventions, he was always in attendance, systematically working his way along, it was said, "according to the numbers in the catalogue."[6]

There were some shows, of course, which engaged Wellington's professional interest. He repeatedly visited and approved of the several panoramas of Waterloo at Leicester Square;[7] he was at the grand reenactment of the battle at Vauxhall Gardens in 1827, when he was said to have "laughed heartily at his representative," and again at the revival of that show in 1849.[8] He was hardly less assiduous in attending exhibitions depicting later battles with which he had had nothing to do. A friend of Benjamin Robert Haydon spotted him at the panorama of the bombardment of St. Jean d'Acre,[9] and he made a notable appearance at Burford's panorama of Sobraon. "The stage on which he stood," wrote an onlooker, "might well be supposed to be a height from which the commander-in-chief was surveying and controlling the fluctuations of the

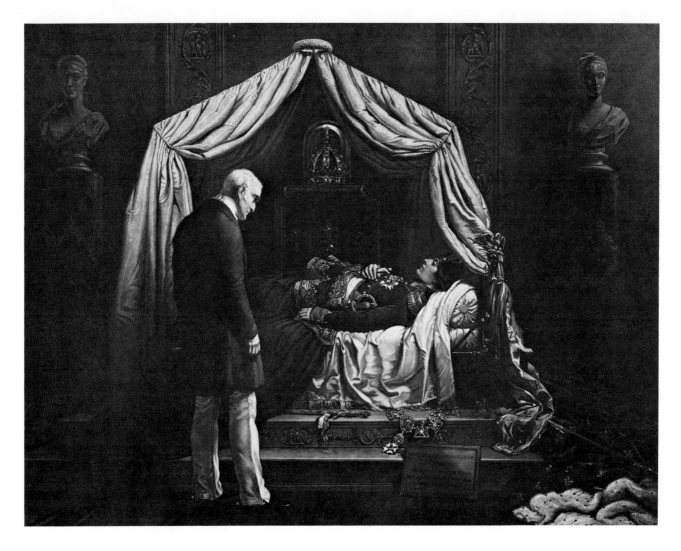

65. *The Duke of Wellington Visiting the Effigy and Personal Relics of Napoleon at Madame Tussaud's* (engraved from a painting, now destroyed, by Sir William Hayter, 1852).

conflict. Contrary to the usual impassiveness of temperament which the Duke exhibited, he became intensely excited, and seemed to chafe against the barriers which restrained him from the field he so distinctly realized." The scene inspired a correspondent in a newspaper the next day to quote Scott's lines:

> As the worn war-horse, at the trumpet's sound,
> Erects his mane, and neighs, and paws the ground;
> Disdains the ease his generous lord assigns,
> And longs to rush on the embattled lines.[10]

The Duke was also a frequent visitor at Madame Tussaud's, where, seeing him contemplating the effigy of Napoleon, the Tussaud brothers commissioned Sir William Hayter to paint the scene. The picture, finished after Wellington's death, hung in the wax museum until it was destroyed in the fire that gutted the building in 1925. On the whole, however, it seems that Wellington was more interested in the Chamber of Horrors, for he left a standing order with the management to be notified whenever a recent sensational crime was memorialized there. According to a print by William Heath (1829), he was sometimes to be observed looking at caricatures of himself in print shop windows. If there had been such a thing, he should have owned a permanent pass to all the rooms in the Egyptian Hall, for he was there constantly: at a private view of Catlin's Indian paintings, at demonstrations of Professor Faber's speaking automaton, and at performances by General Tom Thumb, the celebrated American midget, whose impersonation of Napoleon, it was said, "particularly amused" him. The General, his manager, P. T. Barnum, recalled, marched up and down the platform, "apparently taking snuff in deep

66. The Duke of Wellington inspecting caricatures of himself at McLean's Print Shop (engraving by William Heath, 1829).

meditation. He was dressed in the well-known uniform of the Emperor. I introduced him to the 'Iron Duke,' who inquired the subject of his meditations. 'I was thinking of the loss of the battle of Waterloo,' was the little General's immediate reply. This display of wit was chronicled throughout the country, and was of itself worth thousands of pounds to the exhibition."[11] When a Chinese junk tied up at a Thames wharf in the spring of 1848, Wellington was among the first to go aboard and watch as "the crew went through their pike and shield exercise, illustrating, by a variety of rapid motions, the national method of attack and defence."[12]

Third in social rank among habitual exhibition-goers was William Scott, Lord Stowell (1745–1836), jurist and authority on maritime law, brother of that most reactionary of judges Lord Eldon; friend of Dr. Johnson, *bon vivant* (a two-bottle man) and trencherman (when someone else provided the meal), and by way of recreation, a copious writer of sermons, though he never went to church. In a biography serialized in the *New Monthly Magazine* in 1846, W. E. Surtees said of him:

The curiosity of Lord Stowell was remarkable; there was no subject above or beneath his interest. Superior to the pedantry or bombast which disdains common sources of instruction and amusement, he was the most indefatigable sight-seer in London. Whatever show could be visited for a shilling or less, was visited by Lord Stowell.* In the western end of Holborn, there was a room generally let for exhibitions. At the entrance, as it is said, Lord Stowell presented himself, eager to see "the green monster serpent," which had lately issued cards of invitation to the public. As he was pulling out his purse to pay for his admission, a sharp, but honest, north-country lad, whose business it was to take the money, recognised him as an old customer, and knowing his name, thus addressed him: "We can't take your shilling, my lord; 'tis t' old serpent, which you have seen six times before in other colours; but ye shall go in and see her." He entered; saved his money; and enjoyed his seventh visit to the painted beauty.[13]

Lord Stowell was reputed to have "compiled a *catalogue raisonné* of these cheap entertainments, during a period of fifty years."[14] If he did, and if it were extant, a future historian might have been saved a year or two of work.†

Among the commoners habitually frequenting exhibitions was Charles Mathews, who, wrote his widow, "was all his life a great sight-seer,—that is, if the curiosity was either a human or any other animal." Among his personal acquaintances were the tiny Count Boruwlaski and the huge Daniel Lambert. Until the Zoological Gardens were founded, he haunted Exeter Change, the Tower, and the fairs "for the sole purpose of beholding such beings as were not elsewhere to be found, even of the human as well as other animals." Wellington, encountering him one day at the zoo's aviary, asked whether he came to the gardens "for studies of character."[15]

Wellington, Lord Stowell, and Mathews doubtless often crossed paths with still another devotee, William Jerdan, editor of the *Literary Gazette* from 1817 to 1850—a fact which may account for that journal's frequent attention to London exhibitions—and author of what is surely one of the most twaddle-laden autobiographies in English. "For some twenty-five years [he wrote in one of its more interesting passages] there was not a known show or curiosity, from the charge of a halfpenny to a guinea, that I did not see. . . . I was detected by Charles Kemble peeping into a halfpenny show, in some street about Long-Acre; in short, giants, dwarfs, mermaids, Albinos, Hottentot Venuses, animals with more heads or legs than 'they ought to,' and all other curiosities and monstrosities, were 'my affections.' "[16]

D3✳ξɑ

The outward spread of the city had mixed effects on the exhibition industry. When the population was concentrated in the City, Westminster, and the immediately contiguous region, theatres and exhibitions were within walking distance of most homes (although members of the "superior ranks" ordinarily rode in carriages). But now the metropolis was sprawling at an unprecedented rate, absorbing not only what had been the outer suburbs as late as the end of the eighteenth century but former self-contained country villages as well. Paddington's population increased from 2,000 to 25,000 in forty years; Tyburnia and the Grosvenor estate were built over in the thirties; Brompton and North and South Kensington too were covered with terraces and squares. The building of three new bridges (Vauxhall, Waterloo, and Southwark) between 1816 and 1819 opened a whole large territory to the south for residential development, and in the ensuing decade the population of Lambeth and Camberwell doubled. As a result, by mid-Victorian times the built-up expanse of London was six miles across.

As people moved farther out, the show area in the vicinity of Charing Cross, the Strand, Leicester Square, and Piccadilly became less accessible. Even

* In his reluctance to spend more than a shilling, Lord Stowell was outdone by Jonas Chuzzlewit, who, as a guide to London sights, "had an insurmountable distaste to the insides of buildings; and . . . was perfectly acquainted with the merits of all shows, in respect of which there was any charge for admission, which it seemed were every one detestable, and of the very lowest grade of merit." (*Martin Chuzzlewit,* Ch. 11.)

† At least a few people at the time recognized that exhibitions were a distinct social phenomenon whose records should be preserved. The antiquary Daniel Lysons (d. 1834) compiled seven ponderous volumes of *Collectanea* abounding with advertisements of eighteenth- and early nineteenth-century shows; Sir Joseph Banks's sister Sophia passed the time in their Soho Square mansion making similar scrapbooks, one of which was devoted to "Balloons, Sights, Exhibitions, and Remarkable Characters"; and the nameless "G.S." of Peckham compiled a valuable one on "Exhibitions of Mechanical and Other Works of Ingenuity." All these are now in the British Library.

when we allow for the fact that Londoners of the time were powerful walkers, the distances that now had to be traversed to reach most exhibitions were something of a deterrent until the development of public transport that began in 1829, when Shillibeer's omnibuses appeared on the streets. (His very first vehicles bore advertisements for the Regent's Park Diorama.) At first the fare was too high for persons below the middle class—sixpence for short journeys, a shilling to the end of the line. But as buses multiplied and their capacity increased, fares were much reduced, to threepence or even a single penny (for a trip, say, from Camden Town to Charing Cross). In addition, frequent and cheap steamer services brought central London within reach of Thames-side communities to the east and west. As far as the London showmen were concerned, this increasing ease of transport probably counterbalanced the fact that their middle-class clientele was becoming more widely dispersed. Those living beyond the reach of bus and steamer services were, however, less likely to come into the city for casual entertainment, although they did so for business.

Few artisans or laborers joined the movement to the suburbs until after the year (1862) with which this study ends. Cheap suburban housing and cut-rate workmen's fares on buses and railways, including the new Underground, came only after the sixties. The people who were the mainstay of the cheaper shows thus remained as close to them as ever, in the working-class neighborhoods and slums of inner London. The rise of speculative builders' terraces, rank after rank, on the former fringes of London interposed a wide ring of brick and mortar between central-city dwellers and the country, rendering them in effect a captive audience for commercial entertainment. Their parents and grandparents had had the country within walking distance of their habitations, and on Sundays and holidays they could easily go there to fill their leisure. But now, the transport available to carry the working-class family to the increasingly remote countryside was too expensive to be considered. In 1841, a British Museum official, testifying before a parliamentary committee, declared that as a consequence, for lack of anything else to do on Sundays and holidays, the workingman "leaves his family and gets intoxicated instead of taking rational pleasure with them."[17]

At the other end of the social scale were the grandchildren of the men and women who in their youth had patronized Cox's Museum—the fashionable idlers with ample money and leisure to devote to exhibitions. But their numbers were small, and by all odds the largest potential audience for shows was the rapidly expanding middle class, which also had the money and the leisure to spend on them. Nearly all exhibitions were open during the day, and they must have depended heavily upon the casual drop-in trade. The leading panoramas—Burford's, the Colosseum until the installation of *London by Night,* and the Diorama—were open only during daylight hours. With the spreading use of gas, most other shows kept evening hours as well.

Accessible to all by day and by night, at no charge and with diversified and constantly changing contents, was one famous London exhibition, or congeries of exhibitions: the shop windows. From the middle of the eighteenth century onward, the metropolis was internationally famous for these; one foreign visitor after another praised the skill with which the goods for sale were displayed, the brilliant lighting, and the animation of the scene as window shoppers passed from one establishment to the next. In 1786 Sophie von la Roche was delighted by the "splendidly lit shop fronts" in Oxford Street. "The spirit booths," she wrote, "are particularly tempting, for the English are in any case fond of strong drink. Here crystal flasks of every shape and form are exhibited; each one has a light behind it which makes all the different coloured spirits sparkle. . . . Up to eleven o'clock at night there are as many people along this street as at Frankfurt during the fair, not to mention the eternal stream of coaches."[18]

Robert Southey, adopting the persona of a Spanish visitor, described the shop windows' inexhaustible appeal at the beginning of the nineteenth century:

It must be confessed, that these exhibitions are very entertaining, nor is there any thing wanting to set them off to the greatest advantage. Many of the windows are even glazed with large panes of plate glass, at a great expense; but this, I am told, is a refinement of a very late date; indeed glass windows were seldom used in shops before the present reign . . .

If I were to pass the remainder of my life in London, I think the shops would always continue to amuse me. Something extraordinary or beautiful is for ever to be seen in them. I saw, the other day, a sturgeon, above two *varas* [English yards] in length, hanging at a fish-monger's. In one window you see the most exquisite lamps of alabaster, to shed a pearly light in the bed-chamber; or formed of cut glass to glitter like diamonds in the drawing-room; in another, a concave mirror reflects the whole picture of the street, with all its moving swarms, or you start from your own face magnified to the proportions of a giant's. Here a painted piece of beef swings in a roaster to exhibit the machine which turns it; here you have a collection of worms from the human intestines, curiously bottled, and every bottle with a label stating to whom the worm belonged, and testifying that the party was relieved from it by virtue of the medicine which is sold within. At one door stands a little Scotchman taking snuff,—in one window a little gentleman with his coat puckered up in folds, and the folds filled with water to show that it is proof against wet. Here you have cages full of birds of every kind, and on the upper story live peacocks are spreading their fans; another window displays the rarest birds and beasts stuffed, and in glass cases; in another you have every sort of artificial fly for the angler, and another is full of busts painted to the life, with glass eyes, and dressed in full fashion to exhibit the wigs which are made within, in the very newest and most approved taste. And thus is there a perpetual exhibition of whatever is curious in nature and art, exquisite in workmanship, or singular in costume; and the display is perpetually varying as the ingenuity of trade, and the absurdity of fashion are ever producing something new.[19]

The "large panes of plate glass" Southey mentions were, of course, far better adapted for display purposes than the grid of small panes with which most shops were equipped. At the time he wrote, they were very expensive, partly because the technology for producing sheet glass was only beginning to develop and partly because a heavy tax was levied on glass of all kinds. But thirty years later all the best shops were fronted with plate glass. An American seedsman who visited London in 1833–1834 recorded that in Regent Street, "the emporium of fashion," "many of the bow windows are glazed with panes 24 by 36 inches, 30 by 45, &c. There is a fur shop having a window on each side of the door, the centre pane in each window measuring nine feet by five." The furrier told the visitor that the latter panes, a half inch thick, cost fifty guineas each.[20] Improvements in production and the repeal of the tax in 1851 considerably reduced the cost of such glass, but it was not until the seventies that the shop window composed of several panes, as large as twelve feet high and four or five broad, gave way to a single undivided one.

The windows' attractiveness was further enhanced by improved lighting. London streets began to be illuminated by gas on a regular basis between 1814 and 1820, and the shops themselves acquired the new brightness not too long afterward. Because the deposits left by imperfect combustion soiled the merchandise, however, the gas jets often were mounted outside the windows, with reflectors inside to direct and distribute the light. All in all, it was a brave show; but far from dulling Londoners' appetites for other exhibitions, it must actually have whetted them.

Not only did exhibitions figure prominently on the physical London scene and in the everyday comings and goings of the population: they also reflected some of the period's most characteristic mental habits and attitudes. One of the most noteworthy elements in the early Victorian cultural climate was the sharpening conflict between what the moral vocabulary of the period differentiated as earnestness and frivolity—between the application of the mind to what were regarded as "useful" and "improving" matters and the carefree indulgence of the innate human desire to enjoy oneself, irrespective of any lasting benefit. To oversimplify and certainly to overdramatize the confrontation, it was a neo-Puritan version of the medieval psychomachia, in which good and evil contested for the soul of Everyman. If a choice had to be made, there was no question that instruction commanded a high priority over "mere" enjoyment, of whatever sort. But to arbiters of personal and social morality, there was, as they were happy to think, no absolute Manichean dichotomy between the conflicting claims; as several future chapters will amply illustrate, they assumed that the two might be harmonized into a perfect, universally acceptable and efficacious blend of application and indulgence which they called "rational amusement."

Nowhere in the mass culture of the time was the campaign in behalf of that social good, so easy to formulate on paper, so difficult to realize in practice, more vividly exemplified than in the exhibition business; and nowhere, as it turned out, was the popular resistance to didacticism thinly coated with entertainment more evident. The heightened value placed upon rational amusement as the eighteenth century faded into the nineteenth could be, and was, invoked to legitimize exhibitions of many kinds. How convenient it was to have at hand a thriving form of leisure-time activity, one already deeply ingrained in the habits of the London populace, which might be enlisted in the cause of moral and mental improvement! As the Benthamite conviction that popular enlightenment was the key to the happy society spread, it came to be realized that exhibitions might play a substantial role in the popular education program: that, in conjunction with mechanics' institutes and cheap instructional books and magazines, they might join in the March of the Mind to the profit of the whole nation. Looked at in this sanguine light, they were a welcome commercial adjunct to the Society for the Diffusion of Useful Knowledge, that dedicated, influential, and sometimes fatuous enterprise which was motivated by Bacon's dictum that knowledge is power.

How strong the hunger for education really was among the people to whom early Victorian liberals so confidently attributed it must ever remain a matter for dispute. There is no question that the proponents of free popular instruction oversimplified the situation and minimized the difficulties in the way of their program; on the other hand, it is at least arguable that the ambition for self-improvement then was abroad in a larger section of the lower-middle and working classes than ever before or after came under its stirring, tantalizing spell. These people could have been depended upon to patronize whatever London shows promised to add something to their store of knowledge and their vicarious instructive experience of the world.

The vogue for education in the early decades of the new century—a backwash of the "reformation of manners" crusade that had begun in the late 1780s—was not confined to those who were determined to enlighten the masses in the interests of political stability and economic advantage. Even among the fashionable, such as flocked to the scientific lectures of the new Royal Institution, could be seen a pre-Victorian earnestness which, while it usually stopped short of any inclination toward methodical study, recognized the pleasure and benefits of using the mind. "So many easy and pleasant elementary books," wrote Francis Jeffrey in 1810, "such tempting summaries, abstracts and tables,—such beautiful engravings, and ingenious charts and *coups d'oeil* of information,—so many museums, exhibitions and collections, meet us at every corner,—and so much amusing and provoking talk in every party, that a taste for miscellaneous and imperfect information is formed, almost before we are aware, and our time and curiosity irrevocably devoted to a sort of Encyclopedical trifling."[21] Jeffrey obviously had his reservations about this kind of intellectual frivolity, but the fact remained that "museums, exhibitions, and collections" were gaining in repute among the upper classes.

Widespread though this enthusiasm for rational entertainment was, it also figured in the sporadic criticism leveled against humorless educationists by those free spirits who regarded it as a symptom of middle- or even upper-class priggishness. Some such attitude is at least implied in Charles Lamb's sympathy for the schoolmaster who, far from being freed at holiday time, "commonly . . . has some intrusive upper-boy fastened upon him at such times; some cadet of a great family; some neglected lump of nobility, or gentry;

that he must drag after him to the play, to the Panorama, to Mr. Bartley's Orrery, to the Panopticon."[22] Supposedly, the boy is as reluctant as his mentor, and, Lamb suggests, he cannot be blamed for that. But perhaps most indicative of the disrepute that the fashion for virtuous self-improvement enjoyed in certain skeptical minds is Thackeray's use of it to characterize the "Consummate Virtue" of the stuffy, self-righteous Hobson Newcomes. Rebuking Colonel Newcome for offering her boys tips, Lady Newcome says:

When they go to school they receive a sovereign apiece from their father, and a shilling a week, which is ample pocket-money. When they are at home, I desire that they may have rational amusements: I send them to the Polytechnic with Professor Hickson, who kindly explains to them some of the marvels of science and the wonders of machinery. I send them to the picture-galleries and the British Museum. I go with them myself to the delightful lectures at the [Royal] Institution in Albemarle Street. I do not desire that they should attend theatrical exhibitions.[23]

Not only panoramas but numerous other kinds of exhibitions provided moral alternatives to the theatre. George Mogridge, a prolific writer for the cheap religious press who left behind some little-known but valuable descriptions of early Victorian shows, assured his pious readers that London was well supplied with "places of public interest . . . as may be visited by Christian people in their hours of relaxation, without hampering them in their earthly duties, or hindering them on their way to heaven."[24] It was to such "serious" persons that Thiodon's Grand Original Mechanical and Picturesque Theatre of Arts, Spring Gardens, addressed its unequivocal reassurance: "The Entertainments offered at this Theatre are quite distinct from that of a Theatrical Description, and on this Account, together with its surprising Ingenuity, and harmless Tendency, is peculiarly calculated to attract the Notice and Support of those, whose Religious Tenets forbid their Participation in Amusements of a more marked and decisive Character."[25] A similar appeal to conscience was made in 1838 when the Bayadères (nautch dancers) were appearing in the evenings at the Adelphi Theatre and at matinees at the Egyptian Hall. It was explained, with how much disingenuousness one can scarcely tell, that the "Dancing Priestesses" were at the Egyptian Hall "at the solicitation of many Families and Individuals who are not in the habit of visiting Theatres."[26] Thus a performance which the scrupulous could not view in the theatre was sanctified when transferred to the supposedly purer climate of the exhibition hall.

Presiding over the founding of such eighteenth-century institutions as the British Museum had been the doctrine of natural theology—the current, deistic version of the older "natural religion" springing from Bishop Butler, which looked upon science as the devout study of Creation in the interests of proving the existence of an all-powerful, all-benevolent, and enormously clever First Cause. Science, in this view, served as a supplement to Holy Writ. In his will, Sir Hans Sloane described his great collection not only as contributing to "the use and improvement of physic and other arts and sciences, and benefit of mankind" but, most important, as "tending many ways to the manifestation of the glory of God [and] the confutation of atheism and its consequences."[27] Such sentiments continued to prevail well into the nineteenth century. The prospectus of the Zoological Society (1825) asserted: "Zoology, which exhibits the nature and properties of animated beings, their analogies to each other, the wonderful delicacy of their structure, and the fitness of their organs to the peculiar purposes of their existence, must be regarded not only as an interesting and intellectual study, but as a most important branch of Natural Theology, teaching by the design and wonderful results of organization the wisdom and power of the Creator."[28]

It was on the same basis that some showmen, whether motivated by piety or expediency, recommended their pay-as-you-enter exhibitions as illustrations of divine ingenuity. The display of the Diastrodoxon, or Grand Transparent Orrery, in connection with R. E. Lloyd's astronomical lectures at various London theatres would, the publicity guaranteed, "familiarly explain all the Phenomena of the heavenly bodies, and give the most interesting and comprehensive View of the sublime works of the Creator."[29] To quote the syllabus of the lectures, "The unbounded view of creation which every starry night presents to the enquiring eye of mortals, excites our admiration and wonder! 'What read we here?' — 'The existence of a GOD!' "[30] In publicity for exhibitions of animate nature, too, the theological note was sometimes present. Pidcock's menagerie at Exeter Change was advertised as "not only innocent, but improving, especially to a contemplative person that beholds not the works of Nature, without admiring Nature's God."[31] It seems likely that few people came to see the animals primarily to have their faltering belief in the argument from nature bolstered. Nevertheless, appeals to religious sentiments, even if they were the merest cant, always provided acceptable window dressing.

No matter where they are found in the showmen's publicity, such appeals never seem very heartfelt. But they strike one as being especially perfunctory when they occur in connection with the attractions in and around Leicester Square, which was the heart of the early and mid-Victorian mass amusement industry. Londoners habitually thought of Leicester Square as virtually synonymous with miscellaneous exhibitions and entertainments. In the late forties, when Prince Albert and Henry Cole, a leading civil servant, were first discussing plans for the Great Exhibition of 1851, the question of its site naturally arose. The prince said in effect, "Leicester Square, of course." Only when the scope of the proposed show was enlarged from a national to an international one was the decision made to locate it in Hyde Park.

Leicester Square's association with the show business had begun while it was still Leicester Fields, a fashionable but as yet sparsely built locality.[32] In 1745, it was said, an enterprising man stood there, aimed a telescope at Temple Bar, where the heads of the Scottish rebels were displayed on spikes, and charged a halfpenny a look.[33] At the sign of the Golden Head on the east side, William Hogarth had his longtime residence and studio, where he exhibited his pictures to publicize the engravings to be made of them. In 1775 Sir Ashton Lever took over Leicester House, on the north side, for his Holophusikon. Again on the east side, at number 28, backing onto Castle Street, John Hunter built his celebrated museum of comparative anatomy. Just off the square, in his home in Lisle Street, Loutherbourg first displayed the Eidophusikon in 1781. A dozen years later Robert Barker built his panorama in Leicester Place, perhaps the decisive event that led to a neighborhood hitherto dominated by the residences of gentlemen, well-to-do-artists, and professional men being transformed into a bustling and increasingly raucous center of commercial amusement.

After the Leverian Museum was moved across the river, Leicester House was pulled down (1791–92) and replaced by shops and offices. Following the death of its owner, Sir George Savile, in 1784, Savile House, adjoining Leicester House to the west, had been allowed to deteriorate. In 1805 part of it was leased to Miss Linwood, the needlework artist (Chapter 28), and a pair of Kidderminster carpet makers. After this part was renovated at the considerable cost of £13,290, Miss Linwood installed in it her already famous pictures.

The Linwood Gallery yielded nothing to Barker's —later Burford's—panorama by way of respectability; indeed it would be difficult to conceive of a public exhibition more staunchly decorous than one of famous paintings imitated in colored wool. Nevertheless, the decline of the neighborhood had already begun, and by the forties the square itself, its railings long since removed for firewood, had become one of the ugliest eyesores in London, a spacious dustbin for dead cats, deposits of oyster shells, broken crockery, old bricks, and the miscellaneous refuse of a considerable portion of the West End. Most deplorable, perhaps, was the defaced condition of the gilded equestrian statue of George I, which had surveyed the ongoing degradation since it began. It had endured the attentions of roistering vandals and practical jokers so long that in the public mind it symbolized, in its mutilated state, the debased condition of the square as a whole.[34]

Facing this urban wasteland and in the network of narrow alleys and short streets surrounding it, interspersing the houses tenanted by exhibitions of many kinds, was an assortment of squalid lodginghouses and dubious hotels and restaurants. The round-the-clock inhabitants were chiefly foreigners; according to some not unbiased observers, a fair sample of the scum of Europe, particularly Frenchmen. The pavements resounded to their barbarous voices, their mustachios and swarthy complexions offended Anglo-Saxon sensibilities, and the odor of garlic and onions emanating from the lodginghouses and restaurant kitchens attested to their peasantlike preferences in food.

Even worse, the Leicester Square–Haymarket region was the site of what Hippolyte Taine called "the lamentable Haymarket march-past" of prostitutes. From noon to midnight and beyond, the sidewalks and the seamy eating and drinking places were full of them; in fact, many of the shabby buildings were their business addresses. It may be that Leicester Square did not achieve its maximum potential as a focus of commercial sex until the seventies, but already in the fifties there was certainly enough vice visible, not to say hidden, to make the area unsuitable for family excursions.

Yet—and this is the most striking anomaly in the history of London shows—it was Leicester Square that Prince Albert automatically thought of when the question of locating the Great Exhibition was raised; and although Leicester Square was not a vicinity of which any Londoner had much reason to be proud, the fact remains that it was the center of entertainment for families as much as for fast young Guardsmen and Dickensian "gents" out for a spree. A Punch and Judy showman told Henry Mayhew, the great sociological

journalist, about 1855 that from the special standpoint of his profession "the best pitch of all is Leicester Square; there's all sorts of classes, you see, passing there."[35] There was no more democratic locality in the entire metropolis.

Presiding over the fun was the many-chambered Savile House, where Miss Linwood's unexceptionable display of needlework pictures was soon joined by a motley fly-by-night assortment of what were sometimes advertised as "Exhibitions for the Million."[36] In 1814 one room was occupied by an "Astronomical Panorama." The next year arrived—and soon departed—Miller's Mechanical and Beautiful Representations, the "animated scenery" show noticed in the preceding chapter. In 1818 one occupant was the Papyruseum, a display of paper objects made by one Mrs. Aberdein, now deceased; another was a waxen effigy of Princess Charlotte, young daughter of the Prince Regent, lying in state, her still-born child beside her. Some fourteen years later the same premises housed the alleged body of "a Peruvian woman, perfect as when in life, supposed to have been buried alive at the remote period of 500 years ago."[37]

By 1846, when the Linwood exhibition finally closed—its very rooms now taken, ominously, by Madame Wharton's *poses plastiques* and renamed, for this equivocal attraction, "Walhalla" (Chapter 24)— Savile House had become a warren of rooms cheaply rentable for amusement purposes. Between that year and 1865 at least fourteen different names were applied to various parts of the house, depending on their current occupants. The building was so complexly divided that, according to one writer, "few could tell whether it was a theatre, wine vaults, a billiard-room, a coffee-shop, a gunsmith's, or a Royal Academy; or, if they could, they never knew, amidst the ascending and descending steps, and doors and passages, which one must take to get anywhere. . . . A confusion of sounds further tends to bewilder the visitor: the noise of everything is heard every where else. The click of billiard-balls, the music of *poses plastiques,* the thwacking of single-sticks, the cracking of rifles, and the stamping of delighted Walhallists, all mingle with each other; and it is only by taking refuge in the lowest apartment, which partakes of a coffee-room, a cabin, and a cellar, that you will find repose."[38]

Savile House was largely a masculine domain in these years. A number of enterprises were dedicated to the manly arts: gymnasiums for wrestling and boxing, fencing academies, gunsmiths, and shooting galleries. It was at one of the latter, William Green's "pistol repository and shooting gallery," that Edward Oxford practiced for his fortunately unsuccessful attempt to assassinate the queen in 1840. If Trooper George, in *Bleak House,* did not actually have his own shooting gallery in Savile House, it must have been close by. The house also catered to another masculine interest. In addition to the *poses plastiques* in the "Walhalla" room, there was in 1848 the Salle Valentino, which was advertised to hold two thousand dancers who could there "enjoy the Fashionable Quadrille, and the Graceful Polka, or the Exciting Galop."[39] Nowhere in London show business were the ideals of the Society for the Diffusion of Useful Knowledge and the advocates of rational amusement less in evidence.

❂

We cannot know how many families were deterred from attending some London exhibitions by the unsavory character of Leicester Square or by the stigma that the consciences of the truly rigorous attached to *any* public exhibition, excluding only Holy Land panoramas and models. But reformers had long stressed that a Christian family could best find wholesome entertainment in the home, insulated from the vulgarity, excitement, and possible seduction of crowds and firmly under the control of the resident moralist, usually the father. And so public exhibitors met brisk competition from the fireside, where some of the delights and benefits their shows purported to offer could be enjoyed in comfortable familial intimacy. Improvement, a Victorian adage might have declared, began at home.

Sometimes it was an exhibition device itself, scaled down and simplified for domestic use, which brought the harmless pleasures of the panorama and the Egyptian Hall into the parlor; sometimes it was an older object updated with a new name from show business. Prominent among the latter were what had earlier been called "prospects"—the long fold-out engravings depicting a broad expanse of landscape or cityscape which few eighteenth-century historical or topographical works with a pretense to costliness could be without (some were published and sold separately). The coming of Barker's panorama, which attempted the same wide-scope pictorial treatment on a mammoth scale, lent new popularity to these staples of the book and printselling trade, in addition to providing an up-to-date name which stuck.[40] The subject of Barker's first success, the Thames vista of London, had been anticipated by at least one "prospect," Sam-

uel and Nathaniel Buck's portrayal (1749) of the scene from Westminster to London Bridge, measuring 161 by 16 inches. Almost coincidentally with the opening of Barker's picture and the issue in a continuous strip of the six aquatints made from the original sketches, there appeared a three-inch-wide strip showing the same scene, enclosed in a hollow spool from which it was unwound through a slot. From this time to the middle of the century at least nine other home "panoramas" of London and its vicinity were sold in printshops.

There was enough affinity between Barker's invention and the engraved scenes to justify, though barely, their prompt appropriation of its name. They were also, after all, elongated representations of a wide outdoor view, and their subjects were often those of the canvas panoramas—Rome, for instance, and Constantinople, Paris, and Athens—though they also portrayed English holiday resorts, such as Brighton, Ilfracombe, Hastings, Tunbridge Wells, and the Isle of Wight, where they were sold as souvenirs. But they did not necessarily presuppose a high vantage point and a complete sweep of the horizon, which was the true panorama's unique characteristic. Their only novelty had nothing to do with their namesake, the use of a cardboard cylinder or wooden drum for storage—an innovation which had the practical effect of reducing the width of the strip and increasing its possible length.

But when they turned from representing fixed vistas to depicting a continuous journey, the engraved panoramas became miniature portable counterparts of the moving panorama, which had adopted the tour theme on a small scale when it appeared in the pantomime in the mid-twenties and had made an extended trip the subject of full-length shows in the late forties. Their convenient size gave them a practical use of which the long cloth strips of Banvard, Smith, Marshall, and others were incapable. The latter offered only a form of vicarious travel, whereas the annotated paper strip-engravings sold by publishers like Samuel Leigh, a specialist in this product, were meant also to be taken along on an actual journey, portraying as they did the whole course of the Rhine or an extended trip through the Alps. Each was conveniently folded and packaged in a space advertised as being little larger than that occupied by a quire of letter paper. By taking one . . . in your *sac de nuit,*" remarked a paragrapher, "you obtain on the spot all the information you desire, and by the panoramic picture you may identify every point of interest."[41] Nevertheless, there was some disadvantage to the use of this accessory; especially if there was a stiff breeze, it was not easy to sit on deck and manipulate a thin strip of paper, backed with cloth, that might be as much as sixty feet long.

The great length which a paper panorama might practically attain suggested another use, which engravers had thought of centuries before it occurred to scene painters and exhibitors of peristrephic panoramas: the portrayal of long ceremonial processions such as coronations, state visits, and funerals. Wenceslaus Hollar, the seventeenth-century maker of London prospects, depicted Charles II's coronation in sixteen strips constituting a continuous panorama, and in 1791 William Camden's old view of Queen Elizabeth's funeral was reproduced in the form of a 346-inch strip wound in a cardboard drum. Henceforth, slowly unwinding a representation of a lengthy procession from a cylinder made it possible to suggest (faintly) that the marchers and riders were in fact moving. There were several paper panoramas of Queen Victoria's coronation and wedding processions, and spool-wound pictures of the annual Lord Mayor's Show were hawked along the route for many years. But the classic, and quite possibly the longest, example of the genre was Henry Alken's and George Augustus Sala's sixty-seven-foot aquatint of Wellington's funeral cortège in 1852.

Cheap periodicals quickly took advantage of the improved engraving and printing techniques which permitted the production of such panoramas in large quantities. In 1830 the *Mirror of Literature,* already a pioneer in pictorial journalism, included in one issue a fold-out strip drawing of George IV's funeral cortège. But it was the *Illustrated London News,* the most successful of all picture papers, which went in for fold-out panorama supplements on a large scale. When it began in May 1842, subscribers were promised "a grand panorama print of London, a picture bigger than anything previously issued." Antoine Claudet, the first daguerreotype licensee, took a large number of views from the top of the Duke of York's Column, and by several widely acclaimed technical feats these early photographs were translated into an engraving measuring fifty by thirty-six inches.[42]

This premium was so well received that the paper brought out several more panoramas in the next few years, including pictures of the Thames, Dublin, and Paris in the year of revolution (1848). A short-lived rival, the *Pictorial Times,* produced a bigger picture of the Thames (150 by 5¼ inches), but the *Illustrated London News* eventually won the contest, with a twenty-two-foot strip-engraving of the Great Exhibition. This burst of journalistic gigantism coin-

cided, not surprisingly, with the current rage for monster-mile panoramas in the exhibition halls.

The words "panorama" and "diorama" were as freely applied in the household as anywhere else.* About 1815 children played with a toy called "The Panorama of Europe: A New Game," but all that was new about it was the name. It consisted of a single sheet on which was printed an engraving tracing a rather circuitous journey from Oporto to London by way of Rome, Paris, Amsterdam, Berlin, Vienna, and Moscow—a design which had already appeared in games with different titles. A "Geographical Panorama"—the example in the Bethnal Green Museum is dated 1822—was no more than an ordinary toy theatre, with grooves in the stage and colored cut-out figures and scenic pasteboard flats to insert in them. Contemporary with it was a geographical peep-show named the Areorama.

In 1826 Leigh brought out a toy advertised as being "on the principle of the Diorama in Regent's Park." The principle was not really Daguerre's, but the effect probably was close enough to satisfy the children who put the set together and made it perform. It consisted of a toy theatre box in which were inserted transparencies representing the familiar Diorama scenes. Behind these views were placed, sometimes on rollers as in the Eidophusikon, other transparent strips, painted as clouds, rainbow, moon, sunrise, and so forth; "which," said Leigh, "being placed behind the first-mentioned views, (and occasionally combined with a movable gauze curtain,) impart to them all the changes of morning, evening, dawn, sunset, moonlight, &c., &c., and gratify the spectator with the most picturesque and charming changes." To serve the function of the real Diorama's skylights and windows, a lamp was placed behind the picture box.[43]

Evidently, there were simpler models of the Diorama, lacking rollers and other such sophistications and consisting instead merely of transparencies, six by seven and a half inches, which were inserted into a slotted frame and shown alternately by reflected and transmitted light. The tie-up with the Regent's Park show, in any case, remained close. The 1836 Alagna avalanche production was so popular that a London printseller published a miniature of it. But the changes of program at the Diorama came too seldom (popular shows being rerun for several seasons) to suit the juvenile dioramists' demand for variety, with the result that the list of available subjects went beyond the Regent's Park repertory.[44]

Meanwhile, an older form of pictorial entertain-

* Probably the ultimate instance of this phenomenon was "The Ideal Diorama: A Scientific Cycle for Exercise of the Mind in Imagerial Invention and Descriptive Composition," an example of which is in the British Library (649.c.3.12). "The 'diorama' consists of a small circular card within a larger circular card. The small card has incomplete 'poetic thoughts' and the larger card concluding 'poetic thoughts' radiating from their centers. By turning the inner card one is able to bring the thoughts together, so that by reading any line straight across, 'original poetic thoughts in great variety will be suggested which the readers may modify to their taste by varying the adjectives or verbs, &c. at pleasure.'" (Private communication from Ralph Hyde.) Any resemblance between this device and Daguerre's picture show would seem to be wholly imaginary.

ment, the magic lantern, still flourished in the home, even as it was being adapted for public display.[45] On special occasions, professional assistance might be imported into the parlor, as William Hone describes:

On a Twelfth night, in 1818, a man, making the usual Christmas cry, of "Gallantee show," was called in to exhibit his performances for the amusement of my young folks and their companions. Most unexpectedly, he "compassed a motion of the Prodigal Son;" by dancing his transparencies between the magnifying glass and candle of a magic lanthorn, the coloured figures greatly enlarged were reflected on a sheet spread against the wall of a darkened room. The prodigal son was represented carousing with his companions at the Swan Inn, at Stratford; while the landlady in the bar, on every fresh call, was seen to score double. There was also Noah's Ark, with "Pull Devil, Pull Baker," or the just judgment upon a baker who sold short of weight, and was carried to hell in his own basket. The reader will bear in mind, that this was not a *motion* in the dramatic sense of the word, but a puppet-*like* exhibition of a Mystery, with discrepancies of the same character as those which peculiarized the Mysteries of five centuries ago. The Gallantee-showman narrated with astonishing gravity the incidents of every fresh scene, while his companion in the room played country-dances and other tunes on the street organ, during the whole of the performance. The manager informed me that his show had been the same during many years, and, in truth, it was unvariable; for his entire property consisted of but this one set of glasses, and his magic lanthorn. . . . Expressing a hope that I would command his company at a future time, he put his card into my hand, inscribed, "The Royal Gallantee Show, provided by Jos. Leverge, 7, Ely Court, Holborn Hill:" the very spot whereon the last theatrical representation of a Mystery, the play of Christ's Passion, is recorded to have been witnessed in England.[46]

One must hope that this belated and modernized representation of a mystery play in a Regency home did not have the untoward effect on Hone's children and their friends that the magic lantern had on the susceptible Harriet Martineau. When she was four or five years old she was frightened by a phantasmagoria: "I did not like the darkness, to begin with; and when Minerva appeared, in a red dress, at first extremely small, and then approaching, till her owl seemed coming directly upon me, it was so like my nightmare dreams that I shrieked aloud." The experience could not be forgotten.

A magic-lantern [she wrote in her *Autobiography*] was exhibited to us on Christmas-day, and once or twice in the year besides. I used to see it cleaned by daylight, and to handle all its parts,—understanding its whole structure; yet, such was my terror of the white circle on the wall, and of the moving slides, that, to speak the plain truth, the first apparition always brought on bowel-complaint; and, at the age of thirteen, when I was pretending to take care of little children during the exhibition, I could never look at it without having the back of a chair to grasp, or hurting myself, to carry off the intolerable sensation.[47]

Other optical novelties that were found in the home, however, never figured in London shows despite their seemingly large potential for exploitation. One was the kaleidoscope, invented in 1817 by Sir David Brewster and promptly pirated. It proved a bonanza for tinmen and glass-cutters—everybody in London, from titled ladies to street urchins, had to have one—but no attempts were made to turn it into an audience show. The kaleidoscope principle, with something of the Diorama added, was applied in the Myriorama, which was composed of a number of scenes that could be combined in various ways to form new ones. But this, too, was confined to the nursery and drawing room.

A generation later, the stereoscope caused an even greater stir than had the kaleidoscope.[48] Invented in 1832 by the young scientist Charles Wheatstone, it was originally used only for scientific demonstration. But in 1849 Sir David Brewster improved and simplified the device by making it into a box with two lenses, through which could be viewed two photographs set side by side, producing the illusion of three-dimensional perspective. Brewster had access to the queen, and her reported enthusiasm for the toy set off another craze. These tiny peepshows were inexpensive to make—they could be sold for as little as half a crown, though de luxe models cost up to twenty pounds—and it was reported that within three months 250,000 of them were sold in England and France. "No home without a stereoscope," the announced ambition of the London Stereoscope Company, founded in 1854, was well-nigh realized. The device's popularity was enhanced even more when Oliver Wendell Holmes, finding that box-viewing gave him a headache, invented the familiar hand-held viewer.

The stereoscope was the cosmorama and the panorama finally domesticated. From the London Stereoscope Company's stock of 100,000 views the mid-Victorian family could select all the scenes ever shown in Leicester Square, Piccadilly, Regent Street, and Regent's Park, and countless additional ones. The potential the little instrument had for wholesome instruction was celebrated in terms indistinguishable, except for one crucial difference, from those that still—but hollowly—were used to praise the panorama. The editor of the *Art Journal,* Samuel Carter Hall, called it "a silent Teacher, from which only good can be obtained. In a word, the loveliest scenes of nature, and the grandest monuments of human genius, are, by the magical power of this little instrument, brought in all their reality and beauty, to our own homes and firesides."[49]

The difference, of course, resided in those last few words. The stereoscope picture, along with its parent, the photograph, was destined to help give the *coup de grâce* to the London pictorial entertainment business as it was known in the late fifties: a development to which proper attention will be paid in another chapter.

William Bullock and the Egyptian Hall

18

Of the many London showmen we meet by name in the old records, few can be seen in sufficient detail for us to conceive the sort of persons they were. Only one or two survive distinctly enough to join the company of their peers in the theatre who wrote, or about whom were written, the memoirs that are the basis of nineteenth-century English stage history. Among these obscure exhibitors, William Bullock has particular claims to remembrance. He was no ordinary member of the workaday London amusement trade. He did, it is true, establish the Egyptian Hall, which was to be the center of the miscellaneous-exhibition branch of the trade for almost a century and which, as we have seen, housed several noteworthy moving panoramas at mid-century. He was himself the proprietor of several successful exhibitions. But he was also a traveler and a naturalist of some reputation, as his election to such learned societies as the Linnean Society of London, the Wernerian Society of Natural History at Edinburgh, and the Dublin Society attests. The 149-page "companion" to his natural history collection, acknowledging a debt to Wood's *Zoography*, reflects his serious educational purpose.

Bullock began as a Liverpool jeweler-silversmith whose interest in natural history was stimulated by the opportunities he had to buy rare specimens from the captains and crews of arriving ships. In 1795 he opened a typically eighteenth-century, which is to say highly mixed, exhibition of natural and artificial curiosities. Some of the oddities on display were reputed to have been brought back from Cook's voyages twenty years

earlier, and the arms and armor came from Dr. Richard Greene's museum at Lichfield.* In 1806 Bullock's agent bought extensively in his behalf at the sale of the Leverian Museum. Many of the curiosities he acquired then also came from Cook's voyages, among them specimens that Sir Joseph Banks had given to Parkinson, the museum's late proprietor.

In 1809, emulating Lever, Bullock moved his collection to London, though retaining the name "Liverpool Museum." It was housed at 22 Piccadilly, part of the site now occupied by Swan and Edgar's, which had formerly been occupied by Philip Astley's Chinese Shadows show, auctioneers, and a Baptist congregation.[1] Early in the following year *Bell's Weekly Messenger* reported that the museum had "become the most fashionable place of amusement in London; more than 22,000 have already visited it during the month it has been opened." By June the total had risen to 80,000.[2] Among the visitors from out of town in April 1811 was Jane Austen, who reported to her sister Cassandra that she found "some amusement" at the museum, "tho' my preference for Men & Women, always inclines me to attend more to the company than the sight."[3] If she had attended to the sight, she would have seen what an American visitor noted just a month later: among much else, a thirty-five-foot-long boa constrictor "which makes the story of Laocoön quite probable," a sixteen-foot-high giraffe, "with a very pretty head like a horse, and mild innocent look, at the top of an immensely long, yet graceful, crane neck," and a bear which looked quite small in comparison.[4]

* This was the best known of the provincial collections apart from Sir Ashton Lever's, which had, in any case, been transferred to London in 1774. Greene was a well-liked apothecary-surgeon whose collection, kept in two rooms at his Lichfield home, consisted mainly of contributions from various collectors, including many from Lever himself. (The museum is described in John Nichols, *Illustrations of the Literary History of the Eighteenth Century,* London, 1817–1858, VI, 318–26; see also *Gentleman's Magazine,* 58, 1788, 847.) Greene took pride in being a relative of Dr. Johnson, who mentions him and his museum several times in his letters to Mrs. Thrale and others. Boswell describes a visit he and Johnson made to the museum in 1776. "Johnson," he writes, "expressed his admiration of the activity and diligence and good fortune of Mr. Green, in getting together, in his situation, so great a variety of things; and Mr. Green told me that Johnson once said to him, 'Sir, I should as soon have thought of building a man of war, as of collecting such a museum.' Mr. Green's obliging alacrity in shewing it was very pleasing." (*Life of Johnson,* ed. G. B. Hill and L. F. Powell, Oxford, 1934–1950, II, 465–66.) After Greene's death in 1793 part of the collection, which ranged from Cherokee artifacts and Roman missals on vellum to "an uncommon Musical Alter Clock" and a model of Lichfield cathedral, was sold, the remainder being taken to Bath by his grandson.

67. William Bullock (engraving by an unknown artist, in George Dawson Rowley's *Ornithological Miscellany*, 1875–1878).

By this time, the new home of Bullock's museum was under construction on the south side of Piccadilly (now numbers 170–173) nearly opposite the foot of Old Bond Street.[5] Its official name was to be the London Museum, but its architecture virtually dictated the informal title it would at once acquire and retain for the rest of its long career: the Egyptian Hall. Egypt had been much in the English mind during the past fifteen years as one of the early theatres of the war with the French and as the site of momentous archaeological discoveries. The *Ægyptiana* show at the Lyceum had been only one of many manifestations of the vogue for the hitherto obscure country of the Nile which had enlivened London theatrical, learned, and artistic circles in those years. The new building in Piccadilly was another. It was designed by Peter Frederick Robinson, a "connoisseur of styles" who, as the Prince of Wales's superintendent of works, had advised him on the purchase of Chinese furnishings for the Brighton pavilion and, as an architect, was well known for his Norman villas and Tudor parsonages. Later he would design the Swiss chalet at the Colosseum.

His London Museum building was in the style most cautiously described as Egyptian eclectic. It was nominally inspired by the great temple of Hat-hor at Dendera, a late Ptolemaic and Roman building which then was counted among the most impressive Egyptian monuments, travelers having either not yet seen or not fully appreciated the finer structures that date from earlier dynasties. The Dendera temple epitomized the Egyptian architectural spirit as the Regency conceived it. Robinson used great freedom in re-creating it in London. The central façade was crowned by a huge cornice supported by sphinxes and two colossal nude statues in Coade stone representing Isis and Osiris. These had been carved by an Irishman named Sebastian Gahagan. Alongside the door were stubby lotus columns, and hieroglyphs bespeckled every free surface. What they said, if anything, was a mystery: the Rosetta stone, which broke the code of this ancient language, was not deciphered until 1822. To passersby, it sufficed that the hieroglyphs *looked* Egyptian; and the building's purpose was, in any event, adequately spelled out by the words LONDON MUSEUM carved beneath the feet of Isis and Osiris.

Until the protracted erection of the Colosseum some years later, no London structure destined to be an exhibition place attracted more attention than did this one—an acceptable windfall, of course, to the prospective occupant. Not a few aesthetically sensitive Londoners disliked its strident exoticism, heightened by contrast with the sedate red-brick Georgian shops and dwellings which flanked it, but as Leigh Hunt said, there was no denying that once seen, it could not be forgotten: "Egyptian architecture will do nowhere but in Egypt. There, its cold and gloomy ponderosity ('weight' is too petty a word) befits the hot, burning atmosphere and shifting sands. But in such a climate as this, it is worth nothing but an uncouth anomaly. The absurdity, however, renders it a good advertisement. There is no missing its great lumpish face as you go along. It gives a blow to the mind, like a heavy practical joke."[6]

Under such circumstances, the hall, which opened for business in the spring of 1812, was bound *not* to be known as the London Museum. The printed guide to Bullock's collection of "upwards of Fifteen Thousand Natural and Foreign Curiosities, Antiquities, and Productions of the Fine Arts" said the collection was "open for public inspection in the Egyptian Temple erected in Piccadilly." For "temple," however, was soon substituted "hall," a change perhaps rendered inevitable by the fact that London had long been familiar with the room called the Egyptian Hall at the Mansion House, designed by George Dance the elder and having even less resemblance to the hall of that name described by Vitruvius than Robinson's confection had to the temple at Dendera. On each side of the entrance in Piccadilly was a shop, one occupied originally by a bookseller and the other by a chemist. On the ground floor was a suite of apartments, 170 feet long, and upstairs a gallery measuring 60 by 27 feet.*

Heretofore, little attempt had been made to organize museum materials in any systematic, rational way, let alone to add a touch of showmanship. Sir Ashton Lever seemingly had tried to impose some order upon his miscellaneous accumulation, but according to William Jerdan, when the Leverian collection fell into Parkinson's hands it was notable only for its disorganization and uselessness as an instrument of education. Bullock's collection, Jerdan said, was "quite the reverse of this—admirably preserved and scientifically arranged," and there is substantial evidence to back him up. Although Charles Willson Peale had anticipated him with the clever settings he devised more than a decade earlier in his natural history museum in Philadelphia, Bullock was the first English museum keeper to arrange his specimens in a semblance of what are today called "habitat groups," with careful attention to postures and physical surroundings.[7]

The central display, called the "Pantherion" and housed in a wing west of the main block, was in-

tended, as a contemporary description put it, "to display the whole of the known Quadrupeds, in a manner that will convey a more perfect idea of their haunts and modes of life." Entering through a mockup of a basaltic cavern suggested by Fingal's Cave on the Isle of Staffa,† visitors found themselves in a room fitted up to resemble a tropical rain forest, with an Indian hut prominent in the foreground, a painted panoramic scene in the background to supply the effect of distance, and "exact Models, both in figure and colour, of the rarest and most luxuriant Plants from every clime" to complete the illusion of place, though there was some doubt what the place was. The specimens, dominated by a giraffe, a rhinoceros, and an elephant, were disposed to suggest their natural activity. The lion, panther, and jaguar were seen in dens or on large property rocks; seals were ranged on rocks overlooking the panoramic "Sea-View"; anteaters hovered near the model of "one of the turrets, or nests of the Termites or White Ants of Africa"; a lemur crouched on the branch of a tree; three sloths clung to the stem of an American aloe, near the head of the rhinoceros.

The other parts of the museum were arranged with the same combination of science and free imaginativeness. According to Jerdan, in another room

3,000 birds were set up with similar accuracy, and attended by well-selected accessories, so as to afford sufficient ideas of their motions, food, and mode of feeding, and peculiarities of every description—from eagles to humming-birds (of the latter of which there were ninety distinct species); and, including the collection made by Captain Cook and Sir Joseph Banks, the whole were so perfect in plumage and disposition, that the aviary, if it might be so called, presented a scene of wonderful beauty to the eye. Unwilling the spectator turned from it, to inspect the numerous amphibious creatures in a third spacious room; but these, again, were found to be so remarkable, that the attractions of the fishes, the insects, the marine productions, could scarcely wile the visitor away to contemplate their various structure, clearly indicated action, and striking life-like appearance. The fossil remains of a former world wound up a spectacle of a most comprehensive character, unprecedented novelty, and unexampled utility.[8]

The quadrupeds, birds, fishes, amphibia, and fossils were supported by the usual mixture of curios: African and North American artifacts, weapons, and articles of dress; models (the death of Voltaire executed in rice paste, a mother-of-pearl Chinese pagoda, a sixty-gun man-of-war made entirely of crystal glass by Bullock himself when a boy); ivory objects of art; flowers made of butterflies' wings; and wool pictures of the

* These figures are from the catalogue of the Roman exhibition, 1816 (copy at BL, 7807.aaa.25). Subsequent descriptions are fragmentary and inconsistent, though one of them, a handbill advertising the impending sale of the hall in 1833 (copy in JJ Coll., London Play Places box 10), gives the dimensions and noteworthy features of each room. Stressing the building's almost infinite adaptability, the bill added that "propositions have been made for converting the Edifice into a chapel." In any case, all that can be said with confidence is that during its long existence the building underwent several interior alterations; that one of the rooms was redecorated in 1819 as "the Egyptian Hall"; that one or more of them was surrounded by a gallery and had natural light from either flat skylights or a dome; that the rooms could be occupied *en suite* or divided; and that there was space for at least three separate exhibitions running simultaneously. See *Survey of London,* XXIX (1960), 266–70, and XXX (1960), plate 44.

† Fingal's Cave had nothing at all to do with the contents of the room, but as repeatedly happened in the exhibition business, Bullock borrowed a popular feature from the theatre. At least two Sadler's Wells productions, its 1805 pantomime and the aquadrama *The Spectre Knight* (1810), had Fingal's Cave scenes, with water effects.

68. Bullock's Liverpool Museum, 22 Piccadilly (aquatint in *Ackermann's Repository of Arts,* 1810).

Holy Family. Bullock had himself collected relatively few items, apart from some of the birds; he had acquired most by purchase or by donation, from such diversified sources, in addition to the Leverian Museum, as the Duke and Duchess of York, Princess Charlotte of Wales, Admiral Bligh, and S. Polito, the menagerist of Exeter Change, who had contributed a pair of beavers, a panther, and a Palatine monkey from "the Slave Coast" that died of the London cold in 1808.

In 1816 Bullock, perhaps finding that the museum alone was not rendering him enough profit, decided to diversify his exhibition. One room, named for the occasion "the Roman Gallery," was devoted to a collection of objects of art he had bought as a speculation: "Magnificent Decorations," as the "descriptive synopsis" had it, "consisting of Antique Marbles, Jasper,

Agate, &c. in Vases, Tablets, and Tazzas; and Superb Pictures of the Ancient and Modern Masters" headed by G. F. Le Thière's large painting, *The Judgment of Brutus upon His Sons.*[9]

In another room Bullock exhibited the result of what might have been regarded as a desperate gamble but which turned out to be a lucky coup. The British fascination with Napoleon had already begun to have what would prove to be its strong and lengthy impact upon the exhibition business. Lefèbvre's and David's huge (fifteen by six feet) portrait of the fallen emperor, proclaimed as "the only natural likeness now publicly exhibiting in Europe" and "most probably the last that ever will be painted of him in Europe," had been attracting crowds, at a shilling admission fee, successively to rooms at 53 Leicester Square, the Adelphi, and

a Waterloo Museum newly set up at 97 Pall Mall.[10] This last was the speculation of a St. James's Street cutler named Palmer, who had gathered, in addition to the portrait and a large painting of Waterloo, four eagles awarded to heroic units of Napoleon's army and an array of weapons and armor.[11] In the same neighborhood in 1815 there were at least two other displays of Napoleonana: the Waterloo Exhibition at 1 St. James's Street, featuring the emperor's clothes, "superb dresses from the empress' apartment," and miscellaneous gleanings from the battlefield;[12] and the Waterloo Rooms at 94 Pall Mall, which, as late as 1824, advertised itself as a "fashionable lounge" whose star attraction was Napoleon's white barb charger, Marengo. This battle-scarred animal, announced the proprietor, "has five Wounds which are visible; and a

Bullet still remains in his Tail. The Imperial Crown and the Letter N. are branded on his hind quarters. He is so gentle, that the most timid Lady may approach him without fear."[13] The painter Haydon had a yearning, evidently not realized, to ride this former mount of the conqueror whose portrait he painted some forty times.[14]

But if Pall Mall had Napoleon's horse, Piccadilly had Napoleon's carriage, and the advantage to Bullock was enormous. On the evening after the Battle of Waterloo the emperor's traveling carriage, in which he had ridden during the Russian campaign and on his return to Elba, fell into the hands of the Prussians. The coachman, attacked on the box by a company of lancers, had been severely wounded and left for dead. He survived, however, at the cost of an arm, and from

69. Bullock's London Museum (the Egyptian Hall) (aquatint in *Ackermann's Repository of Arts,* 1815).

70. Napoleon's carriage at the Egyptian Hall: George Cruikshank's *A Scene at the London Museum Piccadilly,—or—A Peep at the Spoils of Ambition, Taken at the Battle of Waterloo—Being a New Tax on John Bull for 1816 &c &c.*

his sickbed he told his captors that Napoleon "had not been in the carriage for some hours before it was taken; but had passed it on horseback about ten minutes before, giving orders that it should follow him—*Sauve qui peut!*" The Prussian major who captured the vehicle passed it on to General Blücher, who in turn arranged to have it taken to England and presented to the Prince Regent. The prince, needing the money more than an extra carriage, sold it to Bullock for £2,500.[15]

The carriage, a luxurious bullet-proof vehicle painted dark blue and gilt, with vermilion wheels, went on display at the Egyptian Hall in the first week of January 1816, along with the now-recovered coachman, two of the horses, Napoleon's folding camp bed, and the contents of his traveling case, "close on a hundred pieces . . . nearly all in solid gold, two leather bottles, one of rum and the other of fine old Malaga, a million francs-worth of diamonds and a cake of Windsor soap."[16] The show attracted more people—10,000 a day—than had any previous London exhibition.* Both Rowlandson and Cruikshank depicted the swarming crowds, whose total reached 220,000 by the time the show closed on 24 August 1816.[17] Then Bullock took the carriage on tour, with equally gratifying results. He wrote shortly afterward that the carriage and its contents had been a veritable Elijah's mantle to him: they "gave me the power of accomplishing, in a few months, what, with all his talents, riches, and armies, he [Napoleon] could never succeed in doing; for in that short period I over-ran England, Ireland, and Scotland, levying a willing contribution on upwards of 800,000 of his Majesty's subjects; for old and young, rich and poor, clergy and laity, all ages, sexes, and conditions, flocked to pay their poll-tax, and gratify their curiosity by an examination of the spoils of the dead lion."[18] When the carriage was shown in Brighton, however, a local bard took a different view of the sensation it had caused:

What wondrous things are daily brought to view,
  Produced by Time, and shown by Fortune's glasses!
Six noble horses the great Napoleon drew,
  Now, one Bullock draws a hundred thousand asses![19]

From an investment of £2,500 Bullock won a return of £35,000.[20]

The sensation in Piccadilly evoked appropriate response from other showmen. No sooner had Bullock withdrawn the carriage from the Egyptian Hall to take it on tour than there went on display at Bartholomew Fair "The Superb and Elegant Pleasure Carriage of Napoleon Buonaparte . . . presented by him to his son Napoleon, King of Rome. At the taking of Paris it was sent, by order of the Allied Sovereigns, among Buonaparte's other valuables, to the Island of Elba, from whence it has lately been purchased, at a very great expence." So said the flyer; admission (half the rate in Piccadilly) was sixpence, working people and children threepence.[21]

Once Bullock had exhausted the potentialities of the battlefield carriage, he sold it to a coachmaker for £168. In 1843 it was purchased by Madame Tussaud and Sons, who installed it in a new display area initially billed as "The Shrine of Napoleon, or Golden Chamber."[22] At the waxwork it remained, the most durable of all the Tussaud exhibits, for over three quarters of a century.

Bullock invested part of the proceeds from the carriage exhibition in another Napoleon-related speculation, a "Museum Napoleon, or Collection of Productions of the Fine Arts executed for and connected with the History of the ex-Emperor of the French, collected at Considerable Expense from the Louvre and Other Places, &c."[23] This collection joined the Roman Gallery as another of the Egyptian Hall's assorted attractions. But by 1818 Bullock seems to have been forced to conclude that he had too much capital tied up in these various collections. He therefore asked the University of Edinburgh if it was interested in buying his entire natural history collection, which included 2,485 birds, 429 amphibia, and 232 quadrupeds valued at £25,000—a figure he arrived at, no doubt, by splitting the difference between the £20,000 he pronounced it worth when at 22 Piccadilly and the £30,000 at which he valued it in the catalogue sold at the Egyptian Hall. His asking price was only £9,000, but the university was not interested.[24] Bullock then approached the British Museum, where he had a powerful advocate, Sir Joseph Banks; but in view of that institution's chronic penury, Banks held out little hope.[25] Bullock decided, therefore, to sell all three of his properties, the original Liverpool/London museum, the Roman Gallery of antiquities and pictures, and the Museum Napoleon, at an auction conducted by himself.[26]

The sale, the largest of its kind since the Leverian, occupied twenty-six days (29 April–11 June 1819) and attracted hundreds of prospective purchasers, including representatives of continental museums as well as private collectors, eager to add to their holdings now that the dislocations and uncertainties of the long war had ended. Most of the ethnographical material went to the Berlin Museum, and most of the arms and armor to Sir Samuel Meyrick, the noted antiquary. The centerpiece of the Museum Napoleon, "the original model of the Colossal Statue of Napoleon, twelve feet high, which was taken from the top of the Column of Peace in the Place Vendôme when the Allies entered Paris in 1814," was knocked down for £33 12s. to William Beckford of Fonthill Abbey, one of the most voracious collectors of curios and objets d'art since Horace Walpole.

But an even more celebrated collector was represented at the Bullock sale.[27] Daniel Terry, an actor-manager lately returned to London after an interval in the provincial theatre, attended in the interests of his friend Sir Walter Scott, whose novels he had been instrumental in adapting for the stage and who was then busily accumulating material for his projected private museum at Abbotsford. In a letter dated 18 April Scott had casually written to Terry, "I see Mr. Bullock (George's brother)† advertises his museum for sale. I wonder if a good set of real tilting armour could be got

* Among the spectators was Lord Byron, who was so taken with the carriage that, for reasons having to do with his personal vanity and possibly with some vague plan to liberate France from the restored Bourbons, he had a duplicate made by a well-known Long Acre coachbuilder. In this version, the drawers, compartments, and equipment intended for the use of a field general were replaced by a library and complete dining facilities. In it Byron crossed the Simplon to Italy, and it carried him on many of his pilgrimages there until in 1819, with its paint beginning to chip, it trailed Count Guiccioli and his wife, Byron's mistress, to Venice. On the eve of his departure for Greece in the autumn of 1823 Byron instructed his Geneva banker to have the carriage "kept in good order." What happened to it is not known. (Leslie Marchand, *Byron: A Biography*, New York, 1957, II, 603, 661, 718, 791, 813; III, 1132.)

† George Bullock, a sculptor, had died in the preceding year. He was represented at the sale by some models in rice paste—presumably not including the one of Voltaire's deathbed, which was attributed to a "M. Oudon" (Houdon?)—and a "beautiful Equestrian Model of Edward the Black Prince in Armour." Of him, too, one would wish to know more. Haydon wrote in his diary (ed. W. B. Pope, Cambridge, Mass., 1960–1963, II, 209) that "George Bullock was one of those extraordinary beings who receive great good fortune & are never benefitted by it, & suffer great evils, and are never ruined, always afloat but never in harbour, always energetic, always scheming, who should have had a frame of adamant, money without end, & a world that was boundless." There must be a story behind such a characterization.

In the foreground are additional Napo-

71. Napoleon's carriage at the Egyptian Hall: Thomas Row-landson's *Exhibition at Bullocks Museum of Boneparts Carriage Taken at Waterloo,* 1816. In the foreground are additional Napoleon relics; in the background, reminders of other Bullock enterprises in the same building (the Natural History Museum and the Roman Gallery), of an attraction Bullock turned down (the Hottentot Venus; see below, Chapter 20), and of that old favorite, the ageless midget Count Boruwlaski.

cheap there." Terry was only too happy to look into the matter, and on 7 June, as the sale neared its end, he wrote Scott:

My dear Sir, I have been doing something for you in the way of Armour with which I hope you will be satisfied. It is true that I have run you a little in debt to Mr. Bulloch; but for about £40 actually £45-6-6 I have obtained what I consider as very well worth from £100 to £130 and given you the power of making a very handsome as well as considerable addition to the walls of the Armoury. Indeed it seemed to me as if Bulloch, to whom I mentioned the destination of my purchases, was pleased at the prospect of their becoming yours; and knocked them down the faster for that purpose.

Terry's purchases ranged from "two very superb Back and Breastplates and arms of the blue & gold armour worn in the Time of Louis 14th" (£18 13s. 6d.) to a foul-weather jacket of an Eskimo made from the intes-

tines of a whale (19s.). A fine haul indeed; except that Scott had not authorized any of these purchases. It was plainly an honest misunderstanding or an excess of zeal on Terry's part, and Scott, whose life in those months was complicated by serious illness and financial troubles, sent him £50 at once, meanwhile expressing to other correspondents his distress over "poor Terry's" embarrassment. The contretemps was settled by mid-August, and at the end of September Scott was writing to thank Terry for "your most acceptable present," a knife, which evidently was intended as a token of Terry's contrition. In the years that followed, Scott often sought his friend's advice on questions relating to the fitting up of Abbotsford.

When the hammer fell for the last time, Bullock had made £9,974 13s. Thus the addition of the Roman Gallery and the Museum Napoleon had brought him about a thousand pounds over what he had sought to get from the sale of his original museum alone. Some of the prices were disappointingly low because a number of the natural history specimens were in bad condition, and a few, to borrow the euphemism of the auction room, were "compound," that is, not as Nature had made them. Among these was a boa constrictor—the same, no doubt, that Jane Austen had overlooked—composed of two serpent skins and a wooden head.[28] The prices some of the works of art commanded suggest that there may have been some dissatisfaction with them, too. A painting of the Virgin and Child and St. Anthony, attributed to Correggio, which Bullock said he had "bought at Tivoli, near Rome, where he found it stopping up the window of a cow-house" and which had cost him "10d. and 5d. carriage," went for a mere £16. A "portrait of Titian, extremely spirited," certified by Benjamin West to be the work of Giorgione, brought twenty-three guineas.

Regardless of the sum realized, Bullock was encouraged to believe he had found auctioneering to be his true métier. No sooner had the sale of his own properties concluded than he was advertising the forthcoming auction, at the Egyptian Hall, of other lots, including a consignment of choice specimens formerly in the Leverian Museum.

ᴅƷ✳Ǝᴅ

At this point occurred the episode in the Egyptian Hall's early history that glows most brightly in retrospect.[29] Benjamin Robert Haydon, whose showmanly instincts were too overdeveloped to win him the esteem of his fellow artists, proposed to exhibit most of his important canvases, including the latest, *Christ's Triumphal Entry into Jerusalem*. Without a shilling in his pocket he approached Bullock, who willingly rented his great room for the purpose at £300 a year. Haydon had his students write out eight hundred invitations to the preview and address them to "all the ministers and their ladies, all the foreign ambassadors, all the bishops, all the beauties in high life, the officers on guard at the palace, all the geniuses in town, and everybody of any note." Then, borrowing £50 from Coutts's Bank on his mere signature, he bought purple-brown fittings at a wholesale merchant's, rushed back to the hall and delivered them to the waiting decorators. "Bullock," he recalled in later years, "was looking at the pictures with all the air of a landlord who scented no rent."

Then came the day of the preview, 25 March 1820. Haydon shuttled back and forth between the Egyptian Hall and Hatchett's Coffee Room across the street. At half-past twelve he went into the hall once more. "Anybody come?" he asked his assistant. "Yes, sir; Sir William Scott [Lord Stowell] is just gone in." "That will do; he always goes to every exhibition on earth and brings everybody." Haydon went back to Hatchett's and treated himself to a good lunch and a couple of glasses of sherry. At 3:30 he emerged, to find Piccadilly choked with the coaches of the quality. If, among them, there was not quite everybody he had invited, enough were in attendance to make a brave show. Inside the hall, Haydon's friends John Keats and William Hazlitt were rejoicing in a corner. Then entered the Persian ambassador and his suite. "His fine manly person and black beard, with his splendid dress, made a prodigious show, and he said, in good English and in a loud voice, 'I like the elbow of soldier.'"

But the climax of that great day was the majestic entry of Mrs. Siddons. The room fell silent. Mrs. Siddons addressed herself to the painting hung most conspicuously—*Christ's Entry*. "After a few minutes," Haydon recounted, "Sir George Beaumont, who was extremely anxious, said in a very delicate manner: 'How do you like the Christ?' Everybody listened for her reply. After a moment, in a deep, loud, tragic tone she said: 'It is completely successful.'"

That did it: Haydon's fortune was, for the moment, made. Not only had the legendary Tragic Muse of Reynolds's portrait given her weighty approval; Sir Walter Scott was in town, and since he and Haydon were both friends of Daniel Terry, they dined together one evening. The next morning, before the Egyptian Hall's doors were opened, the author of *Waverley* was found patiently sitting on the steps outside. His enthusiastic attendance, too, must have been well publicized. The result was that Haydon ended up with £1,547 8s. gate receipts (at a shilling a head, that meant 30,948 visitors) and, after all expenses were paid, a profit of £1,298 2s. Bullock got, in addition to his £300 of rent, an incalculable amount of free advertising of the choicest kind for his exhibition hall.

The Egyptian Hall's prestige remained high the next year when an odd stroke of luck determined that it be occupied by, of all things, a sensational exhibition of Egyptian art and artifacts. The story behind this show was as romantic, in its way, as the exhibition itself.[30] Giovanni Battista Belzoni was a native of Padua who wandered through England during the years of the Napoleonic Wars as a sideshow giant, strong man, and conjuror; he finished as a national legend in the Samuel Smiles tradition. The story of his life was set forth in

72. Giovanni Battista Belzoni (unsigned, undated engraving).

Except for a trip to the Iberian Peninsula in 1812, Belzoni remained in England until the war ended in 1815, when he returned to the continent and thence to Egypt, his mission being to sell Muhammad Ali Pasha a new type of waterwheel to irrigate his parched country. Muhammad Ali proved not to be interested, but Belzoni, stranded, had a brilliant idea, not the least recommendation of which was its strong appeal to British patriotism. In these years, as the presses poured forth a constant stream of works written by members of Napoleon's "army of savants" who had accomplished a great deal of field work during the French occupation of Egypt, Britain had nothing equivalent to show by way of cultural ploughshares. Whatever ambition her scholars had to rival the French as Egyptologists had been frustrated by the fact that her own invasion of the country had lasted for only a few months in 1807. Now that peace had come, Belzoni successfully proposed to the British consul that he be deputed to claim for England and bring down from Thebes the famous colossal head of Rameses II. From this initial scheme, the project broadened so far that in the next three years Belzoni was engaged in a series of intensive explorations and excavations which resulted in the discovery of the buried temple of Abu Simbel and six royal tombs in the Valley of the Kings, the opening of the second pyramid, and the discovery of the lost city of Berenice—the most impressive accomplishment of any single Egyptologist up to that time.

Belzoni brought his accumulated treasures to London in 1820. The perfect site for their display was already in existence in Piccadilly, suitably named and endowed with a façade which advertised the nature of the show so faithfully that no words were necessary. It was as if the Egyptian Hall had been built expressly for Belzoni. To this happy accident the gods of the pharaohs added other gifts. Belzoni had paved the way for his exhibition by publishing soon after his arrival his *Narrative of the Operations and Recent Discoveries within the Pyramids, Temples, Tombs, and Excavations, in Egypt and Nubia; and of a Journey to the Coast of the Red Sea, in Search of the Ancient Berenice; and Another to the Oasis of Jupiter Ammon.* Before the public opening on 1 May 1821 a private preview was held, the guest list having been vetted by Belzoni's publisher, John Murray, who had the power to invite the cream of society and the intelligentsia. They came, they spread the word (assisted by the favorable reviews Belzoni's book was receiving), and the show at the Egyptian Hall was an immediate success—helped in some measure by the fact that more important people than usual

such inspirational works as George Lillie Craik's *The Pursuit of Knowledge under Difficulties,* Thomas Cooper's *The Triumphs of Perseverance,* and a best-selling children's book which went into at least nine editions between 1821 and 1841, Sarah Atkins's *Fruits of Enterprize Exhibited in the Travels of Belzoni in Egypt and Nubia.* "The once starving mountebank," Dickens later wrote, "became one of the most illustrious men in Europe!—an encouraging example to those, who have not only stout heads to project, but stout hearts to execute."

Belzoni was magnificently proportioned, superhumanly strong, and, said Sir Walter Scott, "the handsomest man (for a giant) I ever saw." At Sadler's Wells during his years as a performer this "Patagonian Sampson," as he was billed,* donned an iron frame on which ten or a dozen members of the company would climb. Holding a flag in each hand, he would then walk about the stage, carrying this "huge human candelabrum" weighing about three quarters of a ton. A versatile theatrical craftsman, he also devised scenic effects with fountains and cascades of water.

* Thanks to stories brought back by a number of early travelers, it was widely believed that the Patagonians were a race of giants; cf. the reference to "the giant fair ones of Patagonia" in Goldsmith's *The Citizen of the World,* letter 114.

were in town for the coronation of George IV. On the first day there were 1,900 visitors at half a crown each.

Belzoni had doubtless seen Bullock's imaginatively installed natural history display in these same rooms, and his own exhibition excelled it in brilliance. "Every eye, we think," said the *Times,* "must be gratified by this singular combination and skilful arrangement of objects so new and in themselves so striking."[31] Centrally displayed, under the dome of the Great Room, was a pair of plaster of Paris replicas, made from Belzoni's wax impressions and colored after his drawings, of two of the finest chambers in the tomb of Seti I. One was of the so-called "Room of Beauties," twenty feet by fourteen, lined with "emblematical representations" of the pharaoh and his gods. "The contours," writes a modern biographer of Belzoni, "were fine and delicately traced, the colours rich and glowing. Deep ochrous reds and royal blues lapped the beholder in a warm tide; bright yellows and greens flamed exotically about him. The low roof and the lamp-light sought to re-create Belzoni's first impressions as he entered the tomb." Beyond this was a replica of a much larger room, eerily resplendent with representations of ibis-headed gods, snakes, demons without arms, mummies stretched on couches, a painted group centering on Osiris enthroned.

Ideally, Belzoni should have reproduced, actual size, the whole of Seti's complex tomb; but since the excavation had been 328 feet long, this would have far exceeded the dimensions of the hall. He therefore settled for a one-sixth scale model, and, in an upstairs gallery, drawings "mounted on canvas frames and arranged . . . so that the visitor could see the whole lay-out of the tomb and follow the sequence of passages and chambers from the entrance to the burial-vault." Elsewhere, skillfully deployed, were hosts of objects of kinds seldom before seen in London, and never in such profusion: idols and scarabs, papyri, lion-headed statues of the goddess Sekhmet, a wax model of the second pyramid along with a cross-section, on a scale of 120:1, showing its passages and tunnels. All in all, it was a dramatic exhibition which did much to spread interest in ancient Egypt and in archaeology at large among the general public. The stir it occasioned foreshadowed, at a great distance of time, that caused by the brilliant display of the treasures from Tutankhamun's tomb in London (1972) and the United States (1976–1978).

In many visitors, to be sure, the lamp of learning burned low. The Countess of Blessington, the famous hostess who sometimes worked as a society journalist,

captured the more frivolous aspect of the occasion in an essay she contributed to the *Literary Gazette*—one of the very few extended attempts ever made to portray the company at a London exhibition.[32] The tone of mild satire which was almost obligatory in social descriptions at this time prevents the piece from being thoroughly dependable historical documentation, but there is a residue of recognizable truth. Schoolboys impishly discover likenesses of one another in the monstrous deities. A governess answers her charges' questions by quoting from the guidebook, "not a word of

73. The Great Hall of the Egyptian Hall (outline etching of the room as redesigned by John Papworth).

which the little innocents could understand." Another child asks what a pyramid is, and is told it is "a pretty ornament for the centre of a table, such as papa sometimes has instead of an epergne." Still another demands of his mama, before a model of the ruins of a temple, what place the water represents, and is told that she thinks it is the Red Sea but in any case not to "ask questions, as it would lead people to think them ignorant." A lady asks her companion whether Egypt is near Switzerland; no, she is told, it is near Venice. Some impressionable visitors are made melancholy by all the funereal trappings and proceed to utter platitudes on mutability and the vanity of vanities. Two vulgar-looking old men declare that "it was all a hum, for had there been such a place, Lord Nelson would have said *summut* about it, in his dispatches." Two ladies of fashion enter, escorted by two exquisites, and all four presumably subscribe to the sentiments expressed by one of the ladies: "Do pray let us leave this tiresome stupid place, where there is not a single thing to be seen worth looking at, and where the company is so intolerably vulgar. I really fancied it was a fashionable morning lounge, where one could meet every soul worth meeting in town, for, as to looking at a set of Egyptian frights, it never entered into my head; I have not heard of Egypt since my governess used to bore me about it when I was learning geography; and as to tombs and pyramids, I have a perfect horror of them."

"It was plain," Lady Blessington concluded, "that they came to the Tomb merely to pass away an hour, or in the expectation of meeting their acquaintances. . . . Wrapt up in their own self-satisfied ignorance, the works or monuments of antiquity boast no attraction for them." This may well have been true of the majority of visitors. But whatever their motives or expectations, enough members of the public paid their half-crowns or, later, their shillings to support the show for well over a year. Early in June 1822 the contents were sold at auction and the exhibition closed a few days later. Hungry for new adventure, Belzoni set out again, this time intending to reach the mysterious city of Timbuktu and explore the equally mysterious River Niger. But within a few months he was dead of dysentery.*

◌⧊◌

In December 1822, six months after Belzoni's show closed, Bullock was on his way to Mexico, a country then in turmoil following the overturning of Spanish rule. It is conceivable that the trip was undertaken with the British government's informal blessing as part of the process by which Britain sought to establish trade and diplomatic ties with Mexico, which few Englishmen had entered during the long centuries of Spanish domination. (Britain would officially recognize the new Mexican republic in December 1824.)

While Bullock was at sea, however, war had broken out between the incumbent Imperialists and the insurgent Republicans. Upon arriving at Vera Cruz, fearing that the lives of strangers like himself were in danger, Bullock obtained an interview with Santa Anna, the Republican general. Accepting Bullock's assurance that his mission was "solely to acquire scientific information," the soldier guaranteed his safety. Thus welcomed, Bullock spent the next six months traveling widely in the country. The high point of his stay came when the Mexican congress ceded to him a flooded silver mine, which he had repaired by pumps and machinery brought down from the United States and from which he was said to have made a substantial fortune.[33]

Bullock returned to Piccadilly in November 1823 with a rich haul of exhibits: casts of Montezuma's calendar stone, original carvings, models of tombs, manuscripts, hieroglyphic texts—a broad sampling of the remains of an ancient and, as far as England was concerned, little-known civilization. To these were added materials representing modern Mexico: life-size and miniature models of fruit and vegetables as well as actual specimens wherever possible; over two hundred species of birds, most of them hitherto undescribed; between two and three hundred specimens of fish; a large collection of minerals; and sketches made by Bullock's son, who accompanied him as draughtsman. Public interest having been stimulated, Belzoni-like, by the publication of his *Six Months' Residence and Travels in Mexico,* Bullock opened his show of Ancient and Modern Mexico in April 1824.[34] The installation had the same technical finesse that had distinguished the natural history museum. In an early manifestation of awareness that the technique of exhibitions was worthy of critical appraisal, the *Literary Gazette* commented: "Bullock is certainly matchless in the office of getting up Exhibitions. He forgets nothing; he procures every thing that can be interesting; he suits the times, and he arranges his materials in a way that cannot be surpassed."[35] Downstairs, on entering, one was confronted with a panoramic view of Mexico City made from the same sketches which Burford would use for his next panorama, and in front of it, "in order to heighten the deception, and to bring the spectator

* In April 1825 his widow exhibited at 28 Leicester Square, the former Hunterian Museum, a new model of the famous tomb, reportedly for the benefit of his aged mother and other relatives in Padua. To help the cause along, Sir John Soane, who had bought for his own collection a precious alabaster sarcophagus which Belzoni had tried unsuccessfully to sell to the British Museum, displayed his acquisition at three benefit soirées at his home in Lincoln's Inn Fields. But both this gesture of assistance and the Leicester Square show failed. The tomb model was seized in behalf of the widow's creditors, a fund was begun in her own behalf, letters were written to the *Times,* and an appeal made to the government, but to no avail. (Stanley Mayes, *The Great Belzoni,* London, 1959, pp. 287–90.)

74. Bullock's exhibition of ancient and modern Mexico
(lithographs by A. Aglio, 1825).

actually amidst the scenes represented, a *fac simile* of a Mexican cottage and garden, with a tree, flowers, and fruit; they are exactly the size of their natural models, and bear an identity not to be mistaken." To live in the hut (during opening hours, anyway), Bullock had brought back with him a young Mexican Indian, supposedly the first member of his race to have visited Europe since the days of Cortez, who would, it was announced, "as far as his knowledge of our language permits, . . . describe the several objects to the Visitors."[36]

After disposing of the exhibition following its Egyptian Hall run (the ancient carvings went to the British Museum, to form the nucleus of its pre-Columbian collection), Bullock returned to Mexico for a time, perhaps to attend to his silver-mining interests, then headed back to England by way of the United States. On his cross-country journey in 1827 he stopped at, among other places, New Orleans, where he visited the "Big Bone Museum" which displayed the alleged remains of a 150-foot "crocodile." He tried to buy the exhibit, but the owner said he planned to take it to Europe himself.[37]

During his subsequent brief stay in Cincinnati, Bullock was captivated by The Elms, a thousand-acre estate, stocked with wild turkey, grouse, pheasant, quail, deer, bison, and elk, which extended two and a half miles along the Ohio River opposite the town.[38] He forthwith bought it from its owner, a Kentucky politician with business interests in Ohio, and conceived the idea of founding a model community there, complete with town hall, churches, library, schools, inns—and a museum. Returning to London, he reprinted for English distribution a promotional handbook for Cincinnati issued the year before and bound up with it a twenty-six-page essay of his own, *Sketch of a Journey through the Western States of North America.* Prefacing the sketch was a "Notice to the Public," which read in part: "The Author was so pleased with the country in the neighbourhood of Cincinnati, and convinced of its eligibility, in every respect, for the residence of persons of limited property, that he purchased an extensive estate with a handsome house there, within a mile of the city, to which he is about to retire with his family. The spot is so beautiful and salubrious, and affords such facilities for the erection of pleasurable dwellings, with gardens to them, that, on his arrival in England, with a survey of the estate, he engaged Mr. John B. Papworth, the architect,* to lay out the most beautiful part of it as a town of retirement, to be called Hygeia."

In 1828 Bullock returned to Cincinnati with his fam-

ily, to settle at The Elms and, he hoped, break ground for Hygeia. Shortly after his arrival he gave a dinner party for another newcomer to the region, Mrs. Frances Trollope, who may well have read his *Sketch of a Journey,* with its account of Cincinnati's prosperous present and limitless future, just before she left London.[39] In her chronicle of her American misadventures, *Domestic Manners of the Americans,* she described what she regarded as the Bullocks' ambiguous situation:

He and his amiable wife were devoting themselves to the embellishment of the house and grounds; and certainly there is more taste and art lavished on one of their beautiful saloons, than all Western America can shew elsewhere. It is impossible to help feeling that Mr. Bullock is rather out of his element in this remote spot, and the gems of art he has brought with him, shew as strangely there, as would a bower of roses in Siberia, or a Cincinnati fashionable at Almack's.† The exquisite beauty of the spot, commanding one of the finest reaches of the Ohio, the extensive gardens, and the large and handsome mansion, have tempted Mr. Bullock to spend a large sum in the purchase of this place, and if any one who has passed his life in London could endure such a change, the active mind and sanguine spirit of Mr. Bullock might enable him to do it; but his frank, and truly English hospitality, and his enlightened and enquiring mind, seemed sadly wasted there.

One must allow, of course, for Mrs. Trollope's conviction that no true English soul could escape being stultified by the raw environment—social and physical—of the Ohio Valley. (She said that the Bullocks' broad beans "grew about a foot high and blossomed, but the pod never ripened.")

On one occasion the Bullocks took Mrs. Trollope to witness a camp meeting in the Indiana wilderness. More to her liking, no doubt, were the frequent balls and receptions at The Elms, where Henry Clay, DeWitt Clinton, and James K. Polk were among the guests. But the closest tie that bound the two temporary expatriates was a common interest in showmanship. It has been suggested that the Egyptian Hall's architecture inspired Mrs. Trollope's choice of a mixed Egyptian and Moorish façade for her Cincinnati bazaar,[40] but that is a minor matter. Much more to the point is, Where did she acquire the expertise that made her the inventive and publicizing genius behind the Western Museum in the town? One is tempted to believe her association with Bullock at least brought it to the surface. Owned by an artist named Joseph Dorfeuille, the museum, founded in 1820, had originally been intended as a serious museum of natural history

* Papworth had been responsible for restyling the "great apartment" of the Piccadilly museum into the "Egyptian Hall" in 1819.

† Mrs. Trollope added on a later page: "I heard another anecdote that will help to show the state of art at this time in the west. Mr. Bullock was shewing to some gentlemen of the first standing, the very *élite* of Cincinnati, his beautiful collection of engravings, when one among them exclaimed, 'Have you really done all these since you came here? How hard you must have worked!'"

and Indian artifacts, but the rivalry of another institution with less lofty purposes had required Dorfeuille to vulgarize his own with a mixture of attractions—transparencies, monstrosities, waxworks (thirty figures in all, including Tecumseh in full tribal dress, and an allegorical group of Washington's death), and that durable fraud the Invisible Girl (Chapter 25), whose polyglot voice was supplied from the cellarage by Mrs. Trollope's son Henry.

It was Mrs. Trollope who concocted, along with Hiram Powers, the future sculptor of the celebrated *Greek Slave,* a spectacle that roundly outdid the Loutherbourgian Pandemonium scene.* Without divulging her part in the conception and execution of "The Infernal Regions," she wrote in her book:

He [Dorfeuille] has constructed a pandaemonium in an upper story of his museum, in which he has congregated all the images of horror that his fertile fancy could devise; dwarfs that by machinery grow into giants before the eyes of the spectator; imps of ebony with eyes of flame; monstrous reptiles devouring youth and beauty; lakes of fire, and mountains of ice; in short, wax, paint and springs have done wonders. "To give the scheme some more effect," he makes it visible only through a grate of massive iron bars, among which are arranged wires connected with an electrical machine in a neighbouring chamber; should any daring hand or foot obtrude itself within the bars, it receives a smart shock, that often passes through many of the crowd, and the cause being unknown, the effect is exceedingly comic; terror, astonishment, curiosity, are all set in action, and all contribute to make "Dorfeuille's Hell" one of the most amusing exhibitions imaginable.

Disinterested eyewitnesses agreed. In that spacious replica of a spot in hell (twenty feet long by ten or twelve wide), the like of which was never seen in London, Mrs. Trollope and Powers had put together a macabre *memento mori,* complete with fire-breathing skeletons, disembodied groans (also supplied by Henry), an automated devil seated at center stage with eyeballs rolling and head nodding affably to the onlookers, and a beautiful child frozen fast in agony to the foot of the satanic throne. This mechanical realization of Dante by the banks of the Ohio became one of Cincinnati's great sights, attracting crowds for over a quarter of a century, and was flattered by imitation elsewhere. John Banvard, for example, exhibited a Missouri version of the Infernal Regions in the St. Louis museum he briefly and unsuccessfully operated before devoting himself to the more profitable commodity of a three-mile-long panorama.

When she turned away from showmanship to mer-chandising, however, Mrs. Trollope lost her Midas touch; her bazaar was a catastrophic failure, and she left Cincinnati, most thankfully, in March 1830. Bullock had no better luck with Hygeia, which never progressed beyond Papworth's plans. The following year he sold Elmwood Hall and 710 acres of his estate for $21,000 and moved his family into a small cottage on another part of the property. In 1836 he sold the remaining acreage and returned to England.[41] He is heard of only twice after that. In 1843 he certified the authenticity of the Napoleon carriage, which the Tussauds had just bought from the carriage maker to whom Bullock had sold it.[42] At an uncertain subsequent date, according to Papworth's son, Bullock occupied a house in Golden Square and was engaged in cleaning and relining a number of European paintings he had found rolled up and stored away "in South America."[43] Beyond these not very useful fragments of information, no trace of his career after the Cincinnati episode seems to exist. This is not only surprising, in view of his prominence between 1809 and 1830, but undeserved, in view of his intelligent efforts to extend the scope of popular knowledge. His friend Jerdan reported that George Canning, the foreign secretary, who was then establishing a chain of British consulates in Latin America, "expressed a hope that the consuls he was despatching to the New World might possess half the information Bullock's Museum could afford them"; and elsewhere Jerdan observed, "Such a man does infinite good. He does not set up as a teacher—a showman, if you like—but he conveys more intelligence to the public mind, than a multitude of pseudo-dogmatists, and even able lecturers and writers."[44] Though we know little of his character, apart from Mrs. Trollope's approval, we have Haydon's enigmatic tribute. Bullock, he averred, was "a fine fellow and loved the game of ruin or of success—Westminster Abbey or victory—as well as myself."[45]

॰३·✸·ई॰

If the site of Bullock's grave is unknown, along with the inscription which would give at least the date of his death, he did have a solid monument which endured past the end of the century: the Egyptian Hall itself. Although he ended his connection with it about 1826 or 1827, when he sold his lease to the bookseller George Lackington, his name was long associated with the strange-looking building in Piccadilly. Nothing that appeared on the London exhibition scene in the

* Both native skill and experience made Powers, then in his early twenties, an ideal mechanical waxwork specialist. When he joined Dorfeuille in 1828 he had just spent six years working in a Cincinnati clock and organ factory, and so he was well equipped to construct and repair the mechanisms that moved Satan and the other figures. When called on to make and remodel the wax figures, he proved to have a special talent for modeling, and this discovery determined his life work. Thus the marble *Greek Slave* may be said to have originated in a waxwork devil.

THE THRONE.

75. The Burmese State Carriage ("Rath") as shown at the Egyptian Hall.

nineteenth century was alien to it. When a later occupant, Albert Smith, explored its cellars in the early fifties, he found, in addition to bulky rolled-up panoramas, "the accumulated rubbish of Laplanders, Egyptian mummies, overland emigrants to California, Holy Land Bedouins, electro-biologists, and Ojibbeways," which "had something Augean in its magnitude."[46] Often the Egyptian Hall housed three, perhaps even four, exhibitions at once, competing for the shillings of men and women seeking aesthetic pleasure (paintings and statuary), instruction mingled with the gratification of idle curiosity (Laplanders and deer, American Indians and wigwams), simple amusement (persons with extraordinary gifts), or an unapologetic morbid thrill (freaks). Rooms in the building were available to any impresario or self-managed attraction, on the way up or down, that could pay a deposit on the rent.

Among its other functions, the Egyptian Hall served, in effect, as a cluster of speculative showcases for the miscellaneous entertainers who worked the London circuit; we find them appearing in Piccadilly either before or after their appearance at such other locations as Vauxhall Gardens (in summer), the minor theatres, and, beginning about the 1840s, the concert saloons that were the precursors of the music halls. One advantage of booking a room at the Egyptian Hall was that the exhibition, whatever it was, constituted a separate attraction: it was not part of a bill, and the receipts belonged to the exhibitor alone. There was, of course, more risk involved. A Barnum, with a General Tom Thumb, could make a fortune; a Haydon in another room, with gigantic paintings, could end up penniless. Nonetheless, it was a risk that the backers of hundreds of different exhibitions and acts willingly assumed.

The roster of Egyptian Hall attractions is a motley potpourri of late Regency and early Victorian entertainments for every taste and every social class.[47] There were the freaks, for example: "A Living Male Child,

with four hands, four arms, four legs, four feet, and two bodies, born at Staleybridge, Manchester"; a pair of Bohemian sisters, joined at the pelvis, whom their exhibitor labeled "the Pygopagi Twins" to distinguish them from the more famous Siamese ones, who had also been shown there; a Welsh female dwarf, forty-four years old, thirty-six inches high; a bearded woman from the lower Alps; and German Lilliputians. There were the performers: a six-year-old pianist and vocalist who offered a program, officially described as a "melange," of dramatic, sentimental, and comic songs in her "Louis Quatorze Boudoir"; the Prague and Tyrolese Minstrels; a troupe of Bayadères (nautch girls) about whom an opera and a ballet, the latter still in the classical repertory, were written; and the Modern Samson, or the Wonderful Fistic Stone-Breaker, who, in addition to the accomplishment specified, could lift five hundred pounds of stone with his teeth.[48] There were clairvoyants, too: one or more in the long line of "Mysterious Ladies," and a "Double-Sighted Scotch Youth" named Louis Gordon M'Kean, who could, it was said, "distinguish colour, read either print or manuscript, tell the hour of the day on a watch, or declare any other fact as precisely as the cleverest sighted person, although his eyes are at the same time completely blindfolded, and his back turned to the object of examination."[49]

There were, finally, the unclassifiables, ranging from a huge Pennard cheese on its way to being presented to the queen to the Burmese State Carriage, or Rath, captured in 1824 at Tavoy, during a brief war with the Burmese. Unlike Napoleon's coach, it was designed more for ostentation than for everyday use. Pückler-Muskau was among its many admirers:

It is crowded with precious stones, valued at 6,000 pounds, and has a splendid effect by candlelight; its canopy-like pyramidal form seemed to me in better taste than that of our carriages. The attendants sitting on it were odd enough,—two little boys and two peacocks, carved in wood and beautifully painted and varnished. At the time it was taken, it was drawn by two white elephants; and 15,000 precious stones, great and small, all unpolished, still adorn the gilded wood of which it is made. A number of curious and costly Birman arms were placed, as trophies, round the spacious apartment, which gave a doubly rich and interesting effect to the whole exhibition.[50]

But despite this open-ended miscellaneity, the full extent of which will be apparent in some of the following chapters, the Egyptian Hall retained a slender thread of tradition deriving from Bullock's pioneer shows. For one thing, it continued to serve as a gallery for the exhibition of large, dramatic pictures such as Haydon's; for another, the Napoleonic association it acquired when the Museum Napoleon and the traveling carriage were shown there persisted. The most memorable of the later Napoleon-related exhibitions occurred in 1843, when the room just vacated by George Catlin's Indian collection was refurnished to represent (according to which paper one read) a wealthy gentleman's library or "a state-chamber of the old palace." In a salon now hung with blue velvet under a massive gilt cornice, its ceiling studded with bees (Napoleon's favorite emblem), was displayed the collection of a man of independent wealth, John Sainsbury, who had spent 50,000 guineas for materials bearing not only on the emperor's personal career but on the whole of French history from Louis XIV downward. Although personal relics of Napoleon were few—one suspects most had been snatched up by showmen long since—there was an imposing inventory of other classes of material: "State Papers and Manuscripts, Marbles, Bronzes, Carvings, Gems, Decorations, Medallions, Drawings, Miniatures, Portraits, Pictures, Prints, Vignettes, Coins, Medals, Books, etc."[51] The Duke of Wellington came to the show and expressed his "surprise and satisfaction" and his intention of paying a return visit. He had plenty of time in which to do so: the collection remained on display for eighteen months, after which it was auctioned off. For some reason this huge assemblage—there were 4,000 manuscripts alone, 2,000 letters of Napoleon's principal generals, 2,500 engravings—realized the wretched price of only £1,500.[52] Bullock had made £35,000 exhibiting Napoleon's carriage.

Freaks in the Age of Improvement

19

In olden times, Museums were, doubtless, receptacles for freaks of imposture, and thus they may have greatly extended popular error: in these days, such tricks are out of the question, and every wonder monger must dread the detective police of enlightened public opinion.

—*Illustrated London News,* 3 April 1847

This estimate of the current state of public credulity was no doubt more true than it would have been, say, a generation earlier. But the fact remained that throughout the first half of the nineteenth century, virtually all the kinds of attractions that had enticed pennies and sixpences from the gapers at Bartholomew Fair and in Charing Cross taverns in times past still prospered. Although doubters may have been more numerous than before, the March of Intellect had not progressed so far as to deprive countless Londoners and country visitors of their credulity and their appetite for human wonders, whether natural or contrived—armless artists, hydrocephalic children, fat or pig-faced ladies, spotted men and women, and so on.

Any apprehension that the new zeal for popular education was robbing such marvels of their livelihood would have been quieted by the appearance at the Royal Bazaar, Oxford Street, in August 1828, in a room adjacent to the British Diorama, of a three-year-old prodigy whom it is tempting to call the Girl with the Napoleon Eyes. Just 127 years after Evelyn marveled at the little Dutch boy with the words *Deus*

Meus and *Elohim* written in his eyes, here was a repeat of the same phenomenon; only the text was different. The daughter of a Frenchwoman who was reputed to have been "deeply moved on some occasion during her pregnancy by a piece of twenty sous" on which the critical inscriptions appeared, this little girl, named Josephine, had the rare distinction of possessing, in her left iris, the words NAPOLÉON EMPEREUR, and in her right, EMPEREUR NAPOLÉON. The letters were said to be colored "almost white, but shot through, like what is called shot silk, by the blue of the crystalline humour." Witnesses said that they could decipher the entire words only with difficulty, but that "such parts as NAP and other separate letters are tolerably obvious, without the slightest aid from the imagination of the beholder."[1] Tout ça change, plus ça reste le même.*

In such respects London exhibitions provided a welcome strand of continuity in the midst of quickening physical and social change. Because so many freak shows came and went without leaving any record except possibly for stray handbills, a complete list would be impossible to compile, and the result in any case would be more numbing than illuminating. Still, some prodigies achieved so much fame—were so vividly in Londoners' minds, if only for a brief period—that they cannot be omitted from any conscientious account of the genuine as well as the fraudulent exhibitions that captivated the public.

There was no lack of giants, whether measured horizontally or vertically. The greatest in terms of sheer

* It was reported a fortnight later that at Manchester a baby had been discovered with the name of its father in one iris and the date of its birth in the other. "We should not be surprised," a paper commented, "to see it become the (inconvenient) fashion for every baby to have its papa's initials at least on one of its peepers." (*Literary Gazette,* 23 August 1828, p. 541.)

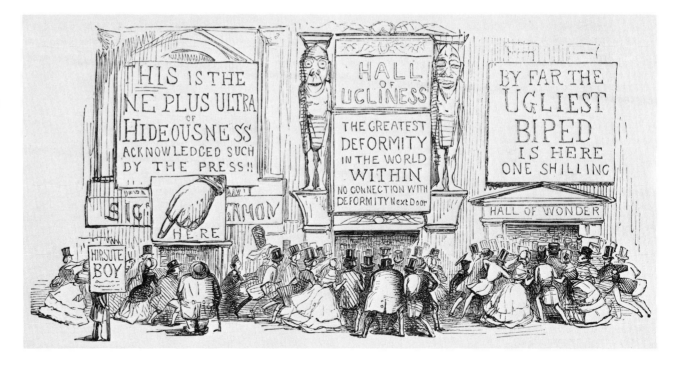

77. "Deformito-mania" (*Punch*, 4 September 1847): "The walls of the Egyptian Hall in Piccadilly are placarded from top to bottom with bills announcing the exhibition of some frightful object within, and the building itself will soon be known as the Hall of Ugliness."

girth and bulk was the celebrated Daniel Lambert: "at the age of 36 weighed above 50 Stone, 14 Pounds to the Stone—measured 3 yards 4 Inches round the Body, and 1 Yard 1 Inch round the leg, 5 feet 11 Inches high."[2] In 1804, before Lambert abandoned his post as keeper of the Bridewell house of correction in Leicester for a wider fame, a writer in *Kirby's Wonderful and Scientific Museum* reported, "When seated, his thighs are so covered by his belly, that nothing but his knees are to be seen; while the flesh of his legs, which resemble stuffed pillows, projects in such a manner as nearly to bury his feet." He was said to be "an intelligent man" who "reads much, and possesses great vivacity" and, less convincingly, to have been active in field sports until the past three years. He was "likewise noted as an excellent swimmer, and as a celebrated feeder of cocks."[3] During his residence in 1806 at 53 Piccadilly, to which he had been transported in a specially built vehicle, he was visited by the cream of London society. Among other distinctions, he was a godsend to the political caricaturists.[4] Rowlandson and others used him as a John Bull figure, personifying the beleaguered nation's indomitable strength and sufficiency in contrast to the meager effeteness of its French adversary.

After his successful engagement in Piccadilly, Lambert returned the next year to display himself in Leicester Square and then went on tour. He died in his

sleep at Stamford in 1809. It took twenty men half an hour to wedge his coffin, six feet four inches long, four feet four inches wide, and two feet four inches deep, into the grave. His tombstone was inscribed:

Altus in Animo, in Corpore Maximus.
In remembrance of that prodigy in nature,
Daniel Lambert, a native of Leicester,
Who was possessed of an exalted and convivial mind;
And, in personal greatness had no competitor.[5]

His survivors evidently had to have their little joke; but then, so did Prince Hal standing over the supposed corpse of Falstaff.

During his first London season, Lambert's fame inspired the billing of an *infant* fat man exhibited only a stone's throw away: "Mr. Lambert in Miniature . . . Master Wybrants the Modern Hercules, who at the age of 4 Months weighed 39 pounds, measured 2 feet round the Body 15 Inches round the thigh and 8 Inches round the Arm."[6] It is not clear from the publicity whether this phenomenon was still living, or what his present dimensions were.

Lambert's adult successors in his peculiar and spacious niche included Thomas Bell, "the Cambridge giant," who occupied the Hog in the Pound tavern, Oxford Street, about 1813;[7] Louis Frenz, a seven-foot four-inch "French giant" in Bond Street, 1822, who was declared, in conformance with his nationality, to

be "most gallant to the ladies, and feels grateful to those who will converse familiarly with him";[8] M. Modaste Mailhoit, "the Celebrated Canadian Giant," five inches taller than Lambert, weighing 619 pounds, seven feet in circumference, with one of his calves alone (three feet four and a half inches) "being larger than a Man's body";[9] and Joseph Gantonio, an Italian with a five-foot-five girth.[10]

Outsize females were almost as numerous. In Piccadilly could be seen, in 1824, a "Swiss giantess" whose beauty, it was candidly admitted, was "of the heavy German caste [and] her limbs thickish or so; but she is altogether well proportioned, about 23 years old, 6 feet five inches high, 24 stone weight [thus 50 percent lighter than Lambert, but then she was a lady], and can lift three hundredweight with one hand!"[11] A twenty-year-old specimen from Pennsylvania, exhibiting at the Royal London Bazaar at an unspecified

date, topped the human Alp by seven inches, but her frame nevertheless was described as possessing "elegant symmetry." She was costarred with "an interesting Female Grecian Child, whose appearance cannot fail to astonish and delight the beholders"—a diplomatic assertion that allowed every patron to frame his own expectations.[12]

At the other end of the scale from the giants, though scarcely outweighing them, were the human miniatures, the most famous of whom, needless to say, was General Tom Thumb, born in America in 1838. His career in England (1844–1846) under Barnum's management has been so often written about as not to require any retelling here.[13] Like Count Boruwlaski, he was a midget, not a dwarf. Three command visits to the royal family and the ensuing adulation by the most fashionable and high-born people in Britain, especially females, turned the talented child into the celebrity of

78. Daniel Lambert: C. Knight's *Bone and Flesh or Iohn Bull in Moderate Condition,* 1806.

ROAST BEEF. and FRENCH SOUP.

Dan! Lambert, who at the Age of 36 weighed about 50 Stone 14 Pounds to the Stone, measured 3 yards 4 Inches round the Body, and 1 yard 1 Inch round the Leg. — 5 feet 11 Inches high.

79. Daniel Lambert: C. Williams's *The English Lamb—and —The French Tiger,* 1806.

the day. (His popularity was due only in part to his winsome minuteness; for the rest, he was, thanks to Barnum's careful grooming, one of the first of what are today called "show business personalities.") As one result, London was visited by a plague of midgets. *Punch,* which gave ample and sardonic coverage to the craze, remarked that "England has taught human nature the exceeding advantage of being little,"[14] and George Cruikshank, borrowing a scene from *Gulliver's Travels,* portrayed "John Bull among the Lilliputians," that worthy being roped to the ground as the General and his rivals relieve his happily complaisant self of watch, purse, and pocket money.*

Among the little people infesting the London showplaces were two brothers and a sister named Mackinlay, who, if they were actually the Highland shepherds the advertising claimed them to be, must have been overshadowed by their sheep dogs; they, too, were invited to the palace.[15] Another was Don Francisco Hidalgo, a forty-two-year-old professional who had been court dwarf to King Ferdinand VII of Spain

for eighteen years. His appearance at the Cosmorama Rooms, succeeding the Highlanders, was heralded by a teaser campaign in the newspapers, but despite his "fine intellectual countenance," his reputed bookish habits, and his ability to speak three languages, he did not succeed.[16] By then London had had its surfeit of intellectual midgets, and the trilingual Spaniard soon gave way at the Cosmorama to a Punjab show.

Bearded women still were dependable attractions. A typical example was the twenty-one-year-old Madame Fortune from Geneva, who was on show in 1852 at Savile House. The beneficiary of "a most brilliant education," she possessed the more valuable occupational asset of a four-inch-long jet-black beard, "as thick and bushy as that of any man . . . which reaches from one eye to the other [and] perfectly encircles the face." Paying customers were invited to tug it to verify its authenticity. The publicity added that "her bust is most finely formed, and leaves not the least doubt as to her Sex." Attended by a Whitechapel accoucheur, whose name, qualifications, and address were given in

* There was also an "Admiral Tom Trump, the Friesland Phenomenon," who was named after an actual Dutch admiral, Von Trump. Ten years old, he reportedly was three inches shorter than his rival, the American general. (Handbill, JJ Coll., Freaks box.)

the handbills, she had given birth only a few months previously to "a child of the female sex" about whose unusual adornments, if any, the handbills said nothing. They extended an invitation to "Fathers and Mothers of Families, and Ladies and Gentlemen who have the direction of Boarding Schools and Academies" to bring their juvenile charges "in order to satisfy their curiosity on the subject of this most Wonderful Phenomenon of Nature."[17]

Possessing a quite different kind of appeal—indeed, her pathetic end briefly engaged the sympathies of all England—was Mademoiselle Caroline Crachami, the "Sicilian Fairy" (or "Sicilian Dwarf," as she was sometimes billed). If Dickens had invented such a story as hers, modern readers would accuse him of intolerable mawkishness; but the documented facts speak for themselves. Exhibited in Bond Street in 1824, the ten-year-old Sicilian Fairy was nineteen and a half inches tall, her feet hardly more than three inches long and her forefingers less than one inch, her waist eleven and a quarter inches around. "She was lively and interesting," reported a journalist who visited her soon after she was put on display; "sat upon a small tea-caddy with infinite grace, and listened to music with evident pleasure, beating time with her tiny foot, and waving her head just as any boarding-school Miss in her upper teens, and conscious of the beauty of her movements, would do. . . . Weak diluted wine and biscuits she relished much, and patted her stomach, saying 'good, good,' as children are sometimes taught to do. For a couple of hours her attention was unrelaxed, and she was observant and animated throughout. She walked a few paces, and expressed many various feelings, of like and dislike, both to persons and things, of impatience, enjoyment, mirth—the latter prevailing."[18] In short, so far as the writer allowed himself to see, a healthy, normal child except for size.

The story given out was that she had been born in or near Palermo to an Italian woman "who, whilst travelling some months before her confinement in the baggage-train of the Duke of Wellington's army on the Continent, was frightened into fits by an accident with a monkey."[19] By great good fortune, more details are available in Mrs. Charles Mathews's memoirs of her husband, who, in his tireless pursuit of sights, went to see "Miss Crackham," as Mrs. Mathews calls her, when she was on exhibition at Liverpool en route to London. Here we have one of the few glimpses which survive of the nineteenth-century show business in an intensely human, unstudied situation. It is a scene from the life of the Crummleses, but a disturbing one,

80. Master Wybrants, "Mr. Lambert in Miniature" (engraving by C. Williams, 1806).

without any of the comfortable geniality that Dickens supplied:

When [Mathews] entered the room, he found her seated on a raised platform, in seeming mockery of regal state, to receive her visiters: she was described to be of foreign birth. The man who attended her, attired in a strange garb, had a tall athletic figure, and formed an admirable contrast to the tiny proportion of his *daughter,* as he called her. . . . The lady was a most disgusting little withered creature (although young), very white, and, what my husband disliked very much in any woman, had a *powdery* look upon her skin. Her voice was pitched in the highest key of childish treble, indeed so thin, and comb-like, that it hardly reached the ear of those to whom she spoke. Her "papa," however, considerably repeated all she said, for the satisfaction of her patrons, adding many particulars not mentionable to ears polite. Mr. Mathews was quite alone with them, for Miss Crackham was not "sought after" by the gentlemen of Liverpool,—an eternal stain upon their gallantry!—and, after some time, during which the man conversed with increased confidence, derived from his visiter's "attentive hearing," my husband startled the foreigner when he spoke of his *birth-place* (Palermo) by asking significantly, whether it was Palermo in the *county of Cork* where he was born? At this inquiry, the man leered at him in an arch manner, scratching his head for a moment, and rubbing his cheek with his hand, as if puzzled

81. Handbill advertising General Tom Thumb, 1844.

how to treat the question. At last, he winked his eye, and putting his finger to the side of his nose, said, "Och! I see your honour's a deep'un! Sure, you're right; but don't *peach*!" And in order to lay my husband under an obligation, that might insure his secrecy, he offered him, *gratis,* what was never allowed to the public without additional fee, the amount of which was announced in large letters over the platform, in the following words: "Those who handle Miss Crackham will be expected to pay another shilling." My husband had forbearance enough to decline this liberality and the opportunity proffered, and never mentioned the ingenious *foreigner's* secret to anybody but his own family, and friends, and acquaintances, &c.[20]

There is enough here for meditation, but the daily and weekly newspapers add more. The author of a series on "The Sights of London" in the *Literary Gazette*—perhaps the editor himself, William Jerdan?—fell abjectly in love with this tiny creature. "I shall visit her again and again," he wrote, "for she is to me the wonder of wonders. I took her up, caressed, and saluted her; and it was most laughable to see her resent the latter freedom, wiping her cheek, and expressing her dislike of the rough chin." This was in the issue of 17 April 1824; a month later (15 May) he described a return bout with her, including particulars of her appearance and behavior. Then (12 June) the stark notice: "Our poor little dwarf is dead. She had been unwell for a few days; and expired on her way home, after enduring the fatigue of receiving above 200 visitors on Thursday last."

The *Times* supplied more details. The Sicilian Fairy had had a cough for some time, and "the untoward changes in the weather during several days of last week" visibly affected her. The newspaper pronounced her—this of course was twenty years before General Tom Thumb arrived in London—"unquestionably the most curious of all the dwarfish candidates for public favour that have visited the metropolis."[21] There was a report, probably deriving, as had Mathews's suspicion, from the name or speech of her exhibitor, a Dr. Gilligan, that the "phenomenon was in reality a native of Ireland." This led the *Literary Gazette* to remark, "The ruse of calling her a foreigner might be adopted to excite public curiosity; needlessly, as we think, for the place of birth could make no difference in the nature of the case. Perhaps it might also be, to a certain extent, to conceal her age; but even in this respect it was unnecessary, for, if only two years old, (and she could not be less), the wonder of so minute a form sustaining the functions of life was sufficiently astonishing."[22] In the case of many London freak shows, such cynicism was well warranted, but this was an exception, as the sequel reveals.[23]

Less than a week after the tiny creature's death in a coach on the brief journey from Bond Street to Duke Street, there occurred an extraordinary scene at the Marlborough Street Magistrates' Court, where two "foreign gentlemen" applied to Mr. Roe, the sitting magistrate, for advice. One identified himself as Fogell Crachami, better known at his present place of residence as Mr. Lewis Fogle. A Sicilian by birth, he was now a member of the "musical department" at the Theatre Royal, Dublin. He was also the father of the

82. *John Bull among the Lilliputians* (etching by George Cruikshank in the *Comic Almanack,* 1847).

child who had lately died. She had resided with him and his wife until a short time ago.

But, having become acquainted with a member of the medical profession, a Dr. Gilligan, that gentleman represented the climate of the country as too cold for the child's constitution, which was then beginning to be rather impaired, and recommended the immediate removal of the child to England, as a more congenial air, and, if that change did not produce the desired effect, ultimately to remove her to the continent. The doctor professed to take such a peculiar interest in the health of the child, that he offered his services to accompany her on her travels, and pay the necessary attentions to her health, provided the parents would consent to his exhibiting her during the short stay they were likely to make in London.

Evidently nothing was said about stopping over in Liverpool, Birmingham, and Oxford to make expenses. At any rate, the parents, whose professional engagements did not allow them to leave Dublin, confided their child to the care of Gilligan, who eventually arrived with her in London and took lodgings in Duke Street, St. James's. There they stayed until the Sicilian Fairy died.

Back in Dublin, her parents had not had word of her since she left in Gilligan's care, and they learned of her

death only from the newspapers. Fogle set off at once for London to take charge of the tiny body. As soon as he arrived at the Saracen's Head, Snow Hill—an inn peculiarly associated with the exploitation of hapless children, for that was where Mr. Squeers was later to recruit prospective victims of Dotheboys Hall education—Fogle went to the exhibition place in Bond Street, where he was referred to the Duke Street lodgings. There he found that Gilligan, his wife, and his brother-in-law, an actor in the Dublin theatre, had decamped with the body, leaving behind, in addition to a bill of £25 for their "splendid suite of apartments," the Fairy's "state bed," and the costume which the landlord, a tailor, had made for her presentation to the king. Gilligan had been heard to say, while she was still alive, that members of the Royal College of Surgeons "had offered, if any misfortune should occur to cause the child's death, to give him 500*l*. for the remains for the purposes of dissection and the use of the college."

Fogle therefore entreated the magistrate's assistance. But that gentleman said with regret that he lacked jurisdiction in the matter. He suggested, however, that Fogle apply to the parish authorities where the child had died, because under the circumstances described, a coroner's jury would have had to hold an inquest. Fogle did so, but found, of course, that the authorities knew nothing of the case, since Gilligan had not reported the death. Fogle and his companion therefore began to make the rounds of the London anatomists. The dean of the profession, Joshua Brookes, told them that Gilligan had offered him the body for £100, but that he had declined. Other "private places of anatomy" and public hospitals yielded no more information. When they returned to Duke Street, Gilligan's former landlord suggested that they try Sir Everard Home, another distinguished anatomist and president of the Royal College of Surgeons, who, it turned out, had been instrumental in having Gilligan show the Fairy to the king. At his house in Sackville Street, Sir Everard said brusquely, "Oh, you have come from Gilligan about the dwarf. The surgeons have not yet held a meeting; therefore I can't say what sum will be voted to him." Fogle, in tears, told the surgeon he was the child's father. Now grasping the situation, Home unbent. He said that shortly after her death, Gilligan had turned up in Sackville Street with the body "and expressed a wish to dispose of it." Sir Everard declined on his own account, but said he would pass along the offer to the Royal College of Surgeons. Meanwhile, the remains could be kept at the anatomical museum in Lincoln's Inn Fields. Gilligan agreed to this arrangement, adding that he was going out of town for a few days but would send a friend around for the "gratuity." Hence Home's assumption that Fogle was the friend.

The distraught father begged to have a last look at his child. Home gave him a ten-pound check and an order to view the corpse at the museum. "But alas!" reported the *Times,* "it was too late. He was shown into a room wherein the first thing that caught his eye was the body of his darling progeny." The dissection evidently was well advanced. "He clasped the corpse in his arms in a manner that excited the feelings of all present, and it was with difficulty he could be prevailed upon to leave the room, which, however, he did, upon the gentlemen promising that nothing further would be done to the infant." Crachami took the Liverpool coach out of town, facing the task of communicating the "dreadful intelligence" to the child's mother in Dublin. We hear nothing more of them or of the absconding Gilligan. Thomas Hood, however, wrote an epitaph of sorts for the Sicilian Fairy when, in his "Ode to the Great Unknown," addressed to Sir Walter Scott, he suspended his flow of banal pleasantries long enough to write,

Think of Crachami's miserable span!
No tinier frame the tiny spark could dwell in
  Than there it fell in—
But when she felt herself a show, she tried
To shrink from the world's eye, poor dwarf! and died![24]

ᴅ᠌ᠵ᠌᠊ᠵ᠊ᠺᴅ

Henceforth the little skeleton was exhibited at the Royal College of Surgeons, access to which was limited to qualified persons, such as surgeons themselves or friends to whom they gave introductions.* A certain portion of London showgoers must have felt aggrieved by being thus excluded, because exhibitions of stunted or malformed children were perennially popular. Sometimes the specimens were living, sometimes dead; in the latter case, the publicity usually suppressed the fact. *Caveat spectator.* Thus, in 1828, a child with two heads was exhibited in Regent Street, admission one shilling for ladies and gentlemen, sixpence for servants and children. The child was, we are told (and can well believe it), "a disagreeable mass in a glass jar of spirits." The following conversation was overheard:

Visitor.	"Is the child alive?"
Show-woman.	"It was alive once."
Visitor.	"Oh, if it is not living, I don't care for it."
Show-woman.	"Only look at it (beginning to uncover the glass); I'm its mother; it was once alive; it is the curusest thing you ever see—quite a curosity, I assure you. I'm the mother of it; never was sich a child seed afore."

But the visitor left, "grumbling at an imposition because the Janus-faced infant was not alive; and if not speaking two different languages, at least sucking two breasts at the same moment."[25] Some people were never satisfied.

Refreshingly, there was no question that the Siamese Twins were alive and well when—the latest and most famous of a line that reached back to the seventeenth century—they went on display at the Egyptian Hall in 1829. Chang and Eng, as they were called, came to England after a prosperous tour of the eastern United States under the joint management of a Massachusetts sea captain and a British merchant in Siam who had contracted with the twins' father for half the profits of the venture.[26] In Bulwer's satirical-sentimental poem, *The Siamese Twins: A Tale of the Times,* we have a description of the sensation they caused in Piccadilly:

From ten, to five o'clock each day,
  There throng'd to see them such a bevy,
Such cabs and chariots blocked the way,
  The crowd was like a new King's levee.

* The skeleton is there still, a silent witness to the bad faith of the surgeons' assurance that "nothing further would be done to the infant," along with the Fairy's tiny slippers, stockings, and death mask. Sharing the same glass case are two "giants'" skeletons—those of Byrne, whose boots and gloves seem all the more huge when laid side by side with her apparel, and of Freeman, an American whose last occupation was tending bar at the Lion and Bull tavern, Holborn, in 1853.

Sir Astley bid high to secure them,
　To cut up when the spring was o'er;
He had, he begg'd leave to assure them,
　Cut up "The Skeleton" before.*

. . . .

In each engraver's shop one sees,
Neat portraits of "the Siamese;"
And every wandering Tuscan carries,
Their statues cast in clay of Paris.
Those statues sell in such a lot,
They play the deuce with Pitt and Scott;
In vain aloft upon the board,
Indignant looks the poet lord;
Unsold, Napoleon now may doze,
And out of joint his conqueror's nose.

Money flocks in, with such profusion,
The door-keepers are all confusion;
"For breathes there one with soul so dead,
Who never to himself hath said,"
When fashion governs all the town,
"Oh, who'd think twice of half-a-crown!"[27]

At the "private levee" held before they went on public exhibition, the twins were examined by leading medical men, whose findings were reported at length in the press. Chang and Eng were joined by "a cartilaginous ligament of several inches in length and in circumference . . . proceeding from the breast-bone, just above the pit of the stomach. . . . [T]he necessities of life have taught them to turn half round, so that they appear side by side, with an inclination inwards, and with each arm about the neck or body of the other."[28] The newspaper coverage stressed the show's wholesomeness: it was not in the least "disgusting or unpleasant," and the twins themselves were lively, cheerful, and intelligent.[29] "They swim across the room with all the ease and grace of a couple skillfully waltzing, and seem never to have any difference of intention or purpose which can give pain to their band of union, by making them draw opposite ways." The "physicians and metaphysicians," as the Times called the experts, had much to chew over, including a paper the twins' "sole medical attendant" read before the Royal Society on the following April first, a date which in this case has no significance. There were provocative questions in profusion, on topics ranging from the anatomical and physiological anomalies involved in the joined bodies to the psychological effects of such unseverable union. Though the twins had "separate purposes, sentiments, and volitions," what about memory, sensation, and the other faculties?[30] The extended public discussion of such unusual problems—one recalls the similar questions Swift had raised a century earlier

about the Hungarian twins—provided the Siamese Twins with unmatchable publicity. It was on this foundation, laid at the Egyptian Hall, that Barnum subsequently built his own expert campaign when he took over the twins' management some ten years later.†

During these years there were a number of such exhibitions which interested the medical profession. If the proprietors had something really genuine to show, they sought public expressions of professional interest because, as always, the cachet of scientific merit would add dignity and box-office potential to what the discerning would otherwise have dismissed as just another fraudulent attraction for the curious and ignorant. But four years earlier (1825) there had been a less fortunate exhibition in a house in Pall Mall called for some reason "the Chinese Gallery" or Saloon. For popular consumption, the show was advertised as "the Living Skeleton," but, as if to justify the high tariff of half a crown, it was also called, more elegantly, "L'Anatomie Vivante."

The specimen on display was a twenty-year-old native of Troyes named Claude Ambroise Seurat, whose mother, rather unexpectedly, was not alleged to have been frightened while he was in the womb, although the publicity did maintain, irrelevantly, that she was short-sighted.[31] A few years earlier, when the political caricaturists were using Daniel Lambert as the colossal model for the well-fed Englishman, Seurat would have been a perfect stand-in for the emaciated Frenchman.[32] Although he was of normal height, five feet seven and a half inches, the circumference of his upper arms was a mere four inches and his waist was less than two feet around. His skin was dry and parchmentlike, and he was shown naked except for a loincloth with holes cut into it "to admit of the hip-bones to pass, for the purpose of keeping it in its proper place." According to one account, "He has a particular passion for music, and even can sing in a faint tone; but conversation must not be kept up for any length of time, as complete exhaustion would be the consequence. When speaking, the rotatory motion through the skin of the neck is perceptible, and the pulsation of the heart conspicuous to the eye."[33] His affliction was diagnosed in The Medical Adviser as "marcores, occasioned by an early obliteration of many of the lacteal vessels and mesenteric glands, or a preternatural deficiency of these vessels and glands, with a consequent early sympathy of the stomach."[34]

A less clinical kind of language was employed to denounce the exhibition. The Lancet, feisty mouth-

* Sir Astley Cooper had recently dissected the "Living Skeleton," whom we are about to meet.

† In the interval they had been toured in the United States and Europe by the sea captain, who had bought out his partner. Barnum acquired them after their proprietor's death and under his management they became one of his most celebrated attractions. Settling between tours on a farm in North Carolina, they married normal-sized sisters and begot a total of twenty-two children. Chang, who had been in bad health for some time and was a heavy drinker, died one night in January 1874, and Eng followed him within hours—dying of shock, the doctors said.

83. Claude Ambroise Seurat, the Living Skeleton (engravings in Hone's *Every-Day Book*, 1826–27).

piece of the medical profession, called it "one of the most impudent and disgusting attempts to make a profit of the public appetite for novelty, by an indecent exposure of human suffering and degradation, which we have ever witnessed."[35] That so wretched a human being should be put on show for gain (including profits from the sale of an "authorized historical" book with three engravings by Robert Cruikshank) offended the lay press as well. A writer in one of the weekly papers leveled a furious attack on this callous undertaking. Shorn of some of his savage epithets, the gist of the complaint was this: "the ingenious owners of this poor sick creature, having six shows-up daily, manage to gather about *thirty pounds a-day,* or nearly 200 pounds a week, or, if they can keep life in so long, *10,000 pounds a-year!*" Their solicitude for the frail source of their livelihood was indicated by their announcement that they would allow him more rest between shows. "Thus he is only required to expose his poor naked frame, in moist or dry, hot or cold,

at one, two, three, four, five, and six o'clock,—to crawl and shuffle round the stage—to have his squalid trunk griped, and his clammy extremities squeezed by hundreds—the beatings of his miserable heart counted, and all his dying symptoms of bone, physiognomy, and distortion commented upon in his hearing, and in terms perfectly clear to his understanding." Perhaps recalling the former profitability of Bethlem Hospital as a London sight, the writer proposed that such exhibitions be opened at hospitals, perhaps at a sovereign a time, with a certain percentage to go to "the Objects or their relatives" and the remainder to the hospitals: the revenue would be sufficient to support "our numerous establishments." Variety could be added by displaying a patient swollen with dropsy alongside one eaten by consumption. It would be a good, highly lucrative show.[36]

To this assault, Seurat wrote—or was represented as having endorsed—a public reply to the effect that, far from being the hapless victim of exploiters, he had been saved by them from a profitless, wandering life of self-exposure in France. The London show was meant to earn him enough money to enable him to "return and live at my ease in my native country"—a rather unlikely prospect, given his condition. He died in London and, pursuant to a transaction concluded before his demise,[37] he ended up as a no longer living skeleton in the museum of the Royal College of Surgeons, alongside the recently acquired Sicilian Fairy.

In the by now familiar pattern of transference from one show medium to another, Seurat's celebrity was promptly exploited elsewhere. Within a few days of his debut in Pall Mall, the very young Douglas Jerrold, just beginning his career as playwright and humorous journalist, wrote a play for the Coburg Theatre entitled *The Living Skeleton,* in which a cadaverous "student of medicine in love and in debt" named Sparerib is asked by a creditor, Sharp, to exhibit himself as a means of getting money to pay off his debt. Sharp observes, accurately, "that the public would rather give half a crown apiece to see a man without flesh than sixpence apiece to put one in good condition." The fun of the play intensifies when "a real skeleton is substituted for Sparerib, and is seized in his name as a victim for the debtor's prison."[38] We need not linger for the denouement.

The Living Skeleton obviously was in no shape to exhibit anything but his miserable self and perhaps croak a faint melody, but it always helped if freaks had some performing talent, as General Tom Thumb did in reasonable abundance, what with his cheerful songs, dances, repartee, and imitations of Napoleon. And then there were, of course, living exhibits whose outward bodies were unremarkable but who were marvelously gifted in one way or another. Fire-eaters were always acceptable entertainment. A female practitioner of the inflammatory art was Signora Josephine Girardelli (1814), who was qualified, it was announced, to bite molten lead, swallow boiling oil, tread on red-hot iron, and wash her hands in sulfuric acid.[39] Another expert, performing at various places in 1818, was Ivan Ivanitz Chabert, "the only Really Incombustible Man," whose advertised repertory was considerably larger than the signora's: he forged a bar of hot iron with his feet and danced on it, drank boiling oil and washed his hands in what was left, put a quantity of burning wax on his tongue and allowed a seal to be taken of it, ate burning charcoal, inhaled the flame of a torch, bathed his feet in molten lead, poured the strongest aqua fortis on steel filings, which he then trampled with his bare feet, rubbed a red-hot shovel on his arms and legs, ate a lighted torch with a fork "as if it were a salad," and poured vitriol, oil, and arsenic into a fire and held his head in the resulting flames.[40] Thus, in part, a handbill. The *Times,* however, added, in the interests of accuracy, that he did not inhale the vapors of arsenic or sulfuric acid as advertised.[41] Skeptics were invited to bring their own chemicals so that there could be no possibility of deception. In a public-spirited postscript to his advertisements, Chabert announced that he would be constantly on call at his lodgings at 27 Leicester Square "to help any Fellow Creature in Danger" at an outbreak of fire.

Chabert's was a popular act. In London and elsewhere "the Fire King" prospered until 1830, when the medical profession, which until then seems not to have been much concerned with his feats, took sudden note of his new prussic acid–swallowing act. Letter writers to the *Times,* signing themselves with such sobriquets as "Chemico-Philosophus," and Dr. Thomas Wakley, the combative editor of the *Lancet,* maintained that if Chabert did in fact have an antidote for so lethal a poison, he should divulge it for humanity's sake.[42] Just before Chabert's announced benefit at his current headquarters, the Argyll Rooms in Regent Street, Wakley prudently inquired at the Bow Street Magistrates' Court what his liability would be if Chabert should die from a dose of the full-strength prussic acid which he, Wakley, proposed to offer him on that occasion. Magistrates' opinion was that Wakley unquestionably would be held accessory to the man's death.

Mr. Wakley, however, having determined to push the Fire King to the utmost lengths, attended with his acid; in doing which he did not take him by surprise, as the application of the former at Bow Street Police-office . . . appeared in all the London newspapers. Mr. Chabert, on being publicly asked by Mr. Wakley if he would swallow the prussic acid he then held in his hand, declined it; but, swallowing his own words, observed, that he had only asserted on a previous day that he would administer that deadly poison to his two dogs, one of whom should die, and the other be saved by taking his antidote. The truth appears to be, that M. Chabert preferred the acid prepared by himself to any other. In consequence of this evasion, the Frenchman was, after a good deal of skirmishing, forcibly ejected from the room by the incensed audience, who imagined that he had received a quietus, which would deter him from again appearing before the public.[43]

They underestimated his pertinacity, however. This was in early February; and in May, responding to popular demand, though possibly with some reluctance,

84. Signora Josephine Girardelli, "the celebrated fireproof female" (engraving by C. Williams, ca. 1818).

Chabert undertook to vindicate his pretensions. At Cox's auction rooms, St. James's Street—the Argyll Rooms having, with delicious suitability, burned down in the interim—he appeared before an audience consisting largely of medical men. To the accompaniment of continual bickering, one dog was given a dose of prussic acid and promptly expired, after which another dog, similarly treated, was apparently saved from death by a timely administration of Chabert's elixir. The result was something of a stand-off, the doctors persisting in their doubts, and Chabert, for his part, accusing them of trying to pillory a foreigner.[44]

Clearly, Chabert's career had passed its zenith. Some weeks later he was on the bill at the Pavilion Theatre with a fresh addition to his repertory, standing "in a temple of fire, composed of five hundred cartridges, which enveloped him in a complete sheet of flame," from which he finally emerged intact. "It appeared to be the general opinion," said the *Times,* "that there was more show than reality in his majesty's last trick. The exhibition was tolerated by the audience."[45] It is conceivable that his decline from favor—and arrival in New York the following year[46]—was directly traceable to his imprudent addition of dogs to his act. A London public that looked on benignly while stunted children and terminally ill adults were exposed for gain was not inclined to favor the mistreatment of dogs, even if they took their prussic acid with equanimity.

Whatever its current status in scientific thought, the hypothesis of the missing link, which had helped sell the Man Teger, the Black Hairy Pygmy from Araby, and the humanoid animal from Mount Tibet to eighteenth-century showgoers, was still cherished by exhibitors. The 1846 version of that elusive creature caused a pleasant stir when it was put on show at the Egyptian Hall. The advertisement bore all the marks of the master, Barnum, as well it might, for he was behind the show:

Is it an Animal? Is it Human? Is it an Extraordinary Freak of Nature? or is it a legitimate member of Nature's Works? Or is it the long-sought for Link between Man and the Ourang Outang, which Naturalists have for years decided does exist, but which has hitherto been undiscovered? The Exhibitors of this indescribable Person or Animal do not pretend to assert what it is. They have named it the WILD MAN OF THE PRAIRIES; or, "WHAT IS IT?" because this is the universal exclamation of all who have seen it. Its features, hands, and the upper portion of the body are to all appearances human; the lower part of its body, the hind legs, and haunches are decidedly animal! It is entirely covered, except the face and hands, with long flowing hair of various shades. It is larger than an ordinary sized man, but not quite so tall. "WHAT IS IT?" is decidedly the most extraordinary being that ever astonished the world. It has the intelligence appertaining to humanity, and can do anything it sees done, or anything which man or animal can do, except speak, read, or write.[47]

This was a bit much, even for Barnum. As he remarked later, even though John Bull "has a most capacious throat and stomach," the What Is It? was "*rayther* too big a pill for John Bull to swallow."[48] And so it proved.

The advertisement appeared on Saturday, 29 August. Those who immediately responded to it found the creature to be a hairy caged beast, somewhat suggestive of a baboon, uttering blood-curdling yells and eating raw meat, including, it was reported, live rabbits. It was a fearsome animal, to be sure. But on Monday, when a representative of the *Illustrated London News* called at the hall, the cage was empty.

The question of "What Is It?" [he wrote] immediately induced another of "Where is it?" and this led to our asking "Why is it?" and "Who is it?" to all of which we in time found a solution. The man told us that What's his name had been taken ill, and was expected to die; and at the same time a person with whom an arrangement had been entered into for some advertising vans was informed that one of the visitors had given Thing-'um-bob an apple stuck with pins, and that the doctors had been called in, but had said that poor What-d'ye-call-him could not live throughout the day. This was all very painful—to those who believed it; but we were not of them.[49]

His suspicion was corroborated when he opened the *Times* the next morning to find a letter signed "Open-Eye":

Being naturally a bit of a naturalist [wrote this correspondent], and consequently anxious to see the "what is it" at the Egyptian-hall in its first wildness, I arose two hours earlier than usual, proceeded thither in a kind of feverish excitement, paid my shilling magnanimously, and was shown into the sanctum of "the wild man of the prairies." Yes, there "what is it" was with its keeper, playing "toss" with an india rubber ball. Oh, the ghost of Buffon! what was my surprise when, at the first glance, I found "what is it" to be an old acquaintance—Hervio Nano, alias Hervey Leech, himself!

I will not take up your valuable space by relating how Mr. Leech sucked raw flesh and cracked nuts, nor how I volunteered (although "what is it" is very savage with strangers) to go alone into his den, which was refused; but I will tell you how the "wild man," finding his hair dress and the fervent expressions of his visitors too warm, shrank into himself and horse cloth, and went to his kennel to argue with the proprietor on the propriety of returning my shilling. The coin was handed back; and as I suppose Mr. Leech will take an early departure for the "wilds of California" again, I hope he will take the comfortable assurance back with him, that The Times won't let Mr. Bull encourage impostors.[50]

And so, according to the *Illustrated London News*'s fancy, the "Wild Man of the Prairies," having changed into street clothes, "went quietly home to dinner in a cab, and slept that night in his usual second-floor wigwam," and his picture looked sadly down from the posters that had been pasted to the walls of the metropolis.

Harvey Leech was well known to London theatregoers as the Gnome Fly.[51] Born in Westchester County, New York, in 1804, when he was fully grown he was but three feet five inches tall. He had a torso of average size but one leg was only eighteen inches from hip to point of toe, and the other twenty-four. "It seems," a newspaper said in the aftermath of the Egyptian Hall fiasco, "as though the thigh-bones and muscles had disappeared, and the knee-joints raised up to the hips." As he waddled along, his hands touched the ground, in the manner of the higher primates. He evidently was as tough as he was misshapen. "His mode of fighting," according to the same account, "was most original; he used to spring in the air, and at the same instant deal the most terrific blow upon his antagonist's head, so that he was a very formidable combatant." Leech's muscular development equipped him to be a spectacular acrobat. He could follow a speeding horse on his hands and feet and then suddenly spring on its back like a monkey, and he could jump ten feet in the air.[52] After working with several circuses he went on the stage, at the Bowery Theatre, New York, in January 1840, portraying successively a gnome, a baboon, and an enormous bluebottle fly in a production of *Tale of Enchantment; or, The Gnome Fly*, a play that had opened at the Adelphi in London two years earlier. Later he went to London, where his grotesque physique and acrobatic feats were much appreciated. In 1843 he was costarred with his compatriot the giant Freeman in a specially written play at the Olympic Theatre, *The Son of the Desert and the Demon Changeling*. His career might have continued to prosper had not someone, in all probability Barnum himself, had the idea of staining his face and hands, fitting him into a hair suit, and thus transforming him from a Gnome Fly into the Wild Man of the Prairies—for the shortest run in London exhibition history.

"They'd have made a heap of money at it," a sidewalk strong man told Henry Mayhew some years later, "if it hadn't been discovered. He was in a cage,

and wonderfully got up. He looked awful. A friend of his comes in, and goes up to the cage, and says, 'How are you, old fellow?' The thing was blown up in a minute. The place was in an uproar."[53] Who was the spoilsport, Leech's perfidious friend "Open-Eye"? According to a plausible account printed long afterward, it was Carter, the American "lion king" who, in the preceding season (late 1845), had been showing "the largest horse in the world," a 2,500-pound animal named General Washington.* A cotenant at the Egyptian Hall was Barnum's Tom Thumb. When the time for Carter's benefit arrived, he wanted Barnum to let the midget ride his mammoth beast, but Barnum, having plenty of publicity schemes of his own and perhaps loath to give Carter so much advantage, declined. Carter thereupon vowed revenge; and it was he who engineered the fatal confrontation.[54]

This account improves on the eyewitness narrative by asserting that, deaf to the pleas of onlookers and "keepers," Carter actually entered the What Is It's cage. The monster cowered in the corner under Carter's fearless gaze. Then, grabbing its forepaw, he "drew the unresisting creature to the centre of the cage—with one strong tug tore the shaggy skin all down its back and sides"—and out, sheepishly no doubt, stepped the Gnome Fly. Carter's punchline was said to have been: "And now, as you've been living on raw meat so long, come down to Craven Street and have a broiled steak with me." This may well be apocryphal; but it is a certainty that Leech died six months later, whether from sheer embarrassment—Mayhew's strong man said, "It killed Harvey Leach, for he took it to heart and died"—or from other causes is not known. The explanation given by an early historian of the New York stage, that he died "from maltreatment received at the hands of the populace," is pure fantasy.[55]

Some years later (1862), the fate of Julia Pastrana brought to a fittingly bizarre conclusion this parade of early Victorian monstrosities. When exhibited in London in 1857 she was said to have come from Central America, specifically the Sierra Madre Mountains of Mexico. The expansive title of a sixteen-page pamphlet sold in connection with her appearance offers some details of her history that are as untrustworthy as they are irrelevant: "Curious History of the Life, Habits, and Adventures of that Strangely formed Being, and Singular looking Creature, the BABOON LADY, MISS JULIA PASTRANA known as the 'Nondescript,' exhibiting at the Regent Gallery. Her Remarkable Formation, and Mysterious Parentage, and how she was Discovered in a Cave, suckled by her

* The 1845–46 season was an eventful one at the Egyptian Hall. On 11 December 1845, as the giant horse was being led around the room before a large audience, the floor gave way and General Washington's legs went into the apartment below, where the porter's wife was sitting. "She screamed and jumped out of the window, while a clock near her was smashed to atoms by the horse's hoofs." The horse, whose off hind leg was much bruised, was extricated with considerable difficulty. (*Times,* 13 December 1845.) Subsequently a double floor was installed. Late in the following June, two months before the What Is It? comedy, the intramural rivalry between General Tom Thumb and the artist Haydon led to the latter's suicide.

Indian Mother. Dwelling only with Baboons, Bears and Monkeys."[56] This wild girl, discovered, it was said, twenty-one years earlier, had learned polite accomplishments in the household of Governor Sanche, of Sinaloa; before coming to London she had been exhibited in the United States and Canada.[57] Her head was described as being "altogether of the oran outan type." Francis Buckland, a naturalist who had a keen interest in this kind of show, adds more particulars:

She was about four feet six inches in height; her eyes were deep black, and somewhat prominent, and their lids had long, thick eyelashes; her features were simply hideous on account of the profusion of hair growing on her forehead, and her black beard; but her figure was exceedingly good and graceful, and her tiny foot and well-turned ankle, *bien chaussé,* perfection itself. She had a sweet voice, great taste in music and dancing, and could speak three languages. She was very charitable, and gave largely to local institutions from her earnings. I believe that her true history was that she was simply a deformed Mexican Indian woman.[58]

Later Julia Pastrana went to Moscow, where she died. The form in which she returned to Londoners' gaze at the Burlington Gallery, 191 Piccadilly, in March 1862 is matter-of-factly stated in an advertisement in the *Illustrated London News:*

JULIA PASTRANA EMBALMED.—This specimen of modern embalming, by a new and hitherto unknown process, has been most critically examined by many of the first scientific gentlemen in London, and pronounced by them to be the most wonderful and marvellously-successful example of embalming ever recorded. The figure being attired in the costume and placed in the attitude of a danseuse, there is nothing in the Exhibition to offend the taste or disturb the sensibility of even the most fastidious lady.[59]

"As regards the history of the embalmment," says Buckland, "there were some queer stories told"—but he does not repeat them, leaving us with only a description of what he saw at the Burlington Gallery for his shilling:

The figure was dressed in the ordinary exhibition costume used in life, and placed erect upon the table. The limbs were by no means shrunken or contracted, the arms, chest, etc. retaining their former roundness and well-formed appearance. The face was marvellous; exactly like an exceedingly good portrait in wax, but it was *not* formed of wax. The closest examination convinced me that it was the true skin, prepared in some wonderful way; the huge deformed lips and the squat nose remained exactly as in life; and the beard and luxuriant growth of soft black hair on and about the face were in no respect changed from their former appearance. There was no unpleasantness, or disagreeable concomitant, about the figure; and it was almost difficult to imagine that the mummy was really that of a human being, and not an artificial model.[60]

Intently examined, the history of the Victorians' involvement with human freaks is a fair index to certain aspects of their psyche. But the macabre return of Julia Pastrana, the bearded Mexican lady who sang in a sweet voice and spoke three languages, perhaps suggests more than do most such tales.

The Noble Savage Reconsidered

20

All else being equal, in the show business it still was advantageous to ascribe foreign origin to a freak or a specialist in an extraordinary line of work. There did not have to be any causal connection between putative country of origin and a freak's freakishness; Chabert's fireproof appetite had nothing to do with his being from France, Caroline Crachami's stunted growth was not attributable to the fact that her parents were Sicilians, and Chang and Eng's peculiarity was not uniquely Siamese. But at the same time that early nineteenth-century showmen continued to exploit the ancient popular association of physical eccentricity with exotic origin, additional value was attached to human show pieces whose attraction lay not in their individual singularity but in the oddity, physical and behavioral, of the whole race to which they belonged. These successors to Omai, the American Indian chiefs, and the other lionized dark-skinned London visitors were savages who had lost their nobility.

No longer did much aura of sentimental primitivism envelop such people. Instead, besides the perennial interest any strange-looking and -acting human being had for the show-going public, and the proof such creatures presented of mankind's variety, they owed their appeal to a new climate of interest in nineteenth-century England. In the preceding century, what small knowledge of human behavior and primitive culture had been obtained from imported savages remained for the most part unorganized and unscientific, like the knowledge the virtuosi derived from the artifacts they so enthusiastically collected. Now appeared the

first stirrings of what would become, by the late 1840s, the infant science of ethnology, for which, of course, living specimens of barbaric or savage races constituted prime raw material. Simultaneously, the imperialism that accompanied the early *pax Victoriana* was weaving ethnology, geography, and the nation's economic and geopolitical aspirations into a single seamless pattern. One significant result was the founding of several organizations which institutionalized these tendencies, providing scientists and interested laymen alike with symposia in which lands and races beyond the sea could be discussed, and giving travelers and explorers additional objectives and sponsorship. The pioneer African Association, founded in 1788, was joined in the next forty years by the Geographical Society (1830) and newly formed sections of the British Association for the Advancement of Science (1831).

To these surges of interest in several related fields the London showmen responded as might have been expected. In addition to the durable basic appeal of the remote and the strange, they now had working for them the strong feeling in favor of rational amusement. Like the proprietors of certain freaks, but somewhat more plausibly, they could claim that their exhibitions contributed to scientific knowledge.

In the case of the Hottentot Venus from South Africa, the first imported savage to win publicity in the new century, such interest as transcended mere titillation derived from the fact that scientists had long regarded her race as the true missing link. To them, the

Hottentots' low state of culture and their uncouth speech, "a farrago of bestial sounds resembling the chatter of apes,"[1] seemed proof enough of their ambiguous and on the whole unenviable position on the ladder of living creation, markedly below man but a little higher than the animals. The "brutal Hottentot" was the epitome of all that the civilized Englishman, happily, was not. At the same time, however, early English missionaries at the Cape of Good Hope felt an obligation to protect these primitive people against the Dutch settlers, whom they accused of innumerable murders and acts of cruelty toward the Hottentots. The move in 1809 by which they were brought into legal subjection to the British government was one of the events that contributed to what was to become the century-long antagonism between the English and Dutch South African settlers.[2] In 1810, therefore, when the Hottentot Venus arrived in London, the name bestowed on her for show purposes embraced a variety of not always harmonious connotations.

Sartje, to call her for the moment by her given name, was unquestionably a valuable show property. Many years earlier, the theologian Richard Baxter had written a tract memorable, if not for its pious argument, then surely for its title: *A Shove for a Heavy-Arsed Christian.* Sartje was something London evidently had not seen before, a heavy-arsed heathen. She may be said to have carried her fortune behind her, for she was steatopygic to a fault. According to her exhibitor, hers was the "kind of shape which is most admired among her countrymen." It was also, in a way, the shape of shapes to come in England itself. As Mrs. Charles Mathews explained to readers in 1839, the novelty of her figure could be sufficiently appreciated only by those aware of the ideal of feminine beauty prevailing in 1810: "In those days, when *bustles* were *not,* she was a curiosity, for English ladies then wore no shape but what Nature gave and insisted upon; and the Grecian drapery was simply thrown upon the natural form, without whalebone or buckram to distort or disguise it."[3] Sartje's bustle owed nothing to the artifice of whalebone or buckram; it was wholly indigenous. As such, it made her, in effect, a grotesque one-woman beauty pageant, conducted under the most degrading circumstances imaginable.

The daughter of a drover who had been killed by Bushmen, Sartje had been brought by Dutch farmers to the Cape, where she became a servant of one Peter Cezar.[4] After two years, Hendrick Cezar, probably Peter's brother, urged that she be taken to England to be exhibited for a period of years, promising to send her back rich. Permission for the trip was obtained from the governor of the Cape, Lord Caledon, who, it was later said, would not have granted it had he known the purpose of the journey.

Preceding Sartje to London was an army surgeon named Alexander Dunlop, who evidently had bought a part interest in her. Upon arrival he made his way to the Liverpool Museum in Piccadilly, where he offered William Bullock a package deal consisting of a camelopard's (giraffe's) skin and the Hottentot Venus. Bullock, a reputable businessman, declined the opportunity to exploit a fellow human being but subsequently bought the skin at a reduced price.* Upon Sartje's arrival Dunlop, to his subsequent regret when he realized how valuable a property she was, relinquished his share in her to Cezar, who proceeded to put her on exhibition in Piccadilly. Among her visitors was Charles Mathews, to whose widow we owe this scene:

He found her surrounded by many persons, some *females!* One pinched her, another walked round her; one gentleman *poked* her with his cane; and one *lady* employed her parasol to ascertain that all was, as she called it, *"nattral."* This inhuman baiting the poor creature bore with sullen indifference, except upon some great provocation, when she seemed inclined to resent brutality, which even a Hottentot can understand. On these occasions it required all the authority of the keeper to subdue her resentment. At last her *civilized* visitors departed, and, to Mr. Mathews' great surprise and pleasure, John Kemble entered the room. As he did so, he paused at the door, with his eyes fixed upon the object of his visit, and advancing slowly to obtain a closer view, without speaking to my husband, he gazed at the woman, with his under-lip dropped for a minute. His beautiful countenance then underwent a sudden change, and at length softened almost into tears of compassion.

"Poor, *poor* creature!" at length he uttered in his peculiar tone,—"very, *very* extraordinary, indeed!" He then shook hands silently with Mr. Mathews, keeping his eyes still upon the object before him. He minutely questioned the man about the state of mind, disposition, comfort, &c. of the Hottentot, and again exclaimed, with an expression of the deepest pity, "Poor creature!"

I had observed that at the time Mr. Mathews entered and found her surrounded by some of our own barbarians, the countenance of the "Venus" exhibited the most sullen and occasionally ferocious expression; but the moment she looked in Mr. Kemble's face, her own became placid and mild,—nay, she was obviously pleased; and, patting her hands together, and holding them up in evident admiration, uttered the unintelligible words, "Oh, ma Babba! Oh, ma Babba!" gazing at the face of the tragedian with unequivocal delight. "What does she say, sir?" asked Mr. Kemble gravely of the keeper, as the woman reiterated these strange words:

* Presumably he rejected the opportunity on humanitarian rather than showmanly grounds. Three years later he had a chance to display Oliver Cromwell's much-traveled head, and was dissuaded from doing so only by the prime minister, Lord Liverpool. (W. S. Shepperson, "William Bullock—An American Failure," *Bulletin of the Historical and Philosophical Society of Ohio,* 19, 1961, 146.)

"does she call me her *papa?*" "No, sir," answered the man: "she says, you are a very fine man." "Upon my word," said Kemble drily, with an inclination of his head, as he took a pinch of snuff for the first time since he entered, which he had held betwixt his finger and thumb, during his suspended admiration and surprise: "upon my word, the lady does me infinite honour!" Whether his fine face in reality struck the fancy of the lady, or whether Mr. Kemble's pitying tones and considerate forbearance of the usual ceremonies, reached her heart, it is certain that she was much pleased with him. The keeper invited him once more to touch the poor woman, a privilege allowed on more liberal terms than in the case of Miss Crackham, as it was without additional fee. Mr. Kemble again declined the offer, retreating, and again exclaiming in tones of the most humane feeling, "No, no, poor creature, no!"—and the two actors went away together; Mr. Kemble observing, when they reached the street, "Now, Mathews, my good fellow, do you know this is a sight which makes me *melancholy*. I dare say, now, they ill-use that poor creature! Good God! how very shocking!"—and away he stalked, as if musing, and totally forgetting his companion until the moment of separation recalled his recollection.[5]

Kemble was not the only humane Londoner to be revolted by this exhibition. Letters of protest appeared in the *Morning Chronicle* and the *Morning Post,* and on 24 November the attorney-general appeared before the Court of King's Bench at the urging of "a Society of benevolent and highly respectable Gentlemen," the African Association. He rose, he said,

to apply to the Court on behalf of this unfortunate female, who was exhibited to the public under circumstances of peculiar disgrace to a civilized country. . . . [The Association] had every reason to believe, that the unfortunate female in question was brought away from her own country without her consent, was kept here for exhibition without her consent, and that the appearance of compliance which she evinced was the result of menaces and ill-treatment. The object of these most humane and respectable Gentlemen was to release her from confinement, put her under proper protection while she remained here, and restore her to her country by the first conveyance that offered.

The attorney-general presented Bullock's affidavit relating Dunlop's visits to him. There were other affidavits, he said, in which persons who had visited the unfortunate woman offered whatever evidence was necessary "to impress the court with an idea of the offensive and indecorous nature of the exhibition . . . But the details would not be fit for the court." He did, however, read the statement of Mr. M'Cartney, secretary of the African Association, who deposed that he had found the Venus enclosed in a cage on a platform raised about three feet above the floor, and that "on being ordered by her keeper, she came out, and that her appearance was highly offensive to delicacy. . . . The Hottentot was produced like a wild beast, and ordered to move backwards and forwards and come out and go into her cage, more like a bear in a chain than a human being. Deponent was confident, from every appearance, that she was totally under restraint; but from his not being able to converse with her, could only judge from appearance. Those appearances, however, were convincing. She frequently heaved deep sighs; seemed anxious and uneasy; grew sullen, when she was ordered to play on some rude instrument of music." A Dutch-speaking visitor asked her whether she had any relations at the Cape, if she was comfortable here, and if she wanted to go back to Africa; but she did not answer. In addition, said the attorney-general, "she is dressed in a colour as nearly resembling her skin as possible. The dress is contrived to exhibit the entire frame of her body, and the spectators are even invited to examine the peculiarities of her form." As the first step toward a habeas corpus proceeding he therefore petitioned the presiding justice, Lord Ellenborough, to order her to be interrogated in Dutch, unrestrained by Cezar's presence. The request was granted.

Several days later a lawyer appeared before the bench on behalf of Sartje's present management, who had taken over from Cezar. His clients, he said, were perfectly willing that the African Association appoint a trustee to care for the money she was earning. A three-hour examination conducted by representatives of the court had elicited from her the free assurances that she was happy in England, which she admired; that she went out in a coach for two or three hours each Sunday; that she had two black boys to attend her, and would like warmer clothes; and finally, that "the man who shews her never comes till she is just dressed, and then only ties a ribbon round her waist." A notary who read to her in Dutch the agreement under which she had been guaranteed half the profits, testified that "she seemed perfectly to understand it."

The attorney-general was forced to concede that the humane and benevolent gentlemen of the African Association had no case. Admittedly, Lord Caledon had erred in granting permission for the Hottentot Venus to be exported from the Cape, but she "was plainly not under restraint, and the only effect of taking her from her keepers would be to let her loose to go back again." Lord Ellenborough agreed, but warned that any "offence to decency in the exhibition" could be grounds for a prosecution. The case was thereupon dismissed.

This well-publicized attempt to mitigate the Venus's alleged suffering called forth several street ballads. One of them was headed "The storie of the Hottentot ladie and her lawful knight who essaied to release her out of captivitie, and what my lordes the judges did therein." Since it runs to a dozen eight-line stanzas and is not a very favorable specimen of what is, at best, an unambitious genre, a single stanza may fairly be allowed to represent the facetious whole. The petitioner before the "Judges grave" alleged

> That in this land of libertie
>   Where freedom groweth still,
> No one can show another's tail
>   Against the owner's will.
> And wished my Lordes to send some one,
>   To know whether or not
> This rare exhibiting was done
>   To please the HOTTENTOT.[6]

In addition to newspaper coverage of the court hearings and the circulation of penny ballads, the exhibition enjoyed the publicity offered by the caricaturists.[7] By a happy quirk of fortune, the Hottentot Venus was displayed in Piccadilly at the moment when it was anticipated—erroneously, as it turned out—that Perceval's weak ministry was about to be replaced by a coalition under Lord William Grenville. In the 1740s a similar coalition government headed by Henry Pelham had been dubbed (by Horace Walpole) "the Broad Bottom Ministry." Now, inescapably, the phrase was revived in order to capitalize upon the Venus's awe-inspiring attribute. Several satirical prints resulted from this latest conjunction of politics and popular exhibitions; another, no less timely, drew a pertinent analogy between the Venus's contours and the amorphous corpulent mass that was soon to become the Prince Regent.

After her London engagement, the Hottentot Venus was shown in the provinces. In December 1811 she was reported to have been baptized at Manchester under the name of Sarah Bartmann. Then she was taken to Paris, where an animal showman exhibited her for fifteen months, causing almost as great a sensation as in London. There, too, she inspired the humorists; in November 1814, at the Théâtre du Vaudeville, was performed Théaulon de Lambert's *La Vénus Hottentote, ou haine aux Françaises,* a vaudeville in one act.[8] French scientists took a greater interest in her than had their London colleagues. The following spring, in the

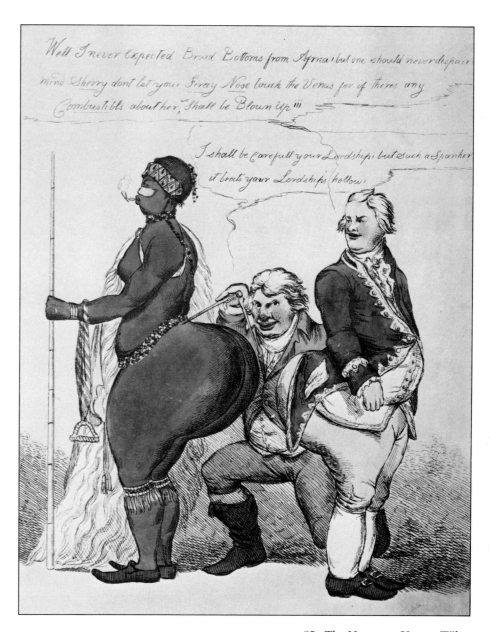

85. The Hottentot Venus: William Heath's *A Pair of Broad Bottoms,* 1810. Lord Grenville is at the right; the playwright-politician Richard Brinsley Sheridan, then a member of Parliament, applies the calipers.

86. The Hottentot Venus: C. Williams's *Prospects of Prosperity, or Good Bottoms Going in to Business*, 1810. Lord Grenville is the figure approaching the Venus; behind him are Lord Perceval, in the gown of the chancellor of the exchequer, and Lord Wellesley, the foreign secretary. The Venus's proprietor is at the right.

interests of the scientific record, she was painted in the nude at the Jardin du Roi and thoroughly examined by the great anatomist Cuvier. These steps were taken just in time, because Sartje was nearing the end of her career. She possessed, in addition to the fondness for trinkets customarily attributed to savages, an even greater one for the bottle. Thus debilitated, she was in no condition to fight the smallpox which, in collaboration with a doctor who mistakenly treated her for "a catarrh, a pleurisy, and dropsy of the breast," killed her at the end of the year.

Cuvier now received official permission to dissect her. Although he paid due attention to her monumental haunches, which he discovered were not composed of muscle but of "une masse de consistance élastique et tremblante, placée immédiatement sous la peau," his chief concern was a peculiarity of her genitalia. Previous medical opinion had held that the so-called *tablier* was a unique attribute of certain African peoples such as Hottentots and Bushmen. Cuvier

found it to be, instead, not a separate organ but an abnormal development of a small structure universally found in females; in witness whereof, he presented to the Académie Royale de Médecine Sartje's own *tablier*, suitably prepared. Thus her unhappy experience of European civilization, which had begun with her whole body going on exhibition in London and her alleged captivity becoming the subject of comic street ballads, ended with an especially intimate fragment of that body being enshrined by the savants and Cuvier's report on it printed in the *Mémoires du muséum d'histoire naturelle* (1817).[9]

Sartje's successor in London, at some remove in time, was Tono Maria, "the Venus of South America" as one paper called her, who appeared in Bond Street in 1822. A Botocudo Indian from Brazil, shown in conjunction with her third husband, Jochina, she seems to have aroused no humanitarian emotions on the part of her beholders, only morbid (and latently sexual) curiosity and disgust. Her attractive peculiarity was the approximately one hundred scars she bore, one for each act of "crim. con." (adultery) ascribed to her. According to the penal code of her tribe, it was alleged, she was entitled to a maximum of 104 such scars, the one hundred and fifth violation being punishable by death. Such glamor as this record invested her with was, however, neutralized by her overall repulsiveness. "Laziness and nastiness," declared one journalist, "are her striking characteristics; and to see her eat is a very emetic spectacle." He described the process in considerable detail, with special attention to the wooden plug which stretched her underlip two inches from the site of her (now vanished) teeth. After eating to satiety, she "lolls back in a fashionable posture, stretches out her feet, fixes her eyes very listlessly on whoever are there, and seems to enjoy a most philosophical luxury." The Venus's less sybaritic husband was reported to be "quite sensible of the value of money, and careful of the receipts of the exhibition. His singing is, for elegance, on a par with his partner's eating, dissonant, loud, and utterly the reverse of musical: it is a mere exertion of the lungs, accompanied by savage expression and fierce and angry gestures." But there was a wholesome lesson in all this. "He whose gallantry thought little of our own fair Countrywomen before, will probably leave the show 'clean an altered man,' and for life after pay the homage due to the loveliest works of creation, enhanced in value by so wonderful a contrast."[10]

D3✳️Ɛᗡ

A much more edifying exhibition this same year (1822), true family entertainment, was the troupe of Laplanders Bullock brought to the Egyptian Hall. Laplanders, like Hottentots, had a special place in the popular imagination, but for a different reason. The uncomplaining, long-lived endurers of a harsh climate and unproductive land, they were, in their frostbitten way, noble savages, whose hardihood was matched by independence and simplicity. A London public brought up on didactic children's books like Thomas Day's widely circulated *Sandford and Merton,* where the Laplanders' austere habit of life was described and their moral virtues celebrated, was well prepared to admire the specimen family—a herdsman named Jens, his wife, Karlina, and their little son—when Bullock brought them to Piccadilly. He had found them in Stavanger in the course of a journey undertaken in his capacity of scientist-entrepreneur rather than of showman. Lapland moss had been discovered on Bag-

shot Heath and at Wimbledon, and someone, perhaps Bullock himself, had got the idea that it would be a profitable venture to domesticate "tens of thousands" of reindeer on English land of no agricultural value. "Excellent venison would be cheaper than mutton in the London markets; furs of the most useful kind would be plentiful; and even in the transport of merchandise, and of persons, a new and extraordinary improvement might be made." Bullock proposed to make a start with a dozen animals he bought in Norway.[11]

It is possible that he did not originally plan to exhibit them, along with Jens, whom he had hired to care for them, and Jens's family; the Egyptian Hall was doing well enough at the moment with Belzoni's Egyptian show. An engaging anecdote told by the playwright Thomas Dibdin suggests that what was to prove another successful Bullock venture came into being by accident. Since quadrupeds happened to be enjoying a vogue on the stage at this moment, Dibdin was commissioned to write for the Haymarket Theatre a two-act afterpiece featuring a herd of reindeer. Bullock undertook to supply these, as well as the chief human performers, who turned out to be the Lapland family themselves—"a little greasy round man who looked like an oil barrel," according to Dibdin; "his correspondingly beautiful wife, in dimensions like a half anker [wine cask]; and their son, about the height of a Dutch cheese, with a hat on: this trio sang, danced, played the fiddle, and displayed their several accomplishments so as to puzzle me amazingly on this point—how I could possibly turn them to any stage account." But workaday writers for the Regency stage were nothing if not adaptable, and in due course the script was written, the music composed, the dances rehearsed, the scenery painted, and the costumes made from models furnished by Bullock. But just as Dibdin prepared to read the piece to the company, Scott's and Bullock's friend Daniel Terry, then stage manager at the Haymarket, arrived with a letter announcing—again in Dibdin's words—"the melancholy fact, that eight of the reindeer had run themselves out of breath;* gone to that bourn, where they would be employed, according to the northern mythology, to draw the shadowy sledges of departed Scandinavian heroes; and (to descend from the romantic fictions of the Edda to plain truth) that the projected piece must be laid aside, and all preparations postponed *sine die,* or, at least, till the arrival of a fresh importation of large horns and long legs from Lapland: the little round man, wife, and child, were, in the mean time, to drive

* According to an independent source, the demise of the animals occurred at Gravesend, where they fell victims to bureaucracy. When Bullock presented the dozen deer for entry into the country, the customs officials were unable to find reindeer in their tariff schedule and therefore felt obliged to send to London for guidance. Bullock offered to pay double the highest rate ever charged for imported animals, including rhinoceroses and giraffes, but this proposal was deemed too irregular to be agreed to. By the time instructions came down from London, eight of the deer had died. (*Literary Gazette,* 1 June 1822, pp. 341–42.)

87. *Mr. Bullock's Exhibition of Laplanders* (engraving by Thomas Rowlandson, 1822).

their sledge round the spacious plains of the Egyptian-hall."[12]

Whether or not the exhibition at the Egyptian Hall was a consequence of the Haymarket fiasco, it was itself a success, taking in £100 a day during the first six weeks.[13] Bullock paid his customary attention to setting. Against a "panoramic" view of snow-covered mountains and ice pinnacles of the North Cape, two tents were erected, one of canvas over poles for summer use, the other of moss for winter. Sledges, snowshoes, weapons, and domestic utensils were ranged around the room.[14] The family made a better impression on the *Times* reporter than they had upon Dibdin. He praised them for "their evident mildness of character, their quick intelligence, their good-natured and easy accommodation of themselves to the novel situation in which they are placed." Inverting the moral his fellow journalist, quoted above, was to draw from the South American Venus only a month later, he added: "By the way, many a lady of rank and fashion might with great advantage take a lesson in manners from the unaffected and graceful self-

possession of the Lapland female." The four surviving deer were "so beautiful, so active, and at the same time so gentle" that they would certainly become "an ornament of parks and pleasure-grounds," though this was not precisely what Bullock had had in mind to begin with.[15] Other news accounts, however, reported them to be dejected and dilapidated.[16]

After reportedly drawing 58,000 visitors in a few months,[17] the Laplanders dropped out of sight for a short while, and when they reappeared in the Egyptian Hall the reindeer were joined by "Wapeti," or "Great Non-descript Elks," which also figured in Bullock's or some other projector's domestication plans. "These extraordinary and beautiful Animals," it was said, "are the size of the Horse, and are so perfectly gentle as to caress their Visitors, and receive food from their hand; they are domesticated by the Indians of the Upper Misuri, whom they supply with the most delicious Venison, and draw in Sledges at the rate of twenty miles an hour. They are now breaking for the Saddle and Harness, and as nine of them have lately been bred near London, not the least doubt remains of their being naturalized in Great Britain."[18] To dramatize their adaptability to social requirements, a "noble-looking male Elk" was harnessed to a two-wheeled carriage and driven around the hall—"a superb hack," said one who had held the reins.[19] Their health and growth were regularly reported in the press through the first half of 1823, particular attention being given to the rapid growth of the males' new antlers.

Although the exploratory voyages of Ross and Parry, which had stirred so much interest from 1818 onward, had occurred on the American side of the ocean, the Lapland exhibition certainly benefited, along with the panoramas and the pantomime, from the vogue of everything associated with the polar regions in those years. By the time a living show with a closer geographical connection with the voyages turned up in London, however, the public appetite for Arctic displays was waning. Thus only the crumbs of patronage remained when a Yankee named Samuel Hadlock, Jr., from the Cranberry Isles, Maine, arrived with a troupe of Eskimos in 1824. The Laplanders proved a hard act to follow at the Egyptian Hall, and as the captain wrote in his diary (an impressive exercise in phonetic spelling), business was so slow that he turned his back on the "great and notid Sittey" and toured the provinces and then the continent. He was later lost while on a sealing expedition in quest of new exhibition material.[20]

D3✳Ɛⅆ

Fifteen years after the Eskimos failed to raise a ripple in London, another American, George Catlin, captured and held the attention of the public for five hectic years. It is quite a story, full of triumphs and reversals, good feeling and bad, honorable intentions and not a little self-seeking.[21]

Catlin was the first great painter of American Indians and a pioneer student and interpreter of their life. Now that the controversy which for so long surrounded his activities and character has ended, his major role in the history of American art and ethnology is universally acknowledged. As Bernard DeVoto wrote, Catlin's "understanding, accuracy, and reliability were attacked during his own time and echoes of the attacks have been repeated down to ours. It is true that he was an enthusiast and even a monomaniac, that he misunderstood much of what he saw, as anyone in his place must have done, that he held some wildly untenable theories, that he never lost his Rousseauian prepossessions about savages in a state of nature, that

he made many mistakes, and even that he falsified or invented some details. Nevertheless, he is in the main reliable and both his books and paintings have been immensely important to American ethnology ever since 1837."[22]

Catlin spent eight years among the Indians of the far West, painting them in all their pursuits and collecting their artifacts in large quantities. Upon returning to the white man's civilization, he exhibited the paintings and the artifacts in Philadelphia and New York to much acclaim, but his attempts to sell the collection to the government failed. He therefore determined to take it to England for exhibition and, he hoped, sale. Smoothing his way was the Honorable Charles Augustus Murray, once a companion of his on the Mississippi and now the Master of the Queen's Household, who booked the show into the Egyptian Hall and added to it the cachet of court interest.

The public exhibition was preceded by a three-day private view, attended, thanks to Murray's court connections, by a large complement of celebrities: dukes and duchesses galore, Wellington of course, the bishops of London and Norwich, "and," Catlin proudly wrote later on, "many others of the nobility, with most of the editors of the press, and many private literary and scientific gentlemen." The show opened to the public on 1 February 1840. Its prospects were distinctly favorable. British interest in the American Indian had been stimulated by Cooper's novels, which were best sellers in pirated London editions, and by the recent travel books of such men as Charles Murray and Captain Marryat. Moreover, there was considerable fear that the Indians were heading toward extinction; and Catlin stressed that in all his work his governing purpose had been to record a native civilization against the time when it would have ceased to exist.

In the middle of the Great Hall was erected a twenty-five-foot-high wigwam from the Crow country at the base of the Rockies, made of over twenty buffalo skins and ornamented with porcupine quills. Ranged about the walls were three hundred portraits of the chiefs of forty-eight different tribes; two hundred other paintings, "comprising," said a handbill, "Landscapes of the Indian Country, the Beautiful Prairie Scenes of the Upper Missouri, Views of Indian Villages, Indian Dances, Buffalo Hunts, Ball-Plays, &c &c. . . . four paintings, containing several Hundred Figures, descriptive of the MANDAN RELIGIOUS CEREMONIES, In which the Mandan Youths are doing Penance, by passing Knives and Splints through their Flesh, and suspending their Bodies by their Wounds, &c. Also a very great variety of Costumes, and other Indian Manufactures and Curiosities."[23] On sale at the door was Catlin's *Notes of Eight Years' Travels amongst Forty-Eight Different Tribes of Indians in America,* which had been published by subscription, the list headed by the queen herself. Later he would also sell, as an elaborate souvenir of the exhibition, his *Hunting Scenes and Amusements of the North American Indians,* with engravings of some of his paintings as well as of artifacts.

During the day, the show was conducted as a purely educational enterprise. Catlin's longtime right-hand man, Daniel Kavanagh, was on hand to answer all questions. It is evident that the clientele who came to the Egyptian Hall show were no better informed than the people who had asked stupid (but sometimes unwittingly revealing) questions in Lady Blessington's hearing during the run of Belzoni's tomb. Kavanagh proposed—the idea unfortunately was not carried out—to post at strategic places throughout the exhibition a list of answers to the hundred questions most frequently asked. The answers included:

"No, there are no tribes that go entirely naked; they are all very decent."
"Mr. Catlin was amongst the Indians eight years, and was never killed during that time."
"The Indians *do* lend their wives sometimes to white men, but it is only their old superannuated ones, who are put aside to hard labour, so it is a sort of kindness all around, and I don't see that there is much harm in it."
"The Indians *don't raise* tea."
"They *never eat* the scalps."
"You *can't come overland* from America."
"Horns on a chief's head-dress have *no bad* meaning."
"The Indians *don't* shave—they pull it out, when they have any beard."
"No, they don't scalp the living—it is not a scalp to count if the man is alive."
"Reason! yes; why, do you think they are wild beasts? to be sure they reason as well as we do."
"Mr. Catlin speaks the English language very well."
"The Indians speak *their own* language."
"The Indians that Mr. Catlin saw are not *near* Chusan, they are 3,000 miles from there, they are in America."
"The Americans are *white,* the same colour exactly as the English, and speak the same language, only they speak it a great deal better, in general."

Three evenings a week, in another room, Catlin put on a performance of what, borrowing the name of a currently popular entertainment, were billed as "Tableaux Vivants Indiennes." Only the middle term of the three was strictly accurate. There was no question that the representations were living; they were, indeed, lively and raucous to a fault. The connotation of "tableaux" therefore was unjustified; and as for the Indians, they were in fact local talent—twenty men and boys (for squaws), probably with Cockney accents but chosen for the presumed Indian cast of their countenances, who, decked out in feathers and war paint, uttered war cries, performed war dances, demonstrated "Indian file," held a war council, and smoked the peace pipe.*

Despite these riches, the show was not a moneymaker. By the end of the first year there had been 32,500 paid admissions at a shilling each. But the rental of the hall was £550 a year, and Catlin's wife wrote home to her parents on 28 February 1841, "much as has been said, London is no place to make money by exhibition. Rent and provisions are just double what they are at home, and the English grudge a shilling more than an American does fifty cents. There are so many shows and exhibitions here, too, that there is no doubt he would do better in some of the large towns."[24]

It was to the larger towns, therefore, that Catlin did move, beginning with Liverpool. But the paintings and Indian gear—there was no live entertainment, as in London—failed to attract profitable audiences or, what Catlin wanted most, a buyer. In the spring of 1843 he was showing at Manchester, on the point of returning to the States, when there arrived in the same city, fresh from America, a showman named Arthur Rankin, with nine genuine Ojibbeways in tow. This was a stroke of luck Catlin immediately took advantage of. What had been lacking all along was the presence of real Indians to add living authenticity to the great collection; the fake warriors recruited from the London pavements obviously had not served that function. Catlin therefore joined forces with Rankin, and after a ten-day run in Manchester the combined show went to London. They cannily delayed their Egyptian Hall opening for a month in order to allow publicity and public suspense to build up and to fit a private performance into the queen's schedule. The fact that the post-show feast at Windsor Castle was laced with champagne brought to an early resolution a problem Rankin and Catlin had anticipated when they laid a strict injunction on their red-skinned charges not to indulge in firewater ("chickabobboo" in the Ojibbeway language, which thereafter became a running motif in Catlin's narrative of his further London adventures among Indians). The braves were given a dispensation to drink champagne on the debatable

* These were not the first bogus living Indians to be seen in London. In 1762, during the excitement over Timberlake's Cherokees, the press reported that three white men, "in Imitation of the Cherokee Kings, and having their Faces painted like them, have been shewn at many of the Places of public Entertainment for the real Indians." (Carolyn Thomas Foreman, *Indians Abroad, 1493–1938,* Norman, Okla., 1943, p. 76.)

88. George Catlin's Ojibbeways seeing the sights of London (*Punch,* 20 April 1844).

ground that it was not spirituous liquor, and henceforth they were allowed to have "an occasional glass of wine or ale." The roistering Cherokees at Vauxhall eighty years earlier could have benefited from so temperate a regimen.

At the Egyptian Hall, the pictures and native objects were eclipsed by the spectacle of Indians performing with immense vigor and total authority routines which their London-bred predecessors had merely imitated under Catlin's direction. The papers praised their warmth, "untutored grace," and lack of affectation, and Rankin was commended for refusing overtures from theatrical managers to put his charges on the stage. One of the high points of the performance was an Indian ball game played under lights—the gas lights of the Egyptian Hall, which, according to one account, hampered the players; they "made more misses than hits."[25]

For a few months, the Indians were all the rage. They received free publicity from the advertising department of E. Moses and Son, whose versified greeting maintained that they had come to London expressly to buy clothing at "the Warehouse by which the whole World appears stirr'd."[26] Whether or not the Indians outfitted themselves at Moses's, they were visible in their native costume at numerous other places in London; Catlin saw to that. In his lively narrative of these years he describes the daily tours he arranged for them to take, painted faces, buckskin leggings, and all, in a chartered omnibus, obviously as much to be seen as to see, and their reactions to the various aspects of London life they observed.

Unluckily, however, the Indians repeatedly got into trouble. Notwithstanding Catlin's stipulation, they seem to have consumed considerable chickabobboo, which led them to precipitate, or at the very least participate in, several disturbances. Worst of all from the English viewpoint, one of them, "Strong Wind," the interpreter, married an English girl who was slated to join the company on the Egyptian Hall platform. The press turned sour, accusing Catlin of exploiting the Indians and Rankin of not keeping a tight enough rein on them. Londoners, initially delighted with these savages and their blood-curdling whoops, now protested against the Wild West atmosphere they took with them everywhere they went. The show itself was far from enchanting everyone who came to see it. Frederic Madden, the Keeper of Printed Books at the British Museum, wrote in his diary on 17 January 1844:

Being so close to the Egyptian Hall we took the opportunity of witnessing the exhibition of the Ojibbeway Indians in Catlin's rooms. One of them was ill, so we only saw eight, viz. the two old men or chiefs, two younger warriors, the interpreter, two women, and a girl. They gave us some of their dances, sham fight, etc. but I must say I was disappointed at the result. The interpreter did not speak a syllable the whole time, and is one of the stupidest looking persons I ever saw. Altogether, it was a very dear five shillings worth. We remained about an hour and a quarter, and as soon as the ceremony of *shaking hands* commenced, we retreated, as I had no ambition to grasp the palm of a dirty savage.[27]

Admittedly, Madden was a pathologically bitter and disputatious man, whose nature did not permit his liking many things; but his reaction to this increasingly shabby exhibition must have been shared by many. Dickens, who was temperamentally prepared to relish any number of things, felt the same way, as we shall see. No doubt the less cultivated side of the Indians became more obnoxious when compared with a more recent American importation who, unluckily for Catlin and Rankin, had taken another room in the Egyptian Hall: General Tom Thumb, the darling of London. "What a contrast," remarked the *Athenaeum,* "is this dapper 'epitome of all that is pleasant to man,' to those fierce gentry the Ojibbeway Indians, who are to be seen and heard on the other side of the staircase!"[28]

To top it all off, declining revenue brought the partners to an acidulous parting of the ways. With three more months remaining on the lease, Catlin advertised at Rankin's behest that the Indians would be on display for only ten more days before going on tour. But when that time expired, Rankin not merely withdrew the Ojibbeways from Catlin's care ("liberated" was the word he used in the press); he promptly put them on show in another room in the Egyptian Hall, advertising that they would be there for two more months.[29] Catlin, left with only the unremunerative paintings and artifacts, renewed his determination to go back to America. But again a new arrival caused him to change his plans. This time it was a delegation of sixteen "Ioways" under the chaperonage of an old acquaintance of Catlin's, G. H. C. Melody. Things seemed to be looking up for the painter, because he had had especially intimate and amiable relations with the Ioways, who, on their native soil, were the Ojib-

beways' mortal enemies. He even was personally acquainted with several members of the present contingent, and his paintings of two of their chiefs had hung in the Egyptian Hall from the beginning of his stay. Now they announced (according to their promoter) that they had "come to dance" at his exhibition.*

The *Times's* tone, when the new tribe arrived in Piccadilly, was at best equivocal. "In personal appearance," it said, "the men are inferior to the Ojibbeways . . . and the women, or squaws, have but little of that sort of female attraction by which men of civilized countries can be charmed . . . Their appearance is between the grotesque and the frightful; but to those who admire the incongruous, even in its disagreeable forms, a sight of them will be a high treat."[30]

Despite this less than consummate enthusiasm in the press, Catlin once more renewed his lease at the Egyptian Hall and, outside business hours, proceeded to expose the Ioways, in turn, to the pleasures and hazards of London life. Like their predecessors, they were treated to the attentions of missionaries, who were no doubt delighted to have the mountain come thus to Mahomet. The Indians received them with tolerance and courtesy but nonetheless reiterated their staunch adherence to their own theology. One morning they breakfasted with Disraeli, who had invited "a large party of the *haut ton* . . . to meet the 'illustrious strangers.'"[31] As the leading mobile London sight of the year, they were taken to visit their permanently rooted competition—the Surrey Zoo, the Tower, and the Polytechnic Institution. En route to these various exhibitions, they amused themselves by keeping count of the gin shops they passed.

Partly to keep them in trim and partly to supply the press with useful items, Catlin took the Indians successively to Lord's cricket grounds, which they called a "prairie," and to Vauxhall Gardens, where, after their run at the Egyptian Hall had ended and they had surrendered their room to General Tom Thumb, they gave afternoon performances against a background of four wigwams.[32] The spectacle of Red Indians encamped and demonstrating their horsemanship on the greensward at Vauxhall, where eighteenth-century beaux had strolled and flirted with the belles of Fanny Burney's set, must have been among the more striking sights of the day. But not even such innovative exposure could forestall the inevitable. Indians—all Indians—clearly had outworn their London welcome. And so, by late autumn, Catlin was touring them in the provinces, where a number of them sickened from the damp climate and the strenuous life they

* It is noteworthy that Catlin's account fails to mention Barnum's main role in bringing over the Ioways. According to Barnum (*Struggles and Triumphs,* I, 399), as compensation to England for its loss of the "Lancashire Campanologists," a troupe of bell-ringers whom he had persuaded to go to America under his management, he "despatched an agent to America for a party of Indians, including squaws. He proceeded to Iowa, and returned to London with a company of sixteen. They were exhibited by Mr. Catlin on our joint account, and were finally left in his sole charge." Catlin's silence concerning Barnum's involvement probably was due to his reluctance to be publicly associated with a showman who possessed none of his—Catlin's—scientific ideals and decorum.

led in the white man's civilization, and two of them died. The survivors then accompanied Catlin to Paris.*

❧✳❧

Although London had tired of Indians themselves, Catlin's charges proved to be the advance guard of a veritable invasion of savages, overlapping and then succeeding the influx of other American curiosities (General Tom Thumb, the monster-mile panoramas) that was the other chief exhibition phenomenon of the forties. In the aggregate, the displays of savages appealed to what was becoming a more and more openly and aggressively displayed aspect of the English character, its complacent assumption of racial supremacy. The several exhibitions were successful, each to its own degree, largely because they fed the national *amour propre*.

The irony is that this effect was quite the opposite of Catlin's intention in the case of his Indians. Part of his trouble, at home as well as abroad, was that he insisted on the social graces, the fundamental morality, the dignity and intelligence which, he was convinced, fully qualified the Indians of the American West for membership in the family of civilized nations. There were sections of the British public, affected by lingering vestiges of the romantic noble savage idea, who were disposed to accept this view, but the more representative Englishman, typified by Dickens, would have none of it. In a noteworthy article titled "The Noble Savage," published in *Household Words* in 1853, he wrote:

Mr. Catlin was an energetic earnest man, who had lived among more tribes of Indians than I need reckon up here, and who had written a picturesque and glowing book about them. With his party of Indians squatting and spitting on the table before him, or dancing their miserable jigs after their own dreary manner, he called, in all good faith, upon his civilised audience to take notice of their symmetry and grace, their perfect limbs, and the exquisite expression of their pantomime; and his civilised audience, in all good faith, complied and admired. Whereas, as mere animals, they were wretched creatures, very low in the scale and very poorly formed . . .[33]

The prejudice Dickens expressed (we shall see additional evidence of it, from the same article, in a little while) was a conspicuous symptom of the general climate of opinion relative to race which had developed by the forties. Although the founding of the Ethnological Society in 1843 would seem to have put such matters on a sound scientific basis, this was not actually the case. The event merely signaled the fact that the general idea of ethnology was increasingly "in the air." But as a scientific discipline it was still obscured by the traditional branches of learning, and even when it was freshly recognized in 1847 by the creation of an ethnological subsection of the British Association for the Advancement of Science, the new group fell under the heading of "Zoology and Botany."

This modest stride toward the formal recognition of ethnology came at a time when the common image of Africa had developed in ways decidedly contrary to the scientific objectivity a learned institution supposedly symbolized. What little reliable and dispassionate information arrived from the field was almost wholly overshadowed by a popular stereotype which the missionary societies had built up across the years and to which the press had given wide circulation. On a somewhat higher level, the discussions of race from scientific, philosophical, and religious viewpoints that occupied the space in serious periodicals formerly devoted to geographical topics had as their leading theme—in contrast to the older view that race was but one among several important factors in determining culture—the conviction that it was the sole cultural determinant. Among the various races in the scale of Creation, according to this body of opinion, there was a wide discrepancy of intellect, and the Anglo-Saxon race was at the very pinnacle of the scale. The old notion of racial egalitarianism and, even more extreme, the view that the savage was actually "nobler" than the civilized European, by now were in utter disrepute, and the new concept of white superiority and nonwhite inferiority, presumably backed by "scientific" evidence, was in the ascendant.[34]

This was the bias which Londoners brought to the successive exhibitions of African and other "savages" in the years around the middle of the century. Although the showmen deemed it advisable to stress the intellectual value of the exhibitions—their contribution to the ongoing discussion of ethnological subjects in the press and the learned societies—in practice their fortune lay not in the scientific implications of the creatures on display but in the vigor with which these creatures confirmed the spectators' prejudices.

The first of the savage procession, after the Indians had vacated the Egyptian Hall, were the Bushmen (Bosjesmen), representatives of a hapless aborigine race who had been the victims in turn of the Hottentots, the Bantu, and the Boers, the last of whom kept them as status symbols and domestic servants— "pathetic elf-like creatures with triangular-shaped faces and slant eyes that gave them a foxy expres-

* Before leaving London, Catlin had been offered £7,000 ($35,000) for his collection, but, still clinging to the hope that it would be bought for the American nation, he refused to part with it. A bill to buy it for $65,000 was laid before Congress in 1846, but no action was taken. Another bill, proposing to buy it for $50,000 spaced over ten years, was defeated by the Senate in 1849. Forced to return to London in the aftermath of the 1848 revolution, he lived an increasingly poverty-stricken life for the next few years, holding an unsuccessful exhibition of his paintings during the Crystal Palace summer.

89. The Bushmen at the Egyptian Hall (*Illustrated London News*, 12 June 1847). The white man is the proprietor who brought the Bushmen to England for a two-year stay.

sion."[35] Two Bushmen children, a fifteen-year-old boy and an unrelated eight-year-old girl, provided "living illustrations" to a paper read before the Ethnological Society in late November 1845, and soon afterward they went on display at the Egyptian Hall.[36] According to the handbills, their respective parents had been murdered by the Kaffirs and they had been rescued by a Boer trader. In the course of each performance, the children first appeared in tribal dress, and the boy did a spear dance; then, "representing a Corporal of the Army," he executed "the Manual and Platoon Exercise, with wonderful precision," and the girl dressed up as a soldier's wife; and in the finale, he was costumed as a gentleman's servant and she as a lady's maid. Little of this seems to have enlarged the nation's store of ethnological information, and perhaps one should not attach significance to the fact that the children from the African bush were costarred with "a fine and curious specimen of the GREAT URSINE BABOON, with some exceedingly rare varieties of the MONKEY TRIBE, from Port Natal."[37] Still, the young Bushmen's routine consisted of the very kind of tricks that monkeys sometimes were taught to perform.

The next year (1847) another, slightly larger troupe of Bushmen arrived at the Egyptian Hall, "that ark of zoological wonders," as one paper called it: the adjective is to be noted. It too was preceded by a bow to the scientific community. A lecture on Bushmen, open to holders of tickets obtainable from a medical bookseller or the office of the *Medical Times*, was delivered at Exeter Hall by Robert Knox, M.D., F.R.S.E., "Corresponding Member of the Académie Royale de Médecine, and Lecturer on Anatomy and Physiology." Though the announcements failed to mention it, Knox was the former Edinburgh anatomist who had won lurid notoriety in 1828 by neglecting to inquire into the provenance of the fresh cadavers that the resurrectionists Burke and Hare were regularly delivering to his demonstration theatre. His discourse, which must have covered a fair amount of ground, was advertised as being "particularly addressed to those interested in the exciting events now going on in South-Eastern Africa, in the Kaffir War, in the great question of race, and the probable extinction of the Aboriginal races, the progress of the Anglo-African Empire, and the all-important questions of Christian mission and human civilization in that quarter of the globe."[38]

The troupe consisted of two men, two women, and an infant, who were exhibited on a raised stage against a painted background of African scenery. Normally, one gathers, they were posed, the mother nursing her "bantling," one man and the other female lying on the floor asleep, and the second man sitting in the corner, smoking. At intervals, however, they went through a variety of "characteristic" performances, punctuated by terrifying yells. No attempt was made to glamorize them; in fact, whereas Catlin had taken pains to preserve the dignity of his savages, the Bushmen's manager seems almost to have gone out of his way to deny his exhibits any connection with the human race. Visitors' first impression on entering the room seems to have been one of revulsion, quickly followed, on the part of newspaper writers at least, by philosophical reflections.

In appearance [said the *Times*] they are little above the monkey tribe, and scarcely better than the mere brutes of the field. They are continually crouching, warming themselves by the fire, chattering or growling, smoking, &c. They are sullen, silent, and savage—mere animals in propensity, and worse than animals in appearance. The exhibition is, however, one that will and ought to attract. The admirers of "pure nature" can confirm their speculations on unsophisticated man, and woman also, or repudiate them, by a visit to these specimens. They are well calculated to remove prejudices, and make people think aright of the times when "wild in his woods the noble savage ran." In short, a more miserable set of human beings—for human they are, nevertheless—was never seen.[39]

These "benighted beings," affirmed the *Illustrated London News,* were "a fine subject for scientific investigation, as well as a scene for popular gratification, and rational curiosity. It was strange, too, in looking through one of the windows of the room into the busy street, to reflect that by a single turn of the head might be witnessed the two extremes of humanity—the lowest and highest of the race—the wandering savage, and the silken baron of civilisation."[40]

Indeed, the Bushmen in particular seem to have administered a powerful boost to the nation's, if not the whole race's, self-esteem. To whatever degree early Victorian confidence had faltered, it was now restored in the spirit of the neurotic hero of Tennyson's "Locksley Hall," which had appeared five years earlier: "I count the gray barbarian lower than the Christian child . . . a beast with lower pleasures . . . a beast with lower pains!" Here, in the disgusting flesh, were examples of the "squalid savage[s]" to whom Tennyson's speaker regarded himself as being inef-

fably superior, and Londoners felt much more content with themselves after looking at them.

In Dickens's view, the Bushmen were the definitive answer to the nonsense, so long mouthed by moral philosophers and romanticists, about the noble savage. In the article already quoted he wrote:

Think of the Bushmen. Think of the two men and the two women who have been exhibited about England for some years. Are the majority of persons—who remember the horrid little leader of that party in his festering bundle of hides, with his filth and his antipathy to water, and his straddled legs, and his odious eyes shaded by his brutal hand, and his cry of "Qu-u-u-u-aaa!" (Bosjesman for something desperately insulting I have no doubt)—conscious of an affectionate yearning towards that noble savage, or is it idiosyncratic in me to abhor, detest, abominate, and abjure him? . . . I have never seen that group sleeping, smoking, and expectorating round their brazier, but I have sincerely desired that something might happen to the charcoal smouldering therein, which would cause the immediate suffocation of the whole of the noble strangers.

In fact, the only (tenuous) connection Dickens saw between these bestial creatures and the human race, properly so called, was their common possession of a trait Dickens almost obsessively dwelt on during one phase of his career: an innate imaginative sense that displayed itself in spontaneous drama. As he wrote on another occasion: "Who that saw the four grim, stunted, abject Bush-people at the Egyptian Hall—with two natural actors among them out of that number, one a male and the other a female—can forget how something human and imaginative gradually broke out in the little ugly man, when he was roused from crouching over the charcoal fire, into giving a dramatic representation of the tracking of a beast, the shooting of it with poisoned arrows, and the creature's death?"[41]

The next African tribe to be represented before this critical London audience was the Kaffirs, who, apart from any ethnological considerations, were topical at the moment; the sixth Kaffir War, this one being between the Cape government and the Xosa Kaffirs led by a medicine man named Umlanjeni, had just broken out. At the Cosmorama Rooms in 1850 an "African Exhibition" featured a Kaffir man, an Amaponda woman, and a Zulu chieftain who had been brought to England by a Mr. Cawood, subject to a bargain made between them and the governor of the Cape Colony by which they would—shades of the Hottentot Venus!—be returned after two years on the English entertainment circuit. "Their behaviour," re-

90. The Africans at the Cosmorama Rooms (*Illustrated London News,* 14 September 1850). The Kaffir man dances before his wife, a member of the Amapondan tribe; the Zulu chief appears to sulk at the right.

ported the *Illustrated London News* (with relief?), "has been unexceptionable; they seem pleased with the change, and enjoy English living, giving preference to mutton as food."[42]

The "savage" theme was soft-pedaled in London exhibitions during the Crystal Palace year, when the emphasis was on the positive—on the progress and amenities of the civilized world. But as soon as the fever of national self-congratulation had subsided the Kaffirs in particular were good business again, the more so because their fellow tribesmen back home were, as the press put it, "giving us more trouble and thought" than any other African race.[43] Of these shows, the most successful (1853) was the one at the St. George's Gallery, Hyde Park Corner. Eleven men, a woman, and a child from Port Natal portrayed "the whole drama of Caffre life" against a series of scenes painted by Charles Marshall. They ate meals with enormous spoons, held a conference with a "witch-finder . . . to discover the culprit whose magic has brought sickness into the tribe," and enacted a wedding, a hunt, and a military expedition, "all with characteristic dances," the whole ending with a programed general mêlée between rival tribes. The *Times* praised

their dramatic talent; "if eleven English actors could be found so completely to lose themselves in the characters they assumed, histrionic art would be in a state truly magnificent."[44] After the performance, the audience was invited to inspect them close-up, shake hands with them, and kiss, stroke, and admire the baby. This proceeding aroused *Punch* to a searing social comment in which the sentimental adulation lavished on the aborigines was contrasted with London's overwhelming indifference to the slum-savages of St. Giles, a notorious rookery in the heart of the city. At the fashionable St. George's Gallery, "Kafirs from Borioboola . . . are delighting the civilised world":

Belles from Belgravia in afternoons come there;
   Thither the fairest of May-fair are whirl'd.
Dowagers craving for something exciting,
   Gentlemen blasé with Fashion's dull round,
Those who find novelty always delighting,
   With those dear Kafirs may daily be found.

And delightful it is there, to see them transacting
   Their business of marriage, and murder, and war;
Delightful to sit there, and know that 'tis acting,
   And not the real thing—which, *of course,* we abhor.

We see in each movement such truth of expression,
    Their stampings and kickings are done with such grace,
That ladies of title e'en make the confession
    That they in the Savage—nobility trace!

But chief the delight, when the acting is ended,
    To go to the room from which CUMMING is gone*
And there inspect closely their figures so splendid,
    And, timidly, even shake hands with each one,
And their dear little baby we smother with kisses,
    And stroke and admire its darling bronze skin,
And think that there ne'er was a baby like this is,
    As a lion of London its life to begin.

It is all very proper to say that a baby
    Might be found nearer home, if we sought for a pet,
And that in the back courts of St. Giles's, it may be,
    Hordes of young savages there we could get:
But, they've no fancy dresses to set off their figures,
    And nothing is thought of an every-day sight;
And "UNCLE TOM"'s roused such a *penchant* for niggers,
    That dark skins must now take precedence of white.

That little dark baby could never have vices
    Like those which degrade us in civilised life;
And though he may p'raps chop his father in slices,
    His country has customs that legalise strife.
But, really—what humbugs call—Civilisation,
    Seems spreading everywhere under the skies,
That soon, I suppose, we shall not have a nation
    To furnish a savage to gladden our eyes.

As the allusions to "Borioboola" and "Uncle Tom" make clear, this poem, published on 23 July 1853, expressed *Punch's* reaction to a dramatic clash of public opinion that had originated the previous year, when the appearance of the first number of Dickens's *Bleak House* (March 1852) had been followed within a few weeks by the first of the many English editions of *Uncle Tom's Cabin*. In Dickens's opening chapters his readers had met Mrs. Jellyby, the philanthropist so devoted to the welfare of the Africans of Borioboola-Gha that she overlooked the sorry plight of her own London family. Surprisingly, however, there is no hint of the Borioboola theme in Dickens's own description, published six weeks before the *Punch* poem, of the Kaffirs at Hyde Park Corner, who, unlike their predecessor savages, mystified rather than repelled him:

Though extremely ugly, they are much better shaped than such of their predecessors as [the Ojibbeways and the Bushmen]; and they are rather picturesque to the eye, though far from odoriferous to the nose. What a visitor left to his own interpretings and imaginings might suppose these noblemen to be about, when they give vent to the pantomimic

expression which is quite settled to be the natural gift of the noble savage, I cannot possibly conceive; for it is so much too luminous for my personal civilisation that it conveys no idea to my mind beyond a general stamping, ramping, and raving, remarkable (as everything in savage life is) for its dire uniformity.

"It is not the miserable nature of the noble savage that is the new thing," Dickens wrote in summing up the whole situation, "it is the whimpering over him with maudlin admiration, and the affecting to regret him, and the drawing of any comparison of advantage between the blemishes of civilisation and the tenor of his swinish life. There may have been a change now and then in those diseased absurdities, but there is none in him. . . . My position is, that if we have anything to learn from the Noble Savage, it is what to avoid. His virtues are a fable; his happiness is a delusion; his nobility, nonsense."[45]

The vehemence with which Dickens excoriated the idea of the noble savage in this piece was due to the way in which events in the past year had completely undercut the point he had meanwhile been making with Mrs. Jellyby's repeated appearances during the serialization of *Bleak House*—that groundless idealization of dirty, subhuman members of other races impeded the far more urgent practice of charity at home. *Uncle Tom's Cabin* had become the most sensational bestseller in English publishing to that date: in one fortnight ten editions appeared, in the first six months 150,000 copies were sold, and in the first year a total of a million and a half. In the spring of 1853 arrived the book's author, Harriet Beecher Stowe—herself, to some minds sympathetic with Dickens's, another ink-stained Mrs. Jellyby—to make a triumphal progress through the country such as had never been enjoyed by queen or saint. Simultaneously with her appeared the Kaffirs. Hence the concurrent, though differently angled, outbursts of *Punch* and Dickens.†

But their adrenalin was wasted. The gush of sentiment at the Kaffir exhibition signaled a dramatic reversal of public sympathy. From fastidious disdain for the African's crudity, as manifested in the response to the Bushmen, the fickle wind of feeling now shifted to the opposite quarter, positive adulation of his simple and defenseless person. The suddenly revived cult of the noble savage gained many recruits in those months, and the Kaffir exhibition and other phenomena related to the *Uncle Tom's Cabin* excitement had much to do with the emerging split in British opinion which, a decade later, would place the sympathies of

* Gordon Cumming's exhibition of African big-game trophies. See below, Chapter 21.

† The Kaffir show was not the only exhibition to figure in the collision between *Bleak House* and *Uncle Tom's Cabin*. In 1853, at 32 Sloane Street, there was a diorama of Christian missions. "Parents," it advertised, "will find this a truly Christian exhibition for their children. Tahiti—New Zealand—The Maori—Island of Tanna—Death of Captain Cook—First Missionary House at Tahiti—Cape Coast Castle—Banyan Tree—Ashanti—Missionary Tombs—The Dungeon, and Rose Madiai." *Punch's* comment (25, 1853, 69) was predictable: "What this Exhibition wants, in order that it may enlist the sympathies of those who are the most earnest promoters of Missionary enterprise, is the addition of a few views of certain savage and heathen regions, the conversation and civilization of whose inhabitants are more particularly important to the British public. The New Cut, Ratcliff Highway, Houndsditch, Whitechapel, and the slums of Westminster, afford fields for the operation of preachers and philanthropists as extensive, as remarkable, and as unknown as the Polynesian Archipelago or the Cannibal Islands." The American slavery issue was the subject of other pictorial shows in these years. At the Cosmorama Rooms, one Rev. W. H. Irwin, for fourteen years a missionary among slaves at an undisclosed location, presented a "narrative panorama" lecture in the course of which he introduced a genuine fugitive slave whose biography, *The Life of Charles Freeman,* was on sale for twopence. (Handbill, JJ Coll., London Play Places box 3.) It was an entertainment at the Royal Victoria Hall (Savile House), however, which squeezed the last drop of sensationalism from this topic of the day: "SLAVERY! SLAVERY! Grand Moving Panorama of the Great African and American Slave Trade, Af-

half the nation with the Union side and those of the other half with the Confederacy.

◁⧁※⧁▷

After the Kaffirs came a fresh importation from the western hemisphere, the Aztec Lilliputians, whose flashy trajectory across the London show firmament in 1853–54, devoid of any controversy relating to the noble savage or the tribulations of Uncle Tom, illustrates how unequal a combatant scientific opinion is when matched against the determination and sheer noise of showmen. It was fitting that at a certain juncture the Lilliputians were advertised in handbills headed "WONDERFUL! WONDERFUL! WONDERFUL! WONDERFUL are thy Ways, Oh, Providence! How wonderful are thy works!"—the very same language the charlatan Katterfelto had used seventy years before.[46]

The so-called Aztecs, a male three feet four inches tall and said to be fourteen years old and a girl two inches shorter and one year younger, arrived in the middle of 1853, after having caused some stir in the United States. Their legend had preceded them. "One can hardly help at first looking upon them," said an American paper, "as belonging to the race of gnomes with which the superstition of former times once peopled the chambers of the earth—a tradition which some have referred to the existence of an ancient race, of diminutive stature, dwelling in caverns, and structures of unhewn stones, which have long since disappeared."[47] The only previous evidences of such a race's having once existed were the sculptures of Yucatan and skulls in Peruvian and Brazilian graves. But here, miraculously, were two living specimens. The American journalist N. P. Willis, who saw them in New York, recorded his impressions:

There was nothing monstrous in their appearance. They were not even miraculously small. But they were of an entirely new type—a kind of human being which we had never before seen—with physiognomies formed by descent through ages of thought and association of which we had no knowledge—moving, and observing and gesticulating differently from all other children—and somehow, with an unexplainable look of authenticity and conscious priority, as if *they* were of the "old family" of human nature, and *we* were the mushrooms of to-day.

Their skin, Willis continued, was of

Indian hue, hair and eyes jet black, the latter, large, brilliant and expressive. The hair is wavy and very beautiful. . . .

They are exceedingly docile and affectionate, and the little girl seemed quite emulous of receiving as much notice as her companion. Their heads are singularly formed—the forehead forming nearly a straight line with the nose, and receding to an apex which it forms with the back of the head—strikingly similar to the sculptured figures on Central American monuments.[48]

The story that accompanied them to England was that they had been discovered in 1849 in Iximaya, an ancient Central American city, hitherto barred to Europeans by the ferocity of the natives.* The discoverers were three adventurers, one of whom, a Spaniard named Pedro Velasquez, had managed to escape with the children after his companions were murdered. This deposition was read before a special meeting of the Ethnological Society, as the subjects of the tale, seated on the table, played with the president's pen, ink, and paper and, it was reported, "exhibited the behaviour of intelligent English children at two or three years of age. They could pronounce only a few English words, which they had been recently taught,—and had evidently no means of communicating with each other by language."[49]

The Ethnological Society's implicit seal of approval gained added luster when the Lilliputians were summoned to Buckingham Palace to meet the royal family. They were off to a promising start. The combination of scientific certification, court favor, and glamor supplied by the romantic story of their affiliation with a lost people and of their personal origins in a forbidden city lent plausibility to the terms in which they were introduced to the public at the Queen's Concert Rooms, Hanover Square: "These unique, strange, and beautiful creatures, so unlike in form and feature to all other members of the human family, have produced the greatest interest amongst the *savans* of the metropolis, and are pronounced to be the greatest living wonders yet discovered, and to have no other alliance in species—traceable by comparative anatomy or otherwise—than to the ancient races whose portraitures are found on the antique Sculptured Obelisks and Hieroglyphical Pictures brought from the ruins of Nineveh, Egypt, and Central America."[50]

Three thousand persons flocked to the Hanover Square rooms in the first two days. Among those early visitors were Professor Richard Owen, the distinguished comparative anatomist, and his wife. The latter wrote in her journal, "Two most extraordinary dwarf children from Peru [*sic*], whose minds seem to go no further than those of ordinary children of two or three years old. These were given out to be about fif-

fecting Land and Thrilling Aquatic Scenes, Views of Noted Places and Picturesque Southern Slavery! British Man of War in Chase of a Slaver! Conflagration of a Slaver! Auction of Slaves. Burial of the Dead. Inauguration Day, Tomb of Washington! Mount Vernon, Underground Railroad to Canada, &c." (Handbill, WCL, StM/LS, I, 181.)

* Central America was a favorite putative source of prodigies in these years. The "nondescript" What Is It? was advertised as having been captured in the mountains of Mexico, and in 1857 the Baboon Lady, Julia Pastrami, would be ascribed to the same region.

teen. I soon attracted the attention of the boy by drawing objects he was likely to know on a piece of paper. He recognised a duck at once, pointing and nodding his head. A cat was not so familiar. They are very strange beings, and the proprietor seems to be making money."[51] Lady Owen's husband, however, found much to doubt in the children's dentition, lack of structural development, and abnormally small cranial capacity, which, according to current anthropological theory, resulted in a stunted intelligence. The conclusion to be drawn was that these alleged representatives of a "lost" race were nothing more glamorous than a pair of severely retarded children belonging to a backward contemporary people.

Thanks to Owen and other skeptics, a cloud soon gathered over this prosperous exhibition. The first point of attack, exemplified by letters in the *Times* on 11 July (only a few days after the children had been introduced to the queen) and in the *Athenaeum* on 16 July, was what one of them called the "fabulous" account of Velasquez's rescue operation. To these, the proprietors—one of whom was a veteran of the entertainment business, an actor and magician named John Henry Anderson, "the Wizard of the North"—responded with a paid advertisement in rebuttal that occupied a column and a half in the *Times*. Immediately after this, in the *Illustrated London News* for 23 July, a brief article considered the case from another viewpoint. Headed "Phrenological View of the Cerebral Organization of the Children Denominated 'Aztec Lilliputians,'" it asserted that "the term 'Lilliputian' does not apply to them. . . . In point of size and shape, their heads are identical with the cast of the head of an oran-outan in the writer's collection. Theirs are not malformed human heads, but Simial heads on human bodies." Because their thick black hair concealed their only deformity—an unnaturally small brain—they were actually rather ingratiating children, "gentle, lively, attractive." But the fact remained that they represented "the zero of moral and intellectual inferiority."

Two days later, the *Times* reprinted a letter the famous naturalist Charles Waterton had sent to the *Leeds Intelligencer*. His main objection to accepting them on their face value, apart from the fact that, as he said, "I really cannot stomach the account given by Velasques de San Salvador," had to do with their language ability. They could understand language even if they could not speak more than a few words. When, on a visit to the exhibition, he had asked one, "Are you a girl?" she nodded; "the boy," he went on, "equally

understood a question of kissing. One would surmise that the faculty which enables them to understand a language would enable them to speak one. How comes it that they have learned nothing of the language spoken by their guardians, the priests?" To this, the exhibitors had a ready reply. The reason that the children did not speak to each other, they said—and that their English vocabulary was limited to forty words—was that "while the children were under the care of the Indian priests in the pagan city of Iximaya, they were kept isolated from the people, and from the other members of their own caste—never spoken to, and never permitted to speak."[52]

These widely circulated aspersions on the little Aztecs' *bona fides*, however, did not diminish the public demand to see them. A month after the show opened, "50,000 of the elite of the metropolis," as the management carefully specified, had visited them.[53] In October they left for an engagement in Dublin. Given the indifference of the public, high and low, to the storm signals in the press, it would possibly be unfair to suggest that their departure was hastened by the belated appearance in the London papers of a report of a meeting held by the Boston Society of Natural History on 1 January 1851. On that occasion Dr. J. M. Warren had read a paper on the Aztec Lilliputians, which concluded: "1. That these children are possessed of a very low degree of mental and physical organization, but are not idiots of the lowest grade. 2. That they probably originated from parents belonging to some of the mixed Indian tribes. 3. That they do not belong to a race of dwarfs, because history teaches us the truth of the doctrine stated by Geoffroy St.-Hilaire, that dwarfs cannot perpetuate their kind." Following Dr. Warren's paper, the Society received a communication from "the Commandant of the Port of La Union, in the State of San Salvador, Central America," to the effect that the Aztecs "were born somewhere near the town of Santa Ana, in that State, of parents, one of whom certainly, if not both, was dwarfed or deformed and imbecile. The Indians residing in the vicinity of Santa Ana are civilized, and centuries ago adopted the Spanish customs and the Spanish language."[54]

Nothing daunted, the management brought the pair back from their provincial tour in time for the Christmas season. The advertisements claimed that 400,000 persons had paid to see them during their previous London engagement and that in a mere three days at the Liverpool Zoo 18,109 persons had crowded in to see the diminutive marvels.[55]

In that same year (1853), still another attraction

* An interesting question was raised in respect to the Aztec Lilliputians which seems not to have occurred to any of the sentimentalists who caressed—physically as well as verbally—the Kaffirs at Hyde Park Corner. In a paper read before the Ethnological Society and subsequently issued as a pamphlet (*The Ethnological Exhibitions of London,* London, 1855), Dr. John Conolly, a well-known medical man and writer on scientific subjects, asked his hearers to consider what would happen to such human exhibits when they had lost their novelty or had "grown too big and troublesome to be carried about. The lives of the Aztecs have been insured by their proprietor, to whom they were sold like sheep; but what support is assured to them? Already they are falling into the class of minor shows, and exhibited in the suburbs. . . . In what workhouse will they end their days? . . . During their long sojourn in this country, it is pitiable to see human beings stared at as mere objects of temporary amusement, to whose subsequent condition all are indifferent." A graver reproach, Conolly continued, was the showmen's utter failure to provide their charges with religious and moral instruction—though, he conceded, the Aztecs, if not the others, were incapable of taking in such ideas. Perhaps "friendly guardians might go back with them, or they might be attached to missions, and protected." It is possible but not provable that the Aztecs escaped the workhouse, at least for the time being. When the Prince of Wales visited Barnum's New York museum in 1860, the "Aztec Lilliputians" were among the curiosities he inspected. (Barnum, II, 515.) But on the same occasion he also saw a Living Skeleton and a "What Is It?" neither of whom could have been the originals, Claude Seurat and Harvey

competed with the Zulu Kaffirs, the Bushmen, two Australian aborigines, and the Aztec Lilliputians. The new arrivals were two juvenile Earthmen, members of a pygmy tribe so called (*Erdermänne*) by the first Dutch settlers in South Africa because they were said to live in burrows in the earth in the same way as did the ground squirrels bearing that name. Actually, the name seems to have been their most questionable attribute, belied as it was by their delicate hands and feet; there was no evidence that they possessed digging tools. Otherwise they appear to have been as represented. The boy of sixteen and girl of fourteen, whose parents were said to have been killed by the Kaffirs, had been taken to Pietermaritzburgh by an agent of a Natal mercantile house, who sent them to England to be educated. Under the guardianship of a Mr. George of Croydon, they evidently had been educated so well that when they went on display in a comfortably furnished room at 71 Quadrant, Regent Street, in May 1853 they were found to speak English with ease but to have "altogether forgotten their own tongue." A deliberate attempt was made to play up the Earthmen's superiority to the Aztecs; "perfect in their kind," it was said, they offered a happy contrast to "the little Central Americans, arrested in their growth."[56] The publicity stressed that they had "lost no time in acquiring the rudiments of European civilization, and they play on the piano and sing in a pretty childish style. . . . They are not set up on a platform to be stared at, and made to perform distasteful feats, but they are in a drawing-room, quite at their ease, so that the visitor literally gives them a call, and becomes one of their society."[57] Shades, this time, of Count Boruwlaski.

When the Aztec Lilliputians returned from their provincial triumph late in 1853, the Earthmen had exhausted the half-crown market. Since they had much in common ("The existence of both Races has always been greatly disputed," ran the new publicity, which was not entirely consistent with earlier claims; ". . . they are unlike any Human beings ever before seen"),[58] the two boy-and-girl acts merged. In a practice otherwise virtually unknown in the London show business, they shuttled between two locales in order to tap two levels of patronage concurrently. Between 11 A.M. and 1 P.M. they were at the Aztecs' former headquarters, the Queen's Concert Rooms, where they catered to the high-class audience at a two-shilling admission charge, with an extra shilling for a reserved seat. Between 3 and 5 P.M. and again in the evening they were billed as "Exhibitions for the Million" at the

Linwood Gallery, Leicester Square, where the scale was sixpence for a place in the gallery, a shilling for one in the body of the hall, and two shillings for a stall. These were gala performances. The advertisements promised that "Miss Clarie Wallworth, Mr. Henry Smith, and Mr. W. J. Morris on the Crystal-Ophonic [undescribed], will assist these human puzzles (concerning whose history, birth, and abiding-place all the world are at variance), forming an Entertainment unlike any before introduced to the London public." It was during this return London engagement, if not earlier, that, as a disgusted witness recorded, "the little [Aztecs] are placed on pedestals, in a supposed temple, to show in what attitude they were found by Velasquez. During that process it is impossible to imagine anything more purely idiotic than the look and actions of poor Maximo, who pulls his large lips, and seems to take no note of anything around him. The scene represents the asserted gods of these asserted Aztecs surrounded by enthusiastic worshippers, and is so patently ridiculous that one knows not whether most to admire the intrepidity of their proprietor, or the amazing gullibility of the spectators."* The latter could buy souvenirs of their gullibility in the form of a shilling *History of the Aztecs,* a sixpenny history of the Earthmen, or sheet music: the *Aztec Polka* (2s.) or Flora and Martin's *Erdmännige's Polka,* dedicated, by permission, to the Duke of Cambridge (2s. 6d.).[59]

Two final troupes of exotic beings fall within our scope, less controversial than their recent predecessors but of some topical interest because they represented a region steadily in the news—the scene of the ongoing search for Sir John Franklin. Early in 1854, mendaciously billed as "the first Natives of the Polar Regions ever seen in London," a trio from the Cumberland Straits, consisting of husband Tickalicktoo, wife Harkbah, and a seven-year-old boy named Harkaluck Joe who belonged to another family, were shown in the Lowther Arcade.[60] They had the honor of being invited to lunch at the deanery, Westminster Abbey, by the dean's son, Francis Buckland. "They were nice, quiet, agreeable people," he recalled, "and were wonderfully struck with the Abbey. Among the monuments, that which most attracted their attention was the figure of a ship; they also fell greatly in love with a marble anchor. I shall never forget their amazement and excessive delight when they first heard the organ's notes rolling along the aisles; the effect was very remarkable upon these poor but innocent people."[61] Two years later, at the short-lived Panopticon, a troupe of Indians from Canada's Lake Huron region—a chief with five warriors, four squaws, and a ten-week-old child—brought back memories of Catlin's redskins, the press commenting, as it had done before the Ojibbeways and Ioways grew tiresome, that "to the artist and ethnologist this exhibition presents peculiar attractions."[62]

But now, by the late fifties, the surge of such exhibitions was over. Londoners' taste for samples of primitive races from the corners of the earth had been abundantly satisfied, and showgoers once more were seeking new sensations, perhaps even new food for thought. Who can tell what reflections the American Indians, the Bushmen, the Kaffirs, and the others stirred in the minds of ordinary beholders? We have Dickens's crisply articulated ideas, but as to the thoughts of those without access to print we can only conjecture. Certainly their reactions were mixed and, in some instances, complicated and even contradictory. Scientific, or what passed for scientific, ideas were inescapably colored by national and racial feeling. As one or two of the press comments quoted above suggest, some spectators may have dwelt upon the indistinct, elusive line that separates civilization from barbarism: a realization to give pause in an era as confident of its own achievement as this one was.

But what invites even more speculation is the fact that this procession of shows passed across the London scene in the years immediately preceding the publication of *The Origin of Species* in 1859. Much scholarly attention has been devoted to the intellectual atmosphere of those years—to the degree and manner in which the English mind was already prepared for the thunderbolt of Darwin's theory. Most of the components of what Darwin formalized as the theory of evolution were abroad in informed circles long before the *Origin* appeared. There can be scarcely any question that the various exhibitions of specimens of other races—so different from, supposedly so inferior to Caucasians—contributed plentifully, in conceptions, prejudices, and stereotypes, to the prevailing climate of those last pre-Darwinian years. Here were excerpts from that scale of Creation whose contents, organization, dynamics, and significance the Darwinian theory was about to revise so drastically. It is not unlikely that at least some of the more thoughtful Victorians, contemplating the Bushmen and the Kaffirs if not the debatable Aztecs, reflected that here, for whatever significance it may have had, they were confronted with possible models of their former selves; or that they murmured with mingled awe and gratitude, "There, but for the grace of the evolutionary process, go we." We cannot know for sure; but to many a mind and sensibility higher than those of the strange beings on display—excluding the frivolous sentimentalists at the Kaffir show—the experience of gazing on such creatures must have induced thoughts too troubling for easy utterance.

Leech being dead long since. Quite conceivably, therefore, the Aztecs Barnum was exhibiting were not the ones who had caused the commotion in London seven years earlier but a replacement pair. In any event, a couple bearing the same title turn up in the London records in 1867, when they were married at the Registrar's Office and held a wedding breakfast at Willis's Rooms, formerly Almack's. (Clipping, GL, Egyptian Hall folder.) One suspects here the devices of a new publicity-hungry impresario, whoever his charges may have been.

The Ancient and the Exotic

21

With the dispersal of the Leverian Museum in 1806 and of Bullock's collection a decade later, the era of museums modeled after the miscellaneous cabinets of the old-time virtuosi ended. Replacing them were commercial shows which, following the precedent set by Bullock's Roman Gallery and Mexican exhibition and Belzoni's Egyptian one, were devoted to a single subject (a nation, a period in time) or, once in a while, to a single object, such as the Burmese State Carriage. In the aggregate, these specialized exhibitions touched on the same fields of interest as had their unsystematic predecessors—ethnology, geography, exotic botany and zoology—but often went beyond them as they reflected new tendencies in public curiosity. There was, for one thing, the broadened sense of history, one of the most influential developments in nineteenth-century culture, which prompted exhibitors to reach into areas of the past not represented in the old conventional collections of "antiquities." For another, there was the expanding geographical interest to which the displays of human beings from remote lands catered; these were now supplemented by separate exhibitions of the *realia*—weapons, costumes, domestic utensils, folk art, religious images and accessories—which such races produced and used.

The enlarging chronological frame in which the modern consciousness was beginning to operate was emblematized by the appearance of a new scientific discipline, paleontology—comparative anatomy with the added dimension of time. Science no longer accepted the larger-than-human thigh bones and teeth cherished from the fifteenth century onward in European churches (and, as we have seen, in London ones) as relics of giants. When large deposits of such bones, sometimes complete skeletons and—most significantly—tusks, were periodically discovered at various continental sites, this hypothesis had been replaced by one that held they were the remains of outsized elephants, or mammoths, that somehow had flourished north of the Alps and even in Siberia. From the 1730s onward, similar bones were also found in North America, and samples of them occasioned much discussion when they arrived at the Royal Society.

In 1801 Charles Willson Peale, erstwhile proprietor of the Philadelphia Eidophusikon and still the enterprising owner of a museum in that city, read in the newspapers of huge bones found two years earlier in a marl pit near Newburgh, New York.[1] Hurrying to the site, he learned that the skeleton, though intact when first unearthed, had been badly damaged when the neighboring farmers and their families who had been invited to join the dig clumsily pulled it out of the clay with oxen. The owner of the land had stacked the broken and disarrayed bones in his granary, hoping, he told Peale, to make a fortune by sending his son on the road to exhibit them. The upstanding museum keeper, it is said, "appealed to his paternal instinct by pointing out that the life of a showman was 'a kind of life very prejudicial to the morals of those who attempted to get maintenance by those means.'" The farmer, accepting his point of view and some cash, gave Peale digging rights, and, equipped with a grant from the American

Philosophical Society, a navy pump, and some army tents, he went to work. In a frequently reproduced painting Peale later illustrated the process by which he drained the swamp with a waterwheel studded with an endless chain of buckets and powered by human energy in the manner of a treadmill. His labors here and at a nearby site produced two mammoth skeletons, the more complete of which Peale took for his museum while he sent his sons Rembrandt and Rubens to London with the other, whose deficiencies Rembrandt had made good by carving substitute bones out of wood.

The exhibition of this skeleton at the Royal Academy's former quarters in Pall Mall in the autumn of 1802, far from prejudicing the Peale brothers' morals, was intended to defray their expenses while Rembrandt attended the Royal Academy school and Rubens, notwithstanding his given name, trained to become a naturalist.[2] This was the first reasonably complete specimen of the extinct creature to be shown anywhere, weighing over a thousand pounds, standing eleven feet high and seventeen and a half long.[3] We do not know how successful the exhibition was, but it had distinguished patronage: the Peales came armed with introductions to two of their father's friends, Sir Joseph Banks and Benjamin West. Rembrandt's *Historical Disquisition on the Mammoth,* published in conjunction with the show, caused considerable interest, although its scientific authority proved small. A plan to tour the skeleton across the continent fell through because of the war, and the brothers returned to the United States with it in November 1803. After being exhibited from 1814 to 1845 at the museum Rembrandt Peale founded in Baltimore, it was at Boston for some time and eventually found its way to the American Museum of Natural History in New York.

A generation later (1841) a room at the Egyptian Hall, christened for the occasion the Antediluvian Museum, contained a skeleton far larger than the Peales', one, according to the publicity, "between whose legs the Mammoth, and even the mighty Iguanodon [the famous native English contribution to vertebrate paleontology, discovered in Sussex in 1825] may easily have crept."[4] Billed as the Missouri Leviathan, this monster, thirty feet long and fifteen high, was the latest enterprise of a German-born scientist-showman named Albert Koch.[5] Koch had made a career of digging up ancient bones, exhibiting them at his St. Louis museum and elsewhere, and then selling them to other museums. In 1839 he had added a chapter to scientific history by unearthing a deposit of "mastodon's" (actu-

ally, ground sloth's) bones alongside which were burned or broken spears, axes, and other artifacts, proof, he maintained, that primitive man coexisted with the mastodon. The next year, at a cost of five months' labor, he excavated in Benton County, Missouri, the skeleton he now brought to London after touring it in the States and winning the approval of the American Philosophical Society. It immediately stirred up controversy, chiefly because the knowledgeable promptly pointed out that the tusks were not only mounted in the wrong place (atop the head) but mounted upside down. Koch, preferring dramatic effect to scientific accuracy, had wanted to produce the effect of fearsome horns, and indeed had succeeded, if at a certain sacrifice of credibility.

Public interest was heightened by an exchange of views between Koch and Professor Owen. Koch maintained that his beast was a *Tetracaulodon missourium;* Owen, at a meeting of the Geological Society, retorted that if it was a tetracaulodon, it was only because Koch had made it so. No particular secrecy was attached to the fact that Koch had made up his specimen from the bones of several distinct animals; if one deducted the extra ribs and vertebrae and the unnatural peculiarities of organization, Owen asserted, the skeleton would revert to what it actually was, a *Mastodon giganteum.* He was right, but Koch made the money. After an extended stay in London Koch took the artificially enlarged mastodon on tour on the continent. The following year he sold the bones to the British Museum, whose experts at once reassembled it in a more scientific pattern, deleting the gratuitous ribs and vertebrae and putting the tusks where they belonged. The reconstructed skeleton occupied a prominent position in Bloomsbury, and today commands the entrance to the fossil mammal gallery at the Natural History Museum, South Kensington.[*]

The jumbo skeleton had been preceded to London by another marvel whose provenance was considerably murkier. George Mogridge wrote of seeing a poster near London Bridge advertising "Wonderful Remains of an Enormous Head, 18 feet in length, 7 feet in breadth, and weighing 1700 pounds. The complete bones of which were discovered in excavating a passage for the purpose of a railway, at the depth of 75 feet from the surface of the ground, in Louisiana, and at a distance of 160 miles from the sea." At the advertised location, the Cosmorama Rooms, Mogridge found the "head," which he thought might have been that of a whale. The proprietors, a pair of Frenchmen, were cautiously noncommittal; they allowed that it might

* Koch then went back to the United States to resume digging. This time, in Alabama, he came up with a "gigantic fossil reptile" which he named the *Hydrarchus sillimani,* after the Yale scientist who appears several times in these pages, and which reputable scientists maintained had been pieced together from the remains of at least five zeuglodons. His attempt to exhibit this newest super-creature in London did not succeed, thanks to lingering memories of the Leviathan controversy and renewed attacks in the press. Again, however, he found the climate of scientific opinion more hospitable on the continent. After another Hydrarchus discovery and other assorted episodes, he retired to St. Louis, where he was revered to the end of his life as a distinguished savant.

have come from a bird, a fish, or a lizard—all colossal, of course.[6] No one seems to have made an issue of the multiple unlikelihoods connected with the Louisiana story, nor is there any clue as to what the macrocephalic object really was.

Less controversial and on a less heroic scale were the collections of objects brought back by professional naturalists and travelers who displayed them either with a view to sale or simply for the sake of the profit that would accrue, popular interest willing, at the gate. At the Egyptian Hall in 1837 Dr. (later Sir) Andrew Smith displayed the assemblage of stuffed animals and birds, along with some artifacts and four hundred drawings, that had resulted from his extensive travels through the then unknown interior of central Africa, in the course of which he had discovered many new species. Proceeds from the sale of the collection the following year were to be devoted to a second expedition, taking up where the first had left off, under the sponsorship of the Cape of Good Hope Association for Exploring Central Africa. Many of Smith's specimens, including three rhinoceroses, were acquired either directly or at second hand by the British Museum.[7]

Two years later, at the Cosmorama Rooms, there was an exhibition stemming from the recent explorations in Guiana of the German-born and -educated Robert Hermann Schomburgk. The room was fitted up as a Guianese hut, in which lived three natives who had formed part of Schomburgk's boat crew and now, clad in waistcloths, jaguar skins, teeth necklaces, and feather caps, danced and demonstrated the art of blowpipe shooting. The collection of natural curiosities and artifacts was a rich one: mammalia, birds, reptiles, fish, furniture, poisoned arrows, a native hammock, and bark shirts. But the most admired exhibit was a full-scale painting of the magnificent *Victoria regia* lily, which Schomburgk had discovered in the jungle.[8] This plant, with a leaf five to twelve feet in diameter, later was grown in a special glass house at the Duke of Devonshire's conservatory at Chatsworth. The duke's gardener, Joseph Paxton, derived from a study of the leaf's rib conformation the idea for the structural design of the Crystal Palace.

Exhibitions of materials relating to Africa, however, were the most numerous, and of these the most celebrated was the one that opened in April 1850, timed to coincide, as Bullock's Mexican and Belzoni's Egyptian shows had done, with the publication of the exhibitor's book. The title of the book in this case, an immediate best seller, was *Five Years of a Hunter's Life in the Far Interior of South Africa,* and the entrepreneur who wrote it was Roualeyn George Gordon Cumming, an Eton-educated "mad sort of Scotchman," as Livingstone called him, who had acquired, seemingly in the cradle, a consuming passion for blood sport. He became, in fact, the veritable archetype of the Big Game Hunter who found a sensual joy in killing. At eighteen he joined the East India Company's Madras Cavalry, but this affiliation evidently did not provide enough challenge to his guns, so after two years he returned to Scotland and devoted himself to deer stalking. When this palled in turn, he obtained a commission in the Royal Veteran Newfoundland Companies, but again his expectations were unfulfilled, and he transferred to the Cape Mounted Rifles, a move which had the advantage (from his point of view, not that of the ecosystem) of taking him to Africa.[9] Here he finally discovered his life work. Resigning his commission at the end of 1843, he bought four wagons, three hundred-weight of lead to make bullets, and 50,000 percussion caps, collected a retinue of servants including a displaced Cockney cabman as valet, and retreated into the bush, where he remained for five years, his guns forever ablaze. According to a contemporary writer:

The whole country figures in his narrative like an immense zoological garden, with all the dens broken up and all the menagerie set free. Springboks, gemsboks, blesboks, wildebeests, oryxes, gnus, buffaloes, antelopes, giraffes, rhinoceroses, lions and elephants, to say nothing of smaller creatures. . . . Mr. Cumming ran riot among them all as freely as they ran riot among one another. He gave chase to everything which could rouse his blood or put him in peril. He fought many a duel with the biggest monsters of the forest. He became as familiar with lions as ordinary British sportsmen are with moor fowl; and often ran after elephants as dauntlessly as ploughboys run after hares; and generally "imbibed" the terrific giant "game" quite as numerously as they had been partridges or trout. His perils, of course, were constant and awful; many of his escapes were hair's-breadth and wonderful; and while all proved him to be one of the bravest of mortals and as mighty a hunter as Nimrod, some excite sickening horror, and provoke sharp questionings as to the moral character of such *sport.*[10]

Cumming's bag in those five years included eighteen lions, twenty-eight black rhinoceroses, thirty-nine white rhinos, seventy-six hippopotamuses, and a hundred elephants.[11] To be sure, the casualties were not entirely on one side. He lost all fifteen of his horses to lions, disease, or the tsetse fly, all thirty of his oxen to the same lethal insect, all twenty of his dogs to lions, panthers, crocodiles, and other predators, and his best wagon driver to a monster lion which a vengeful Cumming had the satisfaction of killing the next day.[12]

Settled in at the St. George's Gallery, Hyde Park Corner, and benefiting from the publicity generated by his book, Cumming became, according to an inevitable waggery later enshrined in the *Dictionary of National Biography,* the lion of the season. His "desert spoils" amounted to thirty tons (ten years earlier, George Catlin had brought a mere eight tons—of artifacts, not stuffed animals—from the Wild West). In the center of the room was the wagon in which he had resided during those productive years, and around it, covering all the walls, was impressive testimony of his stout heart and steady trigger finger. The gallery, commented the *Athenaeum,* "looks like a combination of a baronial hall and a furrier's shop." The lion skins were said to be the finest ever shown in London; over a thousand pounds of ivory were on display; one pair of elephant's tusks, nine feet long, were the largest on record. The place was a bulging repository of hides, teeth, feet, skulls, tails, and horns.[13] All that were missing were representatives of the expendable horses, oxen, and dogs, as well as the unfortunate wagon driver, all of whom, it would seem, had as much right to be stuffed and exhibited as the rest of Cumming's victims.

Benjamin Silliman visited the show and included in his diary a detail that escaped the newspaper accounts—further evidence that the life of hapless exotics attached to a London show was not (as the Hottentot Venus and the Sicilian Fairy could have attested) a uniformly happy one:

A Hottentot boy, who speaks English well, was in the room to give explanations. He is intelligent, and knows much of the history of the animals, and of the adventures in which they were killed. He said, in answer to my inquiries, that he belonged to the christianized Hottentots, but we judged from the odor of gin about him, that he did not very closely observe all the teachings of the gospel. Something of the character of the barbarian still adhered to him; for although small in stature, and not robust, he resented some freedoms that were taken with him by a young man who was present; and, following him around the room, with menaces, he could not be easily appeased.

While admiring "the high degree of romance" in Cumming's narratives of "his perilous warfare against the wild animals" ("romance" seems not to have any deprecatory intent), Silliman nevertheless found it impossible not to feel that the beasts had been "consigned to destruction for the sake of indulging a spirit of reckless adventure."[14] The *Athenaeum* was less moderate, deploring Cumming's "particular form of the spirit of adventure" and declaring, "they are barbar-

ians both—the sporting angler and the sporting lion-hunter." The writer found some comfort in the thought that the show, by attracting other gun-happy adventurers to the African wilds, "gives society a chance that the ranks of an offending class may very probably be thinned by the rough accidents which men who would follow Mr. Cumming's example must confront."[15]

The African exhibition lasted into the late summer of 1852. Strategically situated as it was at Hyde Park Corner, in the intervening year it caught the custom of the throngs passing on their way to or from the Crystal Palace. In August, the humanitarian *Punch* concentrated its pity not on any of the defunct beasts of the jungle but on the suffering pitchman, who, for all we know, may have been the much put-upon Hottentot youth transferred to a new post:

Perhaps there never was a more startling instance of what it is to live, not merely by the sweat of one's brow, but by the perspiration of one's body, than is shown by the individual who stands at the door of CUMMING'S Exhibition in a complete suit of leopard skins. The exhibition is intended to illustrate the triumph of human courage over brute force; but the man in the leopard skins should be endowed with a heart of stone and nerves of iron to resist the furnace heat to which he is daily subjected. If the thermometer is eighty in the sun, we should like to know what it is in the pocket of this poor creature's paletot? We expect to see him drop down some day a mass of human tallow, with the flame of life dimly flickering in his eye by way of socket.[16]

After exhausting the London market, Cumming took his show on tour, adding, somewhere along the way, a formal lecture of his own instead of the explanations of the Hottentot. A report from Dublin in the *Times* (1 March 1858) said that the authorities there had taken over the exhibition to recover a hundred pounds "in which Mr. Cumming was bound in his own recognizance to appear at College-street police-office to answer the charge of indecency preferred against him." The grounds for the charge do not appear, but Cumming got his lion skins back and proceeded to set up at Fort Augustus, on the Caledonian Canal, a museum which became a popular tourist attraction. John Hanning Speke, discoverer of the source of the Nile, was one of the visitors, evidently feeling that he could see Africana in Cumming's Scotland which he had not had the chance to meet in the field.[17] The year before his death—of drink, it is said—in 1866, Cumming sold his whole collection to Barnum, who was then making wholesale purchases to replace the stock lost when his American Museum burned in

91. The Chinese Collection: entrance (*Mirror of Literature,* n.s. 2, 1842, 129).

New York. Barnum complacently noted that although Cumming's was "a great Museum in itself, . . . it was a mere addition to our Museum and Menagerie; and it was exhibited without extra charge for admission." But it was on show in New York for less than three years, perishing, along with all Barnum's other recent acquisitions, in the fire that leveled his new museum on 3 March 1868.[18]

D₃✳£D

The more civilized wonders of another continent, Asia, were not neglected in the London shows. No single Oriental artifact could have been expected to outdo the splendor of the Burmese State Coach seen in 1825, but from time to time the East Indiamen brought back other objects that were promptly put on exhibition for profit. Toward the end of the 1830s there was a spate of these. One, shown for a shilling at the new Exeter Hall, prospectively the headquarters of nonconformist religion, was a twenty-four-foot-square

temple containing numerous images of Buddha.[19] About the same time a newly arrived collection of seventy-eight life-size figures representing "the principal images of Hindu worship" was put on show at St. Katherine's Docks. Though said to be valued at £5,000, the group was knocked down by George Robins, the auctioneer, for a mere £630.[20] At the Crown and Anchor tavern, Strand, in 1840, flanked by a picture of the York Minster fire, a model of King's College Chapel, and three hundred "Ancient Models in Silk" of "the most Superb Dresses of the Various Nations of Earth," was a curious object that had long been in Britain, having been presented to Sir Joseph Banks by the King of Candy (Ceylon). This was an "abridgement" of that monarch's summer tent, "made of the leaves of the Tallipat Palm, so artfully and cunningly joined as to seem only as one Leaf . . . formed by sewing the leaves together with Rushes, and strengthening them by means of lateral Ribs of Split Cane at short intervals, and cementing them with a substance of great tenacity." It was recommended (for purchase?) as "a simple and most durable structure, capable of resisting equally the sun-shine and the storm, and furnishing a high intellectual treat to the Man of Science or the Philosopher of Nature."[21]

With 1839 came the Opium War. The bookshops and periodicals were laden with discourses, learned and light, on the people, customs, and culture of the ancient and still mysterious Chinese civilization. In August 1841, even before news arrived of the Treaty of Nanking, a Chinese Exhibition was ready to illustrate and supplement what the popular mind had so far learned about the vast country which henceforth was to do business with Britain. The collection had been formed by a rich Philadelphian named Nathan Dunn, a lapsed Quaker who had made a fortune in the tea trade during his stay of a dozen years in China.[22] As one of the few Occidental merchants who refused to deal in opium, he had enjoyed the special regard of high Chinese officials, who afforded him a unique opportunity to accumulate his large "cabinet." Prior to being moved overseas, it had been exhibited in Philadelphia (from late December 1838) in a new building erected chiefly to house Peale's museum. In London it occupied a structure built to house it at Hyde Park Corner, a two-story pagoda with green roofs edged with vermilion and supported by pillars of the same color. Visitors entering under an inscription in gilded Chinese characters that proclaimed "Ten Thousand Chinese Things" ascended a flight of stairs which opened on the main exhibition hall, 240 feet long and 50 wide,

dominated by three imposing gilt idols representing
"the three precious Buddhas" or, "past, present, and to
come."[23] The ceiling was hung with varicolored ornaments and large lanterns of green and white, vermilion
and gold. With dragons scowling from the corners of
the ceiling, the whole salon suggested, as a writer in
the *Times* reminisced ten years later, "a sort of
Brighton pavilion with permanent fittings."[24]

From all accounts, this was an exceptionally bountiful display. The 1,341 items described in the catalogue (considerably fewer, to be sure, than the 10,000
advertised outside) represented the Chinese people's
"idols, their temples, their pagodas, their bridges, their
arts, their sciences, their manufactures, their tastes,
their fancies, their parlours, their drawing rooms, their
clothes, their finery, their ornaments, their weapons of
war, their dwellings, and the thousand *et ceteras,* which
make up their moving and living world."[25] "Here,"
wrote John Timbs later in his ever valuable *Curiosities
of London,* "were life-size groups of a temple of idols, a
council of mandarins, and Chinese priests, soldiers,
men of letters, ladies of rank, tragedians, barbers, shoe-
makers, blacksmiths, boat-women, servants, &c.,
amidst set scenes and furnished dwellings. Here was a
two-storied house from Canton, besides shops from
its streets; here were persons of rank in sumptuous
costumes, artisans in their working-clothes, and altogether such a picture of Chinese social life as the
European world had never before seen."[26]

Most people attended the Chinese Exhibition im-
bued with the chauvinistic euphoria that stemmed
from the conclusion of the Opium War on uncompro-
mising British terms. But another, less strident note in
a minor key also was sounded, expressive of a ten-

dency in the early Victorian spirit which is perhaps not sufficiently appreciated. The satisfaction and sanguine expectations generated by the opening of China to western trade were accompanied by a regretful, almost elegiac sense that things would never be the same, now that the white man had forced open the gates of another culture. One journal, the *Art-Union,* drew a suggestive parallel between this show and Catlin's Indians: "It is singular enough, that to Mr. Catlin and Mr. Dunn—both natives of the United States—we are indebted for the most valuable assemblages of modern times; the one rescuing the memory and memorials of the Red Indians from oblivion; the other portraying China as it *was* five years ago, but, most probably, as it will never be again—for the European has entered its sanctuaries, and, the privacy of the Chinese once violated, they must become more assimilated to us in all things."[27] (Contrast the vintage Podsnappery evoked some years later by a panorama of Japan: "Japan, once a sealed book, is now unclasped, and we may freely inspect its treasures. It not only permits travellers to visit it, but has sent its Ambassadors to visit us, and learn how vain were the State precautions that were taken to prevent such a result. The Japanese will learn by these examples, for they are a docile people, and will rapidly improve in civilisation.")[28]

The Chinese Exhibition flourished for two seasons, and then sought a new lease on popularity when the pagoda was completely refurbished in the summer of 1843, the lanterns converted to gas, and the admission price reduced to a shilling. After its years in London, the collection toured the provinces and then returned to America, where Barnum added it to his Broadway Museum in New York. The pagoda, known both as the Chinese Gallery and the St. George's Gallery, remained a conspicuous landmark at Hyde Park Corner for a number of years and was put to several uses, none of them especially appropriate to its original name and function or its architectural style. At various times it housed panoramas—one of the queen's visits to Ireland, another, more successful, of Jerusalem and the Holy Land—as well as Cumming's big-game show and the Kaffir troupe of 1853.*

The focus of London's interest in things Oriental now shifted to the East End. A second Chinese Collection, so called, appeared briefly in 1847 in a field near Bow Church. According to the single advertisement its proprietor placed in the *Illustrated London News,* it was a "complete pictorial epitome of Chinese history, scenery, and customs," housed in "seventeen Monstre Carriages, built by Adams and Company, Bow, char-

acteristically decorated, and forming a spacious Saloon."

It is entered through a Pagoda of exquisite construction, within which are paintings of War Gods, Landscapes, &c. Adjoining this apartment is the Flowery Vestibule of Crystalline Mirrors, and in its rear the GRAND SALOON, 170 feet in length, 30 in height, and 50 in width, lighted from above by numerous windows, and surmounted by a spacious roof, constructed of a material which sheds a golden haze around. In this magnificent apartment, Chinese scenes are so faithfully reproduced, that the huge Golden Gods in their mystic temple—the Emperor on his throne—the Mandarins in their costly homes—the Judge in his Court—the Merchant in his shop—the host of Boatmen, Agriculturists, Street Traders, and Mendicants; together with interesting domestic scenes, and curious paintings, may be seen almost at a glance, although each view affords ample material for hours of study.[29]

Discounting the verbiage, one may doubtless assume that the "seventeen Monstre carriages" were actually ordinary showman's caravans, thrown together as they usually were at fairs, and that the "pictorial epitome" was either a group of crude paintings or a series of peepshows.

Much better documented is the Chinese junk *Keying,* which arrived late in March 1848, after a troubled odyssey that had won her substantial preliminary notice in the press. The *Keying,* it was related, had been clandestinely bought (because Chinese law forbade the sale of native vessels to foreigners) by "a few enterprising Englishmen," who sailed from Hong Kong on 6 December 1846 with a crew of thirty Chinese. Barely surviving a hurricane while skirting the Cape of Good Hope, she arrived at St. Helena intact, and then set sail for England; but adverse winds took her instead all the way across the Atlantic to the United States. During her stay in New York, the sweet mixed with the sour, so to speak. Although "the prettiest women of New York loved to boast" of having visited her, there was labor unrest aboard. The crew, protesting that they had been signed only for a hitch of eight months, for a voyage to Batavia and Singapore, struck for their wages and passage back to China. The court ordered the sale of the vessel and cash payments to the crew.[30]

It was presumably the same complement of seamen who finally brought the gorgeously painted teakwood craft into the East India Docks and readied her for the royal inspection that occurred in May. Billed as the first Chinese vessel ever to round the Cape of Good Hope, let alone to reach Europe, it had three masts and

* In 1847 it displayed a fifteen-by-twelve-foot canvas that had won a prize competition on the subject of Christ's baptism in the River Jordan. (*ILN,* 1 May 1847, p. 127.) More significantly for the history of British art, the next year it took over from the Egyptian Hall, where the first of the series had been held, the "Free Exhibition of Modern Art" organized by a group of independent artists to compete with the five official exhibitions of the day. The show attracted over 22,000 visitors. The second and last of these events to be housed at the Chinese Gallery (1849) was memorable as the occasion of the first display of a Pre-Raphaelite painting, Rossetti's *The Girlhood of Mary Virgin.*

93. The Chinese junk (*Illustrated London News*, 1 April 1848).

94. The saloon of the Chinese junk (*Illustrated London News*, 20 May 1848).

95. The Chin Tee joss from the Chinese junk (*Illustrated London News*, 20 May 1848).

96. The stern and rudder of the Chinese junk (*Illustrated London News*, 20 May 1848).

* Facetiously intended, of course. In the early Victorian vocabulary, "serious" was an epithet applied to evangelical Christians who exuded mildly offensive religiosity.

a burden of between 700 and 800 tons. Both bow and stern were decorated with enormous eyes, "with a view," explained the papers, "to enable the vessel to see her way across the ocean."[31]

Brilliant colours [said the *Annual Register*] shine upon the spectator from every side, with all the formless gaiety which is peculiar to the Chinese. Gaudy shields, as weapons of defence, hang along the deck—and jingalls, a hybrid race between cannon and arquebusses, threaten on each side. If you would take a more concentrated view of Chinese existence, the grand saloon is fitted up as a sort of museum, with all sorts of curiosities; or you may turn into a neat little chapel containing the idols which those serious* Orientals who lounge about the deck are in the habit of worshipping.[32]

Crowds of Londoners made the railway or steamboat trip downriver to see what the *Illustrated London News* called "one of the most rational objects of curiosity

which has ever been brought to our shores."[33] The *Keying* was the floating counterpart of the late exhibition at Hyde Park Corner.

"Talk of the wisdom of our ancestors!" exclaimed the *Examiner*. "Here is a sample of the ship-building wisdom and skill of the ancestors of the Chinese, which may have dated from the earliest ages of the world. Certainly never before did so unwieldy and misshapen a vessel traverse the Indian and Atlantic oceans; and the underwriters, if there were to be found men bold enough to insure a craft of this build, had great need of the pious invocation which is appended to the bills of lading in use amongst Christian nations."[34] Dickens, however, writing in the same paper a month later, failed to share the general enthusiasm. He was more comfortable with the native grotesque than with the exotic, and all the no-nonsense John Bullish side of his nature, all his parochialism and (on some topics) narrowness of sympathy, is revealed in his *Examiner* piece, a sort of warm-up for his disquisition on the noble savage five years later. He marveled that seafarers who knew nothing of shipbuilding or navigation managed to bring the craft to London in the first place.

If there be any one thing in the world that it is not at all like, that thing is a ship of any kind. So narrow, so long, so grotesque, so low in the middle, so high at each end (like a China pen-tray), with no rigging, with nowhere to go to aloft, with mats for sails, great warped cigars for masts, gaudy dragons and sea monsters disporting themselves from stem to stern, and, on the stern, a gigantic cock of impossible aspect, defying the world (as well he may) to produce his equal.

After various space-filling reflections on what life at sea must be like 'in such a conveyance, Dickens concluded on the same complacent note that he struck in connection with other exotics on display in London:

It is pleasant, coming out from behind the wooden screen that encloses this interesting and remarkable sight (which all who can, should see) to glance upon the mighty signs of life, enterprise, and progress that the great river and its busy banks present. It is pleasant, coming back from China by the Blackwall railway, to think that WE trust no red rags in storms, and burn no joss-sticks before idols; that WE never grope our way by the aid of conventional eyes which have no sight in them; and that, in our civilisation, we sacrifice absurd forms to substantial facts. The ignorant crew of the *Keying* refused to enter upon the ship's books, until "a considerable amount of silvered paper, tin-foil, and joss-sticks" had been laid in, by the owners, for the purposes of their worship; but OUR seamen—far less our bishops, priests, and deacons—never stand out upon points of silvered paper and tin-foil, or the lighting up of joss-sticks upon altars! Christianity is not Chin-Teeism; and therein all significant quarrels as to means, are lost sight of in remembrance of the end.[35]

If a diligent Londoner like Lord Stowell visited all these ad hoc commercial exhibitions, he would have acquired, at best, only a spotty idea of what the world beyond the ocean was like. His knowledge of the peoples and natural environments of distant regions would have been no more systematic than if he had spent ten minutes a day reading desultorily in books plucked at random from library shelves. What was needed in London was a permanent central museum in which materials representing most of the fields of interest embraced by the old cabinets would be systematically arranged. The founding of the Ethnological Society, the public interest aroused by the exhibitions of "savages" from Catlin's Indians to the spurious Aztecs, and the general stocktaking that occurred in the wake of the Great Exhibition further underscored this lack. A typical statement on the subject, printed in the *Athenaeum* late in 1851, ran:

our national collections (to our disgrace, as the first maritime nation in the world, be it spoken) are extremely deficient;—in fact, many a second-rate town on the Continent possesses a finer collection, whilst the national museums of Denmark and Holland are pre-eminently rich in this branch. It is, in fact, quite lamentable to think how many tribes first visited by our ships have now either entirely disappeared from the human race, or have so modified their manners as to render it impossible now to obtain specimens of their industrial arts in their aboriginal state. Thanks to our missionaries and naval officers, some slight collections have been formed,—and the comparatively private museums of the United Service Club and of the Missionary establishment in Moorfields, possess the only records of many tribes of which we have now only a traditional or written knowledge. To a small extent, also, the East India Company have formed a museum of the Ethnography of Hindustan.[36]

It is significant that in this survey the British Museum is not even mentioned. The fact was that it possessed, but had no space to display, an extensive ethnographical collection. The specimens in Sloane's own collection, though few in number, were of considerable importance, and their presence at Montagu House had served as a magnet to attract a goodly share of the riches that poured into England as a result of the numerous voyages of exploration and trade in the late eighteenth century. In 1778 a separate room had been fitted up, the "Otaheiti or South Sea Room," with a native mourning dress, cloaks and helmets of feathers, and implements of war from the Sandwich Islands. But thirty years later, in order to make a comprehensive display illustrating "particular Customs of different Nations; their Religion, their Government, their Commerce, Manufactures or Trades," many items not from the South Seas were crowded into the Otaheite room. As more years went by, the problem of space became ever more acute, not least because some of the new acquisitions were of great size—the colossal figure of Buddha, for instance, which Captain Marryat donated in 1825. In 1850 five cases were all that represented the arts and crafts of China and Japan. The great bulk of the museum's ethnological stock, by that time rich in Byzantine, Mexican, and Peruvian material as well as specimens from the South Seas and the Orient,

97. The museum of the London Missionary Society (*Illustrated London News*, 25 June 1859).

was crammed into the basement, where it was of no help to anyone.[37] The Otaheite room itself, still the only one devoted to such exhibits, was, as a critic fulminated in 1848, a scandal:

Never was such a disgraceful jumble of things seen, even in a local museum supported by voluntary contributions and regulated by a batch of half-educated provincial antiquaries. The room reminds us of Don Saltero's verses on his own museum at Chelsea:—

> Monsters of all sorts here are seen;
>   Strange things in nature as they grew so;
> Some relics of the Sheba queen,
>   And fragments of the fam'd Bob Crusoe.

All our early collectors, Tradescant, and Ashmole, and Thoresby aimed at something like arrangement;—but here, in the nineteenth century and in a national museum, we have a collection confounding all the unities of time and place and only worthy of a retired dealer in marine stores. And yet, this is one of the first rooms a foreigner is obliged to see on entering the British Museum.[38]

Of the handful of privately owned exhibitions of exotica mentioned by the *Athenaeum* writer quoted above, the least known and probably the least rewarding to visit was the museum of the London Missionary Society, located successively in the Old Jewry, Austin Friars, and at 8 Bloomfield Street, Finsbury. In 1826 it was open only one day a week, admission being by a ticket signed by a director or officer; twenty years later the days of opening had increased to three, and tickets were no longer required.[39] That its emphasis was something other than scientific is plain from the preface to the catalogue printed in 1826:

the most valuable and impressive objects in this Collection are the numerous, and (in some instances) *horrible*, IDOLS, which have been imported from the South Sea Islands, from India, China, and Africa; and among these, those especially which were actually given up by their former worshippers, from *a full conviction of the folly and sin of idolatry*—a conviction derived from the ministry of the Gospel by Missionaries . . . Many of the articles in this Collection are calculated to excite, in the pious mind, feelings of deep commiseration for the hundreds of millions of the human race, still the vassals of ignorance and superstition; whilst the success with which God has already crowned our labours, should act as a powerful stimulus to efforts, far more zealous than ever, for the conversion of the heathen.[40]

Although it included a fair number of "dresses, manufactures, domestic utensils, implements of war, music, etc." from North and South America, India, and Africa, in spirit the collection was scarcely more than a Christian trophy case. Among the most prized of the witnesses to the power of evangelical religion was a "Virgin Mother and Child from Mysore, that belonged to two Native Roman Catholics, who embraced the Christian religion, and sent the same to the Missionary Society." The specimens of South Sea household goods came from the Queen of Otaheite, who had given them to the missionaries when she was converted to Christianity in 1816. Chinese art was represented by six colored monitory etchings depicting "The Progress of the Opium-Smoker." Obviously the museum's purpose was not to advance learning but to publicize the Missionary Society's success in the field and attract subscriptions for the cause.

There was one exhibit which everybody came to see and nobody, it seems, ever forgot; we have records of its being gazed upon by sightseers as diverse as Prince Pückler-Muskau and Maria Edgeworth.[42] John Keats, who may have seen it when he went to East India House to inquire about a possible opening for a young surgeon aboard one of the company's merchantmen, referred to it in his unfinished "Faery Tale," *The Cap and Bells,* as "a play-thing of the Emperor's choice, / . . . a Man-Tiger-Organ, prettiest of his toys."[43] This was the mechanical man-eating tiger of Tippoo Sahib, part of the booty taken when Seringapatam, the capital of that formidable Mysore potentate, fell in 1799.

Better known was the museum of the East India Company. When the company's headquarters in Leadenhall Street were enlarged at the end of the eighteenth century, rooms were set aside to house the miscellaneous objects already accumulated there. The collection was officially named the "Oriental Repository" and a distinguished Sanskritist, Charles Wilkins, was put in charge. His and his successors' duties were not excessively heavy, because public admission was limited. Originally, a written order from a director of the company was required; later, admission was free for three hours on Saturday, and still later the doors were opened to the ticketless for four hours a day on two days of the week.[41]

Tippoo, who was killed during the final British assault, had had two passions—an obsession for tigers, which were represented everywhere in his courtly emblems, costumes, and even weaponry, and a consuming hatred for the English, who had been steadily reducing his domain. He therefore had had made for him life-size mechanical figures, juxtaposed in fearful symmetry, of a tiger and a man.[44] The latter, a civilian Englishman with black shoes, round black hat, scarlet coat, green breeches, and yellow stockings, lay recumbent in terror; the tiger hovered over him in triumph. Turning a barrel-organ crank in the tiger's side—a duty assigned to a slave in the original setting, and later a privilege enjoyed by visitors to the museum, to the constant annoyance of students in the adjoining library—activated bellows, stops, and other equipment in the respective interiors, producing, on the part of the tiger, deep-throated roars and, on that of the man, heartfelt shrieks and groans. While the tiger moved his head, his prey writhed on the ground and eventually expired.

Thus did one Oriental monarch express his feelings about his enemies. But the toy had a deeper resonance to both Tippoo and the English public, because it reenacted a tragic occurrence in December 1792, when the only son of Sir Hector Munro, a noted general who had earlier humbled Tippoo in battle, had been attacked and fatally mauled by a tiger. His horrible death—he had lingered in agony for twenty-four hours after the tiger leaped on him—had made a strong impression on the English imagination, so much so that many years later Staffordshire chimney ornaments, an early form of popular domestic artware, were produced to commemorate the incident. Little wonder, therefore, that when it was sent from India and installed in Leadenhall Street in 1808, the tiger became one of the most famous individual exhibits in London show history.*

Otherwise, the East India House's museum was noteworthy only because, in default of the British Museum, there was no great competition in its field. The exhibits covered the expectable range: native weapons, specimens or models of agricultural and other occupational implements, Burmese and Javanese musical instruments, Buddhist religious objects, a number of glass cases illustrating Indian natural history, and such star pieces as a silver elephant howdah and a Babylonian stone sent home by Sir Harford Jones in 1801.[45] There was a small assortment of Chinese objects, but nothing like the array Dunn brought from Philadelphia in 1841. Some complained

* Reduced to a heap of several hundred fragments by bombing during the Second World War, it was expertly restored and today occupies an honored position in the Victoria and Albert Museum, where it has been since 1880.

98. Tippoo Sahib's tiger, as it appears today at the Victoria and Albert Museum.

that the museum was unsatisfactorily located and arranged; one had to wind through several passages in East India House and ascend a long stairway, only to find a suite of six or eight ill-lighted rooms with the curiosities stowed on shelves that were too high and in corners that were too dark.[46] Despite these inconveniences, by 1850 the museum was being visited by over 40,000 persons a year.[47]

One other collection, that of the Royal United Service Institution in Whitehall Yard, was also dedicated in part to the relics of empire building. Formed in 1830 to receive the contributions of returned military and naval officers, the museum was normally open only to bearers of tickets signed by members, although the general public was admitted for three days at Christmas and Easter and on the anniversaries of Waterloo and Trafalgar. As it increased year by year, the collection became a microcosm of British military and naval history, with an incidental ethnological-scientific representation consisting of Chinese trophies, a range of minerals and mounted birds and animals, and, most prominently, arms and armor from the Eskimos, New Zealanders, Polynesians, and Africans. In a special Asiatic room were weapons from Borneo, Java, Ceylon,

Punjab, and Afghanistan. There were personal relics in abundance—Drake's walking stick, one of Lord Nelson's hats, Captain Cook's punch bowl and chronometer, the skeleton of Marengo, Napoleon's mount at Waterloo and for a long time, when alive, the star attraction at the Waterloo Rooms in Pall Mall. There were scores of ship models, models of famous fortifications, and relief maps of campaigns and battles; pieces of wood from wrecks dating from various periods, to compare the effects of sea water; all manner of military equipment, from a camp kitchen, reputedly the model for the one Napoleon used on his Russian campaign, to patent sea-rescue apparatus; uniforms and field equipment of not only British but Prussian, Austrian, Belgian and Sardinian soldiers, and the uniform worn by Tippoo Sahib at Seringapatam. One room contained a display of firearms from Henry VIII's time to that of Victoria, with cases containing the swords of heroes; another was devoted to illustrating the successive stages in the manufacture of the Enfield rifle. At the foot of the grand staircase were "pikes, spears, helmets, and long two-handed swords, and on either side shirts of ringed mail of the time of the Crusaders," and elsewhere, in imitation of the ef-

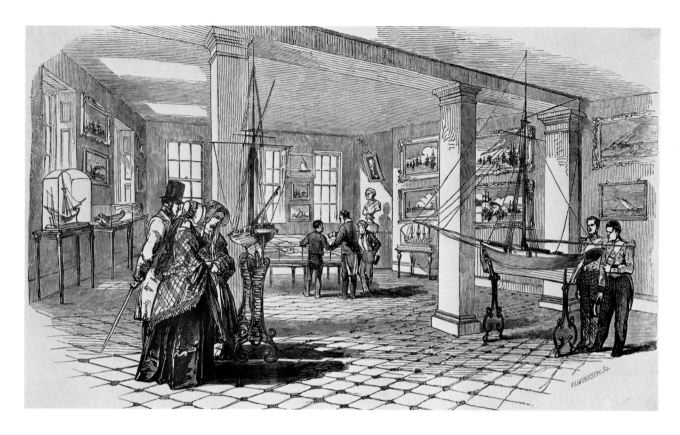

99. The Royal United Service Institution Museum (*Illustrated London News,* 5 February 1848). The room shown was newly arranged to display a bequest of naval paintings and ship models.

fects produced at the Tower armory, two "elegant stars" were composed of arrows.[48]

Of the several early Victorian museums of objects relating to other places and other times, except for the British Museum only this one remained intact down almost to the present, occupying the Banqueting Hall in Whitehall until about 1960. It was the progenitor of the present Imperial War Museum in Lambeth, the National Army Museum on the Chelsea Hospital grounds, and the National Maritime Museum at Greenwich. The other collections were dispersed or divided and, in some cases, reassembled under new auspices, a major development in the general reconstitution of London museums that got under way after the middle of the century.

Life and Death in the Animal Kingdom

22

The fact is, John Bull, though a person of boundless curiosity, has no great taste for the Fine Arts, and would rather spend his time and money in seeing a Calf with two heads than the finest piece of sculpture in the Towneley Collection for nothing.
—Unidentified newspaper, 1805

While cheap treatises like the Society for the Diffusion of Useful Knowledge's four volumes on "the Menageries" popularized scientific information among readers bent on improving their minds, elsewhere in the London public fancy continued to lean toward the zoological freaks that had set former generations agape. At the fairs and in hired stables and halls, besides the ever popular slithering reptiles and playful monkeys, there were still animal dwarfs, giants, and anomalies to be studied. A thirty-three-inch-high "Little Mare from Bengal," allegedly the smallest horse in the kingdom, could be viewed in 1820;[1] and at the other extreme, General Washington, the equine monster shown at the Egyptian Hall in 1845, was followed a few years later (1850) by "SAMPSON, the largest horse in the world, 20 hands two and one-half inches high, and only Four years old." Costarred with him at the Old Burlington Mews was "that wonderful animal, the HYBRID, a cross between the Wild Deer and Pony, visited twice by the Nepaulese Prince and Suite, when his Excellency vaulted several times upon the monster's back: the only individual who ever could, although tried by hundreds of the athlete."[2]

The old show-business premise persisted: there were more things on earth and in the sea than naturalists had yet allowed for, no matter how widespread their searches or how elaborate their taxonomical schemes. In this brave new world of science, faith in the existence of mermaids still lingered among some of the uneducated. Desiccated specimens of this fabled creature had been displayed from time to time in seventeenth- and eighteenth-century fair booths and taverns, and in 1822 a new one turned up at the Turf coffeehouse, St. James's Street. "Three to four hundred people every day," it was reported, "pay their shilling each to see a disgusting sort of a compound animal, which contains in itself everything that is odious and disagreeable"—to wit, a mummified fishlike body standing erect on a curve just above the tail, with a wizened simian head and quasi-human hands, arms, shoulders, and shriveled breasts. In reality it was a sewn-up combination of a blue-faced monkey's torso and the prepared skin and fins of a salmon. It had been shown earlier in Japan by a fisherman who claimed he had caught the mermaid alive in his net.[3] (The probable truth was that it was manufactured in Japan, which was the world headquarters of the mermaid industry.) Eventually it turned up at Batavia, where the captain of an American whaler bought it for $5,000, a transaction which resulted in a dispute over the mermaid's legal ownership being laid before the Court of Chancery on the other side of the globe. After the Lord Chancellor listened to the arguments "with some mirth"—it was not every day that a mermaid exhibited in London was a ward in Chancery—he gave judgment in favor of the ship's owner rather than the captain.[4] The grotesque object was taken to the United States and finally bought by Barnum, who devoted his promotional genius to "the Fee Jee Mermaid," as it was now called, and made a tidy little sum exhibiting it.

The litigated mermaid was not the only member of the apocryphal breed to bid for Londoners' pocket money. No sooner had she worked up adequate publicity than a mer*man* appeared in the Strand. It—or he—had been before the public some twenty-nine years earlier, when a firm of pawnbrokers who had acquired it from a Captain Forster exhibited it in Broad Court. The rivalry between merman and mermaid prompted one paper to recommend that the police look into the matter: "The Society for the Suppression of Vice attack less impious appeals to the public than the declaration of those vagabonds, that it is *a natural production, and one of the wonderful works of God.*"[5] But this did not discourage the exhibition of another merman two years later at 124 Piccadilly. Its authenticity rested, rather insecurely, on "assurances of its owners, and the affidavit of an Indian servant who swears that he has seen a similar creature alive, and on shore for three days." The components of this particular example were analyzed as "a fish tail, an ape body, and the head formed of the jaws of the wolf-fish, the skull of an ape, and the fur of a fox."[6] In a light-hearted appreciation, the *Times* remarked on the modishness of the merman's coiffure, "a fine well-brushed head of hair, rising perpendicularly from the crown of the head in the newest *Dandy* fashion," and recommended that Joshua Brookes assign his anatomy students to make a "cheaper and more perfect" example as evidence of the superiority of British-made goods over those fabricated in the Orient.[7]

During these same years, one of the mermaid's and mermen's leading rivals was a huge beast that was incontestably genuine, even if its novelty was somewhat exaggerated. This was the Bonassus, which was shown in 1821–22, along with a five-legged cow and forty other animals, at a "Grand Repository of Natural History" at 287 Strand, behind St. Clement Dane's. "Take him for all in all," said a handbill, "we ne'er shall look upon his like again." It was not clear why this was so; nor was there more credibility in the further claim that the Bonassus had not been looked upon before, in London at any rate. Under some other name, asserted the exhibitor, he had been mentioned by Aristotle and Pliny the younger, "but, like the

mammoth, he was supposed to be extinct, till revived by the present specimen."[8] What the advertisements carefully suppressed was the fact that under still another name, or names, specimens of the Bonassus had been familiar to earlier generations of London showgoers. *Bison bonasus* (properly so spelled) was merely the scientific name for the European bison, of which the present specimen (*Bison bison,* or buffalo) was the American cousin.*

"Taken near the Stoney Mountains, in the interior of North America, when only six weeks old," this shaggy creature was now fourteen months old. Standing six feet high and weighing two tons, he had been landed at Liverpool and on his roundabout way to the metropolis had been greeted by crowds of "100,000 respectable people" at Manchester, Sheffield, Birmingham, Cambridge, and Oxford. "He has," said the publicity, "the horns of the Antelope, the head of the Elephant, a long beard descending to his knees, the hind parts of a Lion, an immense bunch of hair, like a tiara, upon his head,—his eye is placed upon his cheek bone, and he has an ear like the human species."[9]

The Bonassus's fame, though brief, was intense. As verses affixed to a political cartoon defending Queen Caroline had it,

* In one form or another, this sly use of terms unknown to the common vocabulary was, of course, a favorite device among showmen; one is reminded of Barnum's celebrated trick of making room for newcomers during a crowded day at his American Museum by putting up a sign pointing "To the Egress," which turned out not to be a strange new beast but the exit. According to Thomas Frost (*Circus Life and Circus Celebrities,* London, 1881, p. 78), the menagerist Wombwell later played the identical Bonassus trick at Croydon fair.

101. The Bonassus (engraving by T. Lane (?), *An Old Friend with a New Face or the Baron in Disguise,* 1821). A political satire on the controversy over Queen Caroline. The Bonassus has the head of her alleged lover, "Baron" Bartolomeo Bergami.

An Old Friend with a New Face or the Baron in Disguise

Altho' Bonassus does not roar,
His Fame is widely known,

For no dumb Animal before,
Eer made such noise in Town.

102. The whale skeleton lounge at Charing Cross (engraving in the *Mirror of Literature,* 18, 1831, 104).

Altho' Bonassus does not roar,
His Fame is widely known,
For no dumb Animal before,
E'er made such noise in town.[10]

For some reason, the Bonassus inspired a burst of studiously illiterate *jeux d'esprit* in the press, one of which, purporting to come from a next-door neighbor, complained vividly and at length of the smell and disturbance the exhibition caused.[11] When Lord Stowell turned up for his second look, the managers assured him that he could enter as often as he wished, gratis; in return for which courtesy, they added to their handbills, without his prior knowledge, the proud boldface line "Under the patronage of the Right Hon. Lord Stowell." We are told that "the noble and learned lord's friends" treated him to a ribbing which he accepted with good nature.[12] Even rarer than a mermaid's appearance in Chancery was a judge of the High Court of Admiralty publicly sponsoring a Bonassus.

A trifle more common than Bonassi were carcasses of whales. At the end of March 1809 a favorable specimen, acquired off Gravesend and pronounced by competent judges to belong to the species *Bolena boops,* was loaded on a barge and taken to a point in the Thames between Blackfriars and London bridges, where, its tail projecting four yards over the stern, it did excellent business at a shilling a customer. But the *Times,* while happy that "the public of the metropolis, ever insatiable after raree shows," was having its taste indulged, doubted the wisdom of bringing into "the centre of a populous city, for the mere gratification of gazers, a monster of such bulk, in *a state of putrefaction* . . . the stench," the writer reported feelingly, "was intolerable." He advised visitors to bring along handkerchiefs soaked with strong vinegar. While the show went on, a dispute over its ownership arose, the Lord Mayor claiming the decaying prize in his capacity of Conser-

vator of the Thames, the Admiralty viewing it as a *Droit.* The vendible remains were auctioned at Lloyd's coffeehouse for £75, but it is not clear which party got the proceeds.[13]

A far more elegant whale display was that in 1831, on the site of the King's Mews, Charing Cross, which had been demolished in the course of what were called "metropolitan improvements." This specimen, which was estimated to have weighed 480,000 pounds when alive, had been towed ashore at Ostend in November 1827, after which it was demolished and eventually brought to London as a ninety-five-foot skeleton. Propped on iron supports, it was displayed in a capacious tent, and buyers of two-shilling "saloon tickets" were entitled to enter the whale, even as Jonah had done, but in much more comfort. A platform had been erected inside the rib cage, and here, while a twenty-four-piece orchestra played, visitors could relax at cozily placed chairs and tables, on which were copies of Lacépède's *Natural History* and a guest book inviting epigrams, puns, and other small wit (sample: "Palace of the Prince of W[h]ales"). This, said the *Mirror of Literature* without evident irony, was "one of the pleasantest places we have visited this season."[14] It was certainly one of the most unusual.*

If Albert Koch had delayed a year or two in bringing his suspect *Hydrarchus sillimani* to London, he might have had better luck with it, because in 1848–49 the capital was swept by a sea serpent craze. The captain of H.M.S. *Daedalus,* a corvette returning from East Indian duty, reported upon his arrival at Plymouth that on 6 August 1848, in the south Atlantic off the African coast, he and his crew had observed a creature bearing a strong resemblance to the sea serpent of ancient and medieval myth. This report was taken more seriously than most because the captain was an experienced and trustworthy mariner, and he and his men had a persuasive story to tell. The press and the scien-

* But, in the long run, not unique. Rembrandt Peale had a feast at a skeleton when he held a Philadelphia dinner party inside one of the mammoths he and his father had extracted from the Hudson River Valley clay. The skeleton accommodated a piano and a table seating thirteen guests. One of the toasts on this occasion was: "The ladies of Philadelphia—ere their naked beauties prove as horrible as bare bones, may Virtue behold them clothed in the garments of Modesty." (J. T. Flexner, *America's Old Masters,* rev. ed., New York, 1967, p. 226.) Twenty-five years after the whale's interior was converted into a lounge at Charing Cross, the life-size model of the Iguanodon, one of the several prehistoric creatures built under the guidance of Richard Owen to populate the newly created primordial swamp at the Sydenham Crystal Palace (see below, Chapter 34), was requisitioned for a dinner party. The Crystal Palace Company's public relations officer sent out invitations "on the wing of a pterodactyl" to twenty-one eminent scientists. They came, ate a catered dinner, drank toasts, sang songs ("The jolly old beast / Is not deceased, / There's life in him again"), and returned to London after midnight, much pleased with the novel outing. (Adrian J. Desmond, "Central Park's Fragile Dinosaurs," *Natural History,* 83, no. 8, October 1974, 66.)

tific community took it up with enthusiasm, and the lively discussion continued until Richard Owen put in his authoritative word, declaring that what had been seen from the deck of the *Daedalus* was no serpent—it had none of the characteristics of *any* serpent—but only a great seal or sea lion.[15] *Punch,* which had wedged some sort of joke about the serpent into every issue, professed to find his opinion inconclusive:

MORE LAST WORDS

Who killed the sea-serpent?
 "I," said PROFESSOR OWEN,
 In Zoology so knowing;
"And I killed the sea-serpent!"

Who won't say "die" to the serpent?
 "I," said CAPTAIN McQUHAE,
 "I stick to what I say;
And I won't say 'die' to the Serpent."

Why couldn't it be a serpent?
 'Cause OWEN's never seen one.
 Has there, therefore, never been one?
Why couldn't it be a serpent?

What was't if not a serpent?
 We know it wasn't a seal,
 And 'twas too big for an eel,
And it certainly *was* a serpent.

There's six of us saw the serpent,
 With a mane upon its back,
 And a tail and not a track;
We'll all swear to the serpent.[16]

Shortly afterward, another alleged sea serpent was not only sighted but actually caught off the Northumbrian coast. The Duke of Northumberland sent drawings of it to Owen, who promptly identified it as a ribbonfish, *Regalecus glesne,* a variety seldom seen because it rarely rises to the surface. Still, someone thought it worth exhibiting, because it turned up at the Cosmorama Rooms in May 1849, advertised in abnormally cautious language as "a young specimen, coinciding in its principal features with descriptions of the SEA SERPENT."[17]

Regalecus glesne evidently had no accomplishments, but *Phoca leptonyx,* shown at 191 Piccadilly in 1859, did. This small-tailed seal, captured off Africa in 1854, was reported to have "a fine dog-like head . . . and beautiful eyes, sparkling and rolling with intelligence." Jenny, as she was named, could dance, roll herself in her bath, ring a bell, clasp her fins "in the attitude of supplication," stand on her tail, and say "mama" and "papa" and "John" (her keeper, who may possibly have been a ventriloquist).[18]

Flea circuses remained a durable institution, as befitted an era when popular education was, in some circles, a fashionable cause. Of a troupe of trained fleas in 1833 the *Times* remarked that they had "a spirit well becoming an age when 'the schoolmaster is abroad.' . . . Indeed, from the progress which they have made in improvement [since last season], it would seem that the 'march of intellect' is as rapidly on the advance amongst fleas as with gentry of somewhat larger dimensions." The writer went on to speculate, in the manner of a political economist, what an army of a hundred thousand fleas would be capable of if they were as well educated as the present corporal's guard. They did their mentor proud, enacting the siege of Antwerp with cannon the size of pins, portraying a ballroom scene with four dancers and an orchestra of twelve, and drawing a mail coach in complete harness. A single "whopper" flea pulled a microscopic elephant with a howdah on his back filled with flea-warriors.[19] It was an inspiring spectacle.

One of the largest of these microscopic *manèges,* two hundred strong, was Herr Lidusdroph's company of Industrious and Learned Russian Fleas, whose headquarters in the fifties was at 5 Leicester Square. Through the magnifying glasses mounted around the platform one could see the talented insects firing off artillery and carrying plates in the manner of household servants. One five-year-old star, the Belzoni of the genus *Pulex,* was billed as "the Russian Hercules" who carried twelve of his fellow troupers on his back. Another, in the role of the currently popular Hungarian patriot Kossuth, rode mounted on a Habsburg flea.[20]

Fleas, however, were far from owning a monopoly on education. In 1843 the Cosmorama Rooms echoed with the melodies of a singing mouse, which was reported to warble "incessantly" for a quarter of an hour; "its notes are low but clear, and not unlike that of the nightingale."[21] The nightingale may not have been flattered by the comparison, but the bird kingdom had nothing to apologize for: it too was rich in talent. There were, for example, the "Scientific Java Sparrows" at 23 Bond Street, who, it was announced, had just "finished their Education at the University of Oxford, where they met with the greatest approbation from the Vice-Chancellor, the Collegians, and the Mayor and Inhabitants of that learned City." Three years had been required to complete their schooling—the normal time for undergraduates—and they were perfect in seven languages, which could not be said for all Oxford graduates.[22] At the same location, in another year, was a troupe of canaries under the proprietorship of M. Dujon. Their acts included playing dead, leaping and alighting on their feet again, dancing on a slack rope, carrying two milk pails, roosting peacefully in the midst of a fireworks display, and performing a drama wherein a deserter in a military uniform was tried by court martial, and after being sentenced to be shot was executed by another canary firing a gun from five feet away and carted off in a wheelbarrow by another comrade.[23] A troupe of "Oiseaux Merveilleux," more given to mental gymnastics, appeared at Willis's Rooms in 1852; these birds told the time, solved arithmetic problems in their heads, read minds, and told fortunes, along with "Exercises in Orthography" and "Tours d'Escamotage" (sleight of hand).[24]

Descendants of Dr. Johnson's learned pig were still active in the profession. Among these was Toby, the Sapient Pig, who could be admired at various places in 1818–1823. The property of a person bearing the venerable show-business name of Pinchbeck, he was alleged to have been tutored by "Souchanguyee, the Chinese Philosopher," and earlier to have been "shewn in Spanish America, under the Sanction of the Inquisition, at $5 admittance." It is more credible that his forte was answering questions by "pointing to cards, letters, and persons in the audience."[25] At 248 Regent Street in 1829 was Signor Cappelli of Tuscany with his learned cats, a *corps dramatique* consisting of mother, two sons, daughter, and a "jet-black and maternal-looking negress," who rang bells, worked a rice grinder, hammered on an anvil, drew a bucket up and down a well, roasted coffee, turned spits, played on an organ, and sharpened knives. The *Literary Gazette* was heartened to find feline intelligence vindicated in a field of endeavor too long dominated by fleas, birds, mice, and dogs. "[Cats'] restoration to rational functions," it declared, "is the best proof we have yet met with of the progress of education and the march of mind."[26] Even more impressive evidence, however, was available in the person of Pinkey, a "learned and scientific goose" who confounded those who considered geese to be the stupidest of creatures. In the late twenties and early thirties this prodigy was being toured by a prestidigitator named Hoare. The favored locales for these kinds of entertainment, involving easily portable exhibits of the sort that formerly occupied booths at the now declining or extinct fairs, were taverns and assembly rooms in working-class neighborhoods.[27]

103. Handbill advertising Cappelli's performing cats, 1832.

Apart from the scanty collection of animals at the Tower, the Exeter Change menagerie was the only permanent show of its kind in London. Still under Gilbert Pidcock's proprietorship as the century began, it became one of the city's most celebrated institutions, partly because of its exuberant advertising. One boast, thinly disguised as a news item, declared that "Pidcock, the Terrestial and Aerial Fascinator, is truly called the Modern Noah, and Exeter Exchange his Wonderful Ark. Here the Majestic African Lion roars in concert with the dreadful Bengal Tyger, and the Sol-

104. Handbill advertising the Exeter Change menagerie.

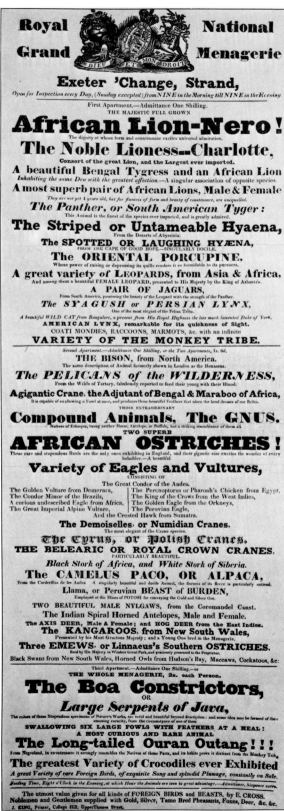

* These were not the only evidences of the menagerie's presence at Exeter Change; in 1826 the *European Magazine* (n.s. 2, 410) remarked that it was "a great annoyance at all times, and a perfect nuisance in warm weather." Many exhibitions throughout the era advertised that their rooms were "well ventilated," but probably no other had as much reason to do so.

omon of Beasts, the stupendous and sagacious Elephant, is contrasted by that minute and most beautiful of all delicate quadrupeds, the Brazilian Sanguin."[28] Deference was paid to the developing sentiment that such exhibitions should be more than mere ways of filling an idle hour or indulging a mindless curiosity. The guidebook to the show as it stood in 1800—illustrated, incidentally, with four engravings by Bewick—specified that its descriptions of the animals were "chiefly extracted from the works of Buffon and Goldsmith."

In 1810 Pidcock died, and another veteran menagerist, S. Polito, bought the animals at auction. About 1817 Polito sold out, in turn, to an able entrepreneur named Edward Cross, who, like his predecessors, was a dealer in wild animals as well as a showman. Under Cross's direction the stock was increased to include such relatively unfamiliar exhibits as gnus, llamas, sea lions, emus, boa constrictors, and a bonassus, perhaps the very one which had caused the stir in 1821–22. The former name, "Royal Menagerie," was first inflated to "Royal Grand National Menagerie" and then became a superlative: "The grandest National Depot of Animated Nature in the World . . . the greatest assemblage of curiosities ever collected together since the days of that primeval collector of natural curiosities, Old Noah."[29]

By now, "Exeter Change" had become virtually synonymous with "menagerie" in the London vocabulary. The Strand façade was distinguished by large colored pictures—"daubs," they were more accurately termed at the time—of the monsters to be viewed within, and, in bold lettering, "Edward Cross, Dealer in Foreign Birds and Beasts." At the entrance stood a barker uniformed as a yeoman of the guard, a gaudily feathered macaw swinging on a perch above him. To the importunities he addressed to passersby, the animals upstairs added a jungle obbligato which sometimes startled horses in the roadway.*

The menagerie was open from nine in the morning until nine at night, a shilling admission being charged for each of the three "apartments" or two shillings for the lot. Every paying visitor was entitled to take a lion cub or two in his arms. Just as the ringing of a bell at Vauxhall Gardens was the signal to assemble for the brief demonstration of the mechanical cascade, so here a bell, rung by an elephant, announced the arrival of feeding time, when, it was said, "nature is displayed in the highest point of animation." The fixed hour originally was 8 P.M., but when social custom decreed a new dining time for human beings, this proved incon-

105. Exeter Change (engraved from a drawing by T. H. Shepherd, 1829).

venient to "many of the Nobility." The obliging proprietor therefore announced that henceforth "the Animals will be Fed at Four O'Clock in the Afternoon."[30]

Among the blue-blooded visitors was Lord Byron, who wrote in his journal on 14 November 1813:

Two nights ago I saw the tigers sup at Exeter 'Change. Except Veli Pacha's lion in the Morea,—who followed the Arab keeper like a dog,—the fondness of the hyaena for her keeper amused me most. Such a conversazione! — There was a "hippopotamus," like Lord L[iverpoo]l in the face; and the "Ursine Sloth" hath the very voice and manner of my valet—but the tiger talked too much. The elephant took and gave me my money again—took off my hat—opened a door—*trunked* a whip—and behaved so well, that I wish he was my butler.* The handsomest animal on earth is one of the panthers; but the poor antelopes were dead. I should hate to see one *here:*—the sight of the *camel* made me pine again for Asia Minor.[31]

Fifteen years later, after Byron's death, this same menagerie would supply the imagery for Thomas

Moore's notorious attack on Leigh Hunt. Published in the *Times* as "Hunting the Dead Lion," the seven-stanza poem castigated Hunt for—as Moore and other friends of Byron saw it—defaming the dead poet in his book *Lord Byron and Some of His Contemporaries*. It began:

> Next week will be published (as "Lives" are the rage)
>   The whole Reminiscences, wondrous and strange,
> Of a small puppy-dog that lived once in the cage
>   Of the late noble Lion at Exeter 'Change.

Hunt, the poetaster-puppy dog, is accused of sycophancy, backbiting, ingratitude, and preference for "his own little bow-wows / To the loftiest war-note the Lion could pour." Finally,

> . . . fed as he was (and this makes it a dark case)
>   With slops every day from the Lion's own pan,
> He lifts up his leg at the noble beast's carcase,
>   And—does all a dog, so diminutive, can.[32]

* Presumably this elephant was the famous and ill-fated Chunee, whose acquaintance we are about to make. But it is important to note for the record that Chunee had a predecessor with the same bag of tricks. Benjamin Silliman saw this earlier elephant at Exeter Change in 1805: "Being asked how many gentlemen there were in the room," he wrote, "he gave as many short breathings as corresponded to the number, and the same for the ladies;—he bolted and unbolted the doors, picked up my cane and gave it to me, took off the keeper's hat and put it on, thrust his proboscis into my waistcoat pocket, and took out a piece of money that was there, etc." (*A Journal of Travels in England, Holland, and Scotland . . .*, New York, 1810, I, 159–62.) When Silliman returned to London in 1851 and saw Chunee's skeleton in the museum at the Royal College of Surgeons, he thought this was the animal he had admired—an understandable mistake, considering that in the interim Chunee had entered English lore as "*the* elephant at Exeter Change." (*A Visit to Europe in 1851,* New York, 1853, p. 438.)

106. The interior of Polito's Royal Menagerie, Exeter Change (aquatint, *Ackermann's Repository of Arts*, 1812).

It was not only leisured poet-aristocrats who frequented Exeter Change; young artists often went there on professional business, as they had in Stubbs's time. From 1803 onward, the Swiss painter Jacques Laurent Agasse made many sketches for his long succession of animal canvases. He was a friend of Mr. and Mrs. Cross, whose portraits he painted, and in 1827 George IV commissioned him to paint the giraffe newly arrived at the royal private zoo near Windsor as a present from the Pasha of Egypt. In this picture, now in the Royal Collection, Agasse again portrays Cross, who is seen with the giraffe's Nubian attendants.[33]

In 1810 Benjamin Robert Haydon recorded in his diary that he was studying the musculature of the lion at Pidcock's, and Charles Bell, the "Painter Anatomist" as Haydon called him, bought a dead specimen from Pidcock for the same purpose.[34] The very young Edwin Landseer haunted Exeter Change (as he also did the Tower menagerie), and his biographer tells us that Cross "took a great interest in the young artist, and gave him every facility for prosecuting his studies. Landseer took to the lion with an alacrity that showed how strongly he realized the art potentialities of the king of beasts." Later Cross further encouraged the

developing artist by giving him and a friend a defunct lion, which they somehow carried to their studio, keeping it there so long, in a leisurely course of drawing and dissecting, that the neighbors complained. An especially congenial subject for Landseer was the devoted pair of a lioness and the bitch which had suckled her, as an orphan cub, from her earliest days aboard a ship off West Africa. "Long after the lioness . . . had ceased to be nursed, she still entertained the warmest affection for her foster-mother."[35] It was peculiarly apt that when Nelson's column was erected in Trafalgar Square, only a few hundred yards from the site of Exeter Change, Landseer, by that time one of Victorian England's favorite artists, should have been commissioned to sculpt the lions.

While the lioness and her little friend were delighting the Exeter Change crowds, from 1812 onward the prime attraction unquestionably was Chunee, the elephant who took Byron's money and then scrupulously returned it to him. Imported from Bengal in 1809, Chunee was just another elephant until 26 December 1811, when he made his stage debut at Covent Garden in the pantomime *Harlequin and Padmanaba*. He was Covent Garden's defiant answer to Sadler's Wells and Drury Lane, both of which had recently made theatrical history of a sort by introducing animals into their dramatic performances—dogs at Sadler's Wells, horses at Drury Lane. A writer in the *European Magazine* described Chunee's first performance:

The Sultan of Cashmire (afterwards Pantaloon) appears returning from a tiger-hunt, mounted on an ELEPHANT. This great animal was preceded by a slave with a dish, from which, we suppose, he was indulged with a *sup* of rum; as he appeared to enjoy it much, and dipped in his trunk with infinite complacency. On his neck sat the Lascar who was ordained to guide him; but whether it was, that like a certain other great performer, now divided from us by the Atlantic, he had indulged too freely in his cups, and could not play;* or whether it was that the tremendous noise of his reception deprived him of *sense* and *recollection;* certain it is, that he did not go through with his part. He just got as far as the centre of the stage, and began to kneel to suffer the terrified Sultan to dismount; when the clamorous sounds from galleries, pit, and boxes, seemed to strike his ear and appal his nerves. He rose hastily, and brushed through the affrighted guards, who made ample way for him to pass out among the wings, which he did hastily, to the dismay of the Sultan and the terror and confusion of his attendants.[36]

Other accounts say that Chunee committed the sin, equally unpardonable whether performed by a stage elephant or by human actors, of "rumping" the audience.[37] But despite cries from the pit of "Shame!" and "Off, Off!" the pantomime had a run of forty nights, after which Chunee retired permanently from the stage and, installed at Exeter Change in a den of oak and hammered iron which reputedly cost the great sum of £350, proceeded to become a national institution. As a youngster, Robert Browning was taken to see Chunee; so, indeed, was every well-brought-up London child. The elephant's drawing power was so great that in a lengthy fit of humorous verse published in the *London Magazine* (July 1825) Thomas Hood depicted him as the rival of Charles Mathews, the latest edition of whose "At Home" entertainment was packing crowds into the English Opera House next door.

But there was a less appealing side to Chunee's character. Some years earlier, after scratching his forehead on some nails his keeper had driven into the wall to prevent his rubbing it there, he had attacked the imprudent attendant and might have killed him on the spot had not other keepers intervened.[38] More serious in its consequences was an incident that occurred only a few months after Hood addressed, on his behalf, the "Remonstratory Ode" to Mathews. On the morning

of 1 November one of the menagerie's keepers, John Tietjen, a special favorite of Chunee, entered the elephant's cage to clean it. As was the custom, a fellow attendant brought him the twelve-foot spear that was flourished to keep Chunee "in awe" during the operation. Tietjen, who had earlier called upon a bystander to "observe the extreme docility and playfulness of the animal," said, "Never mind the spear, the elephant knows me well enough," and threw it on the floor. Chunee took it up in his trunk and playfully whirled it about. Tietjen took up a broom, struck the animal with it, and ordered him to turn round. Chunee obeyed, but in doing so thrust his tusk into the keeper, who fell to the floor and died soon after. At a coroner's inquiry held that same day, a witness testified that as soon as he had wounded Tietjen, Chunee "instantly stood still, and began to tremble, as if conscious of the mischief he had done." All agreed that the killing was an accident. The coroner's jury rendered a verdict in accordance with the evidence and laid a nominal "deodand" (fine) of one shilling on the elephant.[39]

This unfortunate episode did not diminish the affectionate regard in which Chunee was held by the nation. And so it was with profound shock that Londoners opened their newspapers four months later, on the morning of Thursday, 2 March 1826, to learn of their beloved elephant's terrible fate.[40] Throughout his adult life, he had been subject "at certain seasons," as the press delicately put it, to fits of ungovernability—"a madness which [made] him totally untractable." Each succeeding year's visitation was more severe. In anticipation of its onset, the keepers, who apparently believed that the symptoms of libido could be suppressed with measures normally employed against constipation, gave him powerful purgatives. Five years earlier the animal's fury was such as to require the administration of six ounces of calomel and fifty-five pounds of Epsom salts made palatable by mixing with molasses, "a dose which would purge some thousands of his Majesty's liege subjects."† The treacly potion worked, but it did not cure.

On Sunday, 26 February, Chunee, weighing five tons and standing eleven or twelve feet high, began to show "strong proofs of irritability, refusing the caresses of his keepers, and attempting to strike at them with his trunk, also at times rolling himself about his den, and forcibly battering its sides," which were composed of iron-bound oak bars three feet in girth. No carpenter dared attempt the necessary repairs. During the following days and nights, the danger grew that Chunee would escape into the room and

* George Frederick Cooke, a brilliant actor and a notorious lush.

† In the interest of scientific accuracy, it should be noted that an alternative diagnosis of Chunee's complaint gained wide credence: "the tooth-ache,—yes, a tooth-ache, gentle reader,—originating in local injury, and exasperated by the cold blasts of the early year." (*Quarterly Review,* 56, 1836, 323.) This writer repeated a statement printed elsewhere at the time, that "a large quantity of matter was found in the jaw near the base of one of the tusks, on dissection. . . . [W]e have the most unquestionable authority for the diseased state of the parts."

batter down the cages of the lions and other ferocious beasts. His trumpeting aroused them all, and they added their various voices to the uproar, which attracted crowds outside in the Strand. The whole area was cordoned off and two parties of Bow Street patrolmen were stationed inside and outside the building to prevent reckless sightseers from rushing onto the premises.

By Tuesday, the violent elephant was threatening to shake the whole building down. It was clearly too late to attempt purgation. Cross, though faced with the prospective loss of an attraction which had brought him handsome returns, decided to have Chunee killed. But to kill a berserk five-ton elephant in confined upstairs quarters, surrounded by agitated wild animals throwing themselves against the bars of their own cages, and in the midst of a great city, was not easy, and there obviously was no precedent for such an operation. The first stratagem, putting corrosive sublimate (mercuric chloride) in Chunee's hay, failed; he merely smelt it and then rejected it.

For what happened the next day (Wednesday) we have the benefit of a narrative later written by an unnamed gentleman who participated in the event:

I was at the gunmaker's, Stevens of Holborn, when Mr. Hering of the New-road came in to borrow rifles and beg Mr. Stevens to return with him to the 'Change to shoot the elephant. Mr. Stevens was a man in years and full of gout, and I knew directly what would happen; he pointed to me as one for his substitute, and in a very few minutes I had selected the rifles, cast balls, etc., and we were on our way to the Exeter 'Change. We arrived there and found the greatest confusion; beasts and birds most uproarious, set on by witnessing the struggle to keep in order the ungovernable elephant. . . . Mr. Cross was much vexed with his coming loss, and Mrs. Cross in tears.

I was supposed in that day a steady rifle shot, and with Mr. Hering, in my conceit and ignorance, intended to kill the poor brute with our first fire. Dr. Brooks [the anatomist] had tried the poisons, and by his directions we fired into a crease rather below the blade-bone. I expected to see him fall; instead of which he made a sharp hissing noise, and struck heavily at us with his trunk and tried to make after us, and would but for the formidable double-edged spear-blades of the keepers. These spears were ten feet long at least, wielded from a spiked end below, and the trunk wounded itself in endeavours to seize the double-edged blades. It was most fortunate the poor beast stood our fires so long afterwards, for, had he fallen suddenly, and struggled in death, his struggles would have brought him from out of his cage or den, and if he had fallen from the strong flooring built under for the support of his great weight, my belief is, through whole flooring we should have all gone together, lions and men, tigers and birds. He struggled much to come after us, and we were compelled to reload in the passage.

The civilian firing squad having failed in its mission, the next resort was to call in a detail of soldiers from Somerset House. But the British army in turn did not do itself proud. "They had but three cartridges each man. . . . I for a time was compelled to load the muskets for the men; they had not the least notion of a flask; they ran the powder into the musket-barrels in most uncertain quantities, and I was compelled to unload and reload for them, or we should have had some much worse accident."[41] These blundering fusillades had no more effect than if the elephant's head were a bale of cotton. Two surgeons were called in to advise where the riflemen might find the most vulnerable spots. But as the surrounding animals continued to roar and scream, and the whole building trembled with the ferocity of Chunee's assaults on his cage, it was not until about a hundred balls had been fired into him that the first signs of pain appeared, probably because one shot had landed under his ear. "His eyes," according to a newspaper account, "instantly appeared like balls of fire; he shook his head with dreadful fury, and rushed against the front of his den, and broke part of it, and it was expected every moment that the massy pillars, strengthened with plates of iron, would have given way."[42] At this point, as a last desperate resort, a cannon was called for, but before it arrived, a keeper pierced Chunee's vitals with a harpoon. This wound, combined with the cumulative effect of 152 balls, brought him down. "The quantity of blood that flowed from him flooded the den to a considerable depth."

It was a moment that affected all who were present, and, thanks to an attentive press, the millions who read about it in the days and weeks to come. According to our participant, the scene suggested the dignified death of a Roman statesman: "the noble brute seated himself on his haunches; he then folded his forelegs under him, adjusted his trunk, and ceased to live, the only peaceful one among us cruel wretches."[43] Another witness saw Chunee's last moments in a more pathetic light: "He sunk down slowly and majestically on his haunches, and expired, in the posture which is assumed by the elephant when about to be loaded, and which he was most wont to assume when ordered."[44] The obedient Chunee murdered by his friends: that was what hurt. Inevitably, what actually happened was revised in the telling so as to give more play to sentiment. Some years later, a contributor to Charles Knight's encyclo-

107. *Destruction of the Furious Elephant at Exeter Change* (broadside by George Cruikshank, 1826).

pedic *London* apostrophized Chunee in these not untypical terms:

Thine was a sagacious and noble nature. We should not like to have been that one of thy keepers who, after helping to fire into that hapless body some eighty shots, bade thee kneel, little expecting, we may be sure, thou wouldst obey; but thou didst; and beheld thee, in the midst of all thy agony, kneel down. Gradually thou droppest on thy knees, and in calm dignity let the pitiless storm beat on. When they grew tired, they found thee still in that posture, erect, but dead.[45]

As soon as the shooting was over and the elephant lay huge and silent in the blood-spattered wreck of his den, Cross understandably allowed his concern for his ledger books to overrule his feelings and admitted the public, at the usual charge, to view the grisly scene. While he wrestled with his next problem, how to dispose of a dead elephant in the center of London, applications, advice, and distinguished sightseers came from every direction. All the anatomical students in London demanded to be present at the dissection, and offers were made for parcels of elephant meat. Sir Humphry Davy, the Bishop of London, and, of course, Lord Stowell made their inspections; a phrenologist took a mold of Chunee's head, requiring seven and a half hundredweight of plaster of Paris for the job. Another phrenologist, the eminent Spurzheim, it was rumored, was to dissect the brain. But he was not, in the event, allowed that privilege: Cross, for good commercial reasons, wanted to keep the head intact.

On Saturday (4 March) the Bow Street magistrates ordered Cross to get rid of his monstrous public nuisance that very night. Cross did his best to comply. After a major engineering project succeeded in raising the carcass from the floor, nine butchers worked twelve hours to flay the hide, after which a dozen or so surgeons, watched by a corps of medical students, dismantled his innards. By ten o'clock Sunday night, the stench having meanwhile pervaded the whole neighborhood, the operation was completed. At long last, the remains of Chunee, 10,000 pounds of him, were hauled off in a long procession of carts, and quantities

108. Exeter Change: positively the last week (anonymous engraving).

of "perfume" (scented disinfectant?) were doused over the scene of the carnage.

In the aftermath, the *Times* printed a letter from Dr. Brookes denying an evening paper's report that he "dressed and ate part of the putrid elephant." Another letter, signed "Chuny," protested Cross's having confined the elephant in so narrow a box and deprived him of a mate. In the time-honored manner of correspondents to the *Times,* this writer pointed out that they ordered things better at the Jardin des Plantes; that elephants could be cared for more humanely at the Tower of London; and that while Frenchmen could enter the Jardin des Plantes free, Englishmen had to pay to see "our national establishment at the Tower."[46] The press at large catered to the nation's avidity for every particular of Chunee's life and death and everything relating to elephants in general. The *Mirror of Literature* rather insensitively ran recipes for elephant steaks and stew, not thinking to preface them with the necessary condition, "First catch your ele-

phant." The same paper recalled Chunee's attachment to Edmund Kean, whom he had instantly recognized after the tragedian's return from America, and reprinted "anecdotes of elephants" from reference books.[47] Innumerable poems were written on Chunee's passing, one beginning, not unpredictably, "Farewell, poor Chuny! generous beast, farewell!" A tribute of sorts came from Exeter Change's neighbors, the proprietors of Warren's shoe blacking, who preceded E. Moses and Son in the art of versified advertising:

The elephant, lately at Exeter 'Change,
　Poor Chuny, first viewing a well-polished boot,
The sight of his shade in the jet seem'd so strange
　And strongly impress'd that his favourite pursuit
Was, afterwards, curious and minute inspection
Of visiters characterised by reflection
From 30, the Strand, and his voice never slack in
The glad recognition of Warren's jet blacking![48]

AN UPROAR ON CHANGE OR A TRIP FROM EXETER TO CHARING CROSS.

Thomas Hood, following up his former ode, now wrote an equally lengthy "Address to Mr. Cross, of Exeter 'Change on the Death of the Elephant" with an epigraph borrowed from Byron's poem *The Giaour:* "'Tis *Greece,* but living *Greece* no more." A small sample will be enough:

> The very beasts lament the change, like me;
>   The shaggy Bison
> Leaneth his head dejected on his knee!
> Th' Hyaena's laugh is hush'd, and Monkeys pout,
> The Wild Cat frets in a complaining whine,
> The Panther paces restlessly about
>   To walk her sorrow out;
> The Lions in a deeper bass repine,—
> The Kangaroo wrings its sorry short fore paws,
>   Shrieks come from the Macaws;
> The old bald Vulture shakes his naked head,
>   And pineth for the dead,
> The Boa writhes into a double knot,
>   The Keeper groans
>   Whilst sawing bones,
> And looks askance at the deserted spot—
> Brutal and rational lament his loss,

> The flower of thy beastly family!
>   Poor Mrs. Cross
> Sheds frequent tears into her daily tea,
>   And weakens her Bohea![49]

There was an instant catchpenny literature on Chunee. Several dramatic prints illustrating the fatal fusillade were sold in printshops and on the streets; Limbird, the publisher of the *Mirror of Literature,* issued one within forty hours of Chunee's death. A leaflet promised to provide *Every Particular Respecting the Madness of the Tremendous Elephant at Exeter Change, and the Manner Adopted to Destroy That Living Mountain, by Firing Nearly 150 Balls, with Particulars Relating to His Dissection*—a truly mendacious claim, because after page one, which was occupied by the title and a woodcut, only three more pages were left for the exhaustive particulars.[50] Six weeks later, a play entitled *Chuneelah; or, The Death of the Elephant at Exeter 'Change,* was performed with success at Sadler's Wells.

For a while, Chunee dead proved as profitable as Chunee living. Cross exhibited his skeleton, complete with bullet-riddled skull, in his late cage before taking it on tour in the provinces. Later (1829) it was shown at the Egyptian Hall.[51] Then, after a brief stay at the new London University, it wound up in the Hunterian Museum of the Royal College of Surgeons, towering over the diminutive bones of the Sicilian Fairy and the larger ones of the Living Skeleton.*

The martyred elephant remained in the national consciousness for many years. Dickens's contribution to Chuneean mythography was brief and characteristic. Ten years after the event, he wrote in the *Morning Chronicle,* in a passage excised when the piece was reprinted in *Sketches by Boz:* "The death of the elephant was a great shock to us; we knew him well; and having enjoyed the honour of his intimate acquaintance for some years, felt grieved—deeply grieved—that in a paroxysm of insanity he should have so far forgotten all his estimable and companionable qualities as to exhibit a sanguinary desire to scrunch his faithful valet, and pulverize even Mrs. Cross herself, who for a long period had evinced towards him that pure and touching attachment which woman alone can feel."[52]

Dickens obviously failed to share the sentimental hysteria over the great beast's fall; Chunee was not on *his* conscience. Gradually the nation's sense of guilt faded, leaving the elephant, a commanding figure in the modern bestiary, to serve as a vehicle for gentle, wry moralizing. Douglas Jerrold, adopting the persona of an early Victorian Lord Chesterfield in his series "Punch's Letters to His Son" (*Punch,* 1842) reminisced:

You were six years old when I took you to see my friend Mr. Polito's elephant, and gave you a halfpenny. With a nascent generosity, which nearly brought tears to my paternal eyes, you flung down the copper coin at the feet of the majestic animal. Remember you not your first wonder, when the elephant took the halfpenny up? what a curve he gave his trunk! how many bendings and turnings he employed ere he placed the halfpenny cake, purchased with Christian-like sagacity of the tradesman near his den, in his capacious mouth! The same action employed by that elephant to pick up a halfpenny, would be applied to the tearing up by the roots of the forest plane. My son, the elephant is a practical politician: remember him, and if you get exalted, do nothing great or small unless you do it with a twist.[53]

Chunee's martyrdom, the climactic episode in Exeter Change's long career, was a close harbinger of its end. In order to accommodate the widening of the Strand, as part of the urban improvement program that would result in Trafalgar Square, the building was slated for demolition, and in 1828 London witnessed a strange procession, Cross's animals migrating to a new ark only a short distance away—the King's Mews, Charing Cross. Hood wrote:

> Let Exeter Change lament its change,
> Its beasts and other losses—
> Another place thrives by its case,
> Now *Charing* has two *Crosses*.[54]

This relocation, however, was only a stopgap expedient, because the King's Mews also was scheduled to be pulled down; its site, after briefly accommodating the Jonah's Whale lounge mentioned above, would eventually be occupied by the new National Gallery. Cross's next move with his migratory menagerie would be the final one.

* Chunee's skeleton was destroyed by bombing in the Second World War, but, as has been noted, those of the Sicilian Fairy and O'Brien, the Irish giant, survive in the museum. The once "Living" Skeleton has unaccountably disappeared from the Hunterian collection.

Zoos and Pleasure Gardens

23

Less than two months after Chunee's death, Edward Cross, knowing he would eventually have to move from Exeter Change, proposed that the newly founded Zoological Society buy what it wanted from his stock for its as yet unformed menagerie. Receiving no response, he made another overture later in the year, offering to sell his entire collection to the society and in addition to accept appointment as the manager of its menagerie. This time, both offers were declined.[1] Instead of amalgamating, therefore, Cross and the Zoological Society, the two owners of permanent menageries, went their separate ways.

Cross, as we have just seen, found temporary accommodation for his animals at the King's Mews. Meanwhile the Zoological Society moved into its own gardens in the northeastern quarter of Regent's Park in 1828, to the accompaniment of much favorable publicity. Here, in grounds and enclosures designed by Decimus Burton, the architect of the Colosseum then being completed on the other side of the park, wild animals—the smaller ones, at least; the large carnivora were another matter—and birds were exhibited for the first time in London history in accommodations reasonably well suited to their individual requirements. Facilities were provided for their "hybernation" (impossible, one would think, at Exeter Change); monkeys had at their disposal both houses on poles and enclosed cages; eagles and vultures perched in a large aviary; the wolves had a den and large cage, the beavers a dam, the bears a pit—but the Andean llamas, for some inscrutable reason, were installed in a house

of Gothic design.[2] ("These animals," warned the *Picturesque Guide to the Regent's Park,* "usually show their enmity by spitting in your face.")

The original collection of 430 animals and birds, purchased from dealers and contributed by members, soon began to grow. Shortly after George IV's death the new king, William IV, donated the Royal Menagerie from Sandpit Gate, Windsor, including its celebrated giraffe. Shortly thereafter, the Zoo acquired the remaining animals from the Tower of London. This ancient collection, which had dwindled to a few dispirited birds and an elephant and grizzly bear by the first years of the century, had been replenished by a diligent new keeper, Alfred Cops, as a private venture, and by 1830 it included, besides numerous snakes and monkeys, 60 other birds and beasts, among them lions, leopards, a tigress, hyenas, and an alligator. But the facilities at the Tower were dilapidated and inefficient, and the absorption of the old menagerie by the new—the royal animals in 1831–32, Cops's in 1834—was a notable step forward.[3]

The Regent's Park Zoo had over 30,000 visitors in its first seven months.[4] Admission was only by member's order and the payment of a shilling. For a while the gardens were a fashionable place to visit, the society's distinguished board of directors and membership ensuring that they would attract a high-quality clientele. On Sundays especially, it was said, as much influence was needed to obtain a ticket to the Zoo as to get a seat in a box at the opera. But after the novelty wore off, and strict Sabbatarians took exception to the fad of spending Sunday afternoons at the Zoo, the gardens became less popular. Visitors in the mid- and late thirties found the grounds neglected and the animal population meager. For there was, alas, a darker side to the roseate picture originally presented. The grounds and the society's headquarters may have been designed by Burton, but evidently no one but a third-rate traveling showman could have put together the large-animal houses, which, it was said, "were nothing better than caravans dismounted from their wheels." What with their close confinement and the perpetual dampness of the Marylebone clay, the lions, tigers, and pumas lived, on an average, no more than two years after their arrival. Between 1832 and 1836 alone, the Zoo lost nine lions. To replace the wooden huts, the Society built in 1840 a series of outdoor terrace dens which did nothing to lower the mortality rate, because, "rushing from one extreme to the other, tropical animals were left exposed to the full rigour of winter. The drifting rain fell upon their hair, and they were exposed in cold, wet weather to a temperature which even man, who ranges from the torrid zone to the arctic circle, could not resist unprotected." The provision of matting and heating apparatus during the winter was of little avail. Meanwhile, in the monkey house, the heating and ventilation were so wretched that carbon monoxide took a nightly toll; the keepers removed the dead by the barrowful in the morning.[5]

It is to the credit of a few Londoners, at least, that the deficiencies of the Zoological Society's "zeal in behalf of the general interest of knowledge and humanity" were brought to public attention. A writer in the *Quarterly Review* in 1836, adopting a viewpoint that would find acceptance today, declared that in a truly humane zoo "the total alteration of life, the entire disorganization of system which must arise in the case of an animal destined by nature for the most uncontrolled freedom, and to be supported by contingent supplies, few and far between—purchased moreover by laborious roamings, huntings, and watchings,—should be taken into the account. The difference between the desert or the wilderness, and the cage—between the casual prey and the regular supply of beef, would be sufficient to produce disease. . . . Larger and drier dens, well elevated from the soil, and, above all, well ventilated, . . . would enable the animals to take some exercise, and amuse themselves instead of dosing away the monotonous lethargic life to which they are now doomed."[6]

A few months later, Leigh Hunt, who knew what imprisonment was like (he had served two years in jail

for libeling the Prince Regent), went further. Responding to the Zoological Society's argument that if the animals admittedly did not live in ideal conditions in Regent's Park they would be far worse off in other hands, Hunt asked why wild animals should be kept in captivity at all. "Why can we have Acts of Parliament in favour of other extension of good treatment to the brute creation, and not one against their tormenting imprisonment? At all events, we may ask meantime, and perhaps not uselessly even for present purposes, whether a great people, under a still finer aspect of knowledge and civilization than at present, would think themselves warranted in keeping *any* set of fellow-creatures in a state of endless captivity—their faculties contradicted, their very lives, for the most part, turned into lingering deaths?"[7]

Recognizing that such a proposal was bound to get nowhere, Hunt concluded by urging that the least the Society could do would be to enlarge the accommodations so as to give their occupants greater ranging space. Little was done, however, and the Zoo continued to decline. It was saved by an energetic superintendent appointed in 1847, David W. Mitchell, a man of advanced museological principles who was bent on making his exhibition a pleasant and instructive place for the public at large. Even before his appointment, the requirement that each visitor present a voucher from a member had been dropped, and soon after Mitchell took office he reduced the entrance fee to sixpence on Mondays, which immediately became the most popular time to visit, and holidays. He spruced up—and, at long last, drained—the grounds, improved and added to the buildings, arranged special exhibitions, and expanded the collection's scope, adding reptiles in 1849 and fish and mollusca in 1853. In 1852 he instituted Saturday afternoon band concerts.[8]

Most important of all, so far as attracting the general public was concerned, Mitchell introduced what soon became known as the "starring" system, whereby a single new and noteworthy acquisition received special publicity. In 1850 the Zoo acquired a hippopotamus, the gift of the Viceroy of Egypt. Previously it had been considered impracticable, if not impossible, to transport such an animal and then keep it alive in zoo conditions, but Mitchell proved it could be done—and in the process attracted long lines of carriages to the garden's entrance. The hippopotamus was, as one writer put it, the lion of the day, and *Punch* made many cheerful references to it. But stars rise and fall, and eventually the hippo was demoted when the crowds flocked instead to see a newly arrived female elephant

110. *A Prospecte of ye Zoological Societye—Its Gardens. Feedynge ye Beasts* (drawing by Richard Doyle, *Punch,* 19 November 1849).

and her calf, and later an iguana, a chimpanzee, and an anteater. Mitchell's policy of acquiring as many novel specimens as possible and of advertising their arrival in the newspapers bore fruit in steadily increasing patronage.

All was not yet well with some of the animals, however. In 1855, four years before Mitchell left Regent's Park to become superintendent of the Jardin d'Acclimatation in Paris, the miserable condition of the larger carnivora was again deplored in the press.

Why [demanded a writer in the *Quarterly Review*] do we coop these noble animals in such nutshells of cages? What a miserable sight to see them pace backwards and forwards in their box-like dens! Why should they, of all the beasts of the forest, be condemned to such imprisonment? The bear has its pole, and the deer its paddock, the otter his pool, where at least they have enough liberty to keep them in health; but we stall our lions and tigers as we would oxen, till they grow lethargic, fat, and puffy, like city aldermen. With half an acre of enclosed ground, strewn with sand, we might see the king of beasts pace freely, as in his Libyan fastness, and with twenty feet of artificial rock might witness the tiger's bound.[9]

While some improvements gradually were made in this direction, the big animals did not achieve the fullest freedom possible under modern conditions until the development in the early 1930s of the Whipsnade annex to the Zoo, on the Dunstable Downs.*

Ⅾℨ❋℈Ⅾ

As the nineteenth century began, Vauxhall Gardens continued to be the chief site of Londoners' al fresco entertainment, supplemented but never rivaled by the numerous tea gardens and other pocket-sized outdoor amenities offered by suburban taverns. It was still a recreation place for all classes, from aristocrats to artisans. The Prince of Wales was a regular visitor, as other members of his family had been in the past. But even sustained royal patronage could not protect the gardens from less wholesome developments. From the 1770s onward there had been a persistent problem of rowdyism, in an effort to curb which the admission price was raised in 1792 from one shilling to two (three on "gala nights"). It would eventually be raised to four

* The Zoological Society also had a museum, which was intended as a study collection rather than a public attraction. Housed successively in Bruton Street, in John Hunter's former house in Leicester Square, and in Golden Square, it finally was moved (1843) to the old carnivora house in Regent's Park, where it was open to Zoo visitors without extra charge. The British Museum, which had declined to accept the collection as a gift in 1841, received the major part of it in 1853–1855, the remainder going to colleges in Ireland and to provincial museums. The 1,500 specimens acquired by the British Museum were spoken of as "the most important and historical accession ever received" by the Natural History Departments of the museum. (*The History of the Collections Contained in the Natural History Departments of the British Museum,* London, 1904–1906, II, 63.)

on some occasions. Higher prices, however, did not keep out the undesirables, and Vauxhall's developing reputation for occasional riotousness and licentiousness (it became something of a summer retreat for a class of women then known by the erudite euphemism of "Paphians") eventually sped its decline.*

But possibly the most serious problem facing the management was the character of the entertainment offered. Vauxhall had prospered for three quarters of a century by offering a fixed combination of attractions. At long last, people were tiring of them, and it was in danger of becoming an anachronism. Its record from the 1790s onward is largely one of attempting—unsuccessfully in the long run—to cater to new tastes while preserving at least a vestige of the special atmosphere that the name "Vauxhall Gardens" connoted. The major changes occurred in the second decade of the century. The tin cascade was done away with about 1816, and in the same period many trees were cut down and two sides of the grove were roofed in with a vaulted colonnade, drastically reducing what Horace Walpole had called the place's "gardenhood." In the Saloon, Hayman's and Hogarth's pictures, now sadly deteriorated, were joined by a contrivance called, unspeakably, the Heptaplasiesoptron, which consisted of cleverly arranged glass plates producing reflections of "revolving pillars, palm-trees, twining serpents, coloured lamps, and a fountain."[10]

In 1814, two years after the sensational debut of the Siege of Gibraltar show in the Sadler's Wells tank, Vauxhall put on its own naumachia, which, lacking a body of water for the ships to maneuver in, depended for its effectiveness on mechanical devices and fireworks. The latter had been surprisingly late in arriving at Vauxhall, but from this point on they would be as indispensable a feature as the reputed 20,000 lamps that lighted the paths. As often as possible, fireworks were employed in conjunction with the large pictures which represented the management's determination to provide a spectacular outdoor equivalent of the in-town panoramas. In 1823, at the end of the Cross Walk (now renamed the Chinese Walk because of the lanterns lining it), an eighty-foot-high scene of the Bay of Naples erupted nightly. Between that year and 1837 the Vauxhall pictures portrayed Fingal's Cave, the ruins of an Italian abbey, Virginia Water, the burning of York Minster and the Houses of Parliament, Mont Blanc, St. Michael's Mount, Venice, a Gothic abbey, and a Balkan pass.†

In 1827 space was cleared for an open-air theatre accommodating 1,200 spectators on rows of benches

raked forty feet high. Pückler-Muskau was among those who saw the Battle of Waterloo reenacted there as the opening attraction. It seems to have been quite a production. Before the huge red curtain parted, a cannon discharged and the band of the Second Guards Regiment was heard in the distance; then the scene was revealed—the outwork of Houguemont in "artificial daylight," on a gently rising ground amid the old horse chestnut trees of Vauxhall. The French Gardes advanced from the wood, headed by bearded Sapeurs, and as Napoleon rode past in review, "a thousand voices" cried "Vive l'Empereur!" Distant firing was heard, and the French rode off. Wellington and his staff entered, conferred, and rode slowly off in turn. Then the battle began:

whole columns then advance upon each other, and charge with the bayonet; the French cuirassiers charge the Scotch Grays; and as there are a thousand men and two hundred horses in action, and no spare of gunpowder, it is, for a moment, very like a real battle. The storming of Houguemont, which is set on fire by several shells, was particularly well done; the combatants were for a time hidden by the thick smoke of real fire, or only rendered partially visible by the flashes of musquetry, while the foreground was strewed with the dead and dying. As the smoke cleared off, Houguemont was seen in flames,—the English as conquerors, the French as captives: in the distance was Napoleon on horseback, and behind him his carriage-and-four hurrying across the scene. The victorious Wellington was greeted with loud cheers mingled with the thunder of the distant cannon. The ludicrous side of the exhibition was the making Napoleon race across the stage several times, pursued and fugitive, to tickle English vanity, and afford a triumph to the "plebs" in good and bad coats.[11]

This two-hour show was Vauxhall's response to the success of the Battle of Waterloo spectacle at Astley's Amphitheatre three years earlier, in which horses by the score and actor soldiers by the hundred were used. In some ways the outdoor show may have excelled Astley's, if the advertised description of the grand finale was anywhere near the truth: "a superb Display of FIREWORKS will take place, and . . . will assume a novel and appropriate effect: during which MR. COOKE will manoeuvre his War Chariot and Six Horses, then mount his celebrated Charger, Bucephalus, and, at full speed, ride up a nearly perpendicular Rock, to the Temple of Fame, at the summit of the Fire-Work Tower, and there deposit the British and French Colors, as an Emblem of Amity, in the Temple of Concord, a Feat unequalled in the Annals of Horsemanship."[12] The show probably cost too much to be-

* An indication of the continuing attractiveness of the Vauxhall idea as a commercial speculation is the fact that in 1812 some unnamed projectors proposed to take fourteen acres near Regent's Park (then still in the planning stage) and create what was to be called the Royal Elysium. It would be replete with cascades, fountains, walks, Chinese pavilions, and a 400-foot-square sheet of water on which naval victories would be portrayed by "Hydraulic Mechanism." A calculation of the expected receipts and outlays enabled the speculators to conclude that they would clear £32,800 a year. (Prospectus, JJ Coll., London Play Places box 7.) Unfortunately, they never had a chance to test how accurate the projection was.

† One of the few historical inaccuracies in *Vanity Fair* occurs (Ch. 6) in the course of the memorable visit to Vauxhall in 1813 by Becky Sharp, Jos Sedley, George and Amelia Osborne, and Dobbin. Thackeray says that at the "panorama of Moscow . . . a rude fellow, treading on Miss Sharp's foot, caused her to fall back with a little shriek into the arms of Mr. Sedley." There was no panorama of Moscow at Vauxhall until the fifties. (Another Thackerayan scene at Vauxhall, during which Pen pays two shillings to get himself and Fanny Bolton a special vantage point at the fireworks show, occurs in *Pendennis*, Ch. 46.)

111. Picture model of Venice at Vauxhall Gardens (*Illustrated London News,* 12 June 1847). The fearless acrobat Joel Il Diavolo is beginning his descent at the top of the picture.

come a regular feature, but from that time onward the Waterloo Grounds, as the site was called, were the scene of numerous panoramic and pyrotechnic displays. Among these were a three-part show of Captain Ross's Arctic expedition involving seventy-foot-high canvas and wood icebergs (1834) and, coinciding with the Chinese enthusiasm in the early forties, a "dioramic view" of the Golden Temple of Honan, "The Hall of the Celestial Kings," illuminated by colored fire.[13] In 1847 the feature was a view of Venice from the entrance to the Grand Canal; during the fireworks, an acrobat named Joel Il Diavolo descended head-first down a wire from the top of St. Mark's campanile as squibs and crackers exploded from his cap and heels.[14] The addition of acrobats to the fireworks seems to have been a popular innovation. Early in the fifties, after an equestrian show and tableaux of a plaster Napoleon dying and a cardboard Wellington riding to victory, the bill concluded with a pyrotechnic display of the burning of Moscow. A German visitor described the climax: "It is Moscow! It is the Kremlin, and they are burning it! Sounds of music, voices of lamentation, issue from the flames,

guns are firing, rockets shoot up and burst with an awful noise, the walls give way—they fall, and from the general destruction issues a young girl, with very thin clothing and very little of it, who makes her escape over a rope at a dizzy height."[15] This last, at least, was a touch Burford and Daguerre would have scorned to adopt. But Vauxhall was fighting to keep alive.

Another symptom of the management's desperation, appearing in the mid-thirties, was its decision to open the gardens during the day. In a newspaper piece titled "Vauxhall Gardens by Day" (reprinted in *Sketches by Boz,* 1836–37), Dickens wrote:

There was a time when if a man ventured to wonder how Vauxhall Gardens would look by day, he was hailed with a shout of derision at the absurdity of the idea. Vauxhall by daylight! A porter-pot without porter, the House of Commons without the Speaker, a gas-lamp without the gas—pooh, nonsense, the thing was not to be thought of. It was rumoured, too, in those times, that Vauxhall Gardens by day were the scene of secret and hidden experiments; that there, carvers were exercised in the mystic art of cutting a moderate-sized ham into slices thin enough to pave the whole of the grounds; that beneath the shade of the tall trees, studious men were constantly engaged in chemical experiments, with the view of discovering how much water a bowl of negus could possibly bear; and that in some retired nooks, appropriated to the study of ornithology, other sage and learned men were, by a process known only to themselves, incessantly employed in reducing fowls to a mere combination of skin and bone.

Visiting the grounds, Dickens found that in the sunlight the reality belied both the affectionate lore and the well-remembered Elysium-by-night, when "illuminated groves, . . . the temples and saloons and cosmoramas and fountains glittered and sparkled before our eyes" and "a few hundred thousand of additional lamps dazzled our senses." Paying his shilling at the gate, he discovered that the entrance itself was "nothing more nor less than a combination of very roughly-painted boards and sawdust," and the "Moorish tower" on the firework ground a mere "wooden shed with a door in the centre, and daubs of crimson and yellow all round, like a gigantic watchcase!" After the advertised orchestral concert, performed by "a small party of dismal men in cocked hats," he "walked about, and met with a disappointment at every turn; our favourite views were mere patches of paint; the fountain that had sparkled so showily by lamp-light, presented very much the appearance of a water-pipe that had burst; all the ornaments were dingy, and all the walks gloomy. There was a spectral attempt at rope-dancing in the little open theatre. The sun shone upon the spangled dresses of the performers, and their evolutions were about as inspiriting and appropriate as a country-dance in a family vault."[16]

Dickens went on to describe a balloon launching, a popular new form of outdoor entertainment for which Vauxhall Gardens served as the principal site. The most famous of the balloons based there was the Royal Vauxhall, a pear-shaped bag in alternate stripes of red and white. In November 1836 it carried the aeronaut Charles Green on a record 480-mile flight from Vauxhall to Wilburg, in the German duchy of Nassau, after which it was rechristened the Royal Nassau.[17] The next season, the management exploited the gardens' association with the flight by exhibiting, in what was then called the Ballet Theatre, a 400-foot-long moving panorama of the whole trip, beginning with the balloon's launching only a few feet away and showing aeronaut's-eye views of London, Chatham, Dover, the Channel, Calais, Brussels, Coblenz, and Ehrenbreitstein.[18]

From the late 1840s onward the press greeted each new season with complaints about the intensifying vulgarity of both the attractions and the clientele and protests about the multiple payments exacted to see the various individual shows. To this expense were added cab fare and bridge toll from London and the exorbitant prices charged for the infamous Vauxhall ham sandwiches, oleaginous salad, vinegary wines, and skinny fowl.[19] By 1853, the proprietors' application for a renewed amusement license evoked complaints from nearby residents, who were particularly incensed by the all-night *bals masqués* which, they said, were "frequented by many disreputable characters." The license was renewed, but with the stipulation that the revels end at 3 A.M., with no fireworks after 11 P.M.[20] One recurrent misfortune, at least, could not be blamed on the management. Whether or not the meteorological records would bear out the claim, it was widely believed that the special Vauxhall fete days each season, like Ascot Week later on, were the automatic signal for the heavens to open; farmers, it was said, avoided planning to cut their hay on those advertised dates.[21]

There was some pathos in the display during one of the wettest of summers (1848) of a model of a Vauxhall transformed in imitation of Paris's Jardin d'Hiver. The walks would be fully enclosed against the weather and heated as well as lighted by a great number of gas burners, and along the sides would be displayed "a panoramic exhibition of the overland route to India." The rotunda was to become an elegant restaurant, and the Waterloo Grounds were to be converted into an immense hippodrome.[22] This, of course, was nothing but fantasy. Vauxhall sank deeper into ignominy and disrepair, and in 1859 the grounds were sold off for building lots. The movable properties brought a paltry £800 at auction.

⊳₃✳₃⊲

Vauxhall's demise was hastened by the competition provided in its last years by the Cremorne Gardens, opened in 1846 on a twelve-acre tract along the river between Chelsea and Fulham, now the site of the Lots Road power station. Surrounding the chief building, which contained a bandstand and dance floor, were a "Chinese pagoda, a Swiss chalet, an Indian temple, a large theatre, . . . a marionette theatre, concert room, small circus, restaurant, fernery, menagerie, American bowling saloon, shooting gallery, and gypsy's tent"—a sufficiently new and various array of features to lure customers away from shabby, patched-up Vauxhall.[23]

But Vauxhall's more formidable competition had begun much earlier and was also, unfortunately, much closer at hand. At Edward Cross's Surrey Zoological Gardens one could have the best of two worlds—the zoological, as otherwise represented in Regent's Park, and the spectacular, as represented in the Vauxhall pyrotechnic panoramas; and the Surrey gave more for the money than either of those places.[24]

In 1831, having failed to interest the Zoological Society in taking over his dispossessed animals with himself as curator, Cross devised a new plan. At a meeting he initiated at the Horns tavern, Kennington, was founded the Surrey Literary, Scientific and Zoological Institution (soon amended to the Surrey Zoological and Botanical Institution). Cross, reported the *Morning Advertiser,* was "a respectable individual, whose zeal and assiduity in the formation of the contemplated Society could not be surpassed"—as was only to be expected, since he intended himself to be the principal beneficiary of the scheme once it got off the ground. He immediately offered to sell his menagerie to the nascent society for £3,500; Lord Holland offered to let the necessary land for £40 a year; and within a short time an impressive list of patrons was compiled, headed by Queen Adelaide, the Archbishop of Canterbury, and the Duke of Devonshire.

Thus supported, the transpontine rival to the Regent's Park Zoo—"If Oxford has its sausage, / Why not Cambridge have its tart?"—became a reality. The émigrés from Exeter Change moved across the river to the thirteen-acre grounds of the former manor house of Walworth, due east of Vauxhall in the vicinity of the present Penton Place, between Kennington Park and Walworth Roads. Beginning as a commercial imitation of the institutionally owned Regent's Park Zoo, the Surrey initially eclipsed its rival. What was at Regent's Park, demanded the *Mirror of Literature,* "which can be at all compared with the circular glass building of three hundred feet in diameter, combining a series of examples of tropical quadrupeds and birds, and of exotic plants?"[25] This combination conservatory and carnivora house was, in fact, in advance of its time; its 6,000 square feet of glass anticipated, on a modest scale, the Crystal Palace of twenty years later. Adjacent to it were aviaries and an octagon housing zebras, emus, and kangaroos.

The animals represented the most distinct advantage that the Surrey Gardens enjoyed over Vauxhall, so uncomfortably close by, in its first years. Another was the fact that the Surrey grounds, with their promenades, flower beds, statuary, fountains, grottoes, and cascades, were new, with none of the creeping decrepitude that was afflicting Vauxhall. Moreover, the Surrey enjoyed a notable feature that Vauxhall lacked—a three-acre lake with two islets. It was, therefore, in an excellent position to give the older establishment a run for its money. But soon it became apparent that a menagerie alone, however well stocked and housed, and including a giant tortoise on which children could ride, was not enough of an attraction to support an operation of this size.*

The Regent's Park Zoo was subsidized by a well-heeled society, while the Surrey depended wholly on its shilling-a-head admissions and family season tickets costing a guinea (three guineas for a family of more than five). The new gardens therefore faced the same problem Vauxhall had to cope with: the constant one of bringing the customers back, season after season, to see new attractions.

Some of the extra features the Surrey introduced were lastingly successful, others not. From the very beginning until the mid-fifties, it was the scene (as Vauxhall never was) of annual flower shows, which brought it a high-class clientele and much dignified publicity. On the other hand, one notable attempt to emulate Vauxhall backfired. In 1838, two years after the Royal Nassau's first flight, the Surrey Gardens advertised its own ascent, involving a balloon as high as the Duke of York's Column and half the circumference of St. Paul's dome, with a wickerwork car fifteen feet long. A large crowd gathered in the grandstand overlooking the lake. The hours passed, nothing happened, and the spectators grew restive. At seven o'clock a small boat passed along the lake bearing a sign: "The balloon cannot ascend but to compensate for the unavoidable disappointment an eruption will take place at dusk." But the crowd was in no mood to accept a substitute, and so it proceeded to riddle the balloon with stones and bottles, after which it cut the guy ropes of the suspension masts and the balloon collapsed.[26] One can understand why the management thereafter left the aeronautics to Vauxhall and, later, Cremorne.

The eruption which the dissatisfied customers declined to watch that night was a much more dependable item on the Surrey Gardens' bill. In fact, the Vesuvius show of 1837–38, which was the one alluded to, was the first in an extended series of "modelled panorama" and fireworks shows that were the establishment's distinctive specialty, although Vauxhall soon

* It was sometimes said that the Surrey animals kept healthier than those at Regent's Park. (*Quarterly Review,* 56, 1836, 331n.) However that may be, they too aroused the sympathy of some visitors. N. P. Willis wrote: "It is enough to give one the heart ache to see the many shapes of the agony of imprisonment undergone within these pretty shrubberies and hedges. The expression of distress by all manner of creatures except monkeys, is so painful, that I wonder it should be popular as a place of resort for ladies. But there they lounge out the day in great numbers, feeding the elephants, tormenting the monkeys, and gazing in upon the howling bears, tigers and lions, as if the poor creatures were as happy as parlor poodles." (*Famous Persons and Places,* Auburn, N.Y., 1855, p. 376.)

112. The Surrey Gardens: picture model of Vesuvius by day and by night (anonymous water colors).

imitated it. Here the large-scale paintings of Leicester Square and Vauxhall acquired a third dimension. Taking the form of free-standing architectural and topographical models that anticipated modern motion picture sets, these huge constructions of canvas and wood were intended to be admired first for their own sake, by day. The subjects were chosen and the sets designed so as to take maximum advantage of the lake, which served both as a stand-in for specific bodies of water—the Tiber, the Bay of Naples, or even the nearby Thames—and as a reflecting pool for the fireworks. Three or four nights a week the whole ensemble figured in a *son et lumière* spectacle, the sound and illumination being provided by pyrotechnics more elaborate than any seen at Vauxhall, under the direction of J. Southby, self-styled "Chevalier." Southby's collaborator on the scenic side was George Danson, a painter for several London theatres, who later would execute the *Paris by Night* panorama at the Colosseum.

The first major Danson production (1839) was the eruption of Mount Hecla, a welcome change (one assumes it involved more than the name) from the usual Vesuvius and Etna. The set was executed on a scale of a quarter inch to the foot, the "boarded work" towering eighty feet. The performance was so well received that it was held over for a second season, and by the hundredth evening it had been witnessed by 578,000 persons, most of whom shared a journalist's incredulity that "such a scene of wild and rugged barrenness should be existing in the midst of summer, and within a mile of the city of London."[27]

In 1841 the "Colossal Pictorial Typorama, or Modelled View of Rome" was even bigger; the canvas used would have covered three acres, and the cross atop the Surrey version of St. Peter's was 97 feet from the ground. The versatile lake, representing the Tiber, was occupied by a fleet of vividly painted small boats, and the Bridge and Castle of Sant' Angelo were actual structures. The latter had a projecting balcony that served as a box from which favored visitors could watch the fireworks, copied from the Girandola displayed in Rome every Easter Monday. "Here, as at Rome," said one paper,

the striking of a clock is the signal for the illumination; the lights flash on, and, after a time, change from the ordinary tint to a rich roseate hue. The *girandola* commences from the roof of the Castle of St. Angelo, with maroons in rapid succession; followed by Roman candles, with balls of remarkable brilliancy and variety of colour; a superb standard piece of circular design, elaborately beautiful; some effective tourbillions; and several water-wheels upon the surface of the

lake, with which the spectators were especially delighted; a superb cascade of fire, formed by jerbs flowing over the battlemented parapet of the Tower; and, lastly, a volley of rockets, simultaneously fired into the air. . . . At intervals, the whole scene was lit up with blue and red fires, which threw out portions of the Model in bold relief, and admirably aided its vraisemblance.[28]

To some observers, this spectacle exemplified the admirably "rational" nature of the Surrey Gardens' program in general. "It is, beyond comparison," wrote one, "the best entertainment of its class yet produced in this country; it has none of the flaunting, *ad captandum* vulgarity, by which our outdoor exhibitions are too often made attractive for the mental gratification of the public. . . . It is, *per se,* an intellectual amusement, and with the attractions of the Establishment, zoological and botanical, conjoins to render the whole scene a treat of a very superior order."[29] Less pompous and certainly more to the point was the doggerel characterization, by a contributor to the *Comic Almanack* for 1843, of the Surrey's appeal the two previous summers:

At the Surrey menagerie every one knows,
(Because 'tis a place to which every one goes,)
There's a model of Rome; and as round it one struts,
One sinks the remembrance of Newington Butts;
And having a shilling laid down at the portal,
One fancies one's self in the city immortal.

113. The Surrey Gardens: picture model of Rome (*Mirror of Literature,* 37, 1841, 321).

114. The Surrey Gardens: model of old London (*Mirror of Literature,* n.s. 5, 1844, 401).

115. The Surrey Gardens: *Stirring Up the Great Fire of London* (etching by George Cruikshank in the *Comic Almanack,* 1845).

This model so splendid one night was burn'd down,
When, lo! the next day, 'twas announced to the town
That the damage had all been repair'd and put straight,
In time for the next zoological *fête*.
Then who is there henceforth will venture to say
That Rome cannot sometimes be built in a day.

In 1843 the attraction was "Danson's new stupendous Panoramic Model al-fresco of the far-famed excavated TEMPLES OF ELLORA, the greatest wonder of India," the locale of "Pyro-scenic Spectacles, illustrating the splendours of a Burrah-Tamashah, or Hindu Festival, introducing extraordinary Allegorical Tableaux de feu."[30] But probably more to the spectators' taste was the 1844 production, in which the lake was transformed from the Tiber into the Thames: a many-structured display using (it was alleged) 303,000 square feet of canvas and showing London as it was in 1666, including old St. Paul's, old London Bridge, Baynard's Castle, and other landmarks. At night the model was first illuminated and then, by the use of fireworks, subjected to the Great Fire.[31] For the 1846 season, the mimic Thames became the Bay of Naples and served as a reflecting pool for a fresh Vesuvius show, which was singularly well timed because the real volcano was active during the summer.

The next year's subject was the siege of Gibraltar, which had come a long way in the London show world since its modest debut at the Bermondsey Spa more than half a century earlier. This version had a somewhat more elaborate program than did most Surrey Gardens spectacles. As the spectators gathered, they beheld ships of war, with fifty-foot masts, apparently floating on the lake, and behind them, batteries, fortifications, and houses running to the summit of the scenery rock. At nightfall the representation of the siege began: the attack on the garrison by the combined fleets of France and Spain; the return of fire from the town batteries; the burning of houses, with the glow reflected in the water; a general burning of ships, and, according to one account, such an "uproar of infernal noises, that anybody of ordinary nerves may well be excused for feeling uncomfortable at his proximity to the scene of destruction. A droll effect was produced by a squadron of ducks, who, in the hottest part of the siege, gravely followed their leader across the lake, perfectly unmoved by the riot around them, to their roosting place."[32]

In 1849 it was Badajoz that was besieged. A *Punch* writer attended a performance in a less than reverential mood:

That steep castle, which looks like a large Stilton Cheese, or a big yellow Salad-bowl with a lot of green stuff inside, is Badajoz. The two little red soldiers, who are doing sentry in the middle of the mixture may be taken for a couple of spring radishes. You see the bridge which runs across the water—it is so life-like, that the Ducks give themselves a headache every day in knocking against the side, in the hope of getting through it. . . .

The cannons begin to roar, and the animals also. The glass case in which they are kept, is lighted up a glowing red, and it looks so hot you fancy every pane must crack like a roasted chestnut. The trumpets bray their loudest, every drum and every heart is beating quite loud, the Peacock is playing his favourite solo on the railway-whistle, and every now and then, you hear a loud piercing "Oh!" that rises far above the horrible din, and is but a faint echo of the feeling that is filling, almost to a carpet-bag point of bursting, the breast of every man, woman, policeman, and child.

Oh what a crash was that! and no wonder. See one whole side of the castle has fallen in. It is crumbling to pieces like a stout Cheshire that has been undermined by the cheeseknife. The ten soldiers (bless them!) are fighting bravely for their ten shillings; the rockets are drooping in a golden shower over Badajoz, like a large laburnum. . . .

There is a grand explosion—the whole air is hissing hot;—the trees are crimson;—the water is the colour of Tomata sauce,—there is a mighty flash of red fire:—Badajoz is taken. The devoted ten rush once more into the breach, which is burning like a furnace; a figure with a wooden sword, cocked hat, and nose, is pushed forward on rollers,—three cheers rend the sky—it is the DUKE OF WELLINGTON! From this night forth, he is the Hero of a Hundred *and One* Fights. The siege at the Surrey Zoological will not be forgotten amongst his future victories.[33]

(Missing from this description is the detail that the siege of Badajoz was preceded by "an immense Pyrotechnic Representation" of the sea serpent then in the news. The lake was once again put to good use.)

Following the storming of Badajoz in 1849, Napoleon crossed the Surrey Gardens' plank-and-canvas Alps in 1850. The former praise of these outdoor panoramas as "rational" and "intellectual" entertainment could scarcely be sustained now, because, as *Punch* was not loath to point out, this show was a riot of revisionist history. It assumed that Napoleon rode a horse across an Alpine lake, that the horse "had a wonderful talent for standing on his hind legs," and that the momentous crossing was accomplished at night amidst a huge barrage of fireworks whose "reflection must have been seen all over Europe; and the result would have been that MR. BRAIDWOOD [chief of the London Fire Brigade] would have been galloping for days all over England with his engines in search of the

116. The Surrey Gardens: picture model of the siege of Gibraltar (*Illustrated London News*, 3 July 1847).

117. The Surrey Gardens: picture model of the storming of Badajoz (*Illustrated London News*, 26 May 1849).

118. The Surrey Gardens: picture model of the capture of Chusan (*Illustrated London News*, 28 May 1853).

119. The Surrey Gardens: picture model of the eruption of Mount Etna (*Illustrated London News*, 22 May 1852).

fire." None of these historical novelties was to be seen in the "authentic" versions of Napoleon's career mounted at Astley's Amphitheatre or Franconi's in Paris; but so much the worse for them. "[A]s Napoleon did everything different from everybody else, it is very probable that he did as he is represented, or that he would have done so, if there had been a lake"—and, *Punch* might have added, had he enjoyed the creative services of Messrs. Danson and Southby.[34]

In 1852, conforming to the principle of rotation followed by London eruption-mongers, Etna blew up instead of Vesuvius. By a curious atavism, a staple of eighteenth-century volcanic representation was revived—a scene showing "the Pandemonium of the Ancients, with the Caverns and Forges of Vulcan and the Cyclops."[35] The next season, the familiar siege script was rewritten to portray the British attack on Chusan. An American artist left an eyewitness account of the proceedings:

Here a lake suddenly burst upon the view, with lofty mountains stretching many miles into the distance, and raising their heads up to the very heavens. At the base of the hills were the fortifications of an oriental town whose light spires arose behind them. As the sun went down, and it became dark, lights glanced to and fro in the town; and presently, with a grand burst of music, the Chinese Feast of Lanterns was held out on the waves. Boats containing masks, and beautiful with colored lights, were rowed slowly across; rockets fizzed and spluttered, and fountains of fire blazed up from under the water; overhead, the heavens were filled with stars of green and red and blue, bursting and changing color every moment. At a given signal a British fleet is seen off the town, and a bombardment commences; fireships, sent out on their destructive errands, set fire to their own fleets, and flaming and exploding junks are seen floating in the distance. The whole concludes with a grand explosion of different fireworks, and "God save the Queen," by the orchestra; the audience are left to pick their way out, almost in the dark, of the garden so prodigal of light five minutes before. The deception of the scenery is perfect; what appears to be miles away one can walk around in five minutes.[36]

These spectacles, however, although the most fully recorded, were by no means the only major attraction at the Surrey Gardens. As at Vauxhall, there were numerous short-term exhibitions. In 1839–40, for instance, a Mr. H. Carter demonstrated his "New and Extraordinary 'KONIAPHOSTIC,' or 'LIME LIGHT,' a chemical combination of such vivid brilliancy and diffusiveness, as completely to Illumine the Whole Gardens by One Central Light!"—after which the eruption of Hecla must have been almost an anti-climax.[37] Five years later, in the daytime, there was a "Sylvan Fete" consisting, as a *Punch* contributor complained, of "sundry ryghte stupidde freakes of ye grosseste humbugge" —fun and games representative of "Merrie Englande in ye Oldenne Tyme," including an uproariously inexpert demonstration of archery by members of the Toxophilite Club in their forest greens, a performance which it is merciful Sir Ashton Lever did not live to witness.[38] In the summer of 1847, when contributions were being sought to purchase and restore Shakespeare's birthplace, a replica of the house was erected as the headquarters of a fancy fair, the proceeds to go to the national fund.

The Surrey Gardens responded quickly to the fashion for promenade concerts that had begun in London at the Colosseum. One early program (1840) made musical history of a sort when it included Beethoven's *Battle Sinfonia* (*Wellington's Victory*), which had been performed at Drury Lane in 1816 and then had not been heard again until Charles Godfrey, bandmaster of the Coldstream Guards and conductor at the gardens, borrowed the manuscript score from Sir George Smart.[39] But the Surrey's greater musical celebrity began in 1845, when Jullien took over as conductor. At his first concert there, on 20 June, an audience of 12,000 stood before a newly erected shell opposite the giraffe house to hear a 300-piece orchestra perform a program that ended with "God Save the Queen," every phrase of which was punctuated by cannon. For the second concert on 12 July, "The Duke of Leinster lent his *Monstre Contra Basso* to be manipulated by two sturdy players, a monster bass drum, the largest ever constructed, contributed its thunder, and the hundred cornets, trumpets, trombones, ophicleides and serpents . . . blared forth the quintet from *I Puritani* to the huge delight of a vast audience, and, no doubt, to the dismay and discomfiture of the giraffes."[40] (Meanwhile Musard, originator of the Paris prom concerts, was at Vauxhall, conducting a pitiably small orchestra of 100.)

The tireless Jullien, who toured the provinces and conducted at the leading West End theatres the rest of the year, turned up regularly at the Surrey in the following summers, his concerts usually being scheduled between the feeding of the pelicans and white bears at 5:30 P.M. and the fireworks at 9:30. The orchestra normally was no larger than Jullien's minimum requirements, which, to be sure, were not modest, but every season there were several *Concerts Monstres* consisting of either hugely enlarged orchestral forces or gigantic instruments or both. In 1849, for example, they involved a 400-piece orchestra, three military bands, three choirs, and numerous vocal and instrumental soloists, and one memorable number was a Roman march played on twenty trumpets, each of which was three yards long.[41]

With the addition of Jullien and his monstrous music, the gardens reached their prosperous zenith in the late forties, more than ever justifying *Punch*'s tribute delivered some years earlier: "that grand shilling's worth of beasts, flowers, music, and fireworks—the Surrey Zoological."[42] But, like every London show by mid-century, it was at the mercy of tastes which seemed to be changing more quickly with every passing year, and its management became reckless, as was perhaps inevitable when Jullien was at hand, conjuring up his vast projects. The rest of the story is reserved for a later chapter.

The Waxen and the Fleshly

24

As the nineteenth century began, Mrs. Salmon's old-established "perspiring waxwork," as Dickens called it in *David Copperfield,* was still doing business at Prince Henry's house in Fleet Street. On the ground floor was a toy shop; outside, alternating duty day by day, were waxwork figures of a beefeater (a colleague of the living one at Exeter Change) and of a matchwoman, holding out handbills to passersby. Upstairs, in two rooms, were celebrities of all kinds: royalty of course, and Charles James Fox, Pitt, General Wolfe, Dr. Johnson, Nelson, the forger Dr. William Dodd, John Wilkes, John Braham, the singer and future proprietor of the Colosseum, the evangelists Whitefield and Wesley, Dick Turpin, the highwayman, and a familiar London beggar, Ann Siggs. In a third room were groups of "shepherds and shepherdesses with lambs and a goat or two, making violent love," as well as a "miniature wax man-of-war sailing on a sea of crown glass."[1]

Mrs. Clarke, who, with her husband, had taken over the exhibition after Mrs. Salmon's death in 1760, died in 1812, and the contents were sold at auction for less than fifty pounds. The new proprietor moved the display to a house in Water Lane, in the shadow of the Tower. In July 1827 thieving vandals broke into the house, stripped the costumes from the figures, and smashed their heads. The show managed somehow to survive for four more years, and then the mutilated figures were sold for back rent.[2] Perhaps they were bought by one of the itinerant showmen who worked the fairs; waxworks remained a standard attraction wherever cheap amusement was offered. At Bartholomew Fair in 1825, for example, one could see a mixed cast of Mother Shipton, Jane Shore, George IV, Queen Elizabeth, Mary Queen of Scots, the recent murderer Abraham Thornton, and Othello.[3] This may well have been Ewing's venerable show, which was as reliable a fixture at fairs as were the abbreviated live-talent plays of Richardson, who paid Ewing's rent, erected his booth, and took half his profits. As at Mrs. Salmon's and elsewhere, many of Ewing's figures were arranged in groups—waxwork counterparts of the dramatic scenes that were the stock-in-trade of popular early Victorian historical and anecdotal painters: the Earl of Leicester's last interview with Amy Robsart, Louis XVI parting from his family, Lady Macduff and her family slaughtered by direction of Macbeth, and the dying moments of Mark Antony, Anne Boleyn, and Lord Nelson.[4]

There were innumerable waxwork exhibitions under roof. Facing Exeter Change across the Strand in 1812 was the London Grand Cabinet of Figures, seventy of them altogether, including Fox, Pitt, the radical politician Sir Francis Burdett, Daniel Lambert, Bellingham (the assassin of the prime minister, Spencer Perceval), Napoleon, and Mrs. Siddons.[5] Around the year 1830 even such superior amusement places as the Oxford Street Bazaar supplemented their main attractions with "splendidly dressed wax figures" including, in the case of the bazaar, a life-size copy of Rubens's *Descent from the Cross*.[6] On the level of penny shows, there were the Royal Waxwork at 67 Fleet Street (five rooms, 200 figures) and Simmons's in High Holborn.[7] Among the attractions at this last establishment were what the proprietor asserted to be the only true models of the Edinburgh resurrectionists, Burke and Hare. This was a debatable claim, because supposedly authentic figures of this notorious pair were also starred in the collection of the emergent queen of the London waxwork exhibitors, Madame Tussaud, who was advertising, with fractured grammar, "the original figures of BURKE and HARE (taken from their faces, to obtain which the Proprietors went expressly to Scotland); which have excited intense interest from the peculiar nature of their crimes, and their approach to life, which renders it difficult to recognize them from living persons."[8]

At this moment, the early 1830s, Madame Tussaud was about to come in from the road, returning at last to the metropolis where she had begun her British career in 1802 at the Lyceum, alongside Paul de Philipstal's Phantasmagoria.* After leaving London in May 1803, she had toured Britain and Ireland for thirty years, in the manner of Mrs. Jarley in *The Old Curiosity Shop,* stopping for intervals of various lengths at theatres, assembly halls, or whatever accommodations the various towns offered. She and her collection had a narrow escape at Bristol in 1831, when the center of the town was sacked and burned by a Reform Bill mob, and she also had her moments of glory, as when, a little later at Brighton, she was visited by "nearly the whole of the Royal Establishment" and Princess Augusta was said to have declared that she derived "much amusement and gratification" from the exhibition. We do not know what finally determined Madame Tussaud to settle down in London. Perhaps it was her advancing age (she was then in her mid-seventies); it obviously was not a dearth of waxwork exhibitions. In any case, in 1833 she worked her way up from Brighton by way of Dover, Maidstone, Canterbury, Rochester, and Blackheath, arriving at the Royal London Bazaar, Gray's Inn Road, in December. During the following year she had several metropolitan venues, including the new Lowther Rooms in June; the Grove House, Camberwell, in August; and the Mermaid tavern, Hackney, in October. After another stay at the Royal London Bazaar, she finally established her travel-worn troupe at the Bazaar, Baker Street, in March 1835, and proceeded to make these premises one of the most famous entertainment places in London.

Up to this time, apart from the emphasis on French revolutionary and military figures, her range of celeb-

rities had been fairly conventional. Most of the lesser shows had their royalty, their venerable statesmen, their military heroes, their murderers, their characters from literature and legend, and occasionally they would display the effigy of someone currently engaging public attention. But it was Madame Tussaud who made a particular point of keeping up with the headlines. Her governing principle was that "celebrities 'strictly up to date' should be continuously added to every department of her exhibition"—men and women who were in the public eye for whatever reason, their political fame, their bold achievements, their involvement in a tragic accident, their recent marriage or death.[9] A year after the waxworks took over the Baker Street building, the young opera singer Maria Malibran, whom England loved as much for her "sweet, kindly and charitable nature" as for her musical gifts, died during the Birmingham Musical Festival. Madame Tussaud at once made an effigy of her, and crowds came to see it, as they had in 1818 when Princess Charlotte, dead in childbirth at the age of twenty-one, was represented in wax at Savile House.

Thus the exhibition had two classes of figures. The first, built up gradually but steadily, made it in effect a more colorful and better-kept adjunct to Westminster Abbey, the nation's royal burial place and quasi-Pantheon. Here celebrities were seen in postures of apparent life and dressed in suitable garb, not lying piously atop their tombs in the rigidity of marble or frozen in a commanding statesmanlike pose. The second class comprised a running three-dimensional illustration of current events. And so Madame Tussaud maintained a considered balance between the old and the new. The permanent core of historical figures was constantly being refurbished and rearranged, and at the same time there was a constant influx of new personalities to replace those who had faded from the public mind. By this means the establishment ensured that it would never exhaust its potential market: no one could say that he had "seen" Tussaud's and would never have to visit it again.

Furthermore, with few exceptions the new Tussaud figures were *really* new. In his account of Mrs. Jarley's waxworks Dickens poked fun at the duplicity whereby showmen, with only the minimum alteration of appearance, made a single figure do duty successively for several different characters. Inveterate showgoers with long memories must, time after time, have run across familiar figures bearing new names if not always new guises. Albert Smith, writing in 1846

* Did Madame Tussaud exhibit also at 87 Pall Mall in 1802, under the title Grand Salon of Arts and Illustrious Men? According to the catalogue of the show (BL, S.C. 737[2]), the "arts" were represented chiefly by "specimens of pictures in Silk and Worsted, from the collection of Lewis XVI executed at the manufactory of the Gobelins," a portrait of Franklin from the same collection, forty proof-impressions of engravings by "the best French artists," and the same number of waxworks. These last were "executed by an eminent artist, who has invented a chemical composition, which imitates nature with such extreme accuracy, that the figures want nothing of real life, but motion. . . . All the figures have been taken from life, from masks moulded on the persons themselves, or from the best original paintings . . . the body and limbs being moulded on persons as nearly as possible of the size and shape of the originals. Each of the faces of these figures alone cost *fifty Guineas,* from which some idea may be formed of the expence of the whole." While it is true that there was no copyright in showmen's claims, the resemblance between these and Madame Tussaud's is striking. For one thing, the collection featured effigies of such Revolutionary figures as Charlotte Corday, Mlle. de Ste. Amaranthe, and Mirabeau, and these were Madame Tussaud's bread-and-butter line: she had modeled many such celebrities from the heads which were brought to her for the purpose, fresh from the guillotine. For another, her publicity long stressed the secret formula which enabled her to lend the wax a lifelike flesh color instead of (in her words) "the disagreeable hue" which characterized other artists' figures.

120. Madame Tussaud (anonymous engraving).

121. Interior of Madame Tussaud's Waxworks (anonymous engraving).

of a visit to an exhibition set up in a derelict dwelling near Greenwich Fair, reported:

In the recess of a window were placed two figures, evidently intended, originally, for Amy Robsart and the Earl of Leicester, but which represented, we were informed, Queen Victoria and Prince Albert, enjoying the retirement of private life, apart from the pomp of royalty. Why they should have chosen to enjoy retirement in fancy dresses of the Elizabethan period, those best acquainted with the habits of those august personages can possibly inform us. All the characters of the exhibition were, however, old friends. We fancied that we once knew them in High Holborn, where the organ turned at the door, and the monkey sat on the hot gas-pipe. At all events, if they were not the identical ones, the artist had cast two in the same mould whilst he was about it. We do not think he had been happy in the likenesses. Sir Robert Peel was, unmistakeably, Mr. Buckstone grown a foot taller, and wearing a light flaxen wig. Lady Sale we once knew as Queen Adelaide; and Oxford had transmigrated into Wix, the eyes having been manifestly wrenched violently round to form the squint of the latter miserable culprit.* In one point the artist had excelled Nature. He had preserved the apparent dryness and coolness of the skin, whilst the folks looking on were melting with the heat.[10]

Madame Tussaud and her sons, who were gradually taking over the business as its founder aged, would have none of this easy-going attitude toward authenticity. In their exhibition fact was the sternest of task-masters. If the figures could not be modeled from life or from death masks, they were copied from the most dependable pictures. Nor (as the advertising copy regularly insisted) was expense spared to clothe the figures in rich costumes when their station in life required silk, satin, gold lace, or ermine. One of the firm's greatest early coups was the purchase, for a reputed £18,000, of the coronation and state robes of George IV. The satin gown worn by the figure of Queen Victoria in the tableau of her wedding (1840) was commissioned from a group of Spitalfield weavers at a reported cost of £1,000.

Another main reason for the Tussauds' quick ascendancy was the pains taken with the showplace itself, to distinguish their exhibition from the fly-by-night waxworks which, like Mrs. Salmon's in later years, were housed in squalid, dark, cramped quarters repellent to a great portion of the middle-class clientele. The Colosseum's elegance now was matched in Baker Street. One entered through an ornate lobby lined with antique casts and modern sculptures, then went up a flight of stairs decorated with arabesques, artificial flowers, and mirrors. The exhibition room itself, the "Grand Corinthian Saloon" as it was first called, was decorated in the style of Louis XIV and lighted with five hundred gas jets reflected in a wall of mirrors. To provide maximum display space and channel the

* John Baldwin Buckstone was a popular comedian of the time. Lady Florentia Sale was the wife of Sir Robert Sale, second in command during the Afghan War. Her *Journal*, giving a first-hand narrative of the horrors of the British retreat from Kabul, was published in 1843. Both Oxford and Wix had recently made attempts on the queen's life.

traffic flow, there were two aisles, with single figures and small groups arranged along the sides of the room and large groups in the center. Ottomans and sofas were dispersed around the room as in a private art gallery, and over the entrance was a musicians' gallery from which a band discoursed "sweet and ancient airs."[11]

As the Tussaud technique evolved in the next several decades, increasing care was taken with the settings in which the groups of figures were arranged. The waxwork business had a long tradition in this regard. At the best exhibitions, from the early eighteenth century onward, the recumbent effigies of dead royalty were sometimes surrounded with appropriate funereal accessories to add a touch of realism. When Princess Charlotte's effigy was displayed at Savile House in 1818, she was represented as she had lain in state at Windsor, the room "entirely covered with Draperies of black cloth" and the canopied bier flanked with escutcheons, candelabra, and sconces. It was intended to be, as the proprietor advertised, "a *fac simile* of that most splendid and solemn Spectacle."[12] A more elaborate exhibition, turning to good account the Victorians' mournful delight in the trappings of death, was held at the bazaar in St. James's Street in 1841, shortly after the newspapers had given much space to the lavish "second obsequies" of Napoleon, which attended the return of his body from St. Helena to be enshrined in Les Invalides. Like public buildings in Paris on that occasion, the staircase was hung with draperies decorated with huge cypress wreaths and the imperial insignia, and the salon where pictures of the state funeral were shown was dimly lit by gas jets behind colored glasses, which, said one writer, had "a remarkably sombre and funereal effect."[13]

The Tussauds also recognized the value of realistic atmosphere, and now that the show was no longer on the road, where it was difficult or impossible to achieve such effects, they were able to do so. To the outlay for costumes, therefore, was added the expense of appropriate furniture and décor for the various groups, and, most famous of all, the dimly lighted Chamber of Horrors, with its representation of Newgate, the Tower dungeon, and other scenes of crime and expiation.

Typical of the Tussaud showmanship, again, was the effort made to blend the illusory and the real. Certain anonymous wax figures, such as a young Chinaman and a well-dressed English gentleman, were positioned at the very edge of the display as if they were themselves spectators. At one time a figure of the octogenarian Madame Tussaud herself was so located, giving customers something of a turn when they remembered that they had just paid their shilling to an identical old lady, sitting almost as motionless in an armchair at the entrance. A few figures moved by clockwork. One was the famous Sleeping Beauty, converted from Mlle. de Ste. Aramanthe, who had fallen a victim to Robespierre because, as it was explained, "she indignantly refused to become a victim of his lust."* "She breathes," wrote Benjamin Silliman, who saw her in 1851, "and her bust, with her dress, rises and falls so naturally with the respiration, that you instinctively move softly, lest she should be disturbed in her slumber."[14] William Cobbett, the radical journalist in plain farmer's dress, bowed continuously to the onlookers as long as his internal mechanism was kept wound up. When the Chinese Exhibition—itself in large part a wax museum with the figures positioned in replicas of streets, shops, and domestic rooms—was riding the wave of Sinological curiosity, Tussaud's displayed a Chinese couple, the richly dressed wife moving her head as she spoke to her husband.

Madame Tussaud's was also a Napoleon shrine, the most enduring evidence of Britain's ambivalent fascination with the emperor. Two entire rooms at Baker Street were devoted to Napoleonic relics. One held the traveling carriage captured at Waterloo, which had earlier made a fortune for Bullock, the other a collection of 150 personal relics, including Napoleon's camp bed, repeating watch, toothbrush, and table knife, an extracted tooth *and* the instrument his dentist used to extract it, and the clothing he wore in exile.

Once the decision had been made to ensure the frequent return of patrons by keeping the collection in a continuous state of flux, the history of Tussaud's was an uneventful one. By the forties it had acquired the popularity, if not the dignity, of a national institution, a sight of London coequal with the Abbey, the Tower, and St. Paul's. Because it was so familiar, it served as an ever dependable point of reference, an instantaneously intelligible vehicle of allusion. Time after time in the early and mid-Victorian era *Punch* referred to it for a variety of satirical purposes. In 1846, for instance, when a special exhibition of twenty-five court costumes was announced, *Punch,* its social conscience ever acute, suggested that the display area be filled instead by wax figures of wizened, undersized London waifs and beggars modeling their rags.[15]

Popular though Madame Tussaud's was, it was not without its detractors. Though his eyes were jaundiced and his condemnation excessive, Benjamin Moran,

* So went one of the several versions of the Robespierre–Ste. Amaranthe story; it is at least indisputable that the family—mother, daughter, and son—were guillotined. The *Biographie universelle* has a lurid account of their being executed because Robespierre, at a dinner at their house, confided state secrets. Others say the daughter was his mistress. See John Laurence Carr, *Robespierre: The Force of Circumstances* (London, 1972), pp. 82–83.

122. *I Dreamt I Slept at Madame Tussaud's:* an etching by George Cruikshank (*Comic Almanack*, 1847), accompanied by the following verses:

I dreamt that I sle-ept at Madame Tussaud's,
    With Cut-throats and Kings by my si-i-ide;
And that all the Wax-figures in tho-ose abodes,
    At Midnight became vivifi-i-ied. . . .
I dreamt that Napo-le-on Bo-onaparte
    Was waltzing with Madame T-e-ee;
That O'Connell, to study the regicide art,
    Had a gossip with Fieschi-e-ee . . .

(For O'Connell and Fieschi, see the further mention of their presence at Madame Tussaud's, Chapter 30.)

* The practice of segregating the more gruesome subjects, in the interests of an additional entrance fee, began on the road as early as 1822, when a "separate room," later the "Golden Chamber," was set aside for the figures of the French revolutionists. Subsequently, this room was devoted to the Napoleonic relics. Although some writers assert that the name "Chamber of Horrors" was invented by *Punch* in 1845, it was used in the firm's advertising in the *Illustrated London News* as early as 29 July 1843. Despite its having been coined on the premises, it did not always suit the management, which preferred "dead room" or "black room" for internal use, and after "Chamber of Horrors" acquired undesirable connotations it was replaced for publicity purposes by other terms, such as the neutral "extra room." Another alternative, adopted in hopes of giving the display of murderers and their victims the benefit of the current theory that criminal tendencies can be read in the face, was "chamber of comparative physiognomy," but this, not surprisingly, failed to catch on.

secretary to the American legation in the fifties, quite possibly described the show more nearly as it was, rather than as its publicity portrayed it:

The untravelled countryman and his rustic daughters there see the sovereign in regal robes, and her descendants represented in yellow wax, and look with admiring wonder on the stupid show. Wretched figures of more wretched kings and queens are judiciously disposed for exhibition, and the tin spangles on their faded robes glitter in the gas-light, and astonish the delighted and loyal crowd. A whole host of the line of Brunswick stand around like wooden men and women, with eyes agape, staring upon the throng who stare again at them. Miserable caricatures of Napoleon, Washington, Cromwell, Shakespeare, and Byron occupy niches, and the soul sickens at the contemplation of the figures, they so outrage humanity. Each one looks as if ophthalmia were a distemper of the atmosphere, and all suffer from the sad disease. Shakespeare is represented as a modern dandy, "who cultivates his hair"; and Byron as a Greek, with a belt around the waist containing a whole arsenal of arms. . . .

But this is not all. The "room of horrors" invites attention next, as if there were not enough of *horrors* in the first apartments to horrify any decent, well-disposed individual . . .

So much for Madame Tussaud's exhibition of wax figures, the resort of the curious, and a sham to please or alarm children. It is, without misrepresentation, the most abominable

abomination in the great city, and the very audience-hall of humbugs. Barnum ought to have it.[16]

Barnum thought so, too. In 1844 he offered to buy out the Tussauds and move the whole museum to New York, but the proprietors, content with their present prosperity, declined to sell.[17]

In his reference to the "room of horrors" Moran touched on the exhibition's most vulnerable spot: the publicity and, some insisted, the encouragement it gave to crime through its best-known feature, the Chamber of Horrors.* No Victorian murderer of greater than usual notoriety went undepicted in the chamber for longer than Tussaud's craftsmen needed to reproduce his and his victim's likenesses and dress them in appropriate garb (the actual clothes worn when the crime was committed, if they could be bought). As James Russell Lowell put it in 1850, "Madame Tussaud made the discovery that the effigies of a dead criminal would bring in thousands of shillings, while no one would expend a solitary sixpence to look upon the living image of Innocence herself."[18]

Periodically, the clergy and the more self-righteous portion of the press denounced what they took to be the Tussauds' pandering to the public's morbid preoc-

123. *Great Moral Lesson at Madame Tussaud's* (*Punch,* 9 May 1846). A satire occasioned by Tussaud's announcement of the exhibition of "twenty-five male and female magnificent new court dresses, of surpassing beauty, intended to amuse and instruct the middle classes, and to give them an idea of regal splendour." *Punch* commented: "If we were in the place of MADAME TUSSAUD, we would superadd to our collection some twice twenty-five, or more, shabby old working dresses, of surpassing uncouthness, intended to amuse and instruct the superior classes, by giving them an idea of laborious indigence. . . . Thus would one part of the world acquire, agreeably and easily, some little notion of how the other part of it lives."

124. *Madame Tussaud Her Wax Werkes. Ye Chamber of Horrors!!* (drawing by Richard Doyle, *Punch,* 15 September 1849). The accompanying text, in the style of "Mr. Pips his Diary," reads in part: "Then to the Chamber of Horrors, which my Wife did long to see most of all; cost, with the NAPOLEON Rooms, 1s. more; a Room like a Dungeon, where the Head of ROBESPIERRE, and other Scoundrels of the great French Revolution, in Wax, as though just cut off, horrid ghastly, and Plaster Casts of Fellows that have been hanged: but the chief Attraction a Sort of Dock, wherein all the notorious Murderers of late Years; the foremost of all, RUSH, according to the Bill, taken from Life at Norwich, which, seeing he was hanged there, is an odd Phrase. There was likewise a Model of Stanfield Hall, and RUSH his Farm, as though the Place were as famous as Waterloo. Methinks it is of ill Consequence that there should be a Murderers' Corner, wherein a Villain may look to have his Figure put more certainly than a Poet can to a Statue in the Abbey. So away again to the large Room, to look at JENNY LIND instead of GREENACRE, and at 10 of the Clock Home, and so to Bed, my Wife declaring she should dream of the Chamber of Horrors."

cupation with crime. *Punch* was not usually among these moralists, but when the waxworks faithfully illustrated the particularly sensational outburst of murders that occurred in 1848–1850, even it was obliged to protest: "MADAME TUSSAUD offers Scoundrel's Corner, with an immortality in wax. Every day she calls from the columns of the newspapers with a voice of silver (exactly eighteen-pence, 'Horrors' included)—calls to a thoughtful generation to consider and lay well to heart the notoriety, that is the vulgar stimulant of miserable natures. What the statue of NELSON is to the sailor, the Murderer in Wax is to the unblown scoundrel."[19] Despite or, more probably, owing to such assaults, Tussaud's flourished across the decades, and one of the most dependable sights of Victorian London at Christmas, Easter, and Whitsuntide was the long queue in Baker Street, many of whose members, children as well as adults, had been there before.

Tussaud's supremacy did not, however, mean a monopoly. Innumerable small waxwork exhibitions also continued the tradition begun so many years ago at Mrs. Salmon's. In the fifties alone there were a number of shows to which one could repair after having exhausted, for the moment, the delights at Baker Street—or if one had only a penny or sixpence but not a shilling or eighteen pence to spend. At Springthorpe's Waxwork Figures and Grand Cosmoramic Views, 393 Strand, could be seen all the crowned heads of Europe, "warriors clad in suits of real armour, the most celebrated statesmen, poets, divines, heroes, eccentricities, theatricals, orators and other eminent persons," along with a case of mechanical hummingbirds from the Crystal Palace. Springthorpe's had a Chamber of Horrors of its own (and unblushingly appropriated the name); its contents were dominated by two mummies.[20]

Elsewhere in the fifties, Napoleon Montanari exhibited a mockup of the state drawing room at Windsor, with the royal couple, "Surrounded by their Youthful and Illustrious Family," entertaining the Emperor and Empress of France, "with Magnificent and Appropriate State Furniture . . . Together with an interesting Collection of Mexican Wax Figure Models, Illustrating Civilized and Savage Life in Mexico, with the National Sport of Bull Fighting in all its Stages."[21] Another gallery depicted "The Awful Tortures of the Inquisition, with the Authentic Instruments of That Dreadful Institution" and "A Chamber of Horrors, A Collection of French Criminals for the last ten years."[22] Tussaud's Chamber of Horrors may or may

not have inspired Victorian criminals, but it unquestionably inspired other showmen.

Mechanical action, never more than an incidental touch in Baker Street, was the main feature at some other waxwork shows. In 1833–34 two separate exhibitions depicted Napoleon—a French-made figure of him in full uniform, reclining on a couch and breathing as if asleep (at the Cosmorama Rooms), and a "living statue" of him at the tomb of Frederick the Great, attended by three staff officers (at Savile House).[23] At Bartholomew Fair in 1839, Signor Francisco's moving waxworks mingled biblical personalities with scenes of death throes: the decapitation of John the Baptist in the presence of Herod, Herod's tetrarch, Archelaus, and John's jailer, Sergius Paulus, with the Champion of England on Horseback inserted mysteriously in the background; the dying moments of Mark Antony, and of Cleopatra attended by her slaves.[24]

A few years later John Dubourg's Saloon of Arts in Great Windmill Street was wholly automated. A "Splendid Mechanical Museum of 500 Automaton Figures! Lions and Horses! By Sig^r Gagliardi," it contained, among many other figures, a group of Canadian insurrectionists; Judith and Holophernes; an "Avalanche," unidentified but perhaps suggested by the successful one at the Diorama; the perennial Earl of Leicester and Amy Robsart; the slave market at Constantinople; and the brigands' group from the popular opera *Fra Diavolo*. Also on the bill were Androcles and the lion, "the noble beast," according to the catalogue, "raising his paw, turning his head, opening his mouth, lashing his sides with his tail, rolling his eyes, and groaning as in the greatest agony, while the slave wipes the blood from his wound with his pockethandkerchief."[25] Among the visitors to this show was the tract writer George Mogridge. Normally the least captious of observers, Mogridge could not, in this instance, subdue his disbelief. Androcles, the supposed slave, was too well dressed for his condition, and too adequately armed, even to the possession of a white handkerchief, and "though he pretends to wipe the lion's wounded paw, he never once touches it with his handkerchief. The lion roars, and well he may, were I a lion, I would roar myself at such hollowheartedness."[26]

⋈⋇⋈

One specialized branch of the London waxwork trade, which had last been represented by the specimens in Rackstrow's museum, seems to have languished from the later years of the eighteenth century to about 1825. This was the persistently ambiguous exhibition of anatomical waxworks, which in some cases had genuine scientific credentials and purpose and in others used its purported educational value to add a gloss of respectability to what was actually a raree show for the prurient. By a happy accident, at the end of 1828 the word "anatomical" suddenly turned to gold in the show-business vocabulary, when the revelation of Burke and Hare's illicit manufacture of cadavers at Edinburgh endowed it with delectably horrid connotations. As connected with waxwork shows, it recommended itself on two counts. For one, its appearance in advertising might well be taken to promise a display as grisly as the resurrectionists' deeds and the subsequent dissection of the products thereof in Dr. Knox's anatomical amphitheatre; for another, it offered a choice opportunity to add didactic dignity to the much-maligned waxwork exhibitions in general. Now that, as a result of public indignation over the Edinburgh affair, cadavers had become virtually unobtainable at any price, life-size waxen models of the human body became the best substitute, and their suddenly increased desirability as a scientific teaching device was expected to add legitimacy to all waxworks.

Thus, about 1830, there were two cheap shows in High Holborn alone, Simmons's (previously mentioned) at no. 167, and Mrs. Hojo's (or Hoyo's) at no. 172, both of which advertised "anatomical figures" of Samson sleeping on a sofa. Mrs. Hojo, late of the Rotunda, Blackfriars Bridge (the former home of the Leverian Museum), maintained that hers was composed of 300 hundredweight of wax—an unlikely amount, when one stops to consider it—and cost 500 guineas, which is also hard to credit. While the Burke and Hare sensation was not specifically mentioned, and there is, in fact, no evidence that the recumbent Samsons could be taken apart, the bills pointed out that such figures had been prepared "with a view to superseding the use of dead bodies" for medico-educational purposes.[27]

But they were by no means a new invention. Wax models of the human body that could be disassembled to reveal the internal organs were, as we have seen, commonplace in the eighteenth century, and in 1825 they had reentered the London show business with the first of a series of "Florentine Venuses." "Florentine" was a shorthand allusion to that city's famous Istituto di Anatomia Patologica, which had twenty rooms filled with wax models representing in minute detail all the human organs and physiological systems, in health and in a broad diversity of disease.[28] Thus, for show purposes, the adjective "Florentine" was a convenient synonym for "anatomical." But despite this attempt to associate the figure shown in London in 1825 with the center of anatomical teaching through the use of wax, the *Literary Gazette* saw the exhibition in another light: "Under the pretence of imparting anatomical knowledge, this filthy French figure, the property of one Monsieur Esnaut, is exhibited. It is a large disgusting Doll, the alvus of which being taken off like a pot-lid, shows the internal parts, heart, liver, lungs, kidneys, &c as remotely from anatomic precision or utility as any of the sixpenny wooden dolls which you may buy at Bartholomew Fair. . . . The thing is a silly imposture, and as indecent as it is wretched."[29]

In the following years, this crude Venus (or one or more of her sisters: it is impossible to tell how many of these ladies were being publicly disassembled) was on show at several addresses in London, at the Cosmorama Rooms, Dubourg's Saloon of Arts, and in the Strand opposite Exeter Hall, which occupied the site of Exeter Change. Borrowing the odor of sanctity emanating from that new structure, which was largely given over to the offices of charitable and religious organizations, the Venus's owner described her in terms calculated to draw custom from across the road: "The exterior of the Model represents a Female Figure formed from the Venus de Medicis, the interior exemplifies on dissection the various functions of the Human Body, and displays to perfection the order and beauty that prevails throughout the works of the CREATOR, thus affording to those who delight in the contemplation of the sublime productions of Nature an opportunity of doing so without witnessing the disgusting process of the dissection of a natural subject." The Venus therefore possessed as much spiritual as scientific interest. But the tantalizing hint of forbidden knowledge still was there: private showings could be arranged for ladies, at which "every objection that either timidity or delicacy could suggest" would be carefully anticipated and met.[30]

Another Venus (1844)—a "Parisian" one this time—was advertised seemingly with the incidental purpose of evoking the necro-erotic sentiments for which the nineteenth-century psyche had a peculiar fondness. On entering the room where the Parisian Venus lay, readers were told, "we see what seems to be the corpse of a handsome female who has just expired. It is moulded in wax; the face is removed like a mask, and the exterior of the limbs and bosom being lifted, representations of what would appear in a real subject are pointed out. Anatomical explanations are supplied with great clearness by the gentleman who attends. . . . Young medical students would be likely to derive considerable benefit from the inspection."[31]

In 1839, in an exhibition at 27 Margaret Street under the proprietorship of a Florentine named Sarti, Venus was joined by Adonis. The *Times* assured its readers that this show contained "nothing indelicate" and several years later recalled that it was "much and very deservedly admired."[32] Adonis, like Venus, could be taken apart, but from the back rather than the front. Surrounding these figures was a collection of smaller models illustrating the various organs of sense, the structure of the female breast and of the foetus, the pelvic viscera of the male and female, the nature of extrauterine pregnancy, and the appearance of cholera victims.[33] The *Athenaeum* "earnestly recommend[ed] our younger male readers to avail themselves of the opportunity for obtaining a few general ideas on the subject of anatomy, which they may do without labour or disgust." Ladies were admitted for a private view, under the supervision of a female, from 5 to 7 P.M.[34]

Sarti returned to London eight years later, setting up his Museum of Pathological Anatomy in the Cosmorama Rooms. The "Pathological Room" contained three full-length figures and specimens illustrating sixty different diseases; in the "Physiological Room" was a full-length model of a Moorish woman which was divisible into seventy-five sections. Here, Sarti advertised,

the non-professional may comprehend something of the wondrous mechanism by which he "Lives, Moves, and has his Being," and give him the power to communicate intelligibly with his medical adviser respecting the seat and signs of his disordered functions; and to co-operate with him in averting impending danger, or to remove actual diseases; and, finally, to teach him the absolute necessity of putting implicit faith in those men who have made Anatomy and Physiology the study of their lives. Tuesdays and Thursdays for Ladies, who, as mothers and nurses, should be familiar with the Physical and Mental Constitution of that Human Being, the care of which is imposed upon them.[35]

If celebrity is to be measured by persistence of advertisement, however, Dr. Joseph Kahn was the most famous anatomical showman of his era. The quality of his contribution was best summarized by the *Times,* which once commented: "There is a sort of mystery about Dr. Kahn's Museum, where ladies and

gentlemen are only admitted separately, that gives it a charm akin to the fascination of the 'Chamber of Horrors.'"[36] Kahn brought his collection, twelve years in the making, from the continent, where, according to the 1851 catalogue, it had gratified members of the faculty at Leipzig, Elberfeld, The Hague, Amsterdam, and Utrecht and won the approval of the Queen of the Netherlands, who had seen some but not all of the exhibits. Like Rackstrow's museum, this one was composed partly of wax models and partly of specimens preserved in spirits. Kahn's anatomical Venus had eighty-five pieces. What he described as a unique embryological exhibit consisted of 103 microscopical figures "exhibiting the progress of the human ovum in the uterus, from its first impregnation to its birth." The "terrible effects of debauchery under the form of Syphilis" were set forth in seven exhibits relating to the disease in the male, twelve to its manifestations in the female, and ten to its ravages in the face. There was also a demonstration of the "dreadful result of tight lacing" in a model of a pregnant lady of Munich who had dropped dead in her partner's arms "after dancing repeatedly at a ball."[37] (This seems to have been a pet cause of Kahn's. Later, for the sake of a topical tie-in with the Crimean War, the demonstration was amended: "TIGHT LACING in the ARMY. The injurious effects of the pressure of dress upon different parts of the body in both sexes, shown by numerous figures.")[38]

Between 1850 and 1862 Kahn's restless museum had four different addresses: 315 Oxford Street; 232 Piccadilly; 4 Coventry Street, Leicester Square; and 3 Tichborne Street. The early advertising had something of the air of Katterfelto with added intimations of natural theology: "WONDERS OF NATURE AND ART! How marvellous are the works of Nature! Grand! and in their minutiae, inimitable! The nearest approximation to this, however, may be found in DR. KAHN'S MUSEUM . . . where not only are the most beautiful specimens of Human Formation illustrated, but Comparative Anatomy has likewise its representations."[39] As time passed, the publicity laid less emphasis upon the waxen and natural specimens, which came to be taken for granted, and more upon the lectures, whose announced subjects could be changed as often as desirable to attract repeat business. Kahn and his associate, a Dr. Sexton whose professional credentials were equally obscure, discoursed on medical topics, some of them with timely significance: "The Great Tobacco Controversy," "The Phenomena, Curiosities, and Philosophy of the Sense of Sight,"

"The Food We Eat: Its Uses, Preparation, Adulteration, and Digestion," "The Use and Abuse of Air," "Artificial Digestions—Pepsine and Lactic Acid," "Neglected Brain Disease," and "The Mutiny in India: A Question of Race."[40]

From time to time, there were extra attractions. During these very years when the Aztec Lilliputians and the Earthmen were drawing fresh attention to the possibility of races yet unstudied by science, a flurry of reports from travelers in Abyssinia seemed to lend credence to Lord Monboddo's notorious late eighteenth-century hypothesis of an anthropoid race equipped with tails. Kahn therefore advertised the presence in his museum of a family of "Niam-Niams," as the rumored people with the caudal appendages were called. He did nothing to discourage the expectation that the family was alive and walking about, but what the paying customers in fact beheld was a group of waxen figures modeled on the by now familiar lines of African savages, with prominent tails attached. Kahn's lecture argued that there was really nothing remarkable in a human being's possession of a tail, which was "simply an elongation of the vertebral column." His auditors may have believed this, but as a skeptical scientist dryly remarked at the time, "The instruction given on this foundation is at least rather premature."[41] In the summer of 1857 the museum featured the Heteradelph, or Duplex Boy, a monstrosity recently born in Lancashire consisting of the normal one head and chest plus a duplicated torso and legs as well as a rudimentary second pair of arms. It was announced as being "alive and in good health," but how long it remained so is unknown.[42] Kahn's lecture on this *lusus naturae,* a straightforward scientific exposition, was printed in a sixpenny pamphlet.

By the time it opened in Tichborne Street, Dr. Kahn's Museum and Gallery of Science, as it was now called, had shifted its emphasis from waxworks to instruments: an oxyhydrogen microscope, which by now was standard equipment in every London popular science show, Ruhmkorff's electric coil, and something called Guënal's Appareil Uranographique, which, to judge from the name, had to do with astronomy.[43] One constant, however, remained: the subject which required the segregation of the sexes. During its first four years the exhibition held matinees one or two days a week for ladies only, with a "Professional Lady" in attendance to "give the necessary explanations." A set of nine printed lectures on *The Philosophy of Marriage,* Kahn's contribution to the small mid-Victorian library of treatises on human re-

production and marital "hygiene," could be bought on the premises or ordered by mail from Dr. Kahn's professional address in Harley Street. On the whole, the sexological side of the operation represented a sad falling-off from the elegant days of Dr. Graham. Kahn's dingy rooms were no Temple of Health; they housed neither a Celestial Bed nor a corps of ripe-figured, chastely robed Hebe Vestinas. Instead, if American practice at the time is any guide, it may reasonably be supposed that Dr. Kahn's unpleasant exhibits in wax and alcohol and his lectures on "the physiology of marriage" were a come-on for his real trade: that of administering counsel and treatment to the victims of both "secret vice" and promiscuity. Among the visitors to his museum, conveniently situated on the prostitutes' beat, must have been a goodly number of men and youths who either needed—or were easily frightened into believing they needed—the particular kind of confidential medical assistance he offered for a fee.

Kahn was not alone in ministering to the medical curiosity of visitors to the Haymarket–Leicester Square area. In 1853 a portion of Savile House was given over to Reimers's Anatomical and Ethnological Museum, "consisting of upwards of 300 [later increased to 500] superb and nature-like [later: magnificent] Anatomical Figures, in Wax, &c. For gentlemen only."[44] The "clear view of the Delicate Construction of the Human Body" Reimers aimed to present was

effected by hundreds of nature-like Anatomical Figures, Amongst which is particularly observed the Florentine Venus, which is dissectable in all its parts. The Greek Venus, Displaying the Muscular System. Obstetrical Operations, or the various branches of Midwifery, and the Cesarian operation. A Complete Series of Models, illustrative of the Science of Embryology, or the Origin of Mankind, From the smallest particle of vitality, to the perfectly-formed Foetus. The Magnificent Models of the Human Brain and Five Senses tend also to render intelligible the exquisite organization of man's nervous system.

The "Ethnological" in the museum's name referred to a waxwork "Gallery of All Nations," including models of the Aztec Lilliputians, which "exhibits at one glance the varied types of the Great Human Family"—one more evidence of the wave of popular interest in comparative anthropology that rose in the fifties. "Mr. R. observing the great desire of the Working Classes to inspect the Museum, and knowing the great difficulty which they experience in paying the usual price of admission, has reduced the price to

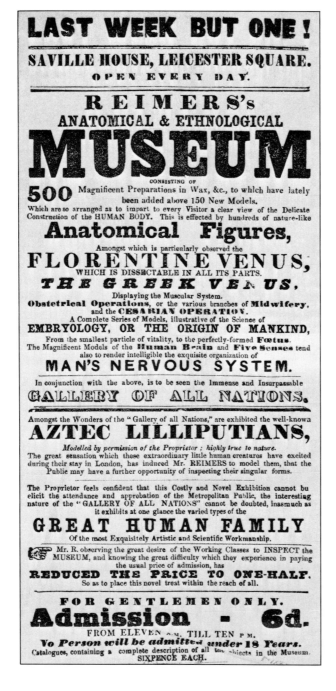

125. Handbill advertising Reimers's Anatomical and Ethnological Museum, 1854.

* There is some reason to believe, though the subject is controversial, that *tableaux vivants* figured in the medieval mystery plays. But they went out of use later on, and their reappearance in the early nineteenth century would seem to have been, in effect, a separate creation.

one-half." But "No Person will be admitted under 18 years"—at any price.[45]

In 1859, at 58 Berners Street, a Madame Caplin opened her "Anatomical and Physiological Gallery (for Ladies only)": the exhibition was open daily, but lectures were given only on Wednesdays.[46] No private matinees were provided for gentlemen. But they were adequately cared for by other rivals of Kahn, the Royal Institute of Anatomy and Science at 396 Oxford Street and Dr. William Beale Marston's Museum of Science, Anatomy, and the Wonders of Nature at 47 Berners Street.[47] By 1862 the fortunes of the Tichborne Street museum were in decline, partly because the conversion of the yard and stables of the adjacent Black Horse tavern into a music hall called the London Pavilion had blocked off its light. Kahn therefore sold his lease and property to Dr. Marston.[48] Eight years later he turned up in New York, operating, not surprisingly, a "Museum for Men only" at 745 Broadway.[49]

Anatomical waxwork shows were most popular, and most vulgarized as well, in the 1850s. It says much about the changing atmosphere of the London show scene at mid-century, especially around Leicester Square, that this development virtually coincided with a similar one in the realm of live entertainment, the *tableau vivant*. In the all-important quest of respectability, both made lofty claims: the anatomical waxwork invoked the dignity of science, the *tableau vivant* the dignity of art. By the early fifties, both pretensions were utterly hypocritical.

The history of the *tableau vivant* as a form of nineteenth-century entertainment has yet to be written. It had a curiously multiple ancestry, part theatrical and part social. In one way, the device of freezing a group of performers in expressive poses represented the principle of the waxwork tableau turned inside out. We have seen that waxwork shows like Mrs. Salmon's had featured groups depicting dramatic moments, and Madame Tussaud had included them in her touring repertory; while still in temporary quarters in Gray's Inn Road before settling in Baker Street she had shown three, the coronation of William IV, the coronation of Napoleon, and, just created, Mary Queen of Scots abdicating the throne.[50] These were waxen representations of real human beings; now, in *tableaux vivants*, real human beings resembled waxen effigies.

But a more direct line of descent was through the drama. Living tableaux were used on the English stage as early as 1811, in William Dimond's *The Peasant Boy* at the Lyceum.* Although moments of suspended action could occur at any time during a play, they were most likely to occur at the very end of a scene or act, when the curtain slowly descended on a suddenly motionless group of players. The late Allardyce Nicoll, the leading modern authority on such matters, was inclined to follow a trade paper of the time in tracing the practice to contemporary German plays where "all the characters are arranged in a picturesque manner, and stand in fixed attitudes, like images on pedestals, when the curtain drops."[51] Some two decades after Dimond's innovation, a refinement was introduced which thereafter differentiated the *tableau vivant* in the stricter sense of the term from the frozen theatrical group in general: the representation of a familiar work of art. (Madame Tussaud's waxen tableau of Napoleon's coronation was modeled after David's painting.) The "living picture" was literally a picture (or statuary) brought to life, though not into motion. In 1829 Planché's Drury Lane melodrama *The Brigand* was interspersed with several tableaux copied from Charles Eastlake's popular series of "banditti" pictures, first exhibited six years earlier: *An Italian Brigand Chief Reposing, The Wife of a Brigand Chief Watching the Result of a Battle,* and *The Dying Brigand.*[52]

Meanwhile another popular kind of theatrical performance was borrowing from the fine arts. In 1813, the versatile Belzoni in his farewell-to-England appearance at Oxford (and possibly in London, though no record of this has been found) performed an act called "the Roman Hercules," described as "several striking Attitudes, from the most admired antique Statues; amongst others, the celebrated Fighting Gladiator; With interesting Groupes from the Labours of Hercules,—The Instructions of Achilles,—and other Classical Subjects, uniting Grace and Expression with Muscular Strength."[53] At almost the same moment, a more celebrated athlete-actor also was becoming identified with this theatrical by-product of the contemporary admiration of the glories that were Greece and Rome. On tour in Belgium during an engagement with Blondin's Cirque Olympique, Andrew Ducrow, the English-born star rider at Astley's Amphitheatre, first performed his *poses plastiques équestres,* striking attitudes as Mercury or Zephyr as he bestrode his galloping horse. The act grew more and more spectacular as, back in England, he worked on it in the next few years; driving as many as nine horses at speed, he won universal applause for both his daring horsemanship and his heroic pantomime impersonations of such diverse figures as a Roman gladiator, a wild Indian hunter, a page troubadour, and a Yorkshire fox hunter.[54] It was for his figures from the antique that he was most admired. As "Timothy Tickler" ("Noctes Ambrosianae," *Blackwood's Magazine,* 1831) rhapsodized:

The glory of Ducrow lies in his Poetical Impersonations. Why, the horse is but the air, as it were, on which he flies! What godlike grace in that volant motion, fresh from Olympus, e'er yet "new-lighted on some heaven-kissing hill!" What seems "the feather'd Mercury" to care for the horse, whose side his toe but touches, as if it were a cloud in the ether? As the flight accelerates, the animal absolutely disappears, if not from the sight of our bodily eye, certainly from that of our imagination, and we behold but the messenger of Jove, worthy to be joined in marriage with Iris.[55]

Eventually the tableaux were presented separately from the equestrian acts. The rise of the curtain—at Astley's and elsewhere—revealed a picture frame in the center of which, on a lofty pedestal against a pictorial background, stood the motionless figure of Ducrow.

It is hardly credible [wrote Pückler-Muskau, who saw the show in Dublin late in October 1828] how an elastic dress can fit so exquisitely and so perfectly represent marble, only here and there broken by a bluish vein. He appeared first as the Hercules Farnese. With the greatest skill and precision he then gradually quitted his attitude from one gradation to another, of display of strength; but at the moment in which he presented a perfect copy of the most celebrated statues of antiquity, he suddenly became fixed as if changed to marble. Helmet, sword, and shield, were now given to him, and transformed him in a moment into the wrathful Achilles, Ajax, and other Homeric heroes. Then came the Discobolus and others, all equally perfect and true. The last was the attitude of the fighting Gladiator, succeeded by a masterly representation of the dying Gladiator. This man must be an admirable model for painters and sculptors: his form is faultless, and he can throw himself into any attitude with the utmost ease and grace.[56]

The German prince declared that Ducrow's performance of "animated statues" "far surpasses the 'Tableaux' which are in such favour on the continent." They existed there in several forms. A correspondent writing in the *Literary Gazette* in 1824 described what he called a new "species of theatrical representation" he had seen at Strasbourg on All Saints Day the year before: the *Mimisch-plastische Darstellung,* translated in the bills as *Tableaux Mimiques,* "an imitation of Pictures by actors on the stage."

In general [he wrote], the subjects are chosen from the Scriptures; and, on the curtain being raised, the performers, in appropriate costume, appear grouped, in suitable positions of person and expression, immovable as statues, presenting the effect of a large painting. Suppose it be the story of Cain and Abel,—they are seen kneeling before their respective altars, exciting the divine response to their sacrifice. This point of time is maintained during a minute and a half or two minutes, when by a signal struck behind the scenes, the fire from heaven descends on the offering of Abel; the attitudes of the brothers change at the same instant; a transport of joy and gratitude, blended with meek humility, depicted on the countenance of the one; rage, jealousy, and vengeance, in that of the other.

The same bill included humorous, secular sequences. After Part I had run its course (Cain and Abel in eight pictures, the Crucifixion in eight, and the Ascension in two), Parts II and III were enacted, the former comprising six scenes illustrating the humors of drunkenness and the battle of the sexes, the latter "Jealousy and Marriage, in eight pictures." The writer reported also that he had seen a similar show at Munich during the preceding Holy Week. The scenes, all of Scriptural subjects in this instance, were performed on a picture stage lighted from behind the frame; each series, "prefaced by a harangue illustrative of the story and characters," represented famous paintings such as Leonardo's *Last Supper* and Rubens's *Descent from the Cross*.[57]

Tableaux vivants quickly became divertissements in the German theatre. When the painter David Wilkie attended a play at Dresden in July 1826 he was enchanted:

The curtain is drawn up between the acts, the stage darkened, and at the back is a scene resembling a picture frame, in the interior of which, most brilliantly lighted from behind, men and women are arranged in appropriate dresses, to make up the composition of some known picture. One I saw the other night was an interior, after D. Teniers. It was the most beautiful reality I ever saw. . . . We were quite delighted with it; but so evanescent is the group, that the curtain drops in twenty seconds, the people being unable to remain for any longer period in one precise position.[58]

Tableaux vivants also figured in entertainments at court, continuing a tradition reaching back to the allegorical groups which often participated in the ceremonial "glories"—processions and pageants—that honored monarchs and other high dignitaries in the Renaissance and later. Sometimes, as in Cardinal Mazarin's gallery in seventeenth-century Paris, ladies of the court were coiffed and costumed to represent figures in the paintings hanging on the walls. During the Grand Duke Nicholas's state visit to Berlin in 1822, *tableaux vivants* portrayed various scenes in Thomas Moore's *Lalla Rookh*.[59]

When Wilkie saw the tableaux at Dresden, he had just come from Rome, where he had spent some time with the English circle. Their favorite diversion that winter had been appearing at masquerades in the costume and pose of individual figures in well-known statues or pictures.* Several ladies had taken the next logical step and formed a group depicting a painting by Raphael, but Wilkie found it "not successful, though it amused." Now, returning to Rome for the winter of 1826–27, he was caught up in a positive fever of what might have been, but was not, called art-acting.

The Countess of Westmoreland, of high rank and splendid establishment, but too ardent, too sensitive, and too indifferent to time, place, and the feelings of other people, has, with my friend Severn, been getting up what we called in Germany *tableaux*. Failures are of course inevitable; yet the night I went with Sir Robert and Lady Liston, some Tableaux with single figures, of which the subjects were very handsome women, succeeded extremely well, and *one*, the Sybil of Guercino, the beautiful Mrs. Cowell, was one of the loveliest visions I ever saw. . . . In order to appease and gratify some friends, a good lady of my acquaintance asked me to try some in her house; invited some beauties on purpose, and after a few rehearsals, we got up four in the simplest manner, in a picture frame, quite as good as those of the wayward Countess. A numerous company was perfectly delighted with them, and the ladies who formed them still more so. We had the Cenci of Guido, the Sybil of Guercino, an Agrippina, and Giorgione's Gaston de Foix in armour, with the Lady placing the order on his breast.

Subsequent living pictures at the home of Wilkie's friend the Honorable Miss Mackenzie "succeeded beyond our most sanguine expectations," he wrote. "We had, besides Sybils and Madonnas from various pictures, various portraits: Lord Darnley, by an early master; Cardinal Bentivoglio, by Vandyke; and, finest of all, a portrait of Titian, by himself."[60]

When, at length, Wilkie returned to England, he found that to his established fame as a painter had been added a new distinction, that of *tableau vivant* producer by appointment to English nobility. In 1833, pursuant to the Duke of Wellington's request that he supervise the program of tableaux from Scott's novels which the Marchioness of Salisbury was planning to present at Hatfield, he devoted much time to making the necessary drawings.[61] In view of his association with *tableaux vivants* it was particularly fitting, and perhaps not accidental, that two of his own paintings, *Rent Day* and *Distraining for Rent,* should have been the subjects of tableaux in Douglas Jerrold's *The Rent Day* (Drury Lane, 28 January 1832). Scarcely a month later the association was again alluded to when a political lithograph

* In this line of descent, the *tableau vivant* can doubtless be traced back to Lady Hamilton, the erstwhile Hebe Vestina at the Temple of Health. Whether or not it was her apprenticeship with Dr. Graham that revealed her talent, as she rose in society she became famous for her "attitudes"—pantomime representations, in full costume and with props, of famous pictures and statues. Draped like a Grecian sculpture, she impersonated Helena, Cassandra, Andromache, and other classic women, to the pleasure of the fashionable company and, in particular, of her elderly husband, who owned a rich collection of Greek marbles. (Horace Walpole: "Sir William Hamilton has actually married his gallery of statues.") See Hugh Tours, *The Life and Letters of Emma Hamilton* (London, 1963), pp. 90, 94, 156–57, 169.

based on one of his paintings was captioned *Un Tableau Vivant. Subject—Mr. Wilkie's Interesting Picture entitled "Calabrian Minstrels Playing to the Madonna."*[62]

By this time, *tableaux vivants* as a self-contained presentation, not a part of a larger production as Ducrow's *poses plastiques* had been, had already made their debut at the Egyptian Hall (August 1830). A reviewer carefully delineated their novelty and what he took to be their immediate antecedents:

It is an art, or rather exhibition of art, not at all known in England, nor indeed generally on the continent. It is a living imitation of a picture, and bears the same relation to one that Ducrow's Statues do to the marble reality. A few years ago, these Tableaux Vivans were the rage with the fashionables at Rome, and among the most admired representations were the famous Sibyls of Raphael, by Mrs. Starkie and some younger friends. We remember, indeed, in this country, to have once seen Malibran, then just budding into all her animated beauty, delight a whole company with a somewhat similar exhibition;—it was merely an interlude—a scene played off but for a few moments, but in such a round of delight, that memory, on recalling it, sorrows in its weakness and humanity, to think such nights will never return. . . . [S]he played the statue which Pygmalion had perfected all but the last few touches. . . .

M. [Ferdinand] Flor's exhibition was somewhat different. It is literally a living representation of a picture. He proposed to give an illustration of the costume, character, and style of the most celebrated of all the schools of painting, beginning with the first dawning of art as exhibited on Etruscan vases and in fresco paintings at Pompeii, proceeding through the Byzantine and Tuscan schools, to its perfection in Raphael and Michael Angelo;—and we are bound to say that in our judgment he was eminently successful.[63]

The critic's regretful conclusion, that this new form of "rational" entertainment would not be widely popular, proved wrong. At Covent Garden in May 1833, for instance, one T. Thompson presented "the Grecian Statues, or Living Models of the Antique," and three years later, at the Pantheon Theatre, Catherine Street, a performance of *King Lear* was followed by "The Celebrated Tableau Vivant of the First Fratricide."[64] In August 1841, Jullien's promenade concerts at Drury Lane gladdened the eye as well as the ear with figures clad in form-fitting white costumes; one selection, the "Quadrille de Venus," was accompanied by five separate groups.[65] During this season, indeed, *tableau vivant* became a vogue term, subject to increasingly elastic usage, and not necessarily implying the imitation of a work of art. Catlin, as we saw, used it to describe the war dances and other demonstrations put on by his troupe of Bow Bells redskins, even though the entire

principle of the tableau was negated by the warriors' furious activity.

Notwithstanding the occasional misapplication of the term, *poses plastiques* were as yet a wholly respectable form of entertainment. They figured prominently in General Tom Thumb's blameless solo act at the Egyptian Hall in 1844, when, in a series of *reductios* (in more than one sense), he posed as Napoleon, Apollo, the Fighting Gladiator, Hercules, Ajax, and Samson Carrying the Gates of Gaza. Douglas Jerrold, purporting to quote him in *Punch,* had him aver that "the 'Erc'les a stranglin the Nimmim Lion was, arter the 'Pollo, the special favorite."[66]

The following autumn (1845) arrived Professor Keller, said to be a teacher of gymnastics at the University of Berlin, with his troupe of "unrivalled artistes, male and female, from the principal Continental Cities in Europe." Performing successively at Vauxhall, the Adelaide Gallery, and Dubourg's Theatre of the Arts in Great Windmill Street, "Professor Keller's Poses Plastiques and Grand Tableaux Vivans" initially had a good press. His Passion Week program could not be faulted; it represented Cain and Abel, Noah building the ark, a scene from the Deluge, Noah offering sacrifices, Abraham relating his dream to his brethren,

126. Handbill advertising Professor Keller's *tableaux vivants* and *poses plastiques,* 1846.

127. Handbill advertising Madame Warton's *tableaux vivants* and *poses plastiques,* 1847?

the funeral of Jacob, Moses delivering the law, and other biblical scenes, with an allegorical representation of Faith, Hope, and Charity added for good measure.[67]

Scriptural tableaux, however, were not Professor Keller's true forte. His regular bill at Dubourg's, rechristened for the occasion "the Ancient Hall of Rome," was more characteristic. Of the seventeen "celebrated Paintings and Sculptures of the Great Masters" portrayed on the first part of the program, the majority—including David's *Prometheus Chained,* Raphael's *Fight for the Body of Patroclus* and *Amazonian Triumph,* Canova's *Three Graces,* Rubens's *Judgment of Paris,* and Thorwaldsen's *Baths of the Dianes*—were noteworthy for the amount of bare flesh the originals depicted.[68] And though on the face of it the second part, "Living Embodiments of the Celebrated Prize Cartoons," would seem innocuous enough, the fact was that in the current controversy over the sketches submitted by artists seeking the commission to paint the frescoes in the new Houses of Parliament (Chap-

ter 29) there was not a little complaint over the relative nudity of some of the figures.

When publicity was given to Professor Keller's inviting a group of artists to a special performance of his "living sculpture," a writer in the *Art-Union,* noting signs of unease, felt obliged to "explain, as these exhibitions are public, that the persons assuming the positions of these famous works are not nude, but wear a dress fitting the person nearly as closely as the skin itself; and moreover, in the groups, which are often composed of a dozen or more of characters, the female figures are fully draped, and the others more or less so, in addition to the covering of which we speak."[69] There obviously was some fear that what had seemed, down to this point, a well-meant effort to popularize fine art by putting it on the stage was in danger of degenerating into a mild form of striptease. It is apparent now, if it was not so at the time, that the entertainment world was taking advantage of the Victorian convention whereby nudity in art, or the suggestion of nudity, was exempt from censure so long as it involved classical subjects. No great effort was needed to stretch the exemption to cover artistic subjects in general. So long as the draperies fitted (and revealed) the form, and the fleshings suggested bare skin, the lubricious potential was there, and, if Professor Keller's own show was comparatively high-minded in intent and execution, in other hands this popular novelty soon courted corruption.

His initial competition came from Walhalla, newly installed in a portion of Savile House. This was the production of Madame Wharton (later spelled Warton), also freshly arrived from the continent, where she had recruited "a Troupe of Eminent Artistes, and been favoured with admission to the studios of several celebrated painters and sculptors."[70] The name Walhalla, whatever else it may have signified to the public mind in 1846—a pagan paradise?—was chosen primarily with a view to its timeliness. The nineteenth-century Walhalla was a replica of the Parthenon built (1830–1842) by Ludwig of Bavaria on an eminence overlooking the Danube near Ratisbon, and Turner's picture of it, *The Opening of the Walhalla,* had been exhibited in 1843. Since the edifice had been intended to house busts of great men, Madame Wharton could scarcely have chosen for her London stand a name more laden with dignity. It was every bit as reassuring as the Ancient Hall of Rome.

Her show, like Keller's at the outset, was designed, ostensibly if not in fact, for family viewing. The opening program included "the unequalled Tableaux of 'A

Grecian Harvest Home' and 'Jephtha's Daughters,'" from a painting that had recently won a prize at the Art Union. For Christmas a matinee bill was devised especially for children: Christmas in the Olden Time, the Queen of the Vintage, the Sleeping Beauty, and the Children in the Wood.[71] The next year, tying in with the current drive to buy Shakespeare's birthplace for the nation, Walhalla presented "A Night with Shakespeare," a selection of illustrations from the plays (Boydell *redivivus*). The program, the first-night proceeds of which were earmarked for the fund, won Madame Wharton golden opinions from the critics, one of whom observed, "The objections which were justly made to these species of exhibition upon their first introduction to this country do not apply to Madame Wharton. . . . Amongst the audience we remarked many of our greatest painters, who all bore flattering testimony to the purely artistic feeling which predominated in the several groups represented."[72]

Such approval, however, did not extend to what was increasingly Madame Wharton's forte, as it was Keller's: the fleshly embodiment of such subjects as were comprehended in "A Night with Canova and Flaxman" and "A Night with Titian." Among the individual works of art illustrated and accompanied by "descriptive music" were Guido Reni's *Venus Attired by the Graces*, Rubens's *Judgment of Paris*, Canova's *Nymph*, and Raphael's *Bacchanalian Triumph*. The Walhalla sensation for Christmas week was a preview of Edwin Landseer's "forthcoming picture" of Lady Godiva. But the house specialty was a full-color enactment of Venus Rising from the Sea.[73]

Meanwhile the Ancient Hall of Rome prospered, the *tableaux vivants* and *poses plastiques* being supplemented by Dubourg's moving waxwork figures and nightly performances by the Ethiopian Serenaders and Ohio Melodists in "a new collection of Nigger Songs."[74] In the summer of 1848, inspired by the competition's Shakespeare festival, Keller advertised "New and splendid Tableaux of Midsummer Night's Dream," which, however, had but a tenuous connection with Shakespeare: "Una on a Moving Lion—Mount Olympus—and Hylas carried away by the Water Nymphs. Also," added the announcement, cryptically, "several other novelties of the most recherché description."[75] A month later were advertised, in somewhat makeshift French, "Tableaux Aerian," a moonlit representation of Diana and Endymion, along with Venus Rising from the Sea.[76] Madame Wharton, it appears, had no monopoly on Venus; nor did she on Godiva, who also turned up at the Ancient Hall of Rome, briefly renamed the Palladium. This Godiva, however, rode a live horse, and was accompanied on the bill by tableaux of Acis and Galatea and the Death of Lucretia.[77]

About this time (1848–49) Madame Wharton, like Professor Keller, disappears from the advertisements. However chaste her portrayals of Venus, Sappho, Innocence, Diana, Ariadne, and Godiva may have been, the Madonna of the *poses plastiques* had personal weaknesses. According to an 1857 issue of *Paul Pry*, a scandal sheet, "Poor Wharton, she met with a sad fate, and payed the debt of nature at a very early age. Let her faults pass away with the bottle to which she became so devotedly attached, 'ere snatched from the scenes of her many triumphs and shame."[78]

Whether chaste and instructive (as the advertisements and some of the reviews insisted) or scandalous (as another body of opinion maintained), *poses plastiques* were the entertainment topic of the day in 1846–1848, and as such, like the monster mile-long panoramas that were about to arrive, they were a prime subject for pantomimes and extravaganzas. In Planché's "fairy extravaganza" *The Invisible Prince; or, The Island of Tranquil Delights* (Haymarket, 26 December 1846), the Princess claimed to have seen a living statue:

Princess: It was alive, and did both sing and speak.
Abricotina: Ah! then it must have been a pose plastique!
Princess: A pose plastique! what's that? You pose me
              now.
Abricotina: An endless exhibition.*
Princess: Endless! how?
Abricotina: Why, how long they may open keep, who
              knows?
              When every day they're less inclined to *close*.
              Group nods at group—each tableau has its
              brother,
              Trying, the wags say, to *outstrip* the other.[79]

Unfortunately (although we are spared further puns), this promising line of discussion was not pursued. But the next year Planché resumed the subject in *The New Planet*, at one point of which, against a backdrop on which posters advertised "The Walhalla" and "The Hall of Rome," Venus exclaimed:

What's this? At the Walhalla, Leicester Square
They shew you Venus rising from the sea!
How dare they take such liberties with me!

After some more lines, she broke into song, to the tune of "Johnny Cope":

* A footnote to Planché's printed text identifies the exhibition as Madame Wharton's.

The Waxen and the Fleshly   347

It's oh, won't I send the rogues marching yet,
The Hall of Rome in a blaze I'll set,
And the Walhalla shall be soon to let,
I give Madame Wharton warning.
They make no doubt of a planet light,
But they seem to have forgotten quite
Though as "Vesper soft" I may rise at night,
I am "Lucifer" in the morning.

Mars: I'll stop this scandal, don't yourself distress—
            I'll make 'em halt!
Harlequin: You'd better make 'em "dress."
Earth: Leave them to Time—he is the great *redresser*.[80]

That the issue of undress was treated so lightly suggests that the *poses* and *tableaux* did not arouse much moral indignation. Certainly in London there was no such furor as occurred in New York in 1847–48, when the police raided the exhibition halls and arrested the performers.[81] Still, there were occasional letters to the papers, such as one from "A Lover of Art" who protested against the *tableaux vivants* "as both offensive to delicacy and eminently injurious to the best interests of *Art*." The writer had no objection to painting from the nude, a subject on which the Society for the Suppression of Vice was currently making representations to the Royal Academy.

But against the wholesale display of female nudity to an indiscriminate mass of people, who view it with (for the most part) anything but . . . high feeling, all real lovers of Art should raise an indignant voice. I do not find fault with the arrangement of their plans, which are conducted with apparent propriety, and got up with much taste: the subjects are, for the most part, moreover, classical and tasteful; but there is an evident preference in the choice of subjects such as, by affording the most opportunity for the display of the form, are the most calculated to attract the worst sort of audience.[82]

To which the *Morning Advertiser* (the newspaper of the licensed victualers, or publicans: but this may be irrelevant) sententiously replied:

The study of the human figure has always been considered by the great masters one of the most important branches of an artist's education. The rules of true art are unchangeable, hence it is that we find the grand lessons inculcated by Raphael, are but re-echoed by Shee [then President of the Royal Academy]. . . . Several of the cartoons exhibited pursuant to the notice issued some time ago by the Fine Arts Commissioners, were remarkable for the rude display of the human subject; some people there were fastidious or prudish enough to pass them with averted eyes. To the pure, all things are pure, and it may be truly said that unless it were to prurient minds, the works of art referred to gave general satisfaction

as far as mere subject and treatment were concerned. . . . In all these [tableaux] there is nothing which can possibly offend even the most refined taste.[83]

A possible reason that the early Victorian public was less disturbed by the *poses plastiques* than one would expect was that in at least a portion of the press there was an informal agreement to ignore them. (By the same token, it is conceivable that there actually was more protest than the papers reported.) The *Athenaeum,* for one, deliberately refrained from commenting on "the tableau mania,—believing it to be a passion which would sink to its proper level" (and therefore out of sight?) "if not protected by persecution."[84] Only when exhibitors went beyond the limits of permissible conduct in other respects might a paper speak out, as did the *Athenaeum* when confronted by an advertisement for a tableau at the Minerva Hall, Haymarket, of "Man's first disobedience" starring a live fifteen-foot anaconda. It was the use of the serpent, which was reputed to feed on live rabbits, and perhaps the suggestion of blasphemy, not the apparent nudity of Adam and Eve, which made the exhibition "so utterly reprehensible."[85] The paper might have saved its ink as far as the anaconda was concerned; the journalist and *bon vivant* George Augustus Sala discovered that it was "a bloated old snake quite sluggish and dozy, and harmless enough, between his rabbits, to be tied in a knot round the tree." But, as it happened, the law did intervene, though for a quite different reason. Sala was there when it happened: "two warriors arrayed in the uniform of Her Majesty appeared on the turn-table, and claimed Adam as a deserter from the third Buffs: which indeed he was, and so was summarily marched off with a great-coat over his fleshings, and a neat pair of handcuffs on his wrists—the which sent me home moralising on the charming efficiency of the Lord Chamberlain and his licensers, which can strike a harmless joke out of a pantomime, and cannot touch such fellows as these, going vagabondising about with nothing to cover them."[86] The *non sequitur* is rather impressive.

The *poses plastiques* reached their lowest level when they arrived at the "night houses" that catered to free-spending, cigar-flourishing men about town— part night clubs, part assignation places, part brothels. There were a number of these crowded, noisy, smoke-filled establishments in the vicinity of Leicester Square and the Strand, the most notorious of them being the Coal Hole tavern, which figures in Thackeray's novels. The Coal Hole was especially known for the scurrilous and not infrequently bawdy "Judge and Jury" audience-participation shows put on by "Baron" Renton Nicholson, the leading impresario of this type of gaslit entertainment. The Baron alleged in his autobiography that it was he who introduced the *poses plastiques* into the world of the concert saloon at the Garrick's Head tavern in 1846, when a group of girl singers, billed as the Female American Serenaders, did double duty by posing while he delivered an "illustrated lecture" on poetry and song.[87] Since one handbill for the Coal Hole, advertising "Mme Pauline and her talented company of female artistes," spoke of "Gems of Art representing Pictures from the Manchester Art Galleries and Scenes from all the principal tragedies, dramas, operas, &c. dresses for which are of the most Magnificent Description," an innocent wandering down the Strand might well have queried why another Coal Hole bill specified "Ladies not admitted."[88] But what the former one did not mention was how long the magnificent costumes remained attached to the female artistes.

The *pose plastique* reached its nadir in the night houses, but, unlike some other forms of popular amusement which suffered corruption, it proved capable of rehabilitation. Walhalla dissolved in flames, along with the rest of Savile House, in 1865; the Ancient Hall of Rome was converted into the Argyll Rooms, one of London's most sin-ridden haunts of prostitutes, and then, in a new career as the Trocadero Palace of Varieties (1882), became once more a home of *poses plastiques*. But by now the advent of the music hall, of which the Trocadero was a leading example, had offered an opportunity for them to be cleaned up and made fit for viewing by whatever portion of the London public—and it was a substantial one—patronized this new institution. Under the somewhat less tarnished name of *tableaux vivants,* the scenes became a fixture of the variety bill, along with acrobats, monologists, conjurors, comedians, and chanteuses, and thus entered the fond memories of many a late Victorian music hall devotee.

More Mechanical Ingenuity

25

The marvels of clockworkmanship that had astonished and delighted Londoners in the last third of the eighteenth century could still be seen in the first decades of the nineteenth, though their appeal was fading as ever more ingenious machines were invented. They descended to the new era in two not wholly separate streams, one originating in Jaquet-Droz's Spectacle Mécanique, the other in Cox's Museum.

Jaquet-Droz's second-generation automatons passed about 1791 to the firm's London representative, Henri Maillardet, who exhibited them at the Great Room, Spring Gardens, between 1798 and 1817, with intervals elsewhere (in 1812, for example, "Philipstal and Maillardet's Automatical Theatre" was showing in Catherine Street).[1] Among the exhibits were the classic musical lady, writer-draftsman, magician, and rope dancer, as well as an assortment of miniature mechanisms—an Ethiopian caterpillar, an Egyptian lizard, and a Siberian mouse—which seem to have been imitations of items in Cox's Museum. In the 1820s the collection, now owned by one Schmidt or Smith, was at the Gothic Hall in the Haymarket, and in 1828 it was advertised for sale.[2] Three years later the much-traveled troupe of artificial men and animals had become part of a typical miscellaneous entertainment. At the Royal Bazaar, Leicester Square, it was supported at matinees by "a grand Udoramic Representation of a Lake and Waterfall in Switzerland" and cosmoramas of Rome, the Cape of Good Hope, Warwick Castle, and the recently completed Menai Straits suspension bridge. At the evening performance there was

a demonstration of laughing gas and, as a finale, a "Physioramic Pyrotechnicon, displaying a series of pleasing and fanciful objects in a manner which cannot fail to excite the highest admiration and amusement."[3] No doubt; but what was it?

Shortly thereafter, the collection was dispersed. The musical lady who had been before the public for so many years was sent to St. Petersburg, and a portion of the other objects went to New York, where they were exhibited under Maillardet's name in 1834–1836.[4] (Separate items from these London automaton shows had already been seen there.) The automaton writer ended up in Philadelphia, where it was destroyed in a fire. The remains of the mechanism, however, were salvaged and a new figure made, which is now in that city's Franklin Institute.[5]

Cox's mantle meanwhile had descended, more or less obliquely, on a jeweler named Weeks (or Weekes), who opened a "Mechanical Museum" about 1803 at 3 Tichborne Street, Haymarket.[6] How many of the exhibits had been in the original Cox museum, how many derived from the Davies who had made miniature replicas of some of Cox's items, and how many Weeks made himself, it is impossible to tell; but Weeks understandably did all he could to emphasize the connection with Cox, whose sumptuous museum was unforgotten despite the lapse of thirty years. Although the exterior at 3 Tichborne Street was unprepossessing—it looked like a common umbrella shop, and the front room actually was one—the visitor who paid the Cox-scale half-crown was ushered into a

128. The automaton exhibition, Gothic Hall, Haymarket (etching by T. Lane, 1826).

spacious salon designed by the noted architect James Wyatt, with a ceiling painted by the artists Biagio Rebecca and Henry Singleton and walls wholly covered with blue satin. Like its prototype, this exhibition hall was filled with sprightly movement and sound: "valuable and superbly ornamented clocks; the striking of the hours of which is followed by the singing of birds, the dancing of peasantry, the flowing of rivers, the passage of boats, the falling of cascades, the revolving of windmills, the fluttering of butterflies, the expanding and closing of flowers, and a number of other musical devices."[7] Cox's pair of seven-foot-high temples, supported by sixteen elephants and embellished with 1,700 pieces of jewelry, was here, along with the silver swan with the articulated neck which swam on "artificial water," a large variety of musical clocks, life-size automaton musicians, a caterpillar that fed on the foliage of a golden tree, a nimble mouse made of Oriental pearls, birds that hopped from stick to stick in their ornate cages, and the figure of an old woman which emerged from a cottage and walked about on crutches. The most publicized mechanism, however, was a 115-piece tarantula spider made of steel, which darted from a box, ran backward and forward on a table, stretched and drew in its slender legs, and moved its "horns" and "claws."[8]

In 1819 the American minister to the Court of St. James's, Richard Rush, visited the museum and was much impressed by it. Weeks told him, said Rush, that "his collection in clocks alone was of the value of £30,000 sterling. It was prepared for the Chinese market, where such articles would be in demand at the prices he put upon them; so he confidently said, though valuing some of his birds at a thousand guineas a piece. He said that the Government of China would not permit the English to have intercourse with them for such purposes, and seemed to be in present despair; but he added, that 'one of these days England will oblige China to receive her wares, by making her feel the strong arm of her power.'" The jeweler's inheritance from Cox seems to have included an overoptimistic estimate of the Chinese voracity for sing-songs. While he waited for the market to open, Weeks hoped that the expense to which he had gone to re-create the flavor of the old museum would be rewarded by a clientele as enthusiastic as Cox's. But although the museum was "a remarkable sample of that exquisite subdivision in mechanical genius, in a field bearing neither upon the useful nor fine arts, to be found only in a vast metropolis," the metropolis did not respond. Perhaps Weeks did not advertise enough; Rush remarked that "although I occasionally spoke of this collection in society afterwards, I hardly met with any one who had as much as heard of it."[9]

Weeks was already seventy-six in 1819. He died in 1834, spared the knowledge that the coercive powers of the Treaty of Nanking (1842) would not specifically require the Chinese to buy expensive mechanical gimcracks. Most of his stock was auctioned off, and the building turned over to other uses; many years later (1857) it became for a while the headquarters of Dr. Kahn's scientific museum. When Weeks's last surviving son died in 1864, the remains of his father's collection, broken, rusted, and clogged with dirt, were sold for trifling sums at Christie's. The silver swan, however, escaped this gloomy fate. Evidently sold separately, it was exhibited at the Paris Universal Exhibition of 1867 by a New Bond Street jeweler. A few years later it was acquired by the collector John Bowes and is now at the Bowes Museum, Barnard Castle, restored to perfect condition.

Kempelen's chess player, whose title to be called an automaton was the subject of lively debate in 1784, returned to London in the autumn of 1818.[10] Its inventor had died in 1804, and its new owner, a Viennese inventor-musician named Johann Nepomuk (or Nepomucene) Maelzel, who had already built two mechanical orchestras, stored it at Schönbrunn Palace. (There is no foundation for the often-repeated story that Napoleon played a game with it in Vienna.) After the war, Maelzel took the chess player to Paris and then to London, exhibiting first at 4 Spring Gardens and then at 29 St. James's Street. During this return engagement it was said to have lost hardly one game in a hundred; and again its claim to be a genuine automaton was challenged, this time in a pamphlet by Robert Willis, a Cambridge undergraduate who was later to become the Jacksonian Professor of Applied Mechanics at the university. Willis went beyond Thicknesse's previous argument by showing conclusively that the complicated machinery which was so ostentatiously displayed was mere pretense, activating nothing, and that the showman's elaborate "proof" that the cabinet was otherwise empty was also a deception. Inside the chest was a human being, who, during the preliminary demonstration that he was *not* there, went through a series of contortions by which he kept one step ahead of the showman as he opened each "empty" compartment in turn. When a game was in progress he could see his opponent's moves through the coat of the Turkish figure.

Willis may have decisively explained the mystification, but Maelzel evidently found his business unimpaired. During the next several years he toured the provinces and the continent with his little troupe of mechanical wonders; besides the (spurious) chess player, he had a mechanical orchestra, an automaton

trumpeter and rope dancer, and a moving picture of the burning of Moscow. At the end of 1825 he took the whole show to the United States, where he moved from town to town for the next ten years. Late in 1835 he was exhibiting in Boston, where Barnum was beginning his career with his first attraction, the moribund but still breathing ancient Negress, Joyce Heth, who, he claimed, had been Washington's nurse. Barnum wrote in his reminiscences that he looked upon Maelzel as "the great father of caterers for public amusement, and was pleased with his assurance that I would certainly make a successful showman. 'I see,' said he, in broken English, 'that you understand the value of the press, and that is the great thing. Nothing helps the showmans like the types and the ink. When your old woman dies,' he added, 'you come to me, and I will make your fortune.'"[11] A few months later the types and the ink illustrated the point, when Edgar Allan Poe's "exposé" of the chess player in the *Southern Literary Messenger* generated fresh interest in Maelzel's long-term asset. (Actually, there was nothing original in Poe's explanation of how the chess player operated; he relied on that in Brewster's *Letters on Natural Magic* [1832], which in turn was no more than a condensation of Willis's pamphlet.)[12] Maelzel died in July 1838 aboard the American brig *Otis* while returning to the United States from Havana. The chess player was bought by a Philadelphia doctor, the father of the neurologist and novelist S. Weir Mitchell, and after an interval in which it was used by a club he had formed for the purpose, he deposited it in the museum that had formerly housed Dunn's Chinese collection. It was destroyed when the building burned in 1854.

Meanwhile the London market for automatons, pseudo-automatons, and mechanical illusions was by no means exhausted. Several kinds of shows continued to cater to the human craving to be baffled. Two automaton draftsmen, or what purported to be such, could be seen between 1826 and 1830. One was the Prosopographus, shown at various locations by a Mr. Herve, which made simple likenesses of visitors for a shilling each, and fancier models at higher prices.[13] The other, at the "Pannus-Corium Establishment," 109 Strand, was the Corinthian Maid, who performed the same feat at the same price but with the advantage of more classically oriented publicity recalling Pliny's "tale from the Archives of Corinth, which relates, that 'the Daughter of Dibutades, a Potter, observing the shadow of her Lover, snatched, in a moment of inspiration, a piece of Chalk, and traced his Likeness upon the Marble Wall.'"[14] The nature of the feat described is cause for suspicion that both "automatons" were impostors.

In one famous instance at the beginning of the century, a variant of the automaton principle supplied the attractive mystery. Here the presence of a human agent, far from being suppressed, was freely admitted. The voice was there, but where was the body? In June 1803 the artist Joseph Farington went to see "the extraordinary contrivance called 'The Invisible Girl'" in a room in Leicester Square and jotted in his diary:*

Four mouths of Trumpet shapes [suspended from a framework] to any of which persons place their ears & hear *as from within* a voice like that of a girl, which answers any question,—describes your person & dress, sings plays on a pianoforte tells you what a Clock it is &c &c. . . . The effect of the voice & the music was surprising, and no conjecture that was made by persons present of the nature of the contrivance seemed satisfactory.—One thought that the sound passed from *below* through Tubes into the mouths of the Trumpets & seemed to the hearer to proceed from the inside of the Ball.—The voice spoke English,—French & German. —The admittance to hear it is 2s. 6d.[15]

When, on the showman's invitation, a spectator proposed a question to the unseen oracle, he spoke into one of the trumpets. The answer seemed to come back from all four, "with sufficient intensity," said Sir David Brewster, "to be heard by an ear applied to any of them, and yet it was so weak that it appeared to come from a person of very diminutive size. Hence the sound was supposed to come from an invisible girl, though the speaker was a full grown woman." The secret of this manifestation of "natural magic" was simple. An india-rubber tube, threaded through the hollow standing frame, conveyed sound underneath the floor to a woman hidden in an adjoining room and returned her answer. A concealed hole in the partition enabled her to see the spectators, whom she could therefore describe as well as converse with.[16]

In time, of course, expositors of science like Brewster revealed the trick, just as they had done with the chess player. The unveiling of this particular mystery was an irresistible invitation to sentimental philosophizing, and Thomas Moore, for one, took full advantage of it. In "To the Invisible Girl," one of his "Cara" poems, he wrote:

They try to persuade me, my dear little sprite,
That you're *not* a true daughter of ether and light,
Nor have any concern with those fanciful forms
That dance upon rainbows and ride upon storms;
That, in short, you're a woman; your lip and your eye
As mortal as ever drew gods from the sky.

But I *will* not believe them—no, Science, to you
I have long bid a last and a careless adieu:
Still flying from Nature to study her laws,
And dulling delight by exploring its cause,
You forget how superior, for mortals below,
Is the fiction they dream to the truth that they know.[17]

The Invisible Girl periodically reappeared (in a manner of speaking) during the next several decades. As late as 1839 she was issuing her ghostly messages at the Cosmorama Rooms.[18] A hybrid creation, with elements of both the Speaking Head of Dr. Johnson's day and the Invisible Girl—one stops short of associating it with the Commendatore's statue in *Don Giovanni*— was the Anthropoglossos, or Mechanical Vocalist, which operated in the early forties in a dimly lighted room in St. James's Hall. Behind a railing was positioned an outsize waxen head which was reputedly meant to be a portrait of Jullien, though other opinion held that it resembled Goliath after David had done his work. Beneath the head, concealed by a sort of petticoat, was a box which the exhibitor periodically wound up. Issuing from the mouth was a funnel from which, one was asked to believe, the spectral voice's program of songs emerged: "Polly Perkins," "The Dark Girl Dressed in Blue," "Annie Lyle," "A Gypsy's Life is a Joyous Life," "God Bless the Prince of Wales," and "God Save the Queen." According to one account, the head was contained in a shallow bowl placed on what seemed to be a tripod; according to another, "like Mahomet's coffin [it] hung suspended in mid-air" by two brass chains. Francis Buckland, then a Winchester schoolboy, reasoning that where there was a voice there must be air, cut off a silk cord inside his hat and held it in front of the funnel while a song was in progress. There was no slightest indication of a draft. Nor should there have been: the illusion of the disembodied head was accomplished by mirrors, and the voice was that of the Cockney ventriloquist who sat behind them. The "mechanism" had no more to do with the performance than did that of the chess player.[19]

❦

By contrast, Professor Faber's Euphonia was a genuine machine, unaided by any human larynx.† Faber, a native of Freiburg, was a former astronomer whom failing eyesight had diverted into the study of anatomy and mechanics. His "Speaking Automaton" was demonstrated to Londoners at the Egyptian Hall in the summer of 1846. The future theatre-manager John

* There was an Invisible Lady in New York as early as March 1800. (Odell, II, 123.) Wordsworth and Lamb encountered another at Bartholomew Fair in 1802. (*The Prelude*, VII, 683.)

† This was not the first actual machine to imitate the human voice, as distinct from the ventriloquial "speaking heads." Kempelen exhibited one of his own devising in 1784, along with the chess player. The *Monthly Review* commented at the time (70, 1784, 308), "it is certain that this ingenious man has carried the powers of mechanism to an amazing degree of perfection, as may be observed in another machine of his invention, which speaks and articulates, distinctly, a considerable number of sentences, in different languages. This *speaking organ* is deemed a much more extraordinary invention than even the wonderful chess-player; notwithstanding the astonishing powers of the latter."

Hollingshead, nineteen years old at the time, attended the show and many years later wrote this touching account of the scene and the performance:

I paid my shilling and was shown into a large room, half filled with boxes and lumber, and badly lighted with lamps. In the centre was a box on a table, looking like a rough piano without legs and having two key-boards. This was surmounted by a half-length weird figure, rather bigger than a full-grown man, with an automaton head and face looking more mysteriously vacant than such faces usually look. Its mouth was large, and opened like the jaws of Gorgibuster in the pantomime, disclosing artificial gums, teeth, and all the organs of speech. There was no lecturer, no lecture, no music—none of the usual adjuncts of a show. The exhibitor, Professor Faber, was a sad-faced man, dressed in respectable well-worn clothes that were soiled by contact with tools, wood, and machinery. . . . The Professor was none too clean, and his hair and beard sadly wanted the attention of a barber. I have no doubt that he slept in the same room as his figure—his scientific Frankenstein monster—and I felt the secret influence of an idea that the two were destined to live and die together. The Professor, with a slight German accent, put his wonderful toy in motion. He explained its action: it was not necessary to prove the absence of deception. One keyboard, touched by the Professor, produced words which, slowly and deliberately in a hoarse sepulchral voice came from the mouth of the figure, as if from the depths of a tomb. It wanted little imagination to make the very few visitors believe that the figure contained an imprisoned human—or half human—being, bound to speak slowly when tormented by the unseen power outside. No one thought for a moment that they were being fooled by a second edition of the "Invisible Girl" fraud. There were truth, laborious invention, and good faith, in every part of the melancholy room. As a crowning display, the head sang a sepulchral version of "God Save the Queen," which suggested, inevitably, God save the inventor. This extraordinary effect was achieved by the Professor working two keyboards—one for the words, and one for the music. Never probably, before or since, has the National Anthem been so sung. Sadder and wiser, I, and the few visitors, crept slowly from the place, leaving the Professor with his one and only treasure—his child of infinite labour and unmeasurable sorrow.[20]

The tiny audience seems not to have merely represented an off day during the Euphonia's run. The machine, to be sure, was a moderate critical success; the *Times,* stressing that "the exhibition is one illustrating mechanical science, and not the raree show of a mountebank," declared it was "almost a duty of all who can afford to see it, to gratify at once their curiosity, and show their encouragement to genius," and the *Illustrated London News,* airily alluding to Roger Bacon's

speaking head, went on to remark that even Vaucanson "must *duck* his diminished head before the Euphonia of our day."[21] Nevertheless, it failed to draw crowds. One visitor who paid a return visit was the Duke of Wellington, who, according to Barnum, initially suspected ventriloquism. "He was asked to touch the keys with his own fingers, and after some instruction in the method of operating, he was able to make the machine speak, not only in English but also in German, with which language the Duke seemed to be familiar. Thereafter, he entered his name on the exhibitor's autograph book, and certified that the 'Automatic Speaker' was an extraordinary production of mechanical genius."[22]

The android aspect of the machine was confined to the torso of a Turk resting on a table, surrounded by crimson drapery concealing the mass of machinery by which his voice was produced. Professor Faber sat at an adjoining small keyboard. By regulating the supply of air to a bellows (the figure's lungs) and by controlling the action of three components—the rubber tube that served as the trachea, the rubber ligaments or ivory reed that served as the larynx, and the movable lower jaw—he could produce a crude semblance of the human voice. Pitch was regulated by turning a small screw. The Turk was capable of halting speech in French, Latin, Greek, and English in addition to his creator's native German. Faber, it was reported, had spent seven years teaching him to pronounce the vowel *e* correctly. The exhibition routine began thus: "Please excuse my slow pronunciation. . . . Good morning, ladies and gentlemen . . . It is a warm day. . . . It is a rainy day. . . . Buon giorno, signiori." Then the spectators were free to ask the figure to speak whatever words or phrases they wished. One interrogator tested it with the Greek word for "sea" ("'thalassee' was very distinctly articulated"), the Greek alphabet, Lachlin Maclachlin ("pronounced with as much accuracy as Englishmen generally attain in the use of the guttural"), Mississippi, Massachusetts, Xerxes, Xenophon, Xantippe, and Hurray for Queen Victoria (Thackeray heard it as "Hourrah for Figdoria") and Prince Albert. The mechanical voice proved generally equal to these demands. Less successful were its attempts to imitate a child's crying, and least impressive of all, as Hollingshead observed, was its singing to the accompaniment of an organ which Faber had also invented. Inevitably, some sounds were not as well managed as others, and some—double *l* in the Welsh "Llangollen" for example—could not be pronounced at all. Nor could intonation be varied, so

129. Professor Faber's Euphonia (*Illustrated London News*, 8 August 1846). Notwithstanding contemporary descriptions, the figure has only a minimal resemblance to a Turk.

that at best the final effect of the performance was one of diligent but unconvincing imitation.[23]

Writing in *Punch*, Thackeray indulged in fancies which strikingly anticipated modern sound recording and reproducing devices. He proposed that the Euphonia be combined with a type-composing machine lately shown at the Society of Arts, so that "as one part of the compound instrument perused each syllable, the phonic part would give it utterance; and thus, by the aid of a simple grinder at the bellows, long speeches might be uttered with all the best benefits of emphasis and oratory" without Lord Brougham's Scottish accent or Sir Robert Peel's "conventicle twang."

A parson [he continued] might set up the Compound Machine in his pulpit, and a clerk or curate work it from the reading-desk, whilst his Reverence was smoking his pipe in the vestry; or an under-secretary might set the bellows going with a speech of LORD JOHN [Russell]'S whilst his Lordship was taking his usual glass of brandy-and-water at BELLAMY'S; or a lawyer in full practice might set a score of them to work, and so actually attend twenty committees at a time; or it might be placed upon THE THRONE, with the august insignia laid upon the top of the machine, and the LORD CHANCELLOR (after kneeling profoundly) might pop the royal speech into the proper receptacle and blow it out again to both Houses in the best style.

A clear saving of 10,000 a year might be effected by setting up a machine *en permanence* in the Speaker's chair of the House of Commons. Place the mace before it. Have a large snuff-box on the side, with rappee and Irish for the convenience of Members, and a simple apparatus for crying out "Order, order," at intervals of ten minutes, and you have a speaker at the most trifling cost.[24]

After failing to make his fortune in London, Faber toured the provinces. According to Hollingshead, his brain child was "even less appreciated" there. "The end came at last, and not the expected end. One day, in a dull matter-of-fact town—a town that could understand nothing but a Circus or a Jack Pudding—he destroyed himself and his figure. The world went on just the same, bestowing as little notice on his memory as it had on his exhibition. As a reward for this brutality, the world, thirty years afterwards, was presented with the phonograph."[25]

This denouement is perfectly suitable to a certain kind of moralized Victorian biography. Working against it, however, are the fact that Faber exhibited the Euphonia in Paris in 1862 and Barnum's statement that in 1873 the professor and his wife were in Philadelphia, where Barnum signed him—and the eloquent Turk—for the coming circus season.[26] But Faber was reported to be already sixty years old when he exhibited in Piccadilly in 1846. Could he have tented with Barnum at the age of eighty-seven? A question beclouded by two unreliable witnesses is hard, perhaps impossible, to settle.

Another mechanical marvel of the forties, the Eureka, purported to realize a long-standing English ambition: the production of a limitless number of Latin hexameter verses unassisted by any muse. Its inventor, John Clark, late of Bridgwater, Somerset, but now residing in Paddington, was said to have been inspired by "an old book, the work of one of the monks of Glastonbury Abbey."[27] He was certainly affected, however, by Brewster's kaleidoscope, a device which could form an indefinite number of geometrical figures, and he cannot have been unaware of Charles Babbage's well-publicized efforts to build a calculating machine.* Babbage's confidence was matched by Clark's. "The nearest approach to a thinking machine ever yet produced," ran an advertisement of the Eureka, " . . . a remarkable and perfectly unique example of the union of metaphysical with mathematical powers."[28]

This latest advance in British technology could be seen in operation at the Egyptian Hall in the summer of 1845.[29] In its front, which resembled a small "bureau" bookcase, it had a slot through which the hexameter lines could be read as they were manufactured. Above this aperture was an inscription:

"Full many a gem, of purest ray serene,
    The dark, unfathom'd caves of ocean bear,
And many a flower is born to blush unseen,
    And waste its fragrance on the desert air."
Full many a thought, of character sublime,
    Conceived in darkness, here shall be unrolled,
The mystery of number and of time
    Is here displayed in characters of gold.
Transcribe each line composed by this machine,
    "Record the fleeting thoughts as they arise;"
A line, once lost, may ne'er again be seen,
    "A thought, once flown, perhaps for ever flies."

When it was set to work, the machine composed one hexameter line at a time, "each verse being perfect in grammar, sense, and prosody." Thus:

Horrida sponsa reis promittunt tempora densa.
Sontia tela bonis causabunt agmina creba.
Bellica vota modis promulgant crimina fusca.
Aspera pila patet depromunt praelia quaedam.
Effera sponsa fere confirmant vincula nequam

—and so forth, *ad infinitum.*† As each line was being composed, a cylinder inside this mechanical Virgil produced background music in the form of "God Save the Queen." Simultaneously, a kaleidoscope mounted on the front of the machine displayed a geometrical figure corresponding to that of the hexameters being created—"every identical verse with its corresponding figure, and every figure with its corresponding verse." When completed, the verse remained in sight through the aperture long enough to be copied. Then the machine gave "an audible notice that the verse [was] about to be decomposed." While the letters were being withdrawn, one by one, the air "Fly Not Yet" was heard from within. If a brake was not applied, the machine would proceed to compose hexameters at the rate of 60 an hour, 1,440 in a day and night, 10,080 in a whole week—a sufficiently nightmarish foretaste of what a robot-equipped future might hold. Each line was guaranteed to be original, "having never been produced before, and never to be repeated again." In the long run, the machine's utility may have been somewhat less than that of Babbage's, but its value to one class of prospective users, Latin-grinding schoolboys, was regarded as incalculable. Thackeray announced in a squib in *Punch* that "several double-barrelled Eurekas were ordered for Eton, Harrow, and Rugby."[30]

⋈⁂⋈

The Eureka was unique among the exhibited inventions of the time in its union of the mechanic and literary arts. But a similar collaboration between machines and other muses had often been attempted during the eighteenth century, in the various musical picture-clocks, automaton birds, and other small devices that produced tunes, and the musical lady at the harpsichord. Beginning in Merlin's day, mechanical music, particularly in the form of elaborate barrel organs, engaged a considerable amount of inventive energy both in Britain and abroad.

Brooding over all such conceptions, miscarriages, and achievements, though in this case the mechanical art was almost overwhelmed by the polite ones, was the most grandiose example of *Gesamtkunst* in English history, the Panathene, which was shown at Spring Gardens in 1822. This "Temple of Arts on a small scale"—a remarkably restrained characterization, since it was twenty-three feet high—represented all five orders of architecture, as well as painting, sculpture, carving, gilding, and music. No picture seems to sur-

* As a correspondent pointed out in the *Athenaeum* (5 July 1845, p. 669), early in the eighteenth century there had been a treatise entitled "Artificial Versifying, shewing any one, though of ordinary Capacity, that can read and write, though he understandeth not a word of Latin, how to make Thousands of Hexameter and Pentameter Verses, which will be good Latin, true Verse, and perfect Sense." The writer unaccountably failed to mention that in the description of the Grand Academy of Lagado in *Gulliver's Travels,* Swift had written of a machine that enabled "the most ignorant person . . . [to] write books in philosophy, poetry, politics, law, mathematics, and theology, without the least assistance from genius or study." Forty pupils, standing at the sides of a twenty-foot-square frame containing bits of wood covered with paper with words and phrases written on them, turned cranks which brought the language elements into ever changing relationships. By working six-hour shifts they produced several folio volumes' worth of broken sentences, which the professor "intended to piece together, and out of those rich materials to give the world a complete body of all arts and sciences."

† Not quite. It was calculated that "the table of hexameters will produce 25,827,165, and the table of pentameters 1,221,756 verses, each of which will differ from its predecessors." (*Athenaeum,* 5 July 1845, p. 669).

vive, and although no summary description can do the Panathene justice, a selection of its principal features doubtless conveys the correct impression. Its frame was of mahogany, and into it, or on it, were laid: an allegorical painting of *Music* by Stothard; a pair of sculptures (Cupid and Psyche, and Antinous); another allegorical painting, *Poetry,* by H. Howard, R.A.; a landscape on velvet, *A Distant View of Eton College,* by C. Town; more sculpture; another work by Stothard, *Painting;* another work by Howard—of *Faith, Hope, and Charity;* more classical statues; another painting on velvet by Town; and this does not exhaust the contents of the lower level alone. The upper part was ornamented with "splendid alabaster vases," and inside—finally—was mechanism: "a self-acting Organ, Harp, and Flageolet" and a musical clock which performed several tunes. "The present sketch," like the handbill from which it has been derived, "will not allow room to describe the protecting Lions, the Eagles, Drapery, Columns, Glass Work, etc. etc." But it may well be believed that, as another throwaway put it, the Panathene was "different in every respect to any thing that has ever been presented to the world."[31] A contemporary paper remarked, in offering its compliments to the "ingenious and enthusiastic" craftsman, reputedly a provincial engraver, "we cannot find much of the cui bono in his magnum opus."[32]

The same witticism was also applicable to the Panathene's only serious rival, the Wonderful Clock (so advertised), shown at the Cosmorama Rooms.[33] Actually it was a relic of long ago, predating Pinchbeck's elaborate timepieces by many years, but only now was it shown in London. Said to have been made over a span of thirty-four years in the late seventeenth century by an Exeter clockmaker named Jacob Lovelace (another source says "Loudan"), it had no fewer than thirteen separate movements. The more prosaic ones reported the hour, the day of the week, and the phases of the moon; the longer expanses of time were indicated by *two* perpetual calendars. The rest of the action took these forms:

"A moving panorama, descriptive of day and night. Day is represented by Apollo in his car, drawn by four coursers, accompanied by the twelve hours; and Diana, in her car drawn by stags, attended by the twelve hours, represents night."

"Two gilt figures in Roman costume, who turn their heads and salute with their swords as the panorama revolves; and also move in the same manner while the bells are ringing."

"Two female figures . . . representing Fame and

Terpsichore, who move in time while the organ plays."

"Saturn the god of time, who beats in movement while the organ plays."

"A circle on the face shews the names of ten celebrated ancient tunes, played by the organ in the interior of the cabinet every four hours."

"A belfry with six ringers, who ring a lively peal *ad libitum.* The interior of this part of the cabinet is ornamented with paintings, representing some of the principal ancient buildings of the city of Exeter."

"Connected with the organ there is a bird-organ, which plays when required." (Some viewer-listeners did not require it. One wrote that it was "the most asthmatical choir of birds it was ever our hard fortune to listen to.")[34]

Less eclectic but quite as formidable, each in its own way, were the several early nineteenth-century contrivances which, dispensing with visual embellishments, were dedicated exclusively to producing or imitating instrumental music. Among the continental builders of music machines was Johann Maelzel, owner of the automaton chess player.[35] This busy musical mechanic (who did not, however, invent the metronome, as he claimed) built two automatic orchestras. The first (ca. 1792) he sold to Archduke Charles of Austria, who, it was said, wanted it for the express purpose of annoying his friends. The second, named the Panharmonicon, was a considerably larger instrument, with a suite of forty-two fictive musicians playing strings, clarinets, trumpets, flutes, drums, cymbals, and triangles. It was in connection with this invention that Beethoven almost joined the ranks of London showmen.[36] He and Maelzel, who had made an ear trumpet for him, were close friends at the time, and in 1813 the two planned to take the Panharmonicon to London. For the projected exhibition Maelzel sketched some music especially designed to reveal the Panharmonicon's capability—a number describing the Battle of Vittoria. From this sketch Beethoven scored the piece for the Panharmonicon and then orchestrated it. *Wellington's Victory,* or the *Battle Symphony,* as it came to be called, was first played in Vienna on 8 December 1813, on a program which also included the Seventh Symphony and the Panharmonicon's execution of marches by Dussek and Pleyel.

The two men, however, fell out over the ownership of *Wellington's Victory;* Beethoven started a lawsuit against Maelzel and wrote to his London musician correspondents warning them that the number, for which Maelzel also possessed an orchestral score, was actually

130. The Wonderful Clock (engraving from the *Official Descriptive and Illustrated Catalogue of the Great Exhibition, 1851*).

his. In the upshot, Beethoven abandoned his suit. He never got to London, but the Panharmonicon did, under the name of Orchestrion, as one of the company of mechanical showpieces which Maelzel exhibited there in 1818–1821. Performing alongside it was the life-size automaton trumpeter already mentioned, which Maelzel had invented at the turn of the century. In the trumpeter's repertory, along with Austrian and French cavalry marches and signals, were tunes by Beethoven. One paper noted with approval that this automaton, unlike his flesh-and-blood colleagues, was wholly without affectation and moreover was consistent in his performance. "Being encored, he displayed none of the *airs* of inflated genius, but readily submitting to be prompted, alias wound up, repeated the tunes with the same brilliant execution, and without introducing new ornaments to spoil what had given so much satisfaction before."[37]

Perhaps the reason that the Panharmonicon was renamed the Orchestrion was that the former name had been preempted—not that there was any rigid protocol in such matters—by an earlier mechanical orchestra shown in London. This was the creation of J. J. Gurk, a landscape painter in the service of Haydn's patron, Prince Esterházy. Gurk spent seven years building a machine which would combine every instrument in a military band, finishing it just before the composer's death in 1809. On being asked to give the invention his blessing and a name, Haydn suggested in a letter that Gurk call it "the PANHARMONICON; and, if any body ask you any questions about it, tell him the name proceeds from old Haydn." "These few lines," said the *Times* when the machine made its London debut, "Mr. Gurk prizes beyond the value of the most precious relicks."[38] Beginning in November 1811, the Panharmonicon gave several hour-long concerts daily in the Great Room, Spring Gardens.

The apparatus, fourteen feet long, seven wide, and four deep, was enclosed in a mahogany frame, decorated with gilt carvings and light blue silk curtains, which reminded some of a four-poster bedstead. On the lower level were thirty-one clarinets, twenty flutes, twenty German flutes, a set of organ pipes, and eighteen bassoons; above these were fourteen brass trumpets and four French horns; and in the background, a pair of cymbals, two kettle drums, a bass drum, a snare drum, and a triangle. All the instruments were real, but each of the brasses and woodwinds was bored to produce only one note. The ensemble was governed by a row of brass keys communicating with a revolving cylinder which was set in motion by clock-

work. A second clockwork operated the bellows for the horns and trumpets, and a third the percussion. The whole business had to be rewound before each selection. There were seven in all, including the overture to Mozart's *La Clemenza di Tito,* the allegretto movement of Haydn's Military Symphony, and (of course) "Rule, Britannia."[39] The engagement was successful enough to encourage Gurk to return with the Panharmonicon in 1817.

The most celebrated English instrument of the kind was the Apollonicon, five years in the making at the organ builders Flight and Robson, in St. Martin's Lane. Completed in 1817 at a cost of £10,000, this mammoth chamber organ had forty-five stops, 1,900 pipes (the largest twenty-four feet long, eight feet longer than the corresponding one in St. Bavo's at Haarlem), and, because it could be played manually as well as by machinery, six keyboards. Its mechanical repertory included the overtures to *The Magic Flute, The Marriage of Figaro, Der Freischütz,* and *Oberon,* and Beethoven's *Creatures of Prometheus,* all of which were performed, it was said, "without omitting a single note of the score, and with all the fortes and pianos, the crescendoes and the diminuendoes, as directed by the composers, with an accuracy that no band can possibly exceed."[40] One can well believe Dr. Thomas Busby, the organist and composer, who wrote in 1825 that the performances "operate[d] on the nerves and feelings of the auditors in a truly surprising manner."[41] However the Apollonicon affected the sensibilities of true music lovers, it became one of London's standard sights and sounds, being demonstrated on the manufacturers' premises for many years. Soon after it was finished, Claire Clairmont, Byron's mistress and a member of Shelley's informal "family," went no fewer than three times to hear it in the course of an eighteen-day stay in London which included one visit each to the British Museum, the East India House museum, the panorama of Rome, exhibitions of stained glass and Canova's casts, and Pidcock's menagerie. Thomas Love Peacock accompanied her on these expeditions, and Shelley may have been along on some.[42] A second Apollonicon, built by a rival firm, was installed at the Colosseum to accompany the Lisbon Earthquake production, but the name had to be dropped when Flight and Robson protested that it belonged exclusively to their instrument.[43]

Contemporaries of the Apollonicon, though of smaller capability, were no less majestically named. One was a barrel organ with a difference, the Componium or Musicalische Improvisator, which was meant to be to music what the Eureka would later be to the composition of Latin hexameters: it improvised variations on a military march without ever repeating itself. First shown in Paris in 1829, it was brought to 160 Piccadilly the following year.[44] It was not a success, some say because the court was in mourning for George IV, but more probably because the run-throughs were so rapid that nobody could tell whether they were truly variations. To one observer it was merely an "amusing bauble" which would satisfy only such people as continued to believe that "the automaton chess-player *really played the game*—that Maillardet's conjuror really conjured."[45] The *Times*'s comment was more philosophical: "Already mechanical science has succeeded in binding down the wings of genius; and carpet-manufacturers and fancy workers no longer consult the taste of artists, but apply to the kaleidoscope to supply them with new patterns. Are musical composers in future to be taught to take their inspiration from such an instrument as is now exhibiting?"[46] The question was merely rhetorical then, but it has deeper significance in a day when music is actually being composed by computer.

In 1837 the Gothic Hall, which had previously housed Maillardet's automatons, M. Louis the seven-foot-six giant, and "the smallest horse in the world," displayed the Euterpeon, another imitation full orchestra. Built over a period of twenty-six years by Martin Blessing of Germany, it was somewhat inferior to the Apollonicon, having but eighteen stops and 1,600 pipes. There were cylinders for the overtures to *Oberon, Masaniello,* and *William Tell,* as well as for four selections from Haydn's *Creation.*[47] A still more modest instrument, the Terpodion, was at the Adelaide Gallery in 1841. No larger than a cottage piano, it was said to "combine the power of an organ (with a sixteen-foot pipe), and the qualities of a bassoon, violoncello, clarionette, and of the Aeolian harp."[48] This was one of numerous versions, all with equally fancy names, of the new class of domestic musical instruments that came to be known generically as harmoniums. They were exhibited primarily to promote sales.

One musical exhibition was particularly noteworthy because it marked the beginning of a distinguished career, that of the inventor-scientist Charles Wheatstone. Wheatstone had come to London from Gloucester to enter the business of musical instrument making. In 1822 he opened Wheatstone's Musical Museum, situated first in the Opera House Colonnade, Charles Street, but shortly thereafter moved to the venerable—and soon to be demolished—Great Room, Spring Gardens. One of his leading exhibits was the Enchanted Lyre, or Acoucryptophone, which had more than a casual resemblance to the Invisible Girl, a version of which, or whom, was also demonstrated. A cluster of horns, suspended from the ceiling and supported by lightweight fixtures from the floor, dispensed a half hour's program of "simple melody and more difficult harmony" without apparent human intervention. (Like the chess player and the Anthropoglossos, the Acoucryptophone was equipped with a clock mechanism which Wheatstone went through the motions of winding up. But the clockwork was there only to enforce the pretense of automatism and actually had no part in the proceedings.) Lady Blessington, who published a description of the museum, was doubtless correct in assuming that the sound came from human performers in an adjoining room and was transmitted by the metallic rods that supported the horns. Another attraction at the Musical Museum was Wheatstone's Grand Central Diaphonic Orchestra, which, an advertisement alleged, "astonishingly augments in richness and power every variety of musical tones." Here again the refractive properties of sound were demonstrated. A glass instrument surmounted by a decorative lyre picked up musical sounds produced in the adjoining room and noticeably increased their sonority.[49]

Punctuating this activity in the field of mechanical or scientific music, or what purported to be such, were several attractions which can only be called retrogressive. Now men imitated machines. In 1834, in the Quadrant, Regent Street, a Mr. Richmond, billed solecistically as "THE MUSICAL PHENOMENA," performed as a musical snuffbox, producing popular airs from a throat that could utter the treble and bass lines simultaneously.[50] At another time, at the Egyptian Hall, a human barrel organ known as the Vox-Bipartitus, or Two Voices in One, imitated a variety of instruments, the Organ Cremona, bassoon, harp, sackbut, hautboy, and double bass, in a range from double G (lowest on the piano) to G on the fifth line of the counter-tenor staff. In the course of performing the overture to Arne's opera *Artaxerxes*—a favorite vehicle of the popular singer-actress Lucia Vestris—this gifted artist brought in every instrument in his repertory, though one assumes *seriatim,* not *tutti.*[51]

The equally gifted Michael Boai, better known as "the Chin Chopper," performed at the Egyptian Hall in 1830 and subsequently at Vauxhall Gardens and Astley's. His specialty was not altogether new. Eustace

Budgell, writing in the *Spectator* in 1712, alluded to a boy "who, tho' he is scarce yet twelve Years old, has with great Industry and Application attained to the Art of beating the Grenadiers March on his Chin," doing so with the laudable purpose of maintaining himself and his mother and equipping himself to join the army as a drummer or color-bearer.[52] Sometime toward the close of the eighteenth century, furthermore, a remarkably ill-favored and negligently dressed busker named Buckland worked the Covent Garden coffee-house circuit with the same brand of eccentric entertainment. W. T. Parke, the first oboist in the Covent Garden orchestra for forty years, had the fortunate opportunity of hearing both Buckland and Boai. The latter, he decided, was the real virtuoso of the two, being capable of more "rapid and articulate execution" than his forerunner.[53] Assisted by his pretty wife on the guitar, the Chin Chopper, having wetted his mouth and fingers, proceeded to strike his chin with the two doubled-up forefingers of each hand, producing a clucking effect that suggested to some the sound of castanets. He could, it was reported, "execute chromatic passages, however difficult, with all the taste, rapidity, and precision of the violin and piano-forte."[54] His scales were remarkably agile, and even his half-notes were distinct; but, added another witness, "the peculiar movements of the performer's head and hands threw an air of the ludicrous over the exhibition."[55]

Which may very well have been. But it was not everyone whose chin, a "musical anvil," had a range of two and a half octaves.

A decade later (1841–1845) another kind of attraction, first at Stanley's Rooms, Old Bond Street, and then at the Egyptian Hall, moved British music for the moment back into the Stone Age.[56] This was the Rock Harmonicon, a xylophonelike contrivance composed of two banks of selected rocks, one row containing the diatonic scale and the other, sharps and flats. Played with mallets whose striking ends were the size and shape of cricket balls, the instrument, as perfected, had a range of five and a half octaves, from the alleged warble of a lark to "the deep bass of a funeral bell," and a repertory that included the overtures to Rossini's *Il Tancredi* and *L'Italiana in Algieri,* selections from *Norma,* and special arrangements of waltzes and galops, quadrilles by Jullien, and various polkas. There were also unspecified selections by Handel, Beethoven, Haydn, Weber, and Donizetti. The Rock Harmonicon, "the resource of a shipwrecked Mozart," was the product of thirteen years' labor by a Cumberland mason, Joseph Richardson, who had quarried its components out of the rock of "mighty Skiddaw" and then hammered and chiseled them to achieve the various tones. It was played by Richardson's three sons, who therefore advertised themselves as "Messrs. Richardson and Sons Original Rock Band." There seems to have been little critical reaction to this novelty, apart from a remark in the *Athenaeum,* a paper which often sought to soften discords, that in the open air "the effect of this primitive dulcimer must be more than commonly picturesque and engaging."

It would be too fanciful to detect in these demonstrations of peculiar human capability an implicit note of defiance—man against the machine. Nonetheless, as the first half of the century closed, old-fashioned automatons clearly possessed little of their former attractiveness. It is true that in 1848–49 Robert-Houdin, the greatest magician of the time, brought to London his popular Soirées Fantastiques, which starred new automatons of his own invention: acrobatic clowns and a pastry-maker who emerged from his shop bearing whatever confections the audience called for, in the manner of Haddock's admired fruiterer.[57] But these were merely fresh refinements, perhaps more sophisticated, of old standbys, and they seem to have caused little stir. The next year the Adelaide Gallery displayed a gathering of jeweled automatons advertised as having originally belonged to George IV when Prince of Wales. "Much money was wasted on these gewgaws," said the *Illustrated London News.* "To the thoughtful, [the exhibition] reads a lesson of Royal vanity, highly instructive."[58] When they could serve only as material for not very fervent moralizing, the day of automatons had clearly passed. In their time—which had spanned a century, beginning with Vaucanson's flute player and duck—they had been marvels of mechanical ingenuity. Now, however, little interest of any kind remained attached to what were, after all, mere adaptations of clockwork or other simple mechanical and physical principles. Vestiges of a past era of primitive technology, they had become more and more obsolete—and uninteresting—as the age of Arkwright and Hargreaves gave way to that of Davy and Faraday.

The Two Faces of Science

26

Absent from all the displays of automatons, speaking and hexameter-composing machines, and mechanical orchestras was any pretense of instruction. Even though Wheatstone's exhibits derived partly from his serious experimentation, his museum was looked upon solely as a place for casual amusement, the occasion, as Lady Blessington put it, "for an agreeable lounge from two to four o'clock in the afternoon."[1] Although its patrons were decidedly more cultivated than those who later frequented Dr. Kahn's anatomical exhibition, the latter got more science for their money, if they wanted science, than did Wheatstone's. The fact was that in this momentous era of English scientific and technical progress, little of the productive activity that was occurring in laboratories and engineering shops was reflected in the popular shows until the late thirties. Even then, the staunch early Victorian confidence that the public was hungry for scientific knowledge proved irreconcilable with the public's stubborn insistence that, first of all, it be amused.

As the century began, "philosophical fireworks" were continuing to harness science to the cause of entertainment in the old way, producing "magical" and spectacular effects from chemical reactions, gas, and rudimentary electrical phenomena. Cartwright's program at the Lyceum was typical of such exhibitions both in its well-advertised avoidance of nuisances like the smoke and smell of gunpowder which attended real fireworks displays and in its inclusion of variety acts such as a program of recitations and songs illustrating "the Seven Ages of Woman" and solos on the musical glasses by Mrs. Ward, late Miss Cartwright.[2] In 1815 another specialist, Mr. Garnerin, at the Great Room, Spring Gardens (renamed for the occasion the "Theatre of Grand Philosophical Recreations"), added to his bill the phantasmagoria and "aerostation," which meant the inflation of gas balloons that would rise and float about the room. The state of the atmosphere permitting, an electrical demonstration concluded with Wellington's portrait being produced "by thunderbolt."[3] One of Garnerin's successors at the same place in 1822, a Mr. Cornillot, promised "Extraordinary Chemical Illustrations, and Feats of Legerdemain" performed in an enchanted garden, "where all kinds of Flowers and Fruits will be made to spring up and expand spontaneously, according to the wishes of the spectators." Featured on this bill was an episode entitled "The Egg in Labour," in which "an animal as large as a melon" would be extracted from "an egg of ordinary size."[4]

But times were changing. The terms advertising a show at the Cosmorama Rooms in 1834 are doubly significant: "Chemical" had now fully replaced the obsolescent "Philosophical," and in the iterated use of "experiments" the promise of instruction was forthright and unqualified. "The beauties and wonders of Chemical Science," said the proprietor, "will be illustrated by an extensive Series of the most interesting and brilliant Experiments, with short and familiar Explanations, so as to render each Experiment easily intelligible. In the entire Series nearly all parts of Practical and Experimental Chemistry will be exhibited,

* But when plays resumed, they too sometimes paid their respects to the planetary system. For the Sadler's Wells Easter show in 1810 the younger Charles Dibdin put together "an Astronomical, and Astrological Pantomime" called *The Astrologer, or Harlequin and Moore's Almanac,* for which he built "a Model of an immense, splendid Orrery of a peculiar nature; with the Zodiacal Signs, Planets, etc.—all the Planets, save the Earth and Moon, being personified, by mechanical figures; . . . when the whole was put into motion, it exhibited the astronomical revolutions in a very perspicacious, amusing, and impressive manner. 'The Man in the Moon' was transformed into Harlequin. The Second Scene represented a grand *Planetarium* (22 feet by 18) and among other astrological notices, I introduced, on a large Scene, a representation of the Heiroglyphic in Moore's Almanack for that Year; the explanation of which was effected by the Clown, and occasioned much diversion." (*Professional and Literary Memoirs of Charles Dibdin the Younger* . . . , ed. George Speaight, London, 1956, p. 103.)

† "The comet of 1811 made a superb entré, and was received with the greatest plaudits," reported the *Literary Gazette,* reviewing Bartley's show ten years later (31 March 1821, p. 206).

‡ Rather surprisingly, this contrivance was not endowed with any elegant name; although "Hydroastrorama," for example, might have been appropriate, it was called simply a "Self Moving Orrery." "Astrorama" later was coined to designate a parasol punched with little holes representing the constellations. The *Athenaeum,* commenting on its novelty in 1848 (24 June, pp. 630–31), remarked that, other considerations aside, it was not a very dependable guide to the firmament: "We doubt if proof sheets were sent." The inventor, a lady named Mary Mathews of Westbourne Street, Hyde Park Corner, showed it at the Crystal Palace.

with the exception of those Experiments which are unpleasant or explosive."[5] But, like all the others, this show attracted trade mainly by its promise of "beauties and wonders," not information.

Another kind of exhibition surviving from the eighteenth century had better credentials as a means of popularizing science. This was the astronomical lecture-demonstration which was for many years a fixture of the Lenten season, especially of Passion Week, when dramatic performances were prohibited and the theatres therefore were available for educational purposes.* Adam Walker's Eidouranion, with its revolving lighted globes representing the planets, continued to be exhibited by his son Deane after his death in 1821. The Eidouranion's chief rival was R. E. Lloyd's Diastrodoxon, another "Grand Transparent Orrery" but "of Superior Science, Splendour, and Magnitude." Standing a foot taller than its prototype, it was equipped with a glass globe, six feet in circumference, representing the earth, its meridians, land masses, and oceans.[6]

Some time about the turn of the century, large transparencies began to be used either in conjunction with the lighted orrery or independently. These "scenes," as they were called, could, of course, portray any aspect of the skies the lecturer desired—the constellations, for instance, and telescopic views of the planets—and a particularly handsome example, shown at the English Opera House in 1817, set forth the signs of the zodiac. It, or a close replica, measured sixty feet in circumference.[7] Even more adaptable to these purposes, however, was the magic lantern, which seems to have been first employed in astronomical demonstrations at the very same time it was also adapted in England for the phantasmagoria. The first lecturer to use painted "sliders" was said to be a Mr. Bartley, who chose the word Ouranologia to distinguish his instrument from others in the field.[8] At mid-century a veteran slide maker whom Mayhew interviewed recalled:

These [diagrams] were made to show the eclipses of the sun and moon, the different constellations, the planets with their satellites, the phases of the moon, the rotundity of the earth, and the comets with good long tails. What a tail 1811 had![†] and similar things that way. . . . Next, moving diagrams were introduced. . . . The moving diagrams were so made that they showed the motion of the earth and its rotundity, by the course of a ship painted on the lantern—and the tides, the neap and spring, as influenced by the sun and moon. Then there was the earth going round the sun, and, as she passed along, the different phases were shown, day here and night there. Then there were the planets going round the

sun, with their satellites going round them. . . . The zodiac made very pretty slides—twelve of them, each a sign.[9]

In 1807–8 another "spheric and transparent Orrery" called the Cosmorama—this was a number of years before the word was used in England to refer to a superior kind of peepshow—was employed in the Abbé Winton's "Sans Pareille Astronomical Exhibition" at the Pantheon. The exhibition may have been intended in part to attract possible purchasers of astronomical transparencies and apparatus which were displayed in adjoining rooms. Of the performance the advertisement said, "the Spectator, placed as it were in the centre of the Universe, contemplates the Starry Firmament, the Constellations of both Hemispheres, and sees nine and twenty Celestial Bodies revolving at once in their orbits and round their own axis"—a description which suggests, surely with no historical foundation, the operation of a twentieth-century planetarium.[10]

One other type of orrery, the work of a man named Busby, was exhibited in 1822, not in conjunction with a regular lecture but in its own ingenious right, as a possible ornament to the conservatory or aquarium of a rich householder who had everything.‡ It consisted, we are told,

of a large trough or tub, filled with water, in the centre of which is a floating basin, with a globe representing the Sun, and the solar motion is caused by a minute stream discharged laterally from a siphon contained in the basin. Round the edge of the tub, the Earth, similarly borne, represented, and acted upon, performs her course; and by a very curious contrivance of machinery, not only her orbicular revolution and polar positions towards the Sun are accurately given, but the Moon (supported on a circular floating ring, and observing the austranical obliquity of orbit, changes of nodes, etc.) is obviously constructed so as to impress the motions of all these heavenly bodies on the mind in the clearest manner.[11]

Press coverage of astronomical exhibitions was more or less evenly apportioned between the representations of the stars and the lecturer's platform style. The visual devices usually were praised, particularly for their illustration of the "picturesque and scientific beauty" and grandeur of the cosmos. Once in a while, however, a reporter in a jocose mood poked mild fun at Bartley, who seems to have been accident prone, for the technical difficulties his orrery had a habit of developing. ("On the first night . . . the harmony of the spheres was not manifest. We doubt not that the motions have since been regulated.")[12] Some lecturers discoursed with admirable lucidity; others went in for

132. Walker's astronomical lecture-demonstration at the English Opera House. The circle of the zodiac framed a succession of transparencies. The picture on the left, taken from a book published about 1826 (Horace Wellbeloved's *London Lions*), evidently is some years earlier than the other, which is dated 21 March 1817.

dramatic effects which may or may not have been successful. A Mr. Goodacre lectured in meter at the Haymarket in 1822,[13] and C. H. Adams, whose "Lenten entertainments" were a fixture of the London calendar for more than thirty years, topped off his explanation of the law of gravity and the earth's diurnal rotation with "Milton's expressive language, which was delivered in a manner that drew forth reiterated applause."[14]

Notwithstanding the visual splendors and the intellectual gratification attributed to them in their advertising and the pronouncements of a friendly press, these astronomical lectures could also be an unmitigated bore, as Dickens, looking back on them from the vantage point of maturity (1863), made plain:

My memory presents a birthday when Olympia and I were taken by an unfeeling relative—some cruel uncle, or the like—to a slow torture called an Orrery. The terrible instrument was set up at the local Theatre, and I had expressed a profane wish in the morning that it was a Play: for which a serious aunt had probed my conscience deep, and my pocket deeper, by reclaiming a bestowed half-crown. It was a vener-

able and a shabby Orrery, at least one thousand stars and twenty-five comets behind the age. Nevertheless, it was awful. When the low-spirited gentleman with the wand said "Ladies and gentlemen" (meaning particularly Olympia and me), "the lights are about to be put out, but there is not the slightest cause for alarm," it was very alarming. Then the planets and stars began. Sometimes they wouldn't come on, sometimes they wouldn't go off, sometimes they had holes in them, and mostly they didn't seem to be good likenesses. All this time the gentleman with the wand was going on in the dark (tapping away at the heavenly bodies between whiles, like a wearisome woodpecker), about a sphere revolving on its own axis eight hundred and ninety-seven thousand millions of times—or miles—in two hundred and sixty-three thousand five hundred and twenty-four millions of something elses, until I thought if this was a birthday it were better never to have been born. Olympia, also, became much depressed, and we both slumbered and woke cross, and still the gentleman was going on in the dark—whether up in the stars, or down on the stage, it would have been hard to make out, if it had been worth trying—cyphering away about planes of orbits, to such an infamous extent that Olympia, stung to madness, actually kicked me. A pretty birthday spectacle when the lights were turned up again, and all the schools in the town . . . were discovered with exhausted countenances, screwing their knuckles into their eyes, or clutching their heads of hair.

But the official view of all this, a blessing laid on every such instructive entertainment in the age, was stated by the head of one of the schools, who came forward and expressed his "entire approval of a lecture as improving, as informing, as devoid of anything that could call a blush into the cheek of youth, as any it had ever been his lot to hear delivered."[15]

D3✳️ƐႳ

To Dickens, this joyless "entertainment" was a prime example of an instrument of popular culture which promised both instruction and delight, and delivered neither. This was what happened to "recreations of the people" on which the cold, heavy hand of educational purpose had fallen. The low-spirited professor's maunderings about the wonders of the universe epitomized the problem that haunted the early Victorian drive to bring science to the people. In an effort to avoid the mindlessness of such leisure-fillers as the philosophical fireworks shows that were 99 percent fireworks and 1 percent philosophy, lecturers and exhibitors had devised a form of didactic entertainment that ran the constant risk—to put it moderately—of being a monumental exercise in boredom.

In the beginning, Adam Walker's astronomical lectures were part of a small but thriving eighteenth-century London institution, the annual courses of scientific lectures that were delivered to subscription audiences largely composed of upper-middle-class men and women. Although there was an element of mere faddishness in their attendance, some, perhaps most, members of such audiences were earnestly bent upon self-improvement, in the same way that the members of the vigorous "literary and philosophical societies" in several provincial centers were intent upon broadening and sharpening their minds.

This impulse was transmitted to a higher social sphere by the lectures on science given, from the first years of the nineteenth century onward, at the Royal Institution in Albemarle Street.[16] Founded by Count Rumford in 1799, the Royal Institution initially was designed, said its prospectus, "for diffusing the knowledge and facilitating the general and speedy introduction of new and useful mechanical inventions and improvements; and also for teaching, by regular courses of philosophical lectures and experiments, the application of the new discoveries in science to the improvement of arts and manufactures, and in facilitating the means of procuring the comforts and conveniences of life." Although in time much important work in pure science was to be achieved in Albemarle Street, at the outset the Royal Institution's purpose was explicitly utilitarian, just as was that of the mechanics' institute movement founded a quarter-century later. According to Rumford's plan, a "repository" (showroom) would contain models of stoves, fireplaces, kitchens, and laundry rooms suitable for the dwellings of the poor, and there would be courses in the mechanic arts suited to the capacities of get-ahead workmen. Such people would be the primary beneficiaries. The secondary ones, from whom the necessary money would be derived, were members of the upper class, who would also attend the institution, but "chiefly for amusement or because it may be fashionable. These," one of Rumford's colleagues told the board of managers at the outset, "it is our business to amuse, while at the same time I hope we shall be able to interest them in the subjects, and communicate considerable knowledge without any trouble to themselves. For these I would propose a popular course of experimental philosophy, in which all abstract reasoning shall be avoided, the most entertaining and interesting experiments introduced, and the whole calculated to afford pleasure and instruction to those who have not had an opportunity of examining these subjects and to refresh the memory of those who have." As things turned out, it was this clientele alone which the Royal Institution came to serve. With Rumford's departure in 1802 went also the emphasis on usefulness to the working class. The heart of the institution became, instead, the laboratory and library for the scientists on the staff and the lectures they delivered to the subscribers.

This shift in direction and emphasis was managed by an enthusiastic young scientist from Bristol, Humphry Davy, who joined the establishment in 1801 as assistant lecturer in chemistry and the next year was made professor. His lectures were an immediate hit. According to a contemporary, "Men of the first rank and talent,—the literary and the scientific, the practical and the theoretical, blue-stockings, and women of fashion, the old and the young, all crowded—eagerly crowded the lecture-room. His youth, his simplicity, his natural eloquence, his chemical knowledge, his happy illustrations and well-conducted experiments, excited universal attention and unbounded applause." Ladies, it was authoritatively reported, "praised the

Scientific Researches! — New Discoveries in PNEUMATICKS! — or — an Experimental Lecture on the Powers of Air.

133. A lecture at the Royal Institution: James Gillray's *Scientific Researches!—New Discoveries in PNEUMATICKS!—or—an Experimental Lecture on the Powers of Air,* 1802. Humphry Davy, who had administered "laughing gas" to several gentlemen during a course in "pneumatical chemistry" the preceding year, is holding the bellows for the lecturer, Thomas Young, a distinguished physicist. Count Rumford faces the table from the right, a little apart from the audience.

lecturer's bright eyes and said they were meant for something other than poring over crucibles; they sent him notes and sonnets."[17] Davy, in short, was a matinee idol as well as a scientist, and by virtue of that fact the lectures at the Royal Institution became a lively topic of the day, sometimes diverting attention from the crises and rigors of the war with Napoleon. The lawyer-politician Francis Horner recorded in his diary on 31 March 1802:

The audience is assembled by the influence of fashion merely; and fashion and chemistry form a very incongruous union. At the same time it is a trophy to the sciences; one great advance is made towards the association of female with masculine minds in the pursuit of knowledge, and another domain of pleasing and liberal inquiry is included within the range of polished conversation. Davy's style of lecturing is much in favour of himself, though not perhaps entirely suited to the place; it has rather a little awkwardness, but it is

that air which bespeaks real modesty and good sense: he is only a little awkward because he cannot condescend to assume that theatrical quackery of manner which might have a more imposing effect.[18]

By the time fame had somewhat turned his head, increasing his devotion to life in high society and concomitantly diminishing his dedication to the spread of scientific knowledge, Davy had put the Royal Institution on the firmest of foundations to hand to his successors. His lectures became more and more infrequent, but now Michael Faraday, a bookbinder's apprentice who had gained entrance to the establishment with tickets given him by one of his employer's customers, was ready in the wings. Initially a laboratory assistant and curator of the mineralogical collection, Faraday became in time a highly successful lecturer as well. The dates of his "Friday Evening

The Two Faces of Science 367

Discourses," inaugurated in 1825–26, were listed in upper-class Londoners' engagement books as religiously as the weeks set for the Royal Academy's summer show. When he retired in 1862 he had delivered over one hundred of these lectures, partly on the results of his own research, partly on the work of others (for example, the revolutionary engineering methods Brunel used as he slowly bored the Thames Tunnel), and partly on applied science, such as the progress of safety in the mines—an especially fitting topic at the Royal Institution, because Davy had invented the miner's safety lamp.[19]

In 1853 the third member of the succession, John Tyndall, joined the Royal Institution. Of the three, he seems to have been the most informal lecturer, sometimes overtly a showman, indulging in excessively dramatic effects, posing, humoring his audience's foibles. Some accused him of vulgarizing science, but the 51 Friday evening discourses and the 307 afternoon lectures he delivered during his thirty-three years at the Royal Institution unquestionably encouraged the public to accept science's new authority.[20]

Besides the lectures designed for ladies and gentlemen with time on their hands, there were the famous annual courses of Christmas lectures for children, which Faraday introduced in 1825. He delivered nineteen of these series himself, and Tyndall gave twelve. It was a standing joke that in the competition for the amphitheatre's three hundred seats the children were virtually pushed aside by their elders. "The 'juveniles,'" commented the *Illustrated London News,* "are worth seeing—Princes of the blood royal, savants of European reputation, future dukes and earls, fair ladies, and grey-headed professors, intense students animated with a love of science, chemists, doctors, poets, lawyers, and wits; these usurp the place of boys, mix with them and crowd them on their seats."[21] Even the Prince of Wales, Victoria's and Albert's unstudious son, heard about electricity here.

On a lower social level the same campaign to popularize science was waged under different auspices. By the third decade of the century it was increasingly recognized that the prosperity of an industrial, world-trading Britain rested upon science and its practical applications. There had to be more inventors, more technicians, more ordinary workers ("mechanics") who understood the scientific rudiments of their various manufacturing occupations so that they would be more efficient and productive. "The people," in a word, had to be taught science. This was the constant cry of those who represented in the national forum the

Manchester industrialists and the merchants whose interest lay in the steady expansion of the factory system and of foreign trade in manufactured goods.

Another, less frequently articulated motive was at work, especially as a wave of popular discontent swept the nation in the 1820s and threatened to engulf it in civil war in 1832: the necessity (as many public men saw it) of wholesomely distracting the people's attention from political inequalities and social injustices. An absorbing interest in science, in addition to furthering the nation's technological and economic interests, might be a social tranquilizer if not an outright opiate of the people.* Though the idea, understandably, was never couched in such blunt terms, for the Romans' diversionary circuses might well be substituted, with untold advantage to the nation's wealth, the cheap, nutritious bread of scientific information.

This, in the late twenties and the thirties, was one of the aims of a highly vocal and politically adept coterie around Lord Brougham, left-wing Whiggish in politics, Benthamite in general orientation—the philosophical radicals, as they were called. Their propagandist, organizing, and publishing arm, the Society for the Diffusion of Useful Knowledge, with its network of mechanics' institutes in the provinces, its mass-circulation *Penny Magazine,* and its catalogue of cheap informational books, spread the new gospel of self-help through adult education. Although it never produced the class of technically skilled industrial workers that was its goal, it unquestionably stimulated the public appetite for easy-to-digest knowledge, above all scientific information with practical application.

Here was a matchless opportunity for public exhibitions to benefit society. In this increasingly materialistic popular culture, interest was concentrated upon physical properties and processes rather than upon, say, philosophical and moral concepts. The practical necessity for visualizing which had asserted itself during the Royal Society's early years, when Baconian science came wholly into its own, now had a crucial bearing on the nation's economic progress. Comprehension of the subjects that engaged the minds of people who were determined to better themselves in workshop and factory depended heavily upon objects rather than words—upon samples of minerals, and working models illustrating the principles of mechanics and hydraulics, and actual examples of new machinery. In such circumstances, exhibitions could fulfill a function which was beyond the power of the printed word, supplementing, extending, and making

* The idea was by no means new, though it now was applied to a lower social class. In the *Spectator* (no. 262, 31 December 1711), Addison had written that the study of natural philosophy "draws men's minds off from the bitterness of party and furnishes them with subjects of discourse that may be treated without warmth or passion. This is said to have been the first design of those gentlemen who set on foot the Royal Society; and had then a very good effect as it turned many of the greatest geniuses of that age to the disquisitions of natural knowledge, who, if they had engaged in politics with the same parts and applications, might have set their country in a flame. The air-pump, the barometer, the quadrant, and like inventions were thrown out to those busy spirits, as tubs and like inventions are to a whale, while he diverts himself with those innocent amusements." In early Victorian times it was not the geniuses of the age who were to have their energies rechanneled; it was the common people.

more concrete and immediate what one could learn, in the abstract, from books and lectures.

Profit-minded showmen and altruistic public men alike responded to this new need for exhibitions that conveyed scientific information in tangible and dynamic form. But their response, when measured against the whole spectrum of science, lacked balance. The former emphasis on "natural history"—botany and zoology in their widest reaches—which had characterized the interests of eighteenth-century collectors now subsided as far as the London exhibition world was concerned. There were, to be sure, many specimens of exotic flora and fauna to be seen in the various exhibitions that reflected the nation's expansionist concerns; and from the thirties onward both Kew Gardens and the Zoological Gardens in Regent's Park were available to Londoners wishing to study living examples of plants and animals. But exhibitions of stuffed or otherwise preserved mammals, birds, reptiles, fish, and plants—apart from the occasional monstrosity—sharply decreased after Bullock's collection was sold and dispersed in 1819. Except at the British Museum, where the collections were uneven, ill kept, and largely out of sight, there was no longer any concentration of natural history materials on the scale of Bullock's or Lever's.

The nearest approach to these collections, not counting a "New Royal Museum" of "upwards of 10,000 different specimens of Natural History from all parts of the world" that briefly occupied quarters in Piccadilly about 1816,[22] was the London Museum and Institute of Natural History in Brydges Street, Covent Garden, formed by the naturalist Edward Donovan, a prolific writer on scientific topics and compiler of the Leverian catalogue. Opened to the public in 1807, with many specimens purchased at the Leverian sale the preceding year, this was a collection representing "the various departments of the animal, vegetable, and mineral creation" with, among much else, four hundred cases of birds and several hundred botanical specimens behind glass.[23] An enthusiastic, and quite probably planted, letter in the *European Magazine* that year declared that "it would be impossible, at this time, for any collector, possessing the most unwearied attention, sanguine wish, and unlimited purse, to form another collection" equal to Donovan's.[24] Actually, the museum seems to have been intended at least partly to attract subscriptions for the proprietor's numerous publications, which, according to the article on Donovan in the *Dictionary of National Biography,* were valuable for their illustrations rather than for their verbose and mediocre text. The museum remained open for many years but finally was caught in the ruin of Donovan's affairs; in 1833, asserting that he had been reduced to poverty by the rascally booksellers who published his works, he issued a public appeal for money to take his case to Chancery. He died four years later, and his collection is heard of no longer.

No other comprehensive exhibition of botanical and zoological specimens would be available to Londoners until the British Museum's collections at long last found satisfactory housing in South Kensington in 1881. The Royal Institution's heavy stress on chemistry, physics, and geology was typical of the age. The applied science on which the nation's expectations of sustained greatness rested had relatively little to do with the animal and vegetable kingdoms; the moving forces of the new industrial civilization were steam and iron, hydraulics and engineering.

D3✳ξฉ

The most publicized exhibition of a technical breakthrough in the years when the March of Mind was getting under way was that of the oxyhydrogen microscope, which contributed little to material progress but was well suited for show business. The microscope, as such, was no stranger to the trade. Katterfelto had long ago realized the solar microscope's power to bring in the shillings, but that power was reduced to nothing on a cloudy day when, as was the case in his time, no adaptable source of artificial light was available to illuminate the microscope's field. Furthermore, there was the problem of achromatic aberration. One Dr. Goring complained in 1827:

We may as well expect to gather figs from brambles, as to get a fine picture from an uncorrected convex lens. The image of a common solar microscope may be considered a mere shadow, fit only to amuse women and children, more especially if we attempt to exhibit brilliant opaque objects, which either become indistinguishable with a limited aperture, or enveloped in a glorious mass of aberration, with an enlarged one. The utmost it can do is to give us the *shadow* of a flea, or a louse as big as a goose or a jackass. . . . The swinish vulgar will always be gratified by such spectacles, because they have no idea that a microscope of any kind is to do more than exhibit objects very much dilated in point of bulk.[25]

Even as Goring wrote, however, part of the solution was already in hand. In 1828 an achromatic microscope went on display under the name of the Microcosm at 24 Regent Street. For two shillings a curious Londoner could view "about Twenty Scenes of Living and other Objects, Magnified from One Thousand Four Hundred to a Million of Times. They are represented on a plane six feet square, and can be seen by a large company at the same time." "All the incantations of the 'Freischütz,'" it was said—Weber's opera was then the rage—"are far surpassed by the monstrous forms in a single drop of water."[26]

The rest of the solution was provided by the invention of the oxyhydrogen light. As a source of illumination for microscope projectors—the familiar magic lantern combined with a scientific instrument—it dramatically outshone the unreliable sun. In 1833 the first oxyhydrogen microscope, built by Messrs. Cooper and Cary, chemist and optician respectively, was displayed at Stanley's Rooms, 21 Old Bond Street. The proprietors' handbill, headed "Solar Microscope Superseded," promised "a grand and interesting spectacle of the Wonders of the Microscopic World." At a preview, such scientists as Faraday, Babbage, and the elder Buckland saw images projected on a screen fourteen feet across. "A few hairs of an infant appeared like tubes two inches in diameter. . . . The sting of a bee was a monstrous barbed weapon, four feet long. The lancets of the horsefly were sabres about two feet in length. . . . Some of the worms found in stagnant ditches, the natural size of which is that of a thread, appeared like the largest-sized boa constrictor."[27]

Competition sprang up at once. Never, indeed, until the advent of the monster mile panorama at the end of the next decade, was the in-fighting livelier than it was among the rival microscopes. Advertisements and news items alike filled the papers with vivid imagery and magnified numbers. Of one show it was said, "To see a flea as large as a camel must gratify every flea-bitten observer, by inducing a satisfaction and sense of security at not having been devoured by the attack of such an animal."[28] An operation at 106 New Bond Street claimed that its instrument made a flea look "as large as the late elephant Chunie." Under competitive pressure, the Stanley's Rooms showmen enlarged their original claim of a 10,000–300,000-time magnification to 2,000,000. The New Bond Street exhibitors responded by escalating theirs to 2,500,000.[29]

Alfred and Mary Tennyson and their friend Arthur Hallam visited one such "great Microscope" in March 1833, Hallam reporting back to his fiancée, Emily Tennyson, that they saw "all the lions and tigers which lie 'perdus' in a drop of spring water."[30] The poet's reaction is not on record, although his son said that later in life he remarked, on looking through a microscope,

"Strange that these wonders should draw some men to God and repel others. No more reason in one than in the other."[31] Perhaps other visitors to the Microcosm had a similar thought. Pückler-Muskau's reaction was more fervent. "What it shows," he wrote, "is really enough to drive a man of lively imagination mad. Nothing can be more horrible,—no more frightful devilish figures could possibly be invented,—than the hideous, disgusting water animalculae (invisible to the naked eye, or even to glasses of inferior power,) which we daily swallow. They looked like damned souls darting about their filthy pool with the rapidity of lightning, while every motion and gesture seemed to bespeak deadly hate, horrid torture, warfare, and death."[32]

Somewhat less apocalyptic but indisputably more picturesque—whatever its deficiencies as sober historical evidence—was the description the visitors from Persia previously mentioned wrote of their encounter with an oxyhydrogen microscope a little later, at the Adelaide Gallery:

The wall opposite to our face was made most elegantly white with paint, so much so, that in the place although dark, yet the face of a man might be seen in this wall; opposite this wall there is just another, which was just behind us, which had several holes in it, where there are several instruments, which had such a power, a thousand times more than the lustre of the sun. Whenever they touched this apparatus, the array of the load-stone came out of the holes, and gave out such a ray of light that no one dared to look at the wall; but when they moderated the power of the instrument, a man might look at it. . . . Afterwards the master brought some water in a glass, which he placed against this light. This drop of water suddenly (praise be to God!) looked as if it were a great sea; in which we observed myriads of animals of different kinds, in forms of leopards, and some as large as elephants, and camels, they were mingled together, and eating each other. All of them had several thousand feet and hands; such a thing had never been thought of, nor would it enter the mind. Indeed, all those that came to see this, had no courage to look at these dreadful beasts. The operator was standing by the wall with a stick in his hand, explaining the nature of every one of these animals, and said in the English language, "This is the pure water that you drink every day, without being sensible of the wonderful power of God of the universe displayed in it; and what food he has given you which you do not understand."[33]

In view of the appalling pollution of Thames water in that epoch, one can only hope the lecturer spoke in irony. For, as medical research was belatedly to prove, it was the lethal connection between sewage and drinking water—the principal London water companies drew their supplies from the Thames directly opposite or below sewer outfalls—that was responsible for the cholera that had killed over 16,000 persons in England and Wales in 1832, and would claim an equal number in London alone in 1849. The controversy over the etiology of the disease, carried on in the lay press as well as scientific journals, was informally and unforgettably illustrated in these microscope exhibitions. No one reading the arguments in behalf of the transmission-by-microorganism theory could fail to remember those "hideous, disgusting water animalculae . . . darting about their filthy pool" as fearsomely magnified on a screen in New Bond Street.

Even apart from its immediate relation to what was then called "the sanitary question," the oxyhydrogen microscope, thus publicly displayed, may have had as stimulating and liberating an effect upon the popular imagination as, say, the panorama's. Except for the very imperfect revelation of the microscopic world that was made possible by Katterfelto's solar instrument, it was not until the oxyhydrogen microscope appeared that London showgoers were directly affected by the wonders of the world that lay beyond the unaided eye. Formerly, people had had to settle for such knowledge of invisible life as they could acquire from unsatisfactory illustrations in books or from scientists' reports of what they saw through their microscope's eyepieces. Now people could see for themselves. They were probably less consciously—or articulately—affected than was Pückler-Muskau, but the impact was there just the same. Perhaps it is most accurate to say that, as was true of certain of their other experiences in the London shows, their imagination was expanded and excited without their knowing it.

ᴆᴣ⁂ᴇᴅ

The imagination was affected, but scarcely the intellect; for, apart from the way in which it made vivid the presence of objectionable matter in London drinking water, the oxyhydrogen microscope seems not to have stirred much popular interest in biology. In the London show business it was represented as an amusing and, in its own way, a spectacular toy, not as an avenue to scientific discovery. Other objects of scientific or technical interest were exhibited in the same spirit, along with, in some cases, the hope of making a sale or of raising subscriptions for a business venture. That had been the motive behind Merlin's museum of invention in Hanover Square, and it was also behind the display, at Wigley's Promenade Rooms in the first

years of the century, of "the original model of a new[ly] invented Travelling Automaton, a machine which can, with ease and accuracy, travel at the rate of six miles per hour, ascend acclivities, and turn the narrowest corners without the assistance of horse or steam, by machinery, conducted by one of the persons seated within."[34]

In 1804 a German entrepreneur named Frederick Albert Winsor (*geboren* Winzer) gave a series of lecture-demonstrations at the Lyceum, home of gas-derived philosophical fireworks, as part of his efforts to establish a joint-stock company to supply London with illuminating gas. His scientific credentials were as questionable as his financial ones, and he spoke such poor English that he left the lecturing to another person, who however was not always available, since he tended to drink. But when all went well, Winsor performed on stage with an assortment of coke ovens, distilling apparatus, and candelabra while the lecturer read the accompanying script from the pit. These Lyceum demonstrations of "the wonderful discovery of refining Smoke, to make it burn more brilliant than gas" generated much public interest in the illuminating possibilities of coal gas, and large crowds attended Winsor's lighting of the garden wall between Carlton House and St. James's Park on the night of the king's birthday in 1807. It was not until 1814, however, that the newly incorporated Gas Light and Coke Company got permission to put mains in Pall Mall and adjoining streets, and in the following year Winsor, who had been demoted to the office of the company's technical advisor, fled to France to escape his creditors.[35]

One of the inventions most publicized through London exhibitions was J. H. Barlow's steam egg hatchery, shown at the Egyptian Hall in 1824, when Bullock's Mexican artifacts were drawing crowds elsewhere on the premises. Two years earlier "the Egg in Labour" had been a featured trick in a magician's show; now—such was the March of Mind—eggs labored by the thousands under scientific auspices. Artificial incubation was not a new idea; the ancient Egyptians had employed the warm rays of the sun for the purpose. In Britain there were obvious climatic handicaps to this method, but an alternative had been found. Billed somewhat obliquely as an "Improved Grapery" though the product was fowl rather than grapes, Barlow's exhibit featured a steam-heated structure composed of forty ovens, each of which contained 1,500 eggs of chickens, ducks, even emus. The ovens were kept at a steady temperature of 101 degrees; the eggs of domestic fowl would hatch in three weeks,

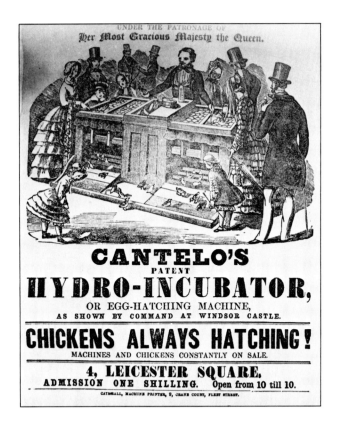

134. Handbill advertising Cantelo's steam incubator, 1851.

those of the emu in seven weeks, six days. The most striking part of the show was a series of twenty-one illuminated vessels demonstrating the entire process of incubation from the first deposit of the egg to the bird's emergence from its shell.[36]

Fifteen years later (1839) an improved hatchery was displayed at several successive locations under the name of Eccaleobion. It was heralded by a broadside of six stanzas entitled "Hatching by Steam!" which began:

Ye merry men of England attend unto my story;
Ye all have heard of Egypt old and her magicians hoary;
How with their reeds of silver bright, on banks of father
　　Nile,
The very stones to chickens' bones they turned in famous
　　style.
　　And they're all a hatching-hatch-hatch-hatching—
　　And they're all a hatching at 121, Pall Mall.[37]

"Life in Countless Thousands of Animal Beings, from a Wren to an Eagle, is Produced by Machinery!" exclaimed the publicity. "This extraordinary Machine which in the ungenial climate of England, realizes the greatest wonder of Egypt, both in the ancient and modern world has already given existence to Several

thousand Chickens and other birds, it stands upon a table, and animal life in its most perfect and healthful state is made to burst into existence in the presence of the visitors. It is capable of containing two thousand eggs, and of hatching about one hundred daily, or Forty thousand per annum!"[38] Unless the machine was converted from steam to gas while on display, the title of the broadside is at odds with a sober description of the Eccaleobion published in a weekly paper, which specified that the heat was "imparted by gas." The room was heated by gas also, to (it was said) an equal temperature; which must have made it the most uncomfortable exhibition on record.[39]

There was still room for both improvement and competition. In 1848 a certain Cantelo exhibited, under the slogan "Poultry for the Million!!" and the patronage of the queen, a "hydro-incubator" which was said to be the only commercially successful machine. This exhibition, first at the Cosmorama Rooms, was merely the town branch of Cantelo's poultry farm at Chiswick, and both the machines and the eggs were constantly on sale.[40] In 1851 Cantelo was relocated at 4 Leicester Square, where, in addition to the spectacle of the birds "liberating themselves" from their shells, the old lineup of bottles was again in evidence—"a series of specimens, whereby the nascent bird is exhibited in every stage of the mysterious process of the organization of a living animal."[41] Embryology was a popular study in the vicinity of Leicester Square at that moment: one recalls that Dr. Kahn had a similar display of human prenatal development.

Some fifteen years earlier, a much bigger bird had been hatched in hopes of attracting financial backing, but it had proved no more capable of sustained flight than one of Cantelo's hens. This was an "Aerial Ship" named the *Eagle,* displayed in the summer of 1835 in Victoria Road, South Kensington, in a wooden enclosure called for the occasion the "Dock Yard" or "Arsenal." Its sponsor was a Frenchman of Scottish extraction named Comte de Lennox, otherwise known as the European Aeronautical Society. In the preceding August 50,000 Parisians, paying a franc a head, had been drawn to the Champ de Mars by heavy publicity promising that the *Eagle* would become airborne on that day. No sooner was it inflated, however, than it broke from its moorings, went up a hundred feet, and burst. The infuriated crowd pounced on the wreckage and completed the destruction. But the European Aeronautical Society still clung to its announced intention of instituting regular air service between London, Paris, and other capitals, and in pursuit of this goal, the fragments of the *Eagle* were brought to London and reassembled in South Kensington. There shilling ticket-holders and two-guinea subscribers beheld a balloon 150 feet long, 50 feet high, and 40 feet wide, pointed at both ends but otherwise suggesting the configuration of a whale. Below it hung a seventy-five-foot-long car shaped like a boat, with a tarpaulin-covered cabin in the center in which twenty passengers could stand or sit. Later the *Eagle* was shown at Vauxhall, but unlike the more orthodox balloons that frequently rose from the gardens, this one never left the ground. Instead, it was seized for debt and carted away, into oblivion, by the sheriff of Middlesex.[42]

Some mechanical exhibits claimed public patronage solely as curiosities, with no commercial overtones. In 1828 the Argyll Rooms in Regent Street housed a model of the Emperor of Austria's salt mine in Galicia,[43] and four years later a father and son exhibited a hydraulically operated twelve-foot-long model of a copper mine near Tavistock.[44] Even the mechanical theatres at the fairs participated in the current enthusiasm for technology. In 1836–37, for instance, Gregory's Mechanical Exhibition, housed in a caravan and powered by a combination of clockwork and steam, showed moving figures of men, women, and children tending the machinery of a silk mill.[45]

One further mechanism displayed at this time had no apparent commercial possibilities, but it did, in a way, reflect the progress of technology. A generation after working models of the guillotine had been exhibited in London, the renewed fervor of French politics made a timely show item of the guillotine's successor, the "infernal machine," or bomb. At 28 Coventry Street, Haymarket, was exhibited in 1835 an exact replica of the "horrific instrument of destruction" which had been used shortly before in an unsuccessful assassination attempt against Louis Philippe and his sons during a military review on the Champ de Mars. (This was shortly before the fiasco, at the same place, of the *Eagle* balloon.) The show was rounded out with wax likenesses of the conspirators as they stood trial and a model of the room in which the ringleader, Fieschi, kept his deadly weapon. Ladies were assured that "the most scrupulous attention has been observed not to wound the most fastidious delicacy."[46] To profess concern for female sensibilities was always good advertising practice.*

The largest manifestation of British engineering genius to have some connection with the London show business was the Thames Tunnel.[47] The tunnel, the first ever built beneath a navigable stream, was among the major projects of the celebrated Brunels, Marc Isambard (father) and Isambard Kingdom (son). Intended to provide a carriageway between Wapping and Rotherhithe—an undertaking fully as ambitious as any railway would be in the years immediately ahead, and fraught with unprecedented problems and risks—it was begun in March 1825. After the shafts were sunk, boring through the Thames mud was commenced with the use of the newly invented tunneling shield. During the early stages of the work, sightseers—as many as six or seven hundred a day—paid a shilling each to be admitted to the eerie gaslit scene, kept at a distance from the shield by a rail. When the company ran out of money in 1828 (despite the £2,000 it had collected from visitors) and the shield was bricked up, a large mirror was placed against it and the silent tunnel became a great peepshow.

At one point (1834) in the years during which construction was suspended, a model, one-eighth inch to the foot, of the tunnel as it would appear when completed was exhibited in King William Street, partly, perhaps, to attract new capital.[48] Two years later work was resumed with a new shield, and sightseers were again invited to descend the spiral staircase at the Rotherhithe end and walk up to the very spot where the navvies were coping with the mud. The tunnel was regularly advertised in the entertainment columns of the press. There, month by month, the progress of the boring was reported—fewer and fewer feet left to go toward Wapping—until, in mid-summer 1841, the project was closed to visitors pending completion of the Wapping stair well. Two years later the finished tunnel was opened to traffic and sightseers. Exclusively a pedestrian thoroughfare because there was no money to build the expensive approaches required for road traffic, it became an obligatory London sight, the only one that was open twenty-four hours a day. In the first year over two million people paid a penny each to pass through on business or pleasure. Catlin took his Ioways there, but the experience of sauntering through the "gloomy halls" only to emerge "in the midst of one of the most unintelligible, forlorn, and forsaken districts of London or the world" elicited little enthusiasm.[49]

Between the two roadways were sixty-four arches, in the bays of which were set up all manner of refreshment and gewgaw stalls and other shoestring enterprises familiar to idlers in the less fashionable of the aboveground bazaars. Among these was a hand press on which a broadside describing the tunnel was printed—a direct descendant of similar presses that

* A handbill announcing the display of a "male Egyptian mummy" at 22 Haymarket about 1827 bore the assurance, "the most delicate Female may attend the Exhibition, as there is nothing to offend decency." A contrary statement in another throwaway, this time advertising "a female child, only 8 months old, with the largest head ever known . . . ¾ of a Yard! from the Chin to the top of the Scull, 12 inches" (Church Street, Shoreditch, 1834), may well have more than compensated for its loss of some feminine trade by the extra men and boys it attracted: "No pregnant women admitted," it warned. (GL, Playbills of London: Circuses and Miscellaneous Entertainments box.)

had been set up on the frozen surface of the river during the old frost fairs. Equally popular souvenirs, for which the subject was well adapted, were cardboard and paper peepshows of the tunnel. One version involved a hand-colored engraving which, when viewed through an oval aperture, showed a long perspective of the two passageways. There were also paper panoramas, one of which, a colored lithograph 126 inches long, showed a continuous longitudinal section of the tunnel's interior.[50]

For a penny or two additional to the one spent to enter, a visitor could see a cosmorama. One such show, in 1848, had views of the Giant's Stairs at Venice, the marketplace at Messina, the interior of Chartres Cathedral, London by night, and the queen's wedding.[51] There was also a "steam cosmorama"— the steam being supplied by a Lilliputian engine to an Italian barrel organ—which had, in addition to the royal wedding, scenes of historical or contemporary interest (Napoleon at Waterloo, Louis Kossuth on a Hungarian battlefield).[52]

Nathaniel Hawthorne, visiting the tunnel in September 1855, wrote a meticulous description of it from which some of the preceding details have been taken.[53] "It would have made an admirable prison, or series of dungeons," he reflected, "according to the old-time ideal of places of confinement. . . . So far as any present use is concerned, the Tunnel is an entire failure, and labor and immensity of money thrown away. . . . Perhaps, in coming ages, the approaches to the Tunnel will be obliterated, its corridors choked up with mud, its precise locality unknown, and nothing be left of it but an obscure tradition." Despite this prophecy, the tunnel was not lost from memory. It was sold in 1865 to the East London Railway Company and eventually became a link in the London Underground system, in whose Whitechapel–New Cross trains it may be traversed today. Beginning as it did, as an exhibition of audacious engineering, and then turning into a cheap miscellaneous bazaar, it offered a paradigm of a process that had, by that time, become all too familiar in the London show trade.

Technology for the Million

27

No better test can be applied, to determine the degree of refinement, intelligence, and education of a people, than the avidity displayed by them for places of instructive amusement, where not only are shows to be seen, but ideas acquired, and whence visiters retire, not only more happy than they entered, but more knowing.

—*Blackwood's Magazine,* 51 (1842), 424

Individual exhibitions of oxyhydrogen microscopes and vehicles that theoretically would fly catered in a small way to the public curiosity about things mechanical which was being stimulated particularly by the easy-to-read articles on invention and engineering printed in the *Penny Magazine* and *Chambers's Edinburgh Journal*. But they failed to meet the principal need, which was for a central, permanent institution where new inventions could be displayed and popular understanding of applied science could be disseminated by lectures and demonstrations. In the former respect, Britain lagged far behind France, where the Conservatoire National des Arts et Métiers, founded in 1796 as an outgrowth of the former "Cabinet des machines de Vaucanson," provided a true technological museum, replete with machines and models for aspiring inventors and industrial workers to study. From 1798 onward, in addition, the French government had sponsored a series of exhibitions of industrial machinery and its products, and these shows were quickly imitated by other continental nations. Even in Ireland, from 1824 onward the Dublin Society of Arts held a

triennial series of such shows. But Britain scorned them, one reason being the inveterate suspicion many cherished of anything French in origin, and another the conviction that British-made products needed no such bush. Their superior quality sold them without any recourse to publicity.[1]

The only approach in London to a regular display of the mechanic and engineering arts had been made by the Society of Arts, beginning in 1761. Originally intended to promote the development of both fine arts and technology, the Society had soon been relieved of the first function by the establishment of the Royal Academy, whose founders had held their first show at the Society's headquarters. Thenceforward it had devoted itself mainly to applied science, holding annual exhibitions of new machines and models in its "repository" and awarding prizes to the entries deemed to contribute most to the nation's technological progress, particularly in agriculture. The Society bought the winning exhibits, kept them on display for a brief period following each annual show, then stored them. But as the years passed and the Society's initial energies flagged, the competition for premiums had become informal and haphazard, and the repository itself had degenerated for the most part into a jumble of dusty, outmoded curiosities which were given away, sold, or thrown out. Since the Society had always been a private institution and the very existence of its collection was known to but a handful of people, its decline caused no great concern.[2]

And so the need remained. The first step toward ful-

135. The National Repository at the King's Mews, Charing Cross (engraved from a drawing by T. H. Shepherd). Cross's menagerie occupies a portion of the same building.

filling it that had any tangible results was taken in 1828, when a group of educationists, stirred by the new mechanics' institute movement, organized the National Repository for the Purpose of Annually Exhibiting to the Public the New and Improved Productions of the Artisans and Manufacturers of the United Kingdom—in short, nineteenth-century London's first industrial show. Sharing quarters in the old King's Mews with Cross's menagerie, which had just emigrated from the doomed Exeter Change, this display case for new inventions and improved old ones contained, among other useful items, silk looms that were worked at certain hours, kaleidoscopes, rain gauges, musical glasses, "crystallo-ceramic ornamental glass," models of improved steam engines, a portable flour dressing machine, and a multipurpose whalebone walking stick containing a mariner's compass, opera glass, telescope, pens, and ink. Special attention was devoted to the proposed "metropolitan improvements" typified by the Charing Cross redevelopment scheme then getting under way. A twenty-two-foot model showed the design of a wrought-iron suspension bridge proposed for erection either at Charing Cross or at Lambeth, and, in response to a growing concern that the obscenely congested graveyards of the city were a health hazard, there was a model of a forty-acre "pyramidal metropolitan sepulchre,"

suggestive of John Martin's more bizarre architecture, that would tower four times as high as St. Paul's and accommodate hundreds of thousands of bodies.[3]

The National Repository was, however, an almost instant failure. When the brief initial expression of public curiosity subsided, the indifference or outright opposition of many influential manufacturers, who were reluctant to expose their newest machinery or products to competitive eyes, made itself felt, and each of the few succeeding shows was more meager than its predecessor. In 1831 the demolition of the King's Mews to make way for the National Gallery provided an excuse, if any were needed, to move the National Repository to a small room at the familiar address of 28 Leicester Square, formerly John Hunter's museum, where it was known as the Museum of National Manufactures and of the Mechanical Arts and derided as a mere "toy shop." Among its sponsors was Charles Wheatstone, then still identified as a "Musical Instrument Maker." But success continued to elude it.[4]

The next try would be luckier, thanks in part to a venturesome Yankee and his steam-operated machine gun.[5] Jacob Perkins, born at Newburyport, Massachusetts, in 1776, had won considerable reputation and fortune in his native country through a number of inventions, especially of nail-making machines and a counterfeit-proof engraving process. Most recently a manufacturer of fire engines in Philadelphia, he had come to London in the second decade of the century to establish a branch of his versatile firm, which he hoped would be awarded the contract to print Bank of England notes. This was not forthcoming, but Perkins, setting up his business in Fleet Street, found alternative sources of profit in printing notes for local banks and manufacturing steam engines. But the neighbors' objection to the constant racket emanating from this "safety steam engine manufactory" led in 1824 to its removal westward—to, of all places, the junction of Albany Street and the New Road, a vicinity with high visibility at the moment because the new Diorama had been attracting crowds for the past several months and the construction of the much-heralded Colosseum was just getting under way. Perkins obviously knew a good showmanly site when he saw one.

It was there, in a specially constructed building, that he first demonstrated his newest invention, a steam gun, to a delegation of high-ranking members of the military establishment headed by the Duke of Wellington (6 December 1825). To prevent accidents such as occurred earlier, when a horse a lady was driving bolted at the explosions inside the structure and she was thrown to the pavement, traffic was diverted for the occasion. During two hours of incessant and thunderous firing, Perkins revealed his novel weapon's capabilities. According to a fellow American, S. G. Goodrich, the author of the famous "Peter Parley" books for children, "The balls were put in a sort of tunnel, and by working a crank back and forth, they were let into the chamber of the barrel—one by one—and expelled by the steam. The noise of each explosion was like that of a musket, and when the discharges were rapid, there was a ripping uproar, quite shocking to tender nerves. The balls—carried about one hundred feet across the smithy—struck upon an iron target, and were flattened to the thickness of a shilling piece."[6] This pilot model fired balls at the rate of at least one hundred a minute; some immediately contemporary evidence places the rate much higher. A simple calculation in the economics of mass destruction led Perkins to assure his military visitors that "to throw 15,000 bullets per hour for sixteen hours would require 15,000 pounds of gunpowder at a cost of £525 while by steam it would not cost more than £4." This assumes a steady firing rate of 250 balls a minute. But in a lengthy poem called "Steam," which was published shortly afterward in the New Monthly Magazine, poetic license doubled the figure:

Five hundred balls, per minute, shot,
   Our foes in fight must kick the beam;
Let Perkins only boil his pot,
   And he'll destroy them all by Steam.[7]

The onlookers, though deafened, were much impressed. According to Goodrich, the king's brother, the Duke of Sussex, kept saying to Wellington, "'Wonderful, wonderful, d----d wonderful'; then again, 'wonderful, d----d wonderful.'" Nevertheless the army declined to adopt the gun, and Perkins, while continuing to make improvements, sought other ways to promote it. About 1832 the steam manufactory was moved from the edge of Regent's Park to an address near Gray's Inn Road, but the gun was installed elsewhere, at the new National Gallery of Practical Science, Blending Instruction with Amusement, soon to be familiarly known as the Adelaide Gallery. This replacement for the moribund National Repository was sponsored by a group of enterprising men that included, in addition to Perkins, Ralph Watson, a wealthy philanthropist, Thomas Telford, a leading engineer, and Thomas Brickwood of the South Sea House.[8] Its announced object was "to promote . . . the adoption of whatever may be found to be comparatively superior, or relatively perfect in the arts, sciences, or manufacturers . . . [and] the exhibition of works of art, and of specimens of the rare productions of nature." Like the National Repository, but on a continuing basis, it was intended particularly to display, "subject to immediate return on demand, and meanwhile protected by every precautionary arrangement, specimens and models of inventions and other works, &c. of interest, for public exhibition, free from charge . . . thereby gratuitously affording every possible facility for the practical demonstration of discoveries in Natural Philosophy, and for the exhibition of any new application of known principles to mechanical contrivances of general utility."[9] In 1834 the organization, now renamed the Society for the Illustration and Encouragement of Practical Science, received a royal charter.

The Adelaide Gallery was on the north side of the Lowther Arcade, a shop-lined passage leading from the Strand to Adelaide Street just east of St. Martin's-in-the-Fields, on the site now occupied by the home office of Coutts's Bank. The arcade with its Nash façades had recently been built (1831) to replace a slum, in conjunction with the same improvement scheme which had required the razing of Exeter a gas mask ("the air is drawn through a sponge moistened with vinegar placed at the bottom of the tube"), a shower bath, a device for desalinating sea water, a working Jacquard loom, a gas meter, a garden-barrow fire engine, a model of Newcomen's steam engine, a collection of Chinese musical instruments, improved patent horse collars, a cattle stomach pump, a "hand grenade for house defence," a "model of the bust of a human figure" ("by a mechanical contrivance a knife can pass through the neck without detaching the head; and at the time a faint cry will be heard, and the eyes will move"), models of various buildings and engineering works, a Gobelin tapestry, a thermometer to be carried in the pocket as a watch, and deposit from the boiler of a brewery. The establishment soon added that requisite exhibition-item of the moment, an oxyhydrogen microscope with three sets of lenses which were said to magnify 16,000, 800,000, and 3,000,000 times, respectively.[11] This was probably the one that Hallam and the Tennysons admired.

But the single attraction with which the Adelaide Gallery was most closely identified in the public mind was the steam gun, which was loudly demonstrated every hour, not always to the comfort of visitors who found in the same room "so many objects requiring a quiet contemplation." Since showing his invention to the military commanders ten years earlier, Perkins, if we are to trust the statement printed in the catalogue, had more than quadrupled the gun's discharge rate; now it could fire "a current of *seventy balls* . . . in *four seconds*," which works out to 1,050 per minute. The artist William Powell Frith recalled in his autobiography a demonstration he attended as a youth: "The man who showed it gave a kind of lecture upon it; assured the audience that the Duke of Wellington came to see it the day before yesterday, and told the speaker that if he could have had the benefit of the steam-gun at the Battle of Waterloo, that engagement would have been over 'in about half an hour, instead of lasting all day.' He also said that all the regiments in our present army would be furnished with steam-guns, and it was expected in consequence that there would be no more fighting."[12] Putting aside the defective prophecy, one notes that Wellington's alleged remark about the hypothetical efficacy of the gun at Waterloo, repeated in every account of Perkins's invention, seemingly has no sounder authority than the spiel of a lecturer, which, given the nature of most such routines, means it has very little authority indeed.

Second in interest to the steam gun was the canal, in which were demonstrated clockwork models of

136. Façade of the Lowther Bazaar (woodcut by C. Wall, 1842).

Change. It was, in effect, a replacement for that landmark insofar as it too had stalls and small shops devoted to the sale of knicknacks, novelties, and luxury wares. By the fifties its specialty had become toys, and from then on to the end of the century (the building was demolished in 1902) it was a children's paradise.[10] The Adelaide Gallery itself was a long, narrow room consisting of two levels, the lower of which had in the middle a seventy-foot-long tank, or miniature canal, holding 6,000 gallons of water. Arranged along the sides of this room and occupying the gallery as well were the machines, devices, and models sent in for display. The seventh edition of the catalogue (1834) lists over 230 exhibits, including much marine equipment,

137. The Adelaide Gallery: interior (etching by Thomas Kearnan).

steamboats driven by paddlewheels of improved design, stated to cause less disturbance in rivers than those in present use. ("We apprehend, however," commented the ever judicious *Penny Magazine,* "that the comparison is hardly fair between little boats slowly revolving in a tub of still water, and a great vessel running at a rate of twelve miles an hour on a rapid river.")[13]

Special attention also was paid to improvements in land and air transport. On display in 1838 was "the much-admired AELLOPODES, Or Carriage for travelling, without Horse or Steam, but propelled by the traveller's own weight, at the rate of from twenty to thirty miles an hour."[14] In 1845 there were lectures on the "atmospheric railway," a vacuum-propulsion line which Isambard Kingdom Brunel was building in south Devon.[15] Charles Green, the famous Vauxhall

aeronaut, lectured on ballooning, and an "aerial machine worked by propulsive machinery" was exhibited.[16] From 1838 to 1842 a leading attraction was a forty-inch electric eel from South America from which Faraday induced "a most intense electric spark."[17] Another source of energy was a galvanic battery kept under a glass bell, where four little figures were kept spinning and would continue to do so, it was promised, "as long as the galvanic action lasts, which may certainly be several years."[18] The Adelaide Gallery, in fact, was the first direct English progenitor of the modern science and technology museum with its working machines and models and its visual dramatization of elementary scientific principles.

It also figured prominently in the earliest days of English photography. Although it is not quite accurate to say, as do some histories of photography, that this was the place where daguerreotypes were first shown in England (there was a prior exhibition at 7 Piccadilly a month earlier, on 13 September), the Adelaide Gallery did house a display and a daily demonstration of the art of picture-taking in October 1839. The exhibitor, M. de St. Croix, was almost immediately put out of business by an injunction obtained by Antoine Claudet, a London importer and dealer in sheet and ornamental glass, who had bought a license direct from Daguerre to sell pictures and picture-making apparatus at his shop in High Holborn. Claudet succeeded St. Croix at the Adelaide Gallery, erecting on its roof a studio where he took portraits—in the open air in fine weather, under a blue glass canopy when it rained. In 1844 Claudet's flourishing business required him to extend his operations to the building next door, and three years later he set up a branch studio at the newly reopened Colosseum. At mid-century his "Temple of Photography" at 107 Regent Street was the center of a whole cluster of daguerreotype studios.[19]

In view of the stated purpose of the National Gallery of Practical Science, the use of its roof as a photographic studio could hardly have been more fitting. Claudet's cumbersome equipment represented the newest thing in science, and his lighthearted sitters certainly participated in the promised amusement. Such a rationale applied, also, to the introduction in 1840 of the Biscenascope, the improved oxyhydrogen dissolving view projector invented by Edward Marmaduke Clarke, one of the founders of the ill-fated National Repository. It too could be—and was—said to blend instruction with entertainment. But already the gallery was in financial trouble. The proprietors, seeking a purchaser in 1841, claimed that they had spent £20,000 on it and that it had drawn half a million visitors in its less than a decade of existence. In putting it up for sale they hoped that "the public may still reap the benefit of their hearty endeavours to carry out the objects for which the Institution was founded."[20] Somehow it survived, but its objects had, perforce, to be compromised. Apart from the apparatus itself, there was not much science in the 1842 Biscenascope program. Accompanied by instrumental and vocal music behind the screen, it consisted of fifteen subjects, including three views of the Tower of London (by day, by night, and the armory burning, as it had just done) and portraits of celebrities such as Faraday, the whole winding up with "an allegorical piece representing Britannia, supported by Scotia and Hibernia, and attended by the arts and sciences."[21] In addition to these

dissolving views there was, in accordance with the fashion that had started at the Colosseum, a "Grand Promenade Concert, Vocal and Instrumental," in the interval of which, on four evenings a week, the gas microscope was demonstrated and, on the other two, magical illusions performed; with the extra attraction of "Laughing Gas every Tuesday and Saturday evening."[22] And all this for one shilling.*

Although the more "scientific" entertainments persisted for a while—the microscope, the demonstrations of electricity, glassworking, pneumatics, and magnetism, the timely lectures on China and the Chinese—the trend was inexorably toward the kind of attractions that meanwhile were drawing customers to establishments unhallowed and unburdened by scientific ideals. In 1844 an automaton writer-draftsman made by Robert-Houdin, which Barnum had bought in Paris and now put on exhibition in the gallery en route to New York, shared the bill with his premier moneymaker, General Tom Thumb.[23] It was at this time that Barnum considered buying the gallery and running it in partnership with a nephew of George Catlin.[24] Two other juvenile entertainers besides General Tom Thumb were then at the Adelaide Gallery: the Infant Thalia ("The Pet of the Petticoats") giving comic impersonations, and the Infant Sappho, a three-and-a-half-year-old musical prodigy, who was said to number among her admirers the elderly Dukes of Sussex and Cambridge and "a great part of the Nobility" and who, furthermore, had collected a diamond from the queen when she performed for her.[25] In 1845 the fact that the gallery was auctioned off for a paltry 490 guineas—sufficient sign that its outstanding debts must have been considerable—went unnoticed inside, as, in this and succeeding seasons, a "Professor of Elocution" delivered a comic lecture "On the Genius and Writings of Boz" and the dissolving views "illustrative of the Holy Writings" gave way to a program devoted to "Humorous and Grotesque Shadows."[26] A German "siffleur" could be heard "imitating the feathered and brute creation to perfection," and Professor Keller's "Poses Plastiques and Grand Tableaux Vivans," alighting here briefly on their way to nearby Leicester Square, represented scenes from "the Ancient Masters," followed by the Ohio Melodists, a belated imitation of the more celebrated Ethiopian Serenaders.[27]

It was the story of the Colosseum all over again, the only difference being the initial premise that had proved untenable. At the Colosseum it had been faith that the public would support indefinitely an institu-

* The changing tone of the gallery's offerings may have been forced to some degree by the appearance of competition at its very door. In the Lowther Arcade extensive remodeling had produced in 1841 the Magic Cave, "the only Subterranean Exhibition in London"—a claim which disregarded both the marine cavern at the Colosseum and the Thames Tunnel. The attractions, available for sixpence as against the Adelaide's shilling, included sixteen cosmoramic views with dioramic effects, "A Splendid Picture of the CRUCIFIXION," and "an original painting, by Mr. Cox, of the Eve of the Deluge." (ILN, 14 January 1843, p. 31; WCL, StM/LS, II, 179, and Box F137/Lowther Arcade.)

tion notable chiefly for its elegant architecture and decoration; here it was confidence that an institution primarily devoted to popularized science and mechanics could make a go of it. By the mid-forties the gallery's atmosphere had come to resemble that of the Royal Colosseum Saloon a decade earlier under Charles Sloman's fleeting management. In addition to everything else, it was the scene of "grandes soirées musicales and dansantes," with refreshments, so the advertisements claimed, "of the most recherché description, with every regard to economy in the prices"[28]—which, being translated, seems to mean cheap liquor. A saxhorn band gave a concert, reputedly the first English appearance of that instrument.[29]

The *Times* failed to detect much gaiety in the proceedings. During a typical evening in this so-called Gallery of Practical Science, it reported, "an elderly and somewhat heavy-looking person" delivered "a tedious narrative of old Americanisms . . . occasionally relieved by the songs of a confederate in his absurdities," to the accompaniment of considerable hissing from the audience. "A bell, similar to that used by dustmen, was then rung by a person who announced that, by the payment of an extra sixpence a piece, each lady and gentleman present might inspect the studies and labours of the industrious fleas. Shortly after this, half-a-dozen of that class of persons who are not inappropriately termed 'snobs,' inhaled the laughing-gas and managed by the display of various antics to make themselves greater fools than nature perhaps designed them to be."[30]

In a pathetic gesture toward retaining a vestige of didactic purpose, as well, no doubt, as in an effort to circumvent the licensing laws, the Adelaide Gallery advertised *lectures* on popular dances from the ancient Greeks' to the reigning polka. There is little reason to suppose that they took up much time, if indeed they actually were delivered. What the customers clearly came to see was the dances demonstrated by "some foreign artistes."[31] In 1846 it was reported that "all the steam-guns and electrifying machines have been cleared away" and "Laurent's Casino," on the model of the Salle Valentine in Paris, had taken over.[32] "Admirable order is maintained by some half-dozen masters of the ceremonies," reported a newspaper,[33] saying more than it perhaps intended: a onetime museum dedicated to the cause of British scientific and technical progress, and even to some degree that of the fine arts, for paintings sometimes were consigned there for sale, now had to employ a whole corps of chuckers-out. One can sense the sadness, or at best the

resignation, felt by the *Mirror of Literature,* one of the first weekly papers published in the cause of popular instruction, as it summarized the state of affairs in 1847: "The Adelaide Gallery, with its chemical lectures, and its electrical machines, has changed its guise, and in lieu of philosophical experiments, and models of railroads and atmospheric locomotives, we have the gay quadrille, the valse à deux temps, and the bewildering polka; in lieu of the reports of air guns and detonating materials, we have the enlivening strains of a splendid orchestra . . . waking the echoes with their soul-inspiring and dance-compelling measures."[34]

Five years later (1852) the gallery became the Royal Marionette Theatre, with puppets from "the theatres of Naples, Rome, Milan, Genoa, etc." and an orchestra drawn from "the two Italian Opera Houses."[35] When the marionettes' successful season ended, the establishment, while retaining its new name, reverted to and solidified its former role of combination variety theatre and exhibition hall for oddities. Along with farces, dancing divertissements, "sagacious" dogs and monkeys, and *poses plastiques,* it offered between 1854 and 1857 a wide spectrum of currently popular attractions. Its answer to Dr. Kahn's Heteradelph was the Edmonton Twins, pronounced by eminent medical authorities "the greatest Natural Curiosity of the Age!": a *lusus naturae* consisting of "Two perfect Heads with beautiful black hair. (Male and Female) united to one Body, with Two Spinal Columns—Three Arms, Four Hands, & Two Legs, Presenting altogether the most Wonderful Anatomical Structure ever offered to the notice of the Public."[36] There was also the "eighth wonder of the world," just arrived from the Crystal Palace in New York, "the Monster of the Forest," "the Vegetable [or Sylvan] Mastodon," a California tree 363 feet high (or 863 according to a handbill) and 31 feet in diameter. How much of it was actually on display went unspecified.[37] From America also came, to exploit the *Uncle Tom's Cabin* rage, "'Prince,' the Giant American Bloodhound! The great Negro Hunter of the South, the largest, the handsomest, the most muscular and powerful Dog in the World," allegedly descended from a race of animals in the Ural Mountains, "spoken of in Pliny's History as THE TERROR OF WOLVES AND BEARS, AND A MATCH EVEN FOR THE LION HIMSELF . . . the great war dog of the ancients," only recently introduced into the United States to hunt down runaway slaves.[38] It was with such sensational attractions—and a "Grand Exhibition of Telescopic Cosmoramic views," "eighty various, magnificent, dioramic, transparent Scenographs," which probably were no more than a routine peepshow—that the Adelaide Gallery became indistinguishable from the miscellaneous shows not far away in Leicester Square.[39]

ᗡꙅ᙭ꙅᗡ

The gallery's transformation from technological display place to amusement hall was due in part to the fact that in 1838, half a dozen years after it was founded, it had acquired a formidable rival. That new institution quickly became so well known that one summer, in the midst of all the swings and roundabouts, games of chance, beer shops, and penny shows at Greenwich Fair, the rowdy resort of Cockneydom, there was a booth named for it (with who knows what wry sense of humor?): "the Polytechnic Institution."[40]

That the Polytechnic was founded so soon after the Adelaide Gallery was partly due to the latter's built-in limitations, which soon became apparent. But, even more, it bore witness to the power the idea of popularized science and technology possessed in those expansive years. The potential for the advancement of practical knowledge that such institutions represented was seemingly as enormous as their supposed constituency, and there appeared to be room for any number of them. So, at least, must have thought the man behind the Polytechnic, Sir George Cayley, who had been one of the Adelaide Gallery's original sponsors. Cayley, a sixty-five-year-old member of an old Yorkshire family, was a dedicated advocate of social reform, particularly as it might be effected by popular technical education. Equally important, he was a busy and intellectually adventurous theoretical physicist and experimental engineer who had invented the caterpillar tractor, numerous safety devices for railways, and an artificial hand. Ever since 1809 he had been publishing in the *Mechanics' Magazine* papers on aerodynamics and its application to the design of aircraft. Rediscovered after the surfacing of his notebooks in 1927, these pioneer contributions to scientific knowledge have resulted in his being belatedly acclaimed as the father of heavier-than-air navigation.[41]

In founding the Royal Gallery of Arts and Sciences, as the Polytechnic was originally called, Cayley was joined by a group of members of Parliament and practical scientists, none of whose names have much significance today. The greater part of the capital was furnished by a builder named Nurse, and prominently involved in the day-to-day operation of the institution was Professor Bachhoffner, "principal of the department of natural and experimental philosophy" until 1855, when he moved to the Colosseum to preside over its last declining years.

Like the Adelaide Gallery when it first opened, the Polytechnic, which received a royal charter in 1839, was a kind of modernized Society of Arts, dedicated to encouraging inventors by giving free space and publicity, though no prizes, to the machines and models they sent in. But it was also intended to have an educational function similar to that which Count Rumford initially envisaged for the Royal Institution and which actually underlay the mechanics' institute movement in the provinces. While the Adelaide Gallery had brief lectures and demonstrations to explain some of its more interesting machines, at the Polytechnic a continuous program of popular lectures was a major attraction. For a brief period at the outset, it also had teacher training classes in chemistry, physics, and other sciences, and classes in engineering and navigation for naval officers. There was even a short-lived school for railway engine drivers. But these activities were soon suspended, and although another service, a well-equipped laboratory and workshop for "private experimentalists and patentees who may require assistance," lasted longer, as far as the public at large was concerned the Polytechnic was devoted to exhibits, demonstrations, and lectures for laymen.

The Polytechnic was (and still is) at 309 Regent Street, near Langham Place. Most of the exhibits were contained in the galleried Great Hall, 120 feet long and 40 wide, where, for his shilling, a visitor could examine a bewildering variety of objects: an orrery, two astronomical clocks, models of the human ear and eye that could be taken apart like a Florentine Venus, a hydrostatic bed (to prevent bed sores: shades of Merlin!), a pneumatic telegraph, fire rescue apparatus, a pin-making machine, a machine to make brick and tile, various designs of steam engines. And, since the old principle of miscellaneity still hovered over such collections, there were curiosities with little apparent relevance to the March of Machinery, such as a waxen tableau of the Resurrection, a stuffed pig, and "a wooden bucket carved by a footman in his leisure moments, when 'his family was dining out.'" In the smaller Hall of Manufactures were, among other pieces of machinery, a printing press, an optical workshop, a glass furnace, an ivory-turning lathe, and power looms. There was also a 500-seat lecture hall whose capacity would later (1848) be doubled or even, according to one source, tripled.[42]

The Polytechnic and the Adelaide Gallery were in

strenuous competition from the day the former opened. Their rivalry was not limited to incidentals (both, for example, displayed models of the Thames Tunnel) but extended to the star attractions. The Polytechnic had its own gas microsope, projecting on a 425-square-foot screen the animal life present in the rich broth that was the metropolitan water supply. In general, the Polytechnic's policy was simply to outdo the Adelaide Gallery at anything the older institution attempted in the way of technical exposition. The Adelaide had one miniature canal for the display of maritime equipment and models of docks, locks, light-houses, paddlewheels, and so forth; the Polytechnic (before it was discovered they took up too much space) had two, with a surface of 700 square feet. The Adelaide had a tiny glass diving bell occupied by a frantic mouse which, when the bell was submerged, had to pump air into it by working its revolving cage. The Polytechnic went the Adelaide two better in this field—diving was much in the public eye because of its importance in the construction of the Thames

Tunnel—by not only installing an actual full-size bell but demonstrating the alternative technique of submersion, that of going down in a diving suit. The Parsee ship architects who went the rounds of the London shows at this time naturally were much taken with this part of the Regent Street exhibition:

A diver, clothed in a patent water and air tight diving dress, goes down a ladder to the bottom of the reservoir of water, being supplied from the air pump with air through a tube that enters into his dress; he is when prepared to descend, the oddest looking creature ever seen, he has an immense helmet of white metal over his head, and in front of his eyes are two large thick pieces of glass protected by bars of metal, this helmet is strongly strapped to his water proof dress, and he then presents a most laughable appearance.[43]

Loaded with weights, the diver walked about the bottom of the tank and picked up coins tossed by the spectators.

Suspended from a crane over the reservoir, the three-ton cast-iron diving bell was submerged several

139. The Polytechnic Institution: two views of the Great Hall, ca. 1838 (lithographs by A. Friedel and G. J. Cox).

times daily with a cargo of five or six people aboard who paid a shilling each for the privilege. Scientifically minded men went down to test the pressure of the atmosphere on their eardrums. Curiosity seekers went down for the sake of the novel sensation. Young blades went down to enhance their standing "in the bright eyes of the pretty girls who are looking on [their] sub-aqueous venture from the galleries above"; the girls could watch through the glass panes let into the top of the bell.[44] The most eminent diver was Prince Albert himself, in 1840.[45] Several years later, Catlin's adventurous Indians followed the queen's husband into the Polytechnic depths.[46] The diving bell, in fact, was to the Polytechnic what the steam gun was to the Adelaide Gallery—a virtual trademark. It brought in a thousand pounds yearly in extra fees.[47]

The Polytechnic participated equally with the Adelaide Gallery in introducing photography to England. Although Claudet had set up his glass house atop the Adelaide Gallery for experimentation in 1840, he did not begin taking portraits professionally until June 1841, whereas John Johnson, the American part-inventor and patentee of the mirror camera, opened his studio on the Polytechnic's roof on 23 March of that year. During the first few months he took in as much as £150 a day from "the nobility and beauty of England" who desired to sit before his camera.[48] After the studio was shut down in 1852, the Polytechnic continued to exhibit samples of the progress the art was making. The Christmas show of 1853 featured photographs "prepared expressly for this Institution by Mr. Ferrière of Paris, exhibited on a surface 35 feet by 28."[49] A later show was of pictures of London prepared by "Mr. Mayall, the photographist," from two-inch-square glass plates and, it was claimed, enlarged 40,000 times by the dissolving-view apparatus.[50]

Almost from the beginning, dissolving views were a Polytechnic fixture, and they remained so throughout the institution's career.* They probably were the main reason, apart from the obvious delights of the working models, for the Polytechnic's reputation as a favorite haunt of children. At the Adelaide Gallery the exhibits came off second best to the limitless delights of the toy shops in the adjoining Lowther Arcade, but at Regent Street all the entertainment was inside the exhibition hall. The presence of children is noted in press reports of Polytechnic programs almost from the beginning; in the summer of 1841, for instance, the *Athenaeum,* reviewing the current dissolving-view show, spoke of "the delight with which the younger part of the spec-

tators saw the grim interior of the vaults of Chillon, or the imposing nave of a cathedral, change, while they were looking, into some marine or lake landscape."[51]

The management's astuteness in this respect was matched by what it called, in a much later advertisement, its "Vigorous Prosecution of Novelty"[52]—not only new inventions that could be adapted for entertainment purposes and new entertainments that could be disguised as inventions, but lectures and demonstrations with a topical angle. Whereas the panoramists, in attempting to provide large-scale illustrations of locales in the news, had to live with a time lag of up to several months between the selection of a current topic and the completion of the canvas, at the Polytechnic it was possible to advertise topical features within a few days after an event broke into the newspapers. There were always fresh subjects to provide pegs on which dissolving-view lectures and demonstrations of elementary scientific principles could be hung. A full list of these would run to hundreds of items. A small sampling will be enough to show how assiduously the management sought to teach science by appealing to the audience's growing interest in the affairs of the day.

In 1845, for example, as at the Adelaide Gallery there were lecture-demonstrations on the principles involved in the atmospheric railway and on the potato disease that had brought mass starvation to Ireland. The following year, topics of interest were the electric telegraph, then finding its first practical application as a railroading device, gun cotton, recently invented by Schönbein of Basel, and the Irish famine. As a character in Planché's extravaganza *The New Planet* sang,

> There science, by the gallon, you may quaff,
> Converse by the electric telegraph,
> Learn to gun cotton how much power the state owes,
> And what on earth has come to the potatoes.[53]

The sequence of lecture topics in the summer of 1848 offers an especially good instance of how the Polytechnic went about popularizing science. The lecture given in July, by one Isham Baggs, Esq., was seasonal rather than strictly topical: "The PHENOMENA of THUNDERSTORMS and the CAUSE of LIGHTNING." But within a few weeks, as the hot weather spread cholera through the London slums, Mr. Baggs's announced topic was amended to "ASIATIC CHOLERA, and Its Dependence on the ELECTRICAL STATE of the ATMOSPHERE, with New and Practical Suggestions for Its Treatment." A month later (2 September) Baggs was succeeded by another

* These caught Barnum's eye in particular. During his first stay in England, in addition to contemplating the purchase of the Adelaide Gallery and Shakespeare's birthplace and drawing up papers to buy Madame Tussaud's waxworks, he spent $7,000 for duplicates of certain main attractions at the Polytechnic. Prominent among these were dissolving views, many slides for which, showing American scenes, he had painted to order. (Barnum, I, 400-401.)

lecturer, whose topic was "The Cause of the FATAL EXPLOSION in ALBANY-STREET, explained, and illustrated by Experiments"—namely, the demonstration of a new patent gas-making apparatus.[54] The Albany Street explosion, which rocked the Colosseum, had occurred less than a month before.

In the early fifties, the widespread adulteration of food and drink, particularly as exposed in a sensational series of articles in the *Lancet,* served as a recurrent topic of scientific discourses. John Henry Pepper, "the chemical professor to the establishment" and its chief lecturer from 1848 onward,* spoke on fermentation, "with especial reference to the bitter ale of Messrs. Allsopp, and other eminent Burton brewers," a commodity that had been singled out as being of questionable purity. Pepper proved that as little as one seventy-thousandth part of strychnine (one of the impurities with which it was alleged the beer was laced) in a gallon was easily detected by analysis and, to the relief of his auditors, concluded that Burton ale was "really a genuine article, and made only of malt, hops, and spring water."[55] Another subject of controversy admirably suited to the Polytechnic's interests, though not necessarily to the season in which it was discussed (Christmas 1853), was that of the spontaneous combustion of the human body as recently exemplified in the oily disappearance of Krook in Dickens's *Bleak House.* Pitting his chemical learning against the authorities Dickens cited, the courageous Pepper declared that there was no scientific basis for the supposition that a body could ignite itself.[56]

Strychnine reentered the agenda in 1856, when the revealed and rumored exploits of the Rugeley poisoner, Dr. Palmer, engrossed the nation. No sooner had the case broken in the papers than Pepper was ready with a lecture on "The Poison Strychnine" with "the Tests used for its Detection exhibited in the Oxy-Hydrogen Microscope."[57] By this time, the instrument must have paid for itself many times over. By this time, too, Pepper must have virtually perfected the art of merging "science," flexibly defined, with a whole range of topicalities in a single lecture. His discourse on "A Scuttle of Coals from the Pit to the Fireside," given in November 1857, employed dissolving views, diagrams, and specimens not only to illustrate principles of geology and mechanics (mining engineering and machinery) but to touch upon social reform (Lord Shaftesbury), safety (Davy's lamp demonstrated), social reconciliation (a banquet given by the Marchioness of Londonderry for her mine workmen), and a news event (a recent disaster at the Lunhill Colliery).[58]

There was double topicality in the 1857–58 feature, "philosophical amusement . . . illustrations . . . experimental, and replete with instruction . . . aimed at some superstitious practices lately revived among us."[59] A Mr. Downes lectured on "natural magic in connection with the mechanical approaches now so extensively employed by modern wizards." By "wizards" was meant both conjurors (stage magic was enjoying a surge of renewed popularity at the moment) and mesmerists, levitators, and mediums like the celebrated Daniel Dunglass Home, who made true believers out of a number of famous Victorians.

Ironically, the Polytechnic, which owed its inception to the Adelaide Gallery's failure to serve its announced serious purpose, found itself increasingly under the same pressures to which the Adelaide meanwhile was succumbing in a somewhat cruder way. The Polytechnic's managers did not abandon their determination to make instruction entertaining, but they were forced to qualify it. If entertainment *could* be combined with instruction, they seem to have reasoned, fine; but, in view of the necessity for balancing the books, there had to be entertainment in any case. As the mid-century was approached and then passed, the lectures and demonstrations, while they continued to be a more prominent part of the total offering at the Polytechnic than they ever had been at the Adelaide Gallery, had to share audiences with popular performers brought in from elsewhere on the London amusement circuit: the Infant Sappho, for example, during whose performances the oxyhydrogen microscope was demoted to the status of an entr'acte filler. In 1852 the multilingual Kransz de Feher, whose music also enlivened the Holy Land panorama at the Egyptian Hall, offered his "New Musical Divertissement" of "twenty National Melodies in twenty different Foreign Dialects."[60] No attempt was made to justify such attractions on the sober grounds of scientific education.

The utilitarian-minded portion of the intellectual establishment deplored this by now well-proved popular appetite for the light, sweet tarts of amusement rather than the nutritious loaf of instruction. But to others, the science-for-the-million fad which had produced the Adelaide Gallery and the Polytechnic was itself to be deprecated, because it was based upon a faulty reading of human nature—an exaggerated estimate of the mass public's appetite for dull facts. The ridicule that had been showered somewhat earlier upon the Society for the Diffusion of Useful Knowledge (parodied by Thomas Love Peacock as the "Steam Intellect Society") was now directed, albeit somewhat more gently, toward these derivative institutions. The future showman Albert Smith, in "A Little Talk about Science and the Show-Folks" (1843?), predicted with tongue more than half in cheek:

The time is fast approaching when our very nurseries will be the schools for science; when our children's first books will be treatises on deeply scientific subjects; and when even their playthings will partake of the change. The Dutch toys will be thrown aside for the Daguerréotype: the doll's house will be a model of the Adelaide Gallery; and the nursery carpets and morning dresses will be burnt full of holes by the acid from the doll's galvanic trough or hydrogen apparatus. Cheap air-pumps will be imported from Holland in chip boxes, with barrels fitted up on the principle of the pop-gun; and dumps [leaden counters used in various games] will be no longer cast in pipe-clay moulds, but turned out fresh and sharp by the electrotype—another type of the advancing age. Noah's arks will assume the form of chemical-experiment boxes: the beasts and birds will turn to rows of labelled reagents, and Noah and his family, sticks, little round hats and all, will be transformed into test-tubes and spirit lamps. The magic-lantern will be cast aside for the gas-microscope; and our old and once-loved friends, the devil and the baker, the tiger that rolls his eyes, and the birds that fly out of the pie, will at last vanish away to nothing in reality, before the magnified attractions of the claws of the *Dytiscus Marginalis,* the wing of the *Libellula,* or the wriggling abominations of a drop of dirty water; of which horrors, collected from standing pools and crammed into the smallest possible quantity of fluid that will allow them to move, people go away from the exhibition firmly convinced that they allow millions to pass down their *oesophagus* (it used to be called gullet) every time they take a draught of water, and they abandon it in consequence, and stick to Guinness and Whitbread. We do not think that any microscopic exhibitor has yet been rash enough to show what species of monstrous animalculae is found in a pot of stout or "half-and-half."[61]

In that final prophecy, of course, Smith failed to anticipate Pepper's analysis of Burton ale.

Reviewing the aims and accomplishments of the Polytechnic a dozen years after its founding, Dickens was torn between his Victorian enthusiasm for practical knowledge and his romantic conviction that it must not be allowed to overrule the imagination and human sympathies:

The Polytechnic Institution in Regent Street, where an infinite variety of ingenious models are exhibited and explained, and where lectures comprising a quantity of useful information on many practical subjects are delivered, is a great public benefit and a wonderful place, but we think a people formed *entirely* in their hours of leisure by Polytechnic Institutions would be an uncomfortable community. We would rather

not have to appeal to the generous sympathies of a man of five-and-twenty, in respect of some affliction of which he had had no personal experience, who had passed all his holidays, when a boy, among cranks and cogwheels. We should be more disposed to trust him if he had been brought into occasional contact with a Maid and a Magpie; if he had made one or two diversions into the Forest of Bondy; or had even gone the length of a Christmas pantomime. There is a range of imagination in most of us, which no amount of steam-engines will satisfy; and which The-great-exhibition-of-the-works-of-industry-of-all-nations, itself, will probably leave unappeased.[62]

The Great Exhibition (the Crystal Palace), which was in one aspect the Polytechnic raised to an exponential power, probably had the result Dickens foresaw: it sated the public appetite for machines, however marvelous, but left the imagination, as he said, unappeased. In its wake, the Polytechnic fought to survive. Pepper took over its management as director and sole lessee in mid-summer 1854. Stoutly reaffirming its first principles, he sent to factory foremen in the London area batches of tickets entitling their workmen and the workmen's families to a reduced admission of sixpence on Monday nights.[63] How many employees took advantage of the offer cannot be known. At first glance it seems odd that one of the several series of Monday night lectures "to the working classes" was delivered by Henry Mayhew on "the CURIOSITIES OF LIFE among the LABOURERS and POOR of LONDON," a topic on which one would think such an audience had little need of enlightenment.[64] It may be that the subject was intentionally chosen to reassure "the working classes" that, low as they were on the social scale and meager and uncertain though their livelihood was, beneath them were people still worse off than themselves. The Victorian social vocabulary harbored such fine distinctions.

Pepper continued to squeeze the last possible drop of entertainment from the scientific demonstrations; thus the limelight was put to work illuminating a "new and beautiful optical Diorama of Sinbad the sailor," and a demonstration of the principles of acoustics took the form of an explanation, by Pepper, of "the beautiful experiments of Professor Wheatstone . . . by which four of Erard's harps play sweet but mysterious music, without visible hands, as the sounds are conducted to them by rods from instruments played upon by performers who are placed several floors beneath the lecture-room."[65] Less ambiguously classified as entertainment was the new "diorama," "Sparks and Specs of

Sam Slick," a travel show proceeding from Liverpool across the Atlantic (with a burning steamer and floating icebergs sighted on the way), arriving at Boston, then proceeding to New York for a look at Jenny Lind's hotel and finally to Philadelphia, Baltimore, and Washington.[66] In the autumn of 1854 Pepper introduced "GOOD DRAMATIC READINGS" from Shakespeare. Miss Glyn read from *The Merchant of Venice, Hamlet,* and *Romeo and Juliet,* and, the next season, Mrs. Chatterley from *Much Ado about Nothing.*[67]

The Christmas bill for 1856 typified the Polytechnic's estimate of what the public currently wanted. Pepper lectured on optical illusions and fireworks, the latter, entitled "THE BRITISH BOUQUET," displaying the portraits of the royal family; "an INGENIOUS JUVENILE MECHANICAL MODEL THEATRE" showed the drama of "ONE O'CLOCK; or, THE KNIGHT and THE WOOD DEMON" and the ghost scene from that old melodramatic favorite *The Corsican Brothers;* a conjuror conjured; in the dissolving views, a series called "THE TRAVELER'S PORTFOLIO" was followed by "YE PITIFULL and DIVERTYNGE HISTORIE of BLEW BEARD" with "original humorous description" by a veteran panorama lecturer, Leicester Buckingham; and the whole festive performance concluded with the distribution to the children in the audience of Christmas tree ornaments and "hundreds of Mappin's Pocketknives"—a reasonably far cry from the holiday lectures on scientific topics which men of Faraday's and Tyndall's stature were meanwhile delivering before packed houses of upper-class "juveniles" at the Royal Institution.[68]

But the juvenile trade at Christmas, no matter how profitable it was or by what means it was attracted, was not enough to keep the Polytechnic solvent. Cayley, who remained its faithful chairman through the many dark days, died in 1857—he had published his last paper on aeronautics only five years before, at the age of seventy-nine—and the next year, when the lease was up for renewal, Pepper declared himself unable to afford the increase of £300 in rent asked by the board of directors and thereupon resigned. On the occasion of his departure (a temporary one, as it turned out), he gave himself a "complimentary benefit" extending over three days, with Albert Smith and other theatrical personalities entertaining and a Grand Fancy Bazaar laid on as well.[69] At the very time these festivities were in progress, the "scientific gentlemen" who constituted the board of directors made a clean sweep,

on paper at least, in their determination to restore the Polytechnic to its pristine dignity. In September the *Illustrated London News* applauded their having "banished from the establishment everything which is not in some way connected with the purposes for which it was originally designed, and substituted in the room of exhibitions fit only for a place of mere amusement lectures on all subjects connected with popular science and natural philosophy." As a result, it continued, visitors were of "a much better class than heretofore," "aristocratic patronage" had been resumed, and the "operative members of the community" were being taken care of through lectures.[70]

The *Illustrated London News* never was much given to irony, and there is no reason to suspect it was being ironical then; but the Polytechnic advertisements that ran in the same pages give no indication that the new management had in fact purged the institution of what sober-sided critics deemed its frivolity. As at the Adelaide, the inclusion of the word "lecture" in the designation of some attractions was hardly more than a token gesture toward an ideal still not wholly abandoned: "Lectures on the Philosophy of Juvenile Amusements," a lecture-demonstration by the Italian Salamander, Signor Buono Core, "who will walk in the midst of flames uninjured in his Patented Prepared Dress"; lectures on "the Humorous Melodies of Old England." But these acts were no more lectures than were the others on the same program—the phantasmagoria, the "brilliant arpeggios" of a harpist, the dissolving views of Don Quixote, and the concluding "Distribution amongst the Juveniles of Gifts from the Wheel of Fortunatus."[71]

The entertaining part of the Polytechnic's bill was entertaining enough to attract 5,000 paid admissions on Boxing Day 1858.[72] But the institution seems to have been fated never to have had its occasional stroke of good luck—or good management—unattended by subsequent disaster. A week later a defective "joggle-joint" caused a stairway to collapse as a crowd of between 700 and 1,000 was leaving the building after the performance.[73] A ten-year-old girl was killed and thirty other casualties were sent to Middlesex Hospital.* A coroner's jury came out strongly for building inspection laws that would prevent such mishaps in the future. The Polytechnic went on for a time, but when damage suits were brought against it, it closed its doors. A new company bought out the old one for £4,000 in August 1859, but needed £4,000 more for necessary repairs.[74] This sum evidently was not raised, because the following March an attempt was

* The casualty list published in the *Times* (5 January 1859) provides a rare opportunity to estimate the social composition of a typical show clientele. Ranging in age from three to eighty-three, the injured gave addresses in Soho; Wilton Place; Charles Street, Westminster; Vauxhall; Blandford Square; Fitzroy Square; Newington Causeway; and elsewhere. On the whole, there seems to have been a fairly even distribution of middle- and working-class patrons.

made to sell the whole establishment, which, it was said, had cost £40,000 all told. The only bidder was E. T. Smith, an ex-policeman and speculator in theatrical properties who at one time or another owned or leased Drury Lane, Her Majesty's Theatre, Astley's, and a number of public houses, wine vaults, and music and dancing gardens.[75] His offer of £3,100 was below the reserve price fixed by the Court of Chancery, and so the property was withdrawn.[76]

Somehow the Polytechnic managed once more to stagger to its feet, and an advertisement in the *Illustrated London News* in April 1861 attempted to put the best face on what, in view of all the Polytechnic had been intended to be and do, can be read only as surrender to the inevitable: "The great success which has attended the new Entertainments at this Institution has induced the Managing Director [a man named John Phene] to make arrangements for continuing the popular and amusing subjects with which Mr. Frederick Chatterton and Mr. George Buckland have delighted crowded audiences during Easter. The inspiring sweep of Mr. Frederick Chatterton on his powerful Harp, and the facetious humour of Mr. George Buckland, form a contrast that few musical entertainments of this description can equal. Dissolving Views and other exhibitions as usual."[77]

A brighter epitaph was written some years later by Edmund Yates, in the fullness of his nostalgia:

Ah me! the Polytechnic, with its diving-bell, the descent in which was so pleasantly productive of imminent head-splitting; its diver, who rapped his helmet playfully with the coppers which had been thrown at him; its half-globes, brass pillars, and water-troughs so charged with electricity as nearly to dislocate the arms of those that touched them; with its microscope, wherein the infinitesimal creatures in a drop of Thames water appeared like antediluvian animals engaged in combat; with its lectures, in which Professor Bachhoffner

was always exhibiting chemistry to "the tyro;" with its dissolving views of "A Ship," afterwards "on fi-er," and an illustration of—as explained by the unseen chorus—"the Hall of Waters—at Constant-nopull—where an unfort—nate Englishman—lost his life—attempting—to discover the passage"—with all these attractions, and a hundred more which I have forgotten, no wonder that the Polytechnic cast the old Adelaide Gallery into the shade, and that the proprietors of the latter were fain to welcome an entire and sweeping change of programme.[78]

It is true that the Polytechnic never turned into a Laurent's Casino, as the Adelaide Gallery had. But Yates describes it only in its palmy days, before it too succumbed to the public's ultimatum that unless places of instruction converted themselves into amusement halls, it would take its shillings elsewhere. The fact was that, in the conditions prevailing in early and mid-Victorian England, the formula for popular scientific education that had inspired such institutions simply did not work. In his *Gavarni in London* (1849) Albert Smith came closer than Yates did to the truth of what had already happened at the Adelaide Gallery and would soon occur at the Polytechnic as well:

The oxy-hydrogen light was slily applied to the comic magic-lantern; and laughing gas was made instead of carbonic acid. By degrees music stole in; then wizards; and lastly talented vocal foreigners from Ethiopia and the Pyrenees. Science was driven to her wit's end for a livelihood, but she still endeavoured to appear respectable. The names of new attractions were covertly put into the bills, sneaking under the original engines and machines in smaller type. But, between the two stools of philosophy and fun, Science shared the usual fate attendant upon such a position—she broke down altogether. Her grave votaries were disgusted with the comic songs, and the admirers of the banjo were bored with the lectures. So neither went to see her; poor Science declined into the *Gazette* [went bankrupt]; and . . . fled to America.[79]

Artifacts and Models

28

In their announced purposes the Adelaide Gallery and the Polytechnic typified the new wave of museological interest as the Victorian age began. Inventions, engineering models, scientific demonstrations were most in harmony with the temper of the moment. But the kinds of nonmechanical manmade objects that had dominated the old-fashioned curio collection were far from losing their appeal. Let the scientific-minded have their steam guns and diving bells; to another sort of taste, the "artificial" rarities once thrown together in the cabinets of the virtuosi, in the hugger-mugger of Don Saltero's coffeehouse and, on a larger scale, at the Leverian Museum retained their fascination. Now, however, they were not shown en masse, but in innumerable temporary displays, each of which was devoted to a particular category of objects or even, not infrequently, a single remarkable example.

The growing popular interest in the history of civilization was responsible for a significant number of such exhibitions. The fame of the Elgin marbles and the success of the Roman, Mexican, and Egyptian exhibitions at the Egyptian Hall resulted in several displays of antique art and architecture. Etruscan sepulchral artifacts (vases, urns, ewers, idols, lachrymatories, recumbent statues, sarcophaguses) were shown at three or more halls between 1830 and 1837;[1] Giovanni d'Athanasi displayed at Exeter Hall in 1836 a collection of antiquities which was said to reveal more of Egyptian everyday life than any previous show;[2] and in 1850 ancient mosaics discovered in Burgundy, including one of the combat of Bellerophon with the Chimera, were exhibited for sale in Pall Mall.[3]

Several temporary shows of arms and armor competed with the famous permanent collection at the Tower, which, however, was drastically reduced when the Small Armoury burned in 1841. About 1817–1820, when enthusiasm for things medieval was being fed by Scott's novels, there was an Exhibition of Military Antiquities at 11 Pall Mall. Here, said the catalogue, were to be seen "numerous examples of the most beautiful and exquisite Workmanship in noble Shields, Helmets, Swords, Guns, &c &c by the celebrated Benvenuti Cellini, and other eminent Artists, &c &c. Among the Royal and most distinguished Suits in this Collection will be Found—the Antient Crusader! Knights mounted for the Tournament, (Upon Their Noble Steeds), the renowned Albert, the Giant of Bavaria, Henry IV of France, &c &c &c." Among the 250 objects on display were 25 complete suits of armor, as well as scores of crossbows, spurs, pistols, powder flasks, maces, and instruments of torture. "An excellent resort for the edification of children," said the *Literary Gazette*. Not all the exhibits came from the age of chivalry, however; one was as topical as the Napoleon carriage. This was a "Cuirass of Scale Armour . . . made for General Bonaparte, on his expedition to Egypt, and worn under his apparel; and there is little doubt," the catalogue declared, "but this secret defence was used by him for a long time afterwards in his own capital, through fear of assassination." Or, as a weekly paper put it more lightly, "the secret armour worn by Buonaparte under his vest, as our Dandies wear their stays." To soften the effect of all this military metal, the walls were hung with sepia drawings by Fragonard.[4] The collection was sold at Christie's in 1821, but it, or a similar one, appeared at the Gothic Hall in 1830.[5]

The best-publicized show of arms and armor was the one Samuel Luke Pratt, a specialist dealer in New Bond Street, put on in 1840. Pratt had had much to do with inspiring, and then equipping, the famous fake-medieval tournament at Eglinton Castle the preceding summer, when the cream of British society played at being caparisoned knights and favor-bestowing ladies as diligently as Marie Antoinette's court had assumed pastoral roles at the Petit Trianon.[6] The lavishly mounted combat, a triumph of archaeological recreation and conspicuous expenditure, received extensive press coverage. The not inconsiderable portion of the public who relished the misfortunes of the aristocracy took special democratic delight in the reports of the Scottish storm which virtually washed out the proceedings on Lord Eglinton's estate.

Six months later, cleansed of mud and rust so far as was possible (some items were irreparably damaged), most of the armor and weapons went on show in an annex to Pratt's shop, a room at 3 Lower Grosvenor Street which he had refitted two years earlier as a baronial apartment and named the Gallery of Ancient Armour. Among the star items were the Knight of the Lion's Paw's polished steel armor, with matching tilting shield, lance, plume, and crest; the Knight of the Burning Tower's shirt of chain mail, emblazoned banner and shield, and polished steel suit; the Knight of the Swan's armor, lances, and horse armor; and the armor worn by Prince Louis Napoleon in his role of Knight Visitor. In the center of the room two of the fourteen equestrian figures on display were represented in the very act of tilting. "The Earl of Eglinton has planted so fierce a blow with his lance on the breast plate of his opponent, that the latter is apparently falling from his horse, and hangs back over the saddle, as if deprived of sensation"—a courteous compliment to the nobleman whose innovative house party had been rained out. Surrounding the figures of men and horses was a large inventory of "lances, pikes, maces, martels, daggers, swords, bows, matchlocks, bills, holy water sprinklers (a curious title for deadly weapons),* shields, targets, and all the implements of slaughter and defense."[7] In July the whole collection was auctioned off at absurdly low prices. Andrew Ducrow,

the only bidder for Louis Napoleon's "geranium robe," got it for seventy shillings.[8] Some of the individual items, such as an outsize "cap-à-pie Giant Armor," reappeared in the so-called Maximilian Collection shown at Savile House in 1851 and sold, in turn, at Christie's in the following year.[9]

There was also an exhibition of what a paper facetiously called "female ancient armour"—a collection of costumes from the Commonwealth and Restoration shown on twenty-two waxen figures successively at the Cosmorama Rooms and the Somerset Gallery, Strand, in 1833–34. Formerly the property of an eccentric named Mrs. Lusons, who had died some fourteen years earlier at the reputed age of 116, these specimens permitted one, as the *Literary Gazette* pointed out, to "trace the vagaries of fashion over horse-loads of horse-hair head-dresses and other equally absurd changes in hoop, and farthingale, and long waist, and stomacher, and train and trumpery, till nature prevails again, and again fashion runs riot through all the phantasies of female masquerading."[10]

Although those proto-museum pieces, the relics of Scriptural personages and saints, understandably did not reappear in nineteenth-century exhibitions, there were a few scattered shows of religious objects. "Charlemagne's Bible," a venerable manuscript of St. Jerome's version "written by Alcuinus Albinus, an Englishman," was at the Cosmorama Rooms in 1836,[11] and at the same place a dozen years later was a crucifix made by an artist-monk, Carol Pesenti.[12] The latter display followed hard upon an exhibition of brass rubbings—quite possibly a show-business attempt to take advantage of the current burst of antiquarian research, stimulated by the Oxford Movement, into medieval church architecture and accessories. Two hundred figures of "noble and distinguished personages, including Priests, Knights, and Civilians," were represented.[13]

The Cosmorama Rooms in those years of the forties played no favorites as between the sacred and the profane. The same premises that at various times housed the Charlemagne Bible, the crucifix, and the brass rubbings also were occupied (1845) by the exhibition of François-Eugène Vidocq, the seventy-two-year-old former chief of the French detective police, who was a walking legend as "the Napoleon of his profession," and prospectively a major inspiration for the archetypal sleuth of fiction. Vidocq was already well known to the English public. His ghost-written, fictionized, and vainglorious memoirs, published in an English translation in 1829–30, had inspired several melodra-

* The *Times*'s own interpolation.

mas on the London stage. Two of these, indeed, whose titles were identical except for an exclamation point, opened within a week of each other: Douglas Jerrold's *Vidocq! the French Police Spy* (Surrey Theatre, 1 June 1829), and Buckstone's *Vidocq the French Police Spy* (Coburg, 7 June). Now this fabled adventurer, who, since leaving the Sûreté for good in 1832, had divided his time between his private investigation business and a paper manufacturing firm, laid out before the London public the memorabilia of his professional career along with some relating to French criminal justice and detention generally. These included a number of his disguise outfits (those of a priest, carter, miller, coachman, and diligence-starter) and the manacles and weighted shoes he had escaped from, or with, in his active days as a *galérien* and escape artist; manacles worn by convicts at Toulon and Brest and the saws and files they used to escape; and relics of several celebrated murderers.[14]

The elderly demi-hero (no one had more adroitly alternated the roles of hunter and hunted than he) was in daily attendance. The *Times* marveled at his extraordinary muscularity, his ability to contract his height by several inches, the flexibility of his features; he would, it said, "make an excellent player in such representations as require an actor to sustain several parts."[15] N. P. Willis, then in London, described him in terms surprisingly prophetic of Agatha Christie's Hercule Poirot: "He is a fat man, very like the outline of Louis Philippe's figure, and his head, enormously developed in the perceptive organs, goes up so small to the top, as to resemble the pear with which the King of the French is commonly caricatured. Vidocq's bow to me when I came in was the model of elegant and respectful suavity, but I could not repress a feeling of repugnance to him, nevertheless."[16] As a whole, commented the *Illustrated London News,* the exhibition resembled "nothing so much as the museum of Jonathan Wild, described by Ainsworth."[17] It is impossible not to wonder what hints the Tussauds took from it for improving their own flourishing Chamber of Horrors.

ᗝᒋ᙭ᘿᗡ

Most of the other kinds of exhibition objects favored during the first half of the nineteenth century were representational; thus to the public they had a double interest, that of their subject and that of the material and craftsmanship which went into their making. Prominent among these holdovers from the private cabinets and public exhibitions of the eighteenth cen-

tury were architectural and topographical models, the most outré of which, no doubt, were the models of the Tuileries, Luxembourg, and the palace of Charles IV, with moving figures, carved from beef bones by some French prisoners of war at Norman Cross barracks, Huntingdonshire, and displayed in 1814 at 42 Old Bond Street.[18]

Dubourg's collection of cork models continued to be a fixture on the London scene, first at 17 Duke Street, Manchester Square, and then at 67–68 Lower Grosvenor Street, for a number of years in the early part of the century. In 1808 there were twenty-eight exhibits, described thus:

Done by Scale, Representing some of the most superb remains of Roman Magnificence, in and near Rome, Naples, Verona, and the South of France; the much celebrated Temple of the Sibyls at Tivoli, executed from a scale of one inch to a foot. Amphitheatres, temples, mausoleums, catacombs, &c. With every decay of time and tint of colour, as the originals, with greatest nicety; taken during actual residence of Nine Years. A model of the Town of Tivoli, with the grand cascade and surrounding country. Mount Vesuvius at the time of a great Eruption, with the flowing of the Lava—A night view of a Torrent of Lava that ran, forming a singular and beautiful Cascade of Fire.[19]

The American diplomat Richard Rush reported seeing the show (he specifically mentions also Virgil's tomb and the Grotto of Egeria) in 1819. "The Neapolitan Minister," he wrote, "had drawn my attention to it by remarking that representations of the ancient buildings in Italy, were thought to be better in Cork than perhaps any other material—particularly of the colour of some of them; a sort of duskiness, or brown this side of it."[20] Among Dubourg's models of English subjects were Somerset House as of 1776, Stonehenge, and the ruins of the chapel at Glastonbury and the church of Godstow Nunnery, Oxfordshire.[21]

Models sometimes appeared as adjuncts to other shows. Several dusty and battered specimens representing both the old and the new St. Paul's were among the extra-charge displays that contributed to the much complained-of cheapjack air of the cathedral. Catlin's Indian exhibition had a model of Niagara, "representing in perfect relief, proportion, and colour, every house, tree, bridge, rocks."[22] At the Polytechnic one could see the Typorama, a three-feet-to-the-mile scale model of the Undercliff on the Isle of Wight, where the collapse of a long section of precipice had produced the unusual geological phenomenon of a pair of cliffs. The details of the exposed stratification could

140. Cork models of ancient temples and other buildings at Dubourg's Museum (mezzo and aquatint by Dubourg, ca. 1818).

be studied with the aid of artificial light and magnifying glasses.[23]

Cathedrals were favorite subjects of models. One of St. Peter's, Rome, was shown in Maddox Street, Hanover Square, in 1840; built by a poor mechanic of Brescia, it measured fifteen by seventeen and a half feet, and contained over one hundred miniature statues.[24] It was soon eclipsed, however, by another of the same building, said to be the life work of a Tuscan artist named Gambasiori. The white marble figures and architecture were imitated in ivory, and the various colored marbles in Oriental woods; the mosaic pavement was also of wood, and the altarpieces were of copper painted in oil. The interior was lighted by a small mirror, but for a better view the whole model could be opened up. Toward the end of the run (the artist, it was announced, had been summoned back by the Grand Duke of Tuscany), models of four Pisan buildings, also in ivory and colored woods, were added to the exhibition.[25] A miniature replica of Cologne Cathedral, reproducing every one of the 128 trac-

eried windows, the 5,000 crocketed pinnacles, and the 376 statues, was at the Cosmorama Rooms in 1849. It was a sign of the times that iron was used in the model, as it was in the building itself. A model of Rouen, illustrating an older conception of cathedral design, was displayed alongside it.[26]

These models were usually advertised as the product of many years of devoted labor. No such claim, however, could be made for two of York Minster which were hastily gotten up for exhibition in the wake of the 1829 fire. One, shown at the Horse Bazaar, Baker Street, was the work of a self-taught artisan whose model of Westminster Abbey was simultaneously on display at the King's Mews.[27] There is no reason to believe that it was any more impressive than the one at the Western Exchange, which was described in the press as a poor thing, made with the aid of only a knife and two small punches, the windows being covered in gauze and other unrealistic materials and a lighted candle under the tower suggesting the arsonist's torch.[28]

Other buildings represented by exhibited models were the Taj Mahal, all in ivory, made by native Indian artists under the direction of two British officers (5 Haymarket, date uncertain);[29] the Roman Colosseum (New Bond Street, 1816; Cosmorama Rooms, 1838), made from wood and showing the building as it was when new;[30] the Théâtre Français (Egyptian Hall, 1831; Leicester Square, 1832), with the back part capable of being opened to reveal the stage machinery;[31] and Scott's Abbotsford, along with Dryburgh Abbey, his burial place (Regent Street, 1835).[32] At rooms in King William Street, in 1834, there was an assemblage of plaster of Paris models of buildings in Egypt, Greece, and Italy, as well as of the Charing Cross redevelopment scheme, which at that time proposed, in addition to works that were actually carried out, the destruction of St. Martin's-in-the-Fields and the erection of two imposing edifices, the National Metropolitan Church and the Senate House.[33]

More complicated, of course, were models of whole cities. A wooden one of the City of London, shown at the Western Exchange in 1831, purported to represent 73,000 houses, 107 churches, and all public buildings.[34] If it did, it was a worthy three-dimensional complement to the panorama recently opened at the Regent's Park Colosseum. A 25-by-15-foot model of Paris was displayed at the Western Exchange in 1825, a 24-by-20-foot one of Edinburgh in Piccadilly in 1843, and an especially elaborate one of Venice at the Egyptian Hall in 1843–44.[35] This last, bathed in limelight imitating the sun, was said, in a barrage of statistics such as no advertisement of an early Victorian model could be without, to show 102 churches, 122 towers, 340 bridges, 135 large palaces, 927 smaller ones, 461 canals, and 18,479 houses.[36]

The Holy Land panoramas of mid-century were anticipated by several models illustrating the topography and settlements of that region. In the late 1830s or early 1840s a model—seemingly not much more than a map—of Palestine, eighteen by nine feet, was at a room near Somerset House. "It is made of cement, and painted of a greenish cast; the sea, lakes, and rivers, are light blue. The eye of the spectator takes in, at one view, the whole of the land of Palestine. The cities are represented by bits of carved cork, and the towns by white circles. The royal cities are signified by Roman letters, the Levitical cities by circles and scrolls, and the cities of refuge by circles and crosses. There are also gilt lines drawn to show the several boundaries of the different cities, and pale lines to mark out the roads."[37]

A Bible was placed at one end of the table for reference.

In 1846–1849 there was a rash of such models in London, assisted perhaps, apart from any religious considerations, by Disraeli's novel *Tancred* (1847), from which one advertisement quoted: "The view of Jerusalem is the history of the world—it is more, it is the history of earth and Heaven—where not a spot is visible that is not heroic or sacred, consecrated or memorable; not a rock that is not the cave of Prophets—not a valley which is not the valley of heaven-anointed kings—not a mountain that is not the mountain of God."[38] The first miniature Jerusalem on the scene, at 213 Piccadilly, was a model of the ancient city constructed by a resident of Dublin named Brunetti. Before arriving in London it had been inspected in other cities by "at least 60,000 persons, including 1,000 clergymen and 300 travellers in the Holy Land."[39] The two latter classes, one must suppose, vouched for the model's accuracy. The descriptive lecture is variously reported. According to one witness, "The deepest hush prevails through the room; and scarcely the rustling of a garment, or the drawing of a breath is heard."[40] But another remarked that "the tone of the speaker is brought into conformity with his subject more entirely than was agreeable to ourselves," which undoubtedly means that for their shilling (children and schools sixpence) those attending the show were treated to a regular sermon.[41]

At the Egyptian Hall, Brunetti's model was rivaled or complemented by "The Jerusalem of Prophecy"—the city as it was at the present time rather than as it had been—executed at the command of Queen Adelaide by an Edwin Smith. This was only half the size of Brunetti's (100 square feet) and seems not to have been on display long.[42] More successful were the Reverend Robert Hartshorn's small models of the tabernacle and the encampment of Israel at 58 Pall Mall in 1848. The tabernacle was especially praised. "The miniature candlesticks, sacred vessels, &c," we are told, "are of gold or silver, the pillars are richly gilt. . . . The curtain of the holy place is exquisitely embroidered, and even the water-vessels have been carefully copied from the specimens in the British Museum."[43]

Some of these models, like so many panoramas, served stay-at-home Londoners who wanted to see the world vicariously. In 1825 William Bullock consolidated his Mexican show in the Egyptian Hall in order to free a room for "Switzerland in Piccadilly," Pro-

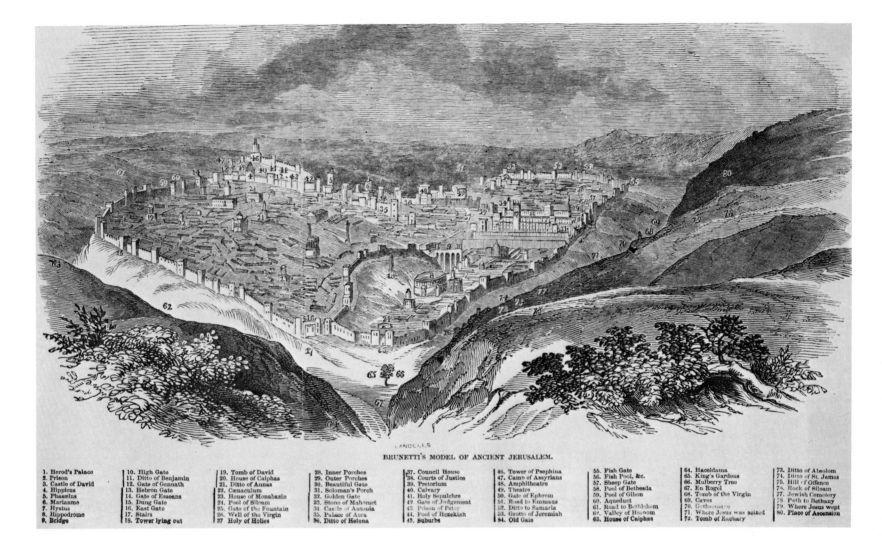

BRUNETTI'S MODEL OF ANCIENT JERUSALEM.

1. Herod's Palace	10. High Gate	19. Tomb of David	28. Inner Porches	37. Council House	46. Tower of Psephina	55. Fish Gate	64. Haceldama	73. Ditto of Absolom
2. Prison	11. Ditto of Benjamin	20. House of Caiphas	29. Outer Porches	38. Courts of Justice	47. Camp of Assyrians	56. Fish Pool, &c.	65. King's Gardens	74. Ditto of St. James
3. Castle of David	12. Gate of Gennath	21. Ditto of Annas	30. Beautiful Gate	39. Pretorium	48. Amphitheatre	57. Sheep Gate	66. Mulberry Tree	75. Hill of Offence
4. Hippicus	13. Hebron Gate	22. Cœnaculum	31. Soloman's Porch	40. Calvary	49. Theatre	58. Pool of Bethesda	67. En Rogel	76. Rock of Siloam
5. Phaselus	14. Gate of Esseans	23. House of Monabazin	32. Golden Gate	41. Holy Sepulchre	50. Gate of Ephrem	59. Pool of Gihon	68. Tomb of the Virgin	77. Jewish Cemetery
6. Marianne	15. Dung Gate	24. Pool of Siloam	33. Stone of Mahomet	42. Gate of Judgement	51. Road to Emmaus	60. Aqueduct	69. Caves	78. Path to Bethany
7. Hystus	16. East Gate	25. Gate of the Fountain	34. Castle of Antonia	43. Prison of Peter	52. Ditto to Samaria	61. Road to Bethlehem	70. Gethsemane	79. Where Jesus wept
8. Hippodrome	17. Stairs	26. Well of the Virgin	35. Palace of Acra	44. Pool of Hezekiah	53. Grotto of Jeremiah	62. Valley of Hinnom	71. Where Jesus was seized	80. Place of Ascension
9. Bridge	18. Tower lying out	27. Holy of Holies	36. Ditto of Helena	45. Suburbs	54. Old Gate	63. House of Caiphas	72. Tomb of Zachary	

fessor Gaudin's twenty-six-by-twenty-one-foot representation of eighteen Swiss cantons, which had previously been shown in Geneva. The model, promised the proprietor as he availed himself of the panoramists' chief selling points, would make visitors to the Egyptian Hall feel "as though they were actually traversing [Switzerland's] stupendous Mountains, or strolling through its fertile Vallies. . . . The historical or literary inquirer will note situations rendered interesting by the names of William Tell, of Voltaire, of Gibbon, and Rousseau; nor will the spot where our favorite Kemble closed an honorable existence be passed without a pause! The accomplished Tourist may likewise here renew his acquaintance with scenes too splendid and romantic to be evanescent, and explain to inquisitive friends, who have not had his opportunities

of seeing the realities, those objects which most attracted his attention on his travels."[44]

Of more sensational interest was the model, displayed at 80 Pall Mall in 1829 and the Cosmorama Rooms in 1831, of the prison of the Holy Inquisition at Coimbra, which had been destroyed by an aroused populace in 1820. Made by a Mr. Young, who was an eyewitness to the event, the model could be disassembled to afford "a perfect idea of the infernal system pursued by that monstrous tribunal." The idea was enlarged by accompanying pictures portraying the fire and water treatments administered to recalcitrants.[45] "Every Protestant," opined the Times, "should see this model; it will confirm him in his adherence to his mode of faith; and every Papist should also indulge in a look at it, as it will show him by what means his re-

141. Brunetti's model of ancient Jerusalem (Illustrated London News, 23 January 1847).

ligious opinions and tenets have been supported for ages on the great continent of Southern Europe."[46] Ten years later, at the Cosmorama Rooms, could be seen a model of the slave ship *Semiramis,* alias *Regulo,* which was captured off the west coast of Africa, with 600 slaves aboard, by H.M.S. *Dryad.* A portion of the upper deck could be removed to show the conditions in which the slaves lived below.[47]

Finally, models, like panoramas, mechanical theatres, and theatrical spectacles, helped perpetuate the glories of Trafalgar and Waterloo. There must have been a continuous succession of these across the whole first half of the century. As late as 1850, at 168 New Bond Street, an "intelligent exhibitor" dressed as a pensioner (which he may in fact have been) showed a Trafalgar model composed of sixty-five ships, with tracings on the sea to show the course of each vessel as she was brought into action, firing broadsides of cotton wool.[48] At some undeterminable date, a penny paid at 246 High Holborn gained admission to a "Grand Military Spectacle of the Battle of Waterloo" which claimed to show "upwards of 50,000 Figures."[49] At the Cosmorama Rooms in 1839 a Mr. Fox of Pimlico exhibited a model of Waterloo which, according to one paper, was "less elaborate and consequently more intelligible to spectators in general than that in Piccadilly."[50]

The model upon which Fox's was alleged to improve was the most famous of all such productions in the nineteenth century. It was the first of two made by Lieutenant William Siborne, Sandhurst-trained son of a captain in the Norfolk Regiment of Foot.[51] According to an acquaintance, "he was a perfect gentleman, and a most accomplished officer, thoroughly scientific, a man of fine intellect and judgment, most unpretending in his manner, and very well informed. Pity that the British Army was then so constituted as to condemn a man like Siborne to an utterly subordinate and inadequate sphere of duty."[52] Ironically, this man who enabled the early Victorian public* to visualize the battle more comprehensively than did a representation in any other medium, missed participating in it by a matter of weeks: it occurred on 18 June, and he was drafted to join Wellington in August. While serving in various military posts, Siborne became an authority on surveying and topographical modeling. In 1830 the army commissioned him to build a model of Waterloo. In preparation for this task, he lived for eight months at a farm on the battlefield and sent printed questionnaires to surviving officers who had participated in the battle. But he could devote only his

leisure to making the model, and he was further handicapped when funds for the project were cut off by the reform ministry that took office in 1833.

The model was eventually finished and placed on display at the Egyptian Hall in the autumn of 1838. Covering an area of 440 square feet and scaled at nine feet to the mile, it depicted the entire region, not only the battlefield proper but the adjoining countryside as well. There were said to be 190,000 metallic figures of soldiers and horses deployed across the fields, so minute that for better inspection a number of magnifying glasses were fixed about the table. Fire and smoke were imitated by tinseled metal and fine wool or flock; and—a feature singled out for praise by nearly all the reviewers—the different crops, rye, potatoes, oats, barley, clover, were represented by appropriately colored silk or floss, and fallow fields by brown cassimere.[53]

Of all the London exhibitions he could have seen, this was one that Wellington could scarcely be expected to have missed. Yet it is the only one which we are positive he did not attend, because in his concern to keep the historical record straight, he knew he should not. In a letter dated 23 April 1840, he told Lady Wilton that he had seen Siborne's preliminary sketch but "understood . . . that the Model would not give an accurate Representation of the Position of the Troops of either or of both the Armies at any particular period of the Day." Instead, Siborne represented "every Corps and Individual of all Nations" as being involved at the same moment, which was not the case. "I was unwilling," the duke continued, "to give any Sanction to the truth of such a representation in this Model, which must have resulted from my visiting it, without protesting against such erroneous representation. This I could not bring myself to do on [any] account; and I thought it best to avail myself of my absence from London, and of Indisposition, never to visit it at all."[54]

Siborne evidently gave out different figures on what the model had cost him to build—£3,000, £4,000, and £10,000.[55] Whatever the true amount, the exhibition barely paid expenses. After Siborne was promoted to captain and retired on half pay in 1840, he devoted himself to writing a two-volume *History of the War in France and Belgium in 1815,* which became a standard textbook in military schools, and to building a second model. This one, on the scale of fifteen feet to the inch, was confined to the portion of the field which witnessed, early in the day, the charge of the Marquis of Anglesey's cavalry and of Sir Thomas Picton's in-

* Evidently not including Thackeray, who met Siborne while staying with the novelist Charles Lever at his home near Kingston, Ireland, in 1842. At dinner they talked about Waterloo, which, according to an unnamed Major D——who was also present, "Thackeray did not pretend to know anything about." Later they attended a military review outside Dublin, and the major noted how ignorant and apprehensive Thackeray was when he witnessed the manoeuvres. "Thackeray," he wrote, "remarked that a great amount of interest still attached to everything connected with Waterloo, the British public seeming never to tire of it; he had been thinking since we met at dinner of writing something on the subject himself, but he did not see his way clearly. . . . From what Captain Siborne had mentioned at Lever's house, added to what he had himself seen on that day at the review, he seemed to have arrived at the conclusion that it would be useless for him to attempt anything in the way of military scenepainting that could lay the slightest claim to correctness. . . . On the whole . . . he seemed much inclined to 'laugh at martial might,' although he still held to the idea that 'something might be made of Waterloo,' even without the smoke and din of the action being introduced." (W. J. Fitzpatrick, *The Life of Charles Lever,* London, 1879, II, 409, 414–15.) The result was the much-admired treatment of the battle by echo, so to speak, in *Vanity Fair.*

fantry. In 1844–45 it was displayed at the Egyptian Hall along with the earlier model, which had been repainted and revised to conform with the account given in Siborne's book. Both were for sale, together with others, still under construction, which would show other phases of the battle. But no one bought them.[56]

Siborne's last five years were spent as secretary and adjutant of the Chelsea Hospital. After he died in 1849, the first model fell into the hands of someone who offered to sell it for considerably less than the £4,000 Siborne had wanted. Sufficient money was raised by subscription and the model was deposited with the United Service Institution in Great Scotland Yard.[57] It accompanied the museum of that institution to its final site, the Banqueting Hall in Whitehall, where it remained on display until the collection was dispersed in 1962. The second model is at the Tower of London.

ᗞᏃ᙭Ꮓᗞ

Whatever their instructional value may have been, models attracted showgoers because they belonged, by courtesy terminology at least, to that capacious category of objects called "works of art." Thus they invited the patronage of whatever portion of the middle class, in its modest aspiration toward humane culture, was beginning to take a sedate, gingerly interest in manmade beauty wherever found. In the first half of the nineteenth century the meaning of the word "art" had not yet contracted to its present scope. Works of "fine" art and works of mere artifice or ingenuity were not as sharply differentiated as they are today, and, in the prevailing condition of public taste, the latter were at least as interesting objects for exhibition as the former. Shows of individual paintings and marble sculptures were less numerous than exhibitions devoted to art objects in other materials.

In the mid-1830s wooden statuary enjoyed a brief vogue. One such show, in Bond Street in 1833, was composed of limewood carvings of "poetical and historical subjects," Joan of Arc receiving the consecrated banner, the execution of Lady Jane Grey, Sir Roger de Coverley going to church, and David and Abigail.[58] The next year a Mr. Rogers exhibited in Church Street, Soho, "several hundred figures, in box-wood and oak, by the most celebrated sculptors of the fourteenth and fifteenth centuries," including also "coffers and stands belonging to the Cenci, of the time of M. Angelo" and "a superb assemblage of the most elaborate carvings of Grenlin Gibbons, of birds, fruit, flowers, and dead game."[59] Twenty-five figures of

Protestant reformers, carved by Brustolina, appeared in Old Bond Street in 1835. Zwingli, Melanchthon, Luther, Erasmus, and others were portrayed "suffering the pains due to them for their heresies." Originally in the library of San Giovanni e Paolo, Venice, this collection was said to have been part of Napoleon's plunder.[60]

Notwithstanding the ineradicable association of wax figures with Madame Tussaud, the Abbey's ragged regiment, dubious anatomical displays, and innumerable wandering exhibitions, waxworks maintained a tenuous respectability in serious art circles. Waxen busts, portraits, groups, and genre scenes, ranging in size from small scale to life, and in style from low relief to "full-roundedness" (three dimensions), continued to appear in regular art exhibitions as well as occasional commercial shows. Some of the work of the well-known late eighteenth-century modeler in wax Samuel Percy was shown posthumously at the Egyptian Hall.[61] At the Cosmorama Rooms in 1846 an exhibition of oil-painted relief models of birds, fruit, and fish, which one assumes to have been made of wax, was recommended to the public on technical grounds, as "overcoming the most difficult question in Art; viz, the combining distant perspective on a flat surface, with a foreground modelled in relief; preserving, at the same time, unity of composition."[62]

Tapestry also was occasionally shown. At the Historic Gallery in 1802 were Gobelin tapestries of Don Quixote, a fishing party, and a fortune teller (among other subjects) from the collection of Louis XVI.[63] A 2,000-square-foot specimen, alleged to have been designed by Rubens and worked by nuns at a Florentine convent over a period of thirty years, was shown at 213 Piccadilly in 1845, and the effect by gaslight was pronounced to be "magnificent."[64] The most extravagantly praised exhibit in this line (if only by its proprietor) was what a handbill called "The Most Superb and Magnificent Assemblage of Tapestried Needlework in the Universe," which formerly "adorned the walls of that voluptuous monarch, Louis XIV." The present owner felt, he said, "that it would be a reflection upon him as an Englishman if he allowed them to leave this country without indulging his countrymen with a sight of them." Negotiations were under way "with a foreign Prince" but the plain implication was that they could be broken off if a patriotic English purchaser turned up.[65]

Most advertised "exhibitions" of tapestries were actually offerings for sale. A needlework "panorama" of the Battle of the Pyramids, 400 square feet with portraits of all of the principal characters, was offered at the Royal Bazaar, Gray's Inn Road, in 1830,[66] and the history of Antony and Cleopatra, in seven scenes, was displayed the next year at 28 Old Bond Street.[67] A handbill in 1837 advertised "600 square feet of classical subjects, worked in silk of unusual quality, gold, silver, pearls, and precious stones" to a claimed value of £10,000.[68]

There was, finally, the biggest objet d'art of them all, exclusive, perhaps, of the Panathene—the elaborate cut-glass Royal Clarence Vase, made by John Gunby and Company of Birmingham and shown successively at the Egyptian Hall and the Royal Bazaar, Oxford Street, in 1831. Valued at 10,000 guineas, it weighed eight tons, stood fourteen feet high, had a circumference of thirty-six feet, held 900 gallons, and could be disassembled and moved from place to place. Its practical usefulness would seem to have been limited, but it was a curiosity fully worthy of its time.[69]

Most numerous and various, however, were the exhibitions devoted to parlor art: the kind of curios found in bibelot cabinets, under glass domes, on mantels, and hanging on the walls of the notoriously cluttered Victorian drawing room. In one way these exhibitions were the equivalent of modern hobby shows, because they displayed elaborate examples of the crafts to which innumerable leisured women devoted their talents. Many visitors came to get ideas for their own creative activity. But it was hoped that they also came to buy, because many such exhibitions evidently were merchandising ventures. They were the most home-oriented of all London exhibitions; their number and the nature of their displays suggest the persistence with which popular artistic taste was, in the quite literal sense, domesticated.

Originally admitted, though sparingly, to regular art exhibitions, most works of craftsmanship now were depreciated by all with some pretension to artistic judgment. Writing in 1808 of the last feeble days of the Society of Artists, the painter Edward Edwards remarked that the articles it collected for its exhibition in 1791 "were very insignificant, most of which could not be considered as works of art; such as pieces of needle-work, subjects in human hair, cut paper, and such similar productions, as deserve not the recommendation of a public exhibition."[70] Perhaps not; but public taste nevertheless continued to run strongly toward such works, the products of unusual techniques applied to out-of-the-ordinary materials.

In this line of popular art, the most venerable exhibition as the nineteenth century opened was the one that

Sophie von la Roche had admired in 1786, the grotto and shellwork curiosities of Mrs. Phillips and her daughter. This show, which had been outside the entrance to the Tower of London for some forty years, had now moved to Exeter Change, where in 1813 it included "Three Grand Pieces illustrative of the Battle of Seringapatam" and models of the ten-storied Kew Pagoda "ornamented with the richest Foreign Shells," Fair Rosamond's Woodstock Bower, Holland House, and the Thatched House on the Kensington Turnpike.[71]

A considerably more bizarre exhibition was Mrs. Dards's at 1 Suffolk Street, Cockspur Street (ca. 1800). This consisted of what a visitor later described as "an immense collection of artificial flowers made entirely by herself with fish-bones, the incessant labour of many years. I remember, in the course of conversation, Mrs. Dards observed, 'No one can imagine the trouble I had in collecting the bones for that bunch of lilies of the valley; each cup consists of the bones which contain the brains of the turbot; and from the difficulty of matching the sizes, I never should have completed my task had it not been for the kindness of the proprietors of the London, Free-Masons', and Crown and Anchor Taverns, who desired their waiters to save all the fish-bones for me.'" Her trade card contained the apposite (though unattributed) lines, "With bones, scales, and eyes, from the prawn to the porpoise, / Fruit, flies, birds, and flowers, oh, strange metamorphose!"[72]

The period also saw an extended fashion for artistic novelties created from plain white paper. The first of a series of paperwork exhibitions (1818) was the Papyruseum made by the late Mrs. Aberdein, who used no tools other than a pair of scissors, a knife, and a pin to make "Flowers, Landscapes, Models of Architecture, 132 Figures of Public Characters of various Nations, representing their peculiar expressions of countenance, customs, costumes, &c."[73] In Soho Square was shown (1824) the work of another ingenious female, the Selenescopia, which evidently sought to produce the effect of the new Diorama in miniature. It consisted of a series of small moonlight views of a lighthouse, a hermit, the interior of a church, lovers under the shadow of trees, and other subjects, made by placing a light behind a sheet of white paper. "By rendering it more or less transparent, and more or less dense," we are told, "she gets all the qualities of intense light, and every variety of shadow." But she obviously did not get the Diorama's qualities of color.[74]

In 1827 Isaac Williams, of 46 Upper Ebury Street, advertised, for private viewing only, a group of models of gentlemen's seats, towers and castles, all made of paper.[75] More accessible to the public was the exhibition of "Trepado, or Cut-Paper Work," at the Oxford Street Bazaar (1829). The unnamed artist displayed sixteen examples of his peculiar craft, among them pictures of the Lord's Supper, the conversion of St. Paul, the Battle of Alexandria, and George IV. The entire show perished in the fire that destroyed the bazaar the same year.[76]

A "celebrated" papyrotomist, Master Hubard, was represented in a show at 48 Cornhill in 1830–31. (He may or may not have been an American; he had earlier exhibited in New York, under the name "the Hubard Gallery," in 1824–25.)[77] His specialty was pictures, in black paper, of celebrities, family groups, sporting and military events, and topographical scenes. These were not mere silhouettes, because within the black mass were contained crosshatching, details of wrinkles, and shadings of light. The exhibition actually was a means of advertising Hubard's studio, where he cut likenesses of visitors at a shilling a head, frame and glass included.[78] Three years later, at 28 Old Bond Street, two young ladies from Hampshire exhibited their Papyro Museum in aid of Queen Adelaide's Charity at Southampton "for the relief of decayed individuals of respectability." Four years in the making, this was a collection of two-inch-high paper figures "of every class, and in all varieties of occupation . . . remarkable for character, expression, and propriety of costume."[79] Evidently they could not be fully appreciated without the use of magnifying glasses, which were supplied; even so, it requires only a moderately cynical imagination to assume that they were hardly more than skillfully wrought paper dolls.

Belatedly (1847), another artist in paper exhibited at the Cosmorama Rooms the "Camera Lunaris." The pictures, of Tintern Abbey and a street in Northampton among other subjects, were reported to be "perfectly colourless, and without any shade or any other outline produced by the pencil or the brush. They have all the appearance of coloured views, the tints being such as moonlight produces, viz. gray and dark slate colours. These tints are also varied, so that no sudden transition is apparent, the tints blending and softening into each other in an artistic style."[80] What they looked like, we can only guess.

In the Strand about 1830 three separate glass-working exhibitions competed with one another. Possibly the leading one was at no. 194, where the firm of J. Andrews and Son combined an exhibition room (admission sixpence) with a salesroom. Andrews and his craftsmen were proclaimed to have discovered the secret of "spinning out of one pound of common window glass, 200,000 Yards, at One Thousand Yards in One Minute." The productions on display included crystalline representations of the late Duke of York lying in state (1827), the Lord Mayor's carriage and suite, Adam and Eve in Paradise, King Charles in the oak, John and Molly kissing under a mistletoe bush, John Gilpin's ride, "off to Gretna Green," Tam o' Shanter's narrow escape, and Moses discovered in the bulrushes. Some of these may have been marvels of miniaturization, as others certainly were: "a complete stag hunt, that will enclose in a nut-shell, fifty-two hounds, a stag, and eight horsemen," and ten dozen silver spoons in a cherry stone.[81] Nearby, at 161 Strand, was another exhibition hall and salesroom, that of one Miles, who doubled as a self-styled "preserver of all species of animated nature to imitate life," in simpler language, a taxidermist. For a shilling, which like sixpence spent at Andrews's bought one also a souvenir from stock, one could see, all in glass, a model of the Monument and another of St. Paul's and a variety of cascades and temples.[82] At a third such exhibition, at 158 Strand, were shown glass models of the *Royal William* steam packet, Nelson's *Victory*, and the Vauxhall balloon with parachute attached.[83] It was perhaps one of these ateliers that produced the fourteen-foot-high glass replica of the tomb of Abelard and Eloise in Père Lachaise, exhibited at the Royal Westminster Bazaar, Leicester Square (1831), along with the Phusithaumaton, "or, Magnificent Revolving Island," which appears to have been a novel means (a decked-out turntable?) of displaying old-fashioned curiosities—gems and 2,000 specimens of insects and birds.[84]

D3✳️Ǝꓷ

From this record of what they were invited to pay to look at under the banner of art, it is clear that as a class London exhibition-goers were credited with little aesthetic discrimination—and rightly so. They were willing to gaze at any mimicry of reality, no matter how grotesque, clumsy, unsuitable, or improbable: shellwork, fishbone flowers, paper constructions, glass work, waxen tableaux.* Such objects were judged on two grounds: the dexterity of their makers and, as with panoramas and other pictorial entertainments, their verisimilitude—despite the palpable incongruity, or at least the unconventionality, of the material employed. This was true, above all, of a major class of

* The true extent of this appetite, or at least exhibitors' estimate of it, is best indicated by the display in 1848 of an alleged inversion of the usual process: not man imitating nature by art, but nature imitating man—whether by art or accident could be left to the theologians. At the Egyptian Hall a stone worker exhibited what he had come upon while preparing a foot-square block of marble for an obelisk: a three-inch-tall figure of a lady clad in the height of early Victorian fashion, with parasol, gloves, ringlets, cottage bonnet, veil, and a muff of Hudson's Bay Company elegance, and a companion bust of a gentleman. These marmoreal miniatures, the advertising suggested, were on a par with the productions of John Martin "or some other celebrated Artist"; the distinguished company who had already seen the show were unanimous in their judgment that the figures were "the inimitable production of nature—and an impossibility to have been the production of art." The *Athenaeum* remarked (11 November 1848, p. 1126) that one could get as good results from applying the imagination to cut fern roots or a blazing fire, and Francis Buckland annoyed the proprietor by refusing to see in the piece of common marble anything but "a bit of fossil coral-like madrepore of a white colour." (*Curiosities of Natural History*, 3rd ser., 2nd ed., London, 1868, II, 164–65.) But the same people who were willing to see "Napoléon Empereur" inscribed in a little girl's eyes and able to find intelligibility in the Euphonia's mechanical speech undoubtedly paid also to see this supposed marvel of natural art.

142. Miss Linwood's Gallery: the main salon.

* Making needlework reproductions of famous paintings, already a popular diversion among eighteenth-century ladies, became a widespread domestic art with the advent of Berlin wool early in the new century. Patterns were provided in women's magazines and sometimes were sold separately. Among the most favored subjects were Raphael's *Sistine Madonna,* Rubens's *Descent from the Cross,* Leonardo's *Last Supper,* Landseer's animal pictures, and innumerable scenes from Scott. At the Crystal Palace there were no fewer than six needlework copies of *The Last Supper* alone. See Molly G. Proctor, *Victorian Canvas Work: Berlin Wool Work* (London, 1972), passim.

popular art, the specific literal imitations, in other media, of well-known works of art. Though not unknown earlier—we have seen that famous pictures were being reproduced in stained glass and needle-work in the late eighteenth century—the taste for transposed copies of classic and familiar paintings and statuary was most characteristic of an era when a steadily enlarging public, intent upon subject matter rather than the subtleties of artistic technique and ever ready to be awed by stunts, repaired to exhibition halls in quest of rational, if not truly aesthetic, pleasure.

The predominant, almost legendary figure here is Mary Linwood, whose gallery of needlework paint-ings was one of the standard sights of early nineteenth-century London, so famous that when David Copperfield took Peggotty about town this was one of the four they visited, the others being Mrs. Salmon's waxworks, the Tower, and the dome of St. Paul's. Miss Linwood, born in Birmingham in 1755, was the daughter of an unsuccessful threadmaker and his schoolmistress wife.[85] She moved to Leicester in her twenties and lived there the rest of her life, but it was in London that her fame centered. Although a composer of some merit, her forte was the copying of

famous paintings in colored worsted wools on linen.* "The needle in her hands," wrote an admiring con-temporary, " . . . became like the plastic chisel of a Praxiteles upon a block of marble; she touched the groundwork and the figures started into form."[86] One of her early productions won a prize at the Society of Arts; in 1785 a selection of them was taken to Windsor to be inspected by the royal family; in the same year and again in 1787, they were shown to the public at the Pantheon. Then the growing collection took to the road, returning periodically to London but not be-coming permanently established there until 1809, when Miss Linwood moved it into a portion of old Sa-vile House, which she renovated for the purpose.[87]

The exhibition rooms, at the back of the first floor, were reached by a magnificent staircase preserved from the days when this was Sir George Savile's town house. The main hall, one hundred feet long, was hung with scarlet broadcloth and imitation gold bullion tassels. The pictures were displayed on one side only; opposite this wall were a fireplace, windows, and sofas and settees matching the hangings—a décor patterned directly after the private galleries of aristocratic col-lectors. Adjoining the principal gallery was "the Scriptural Room" in which were hung copies of Raphael's *Madonna della Seggiola,* Carracci's *Dead Christ with the Two Marys,* and—the star of the entire collection—Miss Linwood's version of Carlo Dolci's *Salvator Mundi,* for which she was reportedly offered 3,000 guineas but which she bequeathed to the queen. Other rooms and corridors held a series of contrived settings designed to enhance the dramatic impact of the pseudo-paintings: entrances to prison cells, through which could be viewed Northcote's *Hubert and Arthur* and the same artist's picture of Lady Jane Grey awaiting execution; a cottage window with Gainsborough's *Children Warming Themselves at the Fire* inside; a rocky recess encasing Westall's *Gleaner and Child* and Gainsborough's *Woodman.* Most memorable of all were two gloomy caverns, one looking upon a representation of a bright sea breaking on the shore, the other containing copies of Stubbs's pictures of a lion and a tiger, so lifelike, said the impressionable Parsee ship architects, "that we actually took them to have been stuffed and placed there for show."[88]

The picture collection, steadily added to until Miss Linwood lost her eyesight when she was about seventy-five, eventually consisted of over sixty reproductions, in addition to a self-portrait she made when she was nineteen. Other subjects included Opie's *Jephtha's Rash Vow* and *Eloisa;* several of Morland's dog pictures; Guido Reni's *St. Peter;* Joseph Wright's *Virgil's Tomb by Moonlight;* Ruysdael's *Sea Piece: Brisk Gale;* and Reynolds's *King Lear, A Laughing Girl,* and *Girl and Kitten.*[*] The catalogue appended to each title an appropriate excerpt from poetry, mostly from favorite eighteenth-century authors like Thomson.[89]

In general, the men who left recollections of visits to Miss Linwood's were not enthusiastic. Thackeray commented:

Your grandmother or grand-aunts took you there, and said the pictures were admirable. You saw "The Woodman" in worsted, with his axe and dog, trampling through the snow; the snow bitter cold to look at, the woodman's pipe wonderful; a gloomy piece, that made you shudder. There were large dingy pictures of woollen martyrs, and scowling warriors with limbs strongly knitted; there was especially, at the end of a black passage, a den of lions, that would frighten any boy not born in Africa, or Exeter Change, and accustomed to them.[90]

Dickens was not as restrained in his judgment, though doubtless he saw the exhibition under less favorable circumstances than had Thackeray. In an apostrophe to Miss Linwood he wrote: "I myself was one of the last visitors to that awful storehouse of thy life's work, where an anchorite old man and woman took my shilling with a solemn wonder, and conducting me to a gloomy sepulchre of needlework dropping to pieces with dust and age and shrouded in twilight at high noon, left me there, chilled, frightened, and alone."[91]

After Miss Linwood died in 1845 the collection was sold at Christie's. The prices they brought were not excessively high: *The Judgment upon Cain,* which took ten years to make, brought £64 1s., and only one picture (the Ruysdael *Waterfall*) went for more than £40.[92] Her portrait of Napoleon, in gratitude for which he was said to have conferred on her the freedom of Paris, is now in the Victoria and Albert Museum, and other pictures are distributed among other galleries; a number, including her self-portrait and her *Nativity* after Carlo Maratti, are in the Newarke Houses Museum, Leicester.

Miss Linwood's name and reputation survived her as a useful commodity in the London exhibition business. Soon after the pictures were removed to Christie's, her gallery was taken over by another specialist in copies of celebrated works of art—Madame Wharton, with her *poses plastiques.* From one viewpoint, this was admirably fitting; from another, of course, the declension from Miss Linwood to Madame Wharton was a precipitous one. But the proprietress of the living statues, like numerous other occupants of the rooms during the next decade, relied as heavily as she could on the aura of respectability which advertising her showplace as "Late Miss Linwood's Gallery" afforded.

In more closely related areas of show business, the name of Linwood was often invoked both to describe and to praise works of artifice which, while having the same general purpose as her needlework pictures, employed different materials or techniques. When a humble gardener exhibited a series of pictures made of moss in 1825, the *Literary Gazette* decided that its readers could visualize them best if they thought of "Miss Linwood's or the Gobelin silks turned into the different coloured mosses of many trees and shrubs, and employed in *mossing* a complete picture."[93] In 1848, an advertisement of a nine-foot-long model landscape done wholly in Berlin wool but without the use of needle or canvas, contrived a posthumous testimonial: "Some of Miss Linwood's intimate acquaintances have said, that had Miss Linwood been living she would have been much gratified to have seen this 'perfect reflection of nature.'"[94]

Several other techniques involving cloth or needles

* Seemingly the only contact, fleeting though it was, that Miss Linwood had with contemporary artists themselves was her employment of John Constable in 1802 to paint a "background to an ox." This is said to have been Constable's first paid commission. (*John Constable's Correspondence,* ed. R. B. Beckett, II, Suffolk Records Society, VI, 1964, 27–28.)

were employed to the same end. At the Lyceum early in the century was Mr. Immanuel's Panoramic Exhibition of Paintings on Velvet. The display space was a "segment of a circle" (hence "panoramic") occupying 2,160 square feet, which evidently was meant to imitate a portion of the wall of an art gallery. On this surface were hung a variety of pictures on velvet, some of them copies of famous paintings like Rubens's *Daniel in the Lion's Den* and others of scenes not associated with specific pictures, such as "Rural Scene" and "African Wilderness."[95]

The eighteenth-century art of copying engravings in needlework persisted. In 1819 a German artist, Miss Pajeken, had an exhibition in Soho Square of reproductions in black silk and hair and in colored silks as well. These, commented the editor of the *Literary Gazette,* "do not seem to deserve notice as belonging to the fine arts."[96] Even less deserving, one would think, though it received kindly press notices, was the exhibition at 15 Soho Square, 1831, of "Copies of Pictures worked in Scraps and Tailors' Parings of Cloth" by the widow of an army officer. Nine were copies of modern pictures, ten of Old Masters.[97] Another imitative technique carried over from the previous century was that of engraving on charred wood. One artist's work in this genre, which included copies of Raphael's cartoons, Morland's *Connoisseur,* and Rubens's *Entombment,* was shown in 1836. The *Observer* likened them to "highly finished Sepia drawings," and the *Morning Advertiser* said they had "the full tone of fine old paintings"; comments which show, if nothing else, that newspaper writers were as easily deluded as the people who paid their shillings to see what were officially billed as "framed engravings."[98]

Still another medium in which celebrated paintings were copied was stained glass, now enjoying renewed popularity with the development of transparent lighting effects in the theatre and, after 1823, at the Diorama.[99] (The advertisement of one such show in 1817 claimed that the effect of the paintings "may be compared to the first burstings of light upon the new created world," which was fairly hyperbolic even for a trade whose publicity seldom erred on the side of understatement.) The *chef d'oeuvre* in Comyns's show in Pall Mall in 1815 was an eight-by-five-foot copy of Reynolds's picture of George III in his coronation robes; that of Joseph C. Backler's exhibition in Newman Street, Oxford Street, in 1817 was a copy of Raphael's *Transfiguration,* made for the east window of St. James's, Piccadilly. In 1837 and 1839, respectively, two versions of the Descent from the Cross were seen

—Rubens's, which was frequently reproduced, and Spagnoletto's. Even when a window was created from fresh designs, stress was laid on the fact that individual portraits in the composition were copied from famous originals. Thus, when Wilmshurst's enormous window (eighteen by twenty-four feet) of the Field of the Cloth of Gold was displayed in an Oxford Street room specially decorated in the style of the reign of Henry VIII, attention was called to the forty (out of a total of one hundred) life-size figures whose portraits were borrowed from Holbein.

Celebrated pictures could also be seen in wax; a life-size copy of the Rubens *Descent from the Cross* was displayed along with Stanfield's and Roberts's British Diorama at the Royal Bazaar in 1828.[100] Two years later, in Old Bond Street, there was a mosaic portrait of George IV, after Lawrence's picture in the Vatican; a labor of four years, it reputedly consisted of over a million pieces of stone. On display at the same time was a mosaic picture of Europa, after Guido, which was said to be suitable for a lady's work table.[101] And at the Egyptian Hall in 1838, shown under the patronage of the Austrian ambassador, Prince Esterházy, with proceeds to go to the relief of Hungarian flood sufferers, was a copy of Lebrun's picture of the Battle of Arbela, executed by a Pesth silversmith named Joseph Szentpetery, on a single sheet of embossed copper measuring three feet by eighteen inches.[102]

Thus in the first half of the nineteenth century, famous paintings were copied in at least eight different substances, not counting the fleshings—or flesh—of Madame Wharton's artistes. The reasons for this abiding enthusiasm for works of art portrayed in extraneous materials lay deep in the collective aesthetic sense of the British public, which was as yet almost totally inexperienced in the appreciation of original art. It was, for one thing, a manifestation of a much wider social phenomenon of the time, the fashion for disguising one substance as another, as in architecture and domestic furniture, or, equally common, for concealing the true function of, say, a piece of household equipment. Hence the innumerable examples of transposed and disguised substance and function displayed at the Crystal Palace, a riot (according to critics like Ruskin) of "insincerity."

But why this demeaning treatment of fine art in particular? There was nothing vulgar or indecorous, after all, in painted canvas or sculptured marble. One explanation might be that this was a way of reducing art to the common understanding. Surely, in any case, no general reverence springing from first-hand knowledge of Raphaels or even of Reynoldses inhibited the encouragement and acceptance of copies in disparate media. On the contrary, such reverence as there was, was culturally inherited; that is, it was accepted as a matter of genteel dogma that Old Masters, as well as the most popular recent and contemporary British artists, were "great." From that reverential acceptance it was an easy step, as the history of hero worship in the same epoch repeatedly demonstrates, to familiarity. Behind the impulse to translate paintings from oil on canvas to worsted on linen, or engravings from ink on paper to hair or silk thread on cloth, lay what might be called, with only slight exaggeration, cozy affection.

It was the subject of the picture, enveloped in the vague aura of its "greatness," not its artistry, that counted, and this could be preserved in copies in whatever substance was chosen, no matter how cruelly the original's inimitable qualities were sacrificed. Compared with the original, a copy might be only a grotesque simulacrum; nevertheless, it preserved the outlines and supposedly the spirit, and that seemingly was enough. If the qualities that made the original picture great art were totally obscured, there was substantial compensation in considering the peculiar expertise and the hours of labor that went into the needlework or the wax molding.

This rage for copying was, on the whole, less defensible than the fashion for cheap plaster replicas and miniature copies of statuary, because it was possible for those to be reasonably faithful representations of their originals. Still, however misguided the impulse was, these crude imitations of pictures catered to a subliminal craving for aesthetic experience. Corrupted though the average onlooker's response was by sentimental or moral considerations and by admiration for mere mechanical skill, these copies (along with increasingly accessible engravings) represented for a long time the limits of most Londoners' experience of art. Only slowly and patchily, beginning in the second quarter of the century, did a first-hand acquaintance with the fine arts—apart from an example or two at a time, in some ad hoc show—cease to be the exclusive privilege of a fortunate or determined minority of the London population.

Fine Art for the People

29

Is it not a disgrace to this country that the leading historical painters should be obliged to exhibit their works like wild beasts, and advertise them like quack doctors!
—Benjamin Robert Haydon, *Table Talk,* undated[1]

As the coronation of George IV approached in the spring of 1821, the *Literary Gazette* remarked on "the glories of London in the Arts" under "a king who promises to do more for literature, and every refined pursuit, than any monarch that ever sat on the British throne."[2] So far as the fine arts were concerned, the praise was not ill bestowed. As the Prince of Wales, the new king had already expressed his ambition to build up a royal collection to rival those of the great art-loving monarchs on the continent as well as that of his own predecessor Charles I. A decent portion of the huge sums he spent on personal indulgences reached art dealers and artists, and at Carlton House he maintained a gallery of substantial quality. Whatever his deficiencies in other respects, therefore, George IV was a suitable monarch for a moment when the fine arts, ceasing to be the exclusive precinct of an establishment centering in the Royal Academy and one or two other artists' groups, the leading dealers, and a socially elite clientele, gradually became the concern of a widening portion of the middle class. Now, for the first time, pictures by Old Masters, hitherto seen only in engraved reproduction, could be admired by some portion of the public on a more or less regular basis. At the same time, benefiting from the surge of patriotism generated by the Napoleonic Wars, the productions of native artists (as well as American-born ones, such as West and Copley, who were members in full standing of the London art world) aroused keener interest and commanded higher prices.

The manifestations of "the glories of London in the Arts" in 1821 consisted of three fixtures, the annual exhibitions of the Royal Academy, the British Institution, and the Society of Painters in Water-Colours, plus: in Soho Square, a display of engravings by living British artists; in Pall Mall, an assemblage of the portraits Sir Thomas Lawrence had painted abroad; in Newman Street, a retrospective show of Benjamin West, who had died the preceding year; at the Egyptian Hall, Belzoni's tombs; in Pall Mall, Haydon's *Christ's Agony in the Garden;* three rich private collections, the Grosvenor, the Stafford, and the Angerstein; and exhibitions of works to be auctioned by Christie, Bullock, and Phillips.[3] So many art shows in a single season would have been inconceivable only twenty years earlier, if only because the public for art then was not large enough to support such a number.

One conspicuous evidence of the way in which the audience was expanding was the increase in the number of organizations specifically designed to bring art, old and new, to its attention. Second in prestige and influence to the Royal Academy was the British Institution, also called the British Gallery, which held its first exhibition in 1806 in Boydell's former Shakespeare Gallery, where the three exhibition rooms were refitted to resemble a sumptuous suite in a private

143. Sir John Leicester's Gallery (engraving in *Ackermann's Repository of Arts,* 1822).

mansion. Frankly intended to promote the sale of new work, the British Institution was not so much a rival to the Academy as a supplement, many artists exhibiting at both shows. In 1813 it presented the first one-man retrospective show, of Reynolds, and two years later the first loan show, of 146 Dutch masters from private collections. For many years its routine consisted of two annual exhibitions, one of living artists and one of Old Masters. The work of living artists was given additional exposure in the gallery of the Society of Painters in Water-Colours (founded in 1805); two other exhibition-sponsoring groups were to come in the next few years, the Society of British Artists (the Suffolk Street Gallery, 1823) and the New Society of Painters in Water-Colours (1831).

These exhibitions were open to the public, usually at the customary charge of a shilling. Much less accessible were two great private collections, although the fact that they were open at all often led their owners to be congratulated on their public spirit. The first to be opened on a limited basis was that of the Duke of Bridgewater, housed in a building constructed in 1797 adjacent to his mansion, Cleveland House, facing St.

James's Palace. This collection was composed of Old Masters, including forty-seven of the Orleans pictures. During the London season the gallery—renamed the Stafford Gallery after the duke's nephew inherited it and added a second room in 1806—was open on Wednesday afternoons to holders of tickets obtained in advance from its owner. Guests were received by a dozen gorgeously attired footmen, each of whom wore a blue coat covered with 120 yards of silver lace, the whole ensemble costing forty guineas per man. Two dozen more servants, out of livery, were deployed on the grand staircase. In the gallery proper, lighted by 263 lamps on eight-foot pillars, the cream of the aristocracy and the celebrities of the art establishment exercised their connoisseurship. This was no place for the man in the street, in the unlikely event that he managed to obtain a ticket.[4]

The second such gallery, opened in 1818, was that of Sir John Leicester (later Baron de Tabley), whose collection reflected the changing taste of the time in that it was limited to eighteenth-century and contemporary English painters. A card was necessary for admission on appointed Thursday afternoons. Although the ticket distribution policy was said to be fairly liberal, in practice the Thursday clientele was socially as exclusive as that in Cleveland Row: "a crowd of taste, talent, and fashion," said a writer at the time, "including many distinguished ornaments of the Peerage, and their ladies; several celebrated members of the Senate [Parliament], and smiling belles who form the enchantment of the first circles."[5] Some among them did not come primarily to inspect the pictures. Anna Jameson, the art historian, later recalled with disapproval "the loiterers and loungers, the vulgar starers, the gaping idlers, we used to meet there—people, who, instead of moving among the wonders and beauties . . . with reverence and gratitude, strutted about as if they had a right to be there; talking, flirting; touching the ornaments—and even the pictures!"[6]

One other London gallery was nominally open to the public at large, though it attracted few visitors. This was the Dulwich College picture gallery, a small but excellent collection opened in 1814. It required only the presentation of a ticket obtainable gratis from printsellers in central London—a stipulation intended, it was said, to prevent overcrowding; but since this was an unlikely contingency in view of the gallery's location in what was then a remote suburb, it could only be interpreted as a device to ensure (as a contemporary writer put it) "that none of an aspect decidedly plebeian come forward."[7]

To the institutional exhibitions and the private art collections that were open on a highly selective basis could be added the growing number of frankly commercial shows, typified by the ones Bullock was providing at the Egyptian Hall. The totality was sufficient proof that interest in art was beginning to spread through a segment of the middle class. The full effect of Hogarth's democratization of the artistic subject, above all his use of scenes and situations from contemporary life, was now being felt. Genre pictures, such as those of the popular David Wilkie, were attracting connoisseurs and the broad public alike away from the grand treatments of classical and historical themes that had hitherto been regarded as the supreme subjects of painting. The sheer amount of reportage guaranteed contemporary art an appreciative audience which was largely indifferent to the erudite and aloof pretentiousness (as some would have regarded it) of "classical" painting. And so Londoners were more eager than they had been in the past to attend art exhibitions; in terms of their unschooled interests and tastes, there was simply more to see. In theory there was no reason why they should not do so if they had the requisite

shilling. But how welcome members of the public at large were made to feel is another matter. The Royal Academy's summer show traditionally was the resort of men and women of title and wealth, of connoisseurs, collectors, and mere elegant idlers. A caricaturist in 1807 depicted the fastidious disgust of fashionable people who, having gone late to the exhibition to avoid "the Canaille," confront "a fry of wretches who have shoaled in (after dinner!) from all the unheard-of holes in the City and suburbs"—eating dinner at noon being then a sure mark of bourgeois habit.[8]

The gradual breakdown of the old exclusiveness was demonstrated by an episode in 1822, when the social composition of the Academy show's clientele took a violently (if temporarily) democratic turn. This was the year when Wilkie's *Chelsea Pensioners Receiving the Gazette Announcing the Battle of Waterloo,* commissioned by the Duke of Wellington, was hung, heralded by newspaper descriptions occupying as many as four full columns. Attracted by the subject, men and women representing all but the lowest walks of life, including the very classes whom the shilling admission charge had originally been designed to exclude, crowded Somerset House day after day. "Soldiers hurried from drill to see it," wrote Allan Cunningham, Wilkie's early biographer; "the pensioners came on crutches, and brought with them their wives and children to have a look; and as many of the heads were portraits, these were eagerly pointed out, and the fortunate heroes named sometimes with a shout." The picture was hung at eye level, with the result that it was in imminent danger from the application of noses and the rims of poke bonnets. The artist, visiting the scene soon after the opening, called on Sir Thomas Lawrence, the president of the Academy, to put up a semicircular railing in front of the painting.[9] This was the first time any such precaution had been required at an Academy exhibition, and the new breed of gallery-goers did not go unnoticed by the press. "To judge by the crowds which poured in," remarked a newspaper, "one might imagine that all Cockney-land was peopled with connoisseurs, as all Italy is said to be inhabited by persons of fine tastes and good voices."[10]

This was an obvious exaggeration. Not "all Cockney-land" was represented there but only the "respectable" portion of it—solid middle-class citizens, at worst artisans and tradespeople. The dismay expressed was due simply to the intrusion of anonymous visitors without social credentials, the bourgeois infiltrating the elite. But their presence led observers

144. The "canaille" at the Royal Academy: etching by John Augustus Atkinson, 1807. One of a series illustrating "The Miseries of Fashionable Life."

145. "All Cockney-land" at the Royal Academy: etching by George Cruikshank (*Comic Almanack*, 1835).

with a more liberal social outlook to assume that they represented a large potential audience for art who failed to attend exhibitions only because they could not afford to. This was the point made in a letter headed "Admission of the Lower Orders to Public Exhibitions" which was printed in the *Literary Gazette* in 1819. The writer described a visit with a (quite possibly imaginary) French friend to Sir John Leicester's gallery, which was unique in that departing visitors were not expected to tip the attendants—a custom that had long prevailed at stately homes in the country. The Frenchman got out his money at the door. "I assured him," said the correspondent, "there was nothing to pay. 'Why, I paid at Mr. ———, and the ———, and ———.' . . . 'Why do not the rest of the Nobility follow his [Sir John's] example?'" The Louvre, after all, was freely open to *les plus bas* of Paris, a fact that caused Englishmen perennial embarrassment. The Frenchman said: "Listen. Allow one free day in each fortnight, or even each month, at the Pall Mall and Somerset House Exhibitions; on that day let an attendant be stationed in each apartment, and put on each door a printed regulation; let the sticks, &c. be left below, and sentinels admit only as many at a time as the rooms may contain. I mistake the character of the populace if you will not find, that if flattered by your consideration for their amusement, and your confidence in their propriety, they do not acquit themselves as they ought."[11]

Liberal opinion held that the original reason that art exhibitions levied a shilling entrance fee—fear of damage, disorder, "impropriety" on the part of the common people—was no longer valid. To exclude them had ceased to be reasonable or just; they could be relied on to behave themselves. This conviction, as we will see later in this chapter, determined the policy of the National Gallery when it was opened at 100 Pall Mall in 1824. But the question was by no means settled. Aside from such isolated incidents as the crush to see the *Chelsea Pensioners,* which were undoubtedly special cases, did the increasing enthusiasm for the fine arts reach—indeed, should it reach?—below the comfortable and relatively cultivated upper middle class?

⊃ϟ✳ϟ⊂

Whatever its precise social scope, that enthusiasm encouraged the development of several kinds of exhibitions apart from the annual shows which were its earliest beneficiaries. One-man shows grew more numerous. A few, though not excluding the hope of sales, were chiefly retrospective, commemorating a leading artist's career. Such was the show Benjamin West's sons prepared in 1821, after their father's death, in a pair of galleries specially built in the garden of his home at 14 Newman Street. Approximately one hundred pictures were on display, one gallery being devoted solely to his *Death on the Pale Horse* and *Christ Rejected by Caiaphas*. During its first twelve months the show attracted 95,000 visitors, and it remained open several more years, benefiting from the popularity a number of West's paintings had enjoyed during his lifetime.[12] Like Gainsborough and his fellow American Copley, he had held exhibitions in direct competition with the Royal Academy; in 1806, 30,000 people had visited his studio to see his *Death of Nelson*.[13] His *Christ Healing the Sick* (1812) attracted such crowds to the British Institution that that body, which had paid the record price of 3,000 guineas for the painting, got back all but 500 in gate receipts.[14]

More common than posthumous retrospectives were the one-man shows primarily intended, like the exhibitions at the Royal Academy and its satellites, to facilitate the sale of new art and invite commissions. They also offered the artist a second prospective source of income, for if he had a popular following, the amount taken in at the door, from those who simply wanted to see the pictures but had no intention of buying, might add substantially to whatever he made from selling the canvases themselves. Blake had such a show in 1809, in his brother's hosiery shop in Broad Street; Turner had begun an annual series five years earlier, in his house in Harley Street, and would continue them for many years, with a hiatus between 1816 and 1822. It was at these exhibitions that Turner disposed of most of his output, only a small portion of which was hung at the Academy. In May 1812 Wilkie, encouraged by the popularity his pictures enjoyed at the Academy to believe that a one-man show would do even better, took a house at 87 Pall Mall and exhibited a collection made up partly of new paintings (for the benefit of prospective buyers) and partly of older ones borrowed from their owners (for the benefit of mere art lovers and loungers). This particular venture was unsuccessful because Wilkie, notwithstanding his general canniness in business matters, did not know how to puff such an exhibition.[15] Wilkie's popularity and the respect in which he was held by his fellow artists did nothing, however, to reconcile conservative opinion to the institution of the one-man show. To many traditionalists, inside as well as outside the Academy, there was something flagrantly unprofessional about putting on, and advertising, a pay-as-you-enter exhibition devoted to one's own works. As late as 1865 Ford Madox Brown's candidacy at the Garrick Club was opposed because he had held one-man shows.[16]

If such exhibitions smacked too strongly of the entertainment world and the crass marketplace, much of the blame had to be laid at the entrance to the Egyptian Hall. In the course of auctioning off the Roman Gallery of Antiquities and the Museum Napoleon (1819) Bullock had discovered that his rooms' spaciousness and their superior and (possibly) flexible lighting—both artificial and from skylights—ideally suited them for the exhibition of works of art, large dramatic paintings in particular. At the very moment that his sale was progressing, in another room was displayed Matthew Wyatt's painting of a recent sensation, the attack on the horses of the Exeter Mail by a lioness escaped from a menagerist's caravan.* "The picture," said one reviewer, "is disposed in a panoramic way, and the spectator looks at it from a darkened room. By this means a still stronger deceptive appearance is given to one of the most surprising effects of light that was ever produced." The light, indeed, was "literally so vivid as to seem real. . . . Considering it as a great curiosity, we recommend it to public attention, for we are sure that without seeing it no one would believe that such a magical splendour could be obtained from mere colours on canvas."[17]

In short (to generalize for a moment, because the observation may well be true of one or two other halls), when exhibition rooms housed large pictures they were arranged, so far as practicable, as panorama rooms. The spectacle inherent in such pictures, especially their dramatic lighting, was enhanced by the showmanly way in which they were presented, with natural or artificial illumination concentrated on them and distracting elements suppressed. Studio paintings thus were given the advantage of display techniques borrowed from the panorama and diorama; in effect, theatrical practices were imported into the temporary art gallery. That paintings inspired by "the cult of immensity" and panoramas were treated similarly in the exhibition hall helps explain why the distinction between the two was often obscured in common parlance. One can only wonder how much the expectation that their pictures would be displayed in such a contrived setting affected the techniques of some contemporary painters.

Next among the pictures to benefit from the arrangements at the Egyptian Hall was Haydon's *Christ's Triumphal Entry into Jerusalem* (1820). While it was drawing crowds to one room, Géricault's *The Raft of the "Medusa"* was equally successful in another.[18] This painting was inspired by a maritime and political cause célèbre—the wreck in July 1816 of a French frigate and the grisly two-week saga, replete with starvation, cannibalism, murder, and insanity, of a makeshift raft only 15 of whose 150 original occupants survived to be rescued. Apart from its considerable artistic interest, Géricault's canvas was a prime document in the uproar that erupted despite the Bourbon government's efforts to suppress the worst aspects of the disaster, above all the incompetence of the landlubber political-appointee captain and the cowardice of the officers.† After the picture caused a sensation at the 1819 Salon, Géricault, hearing from the son of the painter Guillaume Le Thière how profitable the show of his father's *Brutus Condemning His Son* had been at the Egyptian Hall in 1816, wrote to Bullock proposing that he exhibit *The Raft of the "Medusa"* there. Bullock quickly agreed. The public was already well acquainted with the subject, not only through press dispatches from Paris but from an English translation of a book written in protest by two of the raft's survivors, the ship's surgeon and a naval engineer, after a managed trial had got the accused captain off with a light sentence. Bullock proceeded to fan fresh interest by a splashy advertising campaign in the leading newspapers. It is possible that he also had something to do with the fact that just a week after the public opening on 12 June 1820, the Coburg Theatre staged a melodrama by Moncrieff, *The Shipwreck of the "Medusa"; or, The Fatal Raft*. His exertions paid off. Measuring eighteen by twenty-four feet, *The Raft of the "Medusa"* was laden with the kind of psychological and dramatic detail that made it a perfect subject for commercial exhibition. As the leading authority on it observes, it "yields its full effect only to the intimate viewer" who can study it for hours.[19] Some 50,000 persons came to see it before the end of the year.[20]

Then, like other large paintings of the time, Géricault's was taken on tour, and what happened subsequently well illustrates the interplay and rivalry between two popular forms of art. Marshall's "Marine Peristrephic Panorama of the Wreck of the Medusa French Frigate and the Fatal Raft," a painting occupying 10,000 square feet of canvas as against Géricault's mere 432, was already on tour. After a run in Edinburgh, it moved to Dublin, where it came into direct competition with the painting. Despite a reduction in price (from 1s. 8d. to 10d.) the latter exhibition attracted small audiences, while Marshall showed three

* Another painting that was on commercial exhibition in this period also owed its popular appeal to its topicality. This was the portrayal of Napoleon aboard the *Bellerophon* which the young artist Charles Eastlake painted from sketches he had made from a small boat in Plymouth Harbor (1815). Bought by five citizens of Plymouth, the picture was exhibited in London and elsewhere. The £1,000 Eastlake earned enabled him to go to Italy, the first step in a career that eventually led to the presidency of the Royal Academy and the directorship of the National Gallery.

† By coincidence, it was at this moment that political propaganda made one of its very few appearances in London exhibitions apart from the caricature shops. When the controversy over Queen Caroline's right to share the throne of her estranged husband, George IV, was at its height, her partisans arranged to show Carloni's painting of the Princess of Wales—as she then was—entering Jerusalem on an ass: a bizarre event in the scandalous progress of the woman whom Sir Walter Scott called "the Bedlam Bitch." This picture and the several satirical prints it inspired added heat to the political atmosphere. (See George, X, 117–18, 192–93.) Subsequently the turbulent trial of the queen, spiced with testimony relating to her alleged sexual delinquencies, was depicted in a huge painting (35 by 12 feet) shown at 48 Belvedere Place, Borough Road. (Horace Wellbeloved, *London Lions, for Country Cousins and Friends about Town . . .*, 2nd ed., London, 1826? p. 107.) Whatever its artistic merits, its subject placed it among the numerous large pictures of the era which portrayed crowded public events such as momentous sessions of Parliament, coronations, and state funerals—topics that made them particularly suitable for popular exhibition in the days before newspaper photography.

times daily for months on end. Eventually the peristrephic show, now billed as a "French panorama," was brought to the Great Room, Spring Gardens, to capitalize on whatever interest in the topic remained in 1823.[21] The intrinsic merits of the two shows aside, Marshall had the inestimable advantage over Géricault of providing a running pictorial narrative of the dreadful sequence of events, whereas the French painter could portray only one moment.

Henceforth the Egyptian Hall was the chief London site for the temporary display of pictures, either for sale or, in the case of paintings with "sacred, royal, or sensational interest," for the sake purely of the gate receipts. In most seasons at least one of its several apartments was occupied by some sort of art exhibition while the remaining ones housed miscellaneous entertainments, the froth of the London show business. The art exhibitions covered a wide range of contemporary interest, as a sampling of them indicates:

1823: A statuary display including a twenty-foot-high group from Monte Cavallo, casts of Michaelangelo's statues, and Canova's "beautiful and engaging Group of the Three Graces caressing each other."[22]

1826: An altarpiece attributed to Murillo.*

1828: Eighteen of LeJeune's paintings of the most important battles fought by the French army between 1792 and 1812.[23]

1829: Turner's watercolors for a series of engravings, *Views in England and Wales,* exhibited by the engraver and publisher to attract subscriptions and possibly sell the drawings.[24]

1843: Sir George Hayter's 170-square-foot painting of the House of Commons in session. Counting the other historical pictures on display, the number of portraits of contemporary public figures to be seen in the room was said to total 800.[25]

1847: A statue of Venus by an Irish painter lately turned sculptor, John Henry Nelson. The undraped figure, which one critic asserted had more delicacy than any of Canova's Three Graces, was said to have "attracted the notice of many patrons of art who expressed much interest in the future prospects of the sculptor." These proved to be bleak indeed. He took his masterwork, the result of "two years of unremitting toil," to Manchester, and while exhibiting it there, he died, "leaving a widow and four children totally unprovided for."[26]

1848: "Vos Maitino's celebrated altarpiece, the Magnificus," paintings by Rubens, Domenichino, and Titian, and Philippoteaux's timely painting of *Lamartine à l'Hôtel de Ville,* showing the poet, surrounded by members of the provisional government, repudiating the red flag. "Those who have seen this picture," advertised the proprietor, "may well say they have seen the revolution itself."[27]

1860: "Authentic Portraits . . . of the VICTORIA CROSS HEROES—their deeds of daring and chivalry. Many large historical Pictures, illustrating two national epochs—the Russian War and the Indian Mutiny."[28]

For the full chiaroscuro of initial ambition followed by either success or failure that marked the story of art exhibitions in Regency and early Victorian London, records of other display rooms must of course also be consulted. Rubens's picture of Susanne Fourment, the *Chapeau de Poil* (at that time often misnamed the *Chapeau de Paille*), was exhibited in Stanley's Rooms, Old Bond Street, in 1822 by two Englishmen who had bought it at Antwerp for £3,190 in hopes of selling it to the king. Disappointed in that expectation—though he kept it for some time on approval—they put it on display at an admission price of half a crown. During the three or four months it was open, the exhibition netted 1,200 guineas.[29] Some years later (1829–30) statues of Burns's Tam o' Shanter and Souter Johnny, on tour before being installed at the poet's birthplace at Alloway, drew 90,000 persons during their London run and took in nearly £2,000.[30] These were the work of a former builder's apprentice named James Thom, a wholly self-taught sculptor who carved direct from the stone without bothering with preliminary sketches. The critical opinion expressed at the moment, that these pieces "inaugurated a new era in sculpture," may have been unwarranted, but it certainly did Thom no harm. He executed orders for sixteen replicas from various patrons, and went on to carve other popular subjects from Burns and Scott.† In time the original Tam o' Shanter group was reproduced in as many materials as Rubens's *Descent from the Cross.*[31]

Although "benefit" art exhibitions were not as common as they were to become in the twentieth century, there were a few in mid-Victorian times. In 1848 the celebrated Reform Club chef Alexis Soyer opened a display of 140 paintings and drawings by his late wife, who had exhibited at the Royal Academy and the

* This was an age when, the philosophy of art attribution being as yet more imaginative than scientific, misrepresentation was rampant, and shady characters like the Reinagles, father and son, had adequate scope for their operations. Anticipating skepticism, the proprietors of the altarpiece printed in the booklet given out at the door a certificate of authenticity signed by the Capuchin monks at Cadiz, from whom the painting was said to have come. These signatures were attested by certain British merchants at Cadiz and the merchants', in turn, were notarized by the British consul. (*Brief Description of the Picture, A Grand Altar-Piece from the Capuchin Convent at Cadiz . . .* , London, 1826; copy at BL.) None of this documentation, of course, proved that the altarpiece was Murillo's.

† One self-taught Scottish sculptor clearly called for another, and hard on Thom's heels (1831) came John Greenshields, a Lanarkshire mason, who displayed, in the Regent Street Quadrant and at the Queen's Bazaar, Oxford Street, colossal statues of the late George IV and the Duke of York—and eight life-size figures illustrating Burns's "The Jolly Beggars." (Handbill, GL, London Playbills: Circuses and Miscellaneous Entertainments box.)

British Gallery, in aid of a fund to establish a soup kitchen in every London parish that needed one during that year of extreme destitution. Despite his fame, a fancily printed card of invitation to the private view, and a good send-off by the *Times,* Soyer managed to collect only £260, an amount barely sufficient to provide 50,000 helpings of soup in the single district of Spitalfields.[32] A decade later, to raise funds for the Marylebone Literary Institution, a show composed exclusively of animal pictures from the collection of Jacob Bell, a pharmaceutical magnate who specialized in these and sporting pictures, was held at 17 Edwards Street, Portman Square.[33]

To some hopeful owners of art, exhibitions brought nothing but grief. In 1847 a picture that was said to be the long-lost sketch Velásquez made in 1623 of Charles I, then Prince of Wales, was shown for a shilling. Its owner, Mr. Snare, was not a Dickensian lawyer, as his name suggests, but a Reading bookseller; but the alleged Velásquez did involve him in an extended series of legal difficulties. His landlord seized it for nonpayment of rent and Snare had to pay £400 to retrieve it. Then he took it to Edinburgh, where it was again seized, this time by the sheriff on behalf of the Earl of Fife, who claimed it as a family heirloom. The earl died before the courts resolved the issue, but his executors pursued the litigation. Snare ultimately collected £1,000 from them as compensation for the revenue he claimed he would meanwhile have obtained from exhibiting the picture.[34]

An unusual amount of warm human interest attaches to one more of these exhibitions. For many years Charles Mathews the actor had collected portraits of English theatrical celebrities, eventually owning four hundred of them, including paintings by Hogarth, Reynolds, Romney, Zoffany, and Lawrence. To house these he built an informal gallery adjoining his beloved Ivy Cottage in Kentish Town, where Charles Lamb, who had a sentimental passion for "the old actors," saw them. Mathews proposed that Lamb write a catalogue of the collection, but Lamb apologetically declined: "I know my own utter unfitness for such a task. I am no hand at describing costumes, a great requisite in an account of mannered pictures. I have not the slightest acquaintance with pictorial language even. . . . What a feast 'twould be to be sitting at the pictures painting 'em into words; but I could almost as soon make words into pictures."[35] Suffering financial reverses, Mathews sought to sell the collection to the Garrick Club; refused, he put it on exhibition in 1833 at the Queen's Bazaar in the hope it would find a purchaser. Not only did he fail in this; he netted little if anything from the paid admissions, because the public resolutely declined to spend a shilling to see pictures which in easier days Mathews had gladly shown for nothing.[36] (One paying customer was Macaulay, who described the collection enthusiastically and at length in a letter to his sister.)[37] After Mathews's death in 1835 the pictures were sold for a mere £1,000—to the Garrick Club.

⚹

A flourishing phase of the art exhibition business, profitable to artists and dealers alike, was the display of paintings from which engravings were to be made. Of the three interrelated monetary values a canvas might have—its own, as an object to be bought and sold; its power to draw shilling-a-head visitors to an exhibition; and its copyright as the original of an engraving—the last sometimes was the largest in terms of pounds sterling. The owner of the engraving rights, whether he was the artist himself, a dealer, or a print publisher, found public exhibition of the original a highly desirable way of publicizing the engraving and, in the case of a dealer or publisher, an additional means of recouping his investment.[38] W. P. Frith's experience is a good case in point. In 1853 he sold *Ramsgate Sands* to a dealer (Lloyd) for 700 guineas. Lloyd in turn sold it to the queen at cost, but retained the exhibition and engraving rights for a three-year term. Exercise of these rights brought him over £3,000 clear profit, since he had, in effect, paid nothing for the picture. Frith was wiser the next time round. He painted *Derby Day* for Jacob Bell for £1,500, but before finishing it he sold Ernest Gambart, a leading dealer, the engraving rights for a like sum and the right to exhibit it after the Royal Academy show for an additional £750. When, at the Academy show of 1858, the picture had to be railed off—the first to require such protection since the *Chelsea Pensioners*—the success of the subsequent commercial exhibition and engraving was assured. Gambart's investment of £2,250 proved a wise one, and Frith had made 50 percent more from the subsidiary rights than he had from the canvas.[39]

When he entered into that deal with Frith, Gambart was already aware of the profit to be derived from engravings. In 1854 he had bought the copyright of Holman Hunt's *The Light of the World* and cleared £8,000 in a single year from the engraving.[40] When Hunt completed *The Finding of the Saviour in the Temple,* he fixed on the unheard-of asking price of 5,500 guineas. At the urging of his friend Wilkie Collins, he consulted Dickens, a shrewd judge of the monetary worth of popular artistic properties, including his own. Dickens approved, and Gambart willingly paid. He was soon glad he did. At the German Gallery in Bond Street, after the painting had caused a great stir at the Academy show, he collected as much as £40 a day at the door, and in the end made £4,000 from admissions, £5,000 from sales of the engraving, and £1,500 from the sale of the picture.[41]

Beholding his rival Gambart virtually coining money, the flamboyant, illiterate but successful dealer Louis Victor Flatow determined to outdo him. He commissioned *The Railway Station* from Frith, paying £4,500 for the canvas and the reproduction rights (so said Frith in his *Autobiography;* press reports at the time put the figure at 8,000 or even 10,000 guineas) and an additional £750 for the exhibition rights. When the picture was finished, Flatow devoted full time to exploiting it. In the spring and summer of 1862, 80,000 Londoners and visitors in town for the second international exhibition paid a shilling each to see it in a gallery next to the Haymarket Theatre, while Flatow circulated among them taking orders for the engraving. His investment returned him £30,000.[42]

It was in the exhibitors' and printsellers' ledgers that the preferences of the new mass market for art could most accurately be read. If a Victorian painter wanted to be a financial success in the manner of a Landseer, a Frith, or a Holman Hunt, he selected his subjects and cultivated his technique with an eye directed less toward the usual clientele of the Academy shows than toward the larger public who would pay a shilling to see his painting when shown by a dealer or publisher and subsequently a guinea or two, often less, to buy the engraving thus advertised.

Prints themselves continued to provide Londoners with free sidewalk shows. The tone of these displays was drastically different from that of the robustious Rowlandson-Gillray era; nowhere in London was the effect of the long campaign for the reformation of manners more evident. The bold, often scurrilous, and always lively satirical prints that had formerly drawn knots of appreciative spectators to shop windows disappeared quite suddenly at the time of the First Reform Bill. Many years later Thackeray, in his best *eheu fugaces* vein, regretted the passing of the dealers who specialized in them:

Knight's, in Sweeting's alley; Fairburn's, in a court off Ludgate hill, Hone's, in Fleet street—bright, enchanted pal-

aces, which George Cruikshank used to people with grinning, fantastic imps, and merry, harmless sprites,—where are they? Fairburn's shop knows him no more; not only has Knight disappeared from Sweeting's alley, but, as we are given to understand, Sweeting's alley has disappeared from the face of the globe—Slop, the atrocious Castlereagh, the sainted Caroline (in a tight pelisse, with feathers in her head), the "Dandy of sixty" [the Prince Regent], who used to glance at us from Hone's friendly windows—where are they? Mr. Cruikshank may have drawn a thousand better things, since the days when these were; but they are to us a thousand times more pleasing than anything else he has done. How we used to believe in them! to stray miles out of the way on holidays, in order to ponder for an hour before that delightful window in Sweeting's alley! in walks through Fleet Street, to vanish abruptly down Fairburn's passage, and there make one at his "charming gratis" exhibition. There used to be a crowd round the window in those days of grinning, good-natured mechanics, who spelt the songs, and spoke them out for the benefit of the company, and who received the points of humour with a general sympathizing roar.[43]

Writing as he was for a sedate, respectable mid-Victorian audience, Thackeray soft-pedaled the frequent coarseness and bawdry of those high-spirited prints, but no matter. The point is that in the 1830s they disappeared, and illustrated social satire shortly became the province of weeklies like *Punch*. The void thus created in the array of London shop-window shows was promptly filled, however, by the Boydell-descended branch of the trade, the sellers of illustrated books in parts and separate engravings. After the huge success of *Pickwick Papers,* many novels were published in monthly installments, each containing one or more illustrations, and these were duly displayed in printsellers' and booksellers' windows, as were the copperplate engravings that graced the topographical works and drawing room gift books of the period and the large prints intended for framing. "The fine line engravings after Wilkie's popular pictures," wrote Henry Vizetelly, a member of the trade, long afterward, "found many admirers; while the stupendous proportions and theatrical effects of John Martin's architectural phantasies, with their myriads of seething figures and their suggestions of illimitable space, were gazed at with something like wonderment."[44] There were catchpenny outdoor displays as well. Grubby assortments of second-hand or remaindered prints were arranged in umbrellas spread open on sidewalks or strung on fences, just as Silas Wegg daily displayed his ballads on a clothes horse in *Our Mutual Friend.* *

The various devices by which art was brought to the

* Public exhibitions and the distribution of engravings were linked in another manner by the Art Union, founded in 1837. A subscription of a guinea a year entitled a member to participate in a lottery, the cash prizes of which were earmarked for the purchase of original works from any of the five leading galleries. The winners' choices then were displayed at the Suffolk Street gallery of the Society of British Artists for a fortnight in August. In 1843 over 147,000 persons visited the show. All subscribers received a copy of an engraving the union commissioned and distributed annually. See Anthony King, "George Godwin and the Art Union of London 1837–1911," *Victorian Studies,* 8 (1964), 103–30.

home—among them the influential *Penny Magazine,* which printed many illustrations of famous paintings, statuary, and architectural monuments as part of its comprehensive program to enlighten and humanize the masses—eventually diminished the importance of printsellers' windows as poor men's art galleries. In their place, however, appeared windows devoted to the new art of photography. The familiar displays of portrait engravings gave way in the fifties to camera studies of the same celebrated subjects, from prime minister and poet laureate to Ada Menken, the tights-clad star of *Mazeppa.* In 1855 there were sixty-six photographic studios in London; six years later there were two hundred.[45]

In its first decades photography was the subject of a variety of exhibitions apart from those in the studio windows. The popularity of the photographic show at the Great Exhibition of 1851 led to the first independent photographic exhibition, held by the Society of Arts in the winter of 1852–53, and to the first show of the new Photographic Society a year later. At that moment the Crimean War broke out, and this new form of picture making responded to the challenge in the way the panorama had responded to the Napoleonic Wars. Pioneer field photographers, led by Roger Fenton in his mobile darkroom, sent back thousands of scenes—Fenton alone some three or four hundred. Several exhibitions were devoted to these, including one of Fenton's work at the Pall Mall rooms of the Water-Colour Society and one of James Robertson's at 222 Regent Street.[46]

The old and the new overlapped. Paintings and engravings were shown side by side with photographs. Thus at Colnaghi's, canvases to be engraved—T. Jones Barker's *Allied Generals before Sebastopol* and Winterhalter's picture of the Empress Eugénie and the ladies of her court, both crowded with scores of portrait figures—shared wall space with tinted photographs of the Princess Royal's wedding party.[47] Elsewhere, the Victorian insistence on making things seem what they were not resulted in photographs being disguised as conventional oil paintings. At Dickinson's Portrait Galleries in New Bond Street, there was a shilling show of "some hundreds of important and highly-finished portraits of individuals of celebrity, in talent, rank, and fashion," all of which were either photographs retouched and colored to resemble painted miniatures or, in the case of full-length figures, were painted copies of photographs.[48] This ambiguity would, of course, be largely resolved in coming decades. Although photography would not replace con-

ventional art, as had been wildly predicted during the first stir over Daguerre's and Fox Talbot's inventions ("From today painting is dead!" exclaimed the French artist Hippolyte Delaroche), the emergence of pictorial journalism, a commodity designed to be consumed in the home, did doom more than one large class of London exhibitions.

In this web of relationship between nineteenth-century British art and London exhibitions, two artists recurrently figure: Benjamin Robert Haydon, that tempestuous and luckless blend of idealism, megalomania, and paranoia, and John Martin, the master of cataclysm or, as he was dubbed in *Blackwood's Magazine,* "the King of the Vast."[49] Both painters subscribed to the cult of immensity, and by virtue of that fact each had a strong affinity with the panorama mode. Beyond that, however, their connections with the world of London exhibitions took quite different forms and had different consequences.

Haydon's practice of renting a room in London's most famous hall of miscellaneous entertainment to show one or two enormous paintings (sometimes surrounded by smaller ones) while freaks and variety performers were on display elsewhere in the building, made him the most ridiculed artist of consequence in London. His fellow artists as well as the critics had plenty of other objections to him, but the one they most relied upon throughout their long running quarrel was the claim that he had degraded Art by the vulgarities of the raree showman. One or two of his Egyptian Hall exhibitions achieved the dual end he sought—a clear profit at the box office and gratifying publicity—but the last one literally killed him.

Haydon's first triumphal entry into Piccadilly occurred, as we have seen, in 1820. The next show, of *The Raising of Lazarus* (1823), in the room just vacated by the Laplanders, commenced as auspiciously, with receipts of some thirty pounds a day; but Haydon's creditors closed in, an execution was served on the picture, and the artist was deposited in the King's Bench debtors' prison. His next Egyptian Hall venture, *The Mock Election* (1828), was a moderate success, but then his luck ran out for good. Although he returned to Piccadilly several times in the next decade, each of these ventures was a failure. In 1846 he tried once more.[50] Three thousand pounds in debt, depressed by his failure to win a prize in the design competition for the Westminster frescoes, Haydon hired one of the two rooms on the upper floor of the Egyptian Hall to show his newest canvases, *The Banishment of Aristides* and *The Burning of Rome*. Below him were Catlin's Ioways, nearing the end of their run; across the corridor from his own room and booked to open the same day (Easter Monday) was General Tom Thumb, beginning the second of his farewell engagements. As was his custom, Haydon invited four hundred of the quality to a private view. No more than half a dozen appeared. But as soon as Tom Thumb opened for business, Piccadilly was jammed with the carriages of his admirers. Under the best of circumstances Haydon would not have welcomed the midget's competition; as a Napoleonist who had painted an interminable series of pictures of his hero, he had resented Tom Thumb's impudent Napoleonic impersonations during his first London engagement. The new crowds were the last straw. In the *Times* for 21 April he advertised: "*Exquisite Feeling of the English People for High Art.*— GENERAL TOM THUMB last week received 12,000 people, who paid him £600; B. R. HAYDON, who has devoted forty-two years to elevate their taste, was honoured by the visits of 133½,* producing £5 13 6."

On 4 May the proprietor of the Egyptian Hall billed Haydon £30 for unpaid rent; two weeks later, after the exhibition closed, the men carrying the enormous paintings out of the hall had to maneuver them past the queue on the staircase waiting to get inside General Tom Thumb's show. On 22 June, Haydon shot himself in the head and then cut his throat.

Possibly because he had only a minimal association with the hall, John Martin escaped the obloquy from his fellow artists that was Haydon's lot.[51] He exhibited there only once, in 1822, when, already famous as the painter of *Belshazzar's Feast,* he installed a show including most of his major works to date except for the *Belshazzar,* the centerpiece being the large (eight feet three by five feet four) *Destruction of Pompeii and Herculaneum.* Six years later he exhibited his *Fall of Nineveh* separately, at the Western Exchange, and for the same purpose Haydon had: to make money from the gate receipts. But his more significant and characteristic association with the world of popular exhibitions was due to his absorbed interest in the techniques of contemporary pictorial spectacle: his adoption of the panoramist's characteristic viewpoint (surveying a wide tract from a commanding eminence) and especially his dramatic use of light.† As a pupil-assistant at a firm of glass painters, Martin was persuaded, as he later wrote, that painting on glass "is capable of producing the most splendid and beautiful effects, far superior to

oil-painting or water-colours, for by the transparency we have the means of bringing in real light and have the full scale of nature as to light and as to shadow, as well as to the richness of colour which we have not in oil-painting nor in water-colour." This was an enthusiasm that Gainsborough, the admirer of the Eidophusikon, had acquired before him, resulting in the box with the candle-lit glass slides, and Martin's contemporaries immediately recognized the affinity his luminous canvases had with other popular optical shows. Charles Lamb for one, after having seen *Belshazzar* and *Joshua Commanding the Sun to Stand Still upon Gibeon,* dismissed Martin's art as a "phantasmagoric trick," and the same resemblance occurred to Constable. Writing of a conversation he had had with a friend on the art of Martin and Danby he remarked, "The art is now filled with Phantasmagorias."[52]

Belshazzar's Feast, the tour de force of lurid, violent painting which made Martin's reputation, was a kind of art well suited to the taste of a public whose eyes feasted on panoramas. Displayed at the British Institution in February 1821, it created such a sensation that, like Wilkie's *Chelsea Pensioners* the next year at the Academy, it had to be railed off. The exhibition was kept open an extra three weeks to accommodate the throngs, and when it closed the picture was moved to the Strand shop of Martin's former employer, William Collins, who had bought it for a reputed 800 guineas. Five thousand more people paid to see it there. An added attraction was a copy of the picture painted on glass by Martin himself and let into the wall of the shop, so that, as Samuel Redgrave, the Victorian chronicler of British art, said, "the light was really transmitted through the terrible handwriting."[53] Never had the fine arts and the diorama drawn closer than they did at that moment, but they would be associated in another way in 1833 when Hippolyte Sébron, Daguerre's collaborator in the new double-effect diorama, exhibited at the Queen's Bazaar what was misleadingly billed as "Mr. Martin's Grand Picture of Belshazzar's Feast painted with Dioramic Effect . . . five times as large as the late Mr. B. West's celebrated picture of Death on the Pale Horse . . . [occupying] in magnitude the space of Four Dioramic Views."[54] Martin was not flattered. Giving evidence before a parliamentary inquiry on copyright three years later, he said, "It was a most infamous piece of painting, and the public were given to understand that I was the painter; this was ruining my reputation, and at the same time taking from me that which ought to be my own, my copyright. I endeavoured to stop the exhibi-

---

* Haydon explained that the half was a little girl. Though nameless, she has a special place in the history of British art.

† William Feaver, in his recent *John Martin* (London, 1975), constantly uses terms like "panoramic" and "dioramic" in describing Martin's characteristic art, and he repeatedly alludes to such pictorial entertainments as the Eidophusikon, Girtin's Eidometropolis, the panoramas, and the Lisbon earthquake show at the Cyclorama. He prudently stops short, however, of asserting that Martin was directly influenced by any of these shows.

tion by injunction, but was referred to a jury."[55] Martin was the more sensitive on this point because in 1832 he had probably supervised, and thereby sanctioned, another painting of *Belshazzar's Feast* on glass at the Collins shop.* In 1837 glass copies of *The Fall of Nineveh* and *Joshua* were shown at the Cosmorama Rooms, and several years later at the Polytechnic.[56]

The popularity of Martin's huge, nightmarish paintings, full of writhing casualties of God's or nature's wrath and of pinnacled architectural monstrosities that anticipated the more extravagant efforts of Cecil B. DeMille, had other sources besides the peculiar luminosity that reminded spectators of the phantasmagoria and the Diorama. Always eager to pay its shillings to view pictures of panoramic magnitude, the public welcomed these canvases which in some respects, especially the hundreds of figures whose agony was so convincingly depicted that they seemed actually to move, outdid the competition. If Martin's vast palaces and apocalyptic visitations exceeded in melodramatic "sublimity" anything the panoramas themselves attempted—subjects like his were, of course, not their forte—the doomed populations in their throes offered a *frisson* more intense than any number of *Medusa* rafts as portrayed by either Marshall or Géricault.†

D⳹✳⳹D

As public receptivity developed over the decades, the government slowly came to accept the notion that the production and consumption of art should be encouraged by public funds and institutions. This commitment was long in the making. Apart from grants enabling the British Museum to acquire the Towneley and Hamilton collections of antiquities, public money was not provided in any large amount until Lord Elgin prevailed on the government to buy his Parthenon marbles; even then, the £35,000 given was scandalously short of their cost to him. The marbles had arrived in London in a number of lots between 1803 and 1811. As they accumulated they were stored in what Haydon indignantly described as a "damp, dirty penthouse," perhaps a stable, in the yard behind Lord Elgin's house near Hyde Park Corner. Visitors were admitted on Saturdays and Sundays. In 1809 Haydon pleaded with their owner to erect a building worthy of the sculptures, but, intent on selling them to the nation, he refused. Two years later they were moved to the back yard at Burlington House. After the protracted haggling between the government and Lord Elgin was terminated in 1816 and the British Museum

took possession, they were deposited in two frame sheds adjoining Montagu House, firetraps which would have seen the precious booty destroyed if they had ignited.[57] Here Keats saw them, in a mood that was later recalled and preserved in the "Ode on a Grecian Urn," and here they remained, in squalor and peril, until 1831, when they were installed in a room in the new west wing.

The practice of buying art for public enjoyment—it was far from being an established policy as yet—had had an unpromising beginning. The conviction nonetheless was spreading that art, like practical science, might be a valuable expedient in calming the fevers of a nation in which political and social bitterness was reaching dangerous levels. Money spent for the "cultivation of taste" would be well spent if, as some people thought, it "softens men's manners and suffers them not to be brutal." This novel idea was characteristically expressed in the minutes of the Art Union:

The influence of the fine arts in humanising and refining, in purifying the thoughts and raising the sources of gratification in man, is so universally felt and admitted that it is hardly necessary now to urge it. By abstracting him from the gratification of the senses, teaching him to appreciate physical beauty and to find delight in the contemplation of the admirable accordance of nature, the mind is carried forward to higher aims, and becomes insensibly opened to a conviction of the force of moral worth and the harmony of virtue.[58]

So ran the theory as expressed by the middle-class promoters of public culture when they talked among themselves. In 1848 the Reverend Charles Kingsley, addressing working people directly in his radical paper, *Politics for the People,* translated it into terms calculated to touch their hearts:

Picture-galleries should be the workman's paradise, and garden of pleasure, to which he goes to refresh his eyes and heart with beautiful shapes and sweet colouring, when they are wearied with dull bricks and mortar, and the ugly colourless things which fill the workshop and the factory. . . . Those who live in towns should carefully remember this, for their own sakes, for their wives' sakes, for their children's sakes. *Never lose an opportunity of seeing anything beautiful.* Beauty is God's hand-writing—a way-side sacrament. . . . Therefore . . . picture-galleries should be the townsman's paradise of refreshment. Of course, if he can get the real air, the real trees, even for an hour, let him take it, in God's name; but how many a man who cannot spare time for a daily country walk, may well slip into the National Gallery or any other collection of pictures, for ten minutes. *That* garden, at least, flowers as gaily in winter as in summer.[59]

* It is this later version, painted by G. Hoadley and A. Oldfield, which is displayed at Syon House, Brentford. Unfortunately it has several prominent cracks.

† The last of Martin's associations with London exhibitions occurred in 1853–54, when he was one of the founders of the Panopticon in Leicester Square (see below, Chapter 34). Two other fortuitous ones, however, had taken place much earlier. One of his brothers, William, is said to have exhibited a perpetual motion machine at 28 Haymarket in 1803 (Thomas Balston, *John Martin,* London, 1947, p. 27), and another, Jonathan, set the fire that badly damaged York Minster in 1829, thus providing a spectacular subject for more than one dioramist, cosmoramist, and model maker.

Stripped of at least its overt sentimentality, it was this notion which, among others, supplied the justification for supporting the National Gallery with public funds.

London had been the last major European capital to acquire a governmentally sponsored art collection. Vienna had had one since 1781, Paris since 1793, and other cities had followed. Agitation for a public gallery in London had begun among some influential painters, including West, early in the century, but it was only with the receipt of an unanticipated windfall, the Austrian government's partial payment of a twenty-five-year-old war debt, that funds became available. At that moment (1823) John Julius Angerstein's collection of Old Masters came on the market, and the money was used to buy it and the house it occupied in Pall Mall, which was opened to the public in May 1824.[60] There were only thirty-eight pictures to begin with, but this nucleus soon attracted others by gift and purchase, with the result that the house, already proving unsuitable for other reasons, could not hold them all. In 1834, therefore, the National Gallery moved five doors west, to 105 Pall Mall. This larger building also soon lacked sufficient space, and four years later the gallery was provided with its first expressly designed home facing the newly laid-out Trafalgar Square.

This was a step in the right direction, but, as it turned out, a very inadequate one. Half the building was given over to the Royal Academy, which moved there from Somerset House. The nation's paintings—still not numerous or distinguished in comparison with continental galleries; Ruskin called the collection "an European Jest"[61]—were hung in four large galleries and two small ones. The floor space quickly became as crowded as the walls. In the first year at Trafalgar Square the gallery attracted 397,000 persons as compared with a maximum of 127,000 in the former building; the second year's attendance exceeded half a million.[62]

These figures would seem to have vindicated the liberal confidence that the public at large had a serious desire to look at pictures, but the situation was not quite that simple. Entrance was free to all, and when the original building was first opened, Lord Liverpool, the prime minister, expressly hoped that parents would bring their children.[63] They did so, especially on "Saint Monday," the informal working-class holiday, as part of a socially variegated crowd such as had never before been seen at a London art gallery, except, perhaps, when the *Chelsea Pensioners* was hung. "Nobility [came] in their coroneted carriages; gentry in their several vehicles; and tradespeople, country folk, young persons, and well-dressed domestics in their holiday clothes on foot," according to the tract writer George Mogridge, who could not quite decide whether the scene heartened or displeased him.

Three sailors have just walked in with blue jackets. There! I have hit off a sketch of one of them—a veteran, in a canvass hat, as he now sits, with one leg flung across the other, looking as independent as a lord. He is gazing on the Holy Family, by Murillo. Well, a tough sailor has some tender touches of feeling in his heart, and that painting of Murillo is as likely as any that I know to call them forth. There are a few among the company walking about with their hats in their hands, and well would it be could they prevail on the rest, by their more civilized, courteous, and respectful demeanour, to follow their example; but no, it will not do. It is only striving against an irresistible stream.[64]

If Kingsley felt any such ambivalence, he concealed it. "It is delightful," he wrote, "to watch in a picture-gallery some street-boy enjoying himself; how first wonder creeps over his rough face, and a sweeter, more earnest, awe-struck look, till his countenance seems to grow handsomer and nobler on the spot, and drink in and reflect unknowingly, the beauty of the picture he is studying."[65] One would think, however, that transfigured crossing sweepers were moderately rare phenomena in the National Gallery. The more usual behavior of the masses in an art gallery, it appears, was to adopt it as a pleasant picnicking locale, convenient and out of the weather. Parties of country people drew up the benches in a circle and opened their lunch baskets, and when an official expostulated they matily invited him to sit down with them and have a pull at their bottle.[66]

Art lovers and idlers alike complained of the heating and ventilation. An attendant told a Select Committee of Commons in 1841 that the ventilation at Trafalgar Square (to borrow the feeling words of a later critic) was "disgusting and pernicious."[67] Another complaint, touching the gallery's educational role, had to do with catalogues. The shilling which one saved at the entrance might be invested in a catalogue, but this consisted only of a bare list, in large type, of the 163 pictures owned as of 1838—no more matter than could have been printed on a sheet the size of a playbill and sold for a penny. In the busy months of 1840 (April–September) only 4,751 persons out of the 300,000 and more who entered the building bought copies, though many more came equipped with unauthorized reprints which "extraofficial persons," namely hawkers, sold outside the door for threepence.[68] All in all, the principle established by the founding of the National Gallery was more satisfactory than the way it was so far implemented.

A related event which happened to coincide with the move to Trafalgar Square had a significance which was mostly symbolic. At his death in January 1837 the architect Sir John Soane, having forehandedly obtained a special act of Parliament accepting the conditions he laid down, bequeathed to the nation his house and museum in Lincoln's Inn Fields and all their contents, a large and diversified collection of antiquities and works of art, including Hogarth's *Rake's Progress* and *Election Entertainment*. The house was crammed with thousands of artistic and architectural curios, making it, as a writer in the *Penny Magazine* said, "an architectural kaleidoscope, presenting a great variety of combinations within a very small space."[69] At the rear was the museum proper, consisting of an Egyptian sepulchral chamber designed to supply an appropriate setting for the fine sarcophagus Belzoni had tried in vain to sell to the British Museum, and a suite of rooms reminiscent of Walpole's Strawberry Hill: the cell, oratory, monastery, and grave of a hypothetical monk named Padre Giovanni, each room fitted out with the furnishings appropriate to its role in the life of "a man of refined taste as well as severe austerity."

Describing this monastic version of Bullock's habitat display technique, the *Penny Magazine* writer, addressing a reading audience of serious-minded workingmen, found himself somewhat at a loss when he considered the inevitable question of its practical usefulness. The house itself, to be sure, offered no problem: it was "a model-house, intended for architects, artists, and persons of taste . . . more for the benefit of a class, than for the use of the public indiscriminately." Artisans engaged in the interior decorating trade, he was confident, would find it of much interest. But "different minds will form different opinions" of the monk's complex, "accordingly as they may think the idea the product of poetry or quackery." In his effort to create a setting in which his lifelong accumulation of curios would be appropriately and harmoniously housed, Soane had approached the perilous border of the artifice and incongruity which characterized some kinds of exhibitions as well as antiquarian "improvements" on country estates:

Certainly an apology appears requisite for some of its details—for the monastery and monk's abode savour not a little of that trifling spirit which creates mimic waterfalls and builds interesting ruins. Yet one almost fancies that the venerable architect, so sensitive about his character and fame,

frowns, from the monk's parlour, on any attempt to apologize for any creation of his, costing him, as it did, thought, time and money. Let the reader examine them before he condemns. If the idea be sanctioned at all, it must be admitted that, in the present instance, the details are very well executed. Sir John Soane appears to have acted on the maxim—let there be variety, and let each variety be unique of its kind. And great variety there certainly is.

—An observation with which any present-day visitor to the house is bound to agree. But few readers of the *Penny Magazine* or any other periodical found their way to the museum, to examine before they condemned or approved. Unlike the National Gallery, Soane's benefaction to the nation could be visited only by holders of tickets obtained from the trustees, a practice which had effectively held down attendance at the British Museum during its first half century. Some of the income from the £30,000 endowment was devoted to paying six guards, whose duties could hardly have been onerous: the building was open only about 40 or 50 days each year, and was closed entirely for five months out of the twelve.[70] The total annual attendance was never more than 3,000, and even in 1851, when London swarmed with sightseers and as a special concession the museum was open for 108 days, the average daily traffic was only 77 persons.[71]

Other public-spirited gestures at the same time were more fruitful. In 1838 Queen Victoria ordered that twenty-nine rooms at Hampton Court Palace be opened gratis, without the "discretionary amount" formerly paid to the housekeeper.* Although, as a writer in *Fraser's Magazine* pointed out, the arrangements were not ideal, it was a step in the right direction:

The company are led by a guide, who allows them to remain before each picture only during the time spent in pronouncing its subject and painter; a period distributed with the strictest impartiality between the sublimest productions of Raphael and the poorest Dutch performances. In private mansions some slight mitigation may be obtained, but this is precluded by the tone of authority assumed in the royal residences. Lately, however, along with the remission of the moderate fee, the public obtained the more important privilege of being allowed to spend any time they pleased in viewing the pictures. They are only subject to a somewhat capricious limit, that no one shall step back to take a second view of one, even though in the same apartment; yet this is what one feels often inclined to do.[72]

The most impressive demonstration of popular interest in art before the middle of the century occurred in connection with the Westminster fresco

* The palace had received 1,200 paintings of all qualities when George IV dismantled Kensington Palace. Small fees still were charged to see the orangery and the great vine and to get lost in the maze. In 1840 the grounds were visited by 122,339 persons, who were described before a Select Committee of Commons the next year as being, many of them, from "the lower class; they come in vans; sometimes . . . 60, 70, and 80 vans in a day, each van containing nearly 30 persons." Their behavior was generally exemplary despite the temptation to pick the flowers. There was some trouble, however, with "men coming in tipsy, and being sick." (*Report from the Select Committee on National Monuments,* 1841, qq. 2310–34 passim.)

146. Social commentary on the Westminster fresco exhibition: John Leech's *Substance and Shadow* (*Punch,* 8 July 1843). The drawing represents an ordinary picture gallery, not the cartoons for the frescoes as they were actually displayed in Westminster Hall. Leech evidently had made the drawing before the exhibition opened on 3 July and overlooked the fact that the cartoons would be much larger and confined to a certain class of subject.

competition.[73] After their original plan to hire German artists to decorate the new Houses of Parliament stirred protests that the government was neglecting British art, the Royal Commissioners decided to offer ten prizes for the best cartoons submitted by native artists on subjects from British history, Shakespeare, Spenser, or Milton. One hundred and fifty artists competed, their entries being displayed in Westminster Hall beginning on 3 July 1843. During the first twelve days, when a shilling was charged for admission, the show had a daily average of 1,800 visitors.[74] After it was thrown open free (except on Saturday afternoons), it drew large crowds. The size of the cartoons perhaps had something to do with the show's popularity: eyes accustomed to panoramas could appreciate pictures which, by the rules of the competition, had to be "no less than ten nor more than fifteen feet in their longest dimension" and the figures life-size. But there were

also the facts that this art show was free (which was otherwise true only of the National Gallery) and that it was held in a spacious setting (which was not true of the cramped National Gallery).

The crowds that year and the next, when the judges, having failed to award any contracts to the winners of the first competition, decreed a fresh contest for actual frescoes and statuary, evoked considerable comment in the press. When the first show opened, *Punch,* caught in a dilemma between two of its early (radical) principles, the people's right to a free show and their claim to a decent life, including freedom from starvation, reacted savagely. John Leech's drawing "*Substance and Shadow*" was captioned, "The poor ask for bread, and the philanthropy of the State accords . . . an exhibition."[75] The following year *Blackwood's Magazine* published a fourteen-stanza poem entitled "Westminster-Hall and the Works of Art, (On a Free-Admission

Day)'' which expressed a more approving, if senti-mental, view of the phenomenon. Three of the stanzas fairly represent the whole:

O! ye who doubt presumptuously that feeling, taste, are
    given
To all for culture, free as flowers, by an impartial heaven,
Look through this quiet rabble here—doth it not shame
    to-day
More polish'd mobs to whom we owe our annual squeeze in
    May?
Mark that poor Maiden, to her Sire interpreting the tale
There pictured of the Loved and Left, until her cheek grows
    pale:—
Yon crippled Dwarf that sculptured Youth eyeing with
    glances dim,
Wondering will he, in higher worlds, be tall and straight like
    him;—
. . . .
How well they group with yonder pale but fire-eyed
    Artisan,
Who just has stopp'd to bid his boys those noble features
    scan
That sadden us for WILKIE! See! he tells them now the story
Of that once humble lad, and how he won his marble
    glory.[76]

There were more shows in the years following, but the public lost interest as Parliament continued to squabble over the appropriation of funds and the commissioners continued to vacillate. The unexpected popularity of the first two exhibitions, however, gave fresh ammu-nition to those who sought to gain wider free access to art for the people, if necessary through government initiative and subsidy.*

Meanwhile, the free admission policy at Trafalgar Square was running into opposition. In 1850 a Select Committee of Commons received fresh testimony that "the Gallery is frequently crowded by large masses of people, consisting not merely of those who come for the purpose of seeing the pictures, but also of persons having obviously for their object the use of the rooms for wholly different purposes; either for shelter in case of bad weather, or as a place in which children of all ages may recreate and play and not unfrequently as one where food and refreshments may conveniently be taken."[77]

The crowd problem increased as the collection grew. The gallery had to absorb a steady stream of ac-quisitions, notably the Vernon collection of modern British art in 1847. The same five rooms whose walls had barely accommodated 163 pictures in 1838 now were hung with over 300, some of great size, with the inevitable result that many were, for practical pur-poses, out of sight.[78] It was little wonder, then, that still another, this time really satisfactory building to house the national collection figured prominently in the Prince Consort's scheme, unrealized in that form, for a cultural center in South Kensington after the Crystal Palace had helped spread enthusiasm for the arts in general.

It was an enthusiasm which sprang from a vague persuasion that art was "good" (and somehow useful) rather than from any tangible fund of information or perception. The average Londoner's experience of art, as Ruskin found it in the fifties, had been confined to the various kinds of copies described in the preceding chapter; to engravings, which were becoming ever more plentiful and more widely distributed; and to at-tendance at various temporary shows of celebrated individual works of art and, under less than ideal con-ditions, at the National Gallery. The rest of the places where art could be seen—the annual exhibitions, the displays of individual paintings at print publishers' show rooms—were theoretically open to all who had a shilling to spare, but in practice their hospitality did not extend below a certain plainly respectable portion of the middle class. If, as Ruskin lamented, the British public at large had no genuine aesthetic sensitivity, no awareness or respect for great art; if it was, in artistic matters, as Philistine as Matthew Arnold would later join Ruskin in declaring it was; if art simply did not play a significant role in everyday life, there were sufficient reasons (apart from one's personal reading of human nature) why this should have been so.

* At the 1843 show a discovery was made which would have been of interest to the officials at the Na-tional Gallery in connection with their own printed-catalogue problem. Prince Albert and his collaborators, ever eager to popularize information, prepared a sixpenny pamphlet con-taining all the literary quotations which the fresco cartoons illustrated. Mindful of the National Gallery's experience, Charles Eastlake abridged this catalogue into one which sold for a penny, but the poorly dressed visitors preferred to buy the more expensive one. (Winslow Ames, *Prince Albert and Victorian Taste,* New York, 1968, p. 52.) Pioneers in this field often discovered that the behav-ior of the newly enfranchised public defied all logic.

Entr'acte: Inside the Exhibition Business

30

A "moderate calculation" in 1851, referring to past years' experience and not to the unexampled boom of that Crystal Palace year, concluded that some £4,000,000 was spent annually by London sightseers.[1] This can only have been the most speculative of guesses, but it is probably as credible as any such figure from the time can be. Although the total volume of the exhibition business cannot be reliably ascertained, it is obvious that exhibitions were subject not only to the forces that governed all kinds of commercial enterprises but, in addition, to those peculiar to the entertainment world. Wholly dependent as they were on the caprices of public interest, exhibitions were at least as risky investments as theatre pieces. The loss suffered by the unfortunate impresario of the rhinoceros in 1684 foreshadowed innumerable financial disasters in the trade for the next two centuries, although only a few were on the scale of John Braham's at the Colosseum. Bankruptcies, forced sales, and seizures of property were common occurrences. All too typical was the experience of a Mr. Illius, proprietor of a well-thought-of model of Venice at the Egyptian Hall: when he fell behind in his rent, the executors of Lackington, the late proprietor of the hall, seized the model, placed it in a damp cellar, and thus deprived him of the only means he had of paying them. A subscription was begun to rescue his unfortunate family.[2]

On the other hand, some astute or lucky proprietors of London exhibitions earned respectable competences. Henry Aston Barker was well off when he retired from the panorama business in 1822, and William Bullock seems to have made a small fortune from various Egyptian Hall attractions, though it is likely that at least part of the money he used to buy the thousand-acre estate across the river from Cincinnati came from his Mexican silver mine.

Regrettably, there are virtually no specific, let alone dependable, data to support an economic analysis of the exhibition trade.* But from an unattributed report of earnings at the three-day Bartholomew Fair in 1827 we can derive at least an idea of the range of the revenue at various kinds of attractions and their comparative drawing power:

Wombwell's menagerie	£1700
Richardson's theatre	1200
Atkins' menagerie	1000
Morgan's menagerie	150
The pig-faced lady	150
The fat boy and girl	140
The head of William Corder, the "Red Barn" murderer	100
Ballad's menagerie	90
Ball's theatre	80
The diorama of Navarino	60
Chinese jugglers	50
Pike's theatre	40
The fire eater	30
Frazer's theatre	26
Keyes and Line's theatre	20
The Scotch giant	20[3]

The printed records do contain frequent reports, for

* One partial exception is the Surrey Zoological Gardens, whose official archives, or what seem to be such, are contained in eight large scrapbooks in the British Library. They contain a fair amount of business correspondence, from which we learn, for example, that Barnum charged £45 for a single appearance by General Tom Thumb. (To put this price in perspective, it is interesting to note that the famous ballet dancer Taglioni received £120 a night at the same time. But since for a long time Tom Thumb appeared every day at the gardens in addition to his engagements at the Egyptian Hall and elsewhere, Barnum doubtless gave the management a special rate.) Among these records there are, however, no ledgers or other financial accounts.

whatever they may be worth, of the money taken in at various unusually popular indoor shows. These figures have often been cited in the preceding chapters. But although they are reasonably good indications of how large gross income might be over periods of various lengths, they are seldom accompanied by mentions of net profit. There are a few bits of evidence as to expenses. We know, for example, that the Society of Painters in Water-Colours paid £200 each year for its three-month occupancy of the Great Room, Spring Gardens, and subsequently the same amount for the "Roman Gallery" at the Egyptian Hall; and that George Catlin paid £550 a year for the "large room"—they may have been identical—in the same building.[4] The sketches from which panoramists painted their canvases cost them substantial sums. In 1808 Barker was said to have given the artist William Alexander 70 guineas for a view he had drawn of Rio de Janeiro,* and about the same time he paid the Egyptologist Henry Salt 100 guineas for the use of a set of drawings of the pyramids.[5] Almost forty years later, however, Robert Burford paid David Roberts only £50 for the copyright of a panoramic drawing Roberts had made of Cairo. Each of the four-scene dioramas which Thomas Hamlet commissioned from Roberts and Stanfield for the Oxford Street Bazaar brought the pair £800.[6]

The only detailed breakdown of a given exhibition's total receipts and expenditures so far encountered appeared in a paid advertisement, headed "The Papyro-Museum, or, Casting Pearls Before Swine," in the *Times* for 15 September 1832. This venture by two worthy sisters, to which allusion has already been made, had not succeeded, and someone bought space in the paper to exhibit their balance sheet:

déjeuné goers, and ostentatious patrons of virtu. . . . If this be not disgusting, if it be not an eternal disgrace, if it fail to rouse deep indignation, and to justify the bitterest contempt, then what can or ought?"—and much more to the same accusatory effect. But whatever conclusion regarding the state of public taste might be drawn from the guileless paper-cutters' loss of £30 5s. 11d., the inexorable fact remained that, as Mr. Micawber once memorably pointed out, the difference between happiness and misery—or success and failure—was simply the difference between income and outgo. And in the eternally unpredictable circumstances of show business, no one could be sure that the odd shilling would fall on the right side of the balance.

Although the internal affairs of the London shows remain in inscrutable darkness, the efforts exerted to make them turn a profit are a matter of conspicuous public record. Surviving pictures of the crude pictorial banners flaunted before the booths at Bartholomew Fair and the ill-printed handbills of eighteenth-century Fleet Street shows are among the oldest memorabilia of commercial publicity. In addition, some exhibitors bought space in the London newspapers as early as the first years of the eighteenth century. They quickly cultivated the extravagant rhetoric and the devices of wily deception which would mark their descendants' professional language down through the years, to the irremediable corruption of the historical record. In the nineteenth century, established attractions such as the Leicester Square panorama, the Diorama, the Colosseum, and the Polytechnic, and individual exhibitors at places like the Egyptian Hall and the Cosmorama Rooms, advertised both in the daily papers and in such widely circulated middlebrow weeklies as the *Athenaeum* and the *Illustrated London News*. This expense

				£	s	d
Debit	Twelve weeks' rent of room			25	4	0
	Carpenters' and drapers' bills			11	3	1
	Three printers' bills			11	2	0
	Advertisements in daily and weekly papers			27	4	6
	Salaries of receiver, check-taker, placard men			25	19	0
	Sundries, including carriage, insurance, postage, magnifying glasses, stationery			8	5	4
				108	17	11
Credit	Admissions	£71	11s.			
	Catalogues	7	1	78	12	0
			LOSS	30	5	11

"Reflect on this," commanded the advertiser, "ye directors of public taste and opinion, opera goers,

must be considerable, especially in the days when newspaper advertisements were taxed. Lesser

* This does not seem to have been used. Rio de Janeiro was first the subject of a panorama in Leicester Square in 1828.

147. Sign bearers advertising exhibitions (watercolors by George Scharf the elder, various dates).

enterprises, however, seldom went beyond distributing handbills and pasting posters on walls.

In this dawning age of modern advertising, show publicity was by no means restricted to handbills and newsprint. The Diorama and Burford's panorama were among the first London businesses to advertise on the outside of the new omnibuses. In the thirties the puffery that men like Carlyle and John Stuart Mill deplored spread from buses, billboards, and sidewalk inscriptions to sandwich men and men garbed in appropriate and attention-catching costume. In 1835 the *Athenaeum* observed, probably with considerable truth, that "the advertisement is often far more satisfactory than the show itself."[7] Especially conspicuous, if not universally applauded, were the wagons that helped clog traffic in the busiest West End streets. They were described by a German visitor at mid-century:

Behold, rolling down from Oxford Street, three immense wooden pyramids—their outsides are painted all over with hieroglyphics and with monumental letters in the English language. These pyramids display faithful portraits of Isis

and Osiris, of cats, storks, and of the apis; and amidst these old-curiosity-shop gods, any Englishman may read an inscription, printed in letters not much longer than a yard, from which it appears that there is now on view a panorama of Egypt—one more beautiful, interesting, and instructive than was ever exhibited in London. For this panorama—we are still following the inscription—shows the flux and reflux of the Nile, with its hippopotamuses and crocodiles, and a section of the Red Sea, as mentioned in Holy Writ, and part of the last overland mail, and also the railway from Cairo to Alexandria, exactly as laid out in Mr. Stephenson's head. And all this for only one shilling! With a full, lucid, and interesting lecture into the bargain.

The pyramids advance within three yards from where we stand, and, for a short time, they take their ease in the very midst of all the lights, courting attention. But the policeman on duty respects not the monuments of the Pharaohs; he moves his hand, and the drivers of the pyramids, though hidden in their colossal structures, see and understand the signs. . . . The Panorama of the Nile, the Overland Route, the Colosseum, Madame Tussaud's Exhibition of Wax-works, and other sights, are indeed wonder-works of human industry, skill, and invention; and, in every respect, are they superior to the usual productions of the same kind. But, for all that, they must send their advertising vans into the streets; necessity compels them to strike the gong and blow the trumpet; choice there is none. They must either advertise or perish.[8]

In what was probably the most novel of all advertising devices the trade employed, the management of the Nile panorama sent balloons aloft to shower down pink or golden tissue-paper envelopes containing vouchers redeemable for half-price tickets.[9]

Members of the press got their free passes and discount tickets by post or messenger and shared them with friends and relatives. Some entrepreneurs went further and offered refreshments, even whole dinners, in conjunction with their previews. A few editors and reporters seem to have responded to their invitations only with a heavy sense of rectitude. Commenting on the press preview of Kenny Meadows's pictures of the burning of the Houses of Parliament, one journalist wrote:

As we could not, consistently with our sense of public duty, and the respectability of the public press, partake of the good things that were lavishly provided upon the occasion, we admit that we did not stay much above an hour in the room. We are sorry that Mr. Meadows should have formed such an opinion of the Press as to think a feast necessary to secure a favourable report of his exhibition; much more do we regret that the conduct of some of our brethren should serve to justify that opinion. How some of our contemporaries could form a just opinion of Mr. Meadows' pictures, with their heads *full* of Mr. Meadows' wine, is beyond our comprehension.[10]

This was in 1836. Despite such occasional bracing avowals of uncorruptibility, the press continued to be amenable to showmen's hospitality, a fact Vidocq recognized when he maintained a private bar for newspapermen during his exhibition at the Cosmorama Rooms.[11] The press preview, expertly catered and adequately supplied with spirits, was public relations money well used. Albert Smith, always a lavish spender, encouraged favorable notices for his *Ascent of Mont Blanc* show by having oysters and champagne laid on by Rule's, the Covent Garden caterers.[12] Whether a man from the *Athenaeum* attended these free festivities is not on record, but in 1859 the paper proclaimed its integrity when confronted by the following invitation: "The proprietor of the Talking and Performing Fish presents his compliments to the Editor of the Athenaeum, and will be proud of his presence (or representative) at the private Exhibition, on Wednesday, May 4, at any time between the hours of 11 and 5

o'clock. Dinner (to which gentlemen present at the private view are respectfully invited) at the Gordon Hotel, 3, Piazza, Covent Garden, at 6 o'clock." "The purpose of this Fish dinner," the editor (or his representative) wrote, "obviously was to put wine into the ink. The public were to see the Talking Fish under a post-prandial hue. By the higher members of the press we know that such hints at corruption are spurned with anger; and we confidently hope that no English gentleman who wields a pen in the public service could be found to accept so coarse a bribe."[13] But if the writer had presented himself at the Gordon Hotel at six o'clock, he would in all probability have discovered a sizable company of—if not precisely English gentlemen who wielded their pens in the public service—hungry and thirsty London journalists.

The fact was that, however moralistic the tone some papers adopted toward "bought" publicity, much of the attention the exhibitions received in the daily and weekly papers took the form of planted items. Some puffs, posing as news stories or reviews, unquestionably were bought outright. The publicity costs of Wilkie's unsuccessful one-man show of paintings in 1812 were broken down into £72 for advertisements and £16 for what his first biographer delicately called "newspaper paragraphs."[14] This may or may not have been, for the time, a typical cost ratio between acknowledged and covert advertising, but throughout the era access to the entertainment news columns of some papers was a salable commodity. It is equally plain that many if not most routine "reviews" were actually press releases which, even if their translation from manuscript to type was not accompanied by the transfer of money, at least saved the paper the expense of a reporter. Only in the case of negative criticisms can one be fairly sure they did not originate with the proprietor.

The conditions of the exhibition business being what they were—fiercely competitive, with a long tradition of hyperbolic language and almost routine misrepresentation or suppression of facts—ordinary business ethics were at a deep discount. In newspaper advertising, for instance—the palpably excessive claims of such establishments as Vauxhall and the Surrey Gardens are among the exceptions—deceit took the form largely of omission or ambiguity, or the inexact use of words like "panorama" and "diorama." An exhibition of "grand tableaux" might well turn out, on inspection, to be nothing more than a series of peepshows. In handbills and placards, however, the showmen threw off whatever restraints may have governed their statements in the *Times* and the *Athenaeum*. There they drew upon every trick of the trade as well as every font of type in the printer's cases: the declaration of the exhibit's rarity or strict uniqueness; the claim that it had already been shown to admiring multitudes, preeminent among them royalty, the nobility, and the gentry (and, in suitable contexts, the clergy); the often related claim that it had been a sensation on the continent, where it had been visited and approved by the leading savants; the attempt, where there was more than a single attraction, to multiply and magnify the components into seeming to represent a full afternoon's or evening's entertainment; the grave protestation of the exhibit's genuineness, indignantly repulsing any suggestion that fraud was involved; sometimes an extravagant assertion of the cost of the machine or objet d'art.

One customary claim seems to have been calculated to appeal to the prevailing work ethic: the allegation that such-and-such a piece was the product of x years of devoted labor. This was no novelty: as early as 1709 Jacobus Morian's moving picture had been recommended to the public on the ground that it had required five years to build. But this article of Puritan morality—the virtue of single-minded, dedicated labor—had an even stronger and wider sanction in the first part of the nineteenth century, with the result that one exhibit after another was claimed to have been the work of half a lifetime: the Wonderful Clock (thirty-four years), the Euterpeon (twenty-six), the Euphonia (twenty-five), the Eureka and the Rock Harmonicon (thirteen each). Models required as much patience: one of Edinburgh took seventeen years, one of St. Peter's, Rome, fourteen; the Taj Mahal required twelve, and Cologne Cathedral eight years and seventeen days. Compared with these, the ill-fated Papyro-Museum (four years) and Gurk's Panharmonicon (seven) would seem to have been thrown together on a weekend. Whatever aesthetic interest such objects of pseudo-art may have possessed was subordinated to the ethical, if not actually ignored; rooms containing them became in effect secular shrines, the objects being hallowed by the sweat of their artificers' brains and fingers.

No one, of course, ever mistook a showman's handbill for a sworn affidavit. In this world, mendacity was taken for granted and, except by the most naive, automatically discounted. But once in a while an unfettered and vehemently self-righteous press pounced on what it deemed to be an especially egregious attempt to deceive. (Only rarely, in the case of certain anatomical Venuses and the Living Skeleton, for example, was the actual nature of an exhibition denounced. The usual ground for complaint was simply that a show failed to live up to its billing.) In 1820 the *Literary Gazette,* which had a notably sensitive nose for humbug, attacked "the Historical and Allegorical Picture, of the Spanish Inquisition, painted by V. A. Revelli, Professor of Painting in the University of Turin, and Member of the Imperial Academy of Sciences":

A red-hot piece of canvas, designated as above, is on exhibition in Pall Mall; and many as have been the sights of London which we have visited, we must say that this excels them all, for the grossness of its imposition. A miserable, indecent, and offensive daub, as a work of art not superior to the pictures which one sees for a half-penny by looking through the magnifying glass of a peep-show, is placed in a darkened room, and by the paltry trick of lighting it from below, made to look like a bad transparency. And for a view of this hoax, honest Mr. Bull is charged a shilling, besides the purchase of a pamphlet descriptive of the allegory—as if it were pleasant to pay for the particulars of the cheat practised upon his credulity.[15]

Three years later the same journal descended on an exhibition of paintings of mythological subjects by one "Signor Reina," who was advertised (though not in its pages) as "the Modern Correggio":

In our lives we never saw such a waste of canvas. . . . David's Coronation rises in esteem at the view.* The most absurd anomalies; combinations that would disgrace the infancy of the Art and its rudest medleys; naked forms rendered odious and indecent by bad painting: such constitute the merits of this shameful and shamefully bepuffed Exhibition. We know of no visitors for whom it is fit, except the Agents of the Society for the Suppression of Vice; and we have only to add, that a more indelicate, nasty, impudent, trumpery show, was never offered to a British public.[16]

These assaults were aimed only at fly-by-night exhibitions on the fringes of the trade, which probably deserved them. The more substantial shows enjoyed generally amicable relations with the press, which was inclined to praise their virtues and overlook their shortcomings.

Such exhibitions also enjoyed from time to time one other source of free publicity, the topical extravaganzas mounted at the major theatres in the holiday seasons. The most generous dispenser was James Planché, at least four of whose productions were based on, or had scenes alluding to, the exhibitions that were competing with them at the moment. The first of these was *The Drama at Home* (Haymarket, 1844). In the

* Touted as "the largest picture ever painted," this canvas had received a blistering review in the same paper some six months earlier (7 December 1822, pp. 775–76).

finale, entitled "Grand Anomalous Procession of the London Exhibitions," the master of ceremonies, played by the younger Charles Mathews, asked The Drama (Mrs. Glover), "Will you receive the London Exhibitions?"

The Drama: Yes, for I'm told there are such sights to see
The town has scarcely time to think of me.

March. Enter in procession, and preceded by Banner-Bearers and Boardmen, the Ojibbeway Indians, General Tom Thumb, the Centrifugal Railway,* Madame Tussaud, with Commissioner Lin and his favourite Consort,† the Industrious Fleas, Diver and Diving Bell, and the Chinese Collection.

There ensued songs not worth quoting: Puff (a stock character, symbolizing showmanship) on the Ojibbeways, gibberish set to the tune of "Jim along Josey"; Ariel, advancing with Tom Thumb, singing to the tune of "Yankee Doodle," "Every wonder here to send, / Jonathan's a mania"; and Puff again on the Centrifugal Railway to the tune of "A Frog He Would a Wooing Go". Then:

Ariel: (Tune: "Sweet Kitty Clover")
To see you in clover, comes Madame Tussaud,
O, o, o, o, O, o, o, o!
Your model in wax-work she wishes to shew,
O, o, [etc.]
The King of the French and Fieschi the traitor,
Commissioner Lin and the Great Agitator,
Kings, Princes, and Ministers all of them go,
O, o, [etc.]
To sit for their portraits to Madame Tussaud.
O, o, [etc.]

Punch: (Tune: "Gee up Dobbin")
You talk about wonders! just look upon these;
You'd think them two little industrious fleas;
But just through a microscope peep at their mugs,
And these two little fleas become horrid hum*bugs!*
Gee up Dobbin, gee up Dobbin,
Gee up Dobbin, gee up and gee-whoa!

Ariel: ("The deep deep sea")
Oh don't he look a love, (pointing to DIVER)
In his helmet and coatee,
Rendered waterproof to rove,
In the deep deep sea!
Than the wave he dives below,
He can cut a greater swell,
And to match this diving Beau,
Here behold a diving *Bell!*
For a shilling if you please,
You inside may take a seat,
And an ocean sound at ease
In the midst of Regent Street.
Oh, don't he look a love, etc.

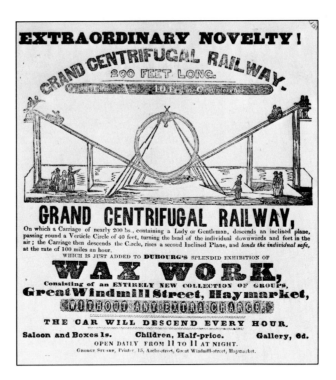

EXTRAORDINARY NOVELTY!
GRAND CENTRIFUGAL RAILWAY.
200 FEET LONG.

GRAND CENTRIFUGAL RAILWAY,
On which a Carriage of nearly 200 lbs., containing a Lady or Gentleman, descends an inclined plane, passing round a Verticle Circle of 40 feet, turning the head of the individual downwards and feet in the air; the Carriage then descends the Circle, rises a second Inclined Plane, and *lands the individual safe,* at the rate of 100 miles an hour.
WHICH IS JUST ADDED TO **DUBOURG'S** SPLENDID EXHIBITION OF
WAX WORK,
Consisting of an ENTIRELY NEW COLLECTION OF GROUPS.
Great Windmill Street, Haymarket,
WITHOUT ANY EXTRA CHARGE.
THE CAR WILL DESCEND EVERY HOUR.
Saloon and Boxes 1s.   Children, Half-price.   Gallery, 6d.
OPEN DAILY FROM 11 TO 11 AT NIGHT.
GEORGE STUART, Printer, 15, Archer-street, Great Windmill-street, Haymarket.

148. Handbill advertising the Centrifugal Railway in Great Windmill Street, 1842.

Puff: ("Chinese Dance")
Ching-a-ring-a-ring-ching! Feast of Lanterns!
What a crop of chop-sticks, hongs and gongs!
Hundred thousand Chinese crinkum-crankums,
Hung among the bells and ding-dongs!
What a lot of Pekin pots and pipkins,
Mandarins with pig-tails, rings and strings,
Funny little slop-shops, cases, places
Stuck about with cups and tea things!
Women with their ten toes tight tucked into
Tiddle-toddle shoes one scarcely sees;
How they all got here is quite a wonder!
China must be broken to pieces![17]

Planché returned to the topic of current exhibitions in *The New Planet; or, Harlequin out of Place* (Haymarket, 1847). The new planet was Neptune, discovered the preceding September, and the action involved Neptune's descending by the stroke of Harlequin's wand, along with the older planets, to the Colosseum and then the Polytechnic. An exhibitor demonstrated, with songs, the electric telegraph and the explosive effects of gun cotton. Then to the Egyptian Hall for "a mysterious lady" and the Ethiopian Serenaders (*Earth:* "Tarnation! / Why, here's another Yankee importation!"), and finally to the opera houses for samples of the singers and airs then in fashion.[18]

There was, in fact, a healthy symbiotic relationship

* An amusement park device demonstrated at Dubourg's Mechanical Theatre and at the Egyptian Hall. A car with a passenger aboard went down an inclined plane, looped the loop at the bottom of the dip, and had sufficient momentum left to climb a plane at the opposite end of the run. The ride was said to last five and a half seconds and the car, it was claimed, reached a speed of one hundred miles an hour. ([George Mogridge], *Old Humphrey's Walks in London and Its Neighbourhood,* London, 1843, p. 211; handbill, GL, Egyptian Hall folder.)

† Commissioner Lin Tse-hsu, the Chinese high official deputed to smash the opium trade, figured prominently in dispatches from the Orient in the early stages of the Opium War. Like two other figures mentioned in the ensuing song— Fieschi, the would-be assassin of Louis Philippe, and "the Great Agitator" (Daniel O'Connell, the Irish patriot, who had recently been released from prison)—"Commissioner Lin and his favourite concubine," as the catalogue called her, were represented by newly installed figures at Tussaud's.

BREES'S
COLONIAL PANORAMA,
LINWOOD GALLERY
LEICESTER SQUARE.

TAR-NAR-OOI   AR-RE-MI

NEW ZEALAND
NELSON   CANTERBURY
OTAGO   AUCKLAND
TERANAKI   HOKIANGA
WELLINGTON   BAY OF ISLANDS
Mornings 1 and 3, Evenings at 8.
"Will do more to promote emi-   "The best thing of the kind
gration than a thousand speeches that has yet been exhibited."—
and resolutions."— *The Times.*   *Morning Post.*
Admission One Shilling.
Reserved Seats 2 shillings, Stalls 3 shillings.
James Carroll, Printer, 275, Strand.

among the leading exhibitions, both commercial and institutional. It rested partly on the spirit of cooperation and partly on the principle that if you can't beat the competition you can at least take advantage of it. Thus the Nile panorama advertised that it illustrated the Egyptian antiquities at the British Museum.[19] The Polytechnic tied in a number of its seasonal attractions with exhibitions elsewhere. In the summer of 1851, for instance, it featured lectures on "All the MOST INTERESTING DEPOSITS at the GREAT EXHIBITION"—lectures not being part of the program at the Crystal Palace itself.[20] And the Christmas bill six years later included a "pictorial entertainment" entitled "Home for the Holydays" which portrayed "the nightmare of a ravenous youth, who, after gorging himself to repletion at the Crystal Palace [now

removed to Sydenham], falls asleep in the Egyptian Court, and is carried up the Nile in his dream."[21]

Far from being always self-contained entities, their purposes confined to the amusement and instruction promised in their advertising, many London shows had commercial relationships extending in several directions outside the entertainment world. Several notable ones—Bullock's Ancient and Modern Mexico, Belzoni's Egyptian tombs, Catlin's Indians, Cumming's safari-spoil—coincided, not by accident, with the publication of books by their proprietors. Vidocq's exhibition, also, was connected with a proposed continuation of his memoirs, though this project fell through.[22]

We have already seen that in addition to promoting the sale of works of art, exhibitions were used as showcases for new inventions. This was the main original purpose of the Adelaide Gallery and the Polytechnic. But exhibitions were used for other kinds of exploitation and propaganda as well. Although George French Angas's exhibition at the Egyptian Hall (1846) of his paintings of scenery and native life in South Australia and New Zealand was intended primarily to attract subscriptions for the two folio volumes on the region he was about to publish, it also served as an advertisement for the South Australia Company, which his father had founded and headed.[23] The publication of Samuel Sidney's best-selling *Handbook to Australia* two years later, along with much concomitant discussion in popular magazines like Dickens's *Household Words,* contributed to the burst of interest in emigration to the Antipodes that marked those years. Of S. C. Brees's Colonial Panoramas at 393 Strand (1851) the *Times* said they would "do more to promote emigration than a thousand speeches and resolutions."[24] But this would have been an incidental effect; Brees's participation in the current attempt to solve the "condition of England question" by shipping the hapless victims of industrialization and urbanization halfway round the world was subsidiary to his effort, as principal engineer and surveyor to the New Zealand Company, to attract investors. Preparing to close his exhibition, he advertised that as he was about to return to New Zealand, he "wishes to be joined by some gentlemen with capital. £1,000 would go as far as £10,000 under his management; £5,000 would be ample. Consignments and agencies undertaken, and land selected. From Mr. Brees's well-known character and knowledge of the subject, this is an opportunity rarely occurring. There would be no risk whatsoever."[25]

From Australia the next year, 1852, after a ten-year stay, came the Plymouth-born watercolorist John Skinner Prout, nephew of the better-known artist Samuel Prout. His panorama of the Australian gold fields at the Polytechnic was not an artistic success—the *Athenaeum* complained that Prout had painted it "with a very yellow brush and a very jaundiced eye"—but it too served the cause. Prout himself did the lecturing, "in order to give the fullest information to those interested in the important question of Emigration to the Australian Colonies."[26] Two years later, in a room adjoining the Polytechnic, Washington Friend's diorama of Canada and the United States served overseas development in another way. It had for its "great object" the promotion of the proposed "Tubular Railway Victoria bridge over the St. Lawrence, a project to dwarf the Menai Straits bridge."[27]

Beginning with eighteenth-century Exeter Change, with its scores of stalls downstairs and its varied entertainments upstairs, exhibitions often shared premises with shops. Their presence in the bazaars that were so distinctive a feature of London in the first half of the nineteenth century signified a mutually profitable arrangement. The best bazaars were meeting places for the carriage trade; men and women came there to pass an idle hour and buy more or less expensive baubles, toys, and *objets de luxe,* and while there they might be inclined to drop into the exhibition room to see whatever was showing. Conversely, patrons initially attracted by the exhibition might well be expected to loiter among the stalls and boutiques. Entertainment thus was an adjunct to what would now be called fun-buying; it appealed to the same open purses. A similar rationale lies behind the location of small cinemas in today's shopping centers. Exhibitions and retail trade cohabited most frequently at the Lowther Arcade (the Adelaide Gallery), the Cosmorama Rooms, and the Royal, subsequently the Queen's, Bazaar in Oxford Street. This last was a superior example of the type. The *Mirror of Literature* said of it shortly after it opened, "There is no similar establishment in London where so much may be seen for so little money"—dioramas, paintings, wax figures, models, and other exhibition material, but also much to buy: "several handsome specimens" of furniture, "many of them fit for the splendid palaces building in Regent's Park," and abundant stocks of *"bijouterie* and nic-nacs, the *Nouveautés de Paris* and Spitalfields—Canton in China, and Leather-lane in Holborn."[28]

In the bazaars as elsewhere, the distinction between merchandising and genuine show-business exhibitions was often obscured. Many of the "exhibitions" of cut-paper work, handicrafts, and other novelties in places like the Cosmorama Rooms were actually sales stalls. Indeed, one measure of the drawing power that the notion of a public exhibition had was the frequency with which such extensible words as "museum," "collection," and "gallery" were applied to displays of goods for sale, substituting, for the crass implication of trade which the word "sale" possessed, the more inviting connotation of an entertaining or instructive show that was worth paying admission to see. From the beginning, of course, when rarities of one kind or another were the commodity in question, the two purposes of exhibition and sale were hardly separable. As early as 1704, David Randall, a dealer in rare birds in Channel Row, Westminster, advertised that several particularly rare specimens, a huge "Casheward" bird from the East Indies that weighed between two and three hundred pounds, and "two Flamingers from the East Indies," were shown "every hour in the Day for Money."[29] Later (1709–10) an added attraction was one of the mechanical pictures then in vogue.[30] The trio of wax modelers, Mrs. Salmon, Mrs. Goldsmith, and Mrs. Mills, maintained their exhibitions not only for the sake of the gate receipts but to advertise their private services to persons wishing, as Mrs. Mills said, to "have their Effigies made, or their deceas'd Friends on reasonable Terms."[31] Wildman's exhibition of feats with bees was, in part, an advertisement for his Bee and Honey Warehouse in Holborn.[32]

After the middle of the eighteenth century, when the annual exhibitions of the Royal Academy had become established as the principal means of bringing artists and prospective buyers together, the word "exhibition" itself, which was first applied specifically to these shows, naturally acquired a frequent connotation of goods offered for sale. From the art world it spread to other areas of trade. One instance out of many was the competing glass-working establishments in the Strand in the 1830's, which were mainly interested in selling—not merely showing—their wares. It is quite possible that such "exhibitions" often waived the stated admission fee.

Sometimes a self-styled exhibition which was actually a salesroom borrowed the materials of genuine shows to lend a color of legitimacy to its use of the word. This was the case in 1823 with the so-called Indian Museum and Exhibition at 80½ Pall Mall, which announced the presence of a cosmorama as bait to lure the customer into what was nothing more than a salesroom—a mere "cabinet of knickknacks" as the *Times* dismissed it, consisting of seventy-nine lots of Indian weapons, musical instruments, and assorted curios. In this instance the cosmorama novelty was itself a fraud, because the pictures—104 of them, valued at £400 and portraying the birth, battles, and other exploits of Raamah—were hung about the walls in the usual way, only a solitary example being shown behind a cosmoramic glass. The reason, the catalogue disingenuously explained, was that "it would occupy too considerable a portion of time to view the whole of the Drawings through the Glass"— time which, no doubt, could be better spent selecting one's purchases.[33]

In other cases it is harder to determine which had priority—the exhibition or the sale. Early in the century the Apiarian Museum at 13 Old Bond Street advertised a gallimaufry of attractions which included "panoramic views" of Edinburgh and London, models of St. Peter's and St. Paul's, shells, needlework, "flowers, insects, birds, cattle, temples, grottos, and rocks, with a representation of the perpetual motion [machine]." All of these may have been for sale, although the handbill does not expressly say so. But what could definitely be purchased here, besides "an instantaneous light machine, or selasphoric invention," whatever that may have been, were (hence the title of the establishment) bees, hives, and honey. "As soon as the season will permit," the proprietor promised, "various experiments will be exhibited, illustrative of [the bees'] great Tractability and Docility."[34] Somewhat later, at Savile House, there was a Calonnian Museum, "originally designed by Mons. De Calonne, when Premier Minister of France,* for the Information of the Curious. . . . Birds, Quadrupeds, Fishes, Insects, Shells, Minerals and other interesting Subjects of Natural History from most parts of the globe." This collection contained another "perpetual motion" along with a "hail storm" (not described) and the usual shell work, glass temples, and Otaheitan artifacts. Again, the handbill gave no hint that M. de Calonne's collection was itself for sale, but the proprietor added, "Natural Curiosities of all kinds Bought, Great Variety of Duplicates for Sale, either Singly or in Collections."[35]

Despite their majestic titles, it is evident that some of these "museums" were nothing more than junk shops whose owners attempted to dignify their miscellaneous, eccentric, battered, and often useless stock by the terms "curios" and "rarities." They were the descendants of the antiquarian shops that served eighteenth-century collectors—George Humphrey's, for example, whose accumulated stock was pretentiously named "Humphrey's Grand Museum" and even the "Museum Humfredianum" when it was exhibited in St. Martin's Lane in 1778–79 prior to sale by auction.[36] Among the dirty, chaotic establishments in this peculiarly Dickensian line of commerce was the one operated by Little Nell's grandfather:

. . . one of those receptacles for old and curious things which seem to crouch in odd corners of this town and to hide their musty treasures from the public eye in jealousy and distrust. There were suits of mail standing like ghosts in armour here and there, fantastic carvings brought from monkish cloisters, rusty weapons of various kinds, distorted figures in china and wood and iron and ivory: tapestry and strange furniture that might have been designed in dreams. The haggard aspect of the little old man was wonderfully suited to the place; he might have groped among old churches and tombs and deserted houses and gathered all the spoils with his own hands.[37]

The trade in natural and artificial rarities to which the Old Curiosity Shop dimly belonged was small, almost wholly undocumented, but steady. The "nicknackatorian" who often served as middle man between collectors was both a broker and a speculator, though sometimes he posed as a collector himself. Such, in all probability, was "P. Dick, Sloane-street," who "collected" the mélange described in a catalogue dating from the 1830s. The title gives a sufficient idea of the range such stocks had: *A Descriptive Catalogue of a Museum of Antiquities and Foreign Curiosities, Natural and Artificial; Including Models Illustrative of Military and Naval Affairs, Armour and Weapons, Instruments of Torture, Polytheism, Sepulchres, with the Manner of Depositing the Dead; the Costume of Different Nations, Manuscripts, Natural History, Including Anatomy, &c &c &c.* More specifically, Dick had in stock many models in cork (including at least one by Dubourg), a sword used by Garrick, and the inevitable curios from Cook's voyages.[38]

These dealers were prime buyers of curios newly brought from distant lands by sailors debarking at the Thames wharves. A certain unnamed "Museum, No. 51 Newman Street," which advertised "a great variety of shells, minerals, and fossils" for sale, summoned customers by a handbill announcing the arrival from New Zealand of an item no lover of curiosities should miss: "Tippohow's Head," the former possession of a chieftain who had lost it in the course of an intertribal fight in 1820. "Very pleasant and perfect" it was, with

* Charles Alexandre de Calonne (1734–1802) was the minister of finance who persuaded Louis XVI to propose to the nobility that they renounce their exemption from taxation. The suggestion was not well received, and Calonne thereafter spent a number of years in England.

428 The Shows of London

"teeth whiter than ivory, the hair flowing in fine black curls" and appropriately tattooed. Along with it were shown native costumes and savage artifacts, including a war club "having several locks of human hair attached to the handle, denoting the number of victims slain by it."[39] The proprietor's plain hope was that persons attracted to his "museum" by these fairly grisly items would linger to buy from his ordinary stock.

One of the principal activities of these curio-mongers was attending auctions at which private and commercial collections were dispersed and buying on speculation properties rejected by the showmen who also were there. Although many rarities left London by this route, numerous others remained, to circulate from one exhibition to another; in the long course of years, compulsive showgoers like Lord Stowell would repeatedly run across old friends in new settings. A sperm whale specimen and an anatomical model of "the Grecian daughter" from Rackstrow's museum turned up at the sale of Gilbert Pidcock's menagerie and museum in March 1810.[40] Many of the items in the Leverian sale of 1806 found their way into other exhibitions, including Bullock's and that of Mrs. Phillips and her daughter.[41] As has been seen, Jaquet-Droz's and Maillardet's famous automatons moved from one owner to another after Maillardet's death; several of them surfaced in New York City in the 1830s.[42]

Some fairly elaborate shows never did so well that their owners would refuse to sell them to buyers who, they guaranteed, would make a fortune from them. In the 1760s a handbill enumerating the wonders of Pinchbeck's "Utile et Dulce, or, the Much Improved Mechanical Exhibition," concluded: "And as, perhaps, there never was an Exhibition, by which an active Person might in travelling win a more genteel or reputable Livelihood, (if not an easy Fortune), as by this most amusing and Instructive One,—the Whole or any Part will be disposed of on easy Terms."[43] A few exhibitors were in effect, like Pinchbeck, manufacturers to the trade. The models of Geneva and Switzerland shown at 20 Frith Street, Soho, in 1819 were samples of the craftsmanship of I. B. Troye, "Modeller to her late R. H. the Princess Charlotte, and pupil of the celebrated Mr. Exchaquet, Geometrician to his Majesty the King of Sardinia," who was prepared to execute similar models, on various scales—presumably for other showmen as well as for schools.[44]

A small entrepreneur hoping to earn a living in the exhibition trade, in London or on the road, had no dearth of properties to choose from. A 400-square-foot worsted needlework "panorama" of the battle of Grand Cairo, shown (1833) at a house in the City Road and declared by "French families and travellers of distinction" to "surpass the Works of the Gobelins of Paris," was advertised as being "very attractive to a Bazaar, Watering Place, or to make the Tour of Europe."[45] The model of London shown at the Western Exchange in 1831 was put up for sale four years later, by which time it had grown even faster than London itself, from 73,000 houses to 120,000. "It has only been exhibited where it now stands," declared the advertiser, "and, it is presumed, this is a sufficient hint to the speculator; for if exhibited in the Country, Paris, or the United States, a splendid fortune must be accumulated."[46]

Pictorial entertainments, too, passed through the market, sometimes to take a new lease on life as a touring attraction.* At the beginning of his career Barker put up his used canvases for sale to any speculators who wished to take them to Dublin, Edinburgh, the continent, or other promising locales.[47] Two moving panoramas, one a thousand-square-foot depiction of Hobart Town, were announced for auction in 1840.[48] The much traveled "Grand Mechanical and Picturesque Theatre of Arts" described in Chapter 16, which had been seen most recently at the Cosmorama Rooms, was up for sale in 1834 and again in 1840, the owner declaring that it "offers to any spirited individual the certainty of realising an ample fortune, either by exhibiting it in the provinces or the American continent."[49] It finally went to America in 1859 (one wonders what its condition must have been after all those years of wandering) when Barnum ran across it at Southampton and bought it for his New York museum.[50]

When exhibitors sought to unload properties from which they had squeezed as much profit as they could, they did not confine their search for buyers to their fellow showmen. Offering his early panoramas to the trade, Barker added that he would be glad to hear from "any Nobleman or Gentleman [who] may chuse to purchase for amusement."[51] No mansion in city or country seems to have acquired a panorama, but it is possible that some cosmoramas in Regent Street found their way there. This is the implication of an imperfectly phrased announcement in the catalogue of the Cosmorama show itself: "Many of the Visitors to the Cosmorama having expressed a desire to fit up their country houses, with one or more Windows and Views similar to those of this Exhibition. The Propri-

* A number of the Leicester Square and Strand panoramas did tour, some of them (Paris, Waterloo, Algiers, Mexico City, Jerusalem, Athens, Geneva, Niagara, Thebes, Lima, Rome, and New Zealand) eventually turning up in America. (Odell, II, 538–40; III, 223, 368, 428, 458; IV, 257, 324, 419–20.) Marshall's panoramas were peripatetic as well as peristrephic, and they too (Navarino, Waterloo, Napoleon's funeral) reached the United States. (Odell, III, 537–38, 541; IV, 43.) Both of the Mississippi shows toured the provinces, as did Gompertz's Arctic regions panorama, which is recorded as having been at Canterbury, Portsmouth, Shrewsbury, Oswestry, Stafford, Nottingham, Grantham, Peterborough, Cambridge, and York, among other places, in 1852–1857. (Advertisements of various dates in *ILN*.) When the full history of the entertainments offered in the provincial towns during the nineteenth century is written, it will be seen that there was a steady flow of London attractions, especially after the building of the railways. Panoramas and dramatic paintings, such as *The Raft of the "Medusa"* and some of Haydon's and Martin's canvases, perhaps predominated, but exhibitions of other kinds toured as well—Catlin's Indians, for example, the Siamese Twins, General Tom Thumb, and Miss Linwood's needlework pictures both before and after their long tenancy at Savile House.

150. The façade of Ferguson's Grand Promenade of Wonders (*Punch*, 13 May 1843).

etors most anxious to further the wishes of those Friends, who have by their Patronage contributed to its success, beg leave most respectfully to Announce that they will be happy to execute any Commands that may be favored, with Views equally interesting and painted by the same Masters."[52]

D⅜✳⅜ᗡ

From used exhibition properties new miscellaneous shows were thrown together—short-run affairs, with no pretense of selection or system, displayed slapdash

in a hired room for whatever pittance they would earn. Thus, in the lower room at Spring Gardens (1824), timed for the school holidays, was shown what was billed as "Five Exhibitions in One," a single shilling covering the lot: a colored model of Palestine from the Society of Arts' repository at Adelphi House, a model "from Piccadilly" "shewing Captain Parry's attempt to explore the North West Passage," stuffed animals from a former show in Pall Mall, the enchanted lyre from Wheatstone's Museum, and the ubiquitous Invisible Girl.[53] Some helter-skelter assemblages of cast-off items, seldom costing more than twopence to enter, led marginal existences in working-class neighborhoods. Pollard's Museum at 25–26 New Cut, Lambeth, was typical. Within its shabby walls were gathered a claimed hundred wax figures, a mechanical transparent orrery, a microscope, a galvanic apparatus, dissolving views, and a phantasmagoria.[54] There probably were scores of such operations in nineteenth-century London, virtually none of which left any trace except for an occasional flimsy, crudely printed handbill preserved in some archive.

One exception was Ferguson's Grand Promenade at 167 High Holborn, which advertised a collection consisting of a Devonshire giant and two dwarfs, all alive; mechanical wax figures of Lady Flora Hastings (the unfairly accused central figure in a scandal at the youthful Queen Victoria's court), John Marchant ("the murderer of his fellow servant in Cadogan Place, Chelsea"), and "the Female School of Nicholas Nickleby"; a mechanical panorama (ex Egyptian Hall?) of the Grace Darling sea rescue; live serpents; a mummy; numerous nonmechanical waxworks; and (a special coup) the fittings and drapery allegedly used at the enthronement of the queen.[55] This show—or at any rate its exterior—had the distinction of being described in the course of a *Punch* series (1843) on "The Gratuitous Exhibitions of London." After dilating on the three-dimensional figure of the giant and an equally imposing painting of two fat boys that almost hid the building's three-story façade, the writer enumerated the contents of the ground-floor show window, which could not be made out in the accompanying drawing: "an elaborate model of 'The Castle of Doune, on the banks of the Forth, Stirlingshire'; from, or in, or near which, somebody or another was beheaded"; "a representation of the Spotted Boy in a glass case, as well as a group of small figures which the spectator will not be able exactly to comprehend; but the triumph of art is shown in a railway-engine and tender, shut up in a bottle, without any visible means of explaining how it got in there. In the Anatomical department, we find two skeletons of cats' heads, and a preparation of a singular pig in spirits."[56]

Punch recommended ironically that the whole collection of marvels be transferred to the British Museum nearby, but it proved to have a different destiny. Three years later the Exhibition of Nature and Art, as it now was called, was at 31 Calcraft Terrace, New Cut. One December night, while Mr. Ferguson and one or two others were sitting in the kitchen drinking rum and water, the premises caught fire. Fed by the wax figures, the flames made such headway that an eighteen-year-old female dwarf died, along with some serpents and monkeys. One other monkey, having wrapped himself in a piece of green baize, was discovered unhurt by firemen searching the ruins.[57]

Below these slum shows in the pecking order, finally, were the street exhibitions. Henry Mayhew's *London Labour and the London Poor* is encyclopedic on this topic as of 1856, providing an incomparably intimate view of the lives, skills, and trade lore of these poverty's-edge public entertainers, expressed in their own words: the men who exhibited Punch and puppet shows, peepshows, trained animals, mechanical figures, telescopes, microscopes, and Chinese shadows ("the proper name," Mayhew was informed, ". . . is *lez Hombres,* . . . for Baron Rothschild told me so when I performed before him"); and the performers—acrobats, strong men, jugglers, conjurors, fire-eaters, snake-, sword-, and knife-swallowers, clowns, reciters, ballet dancers, instrumentalists, ballad singers.[58]

Mayhew offers a long account of the "happy family," a variety of small animals and birds living harmoniously in a single cage.[59] In the 1850s there were five such shows in the metropolis, the largest, and therefore the most peaceable of all, consisting of fifty-four birds and animals in a single cage: three cats, two dogs, two monkeys, two magpies, two jackdaws, two jays, ten starlings, six pigeons, two hawks, two barn fowls, one screechowl, five sewer rats, five white rats, eight guinea pigs, two rabbits, one hedgehog, and one tortoise. The doyen of this branch of the trade was said to be John Austin, a former Midlands stocking weaver whom two of Mayhew's informants credited with discovering the secret of bringing up a menagerie where "dog eat dog" was a mere figure of speech. But the happy family was not really a Victorian invention, however impressively it illustrated the extension of the prevailing ideal of domestic harmony to the animal kingdom. As we have seen, "Batchelor Dick," who traveled about London in his iron house about 1750,

possessed a nuclear happy family in the hawks, pigeons, and owls which, suppressing their mutual antipathies, lived amicably in a single cage. We learn from Francis Buckland that Austin, the putative inventor of the Victorian enlarged version, was only the licensee of a Lambeth workman named Charles Garbett. Garbett's donnée came from his cat who, bereft of her litter of kittens, adopted a litter of baby rats and tenderly reared them to adulthood. After much observation and experimentation Garbett devised the proper technique but, says Buckland, kept it a closely guarded secret.[60] Mayhew, however, derived from one happy-family proprietor a description of the process which can only be called exhaustive and definitive, occupying as it does seven closely printed columns in *London Labour and the London Poor*.

In any event, John Austin set some kind of record in the London show business by occupying a single pitch, outside the Feathers public house in the Waterloo Road, near the foot of Waterloo Bridge, for thirty-six years, "all but five months." When he began in 1820, he made from fourteen shillings to a pound in the late afternoon and evening alone; at the end, he was lucky to make two and six a day. The competition, including one rival outside the National Gallery, had been too much for him.[61] But there had been glorious moments in the happy-family business. Mayhew was told that Austin exhibited his amiable animals at Buckingham Palace in 1833, and the *Times* for 15 August 1842 reported that "a noble Earl" had arranged for such a show, proprietor not named, to be brought to the same palace. Since the cage was too big to be taken upstairs, it was placed in a large room on the ground floor, where the queen and the prince spent three quarters of an hour "witnessing the affection, if such a term may be used, which existed between animals and birds of natures so opposite." One can find what irony one will in the fact that the same issue of the *Times* devoted several anxious pages to reports of the Plug Plot riots in the manufacturing districts which dramatized, as no previous events had done, the perilous and bitter hostility that now existed between the rich and the poor.

Mayhew does not mention the survival in the London streets of clockwork peepshows. Another contemporary witness, however, tells of coming upon such an exhibition, entitled "What was saved in Noah's ark when the world was drowned," in the Blackfriars Road on New Year's Day, 1831. In a box no more than a foot square could be seen, on payment of a halfpenny, a landscape, against which a model of

151. "The Happy Family"
(*Punch*, 20 May 1843).

the ark, activated by a handle, discharged "all the 'birds of the air and the beasts of the field' . . . to their resting place." The same witness describes a "curious piece of mechanism" shown by a mechanic in Hay Hill, Piccadilly, in 1833. Called "the Ocean in Miniature," it "consisted of a square case, about 18 inches long and 12 inches wide; it was handsomely enclosed in a black and gold frame. In the interior was seen a view of a castle or fort in the distance, having the sea in front. The inventor then, with a small handle, wound up some concealed machinery, which immediately put in motion two ships that appeared to sail through the waves, with a proper undulating movement; the waves also seemed to move with natural effect, rising and falling as the vessels passed along to the end of the case; the ships disappearing for a short time, they reappeared on the opposite side: the motion continued for about a quarter-hour." There was no fixed charge for viewing, the exhibitor depending "on the generosity of the passersby."[62]

The most elaborate of these street shows was one described in 1853. It combined farcical with fearsome episodes in the immemorial tradition of the puppet theatre and Punch and Judy shows. In front of a large barrel organ was

a stage about five or six feet in width, four in height, and perhaps eighteen inches or two feet in length. Upon this are a variety of figures, about fourteen inches long, gorgeously arrayed in crimson, purple, emerald-green, blue, and orange draperies, and loaded with gold and tinsel, and sparkling stones and spangles, all doubled in splendour by the reflection of a mirror in the background. The figures, set in motion by the same machinery which grinds the incomprehensible overture, perform a drama equally incomprehensible.

In one corner of the stage was a cavern "containing some supernatural and mysterious being of the fiend or vampire school," and opposite it, the lion's den of the Daniel story, with the lion opening its mouth in six-eight time and an angel pivoting with outspread wings to the same rhythm. On the stage a Turk brandished a dagger over a prostrate slave; Nebuchadnezzar, down on all fours, ate grass; and Queen Victoria, Prince Albert, Napoleon, and Tippoo Sahib and his sons awaited their cues.

After a score or so of bars, the measure of the music suddenly alters—Daniel's guardian angel flies off—the prophet and the lion lie down to sleep together—the Grand Turk sinks into the arms of the death-doomed slave—Nebuchadnezzar falls prostrate on the ground, and the fiend in the gloomy cavern whips suddenly round and glares with his green eye, as if watching for a spring upon the front row of actors, who have now taken up their cue and commenced their performance. Napoleon, Tippoo Sahib and Queen Victoria dance a three-handed reel, to the admiration of Prince Albert and a group of lords and ladies in waiting, who nod their heads approvingly—when br'r'r! crack! at a tremendous crash of gongs and grumbling of bass-notes, the fiend in the corner rushes forth from his lair with a portentous howl. Away, neck or nothing, flies Napoleon, and Tippoo scampers after him, followed by the terrified attendants; but lo! at the precise nick of time, Queen Victoria draws a long sword from beneath her stays, while up jumps the devouring beast from the den of the prophet, and like a true British lion— as he doubtless was all the while—flies at the throat of the fiend, straight as an arrow to its mark. There follows a roar of applause from the discriminating spectators, amidst which the curtain falls, and, with an extra flourish of music, the collection of copper coin commences.[63]

It is surprising that Mayhew seems not to have known of this elaborate show, since it was current at the very time he was interviewing scores of street exhibitors. One other kind of open-air show is absent from his pages, conceivably because it had disappeared by the time he gathered his information: the home-made model. In November 1830 a sailor collected halfpennies by showing a miniature fifty-gun frigate made from a single date-palm leaf. It was, we are told, "carried about the streets in a covered carriage, at the front of which the man sat, and conveyed himself along, by turning various wheels with his hands, and pressing on treadles with his feet."[64] Four years later a Staffordshireman named Isaac Wilkes carried about the streets of Walworth a model, only twelve inches by eight, of the above-ground works of a coal mine, operated by weights attached to strings. "The casual bounty of passersby was the only means of subsistence which he had."[65] The best value in this line, however, was shown in the vicinity of St. George's Fields, Southwark, in January 1837—an exhibit which, incidentally, offers an additional illustration of show-business symbiosis, in this case linking an exalted institution with a humble one. This creation of an "ingenious mechanic" was a tin model of the Regent's Park Colosseum. For a penny one could look through glasses aimed between the Doric pillars of the portico and see the various interior appointments, prominent among which was a stream of real water pumped over a line of rock work to descend in a cataract ten inches high.[66] This was represented as being Niagara Falls, but in the real Colosseum, of course, it was the cascade seen from the window of the Swiss cottage.

However simple their conception and crude their execution, these street exhibitions resembled in kind those routinely presented in hired rooms round about Piccadilly, Old Bond Street, and the Strand. The difference was that their ragged impresarios either were too poor to rent a room or thought they could do better on the pavement. With them, and with such obvious indoor bids for charity as "Wadham's Grand Cosmorama, with Dioramic and Panoramic Effects. Painted by himself—deaf and dumb," at 151 Strand in 1839,[67] the London show trade reached rock bottom, economically as well as artistically. In their own field these street exhibitions were the equivalents of the store-front penny gaffs which constituted the lowest depths of the London stage. But the very fact that there were so many of them demonstrates that among the indigent of the metropolis there were some men shrewd enough to know that charity was most likely to be had from Londoners when appeal was made to their unquenchable curiosity.

National Monuments

31

The Government, strong in its conservative instincts, "slow of heart to believe," and still more sluggish of hand to execute—no longer waits to be "debated" into niggard grants, but, casting aside its *peasant* prejudices, boldly heads the movement, and with a liberal spirit guides its resuscitated energies for the education of the people, the improvement of our industrial products, the monumental record of our acts and heroes, and the general aggrandisement of the state.

—*Illustrated London News,* 11 February 1843

Until the post–Reform Bill era, except for appropriating money to the British Museum and the National Gallery, the British government had played no part in the London exhibition world. The old and still prevailing philosophy of government's proper sphere simply excluded such aspects of the people's life from official concern. In fact, however, four of the most famous London shows belonged to the nation: two obliquely, as the property of the established Church of England (Westminster Abbey and St. Paul's Cathedral) and the others (the Tower of London and the British Museum) as outright public property. In the absence of any official solicitude respecting their management, three of these were operated as mercenary places of public resort. No such extortionate atmosphere distinguished the fourth, the British Museum, but its studied policy of excluding as many members of the general public as possible was equally at odds with the new social thought that began to make itself

felt in the thirties and forties. The story of the controversy involving these well-known London sights in the first half of the century is an exemplary instance of the conflict between conservative tradition and liberalism as the first faint outlines of the so-called interventionist state began to appear. By the early forties, when exhibitions, broadly conceived, were coming to be looked upon as a possible instrument of social reform, and their provision and regulation a proper concern of national policy, there were signs that the government would soon actively involve itself in an aspect of London life which until then had been monopolized by private and vested interests.

The monument-showplace most often complained of was Westminster Abbey. Beginning in 1801, when the building ceased to be a public thoroughfare, a fee was levied for admittance at all times except during divine service, at the conclusion of which the vergers brusquely showed nonpaying worshipers the door. The old practice of farming out particular portions of the building for the benefit of the minor canons, lay clerks, and organists persisted. By 1807, the aggregate charge to see the Abbey was two shillings, on top of which tips were expected at numerous points, though nominally forbidden. A complete tour of the church therefore might cost double the official amount.[1]

To a growing number of Londoners and visitors this was intolerable, the more so after 1821, when the public had been admitted free for a short while to view the magnificent decorations put up for George IV's coronation. The reimposition of the fees led to questions being asked in the press, but with no immediate result. In the *London Magazine* for October 1823, Charles Lamb addressed an impassioned open letter to his friend Robert Southey, begging him to exert his influence to ensure that "the doors of Westminster Abbey be no longer closed against the decent, though low-in-purse, enthusiast, or blameless devotee, who must commit an injury against his family economy, if he would be indulged with a bare admission within its walls." A year and a half later (February 1825) Thomas Hood addressed the dean and chapter directly, using as his epigraph the observation of Goldsmith's Chinese philosopher on the same subject, "Sure the guardians of the Temple can never think they get enough." The tone of the poem is sufficiently represented by these excerpts:

> Oh, very reverend Dean and Chapter,
>   Exhibitors of giant men,
> Hail to each surplice-back'd adapter
>   Of England's dead, in her stone den!
> Ye teach us properly to prize
>   Two-shilling Grays, and Gays, and Handels,
> And, to throw light upon our eyes,
>   Deal in Wax Queens like old wax candles.
>
> Oh, reverend showmen, rank and file,
>   Call in your shillings, two and two;
> March with them up the middle aisle,
>   And cloister them from public view.
> Yours surely are the dusty dead,
>   Gladly ye look from bust to bust,
> Setting a price on each great head,
>   To make it come down with the dust.
> . . . .
> Here many a pensive pilgrim, brought
>   By reverence for those learned bones,
> Shall often come and walk your short
>   Two-shilling fare upon the stones.—
> Ye have that talisman of Wealth,
>   Which puddling chemists sought of old
> Till ruin'd out of hope and health—
>   The Tomb's the stone that turns to gold!
> . . . .
> "Walk in! two shillings only! come!
>   Be not by country grumblers funk'd!—
> Walk in, and see th' illustrious dumb!
>   The Cheapest House for the defunct!"
> Write up, 'twill breed some just reflection,
>   And every rude surmise 'twill stop—
> Write up, that you have no connection
>   (In large)—with any other shop!
>
> And, still to catch the Clowns the more,
>   With samples of your shows in Wax,

> Set some old Harry near the door
>   To answer queries with his *axe*.—
> Put up some general begging-trunk—
>   Since the last broke by some mishap,
> You've all a bit of General Monk,
>   From the respect you bore his Cap![2]

In token response to such criticism, the dean reduced the admission fee to 1s. 3d. in June 1825. When the aggrieved clerical concessionaires protested that this sharply reduced their perquisite, they were threatened with dismissal, the dean maintaining that they had not kept their part of the ancient bargain by dusting the monuments.[3] The House of Commons thereupon demanded an accounting of the funds, which the authorities reluctantly supplied, making clear that they resented any attempt on the part of government to interfere in what was none of government's business. The charter granted by Queen Elizabeth, they asserted, "conferred the church on the Dean and Chapter for ever, and has subjected it to their sole and lawful management. And further, their founder has not only empowered, but required them to defend the privileges and immunities which she has thus bestowed upon them, against all aggression or encroachment."[4]

Although the entrance charge was subsequently reduced to ninepence, once inside, visitors were still at the mercy of the enclosure system. Visiting London in 1835, the historiographer Frederick von Raumer complained that the building was "a labyrinth of wooden partitions, doors, screens, railings, and corners. . . . It seemed as if all these nooks and swallows' nests were contrived merely to increase the number of showmen and key-bearers who lurk in them."[5] Despite the formal prohibition of tips, attendants intimated that there was no rule against leaving coins on a convenient tomb. And as one left, full of the patriotic emotions a sight of the Abbey evoked despite all the mercenary distractions, one was confronted by the filthy but still serviceable relic of past mendicity alluded to in the final stanza of Hood's poem. As the clerical humorist Richard Harris Barham—who was attached to the rival establishment at St. Paul's—put it in one of his *Ingoldsby Legends*,

> I stood alone!—a living thing 'midst those that were no
>   more—
> I thought on ages past and gone—the glorious deeds of
>   yore—
> On Edward's sable panoply, on Cressy's tented plain,
> The fatal Roses twined at length—on great Eliza's reign.

152. Westminister Abbey and St. Paul's Cathedral as showplaces: George Cruikshank's *Clerical Showfolk and Wonderful Layfolk,* 1819. In addition to satirizing the conversion of churches into tourist traps, the engraving alludes to current fads (phrenology and velocipedes), the polar expedition, and a project for establishing a passenger service of steam balloons between London and Paris.

I thought on Naseby—Marston Moor—on Worc'ster's "crowning fight";
When on mine ear a sound there fell—it chill'd me with affright,
As thus in low, unearthly tones I heard a voice begin,
"—This here's the cap of Giniral Monk!—Sir! please put summut in!"[6]

The waxworks, too, survived, more decrepit than ever. In 1828 James Fenimore Cooper joined the long succession of visitors who deplored the show, which was "every way worthy of occupying a box at Bartholomew Fair." Wondering what had "induced the dean and chapter to permit this prostitution of their venerable edifice," he answered his own question: "the very

* The figure, still to be seen today, was widely regarded as an extremely faithful likeness; the Prince Regent, the Duchess of Devonshire, and Lady Hamilton herself praised it. What originated as a pawn in ecclesiastical show-business rivalry has proved to have substantial value as historical evidence.

motive which induced Ananias to lie, and Sapphira to swear to it."[7]

But at least there was one relatively new figure, whose introduction had been necessitated by the intensified competition at St. Paul's. Although the cathedral had had a fair number of visitors in the eighteenth century, mainly to make the long climb to the dome for the view, it did not acquire full standing as an obligatory sight of London until 1805, when Nelson's funeral, the display of his funeral car, and the erection of his tomb focused the nation's attention on it. Even before the majestic ceremony, the crowds coming to see the preparations had netted the vergers £40 a day.[8] In response, the minor functionaries at the Abbey commissioned a counterattraction from the wax portraitist Catherine Andras, who had a studio at the Historic Gallery in Pall Mall. She had earlier made a miniature portrait of Nelson while he was being painted by her foster-father, Robert Bowyer, proprietor of the gallery. Now she produced a life-size effigy (her only work on this scale) for which the gentlemen of the choir paid her £104 14s. 9d.[9] Clothed in garments supplied by Nelson's family, including a hat with a crescent-shaped piece of green silk that could be lowered to protect his remaining eye from the sun, the effigy was installed in a place of honor among the waxworks and the tourist revenue recovered.*

But the Abbey nevertheless had lost its once considerable advantage over St. Paul's. This developing branch pantheon now became a London attraction coequal with the original, and its own century-old entrance fee as much of a public issue as the price scale at Westminster. Immediately after Nelson's funeral a cartoon showed a sailor looking up at a modest memorial to his fallen leader which he had erected in his garden. A scroll at his feet read: "Every person who wishes to see the Monuments in St. Paul's must pay Twopence! Sailors should have free admission," and a legend over his head exclaimed in part, "I'll be no Twopenny Customer at St. Paul's! This shall be poor Jack's Monument, in his little garden, to his Noble Companion." Within a few months, the lifting of the charge became one of the pie-in-the-sky campaign promises attributed to Charles James Fox in a satirical print on the approaching Westminster election. Fox, as "Sancho the Second," was depicted delivering a speech overflowing with Cockaigne mirages—houses roofed with pancakes, streets paved with quartern loaves, and: "you shall see the [Tower] Lions for nothing, the [Abbey] Tombs for nothing, & St. Pauls for

153. Taking country cousins to see the Tower of London: engraving by Thomas Rowlandson, 1807. One of a series of illustrating "The Miseries of Social Life."

nothing—in short all that is rare & beautiful in England for nothing!"[10]

But the authorities were unmoved. So impervious were they to public sentiment, in fact, that on the day of Benjamin West's funeral in the cathedral in 1820, they abruptly raised the entrance fee to a shilling. A correspondent of the *Literary Gazette* seized the occasion to point out their failings both as men of God and as showmen: as churchmen they "set the paltry profit derived from making a show of a national church above the disgrace attached to the traffic," and as exhibitors they allowed the monuments "to be covered with filth and dirt, instead of keeping them clean for the inspection of their customers," and the noble pre-Fire monument to Dr. Donne to fall into ruin.[11]

It became customary to link the two edifices in denunciation. George Cruikshank's caricature of *Clerical Showfolk and Wonderful Layfolk* (1819) showed models of the Abbey and St. Paul's into each of which a boy peered as if at a peepshow. And Lamb, after his assault on the two-shilling charge at the Abbey, went on in the same open letter to assail the twopenny one at the cathedral:

A respected friend of ours, during his late visit to the metropolis, presented himself for admission at St. Paul's. At the same time a decently clothed man, with as decent a wife, and child, were bargaining for the same indulgence. The price was only two-pence per person. The poor but decent man hesitated, desirous to go in; but there were three of them, and he turned away reluctantly. Perhaps he wished to have seen the tomb of Nelson. Perhaps the Interior of the Cathedral was his object. But in the state of his finances, even sixpence might reasonably seem too much. Tell the Aristocracy of the country (no man can do it more impressively); instruct them of what value these insignificant pieces of money, these minims to their sight, may be to their humbler brethren. Shame these Sellers out of the Temple.

As Lamb suggested, although twopence was not a negligible amount of money to a poor man, it was the principle involved that was at issue, not the size of the fee. Still, the very paltriness of the sum made it all the more objectionable, because it cheapened still further

154. The Tower of London: the horse armory, built 1826 (*Illustrated London News,* 22 April 1848).

the show-business atmosphere. Six months after Lamb addressed Southey in the *London Magazine,* a self-styled "stranger, newly come to London," addressed the editor of the *Examiner.* He had had to pay the regulation twopence to see "the inside of Solomon's Temp—no, no,—the interior of St. Paul's Church."

I could not [he wrote] divest myself of the idea that I was looking at a two-penny show, and was indignant on seeing the productions of such masterminds as Wren's and Chantrey's, &c. made the means of wringing beggarly twopences out of the pockets of the natives, and what is infinitely worse, out of foreigners'! Well might the great Napoleon say, we trafficked in every thing; but he was little aware that to "a nation of shopkeepers," he might have added, of showkeepers, and that we made a show even of our St. Paul's Church, and a two-penny one, too! Had the admission been half-a-crown, I would have paid it with comparative pleasure; but this "*only* twopence—walk up!"—it will make me

think more meanly of myself, as an Englishman, as long as I live.[12]

Just as at the Abbey, once inside the building a visitor was subjected to multiple charges to see the individual sights—fourpence here, sixpence there, a shilling somewhere else. An American named Alexander Mackenzie described his arrival at the box office:

Within the door I was encountered, face to face, by a fat porter, whose whole appearance indicated that religion was as good a trade here as in other countries where it is supposed to be better. . . . He offered me tickets for various parts of the buildings, and other attendants, men or women, proffered tickets in like manner for the rest; that for the dome being half a crown, and the whole together about five shillings; each particular object having its particular price set on it; the whispering-gallery, the library, the great bell, down to the remains of the hero Nelson, which are exhibited to Englishmen at a shilling the head.[13]

As at the Abbey, also, there were signs stipulating the official charge for each attraction, and below them visitors were encouraged, indeed almost coerced, by the attendants to give them a substantial tip. Cooper recorded that one female guide, having finished her rote history of the attraction to which she was accredited, slid "without altering the key, or her ordinary mode of speaking," into her final sentence: "By the rules of the church, I am entitled to only two pence for showing you this, and we are strictly prohibited from asking any more, but gentlefolks commonly give me a shilling."[14] Little wonder that Thomas Sopwith, visiting St. Paul's about the same time, found his "pocket sweating pretty freely all the while" as he inspected the ball atop the dome, the library, the models, clock, bell, and crypts.[15]

The Tower of London received less criticism in the first third of the century than it appears to have deserved, perhaps because it was not under clerical management. Its fee structure was as complex as those at the two great churches, and making the complete round cost considerably more—no less than twelve shillings in the 1830s—with the usual gratuities in addition.[16] The earliest attraction, the menagerie, was closed in 1834, when the last of the animals were transferred to the Regent's Park Zoo. What remained, apart from the grim history-haunted buildings themselves, were the crown jewels and regalia and the armories. The old armory was no more than a chaotic lumber room. There was no scholarship behind the exhibits, the various suits of armor and other accouterments being attributed to monarchs and periods almost at random; an Oriental suit of mail, for example, was identified as that of a twelfth-century Norman crusader. In 1825, preparatory to moving part of the collection into a new building (the so-called Queen Elizabeth's horse armory, a Tudor structure with a Gothic cloister inside), Samuel Meyrick, the leading expert on such matters, was brought in to rearrange it according to some rational plan. This aim, however, was frustrated by his being required to assign every suit to some great personage, regardless of whether there was any evidence of the attribution—and in most cases there was none.[17]

The quality of the lecturing was as uninspiring as ever. Alexander Mackenzie, while admiring the "ingenious machinery" by which the crown jewels were rotated on a turntable so that all could see—no longer did the attendant casually hold them up behind bars in a dark room—found "something wonderfully ludicrous in the discourse of the old show-woman."

It was the farce following upon the heels of the tragedy. She has held the same station, and sung the same song, from daylight to dark, during a score of years. It was chanted in a sort of whining recitative, and some parts of it ran as follows. "This is the golden font what baptizes hall the princes and princesses of the royal family; the hampuler, or golden heagle as olds the oly hoil what hanoints the king hat the coronation; the golden fountain what plays the wine at the coronation; the golden saltcellar of state in the form of the White Tower, what stands at the king's table at the coronation; Harmilla, hor bracelets; Curtana, the Sword of Justice and hof Mercy; the Golden Spoon." After an awful pause to prepare for the climax, in a tone of increased earnestness and importance she went on, "This is the Himperial Crown; the pearl upon the top was pawned by Cromwell in Olland for eighteen thousand pounds; the red stone which you see is an uncut ruby of hinesteemable valhew; without the ruby the crown is valued at one million of pounds."

After she finished her recitation, Mackenzie remarked, "How happy you are, to be able to see all these fine things for nothing every day!" She delivered the retort he asked for: "An hi honly got that for my pains, hi should be badly off!"[18]

The British Museum, finally, entered the nineteenth century in a practically comatose condition so far as service to the public was concerned. Of the £120,000 allocated to it between its establishment in 1759 and 1816, half had gone for books and manuscripts and half for two large collections of antiquities, the Towneley and the Elgin. Virtually nothing had been spent for zoological, botanical, mineralogical, or paleontological materials, so that its exhibits in these fields of growing interest, beyond the original Sloane collection, were as yet confined to what it received by gift or bequest. Beginning in 1816 modest grants were made for such purchases, but the museum's holdings only began to expand in a major way four years later, with Sir Joseph Banks's bequest of his great scientific collection.

Unsuitable from the beginning as a museum, the building now became more and more congested as the flow of acquisitions, stimulated by the Banks bequest, swelled in the late twenties and thirties. Under the begrimed painted ceilings the "admired disorder" increased, the unlabeled and uncared-for exhibits being thrown together without regard for logical relationships or effective display. Much material decayed to the point of uselessness, and periodic bonfires consumed the "rubbish" from the several scientific departments. In a losing effort to bring space abreast of content, ill-matched, damp, and otherwise unsatisfactory annexes were added from time to time as part of the long drawn-out process (1823–1852) by which

155. The British Museum: entrance hall of old Montagu House (watercolor by George Scharf the elder, made in 1845, shortly before this portion of the building was demolished).

old Montagu House was replaced by a new structure. For two decades, therefore, visitors wandered through the premises distracted by the dirt and noise of a seemingly permanent construction project.[19]

The administration was in the hands of a few sinecurist officials, chiefly clergymen, who invoked the pressures of their research, which was desultory at best, to justify their extreme reluctance to welcome casual visitors or even, in some cases, those with a serious professional interest in the collections. In the entire year 1805 only 2,500 persons, mostly foreigners, braved the obstacles thrust in their way. Among these was Benjamin Silliman, who after having been repeatedly disappointed in his attempts to get inside, finally succeeded, only to duplicate William Hutton's experience twenty years earlier. "It is really distressing," he wrote, "to be surrounded by a host of things which are full of information, and then to be hurried away from them just as one is beginning to single out particular objects."[20] A small improvement occurred two years later, when the ticket requirement was dropped in favor of admitting "any person of decent appearance" up to a limit of about 120 a day.[21] As a consequence, 13,000 persons entered during the first year under the new policy (May 1807–April 1808).[22] But the single step forward was promptly canceled out by a step backward. In 1810, because of allegedly inadequate staffing, the days of opening to the public were reduced from four to three (Monday, Wednesday, Friday), and this remained the rule for many years.[23]

The pace of the guided tours was unaffected. Another visitor from America, Louis Simond, was in one of the parties that were hustled through the museum in 1810. A guide "took charge of us, and led us *au pas de charge* through a number of rooms full of stuffed birds and animals—many of them seemingly in a state of decay. We had a glimpse of arms, dresses, and ornaments of savages hung around—of a collection of minerals—next of antiquities from Herculaneum and Pompeia, and monstrous Egypt. . . . We had no time allowed to examine any thing; our conductor pushed on without minding questions, or unable to answer

156. The British Museum: the old Sculpture Gallery, 1827 (watercolor by George Scharf the elder).

them, but treating the company with double *entendres* and witticisms on various subjects of natural history, in a style of vulgarity and impudence which I should not have expected to have met in this place, and in this country."[24]

◻❖◻

This, then, was the condition of the four major public monuments in London when the reformist Whigs came to power in 1832. Hitherto, unlike the closely related movements in behalf of free elementary education and scientific education for the adult masses, which had behind them the powerful lobbying and propagandizing force of organizations like the Useful Knowledge Society, the spreading dissatisfaction with the operation of these institutions had been unfocused and unorganized. Now, however, the sentiment for converting three of the monuments into freely accessible places for public enjoyment rather than personal (ecclesiastical) gain or comfort was adopted as a part of the reform bloc's program, not only for its own sake, but to help energize the program as a whole. It proved very useful.

The liberal Whigs were strongly, though selectively, antiestablishment, in harmony with the movement that had recently seen London University founded to challenge the Oxbridge monopoly on English higher education and, in another sphere, with Haydon's (and later Martin's) campaign against the autocratic Royal Academy. The impending attack on the British Museum would be fueled by the not unrelated facts that its trustees, a self-perpetuating body, were drawn from the most conservative elements in contemporary society, and most of its officials were clergymen well paid to do little work. The most powerful vested interest of all was the Church of England, whose lush privileges and unbecoming wealth the secularist politicians in particular were determined to trim. Although the actual sums of money involved at the Abbey and St. Paul's were of little consequence, the assault on the ecclesiastical proprietorship of the shows there neatly dovetailed with the grand scheme to cleanse the Established Church of its manifold corruptions of nepotism, pluralism, and luxury. What the liberals took to be the people's active desire to enjoy the public sights of London unhindered by entrance charges, the importunities of attendants, and obstructive officialdom provided them with a most attractive ground on which to assert the people's interests over the parsons', to challenge the dead hand of outworn, self-serving custom.

The reformers, however, were not so heavily committed to the democratic principle that they failed to share the upper class's long-standing fear of the people as a social and political force with great, though unmeasured, potential for trouble. The Luddite disturbances of 1811–12 and 1816 and the more recent crisis over the Reform Bill were vivid in memory, and from the mid-thirties the ominous clouds of "physical force" Chartism were gathering. An implicit end which giving the people free access to public monuments might serve, therefore, was to provide them, as popularized science might also do, with a peaceable and perhaps even rewarding alternative to talking and thinking subversion and forming militant radical organizations.

Yet beneath these immediate pragmatic objectives resided a substantial layer of idealism which was genuine enough, no matter how glibly it often was invoked —degenerating sometimes into the worst kind of pious cant—in order to conceal less altruistic purposes. A certain influential, if relatively small, body of public men had begun to believe that the intellectual curiosity and constructive mental energy to which exhibitions typified by the British Museum and the Abbey might appeal was a valuable cultural resource. In their view the government was obligated to oversee, if not actually support and manage, such institutions in behalf of the people's moral and social improvement. In the thirties and forties, when the popular education movement reached its peak, there were innumerable expressions of this faith that the ordinary man was capable of participating in the nation's cultural life and should be encouraged to do so. One such statement appeared in *Blackwood's Magazine* in 1842:

Exhibitions, galleries, and museums, are part and parcel of popular education in the young and the adult: they stimulate that principle of inquisitiveness natural to man, and with the right sort of food: they instil knowledge, drop by drop, through the eye into the mind, and create a healthy appetite, growing with what it feeds on: they make the libraries of those who have no money to expend on books, and are the travels of those that have no time to bestow on travel: they are schools in which the best and only true politeness may be taught—politeness that refines the manners by ennobling the heart: they are the best allies of despots, beguiling even slavery of its bitterness; and the surest aids to freemen, since they inculcate tastes and habits that render even freemen still more free.[25]

Among the evidences of the people's presumed interest in visiting the great national monuments was the wide circulation of cheap papers describing and picturing them. Amidst all its other "general information" articles the *Penny Magazine,* for example, ran illustrated descriptions of England's abbeys and churches and the Tower of London. The result of this burst of attention to architecture and native antiquities in the didactic section of the popular press was, according to more than one witness before parliamentary committees, "a laudable curiosity in the hitherto misinformed mind, as well as a greater respect for works of art and antiquity."[26] So wholesome a development should be officially encouraged by enabling the public to visit, without cost or hindrance, the places they read about.

There was also the appeal to patriotism. As travel to the continent increased, some Englishmen were disturbed by what they regarded as their own nation's clear inferiority to France, Italy, and Germany in respect to the accessibility of public buildings. The *Blackwood's* writer just quoted was unequivocal on the point:

If there is one thing in which we fall below foreign nations, it is in the circumscribed and limited utility of our purely national, which should be purely gratuitous, exhibitions. In this we are positively shabby, and more than shabby—we are unwise. From our public exhibitions, we must be estimated by the great mass of foreigners who may not have opportunities of gaining access to select society, and who can see nothing of us but our streets, and the outsides of our houses. The courteous liberality with which they fling open to us their churches, halls, and galleries, we do by no means reciprocate; and whatever estimate they may form of our power, grandeur, and wealth, they have but little to say in favour of our generosity.

The most elevated note of this campaign, however, was struck by those who envisaged the aesthetic, and eventually the moral and religious, benefits that would accrue to a public enjoying free access to places like the Abbey and St. Paul's. A member of Parliament who admitted that he seldom found himself agreeing with the reformist party declared that the difficulties impecunious people had in entering those venerable houses of worship meant that they were being deprived of "the finest works of art in the world." Alluding to Burke's definition of the sublime and its tendency to call forth noble feelings, he expressed the opinion that "fine paintings on religious subjects, good sculpture, and striking architecture, influence and improve the religious sentiments of the lower classes."[27] One of the parliamentary committees involved in the movement took the same line in its report. Free admission, it asserted, "may be made conducive not merely to the

gratification of curiosity and the acquirement of historical knowledge, but to the growth and progress of religious impressions, by leading the mind of the spectator from the contemplation of the building to a consideration of the views with which, and the purposes for which, it was originally erected and is still maintained."[28]

Opposing this idea that every man had an inherent right to enjoy and benefit from the national treasures were, for the most part, the old-line Tories who at the same time were fighting proposals for state-aided elementary education on the ground that teaching working people to read would tempt them into unproductive idleness and, in the extreme view, foment rebellion. They pointed to the menace that the democratization of privilege in such matters as museumgoing exercised over taste. The familiar application of Gresham's law to culture in general in an emerging democracy—that low standards of necessity supersede high ones—was invoked in respect to museums in particular. James Fenimore Cooper, who shared some of the deepest prejudices of his English Tory cousins, doubtless spoke for many when he remarked of the Abbey waxworks that they exemplified the "crude and coarse tastes" which the purchasing power of the people had made a norm for the whole nation; they had "an influence on all public exhibitions that is unfelt on the continent, where the spectacle being intended solely for the intellectual, is better adapted to their habits."[29]

The doughty populist-journalist William Cobbett, sitting in the reformed Parliament as member for Oldham, vociferously opposed grants for the British Museum's annual expenses and a new building for other reasons.

He would ask [reported Hansard] of what use, in the wide world, was this British Museum, and to whom, to what class of persons, it was useful? He found that 1,000 *l.* had been laid out in insects; and surely hon. Members would not assert that these insects were of any use to the ploughboys of Hampshire and of Surrey, and to the weavers of Lancashire! It did a great deal of good to the majority of those who went to it, but to nobody else. The ploughman and the weavers—the shopkeepers and the farmers—never went near it; they paid for it though, whilst the idle loungers enjoyed it, and scarcely paid anything. Let those who lounged in it, and made it a place of amusement, contribute to its support. Why should tradesmen and farmers be called upon to pay for the support of a place which was intended only for the amusement of the curious and the rich, and not for the benefit or for the instruction of the poor? If the aristocracy wanted the Museum as a lounging place, let them pay for it. For his own part he did not know where this British Museum was, nor did he know much of the contents of it, but from the little he had heard of it, even if he knew where it was, he would not take the trouble of going to see it.[30]

This same Cobbett, a few days earlier, had categorically declared that education was useless and that he was completely opposed to the "higher branches" of science. Rebuked though he was by some of his conservative fellow members, his views were not peculiar to him; expressed in more temperate language, they were held by a significant portion of Parliament. Nevertheless, the burden of sentiment lay elsewhere. The prevailing, if not necessarily most realistic, note in this hopeful era of cultural dissemination was that struck by one Whig member in opposition to Cobbett, Thomas Spring Rice: "Let the hon. Member go to the Museum on any public day, and he would find it crowded . . . with members of the poorer classes, who went there to see the works of art and science, which they had read of in the works of information which they had read on the previous Saturday. He would see that the pleasure derivable from the *chefs d'oeuvres* of arts and science was not confined to the higher classes, but was extended even to those whom we were accustomed to consider as the lower classes of the community."[31]

▷⫛✳⫛◁

Clearly, Spring Rice was exaggerating in a good cause: the attendance figures for these years do not permit us to believe that any substantial numbers of "the poorer classes" found their way into the British Museum. But it was in behalf of this body of the population, to which some public men attributed a genuine hunger for knowledge, that several select committees of Commons were appointed to look into the alleged malfeasance, corruption, and antidemocratic management of the noncommercial institutions most familiar to London sightseers. These inquiries constituted forums in which the complaints hitherto aired in the press, with little result, could now be authoritatively restated, amplified, and augmented. The principal subjects of the investigations were the British Museum (1835–36), "national monuments and works of art" (1841), and the National Gallery (1850). Although most of the impetus came from liberals, these were not wholly partisan undertakings. Supporting the inquiry into the British Museum, for instance, was an influen-

tial portion of the scientific community whose spokesman was Sir Humphry Davy, well known to be no "Radical Reformer" but a thoroughgoing Tory. The questioning, however, was ordinarily led by a chairman whose purposes were unmistakable, Joseph Hume, a veteran leader of liberal causes. Indispensable though the voluminous record of evidence is, it must be read with caution. The issues were emotional ones, engaging the witnesses' deepest social convictions and prejudices, and both the vividness and the hyperbole of some of the testimony distort the reality.

The tenor of the examination of hostile witnesses as well as an important line of questioning is typified by this passage in the record of the 1835 British Museum inquiry, when the crusty principal librarian (director) of the institution, Sir Henry Ellis, was giving evidence. The issue at the moment was the museum's practice of closing at Easter and Whitsuntide for annual cleaning and the receipt of a year's accumulation of newspapers from the Stamp Office. "Do you think," Ellis was asked, "that is a sufficient reason for excluding the public at a time when so large a portion of the people are at leisure?" "I think," he replied, "the most mischievous portion of the population is abroad and about at such a time."

Q. Do you think that any mischief would arise to the Museum provided sufficient attendants were present? *A.* Yes, I think the most vulgar class would crowd into the Museum.

Q. Do you not think that one object of the Museum is to improve the vulgar class? *A.* I think the mere gazing at our curiosities is not one of the greatest objects of the Museum. . . .

Q. Do you think there would be any difficulty, supposing the Committee thought that the Museum should be open during the Easter and Whitsun weeks, in accomplishing such a wish? *A.* I think the exclusion of the public is very material, inasmuch as the place otherwise would really be unwholesome. The great extent of cleansing which they enable us to undertake, renders those weeks very necessary to us. . . .

Q. Would it not be desirable, with reference to the great mass of the people, that that cleansing should take place at some other part of the year, and that the Museum should be open during the great public holidays? *A.* I think the inconvenience, generally speaking, is less on those great public holidays than it would be at any other time.

Q. Are there not more people about whom you should be anxious to instruct and amuse during those holidays than at any other portion of the year? *A.* I think the more important class of the population (as far as we are concerned) would be discontented at such a change as the former question contemplates.

Q. Will you describe what you mean by the more important part of the population? *A.* People of a higher grade would hardly wish to come to the Museum at the same time with sailors from the dock-yards and girls whom they might bring with them. I do not think such people would gain any improvement from the sight of our collections.

Q. Did you ever know of an instance of a sailor bringing a girl from the dock-yards? *A.* I never traced them to the dock-yards, but the class of people who would come at such times would be of a very low description.[32]

The eventual consequence of this asperity-laden exchange, and of other lively passages of questioning during the same committee's hearings, was that in 1837 the British Museum was open, for the first time, on holidays. On the first Easter Monday under the new policy, 23,000 persons jammed the building.[33] Despite Sir Henry's black misgivings, no slightest breach of the peace occurred; but this did not soften his and most of his colleagues' resistance to the further proposal that the museum and the other national monuments be opened on Sundays as well. The pressure to provide free places of recreation on Sundays and holidays was growing as city dwellers, deprived of their former easy access to the countryside, were forced to depend on the resources of central London to fill their leisure. On Sundays the Abbey and St. Paul's were open only for services, after which everyone was unceremoniously evicted. Brought back to testify before the National Monuments Committee in 1841, Ellis was as implacably opposed to opening the museum on Sunday as he had been to moving the "closed for cleaning" weeks to nonholiday periods. "The servants of the museum," he declared, "are as much entitled to the quiet of the Sabbath as any others of Her Majesty's subjects." Although Sunday labor was required of some British subjects, in general it was a peculiarity of "catholic countries" and therefore not a precedent to be followed in Britain. One of Sir Henry's colleagues offered another argument against Sunday opening: it would not do to rely on attendants who were willing to take Sunday duty. "I should have less confidence in a man who would be willing to have his Sunday occupied in that way than in one who had scruples upon the subject." A third official, however, John Edward Gray, the keeper of the zoological collection, broke ranks on the issue. Having formerly practiced medicine in Spitalfields, he knew that the residents there were "very fond of works of natural history" and spent their Sundays working in their gardens and botanizing in the country. They would assuredly come to the British Museum if it were open on Sunday afternoons.[34] (The example was as loaded as the reasoning was imperfect, because residents of Spitalfields, the descendants of silk weavers who had come there as Huguenot refugees, were regarded as the aristocrats of London labor, with a markedly superior interest in things of the mind. They constituted a negligible minority of the total population.)

It was a reformist tenet that, as a fellow of the Antiquarian Society told the 1836 British Museum Committee, opening the museum on Sunday "would be one of the very best modes of counteracting the effect of gin palaces," which were then open all day Sunday and, after 1839, would be allowed to do business after 1 P.M. *Q.* "It would tend to give them a taste for objects of natural history, rather than a taste for gin?"[35] *A.* "Unquestionably, it would be one of the best modes of improving the morals of the people."* Sir Henry Ellis bluntly disagreed: "I do not think that the Museum would be an attraction to any party who might be inclined to go into a public-house on the Sunday."[36]

Another subject of the National Monuments inquiry was the fees at Westminster Abbey and St. Paul's. The authorities at the latter place, represented by the clergyman-wit Sydney Smith, who was a canon residentiary, maintained that the twopenny admission fee was absolutely necessary to keep within bounds, if it could not wholly eradicate, the use of the cathedral as a place of assignation and a resort of pickpockets and prostitutes. Small though it was, the charge would separate the earnest visitors who came to see the statuary and architecture from those who had less reputable business. "I think," said Smith, "if it became generally known in the metropolis that anybody without payment might come into the church of St. Paul's, all those evils . . . would take place." Why not, then, he was asked, make doubly sure by doubling the price? "Because we must take some medium between the indulgence to the public and the decorum of the church."[37] As for Westminster Abbey, either it did not have the same problem or the officials were more realistic. Their spokesman did not see how entrance could be denied anyone paying the fee: how were the attendants to "discriminate between a common prostitute and other persons, if she is properly attired, and conducts herself with decency"?[38]

The problem at the British Museum was somewhat

* This may or may not have been overidealistic, but there can be no such doubt in respect to a proposal that employed workingmen be encouraged to pay weekday visits to St. Paul's and the Abbey. Two witnesses before the 1841 National Monuments Committee readily assented to the proposition that if those buildings "were known to be open for a few hours every day . . . parties from the different workshops and factories in the town [would] be formed to go and visit them in succession, instead of, as now, going to a public-house." (*Report from the Select Committee on National Monuments,* 1841, q. 1347.)

different. Children under eight were not admitted on public days. The ineffable Sir Henry Ellis professed surprise when told that parents left their young children at a neighboring tavern while they went through the museum, or that one parent remained in the courtyard with the children while the other entered; he admitted, however, that he had heard the complaint of a nearby upholsterer that "sometimes he had six or eight people at his shop at one time begging to be allowed to sit down with their children till their friends came out."[39] The amenities provided for visitors once they got inside the building briefly concerned one committee. There were, it appears, no indoor sanitary facilities, only two outdoor privies. Q. "Do you not think in the concourse of 20,000 or 30,000 people [who came once the building was opened on holidays] passing in one day through the rooms, instances may occur when great inconvenience arises from want of such places?" Sir Henry Ellis: "No doubt."[40]

Arrangements at the Tower of London were in the charge of the Duke of Wellington, who, as chief constable of the Tower since 1826, was in effect an executive showman. Like Ellis, but less abrasively, he was opposed to admitting the public to his exhibition without severe restrictions. He was, after all, a soldier, and although the Tower had ceased to be used as a military stronghold in 1554, "he saw it," Lady Longford has written, "as the modern revolutionary mob's bastille, for whose possession they and he would never cease to fight. . . . 'What is to prevent some thousands each with a shilling from going there if they please, and when once there from doing what they please? Who is to keep them in order? Or to turn them out?'"[41] The hundreds of thousands of swords, spears, and halberds in the armory, to say nothing of the muskets and ammunition, must, in his estimation, constitute a standing temptation to the mob. Wellington therefore ordered that no more than one hundred visitors be allowed inside the walls at a given time, with the result that on some days there were long lines of people waiting for those already inside to leave. That was one reason why the prescribed parties of twelve (an ideal figure which in practice was often raised to twenty or thirty) were hustled through.[42] Another, of course, was the warders' awareness that the greater the turnover was, the larger the day's total tips would be.

D⅗❋⅗᠌D

Ellis's opposition to opening the British Museum at holiday seasons and Wellington's limitation on the number of persons allowed inside the Tower at a given time exemplified the most deep-seated prejudice that haunted all discussion of free access to public monuments: the fear of the crowd that has already been mentioned. At base it was a political fear, a virtual conviction that large gatherings of lower-class people, if not strictly controlled, always posed a threat to order. The liberals, recognizing the power of such apprehensions in this nervous age of the Chartists, sought to quiet them by arguing that "the million's" capacity for mischief could deftly be diverted into healthy channels by sending them to places like the Abbey and the British Museum. This was another assumption, less explicit than the one having to do with temperance, that lay behind the advocacy of public monuments as alternatives to public houses, because it was at one tavern or another that numerous reform or revolutionary movements in the past two centuries had been launched or had their headquarters.

But in these parliamentary inquiries, as in the surrounding climate of press comment, despite the lowering Chartist threat there was little overt hint of a bread-and-circuses motive. The specifically political desirability of moving crowds from unruly taverns to the calmer environs of churches and museums went largely undiscussed. Instead, attention was centered on the personal and group behavior of the masses, on their capacity for disorder unrelated to political agitation, and how it could be transformed into personal decency, decorum, and responsibility. The extensive testimony received by the committees must be read with an awareness that in the earliest Victorian years the public behavior of the urban population was less restrained than at any time since. "Riotous" conduct, often accompanied by drunkenness, was commonplace, and, in the thickening atmosphere of middle-class propriety, disgusting.

The prevalence of public drunkenness gave pause to even the best-intentioned friends of the people. Not many chose to contemplate the possibility that working-class men and women, failing to appreciate that the British Museum, for example, was a wholesome alternative to the public house, would seize the best of both worlds by stopping in at the latter on their way to the former. Some who were in a good position to know, however, were not unmindful of this contingency. One of the witnesses before the 1835 British Museum Committee was a minor official who was better disposed than most of his colleagues toward the common people who came to the building. "The ignorant," he said, "are brought into awe by what they see about them, and the better informed know how to conduct themselves. We have common policemen, soldiers, sailors, artillery-men, livery-servants, and, of course, occasionally, mechanics; but their good conduct I am very pleased to see." Yet even he was opposed to opening the museum on such holidays as Boxing Day, Easter Monday, and Whit Monday. "We find," he explained, "that the lowest of the low on those days are set at liberty, and get intoxicated, and I would not answer for their conduct." The obvious fear was that if the museums-for-the-people movement succeeded, the tumultuous scenes which marked the Cockney rites of spring down the river at Greenwich Fair would be moved indoors in Bloomsbury. At the very least, urged this witness, if the museum were to be opened on those days, "it would be advisable . . . to have a good watch at the door, that no one in a state of the slightest inebriation or not decently attired should be admitted."[43] On the brighter side there was the thought that if the bibulous were excluded, their respectable friends would enjoy their visit all the more.

While the British Museum struggled to fend off the pollution of the proletariat, the officials of St. Paul's reported that their premises were desecrated by the "fashionable" as well. The most horrendous documentation of the dangers the London populace offered to a national monument—though some of the other testimony suggests it was exaggerated—was delivered to the 1841 committee by Sydney Smith. Four years earlier there had been an unsatisfactory exchange of correspondence between Church and State initiated by the queen's request, transmitted to the dean and chapter of St. Paul's by the home secretary, Lord John Russell, that the cathedral be opened to the public at certain times without the payment of any fee or gratuity.[44] The queen's wish was acceded to for several Sundays, but the experiment ended after Smith received this distraught communication from one of the minor canons:

Rev. Sir,—Your good intention of accommodating the public by throwing open the entire area of the cathedral on the Sunday afternoon, I am sorry to say, has produced an evil of so serious a nature as to require immediate consideration. I should fail were I to attempt to give you even a rough sketch of the disgraceful scene which every Sunday afternoon is being enacted around us. The whole cathedral, excepting the choir and those assembled in it for divine service, is converted into a lobby for fashionable loungers; hundreds of persons meet together for no other purpose than to make an exhibition of this description; so that what with the pacing of feet, the murmur of voices, and the gadding to and fro of fig-

ures, every church-like notion is driven from our minds; the whole thing more resembles a promenade in a ball-room than a congregation in the house of God. I do not hesitate to declare, that in my life I never witnessed such a violation of decency.[45]

It appears from this that a Sunday afternoon open house in the nave of St. Paul's was virtually indistinguishable from a weekday afternoon in an Oxford Street or Regent Street bazaar, one difference being that the cathedral lacked cosmoramas. But the moral tone at St. Paul's was in much greater peril than at those secular meeting places. When the Select Committee on National Monuments sat in 1841, Joseph Hume produced a letter Smith had written to Lord John Russell, reporting the failure of the experiment and warning, "If the doors of St. Paul's were flung open, the church would become, as it has been in times past, a place of assignation for all the worst characters, male and female." Under questioning, Smith was forced to admit that "times past" referred to "the century before last," when, as was notorious, lawyers transacted business, lotteries were drawn, and "all sorts of nuisances took place" in the old cathedral, destroyed in the Great Fire of 1666. Nevertheless, he insisted that the same evils prevailed at the present moment: "beggars, men with burthens, women knitting, parties eating luncheon, dogs, children playing, loud laughing and talking, and every kind of scene incompatible with the solemnity of worship. . . . On one side of a line the congregation are praying; on the other is all the levity, indecorum and tumult of a London mob, squabbling with the police, looking upon St. Paul's as a gallery of sculpture, not a house of prayer, and vindicating their right to be merry and gay, if they abstain from crime."[46]

In the same letter, Smith had stated that "the cathedral is constantly and shamefully polluted with ordure; the pews are sometimes turned into *cabinets d'aisance.*" A later witness, a verger with eight years' service, gave graphic testimony to the same effect; "most of the corners [inside the church]," he asserted, "have been swimming with water."

Q. Do you mean simply urine, or any thing else? A. Both.
Q. Does it take place often? A. Very frequently.
Q. Do you find it out afterwards? A. We find it out afterwards; we caught one person in the act.
Q. How many have you caught, say in the course of the last year? A. I suppose more than 20.
Q. That you have seen do it? A. Yes; but we could not do any thing with them, only let them go.

Q. Were they men or women? *A.* Generally they have been ladies, a good many of them, and men too.[47]

One other acute problem laid before the National Monuments Committee was vandalism. Smith testified that at St. Paul's "the monuments are scribbled all over, and often with the grossest indecency," and he was backed up by his senior verger, an employee of upward of forty years' service, who said that "a man went round only last week to take the writing off the walls in different parts of the church, where there has been gross and vulgar lines, not fit for any person to see."[48] Most of the inscriptions, it appears, consisted of the names of male visitors "and the names of various ladies of their acquaintance." Prevalent though graffiti were, at St. Paul's there had been only two instances of structural damage to monuments, both accidental.[49]

At Westminster Abbey, however, outright destructiveness remained a problem. In his *Letters from England* (1807) Robert Southey, in the character of a Spanish visitor, had observed, "from the mischief which is even now committed, it is evident that, were the public indiscriminately admitted, every thing valuable would soon be destroyed." The English, he said, have a "barbarous habit . . . of seeing by the sight of touch."[50] (Lamb may well have remembered this remark when he came to address his open letter to Southey sixteen years later. As an old Christ's Hospital boy himself, he magnanimously defended the maligned Westminster School boys, who, he said, were permanently blamed for the most celebrated of the many instances of Abbey vandalism, the decapitation of Major André's effigy. No matter who did it, for such an offense, committed long ago, "the people of England are made to pay a new Peter's Pence . . . ; or must content themselves with contemplating the ragged exterior of their Cathedral." Lamb impishly concluded: "The mischief was done about the time that you [Southey] were a scholar there. Do you know anything about the unfortunate relic?")[51]

About 1822 the iron "palisadoes" which surrounded many of the royal and noble tombs had been removed by the order of Sir Francis Chantrey, the Abbey architect, who pointed out that they protected only the pedestals of the monuments and afforded too tempting a platform for miscreants who could, and did, climb up to deface and mutilate the sculpture.[52] But where there was a will there remained other ways, and the monuments continued to be imperiled. Much of the relatively recent damage had been caused during the coronations of George IV, William IV, and Victoria. During preparations for Victoria's ceremony alone, the erection of scaffolding to provide the maximum number of spectators' seats had resulted in twenty-four toes, fingers, and bits of drapery being knocked off. Said one of the laborers: "What! can you expect a man who has only 18s. a week to take care of sculpture?"[53]

Such facts, regrettable as they were in themselves, were elicited for the record in order to counter the assumption that it was the reckless or fun-loving members of the public who did all the damage. Englishmen in general, several witnesses alleged, had less reverence for their religious edifices than did people in Catholic countries. Sydney Smith and Henry Milman, representing the Abbey, agreed that this was one of the less desirable by-products of Puritanism. The latter pointed out that a Roman Catholic entering a church "dips his finger into the holy water, and, as it were, is reminded thereby of the sanctity of the building; but a vast number of the people of England, I regret to say, (and I wish a much more profound feeling could be rooted generally into the people,) will march in with their hats on, and walk about as if it were an ordinary building."[54]

John Edward Gray, the British Museum official quoted earlier, came to the defense of his compatriots, who, he said, had been "most unjustly abused" for their supposed misconduct in public buildings, partly because of "that delight which the English have in complaining of their countrymen, and praising foreigners at their expense, and partly by designing persons, who have profited by places being kept from public view, except on the payment of fees." He maintained that if the English did, perhaps, write on walls more than people did on the continent, it was because "they have not the constant dread of the surveillance of the police, which the French appear always to have before their eyes." This "remnant of barbarism" was the price—a small one, to be sure—that the nation had to pay for the precious freedom of the individual.[55]

As ill luck would have it, two separate incidents soon confirmed the bleakest fears of those who saw the unrestrained public as a threat to the nation's artistic treasures. In January 1844, a lame visitor to the National Gallery suddenly raised his crutch and thrust it through Mola's *Jupiter and Leda*. He maintained that it was an accident—that he had been pointing out the beauties of the painting to a friend and his crutch had slipped.[56] Understandably embarrassed, both Hume and Sir Robert Peel hastened to assure the House of Commons that the incident was an isolated one and that there was now "no tendency among the people in general to do that wanton mischief which had once been apprehended from them."[57] But a year later an even more serious incident gave fresh cause for apprehension. On 7 February 1845 a youth identifying himself as William Lloyd, a student at Dublin University, picked up a large Babylonian sculptured stone in a room at the British Museum and hurled it at the case containing the famous Portland vase, the finest surviving example of Roman cameo glass. The vase was shattered into more than two hundred pieces. Since it was not the museum's property, having been lent by the Duke of Portland, the authorities could prosecute Lloyd only for breaking the case, which was valued at £3. He spent a few days in jail and then was released upon payment of that sum. The *Times* printed fierce letters recommending that a stiff law be passed to cover such crimes and that offenders be sentenced to the pillory and a dose of the cat-o'-nine-tails.[58] In the end, a skillful craftsman restored the vase to almost pristine condition. But the friends of the people had to work harder than ever to persuade public opinion that when ordinary men and women visited national showplaces they were, as a class, devoid of mischievous intent.

Implicit in much of the discussion was the belief that many of officialdom's worries could be resolved by the provision of adequate police. At St. Paul's, officers were on duty only on Sunday, and then mainly to see that the worshipers left as soon as service was over; otherwise the vergers would, as one of them said, be deprived of their "refreshment; we could not all stop there, and it would not do to leave the public by themselves; we do not know what injury they might do."[59] The trouble was that little of what "the public" did actually broke the law. Using the interior of a cathedral as a privy evidently was no more a legal offense than were the Sunday affectations of the fashionable crowd that so distressed the minor canon. A practical difficulty at the Abbey was its layout. The presence of so many chapels and other enclosures, and of huge monuments behind which all sorts of mischief could be committed, made efficient policing almost impossible.

Still, as Colonel Rowan, one of the two original chief commissioners of the Metropolitan Police, testified in 1841, he could do the job if he had enough men. He had sent as many as a dozen constables to the British Museum on holidays, and they had kept perfect order; he could do as well at the Abbey, which, however, offered another peculiar problem—its proximity to St. James's Park, where there might be ten thousand people on a pleasant Sunday; what if they all decided to look at the monuments at the same time? When the Abbey had been thrown open without restriction several days after each of the two recent coronations so that the public might see the decorations, the police had had some difficulty, but only "on account of the numbers; none on account of the disposition of the people." Speaking from twelve years' experience, Rowan declared that the conduct of the London populace had much improved, "especially upon occasions when great numbers assemble," such as the queen's appearing before Parliament and the Lord Mayor's Show.[60]

This was the sort of thing Hume and his liberal colleagues wanted to hear, backed up as it was by a substantial amount of testimony to the same effect from other well-chosen witnesses. The great problem they faced was to reassure the respectable public at large, particularly in view of such an embarrassment as the smashing of the Portland vase. Throughout the forties influential portions of the London press strove to allay any doubts that a general reformation of manners had indeed occurred and that places like the Abbey and the British Museum were no longer in the slightest danger from mischief-makers. Papers like the *Times* and the *Illustrated London News* regularly added to their reports of the holiday attendance at public monuments such statements as "perfect order was maintained" and "there was no single instance of misbehavior."

D3⚹E⊃

The mere prospect of these parliamentary inquiries caused a few reforms to be effected at the institutions due to be scrutinized, and several others followed the hearings and the respective committees' recommendations.* Among the reforms which anticipated the inquiries was the long overdue retirement in 1839 of the ragged regiment, the scandalous epitome of the Abbey's catchpenny atmosphere. As we have seen, in grudging compliance with one or two recommendations, the British Museum was opened on holidays, and the trustees, accepting a suggestion from Sir Robert Peel, decided to issue cheap guides to the contents of the four main departments open to visitors.

The Tower of London prospered as never before, thanks to the publicity it received from Ainsworth's sensationally popular novel of that name (1840). Admission to the armory had been cut to a shilling in 1838 and to sixpence a year later, with the result that attendance in 1840–41 was almost nine times what it

* The queen set an example by opening Hampton Court and Windsor palaces on a more liberal basis and throwing Kew Gardens, hitherto the private property of the sovereign, open to the public. A museum was added at Kew in 1847 and Sunday opening instituted in 1853. Greenwich Hospital, which had been open to visitors since at least 1791, hurriedly revised its fee schedule to correct a glaring anomaly. Although soldiers were admitted gratis, sailors, who after all had a special interest in this stately retirement home for the nation's naval pensioners, had to pay the usual fee of threepence to see the chapel and threepence to see the painted hall. Now they were added to the free list. (*Report from the Select Committee on National Monuments,* 1841, qq. 2028–46.)

157. The British Museum:
Easter Monday crowd in the
Great Zoological Gallery, 1845
(*Illustrated London News*, 29
March 1845).

had been only four years earlier, when the fee was two shillings.[61] Considerable additions were made to the armor collection between September 1839 and May 1841, chiefly suits and weapons lately used at Eglinton. But these accessions were promptly canceled out by the loss of 200,000 stand of arms and an "almost innumerable quantity of trophies" in a fire that swept the Small Armoury and the Grand Storehouse for the Royal Train of Artillery on the night of 30 October 1841.[62] True to London show tradition, the Tower capitalized on its misfortune by charging sixpence to see the ruins. For months thereafter relics of the fire were vended at the site.[63]

Elsewhere, once the committees' reports had been issued and such action taken as the authorities at the various monuments thought desirable, plenty of room for complaint remained. The near-completion of the building program at the British Museum had provided several large new exhibition halls, but the collections

continued to outgrow the available space. Ralph Waldo Emerson, visiting the museum in 1848, dismissed it in a few tart words: "The arrangement of the antique remains is surprisingly imperfect & careless, without order, or skilful disposition, or names or numbers. A warehouse of old marbles."[64] Later evidence makes plain that the other collections were in no better shape. But at least there was no question of multiple fees or intrusive attendants, and it was these stumbling blocks to enjoyment, which the inquiries had done nothing to eliminate, that placed the other monuments under more severe criticism than ever during the forties.

At St. Paul's, where the twopenny entrance fee was stubbornly retained, it was, according to an incensed writer in *Blackwood's,* but the prelude to a process of continuous extortion once the visitor was inside:

There is a fee for the body of the church, a fee for the choir, a fee for the whispering gallery, a fee for the library, a fee for

158. The British Museum: two of the new exhibition halls (*Illustrated London News*, 13 February and 3 April 1847). Above: the Egyptian Room. Below: the Coral Room.

the clock-work, a fee for the great bell, a fee for the little bell, a fee for the ball at the top, and a fee for the vaults at the bottom; wherever an Englishman would put his nose, in any corner of this his own National Church, built by the contributions of his ancestors, he is met by a mob of money-takers, cheque-takers, and the like, vociferating fees—fees—fees! . . . The demands of the money-takers are studiously regulated so as to extort the greatest possible amount of money from the visiters.[65]

We may sacrifice the subsequent elaboration and peroration in favor of a more succinct statement of the case that appeared the next year in the *Athenaeum:* "This tariff, it is manifest, has been arranged with a shrewdness that would not discredit Madame Tussaud, nor any other adroit manager of an exhibition, the entire spectacle being distributed into parts, none of which affords the visitor too much amusement for his money, whilst each decoys him onward from the previous sight to fresh wonders and expenditure." It was not possible even to be selective: to get to a given attraction one had to pass through others, paying at each turnstile en route. The writer bristled: "as each sight finishes, how civil, how sedulous, to inform the visitor —'But two-pence more, and you see the wonderful Clock, sir,'—'You are now half way to the Ball, sir; another eighteen-pence takes you up, weighs 5,600 pounds, holds twelve persons, 'Arrow-on-the-Ill visible from it just now, sir; only eighteen-pence additional.' He that after these illustrations can believe St. Paul's a tabernacle of white-handed human cherubim, guarding the sacred treasures, could swallow a camel."[66]

At the Abbey, the chief cause of complaint was no longer the admission charge per se. Following the unpleasantness between Parliament and the dean and chapter in the mid-twenties, an arrangement was eventually arrived at whereby the canons and singing men renounced their claim on the money collected from visitors in exchange for a collective annual stipend of £1,400.[67] The fees, now earmarked for cleaning and maintenance, were gradually lowered, until by the mid-forties the public was admitted gratis to the south transept, including the Poets' Corner, threepence being charged to see the monuments in the nave and threepence more to see all the rest. Subsequently, the whole nave was liberated. Two disadvantages of the old enclosure system, however, remained: the offense to the eye and the bothersomeness of the now salaried (a guinea a week) corps of "tomb-showers." Describing in this novel *Sybil* (1845) Egremont's first visit to the build-

ing, Disraeli wrote of his disenchantment by "the boards and spikes with which he seemed to be environed, as if the Abbey were in a stage of siege; iron gates shutting him out from the solemn nave and the shadowy aisles; scarcely a glimpse to be caught of a single window; while on a dirty form, some noisy vergers sat like ticket-porters or babbled like tapsters at their ease."[68]

And so the young, impudent *Punch* had plenty of ammunition when it picked up the campaign where the committees of Commons had left off. Between 1844 and 1851 it persistently sniped at the "clerical showmen" of both the Abbey and St. Paul's. In one satiric paragraph and cartoon after another it recommended that the dean and chapter advertise in the newspapers and on placards, as did the Colosseum; that the Poets' Corner accept Byron's body as a counterattraction to the giraffe and chimpanzee at the Zoo; that a circuslike platform be erected on the west porch of St. Paul's, complete with garish posters, band, and barker; that children be admitted to both buildings at half-price, as was done at Madame Tussaud's; that there should be refreshment stalls at both places; that handbills be distributed at Sunday services advertising the weekday attractions; and that the dome of St. Paul's be fitted up as a camera obscura show.[69] Whispers that were reported overheard in the Whispering Gallery included:

> "This building is supported by involuntary contributions."
> "The Bishop expects every Englishman to pay the duty."
> "The Showman has no salary, excepting what he receives from visitors."
> "Persons who are pleased with the exhibition are requested to recommend it to those outside."
> "The Free List is suspended, excepting for Members of the Royal Family."[70]

It was a joyous campaign which even today is entertaining to follow; and it probably did some good, though the evidence is conflicting. At the Abbey, according to a letter to the *Times* in 1847, the chattering *ciceroni* hitherto complained of had disappeared, and one could now see throngs "walking about admiring the architecture, or spelling out the monuments, and enjoying all they saw the more from being free and unattended, with no odious verger dogging their heels and directing them what to look at, and wearying their ears with his humdrum tales a thousand times told."[71] But the writer must have happened into the building at a fortunate moment, when the vergers were taking a break; for seven years later Nathaniel Hawthorne, vis-

159. *Punch*'s vision of sandwich men advertising St. Paul's Cathedral (*Punch*, 17 April 1847).

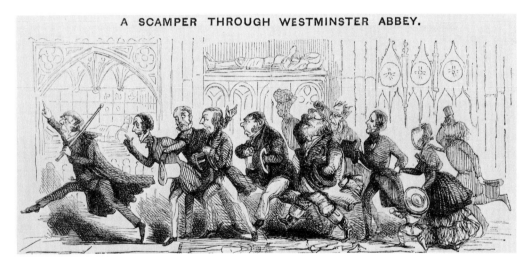

A SCAMPER THROUGH WESTMINSTER ABBEY.

160. Whirlwind tours of Westminster Abbey (two fancies from *Punch*, 25 October 1845 and 5 September 1846).

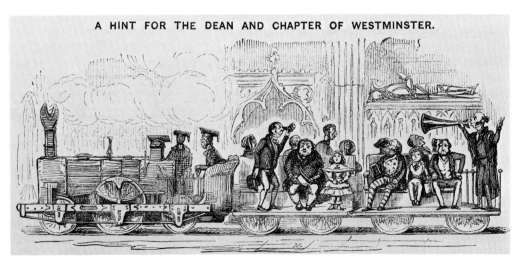

A HINT FOR THE DEAN AND CHAPTER OF WESTMINSTER.

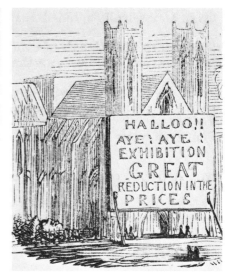

161. *Punch's* comments on "Ecclesiastical Exhibitions" (*Punch*, 11 May 1844; 28 February and 31 May 1846).

iting the Abbey as the bells were ringing to celebrate the capture of Sebastopol, ran afoul of his pet abomination as a conscientious sightseer, the intrusive guide who took his parties through the premises at headlong speed. (He made the same complaint about the Beefeaters at the Tower.) "[We] went through the chapels," he wrote, "at such a pace that we scarcely saw anything, and brought away not a single distinct idea of any one object . . . I so hate to be led round under the auspices of a showman, that I was glad when we got through with the Chapels; though we left behind us immense riches of architecture and monumental sculpture—crowds of royal and knightly tombs—which we appreciated no better than if we had never glanced at them."[72]

One thing, however, is certain. By the time the dust settled in 1851 (the cliché has the sanction of history, because no visitor ever wrote of St. Paul's in those years without deploring its dirt),* these famous London sights now attracted crowds unthought of a mere decade earlier. Comparative annual attendance figures tell the story. In 1827–28 the British Museum had 81,228 visitors; in 1838, 266,000; in 1848, 897,985.[73] In 1837–38 the Tower armory alone (there seem to be no figures on the total number who entered the precincts) had 11,104 paying customers; only four years later, there were 95,231.[74] The National Gallery had the same experience: 397,649 persons entered it during its first year at Trafalgar Square (1838); in 1845 the total attendance was almost 700,000.[75] On one day alone, Boxing Day 1847, 24,191 persons entered the

British Museum—a crowd that would have given Sir Henry Ellis apoplexy, had he still been in charge—and two thirds as many (16,270) were at the National Gallery.[76]

Almost accidentally, both directly and by way of the pressure it exerted upon the church, Parliament had come to participate in the London exhibition business. By more or less cleansing the Abbey and St. Paul's of the grounds for the frequent reproach that they were managed like Madame Tussaud's, it had made them the most popular attractions in London—true rivals of the Baker Street waxwork. It had forced the British Museum to be made accessible to the same public that the Polytechnic had had it in mind to serve. Public monuments now competed with commercial enterprise for the leisure-time custom of the multitude.

Equally important, in the course of the protracted discussion in Parliament and press that had attended these developments, the hopes and fears centering on the people's right to the enjoyment of national monuments had been extensively canvassed. For the first time, also, the broad educational potentialities of exhibitions and the social and cultural implications of certain aspects of show going had been recognized, although more questions were raised than there were decisive answers supplied. When, at the end of the forties, the idea of a great national exhibition to be held in London was broached, all that had been said, proposed, and accomplished in the preceding fifteen years turned out to have been an instructive prologue.

* Benjamin Silliman's complaint in 1851 was typical: "The statues, and the still more numerous allegorical figures which accompany them, appear very sad in their foul drapery of long accumulated dust. On every part where dust will lie, even on sloping arms and limbs, it reposes in a thick and offensive appearance. . . . It would require not only dusting, but thorough cleaning by water, to restore the purity." In contrast, the monuments at the Abbey, though much more numerous than at St. Paul's, were "all clean almost as newly chiselled marble." (*A Visit to Europe in 1851,* New York, 1853, pp. 416–17.)

The Crystal Palace Year: 1851

32

While the Adelaide Gallery and the Polytechnic were contributing in their respective ways to Londoners' scientific and technological education, a similar movement had been progressing in the provinces. Part of the mechanics' institute program was the maintenance of cabinets of natural curiosities and demonstration equipment by which scientific information could be brought to the institutes' clientele, who were initially conceived to be manual workers and machine tenders but who actually came mostly from the artisan and commercial middle class. Few of these mini-museums, however, amounted to much; they were the least successful aspect of the movement. But the temporary large-scale exhibitions arranged by the local organizations in several large towns for publicity and fund-raising purposes were another matter. At Leeds in 1839, for example, an exhibition of "arts and manufactures" attracted 183,913 persons and enabled the local institute to buy itself a large building.[1] At Sheffield about the same time, 436 owners lent 2,654 items for display, including manufactured goods, models, oil paintings, and specimens of the various branches of natural history. The total attendance was 70,000 and, not least important, it was noted in the national press that "the greatest order and decorum were at all times observed."[2] At Liverpool there were three such shows in the early forties. The first (1840), occupying fifteen rooms in the institute's building, netted £3,340 in six weeks. The second, two years later, required twenty rooms, as well as a shed to house Catlin's touring collection of Indian costumes. The third (1844) revealed

that provincial tastes were not much behind London's at the moment; in addition to the usual assortment of instructive exhibits, there now was, in the manner of the Polytechnic, a strong tincture of quasi-amusement: a diving bell, dissolving views, and a panorama.[3]

The success of those provincial exhibitions did not go unnoticed in the metropolis, which had no strong mechanics' institute movement of its own. The *Penny Magazine* and other organs of the adult education crusade reported on them, and the Society of Arts, which acted as an informal headquarters of the institutes after the Society for the Diffusion of Useful Knowledge faltered, funneled information on them to its members. The Society of Arts was, in fact, the chief institution promoting exhibitions of the "practical arts" in the forties.[4] It had sponsored annual displays of new inventions, mainly agricultural implements, since its founding eighty years earlier, but these were routine affairs, seldom noticed in the press. It had also maintained a "repository," mentioned earlier, where prize-winning prototypes and models of machinery were intended to be kept permanently, even though in practice most were given away, sold, or destroyed. The exhibits were more curious than instructive; one visitor noted the dusty presence of prosthetic devices, fire-escape apparatus, turnip slicers, "instruments to restrain vicious bulls," "pans to preserve butter in hot localities," umbrella tips, tail-pieces for cellos, "instruments to draw spirits, and instruments to draw teeth."[5]

At no time, however, had the Society exhibited

manufactured goods. Although Britain was the first industrialized nation, she lagged behind continental countries in displaying the products of her machines. There had been small shows of such articles at Geneva, Hamburg, and Prague as early as 1789–1791, and a larger one at Paris in 1798; thereafter, various governments had sponsored periodic industrial exhibitions. The two held in Paris and Berlin in 1844 provided the belated impetus for a modest show in London, where, in March 1847, the Society of Arts held an exhibition of "select specimens of British manufactures and decorative art"—214 examples of pottery, glass, wallpaper, furniture, and cutlery—which was attended by 20,000 persons. Thus encouraged, the Society put on a second show (March–April 1848), which attracted 700 exhibits from manufacturers and was seen by over 73,000. Attendance in 1849 exceeded 100,000, some being attracted by the two evening "promenades" illuminated by the novel electricity, others by the reduced fee (twopence) offered to artisans during Easter week.

But the most successful of this series was the Exhibition of Ancient and Medieval Art in 1850. Drawn "from the cabinets and galleries of the greatest connoisseurs in the kingdom," and consisting of "those models of early art and excellence in design in which the genius and industry of preceding ages have been embodied," this was advertised as an exhibition "where the manufacturer can correct his taste and refine his judgment, and where all who have a reverence for the past can revive and refresh their impressions."[6] Metalwork was the focus of the display, but it was surrounded with examples of sculpture and carving, enamels, jewelry and personal ornaments, clocks and watches, glass, and fictile manufactures (terra cotta ware, stoneware, and so on). Again "intelligent Artisans and Mechanics" took advantage of a reduced admission fee during the last two weeks. Saluted by the *Times* as "a fitting prelude to the great industrial display" of the coming year, this 1850 show was symptomatic of the Society of Arts' deepening involvement with the Great Exhibition. The Society's president was Prince Albert and one of its leading members was Henry Cole, and between them they used the resources of the Society—its influential leaders, its access to publicity, and its recent experience with such shows—to lay the groundwork of the Great Exhibition of 1851.

The Crystal Palace, as it came immediately, affectionately, and enduringly to be known, rather than by its official title of Great Exhibition of the Works of Industry of All Nations, represented in its quintessen-

tially Victorian way the grand climax of the story told in the preceding chapters. It was the event toward which one main stream of London exhibitions proved, in retrospect, to have been leading; it was the exhibition of exhibitions, the most lavish of shows, the apotheosis of the lofty ideal of "rational entertainment." The palace itself, in all its gemütlich sociability and splendid hugeness—it occupied nineteen acres as against Vauxhall's twelve, and was three times as long as St. Paul's—has been so much written about that only brief mention is required here.[7] Its story has become a virtual legend, but one whose basic truth, insofar as it relates to the palace's success as a show and as an occasion for national pride and momentary class reconciliation, has never been successfully challenged. Despite the presence of such nay-sayers as Carlyle, Dickens, and Ruskin, all of whom deplored the complacent materialism of the "Crystal Palace spirit," the sun-bathed summer of 1851 in London was, in truth, a euphoric one.*

The euphoria was all the more intoxicating because many people had envisaged a quite different result to the project with which Prince Albert, Cole, and their colleagues had busied themselves for the past two years. To the skeptics, it was at once grandiose, hare-brained, and downright dangerous. The perils possibly attending the concentration of large numbers of people in a limited space had been a recurrent theme in the testimony before the select committees on the management of the British Museum and the other national monuments. The Crystal Palace would be such an enclosed space, on a mammoth scale; so also, by extrapolation, might be an entire metropolis congested with throngs of unpredictable visitors. All too recently —on 10 April 1848—Londoners had known the experience of living in a city considering itself in imminent danger of seditious takeover, when hundreds of thousands of workingmen gathered to march under the Chartist banner. Like all other public buildings, the British Museum, which still had its sentries at the gate, was fortified and its employees armed. At the end of that fateful day, when the militant Chartists had been peaceably dispersed and the peril had faded, the museum officials turned in their arms and went to their several homes.

But the unease remained. The bewhiskered Cassandra, Colonel Charles de Laet Waldo Sibthorp, for over twenty years the borough of Lincoln's reactionary gift to Parliament, prophesied robbery, rape, riot, whoremongering, mugging, and military and industrial espionage on a truly cosmic scale. Sibthorp, how-

* The spirit of the occasion was well caught in the program for Jullien's musical panorama, the "Great Exhibition Quadrille," an auditory spectacle of no mean dimensions (it was scored for 207 instrumentalists): "The March of all Nations to London. The morning of the inauguration of the Grand Exhibition is supposed to have arrived. The great city, which for the first time shelters such wonderful masses from all parts of the known world, is as yet still, when at daybreak the festival is ushered in by the sounding of the chimes of London, echoed far and near from each surrounding belfry. Soon the city is in movement, and the multitudes hasten towards the same goal, all eager to behold the most stupendous realisation of human industry recorded in the history of the globe. A tremendous shout burst[s] forth, and the welcomed Nations all join in the glorious cry of 'God save the Queen.'" (Adam Carse, *Life of Jullien,* Cambridge, 1951, pp. 66–67.)

ever, merely reduced to his characteristic and much-derided absurdity what a number of other public men inside and outside Parliament, including the editor of the *Times*, were thinking. The elderly Duke of Wellington, commander-in-chief of the emergency forces raised during the Chartist crisis, also was haunted by phantasms of turmoil and revolution. Unable to understand the point of "an exhibition of Works of Art and Manufacture," especially one to be housed in an enormous building made mostly of glass, he warned, "The glass is very thin."[8] So too would be the tempers of a motley mob attracted to London during the long summer. So many pickpockets, confidence men, cutthroats, prostitutes, foreign spies, stealers of trade secrets, and other illicit practitioners were expected to descend on the metropolis that to dispassionate observers it might have seemed likely that they would be most effectively foiled not by the police but by the law of diminishing returns. The chief commissioner of police, however, was taking no chances. He asked for, and got, a thousand extra men. A Central Working Classes Committee was formed, ostensibly to "interest the millions to visit the Exhibition" but actually to consider ways and means of dealing with the millions once they arrived—a project that went beyond merely finding housing accommodations for them. The Bishop of Oxford was chairman of the committee, and among its members were Dickens, Lord Ashley, John Stuart Mill, Thackeray, and John Forster, the editor of the *Examiner*. Failing to receive official recognition, this body disbanded almost as soon as it had met, but the very fact that it was organized in the first place suggests how active was the fear that something seriously untoward would happen in a London crowded as it had never been crowded before.[9]

The story, as everyone knows, had a fairy-tale ending appropriate to the fairy-tale atmosphere generated by the very appearance of the Crystal Palace. Between 1 April and 30 September 4,237,240 persons arrived in London, 50 percent more than in the same period in the preceding year. Of these, 58,427 were foreigners, an increase of 276 percent (led by 27,000 Frenchmen and 10,500 Germans), although the number was considerably below predictions.[10] The potential for disturbance was there, but nothing happened. Neither the 1,000 extra constables nor the 10,000 troops that Wellington kept in discreetly hidden reserve were needed.

Although there had been some mingling of the classes at certain exhibitions in the past—at the panoramas, for example, and the Polytechnic—it was at the Great Exhibition that social distinctions were, for

the moment, most widely disregarded. A full-page *Punch* drawing captioned "The Pound and the Shilling. 'Whoever Thought of Meeting You Here?'" celebrated the novel fellowship of the gentry and the laboring class inside the Hyde Park enclosure; an article called "The Grand Hatching Year," based on a visit to Cantelo's incubator, now restored to the London show scene in Leicester Square, enumerated all the dreaded eggs—Chartism, Socialism, Red Republicanism, and so on—which had failed to hatch.[11] Indeed, the Crystal Palace Year euphoria took the form, in part, of an immense sigh of relief as proof mounted that the Sibthorps had been wrong.

The exhibits in "this Diorama of the Peaceful Arts," as the inventor Charles Babbage called it,[12] were mainly of kinds hitherto encountered at the Polytechnic, the new Museum of Practical Geology, and the innumerable separate shows, across the decades, of inventions and manufactured or handcrafted objects. There was a great abundance of machinery, inventions, and scientific instruments, including orreries and oxyhydrogen microscopes; musical instruments; weapons; raw minerals and processed materials; models illustrating architecture and civil and mechanical engineering; embroidery, needlework, and all manner of other crafts; "Indian curiosities"; waxwork models and pictures; shell work; sculpture, mosaics, enamels, curios made of every material from ivory to cardboard. The show was all very instructive if taken in moderate doses, and it unquestionably broadened, if only for the moment, the mental horizons of the millions of men, women, and children who passed through the turnstiles. To countless numbers it was the unforgettable high point of their constricted lives. And the fact that so many of the exhibits came from abroad, often accompanied by natives of the countries represented, was an effective though hardly complete antidote to the tight insularity of the period. The Crystal Palace was a better vehicle for vicarious travel than any number of panoramas.*

While the building was being erected in Hyde Park (September 1850–January 1851) its size, the novelty of its design, and the efficient speed with which an army of workmen put it up attracted even more attention than had the rise of the much talked-of Colosseum two decades earlier. "No show within the memory of man," said one paper, "has drawn such crowds to the banks of the Serpentine."[13] Until the building was under roof, admission could be had for five shillings, the proceeds to go to the workmen's accident fund, as had the "staircase money" at St. Paul's at the begin-

* There were no panoramas, however, or any other kind of pictorial entertainment; paintings were excluded from the "Fine Arts" category on the questionable ground that "they were already well provided for in the Academy." A "mechanical picture" listed in the catalogue turned out to be representations of Knox's house in Edinburgh and Balmoral Castle manufactured from colored inlaid wood.

162. General view of the Crystal
Palace (lithograph from *Mighty
London Illustrated*, 1851).

163. The Crystal Palace: a portion of the interior (anonymous etching).

ning of the last century. Then sightseers were excluded until the opening day. For the first three weeks that the completed Crystal Palace was open to the public (1–22 May) the same five-shilling fee was charged, after which it was reduced to a single shilling for the first four days of the week (these were overwhelmingly the most populous) and half a crown on Fridays, the full charge being retained only on Saturday afternoons. Preliminary estimates had been that the maximum daily attendance would be 50,000, but within a few weeks there were 60,000 and 70,000 days. The total number of admissions during the run of the exhibition (1 May–11 October) was 6,093,896. The other London showplaces thus had a vast pool of amusement-seekers to draw from.

ᴅ⒊⁕⒋ᴅ

The exhibitions in Leicester Square and elsewhere constituted in this year a variegated, comprehensive supplement to the supreme one west of Hyde Park Corner. This was the point implied, if not actually intended, by a picturesque episode at the Crystal Palace's opening ceremonies. While high-ranking officers, diplomats, and other personages were awaiting the queen's arrival, a Chinese garbed in a robe of embroidered silk, his long pigtail swinging below a red cap with peacock's feathers, was seen making deep Oriental obeisances to Wellington and his old comrade in arms the Marquis of Anglesey. No one knew who he was; certainly he did not represent the Celestial Empire, which had not even recognized the existence of the Great Exhibition. But he bore himself with conspicuous aplomb, to the amusement of the crowd. According to one account, it was the queen herself, when she arrived, who arranged that he march in the colorful procession, just behind the ambassadors and the Duke of Wellington. It was not realized until the ceremonies were over that the smiling, bowing interloper was one He-Sing, an envoy from a tourist attraction then open for business on the bank of the Thames—the famous Chinese junk.[14]

Every showman in London strove to win his share of the summer crowds' custom in what amounted in the aggregate to a grand reprise of the most popular exhibitions of the past quarter-century.[15] Dominating the list were at least a dozen panoramas and dioramas of various kinds, the most ever displayed in a single season. At the head was good, gray Burford's, now over fifty years at the same location. The most popular of the panoramas as the season began, however, was

the *Overland Route to India* at the Gallery of Illustration, which by the end of March had already had a total of 900 performances, before audiences totaling 200,000.[16]

At the Gallery of Illustration, also, was a diorama that offset the exoticism of the passage-to-India panoramas with a domestic flavor unprecedented in the history of the art, Grieve's and Telbin's *Our Native Land:* "an attempt," as a guidebook put it, "to depict the amusements and employments of a country life during the several varieties of spring, summer, autumn, and winter. The husbandman may be found pursuing his useful toil from seed time to harvest, his occupation in the field from the earliest budding spring to the gathering of the ripe golden crops; the sports of the field, pertaining to the higher classes, as followed by them in the 18th century; the peasant's pastime, his may-pole and rustic dance, enjoyed after the labour of the day, are not omitted."[17] The successive scenes were accompanied by recitations from the poetry of Thomson and Shakespeare by the veteran actor Frederick Vining, father of the Adelaide Gallery's Infant Sappho, and by pianoforte selections such as excerpts from Beethoven's Pastoral Symphony. *Our Native Land* had a rather bad press, one critic complaining that the pictures were too generalized and "pretty" (lacking in realism) and that they, the recitations, and the music got in one another's way.[18] Another reviewer regretted that no room was made for colorful scenes from Wales or Scotland.[19] The subject was not particularly of a kind to draw crowds of country folk, whose experience of rural life as it actually was would have made them unreceptive to these idealized pictures, and it seems not to have lasted into the summer.

The Egyptian Hall, like Burford's, had a triple panorama bill going in its several rooms. One was the second version of the famous trip up the Nile and back; another was Fremont's *Overland Route to Oregon and California,* revised to take account of the gold rush; and the third was another production of the Nile panoramists Warren, Fahey, and Bonomi, a diorama of the Holy Land, the pilgrimage starting at the point where the Israelites began their wanderings and terminating "among the scenes consecrated by the Saviour's presence."

The Holy Land was the single most popular topic of panoramas in the Crystal Palace year; perhaps the entrepreneurs felt it was the safest bet in view of the scruples many visitors from the country brought with them. Whatever stigma attached to other London exhibitions surely was inoperative here. In addition to Burford's Jerusalem panorama and the Holy Land tour

164. Cambon's moving panorama: the fountains of Versailles (*Illustrated London News*, 22 February 1851).

at the Egyptian Hall there was William Beverley's diorama of Jerusalem and the Holy Land at the St. George's Gallery (formerly the Chinese Gallery), Hyde Park Corner—the perfect location to attract families heading back from the Crystal Palace.

Savile House had three panoramas during the season, though not all at the same time. One was Charles Marshall's "GREAT EDUCATIONAL AND PICTORIAL EXHIBITION, GEO-GRAPHICAL, HISTORICAL, AND STATIS-TICAL, OF A GRAND TOUR THROUGH EUROPE"—a title that owed something, by antici-pation, to the Major General in *The Pirates of Penzance*. These canvases illustrated the three routes an English tourist would most likely follow during the present year—the Thames to Constantinople by way of Berlin and Budapest, Rome to Mont Blanc, and the Rhine from Bingen to Cologne. The second Savile House "grand moving diorama" was of a trip up the Ganges from the point where the *Overland Route to India* at the Gallery of Illustration left off, arriving finally at the palace of Agra, "from which is seen the splendid mau-soleum, the Taj Mahal." There was also a three-tableau portrayal of Paris, St. Cloud, and Versailles painted by Monsieur C. Cambon, scene painter for the

Opéra and the Opéra Comique. The *coup de théâtre* here was the use of real jets of water in the scene showing the fountains of Versailles. At the Apollon-icon Rooms, St. Martin's Lane, another French diorama was visible—a twenty-scene biography of Napoleon, including the Bridge of Arcola, the Field of Austerlitz, the coronation in Notre Dame, and other highlights. The proprietors, M. and Mme. Conde, lec-tured alternately in English and French. This show, however, seems not to have lasted long, perhaps be-cause the influx of French sightseers fell below expec-tations.

Those desiring a closer look at Constantinople than Marshall supplied at Savile House could repair to the Polyorama in Regent Street, where Allom's pan-orama of the region depicted various features of Turk-ish life, such as the bazaar, the baths, and the seraglio. A diorama of Nineveh, at the Gothic Hall, Lower Grosvenor Street, exploited the fame of Layard's re-cent excavations, the lecture being delivered by an art-ist who had accompanied the expedition. Gompertz's Polar Regions, at the Partheneum Assembly Rooms, St. Martin's Lane, recalled Burford's two semicircular panoramas of the same subject, which had been with-drawn early in the year. There was a panorama of the

Cape of Good Hope and Natal at the Western Institution, Leicester Square, and at 393 Strand, S. C. Brees showed two series of pictures, one of New Zealand, Australia, and the Brazils, the other of Ceylon, Calcutta, and Wellington, New Zealand. Two of Bouton's double-effect dioramas, St. Mark's and Fribourg, not previously seen in London, were exhibited in a new bazaar, converted from the fish department of Hungerford Market, Charing Cross.

Inconveniently removed from all this activity were the two landmarks at the southern edge of Regent's Park. The Diorama's double bill consisted of the Castle of Stolzenfels and Mount Etna; this continued into the autumn, and then the Diorama closed forever. At the Colosseum, the panorama of the Lake of Thun was replaced for the summer by the old London canvas in the daytime and *Paris by Night* in the evening. (Lisbon was still quaking in the Cyclorama.) At the other end of the park, the Zoological Gardens completed several buildings just in time for the summer crowds (the largest single-day attendance was 14,000, and the year's total was a record-breaking 677,000).[20] The celebrated hippopotamus now enjoyed an enlarged open-air tank, where a thousand spectators at a time could view his submerged bulk, and two large new aviaries also were open, one 175 feet long with a stream of water running through it. A temporary structure housed the ornithologist John Gould's remarkable collection of mounted hummingbirds, which would eventually go to the British Museum. Less relevantly, the Zoo also displayed Salter's huge painting, now ten years old, of *The Waterloo Banquet at Apsley House.*

The Cosmorama, now renamed the Prince of Wales's Bazaar, featured an almost studied lack of novelty: its scenes included the old faithful burning of Edinburgh, St. Peter's, Mont Blanc, Versailles, and the Grand Cairo. The subjects of the cosmorama pictures added to the vertical exhibition rooms in the shafts of the Thames Tunnel were not much more innovative. They included Calcutta, Southampton Water, the Isle of Wight, Grace Darling, and the Eddystone Lighthouse. (In justice, it might be remarked that however old-hat these were to London showgoers, to visitors from the country the dew of novelty was still on them.)

At the Polytechnic Professor Pepper lectured on the exhibits at the Crystal Palace. His colleague Professor Bachhoffner discoursed, with appropriate apparatus, on the total eclipse of the sun which occurred at the end of July. There were dissolving views, including a series on the Holy Land; demonstrations of Foucault's pendulum; "ingenious deposits" (exhibits) by the Gas Fitters Association, which turned out to be new-model cookstoves; and, said a guide to the London attractions of the year, "we would direct the especial attention of such of our readers as are suffering from tender feet, to case 894, containing specimens of elastic boots, the invention of Mr. Sparks Hall, whose establishment is opposite to this institution; these boots having been worn by Her Majesty in ascending the highest hills in Scotland, during her recent visit to that country, sufficiently attest their comfort and utility."[21]

Tussaud's did not install any special exhibition for the year, although one notable addition was made to the waxworks, a model, in full ecclesiastical garb, of Cardinal Wiseman, the central figure in the "papal aggression" furor stemming from the pope's setting up a Roman Catholic hierarchy in Protestant England. The waxwork's advertising, confident that crowds would come, took care that their presence would not deter still more crowds: "The most timid need not fear visiting the promenade with their families, being sure to find ample space and good ventilation." Benjamin Silliman, revisiting London for the first time in forty-five years, found that the throngs who passed through the door in Baker Street "belonged not to the upper ten thousand, but to the lower million."[22]

The Chinese Exhibition, after a stay in New York at Barnum's museum and still under his management, was back for the season. Its former venue, the pagoda at Hyde Park Corner, having been taken over by Beverley's Holy Land panorama, it was now housed in a specially designed structure near Albert Gate, Knightsbridge. The collection was said to have dwindled to less than half its former size in the course of its wanderings, but there were some new features, notably a seventeen-year-old "small footed Chinese Lady (whose Lotus feet are only two and one-half inches in length)," along with her family and suite. She sang songs, accompanied on native instruments, and among her most attentive auditors one day was the composer Hector Berlioz, in London to act as a juror at the Great Exhibition. He left a detailed account of her performance, though he said nothing of the "band of unrivalled Sax-horn performers" who were also on the bill.[23] Business, however, was poor, and at the end of the season the collection was auctioned off piecemeal by Christie's.[24]

The Chinese lady's sea-going compatriots meanwhile were benefiting from the publicity they had received the day the Crystal Palace opened. Their junk was now moored more accessibly, if not more salubriously, at the main outfall of the St. Clement's parish sewer at Blackfriars. Early in July they announced the ascent, during a "Grand Juvenile Fete," of a "gigantic Balloon Residence" titled "The Flying Palace of Aladdin." Two weeks later patrons were invited to "dance on the deck, surrounded by Lanterns, Flying Fish, Fiery Dragons, etc." The social dancing in itself may have been inoffensive, but the sailor hosts went too far when they added to the uproar by dancing in the native manner, singing, and demonstrating feats of arms. Nothing, reported one paper, could have exceeded the effect of their vocalizations "except that impromptu feline discourse which we sometimes hear on housetops at dead of night." The residents of Essex Street, tenants of the Duke of Norfolk, seem to have concurred. A week later, his Grace's solicitor prevailed upon the City Navigation Committee to issue a peremptory order for the "illuminations, with the music and dancing," to cease.[25] The junk disappears from the records at that point.

A weary George Catlin returned to London for the festival year after a misfortune-plagued sojourn in Paris. Still trying to dispose of his Indian collection, he had suggested to more than one government and learned body, without avail, that it be used as the nucleus for a "museum of mankind" (a title adopted a century later for both the ethnological museum in Paris and the ethnographic branch of the British Museum in Burlington Gardens). Now, in rooms in Waterloo Place, Pall Mall, he displayed wax figures of his former Indian troupe, including his interpreter, who had taken his English bride back with him to Canada, where they were said to have "happily established themselves." The walls were hung once again with Catlin's pictures. In August he added to the show a delegation of Iroquois chiefs and warriors who were selling off the "thousands of exquisite fabrics of moccassins, bags, reticules, caps, bracelets, etc.," which they had intended to display in the Crystal Palace but which they now "preferred having the privilege of selling . . . in Catlin's Indian Collection."

As for the three pleasure gardens, the oldest, Vauxhall, was nearing the end of its long decline; apart from a timely Temple of Concord pyrotechnic panorama it seems not to have put on any special show to supplement its facilities for eating, drinking, and assignations. The Nassau balloon ascended as usual. At the Cremorne Gardens there was one more noisy, smoky representation, ten minutes in length, of the siege of Gibraltar, featuring, most anachronistically, miniature steamboats named the *Bride, Bridesmaid, Groom, Wedding Ring, Parson, Beadle,* and *Parish Clerk*.[26] The "Royal Cremorne Cosmorama" was composed of fourteen "Diaphanous Views on an Entirely New Principle" of ships on fire, Venetian canals, a Swiss cottage and waterfall, and views of Nanking, Peking, Innsbruck, Malta, and other such tried and true subjects. There were also panoramas of Nineveh and the Great Exhibition, *tableaux vivants,* the Ethiopian Serenaders, and a female conjuror.

The Surrey Gardens had a characteristic assortment of attractions: a steam hatchery, a Chinese pleasure junk on the ever adaptable lake, and the usual modeled panorama, which this year was billed as "a stupendous novel DIAPHANIC PANOPTICON," a term that was at least as descriptive as Cremorne's "diaphanic cosmorama": "200 feet in length, with figures fifteen feet in height, designed and painted by the Messrs Danson, pourtraying the Horrors of War! And the closing of the Brazen Gates of the Temple of Janus, which becomes the Temple of Concord! Illustrative of the Peace of the World!" The finale was a "Grand Allegorical and Mechanical Pyrotechnic Tableau and Enormous Transparency, set in a jewelled frame . . . Representing Britannia introducing Peace and the Arts and Sciences of the World depositing their Contributions before Her Majesty, the Queen of England, and her Royal Consort!" At this climactic moment, the schedule called for an eruption, which, the publicity averred, was "deserving of the appellation of 'the Kohinoor! Or "Mountain of Light" fireworks.'"[27] No appellation could have been more timely, because the Kohinoor diamond had been presented to the queen only the year before.

Elsewhere, Gordon Cumming's African adventure exhibition shared the St. George's Gallery with the Jerusalem panorama; in Sloane Street an industrious flea show, also borrowing its theme from the news, featured "the fleas in California, digging, washing, and sifting gold," supplemented by lectures on the solar eclipse illustrated by the oxyhydrogen light; General Washington's successor as the largest horse in the world, a steed named Goliath, was at the old Burlington Mews; and in Oxford Street, notwithstanding his frequent warnings that he was about to close, Dr. Kahn continued to dispense information on anatomy and sexual physiology. The original Apollonicon, now owned by another organ builder who had enlarged it to a height of twenty-four feet and a depth and breadth of twenty-one, was to be heard at the Royal Music

Hall, Adelaide Street (the Adelaide Gallery). Here it worked on old melodies and new: the music of the masters (Mozart, Haydn, Handel) and more recent classics like Rossini's *Stabat Mater,* the overture to *Fra Diavolo,* and a medley from *Les Huguenots.* Adjoining it, under the name of the "Grand Exhibition of Art," was a miscellaneous show, obviously thrown together from odd lots, which afforded a retrospective view of the whole range of popular attractions from the century's first fifty years: "Articles of *vertu,* and divers mechanical curiosities, originally belonging to George IV, when Prince of Wales," which reputedly had been made for Lord Macartney to present to the Chinese emperor but had not been finished in time; an automaton female organist, playing "The Blue Bells of Scotland" and "Auld Lang Syne"; an automaton singing bird in a case of pure gold; some miniature wax busts of British worthies; an egg hatchery; tapestries representing Scriptural and other subjects; and cosmoramic views of the private apartments in Windsor Palace.[28] At Savile House, in addition to several panoramas, were the Kaffirs, Cantelo's incubator (whose advertisements were headed, arrestingly, "THE GREAT EXHIBITION INCOMPLETE"), and the Lapland Giantess, "the largest female ever known."

The most important addition to the London entertainment scene this year was Wyld's Great Globe.[29] James Wyld, M.P. for Bodmin and Geographer to the Queen, was a well-known map seller and globe maker at Charing Cross. As plans for the Great Exhibition progressed, he had conceived the idea of erecting inside the building a mammoth globe, nominally to provide additional instruction but, more practically, to advertise his wares. (Nothing except refreshments could be actually sold inside the Crystal Palace.) The Royal Commissioners, however, had no intention of turning the gleaming structure into an extension of a central London street, choked with wagons made up as monstrous replicas of the commodity advertised. Not content merely to exhibit his maps and globes in the paper, printing, and bookbinding section (as he did), Wyld cast about for some other way to publicize his wares. If he could not erect a globe inside a building, why not erect a globe that was itself a building? The ideal location was in the very heart of the amusement district—that deplorable plot of privately owned wasteland called Leicester Square.

Meeting with interested parties of the neighborhood early in February 1851, Wyld proposed to rent the square for a term of ten years and erect thereon a build-

ing that would lend a much-needed touch of dignity and didactic purpose to the show-business center of London. At the end of the ten years, if they approved, he would renew the lease; otherwise he would demolish the structure and convert the square into a garden. The meeting concurred with this scheme and thanked him "for his exertions to rescue Leicester-square"—which the chairman had candidly described as "a public nuisance"—"from its present dilapidated condition."[30] In a year when the metropolis was itself on display, it would be one less eyesore to be ashamed of.

Having obtained a lease from the family who owned the square and, according to *Punch,* sent out parties of intrepid huntsmen to exterminate the starveling cats that had long infested the spot, Wyld moved his builders in. With the opening of the Great Exhibition only two months away, his construction crews worked round the clock, the night shift being assisted by flaring gas torches. As it rose like a fungus from the rubble-filled plot, the building attracted as much attention as had the rise of the Crystal Palace just months before; it was the finest of free London shows. Despite a scare when the builder's storehouse and pay-office burned down, the globe was finished on schedule at a cost of £5,000, and the press preview was held on 29 May.

Actually, this was not the first structure of its kind. As early as 1823 there had been such a building, called the Georama, in the Boulevard des Capucins in Paris.[31] Designed by C. F. P. Delanglard, it was a hollow sphere forty or fifty feet in diameter with a framework of iron circles and arches spaced at intervals representing ten degrees of longitude and latitude. The map of the world, on a scale of between sixteen and seventeen miles to the inch, was spread on the interior of this globe, the portions representing the land being of opaque paper and the water indicated by translucent muslin. Spectators entered at the bottom, through Antarctica, and ascended to three circular platforms projecting from the staircase, very much in the manner of the Colosseum then rising in London. (The close coincidence of dates makes it appear possible that the design of the Colosseum's viewing areas was influenced by the Georama.) Thus the world could be viewed, at a remove of nine or ten feet, successively from the Tropic of Capricorn, the equator, and the Tropic of Cancer.* Of course there was a patent illogicality to all this, as a writer in the *London Magazine* (1828) pointed out: the world was turned outside in, and the viewer had to go through "a difficult and painful process of mind, which we may term the *translation* of all the objects which the attention gathers."[32] There was a pro-

* Pückler-Muskau visited it in January 1829 and wrote (p. 498): "Here you suddenly find yourself in the centre of the globe . . . you find the hypothesis of a sea of light confirmed, for it is so light that the whole crust of the earth is rendered transparent, and you can distinctly see even the political boundaries of countries. . . . The lakes appear, as in reality, beautifully blue and transparent, the volcanoes little fiery points, and the black chains of mountains are easily followed by the eye. . . . I was much displeased at seeing no notice taken of the recent discoveries at the North Pole, in Africa, and the Himalaya Mountains. The whole affair appeared to me somewhat 'en décadence.'"

165. Erecting Wyld's Great Globe at night (*Illustrated London News*, 22 March 1851).

* Other details of the Great Globe's ancestry, not necessarily consistent with those just given, are found in a pamphlet by [Saxe Bannister], *Pictorial Maps for the Illustration of the Land, the Sea, and the Heavens, on the Walls of Large Buildings, Georamas, and Lectures on Geography: A Letter Addressed to C. A. Eastlake, Esq. . . .* (London, 1849) (copy in Forster Collection, Victoria and Albert Museum; abstract in *Athenaeum,* 7 July 1849, p. 697). The author refers to a georama built by Langlois in Paris in 1833 which, after Langlois's death, was taken over by a M. Guérin, "who, a few years ago, proposed its construction in London, by a society." (According to the *Grande Encyclopédie,* s.v. "georama," Charles-Auguste Guérin built a georama on the Champs Élysées. This, like its predecessors, was a failure, despite "d'ingénieux artifices d'optique [qui] donnaient aux terres et aux mers un aspect assez naturel.") "A similar georama," continued Bannister, "with the means of popularly illustrating every branch of geography, is planned for the west end of the town in an edifice admirably calculated for the development of the views set forth in this letter" (mainly the desirability of installing relief maps in the corridors and committee rooms of the new houses of Parliament). His further assertion, that "several years before the georama was constructed in Paris, a vast globe with analogous objects was planned for the Colosseum in the Regent's Park," seems not to be substantiated elsewhere.

posal to erect a similar structure in London, but this had to await the fresh inspiration of James Wyld twenty-three years later.*

The Leicester Square structure was a brick rotunda eighty-five feet in diameter, with blank walls surmounted by clerestories and supporting a zinc-ribbed dome which formed the upper half of the globe, approximately sixty feet in diameter. The globe's exterior was painted blue, with silver stars arranged in the proper constellations. Between the rotunda wall and the lower half of the globe was a circular passage used to exhibit Wyld's globes and maps. Entering through a Doric portico, the visitor found himself at the bottom of a series of staircases which led to a succession of four viewing platforms, from each of which he could inspect portions of the earth with its land masses and oceans. This spherical relief map, made up

of 6,000 plaster casts, had a horizontal scale of ten miles to the inch. Geographical features were distinguished by color and texture. All the world's well-known volcanoes, in simultaneous eruption, had tufts of cotton wool issuing from their red-painted peaks; snow-covered mountains were represented by roughly modeled masses of a glittering white substance; deserts were painted in a tawny color, the oceans blue, the fertile areas green.

As soon as it opened, the globe became the most popular attraction of the year except for the Crystal Palace itself. It found favor even with such strict religionists as the naturalist Philip Gosse, whose son Edmund recalled many years later that this was the only show his father ever took him to. "It was a poor affair," Gosse wrote; "that was concave in it which should have been convex, and my imagination was

166. Wyld's Great Globe: exterior (lithograph by R. S. Croom, 1851).

167. Wyld's Great Globe: cross section of the interior (*Illustrated London News,* 7 June 1851).

deeply affronted. I could invent a far better Great Globe than that in my mind's eye in the garret."[33] But this was a distinctly minority view, and Wyld must have got his investment back in a short time. His main problem came at the end of the season, when he had to find ways of keeping his exhibition profitable during the nine years that remained on the lease. We shall see in the next chapter how he solved it.

D꒓⁘꒒C

No attendance figures exist for the London commercial entertainments during the Crystal Palace season, but the Royal Commissioners did obtain reports from all the public and institutional exhibitions as well as four mansions and galleries opened by their noble owners. A comparison with the number of visitors counted in the preceding year reveals how dramatically in some cases—the exceptions are worth pondering—the crowds increased in 1851:

permitted to gaze your fill at certain tombs not included in the tariff, but should the visitor wish to extend his walk round the more curious portion of the Abbey, the Dean and Chapter meet him Tussaud-wise [i.e., as at the door to the Chamber of Horrors], and exact the extra fee."

The sixpence charged for admission to the chapels was a minor imposition compared with the multiple fees still levied at St. Paul's. In the preceding year, the issue of the despised Paul's pence had become tangled with the hysteria over papal aggression. Responding to urgings that the iron fence in front of the cathedral be removed to provide easier access and reduce traffic congestion, the dean and chapter said, in effect, that the beleaguered Church of England had to take a stand somewhere, and this was the place and the time. The *Athenaeum* declared that they "look on the iron railing as a military out-work of St. Paul's, the surrender of which may lead to fresh attacks on the Church—to the abolition of the two-pences of show-money, and the

	1850	1851
Windsor Castle	31,228	129,400
St. Paul's: Floor	"No account"	"From 600 to 6000 visitors per hour"
Galleries	"No account"	110,250
Westminster Abbey	"No account"	"About 6000 a day"
British Museum	720,643	2,230,242
National and Vernon Galleries	519,745	1,109,364
Hampton Court Palace	208,374	325,774
Kew Botanic Gardens	163,828	184,248
Tower of London: Armory	32,313	233,561
Crown Jewels	32,888	209,000
Greenwich Hospital	66,054	364,680
United Service Museum	33,733	36,470
East India House Museum	18,623	37,490
London Missionary Museum	"No account"	"About tenfold"
Northumberland House	—	240,000
Syon House	—	110,000
Bridgewater Gallery	—	80,000
Lord Ward's art collection	—	20,000[34]

At the beginning of the year, the prospect of those crowds led the press to take up anew the still controversial topic of the fees at the Abbey and St. Paul's. "What," demanded a *Times* leading article on 3 January, "will be the surprise of our visitors, and what should be our own shame, when our guests find themselves stopped at the entrance of these sacred buildings, and pestered for trumpery fees by a pack of importunate vergers? . . . At Westminster Abbey you are

throwing open to the public of the great west door."[35] (Hitherto, in contravention of Wren's plan that the visitor should acquire his first splendid view of the interior from the west door, the public had been required to use a side entrance.) The dean and chapter temporized and finally took the position that nothing could be done about the twopence until something was done about the railings, and this could not be done until the Corporation improved the approaches to the

168. Mr. Punch slaying the dragon of ecclesiastical avarice at St. Paul's Cathedral (*Punch*, 5 April 1851).

PAY HERE

TWO PENCE

THE DRAGON OF SAINT PAUL'S

I SHAL you singe a lytel song
Aboute a Dragon, grete and strong.
Thys Dragonne was a great marvàyle;
He abode in Seinct Powle hys Cathedrale.

A manne's knobbe hys necke hadd on,
Lyke to the hedd of a stout parsòn;
All hys bodye ytt was blacke,
With a longe tail to hys backe.

Hee had a paunche both round and bigge,
Like a Smythfelde-Clubb pryze-pigge;
He cold clutche his clawes with a mighty grippe,
Nothinge he gott awaye mote slipp.

A wide swallòwe hadd thys Dragòn;
Besyde turtèl and venisòn,
And porte wyne and goode stronge bere,
He boltyd evere so moche a yere.

He swallowyd tythès and glebès fatt,—
Down I wys went all he gat;
He gulpyd loaves and fyshes riche,
And wold tucke in tyn like any ostrìche.

Thys Dragon was a mightye boare;
He used to kepe Seinct Powle hys door;
Thereyn, forsothe, mote noe man goe,
But must give hym twopence to se the showe.

He wolde take the twoepence yn hys clawes,
And caste them into his open jawes,
And so quicke he gobbled the copperes browne,
As a smal boye mote cramn jam-tartès downe.

He swallowed the twopence of alle who came,—
The twopence of squier, and the twopence of dame,—
The twopence of lorde and the twopence of knyghte,—
The twopence of knave and the twopence of wryghte.

Of lytel boyes, and girls also,
SIR DRAGON the twopence wolde swallòwe;
And soche as were pore, and no twopence cold paye,
From the doore of Saynt Powle's he wold fright awaye.

The good knyghte *Ponche* ytt sore dyd greeve,
The Dragoune thus sholde rob and theeve;
Soe he toke hys launce, and did on hys mayle,
And hee went att the Dragon tooth and nayl.

He bete the Dragon from black to blue,
He pokyd and thrustyd him through and through,
But colde not hytt his brain or harte,
As yff the Dragon had noe soche part.

He pricked the Dragon in tycklish sorte,
The Dragon bled both sherris and porte,
Yett styll dyd he kepe Saynt Powle hys gate,
And gorged the brownes at his olden rate.

But *Ponche* dyd att him with myghte and maine,
Till he beganne to twiste with pain;
On the hyp he hytt hym sore,
And dugge him in hys rybbes the more.

Ponche the Dragon did soe mawle,
That he colde nether flye nor crawl,
Tyll his last kick anon he kicked,
Saynt Powle hys Dragon soe was lycked.

I wis there was grete jubilie
When the Church of Saynt Powle was opened free,
And all the peopyl cried hoorawe!
For *Ponche* that had the Dragon yslaw.

Ponche tooke the Dragon his scalye hide,
And had ytt stufft with straw insyde,
And sett ytt on hye for a scare-the-crowe
To all parsones that make their Churche a showe.

building.[36] But the pressure soon became irresistible, and at long last, at the end of April 1851, only days before the Crystal Palace opened, the hated twopenny entrance charge was abolished.

It was a famous victory. No longer would divine service end with the vergers' cry "Service is over, and tuppence for all that wants to stay." But the capitulation was more symbol than substance: the financial arrangement between the dean and chapter and the vergers was tidied up, as it had been long since at the Abbey, but the internal fees remained, though slightly reduced. Now, instead of the former charge of 4s. 4d., one could see the whole of the cathedral's attractions for 3s. 6d. The four vergers, deprived of their tuppences at the door, received a salary of £100 a year, and in addition were empowered to sell guidebooks, which they bought wholesale for 3d., at a markup of 100 percent.[37]

Despite a tall fence that happened at this inopportune moment to be erected in front of the British Museum (a gesture that called forth severe words in the press), that institution, still unreconciled to being a place of public resort, admitted over three times as many persons as in the preceding year. Visiting the museum was the thing to do, but it would seem that the crowd's pleasure, let alone its instruction, was minimal. The complaint of a French visitor, uttered a year or two later, supplemented Emerson's curt summary in 1848: "No method in the classing, an indigestible mixture of marble and plaster, no chronological order in the Greek and Roman monuments. It is a sumptuous and uncleanly bazaar. Beautiful busts and statues are covered with dust, the floors are filthy. The walls are dull and colourless, the whole place looks like a warehouse. In a large room painted a dirty yellow are the marbles from the Parthenon."[38]

The dilapidation and congestion in Bloomsbury were all the more to be censured when they were contrasted with the well-kept luxury of the private art galleries several titled collectors threw open during the season. The Bridgewater Gallery, made accessible to the public by courtesy of its present owner, the Earl of Ellesmere, attracted more than 5,000 visitors in a single week. The Duke of Northumberland opened both Northumberland House at Charing Cross and Syon House, his country place near Brentford, and 350,000 persons availed themselves of the chance to see how nobility lived as well as the pictures and statuary they owned. Lord Ward could not extend similar hospitality because his own gallery in Park Lane was not yet built; but he generously compensated for this by installing the whole of his collection of Old Masters in the Egyptian Hall, a resplendent climax to the old building's use as an occasional art salon. The public was admitted three days a week with tickets obtainable at printsellers', Mondays and Fridays being reserved for Lord Ward's friends and Saturdays for artists.[39]

And so 1851, the year of the Great Exhibition, was also the year of the most exhibitions that London had ever seen. From Holy Land panoramas, Lapland giants, and steam hatcheries to galleries of Old Masters, the range of shows was, if possible, broader than it had ever been before, and it would not be matched in any subsequent season. Although there was still a decade left before the London exhibition business was transformed almost beyond recognition, this year marked its apogee.

The Fifties, I: New Patterns of Life and the Decline of the Panorama

33

During the fifties the variegated complex of popular shows which had developed in the preceding half-century began to disintegrate. Superficially, it is true, the change was not immediately apparent. Leicester Square, with its labyrinth of cheap and not infrequently nasty exhibits in Savile House, its Dr. Kahns, Aztec Lilliputians, and vulgarized *poses plastiques,* was as hectic and garish as ever. But in the retrospect of more than a century it can be seen that a deep transformation was well under way. New leisure-time habits, new patterns of city living, above all new popular interests, meant that not only the structure but the whole nature and tone of London exhibitions were undergoing a revolution.

Tendencies in the social life of London which were first evident in the forties now quickened. The building of a dense web of railways in the metropolitan area, carrying mostly local traffic, dispersed the population at a faster pace and more widely. People were settling farther and farther from the long-established locale of entertainment in central London. The hundreds of thousands of families now living in the outlying districts had either to travel a considerable distance into town—such travel, to be sure, was faster, cheaper, and more convenient than before—or find their recreation closer to home. It is significant that the new centers of mass entertainment built during the rest of the century were located at Sydenham, where the Crystal Palace was reerected and enlarged, Muswell Hill (the Alexandra Palace), and Earl's Court (Olympia). Those same railways affected the habits of residents in inner London. Cheap fares, holiday excursion trains, and increased short-trip service made it easier to escape to the suburbs or the open countryside for a day's outing. In 1857 the *Times* observed that the Easter season and Whitsuntide were no longer times of signal prosperity for central London amusements. Wishing "to shake off the dust and bustle of city life and to seek amid the freshness of rural scenes that wholesome recreation which it is vain to look for amid the crowded thoroughfares and murky atmosphere of London," thousands of city dwellers flocked on holidays to the railway stations. At Whitsuntide that year, the London and Brighton Railway alone conveyed no fewer than 57,000 excursionists. Some went to the Crystal Palace, the rest to various other destinations where they could picnic, ramble, and nature-walk.[1]

Simultaneously, Londoners were beginning to enjoy an advantage notoriously denied the tenement-bound masses in the industrial cities, open spaces within convenient walking distance of their homes. The royal parks were made more accessible. Several expanses of fields and gardens were acquired for the public (Primrose Hill, 1842; Victoria Park, 1849; Battersea Park and the Victoria Embankment in the fifties), and successive acts of Parliament forbade the enclosure of common land and encouraged private owners to bequeath recreational land to the nation. Notwithstanding the decline of the old pleasure gardens, Londoners were becoming less dependent on indoor shows to occupy their leisure. Their choices steadily widened.

The completion of railways from all parts of the island meant that London exhibitions now had the whole population of Britain to draw upon. The Great Exhibition owed much of its success to the ease and cheapness with which families could get to London from Wales and Cornwall, the Midlands and East Anglia, Yorkshire and Scotland. London was more of a tourist center than ever, and there is little question that from this time onward a larger proportion of the crowds at Madame Tussaud's and the Abbey, for example, was composed of people who had come up from the country. On the other hand, changed conditions of life in the provinces made it less necessary to come to London in quest of shows. As railways replaced coaches and wagons, attractions which had exhausted their drawing power in London were increasingly likely to migrate to the provinces. Cities like Manchester, Liverpool, Sheffield, and Leeds saw more panoramas, more display-piece paintings, more waxworks, more troupes of savages, now that railways enabled these to be moved from London so readily. Residents of provincial cities and towns also were beginning to be provided with museums of their own, thanks to the lingering influence of mechanics' institutes as freshly stimulated by the Society of Arts and to legislation (1845, 1850, 1855) which allowed local authorities to levy a modest tax to build and maintain museums. Civic pride in these provincial centers—sixteen of them had a population of over 100,000 by 1862—was beginning to be manifested in the establishment of museums and art galleries either by private gift or bequest or by concerted local action. Manchester scored a notable coup in 1857 when it compensated for the Crystal Palace's omission of paintings from its fine arts section by holding the nation's first wide-ranging loan exhibition.

One hastens to add, however, that the extent to which the provinces were supplied with museums and art galleries by 1862 must not be exaggerated, as is sometimes done. Most of the local natural history-cum-curio collections, the property of "literary and philosophical" societies, were small, decrepit, ill housed, and often not accessible at all. They were scarcely better than many old-fashioned private cabinets. Response to the enabling legislation was slight in the early years; only a handful of towns, among them Sunderland, Leicester, Salford, and Warrington, took advantage of it. By 1862 no more than four or five cities possessed museums and galleries important enough to warrant their being called cultural centers. The first big wave of founding such institutions,

inspired in large part by what the government was doing in South Kensington, came only in the seventies and eighties.[2]

Increased mobility was only one of the changing social habits which had a bearing on the London shows in the fifties. The agitation to open public monuments like the British Museum on Sunday afternoons which had threaded through the successive parliamentary inquiries seemed on the verge of bearing fruit when a Select Committee on Places of Public Entertainment recommended in 1854 that "places of rational recreation and instruction" be opened after 2 P.M. on Sunday. But the recommendation was exceedingly ill timed, because at that moment a fever of Sabbatarianism was sweeping the country, and when the proposal came to a vote in 1856, the Commons defeated it by 376 to 48. (Another reform the Select Committee proposed, to encourage attendance if and when the places of rational recreation were opened on Sunday, was reducing the hours of public houses on that day to 1–2 P.M. and 5–9 or 6–10 P.M. There was so much protest that the very next year, 1855—before the museums' Sunday opening was so resoundingly rejected—the pubs' hours were increased to 1–3 P.M. and 5–11 P.M.)

At this moment there was also a campaign, fortunately uncomplicated by the religious issue, to reduce working hours. Many workingmen, as well as tradesmen and their assistants, did not leave their jobs until 8 P.M., and therefore there had not been, up to this point, much discussion of opening museums and similar places in the evening. More immediately in prospect than shorter hours every day of the week, however, was the Saturday half-holiday, which meant quitting work at 3 P.M. Correctly foreseeing that the latter reform would soon take place, the press pointed out that "our places of national resort are nearly all closed on that day," among them the British Museum and the National Gallery, and that the admission fees at other places were forbiddingly high for the working class. (The five-shilling charge, it will be remembered, was retained at the Crystal Palace *only* on Saturday afternoons.) "Thus," said the *Athenaeum,* "a line of prohibition seems to extend round London on the very day which a wise and rational movement promises to make the workingman's holiday."[3] In March 1860 a Select Committee on Public Institutions met to explore the possibility of "promoting the Healthful Recreation and Improvement of the People" by opening publicly supported institutions "at Hours on Week Days when, by the ordinary customs of Trade, such persons are free from toil." Among the witnesses were the liberal clergyman F. D. Maurice, speaking from his experience at the Working Men's College (adult night school); Thomas H. Huxley, in his capacity of lecturer at the Museum of Practical Geology; and Ruskin, whose lengthy testimony was so cloudy that a subsequent witness professed himself quite unable to understand what he was in favor of. The committee concluded that the dangers envisioned, particularly the risk of fire from the gas lighting, were minimal, and that the coming reduction of working hours during the week, not on Saturday alone, would increase the demand for evening hours at public institutions. It therefore recommended that the British Museum and the National Gallery be open from 7 to 10 P.M. at least three days a week. No action was taken.*

Conspicuously absent from the testimony before this committee was the fear, underlying so much of the discussion at the earlier parliamentary inquiries, that indiscriminate admission of the working class would entail disturbances. The crowds' exemplary behavior at the Crystal Palace, it seemed, had permanently disposed of that bogy. It had proved that exhibitions could put the hitherto untrusted "million" on their best behavior, acting indeed as a positive agent for the reformation of manners (in the strict sense of the term) as well as of wholesome entertainment and instruction. Whatever arguments there might be against tailoring opening hours to suit the working class's convenience, fear of disorder was not among them; or at least it was no longer politic to express such a feeling. Yet it must have been a lingering vestige of such a fear, as much as the contrary conviction that the danger of riotous behavior had really passed, that led the press to continue to include in its reports of record-breaking holiday attendance at popular sites the customary assurances that no breach of the peace had occurred. "The strictest order and regularity were observed," reported the *Illustrated London News* when it announced, after Boxing Day 1853, that between 40,000 and 50,000 "well dressed persons" had entered the British Museum and about 2,000 "well dressed persons"—the phrase, significantly, was repeated—were in the National Gallery at any given time during the day.[4] In 1855 a writer in the conservative *Quarterly Review*, noting that the attendance at the Zoological Gardens in the previous year represented a more than threefold increase over the total in 1848, when the "more liberal system of management came into play," observed: "Here, then, we have an increase of 135,712 persons, many of whom were, no doubt, rescued, on those days at least, from the fascinations of the public-house.

With all this flood of life, the greater portion of it undoubtedly belonging to the labouring-classes, not the slightest injury has been done to the Gardens. A flower or two may have been picked, but not by that class of Englishmen who were once thought too brutal to be allowed access unwatched to any public exhibition."[5]

The sense of relief induced by such model behavior is unmistakable; yet it would not do to be overconfident, for an occasional disturbing episode suggested that beneath the placid surface the old danger still lurked. At first glance, the advertisement which Tussaud's placed in the papers after Boxing Day 1858 was nothing more than a pleasant gesture of appreciation, expressing as it did "grateful thanks to the crowds that visited their Exhibition on Boxing Day, being the greatest attendance they have ever had during twenty-four years in Baker-street; the most perfect order prevailed, and the day passed off as if it had been an assemblage of the highest persons in the Court."[6] Whatever the press said editorially, it was almost unheard of for a London showplace itself to utter public thanksgiving that a riot had not broken out when the premises were jammed with a holiday crowd. But the news columns reveal that at that moment the waxwork people had particularly good reason to be grateful to their customers. On the day when perfect order had prevailed in Baker Street, a false alarm of fire at the crowded Old Vic, across the river, had caused a panic resulting in the death of sixteen youths ranging in age from nine to twenty. Even before the corpses were removed from the building, the second performance of the day proceeded on schedule. When the lessee was criticized for this seeming callousness, he had a reply ready. "No one," as the *Illustrated London News* put it, "who has ever seen the mass of ruffianism which collects in the New Cut, especially at holiday time, will doubt that Mr. Towers took the wisest course. The savage yell that would have greeted an announcement that disappointed such an audience, influenced by 'the festive season,' would have been the prelude to a brutal riot that probably would have ended in a far greater loss of life than that we have to record."[7]

D3✳ЄD

The big question of the fifties in the commercial branch of the exhibition trade was how to attract customers whose expectations and standards of value had been radically revised after the pleasure of exploring the inexhaustible Crystal Palace on shilling days. The

* Meanwhile, the Scottish Academy of Art, in Edinburgh, had successfully instituted evening hours. In 1849 its secretary told David Roberts, who was urging the Royal Academy to follow suit, that evening opening had not diminished daytime attendance despite the reduction in the entrance fee, and that "many who go at night are induced to go by day also, and thus a love of art is begun which otherwise might have had no beginning." The Royal Academy adopted evening hours in 1862. (James Ballantine, *The Life of David Roberts, R.A.,* Edinburgh, 1866, pp. 170–71.)

Adelaide Gallery, the Polytechnic, and the Surrey Gardens had already operated on the principle that the greater the variety of exhibits and entertainment obtainable for a single shilling, the greater (other things being equal) the crowd would be. But the same demonstration was made on an incomparably larger scale at the Crystal Palace, after which the Polytechnic's manifold offerings seemed meager indeed. (To some tastes, also, there was greater value in what could be examined in the British Museum and the National Gallery without any charge whatsoever.) The contrast so conspicuously made in 1851 between what a shilling would buy in Hyde Park and what it would buy in Leicester Square was not forgotten in the years to come.

For those who had to be somewhat less careful of their pocket money, the stage had now intensified its competition with the nondramatic shows. Not only did the London theatre cater to a greatly enlarged total population; the proportion of that public who were disposed to enter playhouses was increasing, and there were more playhouses to enter. The improvement in the quality of fare offered, the popularity of the Kean and Phelps spectacles in the fifties, which strove to outdo the panoramas that had inspired them, the drive to exile the prostitutes who used the theatres as a base of operation, and, not least, the relaxation of the moral scruples against playgoing—all these were beginning to shift patronage back toward the theatre and away from the enterprises which had for so long profited from its disrepute. Moreover, the coming of the music hall provided an alternative mode of theatrical entertainment consisting of the very kinds of acts that had hitherto been imported to rescue establishments which had started out as exemplary shrines of rational amusement but had found the going too rough without the aid of musical acts, dissolving views, comic routines, and conjurors. No longer could places like the Polytechnic depend on this sort of fare to bring in customers; patrons who wanted it naturally preferred to go to houses devoted solely to it and devoid of the dull and increasingly incidental paraphernalia of technical and scientific instruction.

The whole situation could be read, in microcosm, in the panorama branch of the industry. The first years of the fifties were, as the comic song had it, "The Age of Panoramas." But how long would this "panoramania" —the word was Albert Smith's[8]—last? The contest between the educational tour and the music hall turn was an uneven one at best, but any doubt of its outcome was dispelled by Smith's sensational success as a panorama performer. His *Ascent of Mont Blanc* was

the most popular entertainment of the whole decade, setting a standard and attracting a volume of box-office business which rivals could only envy and— most ineffectually, as it turned out—try to match.[9]

The son of a Chertsey doctor, Smith was himself a qualified physician, but the ultimate direction of his career was determined when, on his return from a holiday in Switzerland in 1838—he was then twenty-two—he dug out a good-sized toy panorama he had made as a child and equipped it with garishly colored strip-pictures of Alpine scenery on a scale of three feet to the mountain. A carpenter made him a peristrephic mechanism on which to roll them, and he then toured the Thames valley's self-styled literary and philosophical institutions—actually scruffy halls up muddy lanes—with his "Alps in a box," accompanying the show with a lecture he adapted from a printed narrative of an ascent of Mont Blanc in 1827. His brother, who was later to become Dickens's business manager, held a piece of candle behind the moon on the Grands Mulets, a touch that was always applauded.

Soon after this modest but heady taste of show business, Smith gave up his medical career and, gravitating to London's Grub Street Bohemia, became one of *Punch*'s first contributors and a prolific writer of fiction and stage pieces.* One of his first published writings was "The Confessions of Jasper Bubble, a Dissecting-Room Porter," in *The Lancet*, "a series of ghastly grins," as a nonmedical paper characterized it.[10] He quickly gained a circulating-library and railway-station-bookstall following with a number of light satirical novels of London life, notably *The Adventures of Mr. Ledbury and His Friend Jack Jackson* (1844), culminating in a whole series of facetious sketches—*The Natural History of Stuck-Up People*, of ballet girls, of gents, of flirts, of idlers. *The Struggles and Adventures of Christopher Tadpole at Home and Abroad*, illustrated by Leech, was a best seller in 1848. His periodical *The Man in the Moon*, a parody of *Punch*, added to his reputation even though it lasted for only thirty issues.

Smith was an inveterate traveler, and by 1850 he had toured not only Europe but the Levant and the Middle East, a region that had been much in the book news with Kinglake's *Eōthen* (1844), Warburton's *The Crescent and the Cross* (1844), and Thackeray's *Notes of a Journey from Cornhill to Grand Cairo* (1846), all of which had whetted the public appetite for the Nile and Overland Route panoramas. Smith's own contribution to this topical literature of travel was *A Month at Constantinople*, published the month before he first appeared in

* He was also—very briefly—an aeronaut. In 1847 he ascended in a balloon from Vauxhall Gardens to shoot off fireworks over Pimlico, but he got caught in a thunderstorm and fell, with the balloon, into Belgrave Road. This misadventure probably had something to do with his decision to restrict future ascents to the terra firma of Mont Blanc.

169. Albert Smith's *Overland Mail* panorama-lecture (*Illustrated London News*, 8 June 1850).

London as a tour conductor. It was not very well received, but its jocular approach to a subject which customarily was treated with heavy sobriety set the tone of the new form of entertainment which would make him a theatrical celebrity.

Smith's *The Overland Mail*, "A Literary, Pictorial, and Musical Entertainment," opened at Willis's Rooms on 28 May 1850, almost exactly two months after the *Overland Route to India* panorama (Chapter 15) had its first performance. Although the formula was Smith's own, it plainly derived from the part-dramatic, part-narrative monologues and impersonations of Charles Dibdin and the elder Charles Mathews several decades earlier, a kind of variety entertainment then sometimes called the "monopolylogue." (The word was now revived, and in years to come would be particularly identified with the programs performed by Mr. and Mrs. German Reed at the Gallery of Illustration.)[11] Smith's new brand of entertainment combined the monopolylogue with the panorama. His subject was only a portion of the Overland route—the Suez-to-Cairo segment from which the en-

tire route derived its name. As dioramic pictures, painted by William Beverley, were displayed, Smith delivered a fast-paced conversational narrative of the journey, a mixture of impersonations, songs, and anecdotes having mostly to do with the eccentricities and affectations of English travelers and people met along the way: the sort of genial caricature Mark Twain would later employ in *Innocents Abroad*. From beginning to end the performance was low-keyed, with no theatrics or straining for effect; Smith gave the impression of being a raconteur in a private drawing room, spontaneously reminiscing by free association and recreating the amusing incidents and characters of the trip. Thus the novelty that Banvard had introduced into the travel panorama—the entertaining narrator—became the principal feature of the show. The spotlight now was on the performer, the pictures serving only as incidental illustrations of the monologue and the songs. The show lasted for over a hundred performances, closing in mid-July, after which Smith took it on tour.

A year later, accompanied by Beverley, Smith was

back in the Alps, a region which fascinated him. The completion of the railway to Chamonix had made the area easily accessible to Englishmen as a holiday spot, and the presence of Mont Blanc constituted a challenge to their daring, their athletic skill, and their powers of endurance. Now Smith went up himself. It is true that local gossip at the time had it that the intrepid Londoner was "dead beat" long before he reached the top, his guides carrying him the rest of the way in a large provision basket.[12] But one way or another his mission was successfully completed, and the publicity mill began to grind. From Chamonix, Ruskin wrote his father (16 August), "There are an immense number of people here, of course. Effie counted forty mules at one time on the Montanvert, and there has been a cockney ascent of Mont Blanc, of which I believe you are soon to hear in London."[13] London did hear. Assisted by preliminary puffs, such as an article on his climb which Smith planted in the January 1852 issue of *Blackwood's,* the public was well prepared for the opening of his new entertainment, *The Ascent of Mont Blanc,* at the Egyptian Hall on 15 March.

The room had been converted into a little plot of old Switzerland, *bien meublé.* Most prominent was a full-scale representation of the exterior of a chalet, in the center of which was a curtained window through which a cheery light shone; during the scenes the portion representing the wall was raised out of sight. The front of the hall, according to a contemporary description, "was occupied by a large pool of water, surrounded by granite rocks and Alpine plants, and well stocked with some fine live fish; and from this spring clumps of bulrushes and Arum lillies, which throw water and gas from their petals. Chamois skins, Indian corn, alpenstocks, vintage baskets, knapsacks, and other appropriate matters are grouped about the balconies, and vines and creepers slung about the rafters and beams." The room was further decorated with the banners of the various cantons, and "some remarkably elegant lamp-shades of hanging leaves and flowers break the light very agreeably." Mottoes dispersed on the scenery and about the room, quoting the sayings carved on real chalets, may have led members of the audience to wonder whether Polonius had been a Switzer in his youth. On the center drop: "Speak little: Truth say: Want little: Cash pay." Below the private box: "Doing Good, above all Gold; on Love and Kindness keeps a Hold."[14]

After the audience had sufficiently admired the setting, Smith entered from a door of the chalet, not in peasant or Alpinist garb, as might have been expected, but in full evening fig. He mounted a small raised platform, on which stood a small "pianette" laden with a model of a diligence, mule bells, and other props, and the performance began. Like the *Overland Mail* routine, it was a combination of anecdote, impersonation, song, and mild satire, all woven together by Smith's relaxed platform manner. Behind him, during the first act, were shown stationary pictures, from Beverley's sketches, of scenes en route from Geneva to Chamonix; after the intermission, the ascent of the mountain was depicted by a panorama moving vertically. Excellent though these paintings were, however, they were upstaged by the entertainer. Audiences particularly applauded his light songs, some sentimental, some topical. Of the latter, the most famous was "Galignani's Messenger" (the name of an English-language newspaper published in Paris), a tuneful fruitcake filled with allusions to the news of the day. Rewritten almost every night to take advantage of the latest headlines, this patter song remained an indispensable feature of the show from season to season, despite the many changes made to the program surrounding it.

A number of patrons left first-hand accounts of the show. Among these was Henry James, twelve years old at the time he attended *The Ascent of Mont Blanc* in the summer of 1855. Near the end of his life, he described his visit:

I recall in especial our being arrayed, to the number of nine persons, all of our contingent, in a sort of rustic balcony or verandah which, simulating the outer gallery of a Swiss cottage framed in creepers, formed a feature of Mr. Albert Smith's once-famous representation of the Tour of Mont Blanc. Big, bearded, rattling, chattering, mimicking Albert Smith again charms my senses, though subject to the reflection that his type and presence, superficially so important, so ample, were somehow at odds with such ingratiations, with the reckless levity of his performance—a performance one of the great effects of which was, as I remember it, the very brief stop and re-departure of the train at Epernay, with the ringing of bells, the bawling of guards, the cries of the travellers, the slamming of doors and the tremendous pop as of a colossal champagne-cork, made all simultaneous and vivid by Mr. Smith's mere personal resources and graces. But it is the publicity of our situation as a happy family that I best remember, and how, to our embarrassment, we seemed put forward in our illustrative chalet as part of the boisterous show and of what had been paid for by the house.[15]

The Ascent of Mont Blanc was one of the biggest hits of the whole Victorian era.* The word spread throughout the world of fashion; "London," says

* Not the least of Smith's innovations was his efficient management and care for his audience's comfort and convenience—concerns which, one gathers, did not always distinguish London entertainment places. Not only did he give the Egyptian Hall the thorough housecleaning it required after many years of hard use; he forbade gratuities to attendants, placed free programs on the seats before the audience arrived, requested ladies not to wear bonnets at the evening performances, abolished the one-shilling surcharge for advance booking, and in his performance, by expert control of pace, kept so close to schedule that he never deviated more than a half a minute in total time elapsed, yet never abridged a single important sentence. (*Times,* 18 September 1854.)

170. Albert Smith's *Ascent of Mont Blanc* at the Egyptian Hall (*Illustrated London News*, 25 December 1852).

Smith's most recent biographer, "danced to 'The Mont Blanc Quadrille' and 'The Chamouni Polka,' with Beverley's views and a portrait of Smith on the music cover. Ladies cooled themselves with fans decorated with views of the ascent." Jullien now found himself called "the Mont Blanc of Music" as he conducted "Les Echos de Mont Blanc Polka" at his Covent Garden prom concerts. Indeed, the fame of Smith's show, far from hurting the rest of the London amusement industry, sent out waves of prosperity from which other productions benefited. At the Egyptian Hall itself, the Holy Land panorama upstairs, which had been doing poor business despite its musical frills, now found itself playing to full houses made up of those who could not get into Smith's show; "those who failed in ascending Mont Blanc," remarked the *Times*, "consented to endure a pilgrimage to Palestine."[16] (Later, when he continued to have to turn prospective patrons away, Smith saw no reason why someone else should profit from their going upstairs to

see another show. In the winter of 1854, therefore, he rented the room himself and, taking advantage of the Crimean War, replaced the Holy Land with the panorama of Constantinople that Beverley had painted for the Crystal Palace crowds three years before.) The prosperity reached as far as Chamonix itself, where it was said that the route up Mont Blanc had become as crowded as Piccadilly at Smith's show time. Within a few years, according to a disgusted Ruskin, the region became overrun with "English mobs"—to the profit of the local hotel industry and supporting services.

The *Mont Blanc* show also sent waves of inspiration into the London entertainment business. It supplied Planché with a ready-made topic for his new Haymarket attraction, *Mr. Buckstone's Ascent of Mount Parnassus: A Panoramic Extravaganza,* in which the noted comedian Buckstone performed in a replica of the Egyptian Hall chalet. And in 1855, borrowing his title from Charles Mathews and his format from Smith, Gordon Cumming reintroduced himself to the

London public as "The Lion Slayer at Home." In his new role, this Albert Smith of the bush, "a slim gentleman, white of hand and delicate of feature," according to one critic, performed "in a deadly circle of skulls, tusks, antlers, horns, bones, and skeletons,—the remains of a whole forest population; and talks, with the easy familiarity of a boudoir, of life-tussles with cobras and lions, making small drawing-room jokes about his old enemies, and occasionally catching up a date by easy reference to his hundredth elephant encounter." A thirty-scene diorama illustrated the African locales through which Cumming guided his West End safari.[17]

By the end of his second season, August 1853, Smith had performed 471 times before 193,754 people. For the third season the program was revamped, though all the sure-fire features were kept. At the opening night much was made of the appearance at the Egyptian Hall of four chamois and ten St. Bernard dogs, two of which Smith later gave to the Prince Consort and a third to his friend Dickens. The publicity the dogs brought him was worth many times what he had paid for them. One always accompanied him on the street, a much more attention-getting advertisement for the show than the shabby sandwich men Banvard had hired for his; and at the interval at each performance at least one dog came forth, to be petted by young ladies and deliver to children in the front row packets of chocolates instead of their breed's traditional tot of life-saving brandy.

Smith was a master publicist, an astute Barnum with the advantage of good English breeding.* If Barnum had managed to arrange for General Tom Thumb to make visits to the royal family, Smith did no less; to a private performance attended by the Prince Consort and his sons, he was later able to add a command show at Osborne in August 1854 and another at Windsor in 1856. At every landmark performance—the five-hundredth, the one-thousandth—audiences were given a souvenir. Patrons at the Christmas week peformances in 1855 received Mont Blanc Twelfth Night Characters, "a sheet of twenty-four color illustrations of characters from the show, which folded into an envelope decorated with a picture of the proscenium." For each of the characters Smith wrote a descriptive quatrain, and the gaily colored pictures were from lithographs by "Cuthbert Bede" (the Rev. Edward Bradley, author of the current best-selling university novel *The Adventures of Mr. Verdant Green*). Both text and illustrations were redolent of *Punch,* to which their respective creators both had been contributors.†

Add to all this the friendliness of a carefully cultivated press, and it is little wonder that *The Ascent of Mont Blanc* kept drawing crowds month after month to the room where "Albertus Maximus, the boon companion of the metropolis," as the *Times* called him, held forth.[18] When the novelty of the direct route to Mont Blanc finally wore off, Smith and Beverley decided on a circuitous trip for the fourth season (1854–55) and accordingly went to Boulogne, Amsterdam, and Cologne for fresh pictures. These were supplemented by, of all things, a relic of Dr. Gropius' old Pleorama, which had pioneered the panorama tour twenty years earlier: the moving picture of the Rhine between Cologne and Bingen, bought for a pittance from a down-at-the-heel Birmingham theatre.

The show's original title was becoming less and less descriptive of the program. By November 1856 the ascent was relegated to an entr'acte, and attention was shifted to Baden, which Beverley showed in a moonlight view of "Conversation House" while Smith talked about the gambling that went on inside. A year later, the second half of the performance was devoted to Naples and another mountain, Vesuvius, which, whatever the sterling virtues of Mont Blanc, had the considerable advantage of being explosive. At the beginning of the season, Smith observed in his prepared remarks that there would soon be an eruption at Naples. A few days later, there was at least a series of earthquakes.[19]

After 2,000 performances and innumerable versions of "Galignani's Messenger" the Mont Blanc show closed for good on 6 July 1858. Looking for a new world to conquer and bring back to Piccadilly, Smith lighted on China, now in the forefront of the English consciousness by virtue of the recent Anglo-French capture of Canton and the subsequent Treaty of Tientsin, which expanded the gains resulting from the Opium War two decades earlier. After a tour of the Orient, Smith returned to London and prepared a wholly new show, which opened on 22 December. He cautiously retained the magic name of his favorite mountain in the title; now it was *Mont Blanc to China*. The opening night audience entered through a glittering all-Oriental foyer, where willow-pattern plates bearing Smith's picture could be bought for a shilling. Inside the hall, gone were the Swiss mottoes: the new wisdom was contained in Confucian aphorisms. Gone too was the chalet, now replaced by a Cantonese flower-garden pavilion flanked by a pagoda and a portion of a shop. The first part of the performance, beginning with the obligatory views of Mont Blanc,

* Smith, in fact, called Barnum "his teacher in the show business." In the autumn of 1844 the two made a trip to the Midlands, which, as far as Barnum was concerned, was a showman's holiday; he stopped in at various exhibition places—fairs, the porter's "museum" of trumperies at Warwick Castle—in search of ideas and objects for his own use. Smith, he wrote, "often confessed that he derived his very first idea of becoming a showman from my talk about the business and my doings, on this charming day when we visited Warwick." Their friendship was renewed in 1857, when Barnum was back in London; Smith took him to dinner at the Garrick Club and put him on the free list at the Egyptian Hall. Barnum recognized some of the material in Smith's current edition of the Mont Blanc show. Among other episodes and anecdotes, there was that of an American showman named Phineas Cutecraft trying to buy the bones of the 11,000 martyred virgins at Cologne Cathedral. When the horrified sexton refused, Cutecraft replied, "Never mind, I'll send another lot of bones to my Museum, swear mine are the real bones of the Virgins of Cologne, and burst up your show." (Barnum, I, 291–98; II, 450–54.)

† In a manner strikingly modern, children's toys were spun off from this popular entertainment. One was an Ascent of Mont Blanc game, a near relation of Parcheesi with a board, spinner, and three dozen counters for each player. The route shown on the board, illustrated with fifty-three scenes after Beverley's sketches, led from the Egyptian Hall to the mountain. At each stop along the way a player was penalized or given a bonus (for instance, when crossing the Channel, "If you do not feel the least sick here, you may take six [sic!] from the pool as a reward."). The first to reach the summit took the pool. Another Smith-sponsored home entertainment

was a kind of Smith retrospective—material from the old Overland Mail and some of the familiar characters from the Mont Blanc show. For "Galignani's Messenger" was substituted a patter song called "The Home News." The second part of the program was devoted to a panorama of China and ended with the setting of a gigantic willow plate, over which passed a procession of mechanical figures.

It was a brave new beginning, but it did not succeed. Young Kate Stanley, Bertrand Russell's mother, may not have been typical of all Smith's patrons, but her response probably defines one objection the more earnest ones had: "we all went to Albert Smith's China it is very amusing indeed though very vulgar & he really tells one nothing about China that one did not know before, there was a capital political song in which Palmerston was pantaloon knocked over."[20] Political songs, however, did not make up for the absence of the Rhine and "Galignani's Messenger" and the mere token presence of Mont Blanc. Smith readily restored the old favorites, and business picked up. On the two-hundredth night, the willow-pattern plates were given away as mementoes. The second season of the reconstituted entertainment began in November 1859—seven and a half years since Smith had first brought Mont Blanc to the attention of a Piccadilly audience. It prospered in its turn until the middle of May, when Smith, walking from the Egyptian Hall to the Garrick Club in a rainstorm, contracted bronchitis, from the complications of which he died two days later.

⊏ꝫ⁂ꝫ⊐

As the good-humored master guide of London's armchair excursions, Smith initially had felt no great urge to dole out hard information along with his running store of whimsical observations about men and places. In later years, however, he was aware that, with all his power over his audiences, he had not done much to inform them. He brought back from China numerous "specimens of Chinese industry connected with their domestic life and customs, as well as their arts and manufactures," which he tried to ease into his monologue. But he soon discovered, in the words of the *Illustrated London News* shortly after the show opened, that "after endeavouring to force *instruction* in every way—'gilding the pill' as he was best able—his audience did not care one straw about it. They came to hear him solely for amusement, and the instant he com-

menced any matter-of-fact details, however characteristic it might be, he lost his hold over their attention, and they listened to him as listlessly as they would have done to the mere verbal description of a panorama or the demonstration of a geological section, which they do not care to understand."[21] So he withdrew the museum pieces from the performance and arranged them instead in the former "toilette" and waiting rooms, which were kept open and lighted for the public to linger in after the performance. Few chose to stay.

In tardily attempting to add a modicum of instruction to his show, Smith had made one of the few miscalculations of his career. It was true that travel was a reliable topic for popular entertainment. The Crystal Palace with its mammoth assemblage of the products of countries all over the world, followed by such innovations as Thomas Cook's first guided tours of the continent in 1855, had markedly increased the desire to go abroad. For those who were able to do so, now that more of the nation's wealth was trickling down through the middle class, and cheap transport and modestly priced hotels were making continental touring for many a genuine possibility rather than a hopeless dream, London's panoramas served as appetite-whetters, useful preparations for the real thing. Edmund Yates wrote about this time of Whitsuntide trippers "who do Paris, and rush through France, and through Switzerland to Chamounix, [and] compare every place they are taken to with the views which formed part of the exhibition at the Egyptian Hall."[22] For those who were deprived of actual travel, the panoramas, along with the increasingly popular dissolving views, still offered as adequate a substitute as was available in those precinema days. But if the public were to attend these shows, the instruction had to be spiced with a generous dash of entertainment. Their proprietors had to provide raconteurs, assisted if possible by musicians playing or singing popular airs; panoramic tours had now reached the point where they dared not be much more than light-hearted holiday excursions held indoors.

Reviewing the livened-up panoramas that sought to compete with *The Ascent of Mont Blanc* and its Egyptian Hall offspring between 1852 and 1860, one has a heavy sense of uninspired imitation. As Planché complained in his Haymarket production for Easter 1854, *Mr. Buckstone's Voyage round the Globe (in Leicester Square): A Cosmographical, Visionary Extravaganza, and Dramatic Review:*

was a set of seventeen stereoscopic views, Mr. Albert Smith's Ascent of Mont Blanc in Miniature. Before long, the show upstairs also had a tie-in toy, a Diorama of Constantinople in Miniature—a cosmorama equipped with thirteen views for 7s. 6d. or twenty-six for 10s.

         . . . . The fellows never know
When of a thing the town has had enough.
If once they make a hit with any stuff,
They cram the public with the self-same fare
Until the stuff's completely worn threadbare.

. . . .
    Whether strait or in a ring,
    A panorama is the thing
    By which to make your hay
    While the sun shines fair.[23]

Perhaps one or two panoramists besides Smith did make hay; but against the bright background of his creativity, the other pictorial entertainments seem dreary and stale, their search for the right formula seldom extending further than the laying on of more musical and spoken divertissements.

Typical in more than one respect of the panoramas of the fifties was the diorama of Canada and the United States painted and presented by 1854 by a showman named George Washington Friend in a room next to the Polytechnic. The nonpictorial features here were the proprietor-narrator's stories, an "Original Chorus of Canadian Boatmen" and "lyrical accompaniments, some . . . expressly written by Mr. Samuel Lover," the popular Irish composer.[24] Several years later the show returned, its topicality sharpened by the fact that the Prince of Wales was touring North America at the moment. For still more timeliness, however inappropriately, Friend donned the costume of the celebrity of the day, the Hungarian patriot Louis Kossuth. According to the *Times,* the whole performance—the pictures, the songs, the stories—was trite; a public "accustomed to the productions of Beverley, Burford, Grieve, and Telbin" would not be "'struck all of a heap' by this one."[25]

The records of other tour panoramas support this growing sense of déjà vu. In 1854 Charles Marshall's Tourist Gallery showed "the grand routes of a Tour through Europe," commencing with the departure of the *John Bull* steamer from the Tower and winding through Germany, Prussia, Austria, and Bavaria, then down the Danube to Constantinople, and returning by way of Italy, the Alps, Geneva, the Rhine, and Cologne to the welcoming White Cliffs of Dover, with a descriptive lecture and music "selected from the works of the first composers."[26] The next year J. R. Smith, former proprietor of the longest Mississippi panorama, returned with his "Gigantic Tour of Europe" from what strikes one as having been an exercise in delivering coals to Newcastle: "a most successful Tour

on the Continent." This canvas of 30,000 square feet ("the largest in the world!"), with views forty feet across, covered much the same territory as the Tourist Gallery, with the now requisite "Terrific Ascent of Mont Blanc."[27] In 1860 Hamilton's "Excursions to the Continent" also claimed 30,000 square feet of canvas. The guide, said the *Athenaeum,* "hurries them from London to Milan, from St. Petersburg to Sebastopol. All the panoramas which have amazed the London school-boy for a dozen years seem rolled into one."[28] As well they might, because the tour pictures were running out of subjects.

There remained one chief means, apart from songs and humorous narration, by which panoramas might survive. An institution that had outlived its inspiration could at least reflect the concerns of the moment, and topicality had always been the panoramas' strong suit. Salvation might therefore be found in a renewed attempt, more assiduous than ever, to keep up with the headlines; and two or three news-dominating events in the fifties chanced to provide panoramists with the opportunity they needed. In April 1852, with what appears to have been remarkable prescience, the scene painters William Telbin and John Burnett opened, at the Gallery of Illustration, a "Grand National and Historical Diorama, Illustrating the Wellington Campaigns, in India, Portugal, and Spain; Concluding with the Battle of Waterloo."[29] A banal subject on the face of it, especially the Waterloo; but the proprietors could not have been luckier. On 14 September the duke died at Walmer Castle. The London show business, mourning its most eminent regular customer and a man whose military genius had supplied it with a subject upon which it had prospered for almost half a century, quickly prepared its tributes. At the Gallery of Illustration, the Wellington campaigns show was hastily retitled *The Life of Wellington* and two scenes were added as soon as they could be painted—"Exterior of Walmer Castle (by Moonlight)" and "The Duke's Chamber." Then, by one of the quickest jobs in panorama history, in less than a month after the lavish funeral on 18 November three more scenes were tacked on, showing Wellington lying in state, the funeral procession through the streets, and the interior of St. Paul's during the ceremony, with Handel's funeral anthem sung "by an efficient choir, accompanied by the Organ."[30] At Leicester Square, a freshly painted panorama of Waterloo, the third or fourth such at this house, was opened on 17 November. In due course, the St. George's Gallery unveiled "The

GREAT DIORAMA of LONDON, as it appeared on the day of the Funeral, showing the whole of the scenes connected with this magnificent pageant and ceremonial, commencing with Walmer Castle and ending at St. Paul's Cathedral."[31] In March 1854 this exhibition was moved to Hungerford Hall, where Bouton's dioramas had been shown during the Crystal Palace season. It did not survive long in the new location. A month later a fire, caused by boy employees dropping on the floor the flaming paper with which they lighted the gas jets, burned the building to the ground.[32]

An inevitable derivative of the Wellington excitement* was a Napoleon diorama, hastily painted by Charles Marshall for display, beginning at the end of February, in the new Regent Gallery. Apart from certain unspecified but "extremely ingenious" mechanical innovations, the show was noteworthy for the shift in attitude it reflected. Almost forty years after Waterloo, it was no longer necessary to make a panoramic review of the Napoleonic Wars an unbroken recital of English victories. In Marshall's show there were only two such scenes, the battles of the Nile and Waterloo. Otherwise the panorama, like its counterparts in Paris (and the *gloires militaires* which for many years dominated the repertory of theatres like the Cirque Olympique), was devoted to Napoleon's victories. British chauvinism, in this respect at least, was on the decline. But English showmen's indifference to artistic or thematic fitness was still strong, as the advertised "performance of glees and madrigals by artistes of eminence, including the German Quartett Party," at the end of a show devoted to Napoleon would suggest.[33]

In the immediately following years, the panoramas, including those nominally taking the form of grand tours, sought to adjust themselves to a new public expectation. The electric telegraph and cable were bringing London the news of events thousands of miles away within minutes, and with the spirit of "Galignani's Messenger" hovering over every show, panoramists had to be quicker with the brush than ever before. Long before Britain became militarily involved, they had kept a weather eye cocked on the Constantinople region, where clouds were gathering. As soon as Turkey declared war on Russia (October 1853) and the British fleet was ordered into the Black Sea (January 1854) the rush to provide "illustrations of the war" was on.

The career of Telbin's and Grieve's panorama was typical. It had opened at the Gallery of Illustration in the middle of 1853 as *The Overland Mail to India and Australia*. The following February the proprietors added a diorama of Sebastopol, a focal point of the war although it would not come under siege until October.[34] Two months later the trip was detoured to show "the Route of the British Army to the Seat of War," beginning with the embarcation at Southampton and following the troop ships through the Mediterranean to the Black Sea. "As the war proceeds," it was announced, "the proprietors intended to add to the diorama such scenes as would serve to illustrate its progress and results."[35] This promise of continuous revision was kept, the name of the show being changed to "the Danube and the Black Sea" to accommodate the widening theatre of war. The new pictures themselves seem to have been less than satisfactory, one journalist complaining that "even with a lorgnette, we were unable to catch the lines of those terrible fortifications of which Russo-German newspapers have said so much. A mass of white paint, seen through a quantity of rigging, is the only indication we have of the formidable fortress. We have, however, if it be any compensation, a large sheet of water, a clear sky, and a large assemblage of vessels."[36] Despite such cavils, the use of the panorama to provide a running history of the war as well as to supplement the daily telegraphic dispatches kept the Gallery of Illustration in business throughout the war. If the pictorial representation of the military arrangements left something to be desired, the lack was supplied by the lecturer, J. H. Stocqueler, who employed diagrams to explain what entrenchments, bastions, and gabions were and displayed actual Minié rifles and Colt's and Dean's revolvers.[37]

At Leicester Square, Burford rehung his old Constantinople panorama, last shown for two months in 1846. It ran for three months this time, being succeeded at Christmas 1854 by a portrayal of the Battle of the Alma, which had occurred three months before. The climactic event of the war, the siege of Sebastopol, was illustrated (May 1855) while it was still in progress. Still another Sebastopol picture, illustrating the capture of the town, opened in February 1856.

In the upper room at the Egyptian Hall, renamed for the occasion the "New Turkish Room," Albert Smith, as we have seen, revived Allom's and Beverley's moving panorama of Constantinople, with a lecture by a Mr. Kenney. It had no military significance—the concluding tableau was a view of a great fire in the city as seen from the Golden Horn—but it was meant to oblige a popular desire for topographical orientation now that an unpleasant war was being waged not far away from the scene depicted.

* Elsewhere the commemoration took other forms. Within a few weeks of the funeral, Tussaud's installed what was billed as a "Magnificent Shrine of Memorial in honour of the late illustrious WELLINGTON, representing him as in the Olden Times, reposing on a tented couch, under a splendid canopy of the Cloth of Gold, dressed in a Field-Marshal's uniform, wearing various Orders of Knighthood, covered with the Mantle of the Order of the Garter." (*Athenaeum*, 6 February 1853, p. 168.) For five weeks in the summer of 1853 the funeral car was displayed at Marlborough House. Fifty thousand persons availed themselves of the free tickets provided by its manufacturers, Messrs. Bantling and Son. The *Illustrated London News* (27 August 1853, p. 179) seized the occasion to remark on the way times had improved. "A few years since," it said, "such an object of curiosity would have been made the costly sight of a show house"—the allusion is almost surely to the Napoleon carriage at the Egyptian Hall—"whereas, by the present regulation, it is free and accessible to all classes of the people." The monstrous vehicle is now a featured exhibit in the crypt of St. Paul's.

In *Mr. Buckstone's Voyage round the Globe,* Planché inserted not only spoken allusions to the war but a moving panorama of Constantinople, the Golden Horn, Gallipoli, and the actual scene of the fighting. Buckstone, the star, complained of the number of Golden Horns to be seen:

> There's one in Piccadilly, blown by Kenney,
> At the Egyptian Hall, whose notes have long
> Been answered by the echoes of Mont Blanc.
> Another Burford puffs in Leicester Square;
> . . . in short, it's quite Horn Fair;
> And folks who wish to see the best of them are
> Themselves between the horns of a dilemma.[38]

Next came the Sepoy Mutiny of 1857, the last major event to be depicted in the panoramas. By now, the need for haste and sensationalism had come to overrule whatever vestigial taste the showmen still possessed. Charles Marshall's Delhi picture, painted "with surprising alacrity to meet the times," got short shrift in the press. It was lectured on, reported one critic, "by one of those smooth-tongued expositors, with a white wand, that moves like a clock-hand over the surface of the picture, which is painted with the theatrical exaggerations of ultramarine water and plains of burnt sienna, dotted here and there with white and black rebels and red Englishmen."[39] In 1858 the slaughter of women and children at Cawnpore was among the subjects of a Mutiny panorama at the new St. James's Hall; the *Illustrated London News* found it revolting and urged its withdrawal. But the paper did not object to its being on the same bill with a dioramic representation of the crypt of the Holy Sepulcher in daylight, dusk, and lamplight, or to the fact that during the scene changes the audience was entertained by a "sax-tuba" band.[40]

There was every reason to think that the panorama was coming to a dead end. Its demise as a stock form of entertainment might have been staved off by a successful technical innovation comparable to the original Diorama or the Lisbon Earthquake Cyclorama, but none was forthcoming.* Instead, two momentous technical developments which had originated in the 1840s now ended the panorama's presence as a fixture among London shows, uninterrupted since 1792. One was the adaptation of the engraving process to the needs of the time-short periodical press. The success of the *Illustrated London News* in 1842 had led to the establishment of several papers which depicted recent events and newsworthy scenes in sharp, detailed engravings, thus undercutting the panorama in a field in

which it had long specialized. The picture papers covered the Crimean War, the Sepoy Mutiny, and the other events of the fifties more vividly and comprehensively than any number of panoramas could have done. The other development was that of photography, ironically Daguerre's contribution to the demise of an industry in which he had earned the money to support his experiments. Although the direct reproduction of photographs in newspapers and magazines was still a number of years off (meanwhile, engravers would copy them for illustrations), commercial photography had advanced so far by the late fifties that pictures of news events and foreign scenes could be seen in shop windows and taken home. The panoramists thus found themselves in the same situation as portrait painters: their occupation was slipping from beneath them.

Prominent among early photographs were—again ironically—those of scenes which had been the special province of the series of panoramas that began with the Nile journey at the Egyptian Hall. Commencing in 1856, the pioneer Francis Frith made scores of photographs of ancient monuments in Egypt, the Sinai, Palestine, and elsewhere in the Middle East. Gathered into large folios, prints of these pictures supplanted the familiar books of topographical engravings which had been the domestic equivalent of the panoramas. More important, an eight-foot-long view of Cairo, enlarged from seven of Frith's negatives, was shown in 1858 at the Photographic Society's exhibition.[41] Perhaps, instead of being painted, panoramas could be made from vastly enlarged photographs, in the manner of twentieth-century photo murals? This was not attempted, but, just as another Frith—William—was sketching his *Derby Day* from photographs, Burford experimented with photographs instead of drawings as the basis of his panoramas of Hongkong, Canton, and Sebastopol. Success eluded him, however; as a writer remarked in 1860, "For the objects in the foreground, [the camera's] operation is perfect; but it is found that the distance cannot be accurately represented with the same focus. Another difficulty which the painter finds very embarrassing, is the depth of its shadows, which perplex the relations of objects in respect to distance. Thus the painter of the panorama of the Forum at Rome informed the writer, that when he compared certain photographic representations with the sketches which he had made himself on the spot, he found such essential differences between them as to render the former to a great extent inapplicable to his purpose."[42] The result of a similar experiment was shown at the

* One was proposed in 1856, when a group of London journalists and men about the theatre, including Henry Mayhew and Douglas Jerrold, formed the General Exhibition Company to develop the Georama, a panorama on a new principle. (The projectors may not have been aware that the name had already been applied to the Parisian prototype of Wyld's globe.) Instead of moving horizontally from one side of the stage to the other, the canvas would "move from the centre, in front of the spectator, divergingly or obliquely to either side; and as it thus passes, the spectator will fancy himself in the act of moving forwards whilst the scenery will appear to be fixed and stationary." This, it was maintained, was the ideal way to produce the illusion of moving along a street, road, river, or canal. The proposed site was to be the Gallery of Illustration and the artists the busy Telbin and Grieve. The company's prospectus printed a letter from the aged Leigh Hunt, in which, after endorsing the scheme, he went on to draw once more from his by now démodé vein of Fancy. The next step, he said, would probably be a show "giving us a taste of the very climates through which we pass;— now a cold blast from Russia, and now a Zephyr from Greece! Nay, birds may be set singing in trees, bells ringing from steeples, torrents be heard falling, thunders reverberating. Nor would any one be astonished, if we were to stop now and then at the door of an inn or hotel, and be served by some local 'Wizard' of a landlord with cakes *ad libitum,* and drinks out of some interminable bottle. This however," Hunt belatedly concluded, forgetting the "magic barrel" of his youth, "might look a little too fanciful for the sober 'truthfulness' of your operations." (JJ Coll., London Play Places box 7.) The Georama never materialized, but the double-cloth device, though supposedly none of the accessories Leigh Hunt dreamed up, was adopted by the Drury Lane pantomime of Robinson Crusoe many years later, in 1881. (Private information from David Mayer III.)

Polytechnic in the spring of 1862, coinciding with the arrival of a Japanese mission to mark the opening of Japan to western trade: a 9,000-square-foot canvas of Jeddo (Tokyo) and its suburbs painted by native artists after photographs made by a Captain Wilson, who was connected with the British Embassy.[43] Since the publicity concentrated upon the risks all concerned had taken to produce the picture—if detected, they could have been executed for portraying the forbidden scenes—nothing was said about photography's effect upon the fidelity of the pictures.

The arrival of the camera affected the panorama trade in still another way. Heretofore, the magic lantern's manifest advantages as an alternate form of pictorial entertainment had been limited by its cumbersome size and the cost of slides. But now photography made it possible for slides to be reduced from eight inches across to a mere three, and for the projected pictures to be sharper than was possible when the slides had to be painted by hand. The cost of a slide correspondingly fell from as high as twenty pounds to a shilling, and a great stock of photographic views, including all the subjects of topographical panoramas, became available to every exhibitor. The reduced size of the slides in addition made it possible to build smaller, more compact projectors.

Thus there was a distinct air of futility in the *Times*'s attempt at the end of 1861 to argue that the advance of photography had not made panoramas obsolete. Although "every schoolboy" now knew the look of the chief buildings in continental cities through cheap illustrated papers, if not through lantern shows, "there are aspects of soil and climate which neither engraving nor the photograph can represent" but the panorama can, "with a completeness and truthfulness not always to be gained from a visit to the scene itself."[44] Although color was not specifically mentioned, this was one respect in which the panorama did enjoy an unequivocal advantage over the photograph. But such superiorities counted for little. If it was graphic representation of place that people wanted, they could have it conveniently and cheaply at home in engravings, illustrated papers, books, magic-lantern slides, and that newest of home-entertainment inventions, the stereoscope. If, on the other hand, they wanted sheer amusement, they could also find it more dependably and in greater variety outside the panoramas.

Robert Burford died in 1861, and his son, Robert William, kept the Leicester Square establishment going for only two more years. Although panoramas did not vanish wholly from the London scene, as a major genre of popular art they had reached the end of the road. Their history had been long and varied, as filled with failures as with successes, but on the whole it had been a creditable one. Reviewing one of Burford's last shows, the *Athenaeum* pronounced what was in effect a funeral eulogy, and like most eulogies it failed to tell the whole truth:

We English are bated by brave neighbors—who themselves live and die, morally and personally, between the Boulevards and the Palais Royal—with our insular inattention to the business of the big world beyond our shores; and we have ourselves, in that spirit of humorous self-depreciation which our brave neighbours believe to be as real in its sincerity as the confessions of Rousseau, invented in the words Parish-politics and Little Peddlington, phrases of abuse with the same moral. Yet here are we, as our public amusements show, making the very grandest of grand tours. Lucknow, New York, Canton, San Francisco, Delhi, Constantinople, and St. Petersburgh, are all as familiar, even to our children, as Paris or Rome, Brighton or Bath.[45]

True enough, so far as it went. If nothing more, the panorama had helped widen the imaginative horizons of the inhabitants of a tight little island during a time when, for various reasons, cultural insularity was rampant among the great majority of the people. Against this parochialism of intellect and interest the panoramas had served, within modest limits, as a counteragent. But what was forgotten in this twilight of the institution was the high regard in which some had once held it, as prospectively, if not actually, a legitimate, highly promising new form of art. Those initial expectations had finally been obscured, half a century later, by what the *Athenaeum* writer omitted to notice: the way in which "the very grandest of grand tours" had been compromised by their proximity to the music hall and their futile effort to compete with the new speeded-up journalism. The gadgetry and extra attractions the showmen had introduced in their losing effort to keep their pictures competitive in the London amusement world had finally doomed it, and "the age of the panorama" became a mere rueful memory.

The Fifties, II: The Old Order Changeth

34

As the end of the 1851 season approached at Hyde Park, the great topic of public discussion—replacing the controversy over the potential dangers of the exhibition, an issue now fortunately laid to rest—was what to do with the Crystal Palace. The Royal Commissioners had given a firm commitment to remove it from the park, yet it had so enchanted the nation at large that few could bear the thought of its being dismantled, never to rise again. The idea of a winter-garden exhibition hall, however, had been much in the air in the past few years. We have already noted that such a scheme had been proposed in 1848 to restore the fortunes of old Vauxhall; and about the same time, Charles Kingsley, rankled because he had to pay a shilling to visit the tomb of Robert Burton at Christ Church, Oxford, half-jokingly proposed that "those useless relicts," cathedrals at large, be turned into winter gardens for workingmen's enjoyment.[1]

The winter-garden idea, broadened into that of an all-year-round showplace, was the one finally adopted to save the Crystal Palace. The stated purpose of the private company of speculators who bought it and moved it to the South London suburb of Sydenham was to provide "refined recreation, calculated to elevate the intellect, instruct the mind, improve the hearts of, and welcome the millions who have now no other incentives to pleasure but such as the gin-palace, the dancing saloon, and the ale-house afford them."[2] To this end, they enlarged the already enormous iron and glass building by half, creating a total space of 843,656 square feet, at a cost of £1,300,000. Merely to maintain so great a structure, let alone fill it with profitable attractions, was to prove a daunting undertaking.[3]

Initially, however, the enterprise had one advantage that no money could buy: the ready-made fame (the commercial term "good will" is especially appropriate here) that the building brought with it. And, as far as sheer volume of patronage was concerned, the company's original expectation was fulfilled. In the first thirty years after the Crystal Palace was opened (1854) on a hill overlooking—and conspicuous from—both London and the Surrey countryside, an annual average of two million people passed through the doors. Its ready accessibility was guaranteed by the addition of an extra down-line from London Bridge on the London, Brighton, and South Coast Railway, whose chairman happened also to be chairman of the Crystal Palace Company, and by the building of the West End of London and Crystal Palace Junction Railway, which brought crowds from Victoria. (In the sixties one more line began to serve the site at a separate station—the London, Chatham, and Dover, which tapped the traffic arriving from still another direction.)

At this permanent Crystal Palace there was more than enough to see, hear, and do. Most notable, at the outset, were the features designed to serve the announced purpose of elevating the intellect and instructing the mind. In essence, the interior, designed by the company's "joint directors of decoration," Owen Jones and Digby Wyatt, was a hybrid of the Colosseum, the Egyptian Hall in the Belzonian era, and the British Museum's new exhibition rooms, with abundant reminiscences, also, of the most admired parts of the Hyde Park structure. Ten elaborate "courts" purported to offer a complete history of architectural and decorative styles from the Egyptians to the Renaissance by way of Greece, Rome, Pompeii, the Middle Ages (reviving the neo-Gothic spirit of Pugin's medieval court in the original building), Byzantium, China, and Moorish Spain. Among the showpieces here were copies of parts of the Alhambra, of the Vatican Raphael frescoes, and of the Elgin marbles; a model of the Parthenon; and reproductions of ancient Roman baths and of the house of a Pompeian citizen just before the fatal eruption of Vesuvius. Two colossal statues presided over the Egyptian court; the Grecian court was in the form of a temple of Jupiter, and enormous bulls and columns, reflecting the treasures just added to the British Museum from Layard's excavations at Nineveh, dignified the Assyrian one.* There were, in addition, a picture gallery, a waxwork Court of the Kings and Queens of England, a natural history and ethnology collection including "models and tableaux of the various races and ages of man together with hundreds of stuffed birds, beasts, and fishes," and a 4,000-seat concert hall. In the center of the building was space for Jullien-size orchestras and choruses as well as a 4,500-pipe organ. This was the scene of the celebrated Handel festival of 1857, the first of a long series of musical events employing large forces.

In the exhibition halls much effort was made to provide continuity with the Hyde Park show. Here, in profusion, were the kinds of objects first identified with the Adelaide Gallery and the Polytechnic and subsequently with the primary interest of the original Crystal Palace: a gallery of engineering models, a large assortment of machinery in motion (textile machines, lathes, steam hammers, carpet looms, steam engines), a "Raw Produce Collection, and Trade Museum," a display of 300 ship models, and a loan exhibition of porcelain and pottery.[4]

At Hyde Park, nearly all the attractions had been inside the building; little was to be seen on the adjacent grounds except the shed housing the steam engine that worked the machinery within. At Sydenham, however, the spacious grounds contained a combination of attractions—mazes, a lake, islands, grottoes, groves, lawns—that dwarfed anything Vauxhall and the Surrey Gardens ever afforded in their palmiest days. An elaborate system of fountains shot seven million gallons of water an hour through 12,000 jets; there were special displays of the waterworks at appointed times. But the most memorable outdoor feature, preserved today, derived from a suggestion by Prince Albert that in view of the era's interest in the dark backward and abysm of time it would be appropriate to devote some attention to paleontology. On a six-acre island in the artificial lake, a kind of instant prehistoric marsh landscaped with replicas of plants from the Cretaceous period, were placed an array of life-size monsters in the order of their supposed appearance in Britain, from Triassic reptiles to Cretaceous dinosaurs and pterodactyls. These were modeled by the sculptor Benjamin Waterhouse Hawkins from designs approved by the great Victorian authority on such matters, Professor Owen. One iguanodon alone required 4 stout iron columns, 600 bricks, 1,550 tiles, 38 casks of cement, 98 casks of broken stone, and 100 feet of iron hooping.[5] Inaccurate though many of the models and their assigned postures were, they had some part in forming the notions of prehistoric zoology that were afloat in the communal mind which received Darwin's momentous argument in late 1859.

So far, all of this was in the spirit of the Hyde Park exhibition: science, technology, architecture, and sculpture. Lady Eastlake, the art historian, was one of the many who applauded the Crystal Palace in its revised version. "It is now a paradise of flowers and works of art," she wrote. " . . . If many make it only an amusement, it will be an innocent one; but, judging from myself, it must be an improvement and raise the whole standard of education."[6] This was what promoters of improved public taste, figures as different as the late Benjamin Robert Haydon and the superhumanly active Henry Cole, had envisioned, but never in such abundance. From the beginning, however, it was plain that no such enticements alone would bring in the revenue the Crystal Palace Company had to have. With admission only a shilling, except on Saturday afternoons (2s. 6d.) and certain special occasions, and a huge and inefficient building to maintain, the proprietors had no alternative. They had to supply sheer amusement or perish.

As a consequence, within a few years the day-to-day offerings at the Crystal Palace became a potpourri of all the varieties of mass entertainment then in favor. Here was recapitulated, on a scale appropriate to the building's magnitude, the experience of the Colosseum, the Adelaide Gallery, and the Polytechnic; with one or two minor exceptions, this was the last Victorian attempt to mix culture and amusement. Recalling Albert Smith's disillusionment at the time of his Chinese show, *Punch* lamented the fulfillment of his

* The classic statuary in the Greek and Roman courts caused a stir which took some of the bloom from the new exhibition in its first few months. Certain portions of the clergy objected to what was called the "naturalism" of the casts, and the offending parts were removed by hammer and chisel. "The covering of the resultant wound, however, presented problems, for on 8th May, with only a month to go before opening, the *Times* reported that the Directors were having difficulties in finding 'a supply of fig leaves for the nude statues.' The plaster foliage was eventually found or manufactured and riveted on to the emasculated loins of the heroes of old but even this did not assuage the outraged sensibilities of a group of hostile clergymen. The battle continued past the opening date and well into the year, but by 15th December the Directors had had enough" and told the clergy that they had done all they intended to do. (Patrick Beaver, *The Crystal Palace, 1851–1936*, London, 1970, pp. 94–96.)

and other men's prophecy that the programs at Sydenham would become increasingly vulgarized, that "its art from 'High' to 'Low,' / Would sink, until it came to flow / Level with vulgar comprehensions."[7]

By a stroke of bad luck, as the proponents of uplift viewed it, the critical moment when the Crystal Palace's future policy was determined coincided with the rage for "sensation" that characterized the early 1860s. When a seemingly insatiable appetite for thrills intensified the normal human preference for amusement over edification, the well-meant effort to refine the popular taste and nourish the mind was doubly doomed. The show-business counterpart of the best-selling sensational novels (*East Lynne, Lady Audley's Secret*) and the melodramas based on them was the daring acrobat Blondin, world famous for his feats on a rope stretched high above Niagara. Sardonically commenting on his crowd-pleasing engagement at Sydenham, the *Athenaeum* noted that he was paid as much for one performance as a curate or a keeper of manuscripts in the British Museum made in a year; what would the Crystal Palace directors do when he palled? "They must look for something else 'sensational,' and will probably find what they look for."[8] Since Blondin was one of a kind, they found no attraction to measure up to him; but once he had made his mark on the Sydenham scheme of entertainment, the managers were bound to continue in the same spirit. After his breathtaking activities on the wire, medieval courts, picture galleries, and natural history displays were insufferably dull.

It was unfortunate, too, that an especially successful Sabbatarian campaign should have been waged in the Sydenham palace's very first years. The same forces that managed to keep the National Gallery and British Museum closed on Sunday afternoon, despite pressure from less rigorous groups, deprived the management of much valuable revenue. But the people played into the hands of the "Sunday Observance fanatics." On Trinity Sunday, 1861, the management opened the grounds and building on a trial basis to holders of the free passes it had distributed in all the pubs in the surrounding area and to passengers in trains heading toward Sydenham. Forty thousand people swarmed in and behaved so riotously that "the whole affair," as one paper said, " . . . must be denounced in the strongest language by every lover of order and propriety, and indeed of common decency."[9] The experiment was not repeated.

As the years passed, the Crystal Palace became more and more a gigantic variety entertainment. Enough of its fixtures remained to preserve something of the initial intention: the Handel festivals, for example, with Costa conducting and Patti in her prime, and the Saturday evening orchestral concerts, continuing for forty years, that offered music as good as any in central London. The 400-foot-long marine aquarium and the menagerie that were subsequently introduced were, superficially at least, instruments of "rational amusement." So too were the many specialized exhibitions the great building housed from time to time— electrical, art, aeronautical, photographic, mining; the trade fairs; the flower shows; and the shows of dogs, pigeons, poultry, and rabbits. On the side of pure entertainment, there were, among other attractions, the fireworks displays for which the Crystal Palace became famous beginning in 1865. One specialty, the "Niagara of Fire," covered 25,000 square feet and consumed a ton of iron filings; another, outshining and outbanging anything Vauxhall or the Surrey Gardens could have presented, portrayed that deathless subject the Battle of Trafalgar in pyrotechnics 820 feet across. More prophetic of the future of popular entertainment than backward-looking was the Zoetrope, a primitive motion picture machine powered by a gas engine, which showed jerkily animated images of conjurors, acrobats, umbrella men, and Jim Crow.*

The shadow of Sydenham fell across the entire London show business, and especially across those other places which combined indoor and outdoor entertainment. Its effect upon Vauxhall Gardens, to be sure, was negligible, for the sufficient reason that by this time that venerable institution was already terminally ill, so far gone, in fact, that no competition could affect it one way or the other. It closed for good in 1859 and the grounds were covered with terrace housing. Cremorne had a brief season of unaccustomed respectable glory in 1860 when Grieve and Telbin built the Stereorama on the premises. The name obviously was inspired by the current stereoscope fad; the concept just as obviously was derived from the Surrey Gardens' modeled panoramas. A circular structure, 120 feet across, 350 in circumference, and 50 high, housed a panorama of Switzerland as seen by a tourist traveling from Lake Lucerne to Lago Maggiore by way of the St. Gothard pass. The spectators stood on an elevated platform in the middle of the space, as at Leicester Square and the Colosseum. In contrast to those conventional panoramas, the Stereorama set against a painted background in the distance a pictorial composition of solid modeled objects and cut-out sets, such as were used in elaborate theatrical scenes, to pro-

* Even more prophetic was the use made of the building in 1929, when J. L. Baird commenced a low-definition television service from it. By then the Crystal Palace was nearing the end of its career. Despite continued large attendance (John Davidson's poem "The Crystal Palace" offers a vivid description of its attractions and atmosphere at the turn of the century) the company went bankrupt in 1911, and the deteriorating building and grounds were bought for the nation through the Lord Mayor's Fund. The palace was used as a naval depot during the First World War. After it was returned to civilian control in 1920, efforts were made to rescue it from its virtually derelict condition, but these were of no avail. It was just as well, everything considered, that the once resplendent structure was put out of its misery by a fire that consumed all of it but two towers on 30 November 1936.

MADONNA DEL SASSO.   MAGADINO, ON THE LAGO MAGGIORE.   VILLAGE OF AIROLO.   SNOW CAVERN NEAR THE DEVIL'S BRIDGE.

THE DEVIL'S BRIDGE.   AMSTAG.   FLUELLEN.   BAY OF URI, LAKE OF LUCERNE.

171. The Stereorama of the St. Gothard route to Italy at the Cremorne Gardens (*Illustrated London News,* 8 September 1860).

duce a three-dimensional effect. Mechanical ingenuity produced a number of realistic effects: chimneys smoked, and real water, piped at 900 gallons a minute, rushed beneath the Devil's Bridge to be diverted into several channels, turning millwheels along the way.[10] It was a spectacle, said the *Art Journal,* to "charm the simple, and make the uninitiated wonder."[11]

Meanwhile the Surrey Gardens, the most vulnerable of the Sydenham Crystal Palace's competitors, had entered on hard times. After Edward Cross retired in 1844, his secretary, William Tyler, had taken over the proprietorship. Now, ten years later, a proposal was made to reorganize the concern as "The Surrey Gardens Temperance Crystal Palace Company," with George Cruikshank, a rabid teetotal crusader, as artistic director. The assumption seems to have been that the success of the original Crystal Palace had been due,

in part at least, to the refreshments on sale being restricted to the cheering but noninebriating products of Messrs. Schweppes, who held the catering concession. By contrast, liquor had always been sold at the Surrey Gardens, as it now was at Sydenham. Therefore (so the reasoning went), by being converted into a teetotal place of entertainment, the Surrey would appeal to the same millions who soberly enjoyed the Crystal Palace but now were deterred from going to Sydenham because it had bars. This idea proved to have little to recommend it, and a noncommittal name, the Surrey Gardens Company (Limited), was adopted instead.[12]

The 1855 panoramic spectacle, in direct competition with Cremorne's, was the Battle of Sebastopol, performed by a 100-man cast of invalided veterans (Cremorne advertised 500) in a "mimic fight, in sorties,

repulses, attacks, and manoeuvres,'' the whole concluding with the defeat of the Russian army and fireworks.[13] Nathaniel Hawthorne visited the gardens with his son Julian on 3 October. His description of the performance and of the gardens in general, seen through his cool, undeceivable tourist's eyes, is a useful corrective to the abandonate rhetoric and hyperbole that always marked the management's publicity. It is additionally valuable because, even without the advantage we have of knowing what was in store, Hawthorne sensed the air of melancholy which by this time pervaded the grounds:*

They proved to be a rather poor place of suburban amusement;—poor, at least, by daylight, their chief attraction for the public consisting in out-of-door representations of battles and sieges. The storming of Sebastopol (as likewise at the Cremorne Gardens) was advertised for the evening; and we saw the scenery of Sebastopol, painted on a vast scale, in the open air, and really looking like miles and miles of hill and water scenery;—with a space for the actual manoeuvering of ships on a sheet of real water in front of the scene, on which some ducks were now swimming about, in place of men-of-war. The climate of England must often interfere terribly with this sort of performance; and I can conceive of nothing drearier for spectators or performers than a drizzly evening. Convenient to this central spot of entertainment, there are liquor and refreshment-rooms, with pies and cakes, and this sort of thing, in which the English never produce anything very delicious. The menagerie, though the ostensible staple of the Gardens, is rather poor and scanty; pretty well provided with lions and lionesses, also a giraffe or two, some camels, a polar bear, who plunges into a pool of water for bits of cake, and two black bears, who sit on their haunches, or climb poles; besides a wilderness of monkies, some parrots and macaws, an ostrich, various ducks, and other animal and ornithological trumpery; some skins of snakes so well stuffed that I took them for live serpents, till Julian discovered the deception; and an aquarium, with a good many common fishes swimming among its seaweed.

The ground is shaded with trees, and set out with green sward and gravel walks, from which the people were sweeping the withered autumnal leaves which every day now scatters down. Plaister statues stand here and there, one of them without a head, thus disclosing the hollowness of his trunk; there was a little drizzly fountain or two, with the water dripping over the rock-work of which the English are so fond; and the buildings for the animals and other purposes had a flimsy, pasteboard aspect of pretension. The garden was in its undress; few visitors, I suppose, coming hither at this time of day, and only here and there a lady and children,

* Compare Dickens's description of Vauxhall by day, written some twenty years earlier (above, Chapter 23).

a young man and girl, or a couple of citizens, loitering about. I take pains to remember these small items, because they suggest the day-life or torpidity of what may look very brilliant at night;—these corked-up fountains, slovenly green sward, cracked casts of statues, pasteboard castles, and duck-pond bay of Balaclava, then shining out in magic splendor; and the shabby attendants, whom we saw sweeping [and] shovelling, are probably transformed into the heroes of Sebastopol.[14]

Hawthorne was among the last visitors to see the menagerie. On a dull, misty morning a month later the animals were sold. A throng of bidders, including representatives of the Zoological Society, large-animal dealers from Liverpool and the continent, and "showmen great and small, from the Messrs. Wombwell and Maunder [the leading circus owners of the era] to your scantily clad man who owns the penny show," followed the auctioneer as he moved from place to place: "Eight shillings for a wax-bill and two cut-throat sparrows. Yours, sir. A paradise grackle—nine shillings—thank you, sir. The next lot—a red and yellow macaw. No. There is some mistake—a yellow and blue macaw. What shall we say for this fine bird, gentlemen? Three pounds five—you have a bargain, sir. A sulphur-crested cockatoo—two guineas—mind your fingers, sir; that lot is spiteful. The next lot—an armadillo—what shall I say for the armadillo, gentlemen? Ten shillings?—thirty?—yes, that's more like its value. A pair of flying squirrels—one pound—cheap as things go. Now for the snakes." The prices paid for some of the larger, more valuable animals were substantial: £1,000 for two giraffes, £450 for an elephant ("never again to draw his cart full of happy, smiling children round the gravel walks, receiving biscuit contributions from his young employers"), £150 for two "stupid" camels.[15]

Despite this liquidation of the establishment's earliest attraction, in the following season of 1856 the Surrey Gardens resumed its valiant attempt to entice its former clientele back from Sydenham. The public rejoicing over the end of the war in the spring, when all London was illuminated, inspired one more Danson panorama, this time a picture of Constantinople, with the all-purpose lake now serving as the Bosphorus. On its placid surface were reflected the revolving stars of fireworks, after which a spirited bombardment took place; then "a colossal figure of Peace, with extended wings, bearing an olive-branch in either hand, advance[d] to the centre."[16] This proved to be the last of the modeled panorama spectacles.

But the Surrey's novelty that year, its boldest bid to

rival the Crystal Palace, was the new concert hall. Erected at a cost of £18,200, which the sale of the animals probably helped defray, and holding 12,000 persons, this was dedicated with a week-long festival that began with a performance of *Messiah* involving an orchestra and chorus of a thousand. The impresario and conductor was Jullien, who had just signed a five-year contract as director of music for the gardens. During the rest of the season there were numerous symphony concerts. The company gained some extra revenue from renting the hall to the evangelist Charles H. Spurgeon, whose Sunday services had outgrown their former accommodation at his own chapel and Exeter Hall. But this was not an unmixed blessing, because on 19 October, during one such service, a false cry of fire caused a panic in which seven persons were killed and fifty hurt. It was perhaps partly in an effort to neutralize the bad publicity resulting from this incident that the company declared a 5 percent year-end dividend which the state of its books was far from justifying.

The next year, 1857, opened auspiciously enough, with Thackeray delivering his series of lectures on the Four Georges in the music hall on 28 January–3 February. This was the summer of the first Handel festival at Sydenham, and Jullien, not to be outdone, opened his concert season on 11 May with an *Elijah* employing a thousand performers, followed by a month of prom concerts; a ten-day "Grand Musical Congress" timed to coincide precisely with the Handel celebration; a series of Rossini, Verdi, Beethoven, Mozart, and Mendelssohn festivals; a *Messiah* performance; and, at the end of July, a four-day military festival with bands of the Guards, Royal Artillery, Royal Engineers, Royal Marines, and Eleventh Hussars. But this plethora of notes was not readily convertible into cash, and by August the company found itself bankrupt. Jullien, speaking to the shareholders, was bitter: the clear profit of £1,000 his series of festivals produced had disappeared, and neither he nor the artists he had hired were paid. In all, he said, he had personally lost a total of £6,000 by this last phase of his involvement with the Surrey Gardens Company.[17]

Ironically, another problem facing the hard-pressed management during these years seems to have been traceable, in part at least, to Jullien. Although there is no specific evidence of overboisterous crowds after the balloon fiasco of 1838, by the fifties the Surrey Gardens' handbills repeatedly assured the public that "the Attendance of Police will be on an efficient scale." This may have been intended to counteract the bad name the other pleasure gardens, Vauxhall and Cremorne, had acquired as resorts that no respectable London family could risk attending; but Jullien himself seems, for whatever reason, to have attracted an unruly crowd wherever he conducted, at Covent Garden and Drury Lane as well as at the Surrey Gardens. His biographer, citing newspaper reports from 1848, 1856, and 1858, says that "some rowdiness on the opening night of Jullien's concerts was evidently a tradition, and seemed to be expected." "How," demanded the *Illustrated Times,* without any reference to the music, "does it happen that the opening night of Mr. Jullien's concerts is always marked by a disgraceful performance?"[18]

His money gone, Jullien returned to France, went insane, and died in 1860. The following year the concert hall burned to the ground, and although it was rebuilt, the gardens' day was clearly over. When St. Thomas's hospital was looking for temporary quarters while its own new buildings were under construction, the proprietors were only too glad to have it as occupant. When the hospital moved to its permanent quarters in 1871, a feeble attempt was made to revive the gardens as an entertainment spot, but this was foredoomed to failure, and six years later the property was sold to builders.

⁂

In the tawdry, rundown Leicester Square neighborhood the tendency of the fifties was toward ever more sensationalism and charlatanry. Savile House remained the center of the miscellaneous show trade—Bartholomew Fair put under roof, "the greatest booth in Europe," as George Augustus Sala wrote in *Household Words* in 1853:

Serpents both of land and sea;—panoramas of all the rivers of the known world; jugglers; ventriloquists; imitators of the noises of animals; dioramas of the North Pole, and the gold-diggings of California; somnambulists (very lucid); ladies who have cheerfully submitted to have their heads cut off nightly at sixpence per head admission; giants; dwarfs; sheep with six legs; calves born inside out; marionettes; living marionettes; lectures on Bloomerism; expositors of orrery—all of these have by turns found a home in Savile House. In the enlarged cosmopolitanthropy of that mansion, it has thrown open its arms to the universe of exhibitions. One touch of showmanship makes the whole world kin; and this omni-showing house would accommodate with equal pleasure, Acrobats in its drawing-rooms, Spiritual Rappers in its upper rooms, the Poughkeepsie Seer in the entrance

hall, and the Learned Pig in the cellar. . . . Needs must I linger, though, by the peristyle of Savile House, at the foot of its wide exterior staircase; though Mr. Cantelo's acolyte, next door, mellifluously invites me to ascend and see how eggs are hatched by steam; though there is a rival lady with her head undergoing the very process of decapitation next door to him; with a horned lady, a bearded lady, and a mysterious lady, on the other side.[19]

At one time or another in these years, in the bedlam that was Savile House one could view (among many other attractions) Reimers's Anatomical Museum, the Aztec Lilliputians, the Earthmen, Brees's panorama promoting Australian emigration, Risley's American panorama, J. H. Burbank's *The Angel Delivering Daniel from the Mouth of the Lions* ("the largest watercolor drawing ever executed, covering a surface of twenty feet wide by twelve feet high"),[20] George Payne's "Nights in the Lands of Gold" ("a panoramic Tour of America, California, and Australia"),[21] and Auguste Reinham's Industrious Fleas, with a cast of one hundred, the climactic scene being one "in which two ladies and two gentlemen dance a polka. The orchestra is composed of fifteen musicians, playing on different instruments of proportionate size. Four having a game at whist. A little brunette on a sofa is flirting with a fashionable beau, while her mama's mind is intensely engaged in the politics of a newspaper."[22] At Savile House, too, one could see a poor man's version of the show at the Cyclorama, Regent's Park: a "Splendid Moving DIAPHARAMA of the Great Earthquake of Lisbon."[23]

One exhibition there was memorable for the breathtaking way in which it professed to be simultaneously comprehensive and particular: "Atkins' Grand Pictorial Entertainment of Creation, Science, and Civilization," which was divided into two parts: "The Earth from Pole to Pole, Astronomy, the Antediluvian Era, and New System of Emigration, with Model Schools, Towns, Farms, and Workshops, Delineated on 20,000 Feet of Canvass," and a "View of Sebastopol, and model of bomb-proof Steam War Battery, To put an end to War, and establish the Basis of Peace and Progress. Interspersed with Select and Appropriate Music."[24] In at least three respects—the survey of "the Earth from Pole to Pole," the attention to emigration, and the Crimean War display—Atkins was competing with Wyld's Great Globe a few yards away, in the center of the square. After the Crystal Palace crowds disappeared in the autumn of 1851, Wyld was faced with the problem of what to do with his unique building for the nine years remaining of his ground lease.

His first impulse naturally was to make the exhibition more topical. The hourly lectures on geography were turned into lectures on emigration, with particular reference to the sea routes to the colonies and descriptions of the climates, products, and social life of those distant lands as they were pointed out on the globular map.[25] From this it was but a step toward installing (1853) an exhibition of gold nuggets, Australia's most attractive product. The nuggets, however, proved nugatory: they were mere pieces of lead washed with gold. Opinion differed on whether Wyld had been taken in by the owner or had himself, Barnum-like, imposed on human credulity.[26]

There was also talk of turning the edifice into something called "the Cosmos Institute" or—George Catlin's term—the "Museum of Mankind." What with the Aztec Lilliputians and the Earthmen (the latter were actually, and most fittingly, displayed inside Wyld's Earth at one juncture), interest in ethnology continued to run high in the early fifties.* With the addition of suitable galleries, the Cosmos Institute, it was proposed, would offer "lectures and demonstrations . . . in physical geography; upon man, in relation to the world he inhabits; and upon matters of general geographical, hydrographical, and ethnological interest." The usual preliminary committee of patrons was formed, among whom were the Bishop of St. David's, the archaeologist Layard, the explorer Humboldt, and the hydrographer Sir Francis Beaufort, but nothing came of the project.[27]

Notwithstanding this vacillation of purpose, as a London landmark the Great Globe continued to be as topical in 1854 as it had been when it first materialized in the middle of Leicester Square three years earlier. Planché's Easter "revue" for that year at the Haymarket, as we have seen, was *Mr. Buckstone's Voyage round the Globe.* The foot of the staircase inside the Great Globe served as the starting point for a sequence of dream scenes in which Buckstone was transported to Europe as it appeared on the model, to India by the panoramas of the Ocean Mail and the Overland Route, to Africa ("with," as the printed script explained, "Ethnological Notes and Reflections on the Bosjesmans, Zulu Kaffirs, Earthmen and other unnatural curiosities"), and to the Arctic ("Interview with the Esquimaux from Cumberland Straits and the Adelaide Gallery").[28]

The same extravaganza was sprinkled with references to the war, which had just been declared; and as promptly as possible Wyld, like so many of his colleagues, brought the Crimea and Russia into his exhi-

bition. He displayed two sets of dioramas by Charles Marshall, one consisting of forty-three scenes of Russia, its palaces and people, "the site and scenes of the memorable events of the late campaigns," the other being a forty-nine-scene "Grand Moving Diorama of a Tour from Blackwall to Balaclava." As the war progressed, models of Sebastopol, Cronstadt, Sweaborg, the Baltic, and other areas of action, supplemented by Wyld's own maps and brought up to the minute by newspaper dispatches, afforded Londoners a graphic day-by-day narrative of the fighting. There were also a "Military Gallery of the Armies of Europe" with weapons and trophies, and one of ethnological as well as topical interest, illustrating "the people of the East from Bulgaria to Afghanistan."[29]

Once more the fateful pattern: as the Great Globe's initially profitable novelty wore off and its first clear purpose was blunted against the inexorable vagaries of popular taste, it had no choice but to imitate what others were doing. From geography, emigration, ethnology, and war it moved on to join the equally hard-pressed Polytechnic and Colosseum in providing variety entertainment. As the 1850s wore on, the odd-looking building became shabbier and shabbier, acquiring the demoralized air that marked most of the show properties in the vicinity of Leicester Square. When the lease expired in 1861, there was no question of renewal. After the structure was demolished, Wyld's promise to restore the square was fulfilled to the extent that it was restored to its former condition. Again "the unwashed Arabs of Westminster disported themselves at their own wild will among the putrifying remains of dogs and cats," as a contemporary put it, and the statue of George I, now back on its former site, suffered fresh indignities. There were legal and bureaucratic tangles, questions were asked in Parliament, and in a strong editorial *The Builder* denounced the situation as "a scandal to those who have any regard for the proper maintenance of our public monuments, and for the dignity or even the decency of the metropolis of Great Britain."[30] Relief did not come until 1874, when the flamboyant company promoter Albert ("Baron") Grant, as a goodwill gesture toward the public he was so liberally bilking, bought the square, laid it out in gardens, replaced George I with Shakespeare, and ceded the now permanently beautified tract to the Metropolitan Board of Works.

The Great Globe's fortunes had sagged all the more in the mid-fifties because a rival suddenly appeared just opposite it: a spanking new building entitled the Royal Panopticon of Science and Art, an Institution for Sci-

* Which is not to say that, among the population at large, it was on any higher intellectual level than before. According to Dr. John Conolly, in his address to the Ethnological Society printed as *The Ethnological Exhibitions of London* (1855), objects and people from savage lands were then still looked upon "as objects of curiosity or of unfruitful wonder, rather than as manifestations of human intellect and modifications of human development in various parts of the same globe, and illustrative of man's unwritten history and progress. The possible improvement of all the varieties, and the ultimate concentration of all the powers developed among them, in widely different situations and circumstances, upon some ulterior results in civilization, have scarcely occupied the mind of any who gazed on mere varieties of form, and colour, and inventive industry, as curious distinctions, inherent or permanent, and associated with no definite sequence." A decade after the Ethnological Society was founded, it had not noticeably elevated the level of the public's interest in such shows; "very interesting specimens of the inhabitants of countries little known to us arrive nearly in every year, are exhibited for money for a time, are even invited for inspection in fashionable drawing-rooms among the novelties of the Spring, and depart: having gained small notice from the ethnologist, and excited no moral interest even among the most serious or the most philanthropic portion of our countrymen."

entific Exhibitions, and for Promoting Discoveries in Arts and Manufactures. Incredible though it may seem, there were entrepreneurs in London who, refusing to concede that theirs was an idea whose time had passed, set out to create a glorified new Polytechnic at a moment when the original Polytechnic was in deep trouble. But hope springs eternal in the speculative breast. "Experience has shown," the Panopticon's prospectus averred, however disingenuously, "that, with a rapidly increasing population, there has sprung up a growing taste for intellectual pursuits . . . the manufacturer by devoting a few hours weekly to the enunciations of the chemical Professor will be better prepared to meet that competition, which, tho' the very life of Commercial enterprise, is ever fatal to the indulgence of inactivity or ignorance."[31]

This public-spirited scheme, capitalized at £80,000, was undertaken by a group which a longtime habitué of Leicester Square, John Hollingshead, described as "a blameless, Pandemonium-Paving Company, Limited."[32] Among them were a number of noblemen, the Landseer brothers, the artists Daniel Maclise and John Martin (who died before the building opened), Lewis Cubitt, architect of King's Cross station and brother of the more famous building Cubitts, and Samuel Carter Hall, editor of the influential Art Journal. The brain behind the enterprise was the man who became the Panopticon's manager, Edward Marmaduke Clarke, the optician and instrument maker in the Strand who had been one of the backers of the National Repository.

The Panopticon building went up in 1852 at 28 Leicester Square, the site of John Hunter's museum and, since then, of numerous temporary shows. Although its erection caused little stir compared to that which the Great Globe had created nearby, no passerby could miss it, because it was built in what was referred to as the "Saracenic, or Moorish" style. The choice was no more inexplicable than it had been in the case of the Egyptian Hall. Owen Jones's great work on the architecture of the Alhambra had commanded much attention when it was published in 1842–1845, and the Moorish style had been employed for the Kensal Green mausoleum of Andrew Ducrow, the originator of the classical pose plastique. There was some objection on the ground of fitness, one literal-minded architect protesting that "the Saracens had not been in the habit of building Panopticon institutions," to which the answer might have been that they had not built railway bridges or termini either, yet Brunel had used Moorish trimmings in his Clifton suspension bridge and Paddington station. Exotic though the general de-

sign and ornamentation were, however, the façade was decorated in a manner calculated to please the most parochial Englishman. A series of Minton tiles portrayed the arms of Purcell, Davy, Newton, Goldsmith, Herschel, Shakespeare, Barry, Watt, and Bacon, as well as the Panopticon's own armorial bearings, which incorporated Newton's apple, Columbus's egg, and Galileo's lamp.

The central feature of the building was a rotunda ninety feet in diameter and of equal height, with a fountain in the center fed by an artesian well. The fountain, like the one at the Hyde Park Crystal Palace which probably inspired it, was spectacular. When the rotunda was darkened, "the stream of water [was] rendered luminous by means of optical apparatus . . . the fluid appearing now like a liquid stream of fire and again resembling a sparkling shower of silver."[33] When playing at full force its jet reached the top of the building. A second appurtenance, also inspired by the Crystal Palace, was a mighty organ, whose 4,004 pipes were operated by a steam bellows. The walls on the ground floor as well as the galleries were lined with bazaar stalls displaying "articles . . . of a kind to add to the brilliant and motley character of the whole spectacle," as the Times put it.[34] An "ascending carriage" emulated the famous installation in that former palace of elegance, the Colosseum.

Another of the Panopticon's derivations was equally clear. Into a polygonal glass tank some twenty to twenty-five feet deep, a diver descended periodically with a helmet containing enough air for ten to fifteen minutes' immersion, and equipped with a "subaqueous lantern" which was a modification of the limelight. From this point on, the roster of the Panopticon's exhibits was pure Polytechnic: a vacuum flask, an "aurora borealis apparatus," a "thunder house," a pin-making machine, a gas cookstove, cork hats, an ornamental sewing machine, the "Euphantine" (whatever that was), and a "Musical Narrator" (a machine for recording improvised compositions on the piano). In the Adelaide Gallery–Polytechnic tradition, there was also a photographic studio on the roof.[35]

For pictorial shows, Clarke relied heavily on his own invention, the improved magic lantern he called the Biscenascope. At one time, the projection equipment combined with the organ to produce an "Optical Diorama Illustrative of Handel's Acis and Galatea." Even without visual effects, the organ was a main attraction. Newspaper advertisements allude to performances, with "invisible voices," of Elijah, portions of Messiah and The Creation, and (the by-now familiar

173. The Royal Panopticon:
exterior (drawing by T. H.
Shepherd, 1855).

174. The Royal Panopticon: the
rotunda (anonymous engraving).

175. The Royal Panopticon: the luminous fountain and galleries (*Illustrated London News*, 11 November 1854).

176. The Royal Panopticon: a scientific lecture in progress.

177. The Royal Panopticon: the "photographic ascending carriage." The elevator delivered patrons to the studio at the top of the building.

anticlimax toward which so many projects like this tended) the Spanish Minstrels.[36]

For a while after the Panopticon was dedicated with organ music and prayer on 16 March 1854, it was a well-attended sight of London. On some days, the new model turnstile clicked off a thousand customers. But neither the luminous fountain nor the thundering organ could stave off the foregone conclusion. The initial crowds had come to see the bright new building and its equally pristine equipment, but they were novelty seekers only; they did not constitute a dependable repeat-business clientele. Once their curiosity had been satisfied, attendance declined precipitously, and the Royal Panopticon closed its doors after only two years. On 11 May 1857, its worth estimated variously at £80,000 and £100,000, it was auctioned off to E. T. Smith, whose offer of £9,000 was more acceptable to the creditors than his £3,000 would be when he tried three years later to add the Polytechnic to his collection of amusement properties.[37] He sold the organ to St. Paul's Cathedral (it later joined the suspension bridge at Clifton), installed a circus ring, and in April 1858 reopened the building as the Alhambra Palace. Two years later, now equipped with a stage and proscenium and given the expanded name of Royal Alhambra Palace and Music Hall, it began a fairly long and certainly gaudy career as a variety house, with dioramas, music hall turns, and acrobats presided over by the redoubtable Blondin. Prostitutes haunted its bars and promenades, and onstage the ballet danced the can-can. As the most sinful theatrical spot in the West End, it helped blacken Leicester Square's reputation even more. It was with considerable satisfaction that respectable Londoners watched it burn to the ground in September 1882.

The Panopticon's quick failure ended the cycle of large-scale exhibitions of mechanical ingenuity, latterly leavened by pictorial and musical entertainment, which had been ushered in less than thirty years earlier by the equally short-lived National Repository. Its ephemeral popularity plainly did nothing to revive the ailing Polytechnic. Not only did it draw away some people who still occasionally went there: it probably discouraged their return to Regent Street, because the ornate newness of the Panopticon made the Polytechnic seem all the more drab and debilitated by comparison. But the Panopticon's failure also demonstrated that, new building or not, little enthusiasm was left for the kind of exhibition it put on. After the many-acred splendors of the Crystal Palace, even the most elaborate commercial show of technical improvements was bound to seem meager and prosaic. In any case, popular interest by this time was veering away from technology and toward applied art, a development to which, as we shall see, the new South Kensington Museum was related as both symptom and response.

To judge from the declining incidence of newspaper advertisements and handbills, the number of ad hoc exhibitions devoted to single objects or coherent collections diminished in the fifties. Only the galvanic wave of activity that the Crimean War sent through the entertainment industry appears momentarily to have slowed this part of the transformation process. In the summer of 1854, when large contingents of the British army were embarking for the Crimea, the Oriental and Turkish Museum, under the proprietorship of two impresarios named C. Oscanyan and S. Aznavour, opened at the St. George's Gallery, Hyde Park Corner. Its announced purpose was to illustrate "not only the abolished institution of the far-famed Janissaries, the renowned Militia of the Turkish empire, with their ancient uniform and armour, but also . . . the various modes of the present day, with numerous agricultural and mechanical implements of the Osmanlis." Imitating the Chinese Collection for which this pagoda had been built, rooms were fitted up to represent aspects of everyday Turkish life— baths, coffee shops, bazaars, street scenes, a palace, a harem, a wedding, a smoking divan.[38] Each room was populated by wax figures, which won the particular praise of the *Times:* "the arms and legs of males are rough with real hair, most delicately applied—actual drops of perspiration are on the brows of the porters."[39] Despite this sendoff, however, patronage seems to have lagged, and within an unusually short time the management was obliged to cut the admission price.

More closely related to the actual events of the moment were separate exhibitions of photographs and drawings made in the war zones, sometimes to advertise books in which they were to be collected. Naval actions in the Gulf of Finland were brought home to Londoners in the form of models (Cronstadt, at 162 Piccadilly) and trophies (from the Fort of Bomarsund, at 83 Fleet Street).[40] As usual, there were camp-followers among the showmen—exhibitors of items only marginally germane to the topic being exploited at the moment. In 1854 one could see at the Portland Gallery, Regent Street, a large model (which unfortunately had to be divided among three rooms) of St. Petersburg as it was early in the century; the publicity

178. The Oriental and Turkish Museum: "A Turkish Dinner Party" (*Illustrated London News*, 14 August 1854).

179. The Oriental and Turkish Museum: "The Hareem" (*Illustrated London News*, 30 September 1854).

claimed that it had been commissioned in 1826 by Emperor Alexander and had cost £20,000 and three years' labor by one hundred men.[41] Elsewhere a model of Sebastopol was displayed by a Signor Tenicia. Its authenticity was limited to, or by, the fact that he had lived in the town twenty years earlier; as the *Athenaeum* dryly observed, the town shown in the model was "not exactly the Sevastopol conquered by the Allies."[42]

The concurrent interest in ethnology, one of whose manifestations was the debate over the riddles of racial migrations and the theories of the transoceanic origins of Central and South American peoples, was served not only by the controversial Aztec Lilliputians but by a show of Mexican antiquities at 57 Pall Mall in 1855: 526 lots of idols, cinerary and libatory vases, sacrificial and musical instruments, and other artifacts "illustrative of the Mythology, the Religious Rites, and the Sepulture of the Toltec and Aztec Nations." Unearthed in 1849 when the Mexicans dug trenches to protect Mexico City from the United States Army, the collection had been brought to London under special license from the Mexican minister of the interior.[43] If an editorial comment on the occasion is any guide, this show had a somewhat different, perhaps a more serious interest than did Bullock's thirty years before: "Theorists, with knotted brows, walk round the rows of idols and vases, and, to their satisfaction, trace a clear connection between the nation of Montezuema and the races of Egypt, India, China, and even Etruria. The last dogmatist has swept all old arguments aside, and boldly asserts, that the original Toltecs were neither Tartars nor the Lost Tribes, but Tyrians, who fled to a new world when Alexander conquered the old."[44]

D3✳️ƷꝹ

Although the government had had nothing directly to do with the Great Exhibition of 1851—the show was financed and managed by private enterprise under the supervision of a royal commission—it was at this point that its hitherto tentative and isolated efforts to initiate, control, and support exhibition places for the common good were converted into policy. After all the Crystal Palace's debts were paid, a clear balance of £186,000 remained, accruing, as had been arranged, to the Treasury. Now the sentiments and experiences of the last decade—the evidence and conclusions of the committees of Commons, the precedent set by the Westminster fresco exhibitions, the lessons learned at the National Gallery, the reforms urged or instituted at

the Tower of London, the British Museum, Westminster Abbey, and St. Paul's, above all the experience of the Crystal Palace itself—suddenly acquired new pertinence. In addition, the Commissioners of Works had lately built with public funds (1848–49) an entirely new museum, the Museum of Practical Geology.* What better memorial to the Great Exhibition, then, than an institution, or set of institutions, which would permanently serve and expand its purposes?

The windfall initiated a process by which London acquired not merely one great public museum but, in the course of time, a whole cluster of them, with a scope and magnitude not envisaged in 1852, though from the outset Prince Albert had in mind a combination of teaching colleges and closely correlated illustrative collections that would cover every interest represented at the Crystal Palace. The original South Kensington Museum, so called, was opened in the middle of 1857 to house a number of heterogeneous collections that had been hitherto displayed separately, imperfectly, or not at all.[45] In the "Brompton Boilers," as the unlovely structure was immediately dubbed—it was built of cast iron, with the exterior painted in green and white stripes in an attempt to impart the gaiety of a tent at a fair—were housed an assortment of submuseums, each of which had something to do with the ideal of industrial education, broadly construed, that had dominated the Crystal Palace. These included an education exhibition (books, classroom equipment, and so on), a museum of building materials, a museum of architecture (one fourth classical, three fourths Gothic), and a museum of "animal products" (to provide working people with lessons in household management and hygiene, somewhat as had been provided for in Count Rumford's plan for the Royal Institution).

But the most important collection, the one most influential in determining the South Kensington's future direction, was the museum of ornamental art. This had come mainly from Marlborough House, which had been the temporary home of the thousands of objects given by or bought from the exhibitors at the Crystal Palace as well as the site of several special exhibitions, beginning with the display, in 1853, of the Sèvres china Henry Cole had rescued from dead storage at Buckingham Palace. To these were added recent purchases, notably 725 lots from the celebrated Bernals collection of porcelain, glass, ivories, jewelry, medals, armor, and furniture and the complementary Soulanges collection from Toulouse. Bought nominally to provide examples from which industrial and

* Built on a site between Piccadilly and Jermyn Street, the museum was a four-story glass-covered hall surrounded by galleries which displayed "all the materials produced in the British Isles, which are employed in architecture, agriculture, metallurgy, pottery, vitrification, and other arts," along with fossils and models of mining machinery. (See *ILN,* 17, 24 May 1851, pp. 421, 445; *Fraser's Magazine,* 43, 1851, 618–30.) In the early years, at least, there were successful programs of lecture-demonstrations for workingmen. (*Athenaeum,* 12 February 1853, p. 196; 6 May 1854, p. 557.) The building, which also housed the Geological Survey, was demolished in the mid-1920s and the collection transferred to the Geological Museum in South Kensington.

180. The Museum of Practical Geology: the Great Hall (*Illustrated London News*, 24 May 1851).

decorative designers could work, these collections proved to be the wedge whereby the South Kensington's doors were opened wide to the fine arts themselves, for their own nonutilitarian sake. Along with them came, either immediately or within the next few years, considerable overflow from the National Gallery—part of the Angerstein collection, the Vernon gift of 157 modern English pictures, and the Turner and Jacob Bell bequests. Housed in a separate wing, the first public art gallery to be designed expressly for gas lighting (the donor had specified that it was to be open at night), was the great collection of modern British paintings given by the Leeds clothier John Sheepshanks.*

The South Kensington was the first noncommercial London museum that was not only explicitly intended for use by the general public (as the British Museum had been under its articles of incorporation) but was actually devoted to public service. Headed by Henry Cole, a man committed to the proposition that museums should offer pleasure as well as instruction, it was conducted in the spirit of the parliamentary inquiries of the late thirties and the forties, which regarded

museums as instruments of social amelioration. Deliberate efforts were made to attract the mass public. Admission was free on Mondays, Tuesdays, and Saturdays, sixpence on other days. In conspicuous contrast to the British Museum, its hours of opening were set with the convenience of the visitors, not that of the officials, uppermost in mind. In addition to the usual daylight hours, the building was also open two nights a week from seven to ten o'clock. "The working man," said Cole,

comes to this Museum from his one or two dimly lighted, cheerless dwelling-rooms, in his fustian jacket, with his shirt collars a little trimmed up, accompanied by his threes, and fours, and fives of little fustian jackets, a wife, in her best bonnet, and a baby, of course, under her shawl. The looks of surprise and pleasure of the whole party when they first observe the brilliant lighting inside the Museum show what a new, acceptable, and wholesome excitement this evening entertainment affords to them all. Perhaps the evening opening of Public Museums may furnish a powerful antidote to the gin palace.[46]

Speaking as he did in November 1857, less than six months after the building opened, Cole portrayed the

* As early as 1851, Lord John Russell's government had had its eye on a site in South Kensington—the south frontage of Kensington Gore—for a new National Gallery to replace the unpopular one at Trafalgar Square, but it dropped the project during its last days in office (January 1852).

situation in too rosy a hue; workingmen's hours had not yet been curtailed to the point at which they and their families could take supper, travel to the western outskirts of London, and still have time to enjoy the museum. The extended hours were a further instance of a reform, ostensibly meant to benefit the working class, which in practice was mainly of service to their social superiors. In addition, the museum's location limited for some years the number of people who could visit it; it was a long walk from most working-class neighborhoods, and bus fare from central London was a deterrent sixpence. The Underground came to South Kensington a full decade after the building was opened.

Three years' further experience confirmed Cole's optimism on the score of the museum as "a powerful antidote to the gin palace." He told a committee of Commons in 1860 that the evening opening had been rewarded by "irreproachable" behavior; only one person was "excluded for not being able to walk steadily." The museum, he said, had had to endure considerable chaffing when it opened a refreshment room which the press immediately interpreted as a beer shop. But the official accounts spoke for themselves. During the month of February 1860, with 45,354 admissions, the sales of intoxicating beverages amounted to only twenty bottles of wine, five bottles of brandy, six quarts of bottled ale and stout, eighty gallons of draught ale, and twenty gallons of porter, which, Cole solemnly told the committee, averaged out to two and a half drops of wine, fourteen fifteenths of a drop of brandy, and ten and a half drops of bottled ale per capita. Such evidence of the clientele's abstemiousness was sufficient, he suggested, to lay low, once for all, the old bogy of drunkenness as a reason for excluding the public from museums.[47]

The comparative spaciousness of the South Kensington Museum and its liberal schedule of opening hours put the disheveled British Museum in a worse light than ever. Suffering the consequences of a long history of poor relations with Parliament and the press, coping in vain with collections which yearly strained further the capacity of a building that was too small even on the day it was completed, handicapped further by many years of financial neglect, even the dedicated and enlightened members of the staff faced an impossible situation. The role of popular educator had been thrust on the museum by social and political circumstances, not to the uniform delight of the officials; and both facilities and staff were ill adapted for this new purpose. On Boxing Day 1853 alone, between 40,000 and 50,000 "well-dressed persons" passed through the doors, and in 1857 some 621,000 visitors were counted in the course of the year.[48] To be sure, on most days the museum was not overtaxed. The holiday opening was the only concession the officials had made to the unremitting pressure they were under; otherwise the days and hours of opening remained the same. The public could enter only three days of the week, from ten to four in winter, ten to five in spring and autumn, and ten to six in summer. The proposal, renewed by Lord Stanley in 1856, to open the museum on Sunday had been among the victims of that year's Sabbatarian fever. But the holiday crowds three times a year provided a severe test of the institution's ability to serve the public, and in the opinion of the press it failed. In 1853 the *Times*, noting the crowds who had come to Bloomsbury the preceding day (Easter Monday), observed that if persons of "the largest and best-informed mind" were bewildered by the "defective arrangement" and "overcrowding of objects," "what, then, must be the impression produced upon the mass of happy, thoughtless, holyday people who flocked there in the thousands yesterday?"[49]

It was partially in hope of making the ordinary man's visit more rewarding that yet one more select committee of Commons was appointed in 1859 to look into the situation. "Hopeless confusion, valuable collections wholly hidden from the public, and great portions of others in danger of being destroyed by damp and neglect":[50] these were familiar charges, and they were not being heard for the last time. Seven years later (1866), in the course of a furious attack on the trustees, Cole wrote in the *Edinburgh Review:*

The state of the collections is a national disgrace. An overcrowded building, most unsuitable for exhibition, most unhealthy to visitors, and destructive to many objects from insufficient ventilation; ill-cared for and ill-lighted; specimens of sculpture disfigured with dirt; specimens of natural history crowded in cases which are not dust-tight and sluttishly neglected; labels wanting—there is throughout an air of sleepy slatternly shabbiness, except in the libraries and a very few other portions, which renders it imperative that Parliament should transfer the annual vote of 100,000 *l.* from the hands of trustees to a more competent and sensible management.[51]

Relief was to come slowly. Meanwhile, however, despite all these discouragements, attendance at the museum continued to grow—a sign of how persistent and keen was Londoners' hunger for any kind of free exhibition, however poorly presented and maintained, but also, perhaps, evidence of their growing disposition to assert their rights. Some among them may well have shared the radical parson Kingsley's sentiment, addressed to the workers in 1848, shortly after the Chartist menace had been successfully dealt with: "The British Museum is my glory and joy; because it is almost the only place which is free to English Citizens as such—where the poor and the rich may meet together. . . . In the British Museum and the National Gallery alone the Englishman may say— 'Whatever my coat or my purse, I am an Englishman, and therefore I have a right here. I can glory in these noble halls, as if they were my own house.' "[52]

The same interpretation could be made of the experience of the National Gallery, which attracted 790,000 persons in 1859 as against the British Museum's 518,000.[53] Here the issue of unrestricted versus selective access was still alive, and it was being fed in a rather unexpected way. In the course of a lecture before the Royal Academy in 1849 Charles Robert Leslie declared, "Pictures, like ourselves, are not only subject to the inevitable decay of age, but to a variety of diseases caused by heat, cold, damp, and foul air. . . . To this last evil . . . the National Collection will remain exposed as long as the indiscriminate admission of the public is continued, and by which the rooms are often so crowded that none can see the pictures, which, in the mean time, are suffering greatly from the dust carried in, and the atmosphere that is generated." He therefore proposed that tickets, to be given out at an office nearby, be limited to those who could write their names. "It may safely be affirmed," he said, "that fine pictures can afford no instruction to those who cannot."[54] To what extent the deleterious effect which crowded rooms had upon paintings was cited as a cover-up for simple antidemocratic feelings is not, perhaps, for us to inquire. It is certainly true that by mid-century the combination of London smog and "human effluvia" was playing havoc with the pictures. The air at Trafalgar Square was heavy with smoke from the chimneys of baths and wash houses, the steam engine that worked the fountains, and the boats at Hungerford Stairs.[55] Leslie's warning (a century before the same deleterious condition led to the closing of the prehistoric caverns of Lascaux) was confirmed by the report of a commission, including Eastlake and Faraday, to a select committee of Commons that had been appointed to look into the condition of the pictures and weigh the advantages of moving the gallery to a more favorable site. The crowds were said to exude an "impure mass of animal and ammoniacal vapour" which condensed on the surface of the paintings

and hastened their deterioration.[56] Scientists could provide no satisfactory solution to the problem.*

Crowd pollution, then, was no chimera, however handy a means it may have provided of evading the social issue; it was a demonstrable menace to pictures in galleries. But there were those who were disturbed, not as Leslie was by any physical threat to the art on display, but by the sheer presence in the National Gallery of persons who, like Leslie's illiterates, supposedly could not derive any instruction there. Among those advocating limited admission—or exclusion—was Anthony Trollope, who in the middle fifties was outspoken on this touchy subject. He deplored the dirt, which rendered many of the pictures all but invisible. (They could not be cleaned because of an intramural dispute between the pro- and anticleaning factions, the latter declaring, with considerable truth, that some paintings which had been so treated were ruined.) He pointed to the "disgraceful" rooms which, dark as they were, were "ill-adapted to the preservation and exposition of pictures"; he complained of the discomfort of viewing the paintings from "a small cane-bottomed chair on a dirty floor." But most of all Trollope deplored the people. Recommending that the gallery be opened for three days a week "to all the world," and for two days to only those who "choose to pay whatever sum may be stipulated for admittance," he went on:

Were any injury to be done to the poor man, any real harm, by his exclusion from the Gallery for two days a week, there would be something in this argument. It shall be admitted that the fustian coat had better be allowed to have the Gallery entirely to himself than be hurt by the proposed rule.

But no injury would result to the fustian coat, who is in truth remarkably indifferent as to the pictures before which he walks. And great advantage would accrue to that class which does not care very much about them. The National Gallery now is a place of assignation, a shelter from rain, a spot in which to lounge away an idle ten minutes, a nursery for mothers who are abroad with their infants, a retirement place for urban picnics. The place cannot be said to be often crowded,† but it is always clear that of those who are there four fifths care nothing for the pictures.

Such uses for a picture gallery do rob those who really love pictures of much of their pleasure. That the poorer classes, that is, those who are comparatively uneducated and who are doomed to lives of manual toil, should really care for pictures, we believe to be impossible. We believe that some carefulness of education, some of that refinement from which we all know that the mass of the populace is debarred, must be necessary to the appreciation of a work of art. This is not at present a popular doctrine. It is now in vogue to speak

* Henry Cole, who could not be charged with antidemocratic bias, made a similar report on the basis of early experience at South Kensington, and was substantially more explicit than either Leslie or the parliamentary committee. "We find," he said in 1860, "that the mere exhibition of pictures to great multitudes exposes them to accidents which would hardly be dreamt of. The public sneeze upon the pictures, and the saliva runs down and positively eats the surface of them. One of the most valuable of Mr. Mulready's pictures was covered with the coughing and sneezing of the public looking close at the picture and laughing in the presence of it. We have great difficulty in preventing them expressing the emotions they feel in looking at a picture; they will touch it; they say 'Look at that expression,' and the consequence is that they scrape off a little bit of the pigment. We have come to the conclusion that pictures within reach must be put under glass. We have already the experience that glass keeps pictures much cleaner. We all know that though the public is generally becoming very well behaved, and is well behaved, still they very much like to touch things. We had a little bit of sculpture, a mother and a baby, and the baby excited the interest of all the mothers that came to the Museum; they were always measuring their babies by the side of it and touching it till it became quite grubby. It happened to be only a cast, but precautions must be taken to prevent things being damaged." (*Athenaeum*, 8 September 1860, p. 330.)

† This assertion is not borne out by other testimony.

of the poor as if they were in all things equal to the rich except in their poverty. But even those who go with the fashions and teach this doctrine know that it is not so—that it cannot be so—and that the saying that it is so will not bring the poor nearer to so desirable a result. . . .

God forbid that we should use such an argument to the injury of the poor. But God forbid also that we should injure any class by a false argument in favour of the poor. Let the Gallery be open to all the world for three days, and let us and all men have such good results as may be procured thereby. But also let those who wish to see the pictures in comparative quiet be enabled to do so at a small expense. There would be no invidious class admission. The sixpence of the mechanic would be as operative as that of the peer.[57]

Thus Trollope, writing in 1855–56. At that very moment, a reply to his forthright elitism was in the making across the river, in the working-class neighborhood of the Upper Marsh, Lambeth, near the railway bridge over the Westminster Road. The respondent would not have read Trollope's denial of the common man's aesthetic capabilities even if it had been available (it was not to be published for more than a century), because he was not in the habit of reading authors like Trollope, if indeed he read much at all. This was Charles Morton, the first great entrepreneur of the music hall. In 1851 he had leased the Canterbury Arms tavern on the Lambeth site and the next year built on the adjacent green a 700-seat auditorium. The Canterbury Music Hall was the first establishment of the kind to which respectable working-class women were invited, its predecessors having been smoke-filled dives ("free and easies") for men only. A contemporary reformer reported that the clientele was composed of "respectable mechanics, or small tradesmen with their wives and daughters and sweethearts. Now and then you see a midshipman, or a few fast clerks" with their mugs of beer.[58] Architecturally the hall was clearly intended to be a laboring-class Colosseum; the entertainment, likewise, recalled the Colosseum Saloon. Another visitor wrote:

We pay sixpence for admission each, and at once enter a sort of spacious vestibule ornamented with some large oil-paintings, pier-glasses, and with a rich array of refreshments of various kinds on a stall or table of considerable length. Open archways in one of the walls enable us to see that the ground floor of the "hall" is crowded; the balcony above is well filled, and by paying an extra sixpence we gain admission to this narrow gallery, running round three sides of the room. Here we can see the proportions of a stately room painted a light stone colour, and of very chaste and ornamental design. The general effect is exceedingly good, and

for purity of style and elegance of architectural character the Hall might be a portion of a palace. It is brilliantly lighted by glass chandeliers of uncommon magnificence and beauty. Refreshments are supplied of good quality, and at moderate prices, according to a printed tariff. Thus artisans, soldiers, small tradesmen, and others in a similar walk of life can spend the whole evening for a moderate admission fee of sixpence, taking more or less of refreshments, or if so disposed, none at all. A constant succession of performances takes place on the stage, chiefly songs with accompaniments, recitations, dancing, etc. A book of words is sold for a penny; it contains fifty-five selections from operas.* All is in good order and in good taste. The whole might pass for an aristocratic concert, but for the *pipes* on the ground floor and cigars above, which sorely test the admirable ventilating qualities of the room.[59]

The visitor then passed into an annex built in 1856, an eighty-foot-long picture gallery which *Punch* called "the Royal Academy over the water." (In a brief memoir of Morton it was later described as "a lordly pleasure house . . . to contain . . . priceless treasures.")[60] According to the eight-page catalogue, Morton intended this innovation (admission sixpence) as a natural extension of his earlier desire that "the 'Million' might have an opportunity of being acquainted with the works of our great Composers, which until that period had been exclusively confined to the 'Upper Ten Thousand.' "[61] A late edition of the leaflet listed 111 pictures; other accounts place the number at between 240 and 300. Among them at various times were Haydon's *Curtius Leaping into the Gulf,* Maclise's *Noah's Sacrifice,* Vernet's *Death Purifying the Soul,* Frith's *Iachimo in the Bedchamber of Imogen,* Danby's *The Advent of Spring,* Gainsborough's *Lady and Boy in a Garden* and *View in Windsor Forest,* Ruysdael's *A Dutch Canal,* Kneller's *Portrait of a Gentleman,* and Lely's *Portrait of a Lady.* One must assume that some of these were either copies in oil or engravings; it is not likely that a genuine Ruysdael, Kneller, or Gainsborough would have been entrusted to a tavern in Lambeth, although the *Curtius Leaping into the Gulf,* for example, may well have been an original: Haydon painted at least six versions. The pictures were, in any case, sent there by Gambart, the West End art dealer, on a sale or return basis.[62] Again the resemblance to the Colosseum, especially to the Glyptotheka installed at the time of the remodeling (1847), is striking: another Victorian place of entertainment embellished with works of art, at no cost to the management and with the possibility of a commission if any were sold to patrons.

Although it is said that Morton personally bought pictures from his walls, it is improbable that his working-class patrons did. But the very fact that he went to the expense of installing an art gallery next to a lively 700-seat music hall is impressive. He was no idealist, no member of the successive "art for the people" coteries of public men. There is even less likelihood that he was a disciple of Ruskin, although Ruskin once visited the Canterbury in the company of Gambart, who in all probability took him there to see the pictures rather than to hear the songs.[63] But Morton must have known his patrons' tastes and believed that, as the *Illustrated London News* put it, their plebeian eyes had been rendered more appreciative by "the large use made of engraving for the purpose of illustrating the current literature and the living arts of the day," just as their ears had come to prefer "the grand strains of Mozart, Rossini, Donizetti, and Meyerbeer" to their old favorites, "Doings at Bartlemy Fair," "Tippity Witchet," and "Hot Codlins."[64]

The success of the Lambeth art gallery was not so overwhelming as to persuade Morton to make a full-time career of disseminating a taste for art through the working class. In 1860 he leased the Boar and Castle tavern in Oxford Street and converted it into the highly successful Oxford Music Hall. But he also remained proprietor of the Canterbury Music Hall until 1868, and the gallery survived until at least 1866, the date of its catalogue's "thirty-third edition."* At the very least, its existence for a full decade suggests that popular interest in painting had spread far enough to warrant a shrewd businessman's risking a substantial amount of money to cater to it. The Upper Marsh, Lambeth, was a fair distance from the exclusive Stafford Gallery in St. James's, with its magnificent footmen, and 263 lamps on eight-foot pillars.

* The building continued to serve as a music hall–theatre until the 1920s. It was bombed out in 1942.

Epilogue

By 1862, most of the landmarks associated with the exhibition industry during the preceding half-century were about to disappear or be put to other uses. Following its last season of variety entertainment (1863) the Colosseum stood empty and derelict until it was pulled down in 1874. The nearby Diorama building had already been converted into a Baptist chapel. Savile House burned down on the night of 28 February 1865 after a workman went looking for a gas leak with a candle. The Adelaide Gallery, now generally known as the Royal Marionette Theatre after the successful run of the Italian marionette company, returned to miscellaneous light entertainment and later was converted into Gatti's, a popular late Victorian and Edwardian restaurant. Vauxhall's site now was built over, as the Surrey Gardens also would be after St. Thomas's Hospital vacated its temporary quarters. Cremorne Gardens lasted the longest, a resort for London's most dubious types who repaired there after Vauxhall closed. Complained about by neighbors who, like Thomas and Jane Carlyle, were kept awake by the fireworks, shunned by the respectable, and evidently unable to make a profit on the shillings of the demi-monde, Cremorne went into a long period of decline, assisted by the constant attentions of the magistrates and police. It finally expired in 1878, when its license went unrenewed and the winter winds blew through the tattered canvas of the outdoor panoramas.

Of all the major commercial exhibition venues, the Egyptian Hall lasted longest. Still a landmark in Piccadilly after the passage of more than half a century, this building with the exotic façade no longer housed any exhibitions comparable to Bullock's natural history museum or his Mexican exhibition, Belzoni's Egyptian tombs, the Napoleon carriage, or Haydon's vast pictures. Instead, it was increasingly given over to "musical and mimetic entertainments"—ventriloquists, monopolylogists in the German Reed vein, a certain "Ernst Schulz's Masks and Faces; or, Studies of Character and Physiognomy," "Mr. Frank Lincoln in his Unique Imitations assisted by Paganini Redivivus, the Greatest Violinist in the World"—and, above all, to Maskelyn and Cooke's Theatre of Mystery, of which it became the permanent home.[1] Thus in the last phase of its colorful career the Egyptian Hall became as firmly identified with conjuring as the Lyceum had been at the beginning of the century with "philosophical fireworks" and the phantasmagoria. For thirty years Maskelyn and Cooke baffled English families at the hall, leaving for another location only in 1904, when the old building was demolished and the present "Egyptian House" of shops and offices was erected on the site.

The Polytechnic, which we last saw fighting for its life with ever stronger infusions of live entertainment in the late fifties, was temporarily rescued in 1862 when its longtime director and chief lecturer, John Henry Pepper, presented an illusionist novelty that exactly suited popular taste in those years of cheap sensations. Invented by a civil engineer and scientific lecturer named Henry Dircks, the Ætheroscope, as it was initially called, was taken over by Pepper and at once became familiarly known as "Pepper's Ghost." This phantasmagoria on a new principle was an apparatus for producing "spectral optical illusions" by the use of mirrors in conjunction with living actors. First used to illustrate Dickens's ghost story "The Haunted Man" at the Polytechnic on Christmas Eve, 1862, the act caught the public fancy at once. Other presentations were soon added to the program: the "Operatic Mystery" of Faust, "with Gounod's Principal Music"; something called "Proteus! or, We Are Here But Not Here!"; and the "laughable spectral sketch" entitled "The Haunted House."[2]

Later Pepper's Ghost was featured at numerous London theatres as well as in New York and Paris. It played many return engagements at the Polytechnic, but one successful novelty was not enough to save the institution. Sounding a note that was as familiar as their style was stilted, the proprietors announced in August 1881 that "From some cause . . . perhaps that the taste of the present age is in favour of more highly spiced amusements than the management could place before its visitors consistently with the carrying out of the views of the founders of the Institution, or in accordance with its Memorandum of Association—it has failed during the last few years in meeting with the pecuniary encouragement necessary to warrant its further continuance."[3] They had therefore determined to wind up the affairs of the Polytechnic while it was still minimally solvent. The final bill was an authentic sampling of the Polytechnic's offerings over the years: the oxyhydrogen microscope and the diving bell, of course; an electric railway carried on pillars round the hall; a life-size automaton Blondin wheeling a barrow on a tightrope and a similarly mechanized Leotard doing a trapeze act; models of machines and marine engines; a lecture-demonstration of "The Wonders of Light"; a dioramic presentation of "A Trip to the Lakes"; Buckland's "entertainments," including "The Knight Watching His Armour" and "Robinson Crusoe"; musical selections; a magic show. . . .[4]

Unlike all of its by now defunct contemporaries, the Polytechnic was fated to have a glorious resurrection. The building at 309 Regent Street was acquired by Quintin Hogg, the Eton-educated partner in a firm of sugar merchants, whose philanthropic interests had led him twenty years earlier to establish a "ragged school" for boys in Endell Street, Charing Cross. Hogg's new venture was called the Polytechnic Young Men's Christian Institute for Artisans, Apprentices, &c. (The "Christian" in the title was misleading: Jews, Mohammedans, Buddhists, and even nonbelievers were equally welcome.) The great hall, site of the diving bell, was turned into a gymnasium, the famous bell itself having been relegated to an obscure resting place in the grounds of the Albert Palace, Battersea Park.[5] Most of the other rooms were converted into classrooms and workshops for instruction in plumbing, pattern making, tailoring, watchmaking, building construction, civil engineering, and other trades and professions. There were also a reading room, a swimming bath, and a savings bank.[6] In this new Polytechnic originated the technical education movement which became so important an element in lower-middle-class London life as to result in Hogg's being linked in remembrance with such earlier Victorian philanthropists as Lord Shaftesbury.

Burford's panorama closed in December 1863. After serving for a while as a penny news room, the building was converted into a church for the Marist Fathers' mission to the French colony in the neighborhood, the first mass being celebrated there in June 1868.[*] Though the conversion of the first panorama building to different purposes was a strongly symbolic event, it by no means marked the panorama's total disappearance from the London scene. In fact, the durability of this veteran form of pictorial entertainment was proved when it withstood the parody to which Artemus Ward, the American humorist, subjected it. In 1866, six years after Albert Smith had died during the run of his panorama-lecture on China, Ward made his debut at the Egyptian Hall in a performance that combined a comic lecture with a comic panorama, presumably the first and last of its kind. Painted to his order in Boston, Massachusetts, the wretchedly executed canvas extravagantly burlesqued Banvard's Mississippi one, and to round out the effect Ward saw to it that during the performance all the accompanying features went wrong, the rolling cloth sticking or being shown upside down, flames being introduced at the wrong places, the wrong selections worked into the musical accompaniment, and so on. The tone of the whole performance was set by a handbill: "Artemus Ward Among the Mormons. During the Vacation the Hall has been carefully Swept out, and a new Door Knob has been added to the Door.[†] Mr. Artemus Ward will call on the Citizens of London, at their residences, and explain any jokes in his narratives which they may not understand. . . . The Panorama used to illustrate Mr. Ward's Narrative is rather worse than Panoramas usually are." The show opened on 13 November 1866 and closed the following 23 January; Ward died six weeks later.[7]

Nearing the end of his own life, Dickens shared the

[*] The building was bombed out in the Second World War, but the present Église de Notre Dame on the site incorporates the circular wall of the original structure.

[†] A reference to Albert Smith's repeated boasts of the improvements he had made at the hall during his long occupancy.

low opinion of panoramas that the jocose publicity attributed to Ward. Writing two years later in *All the Year Round,* he described his long-time *bête noire,* the humorless archetypal didact here called "Mr. Barlow" (after the man who occupied that role in Day's *History of Sandford and Merton*), as a member of "the Moving Panorama trade," holding forth in the dark with a long wand in hand, his pedantic manner of lecturing "made more appalling . . . by his sometimes cracking a piece of Mr. Carlyle's own Dead-Sea fruit in mistake for a joke." Reason enough, said Dickens, why "I systematically shun pictorial entertainment on rollers."[8]

Presumably this dismal performance was not typical of the panoramas that continued to attract audiences after the first large spate of travel shows subsided. Though their role now was a minor one when compared with their dominance in the early fifties, there were at least a dozen such entertainments in London in 1871, ranging in subject from the topical Franco-Prussian War to "Ireland, Its Scenery, Music, and Antiquities" and "Scotland, Its Scenery and Music."[9] The longest lasting of these shows was the series of "excursions to the continent" presented by Harry H. Hamilton at various London locations, notably the Agricultural Hall, Islington, in the seventies.[10]

By now "panorama" meant, in most cases, a slapdash mixture of wide-screen or moving paintings, dissolving views, music, and talk. But Barker's original conception, a huge circular, stationary picture, was not wholly forgotten even though his old building was now a church. In 1881, on the nearby site of Savile House, a French speculator erected a specifically designed building called the Royal London Panorama, which exhibited a 15,000-square-foot representation of the Charge of the Light Brigade. The foreground between the viewing platform and the painting was filled with real turf, bushes, wrecked wagons, spent cannon balls, and waxen corpses of soldiers and horses. Never before had so much attention been given to the three-dimensional appurtenances of a scene. Even more novel, however, was the introduction of thirty electric lamps "representing the power of illumination of 2700 candles." This innovation almost proved the show's undoing, because only three months after it opened, a live carbon was shot into the straw lying in an ambulance wagon. Prompt action averted a catastrophe, but the show still had a comparatively brief life; the next year the building was converted into the Pandora Theatre, renamed the Empire in 1884.[11]

In 1886 John Hollingshead, then retired from the management of the Gaiety Theatre, was approached for advice by an American syndicate which owned a giant panorama of Niagra Falls painted by Félix Henri Emmanuel Philippoteaux, another of whose works, a panorama of Tel-el-Kebir, was later to be displayed in a special building on the Crystal Palace grounds. Persuaded that modern Londoners would enjoy a panorama only if they could eat and drink while looking, Hollingshead advised the promoters to buy a disused building in York Street, Westminster, and add to it a café-restaurant to be built on the site of five old houses adjoining it. Since no liquor license could be had, they bought the lease of the Black Horse public house across the road and transferred that license to their own building. Thus provided for, with an electric searchlight on the roof and a gas "orchestrion" in position inside, the Niagara show opened to much favorable publicity and good houses. Evidently, it made money for the syndicate, but later, when it was returned to the United States and a Jerusalem picture installed in its place, the owners of a similar Jerusalem panorama in Munich sued for breach of copyright. Rather than contest the suit, the Americans sold the whole business, Jerusalem picture included, to the plaintiffs.[12]

The modern motion picture was first exhibited in London at the Polytechnic, on 20 February 1896. A few days later, it was introduced at the Empire (as the kinetoscope or cinematograph) and at the Alhambra (as the animatograph: the show-business affection for classic-sounding names died hard). With its arrival, the many forms of pictorial public entertainment that have been described in these chapters reached the end of their long obsolescence, and the cinema, toward which several of them proved in retrospect to have been pointing, began its career as the new century's supreme form of popular art.

One more belated attempt was made to succeed where the Polytechnic, the Royal Panopticon, and the relocated Crystal Palace had failed. In 1875 a group of speculators, intent on elevating the public morality "by the contemplation of the wonders of nature," acquired two and a half acres fronting on Tothill Street, Westminster, and erected thereon a large building of glass and Portland stone called the Royal Aquarium.[13] Reportedly costing £200,000, it contained reading rooms, dining rooms, billiard and snooker accommodations, a skating rink, a theatre, and—most germane to the company's cultural affectations—picture and sculpture galleries and a large tank for the study of marine life. This last, though it gave its name to the whole establishment, was actually the least important adjunct. Unoccupied for many months, it eventually held a motley assortment of eels, whitebait, starfish, oysters, turtles, alligators, and even a short-lived creature described as a whale. But the patrons' ichthyological interest proved to be mild, and the tank was given over to aquacades and high-diving performances by scantily clad women. Elsewhere in the building, at various times, were "ethnological" exhibits ("Farini's Earthmen," "The Autochtones from Tierra del Fuego," and Krao, "the living missing link, daughter of a tribe of hairy men and women from Laos"), human projectiles, gorillas, and boxing kangaroos. A "classical entertainment" entitled *The Dream of Michael Angelo* proved to be one more edition of the *poses plastiques,* with half a dozen men and women, in white tights, visible on pedestals. At least one spectator objected to the "matronly exuberance of contour" manifested by the females.

The Royal Aquarium quickly became as raffish a place of entertainment as anything in Leicester Square, some of whose prostitutes seem to have emigrated to the supposedly greener pastures of Tothill Street. Both its performances and its patrons were continually decried, not without reason, by public moralists, who were gratified when, early in the new century, the establishment moved to the East End and became the Royal Albert Music Hall, and the Wesleyan denomination, purchasers of the site, rehabilitated it by substituting for the aquarium the present-day Central Hall.

D3❋£d

In such sporadic and ultimately unsuccessful forms several of the characteristic nontheatrical entertainments of the earlier Victorian years survived to the end of the century. The term "exhibition" itself had acquired added meaning in the wake of the Crystal Palace. The epithet "Great" was now indelibly associated with it, and any new venture calling itself an exhibition was expected to be on a grand scale. The official sequel to the 1851 event was held eleven years later, in a temporary building on a plot facing Cromwell Road, the site now occupied by the Natural History Museum. Inescapably, it was an anticlimax. In the nature of things, no exhibition whatever could have evoked the spontaneous enthusiasm, the heady exhilaration, the sheer wonder, that the first one had done. In 1862 memories of Hyde Park still were strong and the new show, elaborate as it was, inescapably suffered by comparison.

Not the least of the reasons was the building, which was uninteresting by any standard and disastrous when compared with Paxton's fairy palace. The deficiencies of its layout and provisions for traffic flow were aggravated by the prevailing craze for crinolines, and making the rounds was so fatiguing that one eminent London physician was reported as saying that in a single week no fewer than three of his patients had had strokes just after leaving the building.[14] The death at the end of the preceding year of the Prince Consort, the man who had worked so hard and effectively in behalf of the first exhibition, cast a shadow over its successor. The widowed queen, of course, did not attend, and Wellington too was dead. The thousand-years-of-peace theme that had brightened the Crystal Palace now had given way—the Crimean War having intervened and Britain's foreign relations, especially those with France, having grown more tense—to a heavy emphasis on militarism, section after section of the building displaying the whole contemporary range of armaments, from swords and daggers to the newest types of cannon. Furthermore, there was an unpleasantly commercial atmosphere in the new exhibition; whereas the exhibitors at the Crystal Palace had shown their wares primarily, or nominally, as examples of their respective nations' technical and designing skills, their successors were frankly out to promote their individual lines. "A gigantic joint-stock showroom," the 1862 exhibition was called, "The Palace of Puffs." To cap it all, economic distress in the North of England cut the number of incoming excursionists, and the summer was abnormally wet. Although the attendance, thanks to a longer season, slightly surpassed that of the 1851 exhibition (6,110,000 as against 6,093,000), when the show officially closed few tears were shed—a dramatic contrast with the sad-triumphant last day in 1851.

Undeterred, the Royal Commissioners built two large galleries just south of the new Royal Albert Hall and adjacent to the gardens of the Royal Horticultural Society. Here (1871–1874) they held four more international exhibitions. The first drew a million visitors, but attendance steadily declined thereafter, owing, it was said, to the increasingly technical and specialized nature of the exhibits. Another series (1883–1886) was more popular. Devoted successively to fisheries, health and education, inventions and music, and the colonies and India, these annual exhibitions had a total attendance of 16,000,000 and made a clear profit. No further shows could be held on the Horticultural Society's grounds, however, as these acres were now built over with institutions and blocks of flats. The next ones,

181. The East India House Museum (*Illustrated London News*, 6 March 1858). The room shown was devoted to specimens of Indian sculpture. "The architecture reproduces the leading forms of a Mahometan musjid."

farther west at Earl's Court, were privately sponsored and down to the end of the century had national themes: America in 1887, Italy, Spain, France, and Germany in following years, and "Greater Britain" in 1899. On the whole, they were more entertaining than educational.[15]

A second legacy of the Crystal Palace, much more permanent and far-reaching in its effect, was the group of museums of which the South Kensington was the progenitor. South of Hyde Park, in the vicinity of Exhibition and Cromwell roads, the vision of the men who advocated museums as instruments of public instruction was fulfilled, not totally of course, but to the extent permitted by the inclinations and intellectual equipment of the people at large and the way these were interpreted by officialdom. The temporary Brompton Boilers were replaced by the sprawling

Victoria and Albert Museum (completed, after many years of construction, in 1909). Across Exhibition Road, between 1873 and 1881, rose the Natural History Museum, to which the scientific collections of the British Museum were transferred, thus reducing, at long last, the pressure for space at Bloomsbury. Large as the new building was, it had only one third of the floor area desired by Richard Owen, who had been in charge of the natural history collections since 1856. In the continuing debate between those who advocated large-scale displays arranged for the benefit of the general public and those who believed most of the museum's holdings should be relegated to study collections for the benefit of researchers, Owen was strongly on the side of the public. If he did not get all the display space he wanted, in general he carried his point; like Cole's museum, the future Victoria and Albert,

Owen's Natural History Museum was oriented toward public use.[16]

Meanwhile the old East India House Museum had undergone a series of vicissitudes. In 1858, after the company's remaining administrative functions had been transferred to the secretary of state for India, the museum was moved to Fife House, Whitehall Yard, the former residence of Lord Liverpool and more recently a tea auction room. Whatever other purposes the building, as remodeled by Digby Wyatt, may have been suitable for, it was ludicrously unfitted to be a museum. The ethnological specimens were consigned to the entrance hall; mineral products were in the library, silk and jeweled costumes in the drawing room, jewelry and Japan wares in the dining room, stuffed birds in six bedrooms, and antelopes, stags, leopards, and other animals in the kitchen. Still, like other museums in this new epoch, the East India drew more visitors than ever before. In the first two years in Whitehall the collection, now open five days a week from ten to three o'clock, had 175,000 visitors. But in 1865 it was moved to the new India House adjoining St. James's Park, where no display space was available, and it was accordingly stored away. Finally, in 1880, most of it, including Tippoo Sahib's tiger, was given to the South Kensington Museum, and the remaining archaeological and scientific material was divided between the British Museum and Kew Gardens.[17]

Tippoo's tiger to the new South Kensington Museum; Sloane's cabinet to the new Natural History Museum; portions of the South Kensington collection to a new branch built in the East End (1872) with the discarded ironwork of the Brompton Boilers, the Bethnal Green Museum: these migrations were typical of the flux which, in the years following 1862, almost totally dissolved the structure and nature of the London exhibition industry as it had evolved since the seventeenth century. What had happened to bring about this transformation? The sheer weight of old, hardened custom probably had something to do with it. The mass taste which had supported particular kinds of entertainment for centuries had finally lost its vitality; *autres temps, autres moeurs,* and the public discovered other ways of filling its leisure. The drama regained the middle- and upper-class clientele it had lost early in the century, and an immensely popular new form of stage entertainment, the music hall, drew to its bills the variegated acts that hitherto had performed in places like the Egyptian Hall and the Polytechnic. In parallel fashion, the Sydenham Crystal Palace concentrated at one spot, accessible for one low admission fee, the manifold types of exhibition that hitherto had been widely scattered. The advent of photography and of cheap illustrated papers doomed the old-fashioned kinds of public pictorial entertainment, notably the panorama, and while dissolving views replaced them to some extent, the cheapened and improved magic lantern, along with the stereoscope, widened the range of such entertainments available in the privacy and comfort of the home. The pleasure gardens were gone, along with the seasonal metropolitan fairs.

Some of the traditional kinds of entertainment, expelled as if by centrifugal force from their old haunts in central London, survived on the periphery, in the shabby traveling shows that set up their pitches in the suburbs. Waxworks, freaks, mechanical theatres, and panoramas could still be seen there as well as in the provinces, but as far as London was concerned they were mere vestiges of an outdated popular culture. The effects of the slow but steady progress of popular education were being felt; the charlatans and the freaks commanded less and less credence. By contrast, the educational role of exhibitions became more prominent. The two great streams of appeal—amusement and instruction—hitherto had been mingled in a single channel dominated by commercial entrepreneurs. Now they diverged, the entertainment of the people remaining in the hands of the profit makers while responsibility for their intellectual and aesthetic culture came increasingly to be accepted by government. As the focal point of London shows symbolically moved from Leicester Square to South Kensington, the age of exhibitions was succeeded by the age of public museums.

SHORT FORMS OF CITATION

NOTES

INDEX

SHORT FORMS OF CITATION

Barnum — *Struggles and Triumphs: or, The Life of P. T. Barnum, Written by Himself,* ed. George S. Bryant, 2 vols. (New York, 1927).

BL — British Library (Reference Division).

EC — Enthoven Collection, Theatre Museum, London. (Temporarily housed in the Victoria and Albert Museum.)

EMI — *Exhibitions of Mechanical and Other Works of Ingenuity* scrapbook, at BL (1269.h.38).

Evelyń — John Evelyn, *Diary,* ed. E. S. de Beer, 6 vols. (London, 1955).

George — *Catalogue of Political and Personal Satires Preserved in the Department of Prints and Drawings in the British Museum,* 11 vols. (London, 1870–1954). (Vols. 5–11 by M. Dorothy George.)

GL — Guildhall Library.

ILN — *Illustrated London News.*

JJ Coll. — John Johnson Collection of Printed Ephemera, Bodleian Library, Oxford.

Lysons — Daniel Lysons, *Collectanea; or, A Collection of Advertisements from the Newspapers . . . [1661–1840];* five scrapbooks at BL, 1889.e.5. A similarly titled 2-vol. set, 1660–1825, pressmark 1881.b.6, is cited as Lysons (2-vol. set).

Mirror — *The Mirror of Literature, Amusement, and Instruction.*

N & Q — *Notes and Queries.*

Odell — George C. D. Odell, *Annals of the New York Stage,* 15 vols. (New York, 1927–1949).

Pepys — *The Diary of Samuel Pepys,* ed. Robert Latham and William Matthews, 11 vols. (London, 1970–).

Pückler-Muskau — [Hermann Ludwig Heinrich Pückler-Muskau], *Tour in England, Ireland, and France, in the Years 1826, 1827, 1828, and 1829 . . .* by a German Prince (Philadelphia, 1833). (A 1-vol. reprint of the 4-vol. London edition.)

StM/Gen — St. Martin/General scrapbooks at WCL.

StM/LS — St. Martin/Leicester Square scrapbooks at WCL.

Walpole — *The Yale Edition of the Correspondence of Horace Walpole,* ed. W. S. Lewis et al. (New Haven, 1937–).

WCL — Westminster City Libraries, Archives Department.

Notes

INTRODUCTION

1. *N & Q,* 9th ser. 3 (1899), 83.
2. George Rudé, *Hanoverian London, 1714–1808* (Berkeley, 1971), p. 5.
3. Neil Harris, *Humbug: The Art of P. T. Barnum* (Boston, 1973), p. 292.

1. FROM CABINETS TO MUSEUMS, I: 1600–1750

1. G. R. Owst, *Preaching in Medieval England: An Introduction to Sermon Manuscripts of the Period, c. 1350–1450* (Cambridge, 1956), pp. 350–51.
2. Ibid., p. 350.
3. Francis Henry Taylor, *The Taste of Angels: A History of Art Collecting from Rameses to Napoleon* (Boston, 1948), p. 36; Douglas and Elizabeth Rigby, *Lock, Stock, and Barrel: The Story of Collecting* (Philadelphia, 1944), pp. 142–43.
4. G. H. Cook, *Letters to Cromwell and Others on the Suppression of the Monasteries* (London, 1965), pp. 38, 39–40, 66, 188–89, 200.
5. Ibid., p. 144.
6. James Gairdner, *The English Church in the Sixteenth Century* (London, 1904), p. 199.
7. Charles Pendrill, *Old Parish Life in London* (London, 1937), p. 21.
8. John Stow, *A Survey of London,* ed. Charles Lethbridge Kingsford (Oxford, 1908), I, 275.
9. Ibid., I, 292–93. Italics added.
10. Quoted from Howell's *England* (1712), BL, EMI.
11. Poem prefixed to *Coryat's Crudities* (1611), quoted in William Brenchley Rye, *England as Seen by Foreigners in the Days of Elizabeth and James the First* (London, 1865), pp. 139–40.
12. Quoted ibid., pp. 188–89.
13. Material on the early history of museums on the continent and in England is drawn from Taylor and Rigby as cited in n. 3; David Murray, *Museums: Their History and Their Use* (Glasgow, 1904); Alma S. Wittlin, *The Museum: Its History and Its Tasks in Education* (London, 1949) and the same author's *Museums: In Search of a Usable Future* (Cambridge, Mass., 1970); Germain Bazin, *The Museum Age,* trans. Jane van Nuis Cahill (New York, 1967); J. Mordaunt Crook, *The British Museum* (London, 1972), Ch. 1; and Edward Miller, *That Noble Cabinet* (London, 1973), Ch. 1.
14. *Works of Thomas Nashe,* ed. R. B. McKerrow (London, 1904–1910; rptd. Oxford, 1958), I, 182–83.
15. "Diary of the Journey of Philip Julius, Duke of Stettin-Pomerania, through England in the Year 1602," ed. Gottfried von Bülow, *Transactions of the Royal Historical Society,* n.s. 6 (1892), 27. A fuller list of the contents of Cope's collection is in *Thomas Platter's Travels in England, 1599,* trans. Clare Williams (London, 1937), pp. 171–73.
16. See Walter Houghton, "The English Virtuoso in the Seventeenth Century," *Journal of the History of Ideas,* 3 (1942), 51–73, 190–219.
17. Evelyn, III, 110–11.
18. Material on the Tradescants is from Mea Allan, *The Tradescants: Their Plants, Gardens, and Museum, 1570–1662* (London, 1964); C. H. Josten, "Elias Ashmole, F.R.S.," in *The Royal Society: Its Origins and Founders,* ed. Sir Harold Hartley (London, 1960), pp. 221–30; R. T. Gunther, *Early Science in Oxford* (Oxford, 1925–1967), III, 280–92.
19. Izaak Walton, *The Compleat Angler* (World's Classics ed.), p. 43.
20. Gunther, III, Appendix A (pp. 390–435).
21. Evelyn, III, 373–74.
22. E. St. John Brooks, *Sir Hans Sloane: The Great Collector and His Circle* (London, 1954), pp. 180–81.
23. Evelyn, II, 100.
24. Quoted in "London Museums of the Seventeenth Century," *Chambers's Edinburgh Journal,* n.s. 15 (1851), 308.
25. James Peller Malcolm, *Anecdotes of the Manners and Customs of London During the Eighteenth Century* (London, 1808), p. 310.
26. *London in 1710: From The Travels of Zacharias Conrad von Uffenbach,* trans. and ed. W. H. Quarrell and Margaret Mare (London, 1934), pp. 36–37. Campe is not to be confused with John Kemp (1665–1717), a man of private means who built up a "fine museum of antiquities" at his house in St. Martin's-in-the-Fields. It was sold at auction in 1721, the 293 lots bringing somewhat more than £1,000. (*The Diary of Ralph Thoresby, F.R.S.,* ed. Joseph Hunter, London, 1830, II, 31–32, 112–13, 139; *Dictionary of National Biography.*)
27. *The London Spy Compleat,* ed. Ralph Straus (London, 1924), pp. 60–61.
28. *London in 1710,* p. 98.
29. Evelyn, V, 13; see also IV, 531–32.

There is a full account of Courten in Edward Edwards, *Lives of the Founders of the British Museum* (London, 1870), I, 259–73, and a briefer one in G. L. Apperson, *Bygone London Life: Pictures from a Vanished Past* (London, 1903), pp. 104–10.

30. Charles E. Raven, *John Ray, Naturalist: His Life and Works* (Cambridge, 1942), pp. 228–39.

31. *Diary of Ralph Thoresby,* I, 299–300.

32. See Apperson, pp. 96–104, and Edwards, I, 290.

33. Brooks, pp. 179–80.

34. *London in 1710,* p. 127.

35. Brooks, p. 179.

36. Material on Sloane is from Brooks and from G. R. de Beer, *Sir Hans Sloane and the British Museum* (Oxford, 1953). The latter is the fullest biographical source, though Brooks contains some information not in De Beer.

37. De Beer, p. 117.

38. Quoted in Henry C. Shelley, *The British Museum: Its History and Treasures* (Boston, 1911), pp. 41–42.

39. De Beer, pp. 130–31.

40. *The Papers of Benjamin Franklin,* ed. Leonard W. Labaree and Whitfield J. Bell (New Haven, 1959–), I, 54.

41. *Benjamin Franklin's Memoirs,* ed. Max Farrand (Berkeley, 1949), p. 110.

42. Edward Young, *Complete Works: Poetry and Prose* (London, 1854), rptd. *Anglistica and Americana,* ed. James Nichols (Hildesheim, 1968), I, 372.

43. *The Tatler,* ed. George A. Aitken (London, 1899), IV, 112–13.

44. *The London Spy Compleat,* pp. 13–14.

45. *Gulliver's Travels,* ed. Harold Williams (Oxford, 1941), pp. 130–31.

46. *London in 1710,* pp. 81–85.

47. James Peller Malcolm, *Anecdotes of the Manners and Customs of London from the Roman Invasion to the Year 1700* (London, 1811), p. 427.

48. Bryant Lillywhite, *London Coffee Houses* (London, 1963), pp. 194–95, lists contemporary and later references to Don Saltero's. The present treatment is derived from the (highly repetitious) sources cited there, as well as Reginald Blunt, *In Cheyne Walk and Thereabout* (London, 1914), pp. 23–57, and *Survey of London,* II (1909), 61–64.

49. Quoted by Apperson, p. 95.

50. There are copies of the 1732 and 1794 editions at GL. A few items have been added from Apperson, pp. 93–95.

51. *The Tatler,* I, 280–83.

52. *Benjamin Franklin's Memoirs,* p. 122.

53. *Diary of Ralph Thoresby,* II, 376.

54. *Peregrine Pickle,* Ch. 69. (Oxford English Novels ed., pp. 346–47.)

55. Lewis M. Knapp, *Tobias Smollett: Doctor of Men and Manners* (Princeton, 1949), pp. 111–12.

56. Material on the Chelsea Bun House is from John Timbs, *Curiosities of London,* new ed. (London, [1867]), pp. 91–92; Sir Richard Phillips, *A Morning's Walk from London to Kew* (London, 1817), pp. 25–26; and *Mirror,* 33 (1839), 210–11.

57. *Journal to Stella,* ed. Harold Williams (Oxford, 1948), I, 259.

58. Quoted, *N & Q,* 10th ser. 6 (1906), 306.

59. Murray, I, 172–73.

60. Lysons (2-vol. set), II, 14.

61. GL, pamphlet no. 1934.

62. Lysons (5-vol. set), II, 216ᵛ–17.

2. FROM CABINETS TO MUSEUMS, II: 1750–1800

1. *The Yale Edition of the Works of Samuel Johnson* (New Haven, 1958–), IV, 64–76.

2. Advertisements in Lysons (2-vol. set), II.

3. Frits Lugt, *Repertoire des catalogues de ventes publiques,* I (The Hague, 1938), entry 3667.

4. Walpole's description of the collection, written on a sheet bound into his copy of the sale catalogue, is reproduced in *The Duchess of Portland's Museum by Horace Walpole,* with an introduction by W. S. Lewis (New York, 1936). See also Dillon Ripley, *The Sacred Grove: Essays on Museums* (New York, 1969), pp. 32–33.

5. Walpole, XXXVII, 439.

6. *Annual Register, 1802,* Chronicle pp. 445–46.

7. Walpole, XXIII, 211.

8. Ibid., XXXVII, 269.

9. Material on Walpole as a collector and museum keeper is from R. W. Ketton-Cremer, *Horace Walpole: A Biography* (London, 1940), passim, especially pp. 307–10, and Gerald Reitlinger, *The Economics of Taste: The Rise and Fall of the Objets d'Art Market Since 1750* (London, 1963), pp. 75–81.

10. Material on the British Museum down to 1800 is from Edward Edwards, *Lives of the Founders of the British Museum* (London, 1870); Henry C. Shelley, *The British Museum: Its History and Treasures* (Boston, 1911); J. Mordaunt

Crook, *The British Museum* (London, 1972); and Edward Miller, *That Noble Cabinet* (London, 1973).

11. Walpole, XX, 358–59.

12. Crook, pp. 56–62.

13. Miller, p. 65.

14. Crook, p. 65.

15. Conflated from Crook, p. 53, and Miller, p. 62.

16. Quoted in Rosamond Bayne-Powell, *Travellers in Eighteenth-Century England* (London, 1951), p. 70.

17. William Hutton, *A Journey to London . . . ,* 2nd ed. (London, 1818), pp. 111–17.

18. [Richard Ford], "The British Museum," *Quarterly Review,* 88 (1850), 138.

19. *Dictionary of National Biography.*

20. *Survey of London,* XXXI (1963), 49–50; John Kobler, *The Reluctant Surgeon: A Biography of John Hunter* (Garden City, N.Y., 1960), pp. 145–46.

21. Material on John Hunter's museum is from Kobler, passim, esp. pp. 100, 177–79, 227–37, 307–17.

22. The fullest treatment is W. H. Mullen, "The Leverian Museum," *Museums Journal,* 15 (1915–16), 123–29, 162–72. Lysons, II, 110ᵛ–118ᵛ, contains many clippings pertaining to the museum. An admiring biographical sketch of Lever appeared in the *European Magazine,* 6 (1784), 83–85. Other sources will be cited in the following notes.

23. *Gentleman's Magazine,* 43 (1773), 219–21.

24. Rashleigh Holt-White, *The Life and Letters of Gilbert White of Selborne* (London, 1901), I, passim.

25. Quoted from an unspecified source by Ripley, p. 32.

26. *Gentleman's Magazine,* 49 (1779), 319–20.

27. There is a more impersonal room-by-room description in the *European Magazine,* 1 (1782), 17–21.

28. *Early Diary of Fanny Burney,* ed. Annie Raine Ellis (London, 1907), II, 248.

29. Benjamin Silliman, *A Journal of Travels in England, Holland, and Scotland . . . in the Years 1805 and 1806* (New York, 1810), I, 208–209.

30. *Sophie in London, 1786: Being the Diary of Sophie v. la Roche,* trans. Clare Williams (London, 1933), pp. 112–14.

31. *Diary and Letters of Madame D'Arblay,* ed. Charlotte Barrett (London, 1904), II, 167–68.

32. On the lottery, see John Ashton, *A History of English Lotteries Now for the First Time Written* (London, 1893; rptd. Detroit, 1969), pp.

105–107, and William J. Smith, "A Museum for a Guinea," *Country Life,* 127 (1960), 494–95.

33. *Dictionary of National Biography,* s.n. "James Parkinson."

34. For the collection as it then was, see William Hone, *Hone's Every Day Book* (London, 1826–1827), II, cols. 987–91.

35. William Jerdan, *Men I Have Known* (London, 1866), p. 70.

36. *The Life of Thomas Holcroft, Written by Himself* . . . (London, 1925), II, 216–17.

37. Joseph Farington, *The Farington Diary,* ed. James Greig (New York, 1922–1928), III, 273.

38. There is a marked copy of the catalogue at BL.

39. Handbill, GL, Fairs collection.

40. *Boswell: The Ominous Years, 1774–1776,* ed. Charles Ryskamp and Frederick A. Pottle (New York, 1963), p. 111.

41. *Sophie in London,* p. 115.

42. *The Prelude* (1805 version), III, 651–68. (*The Prelude: A Parallel Text,* ed. J. C. Maxwell, Harmondsworth, 1971. All quotations from the poem are from this edition.)

3. MONSTER-MONGERS AND OTHER RETAILERS OF STRANGE SIGHTS

1. *The London Spy Compleat,* ed. Ralph Straus (London, 1924), p. 304.

2. J. P. Malcolm, *Anecdotes of the Manners and Customs of London . . . to the Year 1700* (London, 1811), p. 210.

3. *The London Spy Compleat,* p. 176.

4. *Macaroni and Theatrical Magazine,* January 1773, clipping in EC, Gardens box.

5. *The Prelude* (1805 version), VII, 662–94. Compare Ned Ward's lengthy description of the fair as it was a century earlier (*The London Spy Compleat,* pp. 240–49, 251–69). Hundreds of handbills and newspaper clippings are collected in two scrapbooks which Henry Morley used for his history of Bartholomew Fair (n. 10 below): BL (C70.h.6 (2)) and GL (A.5.2.no.12).

6. Evelyn, III, 197–98.

7. Pepys, VIII, 326.

8. Ibid., VIII, 500.

9. *The Diary of Robert Hooke, 1672–1680,* ed. Henry W. Robinson and Walter Adams (London, 1935), pp. 5, 184, 309, 423, 208, 310.

10. Henry Morley, *Memoirs of Bartholomew Fair* (London, 1880; rptd. Detroit, 1968), p. 189. For a ballad on this topic, see pp. 223–24.

11. Quoted in *Memoirs of the Extraordinary Life, Works, and Discoveries of Martinus Scriblerus,*

ed. Charles Kerby-Miller (New Haven, 1950), pp. 294–96. See the Royal Society's *Philosophical Transactions,* 50, part 1 (1757), 311–22, for contemporary descriptions of the twins, who died at Presburg in 1723.

12. *Correspondence of Jonathan Swift,* ed. Harold Williams (Oxford, 1963), I, 82.

13. Evelyn, IV, 389.

14. Newdigate Newsletters, Folger Library. I am indebted to Professor John Harold Wilson for these notes.

15. Walter George Bell, *Fleet Street in Seven Centuries* (London, 1912), p. 541.

16. Advertisement in *Flying Post,* 6–9 February 1703, quoted in William Bragg Ewald, Jr., *The Newsmen of Queen Anne* (Oxford, 1956), p. 167.

17. Ibid.

18. John Ashton, *Social Life in the Reign of Queen Anne* (London, 1883; rptd. Detroit, 1968), p. 204.

19. Ibid., p. 203.

20. *Morning Herald and Advertiser,* 1793; clipping in EC, Exhibitions (Various) folder.

21. J. P. Malcolm, *Anecdotes of the Manners and Customs of London during the Eighteenth Century* (London, 1808), p. 311.

22. Ashton, p. 202; *The Diary of Ralph Thoresby, F.R.S.,* ed. Joseph Hunter (London, 1830), II, 235.

23. J. Holden Macmichael, *The Story of Charing Cross and Its Immediate Neighbourhood* (London, 1906), p. 63.

24. Material on Exeter Change is scattered through books on eighteenth-century London. The present paragraph is based upon the extensive EC Exeter Change file.

25. Obituary, 9 May 1816, EC, Exeter Change file.

26. Basil Taylor, *Stubbs* (New York, 1971), p. 210 and note to plate 73.

27. Constance-Anne Parker, *Mr. Stubbs the Horse Painter* (London, 1971), p. 86.

28. Newspaper clippings, EC, Exeter Change file.

29. Morley, p. 358.

30. Ibid., pp. 279, 336, 358.

31. Ashton, p. 202.

32. Evelyn, III, 93.

33. Ashton, p. 191.

34. Clipping from *Daily Advertiser,* 1753; Lysons, II.

35. Quoted in Ruth Manning-Sanders, *The English Circus* (London, 1952), p. 23.

36. R. Toole Stott, *Circus and Allied Arts: A*

World Bibliography, 1500–1957 (Derby, 1958–1971), I, 30–31.

37. Clippings, EC, Exeter Change file.

38. Ashton, p. 191.

39. Macmichael, p. 66.

40. *Mirror,* 32 (1838), 441.

41. Lysons, II, 105; *Mirror,* 32 (1838), 441.

42. Joseph Strutt, *The Sports and Pastimes of the People of England,* enlarged ed. by J. Charles Cox (London, 1903), pp. 200–201.

43. Robert Southey, *Letters from England,* ed. Jack Simmons (London, 1951), p. 340.

44. Lysons, II, 86–90.

45. *Life of Samuel Johnson,* ed. G. Birkbeck Hill and L. F. Powell (Oxford, 1934–1950), IV, 373–74.

46. *Diary of Robert Hooke,* p. 309.

47. Bell, p. 541.

48. John Kobler, *The Reluctant Surgeon* (Garden City, N.Y., 1960), pp. 238–44; *Dictionary of National Biography.*

49. *Dictionary of National Biography;* Colin Clair, *Human Curiosities* (London, 1968), p. 35.

50. Ashton, pp. 205–206.

51. Taylor (cited n. 62 below), p. 64.

52. T. W. Baldwin, *William Shakespeare's Five-Act Structure* (Urbana, Ill., 1947), p. 777. I am indebted here to Professor Edwin W. Robbins.

53. Collection of advertisements, BL (551.d.18).

54. Ashton, p. 191.

55. Ibid., p. 190.

56. Morley, p. 248.

57. Collection of advertisements, BL (551.d.18).

58. Morley, pp. 248–49.

59. Ibid., p. 251.

60. Ibid., p. 253. One of the fullest contemporary sources of information on freaks on view in the last years of the seventeenth century and the first years of the eighteenth is a curious manuscript book (BL Sloane MS. 5246) entitled *A Short History of Human Prodigies and Monstrous Births, of Dwarfs, Sleepers, Giants, Strong Men, Hermaphrodites, Numerous Births, and Extream Old Age &c.* Compiled by one James Paris du Plessis, who claimed to have been a servant of Samuel Pepys, it is composed of Du Plessis's descriptions, illustrated by crude colored sketches, of freaks he saw in London, and clippings from the newspapers of 1731–1733. In his poverty-stricken old age, Du Plessis tendered the book to Sir Hans Sloane, who gave him a guinea for it.

61. Pepys, I, 138.

62. See Aline Mackenzie Taylor, "Sights and Monsters and Gulliver's Voyage to Brobdingnag," *Tulane Studies in English,* 7 (1957), 29–82, an article to which the following discussion owes much. I am grateful to Professor Arthur H. Scouten for calling it to my attention.

63. Ibid., p. 30.

64. Ashton, pp. 190–91.

65. Ibid., p. 191.

66. Advertisement in *Daily Courant,* 28 October 1708, quoted in Ewald, p. 169.

67. Morley, p. 314.

68. There are accounts of Boruwlaski in, among other places, John Timbs, *English Eccentrics and Eccentricities* (London, 1875; rptd. Detroit, 1969), pp. 258–69, and *Memoirs of Charles Mathews, Comedian,* by Mrs. Mathews (London, 1839), III, 213–32.

69. *Memoirs of the Life of Sir Walter Scott* (Boston, n.d.), IV, 30n. (Ch. XXVII).

70. *Memoirs of Charles Mathews,* III, 232.

71. Bethlehem Hospital is, of course, described in most standard books on seventeenth- and eighteenth-century London. See also Edward Geoffrey O'Donoghue, *The Story of Bethlehem Hospital from Its Foundation in 1247* (London, 1914), and Max Byrd, *Visits to Bedlam: Madness and Literature in the Eighteenth Century* (Columbia, S.C., 1974).

72. O'Donoghue, p. 235.

73. *The London Spy Compleat,* p. 63.

74. *London in 1710,* trans. and ed. W. H. Quarrell and Margaret Mare (London, 1934), p. 51.

75. *The London Spy Compleat,* p. 67.

76. *Familiar Letters on Important Occasions,* ed. Brian W. Downs (London, 1928), pp. 201–202.

77. Sidney Lee, "The Call of the West: America and Elizabethan England, Part III: The American Indian in Elizabethan England," *Scribner's Magazine,* 42 (1907), 313–30.

78. Morley, pp. 248–49; Evelyn, V, 295.

79. Morley, pp. 254–55.

80. This discussion of the Iroquois sachems is based wholly on Richmond P. Bond, *Queen Anne's American Kings* (Oxford, 1952).

81. Timberlake published his narrative of the visit in 1765. It has been reprinted in *Lieut. Henry Timberlake's Memoirs, 1756–1765,* ed. Samuel Cole Williams (Marietta, Ga., 1948). The following paragraphs are derived from this source and from the fuller treatment in Carolyn Thomas Foreman, *Indians Abroad, 1493–1938* (Norman, Okla., 1943), pp. 65–81.

82. Foreman, pp. 83–85.

83. All information on Cartwright's Eskimos is from *Captain Cartwright and His Labrador Journal,* ed. Charles Wendell Townsend (Boston, 1911).

84. *Life of Johnson,* II, 247.

85. Material on Omai is from Thomas Blake Clark, *Omai: First Polynesian Ambassador to England* ([San Francisco], 1941), and J. C. Beaglehole, *The Life of Captain James Cook* (Stanford, 1974), pp. 447–49.

86. Evelyn, V, 453.

87. John Nichols, *Literary Anecdotes of the Eighteenth Century* (London, 1812–1816), V, 487.

88. Letter 45, *Citizen of the World* (Everyman ed.), pp. 124–26.

4. WAXWORK AND CLOCKWORK

1. Evelyn, III, 612.

2. Thomas Frost, *The Old Showmen, and the Old London Fairs* (London, 1874), p. 31.

3. *The London Spy Compleat,* ed. Ralph Straus (London, 1924), pp. 256–58.

4. *N & Q,* 169 (1935), 405.

5. E. J. Pyke, *A Biographical Dictionary of Wax Modellers* (Oxford, 1973), p. 129.

6. Pyke, p. 55; John Ashton, *Social Life in the Reign of Queen Anne* (London, 1883), p. 213.

7. *London in 1710,* trans. and ed. W. H. Quarrell and Margaret Mare (London, 1934), pp. 81–85.

8. Pyke, p. 13; *Appleby's Journal,* 17 December 1718, clipping in Lysons, II, 129 (an abundant source for eighteenth-century London waxworks).

9. *London in 1710,* p. 118.

10. *The Spectator,* ed. Donald F. Bond (Oxford, 1965), I, 117.

11. Pyke, p. 129.

12. Ashton, pp. 212–13.

13. J. H. Macmichael, *The Story of Charing Cross* (London, 1906), p. 25.

14. *Reminiscences of Henry Angelo* (London, 1904), I, 308–309.

15. *Boswell's London Journal, 1762–1763,* ed. Frederick A. Pottle (New York, 1950), p. 289.

16. Quoted in M. Willson Disher, *Pleasures of London* (London, 1950), p. 200.

17. Note by "G.S.," compiler of EMI scrapbook.

18. Material in this paragraph is from Lysons, II, 129–44.

19. Pyke, pp. 143–44.

20. Handbill, GL, London Playbills: Circuses and Miscellaneous Entertainments box.

21. Pyke, pp. 36, 11.

22. The following passage on Patience Wright is based on Pyke, pp. 158–59; C. H. Hart, "Patience Wright, Modeller in Wax," *Connoisseur,* 19 (1907), 18–22; William Dunlap, *A History of the Rise and Progress of the Arts of Design in the United States,* new ed. (Boston, 1918), I, 150–56; Lewis Einstein, *Divided Loyalties: Americans in England during the War of Independence* (Boston, 1933), pp. 390–95; Paula D. Sampson, "Patience Wright and Her 'New Style of Picturing,'" *Antiques,* 87 (1965), 586–89; and the article by C. C. Sellers in *Notable American Women, 1607–1950: A Biographical Dictionary,* ed. Edward T. James et al. (Cambridge, Mass., 1971), III, 685–87. Additional material, not incorporated here, has recently appeared in Kenneth Silverman, *A Cultural History of the American Revolution* (New York, 1976), pp. 179–80, 267, 382–84, 455.

23. Walpole, XXXII, 98.

24. *Letters of Mrs. Adams . . . ,* ed. Charles Francis Adams, 4th ed. (Boston, 1848), pp. 177–78.

25. Pyke, pp. 38–39, 75–76, 162–63.

26. Advertisement in *Craftsman,* 5 December 1730; clipping in Lysons, II, 133.

27. *Correspondence of Jonathan Swift,* ed. Harold Williams (Oxford, 1966), V, 163.

28. Clippings in Lysons, II, 133–35.

29. Boswell, *Life of Johnson,* ed. George Birkbeck Hill and L. F. Powell (Oxford, 1934–1950), IV, 319.

30. Walpole, XXXVIII, 198–99.

31. Advertisement in Harvard Theatre Collection, Panorama box.

32. Material on the contents of Rackstrow's museum is from a catalogue dated 1787 (GL, pamphlet 2734).

33. W. G. Bell, *Fleet Street in Seven Centuries* (London, 1912), p. 539.

34. Advertisement in Harvard Theatre Collection, Panorama box.

35. Wolfgang Born, "Early Peep-Shows and the Renaissance Stage," *Connoisseur,* 107 (1941), 67–71, 161–64, 180.

36. Evelyn, III, 165.

37. The history of peepshows is briefly treated in Lesley Gordon, *Peepshow into Paradise: A History of Children's Toys* (London, 1953), pp. 217–18, and Olive Cook, *Movement in Two Dimensions* (London, 1963), pp. 25–27.

38. M. Dorothy George, *English Political Caricature to 1792* (Oxford, 1959), pp. 56–57.

39. Alfred Chapuis and Edouard Gélis, *Le*

monde des automates: étude historique et technique (Paris, 1928), I, 143–51.

40. This paragraph is based on George Speaight, *The History of the English Puppet Theatre* (London, 1955), pp. 54–56.

41. Pepys, II, 115–16.

42. Ibid., IV, 265.

43. Ibid., IV, 298.

44. Ibid., VIII, 423.

45. Quoted in C. J. S. Thompson, *The Quacks of Old London* (Philadelphia, 1929), pp. 131–32.

46. Speaight, p. 163.

47. Frost, pp. 123–24.

48. Speaight, p. 163.

49. Ibid., p. 158.

50. Ashton, pp. 193–94.

51. G. L. Apperson, "The Early History of Panoramas," *Antiquary,* 40 (1904), 299–304; Joseph E. Duncan, *Milton's Earthly Paradise* (Minneapolis, 1972), pp. 215–16.

52. Evelyn, IV, 24.

53. Apperson, pp. 299–304; *The Diary of Ralph Thoresby, F.R.S.,* ed. Joseph Hunter (London, 1830), I, 47–48, 158.

54. Advertisements in *Spectator,* nos. 43 and 181, in Lawrence Lewis, *The Advertisements of "The Spectator"* (Boston, 1909), pp. 258–59.

55. *N & Q,* 11th ser. 2 (1910), 456.

56. *Diary of Ralph Thoresby,* II, 41.

57. Sybil Rosenfeld, *Strolling Players and Drama in the Provinces, 1660–1765* (Cambridge, 1939), p. 267.

58. Joseph Strutt, *The Sports and Pastimes of the People of England* (London, 1903), p. 146.

59. Quoted in *The Spectator,* I, 128–29.

60. Ibid.

61. Quoted in *The Tatler,* ed. George A. Aitken (London, 1899), III, 82–83n.

62. Advertisement in *Spectator,* no. 43, in Lewis, p. 259.

63. Rosenfeld, *Strolling Players,* pp. 275–76; Rosenfeld, *The Theatre of the London Fairs in the Eighteenth Century* (Cambridge, 1960), pp. 23, 28, 85.

64. *N & Q,* 188 (1945), 38–39.

65. Ibid.

66. Macmichael, p. 282.

67. Handbill, WCL, StM/Gen, I, 126.

68. Rosenfeld, *Theatre of the London Fairs,* pp. 131–32.

69. Lysons, II, 212, 220. There are further descriptions in Alfred Chapuis and Edmund Droz, *Automata* (Neuchâtel and London, 1958), pp. 128–31, and R. W. Symonds, "A Picture Machine of the Eighteenth Century," *Country Life,* 96 (1944), 336–37.

70. Odell, I, 72.

71. *Oxford Companion to Music,* 10th ed., p. 615.

72. Lysons, II, 211.

73. Henry Morley, *Memoirs of Bartholomew Fair* (London, 1880), p. 354.

74. J. P. Malcolm, *Anecdotes of the Manners and Customs of London during the Eighteenth Century* (London, 1808), p. 331.

75. Rosenfeld, *Theatre of the London Fairs,* pp. 37, 124, 99, 167.

76. Advertisement, EC, Exeter Change file.

77. Another advertisement, ibid.

78. Charles Perregaux and F.-Louis Perrot, *Les Jaquet-Droz et Leschot* (Neuchâtel, 1916), pp. 104–105, and picture facing p. 199.

79. *Public Advertiser,* 1776, quoted in *N & Q,* 11th ser. 3 (1911), 125–26.

80. *Reminiscences of Henry Angelo,* II, 250.

5. EXHIBITIONS OF MECHANICAL INGENUITY

1. In addition to the sources specified in the following notes, especially Brewster's *Letters on Natural Magic,* considerable use has been made in this chapter of two works which are indispensable to any study of the history of automatons: Alfred Chapuis and Edouard Gélis, *Le monde des automates* (Paris, 1928), and Alfred Chapuis and Edmund Droz, *Automata: A Historical and Technological Study,* trans. Alec Reid (Neuchâtel and London, 1958). See also the useful article on the history of English automatons in *Chambers's Journal,* 4th ser. 13 (1876), 87–90.

2. *Yale Edition of the Works of Samuel Johnson* (New Haven, 1958–), IV, 73.

3. Quoted by Chapuis and Gélis, II, 184.

4. [J. T. Desaguliers], *An Account of the Mechanism of an Automaton, or Image Playing on the German Flute, &c. . . . ;* reproduced in Arthur W. J. G. Ord-Hume, *Clockwork Music* (London, 1973), pp. 25–38.

5. Sir David Brewster, *Letters on Natural Magic, Addressed to Sir Walter Scott, Bart.* (London, 1832), p. 205.

6. Ibid., p. 268.

7. Desaguliers, as just cited.

8. *Memoirs of Robert-Houdin, Written by Himself,* ed. R. Shelton Mackenzie (Philadelphia, 1860), p. 160.

9. *Analysis of Beauty* (originally published London, 1753; Pittsfield, Mass., 1909), pp. 133–34.

10. Chapuis and Gélis, II, 152.

11. Charles Perregaux and F.-Louis Perrot, *Les Jaquet-Droz et Leschot* (Neuchâtel, 1916), p. 109n.

12. Chapuis and Droz, pp. 283–84.

13. *Mirror,* 2 (1823), 217–18.

14. Brewster, pp. 284–85.

15. *N & Q,* 12th ser. 10 (1922), 269–70, 331.

16. Ibid., p. 269.

17. Handbill reproduced in Ord-Hume, p. 45.

18. Quoted by Charles Michael Carroll, *The Great Chess Automaton* (New York, 1975), p. 21.

19. Lysons, II, 231.

20. *Letters of Samuel Johnson,* ed. R. W. Chapman (Oxford, 1952), III, 167.

21. There is a large literature, streaked through with myth and contradiction, on the automaton chess player. The bibliography appended to Carroll's *Great Chess Automaton* lists fifty-two books and articles, but still is not exhaustive; it omits, for example, the numerous discussions that *N & Q* published across the years. The present mention and the further discussion later on (Chapter 25) are based upon Carroll's compact and reliable monograph.

22. In addition to the sources specified in the following notes, this discussion draws upon G. L. Apperson, "Some Old London Museums and Collections: James Cox's Museum," *Antiquary,* 35 (1899), 276–79; Clare Le Corbeiller, "James Cox: A Biographical Review," *Burlington Magazine,* 112 (1970), 351–58; Chapuis and Droz, pp. 107–16; and a dozen contributions to *N & Q* between 1867 and 1935.

23. Hosea Ballou Morse, *The Chronicles of the East India Company Trading to China, 1635–1843* (Oxford, 1926–1929), V, 71, 154. For the background, see Jack Beeching, *The Chinese Opium Wars* (New York, 1975), pp. 17–20.

24. Frits Lugt, *Repertoire des catalogues de ventes publiques,* I (The Hague, 1938), entries 2056, 2088.

25. *Boswell for the Defence, 1769–1774,* ed. William K. Wimsatt, Jr., and Frederick A. Pottle (New York, 1959), pp. 52, 95.

26. *Antiquarian Horology,* 2 (1956), 208.

27. *Evelina,* Ch. 19. (Oxford English Novels ed., pp. 76–77.)

28. *Satirical Poems Published Anonymously by William Mason with Notes by Horace Walpole,* ed. Paget Toynbee (Oxford, 1926), pp. 112, 122.

29. Copy at GL (pamphlet 6546).

30. *Annual Register, 1775,* Chronicle pp. 104–105.

31. John Ashton, *A History of English Lotteries* (London, 1893), pp. 75–79.

32. Ibid.

33. Lugt, entry 4854; *Times,* 21 February 1792.

34. WCL, Box F138/Spring Gardens/10.

35. Unless otherwise noted, material on Merlin is from *Kirby's Wonderful and Scientific Museum, or Magazine of Remarkable Characters* (London, 1803–1820), I, 274–79; G. L. Apperson, "Some Old London Museums and Collections: Merlin's Mechanical Museum," *Antiquary,* 35 (1899), 368–70; and Percy A. Scholes, *The Great Doctor Burney* (London, 1948), II, 202–209.

36. *Early Diary of Fanny Burney,* ed. Annie Raine Ellis (London, 1907), II, 58.

37. *Diary and Letters of Madame D'Arblay,* ed. Charlotte Barrett (London, 1904), II, 18.

38. *Morning and Evening Amusements, at Merlin's Mechanical Museum . . .* ; copy at GL (pamphlet 829).

39. Walpole, XI, 242.

40. The whole poem is quoted in *Kirby's Wonderful and Scientific Museum,* I, 279.

41. Scholes, II, 206.

42. *Sophie in London,* trans. Clare Williams (London, 1933), p. 140.

43. Ibid.

44. *Public Advertiser,* 25 November 1776, quoted, *N & Q,* 11th ser. 3 (1911), 125–26.

45. *Early Diary of Fanny Burney,* II, 289–90.

46. Prospectus reproduced in Scholes, II, facing p. 206.

47. Ord-Hume, pp. 23–24.

48. Edward Baines, *History of the Cotton Manufacture in Great Britain* (London, 1835), pp. 229–30.

49. Brewster, pp. 285–86.

6. WATER, FIRE, AIR, AND A CELESTIAL BED

1. Evelyn, II, 47.

2. Robert Chambers, *The Book of Days* (London, [1862]), II, 624.

3. Evelyn, V, 247.

4. *London in 1710,* trans. and ed. W. H. Quarrell and Margaret Mare (London, 1934), pp. 50–51.

5. The following description of the water theatre is based on advertisements quoted in *The Spectator,* ed. Donald F. Bond (Oxford,

1965), II, 163; John Ashton, *Social Life in the Reign of Queen Anne* (London, 1883), pp. 219–21; Lawrence Lewis, *The Advertisements of "The Spectator"* (Boston, 1909), pp. 256–58; and W. B. Ewald, Jr., *The Newsmen of Queen Anne* (Oxford, 1956), pp. 169–70.

6. Newspaper clipping, BL, Burney Collection (938.a.20). I am indebted here to Professor Philip H. Highfill, Jr.

7. Ashton, p. 219; *N & Q,* 12th ser. 10 (1922), 331.

8. *N & Q,* 12th ser. 10 (1922), 269.

9. Handbill, WCL, StM/LS, II, 186.

10. Henry Morley, *Memoirs of Bartholomew Fair* (London, 1880), p. 274.

11. Clipping dated 12 June 1771, EC, Exeter Change file.

12. Advertisement dated 24 February 1772, ibid.

13. *The Englishman,* ed. Rae Blanchard (Oxford, 1955), p. 48.

14. There is a sketch of Walker in the *Dictionary of National Biography.*

15. *Diary and Letters of Madame D'Arblay,* ed. Charlotte Barrett (London, 1904), II, 181.

16. Desmond King-Hele, *Shelley: His Thought and Work,* 2nd ed. (London, 1971), pp. 158–59.

17. Advertisement dated 23 October 1782, EC, Lyceum folder.

18. Thomas Frost, *The Lives of the Conjurors* (London, 1881; rptd. Ann Arbor, 1971), p. 142.

19. Clippings, Lysons, II, 187.

20. All material on Dr. Graham is from Eric Jameson, *The Natural History of Quackery* (Springfield, Ill., 1961), Ch. 6.

21. Frost, p. 136. Frost's account, pp. 135–40, gives the main facts about Katterfelto; a more recent treatment is in Jameson, pp. 62–66. Much contemporary material is gathered in Lysons, I, 192–205, and in one of the nine scrapbooks formed by Miss Sophia Banks (BL, L.R.301.h.3).

22. Advertisement in *Morning Post,* 31 July 1782, quoted in Rosamond Bayne-Powell, *Travellers in Eighteenth-Century England* (London, 1951), pp. 194–95.

23. George, V, 668–69, 698–99, 721, 743–45, 765–68, 780–81.

24. The ballooning craze is well described by L. T. C. Rolt, *The Aeronauts: A History of Ballooning, 1783–1903* (New York, 1966); see especially Ch. IV.

25. Ibid., pp. 64–70.

26. Advertisement, *Daily Universal Register,* 5 July 1785.

27. *Survey of London,* XXXI (1963), 275.

28. Handbill, WCL, StM/Gen, I, 126.

29. Lysons, II, 195–97.

30. BL, EMI.

31. *Times,* 19 September 1794.

32. Handbill, BL (1856.g.16).

33. George, VII, 57.

34. William T. Whitley, *Artists and Their Friends, 1700–1799* (London, 1928; rptd. New York, 1968), II, 179.

7. THE SIGHTS AND RESORTS OF EIGHTEENTH-CENTURY LONDON

1. *The Tatler,* ed. George A. Aitken (London, 1898), I, 247.

2. John Stow, *Survey of London,* ed. Charles Lethbridge Kingsford (Oxford, 1908), I, 48. Some additional information about the Tower menagerie in the early years is found in Audrey Noel Hume, "A Royal Menagerie at the Tower," *Country Life,* 117 (1955), 103.

3. W. B. Rye, *England as Seen by Foreigners* (London, 1865), pp. 19–20. Rye also quotes (pp. 207–208) an extensive description of the Tower in 1598. Another is in *Thomas Platter's Travels in England, 1599,* trans. Clare Williams (London, 1937), pp. 159–63.

4. *The London Spy Compleat,* ed. Ralph Straus (London, 1924), pp. 307–22.

5. *London in 1710,* trans. and ed. W. H. Quarrell and Margaret Mare (London, 1934), pp. 38–39.

6. Ibid., p. 41.

7. *The London Spy Compleat,* p. 321.

8. Ibid., pp. 321–22.

9. *Sophie in London,* trans. Clare Williams (London, 1933), p. 129.

10. Hutton, *A Journey to London,* 2nd ed. (London, 1818), pp. 124–25.

11. Friedrich August Wendeborn, *View of England Towards the Close of the Eighteenth Century* (London, 1791), I, 332.

12. Evelyn, II, 195.

13. Pepys, III, 76.

14. Walpole, XXI, 378.

15. John Britton and E. W. Brayley, *Memoirs of the Tower of London* (London, 1830), p. 362.

16. Pierre Jean Grosley, *A Tour to London,* trans. Thomas Nugent (London, 1772), I, 205.

17. *The London Spy Compleat,* pp. 186–88.

18. Sir John Davies, *Works in Verse and Prose,* ed. Alexander B. Grosart (n.p., 1869), I, 334. The loquacious "man that keepes the Abbey

tombes" is also mentioned in Donne's *Satyre IV*, ll. 74–80.

19. Valentin Arithmaeus, *Notes on London and Westminster* (1617), quoted in Rye, p. 178.

20. Edward Arber, *An English Garner: Ingatherings from Our History and Literature* (Westminster, 1897), VI, 271.

21. Letter to the *Times*, 16 July 1825. See also Mrs. A. Murray Smith, *Westminster Abbey: Its Story and Associations* (London, 1906), p. 329.

22. *Citizen of the World* (Everyman ed.), pp. 32, 35.

23. John Thomas Smith, *Nollekens and His Times* (London, 1949), pp. 85–86.

24. The Abbey effigies are exhaustively described by W. H. St. John Hope, "On the Funeral Effigies of the Kings and Queens of England," *Archaeologia*, 60 (1907), 517–70; L. E. Tanner and J. L. Nevinson, "On Some Later Funeral Effigies in Westminster Abbey," *Archaeologia*, 85 (1935), 169–202; R. P. Howgrave-Graham, "The Earlier Royal Funeral Effigies: New Light on Portraiture in Westminster Abbey," *Archaeologia*, 98 (1961), 159–69; and Lawrence E. Tanner, *Recollections of a Westminster Antiquary* (London, 1969), Ch. XI.

25. Quoted, *N & Q*, 2nd ser. 6 (1858), 11–12.

26. Tom Brown, *Amusements Serious and Comical*, ed. Arthur L. Hayward (New York, 1927), p. 114.

27. E. J. Pyke, *Biographical Dictionary of Wax Modellers* (Oxford, 1973), p. 55.

28. *Sophie in London*, p. 118.

29. Walpole, XXXVIII, 111.

30. Smith, p. 86.

31. *Citizen of the World*, p. 36.

32. Rye, p. 178.

33. John Timbs, *Curiosities of London* (London, [1867]), p. 116. For a German visitor's impressions of St. Paul's toward the end of the century, see *Travels of Carl Philip Moritz in England in 1782* (London, 1924), pp. 90–95.

34. Vauxhall figures prominently in most books dealing with London social life and topography from the late seventeenth century to the mid-nineteenth. Two modern books are devoted to the subject: W. S. Scott, *Green Retreats: The Story of Vauxhall Gardens, 1661–1859* (London, 1955), and James G. Southworth, *Vauxhall Gardens: A Chapter in the Social History of England* (New York, 1941). An older account, still valuable, is in Warwick Wroth, *London Pleasure Gardens* (London, 1896), pp. 286–326. A dozen or more boxes devoted to Vauxhall are in

the Harvard Theatre Collection, and much additional material is at EC, BL, and elsewhere.

35. Benjamin Silliman, *A Journal of Travels . . . in the Years 1805 and 1806* (New York, 1810), I, 220, 323.

36. *Samuel F. B. Morse: His Letters and Journals,* ed. Edward L. Morse (Boston, 1914), I, 50–51.

37. B. Sprague Allen, *Tides in English Taste* (Cambridge, Mass., 1937), II, 235–36.

38. Wroth, p. 316.

39. Lawrence Gowing, "Hogarth, Hayman, and the Vauxhall Decorations," *Burlington Magazine*, 95 (1953), 4–19. See also Charles Mitchell, "Benjamin West's 'Death of General Wolfe' and the Popular History Piece," *Journal of the Warburg and Courtauld Institutes,* 7 (1944), 29, for Vauxhall art in West's time.

40. The part fireworks played for three centuries in London entertainments is well described in Alan St. H. Brock, *A History of Fireworks* (London, 1949). For this period, see especially pp. 57–59.

41. J. P. Malcolm, *Anecdotes of the Manners and Customs of London during the Eighteenth Century* (London, 1808), p. 405.

42. Wroth, pp. 215–16.

43. Lysons, II, 164.

44. Silliman, I, 199–200.

45. Lysons, II, 127.

46. Ibid., II, 150–52.

47. Ibid., II, 152; Wroth, pp. 266–67; John Britton, *Autobiography* (London, 1850), I, 97.

48. Advertisements, EC, Gardens file.

49. Wroth, pp. 268–70.

50. This discussion of the Bermondsey Spa is derived from Wroth, pp. 231–36. For an amusing account of a visit to the establishment in its last years, when it had three idle waiters and no customers, see John Thomas Smith, *A Book for a Rainy Day* (London, 1845), pp. 133–38.

51. *Literary Gazette*, 25 July 1818, pp. 472–73.

8. ART ON DISPLAY

1. Quoted in William T. Whitley, *Artists and Their Friends, 1700–1799* (New York, 1928), II, 104.

2. Ibid., II, 71.

3. John Pye, *Patronage of British Art: An Historical Sketch . . .* (London, 1845), pp. 217–20.

4. Ibid.

5. A substantial account of Charles I, Buckingham, and Arundel as the first English collectors of art on a princely scale is found in

Niels von Holst, *Creators, Collectors, and Connoisseurs,* trans. Brian Battershaw (London, 1967), pp. 117–28.

6. The following sketch of the origins and development of London art exhibitions is based on Whitley, Chs. X–XV, and Pye. A valuable appendix in the latter book displays the somewhat tangled history of the several eighteenth-century artists' organizations in tabular form.

7. Derek Hudson and Kenneth W. Luckhurst, *The Royal Society of Arts, 1754–1954* (London, 1954), p. 38.

8. Ibid., p. 37.

9. Whitley, I, 171.

10. Hudson and Luckhurst, pp. 37–38.

11. Edward Edwards, *Anecdotes of Painters . . .* (London, 1808), pp. xxvii–xxviii.

12. Sidney C. Hutchison, *The History of the Royal Academy, 1768–1968* (New York, 1968), p. 55.

13. Whitley, II, 191.

14. *Plan and New Descriptive Catalogue of the European Museum . . .* (1818); copy at WCL.

15. On the Orleans collection: Whitley, II, 179–81; Frank Herrmann, *The English as Collectors* (London, 1972), pp. 133–45; Gerald Reitlinger, *The Economics of Taste: The Rise and Fall of Picture Prices, 1760–1960* (London, 1961), pp. 26–30.

16. "On the Pleasure of Painting," *Complete Works of William Hazlitt,* ed. P. P. Howe (London, 1930–1934), VIII, 14.

17. Kenneth W. Luckhurst, *The Story of Exhibitions* (London, 1951), pp. 53–56; Bryant Lillywhite, *London Coffee Houses* (London, 1963), p. 423.

18. The following account of Copley's exhibitions is drawn from Jules David Prown, *John Singleton Copley* (Cambridge, Mass., 1966), II, 280–357 passim.

19. Quoted in James Thomas Flexner, *America's Old Masters,* rev. ed. (New York, 1967), p. 155.

20. Prown, II, 312.

21. Reitlinger, pp. 66, 72.

22. Clipping from *Morning Post,* 1 April 1783, in Lysons, II, 161.

23. Material on Boydell is drawn from Thomas Balston, "Alderman Boydell, Printseller," *History Today,* 2 (1952), 544–50; W. Moelwyn Merchant, *Shakespeare and the Artist* (London, 1959), pp. 66–76, 237–40; *Survey of London,* XXIX (1960), 335–38; and T. S. R. Boase, "Illustrations of Shakespeare's Plays in the Seventeenth and Eighteenth Cen-

turies," *Journal of the Warburg and Courtauld Institutes,* 10 (1947), 94–108.

24. John Ashton, *History of English Lotteries* (London, 1893), pp. 133–38.

25. *Letters of Horace Walpole,* ed. Mrs. Paget Toynbee (Oxford, 1903–1905), XIV, 291.

26. *Letters of Charles Lamb,* ed. E. V. Lucas (New Haven, 1935), III, 394. See also Thackeray's memories of a childhood permeated with images derived from the Shakespeare Gallery, in his review of Leech's *Pictures of Life and Character, Quarterly Review,* 96 (1854), 75.

27. T. S. R. Boase, "Macklin and Bowyer," *Journal of the Warburg and Courtauld Institutes,* 26 (1963), 148–55, 164–69.

28. Jack Lindsay, *J. M. W. Turner: His Life and Work* (London, 1966), p. 66.

29. The history of the Milton Gallery is traced in John Knowles, *The Life and Writings of Henry Fuseli, Esq.* (London, 1831), I, 171–236 passim.

30. Ibid., I, 236.

31. Letter of 1800, quoted in David Irwin, "Fuseli's Milton Gallery: Unpublished Letters," *Burlington Magazine,* 101 (1959), 440.

32. Boase, "Macklin and Bowyer," pp. 169–76.

33. Ashton, pp. 138–45.

34. The fullest source on the Temple of Flora is Geoffrey Grigson's introduction to the handsome facsimile of Thornton's book (London, 1951). Clippings relating to it are in Lysons, II, 168ᵛ. Benjamin Silliman, *Journal of Travels . . . in the Years 1805 and 1806* (New York, 1810), I, 183–84, describes a visit to the gallery.

35. Ashton, pp. 192–97.

36. *The London Spy Compleat,* ed. Ralph Straus (London, 1924), p. 100.

37. John Rothenstein, *An Introduction to English Painting* (New York, 1965), p. 46.

38. M. Dorothy George, *Hogarth to Cruikshank: Social Change in Graphic Satire* (New York, 1967), p. 57.

39. George, *Catalogue of Political and Personal Satires,* VI, 475.

40. Ibid., VI, 666.

41. Ibid., VI, 607.

42. Undated advertisement, Lysons, II, 110.

43. George, VI, 663.

44. The following paragraphs on exhibitions of stained glass are based mainly on *N & Q,* 146 (1924), 243–44, 292, 346, 374–77. The *Dictionary of National Biography* has articles on Jervais and the Pearsons.

45. Walpole, XXIX, 301.

46. Handbill, WCL, StM/Gen, I, 123.

47. *N & Q,* 6th ser. 9 (1884), 376–77.

48. Lysons, II, 181–83.

49. Ibid., II, 172, 175.

50. Ibid., II, 109, 126–27.

51. *Sophie in London,* trans. Clare Williams (London, 1933), p. 130.

52. BL, EMI.

53. See Martin S. Briggs, "Architectural Models," *Burlington Magazine,* 54 (1929), 174–83, 245–52.

54. Henry Morley, *Memoirs of Bartholomew Fair* (London, 1880), pp. 221–22.

55. B. Sprague Allen, *Tides in English Taste* (Cambridge, Mass., 1937), I, 150.

56. J. P. Malcolm, *Anecdotes of the Manners and Customs of London during the Eighteenth Century* (London, 1808), p. 310.

57. John Timbs, *Curiosities of London* (London, [1867]), p. 92.

58. *Daily Advertiser,* 29 March 1741; clipping, BL, EMI.

59. Allen, I, 63.

60. Lysons, II, 195–97.

61. John Ashton, *Social Life in the Reign of Queen Anne* (London, 1883), pp. 217–18.

62. BL, EMI.

63. Lysons, II, 195–97, and later.

64. Ibid.

65. Ibid.

66. Clipping, WCL, StM/Gen, II, 175.

67. Lysons, II, 195–97, and later.

68. BL, EMI.

69. Lysons, II, 195–97, and later.

70. Ibid.

71. Ibid.

72. Ibid.

73. WCL, StM/Gen, II, 175.

74. Lysons, II, 197.

75. Silliman, I, 199.

76. *The Prelude* (1805 version), VII, 265–79.

9. THE EIDOPHUSIKON

1. The history of the magic lantern is traced in *Barnes Museum of Cinematography: Catalogue of the Collection,* part 2 (St. Ives, Cornwall, 1970).

2. Pepys, VII, 254; R. P. Bond, *Queen Anne's American Kings* (Oxford, 1952), p. 13.

3. *Dr. Campbell's Diary of a Visit to England in 1775,* ed. James L. Clifford (Cambridge, 1947), p. 122.

4. George, V, 164–65, 746; VI, 484–85, 926–27; VIII, 495.

5. See Austin Dobson, "Chinese Shadows," *Side-Walk Studies* (London, 1902), pp. 93–109; Barnes Museum catalogue cited in n. 1, part 1 (St. Ives, 1967), pp. 5–20; George Speaight, *History of the English Puppet Theatre* (London, 1955), pp. 142–46; Olive Cook, *Movement in Two Dimensions* (London, 1963), Ch. 5.

6. Henry Morley, *Memoirs of Bartholomew Fair* (London, 1880), p. 331.

7. *Reminiscences of Henry Angelo* (London, 1904), I, 8–11.

8. *Three Plays by David Garrick,* ed. Elizabeth P. Stein (privately printed, 1926; rptd. New York, 1967), p. 46.

9. Dobson, p. 100.

10. Speaight, pp. 142–43.

11. Dobson, p. 95.

12. Ibid., pp. 95–97.

13. Alfred Chapuis and Edouard Gélis, *Le monde des automates* (Paris, 1928), I, 340–41.

14. W. T. Whitley, *Artists and Their Friends, 1700–1799* (New York, 1928), II, 352.

15. There is a considerable, though scattered, body of commentary on Loutherbourg's theatrical work. The earliest substantial treatments which still have some value are W. J. Lawrence, "The Pioneers of Modern English Stage-Mounting: Philippe Jacques de Loutherbourg, R.A.," *Magazine of Art,* 18 (1895), 172–77, and Austin Dobson, "Loutherbourg, R.A.," in *At Prior Park and Other Papers* (London, 1912), pp. 94–127. A concise summary of Loutherbourg's career as a stage designer, along with a list of the specialized articles from which the facts in the following discussion are drawn, is in Sybil Rosenfeld and Edward Croft-Murray, "A Checklist of Scene Painters Working in Great Britain and Ireland in the Nineteenth Century," *Theatre Notebook,* 19 (1964–65), 105–12. To the bibliographical list may be added James Laver, *Drama: Its Costume and Décor* (London, 1951), Ch. XI; W. Moelwyn Merchant, *Shakespeare and the Artist* (London, 1959), pp. 60–65; Sybil Rosenfeld, "Landscape in English Scenery in the Eighteenth Century," in *Essays on the Eighteenth-Century English Stage,* ed. Kenneth Richards and Peter Thomson (London, 1972), pp. 171–77; and Rosenfeld, *A Short History of Scene Design in Great Britain* (Oxford, 1973), pp. 87–93.

16. *Reminiscences of Henry Angelo,* I, 11.

17. There is a detailed description of this production in Ralph G. Allen, "The Wonders of Derbyshire: A Spectacular Eighteenth-Century Travelogue," *Theatre Survey,* 2 (1961), 54–66.

18. See especially Ralph G. Allen, "De Loutherbourg and Captain Cook," *Theatre Re-*

search, 4 (1962), 195–211, and Lillian E. Preston, "The Noble Savage: *Omai; or, A Trip round the World,*" *Drama Critique,* 8 (1965), 130–32.

19. *European Magazine,* 1 (1782), 182.

20. Most of the immediately contemporary information on the Eidophusikon is collected in Ralph G. Allen, "The Eidophusikon," *Theatre Design and Technology,* 7 (December 1966), 12–16; see also the appendix on the Eidophusikon in Dobson's *At Prior Park,* pp. 277–81. The sole contemporary authority on the Eidophusikon's mechanism is a minor artist and self-styled "Cockney Grey Beard," William Henry Pyne, who wrote under the name of Ephraim Hard-castle. His description, upon which all subsequent accounts, including this one, necessarily depend, was first published in the *Literary Gazette* in 1821 (31 March and 7 April, pp. 198–200, 216–18), as part of a series of intolerably dull reminiscences and after-dinner gossip, "Wine and Walnuts," collected in book form in 1823 (see vol. I, pp. 281–304). Faith in Pyne's reliability is not enhanced when one discovers that, even in a day when factual accuracy was not overvalued in ordinary journalism, his license was so excessive that the serialization of "Wine and Walnuts" had to be suspended at one point "in order," said the exasperated editor (18 November 1820, p. 751), "to verify some dates, respecting which the memory of the ancient author [Pyne was fifty-one at the time] was not absolutely precise." (There had been egregious errors in the portions already printed.) Pyne claimed that he had been "gratified, through particular favour, by a constant admittance behind the curtain" at the Eidophusikon, but how he acquired this entrée is not known. Born in 1769, he was only twelve years old at the time of the first performances and seventeen when the Eidophusikon had its season at Exeter Change. The latest date at which he could have gained his backstage knowledge would have been 1799–1800, when the Eidophusikon was in Panton Street. Thus he was writing at the remove of at least two decades.

21. Quoted by Whitley, I, 354–55.

22. The most extensive, in the *Whitehall Evening Post,* is quoted in W. J. Lawrence, "A Century of Scene-Painting," *Gentleman's Magazine,* 264 (1888), 291.

23. Pyne, I, 302–303.

24. *European Magazine,* 1 (1782), 180.

25. Dobson, *At Prior Park,* pp. 111–12.

26. Ibid., p. 280.

27. WCL, StM/LS, II, 192.

28. *Times,* various dates, 22 February to 25 June 1793.

29. Advertisement, JJ Coll., Dioramas box 4.

30. Handbill, JJ Coll., Play Places box 8.

31. Advertisement, JJ Coll., Dioramas box 4.

32. *Times,* 24 March 1800; *Gentleman's Magazine,* 70 (1800), 271–72.

33. Advertisement in *True Briton,* 13 June 1799, quoted in Jack Lindsay, *J. M. W. Turner* (London, 1966), pp. 70–71. A number of advertisements are in JJ Coll., Dioramas box 4, and there is a handbill in Lysons, II, 244ᵛ. An eyewitness description was printed in *London und Paris* (Weimar), 5, no.1 (1800), 3–10.

34. Lindsay, pp. 70–71, and John Gage, "Turner and the Picturesque," *Burlington Magazine,* 107 (1965), 24–25.

35. Lindsay, pp. 70–71.

36. John Gage, *Colour in Turner: Poetry and Truth* (New York, 1969), p. 255.

37. *Professional and Literary Memoirs of Charles Dibdin the Younger . . . ,* ed. George Speaight (London, 1956), p. 121 and n.

10. THE PANORAMA IN LEICESTER SQUARE

1. No systematic, formal history of panoramas exists. Most of the scattered sources of information are cited in the notes to this and the following chapters. Two others should be mentioned: Germain Bapst, *Essai sur l'histoire des panoramas et des dioramas* (*Extrait des rapports du jury international de l'exposition universelle de 1889*) (Paris, 1891)—condensed in Bapst's "Les panoramas," *La Nature,* 9, part 1 (1891), 266–68, 293–95; and Heinz Buddemeier, *Panorama/Diorama/Photographie: Entstehung und Wirkung neuer Medien im 19. Jahrhundert* (Munich, 1970). Bapst is chiefly concerned with developments in Paris, though some material on England is included; Buddemeier concentrates on the panorama as a forerunner of photography, uses no English sources, and has little historical material. Most modern books on the prehistory of the motion picture, such as Olive Cook, *Movement in Two Dimensions* (London, 1963) (very unreliable) and C. W. Ceram, *Archaeology of the Cinema* (London, 1965), make some mention of the early panorama.

2. This discussion of the antecedents of the panorama is derived from Edward Croft-Murray, *Decorative Painting in England, 1537–1837* (London, 1962–1970), II, Ch. VI, and

Hubert J. Pragnell, *The London Panoramas of Robert Barker and Thomas Girtin circa 1800* (London Topographical Society, no. 109, 1968).

3. Evelyn, III, 375; Pepys, IV, 26. Pepys also mentions Povey's illusionist paintings elsewhere (IV, 18, 297–98; V, 161, 212).

4. *The Life and Correspondence of the Late Robert Southey,* ed. Charles Cuthbert Southey (London, 1849–1850), VI, 215.

5. Advertisement of the European Museum, *Times,* 23 July 1804.

6. The fullest near-contemporary account of the Barkers and Burfords and their panoramas, from which all later mentions are derived either directly or indirectly, is "The Panorama," *Art Journal,* n.s. 3 (1857), 46–47, based on the obituary of Henry Aston Barker in the *Gentleman's Magazine,* 201 (1856), 515–18, but with a substantial amount of additional information. New material also appeared in "Panoramas," *Chambers's Journal,* 3rd ser. 13 (1860), 33–35. "Panoramas and Dioramas," *Leisure Hour,* 35 (1886), 45–48, and G. L. Apperson, "The Early History of Panoramas," *Antiquary,* 40 (1904), 299–304, added little to the record. The most detailed modern treatment of the panoramas themselves, summarizing information found in the booklets sold at the door, is Herbert C. Andrews, "The Leicester Square and Strand Panoramas: Their Proprietors and Artists," *N & Q,* 159 (1930), 57–61, 75–78. There are large collections of these pamphlets at BL, WCL, GL, Museum of London, EC, and JJ Coll. Reviews of most of the Barker-Burford panoramas regularly appeared in, among other places, the *Times,* the *Examiner,* the *Art Journal,* and the *Athenaeum.*

7. *Repertory of Arts and Manufactures,* 4 (1796), 165–67.

8. *Benjamin Robert Haydon: Correspondence and Table Talk* (London, 1876), II, 350.

9. W. T. Whitley, *Artists and Their Friends, 1700–1799* (London, 1928), II, 106.

10. Advertisement in *World,* 19 April 1790; Lysons, II, 171.

11. Other clippings ibid.

12. See Luke Herrmann, *British Landscape Painting of the Eighteenth Century* (London, 1973), pp. 29–35.

13. For the history of the building see *Survey of London,* XXXIV (1966), 482–84.

14. Advertisements, JJ Coll., Dioramas box 3. A dozen early panoramas by various artists were described in *London und Paris* (Weimar), between 1798 and 1806.

15. Thomas Frognall Dibdin, *Reminiscences of a Literary Life* (London, 1836), I, 143–46n.

16. Ibid., I, 146–48.

17. The fullest treatments of the Eidometropolis are William T. Whitley, "Girtin's Panorama," *Connoisseur*, 69 (1924), 13–20, and Pragnell's *London Panoramas*.

18. W. T. Whitley, *Art in England, 1800–1820* (Cambridge, 1928), pp. 38–39.

19. *Times*, 21 May 1803.

20. Advertisement, Harvard Theatre Collection, Panorama box.

21. Benjamin Silliman, *Journal of Travels . . . in the Years 1805 and 1806* (New York, 1810), I, 197.

22. *Art Journal*, n.s. 3 (1857), 47.

23. *John Constable's Correspondence*, ed. R. B. Beckett, II (Suffolk Records Society, VI, 1964), 34.

24. Souvenir key to the panorama of Oxford at the Strand Panorama; *The Farington Diary*, ed. James Greig (New York, 1922–1928), IV, 188–89.

25. These are enumerated in the second part of Andrews's "Leicester Square and Strand Panoramas."

26. See Victor Wolfgang Von Hagen, *Frederick Catherwood Arch^t* (New York, 1950), pp. 41–42. (An untrustworthy source.)

27. *Chambers's Journal*, 3rd ser. 13 (1860), 34.

28. *Athenaeum*, 22 December 1832, p. 828.

29. *Athenaeum*, 2 January 1841, p. 15.

11. A PANORAMA IN A PLEASURE DOME

1. *Times*, 2 August 1827.

2. Elis Jenkins, "Thomas Hornor," *Stewart Williams' Glamorgan Historian*, VII (Cowbridge, Glamorgan, 1971), pp. 37–50. I am indebted to Ralph Hyde for referring me to this and several other arcane sources.

3. *London Review*, 22 August 1863.

4. Hornor's exploit was widely related at the time in connection both with his proposed engravings and with the Colosseum project. The following summary is based mainly on *Mirror*, 1 (1823), 449–51, and *European Magazine*, 83 (1823), 99–104.

5. *Prospectus. View of London and the Surrounding Country . . . from . . . the Cross of St. Paul's Cathedral. To Be Published in Four Engravings*, by Thomas Hornor (1823). There are copies at GL and JJ Coll. (London Play Places box 5).

6. *Times*, 13 December 1828. On the Colosseum as a paradigm of Regency taste, see John Steegmann, *The Rule of Taste from George I to George IV* (London, 1936), pp. 172–73.

7. The Colosseum building and the painting of the panorama were described in numerous contemporary and somewhat later publications: illustrated surveys of London architecture such as Augustus Welby Pugin and John Britton, *Illustrations of the Public Buildings of London*, 2nd ed. (London, 1838), I, 368–75, and Thomas H. Shepherd and James Elmes, *Metropolitan Improvements* (London, 1827–1831; rptd. New York, 1968), pp. 68–78; London guidebooks between 1830 and 1852, including several dealing solely with the Regent's Park area (e.g., *A Picturesque Guide to the Regent's Park*, 1829, copy at GL); and London topographical encyclopedias, most notably Timbs's *Curiosities of London*. The best, though brief, modern description and history is Hugh Honour, "The Regent's Park Colosseum," *Country Life*, 113 (1953), 22–24. There is a good collection of material at the Marylebone Public Library, and another in JJ Coll., London Play Places box 2. The present narrative is based upon all these sources, as well as the *Times*, 2 August 1827, *Literary Gazette*, 17 and 31 January 1829, pp. 42–43, 74–75, and *Mirror*, 13 (1829), 34–37.

8. Parris's part in the project is described in the contemporary articles just cited, and with some additional details, quoted from his journal, in the obituary in *The Builder*, 13 December 1873, pp. 979–80. There are further details of Parris's artistic career in Maurice Harold Grant, *A Chronological History of the Old English Landscape Painters* (London, 1926–1943), II, 325–26.

9. *Times*, 10, 22 April 1829; 15, 18 June 1830; 17 December 1833.

10. A few of Hornor's drawings of local scenes are listed in I. N. Phelps Stokes and Daniel C. Haskell, *American Historical Prints* (New York, 1932; rptd. Detroit, 1974), pp. 79–80, 84.

11. The rumors are reported by William Wells Brown, *Sketches of Places and People Abroad* (New York?, 1855), p. 131, and the *Times*, 7 July 1913. The date of Hornor's death has been ascertained by Ralph Hyde.

12. *Recollections of the Table-Talk of Samuel Rogers*, 3rd ed. (London, 1856), p. 193.

13. *Examiner*, 27 May 1832, p. 340.

14. *A Brief Account of the Colosseum in the Regent's Park* (1829); copy at GL.

15. *Times*, 5 August 1835.

16. C. S. Stewart, *Sketches of Society in Great Britain and Ireland* (Philadelphia, 1834), I, 145–46.

17. Najaf Koolee Meerza, *Journal of a Residence in England . . .* (privately printed, 1839?), I, 292–93.

18. Undated clipping, JJ Coll., London Play Places box 2.

19. Obituary in *The Builder*, 13 December 1873.

20. David Mayer III, *Harlequin in His Element: The English Pantomime, 1806–1836* (Cambridge, Mass., 1969), p. 195.

21. There is a set of these in the Marylebone Public Library (Ashbridge Coll., 125.2).

22. *Penny Magazine*, 2 (1833), 121–23.

23. *Times*, 21 April 1835; advertisement, *Athenaeum*, 3 May 1834, p. 341; handbill, Marylebone Public Library.

24. *Times*, 13 August 1833.

25. *Times*, 10 July 1835; newspaper clipping, EC.

26. Adam Carse, *Life of Jullien* (Cambridge, 1951), pp. 7–10.

27. Osbert Wyndham Hewett, *Strawberry Fair: A Biography of Frances, Countess Waldegrave, 1821–1879* (London, 1956), pp. 10–15. The countess was Braham's daughter. The date the author gives for the purchase of the Colosseum, 1835, is not supported by other sources.

28. Clipping, EC.

29. *Mirror*, 34 (1839), 18; *Times*, 17 June 1839.

30. *Times*, 21 April 1840.

31. *European Magazine*, 1 (1782), 182.

32. *Times*, 29 December 1843.

33. *Mirror*, n.s. 2 (1842), 82–83.

34. *Punch*, 3 (1842), 252.

35. Title page of catalogue, reproduced in F. M. L. Thompson, *Chartered Surveyors: The Growth of a Profession* (London, 1968), plates 26a–26b.

36. *Times*, 12 May 1843; *ILN*, 23 October 1843, p. 284.

37. The refurbished Colosseum received almost as much publicity as had the building in its first years, though without the spice of rosy-visioned speculators and absconding peculators. Among the more detailed descriptions were: *ILN*, 26 April and 3 May 1845, pp. 264–65, 276–77; *Punch*, 9 (1845), 60–62; *Examiner*, 10 May 1845, pp. 293–94; *Mirror*, n.s. 8 (1845), 34–35, 66; *London As It Is Today: Where To Go, and What To See, during the Great Exhibition* (London, 1851)—typical of many such guidebooks; and *Description of the Royal Colosseum,*

Re-Opened in *M.DCCC.XLV* (1845 et seq.)—copy of 23rd edition at GL. The folio "particulars" printed in anticipation of the sale of the property in 1855 (copy at Marylebone Public Library) has additional information. Two visitors' descriptions are Brown, *Sketches of Places and People Abroad,* pp. 255–58, and Nathaniel Parker Willis, *Famous Persons and Places* (Auburn, N.Y., 1855), pp. 368–73. Bradwell's nephew contributed some reminiscences of the renovation to *N & Q,* 10th ser. 3 (1905), 189–90.

38. *Art-Union,* 6 (1844), 315.

39. *Examiner,* 26 July 1845, p. 468.

40. *The New Planet; or, Harlequin Out of Place* (1847), in James Robinson Planché, *Extravaganzas 1825–1871,* ed. T. F. Dillon Croker and Stephen Tucker (London, 1879), III, 165.

41. *ILN,* 13 May 1848, p. 312.

42. Brown, p. 256.

43. Described in, among other places, *ILN,* 30 December 1848, p. 428; *Description of the Royal Cyclorama, or Music Hall* (1849), copy at BL.

44. *Punch,* 18 (1850), 132.

45. *Edmund Yates: His Recollections and Experiences* (London, 1884), I, 145.

46. *ILN,* 30 December 1848, p. 428.

47. *Times,* 25 December 1848.

48. Catalogue prepared for auction sale, 1868; copy at GL.

49. *Times,* 14 April 1854.

50. *Times,* 15 March 1855; "particulars" as cited in n. 37.

51. Prospectus dated July 1856; copy at Marylebone Public Library.

52. *Athenaeum,* 24 December 1859, p. 855.

53. Ellen Terry, *The Story of My Life* (London, 1908), pp. 32–34.

54. *Punch,* 55 (1868), 107.

55. *ILN,* 3 April 1875, p. 326.

12. THE DIORAMA

1. *Repertory of Arts, Manufactures, and Agriculture,* 2nd ser. 46 (1825), 257–65.

2. Unless otherwise attributed, material on Daguerre is from Helmut and Alison Gernsheim, *L. J. M. Daguerre: The History of the Diorama and the Daguerreotype* (London, 1956; rptd. New York, 1968), passim.

3. In addition to Gernsheim, the following description of the Diorama is derived from *Mirror,* 2 (1823), 245–46; *European Magazine,* 84 (1823), 337–43; *Mechanics' Magazine,* 1 (1824),

358–59; A. W. Pugin and John Britton, *Illustrations of the Public Buildings of London,* 2nd ed. (London, 1838), I, 362–67; *Penny Cyclopedia* (London, 1838), IX, 3; [George Mogridge], *Old Humphrey's Walks in London and Its Neighbourhood* (London, [1843]), pp. 265–71; article by John Saunders in Charles Knight, ed., *London* (London, 1841–1844), VI, 283–85; Frederick C. Bakewell, *Great Facts* (London, 1859), pp. 102–10; and Arthur Pougin, *Dictionnaire historique et pittoresque du théâtre* (Paris, 1885), pp. 295–96. The sources listed in n. 1 to Chapter 10, above, also discuss the Diorama. There are especially good collections of material on the subject at EC and the Marylebone Public Library. Particularly in the earlier years, the Diorama's programs were reviewed at length in the daily and weekly papers. See, for example, the *Times,* 30 August 1824; 21 March 1825; 21 February 1826; 5 June 1827; 5 April 1828; 27 May 1829; 22 April 1830. An informative article on "Daguerre's Pleasure Dome" by David Robinson appeared in the *Times,* 5 February 1977.

4. *Times,* 5 June 1827.

5. Gernsheim, p. 23.

6. *John Constable's Correspondence,* ed. R. B. Beckett, VI (Suffolk Records Society, XII, 1968), 134.

7. There are descriptions in Bakewell, pp. 102–110, and *Times,* 4 October 1823.

8. Pückler-Muskau, p. 63.

9. *A Picturesque Guide to the Regent's Park* (1829), pp. 39–41.

10. *Times,* 21 February 1826.

11. *Times,* 5 June 1827.

12. *Times,* 5 April 1828; see also *Literary Gazette,* 19 January 1828, p. 44.

13. *Mirror,* 11 (1828), 184–85; James Ballantine, *The Life of David Roberts, R.A.* (Edinburgh, 1866), p. 28.

14. Ballantine, p. 33.

15. *Literary Gazette,* 9 May 1829, p. 308.

16. *Times,* 28 May 1829.

17. Handbill reproduced in M. Willson Disher, *Pleasures of London* (London, 1950), p. 174.

18. *Times,* 21 July 1841; see also *Art-Union,* 3 (1841), 139.

19. Handbill, EC, Princess's Theatre folder; *Mirror,* 11 (1828), 184–85.

20. Daguerre described the technique of painting double-effect pictures in his *Historical and Descriptive Account of the Various Processes of the Daguerréotype and the Diorama* (London, 1839; rptd. New York, 1969), pp. 81–86.

21. Helmut Gernsheim, *History of Photography* (London, 1955), pp. 48–49.

22. *Athenaeum,* 13 August 1836, pp. 570–71.

23. Knight, VI, 285.

24. *Athenaeum,* 22 April 1848, p. 419.

25. *Punch,* 18 (1850), 132.

26. Gernsheim, *Daguerre,* p. 42; *Athenaeum,* 9 September 1848, p. 913; *ILN,* 10 August 1850, p. 115; newspaper clippings, 1849–1853, at Marylebone Public Library.

13. PANORAMAS: TOPICS OF THE TIMES

1. *Literary Gazette,* 4 September 1830, p. 579.

2. Handbills in grangerized copy (EC) of passage on Richardson excerpted from Pierce Egan's *The Pilgrims of the Thames in Search of the National;* handbills in GL, Fairs box.

3. Handbill, GL, Fairs box.

4. Albert Smith, "A Little Talk about Science and the Show-Folks," in *The Wassail-Bowl* (London, 1843), I, 85.

5. *ILN,* 18 January 1851, p. 46.

6. Handbill, EC, Empire Theatre folder.

7. *Times,* 28 June 1847.

8. "On the Present State of Modern Art," *Works of Ruskin,* ed. E. T. Cook and A. D. O. Wedderburn (London, 1902–1912), XIX, 218.

9. Material on Astley's is from A. H. Saxon, *Enter Foot and Horse: A History of Hippodrama in England and France* (New Haven, 1968), especially pp. 114–15 and 137–42.

10. W. T. Whitley, *Art in England, 1821–1837* (Cambridge, 1930), pp. 95–96.

11. *Literary Gazette,* 17 April 1824, p. 254.

12. *Times,* 25 October 1834; *Literary Gazette,* 27 December 1834, p. 869.

13. *Literary Gazette,* 19 January 1828, p. 44.

14. *Mirror,* 21 (1833), 182.

15. *Mirror,* 37 (1841), 107.

16. Jehangeer Nowrojee and Hirjeebhoy Herwanjee, *Journal of a Residence of Two Years and a Half in Great Britain* (London, 1841), p. 215.

17. The background of the British involvement in Arctic exploration at this period is described by L. P. Kirwan, *The White Road: A Survey of Polar Exploration* (London, 1959), especially Chs. 4, 13.

18. *Times,* 14 January 1834.

19. Henry Crabb Robinson, *The London Theatre, 1811–1866,* ed. Eluned Brown (London, 1966), p. 191; *Athenaeum,* 16 February 1850, p. 185.

20. *Athenaeum,* 12 January 1850, p. 52.

21. Descriptive pamphlet, WCL.
22. *Athenaeum*, 13 June 1840, p. 476.
23. *Mirror*, 36 (1840), 415.
24. *Literary Gazette*, 22 August 1829, p. 556.
25. Handbill, JJ Coll., Dioramas box 2.
26. *ILN*, 26 August 1848, p. 119.
27. *Times*, 26 May 1848.
28. *Athenaeum*, 16 March 1850, p. 289.
29. *Blackwood's Magazine*, 15 (1824), 472–73.
30. *Athenaeum*, 22 April 1829, p. 253.
31. Robinson, p. 197.
32. *ILN*, 9 August 1851, p. 174.
33. *Mirror*, 37 (1841), 122.
34. *Times*, 3 March 1851.

14. THE THEATRICAL ART OF THE PANORAMA

1. *The Prelude* (1805 version), VII, 244–64.
2. David Mayer III, *Harlequin in His Element* (Cambridge, Mass., 1969), p. 22.
3. Quoted in M. Willson Disher, *Clowns and Pantomimes* (London, 1925), p. 307.
4. *Examiner*, 3 January 1830, p. 4.
5. *Dramatic Essays* [by] John Forster [and] George Henry Lewes, ed. William Archer and Robert W. Lowe (London, 1896), pp. 250–51.
6. T. S. R. Boase, *English Art, 1800–1870* (Oxford, 1959), p. 21.
7. John Thomas Smith, *A Book for a Rainy Day* (London, 1845), p. 278. See also Boase, p. 22; W. T. Whitley, *Art in England, 1821–1837* (Cambridge, 1930), pp. 11–12.
8. *Literary Gazette*, 7 December 1822, p. 775.
9. *Literary Gazette*, 14 May 1825, pp. 315–16.
10. Gerald Reitlinger, *The Economics of Taste: The Rise and Fall of Picture Prices, 1760–1960* (London, 1961), p. 71.
11. *Times*, 30 December 1830.
12. *European Magazine*, 84 (1823), 343.
13. *Times*, 7 April 1827.
14. *John Constable's Correspondence*, ed. R. B. Beckett, VI (Suffolk Records Society, XII, 1968), 134n.
15. E. H. Gombrich, *Art as Illusion* (New York, 1960), pp. 253–54.
16. *Literary Gazette*, 4 September 1824, p. 573.
17. *Blackwood's Magazine*, 14 (1823), 472–73.
18. *European Magazine*, 84 (1823), 342.
19. *European Magazine*, 84 (1823), 343.
20. *Literary Gazette*, 4 September 1824, p. 573.
21. *Literary Gazette*, 29 March 1828, p. 202.

22. Quoted by Helmut and Alison Gernsheim, *L. J. M. Daguerre* (London, 1956), p. 26.
23. *Times*, 27 December 1832; clipping in Harvard Theatre Collection, Panorama box.
24. *Athenaeum*, 29 December 1832, p. 845.
25. *Times*, 22 April 1830.
26. *Athenaeum*, 17 February 1849, p. 173; reprinted in Leslie, *A Hand-Book for Young Painters* (London, 1855), p. 4.
27. *Examiner*, 30 November 1828, p. 775.
28. *Examiner*, 21 December 1828, p. 821.
29. *Literary Gazette*, 29 March 1828, p. 202.
30. *Times*, 5 June 1827.
31. *Literary Gazette*, 28 February 1824, p. 141.
32. *Times*, 2 April 1836.
33. *Times*, 26 March 1838.
34. Gernsheim, p. 30.
35. Benjamin Ward Richardson, *Thomas Sopwith, M.A., C.E., F.R.S.* (London, 1891), p. 66.
36. Olive Cook, *Movement in Two Dimensions* (London, 1963), p. 39.
37. Handbill, Marylebone Public Library.
38. Descriptive pamphlet, WCL.
39. *Times*, 30 December 1824.
40. *Mirror*, 37 (1841), 216.
41. *Athenaeum*, 19 July 1845, p. 718.
42. *A Picturesque Guide to the Regent's Park* (1829), p. 40.
43. *ILN*, 13 May 1854, p. 443.
44. *Athenaeum*, 4 March 1843, p. 214.
45. *Athenaeum*, 5 April 1845, p. 335.
46. Louis Simond, *An American in Regency England: The Journal of a Tour in 1810–1811*, ed. Christopher Hibbert (London, 1968), p. 139.
47. *N & Q*, 1st ser. 3 (1851), 406–407; 4th ser. 7 (1871), 432.
48. *Gentleman's Magazine*, 201 (1856), 517.
49. *N & Q*, 159 (1930), 60.
50. *N & Q*, 1st ser. 3 (1851), 526. (The writer speaks of "Girtin's" panorama, but as W. T. Whitley pointed out long afterwards [*Connoisseur*, 69, 1924, 20], the reference, for whatever it is worth, must be to Barker's panorama.) For the report that the London picture was taken to Paris, see above, p. 134.
51. Odell, II, 239.
52. V. W. Von Hagen, *Frederick Catherwood Arch^t* (New York, 1950), pp. 82–84.
53. Eric Adams, *Francis Danby: Varieties of Poetic Landscape* (New Haven, 1973), pp. 65, 74, 129.
54. C. R. Leslie, *Memoirs of the Life of John Constable, R.A.*, ed. Andrew Shirley (London, 1937), p. 24n.
55. *Praeterita*, in *Works of Ruskin*, ed. E. T.

Cook and A. D. O. Wedderburn (London, 1902–1912), XXXV, 117–18.
56. Marcel Brion, *Art of the Romantic Era* (New York, 1966), p. 254.
57. *London As It Is Today* (London, 1851), p. 278.
58. Ibid., p. 281.
59. James Baillie Fraser, *Narrative of the Residence of the Persian Princes in London, in 1835 and 1836* (London, 1838; rptd. New York, 1973), I, 123–24.
60. William Dunlap, *A History of the Rise and Progress of the Arts of Design in the United States*, new ed. (Boston, 1918), II, 165.
61. *Examiner*, 22 April 1832, p. 262.
62. Smith's own statement: *Times*, 18 September 1854.

15. PANORAMAS IN MOTION

1. Handbill, WCL, box 42, no. 4.
2. Odell, II, 303.
3. Clipping from *Bell's Weekly Messenger*, May 1814, EC, Catherine St. folder.
4. JJ Coll., Dioramas box 4.
5. *European Magazine*, 39 (1801), 41.
6. M. W. Disher, *Clowns and Pantomimes* (London, 1925), p. 286.
7. Information on the *Ægyptiana* show is derived from handbills in EC, and an eyewitness account in *London und Paris* (Weimar), 9, no. 1 (1802), 3–10.
8. John Britton, *Autobiography* (London, 1850), I, 81–82.
9. The fullest discussion of the diorama in pantomime, from which otherwise unattributed material in the following passage is drawn, is David Mayer III, *Harlequin in His Element* (Cambridge, Mass., 1969), esp. pp. 69–73 and Ch. IV.
10. *European Magazine*, 79 (1821), 68.
11. *European Magazine*, 81 (1822), 73.
12. H. C. Robinson, *The London Theatre, 1811–1866* (London, 1966), p. 104.
13. A. H. Saxon, *Enter Foot and Horse* (New Haven, 1968), pp. 175–89 passim.
14. The Harvard Theatre Collection, Panorama box, has several bills advertising the show's engagements in the provinces. It was at Newcastle in 1819.
15. Descriptive pamphlet, WCL.
16. Clippings, WCL, StM/Gen, pp. 177–78.
17. Horace Wellbeloved, *London Lions, for Country Cousins and Friends about*

Town . . . , 2nd ed. (London, 1826?), pp. 57–60.

18. Handbill, Harvard Theatre Collection, Panoramas box.

19. Pückler-Muskau, p. 325.

20. Handbill, GL, Fairs box.

21. Another handbill, ibid.

22. Helmut and Alison Gernsheim, *L. J. M. Daguerre* (London, 1956), pp. 46–47.

23. *Literary Gazette,* 24 May 1834, p. 365.

24. *Times,* 12 May 1834.

25. *Athenaeum,* 5 July 1834, p. 509.

26. No full-scale history of panoramas in nineteenth-century America has been written, although materials abound at Harvard, the Boston Public Library, the New York Public Library, and elsewhere. The Mississippi pictures have received the most attention, notably in John Francis McDermott, *The Lost Panoramas of the Mississippi* (Chicago, 1958), and Perry T. Rathbone, *Mississippi Panorama* . . . (St. Louis, 1950). A review article by Roy A. Boe in *Mississippi Quarterly,* 16 (1963), 203–211, adds some data not given by McDermott. Most recent histories of nineteenth-century American art, especially landscape painting, have brief passages on panoramas (e.g., James Thomas Flexner, *That Wilder Image,* Boston, 1962, pp. 248–49), but the largest general treatments thus far are found in Richard McLanathan, *The American Tradition in the Arts* (New York, 1968), pp. 229–30, 302–10, and Lee Parry, "Landscape Theatre in America," *Art in America,* 59 (November–December 1971), 52–61. Other useful sources on particular aspects of the American panorama will be mentioned below.

27. William Dunlap, *A History of the Rise and Progress of the Arts of Design in America* (Boston, 1918), II, 77.

28. Parry, pp. 52–61.

29. See James T. Callow, *Kindred Spirits: Knickerbocker Writers and American Artists, 1807–1855* (Chapel Hill, 1967), pp. 148–49; Odell, III, 407.

30. Biographical material on Banvard is from McDermott.

31. J. F. McDermott, "Banvard's Mississippi Panorama Pamphlets," *Papers of the Bibliographical Society of America,* 43 (1949), 48.

32. On the numerous reflections of the panorama in American literature, see Dorothy Dondore, "Banvard's Panorama and the Flowering of New England," *New England Quarterly,* 11 (1938), 817–26; Curtis Dahl, "Mark Twain and the Moving Panoramas," *American Quarterly,* 13

(1961), 20–32, and Robert L. Carothers and John L. Marsh, "The Whale and the Panorama," *Nineteenth-Century Fiction,* 26 (1971), 319–28.

33. *ILN,* 9 December 1848, pp. 364–65.

34. Handbill, GL, London Playbills and Miscellaneous Entertainments box.

35. There is a sketch of Smith's life in the *Dictionary of American Biography.*

36. See Hershel Parker, "Gansevoort Melville's 1846 London Journal," *Bulletin of the New York Public Library,* 70 (1966), 114–15.

37. *Athenaeum,* 17 March 1849, p. 280.

38. *Athenaeum,* 14 April 1849, p. 303.

39. *Times,* 11, 17 April 1849.

40. *Times,* 28 May 1849.

41. Quoted in McDermott, *Lost Panoramas,* p. 46.

42. One measure of the moving panorama craze is the number of allusions to it in *Punch.* See, for instance, 17 (1849), 14, 20; 18 (1850), 87, 208; 19 (1850), 97; 21 (1851), 138–39.

43. Handbill, WCL, D137/Egyptian Hall; *ILN,* 28 July 1849, p. 55. See also Curtis Dahl, "Panoramas of Antiquity," *Archaeology,* 12 (1950), 261.

44. *Athenaeum,* 28 July 1849, pp. 769–70.

45. *Examiner,* 16 December 1848, p. 805.

46. *ILN,* 30 March 1850, pp. 220–22.

47. *ILN,* 17 August 1850, p. 147.

48. *Athenaeum,* 27 April 1850, p. 457.

49. *ILN,* 30 March 1850, p. 221; *Edmund Yates: His Recollections and Experiences* (London, 1884), I, 145–46.

50. *Athenaeum,* 29 March 1851, p. 219.

51. John Timbs, *Curiosities of London* (London, [1867]), p. 308.

52. *Works of Thackeray* (London, 1898), V, 713.

53. *Times,* 26 March 1850.

54. *ILN,* 30 March 1850, p. 221.

55. Michael Edwardes, *Bound to Exile: The Victorians in India* (New York, 1970), p. 36. For more information on Stocqueler, who claimed to be a boyhood chum of Dickens, see Anne Lohrli, *Household Words* . . . (Toronto, 1973), pp. 427–28, and J. A. Carter, Jr., "Memories of 'Charley Wag,'" *The Dickensian,* 62 (1966), 147–51.

56. *Edmund Yates,* I, 145–46.

57. *ILN,* 17 August 1850, p. 147.

58. *Household Words,* 1 (1850), 73–77.

59. *ILN,* 2 March 1850, p. 146.

60. *Athenaeum,* 2 March 1850, p. 241.

61. McDermott, *Lost Panoramas,* pp. 41–42.

62. *ILN,* 28 July 1849, p. 55.

63. *ILN,* 1 May 1852, p. 334.

64. *London As It Is Today* (London, 1851), pp. 278–81.

65. Printed in a sixpenny pamphlet, *Comic Songs: A Collection of Originals, Sung with Applause at the London Concerts, Written by John Labern* (1852?); copy in Museum of London library.

16. SCENES OPTICAL, MECHANICAL, AND SPECTRAL

1. The Cosmorama's early stay in St. James's Street is mentioned in *Literary Gazette,* 19 May, 15 September 1821, pp. 318, 587; 12 January 1822, p. 31.

2. An illustrated "popular description" of the Cosmorama appeared in *La Belle Assemblée,* 24 (1823), 232–33.

3. *Literary Gazette,* 10 May 1823, p. 301.

4. *Literary Gazette,* 15 September 1821, p. 587.

5. *Descriptive Catalogue of the Cosmorama Panoramic Exhibition* (London, 1825); copy at BL.

6. Catalogue dated 1828 (copy at GL); handbills, EC, Cosmorama folder. A number of other handbills are in JJ Coll., Dioramas boxes 2 and 3.

7. Quoted from Arnott's *Elements of Physics* in *Mirror,* 14 (1829), 430–31.

8. Pückler-Muskau, p. 103.

9. Quoted in *Mirror,* 37 (1841), 253n.

10. Pückler-Muskau, p. 102.

11. *Athenaeum,* 26 May 1838, p. 376.

12. *Literary Gazette,* 18 February 1826, p. 108.

13. Pückler-Muskau, p. 56.

14. *Description of the Views of the British Diorama and Physiorama* (1832); copy at GL.

15. *Literary Gazette,* 20 March 1824, p. 188.

16. George Raymond, *Memoirs of Robert William Elliston, Comedian* (London, 1846), II, 232–33.

17. Joe Cowell, *Thirty Years Passed among the Players in England and America* (New York, 1844), p. 47.

18. Allardyce Nicoll, *A History of English Drama, 1660–1900* (Cambridge, 1952–1969), IV, 27; Moncrieff, *Zoroaster; or, The Spirit of the Star* (London, 1824).

19. Handbill, WCL, box 42.

20. *Literary Gazette,* 16 August 1817, pp. 109–110.

21. *Times,* 23 June 1826; clippings, JJ Coll., London Play Places box 7.

22. Handbill, BL, EMI.

23. *Athenaeum,* 28 August 1830, p. 541.

24. Handbill, WCL, StM/LS, I, 181.

25. See Richard Armstrong, *Grace Darling: Maid and Myth* (London, 1965).

26. Handbill, WCL, D137/Egyptian Hall.

27. *Mirror,* 33 (1839), 80.

28. Handbill, WCL, StM/LS, I, 112.

29. Ibid.

30. *ILN,* 25 January 1845, p. 62.

31. *ILN,* 4 October 1845, p. 222.

32. *Times,* 14 October 1845.

33. Handbill, GL, Fairs box.

34. Another handbill, ibid.

35. See Martin Quigley, *Magic Shadows: The Story of the Origin of Motion Pictures* (New York, 1969), pp. 75–78.

36. Sir David Brewster, *Letters on Natural Magic* (London, 1832), pp. 80–81.

37. Handbill, EC.

38. *European Magazine,* 43 (1803), 186–88.

39. Stanley Mayes, *The Great Belzoni* (London, 1959), p. 66.

40. Ibid.

41. H. C. Robinson, *The London Theatre, 1811–1866* (London, 1966), p. 47.

42. Advertisements, WCL, StM/LS, II, 186–87.

43. Thomas Frost, *Lives of the Conjurors* (London, 1881), p. 206.

44. "A Railer" (Rev. Edward Stanley), *Blackwood's Magazine,* 28 (1830), 825.

45. Nicoll, IV, 113–15.

46. On the improvement of the magic lantern, see T. C. Hepworth, "The Evolution of the Magic-Lantern," *Chambers's Journal,* 6th ser. 1 (1897–98), 213–15, and the interesting evidence Henry Mayhew gathered from a lantern maker: *The Unknown Mayhew,* ed. Eileen Yeo and E. P. Thompson (New York, 1971), pp. 295–98. There is a brief article on Childe in the *Dictionary of National Biography.*

47. Handbill, WCL, StM/LS, I, 62.

48. *N & Q,* 11th ser. 2 (1910), 503.

49. Ibid.

17. ENTR'ACTE: EXHIBITIONS AND LONDON LIFE

1. *ILN,* 23 December 1843, p. 415.

2. Most of the hundreds of travel accounts by foreigners whose journeys included stays in London mention and not infrequently describe in some detail the various standard exhibitions they visited. Occasionally they supply particulars, and more often fresh perspectives, which have been used in the present pages to supplement the native sources. Two extended narratives of London show going are somewhat out of the ordinary. One is *Journal of a Residence in England, and of a Journey from and to Syria . . . originally written in Persian,* by H. R. H. Najaf Koolee Meerza, son of Prince Firman Firman, Grandson of H. M. Fathali Shah, the Late Emperor of Persia (privately printed, [1839]). The author was one of three Persian princes then exiled from their homeland for political reasons. James Baillie Fraser, the Briton who served as their escort and interpreter during their stay, wrote his own account in *Narrative of the Residence of the Persian Princes in London, in 1835 and 1836* (London, 1838; rptd. New York, 1973), which offers a rare opportunity to observe the observers. Another noteworthy book by exotic visitors from this period is *Journal of a Residence of Two Years and a Half in Great Britain* by two Parsee naval architects, Jehangeer Nowrojee and Hirjeebhoy Merwanjee (London, 1841). Both books are permeated with a naif-Oriental flavor which has the merit of distinguishing them from more prosaic accounts by Europeans and Americans. They are, however, overflowing with romantic fancy and misinformation, and for that reason have been used sparingly in what aspires to be a factual study.

3. *Quarterly Review,* 96 (1854), 76.

4. *Sketches from Mr. Mathews at Home* (London, n.d.).

5. B. W. Richardson, *Thomas Sopwith* (London, 1891), pp. 81–82.

6. *ILN,* 1 May 1851, p. 383.

7. *ILN,* 13 November 1852, p. 407.

8. Pückler-Muskau, p. 157; A. St. H. Brock, *A History of Fireworks* (London, 1949), p. 60.

9. *Benjamin Robert Haydon: Correspondence and Table-Talk* (London, 1876), II, 405.

10. Quoted in *Chambers's Journal,* 3rd ser. 13 (1860), 34–35.

11. Barnum, I, 257.

12. *ILN,* 27 May 1848, p. 348.

13. *New Monthly Magazine,* 76 (1846), 94–95. There is more on Lord Stowell in John Timbs, *English Eccentrics and Eccentricities* (London, 1875), pp. 277–79.

14. *Blackwood's Magazine,* 51 (1842), 419.

15. *Memoirs of Charles Mathews* (London, 1839), IV, 133–34, 129.

16. William Jerdan, *Autobiography* (London, 1852–1853), II, 88.

17. *Report from the Select Committee on National Monuments* (1841), q. 3171.

18. *Sophie in London,* trans. Clare Williams (London, 1933), pp. 141–42.

19. Robert Southey, *Letters from England,* ed. Jack Simmons (London, 1951), pp. 69, 77–78.

20. Grant Thorburn, *Men and Manners in Britain; or, A Bone to Gnaw for the Trollopes, Fidlers, etc. . . .* (New York, 1834), pp. 35–36.

21. *Edinburgh Review,* 17 (1810), 169.

22. "The Old and the New Schoolmaster," *London Magazine,* 3 (1821), 495.

23. *The Newcomes,* Ch. XVI.

24. [George Mogridge], *Old Humphrey's Walks in London and Its Neighbourhood* (London, [1843]), p. iv.

25. Handbill, WCL, StM/Gen, p. 179.

26. MS note quoting *Weekly Dispatch,* 4 November 1838, in GL, Egyptian Hall folder.

27. E. St. John Brooks, *Sir Hans Sloane* (London, 1954), p. 219.

28. P. Chalmers Mitchell, *Centenary History of the Zoological Society of London* (London, 1929), p. 10.

29. Clipping, EC, Catherine St. folder.

30. *A Syllabus of a Course of Lectures on Astronomy . . .* (Oxford, 1818); copy in Science Museum Library.

31. Clipping, EC, Exeter Change folder.

32. The most authoritative modern history of Leicester Square and its neighborhood is in *Survey of London,* XXXIV (1966); see especially the section on "The Social Character of Leicester Square," pp. 428–31. The following passage is based also on several of the numerous contemporary descriptions.

33. Tom Taylor, *Leicester Square: Its Associations and Its Worthies* (London, 1874), p. 272n. "Quite incredible to me," says Taylor, pointing out that the authority for the story was an eighty-seven-year-old man, reminiscing in 1825.

34. See, for example, *Punch,* 12 (1847), 71, 190.

35. Henry Mayhew, *London Labour and the London Poor* (London, 1861–1862; rptd. New York, 1968), III, 46.

36. The history of Savile House is recounted in detail in *Survey of London,* XXXIV (1966), 462–64.

37. Handbill, WCL, StM/LS, I, 114.

38. Quoted in *Survey of London,* XXXIV (1966), 464, and in Raymond Mander and Joe Mitchenson, *The Lost Theatres of London* (London, 1968), pp. 59–60. In neither place is the source of the passage given.

39. Mander and Mitchenson, p. 60.

40. The fullest source on paper panoramas,

on which this discussion is based, is *Life in England in Aquatint and Lithography, 1770–1860 . . . from the Library of J. R. Abbey* (London, 1953), pp. 373–410.

41. *Mirror*, 16 (1830), 231.

42. Helmut and Alison Gernsheim, *The History of Photography* (New York, 1969), p. 142.

43. *Literary Gazette*, 28 January 1826, pp. 61, 63; Janet Dunbar, *The Early Victorian Woman: Some Aspects of Her Life (1837–57)* (London, 1953), p. 37.

44. Helmut and Alison Gernsheim, *L. J. M. Daguerre* (London, 1956), p. 39.

45. On the magic lantern in the Victorian home, see David Francis, "Pictures on the Christmas Wall: Two Hundred and Fifty Years of the Magic Lantern," *Country Life*, 142 (1967), 1454–58.

46. William Hone, *Ancient Mysteries Described* (London, 1823), pp. 230–31.

47. *Harriet Martineau's Autobiography . . . ,* 2nd ed. (London, 1877), I, 15, 20.

48. This paragraph is based on B. E. C. Howarth-Loomes, *Victorian Photography* (New York, 1974), pp. 69–70.

49. *Art Journal*, n.s. 2 (1856), 120.

18. WILLIAM BULLOCK AND THE EGYPTIAN HALL

1. *Survey of London*, XXXI (1963), 62.

2. Abrahams, cited in n. 5 below, pp. 61–62.

3. *Jane Austen's Letters to Her Sister Cassandra and Others*, ed. R. W. Chapman (Oxford, 1952), p. 267.

4. Louis Simond, *An American in Regency England* (London, 1968), p. 139.

5. The most extensive historical description of the building itself is in *Survey of London*, XXIX (1960), 266–70. Fuller treatments of the Egyptian Hall as an entertainment center are Aleck Abrahams, "The Egyptian Hall, Piccadilly, 1813–1873," *Antiquary*, 42 (1906), 61–64, 139–44, 225–30; W. H. Mullens, "William Bullock's London Museum," *Museums Journal*, 17 (1917–18), 51–56, 132–37, 180–87; and Hugh Honour, "Curiosities of the Egyptian Hall," *Country Life*, 115 (1954), 38–39. Across the years, *N & Q* printed numerous notes on the hall and its exhibitions and entertainments; see especially 5th ser. 3 (1875), 249, 284–85, 297, 302–303, 396, 451; 10th ser. 3 (1905), 163–64, 236–37, 297, 334, 411–12, 451–52; 4 (1905), 37, 65–66; 11th ser. 5 (1912), 514; 6 (1912), 92, 158. As I was concluding my research, Dr. Anthony

Burton of the Victoria and Albert Museum library kindly called my attention to still another article, Gertrude Bacon, "The Story of the Egyptian Hall," *English Illustrated Magazine*, 23 (1902–1903), 298–308, which drew upon a "complete and most valuable" collection of handbills owned by the hall's last lessee. There are collections of handbills and other documents at WCL, GL (scrapbook, Granger 2.5.7), and EC (Egyptian Hall folder).

6. Leigh Hunt, *A Saunter through the West End* (London, 1861), p. 43.

7. William Jerdan, *Men I Have Known* (London, 1866), p. 70.

8. Ibid., p. 71.

9. *Descriptive Synopsis of the Roman Gallery . . .* (London, 1816); copy at BL.

10. Clippings in Harvard Theatre Collection, Panorama box. See also E. Tangye Lean, *The Napoleonists: A Study in Political Disaffection, 1760–1960* (London, 1970), p. 63.

11. "David Hughson" (Edwin Pugh), *Walks through London* (London, 1817), II, 329–40.

12. *N & Q*, 9th ser. 1 (1898), 327; 10th ser. 12 (1909), 211. There is a ten-page catalogue of this show in JJ Coll., London Play Places box 4.

13. Handbill, JJ Coll., London Play Places box 4.

14. Benjamin Robert Haydon, *Diary*, ed. Willard Bissell Pope (Cambridge, Mass., 1960–1963), II, 451.

15. William Jerdan, *Autobiography* (London, 1852–1853), II, 87–88.

16. Elizabeth Longford, *Wellington: The Years of the Sword* (London, 1969), p. 482. The carriage is described in detail in *Repository of Arts, Literature, and Fashion*, 2nd ser. 1 (1816), 99–103.

17. *The Farington Diary*, ed. James Greig (New York, 1922–1928), VIII, 88.

18. Quoted in Jerdan, *Autobiography*, II, 87–88.

19. *N & Q*, 10th ser. 7 (1907), 393.

20. Abrahams, p. 62.

21. Handbill, GL, Fairs box.

22. John Theodore Tussaud, *The Romance of Madame Tussauds* (London, 1920), pp. 82–93.

23. Abrahams, pp. 63–64.

24. Jessie M. Sweet, "William Bullock's Collection and the University of Edinburgh, 1819," *Annals of Science*, 26 (1970), 23–32.

25. *The Banks Letters: A Calendar of the Manuscript Correspondence of Sir Joseph Banks . . .* (London, 1958), p. 185.

26. Except as noted, this passage on the sale of the Bullock collection is derived from *The

History of the Collections Contained in the Natural History Departments of the British Museum (London, 1904–1906), II, 208–45, which reprints a marked catalogue.

27. The Scott-Terry correspondence is found in *Letters of Sir Walter Scott*, ed. H. J. C. Grierson (London, 1932–1937), V, 361–65, 457–58, 462, 499–500, and Wilfred Partington, *Sir Walter's Post-Bag . . .* (London, 1932), pp. 133–34.

28. Sweet, p. 27.

29. The first-hand account, followed here, is in *The Autobiography and Memoirs of Benjamin Robert Haydon*, ed. Tom Taylor (New York, 1926), I, 279–88.

30. The best of several modern biographies of Belzoni is Stanley Mayes, *The Great Belzoni* (London, 1959), on which this passage is based.

31. *Times*, 30 April 1821.

32. *Literary Gazette*, 9 March 1822, pp. 152–54; reprinted in *The Magic Lantern; or, Sketches of Scenes in the Metropolis* (London, 1822), pp. 39–51. A somewhat similar description of the spectators at a panorama of Waterloo had appeared in the *Literary Gazette*, 29 August 1818, pp. 556–58.

33. William Bullock, *Six Months' Residence and Travels in Mexico* (London, 1824), pp. 27–28, 424–28.

34. See *A Descriptive Catalogue of the Exhibition, Entitled Ancient and Modern Mexico* (London, 1824); copy at BL. There is an extended description of the exhibition in the *Literary Gazette*, 3, 10 January 1824, pp. 9, 25–26.

35. *Literary Gazette*, 10 April 1824, p. 237.

36. Advertisement, GL, Egyptian Hall scrapbook.

37. William Bullock, *Sketch of a Journey through the Western States of North America* (London, 1827).

38. The estate is described in *Cincinnati: A Guide to the Queen City and Its Neighbors* (Cincinnati, 1943), pp. 527–28.

39. All that follows on Mrs. Trollope and Bullock in Cincinnati is from her *Domestic Manners of the Americans*, ed. Donald L. Smalley (New York, 1949), especially pp. xxiv–xxviii, 50–51, 61–63, 67, 167ff. I am indebted to Professor Andrew Wright for reminding me of this valuable source.

40. See Clay Lancaster, "The Egyptian Hall and Mrs. Trollope's Bazaar," *Magazine of Art*, 43 (1950), 94–99, 112.

41. Wilbur S. Shepperson, "William Bullock—An American Failure," *Bulletin of the*

Historical and Philosophical Society of Ohio, 19 (1961), 151–52.

42. Tussaud, p. 84.

43. *N & Q,* 5th ser. 3 (1875), 303.

44. Jerdan, *Autobiography,* II, 85.

45. Haydon, *Autobiography,* I, 280.

46. *Times,* 18 September 1854.

47. There is an extensive but not exhaustive list in John Timbs, *Curiosities of London* (London, [1867]), pp. 320–21. It can be supplemented from the primary materials on the Egyptian Hall found at EC, GL, WCL, and JJ Coll.

48. The first attraction, the double male child, is cited in Timbs; the rest are represented in JJ Coll., London Play Places box 9.

49. Handbill, WCL, D137/Egyptian Hall.

50. Pückler-Muskau, p. 56.

51. *Catalogue of the Napoleon Museum or, Illustrated History of Europe . . .* (London, 1843), copy at GL; *Times,* 13 April 1843.

52. *Times,* 24–27 June 1845.

19. FREAKS IN THE AGE OF IMPROVEMENT

1. *Literary Gazette,* 9 August 1828, p. 508.

2. Legend reproduced in several of the prints depicting him.

3. *Kirby's Wonderful and Scientific Museum* (London, 1803–1820), II, 408–409.

4. See George, VIII, 426–27, 437, 484.

5. John Timbs, *English Eccentrics and Eccentricities* (London, 1875), pp. 250–53.

6. George, VIII, 485.

7. "Giants and Dwarfs," *Strand Magazine,* 8 (1894), 263.

8. Ibid., pp. 432–33; *Literary Gazette,* 16 February 1822, pp. 105–106.

9. Handbill, WCL, C138/Old Bond St.

10. Handbill, WCL, StM/LS, I, 463.

11. *Literary Gazette,* 13 March 1824, p. 172.

12. Handbill, EC, Exhibitions (Various) folder.

13. General Tom Thumb figures prominently, of course, in the contemporary and modern literature about Barnum, including the impresario's own *Struggles and Triumphs* (I, 240–58, 284–90). A recent popular treatment occurs in Raymund Fitzsimons, *Barnum in London* (New York, 1970).

14. Fitzsimons, pp. 133–35.

15. Ibid.

16. *ILN,* 21 February 1846, p. 135.

17. Handbill, WCL, A138/Leicester Square.

18. *Literary Gazette,* 15 May 1824, pp. 316–17.

19. Charles Knight, *London* (London, 1841–1844), III, 206.

20. *Memoirs of Charles Mathews* (London, 1839), IV, 135–36.

21. *Times,* 10 June 1824.

22. *Literary Gazette,* 19 June 1824, p. 398.

23. The following narrative is based chiefly on the *Times,* 15, 17 June 1824, and *Annual Register, 1824,* Chronicle pp. 70–71.

24. *The Complete Poetical Works of Thomas Hood,* ed. Walter Jerrold (London, 1906), p. 16.

25. *Literary Gazette,* 5 July 1828, p. 428.

26. The whole history of Chang and Eng is told in Kay Hunter, *Duet for a Lifetime: The Story of the Siamese Twins* (New York, 1964).

27. *Poetical Works of E. L. Bulwer* (Paris, 1836), pp. 147–49.

28. *Literary Gazette,* 28 November 1829, p. 780.

29. *Times,* 23 November 1829.

30. *Times,* 25 November 1829; *Philosophical Transactions of the Royal Society of London, 1830,* part I, pp. 177–86.

31. Seurat is extensively described in *Hone's Every Day Book* (London, 1827), I, cols. 1017–34, and more tersely in the *Times,* 1, 9 August 1825, and *Annual Register, 1825,* pp. 239*–241*.

32. George, X, 525–27, lists five prints featuring Seurat.

33. *Annual Register, 1825,* p. 240*.

34. *Times,* 12 August 1825.

35. Quoted in *Examiner,* 21 August 1825, pp. 530–31.

36. *Literary Gazette,* 27 August 1825, p. 558.

37. Pückler-Muskau, p. 179.

38. Walter Jerrold, *Douglas Jerrold, Dramatist and Wit* (London, [1914]), I, 75.

39. *Examiner,* 28 August 1814, p. 555.

40. Handbill, EC, Strand folder.

41. *Times,* 27 February 1818.

42. See *Times,* 30 September; 2, 10, 31 October; 26 December 1829.

43. W. T. Parke, *Musical Memoirs* (London, 1830; rptd. New York, 1970), II, 290–92.

44. *Times,* 8 March 1830.

45. *Times,* 25 June 1830.

46. Odell, III, 593–94.

47. *ILN,* 29 August 1846, p. 143.

48. Neil Harris, *Humbug: The Art of P. T. Barnum* (Boston, 1973), p. 98.

49. *ILN,* 5 September 1846, p. 154.

50. *Times,* 1 September 1846.

51. For Leech's early career, see Odell, IV, 368. There is further information in an undated newspaper clipping in GL, Egyptian Hall folder.

52. *Times,* 27 April 1847.

53. Henry Mayhew, *London Labour and the London Poor* (London, 1861–1862), III, 103.

54. This story is from the clipping mentioned in n. 51.

55. Joseph N. Ireland, *Records of the New York Stage from 1750 to 1860* (New York, 1866; rptd. New York, 1966), II, 318–19.

56. Title quoted in R. Toole-Stott, *Circus and Allied Arts* (Derby, 1958–1971), II, 162.

57. *ILN,* 4 July 1857, p. 11.

58. Francis T. Buckland, *Curiosities of Natural History,* 3rd ser., 2nd ed. (London, 1868), II, 40–42. There is a fuller description in an advertisement in the *Athenaeum,* 11 July 1857, p. 885.

59. *ILN,* 29 March 1862, p. 316.

60. Buckland, II, 40–42.

20. THE NOBLE SAVAGE RECONSIDERED

1. Loren Eiseley, *Darwin's Century* (Garden City, N.Y., 1961), p. 260.

2. See Sir Harry Johnston, *A History and Description of the British Empire in Africa* (London, 1910; rptd. New York, 1969), pp. 72–73.

3. *Memoirs of Charles Mathews* (London, 1839), IV, 136–37.

4. Except as indicated, this narrative of the Hottentot Venus in London is drawn from the *Times,* 26, 29 November 1810, and material in Lysons, I, 101–103.

5. *Memoirs of Charles Mathews,* IV, 136–39.

6. R. Toole-Stott, *Circus and Allied Arts* (Derby, 1958–1971), III, 334–36.

7. George, VIII, 947–49, 959; IX, 654–56.

8. Toole-Stott, II, 152.

9. Reprinted in Cuvier's *Discours sur les révolutions du globe, étude sur l'ibis et mémoire sur la vénus hottentote . . .* (Paris, 1864), pp. 211–22.

10. *Literary Gazette,* 23 February 1822, pp. 123–24.

11. *Literary Gazette,* 19 January, 9 February 1822, pp. 45, 87.

12. *Reminiscences of Thomas Dibdin* (London, 1837), II, 194–97.

13. John Timbs, *Curiosities of London* (London, [1867]), p. 320.

14. *Literary Gazette,* 19 January 1822, p. 45.

15. *Times,* 21 January 1822.

16. *Literary Gazette,* 19 January 1822, p. 45.

17. *Literary Gazette,* 9 March 1822, p. 156.

18. *Literary Gazette,* 5 October 1822, p. 638.

19. *Literary Gazette,* 16 November 1822, p. 733.

20. Rachel Field, *God's Pocket* (New York, 1934), pp. 52–54.

21. Except as noted, the following narrative of Catlin's London adventures is drawn from his *Notes of Eight Years' Travels and Residence in Europe, with His North American Indian Collection* (New York, 1848).

22. Bernard DeVoto, *Across the Wide Missouri* (Boston, 1947), p. 392.

23. Handbill, WCL, D137/Egyptian Hall.

24. Marjorie Catlin Roehm, *The Letters of George Catlin and His Family: A Chronicle of the American West* (Berkeley, 1966), pp. 207–208.

25. *Athenaeum,* 10 February 1844, pp. 135–36.

26. *ILN,* 13 January 1844, p. 31.

27. Quoted in A. N. L. Munby, *The Formation of the Phillipps Library from 1841 to 1872,* Phillipps Studies no. 4 (Cambridge, 1956), pp. 53–54.

28. *Athenaeum,* 20 April 1844, p. 360.

29. *Times,* 3 April 1844.

30. *Times,* 8 August 1844.

31. *Times,* 17 August 1844.

32. *ILN,* 10, 24, 31 August, 21 September 1844, pp. 91, 126, 129–30, 190.

33. *Household Words,* 7 (1853), 168.

34. See Philip D. Curtin, *The Image of Africa: British Ideas and Action, 1780–1850* (Madison, 1964), esp. pp. 328–31, 338, 364.

35. Timothy Severin, *The African Adventure: A History of Africa's Explorers* (London, 1973), p. 146.

36. *Athenaeum,* 6 December 1845, p. 1177.

37. Handbill, WCL, D137/Egyptian Hall.

38. *Athenaeum,* 15 May 1847, p. 521.

39. *Times,* 19 May 1847; see also John Conolly, *The Ethnological Exhibitions of London* (London, 1855) (copy in Forster Collection, Victoria and Albert Museum), pp. 8–11.

40. *ILN,* 12 June 1847, p. 381.

41. "The Amusements of the People," *Household Words,* 1 (1850), 58.

42. *ILN,* 14 September 1850, p. 236.

43. *Athenaeum,* 28 May 1853, p. 650.

44. *Times,* 18 May 1853.

45. "The Noble Savage," *Household Words,* 7 (1853), 168.

46. Handbill, WCL, StM/LS, I, 81.

47. Quoted in N. P. Willis, *Famous Persons and Places* (New York, 1855), p. 436.

48. Ibid., pp. 439–41.

49. *Athenaeum,* 9 July 1853, pp. 824–25.

50. Advertisement ibid., p. 828.

51. Richard Owen, *The Life of Richard Owen* (New York, 1894), I, 402.

52. *ILN,* 30 July 1853, p. 66.

53. *ILN,* 13 August 1853, p. 121.

54. *Athenaeum,* 1 October 1853, p. 1170.

55. Handbill, WCL, StM/LS, I, 81.

56. Conolly, pp. 25–28; tearsheet from *Illustrated Magazine of Art,* JJ Coll., Human Freaks box 4.

57. *Times,* 7 May 1853.

58. Handbill, WCL, box 42, no. 3.

59. *Athenaeum,* 23 December 1854, p. 1561; *ILN,* 6 January 1855, p. 15.

60. *ILN,* 18 February 1854, p. 148; *Athenaeum,* 28 January 1854, p. 121.

61. Francis T. Buckland, *Curiosities of Natural History,* 3rd ser., 2nd ed. (London, 1868), II, 57n.

62. *ILN,* 12 July 1856, p. 41.

21. THE ANCIENT AND THE EXOTIC

1. The story of the Peales' mastodons has been told in numerous places. The present summary is based mainly on George Gaylord Simpson, "The Beginnings of Vertebrate Paleontology in North America," *Proceedings of the American Philosophical Society,* 86 (1942), 158–61, and James Thomas Flexner, *America's Old Masters,* rev. ed. (New York, 1967), pp. 222–27.

2. *The Banks Letters: A Calendar of the Manuscript Correspondence of Sir Joseph Banks . . .* (London, 1958), p. 657.

3. *The Farington Diary,* ed. James Greig (New York, 1922–1928), II, 106.

4. Handbill, GL, Egyptian Hall folder.

5. Like Peale's, Koch's story is found in most books on the history of paleontology. The following account is derived from Robert Silverberg, *Scientists and Scoundrels: A Book of Hoaxes* (New York, 1965), pp. 55–60, and M. F. Ashley Montagu and C. Bernard Peterson, "The Earliest Account of the Association of Human Artifacts with Fossil Mammals in North America," *Proceedings of the American Philosophical Society,* 87 (1944), 407–19.

6. [George Mogridge], *Old Humphrey's Walks in London and Its Neighbourhood* (London, [1843]), pp. 245–46.

7. Handbill, GL, Egyptian Hall folder; *The History of the Collections Contained in the Natural History Departments of the British Museum* (London, 1904–1906), II, 55, 247, 485.

8. Handbill, EC, Exhibitions (Various) folder; John Timbs, *Curiosities of London* (London, [1867]), p. 596; *Athenaeum,* 25 January 1840, pp. 77–78.

9. *Dictionary of National Biography.*

10. Quoted in Timothy Severin, *The African Adventure* (London, 1973), pp. 186–87.

11. *Athenaeum,* 11 May 1850, p. 504.

12. *Times,* 9 June 1848.

13. *Athenaeum,* 11 May 1850, p. 504.

14. Benjamin Silliman, *A Visit to Europe in 1851* (New York, 1853), II, 445–46.

15. *Athenaeum,* 11 May 1850, p. 504.

16. *Punch,* 23 (1852), 71.

17. Severin, p. 189.

18. Barnum, II, 639, 645.

19. Handbill, GL, Playbills of London: Miscellaneous Entertainments box.

20. Printed prospectus, BL, EMI.

21. Handbill, JJ Coll., London Play Places box 3.

22. See Arthur W. Hummel, "Nathan Dunn," *Bulletin of the Friends Historical Association,* 59 (1970), 34–39. For this and other references I am indebted to John H. Platt, librarian of the Historical Society of Pennsylvania.

23. Mogridge, pp. 328–30.

24. *Times,* 9 August 1854.

25. There are copies of the *Descriptive Catalogue* at WCL and GL (S.L.26/51). See also *ILN,* 6 August 1842, pp. 204–205; *Mirror,* n.s. 2 (1842), 129–34; and *Athenaeum,* 6 August 1842, p. 711.

26. Timbs, p. 491.

27. *Art-Union,* 4 (1842), 282–83.

28. *ILN,* 31 May 1862, p. 545.

29. *ILN,* 21 August 1847, p. 127.

30. *Times,* 10 July, 15 October 1847.

31. *ILN,* 1 April 1848, pp. 220–22. There is also a full description of the craft in *ILN,* 20 May 1848, pp. 331–32.

32. *Annual Register, 1848,* Chronicle p. 63.

33. *ILN,* 20 May 1848, p. 332.

34. *Examiner,* 20 May 1848, p. 333.

35. *Examiner,* 24 June 1848, p. 403.

36. *Athenaeum,* 29 November 1851, pp. 1253–54.

37. Edward Miller, *That Noble Cabinet* (London, 1973), pp. 74–76, 221–22.

38. *Athenaeum,* 26 February 1848, pp. 216–17.

39. It is described in *ILN,* 25 June 1859, p. 620, and Timbs, p. 599.

40. *Catalogue of the Missionary Museum, Austin Friars* (1826); copy at BL.

41. William Foster, *The East India House: Its History and Associations* (London, 1924), pp. 148–51.

42. Pückler-Muskau, p. 234; Maria Edgeworth, *Letters from England, 1813–1844,* ed. Christina Colvin (Oxford, 1971), p. 539.

43. See Phyllis G. Mann, "Keats's Indian Allegory," *Keats-Shelley Journal,* 6 (1957), 4–9.

44. The fullest history and description of the tiger is Mildred Archer, *Tippoo's Tiger* (Victoria and Albert Museum Monograph no. 10, 1959). See also *Penny Magazine,* 4 (1835), 319–20.

45. There are descriptions of the contents at different dates in Charles Knight, *London* (London, 1841–1844), V, 62–64, and *ILN,* 9 January 1858, p. 29.

46. *All the Year Round,* n.s. 2 (1869), 209–11.

47. *Art Journal,* n.s. 3 (1851), 183.

48. *Penny Magazine,* 10 (1841), 275–77, 286–88; *ILN,* 9 March 1844, p. 149; 5 February 1848, p. 67; 9 June 1860, p. 563.

22. LIFE AND DEATH IN THE ANIMAL KINGDOM

1. *Literary Gazette,* 2 September 1820, p. 575.

2. *ILN,* 10 August 1850, p. 114.

3. *Mirror,* 1 (1822), 17–19.

4. *Times,* 21 November 1822.

5. *Literary Gazette,* 4 January 1823, p. 13.

6. *Literary Gazette,* 26 June 1824, p. 411.

7. *Times,* 26 June 1824.

8. Handbills, GL, London Playbills: Circuses and Miscellaneous Entertainments box; Lysons, V, 5; EC, Strand file.

9. Ibid.

10. George, X, 224.

11. *Mirror,* 16 (1830), 80.

12. John Timbs, *English Eccentrics and Eccentricities* (London, 1875), p. 278.

13. *Times,* 31 March, 4 April 1809.

14. Clippings and handbills, WCL, F138/Charing Cross; *Mirror,* 18 (1831), 104–107.

15. Richard Owen, *Life of Richard Owen* (New York, 1894), I, 323–25.

16. *Punch,* 15 (1848), 243.

17. *ILN,* 19 May 1849, p. 318; 2 June 1849, p. 384.

18. *ILN,* 7 May 1859, p. 443; Francis T. Buckland, *Curiosities of Natural History,* 3rd ser., 2nd ed. (London, 1868), II, 128.

19. *Times,* 13 March 1833.

20. Handbill, WCL, StM/LS, I, 80.

21. *Athenaeum,* 16 September 1843, p. 845.

22. Handbill, WCL, C138/New Bond St.

23. Another handbill, ibid.

24. *ILN,* 10, 24 July 1852, pp. 22, 62.

25. Lysons, II, 90–91.

26. *Literary Gazette,* 21 February 1829, p. 132.

27. Handbills, GL, Playbills of London, Circuses and Miscellaneous Entertainments box, and folders of tavern bills.

28. Clipping, EC, Exeter Change folder.

29. Handbill, BL, Playbills 366.

30. Clippings, etc., in EC, Exeter Change folder, and WCL, StM/LS, II, 189–93.

31. *Byron's Letters and Journals,* ed. Leslie A. Marchand (London, 1973–), III, 206–207.

32. *Times,* 10 January 1828.

33. Frederick Cummings and Allen Staley, *Romantic Art in Britain: Paintings and Drawings, 1760–1860* (Philadelphia, 1968), pp. 172–73; C. F. Hardy, "The Life and Work of Jacques Laurent Agasse," *Connoisseur,* 45 (1916), 195.

34. Benjamin R. Haydon, *Diary,* ed. Willard Bissell Pope (Cambridge, Mass., 1960–1963), I, 128, 130.

35. James A. Manson, *Sir Edwin Landseer, R.A.* (London, 1914), pp. 22, 44–45.

36. *European Magazine,* 61 (1812), 53.

37. *Times,* 18 January 1812.

38. *Annual Register, 1826,* Chronicle p. 25.

39. *Annual Register, 1825,* Chronicle pp. 153–55.

40. The following narrative is based on the extensive contemporary coverage represented in the Exeter Change files at EC and WCL, as well as the *Times* for the relevant days, *Mirror,* 7 (1826), 145–52, and *Examiner,* 5 March 1826, pp. 147–48.

41. This account from "a correspondent" is in Buckland, I, 118–20.

42. *Mirror,* 7 (1826), 152.

43. Buckland, I, 118–20.

44. *Mirror,* 7 (1826), 152.

45. John Saunders in Charles Knight, *London* (London, 1841–1844), III, 206–207.

46. *Times,* 8, 10 March 1826.

47. *Mirror,* 7 (1826), 152.

48. Clipping, EC, Exeter Change folder.

49. *New Monthly Magazine,* n.s. 16 (1826), 343–44.

50. Copy in EC, Exeter Change folder.

51. *Times,* 13 December 1828; *Literary Gazette,* 25 April 1829, p. 276.

52. Quoted in John Butt and Kathleen Tillotson, *Dickens at Work* (London, 1957), p. 55.

53. *Punch,* 3 (1842), 209.

54. *The Complete Poetical Works of Thomas Hood,* ed. Walter Jerrold (London, 1906), p. 435.

23. ZOOS AND PLEASURE GARDENS

1. P. C. Mitchell, *Centenary History of the Zoological Society of London* (London, 1929), pp. 21, 31. Information on the Zoological Gardens in the following passage is from this source unless otherwise attributed.

2. *Mirror,* 12 (1828), 148–50, 408–409. There is more on the first buildings in Gordon Winter, "Early Days of the London Zoo," *Country Life Annual, 1966,* pp. 50–52.

3. John Britton and E. W. Brayley, *Memoirs of the Tower of London* (London, 1830), p. 362.

4. John Timbs, *Curiosities of London* (London, [1867]), p. 838. Detailed descriptions of the Zoo as it was between 1836 and 1852 are found in the *Quarterly Review,* 56 (1836), 309–32, and 98 (1855–56), 220–48; Leigh Hunt, *Men, Women, and Books,* new ed. (London, 1891), pp. 36–53; and *Bentley's Miscellany,* 31 (1852), 622–28.

5. *Quarterly Review,* 98 (1855–56), 222, 228; Hunt, p. 52.

6. *Quarterly Review,* 61 (1836), 318–19.

7. Hunt, pp. 51–52.

8. *Bentley's Miscellany,* 31 (1852), 622–28; *Athenaeum,* 5 October 1850, p. 1041; 28 May 1859, p. 714.

9. *Quarterly Review,* 98 (1855–56), 223.

10. Warwick Wroth, *London Pleasure Gardens* (London, 1896), p. 318. This book, James G. Southworth, *Vauxhall Gardens* (New York, 1941), and W. S. Scott, *Green Retreats* (London, 1955), are the fullest sources on the gardens' declining years.

11. Pückler-Muskau, p. 157.

12. Southworth, p. 102.

13. Handbill, EC, Vauxhall box.

14. *Edmund Yates: His Recollections and Experiences* (London, 1884), I, 140.

15. Max Schlesinger, *Saunterings in and about London,* trans. Otto Wenckstern (London, 1853), p. 40.

16. *New Oxford Illustrated Dickens* (London, 1957), pp. 126–29. Compare Albert Smith's description of Vauxhall out of season in his *Sketches of London Life and Characters* (London, 1859), pp. 149–58.

17. L. T. C. Rolt, *The Aeronauts* (New York, 1966), pp. 121–36.

18. Southworth, p. 65.

19. *Edmund Yates,* I, 141.

20. Wroth, p. 323.

21. *Athenaeum,* 16 July 1859, p. 83. This article was one of several obituaries of Vauxhall published when it closed for good; another was in *Chambers's Journal,* 3rd ser. 12 (1859), 158–60.

22. *Athenaeum,* 23 September 1848, p. 962.

23. Eric de Maré, *The London Doré Saw* (London, 1973), p. 185.

24. Material on the Surrey Gardens not otherwise attributed is from eight scrapbooks at BL (TC 51–58) and from EC, Surrey Gardens file. There is a chapter on the gardens in Warwick Wroth, *Cremorne and the Later London Gardens* (London, 1907), pp. 83–92.

25. *Mirror,* 19 (1832), 1.

26. Rolt, pp. 138–39.

27. *Mirror,* 33 (1839), 321. A detailed description of the performance appeared in the *Times,* 26 June 1839.

28. *Mirror,* 37 (1841), 322–24, 372.

29. *Mirror,* 37 (1841), 370.

30. *ILN,* 3 June 1843, p. 394.

31. *ILN,* 1, 8 June 1844, pp. 345, 374.

32. *ILN,* 22 May 1847, p. 331.

33. *Punch,* 16 (1849), 236.

34. *Punch,* 19 (1850), 42.

35. Handbill, EC, Surrey Gardens file.

36. [John R. Tait], *European Life, Legend and Landscape* (Philadelphia, 1859), pp. 32–33.

37. Handbill, GL, Egyptian Hall folder.

38. *Punch,* 9 (1845), 81.

39. *Theatrical and Concert Companion #514* (playbill), BL, Surrey Gardens scrapbook no. 3.

40. Adam Carse, *Life of Jullien* (Cambridge, 1951), pp. 52–54.

41. Ibid., pp. 61–63.

42. *Punch,* 19 (1850), 42.

24. THE WAXEN AND THE FLESHLY

1. "Aleph" (W. Harvey), *London Scenes and London People* (London, 1863), pp. 58–67.

2. John Timbs, *The Romance of London . . .* (London, 1865; rptd. Detroit, 1968), II, 281.

3. Samuel McKechnie, *Popular Entertainments through the Ages* (London, n.d.), p. 48.

4. Handbill, GL, Fairs box.

5. Handbill, WCL, StM/LS, II, 184.

6. *Mirror,* 11 (1828), 185.

7. JJ Coll., Waxworks volumes.

8. Placard quoted in J. T. Tussaud, *The Romance of Madame Tussauds* (London, 1920), p. 110. Unless otherwise noted, this book and the (superior) history by Leonard Cottrell, *Madame Tussaud* (London, 1951), are the sources of the following pages on the waxwork museum.

9. Catalogue, EC, Tussaud folder.

10. Albert Smith, *Sketches of London Life and Character* (London, 1859), pp. 130–31.

11. David W. Bartlett, *What I Saw in London . . .* (Auburn, N.Y., 1852), pp. 51–53.

12. Advertisement, WCL, StM/LS, I, 105.

13. *Mirror,* 37 (1841), 216–18.

14. Benjamin Silliman, *A Visit to Europe in 1851* (New York, 1853), II, 431.

15. *Punch,* 10 (1846), 210.

16. Benjamin Moran, *The Footpath and Highway; or, Wanderings of an American* (Philadelphia, 1853), pp. 217–18.

17. Barnum, I, 400–401.

18. *Letters of James Russell Lowell,* ed. C. E. Norton (Cambridge, Mass., 1904), I, 244–45.

19. *Punch,* 18 (1850), 153.

20. Handbill, WCL, StM/LS, II, 184.

21. Ibid., I, 181.

22. Handbill, WCL, F137/Panopticum.

23. Handbills, BL, EMI.

24. Handbill, GL, Fairs box.

25. Handbill, EC, Trocadero file.

26. [George Mogridge], *Old Humphrey's Walks in London and Its Neighbourhood* (London, [1843]), pp. 208–11.

27. Handbills, BL, EMI.

28. See E. J. Pyke, *A Biographical Dictionary of Wax Modellers* (Oxford, 1973), p. lx. The *Mirror,* 4 (1824), 318–19, brought the Florentine museum to the attention of its readers.

29. *Literary Gazette,* 31 December 1825, p. 843.

30. Handbill, EC, Strand folder.

31. *Mirror,* n.s. 5 (1844), 231.

32. *Times,* 28 March 1839; 2 July 1847.

33. Handbill, EC, Exhibitions (Various) folder.

34. *Athenaeum,* 13 April 1839, p. 279.

35. *Athenaeum,* 19 June 1847, p. 647; *Times,* 2 July 1847.

36. *Times,* 27 December 1854.

37. Catalogue of Kahn's museum (1851); copy at BL.

38. *Athenaeum,* 10 June 1854, p. 721.

39. *Athenaeum,* 4 March 1854, p. 280.

40. Advertisements in *Athenaeum,* various dates.

41. John Conolly, *The Ethnological Exhibitions of London* (London, 1855), pp. 34–38; *Times,* 27 December 1854.

42. *Athenaeum,* 18 July, 8 August 1857, pp. 913, 1009.

43. *Athenaeum,* 5 December 1857, p. 1520.

44. *ILN,* 4 June 1853, p. 447.

45. Handbill, WCL, box 42, no. 4.

46. *Athenaeum,* 21 May 1859, p. 682.

47. *Athenaeum,* 14 May 1859, p. 650; *ILN,* 23 January 1858, p. 78.

48. *Survey of London,* XXXI (1963), 55–56.

49. Odell, VIII, 652.

50. *Times,* 4 January 1834; Tussaud, p. 73.

51. Allardyce Nicoll, *A History of English Drama, 1660–1900* (Cambridge, 1952–1959), IV, 46–47.

52. Robertson Davies in Michael Booth et al., *The Revels History of Drama in English* (London, 1975–), VI, 219–20.

53. Stanley Mayes, *The Great Belzoni* (London, 1959), pp. 69–70.

54. A. H. Saxon, *Enter Foot and Horse* (New Haven, 1968), pp. 35–38; "Andrew Ducrow," *All the Year Round,* n.s. 7 (1872), 223–29.

55. *Blackwood's Magazine,* 29 (1831), 263.

56. Pückler-Muskau, pp. 426–27.

57. *Literary Gazette,* 20 November 1824, p. 749.

58. Allan Cunningham, *The Life of Sir David Wilkie* (London, 1843), II, 333.

59. Moore's preface to vol. VI of his *Poetical Works* (London, 1841), pp. xxiii–xxvi.

60. Cunningham, II, 243, 406–408, 415.

61. Ibid., III, 67.

62. George, XI, 585.

63. *Athenaeum,* 28 August 1830, p. 541.

64. Handbill, EC, Catherine St. folder.

65. Adam Carse, *Life of Jullien* (Cambridge, 1951), p. 44.

66. *Punch,* 12 (1847), 95.

67. *Times,* 13 April 1846.

68. Handbill, EC, Catherine St. folder.

69. *Art-Union,* 8 (1846), 73.

70. *ILN,* 17 October 1846, p. 254.

71. *ILN,* 14 November, 19 December 1846, pp. 318, 398.

72. *Mirror,* 3rd ser. 2 (1847), 253–54.

73. Advertisements, *ILN,* various dates, 1847; EC, Empire folder.

74. *ILN,* 10 April 1847, p. 238.

75. *ILN,* 26 August 1848, p. 127.

76. *ILN,* 30 September 1848, p. 207.

77. *ILN,* 12 February 1848, p. 92.

78. WCL, box 42, no. 3.

79. J. R. Planché, *Extravaganzas, 1825–1871* (London, 1879), III, 139.

80. Ibid., III, 178.

81. See Odell, V, 378–80, and Meade Minnigerode, *The Fabulous Forties: 1840–1850 . . .* (New York, 1924), pp. 140–46.

82. *Art-Union,* 9 (1847), 24.

83. Clipping, EC, Catherine St. folder.

84. *Athenaeum,* 3 February 1849, p. 118.

85. Ibid.

86. *Household Words,* 7 (1853), 64.

87. *Rogue's Progress: The Autobiography of "Lord Chief Baron" Nicholson,* ed. John L. Bradley (Boston, 1965), pp. 298–99.

88. Handbills, Harvard Theatre Collection, Panorama box; JJ Coll., London Play Places box 1.

25. MORE MECHANICAL INGENUITY

1. Clippings in WCL, StM/Gen, p. 177, and F138/Spring Gardens; Harvard Theatre Collection, Panorama box.

2. Alfred Chapuis and Edmund Droz, *Automata* (Neuchâtel and London, 1958), pp. 342–44; *Literary Gazette,* 6 December 1828, p. 782.

3. Handbill, WCL, StM/LS, I, 62.

4. Odell, IV, 42, 176.

5. Arthur W. J. G. Ord-Hume, *Clockwork Music* (London, 1973), pp. 18–19. (This source is not always to be relied upon.)

6. This passage on Weeks's museum is based on Ord-Hume, pp. 22, 44–45, 49; *Survey of London,* XXXI (1963), 55; *N & Q,* 3rd ser. 6 (1864), 46, and 7th ser. 5 (1888), 295.

7. *Literary Gazette,* 31 July 1830, p. 499.

8. *Times,* 4 January 1832.

9. Richard Rush, *The Court of London from 1819 to 1825* (London, 1873), pp. 19–21.

10. The chess player's career from this point onward is narrated in detail in C. M. Carroll, *The Great Chess Automaton* (New York, 1975), pp. 42–92.

11. Barnum, I, 113–14.

12. See William K. Wimsatt, Jr., "Poe and the Chess Automaton," *American Literature,* 11 (1939), 138–51.

13. Advertisements, WCL, StM/LS, II, 183.

14. Handbill, BL, EMI.

15. *The Farington Diary,* ed. James Greig (New York, 1922–1928), II, 116.

16. Sir David Brewster, *Letters on Natural Magic* (London, 1832), pp. 161–64.

17. Moore, *Poetical Works* (London, 1850), p. 71.

18. John Timbs, *Curiosities of London* (London, [1867]), p. 596.

19. Ord-Hume, pp. 19, 53; Francis T. Buckland, *Curiosities of Natural History,* 3rd ser., 2nd ed. (London, 1868), II, 170–73.

20. John Hollingshead, *My Lifetime* (London, 1895), I, 67–69.

21. *Times,* 12 August 1846; *ILN,* 8 August 1846, p. 96.

22. Barnum, I, 400.

23. *Chambers's Edinburgh Journal,* n.s. 6 (1846), 168–71. See also *Athenaeum,* 25 July 1846, p. 765.

24. *Punch,* 11 (1846), 83.

25. Hollingshead, II, 69.

26. *Athenaeum,* 6 December 1862, p. 739; Barnum, I, 400n.

27. *Athenaeum,* 21 June 1845, p. 621.

28. *ILN,* 28 June 1845, p. 414.

29. The following description is based on *ILN,* 19 July 1845, p. 37; *Athenaeum,* 21, 28 June, 5 July 1845, pp. 621, 638, 669–70; *Times,* 19 June 1845; *Annual Register, 1845,* Chronicle pp. 86–87; handbill, WCL, D137/Egyptian Hall.

30. *Punch,* 9 (1845), 20.

31. Handbills, WCL, F138/Spring Gardens.

32. *Literary Gazette,* 13 April 1822, p. 235.

33. *Literary Gazette,* 1 March 1834, p. 157.

34. *Athenaeum,* 1 March 1834, p. 167.

35. See Carroll, pp. 48–51.

36. The fullest account of Maelzel, Beethoven, and the Panharmonicon is in Alexander Wheelock Thayer, *Life of Beethoven,* ed. Elliot Forbes (Princeton, 1964), I, 543–45, 559–80; II, 686–88, 1094–99.

37. *Literary Gazette,* 26 September 1818, p. 622.

38. *Times,* 28 November 1811.

39. Ibid.; Ord-Hume, pp. 43, 194–95.

40. Ord-Hume, pp. 21, 54–55; handbills, WCL, StM/Gen, I, 101, 199.

41. *Oxford Companion to Music,* 10th ed. (London, 1970), p. 615.

42. *The Journals of Claire Clairmont,* ed. Marion Kingston Stocking (Cambridge, Mass., 1968), pp. 82–85.

43. Ord-Hume, p. 55.

44. See Robert-Houdin, *Memoirs,* ed. R. Shelton Mackenzie (Philadelphia, 1860), p. 172.

45. *Athenaeum,* 22 May 1830, p. 317.

46. *Times,* 20 May 1830.

47. Handbills, WCL, StM/LS, II, 159–60.

48. *Mirror,* 37 (1841), 349.

49. *Literary Gazette,* 23 March, 22 June 1822, pp. 185–86, 396.

50. Ord-Hume, p. 24.

51. Handbill, JJ Coll., London Play Places box 9.

52. *The Spectator,* ed. Donald F. Bond (Oxford, 1965), III, 3–4.

53. W. T. Parke, *Musical Memoirs* (London, 1830), II, 300–302.

54. *Literary Gazette,* 19 June 1830, p. 405; see also the issue for 5 June, p. 372, and *Athenaeum* of the same date, p. 349.

55. Parke, II, 300–302.

56. *ILN,* 23 May 1842, p. 39 and 26 July 1845, p. 63; handbill, Harvard Theatre Collection, Egyptian Hall folder; *Athenaeum,* 24 July 1841, pp. 559–60.

57. Robert-Houdin, p. 179.

58. *ILN,* 21 September 1850, p. 247.

26. THE TWO FACES OF SCIENCE

1. *Literary Gazette,* 23 March 1822, p. 186.

2. *Times,* 14 March 1801. For Cartwright's American engagements, 1817–1824, see Odell, II, 506–507, III, 73, 124.

3. Clippings, WCL, StM/Gen, p. 175, and F138/Spring Gardens.

4. WCL, F138/Spring Gardens.

5. *Literary Gazette,* 15 February 1834, p. 123.

6. Clipping, EC, Catherine St. folder; R. E. Lloyd, *An Epitome of Astronomy, Its Origin and Progress . . .* (Nottingham, 1810?), copy at BL. A description of the lecture-exhibition appeared in *London und Paris* (Weimar), 13, no. 3 (1804), 190–94.

7. Handbill, EC, unclassified.

8. Horace Wellbeloved, *London Lions . . . ,* 2nd ed. (London, 1826?), pp. 2–3.

9. *The Unknown Mayhew,* ed. Eileen Yeo and E. P. Thompson (New York, 1971), p. 296.

10. *An Explanatory Catalogue of the Cosmorama, and of Various Pieces of Mechanism and Transparencies* (London, n.d.), copy at BL; advertisement, Harvard Theatre Collection, Panorama box; *Times,* 7 May 1807.

11. *Literary Gazette,* 22 June 1822, p. 392.

12. *Literary Gazette,* 2 March 1822, p. 140.

13. *Literary Gazette,* 12 January 1822, p. 29.

14. *Literary Gazette,* 23 March 1833, p. 184.

15. *All the Year Round,* 9 (1863), 349.

16. Material on the Royal Institution's early history is drawn from Bence Jones, *The Royal Institution: Its Founder and Its First Professors* (London, 1871).

17. Anne Treneer, *The Mercurial Chemist: A Life of Sir Humphry Davy* (London, 1963), p. 86.

18. Ibid., p. 87.

19. L. Pearce Williams, *Michael Faraday: A Biography* (New York, 1965), pp. 323, 329–32.

20. D. Thompson, "John Tyndall and the Royal Institution," *Annals of Science,* 13 (1957), 9–21.

21. *ILN,* 12 January 1861, p. 29.

22. Handbill, Harvard Theatre Collection, Panorama box.

23. *Dictionary of National Biography; European Magazine,* 52 (1807), 448–49; handbill, JJ Coll., London Play Places box 3.

24. *European Magazine,* 52 (1807), 448–49.

25. Quoted in S. Bradbury, *The Microscope Past and Present* (Oxford, 1968), p. 117.

26. *Literary Gazette,* 19 July 1828, p. 463.

27. Handbill, EC, Exhibitions (Various) folder; *Mirror,* 21 (1833), 138–39.

28. *Literary Gazette,* 7 September 1833, p. 573.

29. *Athenaeum,* 10 August, 14 December 1833, pp. 533, 861.

30. Hallam Tennyson, *Alfred Lord Tennyson: A Memoir* (New York, 1898), I, 102; Christopher Ricks, *Tennyson* (New York, 1972), p. 114.

31. Hallam Tennyson, I, 102.

32. Pückler-Muskau, p. 172.

33. Najaf Koolee Meerza, *Journal of a Residence in England . . .* (privately printed, 1839), I, 304–305.

34. J. H. Macmichael, *The Story of Charing Cross* (London, 1906), p. 26.

35. *Survey of London,* XXIX (1960), 352–54; W. T. O'Dea, *Lighting 2: Gas, Mineral Oil, Electricity* (Science Museum Illustrated Booklet, 1967).

36. *Mirror,* 33 (1839), 249–50; *Literary Gazette,* 8, 15, 29 May 1824, pp. 300, 317, 345.

37. BL, EMI.

38. Handbill, EC, Exhibitions (Various) folder.

39. *Mirror,* 33 (1839), 249–50.

40. *ILN,* 8 January 1848, p. 3.

41. *London As It Is Today* (London, 1851), p. 275.

42. *Athenaeum,* 25 July 1835, p. 573; *Times,* same date; L. T. C. Rolt, *The Aeronauts* (London, 1966), pp. 207–208.

43. *Athenaeum,* 21, 28 March 1828, pp. 272, 299; descriptive pamphlet, GL (5486).

44. *Literary Gazette,* 30 June 1832, pp. 412–13.

45. Handbill, GL, Fairs box.

46. Handbills, WCL, StM/LS, II, 130–31.

47. Facts and figures relating to the Thames Tunnel as a tourist attraction are found in Charles E. Lee, *The East London Line and the Thames Tunnel,* a London Transport publication (London, 1976), pp. 8–11. See also n. 53 below.

48. *Times,* 31 January 1834; *Literary Gazette,* 8 February 1834, pp. 99–100.

49. George Catlin, *Notes of Eight Years' Travels . . .* (New York, 1848), II, 112–13.

50. *Life in England in Aquatint and Lithography . . . from the Library of J. R. Abbey* (London, 1953), p. 397.

51. Handbill, JJ Coll., Dioramas box 2.

52. Max Schlesinger, *Saunterings in and about London* (London, 1853), pp. 144–45.

53. Hawthorne, *English Notebooks,* ed. Randall Stewart (New York, 1941), pp. 232–33. A few additional details have been taken from descriptions by other Americans: David W. Bartlett, *What I Saw in London* (Auburn, N.Y., 1852), pp. 163–69, and Bayard Taylor, *Views A-Foot; or Europe Seen with Knapsack and Staff* (New York, 1860), p. 85.

27. TECHNOLOGY FOR THE MILLION

1. A useful source on the history of national and international exhibitions is Kenneth W. Luckhurst, *The Story of Exhibitions* (London, 1951).

2. Derek Hudson and Kenneth W. Luckhurst, *The Royal Society of Arts* (London, 1954), pp. 187–88, 294–95.

3. Luckhurst, *The Story of Exhibitions,* pp. 81–82; John Timbs, *Curiosities of London* (London, [1867]), p. 599; *Literary Gazette,* 28 June, 20 September 1828, pp. 401, 600–601.

4. JJ Coll., London Play Places box 3.

5. Material on Perkins otherwise unattributed is from Greville and Dorothy Bathe, *Jacob Perkins: His Inventions, His Times, and His Contemporaries* (Philadelphia, 1943), passim.

6. S. G. Goodrich, *Recollections of a Lifetime* (New York, 1857; rptd. Detroit, 1967), II, 226.

7. *New Monthly Magazine,* 13 (1825), 194–95.

8. Thomas Balston, *John Martin* (London, 1947), p. 146.

9. *National Gallery of Practical Science, Catalogue,* 7th ed. (London, 1834). I am indebted to Graham Fyffe for a photocopy of this publication.

10. See M. Veronica Stokes, "The Lowther Arcade in the Strand," *London Topographical Record,* 23 (1974), 119–28.

11. *National Gallery of Practical Science, Catalogue* passim; WCL, Pamphlet D-33. For more details, see *Mirror,* 26 (1835), 113–16, 135–38, 150–51, and Timbs, p. 589.

12. W. P. Frith, *My Autobiography and Reminiscences* (London, 1887), I, 27.

13. *Penny Magazine,* 4 (1835), 418.

14. WCL, StM/Gen, I, 160.

15. *Athenaeum,* 24 May 1845, p. 518.

16. Handbill, EC, Adelaide Gallery file.

17. Timbs, p. 589.

18. *Penny Magazine,* 4 (1835), 417.

19. Helmut and Alison Gernsheim, *L. J. M. Daguerre* (London, 1956), pp. 145–57, 162–63.

20. *Athenaeum,* 7 August 1841, p. 585.

21. *Mirror,* n.s. 1 (1842), 47, 101.

22. *ILN,* 1 October 1842, p. 335.

23. WCL, F137/Lowther Arcade; Barnum, I, 260.

24. Neil Harris, *Humbug* (Boston, 1973), p. 98.

25. Handbill, EC, Adelaide Gallery file; *Athenaeum,* 1 August 1840, p. 612.

26. EC, Adelaide Gallery file; WCL, StM/Gen, I, 170.

27. WCL, StM/Gen, I, 167–69.

28. EC, Adelaide Gallery file.

29. Ibid.

30. *Times,* 15 December 1843.

31. EC, Adelaide Gallery file.

32. Unidentified clipping, ibid.

33. Ibid.

34. *Mirror,* 3rd ser. 2 (1847), 322. The Adelaide Gallery's vulgarized atmosphere and clientele at this time were described in Albert Smith's sketch "The Casino," in his *Gavarni in London* (London, 1849), reprinted as *Sketches of London Life and Character* (London, 1859), pp. 26–31.

35. See George Speaight, *History of the English Puppet Theatre* (London, 1955), pp. 240–44.

36. WCL, F137/Lowther Arcade.

37. WCL, StM/Gen, I, 165; *ILN,* 5 July 1856, p. 23.

38. WCL, F137/Lowther Arcade.

39. *ILN,* 22 March, 12 April 1856, pp. 303, 374.

40. *Times,* 29 March 1842.

41. See J. Laurence Pritchard, *Sir George Cayley: The Inventor of the Aeroplane* (London, 1961). Cayley's connection with the Polytechnic is discussed briefly on pp. 125–27. The short treatment of the Polytechnic's early history in Ethel M. Wood, *A History of the Polytechnic* (London, 1965), Ch. 1, draws upon Pritchard.

42. Wood, pp. 20–21; *Athenaeum,* 4 August 1838, pp. 554–55. The steady inflow of new

exhibits and the topics of current lectures and demonstrations were recorded week by week in the Polytechnic's advertisements in the *ILN, Athenaeum,* and elsewhere.

43. Jehangeer Nowrojee and Hirjeebhoy Merwangee, *Journal of a Residence of Two Years and a Half in Great Britain* (London, 1841), pp. 117–18. An extensive description of the Polytechnic's other exhibits follows this passage.

44. *Comic Almanack for 1842.* See also the mildly facetious description of the Polytechnic in *Punch,* 5 (1843), 91.

45. *Athenaeum,* 12 December 1840, p. 990.

46. George Catlin, *Notes of Eight Years' Travels . . .* (New York, 1848), II, 118.

47. Pritchard, p. 127.

48. Gernsheim, pp. 151–52, 155.

49. *Athenaeum,* 31 December 1853, p. 1596.

50. EC, Polytechnic box.

51. *Athenaeum,* 24 July 1841, p. 560.

52. *Athenaeum,* 15 May 1858, p. 628.

53. J. R. Planché, *Extravaganzas, 1825–1871* (London, 1879), III, 166.

54. *Athenaeum,* 22 July, 12 August, 2 September 1848, pp. 729, 808, 884.

55. *ILN,* 26 June 1852, p. 503.

56. Unidentified clipping, EC, Polytechnic box.

57. *ILN,* 19 January 1856, p. 71.

58. *Times,* 16 November 1857.

59. *ILN,* 10 October 1857, p. 363.

60. *Athenaeum,* 27 March 1852, p. 356.

61. Albert Smith, *The Wassail-Bowl* (London, 1843), I, 75–76.

62. "The Amusements of the People," *Household Words,* 1 (1850), 13.

63. *Athenaeum,* 29 July 1854, p. 945.

64. *Athenaeum,* 14 June 1856, p. 748.

65. *ILN,* 3 February 1855, pp. 117–18.

66. *ILN,* 14 April 1855, p. 347.

67. *Athenaeum,* 28 October 1854, p. 1306; 12 May 1855, p. 556.

68. *Athenaeum,* 27 December 1856, p. 1612.

69. *ILN,* 26 June 1858, pp. 626, 631.

70. *ILN,* 11 September 1858, p. 241.

71. *ILN,* 15 January 1859, p. 63.

72. *Times,* 5 January 1859.

73. *Times,* 5, 14, 25 January 1859.

74. *Times,* 15 May 1860.

75. John Hollingshead, *My Lifetime* (London, 1895), I, 120; *Survey of London,* XXXIV (1966), 495.

76. *Times,* 9 March 1860.

77. *ILN,* 30 April 1861, p. 364.

78. *Edmund Yates: His Recollections and Experiences* (London, 1884), I, 136.

79. Reprinted in Smith's *Sketches of London Life and Character,* p. 27.

28. ARTIFACTS AND MODELS

1. *Literary Gazette,* 10 April 1830, p. 245, and 14 July 1832, p. 446; *Times,* 26 January 1837; *Athenaeum,* 22, 29 April 1837, pp. 287, 306.

2. *Athenaeum,* 12 November 1836, p. 801.

3. *ILN,* 17 August, 16 November 1850, pp. 147, 378.

4. Catalogue in Museum of London library; *Literary Gazette,* 5 June 1819, pp. 363–64; *N & Q,* 12th ser. 9 (1921), 288–89.

5. Gerald Reitlinger, *The Economics of Taste: The Rise and Fall of the Objets d'Art Market since 1750* (New York, 1965), pp. 297–98; advertisement, WCL, StM/LS, I, 167.

6. See Ian Anstruther, *The Knight and the Umbrella: An Account of the Eglinton Tournament, 1839* (London, 1963). Pratt's connection with the tournament is described on pp. 128–32, 235.

7. *Times,* 4 February 1840.

8. John Ashton, *Gossip in the First Decades of Victoria's Reign* (London, 1903; rptd. Detroit, 1968), pp. 106–108; Anstruther, p. 235.

9. *ILN,* 17 May 1851, p. 412; Reitlinger, p. 299.

10. *Literary Gazette,* 1 June, 7 September 1833, pp. 349, 573.

11. *Athenaeum,* 14 May 1836, p. 344.

12. *ILN,* 18 March 1848, p. 189.

13. *Athenaeum,* 3 April 1847, p. 366.

14. See Philip John Stead, *Vidocq: A Biography* (London, 1953); the London exhibition is dealt with on pp. 213–17. There are more details in Samuel Edwards, *The Vidocq Dossier* (Boston, 1977), pp. 174–80. See also *ILN,* 14 June 1845, p. 375.

15. *Times,* 9 June 1845.

16. N. P. Willis, *Famous Persons and Places* (Auburn, N.Y., 1855), p. 352.

17. *ILN,* 14 June 1845, p. 375.

18. Advertisement in BL, EMI.

19. *Descriptive Catalogue of Du Bourg's Museum* (copy at GL).

20. Richard Rush, *The Court of London from 1819 to 1825* (London, 1873), p. 59.

21. Pamphlet, probably older than the one cited in n. 19, at GL.

22. *Athenaeum,* 4 December 1841, p. 935.

23. *Athenaeum,* 2 June 1838, p. 392; 16 January 1841, p. 55.

24. *Times,* 10 February 1840.

25. *ILN,* 5 November 1842, p. 415, and 24 February 1844, p. 127; *Times,* 2 August, 29 September 1842; [George Mogridge], *Old Humphrey's Walks in London and Its Neighbourhood* (London, [1843]), pp. 216–17.

26. *Art Journal,* 11 (1849), 162–63; *ILN,* 14 April 1849, p. 238.

27. BL, EMI. (This source has much material on exhibitions of models.)

28. *Literary Gazette,* 25 July 1829, p. 492.

29. Handbill, GL, Playbills of London: Circuses and Miscellaneous Entertainments box.

30. *Examiner,* 27 October 1816, pp. 682–83.

31. BL, EMI.

32. *Athenaeum,* 2 May 1835, p. 338.

33. *Literary Gazette,* 8 February 1834, pp. 99–100; *Times,* 31 January 1834.

34. BL, EMI.

35. *Times,* 24 February 1825; *Mirror,* n.s. 3 (1843), 299, and n.s. 5 (1844), 382.

36. JJ Coll., London Play Places box 9.

37. Mogridge, pp. 177–78.

38. *Athenaeum,* 17 April 1847, p. 415.

39. *ILN,* 19 December 1846, p. 398.

40. *Mirror,* 4th ser. 1 (1847), 342–43.

41. *Athenaeum,* 2 January 1847, p. 20.

42. *Athenaeum,* 19 June 1847, p. 647.

43. *ILN,* 22 January 1848, p. 44; *Athenaeum,* same date, p. 89.

44. *Literary Gazette,* 20 November 1824, p. 749, and 16 April 1825, p. 255.

45. *Literary Gazette,* 25 April 1829, p. 276.

46. *Times,* 3 June 1842.

47. *Mirror,* 33 (1839), 337; BL, EMI.

48. *ILN,* 20 April 1850; *Times,* 21 May 1850.

49. Harvard Theatre Collection, Panorama box.

50. BL, EMI.

51. The fullest treatment of the models is Charles ffoulkes, "Captain Siborne's Models of the Battle of Waterloo," *Journal of the Society for Army Historical Research* (London), 14 (1935), 201–205. There is contemporary material in BL, EMI.

52. Quoted in W. J. Fitzpatrick, *The Life of Charles Lever* (London, 1879), II, 408.

53. *Mirror,* 32 (1838), 249.

54. *Wellington and His Friends,* ed. the Seventh Duke of Wellington (London, 1965), pp. 133–34.

55. *N & Q,* 11th ser. 8 (1913), 393–94.

56. *Times,* 25 December 1844; *ILN,* 14 June 1845, p. 382; handbill, WCL, D137/Egyptian Hall.

57. *ILN,* 16 March 1850, p. 179, and 23 August 1851, p. 231.

58. *Literary Gazette,* 16 March 1833, p. 172.

59. *Literary Gazette,* 12 April 1834, p. 268.

60. *Athenaeum,* 5 January 1835, p. 16.

61. See E. N. Stretton, "Samuel Percy, Wax Modeller," *Apollo,* 73 (March 1961), 63–66.

62. *Athenaeum,* 28 March 1846, p. 321.

63. *Grand Salon of Arts and Illustrious Men* (pamphlet, 1802), copy at GL.

64. *ILN,* 4 October 1845, p. 222.

65. JJ Coll., London Play Places box 3.

66. BL, EMI.

67. Ibid.

68. Ibid.

69. Ibid.; handbill, EC, Egyptian Hall folder.

70. Edward Edwards, *Anecdotes of Painters* (London, 1808), p. xxxix.

71. Handbill, EC, Exeter Change folder.

72. John Thomas Smith, *A Book for a Rainy Day* (London, 1845), pp. 214–15n.

73. WCL, StM/LS, I, 97–98.

74. *Literary Gazette,* 7 August 1824, p. 509.

75. BL, EMI.

76. *Mirror,* 13 (1829), 266.

77. Odell, III, 166, 223.

78. BL, EMI.

79. *Literary Gazette,* 30 June, 25 August 1832, pp. 413, 541.

80. *Athenaeum,* 22 January 1847, p. 97.

81. Handbills, GL, London Playbills: Circuses and Miscellaneous Entertainments box.

82. Ibid.

83. Ibid.

84. BL, EMI.

85. For a general sketch of Miss Linwood's life, based on the numerous contemporary sources, see Caroline P. Ingram, "Miss Mary Linwood," *Connoisseur,* 48 (1917), 145–48; also *Dictionary of National Biography* and Norma R. Whitcomb, *Mary Linwood* (exhibition catalogue, City of Leicester Museums and Art Galleries, 1951). An unsigned manuscript by a former schoolmate, giving particulars of Linwood's early life, is at WCL, box 42, no. 1.

86. Quoted by Ingram.

87. *Survey of London,* XXXIV (1966), 462–64. This source has a full account of the gallery's arrangement and décor. Additional details in the following description are from Tom Taylor, *Leicester Square: Its Associations and Its Worthies* (London, 1874), pp. 459–61.

88. Jehangeer Nowrojee and Hirjeebhoy Mervanjee, *Journal of a Residence of Two Years and a Half in Great Britain* (London, 1841), p. 214.

89. Copies of the Linwood catalogue, of various dates, are at WCL and GL.

90. *Quarterly Review,* 96 (1854), 76.

91. "A Plated Article," *Household Words,* 5 (1852), 117.

92. *ILN,* 25 April 1846, p. 278.

93. *Literary Gazette,* 7 May 1825, p. 301.

94. *ILN,* 3 June 1848, p. 356.

95. Booklet, JJ Coll., Dioramas box 4; Harvard Theatre Collection, Panorama box.

96. *Literary Gazette,* 1 May 1819, pp. 283–84.

97. BL, EMI; *Athenaeum,* 23 April 1831, p. 270; *Examiner,* 15 May 1831, pp. 309–10.

98. Clippings in JJ Coll., London Play Places box 3.

99. This paragraph is drawn entirely from *N & Q,* 146 (1924), 376–77.

100. *Mirror,* 11 (1828), 184–85.

101. *Athenaeum,* 6 March 1830, p. 144.

102. *Athenaeum,* 31 March 1838, p. 237; *Times,* 24 May 1838.

29. FINE ART FOR THE PEOPLE

1. *Benjamin Robert Haydon: Correspondence and Table-Talk* (London, 1876), II, 293.

2. *Literary Gazette,* 7 April 1821, p. 220.

3. Ibid.

4. W. T. Whitley, *Art in England, 1800–1820* (Cambridge, 1928), pp. 108–10; Frank Herrmann, *The English as Collectors: A Documentary Chrestomathy* (London, 1972), pp. 125–26, 432; *Survey of London,* XXX (1960), 494–96.

5. Quoted in Whitley, pp. 296–97.

6. Herrmann, pp. 125–26.

7. *Fraser's Magazine,* 29 (1844), 263.

8. George, VIII, 596.

9. Allan Cunningham, *The Life of Sir David Wilkie* (London, 1843), II, 70, 74; W. T. Whitley, *Art in England, 1821–1837* (Cambridge, 1930), pp. 30–31.

10. *Literary Gazette,* 11 May 1822, p. 296.

11. *Literary Gazette,* 3 April 1819, p. 220.

12. Whitley, *Art in England, 1821–1837,* pp. 9–11.

13. J. T. Flexner, *America's Old Masters* (New York, 1967), p. 90.

14. Ibid., p. 93.

15. Richard and Samuel Redgrave, *A Century of British Painters* (London, 1947), p. 311.

16. A. Paul Oppé in *Early Victorian England,* ed. G. M. Young (Oxford, 1934), II, 108.

17. *Literary Gazette,* 20 March 1819, p. 186.

18. Material on *The Raft of the "Medusa"* oth-

erwise unattributed is from Lorenz Eitner, *Géricault's "Raft of the Medusa"* (London, 1972), especially pp. 62–64, and Lee Johnson, "The *Raft of the Medusa* in Great Britain," *Burlington Magazine,* 96 (1954), 249–54.

19. Eitner, p. 40.

20. So the advertisements claimed; but Johnson (p. 253) estimates the attendance at 40,000.

21. *Literary Gazette,* 13 December 1823, p. 798.

22. *Literary Gazette,* 19 April 1823, p. 254.

23. Catalogue in Victoria and Albert Museum library.

24. A. J. Finberg, *The Life of J. M. W. Turner, R.A.,* 2nd ed. (Oxford, 1961), p. 315.

25. *ILN,* 20 May 1843, p. 346.

26. *Athenaeum,* 8 May 1847, p. 494; Rupert Gunnis, *Dictionary of British Sculptors,* new rev. ed. (London, [1968]), p. 271.

27. *ILN,* 8 July 1848, p. 6.

28. *ILN,* 2 June 1860, p. 518.

29. Whitley, *Art in England, 1821–1837,* pp. 37–38.

30. GL, London Playbills: Circuses and Miscellaneous Entertainments box.

31. *Dictionary of National Biography;* Gunnis, pp. 387–88.

32. Helen Morris, *Portrait of a Chef: The Life of Alexis Soyer* (London, 1938; rptd. Chicago, 1975), pp. 81–82; *Times,* 13 May 1848.

33. *Punch,* 36 (1859), 168.

34. *Art Journal,* 11 (1849), 99, 163, and n.s. 3 (1851), 263, and 4 (1852), 98; *Times,* 4 August 1851; Randall Davies, *Velásquez* (London, 1914), pp. 11–12.

35. *Letters of Charles Lamb,* ed. E. V. Lucas (New Haven, 1935), III, 136–37.

36. *Memoirs of Charles Mathews* (London, 1839), IV, 157–59; *Literary Gazette,* 4 May 1833, p. 284.

37. *Letters of Thomas Babington Macaulay,* ed. Thomas Pinney (Cambridge, 1974–), II, 308–10.

38. The importance of exhibitions in popularizing interest in art is well described in Jeremy Maas, *Gambart: Prince of the Victorian Art World* (London, 1975), esp. Ch. 5 ("The Exhibition Mania").

39. Gerald Reitlinger, *The Economics of Taste: The Rise and Fall of Picture Prices, 1760–1960* (London, 1961), pp. 149–50; Maas, pp. 99–102.

40. Maas, p. 161.

41. *ILN,* 13 October 1860, p. 337, and 3 May 1862, p. 457; Reitlinger, p. 147; Maas, pp. 115–22, 126.

42. W. R. Frith, *My Autobiography and Rem-*

iniscences (London, 1887), II, 233–38; *Art Journal,* n.s. 1 (1862), 95, 122–23, 210; Maas, pp. 135–37.

43. "George Cruikshank," *Westminster Review,* 34 (1840), 6–7.

44. Henry Vizetelly, *Glances Back through Seventy Years* (London, 1893), I, 88–89.

45. *"From Today Painting Is Dead": The Beginnings of Photography* (catalogue of exhibition at Victoria and Albert Museum, 1972), p. 14.

46. Helmut and Alison Gernsheim, *The History of Photography* (New York, 1969), p. 270; *ILN,* 22 September 1855, p. 359; *Art Journal,* n.s. 2 (1856), 62.

47. *ILN,* 6 February, 6 March 1858, pp. 150, 230.

48. *Athenaeum,* 28 March 1857, pp. 408, 411.

49. "Noctes Ambrosianae," *Blackwood's Magazine,* 32 (1832), 857.

50. The story of Haydon's last show is told in detail in Alethea Hayter, *A Sultry Month* (London, 1965), passim, and Eric George, *The Life and Death of Benjamin Robert Haydon,* 2nd ed. (Oxford, 1967), pp. 280–93.

51. The following account of Martin's connection with the exhibitions of his time is based upon Thomas Balston, *John Martin, 1789–1854: His Life and Works* (London, 1947). William Feaver's recent *John Martin* (Oxford, 1975) adds few facts to the artist's biography.

52. *Letters of Charles Lamb,* III, 98; *John Constable's Correspondence,* VI (Suffolk Records Society, XII, 1968), 249.

53. Redgrave, p. 396.

54. Balston, p. 61.

55. Ibid., pp. 61–62.

56. Ibid., p. 112.

57. Whitley, *Art in England, 1800–1820,* pp. 135–36; J. M. Crook, *The British Museum* (London, 1972), pp. 108–109, 130–32.

58. Minutes of Art Union, 1841, quoted in Anthony King, "George Godwin and the Art Union of London, 1837–1911," *Victorian Studies,* 8 (1964), 107.

59. *Politics for the People,* 6 May 1848.

60. An exhaustive history of the National Gallery's early years is Gregory Martin, "The Founding of the National Gallery in London," *Connoisseur,* 185 (1974), 280–87; 186 (1974), 24–31, 124–28, 200–207, 272–79; 187 (1974), 48–53, 108–13, 202–205, 278–83.

61. *Works of Ruskin,* ed. E. T. Cook and A. D. O. Wedderburn (London, 1902–1912), XII, 398.

62. Attendance figures, 1826–1840, are given in *Art-Union,* 3 (1841), 186.

63. Whitley, *Art in England, 1821–1837,* p. 348.

64. [George Mogridge], *Old Humphrey's Walks in London and Its Neighbourhood* (London, [1843]), pp. 70, 77–78.

65. *Politics for the People,* 6 May 1848.

66. Whitley, *Art in England, 1821–1837,* p. 348; *Report from the Select Committee on the National Gallery* (1850), qq. 82–83.

67. *Report from the Select Committee on National Monuments* (1841), qq. 2658–60; [Henry Cole], "Public Galleries and Irresponsible Boards," *Edinburgh Review,* 123 (1866), 73.

68. [J. F. Murray], "The World of London," *Blackwood's Magazine,* 51 (1842), 421–22; *Report from the Select Committee on National Monuments* (1841), q. 2608.

69. *Penny Magazine,* 6 (1837), 457–64. For an earlier description of the museum, see *Mirror,* 21 (1833), 210–14.

70. *Athenaeum,* 15 September, 22 December 1860, pp. 357–58, 873.

71. *A New Description of Sir John Soane's Museum,* 3rd rev. ed. (London, 1972), p. 65.

72. *Fraser's Magazine,* 29 (1844), 263.

73. The authoritative history of the Westminster frescoes is T. S. R. Boase, "The Decoration of the New Palace of Westminster, 1841–1863," *Journal of the Warburg and Courtauld Institutes,* 17 (1954), 319–58. A briefer treatment is in John Steegmann, *Consort of Taste, 1830–1870* (London, 1950), pp. 129–36.

74. *Athenaeum,* 22 July 1843, p. 674.

75. *Punch,* 5 (1843), 23.

76. *Blackwood's Magazine,* 56 (1844), 652–53.

77. *Report from the Select Committee on the National Gallery* (1850), p. 68.

78. *Report from the Select Committee on Public Institutions* (1860), q. 287.

30. ENTR'ACTE: INSIDE THE EXHIBITION BUSINESS

1. *Art Journal,* n.s. 3 (1851), 287.

2. *Mirror,* n.s. 5 (1844), 382.

3. Cornelius Walford, *Fairs, Past and Present: A Chapter in the History of Commerce* (London, 1883; rptd. New York, 1968), pp. 239–40.

4. John Lewis Roget, *A History of the "Old Water-Colour" Society* (London, 1891), I, 231, 402; George Catlin, *Notes of Eight Years' Travels . . .* (New York, 1848), I, 31.

5. *The Farington Diary,* ed. James Greig (New York, 1922–1928), V, 10–11.

6. James Ballantine, *The Life of David Roberts, R.A.* (Edinburgh, 1866), pp. 28, 165.

7. *Athenaeum,* 28 February 1835, p. 169.

8. Max Schlesinger, *Saunterings in and about London* (London, 1853), pp. 18–20.

9. *Athenaeum,* 16 November 1850, p. 1192.

10. Unidentified clipping, JJ Coll., Dioramas box 4.

11. P. J. Stead, *Vidocq: A Biography* (London, 1953), p. 216.

12. G. A. Sala, "Shows," *Temple Bar,* 8 (1863), 270–72.

13. *Athenaeum,* 7 May 1859, pp. 613–14.

14. Allan Cunningham, *The Life of Sir David Wilkie* (London, 1843), I, 353.

15. *Literary Gazette,* 25 March 1820, p. 207.

16. *Literary Gazette,* 24 May 1823, p. 332.

17. J. R. Planché, *Extravaganzas, 1825–1871* (London, 1879), II, 293–95.

18. Ibid., III, 165–71.

19. Handbill, WCL, D137/Egyptian Hall.

20. *Athenaeum,* 14 June 1851, p. 635.

21. *Times,* 28 December 1857.

22. Stead, pp. 211, 219.

23. *ILN,* 18 April 1846, p. 253. There is a substantial notice of Angas in the *Australian Dictionary of Biography.*

24. Quoted in the "Press Order" to the exhibition, WCL, box 42, no. 3.

25. *Times,* 20 May 1851.

26. *Athenaeum,* 14 August 1852, p. 876.

27. *ILN,* 22 April 1854, p. 367.

28. *Mirror,* 13 (1829), 266.

29. W. B. Ewald, Jr., *The Newsmen of Queen Anne* (Oxford, 1956), pp. 167–68.

30. *The Spectator,* ed. Donald F. Bond (Oxford, 1965), I, 128–29.

31. E. J. Pyke, *A Biographical Dictionary of Wax Modellers* (Oxford, 1973), p. 92.

32. John Timbs, *English Eccentrics and Eccentricities* (London, 1875), p. 277.

33. *Catalogue of the Curiosities in the Indian Museum and Exhibition* (copy at BL); *Times,* 9 January 1823.

34. Handbill, GL, London Playbills: Circuses and Miscellaneous Entertainments box.

35. Hand-copied bill, JJ Coll., London Play Places box 1.

36. Clippings, Lysons, II, 110.

37. *The Old Curiosity Shop,* Ch. 1.

38. Copy at GL (A.6.6.no.2).

39. Handbill, JJ Coll., London Play Places box 9.

40. Catalogue of sale, EC, Exeter Change file.

41. Handbill, ibid.

42. Odell, IV, 42, 176.

43. WCL, StM/Gen, I, 126.

44. GL, London Playbills: Circuses and Miscellaneous Entertainments box.

45. Clipping, unidentified source.

46. BL, EMI.

47. Clipping, Harvard Theatre Collection, Panorama box.

48. BL, EMI.

49. Ibid.

50. Barnum, II, 492.

51. Clipping, Harvard Theatre Collection, Panorama box.

52. Copy at GL (2022).

53. Handbill, WCL, F138/Spring Gardens.

54. Handbill, GL, London Playbills: Circuses and Miscellaneous Entertainments box.

55. Another handbill, ibid.

56. *Punch*, 4 (1843), 195.

57. *ILN*, 5 December 1846, p. 359; *Times*, 2 December 1846.

58. Mayhew, *London Labour and the London Poor* (London, 1861–1862), III, 43–158.

59. Ibid., III, 214–19.

60. Francis T. Buckland, *Curiosities of Natural History*, 3rd ser., 2nd ed. (London, 1868), I, 88–92.

61. Mayhew, III, 215.

62. BL, EMI.

63. Charles Manby Smith, *Curiosities of London Life* (London, 1853), pp. 8–9.

64. BL, EMI.

65. Ibid.

66. Ibid.

67. Handbills, JJ Coll., Dioramas box 2.

31. NATIONAL MONUMENTS

1. Mrs. A. Murray Smith, *Westminster Abbey: Its Story and Associations* (London, 1906), p. 329; see also the letter of protest from "An Architect," *Gentleman's Magazine*, 71, part 1 (1801), 328.

2. *The Complete Poetical Works of Thomas Hood*, ed. Walter Jerrold (London, 1906), pp. 728–29.

3. *Times*, 16 July, 18 August 1825.

4. *Annual Register, 1826*, Chronicle pp. 46–47; *Gentleman's Magazine*, 96, part 1 (1826), 359–62.

5. Frederick von Raumer, *England in 1835 . . .* , trans. Sarah Austin and H. E. Lloyd (Philadelphia, 1836), p. 141.

6. R. H. Barham, *The Ingoldsby Legends*, 2nd ser. (London, 1843), pp. 119–20.

7. James Fenimore Cooper, *Gleanings in Europe: Vol. II: England*, ed. Robert E. Spiller (New York, 1930), pp. 38–39.

8. *Annual Register, 1806*, Chronicle pp. 353–54.

9. E. J. Pyke, *A Biographical Dictionary of Wax Modellers* (Oxford, 1973), pp. 5–6. See also L. E. Tanner, *Recollections of a Westminster Antiquary* (London, 1969), pp. 135–36.

10. George, VIII, 372, 420.

11. *Literary Gazette*, 15 April 1820, p. 252.

12. *Examiner*, 7 March 1824, p. 146.

13. Alexander S. Mackenzie, *The American in England* (New York, 1835), I, 224–25.

14. Cooper, pp. 47–48.

15. B. W. Richardson, *Thomas Sopwith* (London, 1891), p. 71. Benjamin Silliman (*A Journal of Travels . . . in the Years 1805 and 1806*, New York, 1807, I, 139–52) describes the Tower as it was in the first years of the century.

16. *Mirror*, 31 (1838), 275; *Report from the Select Committee on National Monuments* (1841) (hereafter cited as *National Monuments Committee*), q. 2679.

17. Walter Thornbury, *Old and New London* (London, n.d.), II, 81–87.

18. Mackenzie, II, 65–68.

19. J. Mordaunt Crook, *The British Museum* (London, 1972), pp. 109–10; [Richard Ford], "The British Museum," *Quarterly Review*, 88 (1850), 139–54.

20. Silliman, I, 297.

21. Crook, p. 66.

22. Robert Cowtan, *Memories of the British Museum* (London, 1872), p. 305.

23. Crook, p. 66.

24. Louis Simond, *An American in Regency England* (London, 1968), pp. 43–44.

25. [J. F. Murray], "The World of London," *Blackwood's Magazine*, 51 (1842), 419.

26. *National Monuments Committee*, q. 2146. The witness quoted was John Britton.

27. *Hansard's Parliamentary Debates*, 3rd ser. 57 (1841), col. 952.

28. *National Monuments Committee*, p. vi.

29. Cooper, pp. 38–39.

30. *Hansard*, 3rd ser. 16 (1833), col. 1003.

31. *Hansard*, 3rd ser. 20 (1833), col. 618.

32. *Report from the Select Committee on . . . the British Museum* (1835), qq. 1320–30.

33. *Times*, 30 May 1837.

34. *National Monuments Committee*, qq. 2957–58, 3092, 3158.

35. *Report from the Select Committee on the British Museum* (1836), qq. 3408–10.

36. *National Monuments Committee*, q. 2961.

37. Ibid., qq. 91, 93.

38. Ibid., q. 796.

39. Ibid., qq. 2927–30.

40. Ibid., q. 2880.

41. Elizabeth Longford, *Wellington: Pillar of State* (London, 1972), p. 247.

42. *National Monuments Committee*, q. 2734.

43. *Report from the Select Committee on . . . the British Museum* (1835), qq. 3916–22.

44. *National Monuments Committee*, qq. 1–5. Part of the correspondence was printed in the *Times*, 10 January 1838.

45. *National Monuments Committee*, q. 6.

46. Ibid., qq. 16–34.

47. Ibid., qq. 524–34.

48. Ibid., qq. 43, 340.

49. Ibid., qq. 544, 549, 344.

50. Robert Southey, *Letters from London* (London, 1951), pp. 132–33.

51. *London Magazine*, 8 (1823), 406.

52. *National Monuments Committee*, q. 1796.

53. Ibid., qq. 1806, 1810.

54. Ibid., qq. 99, 937, 944, 948.

55. *Penny Magazine*, 6 (1837), 46–47.

56. *Athenaeum*, 27 January 1844, p. 88; *Times*, 24, 25 January 1844.

57. *Athenaeum*, 20 April 1844, p. 360.

58. Edward Miller, *That Noble Cabinet* (London, 1973), pp. 207–208; *Times*, 8 January–24 March 1845, passim.

59. *National Monuments Committee*, q. 615.

60. Ibid., qq. 1359–1430 passim.

61. *ILN*, 22 April 1848, pp. 266–68. For an assault on the conduct of the Tower as a showplace, see *Athenaeum*, 13 September 1845, p. 906.

62. *Mirror*, 38 (1841), 290–94; *Times*, 1 November 1841.

63. *Times*, 4 January 1842.

64. *The Journals and Miscellaneous Notebooks of Ralph Waldo Emerson* (Cambridge, Mass., 1960–), X, 239.

65. *Blackwood's Magazine*, 51 (1842), 422.

66. *Athenaeum*, 23 September 1843, p. 868.

67. *Art Journal*, n.s. 6 (1860), 21.

68. *Sybil*, Book IV, Ch. vi. (Bradenham edition, London, 1927, p. 269.)

69. *Punch*, 6 (1844), 206–207; 9 (1845), 156; 10 (1846), 34, 248.

70. *Punch*, 9 (1845), 252.

71. *Times*, 26 May 1847.

72. Hawthorne, *English Notebooks*, ed.

Randall Stewart (New York, 1941), pp. 219–20.

73. Cowtan, p. 305.

74. *ILN*, 22 April 1848, pp. 266–68.

75. *Art-Union*, 3 (1841), 186; 8 (1846), 313.

76. *Athenaeum*, 1 January 1848, p. 15.

32. THE CRYSTAL PALACE YEAR

1. J. W. Hudson, *The History of Adult Education* (London, 1851; rptd. London, 1969), p. 91.

2. *Penny Magazine*, 9 (1840), 74–75.

3. Hudson, pp. 103–104.

4. Material on the Society of Arts otherwise unattributed is from Derek Hudson and K. W. Luckhurst, *The Royal Society of Arts* (London, 1954), pp. 188–97, 294–95.

5. Charles Knight, *London* (London, 1841–1844), V, 356–57.

6. *Times*, 20 March 1850.

7. The best histories of the Crystal Palace are Yvonne ffrench, *The Great Exhibition: 1851* (London, 1940); C. H. Gibbs-Smith, *The Great Exhibition of 1851* (London, 1950); C. R. Fay, *Palace of Industry, 1851: A Study of the Great Exhibition and Its Fruits* (Cambridge, 1951); and Utz Haltern, *Die Londoner Weltausstellung von 1851: Ein Beitrag zur Geschichte der Bürgerliche-Industriellen Gesellschaft im 19. Jahrhundert* (Münster, 1971).

8. Elizabeth Longford, *Wellington: Pillar of State* (London, 1972), p. 388.

9. Henry Cole, *Fifty Years of Public Work* (London, 1884), I, 187–92.

10. *Official Catalogue of the Great Exhibition* (London, 1851), supplementary volume, pp. 112–13.

11. *Punch*, 20 (1851), 247, and 21 (1851), 14.

12. Charles Babbage, *The Exposition of 1851 . . .* (London, 1851), preface.

13. *Athenaeum*, 15 February 1851, p. 191.

14. *Times*, 2 May 1851; *Examiner*, 3 May 1851, pp. 280–81. See also ffrench, p. 191.

15. Unless otherwise ascribed, all information in this chapter on the London exhibitions of 1851 is derived from advertisements and reviews in the *Times*, *ILN*, and *Athenaeum*, and from the London guidebooks published that year.

16. *ILN*, 29 March 1851, p. 252.

17. *London As It Is Today* (London, 1851), p. 269.

18. *ILN*, 25 January 1851, p. 61.

19. *Athenaeum*, 25 January 1851, pp. 114–15.

20. *Athenaeum*, 2 August, 13 December 1851, pp. 831, 1316.

21. *London As It Is Today*, p. 274.

22. Benjamin Silliman, *A Visit to Europe in 1851* (New York, 1853), II, 432.

23. Hector Berlioz, *Evenings with the Orchestra*, trans. Jacques Barzun (Chicago, 1973), pp. 246–50.

24. *Art Journal*, n.s. 4 (1852), 33.

25. *ILN*, 2, 9 August 1851, pp. 148, 179.

26. An irreverent description was published in *Punch*, 21 (1851), 93.

27. Handbill, EC, Surrey Gardens file.

28. *ILN*, 21 September 1850, p. 247.

29. This account of the Great Globe is based on Ralph Hyde, "Mr. Wyld's Monster Globe," *History Today*, 29 (1970), 118–23.

30. *Times*, 5 February 1851.

31. *Literary Gazette*, 20 October 1827, pp. 685–86.

32. *London Magazine*, 3rd ser. 1 (1828), 501–504.

33. Edmund Gosse, *Father and Son: Biographical Recollections* (New York, 1909), pp. 42–43.

34. *First Report of the Commissioners for the Exhibition of 1851* (1852), p. 121.

35. *Athenaeum*, 18 May 1850, p. 536.

36. *Athenaeum*, 30 November 1850, p. 1252.

37. *Times*, 17 September 1851.

38. [Francis Wey], *A Frenchman Sees England in the 'Fifties*, "adapted from the French" by Valerie Price (London, 1935), p. 226.

39. *Art Journal*, n.s. 3 (1851), 149–50, and 4 (1852), 198.

33. THE FIFTIES, I: NEW PATTERNS OF LIFE AND THE DECLINE OF THE PANORAMA

1. *Times*, 2 June 1857.

2. See Thomas Greenwood, *Museums and Art Galleries* (London, 1888).

3. *Athenaeum*, 2 September 1854, p. 1067.

4. *ILN*, 31 December 1853, p. 591.

5. *Quarterly Review*, 98 (1855–56), 248.

6. *ILN*, 1 January 1859, p. 6.

7. Ibid., p. 7.

8. *ILN*, 25 May 1850, p. 363.

9. The following account of Albert Smith's career is based upon J. Monroe Thorington, *Mont Blanc Sideshow: The Life and Times of Albert Smith* (Philadelphia, 1934) (the fullest treatment), and Raymund Fitzsimons, *The Baron of Piccadilly: The Travels and Entertainments of Albert Smith, 1816–1860* (London, 1967). Some details

are added from the *Times*'s appreciative review of the Mont Blanc show, 6 December 1853, and further *Times* notices, 6 December 1854, 4 December 1855, 25 November 1856, 24 November 1857, 13 January and 23 December 1858, and 7 November 1859.

10. *Athenaeum*, 26 May 1860, p. 719.

11. See Edmund Yates, "Bygone Shows," *Fortnightly Review* (Philadelphia ed.), n.s. 39 (1886), 633–47.

12. Henry Vizetelly, *Glances Back through Seventy Years* (London, 1893), I, 320–21. As the passage in which this remark occurs makes clear, Vizetelly did not like Smith; neither, he says, did Thackeray. For more on Smith as a London Bohemian, see *Edmund Yates: Recollections and Experiences* (London, 1884), I, 227–29.

13. *Works of Ruskin*, ed. E. T. Cook and A. D. O. Wedderburn (London, 1902–1912), XXXVI, 117.

14. *ILN*, 25 December 1852, p. 565; Thorington, p. 165.

15. Henry James, *A Small Boy and Others* (New York, 1913), pp. 317–18.

16. *Times*, 3 February 1854.

17. *Athenaeum*, 1 September 1855, p. 1005.

18. *Times*, 4 December 1855.

19. *Times*, 13 January 1858.

20. *The Amberley Papers: The Letters and Diaries of Bertrand Russell's Parents*, ed. Bertrand and Patricia Russell (New York, 1937), I, 57.

21. *ILN*, 24 December 1859, p. 625.

22. Edmund Yates, *The Business of Pleasure* (London, 1865), I, 101.

23. J. R. Planché, *Extravaganzas, 1825–1871* (London, 1879), V, 11–19.

24. *ILN*, 22 April 1854, p. 367.

25. *Times*, 11 June 1860.

26. [John Weale], *The Pictorial Handbook of London* (London, 1854), p. 700.

27. Handbill, WCL, StM/LS, I, 182.

28. *Athenaeum*, 6 October 1860, p. 453.

29. Handbill, EC, Gallery of Illustration file.

30. Ibid.; *ILN*, 16 October, 18 December 1852, pp. 322, 551.

31. *ILN*, 4 February 1854, p. 99.

32. *ILN*, 8 April 1854, p. 321; *Times*, 1 April 1854.

33. *Athenaeum*, 21 May 1853, p. 619.

34. *ILN*, 25 February 1854, p. 167.

35. *ILN*, 15 April 1854, p. 339.

36. *Athenaeum*, 18 February 1854, p. 214.

37. *Times*, 14 December 1854.

38. Planché, V, 22.

39. *Athenaeum*, 26 September 1857, p. 1213.

40. *ILN*, 8 May 1858, p. 462.

41. Helmut and Alison Gernsheim, *The History of Photography* (New York, 1969), pp. 285–87.

42. *Chambers's Journal*, 3rd ser. 13 (1860), 35.

43. *ILN*, 31 May 1862, p. 545.

44. *Times*, 27 December 1861.

45. *Athenaeum*, 12 March 1859, p. 357.

34. THE FIFTIES, II: THE OLD ORDER CHANGETH

1. Susan Chitty, *The Beast and the Monk* (London, 1974), p. 110.

2. Quoted in Eric de Maré, *London 1851: The Year of the Great Exhibition* (London, 1973), p. 102.

3. Most of the material in the following discussion of the Crystal Palace at Sydenham is from Patrick Beaver, *The Crystal Palace, 1851–1936: A Portrait of Victorian Enterprise* (London, 1970).

4. Advertisement of 1857 attractions: *Athenaeum*, 18 April 1857, p. 511.

5. Adrian J. Desmond, "Central Park's Fragile Dinosaurs," *Natural History*, 83, no. 8 (October 1974), 65. I am indebted to Ms. Mary Rosner for this reference.

6. John Steegmann, *Consort of Taste, 1830–1870* (London, 1950), p. 231.

7. *Punch*, 40 (1861), 258.

8. *Athenaeum*, 2 November 1861, p. 584.

9. *Art Journal*, n.s. 7 (1861), 221.

10. *Times*, 13 August 1860; *ILN*, 8 September 1860, pp. 227–28.

11. *Art Journal*, n.s. 6 (1860), 350.

12. The financial troubles of the Surrey Gardens are amply documented in BL, Surrey Gardens scrapbooks, vols. 7–8.

13. *ILN*, 2 June 1855, p. 533.

14. Hawthorne, *English Notebooks*, ed. Randall Stewart (New York, 1941), pp. 251–52.

15. Francis T. Buckland, *Curiosities of Natural History*, 3rd ser., 2nd ed. (London, 1868), I, 72–79. The prices of the animals, taken from BL, Surrey Gardens scrapbook vol. 7, are sometimes at variance with those Buckland gives.

16. *ILN*, 19 July 1856, p. 68.

17. Adam Carse, *Life of Jullien* (Cambridge, 1951), pp. 91–92.

18. Ibid., p. 119.

19. *Household Words*, 7 (1853), 64–65.

20. WCL, StM/LS, I, 127.

21. WCL, box 42, no. 3.

22. Tom Taylor, *Leicester Square: Its Associations and Its Worthies* (London, 1874), p. 463.

23. WCL, box 42, no. 3.

24. WCL, StM/LS, I, 181.

25. *Athenaeum*, 7 August 1852, p. 849.

26. Ralph Hyde, "Mr. Wyld's Monster Globe," *History Today*, 20 (1970), 122.

27. *ILN*, 27 August 1853, p. 179. The prospectus is quoted at length in the *Examiner* of the same date, p. 554.

28. J. R. Planché, *Extravaganzas, 1825–1871* (London, 1879), V, 9–34.

29. Handbills, EC, Leicester Square folder; WCL, StM/LS, I, 188–94.

30. *Survey of London*, XXXIV (1966), 437.

31. Quoted in Harold Scott, *The Early Doors: Origins of the Music Hall* (London, 1946), p. 187.

32. John Hollingshead, *My Lifetime* (London, 1895), I, 210. Otherwise unattributed material on the Panopticon in the following passage is from *Survey of London*, XXXIV (1966), 492–95. The building was described in detail in *ILN*, 31 January 1852, p. 96, and 18 March 1854, p. 235. There is a good collection of material in WCL, StM/LS, II, 1–17.

33. *ILN*, 7 October 1854, p. 342.

34. *Times*, 12 August 1854.

35. *Illustrated Handbook of the Royal Panopticon of Science and Art* (London, 1854); copy at WCL.

36. WCL, StM/LS, II, 13, 17.

37. Hollingshead, I, 210.

38. *ILN*, 17 June 1854, p. 585.

39. *Times*, 9 August 1854.

40. *ILN*, 19 January 1856, p. 71; handbill, GL, London Playbills: Circuses and Miscellaneous Entertainments box.

41. JJ Coll., Dioramas box 1.

42. *Athenaeum*, 15 December 1855, p. 1467.

43. *ILN*, 27 January, 10 February 1855, pp. 87, 142, 144.

44. *Athenaeum*, 10 March 1855, p. 297.

45. The following account of the early days of the South Kensington Museum is derived mainly from *Survey of London*, XXXVIII (1975), Chs. IV–V—the fullest and best documented treatment pending the appearance of a promised official history.

46. "Introductory Address on the Functions of the Science and Art Department," 16 November 1857, in Cole, *Fifty Years of Public Work* (London, 1884), II, 293.

47. *Report from the Select Committee on Public Institutions* (1860), q. 8.

48. *ILN*, 31 December 1853, p. 591; *Times*, 3 September 1860.

49. *Times*, 29 March 1853.

50. Quoted by Cole in *Edinburgh Review*, 123 (1866), 64.

51. Ibid., p. 69.

52. *Politics for the People*, 1 July 1848.

53. *Times*, 3 September 1860.

54. *A Hand-Book for Young Painters* (London, 1855), p. 216.

55. *Report from the Select Committee on the National Gallery* (1850), qq. 48–57, 341, and passim.

56. Ibid., p. 66. Faraday's testimony occurs at qq. 654–702.

57. Anthony Trollope, *The New Zealander*, ed. N. John Hall (Oxford, 1972), pp. 203–206.

58. Quoted in Laurence Senelick, "Politics as Entertainment: Victorian Music-Hall Songs," *Victorian Studies*, 19 (1975), 154.

59. B. W. Richardson, *Thomas Sopwith* (London, 1891), pp. 273–74.

60. *Sixty Years' Stage Service, Being a Record of the Life of Charles Morton, "The Father of the Halls,"* comp. W. H. Morton and H. Chance Newton (London, 1905), p. 44.

61. A copy of the 1866 edition is at EC, Canterbury Hall file.

62. Jeremy Maas, *Gambart* (London, 1975), p. 69.

63. E. T. Cook, *The Life of John Ruskin* (London, 1912), II, 27.

64. *ILN*, 6 November 1858, p. 440.

EPILOGUE

1. Handbills, EC, Egyptian Hall folder.

2. *Dictionary of National Biography, Supplement One;* handbills, EC, Polytechnic box.

3. Program dated August 1881 in archives of the Polytechnic Institution.

4. Ibid.

5. *N & Q*, 10th ser. 5 (1906), 454.

6. The Polytechnic as it was in 1884 is described in *All the Year Round*, n.s. 34 (1884), 172–76.

7. Curtis Dahl, "Artemus Ward: Comic Panoramist," *New England Quarterly*, 32 (1959), 476–85; playbill, GL, Egyptian Hall file.

8. "Mr. Barlow," *All the Year Round*, n.s. 1 (1868–69), 156–59.

9. Ernest Reynolds, *Early Victorian Drama, 1830–1870* (Cambridge, 1936), p. 31.

10. H. Southern, "The Centenary of the Panorama," *Theatre Notebook*, 5 (1950–51), 67–69;

clippings in Harvard Theatre Collection, Panorama box.

11. Handbill, WCL, StM/LS, I, 185–87; *Survey of London,* XXXIV (1966), 464–65.

12. Hollingshead, *My Lifetime* (London, 1895), II, 218–19, 223–38.

13. This description of the Royal Aquarium is based on John M. Munro, *The Royal Aquarium: Failure of a Victorian Compromise* (American University of Beirut, 1971). JJ Coll., London Play Places box 1, has a good assemblage of material relating to the establishment.

14. *Survey of London,* XXXVIII (1975), 145–46.

15. *N & Q,* 168 (1935), 233.

16. *Survey of London,* XXXVIII (1975), 201–202.

17. *ILN,* 6 March 1858, pp. 228–30, and 3 August 1861, pp. 125–26; *Art Journal,* n.s. 7 (1861), 274; *Times,* 22 July 1861; *All the Year Round,* n.s. 2 (1869), 209–11.

Index